W9-BOF-855

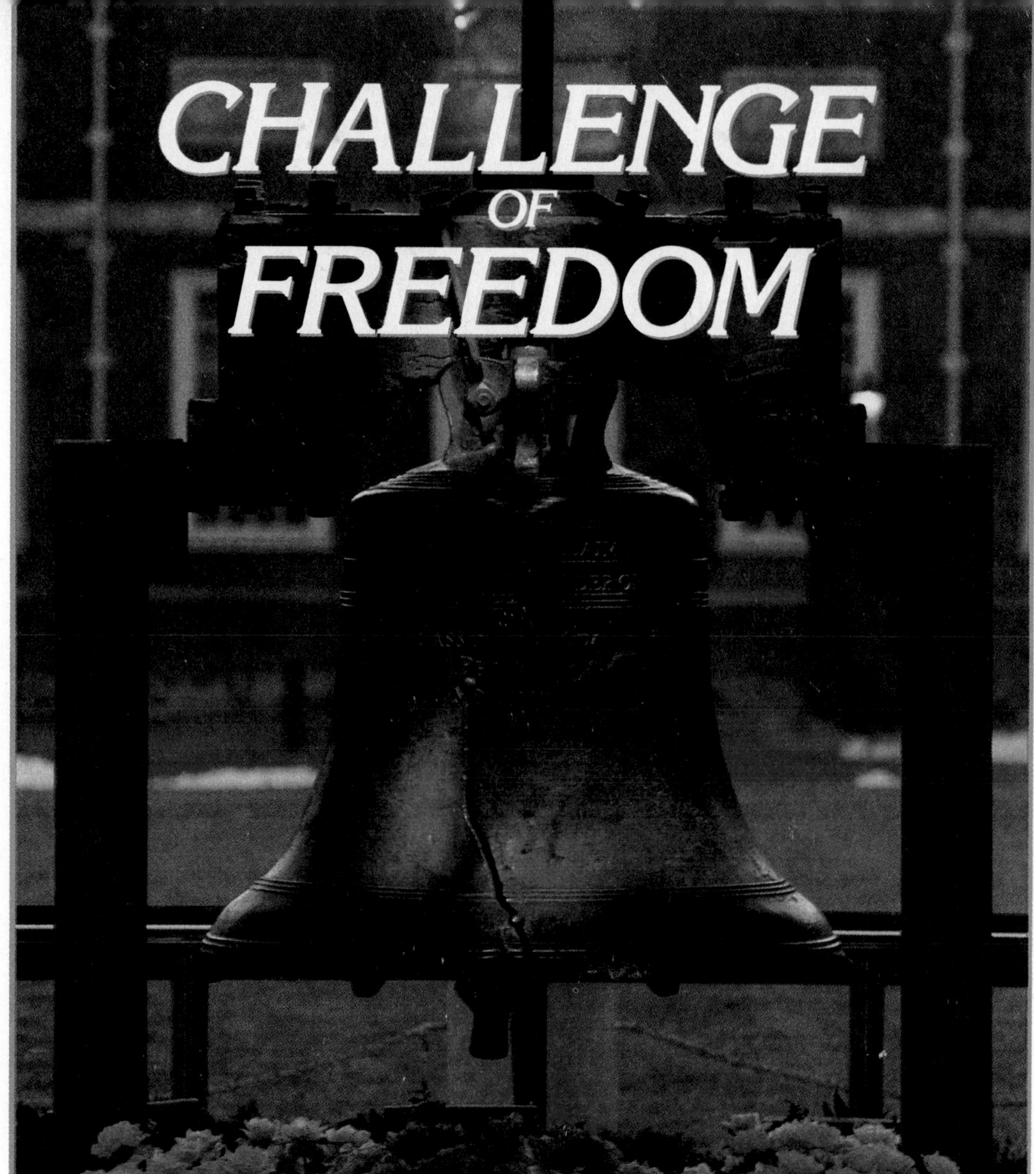

The Liberty Bell, above, is an object of great importance to the American people. Because of its association with the American Revolution, it symbolizes our challenge of freedom.

Cast in London in 1752, it bears the inscription from Leviticus 25: "Proclaim liberty throughout all the land unto all the inhabitants thereof." The bell was placed in the old statehouse, Independence Hall, to commemorate the 50th anniversary of the Commonwealth of Pennsylvania.

The bell was in use when the Continental Congress was in session in Philadelphia. It rang out against British tax and trade restrictions. It was also rung on news of the Boston Tea Party and at the first public reading of the Declaration of Independence. The bell was removed for safekeeping when the British occupied Philadelphia, 1777–1778.

While tolling for the funeral of Chief Justice John Marshall in July, 1835, the bell cracked. Because of its association with the Revolution, it was not recast. In 1846 during the Mexican war it was placed on exhibition at Independence Hall where it remains today. It was given a new glass and steel pavilion for the 1976 Bicentennial year.

Contributing Writers

David Eller
Educational Consultant
Elgin, Illinois

Barbara Kirby
Educational Consultant
Villa Park, Illinois

Denny Schillings
Teacher, Social Studies Dept.
Homewood-Flossmoor High School
Flossmoor, Illinois

Ursula Szwast
Educational Consultant
La Grange, Illinois

Consultants and Reviewers

Loyal L. Darr
Supervisor, K-12 Social Studies Education Curriculum Services
Denver Public Schools
Denver, Colorado

Sonya Heckman
Department Chairman and 8th grade Social Studies Teacher
Greencastle-Antrim Middle School
Greencastle, Pennsylvania

Helen W. Richardson
Executive Director for Secondary Curriculum
Fulton County School System
Atlanta, Georgia

Gail Riley
Social Studies Consultant
Hurst-Euless-Bedford ISD
Bedford, Texas

Michael Solliday
Curriculum and Instruction Dept.
Southern Illinois University
Carbondale, Illinois

Warren Tracy
Director of Social Studies
Duval County School District
Jacksonville, Florida

Marianne Wachholz
Elmhurst College
Elmhurst, Illinois

CHALLENGE OF FREEDOM

Third Edition

Roger LaRaus
Curriculum Coordinator, Evanston Public Schools, Evanston, Illinois

Harry P. Morris
Social Studies Teacher, John Burroughs Junior High School, Los Angeles, California

Robert Sobel
Professor of History, Hofstra University, Hempstead, New York

GLENCOE

Macmillan/McGraw-Hill

New York, New York   Columbus, Ohio   Mission Hills, California   Peoria, Illinois

Special Acknowledgments and Credits—For excerpts and quotations that appear on pages indicated: Page 75: from *The New World*, Stefan Lorant, editor; © 1946, Hawthorne Books, a Division of Elsevier-Dutton Publishing Company, Inc./Page 88: from *Towards One World*, by George Pearson; © 1962, Cambridge University Press. Reprinted by permission of Cambridge University Press./Page 307: from *I Reported The Gettysburg Address*, by Joseph I. Gilbert; *Chicago Tribune Magazine*, November 19, 1978; reprinted by permission of the National Shorthand Reporters Association./Page 326: from *Plunkitt of Tammany Hall*, by William L. Riordon; Copyright © 1963, reprinted by permission of the publisher, E. P. Dutton./Page 341: from *Frontier Mother: The Letters of Gro Svendsen*, by Pauline Farseth and Theodore C. Blegen, editors; the Norwegian-American Historical Association./Page 350: from *Touch the Earth*, by T. C. McLuhan, editor; © 1971, E. P. Dutton./Page 383: from *Across the Plains*, by Robert Louis Stevenson; © 1892, Charles Scribner's Sons./Page 400: from *The Bitter Cry of the Children*, by John Spargo; © 1906, reprinted by permission of Macmillan Publishing Co./Page 456: from *We Were There: The Story of Working Women in America*, by Barbara Mayer Wertheimer; © 1977, Pantheon Books, Inc., A Division of Random House, Inc./Page 476: from *Eyewitness: The Negro in American History*, Third Edition, by William Loren Katz; Copyright © 1974, by Fearon-Pitman Publishers, Inc., 6 Davis Drive, Belmont, California, 94002. Reprinted by permission./Page 478: from the *Chicago Daily Defender*, 1917. Reprinted by permission of the *Chicago Daily Defender*./Page 489: from *The Second Twenty Years At Hull House*, by Jane Addams; © 1930 by Macmillan Publishing Co., Inc., renewed 1958 by John A. Brittain./Page 527: from *This I Remember*, by Eleanor Roosevelt; © 1949, Harper & Row, Publishers, Inc./Page 538: from "Letters From The Dust Bowl," by Caroline A. Henderson; *Atlantic Monthly*, May, 1936. Copyright © 1936 by Atlantic Monthly Company, Boston, Mass. Reprinted with permission./Page 555: from *Farewell to Manzanar*, by Jeanne Wakatsuki Houston and James D. Houston; Copyright © 1973 by James D. Houston. Reprinted by permission of Houghton Mifflin Company./Page 571: from "Boycott the Olympics," *The Nation*, August 21, 1935. Reprinted by permission of *Nation*. And from "Communications," *The Commonweal*, December 6, 1935. Reprinted by permission of *Commonweal*./Page 590: from *An Unsettled People: Social Order and Disorder in American History*, by Rowland T. Berthoff; © 1971, Harper & Row, Publishers, Inc. Reprinted by permission of the author./Page 598: from "What's McCarthyism." Reprinted from *U.S. News & World Report*, September 26, 1952. Copyright © 1952, U.S. News & World Report, Inc./Page 612: from *I Have a Dream*, by Martin Luther King, Jr.; Copyright © 1963 by Martin Luther King, Jr. Reprinted by permission of Joan Daves./Page 633: from "An Expert's Warning On Weapons In Cuba," reprinted from *U.S. News & World Report*, November 5, 1962. Copyright © 1962, U.S. News & World Report, Inc./Page 651: from "Voice of the People," the *Chicago Tribune*, April 3, 1968./Page 664: from *Superpower*, by Robert Hargreaves; © 1973. Reprinted by permission of St. Martin's Press, Inc., and Hodder & Stoughton, Ltd./Page 683: from *Energy: Global Prospects, 1985–2000*, by the Workshop on Alternative Energy Strategies. Copyright © 1977, McGraw-Hill Book Company. Used with permission of McGraw-Hill Book Company.

For Photos see page 796

Cartographer: Susan Mills

Photo Research: Toni Michaels

Cover photo: Kenneth Garrett/Westlight

Send all inquiries to:
GLENCOE
15319 Chatsworth Street
P.O. Box 9609
Mission Hills, CA 91346-9609

ISBN 0-02-650062-0 Student Text
ISBN 0-02-650065-9 Teacher's Annotated Edition

Printed in the United States of America

5 6 7 8 95 94 93

CHALLENGE OF FREEDOM

UNIT ONE

A NEW LAND, A NEW PEOPLE

UNIT TWO

A NEW NATION IS ESTABLISHED

UNIT THREE

UNIT FOUR

PROGRESS AND PROBLEMS

UNIT FIVE

THE UNION IS TESTED

UNIT SIX

THE GROWTH OF THE NATION

UNIT SEVEN

A MODERN NATION IN A NEW CENTURY

UNIT EIGHT

THE DEPRESSION AND WORLD WAR II

UNIT NINE

UNIT TEN

CHAPTER 37 YEARS OF TURMOIL 638

CHAPTER 38 YEARS OF CHANGE 656

AMERICA FACES NEW CHALLENGES

REFERENCE MATERIALS

FEATURES

MAPS

CHARTS, GRAPHS, AND TABLES

KNOWING YOUR BOOK

The authors of CHALLENGE OF FREEDOM have developed and written a history of the United States that is easy to read and to understand. The book is divided into 10 units and 40 chapters. Each unit discusses and explains the different factors that have influenced our country's history. The chapters in each unit present and explain the political, economic, and social changes and events that took place during a certain period of time. By studying these changes and events you will gain a more complete understanding of our country and its people.

The discussion and explanation of the ideas and decisions of earlier Americans will add to your knowledge of American society today. You will also be better able to see what part the United States has in world affairs.

THE UNIT

Unit Opener. Each of the ten units in CHALLENGE OF FREEDOM contains four chapters. Each unit opens with two pages that list the titles of the four chapters. The pages include a time line that lists the important events that are discussed in the unit. The pages contain four captioned pictures that depict some topic covered in each of the four chapters of the unit. The unit opener also includes a brief introduction to the unit.

Unit Review. Each unit ends with two pages called the Unit Review. The unit review contains a summary of the unit. The summary is followed by a review of vocabulary words and questions that check the facts covered in the unit. The review includes questions that review the concepts in the unit and questions that involve critical thinking. The review also includes chronology questions as well as an activity that is designed to build citizenship skills. Each unit review ends with a geography activity that expands your geography skills.

CLOSE-UP CHAPTERS

The fourth chapter of each unit in CHALLENGE OF FREEDOM is a close-up chapter. These chapters are written to give you further detail and greater insight into some topic discussed in each unit. The close-up chapters will help you learn more about the people and events that have played an important part in our nation's history. Each close-up chapter begins with an introduction to the topic covered in the chapter. Each close-up chapter ends with a Chapter Review. The review includes a chapter summary and questions covering the concepts discussed in the chapter. The review also includes questions that involve critical thinking as well as projects that will give you more information about some aspect of the topic covered in the close-up chapter.

THE CHAPTER

Chapter Opener. Each chapter of CHALLENGE OF FREEDOM, except the close-up chapters, begins with a one page opener that includes a time line of the events discussed in the chapter. The chapter opener lists the numbered sections of the chapter. The opener also includes the learning objectives of the chapter.

Chapter Review. Each chapter ends with a two page Chapter Review. The review includes a skills activity and a vocabulary activity that deals with the words introduced in the chapter. The vocabulary activity is followed by questions that deal with the facts and concepts discussed in the chapter. The chapter review contains questions that deal with some of the illustrations used in the chapter. This is followed by several critical thinking questions that ask you for your opinion about various topics presented in the chapter. The chapter review ends with two enrichment activities. These activities are designed to help you expand on the concepts covered in the chapter.

Chapter Features. There are a number of features in each chapter, except the Close-Up Chapter, that will aid you in learning about the United States. Each chapter has a feature called *Recalling the Times*. This feature will give you a first-hand view of some idea or event discussed in the chapter. The feature called *Profiles* will give you insight into a particular person who was important in the history of our country. The feature called *Viewpoints Differ* presents contrasting points of view about a particular topic. Each chapter also includes a feature called *Using Your Skills*. This feature will help to improve your social-studies skills. Through maps, charts, graphs, tables, and other means, you will learn to gather information and to form conclusions. Each chapter also contains a feature called *Do You Know?* This feature presents interesting but little-known facts about some of the people and events in each chapter.

The authors of CHALLENGE OF FREEDOM hope these features will help you in your study of American history. The features have been included to help make the study of history more meaningful and enjoyable.

INDIVIDUAL SECTIONS

Each chapter of CHALLENGE OF FREEDOM includes at least three individual sections. Each section begins with an overview to the section as well as with the learning objectives of the section. The objectives help you to focus on the main concepts presented in each section. Each section ends with a Section Review that review the main concepts of each section.

REFERENCE SECTION

The end of CHALLENGE OF FREEDOM contains a *Reference Materials* section which includes several aids to help you in your study of American history. At the beginning of this reference section there is an illustrated list of the Presidents that gives some important facts about each President. The list of Presidents is followed by a table showing facts and figures about the fifty states as well as the territories, possessions, and commonwealths of the United States. The *Atlas* includes a map of the world, of North America, and six maps of the United States. The *Gazetteer* presents useful information about important places. The Declaration of Independence and the Constitution are presented with comments to help you understand these documents. There is also a *Reference Bibliography* listing books and computer software that you may use to supplement your reading. The *Glossary*, which begins on page 773, includes definitions of words and terms from the book. Finally, the *Index* will help you to find specific information in the text.

0 1000

25,000 BC First people in North America

17,000 BC Desert culture Indians develop agriculture

8,000 BC End of last Ice Age

AD 50 First Mayan writings

250 "Mound Builders" settle in Mississippi Valley

1000 Leif Ericson reaches North America

1492 Columbus lands at San Salvador

UNIT ONE

A New Land, A New People

Earliest times to 1763

The ruins of the walled city of Machu Picchu are a reminder of the once-great Inca civilization.

Sturdy and seaworthy vessels carried adventurous Vikings across the North Atlantic Ocean.

1600 1700

1500 Height of Aztec and Inca empires

1520's and 1530's Spanish crush Aztec and Inca empires

1557 Iroquois League of Five Nations formed

1607 Founding of first permanent English colony at Jamestown

1608 Founding of first permanent French colony at Quebec

1619 First African slaves arrive in Virginia

1620 Separatist Pilgrims land at Plymouth

1630s Great Migration to Massachusetts

1733 Founding of Georgia, last of the original thirteen English colonies

1754 to 1763 French and Indian War

1775 Beginning of American Revolution

CHAPTERS

The first Americans—the ancestors of the American Indians—were Stone Age people. They crossed the Bering Strait land bridge from Asia into North America thousands of years ago and migrated throughout the Americas. Many advanced Indian societies had developed in the Americas by the time the first Europeans came to the new lands.

Spain was the first European country to set up colonies in the Americas. As these settlements brought new wealth to Spain, other countries sent explorers to the new lands. England and France, for example, both claimed large areas of North America. The English colonies in North America grew quickly and brought new wealth to England. However, by 1763, it began to appear that the English colonies in North America were no longer dependent upon Great Britain for support.

"Jamestown About 1614" was painted by Sidney King.

Indians such as the one pictured here are believed to have inhabited the colony of Roanoke.

0 1000

- 25,000 BC First people in North America
- 8000 BC End of last Ice Age
- 7000 BC Desert culture Indians develop agriculture
- AD 50 First Mayan writings
- 250 "Mound Builders" settle in Mississippi Valley
- 600 Height of Mayan civilization
- 1000 Apache and Navaho move into Southwest
- 1492 Columbus lands in the New World
- 1500 Height of Aztec and Inca empires
- 1557 Iroquois League of Five Nations formed

CHAPTER 1

The Earliest Americans

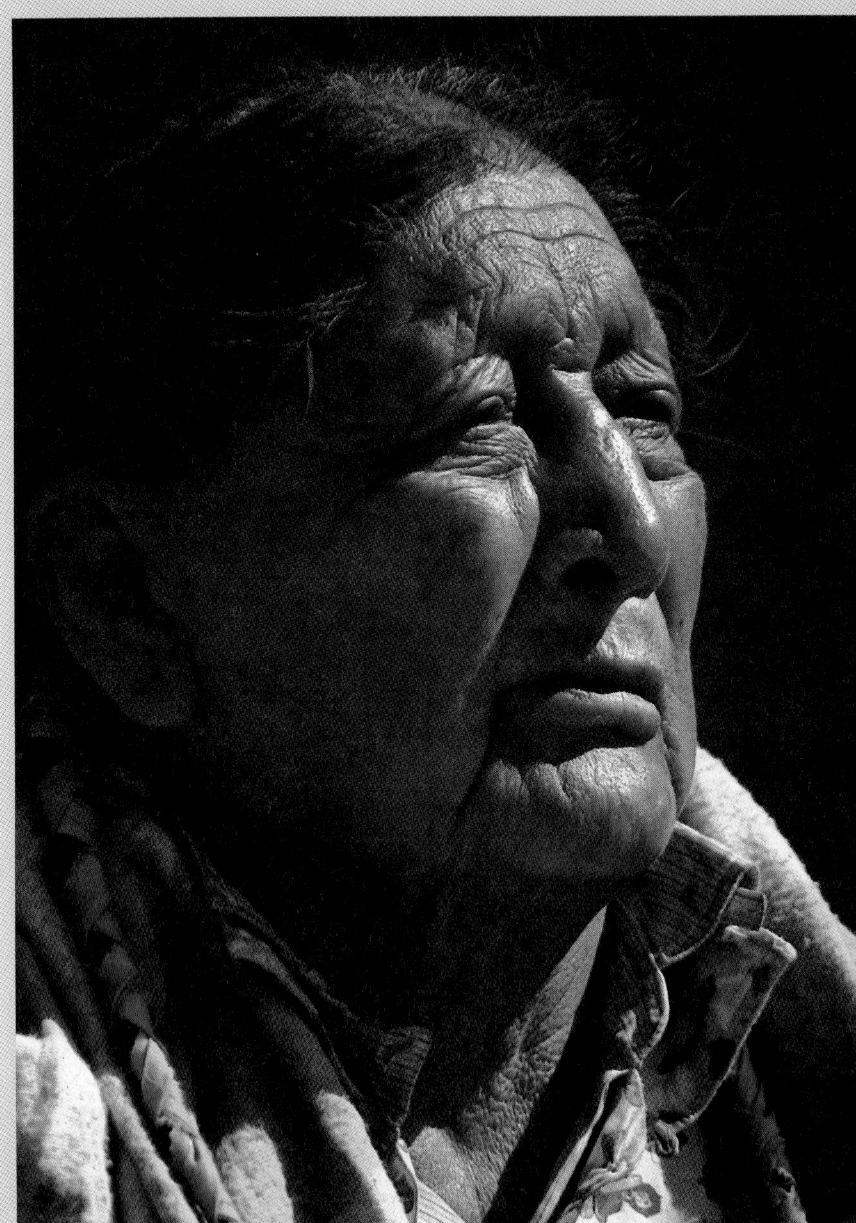

Chapter Objectives

After studying this chapter, you will be able to:

- explain the role that natural environment had in shaping various Indian cultures;
- identify the major North American Indian cultures by their geographic region;
- describe several achievements of the Indian civilizations in North, Central, and South America.

1 The New Land and the New People

Overview People lived in the Americas for thousands of years before the first Europeans discovered these new lands. The earliest Americans—the early Indians—were hunters and followed herds of animals. They were probably unaware that they were entering a new territory. *Archaeologists*—scientists who study the Indians' tools and other remains—have been able to learn much about the way they lived.

Objectives After you read this section, you will be able to:

- name two ways archaeologists use to determine the age of ancient materials;
- explain how and when the earliest Indians arrived in North America;
- describe how the environment of North America shaped the way the early Indians lived.

Dating the Past. Archaeologists can look into the past by using *radiocarbon dating* and by the close study of a certain volcanic stone called *obsidian*. Radiocarbon dating measures the amount of radioactive carbon in things that were once alive. It can measure things as old as 30,000 years.

Plants, animals, and people take in radioactive carbon during their life. After their death, atoms of carbon 14 fall apart at a constant rate. By measuring the amount of atoms that disappear, scientists can estimate the age of many *artifacts*—things left behind by early peoples.

The other means of dating ancient things is through the careful study of the volcanic stone obsidian. This stone takes in moisture from the air. The moisture leaves marks much the same as tree rings. By counting these marks, scientists can learn the approximate age of many things that have been found with obsidian. But radiocarbon dating is still the most widely used means of dating the past up to 30,000 years ago because obsidian is not often found in areas north of present-day Mexico. Rather, it is more often found in South America, where it was used for weapons, for decoration, and for trade by the early South American Indians.

■ *What are two methods scientists use to estimate the age of ancient materials?*

The Ice Ages. The earth has had four periods during which *glaciers*—large sheets of ice—formed. These periods are known as the Ice Ages. Scientists believe that the first Ice Age began as long as 1,500,000 years ago. The fourth and last Ice Age ended as recently as 10,000 years ago. This Ice Age lasted for more than 60,000 years. During the Ice Ages, glaciers sometimes more than one mile deep covered up to 32 percent of the northern regions of the earth (see maps on page 20).

These ice sheets changed the way the earth looked. The depth of the oceans, the temperatures and seasons of the earth, and the places where early Americans lived also were changed. For example, as the ocean water froze and the ice sheets grew, the surface level of the oceans dropped about 460 feet. Average summer temperatures in North America dropped about 10 degrees. And as the glaciers moved slowly southward—only inches each year—they changed the surface of the earth by grinding out great holes in the surface of the earth.

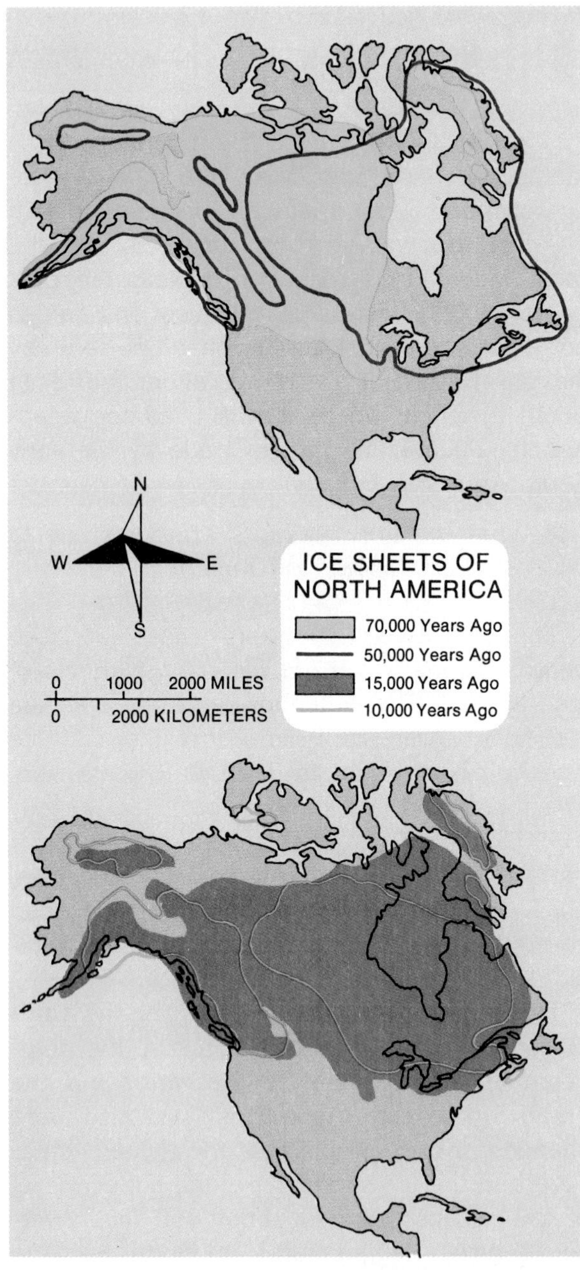

Huge sheets of ice once covered great areas of North America. As these ice sheets moved over the earth, they changed the landscape by carving out high-walled valleys and deep, fresh-water lakes. At which two times were the ice sheets greatest in America?

When the surface level of the oceans dropped, shallow undersea land areas such as the Bering Strait land bridge appeared (see the map on page 21). This was a strip of land that connected Asia with North America. Over a period of 60,000 years, the Bering Strait land bridge changed from a marsh to a grassland. This fertile grazing land attracted herds of animals. Soon, many herds of animals, such as camels, horses, and mammoths, crossed back and forth across the Bering Strait land bridge. Early hunters followed these herds. As a result, groups of people crossed the Bering Strait land bridge from northeastern Asia to North America. These people became the first Americans. They were the ancestors of the American Indians.

■ *How many Ice Ages has the earth experienced?*

The New Americans. No one knows exactly when the first hunters from Asia came to North America. But by studying such things as the tools, weapons, and utensils made by the early Americans, archaeologists are able to understand how they lived. *Clovis points*—spearpoints made from chipped flint that have been found at many early campsites in the Arctic Circle—seem to show that people came to northern North America at least 25,000 years ago. But other discoveries have caused some people to think that the earliest people arrived in North America much earlier—perhaps between 40,000 and 100,000 years ago.

One of the first discoveries about early American life came in 1915. That year, George McJunkin, a black cowboy, found old bones while searching for lost cattle near Folsom, New Mexico. He told a friend about his unusual find and showed him a spearpoint that he had found at the site. Later, the bones of

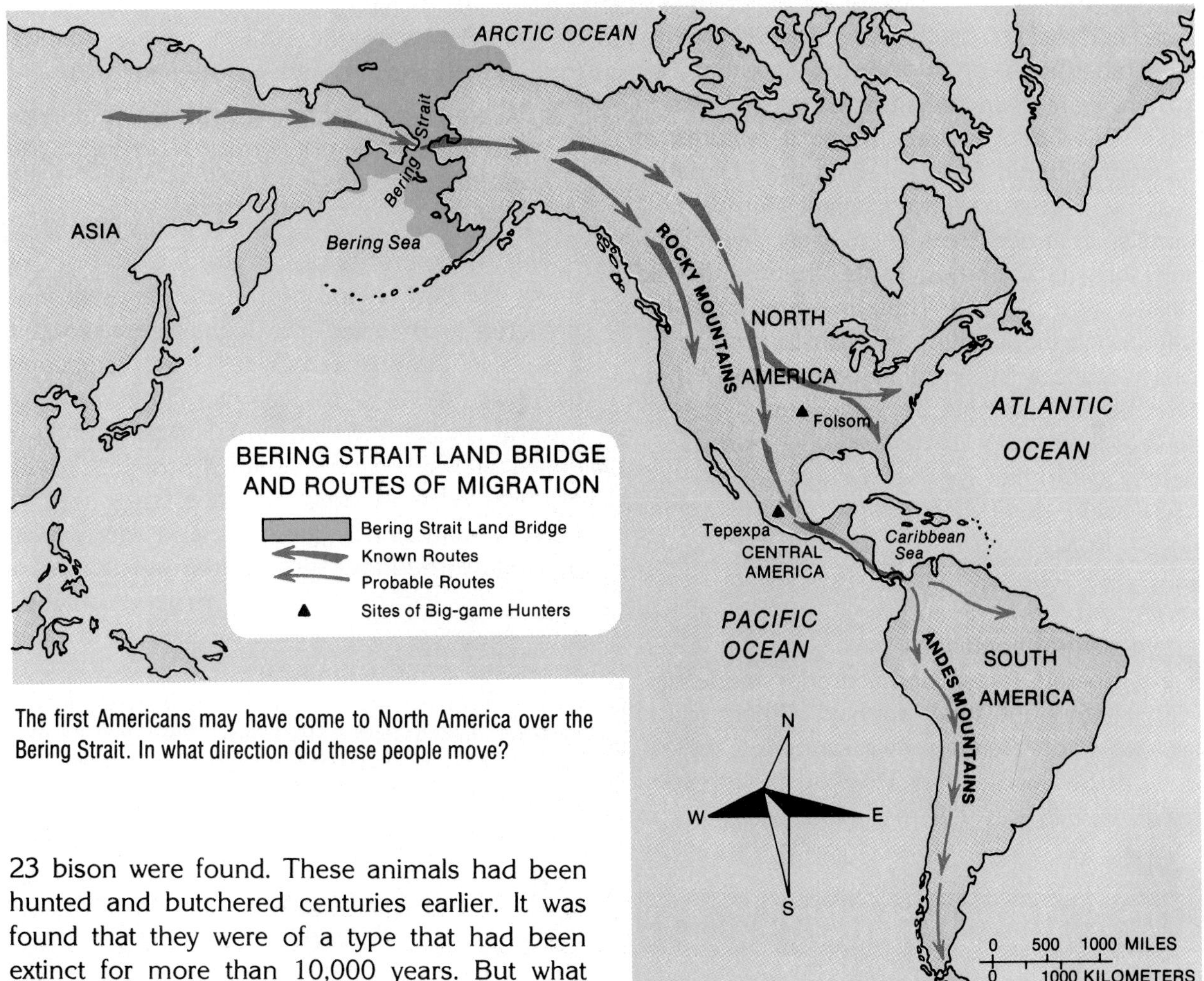

The first Americans may have come to North America over the Bering Strait. In what direction did these people move?

23 bison were found. These animals had been hunted and butchered centuries earlier. It was found that they were of a type that had been extinct for more than 10,000 years. But what caused the most excitement was not the bones but a spearpoint.

The spearpoint was wedged between two bison ribs. This proved that people were in southwestern North America by 10,000 B.C.—that is, 10,000 years before the birth of Christ. Many experts have suggested that this proved that earlier generations of hunters must have arrived in North America at least 25,000 years ago.

What are Clovis points, and where were they found?

Early Migrations. At first, the earliest Americans lived in what is present-day Alaska. The early hunters then followed animal herds as the animals grazed farther south each year. Most archaeologists believe that these migrations lasted about 15,000 years. By about 10,000 years ago (about 8000 B.C.) people were living in most areas of the Americas. Evidence shows that by this time groups of people were living as far north as the Arctic

Circle and as far south as Tierra del Fuego, the southernmost point of South America.

There were many differences in the lands in which these people lived. Physical features of the lands differed greatly, as did their climates. In some areas there were great numbers of animals. In other areas there were fewer animals; but nuts, berries, roots, fruits, and wild grasses were plentiful. Thus, in some areas the early people could hunt and fish to provide for their livelihood. But in other parts of the Americas, the early people depended upon gathering as many types of *vegetation*—plant life—as they could find for their living.

As each generation of the early Indians moved into new, unexplored regions, the Indians had to *adapt*—fit in—to new *environments.* An environment is a place that has certain natural conditions such as a dry desert or a temperate forest. Some groups made new weapons to hunt small animals. Others found new ways of planting and gathering grains, roots, or berries in order to have enough food to eat. In this way different *cultures*—ways of life—developed as the earliest settlers adapted to the many environments in the Americas.

■ *What major factor led to the development of different cultures among the earliest Indians?*

The Early American Indian Cultures. By about 10,000 years ago, early hunters and gatherers had settled into 5 major areas within the present-day United States. The first people to cross the land bridge into North America formed the early *Arctic* and *Subarctic* culture areas. These people settled in the northernmost lands of North America. They lived by hunting animals because the land was usually too cold throughout most of the year for farming. Their *technology*—the making of tools and weapons—was limited at first to making spearpoints and darts.

As other groups moved southward, newer culture areas were formed. The *Big-Game Hunters* made up the largest group of early Americans. They lived on the Great Plains of North America. They hunted mammoths, mastodons, and bison for food and used the skins of these animals for shelter and for clothing.

The people who formed the early *Mountain and Plateau* culture area lived in the Pacific Northwest. These people relied mainly upon fishing for their new way of life. Their culture did not spread to other areas of the new lands because fishing was not always available in other places.

Members of the early *Desert* culture area lived in what is now part of the southwestern region of the United States. These people were mostly food-gatherers rather than hunters. They also made baskets to hold the seeds that they had gathered. And they shaped stones to grind the seeds into flour. In addition, they made throwing sticks and darts to hunt small

DO YOU KNOW?

When did American Indians first use horses?

Indians of the Southwest were the first Americans to use horses. This took place in the late 1500's. At one time, wild horses had roamed North America. But about 100,000 years ago or earlier, all horses disappeared from the American continent. No one knows why this happened, but the changing climate was probably responsible. Horses did not return to the Americas until they were brought by Spanish explorers in the 1500's.

The main activity among the early Indians centered on providing and preparing food for the tribe. Indians of the Eastern Woodlands, such as these people of the Hopewell culture, lived near present-day St. Louis and hunted and gathered nuts, berries, and grasses. What do the figures in this illustration appear to be doing?

The Glass Image

animals. Some people in this culture area later developed *agriculture*—the raising of crops for food—in the Americas about 7000 B.C.

The people of the early *Eastern Woodland and Valley* culture area were the most advanced of the early cultures in North America. They lived in a rich fertile land that was mainly forest. From the trees in the forest they made farming tools and such weapons as bows, arrows, and spears for hunting. They made canoes to cross rivers and lakes. They also traded goods with neighboring groups and, thus, shared new ideas. This helped to spread their way of life.

These earliest American *societies*—groups of people who share many of the same traditions, institutions, and interests—in time developed more-advanced Indian cultures. Each group's way of life continued to change with its needs and because of the conditions of the regions where the group lived.

■ *Which early Indian culture developed agriculture about 7000 B.C.?*

SECTION 1 REVIEW

1. *What two ways are used to determine the age of ancient materials?*
2. *How did the earliest people arrive in North America?*
3. *Why did the early Indian societies develop different cultures?*

2 North American Indian Cultures

Overview Nearly one million Indians lived in North America before the arrival of the Europeans. This number constituted seven major Indian culture areas of North America.

Five of these major culture areas were located in what is today the continental United States. Largely because of their natural environment, these Indian cultures were different from one another in many ways.

Objectives After you read this section, you will be able to:

- list ways in which the major Indian culture groups were similar;
- identify and locate the five major Indian cultures of the United States;
- describe how the environment affected the ways in which the various groups of North American Indians provided for their livelihood.

Similarities Among North American Indian Cultures. There were a number of similarities among the Indian cultures of North America. For example, most of the Indian societies in North America were divided into *tribes.* In general, a tribe was made up of a group of people who lived in the same area. They spoke the same language, and they held the same religious beliefs. Some tribes were also divided into smaller sections called *bands.* A band was usually made up of no more than ten people because there was often not enough food in one area to support an entire tribe. Therefore, by organizing into small bands, the people were better able to roam about hunting and gathering food.

Another similarity among most Indians was a belief in spirits. Many Indians thought that spirits could be found in nature. For example, some Indians believed that spirits dwelt in the sun, in the moon, in rain, and in some plants and animals.

In general, wars were not common among most Indian tribes. When war did break out, battles could bring great honor to the *braves*—the warriors. But war was often just a ceremony to show bravery. Touching the enemy with a *coup stick*—a ceremonial spear without a point—during battle often brought more honor than the killing of an enemy. This was because the warrior showed both courage and mercy.

Most tribes were organized in a somewhat democratic way. Councils were often selected by the people. These councils made the most-important decisions for all the people by giving advice to the chief.

■ *How were some Indian tribes divided?*

Indians of the Eastern Woodland. More than 35 tribes lived in the Eastern Woodland and Valley culture area. Some tribes in this part of the country were the Delaware, the Iroquois, the Fox, and the Cherokee.

There were many resources in the Eastern Woodland area. There was much small game and fish, and the soil was good for farming. For many Indians, farming was the major way to make a living. The Indians grew such crops as corn, tomatoes, squash, wheat, and peanuts.

The Eastern Woodland Indians used *slash-and-burn* agriculture. That is, they cleared the land of trees by cutting them down with crude saws. The tree stumps and underbrush that

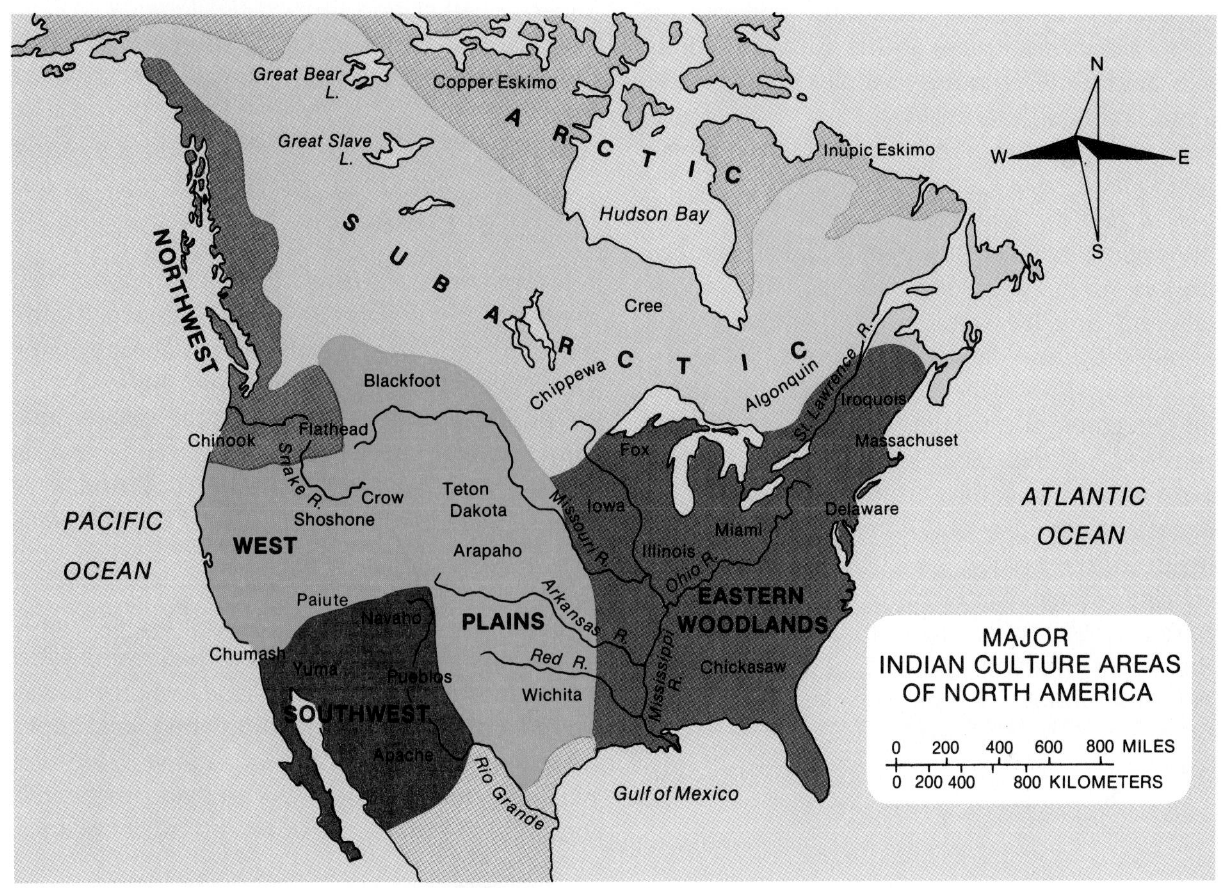

Although the seven basic North American Indian cultures varied greatly, they shared similarities in political and social organization. Alaskan Eskimos, or Inuit, are part of the Arctic culture and arrived from Asia by boat about 2000 B.C.

were left were then burned. This kind of land clearance was fast, but it quickly wore out the land. The Indians would then slash and burn other areas when their fields became worn out.

Because the Eastern Woodland area had rich soil, a *food surplus*—extra food—could be grown. Surplus food was often traded with neighboring tribes. In this way an economic system based on trade began.

Farming led to other changes in the Eastern Woodland area as well. No longer did all people in a tribe need to search for food. They could perform other tasks for the tribe. For example, some people became *shamans*—medicine men who also had political and social power. Still others had time to become warriors, builders, or *artisans*—people who make things by hand. As the Eastern Woodland tribes developed new ways of life, they increased their trade with other tribes. In this way new ideas and new ways of hunting, farming, or building were shared.

The Iroquois people made up one of the most advanced societies in the Eastern Woodland area. The Iroquois people lived in the central part of present-day New York State. Their society was made up of five tribes: the Mohawk, the Cayuga, the Onondaga, the Oneida, and the Seneca.

Women held real power in Iroquois society. Iroquois men were the hunters, the food-gatherers, and the warriors. The women raised the children and tended the crops. However, the women also owned the houses, the fields, and the crops of a village. They also chose the members of the tribal council. If a council member did not behave in the way the women believed he should, the women could remove him from the council.

Unlike many North American Indians, the Iroquois tribes often fought wars with other tribes over hunting grounds. To help make decisions about warfare, the Iroquois tribes joined together and formed the League of Five Nations in the mid-1500's. This group became the largest organization of Indians north of Mexico.

■ *What effect did a food surplus have upon the way of living among the Eastern Woodland tribes?*

Indians of the Plains. Nearly 40 tribes lived on the Great Plains of North America. Some tribes of the Great Plains were the Cheyenne, the Comanche, the Arapaho, and the Iowa.

The Plains Indians lived in small villages that were usually built near rivers and creeks. Houses were made of sod and wood and were then covered with mud. The Plains Indians raised many crops, such as corn, squash, and beans, in the rich, soft soil near the rivers.

The men of the tribes followed buffalo herds in the summer. A buffalo that had been killed was taken back to the village, where it was butchered for food. Clothing, bedding, tools, weapons, and utensils were made from the hide and the bones of the buffalo. In the fall, the Indian hunters returned to their villages.

Ceremonial buffalo dances were often held to assure a good hunt. How did the Indians dress for the dances?

Historical Pictures Service

They helped to pick the crops that the women had planted and had cared for during the summer.

■ *How did the Plains Indians use the buffalo that they had killed during summer hunting?*

Indians of the Northwest. Ten major Indian tribes lived along the northwest coast of North America. The Northwest Coast Indians included tribes such as the Chinook and the Kwakiutl. These Indians hunted game. They also gathered wild berries and fruit. Fishing, however, was the basis of their way of life. The Indians fished in the Pacific Ocean and in rivers and streams. They built their villages near the ocean or near rivers—close to the basis of their way of life.

The Indians made their houses out of wood because much of the northwest coast was covered by forestland. Many tools, utensils, and weapons were also made from wood. Large fishing ships were built by digging out or by burning out the trunks of giant redwood trees. And, as their ancestors had done, they made large *totem poles*—tall, hand-carved poles that told about the leader of a family.

Most tribes of the Northwest were not democratic. The wealthiest families made the important decisions for each village. People who owned many things were thought to be wealthy. They proved their wealth by holding a *potlatch*—a party that lasted many days. It was a chance for the party giver to prove his wealth by giving away many presents. Holding expensive potlatches was necessary to maintain the position as one of the village's most powerful families.

■ *What was the main food supply of the Northwest Coast Indians?*

Indians of the West. There were more than 20 major tribes in the West. These tribes belonged to the *California Indian* society or to the *Great Basin* society. The California Indians lived in the area of what is today California. The Great Basin Indians lived in the land between the Rocky Mountains and the Sierra Nevada and Cascade mountain ranges.

The California Indians lived in an area that had a mild climate. It was rich in foods that could be gathered, such as nuts, berries, and wild grains. As a result, the California Indians did not have to struggle to live. They ate the foods they could easily find. They also hunted small animals, and they fished in the many streams and rivers in their area.

The Great Basin tribes lived in a more difficult place than did the California Indians. The land was hot and had very little water. Few plants could grow there, and few animals could live in the area. Thus, the Great Basin Indians had to move their campsites often to search for food.

■ *What effect did the environment have on the life-style of the Great Basin Indians?*

Indians of the Southwest. More than 15 major tribes lived in the lands that are now northern Mexico, New Mexico, Arizona, and southern Utah. The earliest Indians in this part of the new lands were the Desert people. Some of their descendants were the people of the Pueblo tribes, which included the Hopi, the Taos, and the Zuni peoples. Later Indian settlers in the Southwest were the Apache and the Navaho.

The Pueblo tribes built one of the most advanced societies in North America. Their society was very democratic in that everyone was considered equal. Decisions were made by the group. Work was shared by all the Indians. In part, this is why Pueblo society was very peaceful.

Although the land where the Pueblos lived was very dry, the Pueblo Indians were farmers. They were able to farm because they had learned to *irrigate* the land. That is, they brought in water from nearby rivers and streams for growing crops. The Pueblos then traded their surplus food with other tribes. They also stored corn and other foods in artistic pottery jars. In addition, the Pueblos wove cotton into cloth, which was then used in making their clothing.

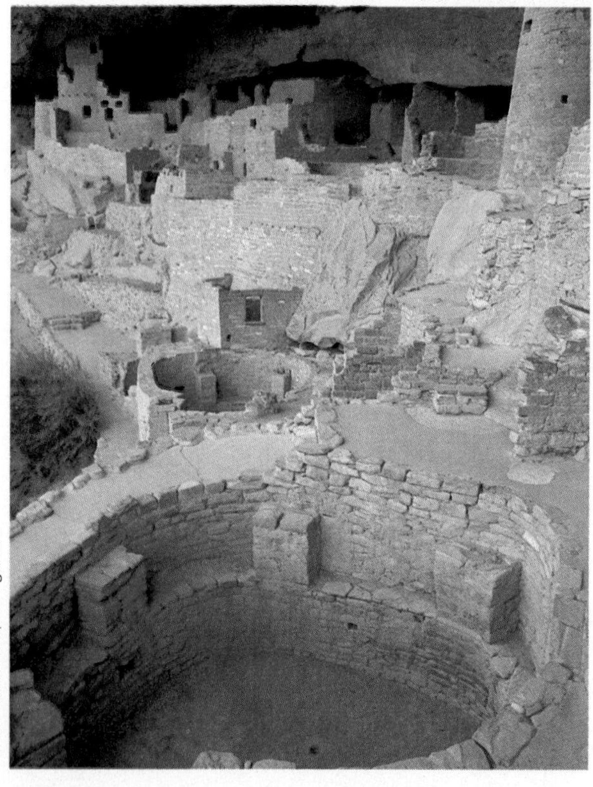

Martin Vanderwall/De Wys, Inc.

The Indians of the Southwest often built dwellings under the protection of the region's sandstone cliffs.

Pueblo Indian villages were often built within cliff walls. Other villages were built at the tops of high plateaus. In these ways the villagers were protected from attack. Sometimes all the people in a village lived in only one building. These buildings, however, might be four stories high, and hundreds of people might easily live in them.

Tribes such as the Apache and the Navaho came into the Southwest from the north about A.D. 1000. They were hunters and gatherers, who followed animals southward. The Apache became a fierce and warlike tribe, however. In part, this was because they attacked other Indian villages for food when hunting was poor. About the time that the Apache and the Navaho peoples moved into the Southwest, Pueblo society began to decline. Many experts believe that this decline was caused by the arrival of the Apache.

■ *Why were Pueblo villages built within cliff walls or at the tops of high plateaus?*

SECTION 2 REVIEW

1. *In what ways were the major North American Indian culture groups similar?*
2. *What were the five major Indian culture areas in what is today the United States?*
3. *Why did a trading system develop among the Indians of the Eastern Woodland?*

3 Civilizations in Central and South America

Overview The Maya and Aztecs of Central America and the Incas of South America developed remarkably advanced civilizations. These civilizations created strong economic systems that supported millions of people.

Objectives After you read this section, you will be able to:

- list some of the major contributions of the Mayan, Aztec, and Incan cultures;
- explain how the Aztecs and Incas enlarged their empires;
- describe the importance of religion to the people of these civilizations

The Mayan Civilization. The Mayan people belonged to one of 12 major tribes living in Central America before the Europeans arrived. The Maya lived in what today are the countries of Mexico, Belize, El Salvador, Guatemala, and Honduras (see map on this page). The Mayan people built an advanced civilization that reached its height between A.D. 300 and A.D. 900. At one time more than 15 million people are thought to have lived in this civilization.

Mayan civilization was based on farming. Many Mayan farmers grew surplus food each year. Therefore, some Indians no longer had to hunt or farm for their own food. Instead, some Mayan Indians were free to trade; to make handmade goods; and to make advances in learning, in government, and in religion.

The Maya also were great builders. They built cities that were used for religious ceremonies and for the buying and selling of goods. Huge stone pyramids and palaces were built in the center of the cities. Smaller temples were then built on the tops of the pyramids. These temples were used by the priests during religious services. However, most of the Mayan people lived in small, mud-covered huts in the countryside close to their crops.

Why did the Maya build cities?

The Mayan Way of Life. Religion was probably the most important part of Mayan life. The Mayan people believed in many gods. They honored a rain god so that the god would bring rain. They prayed to a god of

Advanced civilizations existed in the Americas long before the arrival of Europeans. What was the principal city of the Aztec empire?

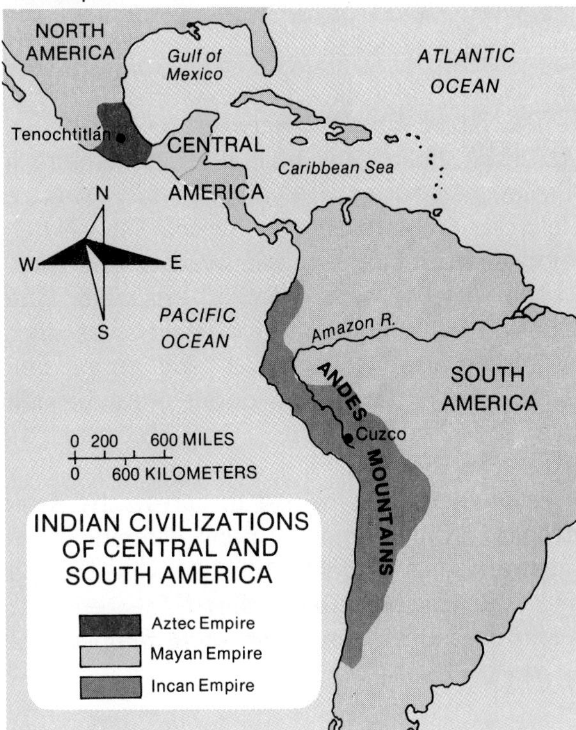

the earth to make the soil rich and good for farming.

Mayan religious leaders—the priests—held great power in Mayan society. They were political as well as religious leaders. The Mayan people provided food for the priests. As a result, the priests had time to study. This study led to a number of important inventions. The priests adapted a numbering system and developed calendars to better understand the passage of time. One of these calendars was a 365-day calendar, much like the calendar used in the United States today.

No one knows why Mayan civilization declined. Some historians believe that slash-and-burn agriculture wore out the land, causing a food shortage. Other authorities think that sickness killed many people. Still others feel that the people revolted against the ruling priests. Nevertheless, as the Mayan way of life began to decline, another civilization was growing in Central America.

■ *What group became the leaders of the Mayan people?*

The Aztec Empire. Between A.D. 1300 and A.D. 1519, the Aztecs built a strong empire in Central America. The capital city was at Tenochtitlán—present-day Mexico City—where more than 300,000 people lived at one time.

The Aztecs were warlike. Prisoners were taken in battle and used for religious sacrifice. As tribes were taken over and more land gained, more taxes and goods were brought into the Aztec Empire. Through wars, the Aztec Empire grew.

Aztec merchants helped to spread the Aztec Empire. By trading with many different tribes, great amounts of gold and silver were brought into the major Aztec cities. The empire's wealth was one reason that great temples and

Historical Pictures Service

The Maya, Aztecs, and Incas developed writing, studied astronomy, and made accurate calendars long before Europeans came to the Americas. The Mayan manuscript (left) was written with pictures and symbols. The Aztec calendar stone (right) was based on careful astronomical observations. And the Incan knot numbering system (far right) was helpful to Incan farmers.

pyramids could be built in the Aztec cities. These buildings were important to the Aztecs because they were often used to honor the sun-god—the most important of the Aztec gods.

■ *Why did the Aztecs fight wars?*

Aztec Society. Religion was the basis for the Aztec way of life. The Aztecs prayed to many gods, but they believed that they were the chosen people of the sun-god. The Aztec ruler was thought to be the child of the sun-god.

The most important group of Aztec society was made up of the religious leaders. These people were the priests of the sun-god. In addition to their religious duties, they kept a history of the Aztec people. Important events and other records were kept on paperlike scrolls. Aztec priests were also teachers. Priests taught children history, craft making, and religious traditions.

Aztec priests made human sacrifices to

Photri

Artstreet

please their gods. The Aztecs feared that the sun would not rise in the morning if human sacrifices were not made. This was because it was also believed that the sun-god needed fresh blood every day in order to remain strong enough to make the crops grow.

Farming was the basis of the Aztec *economy*—a system in which goods are made, divided, and used. Corn was the main crop, but beans, peppers, cotton, and hemp were also grown. Aztec farmers usually grew enough food to support themselves, the priests, and the other people of the cities. In this way many Aztec people could spend more time to better their way of life.

■ *Why did the Aztecs practice human sacrifice?*

The Incan Civilization. About A.D. 1200 the Incas began to build a large empire in South America, which reached its peak between A.D. 1450 and A.D. 1532. In that time the population grew to more than seven million people, and the Incan Empire became the largest Indian civilization in the Americas. The empire took in parts of such present-day countries as Ecuador, Chile, Bolivia, Argentina, and Peru (see map on page 29).

Incan leaders used the empire's natural resources and its workers wisely. Most people had to work for the government on government projects. These projects included the building of palaces, temples, irrigation canals, and roads. They also included the digging of hillside terraces to improve farming.

Stone-covered roads connected all parts of the empire. Merchants used these roads to trade, and government runners provided daily mail delivery. Suspension bridges and baskets on pulleys crossed wide rivers and deep valleys. In these ways trade and communication improved the Incan way of life.

■ *What did the Incan leaders use to help build the empire?*

RECALLING THE TIMES

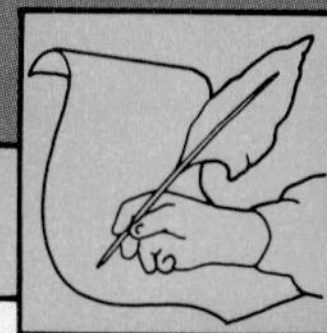

The Inca Empire

The following description of the Inca civilization was written by Pedro Cieza de León, a Spanish soldier, in 1551.

"Since these kings ruled over a land of such great length and vast provinces, and in part so rugged and full of snow-capped mountains and sandy, treeless, arid plains, they had to be very prudent in governing so many nations that differed so greatly in language, law, and religion, in order to maintain them in tranquility and keep peace and friendship with them. Therefore, although the city of Cuzco was the head of their empire, . . . they stationed deputies and governors at various points; these men were the wisest, ablest, and most courageous that could be found . . .

"The Incas always did good works for their subjects, not permitting them to be wronged or burdened with excessive tribute or outraged in any way. They helped those who lived in barren provinces, where their forefathers had lived in great need, to make them fertile and abundant, providing them with the things they required; and to other provinces where they had insufficient clothing, for lack of sheep, they sent flocks of sheep . . . It was understood that these lords knew not only how to be served by their subjects and to obtain tribute from them but also how to keep up their lands and how to raise them from their first rude condition to a civilized state and from destitution to comfort."

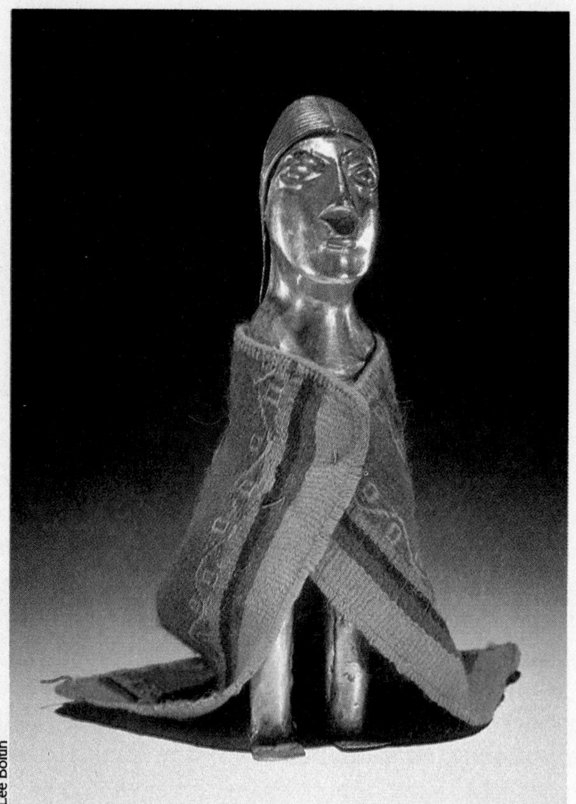

Lee Boltin

Thinking Critically

Why did the kings who ruled over the Inca civilization need to be prudent in governing?

In your opinion, why did the Incas always do good works for their subjects?

Life Among the Incas. The Incan economy was based on farming. Incan farmers were the first people to grow white potatoes. Potatoes were the main food of the Incas; but corn, beans, tomatoes, and several kinds of grain were also raised. All food was kept in special places throughout the empire. The Incan government then divided this food among all the Incan people. In this way, priests, warriors, builders, and artisans did not have to spend time hunting or farming for their food. Rather, they could use their time at the tasks they were trained to do.

Like many other Indian groups, the Incas believed in many gods. They prayed to these gods to provide large crop harvests and to foretell the future. Incan priests, however, did not have as much power as the priests in other Indian societies in Central and South America. This was largely because Incan priests served mainly as medicine men. Thus, they did not have as much political power as did priests in other Indian societies.

■ *What were some of the major achievements of the Incas?*

SECTION 3 REVIEW

1. *What were some major contributions of the Mayan, the Aztec, and the Incan cultures?*
2. *How did the Aztecs enlarge their empire?*
3. *Why was religion important to the people of these cultures?*

CHAPTER 1 SUMMARY

The earliest Americans followed animal herds from northeastern Asia across a land bridge into what is today Alaska. Some evidence found by archaeologists seems to show that the first Americans—later called Indians—may have been in the Americas as early as 100,000 years ago.

As the last Ice Age ended, the early Indians followed herds of animals farther south each year. Over thousands of years, Indians were living in most areas of North, Central, and South America. As the Indians adapted to the many environments of the Americas, new ways of life came about, and different Indian cultures developed. These Indian cultures have made many contributions to our present-day way of life.

Most North American Indians were organized along democratic lines and made their living by farming and hunting. The Indians of Central America and South America also provided for their living mainly by farming. However, better ways of farming helped some Indian groups to use their time for study. In this way three Indian civilizations in Central America and South America made progress in mathematics, in government, in the arts, and in architecture.

CHAPTER 1 REVIEW

USING YOUR SKILLS

Studying a Vegetation Map

The map on this page is a *vegetation map*. That is, it shows the vegetation—plant life—of the North American continent. Study the vegetation map below and answer the following questions.

1. What area of vegetation is found farthest north?
2. What mountain range is found in the eastern part of the continent?
3. In what part of the continent is shrub the most common vegetation?
4. Using the distance scale, what is the distance between the Gulf of Mexico in the south and Hudson Bay in the north in miles? In kilometers?
5. Which vegetation area of the continent, in your opinion, would have been best suited for the early Indians to farm?
6. What geographic factors would have made it difficult for the earliest Indians to migrate southward from Alaska?

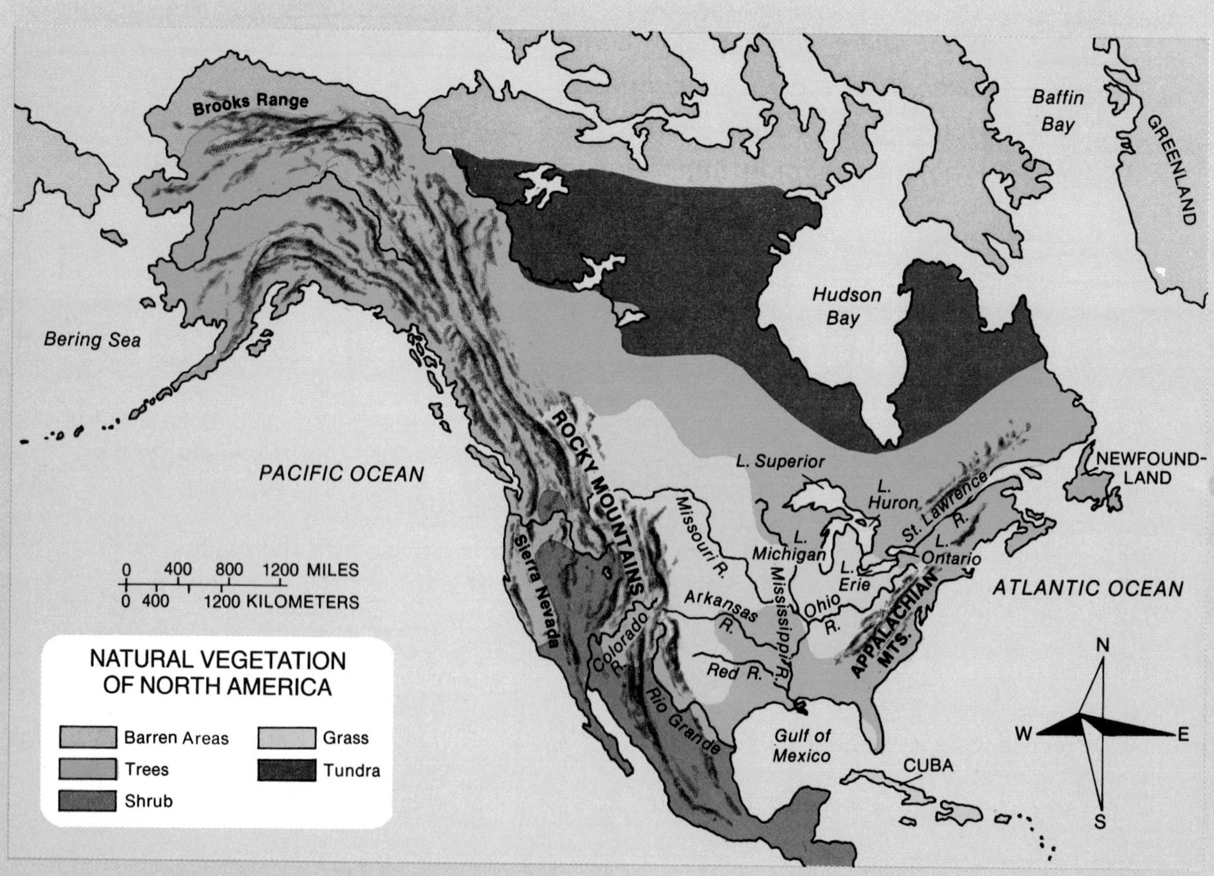

CHAPTER 1 REVIEW

YOU SHOULD KNOW

Identify, define, or explain each of the following:

archaeologists
radiocarbon dating
environments
cultures
technology
agriculture
food surplus
economy

CHECKING FACTS

1. Where did the first settlers to America come from?
2. Name the earliest Indian cultures in North America.
3. What type of agriculture did the Eastern Woodland Indians use?
4. Who made up one of the most advanced societies in the Eastern Woodlands?
5. What Indian tribes made up the Iroquois society?
6. What animal was very important to the Plains Indians?
7. Where did the California Indians and the Great Basin Indians live?
8. Where were Pueblo Indian villages often built?
9. What was the most important part of life in Mayan society?
10. What was the basis of the Aztec economy?

UNDERSTANDING CONCEPTS

1. Why is radiocarbon dating still the most widely used method of dating the past up to 30,000 years ago?
2. How did separate Indian culture areas emerge in North, Central, and South America?
3. In what way did women hold political power in Iroquois society?
4. How did having surplus food affect the Mayan, the Aztec, and the Incan civilizations?

LEARNING FROM ILLUSTRATIONS

1. Study the illustration on page 23. According to the illustration, what were some of the activities needed to provide food for an Indian tribe?
2. In what ways does the buffalo dance, pictured on page 26, depict a buffalo hunt?

CRITICAL THINKING

1. The earliest settlers in the Americas had to adapt to their environment in order to survive. How do the people living in your area adapt to their environment today?
2. Do you think that having a food surplus is important for a culture to advance? Give reasons for your answer.
3. The Plains Indians used every part of the buffalo that they killed. What does this tell you about the importance of the buffalo to the Plains Indians?
4. Do you think learning about cultures such as the Maya, the Aztecs, and the Incas is important to people today? Why do you think so?

ENRICHMENT ACTIVITIES

1. To better understand the many different American Indian cultures, it would be interesting to make a comparative exhibit of clothing, housing, and food found in several American Indian societies.
2. Write a letter to your state or local historical society, and ask for information about the Indian societies that have lived in your area. You could then share this information with your class.

1500 1600 1700

- c. 1000 Leif Ericson, Vikings reach North America
- c. 1300 Renaissance begins in Italy
- 1492 First voyage of Columbus to the New World
- 1497 Cabot leads expedition to the Americas
- 1498 Vasco da Gama finds the ocean route around Africa to the Far East
- 1513 Balboa crosses the isthmus of Panama and sees the Pacific Ocean
- 1519 Cortes captures the Aztec capital city of Tenochtitlán
- 1533 Spanish destroy Cuzco—the Incan capital city
- 1534 Cartier discovers Gulf of St. Lawrence
- 1588 English defeat the Spanish Armada
- 1608 Quebec founded—first French colony in North America
- 1609 Henry Hudson explores the northeastern coast of North America
- 1663 Canada made a French province by King Louis XIV
- 1664 Peter Stuyvesant surrenders all Dutch landholdings to the English troops

CHAPTER 2

The European Exploration of America

Chapter Objectives

After you study this chapter, you will be able to:

- describe the changes in European social, economic, and political systems that helped to bring about a rebirth of learning;
- list the reasons for the decline of Spanish power in the Americas;
- identify the ways European trappers, missionaries, and explorers helped their home countries to colonize large areas of North America.

1 Reasons for the Voyages of Exploration

Overview Many changes took place in Europe during the 500 years before Columbus's discovery of the Americas in 1492. These changes led to voyages of exploration, which in turn led to the discovery of new lands.

Objectives After you read this section, you will be able to:

- identify the changes that occurred in Europe between A.D. 1000 and A.D. 1500;
- discuss how the Renaissance led Europeans to make voyages of exploration;
- explain why many European nations wanted to explore new lands.

Early Explorations. Some people believe that *Viking raiders*—fierce warriors from Scandinavia—and Irish missionaries may have sailed to the Americas hundreds of years before the first voyages of Columbus. According to Irish legends, Irish monks sailed the Atlantic Ocean in order to bring Christianity to the people they met. One Irish legend in particular tells about a land southwest of the Azores. This land was supposedly discovered by St. Brendan, an Irish missionary, about A.D. 500.

Unlike the Irish, who had religious reasons for exploration, the Vikings wanted to gain new lands. In fact, the Vikings received their name from a Norse phrase, *i viking.* This meant "to go raiding."

According to Viking *sagas*—stories about Norse heroes and explorers—Eric the Red sailed westward from the Viking colony at Iceland in A.D. 982. He sailed into the "Sea of Darkness"—the Viking name for the Atlantic Ocean.

Eric and his followers landed in a cold, snow-covered land that had green coasts at its southern tip. Eric named this land *Greenland.* From this base, Leif Ericson—*Eric's son*—led several voyages to lands even farther to the south and to the west. Freydis, Eric's daughter, led one of the last Viking voyages to these lands.

During one voyage to the lands west of Greenland, Leif Ericson made three separate landings. The first landing was at "Helluland." This is thought to have been the southern part of Baffin Island. The second landing was at "Markland." Some experts believe this could have been Newfoundland. The third landing was at "Vinland." This could have been either Newfoundland or Cape Cod.

No permanent colonies were set up at these landings. Some experts believe this was because the people living there—the Indians—were not friendly. For example, Thorwald, Leif's brother, was probably killed by Indians in "Vinland."

No firm archaeological evidence of the Vikings has yet been found in North America. However, remains of houses much like those built by the Vikings have been found in Newfoundland.

■ *Why did the Vikings sail into the "Sea of Darkness"?*

Changes in Europe. After the fall of the Roman Empire in A.D. 476, political and economic conditions in Europe were very unstable. This period of time is called the Middle Ages. The Middle Ages lasted from about A.D. 500 to about A.D. 1300.

During the early Middle Ages warfare among landholding nobles was common. Because of frequent warfare, travel was unsafe and trade became difficult. As a result, many people sought protection of landholding nobles. In return for protection, the people lived on the nobles' estates and helped to farm the land. Gradually, most of these estates—called *manors*—became self-sufficient. That is, the people were able to provide for most of their own needs. Therefore, there was little need for widespread trade.

About A.D. 1000, however, economic conditions in Europe began to change. Trade began to increase. In part, this increase in trade was brought about by the *Crusades.* The Crusades, which began in A.D. 1096, were a series of wars between European Christians and Middle Eastern Moslems. These wars were fought to regain the Holy Land from Moslem control. Crusaders, returning to Europe, brought back such goods as spices, silk, and ivory from the Middle East. This flow of new goods into Europe led to increased trade.

As trade began to increase in Europe, a new social class—the middle class—developed. In general, the middle class was largely made up of *merchants*—people who make their living by buying and selling goods.

Political conditions in Europe also began to change about this time. The growing middle class began to give their support to kings by paying taxes. In return, the kings raised armies to protect the middle class from warring nobles. The kings' rise to power helped to bring

The Bettmann Archive

European life in the Middle Ages was characterized by hard work and isolation. Peasants—members of the lowest social class—farmed the nobles' land in return for protection. But this way of life began to change after A.D. 1000, as trade and contact increased.

greater political stability to Europe. Gradually, nations under the leadership of kings began to take form. As a result of the changes that took place in Europe during the late Middle Ages, a period known as the *Renaissance*—a period of rebirth in learning—occurred.

■ *What economic changes began to take place in Europe, beginning about A.D. 1000?*

The Impact of the Renaissance. The Renaissance began in Italy in the 1300's and quickly spread to most other areas of Europe. During the Renaissance scholars were employed by kings and by nobles to study the arts and the sciences. As a result, great works of art and architecture were created. In addition, many advances in the sciences were made.

Prince Henry of Portugal was a leader who was affected by the new interest in learning. For this reason he started a school to study navigation. He believed that Portugal could increase its trade with countries of the Far East if an ocean route around Africa could be found. Therefore, in 1418 Prince Henry decided to begin a program of exploration. He gathered together people who knew much about such subjects as astronomy, mathematics, and geography. From their studies, Henry could then train sea captains who would make new explorations for Portugal.

Henry had three goals for his school of navigation. First, he wanted the newly trained captains to explore and chart Africa's entire coastline. Second, he wanted to begin a profitable trading system. And third, he wanted to spread Christianity throughout the world. Prince Henry did not live to see his goals met. However, the new ideas of the Renaissance and the new technology of Henry's school of navigation led to many advances. For example, by adapting inventions created by the Chinese centuries before—the magnetic compass, printed maps, and the sternpost rudder—Europeans began a new age of exploration.

■ *What were the three goals of Prince Henry?*

The Age of Exploration. Between A.D. 1400 and A.D. 1600 many European countries began to sponsor voyages of exploration. As a result, this period of time is often called the *Age of Exploration*. The king and queen of Spain, Ferdinand and Isabella, wanted to find an ocean route to the Far East. They paid for several voyages of exploration, led by an Italian sailor named Christopher Columbus.

Columbus sailed westward from Palos, Spain, on August 3, 1492. This was the first of his four voyages sponsored by Spain. After more than two months at sea, the crews of the *Niña*, the *Pinta*, and the *Santa María* saw land. Columbus landed on what is today Watling Island in the Bahamas on October 12, 1492. Columbus called the island "San Salvador" and claimed the land for Spain.

Portugal sponsored more voyages of exploration than any other country in Europe in the years before Columbus's discovery. However, the Portuguese were mainly concerned with finding an ocean route around Africa to India and to China. Vasco da Gama, a Portuguese sailor, sailed around Africa to the Far East in 1498. At the same time, there were few Portuguese voyages to the Americas. Pedro Alvares Cabral, however, landed in what is today Brazil in 1500. This land became Portugal's only major colony in the Americas. By 1500 Portuguese sea power began to decline as the power of other European countries began to grow.

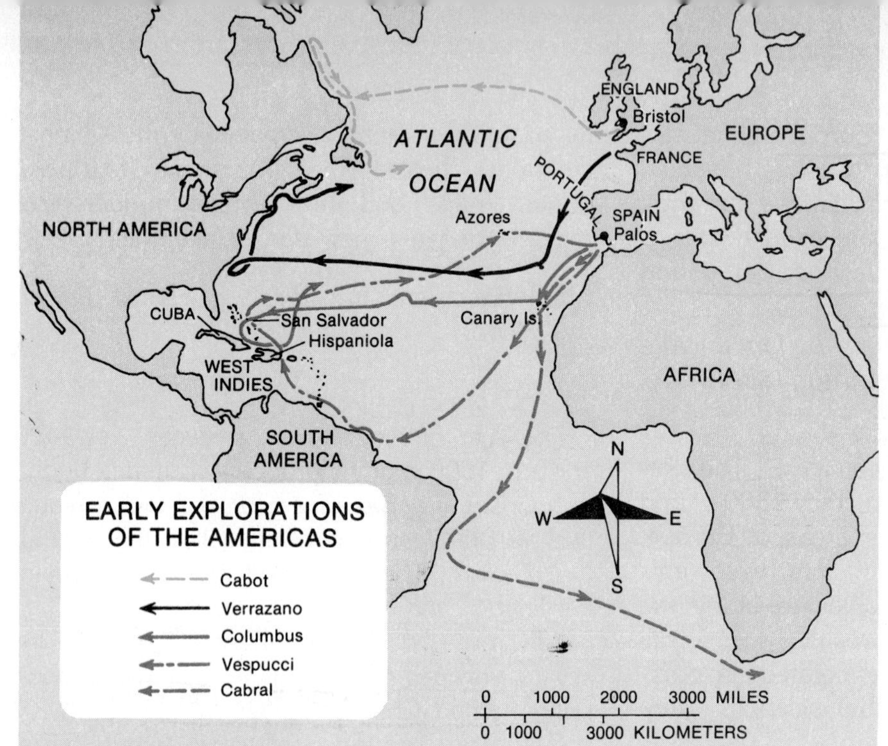

Early European explorers faced many hazards. Food and fresh water often ran short during long sea voyages. And the threat of violent weather plus the lack of accurate charts and other navigational aids added to the explorers' dangers. What two explorers followed the coastline of North America?

England sent its first expedition to the Americas in 1497. This expedition was led by an Italian, John Cabot. Cabot probably landed in Newfoundland. Several years later, in 1509, his son, Sebastian Cabot, discovered the Hudson Straits (see map on this page). Sir Martin Frobisher and Henry Hudson also made voyages to North America for the English in the late sixteenth and early seventeenth centuries.

French expeditions to North America also began in the early 1500's. Giovanni da Verrazano, an Italian, was sent to North America by the French to search for a northwest passage to the Far East. No such passage existed. However, Verrazano charted the North American coast from Maine to the Carolinas. Jacques Cartier led three voyages to North America between 1534 and 1542. He explored the St. Lawrence River and the area near present-day Montreal.

■ *Name four European countries that sponsored voyages of exploration in the late 1400's and early 1500's.*

SECTION 1 REVIEW

1. *What changes took place in Europe between* A.D. *1000 and* A.D. *1500?*
2. *How did the Renaissance lead Europeans to make voyages of exploration?*
3. *Why did many European nations begin to sponsor voyages of exploration in the late Middle Ages?*

PROFILES

The Cabots

Giovanni Caboto, an Italian navigator and trader, was born in Italy in 1450. In the late 1400's, he emigrated to England. Caboto had become an experienced sailor while involved in trade between the eastern Mediterranean Sea and Venice. In England he changed his name to John Cabot. Like Columbus, Cabot believed that a sea route to Asia might be found by sailing west from Europe.

Cabot received the support of a group of merchants from Bristol, an English port city. They financed a crew and a small ship—*the Mathew*—for Cabot. In 1496, King Henry VII of England gave Cabot a license to sail westward in search of wealth.

Cabot and a crew of 18 men set sail from Bristol in May 1497. They landed somewhere along the coast of North America, probably near present-day Newfoundland. Cabot, however, thought that he had reached part of Asia. After claiming the land for England, Cabot explored the area for three weeks and then returned to England. King Henry rewarded Cabot with money and a yearly pension. However, Cabot wanted to go on exploring. In 1498, he set out from Bristol with several ships. John Cabot did not return from this voyage. He most probably went down at sea.

John Cabot's son Sebastian may have sailed on his father's first voyage to America. In 1508 the brave younger Cabot sailed west with two ships. He probed into present-day Hudson Strait and then explored the eastern coast of North America. Sebastian also failed to find a sea route to Asia. Despite the Cabots' failure to find a northwest passage, the Cabot exploration gave England a claim to land in North America.

The Bettmann Archive

Thinking Critically

Why do you think a group of merchants would have been interested in financing a voyage for John Cabot?

What similarities are there between the Cabots and today's astronauts?

In your opinion, what kinds of qualities would John and Sebastian Cabot have possessed?

2 The Spanish in the Americas

Overview Spain was the first European nation to undertake widespread exploration of the Americas. The riches the Spanish found in Central and in South America also paid for more explorations in North America. As the amount of silver and gold declined in Central and South America, so did Spain's power.

Objectives After you read this section, you will be able to:

- identify the main source of Spanish wealth during the 1500's;
- contrast the colonization methods of Spain in South and North America;
- explain why the Spanish Empire began to decline in the late 1500's.

Spain's Dominance in Europe. Spain had become an important power in Europe by 1500. By that time Spain had the strongest army and navy in Europe and took over many parts of Europe. For example, Spain ruled the Netherlands, parts of Italy, and many areas of central Europe. Spain also took over Portugal in 1580.

The Spanish *monarchs*—the kings and queens—held strong beliefs about their country. They were also very religious. Philip II was king of Spain in the mid-1500's. He believed that God had chosen Spain to defend Roman Catholicism in Europe. He also believed that the Spanish should bring their religion to the people of the Americas. Philip II and other Spanish kings and queens sponsored many voyages of exploration to the Americas in the 1500's. They did this to gain new lands and to spread Christianity throughout the Americas.

Because Spain was the strongest power in Europe at this time, other European countries did not want to go to war with Spain. Therefore, few countries were willing to challenge Spain's power in Europe or Spain's exploration and colonization of the Americas in the 1500's.

- *Why did Spain explore the Americas during most of the 1500's?*

Spanish Conquests in Central and South America. During the early 1500's, many Spanish explorations were under way throughout the Americas. In 1513, Vasco Núñez de Balboa sailed to Central America and led his troops across the disease-ridden jungle of the Isthmus of Panama. He became the first European explorer in the Americas to cross this narrow strip of land and to see the Pacific Ocean. Balboa called it the "South Sea."

In 1517, Fernández de Córdoba discovered Yucatán. There he found the descendants of the Mayan Indians. These Indians told him about the great riches of the Aztecs who lived farther north in what is today Mexico. Soon after, Hernando Cortes, also exploring for Spain, led an army into present-day Mexico where he was greeted by Montezuma II, the Aztec leader. The Aztecs believed that Cortes was the fair-skinned god that their religious legends spoke of. Therefore, the Aztecs were not well prepared to fight.

Cortes captured the Aztec capital city, Tenochtitlán, in 1519 after a fierce battle. Cortes destroyed the city in order to build a new, Spanish city. The new city was called Mexico City, and it became the center of the

Spanish Empire in the Americas. By taking over the Aztec Empire, Cortes took great amounts of gold, silver, and jewels for Spain. Land that was good for farming and mines that were rich in gold and silver came under Spanish control. The Spanish also conquered many Indian tribes. The Indians were then made to work for the Spanish.

Francisco Pizarro, another Spanish explorer, led an army into the Incan Empire of South America in 1531. Pizarro destroyed many Incan cities—as Cortes had done to Aztec cities. Finally Cuzco—the Incan capital city—was destroyed by the Spanish in November 1533. The Spanish held Atahualpa, the Indian king, for *ransom*—a demand for riches. In exchange, the Spanish promised to return the king safely to his people. However, Atahualpa was killed by the Spanish while he was held in prison. The Incan Empire then became a part of Spain's landholdings in the Americas.

The conquests of Cortes and Pizarro brought great wealth to Spain (see chart on this page). This wealth helped to pay for more Spanish voyages of exploration and for wars in Europe. Although the amounts of gold and silver in the Spanish-held mines in the Americas began to decrease in the late 1500's, the Spanish believed that their wealth would never fail. As a result, the Spanish did not build a system of *commerce*—the exchange of goods on a large scale—like other European countries were doing at this time. Instead, Spain relied heavily upon taking mineral wealth from its colonies in the Americas.

How did the explorations of Pizarro and Cortes bring new wealth to Spain?

Throughout the 1500's, riches from the Americas poured into Spain. In what year were the riches for Spain the most? What happened to the value of the riches after the year 1600?

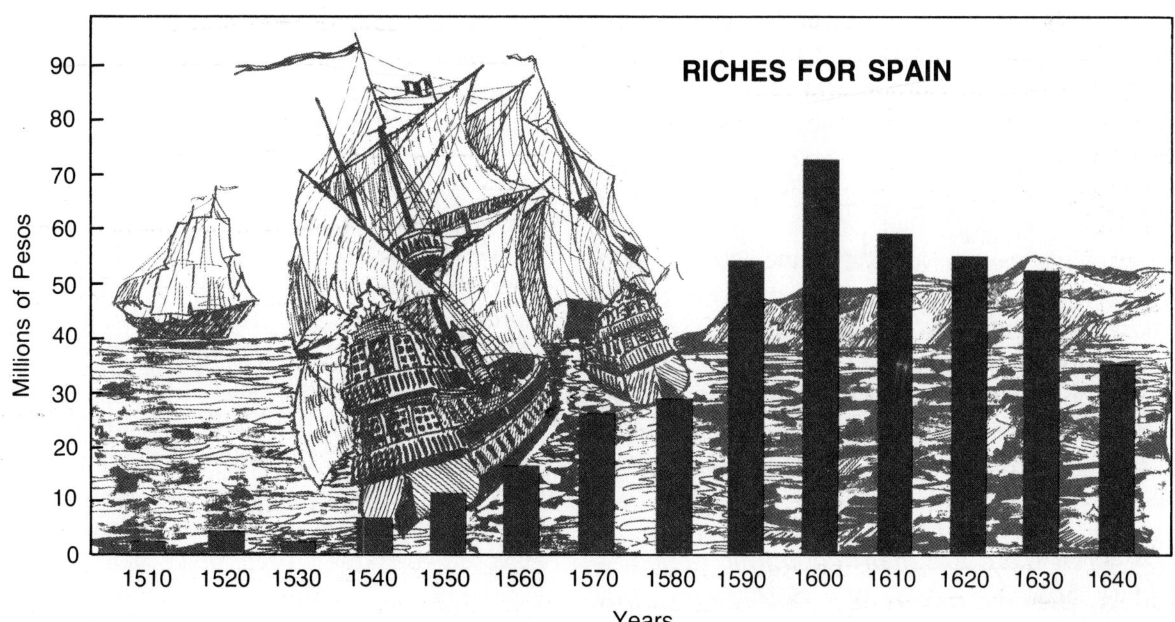

Spanish Colonial Policy. Most parts of Central and South America had been taken over by the Spanish by the mid-1500's. The Spanish Empire in the Americas was then divided into four political divisions called *Vice Royalties* (see map on this page). These were New Spain, New Granada, Peru, and La Plata. In general, these areas were ruled by the Spanish monarch through appointed governors.

Agriculture and mining became the main economic activities of the Spanish colonies in Central and in South America. These colonies supplied Spain with raw materials such as gold, silver, and copper. The colonies also sent farm products, such as wheat and corn, to Spain. In part, this is why Spain became the richest and the most powerful country in Europe throughout most of the 1500's.

Many Spanish explorers and settlers wanted to become wealthy. To do this, many settlers and explorers abused the land. For example, good farmland was overplanted for several years. Also, forests were burned down so that gold and silver could more easily be mined. As a result, the soil was quickly worn out.

Some Spanish explorers and settlers treated the Indians in the Spanish colonies harshly as well. This happened partly because many Europeans thought that people who were different from themselves were not civilized. As a result, many Indians were forced to work long hours in Spanish mines and on Spanish farms. In return for their labor, the Indians were poorly paid—if they were paid at all. Because of such conditions, many Indians died in the years following the arrival of the Spanish to Central and South America.

■ *What were the main economic activities of Spain's Central and South American colonies?*

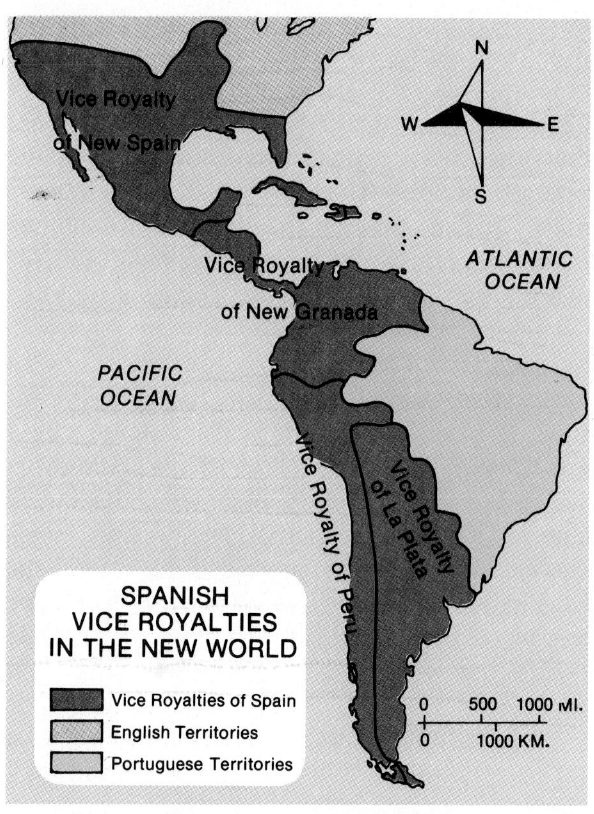

The Spanish Empire in the Americas was divided into Vice-Royalties. This was done so that each area could be governed more efficiently. What were the names of the Vice Royalties of Spain?

Spanish Explorers of North America. Spanish explorers claimed many parts of North America for Spain throughout the 1500's. Ponce de León explored Florida in 1513. He was searching for the legendary Fountain of Youth. In 1528, Pánfilo de Narváez explored western Florida and the northern coast of the Gulf of Mexico. Also in 1528, Cabeza de Vaca and Estevanica—a black explorer—became the first Europeans to explore what is today the southwestern United States.

Hernando de Soto explored the present-day southeastern United States between 1538 and 1542. As he traveled farther west, De Soto began to search for the legendary Cíbola—seven cities made of gold. These probably were Pueblo Indian dwellings that looked as if they were made of gold when the sun shone on their brown adobe walls. De Soto did not find Cíbola, but he became the first European to see the Mississippi River.

Francisco Coronado was also looking for the Seven Cities of Cíbola. He explored as far north as present-day Kansas and became one of the first Europeans to see the Grand Canyon. Juan de Oñate explored the present-day southwestern United States between 1598 and 1605 in an attempt to find the Indian treasures that Estevanica had reported seeing 70 years earlier. However, by the early 1600's, the Spanish knew that large amounts of gold and silver were not easily found in North America.

■ *What were Hernando de Soto and Francisco Coronado looking for in North America?*

The Spanish Empire in North America. By the mid-1600's, the king of Spain believed that Spanish priests could gain new land in North America more easily and less expensively than

Spanish explorers such as Juan Ponce de León (left) and Francisco Coronado (right) claimed all the lands that they explored for Spain. These adventurers also wanted to spread Christianity throughout the Americas and to acquire great wealth for Spain and for themselves.

Photri

The Bettmann Archive

could Spanish soldiers. As a result, land was gained more peacefully in North America than in Central or in South America.

Spanish priests began to set up missions on the *frontier*—the edge of explored land in the late 1600's. Missions were set up in the Carolinas and along the coast of the Gulf of Mexico, as well as along the California coast. The California missions eventually formed a chain that extended from present-day San Diego to as far north as San Francisco.

Indians were attracted to the missions by gifts. The priests then taught the Indians European ways of farming and building. The priests also taught the Indians the Roman Catholic religion and the Spanish language.

The Indians worked for the Spanish, and many Indians lived at the missions. Farm products and items made by hand were sent to Mexico City and to Spain to be sold. Although the Indians were rarely paid for their work, the Indians of North America were not slaves. This was because the Spanish governors of New Spain were influenced by Spanish priests who tried to stop the mistreatment of Indians. Therefore, the Indians who lived in the lands north of Mexico were often given greater control over their own governments than the Indians of Central and of South America. The North American Indians were also allowed to keep some of their own ways of life. Nevertheless, many restrictions were put upon the Indians. For example, Indians were not allowed to ride horses or to use guns.

■ *What did Spanish priests try to teach the American Indians?*

Decline of the Spanish Empire. Changes in European forms of government and in religious thought in the late 1500's brought about many changes in the European economy. One result of these changes was that Spain's economy began to weaken. This was because Spain, unlike many other European countries, had never built up a strong system of trade. Instead, Spain had relied upon the supply of gold and silver from its colonies in the Americas.

As the supply of gold and silver declined, so did Spain's power. In 1588 the Spanish fleet that was to invade England—the Armada—was defeated by the English navy. This defeat caused Spain to lose its position as the strongest country of western Europe. Other western European countries then began to question Spain's claim to land in North America. In particular, the Dutch, the English, and the French began to challenge Spain's power in North America.

■ *Why did Spain's economy begin to weaken in the late 1500's?*

SECTION 2 REVIEW

1. *What was the main source of Spanish wealth during the 1500's?*
2. *In what ways did Spanish colonization of North and South America differ?*
3. *What caused Spanish power to decline in Europe and in the Americas at the end of the 1500's?*

3 The French and Dutch in North America

Overview The French and Dutch built empires in North America from the sixteenth through eighteenth centuries. Missionaries, fur trappers, traders, and adventurers helped build these empires.

Objectives After you read this section, you will be able to:

- identify the main form of commerce in the French and Dutch colonies in North America;
- explain how the Dutch lost their empire in North America;
- describe how the arrival of the Europeans to North America affected the Indian population of the Americas.

French Explorations in North America. French explorers claimed many parts of North America for France throughout the 1500's and the 1600's. Giovanni da Verrazano explored the eastern coast of Canada for France in 1524. In 1534, Jacques Cartier became the first European to reach the gulf of the St. Lawrence River. Cartier was also the first European to sail up the St. Lawrence River as far as present-day Montreal. Cartier claimed these lands for France.

Samuel de Champlain explored large areas of land in the northern parts of North America in the early 1600's. He has been called the *Father of New France,* the name given to the French Empire in North America.

New France consisted of present-day Canada and most areas of the central part of North America. The empire also took in the St. Lawrence River and the entire length of the Mississippi River as well as the Great Lakes. In 1608, Champlain founded Quebec—the first permanent French settlement in North America.

■ *Who established the first permanent French settlement in North America?*

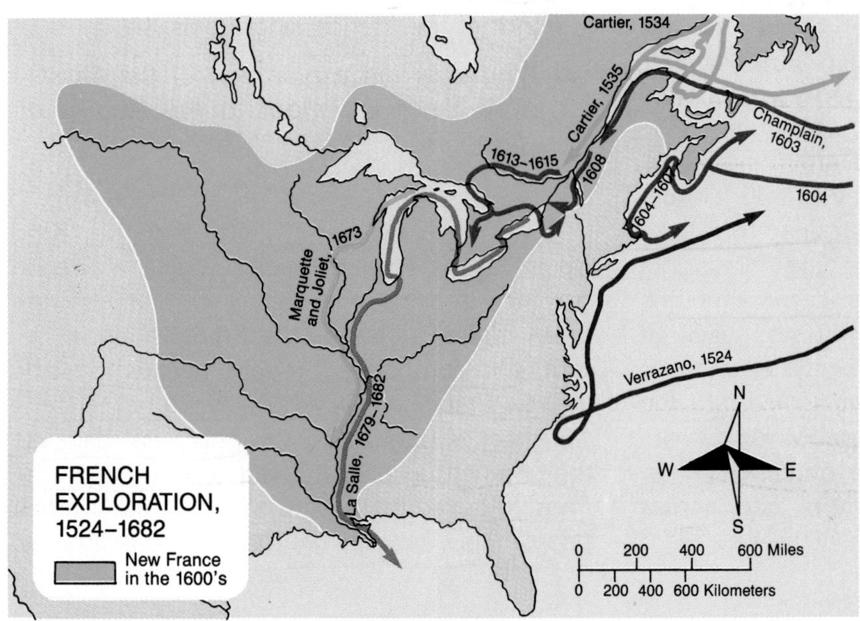

Most French explorers centered their efforts on the St. Lawrence and Mississippi rivers and on the Great Lakes. How are the routes of the explorers distinguished on this map?

The Bettmann Archive

Jacques Marquette, a Catholic missionary priest from France, and Louis Joliet, a French fur trapper, explored large areas of New France in search of a water route to the Pacific Ocean. Marquette and Joliet found the Mississippi River, which became a major artery for the profitable French fur trade. What kind of boats are the explorers using?

French Explorations of the Mississippi River Valley. For many years, French traders had heard the Indians tell about the "Great River"—the Mississippi. It was thought that this river might lead to the Pacific Ocean. The leaders of New France believed that if a passage to the Pacific Ocean could be found by French explorers, France would then control a major trade route to the Far East. In part, this is why Louis Joliet, a trapper, and Jacques Marquette, a Catholic priest, were sent to find a water passage to the Pacific Ocean in 1673.

Marquette and Joliet traveled in birch-bark canoes more than 2,500 miles [4 000 kilometers] from the Straits of Mackinac on Lake Michigan to the point where the Mississippi River and the Arkansas River come together. These French explorers then turned back at that point because it had become clear to them that the Mississippi River flowed into the Gulf of Mexico and not into the Pacific Ocean. They returned to New France by canoeing up the Mississippi and Illinois rivers and across Lake Michigan.

Robert Cavelier, also known as the Sieur de La Salle, explored the lands around Lake Michigan between 1679 and 1682. He was also the first French explorer to explore the entire length of the Mississippi River and to reach the Gulf of Mexico. La Salle then claimed the entire Mississippi River valley for France in 1685. He called the area *Louisiana* in honor of the French king, Louis XIV.

■ *Why was the exploration of the Mississippi River important to the leaders of New France?*

The French Empire in North America. King Louis XIV of France made Canada a French province in 1663. Fur-trading companies were given trading rights by the French king. In return, the companies brought people to settle in New France. However, many French citizens were not willing to move. This was because the French economy was sound and the French government was stable. Most French people were satisfied with their lives in France.

They were not willing to risk losing their possessions or their lives for the uncertain and dangerous way of life in North America. By 1660, there were no more than 2,500 French colonists living throughout New France. Forty years later, only 16,000 people lived in New France. And by 1760, there were no more than 60,000 French colonists living in the vast French Empire in North America.

Montreal was the main trading center of New France. And fur trading was the main economic activity. Farming did not become a major economic activity in New France partially because many French settlements were located in areas of Canada where the growing season was short. As a result, farming was difficult. In other areas of New France, the French settlers were more interested in fur trading than in farming because more money could be earned by fur trading than by farming. In fact, fur became known as French gold.

French fur trappers and traders helped to gain new land for the French Empire. They did this by setting up trading posts along the empire's frontier. In later times many of these posts became cities. Detroit, St. Louis, Green Bay, and New Orleans were once French trading posts.

The government of New France was run by a governor and by an intendant. A governor was a soldier who represented the king of France. The intendant was the head of the colony's Sovereign Council. This council became the lawmaking body of New France as well as its court. The council also carried out the business of the government.

In general, the people of New France did not take part in their government. For the most part, the people trusted their leaders to make decisions for them.

■ *How did French fur trappers and traders help to gain new lands for the French Empire in North America?* By

The Dutch in North America. Dutch merchants also wanted to find a water route through North America to the Far East. In 1609, Henry Hudson, an English sailor, was hired by Dutch merchants to explore the northeastern coast of North America. Hudson sailed into present-day New York Harbor on September 3, 1609, aboard his ship, the *Half Moon.* He sailed nearly 150 miles on what was later named the Hudson River to present-day Albany, New York. Later Dutch land claims in North America were based on this voyage.

Adriaen Block, a Dutch merchant, visited the mouth of the Hudson River in 1614. He then

Henry Hudson, an English explorer sailing under the Dutch flag, traded with the Indians in 1610. What items are the Indians using for trade? Where is the bargaining taking place?

Historical Pictures Service

DO YOU KNOW?

How did America get its name?

The continents of North and South America were named for an Italian explorer, Amerigo Vespucci, by a German mapmaker, Martin Waldseemüller. Vespucci had traveled to the Western Hemisphere in 1499. But unlike Columbus, he did not think the lands he had reached were part of Asia. Vespucci believed these places were a new world. Waldseemüller, the mapmaker, thought that Vespucci had been the first European to reach the new lands. The mapmaker therefore labeled the new lands that he drew on his maps *America* in honor of Vespucci.

sailed north and discovered the Connecticut River. He claimed these lands for the Netherlands. Ten years later, Dutch fur traders founded Fort Orange at what is today Albany, New York.

Throughout the next 50 years, Dutch fur traders set up many trading posts between the Connecticut Valley in the north and Delaware Bay in the south. As a result, Dutch fur traders and settlers took over parts of what would become the states of New York, New Jersey, Connecticut, and Delaware. This area, controlled by the Dutch, was called *New Netherland.*

Fur trading was the main economic activity of New Netherland. A Dutch colony, later called *New Amsterdam*, was set up on Manhattan Island in 1625 by the Dutch West India Company. New Amsterdam was a part of New Netherland and carried on fur trading with the Indians. In 1626, Peter Minuit bought Manhattan Island from the Algonquin Indians for 24 dollars worth of *wampum*—shells and beads used for money. Fur trading between Dutch merchants and the Indians flourished until the mid-1660's.

England had colonies to the north and to the south of New Netherland. King Charles II of England also wanted the Dutch landholdings. In order to take them, King Charles granted the Dutch landholdings to his brother James, Duke of York. The duke then sent his troops to take over New Amsterdam by force. Because New Amsterdam had no more than 1,000 people, the city was not able to defend itself. Therefore, in September 1664, Peter Stuyvesant, the Dutch governor, surrendered all Dutch landholdings to the English troops without fighting.

■ *What was the main economic activity of New Netherland in the early 1600's?*

Dutch Governor Peter Stuyvesant reacted angrily to British demands for New Amsterdam's surrender, but gave up without fighting.

The Granger Collection

The Early European Impact on the Americas. North America was greatly changed by the arrival of the Europeans. By the early 1700's, there were more Europeans living in the Americas than Indians. In part, this was because the Indians did not have natural *immunity*—resistance to infection—against European diseases. European diseases such as measles, smallpox, and typhus killed many native Americans in the 1600's and 1700's.

Also, Indian lands were taken over by Europeans. This brought great wealth to many countries of Europe. However, the land was often abused, and the Indians were frequently pushed off their land and treated badly.

The British eventually took over most of the land in North America that had been held by France, Spain, and the Netherlands. Nevertheless, the presence of each of these nations can be felt in North America today. For example, many people of Quebec, Canada, still speak the French language. In the United States, the influence of France can still be seen in the buildings and in the street names of New Orleans and of St. Louis. Dutch names are still used in New York State. And the Spanish language is spoken throughout many parts of our country today.

The European impact can still be felt in Central and in South America as well. Brazilians, for example, speak Portuguese. And the language of the former Spanish colonies in Central and in South America is Spanish.

■ *What was one impact the Europeans had on the Americas?*

SECTION 3 REVIEW

1. *What was the main economic activity in New France?*
2. *Why did Peter Stuyvesant surrender all Dutch landholdings to the English troops in 1664?*
3. *How did European diseases affect the Indian population of the Americas?*

CHAPTER 2 SUMMARY

Many changes took place in Europe about A.D. 1000. These changes led to a rebirth in learning, known as the Renaissance, about A.D. 1300. Beginning about this time, sea voyages of exploration were sponsored by many countries of western Europe, such as Portugal and Spain. The monarchs and the merchants of these countries wanted to find an ocean route to the Far East.

The Age of Exploration resulted in the discovery of the Americas by Columbus in 1492. Because Columbus had sailed for the king and queen of Spain, all the lands he discovered were claimed for the Spanish Empire. As a result of his voyage, many parts of the Americas came under Spanish control.

As Spanish power weakened in Europe and in the Americas, the French, the Dutch, and the English set up colonies throughout North America. The British eventually became the largest and the strongest European power in North America.

CHAPTER 2 REVIEW

USING YOUR SKILLS

Interpreting Historical Illustrations

The painting on this page is a *historical illustration*. That is, it is a painting that tells a story about an actual event in history. Historical illustrations may be paintings, drawings, sketches, or photographs. This painting tells the story of the Dutch surrender of New Netherland to the English navy in September 1664. The man with the wooden leg is Peter Stuyvesant, the governor of the Dutch colony. He had to decide whether his people should fight the English or surrender without fighting. He finally surrendered without fighting. Study the historical illustration and then answer the following questions:

1. What evidence has the artist included in this picture to indicate that it is of a Dutch colony?
2. What persons—other than the Dutch and the English—has the artist included in the illustration?
3. How do we know that a battle may soon begin?
4. What, in your opinion, might the people be saying to Peter Stuyvesant?
5. In your opinion, does Peter Stuyvesant seem to be agreeing with the men and women in the painting?
6. What elements in this painting might suggest that Stuyvesant was prepared to fight off the English?

The Bettmann Archive

CHAPTER 2 REVIEW

YOU SHOULD KNOW

Identify, define, or explain each of the following:

sagas
manors
merchants
Renaissance
monarchs
ransom
commerce
frontier
immunity

CHECKING FACTS

1. What present-day countries did the Viking raiders come from?
2. What were the Middle Ages?
3. What social class developed in Europe around A.D. 1000?
4. What present-day South American country was once a Portuguese colony?
5. What Spanish explorer was the first European explorer to cross the Isthmus of Panama and to see the Pacific Ocean?
6. What Indian civilizations in Central and in South America were conquered by Cortes and by Pizarro?
7. What Spanish explorer explored Florida in 1513?
8. Which country defeated the Spanish Armada in 1588?
9. Who was called the Father of New France?
10. What was the main economic activity of New Netherland?

UNDERSTANDING CONCEPTS

1. Why did many European rulers and merchants want to find an ocean route to the Far East?
2. How were the Indians of Central and of South America usually treated by the Spanish settlers?
3. Why did Joliet and Marquette explore the Mississippi River?
4. Why were Dutch merchants interested in exploring the northeastern coast of North America in the early 1600's?

LEARNING FROM ILLUSTRATIONS

1. Based upon your study of the illustration on page 36, describe the type of ships used in the 1400's and the 1500's.
2. Study the illustration on page 48. What examples of Indian and of European cultural influences can you find?

CRITICAL THINKING

1. Do you think that the Age of Exploration would have happened without the occurrence of the Renaissance? Give reasons for your answer.
2. What do you think was the main motive for the explorations of the Americas? Why do you think so?
3. Why do you think that the French and the Dutch chose to explore and to colonize the northeastern area of North America?

ENRICHMENT ACTIVITIES

1. Make a bulletin-board display of foreign words and phrases that are commonly used in the English language today. You could include the word, the original meaning, and the country or language from which the word is taken.
2. To understand some of the directional skills the early explorers in the Americas needed, you might like to make a map of your own neighborhood or town.

1600 1700 1800

- 1534 King Henry VIII of England founds the Church of England
- 1606 London Company given charter to set up colony
- 1607 Founding of first permanent English colony at Jamestown
- 1619 First African slaves arrive in Virginia; House of Burgesses formed
- 1620 Separatist Pilgrims land at Plymouth; Mayflower Compact signed
- 1630's Great migration to Massachusetts
- 1681 William Penn founds colony of Pennsylvania
- 1754 to 1763 French and Indian War

CHAPTER 3

The English Colonies in North America

Chapter Objectives

After studying this chapter, you will be able to:

- name the English colonies that were established in North America;
- describe the effect mercantilism had on English society and its need for colonies;
- discuss English colonial policy and how it led to a growth of colonial self-government.

1 Settlement of the English Colonies

Overview Widespread English exploration of North America did not begin until the late 1500's. During this time English adventurers tried to set up colonies in North America. However, they were unsuccessful in their attempts. Between 1607 and 1733, thirteen permanent English colonies were started in North America.

Objectives After you read this section, you will be able to:

- list the reasons for English colonization;
- explain the purpose of the Mayflower Compact;
- compare and contrast the three types of English colonies in America.

Reasons for English Colonization. Many changes took place in England during the 1500's. These changes brought about a greater desire in England for colonies in North America. One of these changes was in farming. English farmers began to use more land for raising sheep than for growing crops in the mid-1500's. This was done because the sale of wool throughout Europe brought in more money than the sale of crops.

Another change that took place in England during the 1500's was in religion. Until the 1530's, most English people belonged to the Roman Catholic Church. In 1534, however, King Henry VIII of England broke away from the Roman Catholic Church and founded the *Church of England*—the Anglican Church. Many English people did not like this change because they wanted to remain Roman Catholics. Other people wanted to *purify*—reform—many practices of the Anglican Church. These people were called *Puritans*. Some Puritans, however, wanted to break away from the Church of England. These people were called *Separatists*.

During the 1500's and the 1600's, the English people who did not support the Church of England were often *persecuted*—punished. Roman Catholics, Jews, Puritans, and Separatists, for example, were sometimes fined, jailed, or put to death for their religious beliefs. Because of this persecution, many of these people wanted to set up colonies in America where they could practice their religion openly. Thus, some English colonies in America were set up as places of *refuge*—safety—for certain religious groups.

■ *Why did the Puritans want to set up a colony in America?*

The First Permanent English Colony in North America. Under English law, all land belonged to the king. King James I *chartered*—gave a permit to—the London Company in 1606. Thus, the London Company was allowed to set up a colony. On May 14, 1607, 100 colonists set up the first permanent English colony in America. The Virginia colony was set up in the area of present-day Virginia. The settlement was made at present-day Jamestown Island and was called Jamestown (see map on page 57).

The Jamestown settlement in the Virginia colony barely survived during its first year in America. This was because many colonists spent their time looking for gold instead of planting crops. Disease and hunger killed about two thirds of the colonists during the first year. However, under the leadership of

John Smith, the colonists were forced to plant crops. Then in 1610, new settlers and fresh supplies were sent by the London Company. In this way the survival of Jamestown was assured.

■ *What was the first permanent English settlement in North America?*

The Pilgrims Settle in Plymouth. The first permanent English settlement in what became known as New England was set up in December 1620. The settlement was called Plymouth and was formed by *Pilgrims*—a group of English Puritans. These people were also called Separatists. The Pilgrims landed on Cape Cod—the eastern-most part of present-day Massachusetts.

Before leaving their ship, the Pilgrims wrote the *Mayflower Compact.* The compact was an agreement about the government of the settlement. The signers agreed that they would obey the laws passed by the majority. The Mayflower Compact was the first written agreement about self-government in America.

Soon Plymouth became a small farming settlement. Its location was poor, however, both for farming and for trade. As a result, its growth was limited.

■ *What was the Mayflower Compact?*

The Types of English Colonies. Three areas of English settlement developed along the eastern coast of North America between 1607 and 1733. These areas became known as the *New England Colonies,* the *Middle Colonies,* and the *Southern Colonies* (see map on page 57).

There were three kinds of English colonies in America as well. *Corporate* colonies were owned by joint-stock companies as *investments*—sources of income or profit. Joint-stock companies were similar to modern corporations. Colonies were controlled by the company that owned them. *Proprietary* colonies were founded and led by individuals who were given grants of land. Pennsylvania and Maryland, for example, began as proprietary colonies. *Royal* colonies were ruled by the

A group of Separatist Puritans in the Plymouth Colony walk through winter snow to church services. Why do you think the men are carrying guns?

The Bettmann Archive

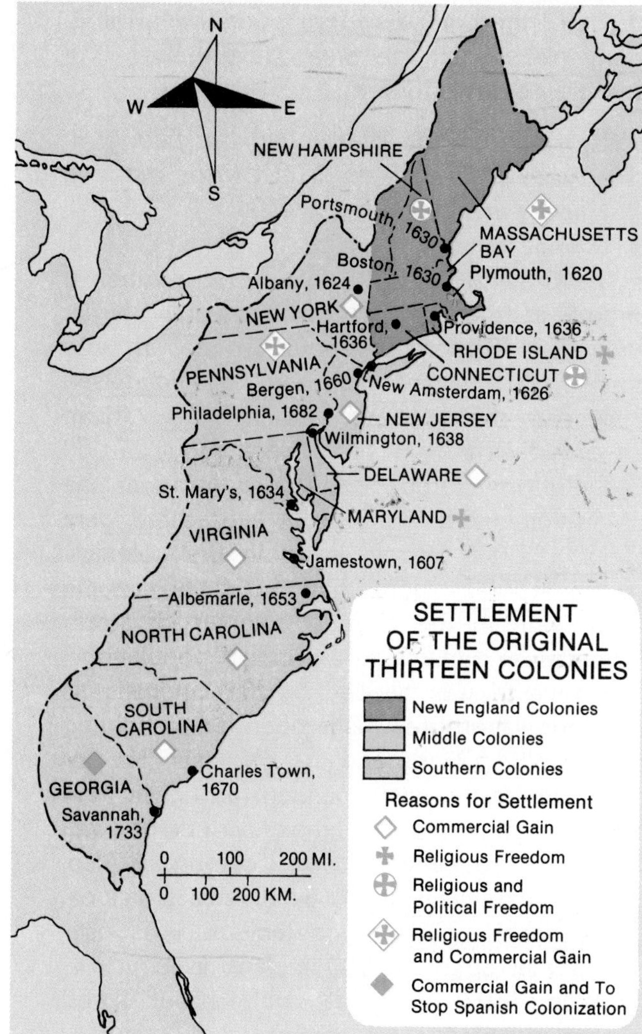

The English colonies in America offered hope for a better way of life to many Europeans. Why was New Hampshire settled? Why was New Jersey settled? Why was Georgia settled?

king or queen. Some royal colonies were set up when the king or queen felt that the proprietor or the company could no longer govern the colony effectively.

■ *What were the three kinds of English colonies in North America?*

The New England Colonies. Most of the New England Colonies were founded in the mid-1600's. For the most part, the New England Colonies were settled by people who wanted religious freedom. The first settlement at Plymouth was made by Pilgrims in 1620. Almost ten years later, a group of English Puritans founded the Massachusetts Bay colony, which eventually took in the Plymouth colony. Within a few years the Massachusetts Bay colony became one of the largest and richest of the English colonies.

For all its success, however, unrest developed in the Massachusetts Bay colony. This unrest led to the establishment of other colonies. Roger Williams and his followers set up the town of Providence in what became the Rhode Island colony.

Connecticut was founded by Thomas Hooker, a Puritan minister, because he and his followers wanted to gain better farmland. New Hampshire and Maine were also settled by people from the Massachusetts Bay colony.

■ *What was the main reason for the settlement of the New England Colonies?*

The Middle Colonies. Four colonies developed in the territory between the Maryland colony in the south and the New England Colonies in the north. These colonial settlements have been called the Middle Colonies (see map on this page).

The Middle Colonies of New York and New Jersey were formed largely from the lands of *New Netherland*—the Dutch empire in North America. Many people who belonged to the *Quaker religion*—the Society of Friends—first settled in New Jersey.

William Penn, a wealthy English Quaker, founded the colony of Pennsylvania in 1681 to provide religious freedom and commercial opportunities for its settlers. The colony was a gift to Penn from the king of England. Delaware, first settled by people from Sweden, became part of Pennsylvania in 1682. Delaware remained a part of Pennsylvania until after the Revolutionary War.

■ *Why was Pennsylvania founded?*

The Southern Colonies. The Virginia colony at Jamestown was the first permanent English colony in America. Later, Maryland was settled by Sir George Calvert—Lord Baltimore—as a place where Catholics and other religious groups could freely practice their beliefs. Religious freedom in colonial Maryland was set forth in the Toleration Act.

During the 1600's, people from Virginia—mainly commercial farmers—settled in lands to the south called the Carolinas. The northern area became North Carolina in 1712. The southern half became the royal colony of South Carolina in 1719.

Georgia was the last of the original Thirteen Colonies to be settled. It was founded in 1733 by James Oglethorpe as a place for prisoners from English debtors' prisons to live. Fifty acres (20 hectares) of farmland were given to each white male settler for commercial farming use. However, because much of the soil was often poor for farming, many people left the area. Nevertheless, the Georgia colony survived.

■ *What was the main way the people in the Carolinas and in Georgia made a living in the early 1700's?*

The Growth of the Colonies. The number of people in the English colonies grew larger each year. The rapid population growth was caused by natural increase, by increased European immigration, and by the African slave trade. By 1640 there were about 27,000 people from Europe and Africa living in the English colonies. Thirty years later, there were about 112,000 people living in the colonies. By the 1750's, more than 1,000,000 people were living in the English colonies of North America—in addition to the Indian population.

More land was needed by the colonists as their population grew. This often led to fighting between the Indians and the colonists. The Indians were often easily pushed from their land because they had no guns or horses with which to counterattack the colonists. Also, European diseases, such as typhus, smallpox, and measles, killed many Indians. It is estimated that about 30,000 Indians lived in Virginia in 1607. By 1669, only about 2,000 Indians still lived in the colony.

■ *What were three reasons for the population growth in the English colonies?*

SECTION 1 REVIEW

1. *What changes in England brought about a greater desire for English colonies in North America?*
2. *Why did the Pilgrims write the Mayflower Compact?*
3. *How did royal colonies differ from proprietary colonies?*

VIEWPOINTS DIFFER

The Legacy of Roger Williams

Roger Williams was a minister at Salem, Massachusetts. He objected to the strong ties between the Puritan church and civil authorities. No government, he held, should have control over religious matters. Williams also believed that the colonists should pay for lands taken from the Indians. For spreading these and other ideas, Williams was forced to leave the colony in 1636.

Historian James Trustlow Adams maintains that Williams was a threat to the existing political and religious welfare of the colony:

His [Roger Williams's] subsequent prominence as the founder of that state [Rhode Island], and his written advocacy of the principle of toleration, have tended to overemphasize the contemporary importance of the proceedings [against him]. The authorities had a fair basis for their action, on civil grounds alone; and although the religious aspect undoubtedly entered largely into the case, it marked, in that respect, no new departure in policy. It merely showed somewhat more clearly, perhaps, that... the magistrates and clergy could be counted upon to act rigorously together. Although personally popular, Williams had acquired few adherents who were willing to follow him beyond a certain point in his struggle, and the victory of the court created but a slight disturbance. The colony, however, in order to avoid even the possibility of strife, had lost what it could ill afford to spare—a mind of wider vision than its own.

Curtis Nettles, by contrast, is sharply critical of the Puritan leaders and views Williams as the victim of persecution:

The stern, inflexible Puritanism of Massachusetts drove into exile four courageous leaders of independent spirit who founded the colony of Rhode Island. Roger Williams, the foremost liberal of seventeenth-century America,... was essentially a humanitarian—a man who could see the good in all sorts of people and who was prone to resist oppression of the weak and lowly by the powerful. Combining the traits of martyr and prophet, he judged issues by the test of justice and equity rather than by expediency or legality, and threw petty considerations of personal advantage and comfort to the winds. Insight and intuition moved him to eloquent, passionate utterance of truth as he felt it, irrespective of logic and authority....

In championing the cause of religious toleration Roger Williams declared war upon the most powerful forces of his time. Persecution was an instrument which all the entrenched churches employed to uphold their supremacy.

Think About It

1. According to Adams, were the authorities right in bringing Williams to court?
2. According to Nettles, why was Williams persecuted?
3. In your opinion, which historian—Adams or Nettles—is more sympathetic towards Williams? Explain your answer.

2 Early Colonial Growth

Overview Most colonists farmed or worked in jobs connected with farming during the 1600's and 1700's. Gradually, however, industries developed. Jobs related to trade and commerce became more common. And colonial society changed.

Objectives After you read this section, you will be able to:

- discuss the effects of the Navigation Acts on the colonies;
- compare and contrast the economic systems of the colonies;
- explain why blacks were brought to America against their will.

The Economic Importance of the Colonies. During the 1500's and the 1600's, the English economy was based on a system called *mercantilism.* Mercantilism was a policy by which a country tried to gain as much wealth as it could. A country could sometimes increase its wealth by becoming as self-sufficient as possible. One way in which countries such as England tried to become self-sufficient was to set up colonies. Colonies provided raw materials that were usually not available in the home country. Colonies also served as a market where goods from the home country could be bought and sold. In this way, the colonists became *consumers*—buyers—as well as workers.

The English government passed laws during the 1600's and 1700's that protected English businesses from competition with other countries and with the colonies. These laws were known as the *Navigation Acts* (see chart on this page). The Navigation Acts were used to control colonial trade, thereby making the colonies more profitable to England.

■ *What was one way the English attempted to make their economy self-sufficient?*

According to the chart below, where could colonial products be sent?

TRADE RESTRICTIONS

Acts	Provisions
Navigation Acts 1650, 1651, 1660–61, 1696	Only English and colonial ships could carry on colonial trade. Goods from Europe first had to pass through English ports. Tobacco, cotton, indigo, and other colonial products could be sent to England only.
Woolen Act 1699	Colonial export of wool or wool cloth forbidden
Hat Act 1732	Export of colonial-made hats forbidden
Molasses Act 1733	Colonies forced to pay high duty on foreign sugar, on molasses, and on rum
Iron Act 1750	No new iron plants allowed in colonies. No duty on iron imported from England into colonies.

Agriculture in the New England and in the Middle Colonies. Farming was the main way of life for the colonists in the New England and in the Middle Colonies. In New England, however, much of the land was often difficult to farm because the soil was rock filled and hard to plow. Also, New England winters were long and cold, which resulted in a short growing season.

Crops such as European wheat often did not grow well in New England. Therefore, the colonists raised corn and other American foods, such as pumpkins, squash, and beans. The Indians had taught the colonists how to grow these foods. Because farming conditions were not ideal, most New England farmers could grow only enough food for their own families. This kind of farming was called *subsistence farming.* Little *surplus food*—extra food—was grown.

The growing season was longer in the Middle Colonies, and the land was more suitable for farming. Grains such as oats and rye grew well in the Middle Colonies. These colonies were sometimes called the breadbasket colonies. Farmers in these colonies could usually grow surplus food, which could then be sold. This kind of farming was called *commercial farming*. Thus, the farmers of the Middle Colonies could earn more money from farming than could New England farmers.

■ *What is the main difference between subsistence farming and commercial farming?*

The Southern Colonial Economy. Farming was more profitable in the Southern Colonies than in the other English colonies in North America. Both subsistence farming and commercial farming were practiced in the South. Commercial farming was done on large farms called *plantations.* This kind of farming gradually became known as the *plantation system. Planters*—the plantation owners—grew crops for their own use. They also grew several cash crops such as tobacco, rice, and indigo. Thus, the development of the plantation system and the introduction of new farm crops helped the southern economy grow.

■ *What main cash crops were grown in the Southern Colonies in the 1600's and 1700's?*

Landowners in the Middle Colonies often lived comfortable lives as farmers. The fertile land produced surplus grain, such as oats, rye, and barley.

New York State Historical Association, Cooperstown

Colonial Economic Growth. Farming continued to be the main source of livelihood for most colonists during the 1600's and the 1700's. However, other industries also developed during this time. Fishing became a profitable way of life in several colonies. By the early 1640's, colonists began to sell large amounts of fish to England and to the West Indies. By the late 1600's, towns in Massachusetts, such as Gloucester, Salem, and Boston, became port cities for large fishing fleets. For example, 430 large ships sailed from Massachusetts in 1676. One hundred years later, more than 2,000 large ships were based in New England. *Whaling*—the hunting of whales—also became a large industry during the 1700's.

As more ships were needed, the lumber industry grew. Forests in most colonies provided wood for shipbuilding. This wood was needed in the English colonies, in England, and in Europe. In addition to shipbuilding, wood was needed to make barrels. In the Southern Colonies, sap from pine trees was made into *naval stores*—tar, pitch, and turpentine.

A trade-route pattern developed among the American colonies, Africa, and the West Indies during the 1600's. This pattern became known as the Triangular Trade (see map on this page). Molasses from sugar plantations of the West Indies was shipped to New England where it was made into rum. In turn, rum and other New England products were sent to Africa. Slaves were bought in Africa with the New England products and were then sent to the West Indies where they were traded for more molasses. In this way, the triangular trading pattern began again. The Triangular Trade was responsible for millions of slaves being brought to the Americas over a period of 200 years.

Trade among the colonies and with other countries grew quickly despite the Navigation Acts. Many new industries, such as iron mak-

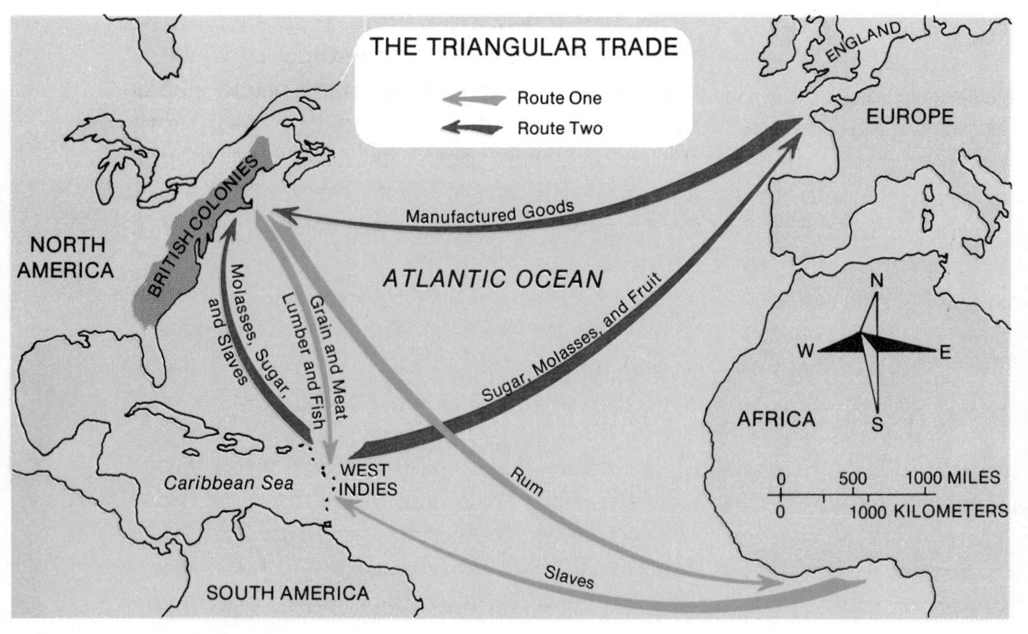

The trade-route pattern known as the Triangular Trade was based upon slavery. Men, women, and children, kidnapped in western Africa, were sold to slave traders in the West Indies and in the American colonies in exchange for raw materials and manufactured goods. What did traders in Africa receive for slaves?

DO YOU KNOW?

Which of the Thirteen Colonies was planned as a silk-producing colony for Great Britain?

Georgia was intended to become Great Britain's silk-producing colony in the early 1700's. Shiploads of settlers and silkworms were sent to the colony to start an industry that would rival the rich silk trade of the Far East. Investors were told that the colony was thickly covered with mulberry trees—the silkworms' food supply. What was not known was that silkworms need the leaves of *white* mulberry trees—not of *black* mulberry trees, which grew in the colony. As a result, Georgia failed as a silk-producing colony.

ing and distilling, also began in the New England and in the Middle Colonies during the late 1600's and the 1700's.

■ *What colonial industry developed as a result of the growth of the colonial fishing industry?*

A Shortage of Labor. The colonies did not have a large labor supply. As a result, many workers from Europe were brought into the colonies during the 1600's and 1700's to fill this need. High wages were promised to people in Europe. However, most people did not want to work for someone else because land in the colonies was often free or inexpensive. Thus, many people could own their own farms.

The major means of obtaining workers was through an *indenture*—a contract to work for a certain period of time. Many people in England did not have enough money to travel to the colonies. Therefore, these people promised to work without wages for those in the colonies who paid for the trip. These workers were called *indentured servants*. At the end of the servants' indenture—usually a period of three to seven years—the servants were free to work for themselves.

■ *How long was the usual period of indenture?*

Involuntary Labor. Some people were put to work in the colonies against their will. This practice was called *involuntary labor*. It was used in every colony. English criminals, for example, were sometimes sent to the colonies for punishment. Some English children were kidnapped and sold as indentured servants. *Debtors*—people who could not pay their debts—were sometimes sold as indentured servants. Indians were sometimes captured and sold into slavery.

The first blacks in America were brought to Jamestown from Africa in 1619 by Dutch traders. These black persons were called "Christian servants." They were treated in the same way as English indentured servants. At the end of their indenture, many blacks gained their freedom and worked on their own farms. William Tucker, born in 1619, is thought to have been the first black child born in America. Thus, the first black people in America were not slaves.

However, there were few available workers in the Southern Colonies during the mid-1600's. It was during this time that the southern economy began to grow, so there was a great demand for workers. Laws were passed in Virginia and in Maryland that made black people slaves for life. This was done because many planters and merchants saw slavery as a source of inexpensive workers. Also, many white people thought that they were better

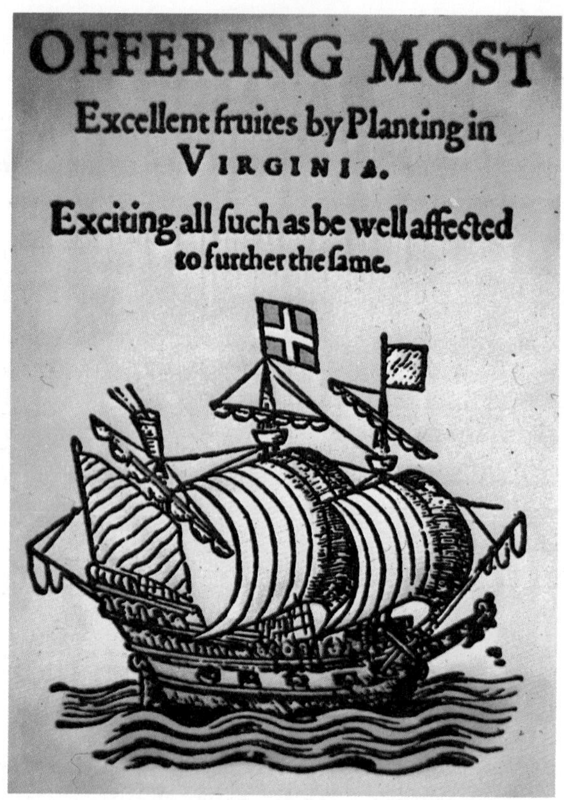
OFFERING MOST
Excellent fruites by Planting in
VIRGINIA.
Exciting all ſuch as be well affected
to further the ſame.

The Bettmann Archive

Many people were drawn to America by advertisements like this. Such announcements were posted throughout England and attracted people hoping to start a new life. What agricultural product is advertised here?

than black people. As a result, slavery grew quickly in the English colonies.

■ *What colonies used the greatest amount of involuntary labor?*

Early Colonial Society. In Europe, society was usually made up of three separate groups of people. A person's *social status*—rank in society—and the social class one belonged to were set by family background and by the job one had. For example, in Europe the upper class was made up of nobles and wealthy landowners. Merchants, teachers, and skilled workers made up the middle class. Unskilled workers and some farm workers—peasants—usually belonged to the lower class.

There were separate social classes in colonial society as well. Wealthy planters and merchants made up the upper class. Farmers, teachers, and skilled workers belonged to the middle class. Indentured servants and unskilled workers made up the lower class. Finally, slaves were at the bottom of the social order in colonial society.

Colonial society in America, however, was less structured than European society. Most colonists believed that the status of people in America could be changed, usually by earning money, by buying land, or by gaining an education. Thus, there was greater *social mobility*—ability to move from one social class to another—in America. However, there was little social mobility for black slaves.

■ *What were the main social classes in colonial society?*

SECTION 2 REVIEW

1. *How did the Navigation Acts strengthen the English economic policy of mercantilism?*
2. *How did the economy of the Southern Colonies differ from the economies of the New England and Middle Colonies?*
3. *Why were blacks first brought to the English colonies in North America?*

3 Political Changes in the Colonies

Overview Great Britain placed few controls on the American colonists. This was largely because between 1607 and 1763, the government of Great Britain did not have an effective plan for ruling the colonies. However, by the mid-1700's, Great Britain began to tighten its control over the colonies in North America.

Objectives After you read this section, you will be able to:

- analyze the English colonial policy in America;
- explain reasons for political unrest in the American colonies during the mid-1700's;
- discuss the importance of the Albany Plan of Union.

English Colonial Policy. The British government placed few controls on its colonies in America until the mid-1700's. Some historians call this a time of *benign neglect.* There were four main reasons for such neglect. First, the king and Parliament were fighting over political power in Great Britain. Second, British leaders were usually too busy with European problems to have much time for colonial interests. Third, the distance between Great Britain and the American colonies made the sending of messages and the shipment of troops and supplies difficult. And fourth, no effective plan for colonial rule was made by the British government before 1763.

During the seventeenth century, the colonies were controlled by many groups within the British government. In 1650, for example, the Council of State was given control of the colonies. Ten years later, however, the Board of Trade took control of all colonial commerce. In 1674, most businesses in the colonies were regulated by the Lords of Trade. In addition, the king's Privy Council—the king's advisers—also wanted control of the colonies.

Many colonists worried that each group within the British government was concerned only with problems of trade and business. Therefore, many colonists began to feel that the English government did not care about the people of the colonies. Also, the lack of colonial control led to a strong colonial belief in *home rule*—a colony's right to govern itself.

■ *What groups within the British government were given some control over the colonies in America?*

The Growth of Self-Government. Every English colony had some form of self-government by the mid-1700's. Early self-government came about partly because most joint-stock companies were allowed to govern themselves. In turn, the companies often let colonists set up their own governments in order to take care of everyday problems. The London Company, for example, in 1618 granted colonists in Virginia the right to set up a lawmaking assembly. The next year, in 1619, Virginia landowners formed the *House of Burgesses,* the first legislative assembly in America. Over the years, colonial governments gained greater control over local affairs.

Not all colonial governments were formed in the same way, however. Nevertheless, by the mid-1700's each colony had a governor, a council, and an assembly. A colony's charter—royal, proprietary, or corporate—set the ways in which people were chosen for office in colonial government. For example, in

Virginia State Library and Archives

Representative government in America grew out of colonial assemblies, such as the Virginia House of Burgesses. The House of Burgesses, founded in 1619, was America's first lawmaking body.

a royal colony the governor was appointed by the king, in a proprietary colony by the proprietors, and in a corporate colony by the stockholders. Only in Rhode Island and in Connecticut was the governor elected by the people. By the mid-1700's, however, most colonies had become royal colonies, and the governors were chosen by the king. The governor then appointed a council whose role was to provide the governor with advice.

Colonial assemblies, on the other hand, were made up of people who were elected directly by the voters of each colony. The right to vote, however, was usually given only to adult, white males who owned land. Later, these colonial assemblies became the basis for representative government in America.

As the colonies grew, most colonists came to have little direct contact with their colonial government. Instead, the colonists came to rely upon local governments for such services as maintaining law and order; for surveying new areas of land; and for building and taking care of public roads, buildings, and bridges.

Two kinds of local government developed in the colonies. *County courts* became the most common kind of local government in the Southern Colonies. *Town meetings* became the most common kind of government in the New England Colonies. Both kinds of local government were used in the Middle Colonies. These local governments came about because they met the needs of the people.

Throughout the colonial period local governments had contact with the colonial governments. However, neither kind of local government was strongly tied to the government of Great Britain—the Crown. Local governments, therefore, became more important to the colonists as unrest between the colonies and Great Britain grew.

■ *Why did the American colonists favor their local governments more than the colonial governments of Great Britain?*

Growing Political Unrest. During the mid-1700's Great Britain tried to tighten its control over its colonies in America in order to make the colonies more profitable. In part, this was because many colonists had ignored the British laws controlling trade. Also, by this time, the British Parliament had gained greater control of the British government. Therefore, the king had less power, and the Parliament was able to establish a stronger colonial policy. Many colonists had grown used to controlling their own trade. In addition, many colonists felt that their local governments could take care of colonial problems better than the British government could. Many colonists also believed that the British Parliament did not really represent American interests. The colonists felt this way, in part, because American colonists could not vote for members of Parliament.

Unrest also arose because many colonists had begun to think of themselves more as Virginians, Rhode Islanders, and so on, rather than as British people. This change came about because most colonists by the mid-1700's had been born in America. Therefore, their loyalty was greater to their colony than to Great Britain. This feeling grew stronger when European problems and conflicts over land in North America caused fighting to break out between France and Great Britain.

■ *Why did the colonists begin to think of themselves as "Americans"?*

The Colonial Wars. Great Britain fought a series of major wars against its old enemy, France, between 1689 and 1763. These wars were fought in Europe and in North America. In part, the colonial wars grew out of European political problems. However, control over land in North America also led to the fighting. For example, both France and Great Britain claimed the land of present-day Nova Scotia. Lands near the Great Lakes and lands between the Appalachian Mountains and the Mississippi River were also claimed by both countries. The Ohio Valley was especially important because fur trapping there was a profitable industry for Great Britain and for France.

Some American Indians also became involved in the colonial wars. British soldiers and colonists were often helped by the Iroquois Indians because the Iroquois Indians did not like the French. Early French explorers, such as Samuel de Champlain, helped other Indian tribes fight against the Iroquois Indians in the early 1600's. However, the French had Indian *allies*—friends—as well. The Algonquin Indians

Land, raw materials, and political alliances were most often the reasons why Britain and France fought four wars in less than a century.

BRITISH–FRENCH WARFARE 1689–1763

In America	In Europe
King William's War 1689–1697	War of the League of Augsburg 1689–1697
Queen Anne's War 1702–1713	War of the Spanish Succession 1702–1713
King George's War 1744–1748	War of the Austrian Succession 1740–1748
French and Indian War 1754–1763	Seven Years' War 1756–1763

were afraid of losing their lands to the British because British settlements spread westward more quickly than did French settlements. Thus, the Algonquin Indians joined with the French to fight against the spread of British settlements in North America. Nevertheless, European settlers continued to take over Indian lands as the wars in North America went on.

The last colonial war between France and Great Britain broke out in 1754. It has come to be known as the *French and Indian War.* At that time the French had built a line of forts throughout the Ohio Valley to protect their land claims. The British, however, wanted to drive out the French. As a result, fighting broke out in 1754 and lasted until 1760. The fighting between the two countries lasted until 1763 in Europe.

British soldiers in America did not fight well during the early part of the war because they were not trained to fight under frontier conditions. However, as the British learned how to fight more effectively on the frontier, they began to win the war.

What was one reason why France and Great Britain fought four wars in North America?

Impact of the French and Indian War. The outcome of the French and Indian War was important to Great Britain and to the English colonies in America. British troops captured Quebec—the capital of New France—in 1759. Montreal—the center of French trade in America—was captured soon after. Because of these battles, the French Empire in North America came to an end. The Treaty of Paris gave Great Britain control of all the land east of the Mississippi River as well as all lands of present-day Canada.

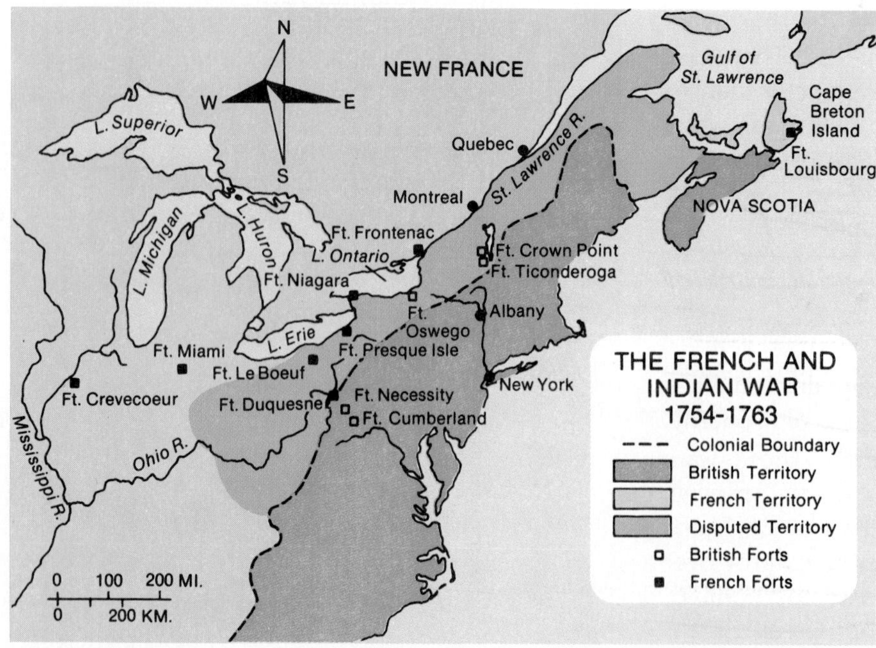

The British army joined with the Iroquois Indians in a war to take over the rich French fur trade and the large land area of New France. The British victory in 1763 provided the British colonies with great room for expansion. What is the closest French fort to British territory? How many British forts were built in disputed territory?

English colonists in America benefited from the French and Indian War as well. More unity among the colonies resulted from the war. In 1754, for example, seven British colonies sent representatives to a meeting in Albany, New York. These people drew up a plan to defeat the French. They also voted on a plan to form a union of the colonies. This plan for union was proposed by Benjamin Franklin and was called the Albany Plan of Union. Although the plan was never agreed upon, it was important because it showed that the colonists were beginning to think about joining together.

The French and Indian War also was important because it was a training ground for many colonists who later fought in the American Revolution. George Washington, for example, led British and colonial troops in one of the first battles of the war. In addition, when the war ended, British settlers were able to move westward without fear of the French.

Following the French and Indian War, Great Britain again began to try to exercise greater control over its colonies in America. In part, this was because many colonial governments had refused to help pay for the war. At the same time, many colonial merchants had traded with France during the war. However, within a few years Great Britain's policies began to anger many colonists.

■ *What lands did Great Britain gain from France as a result of the French and Indian War?*

SECTION 3 REVIEW

1. *Why did the British government neglect the colonies in America until the mid-1700's?*
2. *Why was there growing political unrest in colonial America during the mid-1700's?*
3. *Why was the Albany Plan of Union important?*

CHAPTER 3 SUMMARY

Thirteen English colonies were established in North America between 1607 and 1733 for several reasons. Some early colonists wanted to practice their religion freely. Other colonists wanted to find a place to make a living. Still other colonists hoped to find great wealth. These people helped the colonies to grow—both economically and geographically.

During the 1600's and the 1700's the economies of the colonies grew. New industries arose, and trade increased. The population of the colonies also became larger at this time. The society that came about in the English colonies, however, was less structured than European society.

English control over its colonies in America was not strong until the mid-1700's. However, when the British government eventually began to tighten its control over colonial trade and government, unrest began to grow. At the same time, the colonies in America benefited from fighting a series of four wars with France—the last of which has become known as the French and Indian War.

CHAPTER 3 REVIEW

USING YOUR SKILLS

Interpreting a Time Line

The illustration on this page is called a *time line*. Time lines tell when certain events took place. They also help to put events in *perspective*. That is, by looking at a time line, one can see events in the order in which they took place. The time line below is made up of two parts. The top part of the time line is a series of events that took place in England between 1600 and 1620. The bottom part of the time line lists events that took place in America. Study the time line below, and then answer the following questions:

1. Based on the time line, which event took place first: the founding of Quebec or the arrival of the Pilgrims in America?
2. How many years did it take the Pilgrims to arrive in America after they left England for Holland?
3. Based on the time line alone, which nationality groups founded settlements in America between 1600 and 1620?
4. When was the right to form America's first legislative assembly granted?
5. How many years passed between Champlain's exploration of the St. Lawrence River and his founding of Quebec?

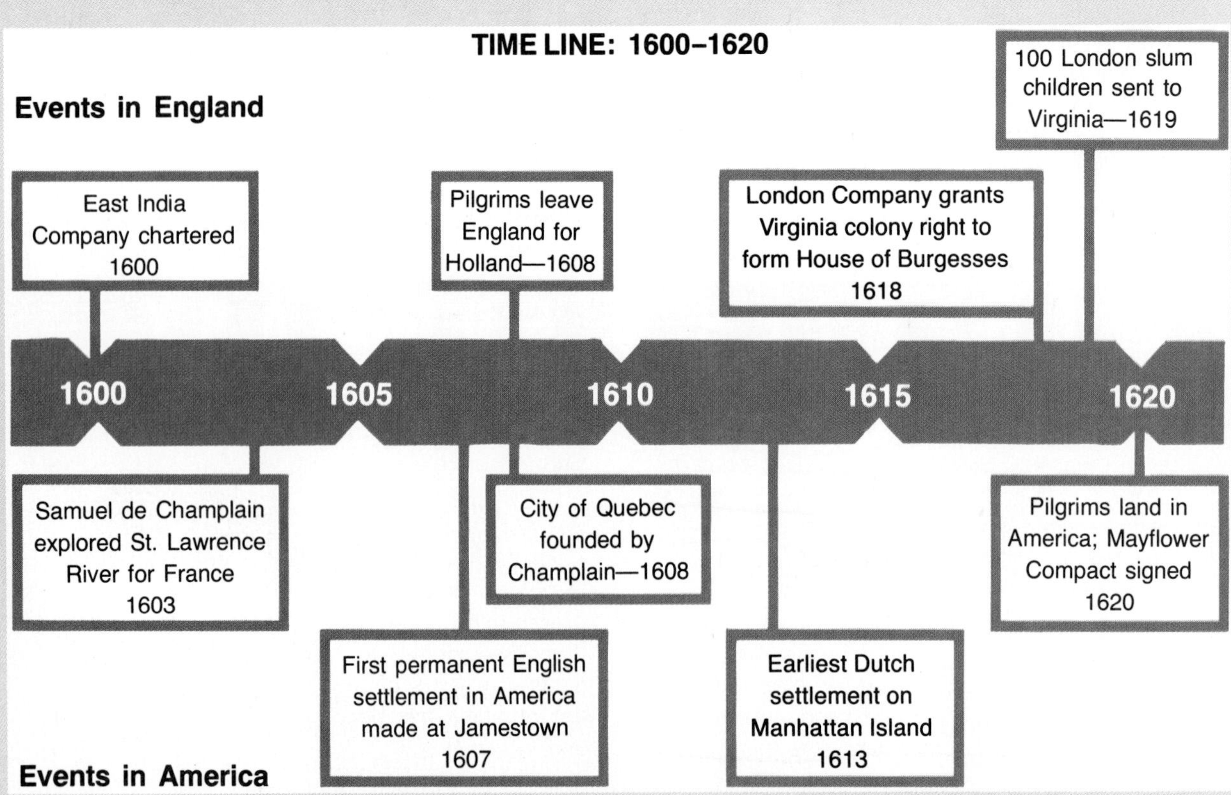
TIME LINE: 1600–1620
Events in England
East India Company chartered 1600
Pilgrims leave England for Holland—1608
London Company grants Virginia colony right to form House of Burgesses 1618
100 London slum children sent to Virginia—1619
1600
1605
1610
1615
1620
Samuel de Champlain explored St. Lawrence River for France 1603
First permanent English settlement in America made at Jamestown 1607
City of Quebec founded by Champlain—1608
Earliest Dutch settlement on Manhattan Island 1613
Pilgrims land in America; Mayflower Compact signed 1620
Events in America

CHAPTER 3 REVIEW

YOU SHOULD KNOW

Identify, define, or explain each of the following:

refuge	indentured servants
chartered	social mobility
consumers	benign neglect
commercial farming	home rule
plantations	allies

CHECKING FACTS

1. What church did King Henry VIII of England found?
2. Who were Separatists?
3. What was the first permanent English colony in America?
4. Why was Georgia founded?
5. What was mercantilism?
6. What is subsistence farming?
7. What four social classes made up colonial society?
8. What were the main reasons for the British government's benign neglect of its colonies in America?
9. What two kinds of local governments developed in the colonies?
10. What did the French build to protect their land claims in the Ohio Valley?

UNDERSTANDING CONCEPTS

1. Why did the Pilgrims write the Mayflower Compact?
2. How were corporate, proprietary, and royal colonies different?
3. Why did Parliament pass the laws known as the Navigation Acts?
4. Why did political unrest grow in the colonies in America during the mid-1700's?
5. How did the French and Indian War benefit the English colonists in America?

LEARNING FROM ILLUSTRATIONS

1. According to the map on page 57, for what reason were the majority of the Thirteen Colonies settled?
2. Study the map on page 68. How did the French attempt to extend their influence from Montreal to the Mississippi River? How did the English defend their colonial frontier?

CRITICAL THINKING

1. If you had been a Pilgrim on the *Mayflower*, would you have signed the Mayflower Compact? Why or why not?
2. Do you think an indenture was a fair way to obtain workers? Give reasons for your answer.
3. Why, do you think, did the Algonquin Indians prefer that the French control the Ohio Valley rather than the British?

ENRICHMENT ACTIVITIES

1. Make a model of a seventeenth-century New England or Virginia village, using papier-mâché and cardboard. Your model could be based on sketches found in encyclopedias or history books.
2. Imagine that you are an English colonist living in America in 1754. Write fictional letters to your friends in England telling about such things as your daily life, your government leaders, your dealings with the Indians, and other aspects of colonial life.

CHAPTER 4

CLOSE-UP: The Lost Colony of Roanoke

INTRODUCTION

Early in the summer of 1585, 108 men set up the first English colony in North America. The colony was set up on Roanoke Island (see map on page 74). Within a year of establishment, many of these men were dead, having died of hunger and disease. In June, 1586, Sir Francis Drake—an English adventurer—stopped at Roanoke Island and took the remaining colonists back to England. The colony had failed.

It so happened that a month after Drake's rescue, a relief ship filled with supplies for the Roanoke colonists arrived at the island. Finding no one there, the captain ordered the ship to sail on. Nevertheless, the ship's captain left 17 men on the island to protect England's claim to North America. This was the second attempt by the English to establish a permanent colony in America.

The third attempt to establish a permanent English colony in America was led by John White and was also made at Roanoke. White, and the colonists who accompanied him, arrived at Roanoke Island in July, 1587—nearly a year since the relief ship left the 17 men on the island. But when White and the other settlers came ashore at Roanoke, no one was there to meet them. The 17 men had vanished—a hint, perhaps, of what would become of John White's Roanoke Colony—the Lost Colony of Roanoke.

1 Founding the City of Ralegh

John White, the leader and governor of the third attempt to colonize Roanoke, was hopeful. When he came to Roanoke Island, he brought with him his daughter, Eleanor, and her husband, Ananias Dare. In the years that followed White's landing at Roanoke, however, White was to experience a long separation from his family. He was also going to confront the unknown.

The City of Ralegh. In July, 1587, a group of English men, women, and children founded a colony on Roanoke Island—a small island off the coast of present-day North Carolina. The English colonists called their settlement the "City of Ralegh." Although it was spelled differently, the settlement was named after Sir Walter Raleigh—a wealthy English noble who supported the establishment of colonies in America.

The City of Ralegh—the Roanoke Colony—was made up of 119 colonists. There were 91 men, 17 women, and 9 children. Also, two babies were born on Roanoke Island between July 16, 1587, and August 27, 1587. One of these babies was Governor John White's granddaughter, Virginia Dare. Virginia was born on August 18, 1587. She was the daughter of Eleanor and Ananias Dare. Virginia was the first baby born of English parents in America.

After only a few weeks on Roanoke Island, the colonists knew that they would need more supplies from England. They did not have enough food to last the winter, and it was too late in the season to plant new crops. Because of these problems, the colonists voted to send Governor White back to England to get more supplies for the Roanoke Colony.

John White's map of the coast of present-day North Carolina provided accurate information for generations of sailors.

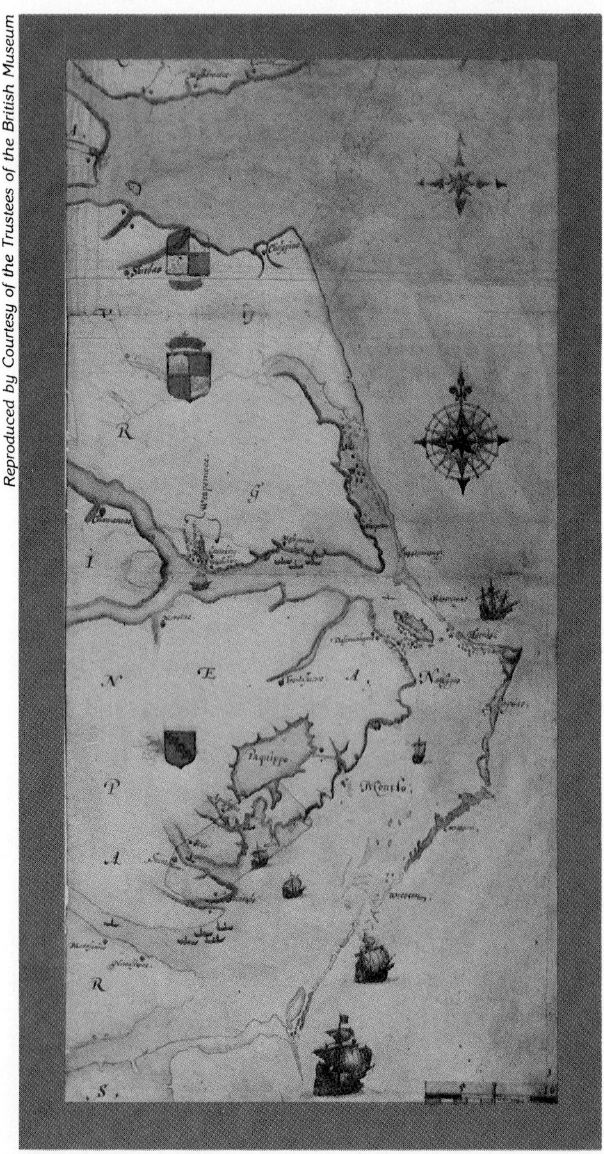

The first attempt at settlement in 1585 had failed. This made Governor White even more determined that his colony would not fail. Although he did not want to leave his family, Governor White sailed back to England in August, 1587. He believed that he could return to Roanoke—and to his family—within six months. However, he soon discovered that this was not to be. John White was the last English person to see the Roanoke colonists alive.

Why did Governor White sail back to England in August, 1587?

The Spanish Threaten England. After his return to England, Governor White twice tried to sail back to Roanoke with supplies. Both attempts failed because of attacks on his ship by Spanish warships. Hundreds of Spanish ships were being fitted out to attack England. And by 1588, every able English ship was being prepared to defend England against the Spanish Armada—an invasion force determined to conquer England. This is why no ship was available to take Governor White back across the Atlantic Ocean to the Roanoke Colony. But John White did not give up hope. He knew that he would return to Roanoke after the Spanish invaders were beaten.

Why did Governor White find it difficult to get back to America?

Return to Roanoke. Three years after leaving Roanoke to return to England, Governor White was finally able to obtain a ship to take him back to his family.

John White sighted Roanoke Island on the evening of August 17, 1590. Sea gulls shrieked under the setting summer sun. Mists, rolling in from the sea, gently shrouded the shoreline. The governor was happy. He later wrote, ". . . [W]e saw a great column of smoke rising from Roanoke Island, near the spot where I had left our colony in the year 1587. The smoke gave us good hope that some of the colony were still there, awaiting my return from England. . . .

"We hailed the shore with friendly greetings, but got no answer. At daybreak we landed, and when we approached the fire we found the grass and some rotten trees burning." This was the first disappointment Governor White was to have. The Roanoke Colony—and the governor's family—was not there. The entire colony had disappeared.

Although the governor was saddened that his family was not at Roanoke, he did not give up hope of finding them. Before the governor had left Roanoke in 1587, he and the colonists had worked out a way to leave messages in the event the colonists had to leave Roanoke for any reason. The colonists had agreed to carve the name of the place they were going to into a tree or some other structure that could easily be seen. If there was danger, the colonists would also carve a cross over the word. Governor White and the sailors from his ship searched the colony for any signs the settlers may have left.

Two signs were found. The word *CROATOAN* was found, carved into the bark of a tree near the settlers' fort. Also, the letters *CRO* were carved into another tree nearby. No cross—the signal of danger—was found. John White was relieved.

■ *What sign made John White think, as his ship came near the island, that the colonists were still on Roanoke Island?*

The Search for the Colonists. Croatoan was an island off the coast of present-day North Carolina close to Roanoke Island. Croatoan was part of the Outer Banks off the eastern coast of North America. Governor White knew

Finding the name CROATOAN—a name that referred to a group of Indians and also to a nearby island—carved into a tree brought new hope to John White that the Roanoke colonists would be found alive and safe. The colonists' signal for danger—a cross—was not found.

Historical Pictures Service

The Bettmann Archive

John White sketched many of the things that he saw in the New World. This drawing shows Pomeioc, an Indian village. How is the village protected from attack?

that friendly Indians lived there. He was sure that his colony—and his family—had moved there in order to have enough food to eat or in order to escape from unfriendly Indians. Although no proof of fighting was found at Roanoke, it seemed possible that Indians had looted some of the materials the colonists—and Governor White himself—had left behind on Roanoke Island. But whatever reasons the colonists had for leaving, John White was happy to know that they had left a message telling where they had gone. He was also sure that he would see his family soon. He thought about his granddaughter, Virginia, who would have just had her third birthday.

As the governor's ship left the harbor at Roanoke on its way to Croatoan, the ship lost all its anchors during a fierce tropical storm. As a result, the ship was almost grounded several times. The sailors became worried. Without anchors to secure the ship in a harbor, it would be too dangerous to land at Croatoan. The ship had to be refitted first with anchors before the sailors would sail into a harbor as dangerous as the one at Croatoan. Governor White knew that refitting the ship meant a delay of at least a year. This was because the ship had to return to England to receive proper fittings. The governor was told that he would have to wait to rejoin his family and his colony. Sadly, the governor watched the sandy shoreline of Croatoan Island pass by as his ship, the *Hopewell,* set sail for Trinidad—where fresh food and water would be taken aboard—and then for England.

■ *Why did the governor's ship, the* Hopewell, *have to return to England?*

SECTION 1 REVIEW

1. *Why, in your opinion, did the Roanoke colonists carve the word CROATOAN and the letters CRO into trees on Roanoke Island?*
2. *In your opinion, why would the loss of anchors have put John White's ship in danger?*
3. *Why might the Roanoke colonists have left Roanoke Island before John White's return?*

2 The Mystery of Roanoke

John White was unable to make a fourth trip to Roanoke Island to search for his colony and for his family. Nevertheless, the Roanoke colonists became a topic of conversation throughout England in the early 1600's. Even today, a great deal of mystery still surrounds the third attempt to set up an English colony on Roanoke Island.

Solving the Mystery. Sir Walter Raleigh sent out five search parties to look for the Roanoke colonists. The last search took place in 1602. Because Spain and England were fighting during the time of the Roanoke colony's disappearance, some people believe that Spanish soldiers captured the people of Roanoke and killed them. However, no records from Spain mention such an event. Some Spanish records do show, however, that Spanish soldiers did land at Roanoke Island sometime in late 1590—after Governor White had returned to England in the *Hopewell*. The Spanish, like Governor White, did not find the Roanoke colonists. Governor White—like all England—never learned what became of his family or of his colony.

A second theory holds that the colonists—believing that Governor White might not return from England with the needed food and supplies—built small boats and tried to sail back to England. If so, their boats were probably much too small for an ocean crossing. The boats may have turned over in a storm at sea, and all the colonists may have drowned. A similar idea is that the colonists were drowned as they sailed from Roanoke Island to Croatoan Island.

The area of ocean just east of the Roanoke and Croatoan islands is still known as the Graveyard of the Atlantic. This is because shipwrecks and other accidents—many unexplained—have taken place in this part of the ocean. In fact, so many accidents have taken place in and near this part of the Atlantic Ocean that some people in modern times have called this area and areas to the southeast of Roanoke Island the Devil's Triangle. Hundreds of people have been lost at sea in this area.

In England in the early 1600's, however, many people believed that the Roanoke Island colonists were captured by unfriendly Indians. If so, the Indians may have taken the colonists inland, away from the coast. Then, it was believed in England, the Indians made slaves of the English colonists. This particular theory was talked about widely in England after the disappearance of the colonists became known. Many people in England believed this theory to be true, even though on his last trip to Roanoke Island John White stated that he found no signs of fighting between the colonists and the Indians. One result of this widespread belief was that English adventurers did not try to set up other colonies in America for more than ten years. And when colonization did start up again, the English settlers landed north of the Roanoke Island colony and away from the Outer Banks.

One final theory is that the colonists went to live with the nearby Croatoan Indians—as the signals carved into the trees on Roanoke Island indicated. The Roanoke colonists may have given up hope of being rescued. The colonists may have needed food, or they may have been escaping from unfriendly Indians. The colonists may have been fleeing from Spanish soldiers or even from English pirates, who often used the harbors and inlets of this region to hide from Spanish ships.

Eventually, however, it is believed that the colonists of Roanoke became part of the Croatoan Indian tribe. The colonists could have traveled away from the seacoast of present-day North Carolina. Some people believe that as the surviving colonists went farther and farther west, and as several years passed, the colonists eventually married into the Croatoan tribe. Amazingly, there seems to be some evidence of such an occurrence.

■ *Why would people in England have hesitated to come to America after learning of the Roanoke colony's disappearance?*

Finding the Lost Colonists. When white hunters first came to the area of present-day Robeson County, North Carolina, in 1719, they found an unusual tribe of Indians living 200 miles [322 kilometers] from Roanoke Island. The Indians of Robeson County called themselves the Croatoan tribe. But more important, they were light skinned. Some of the Indians had blue eyes. Others in the tribe had gray eyes. Usually, Indians have copper-colored skin and dark eyes. Of even greater surprise to the hunters, the Indians spoke English. Later study showed that 54 Indian family names were the same as those of the Lost Colonists. A 1935 study showed that the kind of English still being spoken by about 12,000 Indians in North Carolina was the same kind of English spoken by William Shakespeare and by Queen Elizabeth I of England in the late 1500's—the time of the colony's disappearance.

The evidence gathered by the searchers and from the later study seemed to show that these Indians might have been descendants of the Lost Colonists. Nevertheless, no direct link has ever been made that conclusively proves that these Indians were related to the Lost Colonists. And to this day, no one has discovered what really became of John White's colony—the Lost Colony of Roanoke.

■ *How were the Robeson County Indians different from most other American Indian tribes?*

SECTION 2 REVIEW

1. *Why, in your opinion, might many people in England in the early 1600's have thought that Indians enslaved the Roanoke colonists?*
2. *In your opinion, why do some people believe that the Croatoan tribe might have included descendants of the Roanoke colonists?*
3. *What do you think caused the disappearance of the Roanoke colonists? Why?*

CHAPTER 4 REVIEW

SUMMARY

In 1587, John White and the colonists who came with him from England made the third attempt to set up the first permanent English colony in North America on Roanoke Island. After only a few weeks on Roanoke Island, the colonists knew that they would need more supplies from England. They did not have enough food to last the winter, and it was too late in the season to plant new crops. Because of these problems, the colonists voted to send Governor White back to England to get more supplies for the Roanoke Colony.

More than three years after leaving Roanoke to return to England for supplies, Governor White landed on Roanoke Island. He found that the entire colony had disappeared. Two signs, *CROATOAN* and *CRO*, carved into the barks of trees, gave John White hope that the colonists would be found safe and alive. Croatoan was an island that was close to Roanoke Island where friendly Indians lived. Several search parties looked for the Roanoke colonists, but they were never found.

There are several theories about the disappearance of the Roanoke colonists. Some people think that Spanish soldiers killed them. A second theory holds that the colonists drowned at sea while they attempted to sail back to England or to Croatoan Island. Some people believe that the colonists were captured by unfriendly Indians. Another theory is that the colonists went to live with the nearby Croatoan Indians. Part of the reason for this theory is that evidence seems to show that present-day Croatoan Indians might have been descendants of the Lost Colonists. However, no one has discovered what really became of the Lost Colony of Roanoke.

UNDERSTANDING CONCEPTS

1. Why did the first attempt to set up a permanent English colony in North America fail?
2. Why did Governor White return to England so soon after arriving at Roanoke Island?
3. Why did it take three years for Governor White to return to Roanoke Island from England?
4. What two signs were found near the settler's fort that gave Governor White hope that the colonists would be found?
5. What are four theories concerning the disappearance of the Roanoke colonists?

CRITICAL THINKING

1. In your opinion, what factors made it difficult to set up the first permanent English settlement in North America?
2. Why, do you think, did the disappearance of the Roanoke colonists become a topic of conversation throughout England in the early 1600's?
3. What theory concerning the disappearance of the Roanoke colonists seems most believable to you? Why?

PROJECTS AND ACTIVITIES

Many things about the Roanoke environment in the late 1500's are known as a result of the several detailed sketches and paintings done by John White. Use encyclopedias, art-history books, and other books about early English colonization in North America to find examples of White's work. Examine the artwork. Write a paragraph explaining what you learned about the Roanoke environment from White's work.

UNIT ONE REVIEW

UNIT SUMMARY

The earliest Americans followed animal herds from northeastern Asia across a land bridge into what is today Alaska. As the last Ice Age ended, the early Indians followed herds of animals farther south each year. Over thousands of years, Indians were living in most areas of North, Central, and South America. As the Indians adapted to the many environments of the Americas, new ways of life came about, and different cultures developed. These Indian cultures have made many contributions to our present-day way of life.

The Age of Exploration resulted in the discovery of the Americas by Columbus in 1492. Because Columbus had sailed for the king and queen of Spain, all the lands he discovered were claimed for the Spanish Empire. As a result of his voyage, many parts of the Americas came under Spanish control. As Spanish power in the world weakened, the French, the Dutch, and the English set up colonies throughout North America. The British eventually became the largest and strongest European power in North America.

Thirteen English colonies were established in North America between 1607 and 1733 for several reasons. Among the reasons were freedom of worship, commercial gain, and political freedom. During the 1600's and the 1700's the economies and population of the colonies grew. The society that came about in the English colonies was less structured than European society. At first, the English control over its colonies in America was not strong. However, when the British government eventually began to tighten its control over colonial trade and government, unrest began to grow in the colonies.

In 1587, John White led a group of colonists in an attempt to set up the first permanent English colony in North America on Roanoke Island. There are several theories concerning the disappearance of the Roanoke colony.

YOU SHOULD KNOW

Identify, define, or explain each of the following:

environment	mercantilism
culture	commercial farming
technology	home rule
commerce	John White
frontier	Lost Colony of Roanoke

CHECKING FACTS

1. What influenced the development of different Indian cultures in North America?
2. In what way were most Indian societies in North America divided?
3. What kind of agriculture did the Eastern Woodland Indians use?
4. What were some of the major achievements of the Incas?
5. What new social class developed in Europe during the Middle Ages?
6. What occurred as a result of the changes that took place in Europe during the Middle Ages?
7. What caused Spain to lose its position as the strongest country in Western Europe?
8. What was the first lawmaking body in America?
9. What did the French build to protect their land claims in the Ohio Valley?
10. Who was the "City of Ralegh" named after?

UNDERSTANDING CONCEPTS

1. How were the Indian civilizations in Central and in South America affected by their ability to grow surplus food?
2. Why did many European leaders and merchants in the 1200's through the 1400's want to explore new lands?
3. Why did many early English colonists come to America?

UNIT ONE REVIEW

4. How did the three types of English colonies in North America help the English government rule effectively?
5. Why did the first three attempts to set up a permanent English colony in North America fail?

CRITICAL THINKING

1. In your opinion, why did European colonists often take advantage of the Indians of the Americas?
2. Why, do you think, did three distinct areas of English settlement develop along the eastern coast of North America?
3. If you could choose one of the Thirteen Original colonies to live in, which one would you choose? Why?

CHRONOLOGY

Arrange the following events in the order in which they happened.

a. French and Indian War begins
b. Jamestown founded
c. Leif Ericson reaches coast of North America
d. First Mayan writing developed
e. First voyage of Christopher Columbus to the New World
f. Development of agriculture

CITIZENSHIP IN ACTION

During the Age of Exploration, explorers sailed into unmapped waters. Today American space explorers are making voyages into new areas. What characteristics did early explorers have that space explorers of today have?

GEOGRAPHY

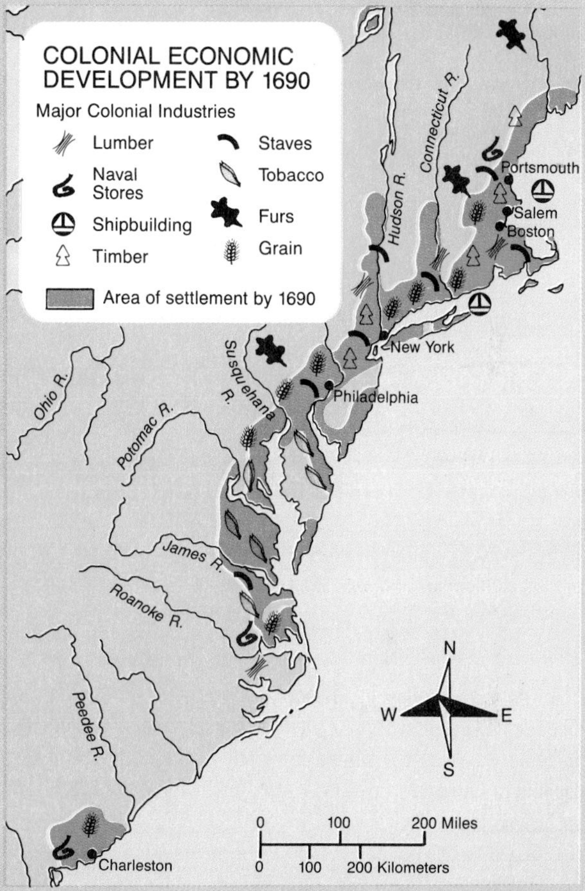

COLONIAL ECONOMIC DEVELOPMENT BY 1690

Major Colonial Industries

Lumber
Naval Stores
Shipbuilding
Timber
Staves
Tobacco
Furs
Grain
Area of settlement by 1690

Connecticut R.
Hudson R.
Portsmouth
Salem
Boston
New York
Philadelphia
Susquehanna R.
Ohio R.
Potomac R.
James R.
Roanoke R.
Peedee R.
Charleston
N
W
E
S
0 100 200 Miles
0 100 200 Kilometers

1. What colonial industries were the most common by 1690?
2. What cities had shipbuilding industries by 1690?
3. What was the major crop grown in the southern colonies in 1690?
4. On the basis of the number of industries near a city, which cities had the most industries in 1690?

1765 1770 1775

1763 Parliament passes the Proclamation of 1763

1765 Parliament passes the Stamp Act

1770 Boston Massacre occurs

1773 Parliament passes the Tea Act

1774 Parliament passes the Intolerable Acts

1775 The Second Continental Congress begins

1776 The Second Continental Congress approves the Declaration of Independence

1777 Articles of Confederation adopted

UNIT TWO

A New Nation Is Established

1763 to 1800

The Old State House in Philadelphia was the site of the First Continental Congress in 1774. In the years that followed, this building was also the setting for many of the important events leading to America's freedom. Later, the building became known as Independence Hall.

Lord Cornwallis surrendered to General Washington at Yorktown, Virginia, on October 17, 1781. The Revolutionary War was over, and America had won its independence.

1780 | 1785 | 1790 | 1795

1781 The British surrender at Yorktown

1787 Congress passes the Northwest Ordinance
The Constitutional Convention meets in Philadelphia

1788 The Constitution becomes the supreme law of the United States

1789 George Washington becomes the first President of the United States

1793 Washington issues a Proclamation of Neutrality

1797 John Adams becomes the second President

CHAPTERS

Great Britain's colonies in North America had developed their own ways of life as well as their own local governments by 1763. When the British tried to tighten controls on the colonies, they met with protest and resistance. The British, however, insisted on their right to govern and to tax the colonies. Fighting then broke out between British soldiers and American patriots in April 1775. This fighting touched off the American Revolution.

The colonists' struggle for independence lasted for eight years. The signing of the Treaty of Paris brought final independence to the Thirteen Colonies. However, with independence came new problems. Nevertheless, the American nation was able to survive and prosper. This was largely because of the Constitution that was written in 1787.

Revolutionary leaders, such as Alexander Hamilton and Benjamin Franklin, were involved in the signing of the Constitution in September, 1787.

British soldiers practice drills on the Boston Common in 1768.

1760 | 1770 | 1780

- 1763 British defeat the French in the French and Indian War
  Parliament passes the Proclamation of 1763
- 1765 Parliament passes the Stamp Act
- 1766 Parliament passes the Declaratory Act
- 1767 Parliament passes the Townshend Acts
- 1770 Boston Massacre occurs
- 1773 Parliament passes the Tea Act
- 1774 Parliament passes the Intolerable Acts
  The First Continental Congress meets
- 1775 Fighting between the British and Americans breaks out at Lexington and Concord

CHAPTER 5

Development of Colonial Unrest

Chapter Objectives

After studying this chapter, you will be able to:

- explain how increased manufacturing in the colonies brought about an increase in colonial trade;
- list several acts of Parliament that angered many colonists in America;
- summarize the reasons for the First Continental Congress.

1 The American Colonies in the Mid-Eighteenth Century

Overview By 1763 British landholdings in North America had become some of the most valuable of Britain's colonial possessions. Good farmland, many natural resources, and a growing population led to the start of the colonial economy. Farming was the base of the economy. Most colonists were farmers. Nonetheless, during the mid-1700's, some manufacturing began to take place. As this happened, trade grew.

Objectives After you read this section, you will be able to:

- identify areas of the world that belonged to the British Empire;
- explain how increased manufacturing in the American colonies brought about greater colonial trade;
- analyze the reasons for British opposition to colonial trade with other nations.

America's Place in the British Empire. By the mid-1700's Great Britain ruled a large empire. It was made up of lands in nearly every part of the world. The British East India Company had been given a charter by Queen Elizabeth I to form settlements in India in 1600. Sir Walter Raleigh had been allowed to set up a colony in North America in 1607. One hundred years later, the British Empire had spread throughout the world. By the early 1700's islands in the West Indies, settlements in Africa, and colonies in Burma and in India had come under the regulation of Great Britain. Later, Australia, New Zealand, and many Pacific islands joined the British Empire. By 1733, 13 colonies had been set up in North America. However, after 1763 the Thirteen Colonies were only a small part of the total British landholding in North America.

Nevertheless, the colonies in America were among the most valuable lands in the empire. This was because land in America was rich in natural resources. These resources were needed by Great Britain. In large part, the actions of the British government toward the colonies were based on the amount of goods the people in America sent back to Great Britain.

Which colonies in the British Empire were the most valuable by the mid-1700's?

Mercantilism and Britain's Colonies. During the 1700's the British government expected its colonies throughout the world to make new wealth for Great Britain. This was the basis of the system called *mercantilism* (see Chapter 3, page 60). The colonies were expected to furnish raw materials for British manufacturing. For example, South Carolina sold about 292 tons [262.8 metric tons] of indigo to Great Britain each year between 1763 and 1775. During the same years, the Southern Colonies alone sold, on a yearly average, about 1,438 miles [2 300.8 kilometers] of wood products to Great Britain. Goods made in Great Britain, such as furniture and ink, were made out of the wood and indigo grown in America.

British colonies elsewhere in the world also sent the home country many goods. Some of these goods were silk, ivory, gold, and precious stones, such as diamonds. In return for colonial raw materials, Great Britain sold British-made goods to the colonies. In part, this is why large-scale manufacturing did not take place in most British colonies during the 1700's. Nevertheless, some industries were set up in the American colonies. This industrial growth had an impact on life in the Thirteen Colonies.

What British-held belief was the basis of the system called mercantilism?

Life in Colonial America. Most people who lived in the British colonies in North America in the mid-1700's had been born in Great Britain or were the children of British parents. Many people from other countries in western Europe also came to America during the mid-1700's. As a result of immigration and of births, the colonial population grew quickly. In 1750 more than one million people were living in the Thirteen Colonies in America. By 1775, more than one and a half million people lived in the colonies. About 20 percent of the colonial population was made up of black people. The vast majority of black Americans had been brought to the colonies as slaves.

Although most colonists lived on farms or in farm areas during the 1700's, five major cities of considerable size had developed in the American colonies by the mid-1700's. These cities were Philadelphia, New York, Boston, Charles Town (later called Charleston), and Newport. One of these cities, Philadelphia, became the second-largest city in the British Empire by 1775. Its population was about 40,000, and it was a leading trade and manufacturing center. Some colonial leaders, such as Benjamin Franklin, lived in Philadelphia.

By 1770, colonial society was made up of

Historical Society of Pennsylvania

The city of Philadelphia was typical of many colonial cities in that it was established at a natural harbor on the Atlantic seaboard. Its growth was largely the result of the increase in trade between Great Britain and the American colonies.

The kitchen was often the workroom of the colonial home, where many special skills—such as spinning yarn and cooking—were needed.

The Bettmann Archive

four classes. Lawyers, doctors, wealthy merchants, planters, and ministers belonged to the highest class. Artisans, farmers, shopkeepers, and teachers made up the middle class. Unskilled workers and indentured servants made up the next-lower class. Slaves belonged to the lowest class in colonial society. However, most people in the colonies—except slaves—could move from one social class to another. Most often, by increasing their income or education, people could move into a higher social class.

■ *What major cities had developed in the British colonies in America during the 1700's?*

Education in the American Colonies. Education was important in colonial society. However, many children were not able to go to school because they were needed as workers. Also, more boys were allowed to go to school than girls. This was because many people believed that women could not understand important matters.

Many children in the colonies did not have a formal education. Instead, they took part in their family's daily work. In this way colonial children learned many of the skills that were needed in the mid-1700's. In some cases, children were taught how to read, how to write, and how to do some arithmetic functions by their parents. For the most part, however, colonial children were taught specific skills and crafts that were needed in day-to-day colonial society.

Crafts and skills were taught largely through *apprenticeships*—working directly with experienced craft workers. Boys were taught how to make such things as furniture, silverware, pewter, glass, and iron instruments, such as farming tools. Girls were often taught how to cook, how to keep foods fresh, and how to make many of the things needed by colonial families. Although their opportunities were limited, many women also worked as innkeepers, as furniture makers, and as owners of small businesses. Through their work, colonial men and women were able to build a strong economy in America during the mid-1700's.

■ *How did most colonial children learn the skills that were needed in the mid-1700's?*

(Text continues on page 89.)

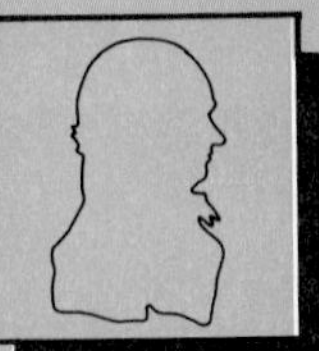

PROFILES

Benjamin Franklin

Few colonial citizens, if any, capture the emerging American character and spirit better than Benjamin Franklin (1706–1790). Born into a poor family in Boston, young Franklin was denied a formal education. Yet he became an avid reader and soon developed a practical, common sense approach to life based on observation and reason.

At seventeen Franklin moved to Philadelphia. By the time he was twenty he had become a successful printer and newspaper publisher. His *Poor Richard's Almanack*, begun in 1732, became a best seller. It contained wise sayings, practical advice, and homespun philosophy—all centering on the virtues of hard work and thrift.

By the time Franklin was 42 he retired from business matters to pursue other interests. He was an inventor and developed such items as bifocal glasses, the lightning rod, an iron stove, and numerous other devices. Franklin was also a scientist and conducted important experiments on electrical current. His inventions and scientific work made him famous in the colonies and in Europe as well.

Perhaps most important, Franklin was a dedicated public servant. He served fourteen years in the Pennsylvania legislature and represented the colony's interests in London. As Philadelphia's most famous citizen, he founded a debating club, a public library, and a philosophical society. He also helped organize an academy, a volunteer fire fighting company, and Philadelphia's first hospital.

During the Revolution Franklin was a staunch patriot and member of the Continental Congress. He later served as a skilled diplomat in England and France. Franklin's final act of public life was as a delegate to the Constitutional Convention in 1787.

The Bettmann Archive

Thinking Critically

Why do you think Franklin was one of America's first national heroes? Explain.
How do you know that Benjamin Franklin was a good American citizen?

The Colonial Economy. Farming remained the main way of life in America during the mid-1700's. Large amounts of farm goods were sent to Great Britain from each colony in America during these years. Between 1763 and 1775, the Southern Colonies alone sent to Great Britain more than 318,206 tons [286 385.4 metric tons] of tobacco, 44,240 tons [39 816 metric tons] of rice, 3,800 tons [3 420 metric tons] of indigo, and 2,221 tons [1 998.9 metric tons] of raw, Georgia-produced silk. Other colonies shipped wood, naval stores, and furs to Great Britain. At the same time, manufacturing developed in cities such as Philadelphia. This, in turn, led to a growth in trade among the colonies, between the colonies and Great Britain, and between the colonies and other countries of the world.

When this trade increased, manufacturing in the colonies was discouraged by the British government and by British business leaders for two reasons. First, British business leaders did not want the Americans to compete with British industries. Second, in an economy based on mercantilism, the Americans were expected to send raw materials to Great Britain. In exchange, the home country sent manufactured goods to the colonies. Colonial manufacturing, therefore, threatened Britain's economic way of life.

Nevertheless, industries grew in some of the American colonies, especially in New England. Despite opposition from Great Britain, iron was made in American foundries. The colonists sent to Great Britain more than 3,222 tons [2 899.9 metric tons] of finished iron in 1763. By 1775, shipments of finished iron had grown to about 4,326 tons [3 893.4 metric tons]. In this way the Americans made Great Britain depend upon the colonies for finished iron. Raw materials continued to be shipped to Great Britain as well. Large amounts of American wood, coal, copper, and furs were sent to Great Britain between 1763 and 1775.

■ *Why did British leaders oppose manufacturing in the English colonies?*

The Colonies and Home Rule. By 1763 home rule had become well-established in the Thirteen Colonies. Colonial governments passed laws and set taxes for the colonies. Therefore, the Americans came to depend more upon colonial governments than upon the British government. Also, local governments allowed many people to take part in running their government. However, the belief in home rule on the part of the Americans led to problems with Great Britain.

As the amount of American goods and products sold outside of the colonies grew

DO YOU KNOW?

Who is generally considered the greatest portrait painter in colonial America?

John Singleton Copley painted portraits that captured the character of Americans in settings that portrayed everyday life. His paintings were straightforward and made use of color, texture, light, and shade. In 1766 Copley sent his painting *Boy with a Squirrel* to an exhibition in London. The painters there praised his paintings and recommended that he study in Europe. In 1774 Copley settled in London permanently. In 1778 he fulfilled a lifelong ambition by becoming a painter of historical subjects. Today critics still praise his straightforward vivid American portraits.

Courtesy of the New York Historical Society

The thriving colonial port of New York City was often crowded with British merchant ships and naval vessels during the mid-1700's.

larger, the American shipping industry grew larger as well. There were 447 ships registered in the American colonies in 1768. Four years later, there were 594 ships to carry American goods around the world—an increase of about 33 percent. This growth of trade and shipping upset British leaders because they were opposed to direct colonial trade with other countries. They were against this trade because Great Britain would not receive any *duties*—taxes on trade goods—if the colonists traded directly with other countries. As a result, Parliament passed a series of laws limiting trade. These laws angered many colonists, but Great Britain was determined to tighten its control over its colonies in North America.

■ *Why were British leaders opposed to direct colonial trade with other countries?*

SECTION 1 REVIEW

1. *When did Great Britain begin to set up colonies throughout the world?*
2. *How did the growth of colonial manufacturing help to increase colonial trade?*
3. *Why, in your opinion, did Great Britain want to tighten its control over its colonies in America in the mid-1700's?*

2 Changes in British Colonial Policy

Overview After the French and Indian War ended in 1763, new land was added to the British Empire in North America. As a result, some colonists began to move westward across the Appalachian Mountains. At the same time, the British government began to change its policy toward the American colonies. This change in policy was met with resistance from the colonists.

Objectives After you read this section, you will be able to:

- list the taxes placed on the American colonists by Parliament;
- describe the effect of the Stamp Act on the American colonies;
- explain why a boycott on all British goods was effective in repealing the Stamp Act.

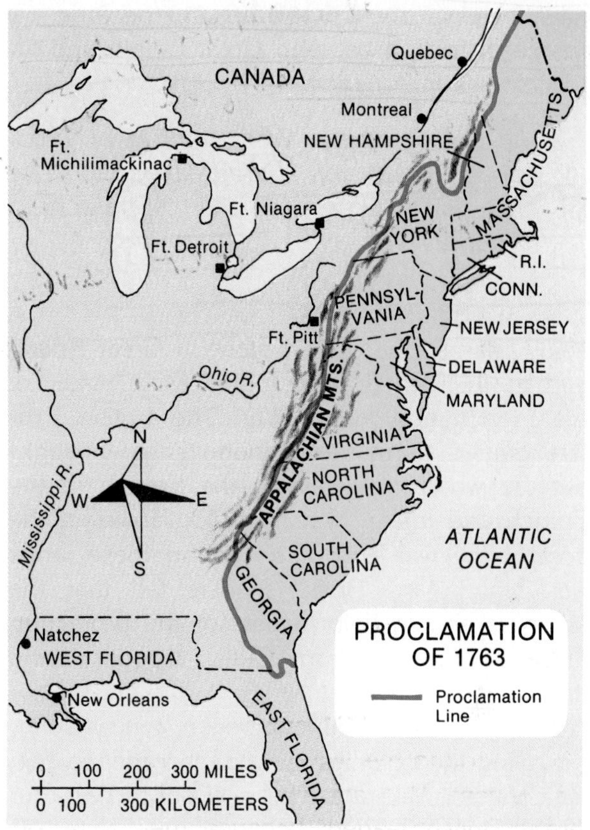

The Proclamation of 1763 restricted settlement to the land east of the Appalachian Mountains. On what geographic features were most of the forts and cities west of the Appalachian Mountains located?

The Proclamation of 1763. In 1763, Parliament passed a law to keep American colonists out of the Ohio Valley. The Proclamation of 1763 declared that all land west of the Appalachian Mountains was not to be settled by the colonists (see map on this page). Rather, this land was to be set aside for the Indians. In part, the proclamation was passed to stop Indian attacks on the *western frontier*—land on the western border of the Thirteen Colonies. These attacks had often been led by Chief Pontiac, an Ottawa Indian chief, who brought together several Indian tribes. These united tribes had then raided British forts and settlements.

The Proclamation of 1763 was made for other reasons as well. By keeping large numbers of colonists out of the closed area, the British government helped British companies keep control of the fur trade in the Ohio Valley. More important, the proclamation caused most colonists to stay close to the eastern coast of North America. The colonists, therefore, would find it easier to carry on more trade with Great Britain. The colonists would also more easily be made to obey British trade laws, such as the Navigation Acts (see Chapter 3, page 60).

The proclamation was not very successful,

however. Large numbers of settlers and many land-settlement companies continued to push back the western frontier of North America. Nevertheless, the proclamation became a source of friction between Great Britain and its 13 colonies in America.

■ *According to the Proclamation of 1763, what group of people was to use the land west of the Appalachian Mountains?*

Great Britain's Need for New Revenue. Many changes had taken place in Great Britain and in the American colonies as a result of the French and Indian War. The British Empire gained many new landholdings throughout the world by defeating the French in the French and Indian War in 1763. However, the cost of the war and of governing these lands was high. Many British leaders felt that the colonists should help to pay for the protection they had received from British troops during the war.

The British government began a new policy for ruling the colonies in 1763 in order to better control its empire. The new policy had four goals. First, the British government wanted to continue to control all colonial trade. Second, many British leaders wanted the American colonists to pay for their share of the debt brought about by the French and Indian War. Third, the British government wanted to strengthen the British Empire. And fourth, British leaders wanted the colonies to bring greater wealth to Great Britain.

To achieve the goals of its new colonial policy, Great Britain did several things. For example, British troops were ordered to stay in the colonies after the war with France to enforce the British trade laws. British warships were ordered to sail near American harbors in order to catch smugglers. Also, *Writs of Assistance*—court orders—let British soldiers search houses, ships, and warehouses for smuggled goods. When the colonists were accused of smuggling, they were put on trial in British courts—not in colonial courts.

Many people in the colonies believed these changes in British policy were dangerous threats to their rights. Therefore, resentment toward Britain's new colonial policy grew. Patrick Henry, a member of the Virginia House of Burgesses, for example, challenged the king's right to make laws for the colonists. Nevertheless, Great Britain continued to tighten its control over the Thirteen Colonies largely by placing new taxes on the Americans.

■ *Why did British leaders want the American colonists to help pay for the French and Indian War?*

Parliament Places New Taxes on the American Colonists. In the years before 1764, Parliament had placed many taxes on colonial goods. These taxes, however, had been used to regulate trade within the British Empire—not to raise new revenue. On April 5, 1764, however, Parliament passed the first of three acts intended solely to raise money for the British Empire.

The *Sugar Act* raised taxes on cloth, wine, and coffee. It also raised taxes on sugar and molasses—the main ingredients needed to make rum in the New England Colonies. However, the Sugar Act did not raise enough money to help the British Empire. This was largely because many colonists continued to smuggle their goods past the British navy.

The *Currency Act,* passed on April 19, 1764, made it illegal for the colonists to print their own paper money. The colonists were also ordered to use only gold or silver to trade with Great Britain. The Currency Act was also largely ignored by the colonists. Because these laws were, for the most part, unsuccessful, George Grenville, Prime Minister of Great Britain, asked Parliament to pass a new law that the colonists could not avoid. Thus, Parliament passed a third law—the *Stamp Act*—on March 22, 1765.

The Stamp Act required the colonists to pay a tax on many kinds of printed materials. These materials included newspapers, licenses, legal papers, books, almanacs, and playing cards. When the tax was paid, a stamp was then placed on these materials. This tax increased the costs on many items in the colonies. The Stamp Act also directly lowered the incomes of colonial newspaper owners, lawyers, merchants, and ministers. Because these people were often leaders in the American colonies, reaction to the acts of Parliament came quickly.

■ *What three acts were passed by Parliament between April 5, 1764, and March 22, 1765, to raise money for the British Empire?*

Colonial Reaction to the Acts of Parliament. Many American colonists were angered by the Stamp Act. Some colonists formed protest groups. Members of these groups worked against British taxation throughout the Thirteen Colonies.

One such protest group, the Sons of Liberty, wanted all American colonists to stop paying taxes to Great Britain. The Sons of Liberty were often violent in their actions. For example, some colonial officials who sold British tax stamps were threatened with death. Some British tax collectors were covered with tar and feathers. Most other protest groups were less violent than the Sons of Liberty.

On October 7, 1765, leaders from 9 of the 13 American colonies met in New York City. This group later became known as the Stamp Act Congress. The Stamp Act Congress sent a letter to Parliament. In the letter, the Congress asked Parliament to *repeal*—end—the Stamp Act. The members of the Stamp Act Congress told Parliament that only colonial governments had the right to tax the colonists. Further, these leaders believed that there should be "No taxation without representation." That is,

An early cartoon drawn in 1773 depicted the strong reaction of many American colonists against British tax policies during the late 1760's and the early 1770's.

The Bettmann Archive

Library of Congress

This illustration from the eighteenth century shows the colonists' opposition to the Stamp Act, which surprised many British leaders. By November 1, 1765—the date when the law was to take effect in the colonies—most of the tax collectors had already resigned their posts.

because the colonists did not have a representative in Parliament, Parliament could not pass laws to tax the colonists.

Members of the Stamp Act Congress knew that Parliament would not repeal the Stamp Act solely because of their letter. Therefore, the representatives asked all colonists to *boycott*—to not buy or use—all British goods until Parliament repealed the Stamp Act. The boycott was successful. Colonial trade with Great Britain was reduced by about 10 percent by 1766.

The colonial boycott was successful because it caused many British business leaders to lose money. They, in turn, asked Parliament to repeal the Stamp Act, which it did on March 18, 1766. However, Parliament then passed the *Declaratory Act* on the same day. This act stated that Parliament had the right to tax the colonists. At the time most colonists did not disagree with this act. However, a growing number of colonists were beginning to feel that the American colonies should be totally free of British control. In the years that followed, a desire for independence began to grow.

■ *What action by the Stamp Act Congress brought about the repeal of the Stamp Act?*

SECTION 2 REVIEW

1. *When did Parliament pass the Sugar Act?*
2. *How did the Stamp Act help to unite the American colonies?*
3. *Why was a boycott more effective in bringing about the repeal of the Stamp Act than a letter from the Stamp Act Congress?*

3 Reaction and Resistance

Overview Following 1766, American colonists who wanted to be free of British rule became known as *patriots*. The colonists who wanted to remain British citizens were called *loyalists*. Most colonists were loyalists. However, as Parliament passed new laws for the colonists in the 1760's and the 1770's, the number of people who favored independence from Great Britain grew larger.

Objectives After you read this section, you will be able to:

- identify the purpose of the Townshend Acts;
- describe the reasons for and the effects of the Boston Tea Party;
- explain the purpose of the First Continental Congress.

Parliament Tightens Controls on the American Colonies. It was not long before Parliament again tried to tighten its hold over the colonies. On June 15, 1767, Parliament suspended New York's government because the New York Assembly had not carried out the Quartering Act of 1765. This act had stated that each colony was to provide *quarters*—a place to live—for British troops. The suspension of their local government came as a serious blow to the people of the New York colony. Many New York people believed that Parliament had taken away their rights as free citizens. Two weeks later, Parliament passed the Townshend Acts. These acts affected almost all Americans.

The Townshend Acts, passed on June 29, 1767, put taxes on many things that had never been taxed in the American colonies. New taxes were placed on paint, glass, lead, paper, and tea. Colonial merchants paid the taxes aboard ship in colonial ports before the merchandise was moved into colonial towns. The taxes were then included in the price of the products. In this way, British leaders hoped to avoid widespread colonial opposition to the new taxes. These taxes were then used to help pay the salaries of British government leaders in the colonies. Also, part of the money was to be used to help pay for keeping British troops in the American colonies. Loyalists and patriots alike were angered by the Townshend Acts.

Why was the New York Assembly suspended by Parliament in 1767?

Colonial Reaction to the Townshend Acts. The Townshend Acts angered many American colonists. This was because before the acts were passed, local governments usually paid, and thus controlled, the salaries of British officials in the colonies. In this way the American colonists had control, at least in part, over the actions of some British colonial officials. The Townshend Acts took away much of this power.

Many Americans became alarmed about the loss of their rights. In response, British-made goods were again boycotted by many American colonists—as they had been before the repeal of the Stamp Act. Once again, the Americans' boycott worked well. Parliament removed the Townshend Acts on April 12, 1770. However, Parliament did not remove the tax on tea. Parliament kept the tax on tea to show that it had the right to place taxes on the colonists. There was little colonial objection to this tax at the time. Nevertheless, many colonists began to form groups to protect their rights as free British citizens.

■ *What action did the colonists take to force Parliament to repeal the Townshend Acts?*

Tension Grows Within the Colonies. Relations between the American colonies and the home country generally improved between 1770 and 1773. Nevertheless, two great problems remained. First, more American colonists questioned Great Britain's right to tax the colonies. These people believed that representatives from America should be admitted to Parliament before any taxes were placed on the colonies. Second, the belief in home rule continued to grow as Americans became involved in their government. These two beliefs led to greater tensions. These tensions, in turn, led to two major incidents that further angered many colonists.

The Boston Massacre was the first major incident. It was touched off when a small group of colonists began to throw snowballs at a British soldier. It took place on the night of March 5, 1770. As the crowd of colonists grew larger, the soldier called for help. More British troops moved into the street. The crowd shouted insults at the British soldiers, and more snowballs, then rocks, were thrown at the troops. When a soldier was knocked down, the troops fired into the crowd, killing five colonists—including Crispus Attucks. Crispus Attucks was one of the first colonists—and the first black person—to die in the conflict between Great Britain and the American colonies. Some of the British troops were later put on trial and found not guilty. Many colonists remained angry.

Two years later, on June 10, 1772, a small group of Rhode Island merchants set fire to the H.M.S. *Gaspee.* The H.M.S. *Gaspee* was a British ship that patrolled the coastline of the New England Colonies searching for colonial smugglers.

British officials in the colonies reacted strongly to the burning. British trade laws were enforced even more strongly. As a result,

Historical Pictures Service

Under the cover of night, many angry colonists burned the H.M.S. *Gaspee* after it had run aground. This burning was in retaliation for the captain's enforcement of antismuggling laws.

Committees of Correspondence were set up throughout the colonies. These committees had two purposes. The first purpose was to tell all Americans of British actions throughout the American colonies. The second purpose was to unite the Thirteen Colonies against further British control of trade.

The first committee was set up in Massachusetts on November 2, 1772, by Samuel Adams and Joseph Warren. Patrick Henry and Thomas Jefferson set up a group in Virginia soon after. The committees increased their work when Parliament passed the Tea Act of 1773.

■ *What were the two purposes of the colonial Committees of Correspondence?*

Colonial Reaction to the Tea Act of 1773. The Tea Act of 1773 allowed the British East India Company to sell its tea in the American colonies without having to pay taxes on it. The law was passed to help the financially weak British East India Company and to lower the price of tea in the American colonies. In this way, the American colonists could buy more tea at lower cost. Members of Parliament expected the colonists to be pleased. Instead, many colonists were angry. This was because many colonial tea sellers were forced out of business. They could not sell tea as inexpensively as could the British East India Company.

Many colonists reacted to the Tea Act and to pressures by the Sons of Liberty by boycotting tea. Ships loaded with tea were often not allowed to unload their cargoes in many American harbors. In Boston, radical colonists disguised themselves as Mohawk Indians and boarded British ships, dumping the British tea into the ocean. This action took place on December 16, 1773, and became known as the Boston Tea Party.

■ *How did the Tea Act of 1773 affect many colonial tea merchants?*

The Intolerable Acts. Members of Parliament saw the Boston Tea Party as open disobedience of British law. The British East India Company saw the incident as an expensive loss of goods. As a result of this action, the British government placed the colony of Massachusetts under British military rule. In early 1774, Parliament passed four new laws to tighten its control over the colonies. In part, these laws were also meant to punish the colonists.

The new laws were known as the Coercive Acts. The Boston Port Bill, passed on March 31, 1774, closed Boston Harbor to all shipping. This hurt the people of Boston because shipping was one of the main ways of earning money in Boston at the time. The Massachusetts Government Act, passed on May 20, 1774, changed the colony's charter, limiting self-government in Massachusetts. Also, colonists were ordered to give housing to British soldiers by the Quartering Act of June 2, 1774. Another law stated that British officials charged with crimes in Massachusetts had to be sent to Great Britain for trial. These four laws made it clear to the colonists that Great Britain would no longer tolerate any colonial disobedience.

Parliament then passed the Quebec Act on June 22, 1774. This act made all land north of the Ohio River and east of the Mississippi River to the Appalachian Mountains part of Quebec. The act was passed to take care of the French-speaking people who came under British rule as a result of the British victory in the French and Indian War. However, this act also limited the westward growth of the colonies. The Coercive Acts and the Quebec Act together were called the Intolerable Acts by the American colonists. Many colonists joined together in protest against these acts.

■ *Why did Parliament pass the Coercive Acts?*

The First Continental Congress. The colonists' Committees of Correspondence reacted quickly to the Intolerable Acts. The committees called for a meeting of all the colonies. In response, representatives from twelve colonies met at Philadelphia on September 5, 1774. This meeting has been called the First Continental Congress.

Every American colony except Georgia was represented at the First Continental Congress. For the most part, the representatives and the people they represented wanted a peaceful settlement with Great Britain. Radical leaders, however, such as Samuel Adams, took control of the Congress. A letter was sent to King George III and to Parliament, stating that the colonists would not obey the Intolerable Acts. The letter also threatened to break off all trade between the colonies and Great Britain.

In response, King George III sent more British troops into the American colonies. This action, in turn, caused many colonists to believe that open war would soon break out. As a result, some colonists began to prepare their colonies for war.

■ *How many American colonies sent representatives to the First Continental Congress?*

Fighting Breaks Out. John Hancock and Samuel Adams of Massachusetts stored a small supply of guns and ammunition near Lexington in case fighting broke out between the colonists and British troops (see map on page 99). Other colonists, such as John Parker of Massachusetts, trained their friends and neighbors to fight. John Parker's soldiers became known as *Minutemen* because they were ready to fight the British at a minute's notice.

General Thomas Gage was the British military governor in Boston. He knew that some colonists were preparing to fight. General Gage had also been told about the colonists' weapons that were hidden near Lexington. Thus, on April 18, 1775, General Gage ordered Major Pitcairn to lead British troops to Lexington to arrest John Hancock and Samuel

The colonial soldiers known as the Minutemen were often local farmers and townspeople.

Historical Pictures Service

Adams. The soldiers were also ordered to capture the colonists' weapons.

Paul Revere and William Dawes were patriots who had learned that British troops were marching to Lexington. They warned John Hancock and the other colonists. Because of the warning, John Parker's Minutemen were waiting for the British soldiers at Lexington and, later, at Concord (see map on this page). Fighting broke out in both villages on April 19, 1775, resulting in the deaths of 273 British soldiers and 93 Minutemen. The British troops were forced to retreat to Boston. The War for Independence had begun.

■ *Why did General Gage order British troops to march to Lexington, Massachusetts?*

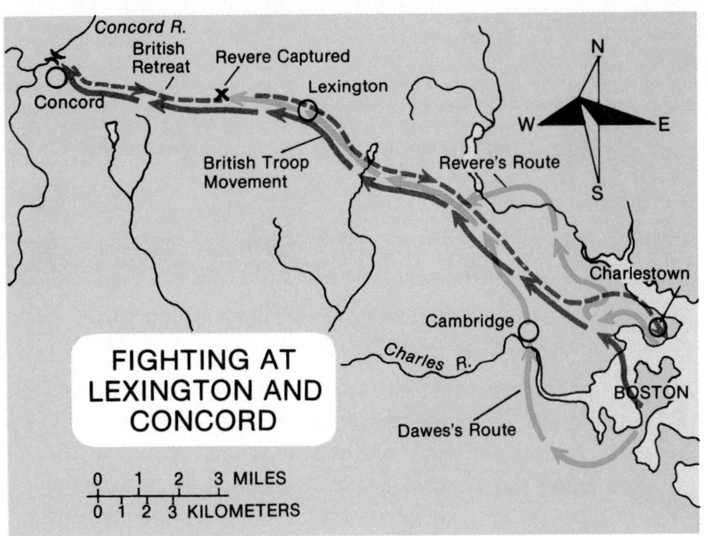

The American Revolution began in April 1775 when British troops marched on Lexington and Concord. Whose route—Dawe's or Revere's—most closely coincided with the British troop movement?

SECTION 3 REVIEW

1. *What items were taxed for the first time by the Townshend Revenue Acts?*
2. *How did Parliament react to the news of the Boston Tea Party?*
3. *Why did the First Continental Congress meet in 1774?*

CHAPTER 5 SUMMARY

The population and the economy of the American colonies went through a time of rapid growth during the 1700's. This was also a period in which many colonists came to believe in home rule.

The British Empire also went through many changes during this time. Because of the French and Indian War, for example, Great Britain gained many new landholdings. In turn, British leaders changed many government policies so that more money could be raised to pay for the Empire. These changes caused some American colonists to question Britain's right to place taxes on the colonies and to take away or change some colonial governments.

As Parliament passed more laws that tightened British power over the American colonies, resistance grew. However, many American colonists still remained loyal to Great Britain. Nevertheless, colonial groups prepared for war. And following the passage of the Intolerable Acts, fighting broke out.

CHAPTER 5 REVIEW

USING YOUR SKILLS

Differentiating Between Primary and Secondary Sources

Source material is information. There are two kinds of source material. *Primary source material* includes documents and accounts written at the time the historic event took place. It also can be an account written by someone who observed the event. *Secondary source material* is usually a description or an interpretation written some time after the event took place. For example, the secondary source materials below were taken from recent history textbooks. Both excerpts discuss the Boston Massacre. However, the column on the left is taken from a British textbook. The column on the right is from an American textbook. Read both columns below and then answer the questions that follow.

1. According to the British text, how many Bostonians were killed in the Boston Massacre?
2. According to the American text, how many Bostonians were killed in the Boston Massacre?
3. Which text gives the exact name that the Bostonians called the British troops?
4. Which text names the leader of the Bostonians?
5. In your opinion, which text gives a more accurate and complete explanation of the Massacre? Explain.
6. In your opinion, is either text written from a strictly American or a strictly British point of view? Explain.

British Textbook

The "radical" or "patriotic" element grew bolder and more extravagant. In Boston the jeering and baiting of the British "lobsterbacks" as they guarded the customs house reached a violent climax when, on March 5, 1770, snowballing turned into a mob attack. Largely in self defense, shots were fired and three Bostonians fell dead in the snow. The incident was promptly transformed by the colonial agitators into the "Boston Massacre" and was solemnly celebrated each succeeding year.

American Textbook

... About the same time that Parliament repealed the Townshend duties, a group of Bostonians, who of course could not know of the repeal, threatened a British sentry, and Captain Thomas Preston and several soldiers came to his aid. Led by Crispus Attucks, the townspeople refused to disperse. Instead they threw snowballs and called the soldiers names. In the confusion that followed, soldiers fired into the crowd, killing five persons and wounding six others.

CHAPTER 5 REVIEW

YOU SHOULD KNOW

Identify, define, or explain each of the following:

apprenticeship	boycott
duties	patriots
repeal	loyalists

CHECKING FACTS

1. When was the British East India Company given a charter to set up colonies in India?
2. What were the five largest cities in the American colonies in the mid-1700's?
3. What four classes made up colonial society?
4. What did the Proclamation of 1763 declare?
5. What did the Stamp Act do?
6. Who were the Sons of Liberty?
7. What did the Quartering Act of 1765 state?
8. How many colonists were killed in the Boston Massacre?
9. What was the Tea Act of 1773?
10. Who were the Minutemen?

UNDERSTANDING CONCEPTS

1. Why did Great Britain expect its colonies to provide it with new wealth throughout the 1700's?
2. What effect did education and income have upon the class system in the American colonies?
3. Why were British government and business leaders against manufacturing in the American colonies?
4. Why were many American colonists angered by the Townshend Acts?
5. Why did Parliament pass the Coercive Acts?

LEARNING FROM ILLUSTRATIONS

1. Study the illustration on page 87. How was much of the cooking done in a colonial home? What other tasks were performed in the kitchen?
2. Study the political cartoon on page 93. What symbols can you find of the colonists' opposition to British taxation?

CRITICAL THINKING

1. Fewer girls than boys attended school in colonial America. This was because many people believed that women could not understand important matters. How do you feel about this belief?
2. If you were a colonist, how would you feel about the various acts of Parliament imposed on the colonists? Give reasons for your feelings.
3. Do you think that Parliament had the right to tax the colonists without any representation from the colonies? Why do you think so?

ENRICHMENT ACTIVITIES

1. You might like to do research in an encyclopedia and then create a bulletin-board display showing the growth of the British Empire in the eighteenth century and America's place in it.
2. You might like to create a series of posters similar to the ones the colonists might have made that encouraged the American colonists to boycott British goods.

1770 1780 1790

- 1775 The Second Continental Congress begins
- 1776 The Second Continental Congress approves the Declaration of Independence
- 1777 Articles of Confederation adopted Americans win the Battle of Saratoga
- 1781 The British surrender at Yorktown Thirteen states form the United States of America
- 1785 Congress passes the Land Ordinance of 1785
- 1786 Shays' Rebellion breaks out
- 1787 Congress passes the Northwest Ordinance

CHAPTER 6

The Struggle for Independence

Chapter Objectives

After studying this chapter, you will be able to:

- compare the strengths and weaknesses of the British and American armies;
- explain how the help of European nations benefited the Continental Army;
- summarize the weaknesses of the Articles of Confederation.

1 A Declaration of Independence

Overview Throughout 1775, a small group of Americans led by Benjamin Franklin had worked in England. This group had hoped to get the British prime minister, Lord North, and King George III to discuss the American colonists' problems. This was because many Americans wanted to avoid war with Great Britain. The king and the prime minister, however, would not meet with the Americans. The refusal led to the Second Continental Congress.

Objectives After you read this section, you will be able to:

- identify the purpose of the Second Continental Congress;
- list the reasons why some Americans believed that the British army could be beaten;
- explain why the Declaration of Independence was written.

The Second Continental Congress. The Second Continental Congress began on May 10, 1775, in Philadelphia. It was called because members of the First Continental Congress had agreed to meet again if Great Britain did not take care of the many problems that existed between the English colonies in America and the home country.

Most members of the Second Continental Congress did not expect to stay long in Philadelphia. But it was clear that there was a great deal of work to be done. The fighting at Lexington and Concord had led Great Britain to take action. British soldiers, led by General Gage, took over Boston on April 19, 1775. About one month later, on May 25, 1775, British generals Howe, Burgoyne, and Clinton reached Boston with more soldiers. Because of these events, the members of Congress agreed to set up an army—the Continental Army—on June 14, 1775. Congress chose George Washington of Virginia to lead the new army.

It appears that most members of Congress did not want to go to war with Great Britain. In an effort to avoid fighting, the Congress sent a letter to the king and to Parliament on July 8, 1775, stating that the Americans did not want war. The letter noted, however, that problems between Great Britain and the colonists over taxation and British trade laws had to be worked out. The letter also pointed out that most Americans remained loyal to Great Britain and to King George III.

King George would not read the letter. Instead, the king wrote the Proclamation of Rebellion on August 23, 1775. This statement declared the colonies to be in revolt. The British army was then ordered to put down the rebellion in America.

■ *Why did the Second Continental Congress meet?*

Colonial Leaders Take Action. The Second Continental Congress had become the acting government of the Thirteen Colonies in May 1775. John Hancock of Massachusetts was chosen as president of Congress. Under Hancock's leadership, Congress began to pass laws for the colonies. Congress also began to tax the colonists. This was done because money was needed to run the new government and to pay for its army. Military leaders began to carry out the orders of Congress. General Washington was chosen as the commander of the Continental Army. His job was to set up and train the army—all within a short period of time and with little money.

For what two reasons did the Second Continental Congress begin to tax the American colonists?

Moving Toward Independence. Most leaders of colonial militias believed that the British Army could be beaten. These leaders felt that their militias had several advantages. First of all, they were fighting for their own land. Second, they were familiar with the area. And third, the American troops used new ways of fighting. Instead of fighting in formation as the British troops often did, the Americans often carried out surprise attacks.

Fighting between British and American troops broke out in several places after May 1775. For example, colonial troops on high ground outside Boston were attacked by British troops on June 17, 1775. As the long lines of British troops advanced, the Americans defended their position on Breed's Hill. They were forced to retreat only after their ammunition ran out. Then, the British won the hill but at a great price. About 400 American soldiers were killed in the battle, but nearly 1,500 British soldiers were killed or wounded. In history books, this battle has become known as the Battle of Bunker Hill.

What was the actual site of the Battle of Bunker Hill?

The Declaration of Independence. The Americans had been at war with Great Britain since April 1775. Nevertheless, some Americans still did not want to fight a war with their home country. But there were many influential Americans who wanted to set up an indepen-

Historical Pictures Service

On June 17, 1775, British troops stormed the American trenches on Breed's Hill, outside Boston. The British attacked the position, just east of Bunker Hill, three times before they could drive the Americans back.

dent government. Thomas Paine, an immigrant from Great Britain, was one of those who believed Americans should fight for their freedom from Great Britain.

On January 10, 1776, Thomas Paine published a pamphlet called *Common Sense.* The pamphlet called upon all Americans to fight for their independence from Great Britain. In *Common Sense* Paine pointed out the wrongdoings of the king. In this way Paine helped to convince many Americans that they should be free of all ties with Great Britain.

By June 1776, most members of Congress also believed that the time had come for the colonies to break away from Great Britain. Congress, therefore, set up a committee led by Thomas Jefferson of Virginia to write a public notice of independence. This statement has become known as the *Declaration of Independence* (see Appendix, page 738).

In the Declaration, Jefferson told why the colonists had to break away from Great Britain. He also told the people of the world why the Americans wanted to set up their own government. Jefferson used many ideas about freedom and about government that were being talked about during the mid-1700's. In particular, Jefferson used many ideas of John Locke. Locke was a British writer who studied and wrote about government and about the rights of all people. Jefferson, however, stated the ideas more clearly and more forcefully than had ever been done before.

The Second Continental Congress approved the *Declaration of Independence* on July 4, 1776. By signing the Declaration, members of Congress told Great Britain that the American colonies were no longer part of the British Empire. However, the king and Parliament would not give up the British colonies in America so easily.

What popular pamphlet urged the colonists to fight for independence?

DO YOU KNOW?

When was the Liberty Bell cracked?

The Liberty Bell was cracked twice. The first crack happened shortly after the bell arrived in Philadelphia in 1752. This damage was erased because the bell was recast from the same metal in 1753. This one-ton bell became an important symbol of our independence because it was sounded on July 8, 1776, to hail the adoption of the Declaration of Independence. It was rung each year thereafter in honor of the Declaration. This practice ended in 1835 because the bell had cracked again as it was sounded during the funeral of Chief Justice John Marshall.

SECTION 1 REVIEW

1. *When did the Second Continental Congress establish the Continental Army?*
2. *What reasons did some Americans have for believing that the British army could be beaten?*
3. *Why did Thomas Jefferson write the Declaration of Independence?*

2 The War for Independence

Overview The British army was believed to be the strongest army in the world in 1775. Nevertheless, the much smaller American army was able to defeat the British by 1783. This happened for several reasons. First, the British were fighting far from home. Second, the Americans were fighting in areas they knew. Third, the Americans received help from several European nations. And fourth, the British were at war with several European countries while fighting the Americans.

Objectives After you read this section, you will be able to:

- identify the battle that was the turning point of the war for the Americans;
- analyze how the help of European nations benefited the Continental Army;
- describe the provisions of the Treaty of Paris.

Armies of the Revolution. Many groups took part in fighting the Revolutionary War. For the most part, the American side was made up of the Continental Army and of state militias. The Continental Army was the thirteen states' full-time, professional army. Soldiers of the Continental Army came from every state. These soldiers signed up for three years, or until the war ended. On the other hand, the militias, which were the volunteer armies of each state, were made up of soldiers who enlisted for no longer than three months at a time.

The British army was larger and better trained than the Continental Army or the state militias. There were about 42,000 British soldiers in the American colonies in 1776. However, British military leaders quickly increased the size of the army by hiring German *mercenaries*—soldiers for hire. About 30,000 of these soldiers, called Hessians, were hired and sent to America.

For the most part, the Continental Army was made up of young, white men. However, more than 5,000 black soldiers fought in the Continental Army and in the state militias. Peter Salem was a black soldier who became a hero in the Battle of Bunker Hill. Women also took part in the fighting of the Revolutionary War. Deborah Sampson, for example, disguised herself as a man in order to fight with the Massachusetts State militia. And Margaret Corbin took her husband's place in battle when he was killed. Although only a small number of colonists actually fought, the American Revolutionary War affected the lives of men and women in all the colonies.

■ *How did the Continental Army differ from the state militia?*

Fighting for Independence. The Revolutionary War took place between 1775 and 1783, with most of the early fighting centered in the Middle Atlantic States. The early battles of the war were most often won by the British. Nevertheless, American soldiers continued to fight against the larger and better-equipped British army.

In mid-July 1776 the British fleet under the command of Lord Howe anchored off the coast of Staten Island, waiting to attack the Continental Army led by General Washington. Two weeks later, this British army was strengthened by the arrival of troops from Charleston, South Carolina, led by Sir Henry Clinton. By late August 1776 the combined

British forces were strong enough to attack the rebellious Americans at Long Island, New York.

The Battle of Long Island began on August 27, 1776, and was won by the British within two days. This British victory forced General Washington and his army to make a long retreat. Washington first withdrew to New York City. However, a series of British victories in the months following the Battle of Long Island forced the Americans across New Jersey and across the icy Delaware River and into Pennsylvania on December 8, 1776.

The Americans had been closely followed in their retreat by a strong British army under the command of General Cornwallis. This army reached Trenton, New Jersey, on the same day as General Washington, narrowly missing the Americans. General Washington, aware of the British position, shrewdly waited for the right moment to counterattack. General Cornwallis, however, pulled back his main army, leaving only a small force to keep watch over the Americans.

Seventeen days after escaping into Pennsylvania, General Washington reentered New Jersey. On Christmas night, 1776, Washington's forces secretly crossed the Delaware River into Trenton and soundly defeated the British army in a surprise attack. More than 1,000 Hessian troops were captured by General Washington's soldiers. By January 3, 1777, Washington's troops were still on the attack, defeating three British regiments in the Battle of Princeton, New Jersey.

■ *How did the Battle of Long Island affect the positions of the Continental Army?*

At the Battle of Monmouth, Mary Ludwig Hays saw her husband fall as she carried pitchers of water to the American soldiers. She took his place at the cannon until the battle ended. In stories that were later told of her heroic acts, she was known as "Molly Pitcher."

The Bettmann Archive

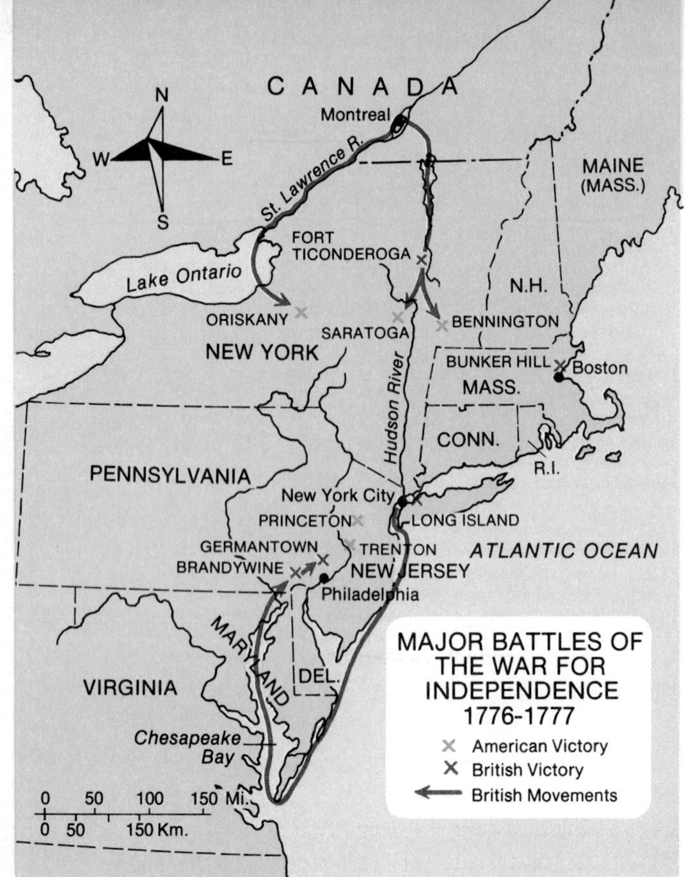

At first, British victories nearly overwhelmed the Americans. But an American victory at Saratoga in 1777 turned the tide in America's favor. Who won the battle at Bennington?

Foreign Aid for the Americans. In October 1777, British troops under General Burgoyne and American soldiers led by Horatio Gates met in the Battle of Saratoga, New York. This ten-day battle later proved to be the turning point of the war for the Americans. The American victory at Saratoga caused several European countries to believe that the Americans would win the war. Because of this belief, some foreign countries began to help the Americans. These countries sent money, goods, and war materials. Experienced leaders also volunteered to help the Continental Army defeat the British. Baron de Kalb and Baron von Steuben volunteered to come to America from what later became the country of Germany. Casimir Pulaski and Thaddeus Kosciusko came from Poland. Major General Lafayette, General de Rochambeau, and Admiral de Grasse came from France.

In what four ways did the Americans receive support from foreign countries?

Loyalists During the Revolutionary War. Loyalists were colonists in America who wanted to remain loyal to Great Britain. They were large landowners, rich merchants, and successful doctors and lawyers who feared major government changes. Many church leaders also remained loyal to British rule.

Patriots often treated the loyalists harshly. Some loyalists were covered with tar and feathers. Others were killed by mobs of angry patriots. Because some loyalists were treated so severely, many loyalists fled to Canada or to Great Britain. Other loyalists, however, stayed in America, where they worked against the War for Independence. Some of these people tried to get patriots to return to British rule by distributing pamphlets that argued against colonial independence. Other loyalists, known as Tories at that time, fought together with British troops against the patriots.

Treatment of the loyalists became even harsher when word of Benedict Arnold's actions became known to the patriots. Benedict Arnold was an American war hero throughout most of the Revolutionary War. But in autumn of 1780 the Americans learned that he was a traitor. Arnold was the commander of West Point, an important American fort. He planned to turn the fort over to the British in exchange

(Text continues on page 110.)

RECALLING THE TIMES

Valley Forge

The Continental Army under General George Washington spent the harsh winter of 1777–1778 at Valley Forge, Pennsylvania. The following account of life at Valley Forge was written in the diary of Albigence Waldo, a doctor who spent the winter caring for the American soldiers.

Dec. 14th [1777]—... The army who have been surprisingly healthy hitherto—now begin to grow sickly from the continued fatigues they have suffered [on] this Campaign. Yet they still show spirit of Alacrity & Contentment not to be expected from so young Troops.... Poor food—hard lodging—Cold Weather—fatigue—Nasty Cloaths—nasty Cookery—Vomit half my time... Why are we sent here to starve and freeze... [A soldier's] bare feet are seen thro' his worn out Shoes—his legs nearly naked from the tatter'd remains of an only pair of stockings...

Dec. 25th, Christmas.—We are still in Tents—when we ought to be in huts—the poor Sick, suffer much in Tents this cold Weather...

Dec. 31st.—Ajutant Selden learn'd me how to Darn Stockings—to make them look like knit work...

Sunday, Jan. 4th. [1778]—... I was call'd to relieve a Soldier tho't to be dying—he expir'd [died] before I reach'd the Hutt. He was an Indian—an excellent Soldier—and an obedient good natur'd fellow....

Thinking Critically

Why did the Continental Army begin to grow sickly?

In your opinion, how did the soldiers feel about enduring the hardships at Valley Forge? Give reasons for your answer.

Courtesy of the Valley Forge Historical Society

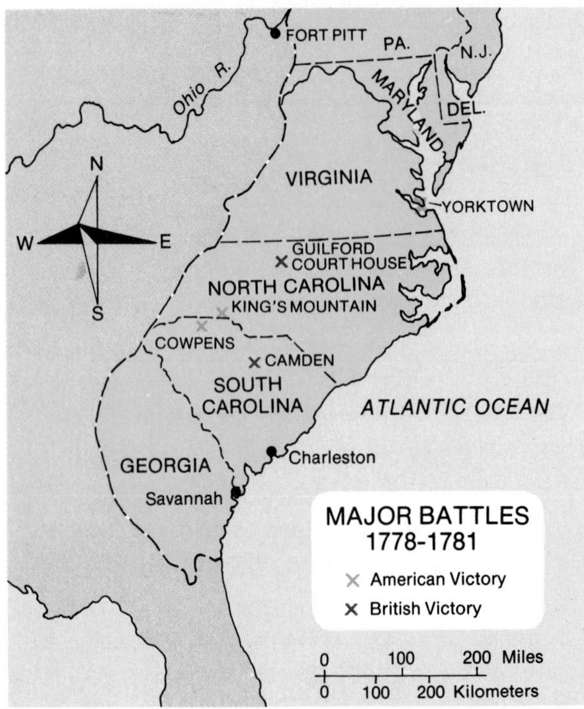

After 1778, the British leaders concentrated their attacks on the southern states. In 1781, the British army was trapped on a peninsula near Yorktown, Virginia. What American victory occurred in North Carolina?

for a large amount of money and a promise of great wealth after the war. His plan was discovered, however, before he could take any action. General Arnold escaped from the Americans and fought on the side of the British until the end of the war. He then escaped to Great Britain.

■ *What groups of colonists tended to be loyalists?*

Fighting in the Last Years of the War. The major battles after 1778 took place mainly in the West and in the South. George Rogers Clark led an American army to the western frontier. There he captured Kaskaskia in what later became the state of Illinois on July 4, 1778. Turning east, Clark's forces captured Vincennes on February 25, 1779. The capture of these important British positions gave the new American government a claim to the British-held lands west of the Appalachian Mountains.

The British army controlled much territory in the South throughout most of 1780. On May 12, for example, Charleston, South Carolina, was taken by the British. This forced the Americans to retreat to the north. On August 16, the Americans were severely defeated at Camden, South Carolina. Two months later, however, a British force—largely made up of loyalist Tories—was defeated by a group of American patriots at the Battle of King's Mountain on the border between South Carolina and North Carolina.

Military activity in the South continued in 1781. Early in January, American troops defeated the British at the Battle of the Cowpens in South Carolina. Less than two months later, American forces, led by Nathanael Greene, inflicted heavy losses on the British army, led by General Cornwallis, at the Battle of Guilford Court House in North Carolina. The British then marched to Yorktown, Virginia, where they expected to meet the British fleet.

The Revolutionary War was also fought at sea. The Second Continental Congress established the Continental Navy shortly after it set up the Continental Army. The navy, however, was no match for the stronger British navy. The American navy was primarily made up of about 2,000 privately owned ships and boats. Nevertheless, the Americans sank or seized about 200 British ships during the Revolutionary War. At one point, Captain John Paul

Jones even sailed his ship, the *Bonhomme Richard,* into waters near the coast of Great Britain. On September 23, 1779, Jones captured the British ship *Serapis* off the coast of Scotland. Such naval attacks were possible because the Americans were allowed to use France as a supply base. The French navy itself also played an important part in the final major battle of the Revolutionary war.

■ *Where did most fighting after 1778 take place?*

Yorktown. The British army under General Cornwallis depended on the British fleet for their supplies. In late September 1781, the French fleet blocked the British navy from reaching Yorktown, where Cornwallis and his troops were waiting. At the same time, General Washington, General "Mad Anthony" Wayne, Baron von Steuben, and Major General Lafayette led more than 16,000 American and French soldiers against the 8,000 British soldiers stranded at Yorktown. More British troops should have been positioned at Yorktown to take on the American and French troops. However, British army leaders could not agree on their planning. The British, therefore, were forced to surrender on October 19, 1781.

King George III and Prime Minister Lord North wanted to continue the war against the patriots, but many members of Parliament wanted peace. As a result, a conditional peace treaty was signed on November 30, 1782, in Paris. However, the formal treaty, called the Treaty of Paris, was not signed until September 3, 1783.

■ *Why were only 8,000 British troops present at Yorktown in 1781?*

The Treaty of Paris. The Treaty of Paris was signed in 1783. It was largely the result of the work of America's representatives—John Adams, Benjamin Franklin, John Jay, and Henry Laurens. In the treaty the United States gained its independence plus the rights to a large amount of land. All the land from the Appalachian Mountains west to the Mississippi River and from the Great Lakes south to Florida was granted to the United States. In return, it was agreed that Congress would recommend to the states that property that had been seized from the loyalists should be returned or paid for. The payment of debts owed to British merchants was also to be encouraged.

Overall, the Treaty of Paris was a victory for the United States. And with its gain of vast new lands, the United States began to build and grow.

■ *What did the United States gain through the Treaty of Paris?*

SECTION 2 REVIEW

1. *Why was the Battle of Saratoga, New York, the turning point of the war?*
2. *How did the Continental Army benefit from the help of European nations?*
3. *What were the provisions of the Treaty of Paris?*

3 A New Nation

Overview The leaders of the new United States of America faced many problems. Perhaps the most pressing problem was the need for a new form of government—a government that could meet the needs of the people of the new nation.

Objectives After you read this section, you will be able to:

- identify the central government that brought the thirteen states together into the United States of America;
- explain why the economy of the United States was weak in the first years under the Articles of Confederation;
- describe the weaknesses of the Articles of Confederation.

Changes in Government. The Second Continental Congress was the body through which the thirteen American states joined together to state their freedom from Great Britain. While the Americans were at war with Great Britain, representatives from each state continued to meet as the Second Continental Congress. Before long, however, it became clear that in order to defeat the British, the Americans had to set up a form of government with greater power. Thirteen members of the Second Continental Congress—one from each state—began to write a plan of government.

The *Articles of Confederation* was the name of the new plan of government. The Second Continental Congress approved the plan on November 15, 1777. Then, the Articles of Confederation were approved by each of the thirteen states. In this way the thirteen states joined together to form the nation called the United States of America. This was done March 1, 1781.

The Articles called for a Congress to be elected to serve as the central government of the United States. However, this Congress could make no laws without the approval of all thirteen states. The thirteen states, proudly independent, were not willing to give up their power to a central government. Thus, the United States government under the Articles of Confederation remained weak.

■ *Why did the government under the Articles of Confederation remain weak?*

Life Under the New Government. The way of life in the United States did not change greatly immediately after the Revolutionary War. The national government under the Articles of Confederation had little impact upon the lives of most Americans. Nevertheless, some changes had begun to take place in American society during the war. And these changes continued in the years that followed. New ideas about government began to emerge. Many Americans, for example, came to believe that religion and government should be separated.

Land use and ways of earning a living also underwent change during this time. New farms were set up in the thirteen states and in the land west of the Appalachian Mountains. This came about because many state governments took over lands that had belonged to loyalists during the Revolutionary War. These landholdings were then broken up and sold in order to help pay war debts. More persons were then able to make a living by farming. Also, more persons traveled beyond the Appalachian Mountains. In this way the frontier of the United States was pushed farther west. However, this was often done at a great cost to Indian groups living between the Appalachian Mountains and the Mississippi River. Nevertheless, few white Americans showed much concern for Indian rights to the lands that the white settlers claimed as their own.

At the same time many Americans began to believe that slavery should be outlawed. The New England states and most of the Middle Atlantic States outlawed slavery within a few years after the Revolutionary War. Slavery continued, however, in places where farming was done on large plantations and where many farm workers were needed. In fact, by the mid-1780's slavery had become a major part of the new nation's farming economy in the South.

■ *What was one new idea about government that began to emerge after the Revolutionary War?*

The Economy of the New Nation. The economy of the United States was very weak in the first years under the Articles of Confederation. This was, in part, because the United States owed many war debts to other countries. In fact, by 1781 the public debt of the United States was already more than 75 million dollars. Also, under the Articles of Confederation the Congress did not have the power

(Text continues on page 115.)

No longer prohibited by British laws from moving west of the Appalachian Mountains, new settlers rapidly began to expand the American frontier.

"Daniel Boone Escorting Settlers Through the Cumberland Gap" by George Caleb. Bingham, Washington University Gallery of Art, St. Louis.

Courtesy of the Essex Institute, Salem, MA

Sandak, Inc.

A uniquely American style of painting developed as artists broke away from European traditions. Benjamin Blythe's "Samuel Curwen" (above left) and Francis Guy's "Tontine Coffeehouse" (above right) were completed before 1800. Charles B. King painted "Young Omahaw, War Eagle, Little Missouri, and Pawnees" (below left) in the 1820's. Thomas Cole painted "Mountain Landscape With Waterfall" (below right) during the 1840's.

National Collection of Fine Arts, Smithsonian Institution

Museum of Art, Rhode Island School of Design, Jesse Metcalf Fund needed to deal with the economy. This power remained with each state. However, the economy in general improved after 1787 as American merchants increased trade with other nations, such as France, Holland, and several countries of the Orient. Moreover, trade between the United States and Great Britain grew slowly but steadily in the years after the Revolutionary War.

American farm products, such as tobacco, indigo, cotton, and rice were sold in foreign countries. Manufactured goods were then often taken in payment. As American manufacturing grew, however, trade payments were made in *specie*—gold and silver. This gave the United States a stronger backing for its paper money. Thus, American paper money rose in value, and the American economy became prosperous for some American merchants and manufacturers. Farmers, however, continued to face economic problems.

■ *Why was the United States economy very weak in the first years under the Articles of Confederation?*

Shays' Rebellion. Massachusetts farmers were very hard hit with economic problems. As the state government tried to repay its war debts, it placed heavy taxes on farmers. Those who could not pay their taxes lost their farms to the state. This angered many farmers, including Daniel Shays.

In 1786, Shays led a group of about 2,000 angry farmers. The group took over a federal arsenal and a state court in the Worcester-Springfield area of Massachusetts. The rebellion was short-lived, however. The state's governor ordered the militia to end the uprising. The group of farmers was broken up, and Daniel Shays was captured. However, because most people in the state were farmers who supported Shays, he was never punished. Nevertheless, the uprising upset many people throughout the country. They came to believe that a stronger central government might prevent such outbreaks from taking place.

■ *Why did the state of Massachusetts place heavy taxes on farmers?*

Early Government Achievements. Under the Articles of Confederation, the central government of the United States accomplished two major goals. First, the government under the Articles ended the Revolutionary War. It did this by signing the Treaty of Paris with Great Britain in 1783. Second, the new government set up a land policy and a structure of government for the Northwest Territory.

By the mid-1780's it was clear to many members of Congress that laws dealing with the western lands had to be made. There were two major reasons for this. First, it was widely accepted that Americans would continue to move westward, settling new areas. Second, several of the thirteen states had made claims on parts of the Northwest Territory. These claims could lead to fighting if the matter was not taken care of by the central government. Overall, the Congress believed it would be better for the central government, rather than the separate state governments, to govern the western lands.

Congress first acted on these problems in 1785. In that year the first national land policy in the United States was passed. The Land Ordinance of 1785 set up the way public land was to be surveyed and subdivided for sale to the public. This law also stated how the land was to be sold. Two years later Congress passed the Northwest Ordinance. This law outlined the steps that had to be taken for a territory to become a state and to enter the Union

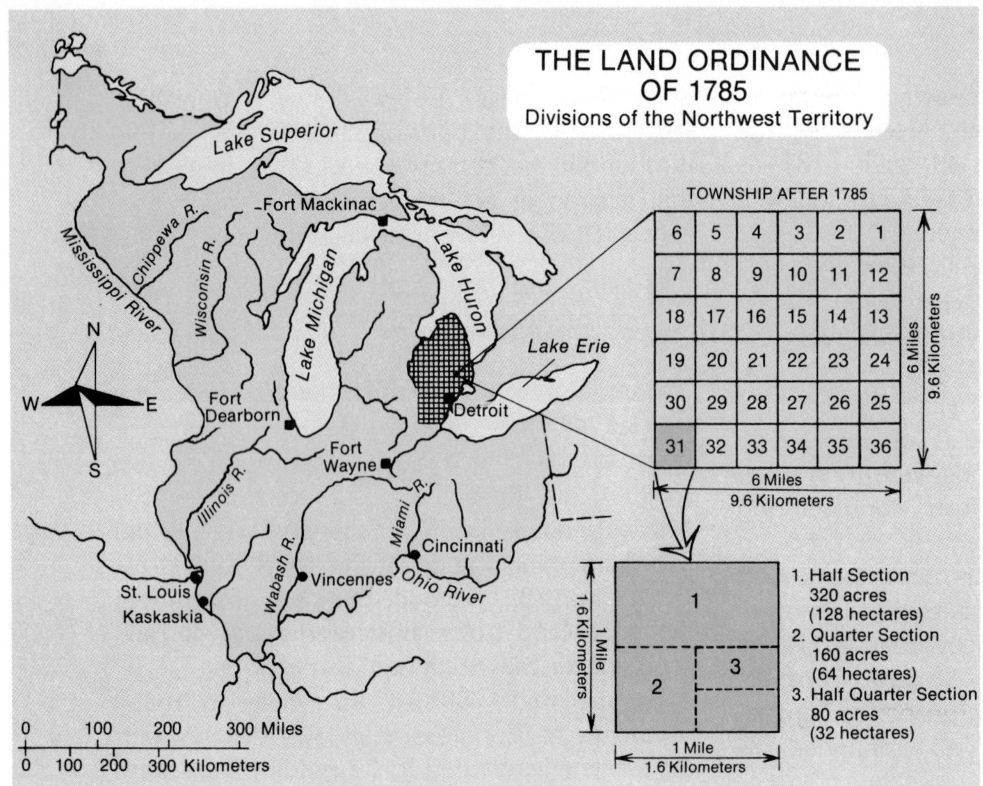

The Land Ordinance of 1785 provided a practical way to organize the western lands. The law aided the laying out of roads, the locating of towns and cities, and the selling of land. Also one section in every township was set aside for the support of public education. According to the map, how many sections make up a township?

on an equal basis with the original thirteen states. This act also outlawed slavery throughout the Northwest Territory.

■ *What were the two major reasons why a national land policy was needed in the mid-1780's?*

Limits of Power. The government under the Articles of Confederation was planned to be weak. This was because members of Congress were against setting up a strong central government, such as the one in Great Britain. Thus, the American Congress was given very limited powers.

There were four major weaknesses in the government under the Articles. First, with no executive leader, such as a king, prime minister, or president, even small problems took months to solve. Major decisions could not be made without the consent of all the states. Second, Congress could not levy taxes. Tax money had to come from each state. Third, trade laws rested with the states. Each state had the power to control its own trade. The central government had no economic power of its own. And fourth, Congress could not enforce the laws that it passed. This was left to the states. Many of the states, however, tended to carry out only a part of many laws.

■ *Why were the Articles of Confederation planned to be weak?*

Attempts at Change. Three attempts to change the Articles of Confederation were made by government leaders who favored a stronger central government. The first attempt grew out of a trade meeting held at Mount Vernon, Virginia, early in 1785. This meeting included persons from Virginia, Maryland, Delaware, and Pennsylvania. Because of the success of this meeting, James Madison of Virginia urged that another meeting be held to discuss trade problems among all states.

The second meeting took place in Annapolis, Maryland, the following year. However, only five states were represented. Alexander Hamilton, the representative from New York, took advantage of the poor attendance. He drew up a report calling for an even larger meeting—a convention of all states—to be held in mid-1787. This convention, Hamilton said, was to be called to revise the weak Articles of Confederation. Hamilton and other government leaders knew that the central government of the United States was not able to deal with emergencies, such as an attack by a foreign country. With James Madison's aid, Hamilton's report was supported by Congress. The call then went out to all states that a convention would be held in Philadelphia, Pennsylvania, in May 1787.

■ *Why were attempts made to change the Articles of Confederation?*

SECTION 3 REVIEW

1. *When did the thirteen American states form the union called the United States of America?*
2. *Why was the economy of the United States weak in the first years under the Articles of Confederation?*
3. *What were the four major weaknesses in the government under the Articles of Confederation?*

CHAPTER 6 SUMMARY

During the 1770's political and economic differences between the American colonists and the British government grew. Nevertheless, many Americans hoped to keep the colonies within the British Empire. However, greater use of military force by Great Britain caused more Americans to think that the colonies should be free from their home country. As a result, the Second Continental Congress—the acting government of the Thirteen Colonies—declared the colonies' independence from Great Britain on July 4, 1776.

The Americans had to fight for their freedom. Often, American soldiers did not have enough food, ammunition, and other supplies to fight effectively against the British army. Nevertheless, the Continental Army, led by General George Washington, was able to defeat the larger British army and to win independence from Great Britain.

The new nation was called the United States of America. It was made up of thirteen states. These states were loosely joined together under a weak central government. The central government was too weak to deal with the problems facing the new nation. Thus, many Americans knew that a stronger central government was needed.

CHAPTER 6 REVIEW

USING YOUR SKILLS

Interpreting Political Cartoons

Political cartoons are drawings that make statements about people, places, or events in the news. Political cartoonists want to show their point of view to their readers often by poking fun at their subjects. For the most part, political cartoonists use easily recognizable symbols for famous people, places, or events. For example, in the United States the elephant has become the symbol of the Republican party. The donkey symbolizes the Democratic party. The political cartoon below was published in Great Britain in 1782. It shows the cartoonist's view of the settlement of the War for Independence. The cartoon also shows that Holland, Spain, and France wanted to keep Great Britain and the United States apart. Examine the cartoon carefully and then answer the following questions:

1. Which country does the white female figure stand for?
2. Which cartoon figure is used as a symbol for the United States?
3. Which cartoon figure symbolizes the country of Holland?
4. Which cartoon figure is used as a symbol for France?
5. To what person might the words on the shield—"George for ever"—refer?
6. What is the cartoonist saying about the relationship between the United States and Great Britain?
7. How does the cartoonist show that three European countries want to keep the United States and Great Britain apart?

Culver Pictures

CHAPTER 6 REVIEW

YOU SHOULD KNOW

Identify, define, or explain each of the following:

Breed's Hill	Deborah Sampson
Common Sense	Casimir Pulaski
Thomas Jefferson	specie
mercenaries	James Madison

CHECKING FACTS

1. When did the Second Continental Congress agree to set up the Continental Army?
2. Who was chosen as president of the Second Continental Congress in 1775?
3. Who was Thomas Paine?
4. Who were the Hessians?
5. To where did many loyalists flee during the Revolutionary War?
6. Who was Benedict Arnold?
7. Where did the British Army surrender?
8. What were the Articles of Confederation?
9. What was Shays' Rebellion?
10. What was the purpose of the Northwest Ordinance?

UNDERSTANDING CONCEPTS

1. Why did the Second Continental Congress meet on May 10, 1775, in Philadelphia?
2. Why did most leaders of colonial militias believe that the British army could be defeated?
3. What groups of colonists remained loyal to British rule, and in what ways did they work against the War for Independence?
4. How did the Land Ordinance of 1785 and the Northwest Ordinance help to organize the western lands?

LEARNING FROM ILLUSTRATIONS

1. Based upon your study of the illustration on page 107, do you think that the artist was pro-American or pro-British? Why?
2. Study the map on page 116. Why are property and boundary lines probably more regular today in states west of the Appalachian Mountains than they are in the thirteen colonies?

CRITICAL THINKING

1. Pretend you are living during the Revolutionary War. Would you be on the side of the patriots or of the loyalists? Give reasons for your answers.
2. After the Revolutionary War, many Americans came to believe that religion and government should be separated. In your opinion, should religion and government be separated? Give reasons for your opinion.
3. If you were living in the United States after the Revolutionary War, would you have been interested in expanding the American frontier? Why or why not?

ENRICHMENT ACTIVITIES

1. To better understand military history, divide into groups and make bulletin-board maps that show the major battles of the American War for Independence as well as British army and Continental Army troop movements.
2. It is interesting to learn more about the individuals who have shaped our history. Use encyclopedias and biographical books to find information about the signers of the Declaration of Independence. Then share this information with your class.

1780 1790 1800

1787 The Philadelphia Convention meets

1788 The Constitution becomes the supreme law of the United States

1789 George Washington becomes the first President of the United States

1791 The first Bank of the United States is set up

1793 Washington issues a Proclamation of Neutrality

1794 United States troops end the Whiskey Rebellion

1797 John Adams becomes the second President

CHAPTER 7

Creating a New Government

Chapter Objectives

After studying this chapter, you will be able to:

- identify the two plans of government introduced at the Constitutional Convention and explain their major differences;
- list several freedoms that are protected under the Bill of Rights;
- name and distinguish between the two earliest political parties.

1 The Constitution Is Written

Overview The national government under the Articles of Confederation was weak. In order to improve the Articles, many government leaders called a meeting in Philadelphia. The meeting became a constitutional convention when it was decided to write a new plan of government that would be stronger than the Articles of Confederation.

Objectives After you read this section, you will be able to:

- identify the differences between the New Jersey plan and the Virginia plan of government;
- describe the plan of government that was finally accepted by the planners of the Constitution;
- explain the differences between the Federalists and the Anti-Federalists.

The Philadelphia Convention. The meeting of the 13 American states was to begin on May 14, 1787, at the Pennsylvania State House—now Independence Hall—in Philadelphia. The meeting was called to strengthen the Articles of Confederation. But because transportation was so poor, few delegates arrived on time. Delegates from Rhode Island never came at all. This was because Rhode Island was against the idea of a stronger central government.

The convention began late—on May 25, 1787—with delegates from 11 states present. However, 55 delegates from 12 states eventually took part in writing the Constitution. The convention continued for 116 days throughout a very hot summer, ending successfully in mid-September 1787.

Many delegates to the convention were well-known people of the time because of their roles in the Revolutionary War or because of the offices they held in their state governments. George Washington of Virginia was chosen as president of the convention. His strong leadership often kept the meetings from breaking up during the many disagreements that took place. Benjamin Franklin, at 81 years of age, was also present as a delegate from Pennsylvania. James Madison of Virginia kept careful notes on the secret daily meetings of the convention. Alexander Hamilton was a representative of New York.

Several well-known Americans did not take part in the convention, however. Samuel Adams, John Hancock, and John Jay were not chosen as delegates by the voters in their states. Patrick Henry was against a strong central government and would not attend. And John Adams and Thomas Jefferson were in Europe on government business.

How many states were represented at the Constitutional Convention at Philadelphia?

The Virginia Plan of Government. Many delegates to the Constitutional Convention held strong ideas about the kind of government the United States should have. Fortunately, the delegates also believed in *compromise*—an agreement in which both sides give up some demands. The Constitution of the United States was developed in this way.

Two plans of government were considered during the Constitutional Convention. The first plan, called the Virginia plan, favored a strong central government. It was probably written by

James Madison. Edmund Randolph of Virginia submitted the plan on May 27, 1787. This plan became the basis of the Constitution of the United States—but only after much debate and compromise.

The Virginia plan favored a government made up of three separate branches. The first branch, Congress, would make the laws for the country. The second branch, the executive, would carry out the laws. And the third branch, the court system, would review the laws made by Congress and deal with persons accused of breaking the laws.

According to the Virginia plan, Congress was to be made up of representatives from each state. The number of persons elected to Congress from each state would be based on the number of people in that state. Thus, a small state, such as New Jersey, would have fewer representatives in Congress than a larger state, such as Pennsylvania. This part of the Virginia plan was favored by states with large populations. States with fewer people, however, did not like the plan.

■ *What were the three branches of government proposed as part of the Virginia plan of government?*

The New Jersey Plan. The smaller states submitted their own plan—the New Jersey plan—in mid-June. It was written to protect the interests of the smaller states. The New Jersey plan favored a government much like the government under the Articles of Confederation. It would be made up of only one branch—Congress. However, Congress was to be given new powers under this plan—powers that the Congress under the Articles did not have. For example, under the New Jersey plan, Congress could levy taxes, put restrictions on trade with other countries, and regulate all trade among states. Under this plan, however, state representation in Congress would not be based on population. Instead, each state would have an equal number of representatives in Congress. Thus, larger states could not outvote the smaller states. The larger states were against this plan.

By early July 1787 it was clear that the Convention was deadlocked over the form the new government was to take. It was also clear that a compromise was needed if the Constitutional Convention was to continue.

■ *What new powers were to be given to Congress under the New Jersey plan of government?*

The Need for Compromise. Four compromises had to be made before the Constitution was completed. The *Great Compromise* solved the differences among those delegates who backed the New Jersey plan of government and those who favored the Virginia plan. This compromise set up a *bicameral legislature*. That is, Congress was to be made up of two houses—the House of Representatives and the Senate. Representation in the House of Representatives was to be based on the number of people living in each state. Larger states would therefore have more representatives than the smaller states. However, the number of representatives in the Senate was to be set at two senators from each state. Therefore, all states would have equal representation in the Senate and have representation based on population in the House of Representatives. Through the Great Compromise the planners of the Constitution also decided upon a government divided into three branches—the executive, the legislative, and the judicial.

The delegates also had to work out a compromise on a matter that caused great disagreement between the northern and southern sections of the country. The problem dealt with the way in which a state's population was determined. This was important because taxation and representation in Congress were based on the number of persons living in each state. Northerners believed that slaves should be counted among the population of a state for tax reasons but not for representation in Congress. Southerners, however, wanted slaves counted for representation but not for taxation. To overcome this problem, the members of the Constitutional Convention agreed to count five slaves as three free persons for both taxation and representation. This became known as the Three-Fifths Compromise.

Many delegates wanted Congress to have the power to end the slave trade. Delegates from states that depended heavily on slave labor, however, did not want the government to have this power. A compromise was reached by giving Congress the power to end the slave trade—but only after a 20-year delay. The government was not given any other power over slavery.

Two problems concerning the election of a President were also settled through compromise. First, the President's term of office was set at four years. And second, it was decided that the President and the Vice-President would not be elected directly by the people. Instead, they were to be chosen by persons called *electors*. The electors were to be chosen by the state legislatures.

■ *How did the Great Compromise satisfy the larger and smaller states?*

The Fight for Ratification. The Constitutional Convention closed on September 17, 1787. On that day 39 delegates signed their names to the new Constitution. However, for one reason or another, 16 delegates would not sign the Constitution. This showed that *ratification* of the Constitution—approval by the states—would be difficult.

Two main groups were involved in the ratification fight. These groups became known as the *Federalists* and the *Anti-Federalists.* The Federalists supported the idea of a strong central—or federal—government. The Federalists worked hard to gain support for the Constitution in each of the 13 states. They did this, in part, by printing newspaper articles that

Virginia State Library and Archives

Roger Sherman proposed what later became known as the Great Compromise as a way to settle the dispute between the large and small states.

Historical Pictures Service

The Ninth PILLAR erected !
" The Ratification of the Conventions of nine States, shall be sufficient for the establishment of this Constitution, between the States so ratifying the same." Art. vii.
INCIPIENT MAGNI PROCEDERE MENSES.
If it is not up it will rise.
The Attraction must be irresistible
DEL.
PEN.
N·JER.
GEOR.
CON.
MASSA.
MARY.
S^o. CARO.
N.HAMP.
VIRG.
N.YORK

Nine states were needed for ratification of the Constitution. However, it was generally believed that the support of Virginia and New York was needed for the union's success.

explained the Constitution to the people. In many of these papers the Federalists stressed the importance of a strong central government for the well-being of the United States. The articles were written by James Madison, Alexander Hamilton, and John Jay. Later, the articles were bound together in a book called the *Federalist.*

The Anti-Federalists were against the Constitution. This was because they feared having a powerful central government. They fought hard against the proposed form of government by bringing their arguments to the people and to the state legislatures. Nevertheless, the Federalists were able to overcome these arguments. In large part, this was because they were better organized than the Anti-Federalists. Also, Federalist leaders, such as George Washington and Benjamin Franklin, were well-known and respected throughout the country. As a result, the Constitution was eventually ratified by all 13 states.

The Constitution became the supreme law of the United States on June 21, 1788. This was the day that New Hampshire became the ninth state to ratify the Constitution. Several states ratified only after being promised that a *bill of rights*—a list of guaranteed freedoms—would be immediately added to the Constitution upon ratification. The writing of the Bill of Rights, as you will read, was one of the first actions taken by the new Congress under the Constitution of the United States.

■ *What main groups were involved in the fight for ratification of the Constitution?*

SECTION 1 REVIEW

1. *What two plans of government were considered during the Constitutional Convention in Philadelphia?*
2. *How did the Great Compromise solve the differences among those delegates who backed the New Jersey plan and those who favored the Virginia plan?*
3. *Why were the Anti-Federalists against the Constitution?*

2 The Design of Government

Overview The Constitution of the United States is one of the most remarkable documents of its kind ever written. The delegates to the Philadelphia Convention based their work on earlier constitutions, such as state constitutions, and on writings from British history. The result was a Constitution that set up a framework of government that has lasted over two centuries.

Objectives After you read this section, you will be able to:

- identify the Bill of Rights;
- describe how the Constitution provides for a separation of powers in government;
- analyze the ways in which the Constitution is flexible and elastic.

The Bill of Rights. When the new Constitution was sent to the states for ratification, many Americans did not think it was complete. This group, which included some delegates to the Constitutional Convention, believed that these rights should be listed to make certain that all Americans would always have these freedoms.

Some Anti-Federalists tried to stop the states from ratifying the Constitution. They did this by pointing out that the citizens' freedoms had not been listed. Those who supported the Constitution, the Federalists, convinced the states that this list would be added by the first Congress. Several states accepted the new Constitution only with this promise.

The first Congress met in early April 1789. It spent much of its first six months in session drawing up this list of freedoms. James Madison, a member of the first Congress, took a major part in writing these changes. By September 1789, Congress had drawn up 12 amendments to the Constitution out of a list of 78 submitted by the states. These were then sent to the states for ratification.

Three fourths of the states—11 states—had to ratify the amendments for them to become part of the Constitution. Of the 13 states, Virginia became the eleventh state to ratify the

James Madison's farsighted ideas, originally laid out in the Virginia Plan, provided a lasting foundation for the Constitution. He later served as President from 1809 to 1813.

Thomas Gilcrease Institute of American History and Art, Tulsa, Oklahoma

first 10 of the 12 proposed amendments on December 15, 1791. The proposed Eleventh and Twelfth amendments dealt with the number of representatives in the House of Representatives and with ways of paying them. These amendments were never ratified and never became part of the Constitution.

The first 10 amendments became known as the Bill of Rights. The first eight amendments listed the rights that members of the first Congress believed to be the most-important rights of people living in a free country. The Ninth and Tenth amendments prevented Congress from passing laws that could take away these rights. To find out all the rights that you have as a citizen of the United States, read the Bill of Rights on page 755 and see the chart on this page.

■ *Which amendments make up the Bill of Rights?*

The Framework of Government. The government of the United States is based on

The first ten amendments to the United States Constitution—also known as the Bill of Rights—guarantee the basic freedoms of all Americans.

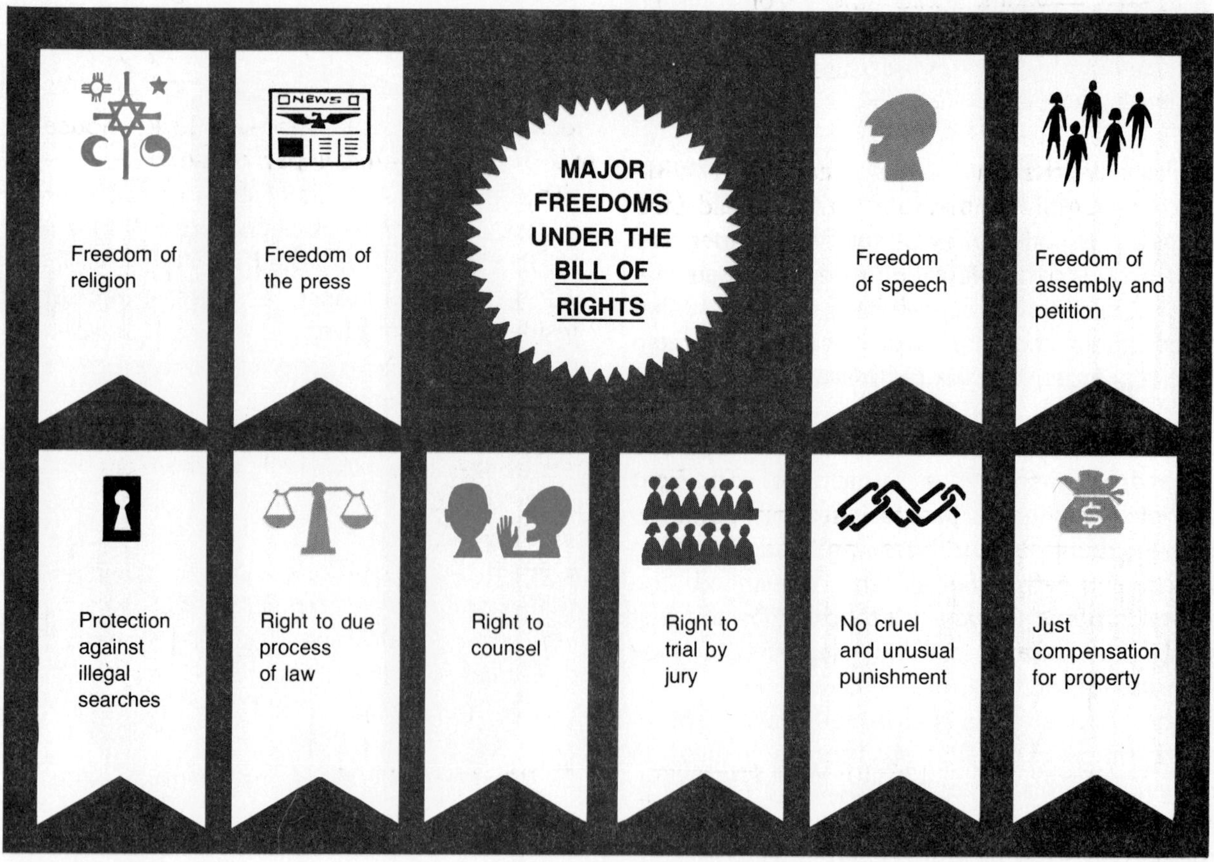

the principle of *constitutional supremacy.* That is, the Constitution is the highest law in the country. Any laws passed anywhere in the country must agree with what is written in the Constitution [*82-*83].[1]

The Constitution provides for the United States to have a federal system of government. In this plan, lawmaking powers are divided between two levels of government—the state governments and the federal government. The duties of government are then shared between these two levels.

The powers that belong solely to the federal government are listed in the Constitution. These powers are called the *delegated,* or *expressed, powers.* This is because they are "expressed"—written into—the Constitution. They include the power to regulate trade and the power to declare war on other countries.

The Constitution does not list the powers given to the states. It does, however, set out what powers the states do *not* have [*51-*53]. This was done so that the states would not take on as much power as they had under the Articles of Confederation. However, through the Tenth Amendment in the Bill of Rights [*94] the people or the states have *reserved powers.* That is, whatever powers have neither been given to the federal government nor been prohibited by the states are reserved for the people or for the state governments. For example, state governments can make laws to license automobile drivers and to regulate hunting and fishing.

Governmental powers are sometimes shared by the federal and state governments. These jointly shared powers are called *concurrent powers.* Road building, dam building, and tax collecting are three examples.

■ *What is the highest law in the United States?*

The Separation of Powers. The United States government is separated into three distinct branches. These are the legislative, the executive, and the judicial branches of government. Each branch has separate duties and powers. This separation was made because the delegates to the Constitutional Convention did not want all governmental powers centered on one person or one branch of government.

The legislative branch—Congress—makes all federal laws [*1-*53]. Congress, as you have read, is made up of two houses. These are the House of Representatives—the lower house—and the Senate—the upper house.

The executive branch of government carries out the laws made by Congress [*54-*64]. The President of the United States is the head of the executive branch of government. The President is also given a number of special powers [*62-*64]. These special powers are called the *enumerated powers.*

The judicial branch of government interprets and applies our Constitution and the laws passed by Congress [*67-*70]. This branch also judges whether or not people accused of breaking the country's laws are guilty. The federal-court system makes up this branch of government. The Supreme Court is the highest federal court and, therefore, the highest court in the country.

■ *What are the three branches of government under the Constitution of the United States?*

[1]Reference numerals such as [*82-*83] above appear from time to time in this chapter and in later chapters. These numerals refer to paragraphs of the Constitution of the United States, which is reprinted on pages 743–764.

Checks and Balances. The planners of the Constitution wanted to make certain that no one branch of government would ever become more powerful than the other two. To maintain this separation of powers, a system of *checks and balances* was added to the Constitution (see chart on this page). Under this system, each branch of government is able to *check*—curb—the powers of the other two branches.

The power of the President may be checked by Congress or by the courts. In the same way, the power of Congress and the courts can be checked by the President. For example, the President can *veto*—block—a law passed by Congress. The President may also appoint persons to become federal judges. Therefore, the powers of the three branches of government are controlled by one another. As a result, the power of government remains

Because governmental powers are separated among three branches, each branch is able to check on the actions of the other two branches. How does the legislative branch check on the judicial branch?

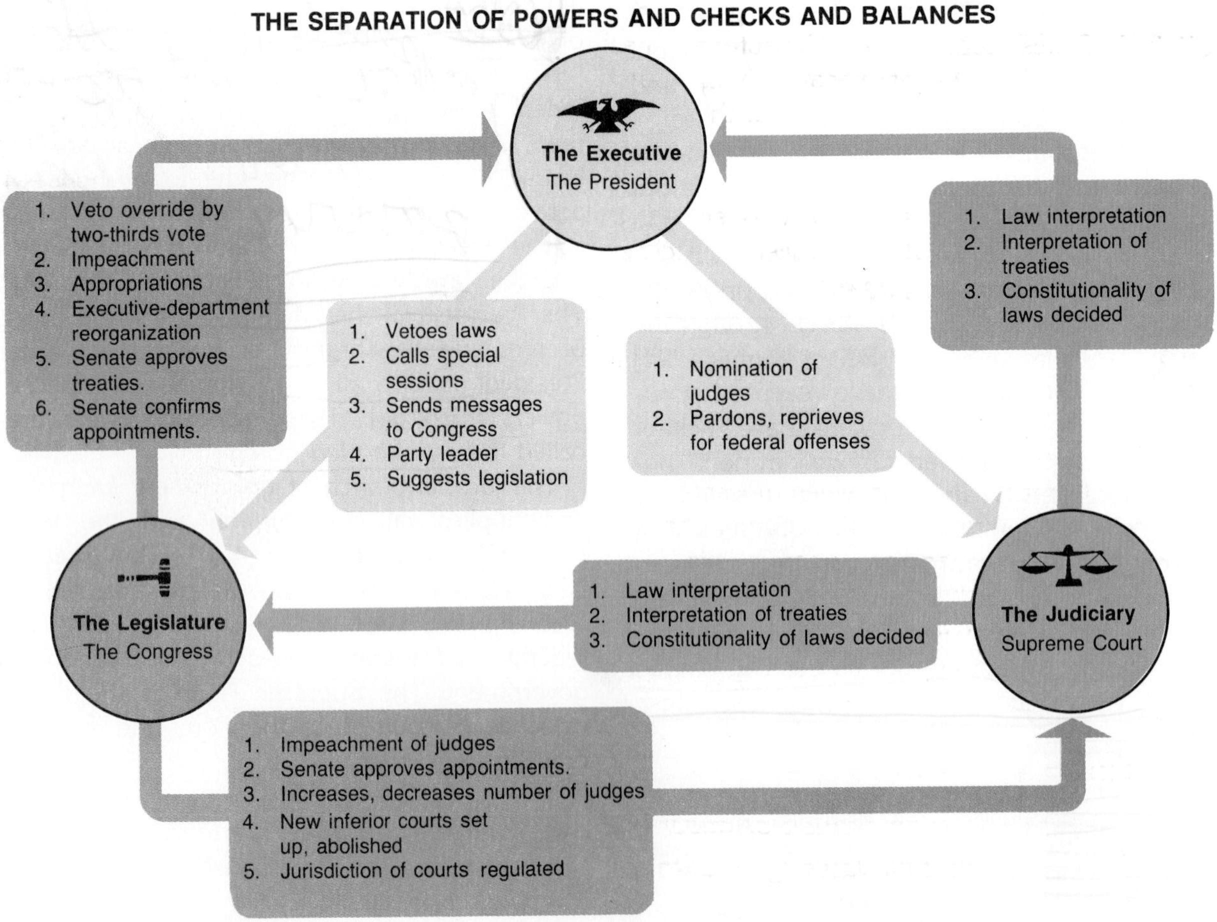

THE SEPARATION OF POWERS AND CHECKS AND BALANCES

The Executive
The President

The Legislature
The Congress

The Judiciary
Supreme Court

Legislature checks Executive:
1. Veto override by two-thirds vote
2. Impeachment
3. Appropriations
4. Executive-department reorganization
5. Senate approves treaties.
6. Senate confirms appointments.

Executive checks Legislature:
1. Vetoes laws
2. Calls special sessions
3. Sends messages to Congress
4. Party leader
5. Suggests legislation

Executive checks Judiciary:
1. Nomination of judges
2. Pardons, reprieves for federal offenses

Judiciary checks Executive:
1. Law interpretation
2. Interpretation of treaties
3. Constitutionality of laws decided

Judiciary checks Legislature:
1. Law interpretation
2. Interpretation of treaties
3. Constitutionality of laws decided

Legislature checks Judiciary:
1. Impeachment of judges
2. Senate approves appointments.
3. Increases, decreases number of judges
4. New inferior courts set up, abolished
5. Jurisdiction of courts regulated

Former Vice-President Aaron Burr was acquitted of treason at his trial in 1807. The writers of the Constitution took great care to define treason [*71] because the British had used it as a weapon against the colonists.

Aaron Burr by John Vanderlyn, Yale University Art Gallery, Bequest of Oliver Burr Jennings

balanced among the three branches of government, with no one branch becoming too powerful.

Why was the system of checks and balances added to the Constitution?

Elastic and Flexible Features. The Constitution, written during the Convention in Philadelphia in 1787, still serves the people of the United States today. The Constitution has lasted for so long largely because it has been able to meet the changing needs of the American people. The Constitution does this in two ways.

The Constitution has a clause often called the *elastic clause* [*42]. It is called elastic because it stretches the power of government. This clause gives Congress the power "to make all laws which shall be necessary and proper for carrying into execution the foregoing powers."

The Constitution is also flexible. That is, it can be formally changed when necessary as the needs of the people in the country change. This is done by adding amendments. The process to be followed for making amendments was written into the Constitution itself. However, only very few amendments have been added to the Constitution since 1787. (Constitutional amendments may be found on pages 755–764.)

How can the Constitution be changed to meet the changing needs of the nation?

SECTION 2 REVIEW

1. *What is the Bill of Rights?*
2. *Which branch of government reviews laws to make certain that the laws agree with what is written in the Constitution?*
3. *Why was the elastic clause added to the Constitution?*

3 The Growth of Democracy

Overview Leaders of the United States under the new Constitution had to set up a workable way of running the government. They also had to face a number of problems. For the most part these leaders relied upon the Constitution and upon their own abilities.

Objectives After you read this section, you will be able to:

- identify the branch of government that had the power to enlarge the court system;
- compare the views of Jefferson and Hamilton toward the establishment of a national bank;
- describe the problems with foreign countries the new government had to face.

The First Presidency. George Washington was unanimously elected to be the first President of the United States in February 1789. John Adams was elected as Vice-President. Road conditions, poor communications, and other problems slowed down the schedule of taking office that was set out in the Constitution. As a result, the first President took the oath of office on April 30, 1789, in New York City, almost two months later than expected.

A major task that President Washington faced was the organization of the executive branch of government. President Washington began this task by forming a group of four close advisers. This group later became known as the President's *cabinet.*

President Washington chose well qualified persons to advise him. Thomas Jefferson was chosen to lead the Department of Foreign Affairs—later called the Department of State. Alexander Hamilton became the first Secretary of the Treasury. Henry Knox was named as head of the War Department. And Edmund Randolph became the first Attorney General—the President's adviser on legal matters.

President Washington knew that his actions would set a *precedent.* That is, what President Washington did as the head of the executive branch of government would become a model to be followed by later Presidents. For example, President Washington worked to maintain the separation of powers established in the Constitution.

■ *How did President Washington first begin to organize the executive branch of government?*

The Court System. According to the Constitution, the six-member Supreme Court would be the highest court in the country. It would also head the judicial branch of government. This was noted in the Constitution [*67]. However, the Constitution gave the power to enlarge the federal court system to Congress. This was done because of the Constitution's system of checks and balances.

The first Congress used this power to set up a court system for the country. This was done largely through the Judiciary Act of 1789. This act created three circuit courts and 13 district courts (see map on page 132). The Judiciary Act of 1789 also made clear the Supreme Court's power over state courts. The act gave the Supreme Court the power to rule on state-court judgments insofar as the constitutionality of the laws was concerned. That is,

(Text continues on page 132.)

VIEWPOINTS DIFFER

The Constitution: An Economic Document?

Historian Charles Beard in 1913 sharply challenged the traditional, democratic interpretation of the origins of the Constitution. His research suggested that the men who framed the Constitution had important economic interests to protect. They created a strong central government that would make safe and increase their financial holdings.

From: *An Economic Interpretation of the Constitution* (1913):

To carry the theory of the economic interpretation of the Constitution out into its ultimate details would require a monumental commentary, such as lies completely beyond the scope of this volume. But enough has been said to show that the concept [idea] of the Constitution as a piece of abstract [not dealing with anything specific] legislation reflecting no group interests and recognizing no economic antagonisms [conflicts] is entirely false. It was an economic document drawn with superb skill by men whose property interests were immediately at stake; and as such it appealed directly and unerringly [without mistake] to identical interests in the country at large.

Many historians accept Beard's interpretation, or a modification of it. Others, such as legal scholar Charles Warren, have maintained that the Constitution was born out of political concerns. The following passage is taken from his *The Making of the Constitution* (1947):

... the men who urged and framed and advocated the Constitution were striving for an idea, an ideal—belief in a National Union, and a determination [resolution] to maintain it.... Historians who leave these factors out of account and who contend that these men were moved chiefly by economic conditions utterly fail to interpret their character and their acts. To appreciate the patriotic sincerity of the motives which inspired the framing of the Constitution, it is necessary to read the hopes and fears of the leading American statesmen prior to 1787...

Think About It

1. According to Beard, to whom in the nation did the new Constitution have appeal?
2. In Warren's opinion, what was the primary motivation of the delegates to the Constitutional Convention?
3. Could the interpretations of Beard and Warren both be correct? Explain your answer.

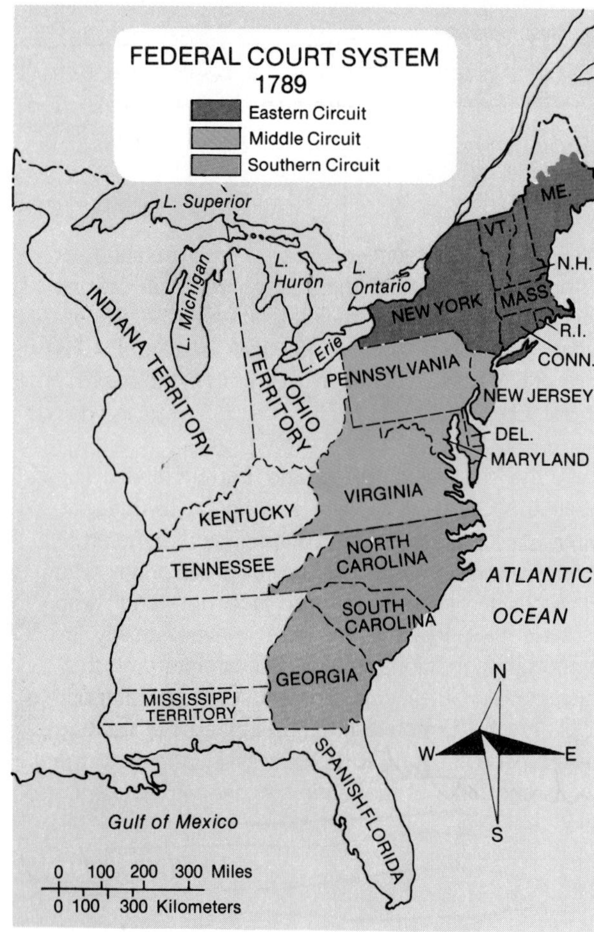

The Judiciary Act of 1789 established three federal circuit courts. Which states made up the southern circuit of federal courts?

the Supreme Court was given the power to decide whether any laws were *unconstitutional*—against what is written in the Constitution.

■ *Which branch of government was given the power to enlarge the federal court system?*

Hamilton and the Money Problem. The United States was deeply in debt in the early 1790's. Debts dating back to the days of the Continental Congress came to more than 56 million dollars. Many state governments were also deeply in debt. State debts came to about 25 million dollars.

Alexander Hamilton, President Washington's Secretary of the Treasury, developed a plan that would pay off these debts and set up a sound base of credit for the country. His plan was to have the federal government *fund* the entire debt. That is, Congress would pay off all debts. The money needed to do this would be raised by levying taxes and by placing high *tariffs* on goods made outside the country. A tariff is a tax on goods brought into the country.

Hamilton's plan was not well liked in the South. This was because most southern states had paid off their debts by this time. They did not want to be taxed to help pay the debts of the other states. However, a compromise was made. Southern lawmakers agreed to accept Hamilton's plan if the nation's capitol would be built in the South. Hamilton's plan was passed by Congress. And Washington, D.C.—the capital of the United States—was soon built in Maryland across the Potomac River from Virginia.

■ *Why was Hamilton's plan not well liked in the South?*

The First Bank of the United States. Alexander Hamilton advised President Washington to set up a national bank. The bank that Hamilton planned was to have four main duties. The first was to hold money. The second was to help collect tax money. The third was to issue paper money. And the fourth was to give out loans to help the growth of American business. The federal government was to own 20 percent of the bank. Private citizens would own the other 80 percent. Thus, the bank would be controlled by the private owners.

This idea caused much argument in the country. It also helped to bring about the formation of political parties in the United States. Some people, such as Thomas Jefferson, were against a national bank. Jefferson based his argument, in part, on the Constitution which does not mention a national bank. Thus, Jefferson and the people who agreed with him believed that the federal government did not have the power to set up a bank. The people who agreed with Jefferson became known as strict constructionists. The political party later formed by these persons became known as the *Republicans.* They were also called *Democratic Republicans.*

Alexander Hamilton and his followers believed that the federal government had the power to set up a national bank. Hamilton based his belief on the elastic clause of the Constitution. Hamilton and his followers became known as the *Federalists.*

Thomas Jefferson (left) and Alexander Hamilton (right) clashed over many issues. Jefferson believed in democracy and in strong state governments. Hamilton favored commerce and a strong central government.

Photri

The Bettmann Archive

DO YOU KNOW?

When was Thanksgiving Day first celebrated as a national holiday?

Thanksgiving Day was first celebrated as a national holiday on November 26, 1789. President Washington created the day to give thanks for the new Constitution. But many Americans also thought of the day as a time to give thanks for a good growing season. For many years, Americans had often come together in autumn to enjoy the foods they had worked so hard to grow. By 1789 such gatherings had become a tradition. It is believed that the Pilgrims of Plymouth Colony held the first Thanksgiving feast in the summer of 1623.

President Washington and most members of Congress agreed with Hamilton to set up a national bank. The first Bank of the United States was set up in February 1791. It was given *assets*—financial resources—of 10 million dollars by Congress.

■ *What were the four main duties of the national bank proposed by Alexander Hamilton?*

The Whiskey Rebellion. During Washington's first term as President, he had to find ways to solve several problems facing the new nation. His Secretary of the Treasury was one of his most important advisers because the country needed money. In order to deal with this problem, Secretary Hamilton asked Congress to put an *excise tax* on whiskey. An excise tax was a tax on many kinds of items made and sold within the country. Many farmers on the western frontier made whiskey from their corn crop. This was because whiskey would not spoil during shipment from frontier fields to eastern markets. Also, whiskey could be sold for more money than could corn.

Hamilton's tax brought great hardship to these farmers. Many farmers would not pay the tax. Some frontier farmers began to plot against the government. And rioting broke out near Pittsburgh, Pennsylvania, in mid-1794.

The Pennsylvania governor and others believed that the courts could end the trouble. Nevertheless, Secretary Hamilton asked the President to send an army to stop the rioting. Washington sent 15,000 troops to end the *Whiskey Rebellion* in October 1794. This action ended the fighting and the tax protest. It also showed the government's ability to carry out federal laws.

■ *What was the main cause of the Whiskey Rebellion?*

Problems With Foreign Countries. After 1793 President Washington had to deal with many problems involving foreign countries, particularly France and Great Britain. The French Revolution had begun in 1789. Most Americans at that time favored this revolution. However, in 1793 the revolution turned into the bloody series of executions called the Reign of Terror. In the same year France and Great Britain went to war. Thomas Jefferson and the Republicans wanted the United States to side with France against Great Britain. Alexander Hamilton and the Federalists, however, wanted the United States to stop all dealings with France.

President Washington issued a Proclamation of Neutrality in April 1793. This stated that the United States would favor neither France nor Great Britain. However, Great Britain would not honor America's neutrality. British warships seized many American trading ships at sea. This led the President to send John Jay, the Chief Justice of the Supreme Court, to England to work out a treaty with Great Britain.

The Jay Treaty increased trade between Great Britain and the United States. It also made Great Britain promise to take its troops out of the Northwest Territory—now United States property. Otherwise, the treaty did not work well for the United States. Great Britain was slow to remove its troops from the Northwest Territory. The British still would not honor American neutrality at sea. And many Americans believed that President Washington had neglected America's closest ally, France.

At the same time, Spain and the United States signed a treaty. The treaty set the boundary between Spanish-owned Florida and the State of Georgia. Spain also gave the United States the right to use the Mississippi River and the port of New Orleans. This treaty was named for Thomas Pinckney, the American who signed it for the United States.

■ *How did Great Britain violate American neutrality?*

The Presidency of John Adams. President Washington did not want to run for a third term as President in 1796. He retired at the end of his second term. To replace Washington, the Federalists backed John Adams of Massachusetts as their candidate for the presidency. Thomas Pinckney of South Carolina was named to run for the vice-presidency. The Republicans backed the election of Thomas Jefferson for President. Aaron Burr ran for Vice-President.

The election was close. Adams received the largest number of electoral votes (71). Therefore, he became the country's second President. Thomas Jefferson received the second-largest number of electoral votes (68). He became the Vice-President although he was from a different political party. Adams and Jefferson were *inaugurated*—took office—in March 1797.

President Adams faced problems with France. France had been taking over American ships at sea. This was being done because America had signed the Jay Treaty with Great Britain, which France opposed. In response, President Adams sent three Americans to France in October 1797. Their mission was to improve relations between France and the United States. Once in France, they were met by three French officials—called only X, Y, and Z—who asked for a *bribe.* They demanded $240,000. The Americans reported the demand to the President, who told Congress. The XYZ Affair, as it became known, caused the relationship between France and the United States to worsen.

The election of 1796 showed how quickly political parties had become important. In which states were the Federalists the most popular?

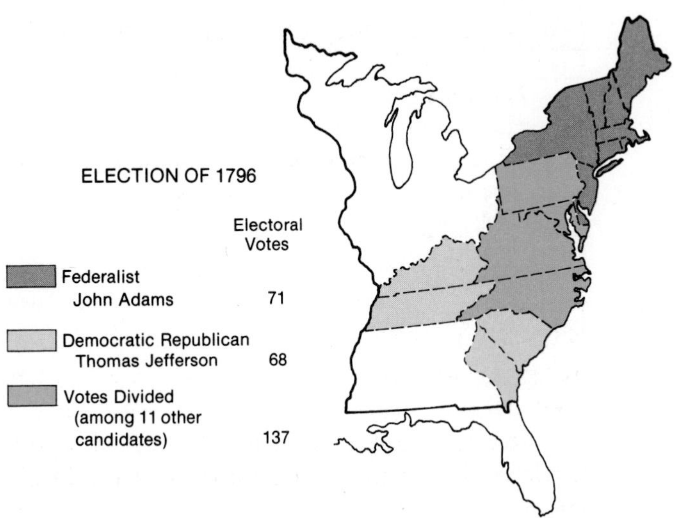

In America, the Republicans, who had favored helping France, were now very unpopular. President Adams and the Federalists used this opportunity to strengthen their stand against the Republicans. The Federalists did this by passing four laws. These laws are often called the Alien and Sedition Acts. Three of these four laws were passed to limit the political activities of new *immigrants*—persons who moved from one country to take up residence in another. This would weaken the Republican party because most new immigrants to the United States favored the Republicans. However, these laws were not carried out.

The fourth act was called the Sedition Act. This was a very harsh law that was passed to stop the Republicans from criticizing the Federalists. The law made it illegal to write, to print, or to say anything that might be harmful to the government or to the President. This law was given an expiration date. That is, it was set to expire when it would no longer be needed. Its date of expiration was set for one day before the inauguration of the third President of the United States, March 4, 1801.

■ *Why was the Sedition Act passed by Congress?*

SECTION 3 REVIEW

1. *What power did the Judiciary Act of 1789 give to the Supreme Court?*
2. *Why was Thomas Jefferson opposed to the establishment of a national bank?*
3. *Why did President Washington issue a Proclamation of Neutrality Act in April 1793?*

CHAPTER 7 SUMMARY

The Constitution of the United States was written during the Philadelphia Convention in 1787. The Convention had been called together to revise the Articles of Confederation. When 55 delegates from 12 states met, they decided to design a completely new framework of government.

The Constitution became the highest law in the country. It also created a federal form of government. In this system, the federal government was given certain powers. Other powers were reserved for the states. The Constitution lists the duties of the three branches of the federal government. In addition, in the Bill of Rights, Congress listed the personal freedoms that are guaranteed to American citizens.

George Washington became the country's first President. During his two terms in office the government undertook several actions that shaped the country's future. The federal court system and the first Bank of the United States were begun at this time to serve the needs of a growing nation. With the election of John Adams as the second President, a two-party political system began.

CHAPTER 7 REVIEW

USING YOUR SKILLS

Interpreting Organizational Charts

Organizational charts are drawings that can show the development of several groups within an organization. Such charts can also show the relationships among various organizational groups. Charts such as the one below are able to show at a glance the makeup of a complex structure or system. The organizational chart below shows the various courts that make up the judicial system of the United States. The chart also shows the relationships among the courts. Examine the chart closely and then answer the questions that follow.

1. How many separate levels make up the state judicial system?
2. What is the highest court in the American judicial system?
3. From how many different courts does the Supreme Court receive direct appeals?
4. Which is the only state court to have power of appeal to the Supreme Court?
5. Federal district courts may appeal to which higher courts?
6. Which federal court would most likely hear a special-appeals case involving a soldier?

THE UNITED STATES JUDICIAL SYSTEM

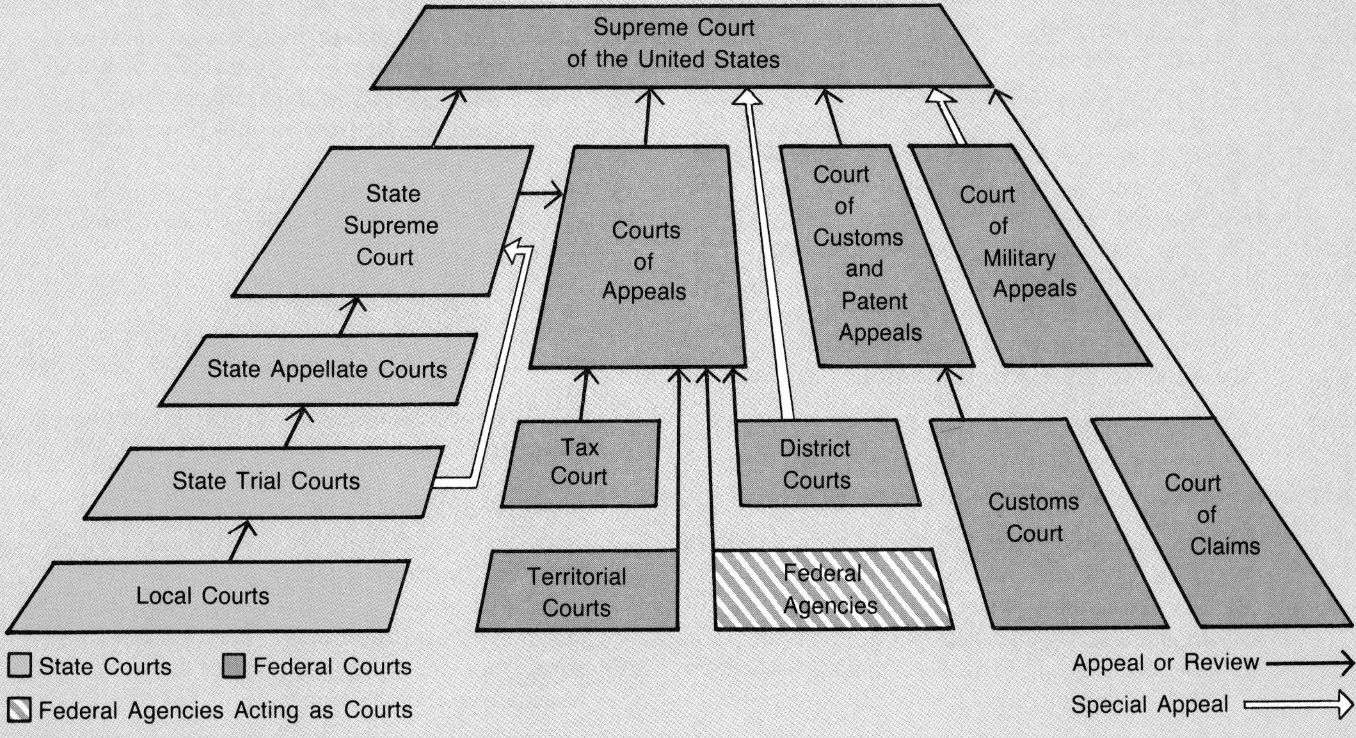

CHAPTER 7 REVIEW

YOU SHOULD KNOW

Identify, define, or explain each of the following:

compromise
bicameral legislature
electors
ratification
Bill of Rights
separation of powers
veto
cabinet
tariffs
immigrants

CHECKING FACTS

1. How many delegates eventually took part in writing the Constitution of the United States?
2. Who was chosen as president of the Philadelphia Convention?
3. What was the Three-Fifths Compromise?
4. What two groups were involved in the fight over the ratification of the Constitution?
5. What is the principle of constitutional supremacy?
6. What are the three branches of government?
7. Who was the first Vice-President of the United States?
8. What four positions made up President Washington's first cabinet?
9. What political party was formed by people who were known as strict constructionists?
10. What were the provisions of the Jay Treaty?

UNDERSTANDING CONCEPTS

1. Why did Rhode Island refuse to send delegates to the Constitutional Convention?
2. Why did smaller states, such as New Jersey, oppose the Virginia plan of government?
3. Why did the Anti-Federalists oppose ratification of the Constitution?
4. Why was a system of checks and balances added to the Constitution?
5. Why was Hamilton's plan to pay off the debts of the United States not well liked by the South?

LEARNING FROM ILLUSTRATIONS

1. Study the chart on page 128. How can the judiciary check the power of the legislature?
2. George Washington was opposed to political parties partly because he believed that they would split the nation geographically. How does the map on page 135 support his fears?

CRITICAL THINKING

1. Do you think the Bill of Rights is an important part of the Constitution? Why do you think so?
2. What problems, do you think, might have resulted had the Constitution not contained an elastic clause?
3. Do you think the United States should have helped France in its war against Great Britain in 1793? Why do you think so?

ENRICHMENT ACTIVITIES

1. To better understand some of the problems faced by the planners of the Constitution, you could work on a list of school rules or on a school constitution. Copies of this document could then be given to the class for discussion.
2. Make an illustrated chart for your class bulletin board that shows major offices of the federal government and the people who now hold them. Your chart can use pictures from newspapers and magazines.

CHAPTER 8

CLOSE-UP: The Boston Massacre

INTRODUCTION

Five persons died and six others were seriously wounded in a clash between British soldiers and the townspeople of Boston in early March 1770. This incident was later called the "Boston Massacre" by Samuel Adams. This incident helped to unite the colonists and to make them aware of the ever-tightening controls that Great Britain held over its colonies. Crispus Attucks, a black man, was one of the five killed in the massacre. He has become, in the opinion of many people, one of the first heroes of the American Revolution.

The incident on King Street in Boston seems to have grown out of the rising tension in Boston that had begun years earlier. Bostonians had been forced to provide food and lodging for British troops since the end of the French and Indian War in 1763. The Quartering Act of 1765 continued the practice, much to the annoyance of many Bostonians. In addition, constant competition over scarce jobs often led to fighting between Boston workers and off-duty British soldiers who were looking for ways to add to their low pay. The Boston Massacre of March 5, 1770, has been called the first battle of the American Revolution.

1 Groundwork for Trouble

Monday, March 5, 1770, was a cold, wintry day in Boston. The temperature ventured above freezing for only a few hours during the day. After sunset, a first-quarter moon came out, providing the only outdoor lighting on Boston's snow-packed streets. Most of Boston's 16,000 people remained indoors. Nevertheless, groups of townspeople, as well as groups of soldiers, walked the streets that night.

Fistfight at the Ropewalks. Problems had been mounting in Boston for years. Fighting between Boston workers and British soldiers had taken place many times. Most recently, fighting had broken out on Friday, March 2, 1770. On that day, an off-duty soldier of the 29th British Regiment went to the town's *ropewalks*—a rope-making factory—hoping to earn some extra money.

Many Bostonians believed that off-duty soldiers were taking scarce jobs away from poor townspeople. A fistfight broke out at the ropewalks between the soldier, Patrick Walker, and a rope maker. It is believed that a rope maker insulted the soldier, touching off the fight.

Private Walker lost the fight. Beaten, he returned to the Main Guard—Boston's military headquarters. There he rounded up several other off-duty soldiers to return with him to the ropewalks to continue the fight. However, a corporal of the Main Guard was able to hold back the soldiers. The rope makers were held back as well by John Hill, justice of the peace in Boston.

■ *Why did Private Walker go to the ropewalks?*

A Feeling of Danger. The weekend was disrupted by several fights between off-duty soldiers and Boston rope makers and dock-workers. In one case, a soldier of the 29th Regiment was not present at morning roll call. Rumor quickly spread through the soldiers' ranks that the missing soldier had been killed by the Bostonians. Friends of the missing soldier began to search the town, often starting fights as they looked. The absent soldier was not dead. He had been with friends.

Although there were strained feelings between the British soldiers and the people of Boston, many soldiers had made friends in the town. Both groups had many things in common. Both groups were British citizens, sharing a language, a history, and a culture. Both groups were also subjects of King George III. However, both groups felt that violence might take place in Boston between the soldiers and certain groups of Bostonians. Several Bostonians later stated that they had heard rumors—from soldiers as well as from their neighbors—that something was to take place on Monday night, the fifth of March. No one, however—neither soldier nor Bostonian—seemed to know what was in store for them.

■ *What groups of people were involved in the fighting during the weekend?*

Samuel Adams and Acts of Parliament. The tensions between Bostonians and soldiers had grown over the years. Various British laws had angered the colonists. In Boston, colonial leaders such as Samuel Adams called out for an end of British control. Samuel Adams had become a powerful voice among Boston's patriots. He had risen to this position more than five years earlier, when Britain's Parliament

Historical Pictures Service

This illustration is an artist's interpretation of one of the several fights that occurred between the British soldiers and the townspeople of Boston between March 2, 1770, and March 5, 1770. How are the tensions depicted in this illustration?

began to pass a series of laws that were intended to raise money for the British government. The first of such laws to draw Samuel Adams's attention was the Stamp Act. It was passed in March 1765. This law stated that a tax stamp be placed on all printed matter: books, newspapers, playing cards, and so on.

Adams and many others were against this law. They believed that Britain should not make money at the colonists' expense. They also believed that Parliament had no right to pass any laws for the colonists. This was because colonists were not represented in Parliament. Despite widespread protests from the colonies, the Stamp Act became law.

The passage of the Stamp Act actually worked to the colonists' advantage. By boycotting certain British-made goods, the colonists throughout North America came together and eventually succeeded in overturning the Stamp Act. The Stamp Act problem also led many colonists to form a new group, the Sons of Liberty. This group, led by Samuel Adams, worked against further British controls over the colonies.

■ *Why were Samuel Adams and many other colonists opposed to the Stamp Act?*

Historical Pictures Service

Tensions increased in Boston on February 22, 1770, after a crowd found the body of a small boy who had been murdered by a British loyalist.

The Effect of the Quartering Act on Boston. Not long after Parliament passed the hated Stamp Act, it passed a law that affected some colonists even more sharply. The *Quartering Act of 1765* forced many colonists to provide British troops with a place to sleep and with food. This law often created a hardship for poor colonists.

The people of Boston, in particular, were greatly affected by this law. Boston was the seat of colonial Massachusetts government, and three large encampments of British troops were positioned in the town by 1770. They had been there ever since the end of the French and Indian War in 1763. Many Bostonians wanted nothing more than to see the last British soldier leave the town.

Boys and girls of Boston had grown up listening to their parents talk about the British soldiers in the town. They had heard the insults that were often spoken to the British soldiers, who dressed in bright-red uniforms. "Lobsterbacks! Lousy rascal lobsterbacks!" the children's parents had called the soldiers.

Historical Pictures Service

This engraving, entitled "The Officer and the Barber's Boys," depicts the taunting of British officers and soldiers in Boston between 1767 and 1770. This type of action led to increased tensions between the British soldiers in Boston and the townspeople.

So it was not unusual to find a group of boys gathered on King Street near the Custom House—the place where trading taxes were paid—on that cold, March night in 1770, teasing the British guard. What was unusual, however, was the feeling of trouble in the air—a feeling shared by the townspeople and the troops.

Private Hugh White of Boston's Main Guard could sense the trouble almost at once. The boys' name-calling suddenly became harsher. Then snowballs and sticks began to rain down on him. Private White ran back to the steps of the Custom House. He placed the bayonet on his musket and readied himself for more trouble.

What did the Quartering Act force many colonists to do?

SECTION 1 REVIEW

1. *When did fistfighting first break out between Boston rope makers and British soldiers?*
2. *In what ways were the Bostonians and the British troops similar?*
3. *Why did the guard at the Custom House place a bayonet on his musket?*

2 The King Street Shootings

Shortly after 9:00 P.M. on the night of March 5, 1770, the bells in several Boston churches were rung. Church bells in the night, in a town where houses were made almost totally of wood, meant only one thing: fire! Townspeople poured into the streets, some carrying water buckets; but others were carrying sticks and clubs. Later, some witnesses stated that they thought it was very strange ". . . to come to put out a fire with sticks and bludgeons [clubs]." The fear of the troops and the townspeople that violence would erupt soon came true.

A Crowd Gathers. The group of teasing boys on King Street soon grew into a crowd of nearly 500 people. Private White, struck by snowballs and sticks, kicked at the Custom House door, hoping to get in away from the crowd. Although a customs officer and his family lived there, no one answered. At the same time in Dock Square, about a half mile from the Custom House, another crowd listened to a man dressed in a white wig and a red cape. Witnesses could not tell what was said, although they later testified that the mysterious man seemed to be stirring up the crowd. Some witnesses thought the man was Samuel Adams. Others believed him to be William Molineaux, also a member of the Sons of Liberty. But still others claimed that the man was a stranger to Boston.

Groups of soldiers had also been roaming the streets of Boston. There were reports that they had attacked some townspeople for little or no reason. Some groups of soldiers were armed with swords and clubs. Other groups were unarmed.

The noise in the streets of Boston continued to attract even more people. Young Samuel Maverick, an apprentice, hurriedly finished his dinner and ran to King Street to see what was happening. Crispus Attucks, believed by many historians to have been a runaway slave, finished eating his dinner at a nearby inn. He, too, was attracted to the activity on King Street. Samuel Gray, the rope maker who was involved in the fighting several days before, was also in the crowd, as were two visiting sailors.

■ *What did the man in the red cape seem to be doing?*

Musket Fire. Private White struck a young man in the crowd with the butt of his musket. The man's cries could be heard above the crowd on the icy street. The crowd became even more restless. "Kill him, kill him, knock him down," they screamed. The guard, terribly afraid, shrieked, "Turn out, Main Guard," in the hope that the 29th Regiment would save him.

Seven soldiers led by Captain Thomas Preston suddenly appeared with their bayonets fixed on their muskets. At the captain's order, the line of soldiers walked steadily, with their bayonets at the ready, to the sentry box in front of the Custom House. At their captain's order they then formed a semicircular line, to protect themselves as best they could. They also double loaded their muskets. However, this was done without a direct order, witnesses later testified.

Voices in the crowd shouted at the soldiers. "Fire!" one faceless voice said. "You can't kill us all." But the soldiers held their fire. Captain Preston stood behind the line. He needed a plan that would hold back the crowd and, at the same time, one that would also protect himself and his troops. Suddenly, a soldier's musket exploded in deadly fire, killing Crispus Attucks, who stood nearby. Then, with no command, the other troops in the line also fired into the crowd. Samuel Gray, the rope maker, fell near the body of Crispus Attucks. Both were killed instantly, as was a nearby Irish sailor. Samuel Maverick was also struck as he watched the excitement. He died hours later, at home, as did another victim. In all, 11 persons had been shot; 5 were killed.

■ *Who ordered the soldiers to load and fire their weapons?*

The Outcome. Captain Preston and the soldiers who had taken part in the shooting were placed under arrest by the British governor. They were charged with murder. Within hours an investigation was started to determine how such an incident could have taken place in Boston—or anywhere else in the British Empire. Hundreds of witnesses came forward, and their statements were written down.

The people of Boston were shocked at what had happened. At the same time, however, they wondered if someone had wanted a serious incident to take place. They remembered seeing groups of off-duty soldiers roaming the streets, clearly looking for trouble. They also remembered hearing Boston's church bells

The Bettmann Archive

Crispus Attucks (center), one of the leaders of the crowd that gathered in King Street on March 5, 1770, was shot and killed by British soldiers during the confusion of the first few moments of the Boston Massacre. By the time the shooting stopped, the death toll had reached five.

The Bettmann Archive

The Bettmann Archive

John Adams (left), a lawyer and patriot leader, successfully defended the British soldiers accused in the Boston Massacre. Samuel Adams (right), his cousin, helped to lead the opposition to British colonial policies in Boston between 1765 and 1775.

ring out a fire warning when there was no fire—adding to the confusion among the crowd on King Street.

Samuel Adams appealed to the British colonial governor to remove all troops from Boston. Although Adams had often demanded this in the past, it was because of the shootings that the request was finally granted—at least temporarily.

Captain Preston and his soldiers had a trial by jury seven months after the shootings took place. Their lawyers were John Adams—a cousin of Samuel Adams and a future President of the United States—and Josiah Quincy. Both men were members of the Sons of Liberty. Surprisingly, all but two soldiers were found to be innocent. Two were found guilty only of minor offenses.

Samuel Adams began to popularize the shootings throughout the colonies. He called the events of March 5, 1770, the Boston Massacre. His efforts helped to bring the Thirteen Colonies together. Samuel Adams's statements also made the colonists more aware of British controls. In this way, Samuel Adams and the Sons of Liberty stepped up their work against British rule.

What verdict did the jury reach in the trial of Captain Preston and his troops?

SECTION 2 REVIEW

1. *Who was the first person killed in the Boston Massacre?*
2. *How many people were killed and wounded in the Boston Massacre?*
3. *Why were British troops finally removed from Boston?*

CHAPTER 8 REVIEW

SUMMARY

On March 2, 1770, an off-duty British soldier, Patrick Walker, went to Boston's rope-making factory to earn some extra money. Many Bostonians believed that by doing this, British soldiers were taking jobs away from the poor people of the town. A fistfight broke out between Patrick Walker and a rope maker. Tension between the British soldiers and Bostonians increased.

Several acts of Parliament, such as the Stamp Act, had angered the colonists. By boycotting British-made goods, the colonists succeeded in getting the Stamp Act repealed. Soon after the passage of the Stamp Act, Parliament passed the Quartering Act of 1765. This act forced many colonists to provide British troops with food and lodging, causing a hardship on many poor colonists. Because the colonists became resentful of this situation, teasing of British soldiers became very common in Boston, and it was especially troublesome on March 5, 1770.

On that day, a crowd of about 500 people, including British soldiers, began to gather on Boston's King Street. They grew louder and louder, throwing snowballs and sticks on the soldiers. One of the British soldiers, Private White, struck a man in the crowd with the butt of his musket. The soldier called for help, and seven soldiers appeared with their bayonets on their muskets.

Suddenly, a soldier's musket exploded, killing Crispus Attucks. Then the other troops fired into the crowd. Eleven persons had been shot; five were killed. The soldiers who took part in the shooting were placed under arrest. Seven months later they had a trial by jury. Their lawyers were John Adams and Josiah Quincy. All but two soldiers were found innocent. Two were found guilty of minor offenses. The Boston Massacre stepped up the colonists' work against British control.

UNDERSTANDING CONCEPTS

1. Why were Bostonians opposed to British soldiers working in the rope-making factory?
2. Why were Samuel Adams and other colonists opposed to the Stamp Act?
3. Why were Bostonians particularly affected by the Quartering Act of 1765?
4. Why were British troops finally removed from Boston?
5. How did the Boston Massacre step up the colonists' work against British rule?

CRITICAL THINKING

1. Do you think British soldiers should have been able to get jobs at the ropewalks? Why do you think so?
2. In your opinion, did Bostonians have a right to be against the Quartering Act of 1765? Give reasons for your answer.
3. In their trial, Captain Preston and the soldiers who were involved in the Boston Massacre were defended by John Adams and Josiah Quincy, both patriots. What does that tell you about the two men's belief in a fair trial?

PROJECTS AND ACTIVITIES

Samuel Adams was very important in organizing the colonial movement against Great Britain. Research the life of Samuel Adams by using encyclopedias, history books, and biographies of Samuel Adams. Find out about his early life, about his role in the American Revolution, and about his life after the American Revolution. You might present your research in the form of a written report.

UNIT TWO REVIEW

UNIT SUMMARY

The British Empire went through many changes during the 1700's. Great Britain gained many new lands. British leaders changed many government policies in order to raise more money to pay for the Empire. As Parliament passed more laws that tightened British control over the colonies, resistance grew. Many colonists remained loyal to Britain, but some colonists prepared for war.

The Second Continental Congress declared the colonies' independence from Great Britain on July 4, 1776. Although the American soldiers had to overcome great obstacles, the Continental Army was able to defeat the larger British army and to win independence from Great Britain. The United States of America was made up of thirteen states. These states were loosely joined under a weak central government. In time, many Americans knew that a stronger central government was needed.

In 1787 the Philadelphia Convention was called to revise the Articles of Confederation. Instead, a completely new framework of government, the Constitution of the United States, was written. The Constitution created a federal form of government. George Washington became the country's first President. During his two terms, the federal court system and the first Bank of the United States were begun. A two-party political system began with the election of John Adams as the second President.

Tension between Bostonians and British soldiers increased until March 5, 1770. On that day, a crowd of about 500 people, including British soldiers, began to gather on Boston's King Street. Some people in the crowd began throwing snowballs and sticks on the British soldiers. One of the soldier's musket exploded, killing Crispus Attucks. Other troops fired into the crowd, killing 5 people. The soldiers involved were arrested. After a trial by jury, all but two of them were found innocent. The Boston Massacre stepped up the colonists' work against British rule.

YOU SHOULD KNOW

Identify, define, or explain each of the following:

boycott
patriots
mercenaries
specie
compromise
ratification
cabinet
Samuel Adams
Crispus Attucks

CHECKING FACTS

1. What was the Stamp Act?
2. What four new laws were passed by the British Parliament following the Boston Tea Party?
3. Where was the First Continental Congress held?
4. What pamphlet called upon the colonists to fight for independence?
5. What plan of government was approved by the Second Continental Congress after the American Revolution?
6. What was the purpose of the Land Ordinance of 1785?
7. What were the New Jersey and the Virginia plans of government?
8. Which branch of government makes the laws?
9. What political party was formed by Alexander Hamilton and his followers?
10. What did the Sons of Liberty do?

UNDERSTANDING CONCEPTS

1. Why did the Stamp Act Congress want Parliament to repeal the Stamp Act?
2. Why did the United States government under the Articles of Confederation remain weak?
3. Why was ratification of the Constitution difficult?

4. Why was a system of checks and balances added to the Constitution?
5. How did Samuel Adams's popularization of the Boston Massacre affect the colonies?

CRITICAL THINKING

1. Do you think the British government had a right to make the colonists pay their share of the debt brought about by the French and Indian War? Give reasons for your answer.
2. If you were living in the colonies in 1776, would you have agreed with the ideas in Thomas Paine's *Common Sense*? Why or why not?
3. Do you think the idea of separation of powers contained in the Constitution is important? Why do you think so?

CHRONOLOGY

Arrange the following events in the order in which they appear.

a. The Second Continental Congress meets
b. Parliament passes the Townshend Acts
c. Five people die in the Boston Massacre
d. Colonists stage the Boston Tea Party
e. The Constitution becomes the supreme law of the land
f. Parliament passes the Stamp Act
g. The Second Continental Congress approves the Declaration of Independence

CITIZENSHIP IN ACTION

Average citizens did not attend the Constitutional Convention. How could they make their opinions known to the delegates who did attend? How can you make your opinions and concerns known to those who are now responsible for our nation's government?

GEOGRAPHY

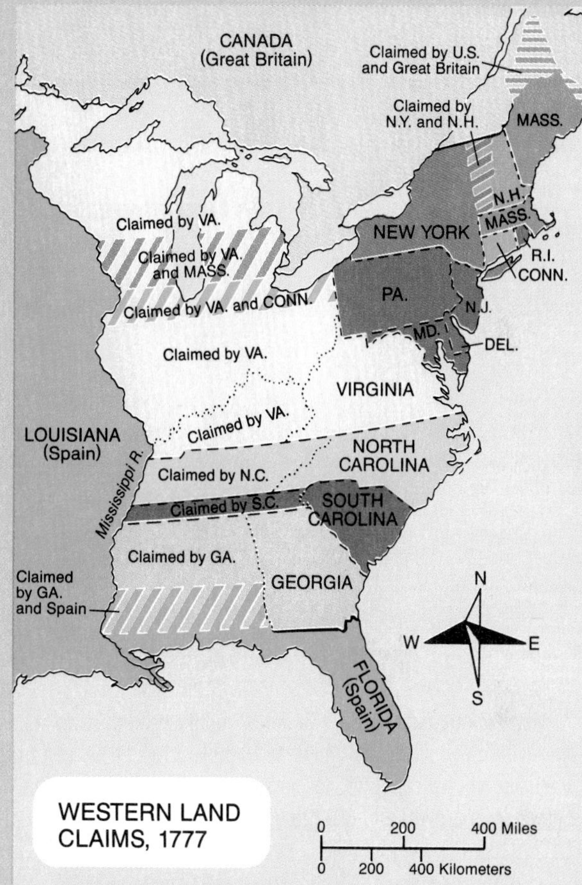

1. Which states claimed land in the west?
2. What foreign country claimed land in the west?
3. What natural feature made up the western border of the western land claims?
4. Which state claimed the largest amount of land?

1800 — 1810

- 1800 Thomas Jefferson elected President
- 1803 Louisiana Purchase; *Marbury* v. *Madison*
- 1804 Lewis and Clark expedition
- 1807 Embargo Act
- 1808 James Madison elected President
- 1812 War declared against Great Britain
- 1814 Treaty signed to end the War of 1812; Francis Lowell builds first factory
- 1816 James Monroe elected President
- 1819 *McCulloch* v. *Maryland*; Panic of 1819

UNIT THREE

The Growing Republic

1800–1837

"Second Street North from Market St. with Christ Church" is an engraving of Philadelphia that was completed in 1799, at a time when the young republic was at the threshold of a new era of tremendous growth and change.

"The Lackawanna Valley" by George Innes, shows how the Industrial Revolution was beginning to change the countryside beauty of America during the first half of the nineteenth century.

1820 · 1830 · 1840

- 1820 Missouri Compromise
- 1823 Monroe Doctrine established
- 1824 John Quincy Adams elected President
- 1825 The Erie Canal opens
- 1828 Andrew Jackson elected President; Tariff of Abominations passed
- 1830 Indian Removal Law enacted
- 1831 McCormick invents reaper
- 1832 President Jackson vetoes Charter of Second Bank
- 1833 Henry Clay's Compromise Tariff enacted
- 1837 Mary Lyon founds Mount Holyoke Seminary—the first women's college

CHAPTERS

The course of American events during the years between 1800 and 1837 did much to shape the character of our country. New social, political, and economic ideas came about to meet changing conditions and different life-styles. Furthermore, the country rapidly grew westward as new waves of American settlers crossed the Appalachian Mountains and the Mississippi River in search of land and wealth.

Americans in the early 1800's were fortunate to have able leaders in charge of the country's government. Outstanding presidents—such as Thomas Jefferson and Andrew Jackson—helped to form many of the political ideas that guide our country today. Among the major challenges of the early 1800's were the coming of industrialization, the War of 1812, and the rise of sectional conflict.

By the 1830's, political campaigns and elections had become exciting contests in which office seekers attempted to appeal to a wide range of voter interests

"The Underground Railroad," by Charles T. Webber, illustrates a stop on the network of stations established to aid fugitive slaves.

1800

1810

1793 Eli Whitney invents the cotton gin

1800 Thomas Jefferson elected President

1803 Louisiana Purchase
Marbury v. *Madison*

1804 Lewis and Clark expedition

1807 British fire upon the American navy ship *Chesapeake*
President Jefferson sets up the Embargo Act

1808 James Madison elected President

1812 War declared against Great Britain

1814 Treaty signed to end the War of 1812
Hartford Convention meets

CHAPTER 9

The Early Years of the Republic

Chapter Objectives

After studying this chapter, you will be able to:

- identify the social and political changes that took place in America during the early 1800's;
- explain the causes of the United States expansion in the early 1800's;
- list the ways in which Americans during the early 1800's were influenced by and reacted to the changing international scene.

1 The Age of Jefferson—1800 to 1815

Overview The Age of Jefferson was a time of far-reaching change. This was because Americans were working to build their country. New ways of living, new ideas about government, and new economic developments rapidly came about. And because of these changes, the United States grew in size, in power, and in wealth.

Americans in the early 1800's faced the new century with high hopes. But many obstacles had to be overcome if the new country was to enjoy its promising future.

Objectives After you read this section, you will be able to:

- describe how Jefferson's ideas differed from those of the Federalists;
- explain how the Supreme Court became strengthened;
- compare and contrast the economy and society of the North and the South.

The Election of 1800. During the late 1700's, the Federalist party, of which Alexander Hamilton was a member, led the country's government. But by 1796, a new political party led by Thomas Jefferson began to challenge the Federalists' power. This party was called the Democratic-Republican party.

The election of 1800 was unusual. In this election, Thomas Jefferson and Aaron Burr—of the Democratic-Republican party—ran against John Adams and Charles C. Pinckney of the Federalist party. At this time, there was no distinction on the electoral ballot between President and Vice-President. The candidate who received the greatest number of electoral votes became President. The person who won the second-largest number of votes became Vice-President. Although the new Democratic-Republican party won the election, both Jefferson and Burr received the same number of electoral votes. As called for in the Constitution, the House of Representatives broke this tie. Jefferson won the presidency, while Burr became Vice-President.

In 1804, the Twelfth Amendment [*96] was passed. This amendment stated that electors would have to cast their votes separately for a President and a Vice-President. Thus, an electoral tie could not happen again.

■ *Why was the Twelfth Amendment passed?*

Jefferson's Policies. Long before the campaign of 1800, Thomas Jefferson had attacked the Federalists' political ideas. Under the Federalists, Jefferson believed, the national

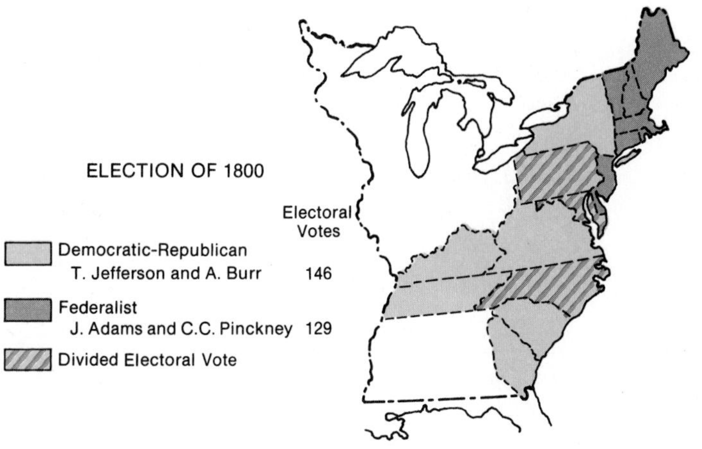

What part of the country voted for the Federalist Party?

Photri

Thomas Jefferson was one of the most talented leaders of his time and was an accomplished musician, inventor, architect, and farmer.

government had become far stronger than the Constitution allowed. Jefferson distrusted strong central governments. He felt that such governments lessened personal freedoms and weakened democracy.

Jefferson felt that a strong national government was only a step away from monarchy. This led him to demand a narrow *construction*—or interpretation—of the Constitution. In Jefferson's view, a narrow construction would lessen the powers of the federal government.

Jefferson also favored the idea of *states' rights*—increased power for the states. He felt that state governments were closer to the people than the national government. As a result, he worked to increase the states' powers.

Jefferson, who had wide support among the voters, did not agree with many Federalist ideas. But he believed that some Federalist policies had been good for the country. Thus, Jefferson continued some Federalist programs, such as government building projects and the United States Bank.

■ *Why did Jefferson support a narrow construction of the Constitution?*

The Supreme Court Is Strengthened. President Jefferson's aim was to lessen federal power. To reach this goal, he worked to cut back the size of the federal government. But Jefferson's attempts to lessen federal power did not always work. And in part, they did not work because of the influence of Chief Justice John Marshall of the Supreme Court.

Marshall wanted to prove that the Supreme Court had broad constitutional powers. Under his leadership the Supreme Court showed its strength and became known as the Marshall Court.

First, the Marshall Court proved its right to rule on the constitutionality of laws passed by Congress. In the case of *Marbury* v. *Madison* (1803), the Court declared a federal law *unconstitutional*—illegal under the Constitution. This ruling established the Supreme Court's power of *judicial review.* This meant that the Supreme Court could decide if a law agreed or disagreed with the Constitution. Thus, the Supreme Court had the power to overturn any law that it felt was unconstitutional.

Then, in the case of *Fletcher* v. *Peck* (1810), the Marshall Court used its power of judicial review to find a state law unconstitutional. This case proved that the Supreme Court had the power to overturn state—as well as federal—laws. The case of *Fletcher* v. *Peck* also showed that Jefferson's doctrine of states' rights was unconstitutional. This was because it was ruled that a branch of the federal government had the right to overturn state laws. In effect, the Supreme Court said that the federal government was constitutionally stronger than state governments.

What is meant by the power of judicial review?

The Growth of Northern Cities. Just as changes took place in government, many changes also took place in the ways Americans lived and worked. These changes helped to shape new and different life-styles in America.

By 1800, many northern people began to live in cities. Thus, an *urban* society—a society in which people live in or near cities—slowly began to appear in the North. This was especially true in the northeastern states—New England, New York, and Pennsylvania.

The large cities of the Northeast strongly influenced northern life. The cities drew people of different backgrounds and interests. And since city dwellers lived near one another, new ideas and new ways of doing things were easily shared. Also, the northeastern cities became centers of American culture. Theaters, schools, and libraries were built in ever-growing numbers. Within a short time the cities of the Northeast became commercial centers, where manufactured goods and farm products were brought for sale or for shipment. These goods were readily available to city people.

What sort of society began to develop in the North by 1800?

The Origins of Northern Industry. The North, with its growing cities, began to *industrialize*—to build businesses and factories—in the early 1800's. Many people in the

Historical Pictures Service

Boston, like many cities in the northeastern United States, grew rapidly during the early 1800's. These cities became centers for commercial, educational, and cultural activities. What structure appeared to be the center of the city?

North—especially in New York and in Pennsylvania—still lived by farming. But in the Age of Jefferson, trade and manufacturing were also becoming important.

Many things helped to encourage the growth of industry in the North. For one thing, some parts of the North—particularly the New England States—were not well suited for farming. People sometimes had to find other ways to make a living. Also, the states in the North often had the resources needed for industry. These resources included waterpower, good transportation, fine harbors, and raw materials. Finally, the cities of the North had a labor force for America's growing industry. This labor force was made up of skilled workers from Europe and Americans searching for new jobs. As a result, during the early 1800's, many small industries, such as ironworks and textile mills, began to appear in the North.

■ *What resources helped to encourage northern industry during the Age of Jefferson?*

The Southern Life-style. In contrast, life in the South was much different than life in the North. This was because southern life-styles in the Age of Jefferson were generally rural. In the South, farming was a traditional way of life that dated back to colonial days. Also, the southern economy was based, in part, upon a thriving trade in *cash crops*—farm goods grown to be sold. The South had several large cities, such as Charleston, Raleigh, and Richmond. But most southern cities were agricultural trade centers rather than manufacturing cities.

Much of the rural South in the early 1800's was broken into small family farms. Most often, each family farm was *self-sufficient*—able to produce enough food and livestock to meet its needs. Any *surplus*—or unused—goods would often be sold or traded at the nearest village market.

The local villages of the rural South usually were much smaller than the cities of the North. But they often served many of the same needs. For example, many southern villages had small markets where farm goods could be bought and sold. And the southern villages—like the cities of the North—brought people together. This meant that news and ideas could be shared. However, rural life in the South often produced small, closely-knit communities rather than large and busy cities.

■ *Why was the South primarily rural in 1800?*

Cotton Becomes King. During the Age of Jefferson, cotton became the major product of the South. But cotton farming had not always been so widespread. In 1792, for example, only 1,500 tons [1 363 metric tons] of cotton were raised. This was because many southern farmers did not feel that cotton was a worthwhile crop. Cotton also needed large areas of fertile land in which to grow. And it had to be harvested, cleaned, and readied for market by hand. Therefore, little income could be gained from cotton sales.

But in 1793, Eli Whitney invented the cotton gin. This machine cut the time and the work needed to prepare cotton for market. As a result, it became profitable to raise cotton.

With the invention of the cotton gin, cotton production quickly increased. In 1800, for example, over 18,000 tons [16 363 metric tons] were raised. At the same time, the demand for cotton cloth grew rapidly in Europe and in America. Soon, more and more southern farmers began to raise cotton. And by the early 1800's, cotton had become "king" in

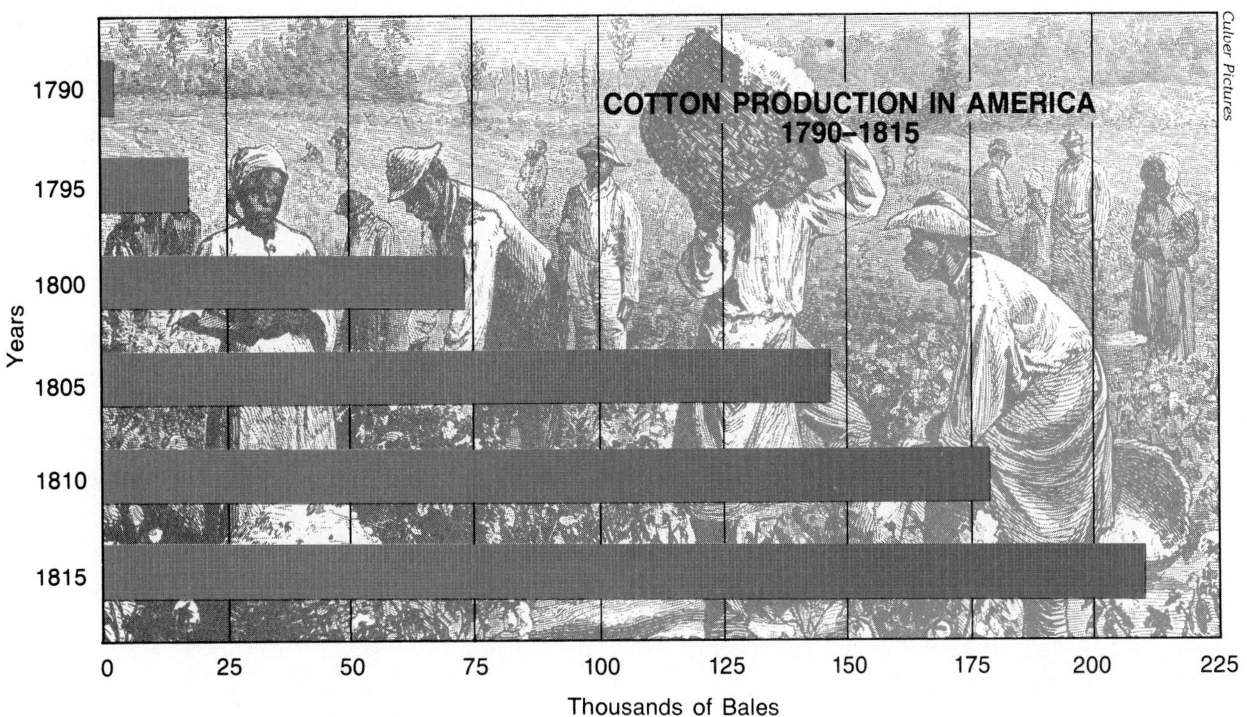

During the early 1800's, cotton became "king"—the most important southern cash crop. About how many bales of cotton were produced yearly by 1815?

the South. Thus, the southern economy in the Age of Jefferson became more dependent upon farming than ever before.

The Age of Jefferson was a time of change in America. The country's society, its economy, and its government grew rapidly. Many other important changes took place as well. Americans moved westward, and the United States gained new lands. And as western settlement continued, the country faced many new challenges.

■ *How did the cotton gin affect the southern economy in the early 1800's?*

SECTION 1 REVIEW

1. *What political changes did Jefferson hope to make?*
2. *How did the principle of judicial review increase the Supreme Court's power?*
3. *Why did America's earliest industries develop in the North and not in the South?*

2 The Nation Grows

Overview During the early 1800's, America grew in size and wealth. By 1803, four new states had been added to the Union. During the first fifteen years of the new century, many Americans moved west in search of new land.

Objectives After you read this section, you will be able to:

- describe how the development of the East encouraged the settlement of the West;
- explain why the western frontier grew in importance during the early 1800's;
- discuss the reasons for opposition to America's expansion westward.

The Search for New Land. Americans began to move west even before the country won its independence. But throughout most of the late 1700's, the country remained closely tied to the Atlantic Seaboard. The great majority of Americans continued to live in the seaboard states of the East. Moreover, the country's economy still depended, in part, upon overseas trade with Europe. Thus, during the late 1700's, the attention of most Americans was centered upon the states of the Atlantic Seaboard.

In the early 1800's, however, a growing number of Americans turned their attention to the lands of the West. Even the term "West" took on a new meaning. Americans had once thought of the West as the land from the Allegheny Mountains to the Mississippi River. In the early 1800's, however, people began to think of the West as the land beyond the Mississippi. This was because America's need for land had become greater by the early 1800's.

The population of the United States grew rapidly during the early 1800's. For example, in 1790, there were less than 4 million Americans. But by 1810, because of immigration and natural growth, the United States had well over 7 million people. As a result, some Americans believed that the seaboard states had become overcrowded. Also, some felt that as the East became more settled, the chances for a good life there became less. Many Americans, therefore, moved west in order to escape overcrowding. Others moved west in search of a better way of life. But until 1803, the United States ended at the Mississippi River.

■ *Why did many Americans move west during the early 1800's?*

The Louisiana Purchase. In 1800, the land that belonged to the United States ended at the Mississippi River. Much of the land west of the Mississippi was owned by Spain. A large part of this land was known as the Louisiana Territory. In 1800, Spain signed a treaty with France that *ceded*—gave—the Louisiana Territory to the French.

The ruler of France during the early 1800's was Napoleon Bonaparte. Napoleon hoped to use the Louisiana Territory to start a new French empire in North America. But if he carried out his plan, America's desire for more land in the West would be blocked.

The treaty that gave Louisiana to France also gave the French control of the Mississippi River. The Mississippi was important to America's growing trade. Several busy commercial cities—such as St. Louis, Natchez, and New Orleans—lay along the Mississippi. These river cities offered large markets for American trade. The river cities also had fine harbors and places where Americans could store their trade goods. In addition, New Orleans served as an important center for America's overseas trade.

Many Americans, including President Jefferson, felt that French control of the Mississippi and of Louisiana would be an obstacle to America's development. As long as Louisiana belonged to France, the United States could not grow west of the Mississippi River. Also, the French could close the Mississippi River to American trade and travel at any time. For these reasons, President Jefferson moved to buy parts of the Louisiana Territory from France.

In the early 1800's, France was involved in a series of wars in Europe. Thus, Napoleon knew that his desire to build an empire in North America would be too costly in terms of lives and of money. As a result, Napoleon was soon willing to sell the Louisiana Territory—except the Floridas—to America. President Jefferson pressed Congress to approve the sale. And in 1803, the United States bought the Louisiana Territory from France for about 15 million dollars. As a result of this sale, the country's size was doubled, and the West was opened to American settlement (see map, page 161).

Why was French control of Louisiana a threat to many Americans?

The West Is Explored. The United States gained a great deal of new land through the Louisiana Purchase. But much of this land was unknown to Americans. In 1803, only a few Americans had been west of the Mississippi River. President Jefferson was therefore eager to learn more about the new lands of the Louisiana Territory.

Photri

Explorers William Clark and Meriwether Lewis were guided through the Louisiana Territory by a Shoshone Indian named Sacagawea, or "Bird Woman," and by York, a slave. The expedition proved to be a great success, as many valuable observations of the new land were made by the explorers.

In 1804, Jefferson asked William Clark and Meriwether Lewis to chart some of the Louisiana territory. Lewis and Clark were to explore the land in the north of the new territory. When they returned, an account of their expedition was to be made public. In this way, President Jefferson hoped to open Louisiana to American settlement.

Lewis and Clark explored the Northwest for two years. They were aided by Sacagawea, an Indian princess, and by a black slave named York, both of whom served as guides and as translators for the expedition. The explorers crossed the Rocky Mountains, mapped the Oregon Country, and reached the Pacific coast. The party followed a somewhat different route when they returned east in 1806.

The journey of Lewis and Clark helped to give Americans a clear picture of the Louisiana Territory. Moreover, because Americans had mapped the Oregon Country, United States claims to this land were strengthened.

Lewis and Clark helped to open the Far West to American settlement. However, the Southwest was not settled by Americans at this time. Another American, Zebulon Pike, had explored the Southwest. But Pike's accounts led many Americans to believe that the land in the Southwest was largely desert. Also, much of this land was owned by the Spanish. Most Americans in the early 1800's, therefore, chose to settle in the West rather than in the Southwest.

■ *How did the explorations of Lewis and Clark help America to grow?*

The West Gains Influence. The Louisiana Purchase helped the West to gain added importance in the eyes of many Americans. This was because some people began to feel that the settlement of the West was the key to America's future. Also, the number of Americans who settled in the West grew rapidly after 1803. As a result, the West and its people won growing political and economic power.

The voters of the West called for the government to take more interest in their needs and their aims. As the population of the West grew, so did its voting power. Government leaders therefore began to give more attention to western ideas and goals.

As more Americans moved to the frontier, the West became economically important as well. Frontier people needed the manufactured goods made in the East. As a result, the West quickly became a market for the goods of the East. Moreover, as people settled the frontier, the West became a farming center. Soon, a lively trade between the East and the West grew. This trade helped to cause a growing desire for more land to settle and to farm.

■ *What changes helped the West to gain economic and political power?*

Objections to Growth. The United States grew rapidly during the early 1800's. But some people believed that such growth was dangerous. Moreover, some Americans, including a small number of New England citizens, were greatly angered by the Louisiana Purchase. This New England group—known as the Essex Junto—worked against President Jefferson's plan to buy Louisiana. They feared that the growing number of voters in the West would soon outnumber the voters of the East. In that case, they felt, the country's government would no longer give equal attention to the needs of the New England states.

The Essex Junto decided upon a plan to build a *Northern Confederacy* made up of the New England states. The Northern Confederacy plan called for New England to

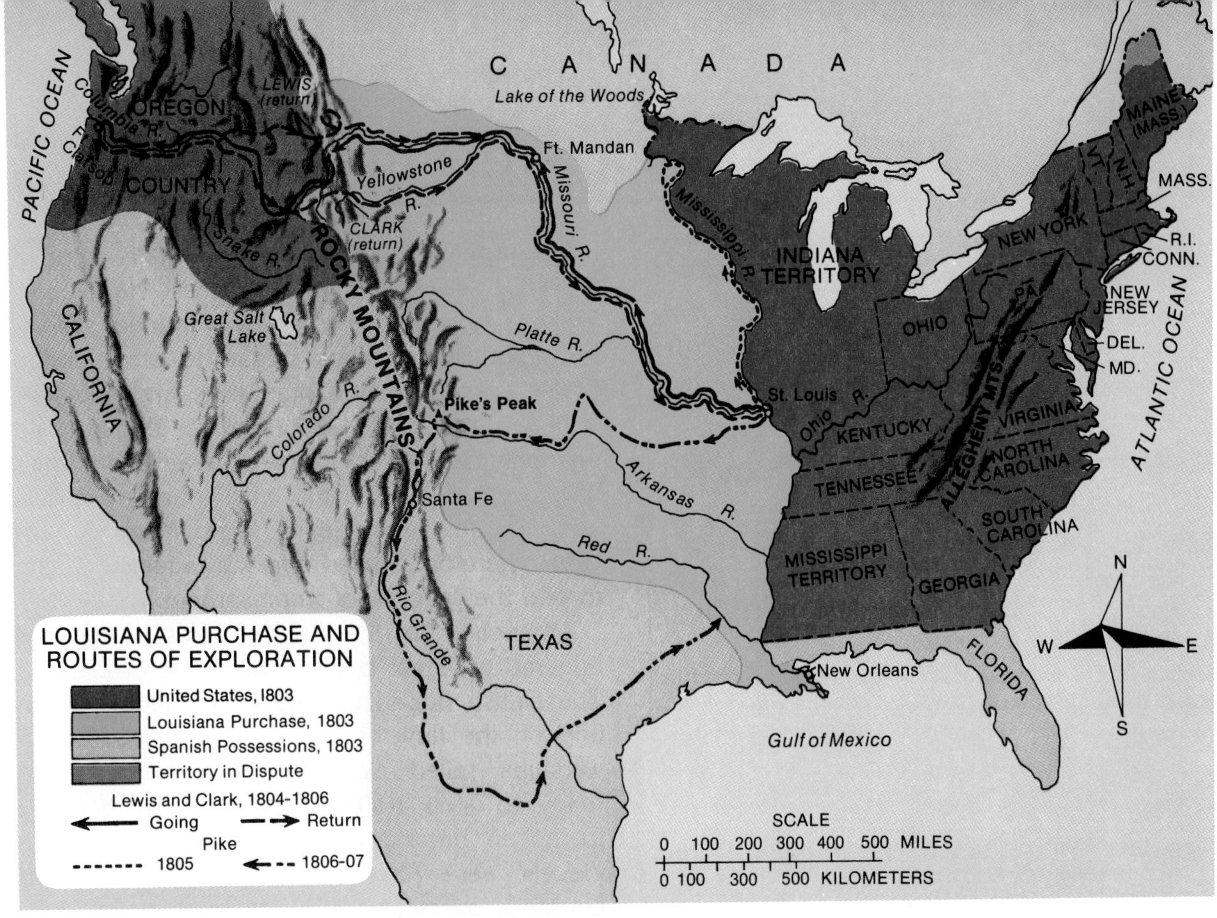

The Louisiana Purchase prompted several government-sponsored explorations of the West between 1804 and 1807. What geographic feature did most of the exploration routes follow?

secede—break away—from the United States. Then, the people of New England could govern themselves. But some leaders of the East—especially Alexander Hamilton of New York—attacked the plan. Hamilton's strong attack helped to defeat the aims of the Essex Junto. Thus, the Northern Confederacy plan was defeated, and New England remained in the Union.

■ *What was the Northern Confederacy plan?*

SECTION 2 REVIEW

1. *When did American interest in western settlement begin to grow?*
2. *How did the movement to the frontier make the West economically important?*
3. *Why did some Americans oppose the Louisiana Purchase?*

3 America and World Affairs

Overview During the early 1800's, America was still closely bound to western Europe. As a result, many of the changes seen in America in the early 1800's came about because of changes in Europe.

Objectives After you read this section, you will be able to:

- describe the changes in Europe that affected Americans in the early 1800's;
- explain how the United States government responded to these changes;
- analyze the effects of the War of 1812 on the United States.

Troubles With France and Britain. During the late 1700's, many Americans' attitudes toward France changed. Most Americans had been sympathetic to the democratic ideas expressed in the French Revolution of 1789. However, with Napoleon's rise to power in the early 1800's, some Americans began to turn against France. This was because many of the ideas of the French Revolution gave way to Napoleon's efforts to build a large empire in Europe. By 1800, most of Europe was at war with France. Thus, by the early 1800's, some Americans no longer favored the French cause.

Other Americans, however, were equally against Great Britain at this time. This was because several British policies of the early 1800's worked directly against American rights and goals.

One British policy that angered Americans was called *impressment*—the seizure of sailors from American ships. Great Britain kept a powerful navy to fight against Napoleon's France. But the navy needed trained sailors. Thus, British warships began to stop United States vessels on the high seas and take—or impress—American sailors. The British said that only sailors who had deserted from their navy were taken in this way. In many cases, however, this was clearly false. Many Americans, therefore, called for war against Britain to end the practice of impressment.

Americans in the early 1800's were also angered by Great Britain's blockade of Europe. The British hoped to defeat Napoleon by cutting off the flow of trade with Europe. British warships sailed along the coast of Europe, ready to stop trading vessels from entering European harbors. But since many of these vessels were American merchant ships, our country's overseas trade was hurt. In the early 1800's, then, grave problems once again arose between America and Great Britain.

■ *What were the causes of American anger toward Great Britain in the early 1800's?*

Problems of Neutrality. In the early 1800's, many Americans called for war against Great Britain. Others, however, wanted the United States to side with Britain in the battle against Napoleon.

While Jefferson was angered by some British acts, he did not believe that America was prepared for war. Also, Jefferson did not feel that the United States should side with Britain in the struggle against France. For these reasons, Jefferson followed a course of *neutrality*. That is, America refused to support either side in the struggle.

President Jefferson, however, soon found that American neutrality was hard to protect. In 1807, for example, the American navy ship *Chesapeake* was fired upon by the British warship *Leopard*. This happened because the *Chesapeake's* captain would not allow British officers to board his ship in search of "deserters." Several Americans were killed or wounded, and four sailors were impressed. The *Chesapeake-Leopard Incident* brought the two countries to the edge of war.

Moreover, the British refused to end their blockade of Europe. In answer, Napoleon ordered his navy to cut Britain off from overseas trade. United States ships were therefore being boarded not only by the British but by the French as well. In addition, United States goods for trading were taken illegally, and American sailors were put into prison. Once again, American merchants and farmers were hurt, and our country's trade suffered.

■ *Why was American neutrality difficult to protect?*

Jefferson Takes Action. Clearly, neither Great Britain nor France intended to honor America's neutrality. President Jefferson decided to act against the two countries. In 1807, he placed an *embargo*—a halt—on all American trade with Britain and France. In this way, Jefferson hoped to make the two countries honor American trade rights.

The Embargo Act of 1807, however, hurt America far more than it did Britain or France. When the Embargo Act halted overseas trade, many Americans suffered from the loss of money and of jobs. The New England states, where much of the country's overseas trade was centered, were especially hard hit. Also, the Act failed to make either France or Britain agree to honor American trade rights. For these reasons, President Jefferson asked Congress to remove the Embargo Act in 1809.

■ *Why did the Embargo Act of 1807 fail?*

The Coming of War. James Madison entered the White House in 1809. President Madison intended to follow Jefferson's policies

During the summer of 1807, the British warship *Leopard* fired three rapid broadsides into the USS *Chesapeake*, an American ship, forcing the commander to surrender. The attack came after the Americans refused to let the British search the *Chesapeake* for British deserters.

Mariners Museum, Newport News, Virginia

of peace and neutrality. At the same time, however, new calls for war with Great Britain were heard. Many Americans believed that our country's economic troubles were largely due to Britain's blockade of Europe. Moreover, many people in the West and the South felt that the United States could easily defeat Great Britain. Then, they believed, our country could take the British lands in North America and gain new trade in Europe as well.

A powerful group in Congress—called the War Hawks—agreed with these ideas. The War Hawks, led by Henry Clay and John C. Calhoun, put growing pressure on President Madison to go to war. The New England states did not want war with Britain, however, and fought against the aims of the War Hawks. Many New England citizens felt that America should go to war against France instead. But in 1812, President Madison finally decided to ask Congress to declare war against Great Britain.

■ *Why were many Americans eager to declare war against Britain?*

The War of 1812. The United States was not prepared to fight a major power such as Great Britain. But until 1814, the British had to give most of their attention to the war against Napoleon. Thus, Americans won several important battles in 1812 and 1813. For example, a small fleet led by Oliver Hazard Perry defeated the British on Lake Erie. This victory gave America control of the Great Lakes. In addition, the United States victory at the Battle of the Thames helped to open the Northwest Territory to American settlement (see map on this page).

The British, however, also won major vic-

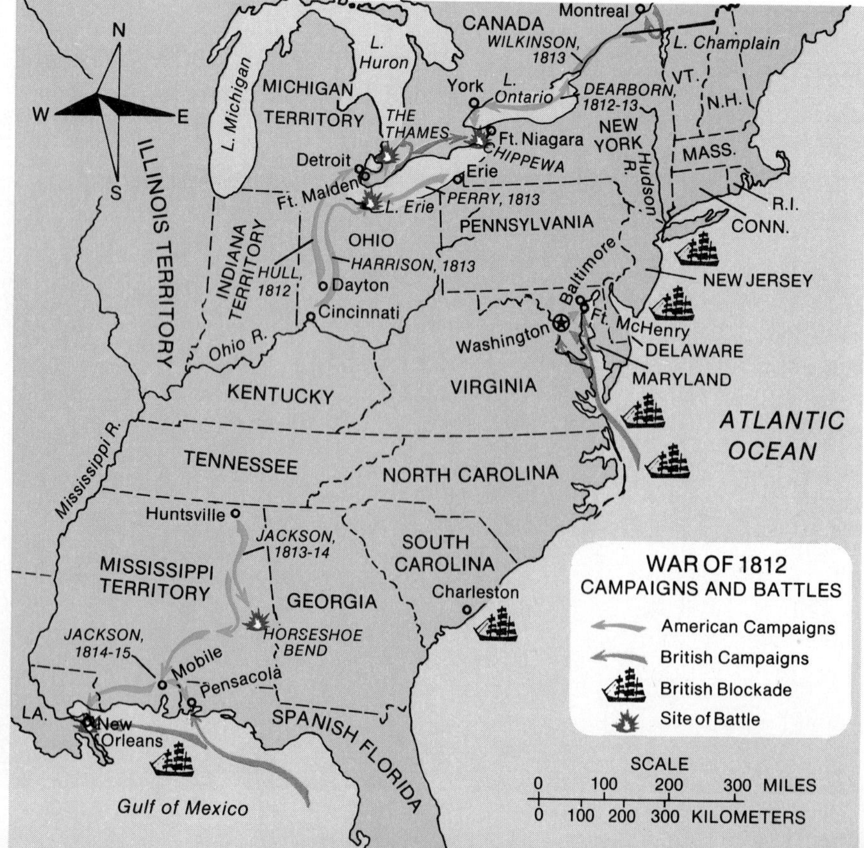

In January 1815, the Battle of New Orleans—a brilliant victory for the Americans and terribly costly for the British—took place two weeks after the war had ended. Where did most of the British campaigns take place?

DO YOU KNOW?

Who was the first American President to be inaugurated in Washington, D.C.?

Thomas Jefferson became the first President to be inaugurated in Washington, D.C. The city had been our nation's capital for less than one year when Jefferson was inaugurated on March 4, 1801. Construction of the city had begun in 1793, after President Washington commissioned Pierre Charles L'Enfant, a French architect, to build a new national capital. At the time of President Jefferson's inauguration, the White House and many other government buildings were still incomplete. In 1814, during the War of 1812, much of the city was destroyed by the British. But by 1819, Washington, D.C. had been rebuilt and enlarged.

tories during the war. British soldiers attacked and burned Washington, D.C. Some other American cities also suffered from British attacks.

Early in 1815, the last battle of the war—fought at New Orleans—was won by Americans under General Andrew Jackson. The Battle of New Orleans was a terrible waste of lives. For on Christmas Eve of 1814—two weeks before Jackson's victory—a treaty had been signed to end the war. However, because messages traveled slowly in the early 1800's, word of the treaty did not reach America until *after* the battle was fought.

The War of 1812 was largely a military draw. But the war did help Americans to reach some important goals. The war ended British impressment, and the United States once again became a major trading power. Just as important was the fact that the war helped Americans to win European respect. Finally, after the War of 1812, the United States did not become involved in European wars for almost 100 years. The long years of peace with Europe helped America to grow and to become strong.

■ *What gains did America make as a result of the War of 1812?*

Protests in New England. Not all Americans favored their country's war with Great Britain. The New England states had hoped to build closer ties with the British. This was because many New England citizens depended upon trade with Britain. The Embargo Act of 1807 had hurt this trade. When the Act was removed in 1809, New England traders were eager to build their businesses once again. But the War of 1812 made this impossible. Thus, New England once again faced major economic troubles.

In 1814, some New England leaders met in Hartford, Connecticut. This meeting—the Hartford Convention—called for New England to make peace with Great Britain. This meant that New England was prepared to act as a country separate from the United States.

The Hartford Convention based many of its ideas and demands upon the principle of states' rights, which is increased power for the states. But the War of 1812 ended before the New England leaders could act further. The Hartford Convention, however, showed how much New England depended upon overseas trade. The convention also proved that the matter of states' rights could become an important problem.

■ *Why did some New England leaders wish to break away from the United States in 1814?*

(Text continues on page 167.)

VIEWPOINTS DIFFER

Angry Journalism in the War of 1812

One interesting aspect of the War of 1812 was that negotiations for peace started almost as soon as the fighting began. Negotiations continued throughout the course of the war. Such peace talks did not, however, stem the feeling of hostility on both sides. British and American bitterness over the war can be seen in contemporary newspaper articles.

The *Niles' Weekly Register* was published in Philadelphia. The following excerpt was taken from the April, 1812, issue—shortly after the war began:

Accursed be the American government, and every individual of it who . . . shall agree to make peace with Great Britain, until ample provision shall be made for our impressed seamen, and security shall be given for the prevention of such abominable [disgusting] outrages in the future.

The viewpoint of the British newspaper, the *London Times*, was equally harsh. This excerpt from May 24, 1814, sharply criticizes the peace treaty that ended the War of 1812:

. . . [N]o weak and cowardly policy interpose [step in] to save them [the Americans] from the blow! Strike, Chastise [punish] the savages; for such they are. . . . With Madison and his perjured [lying] set, no treaty can be made; for no oath can bind them.

The Bettmann Archive

Think About It

1. According to the *Niles Register*, what prevented peace with Great Britain?
2. In the *London Times*, how are Americans described?
3. What do you think is the role of newspapers in shaping public opinion?

Social Problems in America. During the postwar years, Americans tried to build a better society. Their work helped to bring a new spirit of freedom to the country.

But there were still many injustices in the American society of the early 1800's. Most blacks in America were slaves and had few, if any, rights under the law. Also, slavery grew as cotton became more important to the economy of the South. More black slaves were needed to work in the fields and to prepare cotton for market. As the cotton industry grew during the early 1800's, the problem of slavery became greater.

At the same time, however, some Americans began to give more attention to the problems of black slaves. And during the early 1800's, a new movement to free blacks began to gain power in America.

Women, too, did not enjoy equal rights during the early 1800's. American women were not allowed to take part in government or in many businesses. But American women did make some progress during this time. Greater attention was given to women's education. As a result, some women—such as Sarah Hale and Lydia Child—were able to become writers, artists, and teachers. Thus, the needs of women, like the needs of blacks, began to receive some notice in the years after 1812.

■ *What were some important social problems in America during the early 1800's?*

SECTION 3 REVIEW

1. *What was the British policy of impressment?*
2. *How did the Embargo Act of 1807 affect many Americans in New England?*
3. *How was the United States made stronger by the War of 1812?*

CHAPTER 9 SUMMARY

The years from 1800 to 1815 were marked by change and by growth in America. Our country's government became stronger under able leaders such as Jefferson and Marshall. Also, new ways of living and of working began to appear during the early 1800's. In the North, Americans began to build small industries while in the South, farming became more important than ever before.

The United States grew rapidly in size as well as in power and wealth. The Louisiana Purchase of 1803 opened new lands in the West to American settlement. As more people moved across the Mississippi River, the West became an important part of America's growing economy. Also, the West gained a greater voice in our country's government as frontier voters made their wishes known.

During the early 1800's, the United States fought another war with Great Britain. Once again, Americans were able to defend their right to build a free and separate country. As a result, the United States won not only a lasting peace with Europe but world respect as well.

CHAPTER 9 REVIEW

USING YOUR SKILLS

Studying Primary Sources

The excerpt on this page is an example of a *primary source.* A source is said to be primary when it comes directly from the period of time being studied. A primary source may take the form of a firsthand account of a person, an event, or a historical trend. A painting or an illustration might also be a primary source. Another kind of primary source is an *artifact*—a material object such as a tool, a weapon, or an ornament—that comes from the time being studied. Primary sources are relied upon by historians and by other social scientists to give information about a person, an event, or a trend. For example, a letter written by George Washington during the Revolutionary War would tell something about Washington's thoughts, views, and goals. Such a letter might also give information about some aspect of the Revolutionary War itself. The primary source below describes early pioneers in the United States. It was written by a French traveler who visited America in 1802. Study the excerpt and then answer the questions below.

1. According to the excerpt, what were more than half of the first inhabitants of the Ohio Territory called?
2. Based on the description, what characteristic did the first inhabitants of the Ohio Territory share with the first inhabitants of Kentucky and Tennessee?
3. What reasons did more than half of the first inhabitants of the Ohio Territory give for moving westward?
4. According to this account, why were only a few of the first inhabitants of Kentucky and Tennessee still remaining in those states in 1802?
5. What does the author of this account predict will happen to most of the first inhabitants of the Ohio Territory?
6. In your opinion, why were the first inhabitants described in the excerpt necessary to America's westward expansion?

More than half of those who inhabit the borders of the Ohio, are again the first inhabitants, or as they are called in the United States, the *first settlers,* a kind of men who cannot settle upon the soil that they have cleared, and who under pretence [excuse] of finding a better land, a more wholesome country, a greater abundance of game, push forward, incline perpetually [move continuously] towards the most distant points of the American population, . . .

Such were the first inhabitants of Kentucky and Tennessea [Tennessee], of whom there are now remaining but very few. . . . They have emigrated [moved] to more remote parts of the country, and formed new settlements. It will be the same with most of those who inhabit the borders of the Ohio.

CHAPTER 9 REVIEW

YOU SHOULD KNOW

Identify, define, or explain each of the following:

construction
judicial review
urban
industrialize
cash crops
ceded
secede
neutrality
embargo

CHECKING FACTS

1. What was unusual about the election of 1800?
2. What was the Twelfth Amendment?
3. Where did industry first develop in the United States?
4. What kind of life-styles generally existed in the South?
5. What was the population of the United States by 1810?
6. Why did President Jefferson sponsor the Lewis and Clark expedition?
7. Who was Zebulon Pike?
8. What was the Northern Confederacy Plan?
9. Who were the War Hawks?
10. Why did the problem of slavery become greater in the United States during the early 1800's?

UNDERSTANDING CONCEPTS

1. Why did President Jefferson support the principle of states' rights?
2. In what ways did the North differ from the South during the early 1800's?
3. How did the country's growing population affect many Americans in the early 1800's?
4. What were the causes of the Hartford Convention of 1814?

LEARNING FROM ILLUSTRATIONS

1. Study the chart on page 157. What general trend regarding cotton production in America does the chart show?
2. According to the map on page 164, how did the British attempt to prevent the Americans from trading with other nations?

CRITICAL THINKING

1. The North and the South developed different life-styles by the early 1800's. If you had lived at that time, would you rather have lived in the North or in the South? Why?
2. Not all American citizens approved of the Louisiana Purchase. If you were living in the early 1800's, would you have approved of the Louisiana Purchase? Why or why not?
3. In the early 1800's, the United States faced problems with both France and Great Britain. Do you think the United States should have sided with France or Great Britain? Give reasons for your answer.

ENRICHMENT ACTIVITIES

1. With several other students, gather information about the first four presidents of the United States. Based on this information, write short, biographical sketches of these presidents.
2. It may be interesting to find out more about the War of 1812 by looking for information in books and in encyclopedia articles about the war. Using this information, draw maps to show where the major battles of the War of 1812 were fought. Maps could then be displayed on the class bulletin board.

1810 1820

- 1793 Samuel Slater builds America's first machine-driven cotton mill
- 1814 Francis Lowell builds first factory
- 1816 James Monroe elected President
- 1819 *McCulloch* v. *Maryland*
- 1820 Missouri Compromise
- 1823 President Monroe issues the Monroe Doctrine

CHAPTER 10

The New Nation Faces Problems

Chapter Objectives

After studying this chapter, you will be able to:

- list the factors involved in the development of social classes in America;
- explain the relationship between frontier settlement and the rise of American nationalism after 1815;
- identify the forces that resulted in sectional differences during the early 1800's.

1 Social and Economic Growth

Overview In the years after the War of 1812, Americans worked to make their country a better place in which to live. The ways in which America's society grew helped to build a stronger and wealthier United States. But many important problems remained to be solved.

Our country's economy also grew rapidly in the years after 1815. This economic growth brought new ways of working and of living to the people of the United States.

Objectives After you read this section, you will be able to:

- describe how the growth of the middle class affected America;
- identify some of the social problems that faced Americans after 1815;
- explain how the coming of the Industrial Revolution influenced the nation's economy during the early 1800's.

America's New Society. The society that grew in America during the early 1800's was well suited to life in a new country. The ideas and the values that shaped our society gave many Americans the freedom to make a better life for themselves.

By 1815, America was a country of middle-class people and of middle-class goals. That is, most Americans were neither very poor nor very rich. For this reason, the middle class had become the largest and most powerful of America's social classes. A *social class* is a group of people who share the same general status—or position—in a society. In some societies, a person's social standing—or class—was fixed by birth or by family background. But in America, one's social class was often determined by one's income.

The fact that most Americans belonged to the middle class meant that, to some degree, they felt socially equal to one another. In general, they had about the same earning power and about the same living standards. Of course, ways of life depended greatly upon where people lived and upon the jobs they held. That is, life for a settler on the western frontier was much different from life for a worker in an eastern city. But within any one part of the country, middle-class Americans generally followed similar ways of life.

Middle-class Americans of the early 1800's also shared many of the same social values and aims. Most wanted to build a better life for their families. And most believed that hard work was the key to reaching this goal. In addition, many middle-class Americans were eager to have their children attend schools. They felt that education was one way to gain better jobs and a higher standard of living. Thus, the number of schools in America increased as the country's middle class became larger.

During the earliest years of the 1800's, most middle-class Americans were landowners. This meant that the middle class was strongest in the rural parts of the country. But by about 1815, city people had begun to enter the middle class as well.

■ *What was the dominant social class in America during the early 1800's?*

The Spread of the Middle Class. During the early 1800's, most middle-class Americans lived on farms or in country towns and villages. Our society at this time could best be described as both rural and middle class.

By about 1815, however, America's *urban* —or city—population underwent a slow but steady increase as more and more people were attracted to cities. This was because the number of businesses and factories built in America's cities grew rapidly after 1815. And with the growing number of businesses and factories came a growing need for workers.

Most city workers in the early 1800's were poorly paid and could not enjoy good living conditions. Some city workers, however, were highly skilled. Often, they received better pay than did less-skilled workers. Their greater earning power meant that skilled workers were able to become members of the urban middle class. Thus, because America's social classes were based upon income, more people were able to move upward in society. That is, as people earned more money, they were able to move into a higher social class.

The spread of the middle class in both urban and rural America helped our society to become more democratic. This was because middle-class Americans were roughly equal to one another in social and economic terms. The middle class was politically strong as well. Government leaders began to listen to the needs and the wants of middle-class voters. Because of this, many Americans felt that their society—as well as their government—was based upon democratic ideas.

■ *Why were some city workers in America able to enter the middle class by about 1815?*

Winter Scene in Brooklyn, 1817–1820, 97.13, The Brooklyn Museum

Life in the early cities of the United States was still quite similar to life in the rural areas. This painting of Brooklyn shows that people in the city still had to split their own firewood and draw their own water.

Social Problems. By 1815, many Americans believed that they lived in a democratic society. Not all people, however, enjoyed equal rights or an equal chance to improve their way of life. Throughout the early 1800's, a number of Americans were faced with social injustice and with unfair treatment.

During the early 1800's, American women had little real social freedom. They were not thought to be equal to men. Also, women had few economic or political rights. For example, women could not vote, nor could they run for government office. And in many cases, women could not own land or other kinds of property. When a woman married, her belongings usually became the property of her husband. Thus, women had little power or freedom in American society.

Black Americans were among those who suffered most from social injustice during the early 1800's. At this time, most blacks in America were slaves. Black slaves had few rights and little, if any, freedom. Under the law, they were viewed as the property of their white owners. Generally, slaves could be treated with kindness or with cruelty, depending upon the wishes of their masters.

During the early 1800's, slavery was most widespread in the South. This was because workers were badly needed for the growing southern cotton business. And slaves were seen as the cheapest way to meet the labor needs of a growing cotton industry.

At one time, slavery had been present in the North, as well as in the South. But by the early 1800's, the northern states had outlawed slavery. During this time, some northern whites began to be troubled by the hardships of black slaves. Because of this, a movement was started to help slaves and to bring an end to slavery in the South. The *abolitionist movement,* as it came to be called, worked to outlaw slavery throughout the United States. Some northern whites also acted to help slaves escape to the North. These people eventually formed the *Underground Railroad*—a network of safe houses along the route that runaway slaves used to travel north. The Underground Railroad helped to guide thousands of escaped slaves to freedom in the years after 1815. But until the mid-1860's most blacks in America remained slaves.

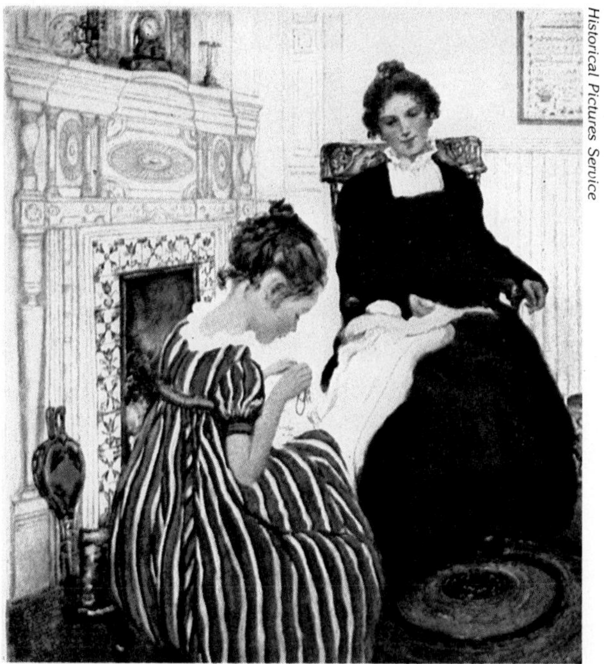

Historical Pictures Service

In the early 1800's, women were expected to learn skills at home. Few attended school.

■ *What was one way in which women were discriminated against in the early 1800's?*

(Text continues on page 175.)

RECALLING THE TIMES

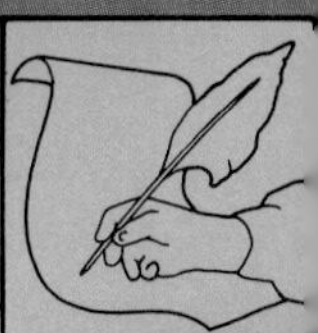

A Quaker's Response to Slavery

One of the first groups to speak out against the institution of slavery was the Quakers—a religious group. Even before the Revolutionary War, the Quakers called for an end to slavery on moral grounds. And by the early 1800's, many Quakers had begun to take an active role in helping slaves escape to freedom. In the excerpt below, Levi Coffin, a Quaker who lived in Indiana, described how he helped runaway slaves.

In the winter of 1826–27 fugitives [runaway slaves] began to come to our house, and as it became more widely known on different routes that the slaves fleeing from bondage would find a welcome and shelter at our house and be forwarded safely on their journey, the number increased. Friends in the neighborhood who had formerly stood aloof from the work, fearful of the penalty of the law, were encouraged to engage in it when they saw the fearless manner in which I acted and the success that attended my efforts. They would contribute to clothe the fugitives and would aid in forwarding them on their way but were timid about sheltering them under their roof; so that part of the work devolved [was left] on us....

I soon became extensively known to the friends of the slaves, at different points on the Ohio River where fugitives generally crossed, and to those northward of us on the various routes leading to Canada....

The pursuit was often very close, and we had to resort to various stratagems [strategies] in order to elude [hide from] the pursuers. Sometimes a company of fugitives were scattered and secreted in the neighborhood until the hunters had given up the chase. At other times their route was changed and they were hurried forward with all speed....

Many of the fugitives came long distances,... in fact from all parts of the South. Sometimes the poor hunted creatures had been out so long, living in woods and thickets, that they were almost wild when they came in and so fearful of being betrayed that it was some time before their confidence could be gained and the true state of their case learned....

Thinking Critically

Why were some Quakers at first reluctant to help the slaves flee?

Do you think the Quakers should have helped the runaway slaves even though it was against the law to do so? Give reasons for your answer.

Industrial Growth. The years after 1815 were times of widespread economic growth in the United States. A major cause of America's strong economic growth during this time was the coming of the Industrial Revolution.

During the mid-1700's, British business leaders had begun to use water-powered machines to make goods for market. Soon, American manufacturers began to copy British machines and to borrow British methods.

In 1793, Samuel Slater of Rhode Island built America's first machine-driven cotton mill. Slater found that New England offered the waterpower and the other resources needed to drive his machines. For this reason, the Northeast became the birthplace of America's Industrial Revolution.

Slater's mill proved that machines were an economical way to make cloth goods for market. Within a few years, machine-powered cotton mills were soon at work throughout the Northeast. At the same time, another northeastern business leader, Eli Whitney, the inventor of the cotton gin, helped to bring about new industrial methods. In 1798, Whitney discovered a way to make each part of a product by machine rather than by hand. Hundreds of parts could be made quickly and cheaply. Finished goods could then be put together in a step-by-step process. Thus, Whitney was the first manufacturer to use the *mass-production* method to make goods for market. Whitney's idea of mass production quickly spread throughout the manufacturing centers of the Northeast.

Francis Lowell, another American, was the first manufacturer to build a *factory*. The factory that Lowell built in 1814 housed all the machines needed to make a finished product. This meant that the step-by-step process used in mass production could be carried out at one time and in one place.

The early Industrial Revolution caused major economic changes in America during the

Rhode Island Development Council

Slater's Mill, built at Pawtucket, Rhode Island, in the early 1790's, was America's first machine-powered cotton spinning mill. The mill, with its water-powered machines, signaled the coming of the Industrial Revolution in America.

DO YOU KNOW?

When was the first high school opened in the United States?

America's first high school, the English Classical School, was opened in Boston, Massachusetts, in May 1821. The school provided a liberal education in literature, history, mathematics, and science. It also prepared students for further instruction on the university level. The school's name was later changed to the English High School. Six years later, in 1827, Massachusetts enacted the country's first state high-school law, calling for tax-supported public high schools in communities numbering 500 families or more.

years after 1815. And in turn, these changes brought new ways of living and of working to people throughout our country.

■ *What developments contributed to the coming of the Industrial Revolution in America?*

Economic Changes. The Industrial Revolution brought about many changes in America during the early 1800's. The use of machines to make goods for market gave Americans a wider choice of things to use and to buy. This was because machines were better able to make a greater number and variety of goods than people could make producing goods by hand. In addition, new manufacturing methods often made goods cheaper to make and to buy. As a result, more Americans were able to buy things, such as cloth, tools, and household goods.

The Industrial Revolution also brought new wealth to many American manufacturers. Using newly developed production methods and machinery, enterprising business leaders were able to make and sell goods that once had to be brought from overseas. For this reason, America's manufacturers during the early 1800's became more able to meet the needs of their country's growing markets. In addition, they were able to increase their overseas trade by selling more manufactured goods to other countries.

In the years after 1815, America became a stronger and wealthier country. At the same time, people began to have new ideas about the meaning of America, about citizenship, and about the role of their government.

■ *In what ways did the Industrial Revolution bring better economic conditions to America?*

SECTION 1 REVIEW

1. *What major factor determined an American's social class during the early 1800's?*
2. *In what ways was democracy limited in our society in the early 1800's?*
3. *How did the Industrial Revolution influence America's economy during the early 1800's?*

2 Nationalism and the Frontier

Overview In the years between 1815 and 1828, the idea of being an American took on a new meaning. Our government began to play a larger role in American lives. Many people began to see the relationship between themselves and their country in a different light. New ideas toward government and toward the country as a whole were also shaped by ongoing western settlement.

Objectives After you read this section, you will be able to:

- discuss the ways the arts reflected a new sense of nationalism in America;
- describe the ways the federal government and continued frontier settlement helped to strengthen national loyalties after 1815;
- explain why the Monroe Doctrine was established.

The Beginnings of Nationalism. Throughout their history, Americans had felt pride in their country. But in the years after 1815, this feeling of pride became stronger and more widespread than ever before. The feeling of pride and loyalty toward one's country is called *nationalism.* Between 1815 and 1828, a wave of nationalism spread throughout America.

Strong feelings of nationalism grew in America for many reasons. One reason had to do with the outcome of the War of 1812. Even though there was no clear-cut winner in the war, many Americans believed that they had defeated the British. Americans were proud of their victories during the war. And this made them feel greater pride in their country. Also, many people began to feel that America offered them a bright and promising future after the war. Because of this, Americans began to have stronger feelings of loyalty to their country.

Another cause of nationalism in America had to do with the arts—such as painting and literature. Many American artists painted pictures that showed our country's beauty and promise. Moreover, writers such as Washington Irving and James Fenimore Cooper portrayed America as an ideal land. Irving's stories, such as "Rip Van Winkle" and "The Legend of Sleepy Hollow," have become great American folktales. Cooper wrote about the early settlement of the West. In books such as *The Leatherstocking Tales,* he described the settlers, their values, and their way of life. Thus,

The defense of Fort McHenry inspired the writing of "The Star-Spangled Banner" in 1814.

Photos courtesy of the Peale Museum

"The Return of Rip Van Winkle" (detail) by John Quidor/National Gallery of Art, Washington, D.C., Andrew W. Mellon Collection

After a 20-year sleep, Rip Van Winkle awakened to learn how many things had changed. The story, set in the state of New York, was written by Washington Irving in 1820.

artists and writers often showed the United States in an ideal light. Because of this, many Americans felt a greater sense of pride in their country.

■ *How did artists and writers contribute to the growth of nationalism in America?*

Nationalism and the Government. There were many other reasons for the growth of nationalism in America. One of the most important of these was the rise of a strong federal government.

Throughout the early 1800's, government leaders acted to build a stronger America. The work of these leaders helped to make our federal government more powerful and more responsive to public needs. Feelings of pride and of faith in the national government grew in America. Because government leaders won the trust of many Americans during the early 1800's, this period has become known as the *Era of Good Feelings.*

One way in which government leaders served their country was by acting to protect its growing economy. In 1816, President James Madison, who had been elected in 1808, asked Congress to pass a tariff on European goods sold in America. A *tariff* is a tax—or a *duty*—on goods made in one country and sold in another. The Tariff of 1816 made European goods brought into our country more costly to buy than American goods. In this way, the government aided manufacturers by helping them to sell more goods. Factory owners were protected and jobs were saved. For this reason, the Tariff of 1816 was a *protective tariff.*

The Tariff of 1816 proved that our government was willing to help Americans build a stronger economy. And the government acted further when it set up the second Bank of the United States.

The first Bank of the United States was started in 1791 by an act of Congress. The Bank helped to set the value and the supply of America's money. For this reason, the Bank was very important to our growing economy. But the Bank closed in 1811 when Congress refused to renew its charter.

Americans soon discovered that without the

Bank, the country's economy was weakened. In some cases, money lost much of its value. Because of this, many Americans called for new laws to start a second Bank. And in 1816, Congress once again acted to open the Bank of the United States.

The second Bank, like the Tariff of 1816, helped to make America's economy stronger. These acts caused many people to gain added faith in their government. But just as Congress helped to build a strong government, so did the Supreme Court add to its constitutional powers.

■ *What were two major examples of nationalistic legislation passed after 1815?*

Nationalism and the Supreme Court. The Supreme Court under Chief Justice John Marshall also worked to build a strong national government. Several major Supreme Court rulings, such as *Marbury* v. *Madison* and *Fletcher* v. *Peck,* gave the federal government power over state governments (see page 154).

One of the most important rulings of the Supreme Court under Marshall was the case of *McCulloch* v. *Maryland* (1819). This ruling said that the Constitution gave the federal government two kinds of power. The first kind of power was that which was clearly stated in the Constitution. The second was that power which was *implied*—meant but not stated. Because of this ruling, the federal government gained broad new powers under the Constitution.

The Supreme Court under Chief Justice Marshall helped to make our country's government stronger. And this, in turn, helped to build a greater spirit of nationalism in America. This new sense of pride and of faith in the country and its government became even greater as the West was settled.

■ *What is an* implied *constitutional power?*

An Expanding Frontier. In the years after 1815, our country grew rapidly as more and more Americans moved west. By 1820, one out of every four Americans lived west of the Appalachian Mountains. By 1828, six new states had been added to the United States.

The settlement of the West after 1815 helped to make America's economy stronger. This was because the West soon became one of the country's most important farming centers. Many western settlers became wealthy by raising food and livestock to be sold in the East. After 1815, Americans came to depend heavily upon the West for food and for other farm goods.

The new markets that grew as the West was settled helped eastern trade and manufacturing to grow. Western people needed the new machine-made goods—cloth, tools, and household goods—of the East. At the same time, the West became economically strong as the need for western farm goods became greater. Soon, a growing two-way trade between the East and the West came about. For this reason, the ongoing settlement of the West was good for America's economy.

As Americans moved west, the spirit of nationalism grew. Loyalty to one's state often decreased as a settler moved west. As a result, many western settlers felt a strong sense of belonging to their country rather than to the states they had left.

The settlement of the West made America stronger in terms of both its economy and its feelings of nationhood. But the settlement of

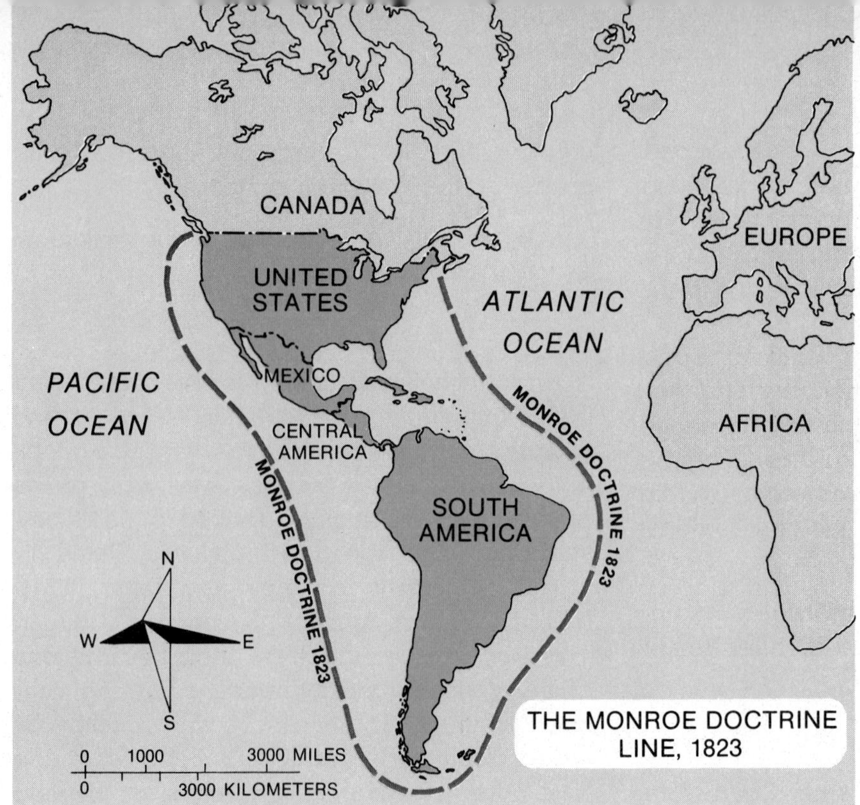

In 1823 President James Monroe issued the Monroe Doctrine. In this doctrine, Monroe stated that the independence of Latin American governments would be protected by the United States. What continents were affected by the Monroe Doctrine?

the West also brought new troubles to America. One of the most important of these new troubles was the Panic of 1819.

■ *In what ways did western settlement help to make America stronger?*

The Panic of 1819. The Panic of 1819 was America's first true *depression*—an economic slowdown accompanied by widespread business failures and by large-scale unemployment. There were many reasons for this depression. One of the chief causes was an outgrowth of the rush to settle the West.

The growing importance of western farming after 1815 helped to cause a *land boom*—a widespread desire for land—in the West. Land prices skyrocketed. Many settlers had to borrow the money needed to pay the rising costs of western land.

By 1819, many state banks had loaned money to settlers. Often, settlers borrowed more money than they could repay. They needed time to build their farms and to raise enough crops to meet their loans. Bankers were frightened when it became clear that settlers could not repay their loans by the promised dates. When banks began to call in their loans, many farmers had to give up their lands in order to make payment. Soon, land prices dropped, farmers went out of business, and banks had to close their doors.

As the Panic of 1819 spread throughout the West, other parts of the country were hurt. Eastern manufacturers lost their markets as trade with the West dropped. Factories were closed and jobs were lost.

The panic lasted for several years. During this time, America's economy was greatly weakened. By about 1825, trade, business, and farming became healthier again. But the panic had caused bad feelings to grow between the different *sections*—parts—of the country. This was because people in one section often blamed people in another section for the panic. And even though the government had worked to end the panic, some Americans lost faith in the government's ability to solve major economic problems.

What was a major cause of the Panic of 1819?

Political Doctrines in the 1820's. During the 1820's, many government plans were based upon nationalistic ideals. One of the most far-reaching of these plans was begun by President Monroe.

Many Americans in the early 1820's feared that European powers were once again interested in gaining land in the Americas. In part, this fear arose because of Russian interests in Alaska and because of British moves into Oregon. Also, several Spanish colonies in Latin America were fighting to gain independence from Spain. Some European powers appeared eager to use these Latin American revolutions as an excuse to move soldiers into the Western Hemisphere.

In 1823, President Monroe stated that a European attack anywhere in the Americas would be viewed as an attack upon the United States. This has since become known as the *Monroe Doctrine.* The Monroe Doctrine stated that European powers were no longer free to take land in the Western Hemisphere. It also showed that Americans were confident in the strength of their country.

Another nationalistic government plan of the 1820's was put forward by Henry Clay, who was Speaker of the House of Representatives. Clay's plan was called the *American System.* The plan called for the government to use stronger tariffs to protect America's growing trade and manufacturing. In addition, government money would be used to build roads and canals. In this way, trade and travel would be made easier, and the country's economy would be helped to grow. Also, Americans would be more closely tied to one another through the planned network of roads and canals.

Clay's American System failed to be voted into law. But it helped many Americans to become more interested in their country. And it showed that nationalistic ideas were a powerful force in the United States.

Strong feelings of nationalism grew in America during the years between 1815 and 1828. But at the same time, many Americans became more interested in the needs of their part of the country. Thus, even as nationalism worked to draw Americans closer together, growing regional loyalties began to divide them.

How did the Monroe Doctrine reflect the idea of nationalism?

SECTION 2 REVIEW

1. *How did writers such as Washington Irving and James Fenimore Cooper contribute to the feelings of nationalism?*
2. *In what ways did the settlement of the West help to strengthen nationalism?*
3. *Why was the Monroe Doctrine established?*

3 The Origins of Sectionalism

Overview During the years between 1815 and 1828, a new and powerful spirit of nationalism spread throughout the United States. At the same time, however, important differences between the major geographic parts of the country served to divide Americans. Growing sectional differences soon brought new troubles to the young country.

Objectives After you read this section, you will be able to:

- identify the three major geographic parts of the United States and the different sectional interests that came about;
- analyze the ways the Missouri Compromise sought to reduce sectional rivalries;
- explain how the development of sectionalism influenced the United States.

Sectionalism and Sectional Interests. Long before 1815, Americans began to see that their country was made up of three major geographic parts. Each of these parts was called a section. The three major sections of America were the North, the South, and the West.

The sections were different in many ways. Each section had its own political and economic needs and goals. That is, each section expected different things from the government. And each section offered different ways for people to make a living. For example, many people in the North depended upon trade and manufacturing for their living. People in the South and in the West, however, were chiefly interested in farming and in the settlement of new lands. In addition, growing numbers of people in the North lived in cities. But most Americans in the South and in the West lived on farms or in small country villages. Because of this, many differences in ways of living and of working came about between the sections.

Different ways of life and different political and economic goals sometimes caused sectional conflicts. After 1815, these sectional rivalries led to many new problems in America.

What were two ways in which people in the South and in the West had similar life-styles?

Museum of the City of New York

New York City, like many northern cities, became a bustling commercial and manufacturing center in the early 1800's.

Northern Natural Gas Co. Collection, Joslyn Art Museum, Omaha, Nebraska

This painting of an Illinois farm by Karl Bodmer depicts the isolation and loneliness faced by many farmers on the western prairies during the early 1800's. Americans had to overcome many hardships as they moved west in search of better farmland.

Growing Sectional Rivalries. After 1815, sectional differences became more apparent. And as time went on, many of these sectional differences caused anger and bitterness to spread throughout America.

One important sectional difference after 1815 had to do with the question of tariffs. The Tariff of 1816, which was a tax on goods coming into the country from overseas, was passed in order to protect America's growing industry. But most of the country's factories were in the North. Because of this, the Tariff of 1816 soon became a sectional question.

Many people in the South and in the West were angered by the Tariff. They believed that it had been passed solely to help the factory owners of the North. The Tariff protected northern factory owners by making overseas goods too costly for most Americans to buy. Since the South and the West had few factories, people from these sections had to pay the prices for manufactured goods that were set by factory owners in the North. For this reason, consumers throughout the country, especially in the South and the West, resented the Tariff.

Another major cause of sectional conflict had to do with the question of slavery. By the early 1800's, all the northern states had outlawed slavery. Many people from the North called upon southern farmers to do the same.

Much of the South's economy, however, was based upon the cotton trade. Southern planters felt that slaves were needed to raise their cotton and to ready it for market. Many southern farmers believed that their way of life would not be possible without slaves. This was because southerners felt that slaves were a cheap form of labor.

After 1815, many southern farmers moved west in search of new land on which to raise cotton. As they moved west, these planters took their slaves with them. Because of this, slavery spread farther across America.

Many northerners were angered by the spread of slavery into new states. These people believed that all new states should be free rather than slaveholding. But southern farmers refused to free their slaves. By 1820, the question of slavery had become a major sectional conflict.

■ *Why was slavery a sectional issue?*

The Missouri Compromise. Slavery caused many political differences between the sections of the country after 1815. The conflict over slavery became even more important when new states were brought into the Union.

During the early 1800's, several new states were formed. Some of these were free states, and some were slave states. Government leaders worked to make certain that the number of free and slave states in America remained equal.

Northerners and most westerners fought against the spread of slavery into the new states. But southern slaveholders fought equally hard against moves to outlaw slavery in America.

By 1819, there were 22 states in the Union. They were equally divided between free and slave states. But in that year, the Missouri Territory became ready for statehood (see map on this page). Missouri wanted to join the United States as a slave state. This meant that the slave states would have outnumbered the free states. Thus, the Senate would be made up of more southern states than northern states. And the South would then become the country's most powerful section.

In 1820, Henry Clay, a leading member of

The Missouri Compromise of 1820 temporarily settled the issue of slavery by forbidding slavery in lands north of the line 36′30°. What states made up the free states?

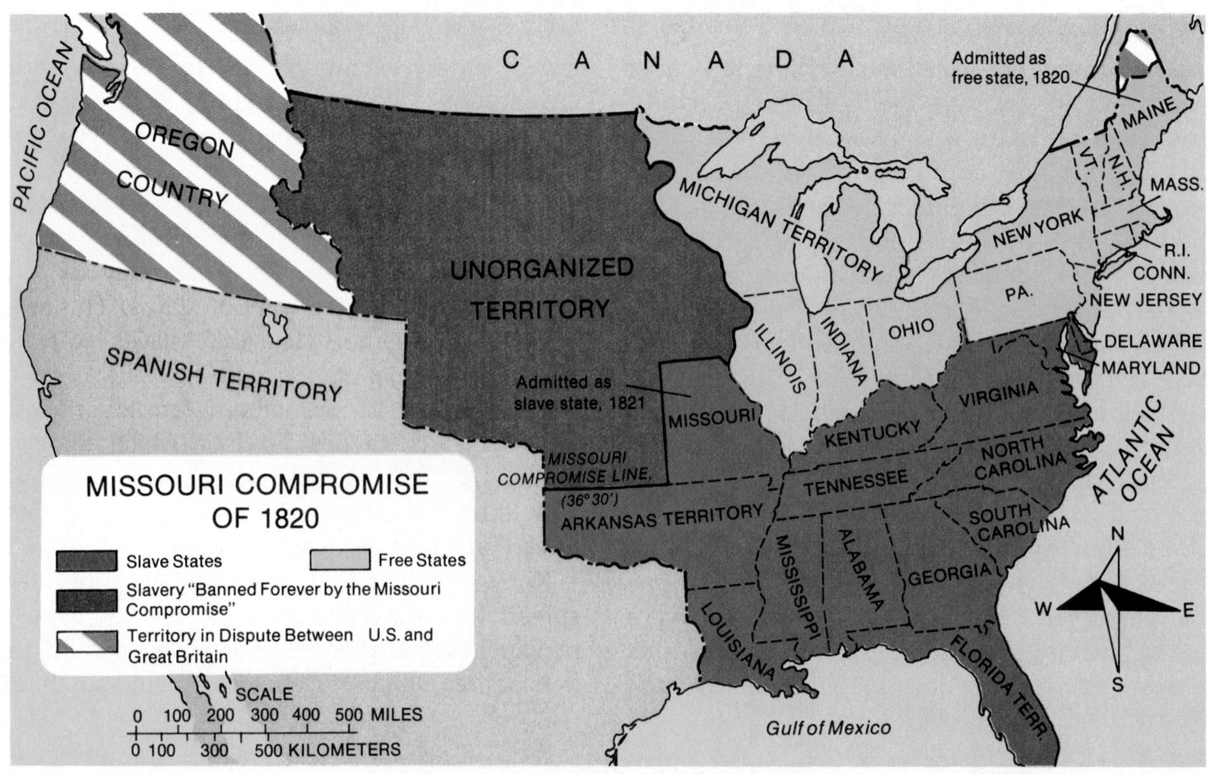

Congress, found a way to keep the number of free states and slave states equal. Under Clay's plan, Maine—once a part of Massachusetts—was given statehood. Then, Missouri was also made a state. Maine entered the Union as a free state, while Missouri entered as a slave state.

Because of Clay's plan, known as the *Missouri Compromise,* the number of free states and of slave states remained evenly divided. But the plan did not end sectional conflict.

■ *How did Clay's plan help to maintain a balance between free states and slave states?*

The Impact of Sectional Conflict. Between 1815 and 1828, sectional differences brought about many changes in the ways that Americans viewed one another. Some of these changes helped to bring needed attention to major problems, such as slavery. But for the most part, sectional differences hurt Americans and their country.

The sectional conflicts that grew after 1815 sometimes caused Americans to become divided against one another. Moreover, such conflicts helped to bring about dangerous feelings of intolerance and of fear. Some Americans came to dislike people or ideas from sections other than their own. For these reasons, sectional differences often served to weaken the unity of our country.

■ *What was the overall result of sectional conflict?*

SECTION 3 REVIEW

1. *What were the three major geographic sections in America?*
2. *How did the Missouri Compromise hope to reduce sectional conflict?*
3. *Why did sectional conflicts often serve to weaken the unity of the country?*

CHAPTER 10 SUMMARY

Between 1815 and 1828, the people of the United States began to shape a new society, one that mirrored their values and their goals. Moreover, some Americans began to see that there was much to do and to improve if their society was to be just and free. At the same time, a growing number of Americans helped to build their country's economy.

After 1815, many people in America began to take more pride in their country and in their government. And the government, in turn, worked to earn the faith and trust of the American people. In addition, our country grew faster than ever before, as new settlers moved west. The ongoing settlement of the West caused many Americans to face new economic hardships.

Just as America grew and changed, so did each of its parts. The North, the South, and the West were different from one another in many important ways. And these differences often led to conflict between the country's sections.

CHAPTER 10 REVIEW

USING YOUR SKILLS

Interpreting Tables and Line Graphs

The table and the line graph on this page depict two different ways of portraying the same information. Both are examples of *statistical information*. Social scientists often use statistical information to determine social or historical trends. The table, below left, and the line graph, below right, show the urban—or city—population of America between 1790 and 1840.

1. According to the *table*, what was the urban population of the United States in 1790? In 1810? In 1830?
2. According to the *line graph*, in what year was America's urban population the lowest? The highest?
3. According to the *table*, was there any one year in which America's urban population decreased? During what ten-year span did the population show the greatest percentage of increase?
4. According to the *line graph*, between what two periods did America's urban population increase the most? The least?
5. Study the *table*. By how many people did the urban population grow between 1830 and 1840? Between 1790 and 1810?
6. Study the *graph*. Is there a trend—a pattern—of change in the urban population between 1790 and 1840? Explain your answer. According to the chapter, what caused the changes in urban population?

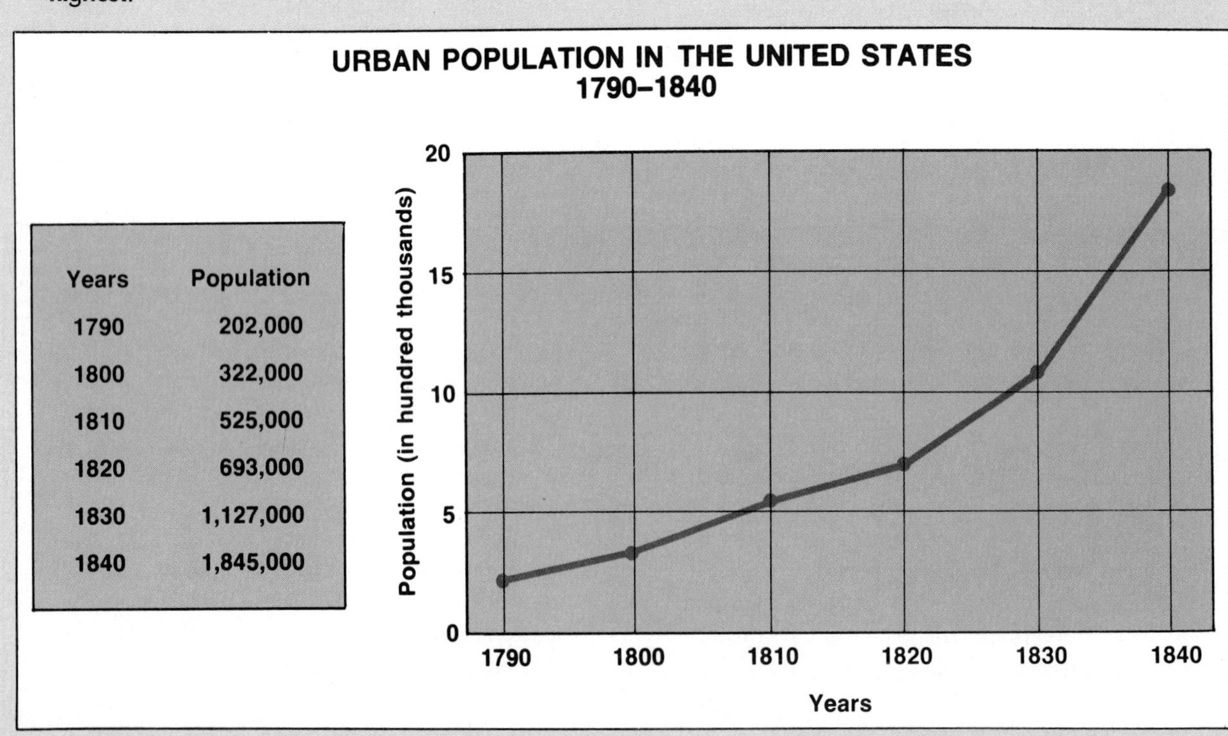

Years	Population
1790	202,000
1800	322,000
1810	525,000
1820	693,000
1830	1,127,000
1840	1,845,000

CHAPTER 10 REVIEW

YOU SHOULD KNOW

Identify, define, and explain each of the following:

social class
abolitionist movement
mass production
nationalism
protective tariff
implied
depression
land boom

CHECKING FACTS

1. What was America's largest social class by 1815?
2. What was the Underground Railroad?
3. Who was Samuel Slater?
4. Where did the Industrial Revolution begin in America?
5. What did the Tariff of 1816 do to European goods?
6. What was the ruling in the *McCulloch v. Maryland* case?
7. What was the Panic of 1819?
8. What did Henry Clay's American System call for?
9. Which of America's sections were generally rural?
10. Which state entered the Union as a free state under the Missouri Compromise?

UNDERSTANDING CONCEPTS

1. Why did the rise of the middle class help our society to become more democratic?
2. In what ways did the Industrial Revolution help to improve standards of living in America?
3. How did western settlement help to cause major economic problems after 1815?
4. What effect did the Tariff of 1816 have upon the growth of sectional differences in America?

LEARNING FROM ILLUSTRATIONS

1. Based upon your study of the picture on page 182, what was probably an important commercial activity in New York City during the early 1800's?
2. Study the map on page 184. In what territory of the United States was slavery allowed by the Missouri Compromise?

CRITICAL THINKING

1. In the early 1800's, most people in the United States belonged to the middle class. To what social class do most Americans belong today? Give reasons for your answer.
2. In your opinion, why did many Americans leave their homes in the East to settle the West?
3. Do you think the people who lived in the South and in the West during the early 1800's had reasons to be angered by the Tariff of 1816? Why do you think so?

ENRICHMENT ACTIVITIES

1. With several other students, gather information about the growth of sectionalism after 1815. Based on this research, draw a map that shows the different sections and the states and territories contained within each section.
2. It may be interesting to find out more about the lives of America's earliest industrial leaders. Information on Slater, Whitney, Lowell, and others can be found in most encyclopedias. This information can be used for brief classroom reports on the contributions of these people to American industrial growth.

1825 | 1830 | 1835

- 1824 John Quincy Adams elected President
- 1825 The Erie Canal opens
- 1828 Andrew Jackson elected President; Tariff of Abominations passed
- 1830 Indian Removal Law enacted
- 1831 First national nominating convention held; First copy of *The Liberator* printed
- 1832 President Jackson vetoes Charter of Second Bank
- 1833 Henry Clay's Compromise Tariff enacted
- 1837 Mary Lyon founds Mount Holyoke Seminary—the first women's college

CHAPTER 11

The Jacksonian Era

Chapter Objectives

After studying this chapter, you will be able to:

- identify the ways that democracy grew in the United States during the Age of Jackson;
- analyze the economic conditions that led to growing sectional competition during the Age of Jackson;
- explain how changing social needs in the early 1800's resulted in a growing trend toward social reform in America.

1 Jacksonian Democracy

Overview The years from 1828 to 1837 are sometimes known as the Age of Jackson. During these years, President Andrew Jackson did much to shape ideas about government in America. Many new political ideas grew out of the Age of Jackson. But Americans did not always agree on the value of these ideas. Some people believed that democracy became stronger and more widespread in our country between 1828 and 1837. Others, however, felt that the ideas that grew under Jackson's leadership helped to weaken America's democratic spirit.

Objectives After you read this section, you will be able to:

- identify the ways that democracy grew in America during the Age of Jackson;
- explain how the strength of democracy strengthened feelings of sectionalism in the 1820's;
- analyze the effects of Jackson's presidency upon the nation's political scene.

A Growing Democracy. The 1820's and the 1830's were years of major change in America. Many of these changes came about as the country became larger and as Americans formed new ideas about their government.

Between 1828 and 1837, the number of Americans rose by over 25 percent to nearly 16 million people. During these years, two new states—Arkansas in the Southwest and Michigan in the Northwest—entered the Union. In addition, Wisconsin became a territory in 1836. Texans won their independence from Mexico in the same year, and Texas was later granted statehood. Thus, the size and the population of the United States grew rapidly in the 1820's and the 1830's.

By the 1820's, new ideas about political rights and freedoms had come about in America. These ideas helped democracy to grow in our country. Two of the most important new ideas had to do with voting rights and with the selection of political candidates.

Throughout the late 1700's, most states limited *suffrage*—the right to vote—to wealthy landowners and property holders. Many states allowed only those people who paid a certain amount of taxes or who followed certain religious ideas to vote. At this time, no states allowed women to vote. In addition, members of Congress—rather than the voters themselves—selected candidates to run for the presidency.

During the early 1800's, however, more and more Americans called for the right to vote and to choose their own political leaders. Because of this, most states slowly did away with many of the laws that had limited suffrage. By the 1820's, for example, voters in most states no longer needed to own property in order to vote. As voting rights became more widespread, the growing number of voters gained more political power.

During the early 1800's, members of Congress, representing the country's political parties, formed *caucuses*—groups—for the purpose of nominating presidential candidates. The public had little voice in this important selection process. But as voters demanded a greater role in government during the 1820's, a more democratic way of choosing presidential candidates came about. In 1831, the first national nominating convention was held. Delegates to this convention were chosen directly by voters. The delegates acted as the voters' representatives at the convention. And by 1836, all political parties were using national conventions to nominate their presidential candidates. For the first time, individual voters throughout the country took part in the selection of their government leaders.

As more Americans gained a voice in their government, our democracy became stronger. But many Americans could still not take part in their government. For example, Indians, women, and slaves did not have any voting rights. Thus, many Americans could not enjoy the democratic reforms that came about during the 1820's. At the same time, however, more people than ever before felt that they had a role in their country's government.

■ *What two factors led to the growth of democracy during the 1820's?*

DO YOU KNOW?

When was the first voting machine invented?

America's first voting machine was invented by Thomas A. Edison in 1868. Edison's early voting machine was designed to record legislative votes, rather than ballots cast by voters in national and state elections. Edison attempted to sell his machine to the United States Congress, but congressional leaders refused his offer. They feared that the machine would prevent the trading of votes during congressional roll calls. A voting machine was first used in a public election in 1892. Today, voting machines are used by more than three fourths of the states at election time.

Effects of Democratic Reform. Many Americans were able to take part in their government for the first time during the 1820's. As suffrage became more widespread in our country, new groups of voters—each with different needs and goals—appeared.

One important voting group that began to emerge in the late 1820's was made up of northern factory workers. Many of these workers wanted the government to enact economic and social reforms. This was because the greatest number of northern factory workers lived in the growing cities of the Northeast. And the cost of living was generally much higher in these cities than elsewhere. But many factory workers were poorly paid and had to live in crowded and unpleasant surroundings. Workers often had to spend long hours on the job to earn enough money to live from week to week. During the late 1820's, then, a growing number of northern workers began to vote for candidates who reflected their concerns. These northern workers soon formed a powerful voting group—or voting block.

Another voting block that gained influence during the late 1820's was made up of middle-class western farmers. The western farmers, like the factory workers of the North, wanted the government to enact economic and social reforms. Both the farmers and the factory workers agreed that such federal action would help them to gain better working and living conditions. Farmers also wanted the government to set low prices on the cost of public lands in the West. In this way, middle-class western farmers could build larger farms and raise more food and livestock. Finally, western farmers called for easy credit on bank loans. This would enable farmers to borrow money to buy land and to improve their farms.

The Library of Congress

President Andrew Jackson's inauguration attracted many Americans from all walks of life and all social classes. Jackson was hailed as the President of the common people.

The growth of new and powerful voting blocks during the late 1820's helped to build democracy in America. This was because people found that by voting as a block, they could better make their wishes and their needs known to government leaders. Thus, individual members of voting blocks found that they had a stronger voice in political affairs.

Political issues that were important to one voting block, however, were not always important to other groups. Moreover, the demands made by voting blocks were often based upon sectional needs and goals. For example, western farmers called for lower prices on land. But northern factory owners were against cheap western land. They feared that northern workers would be drawn west by the promise of cheap land. This would cause worker shortages in the North. Thus, the spread of democracy was in part responsible for growing sectional differences during the 1820's and the 1830's.

■ *What were two of the new voting blocks that began to develop in the late 1820's?*

A Popular President. In 1828, General Andrew Jackson, hero of the Battle of New Orleans, ran for the presidency. Jackson was one of America's leading public figures because of his role in the War of 1812. He had been elected to Congress by the people of Tennessee in 1796 and again in 1823. He had also run for the presidency in 1824. But Jackson lost the election of 1824, which was so close that it had to be decided by the House of Representatives. Speaker of the House Henry Clay favored Jackson's opponent, John Quincy Adams. With Clay's support, Adams won the presidency. The next presidential election, however, in 1828, proved an easy victory for the 61-year-old Jackson. Jackson received 178 electoral votes, while Adams received only 83. This outcome clearly proved that Jackson enjoyed the support of the people.

Andrew Jackson was the first American from west of the Appalachian Mountains to be elected President. Also, he was one of America's most popular leaders. He was often pictured as a man of the people. And many voters believed that Jackson was interested in the well-being of the middle and lower classes.

Jackson was himself a wealthy planter, a slaveholder, and a business leader. Yet he seemed to understand the needs and the wants of the common people. For this reason, the important changes that Jackson made in our government had the support of many Americans. And during his two terms in office—1829 to 1837—he became one of America's most outstanding leaders.

- *Why was Jackson so popular a candidate?*

Jackson's Policies. One of President Jackson's first acts after taking office in 1829 was to reward his political friends. He did this by placing them in government jobs. This practice became known as the *spoils system* because it was based upon the idea that "to the victor belong the spoils." Jackson reasoned that the people who had worked for his election deserved to share in the results of his victory. He also believed that his administration would be stronger if the people who worked for him agreed with his views. Finally, Jackson felt that by rewarding workers with government jobs, more Americans would be able to take part in their government.

The Bettmann Archive

Many present-day historians feel that Jackson's spoils system was truly a step forward for democracy. Others do not agree. These people believe that Jackson's system gave government jobs to unqualified workers.

Most of today's historians agree, however, that a second Jackson policy—that of Indian removal—was cruel and unfair. Under President Jackson, our government forced thousands of American Indians to leave their homelands to make room for white settlers. The Indian Removal Law of 1830 allowed Jackson to take the lands of several major Indian tribes. In return, these tribes were given new land farther west. But the lands given to the Indians were generally poor and ill suited for farming or for hunting. Thus, many thousands of Indians had to leave their homes, their farms, and their businesses for a life of hardship in the Southwest.

Some tribes—including the Seminole in the Southwest and the Sauk and the Fox in the Northwest—resisted the Indian Removal Law. The Seminole Indians fought a bitter seven-

How does this cartoon by Thomas Nast show that some Americans believed that President Jackson's spoils system led to a corrupt government?

This painting, entitled "Trail of Tears," depicts the heartbreak of the Cherokee as they were forced to leave their lands during the winter of 1838–1839. In the move to the Indian Territory of the West, nearly one fourth of the entire Cherokee population died.

year war to defend their homes from the land-hungry American settlers. But Jackson used the United States Army to enforce the law and to finally defeat the Seminole. At the same time, the Cherokee fought the Indian Removal Law in the Supreme Court. They won their case, but President Jackson refused to honor the Court's ruling and illegally drove the Cherokee west. So many Cherokee suffered or died during their westward flight that the route they followed became known as "the trail of tears."

By the mid-1830's, many Indian tribes had been pushed westward. The Indian Removal Law opened much new land to American settlement, but at a cost of thousands of Indian lives.

What were two important Jacksonian policies between 1828 and 1837?

SECTION 1 REVIEW

1. *What groups of Americans still did not have voting rights by the 1820's?*
2. *How did the growth of voting blocks affect sectionalism in the 1820's?*
3. *Why did President Jackson establish the spoils system?*

2 Economic Sectionalism

Overview The Age of Jackson was a time of greater public participation in government. However, it was also a time of growing sectional conflict. This was because some people were more interested in the needs of their sections than in the country as a whole. Between 1828 and 1837, several major sectional conflicts arose because of economic differences among the parts of the country.

Objectives After you read this section, you will be able to:

- identify the economic differences in the country's sections;
- describe how the federal government became involved in the nation's economy;
- analyze the results of President Jackson's economic policies.

Northern Economic Interests. The industrial power of the North became steadily greater throughout the Age of Jackson. By the 1820's and the 1830's, the North was clearly America's leading industrial section.

The coming of the Machine Age and the spread of factories in the North helped many workers to find jobs. As manufacturing became more important to the North, many northern voters worked to gain the government's help for their growing economy.

Many northerners—factory owners and workers alike—favored parts of Henry Clay's American System. This plan had two main goals. First, Clay wanted to bind Americans closer together through a network of roads and canals. Trade and travel throughout the country would become easier, faster, and safer. Second, Clay called for higher tariffs—taxes—on European goods sold in America. This would protect our country's growing industry by making American goods cheaper to buy than European goods.

Clay's plan received widespread support in many parts of the country. However, the plan failed to win approval in Congress, largely because of southern opposition to higher tariffs. But several northern states acted upon some of Clay's ideas. For example, the state of New York under Governor De Witt Clinton built the Erie Canal that stretched from Albany to Buffalo. When it was finished in 1825, the Erie Canal opened Lake Erie to steamboat traffic from as far away as New York City. During this time, the question of tariffs also became important and soon led to bitter sectional conflicts.

■ *What were two major goals of Clay's American System?*

Economic Issues in the South. During the 1820's and the 1830's, the South grew to depend more and more upon the raising of farm goods for sale. Although tobacco was an important crop, cotton was the South's economic mainstay. A large part of the yearly southern cotton crop was sold in the North. There, it was spun into yarn and made into clothing and other cloth goods in the northern mills and factories. Thus, the South depended upon northern industry to turn its cash crops into finished goods for market.

Many southern farmers did not like to depend so much upon the North. And many southerners felt that their cotton and other crops did not sell for high-enough prices on northern markets. But the South had fewer

Courtesy of the New York Historical Society

The Erie Canal became a major transportation-and-trade route after it was completed in 1825. Its construction, which then spurred a canal-building boom, helped to train engineers who designed a series of locks for raising and lowering the canalboats through the hilly New York terrain.

cotton mills and factories than did the North. Southerners who tried to build cotton mills often found that their costs were too high. For this reason, many southern mill owners could not compete with their northern counterparts. This caused much bitterness and anger in the South and led to new sectional differences.

Many southerners in the Age of Jackson also felt that northern ideas toward the use of slaves were unfair. By 1820, the northern states had outlawed slavery. This came about, in part, because antislavery—or *abolitionist*—groups were strong in the North. Also, the North—with large numbers of workers—had no need for slaves. In the South, however, many farmers had come to rely upon slaves as a major form of labor. And throughout the Age of Jackson, the worldwide market for cotton and for other farm goods grew. Because of this, southern farmers depended more and more upon slave workers during the 1820's and the 1830's.

The antislavery activities of northern abolitionists angered many southerners. These people felt that the abolitionists wanted to destroy the South and its way of life. Another cause of southern anger during the Age of Jackson was the tariff question. Many southerners believed that tariffs greatly hurt the South and its economy. This was because such taxes made the cost of European goods on American markets very high. Most people could not buy these goods and chose to buy American-made things instead. But as the need for American factory goods rose, so did their prices. Thus, tariffs were good for sellers—generally northern factory owners—but bad for buyers. And because the South had few factories during this time, southerners were often hurt most by tariffs.

■ *What were two causes of sectional conflict between the North and the South?*

Economic Conditions in the West. During the Age of Jackson, the West—like the South—had few factories. Most westerners made their living through farming rather than through manufacturing. Western cities served chiefly as centers for farm trade and for the shipping of goods to and from the East. For these reasons, westerners grew to depend upon the North for their manufactured needs.

As the West became wealthier and more settled, westerners became more interested in economic developments in the East. This was because economic changes in the East—higher prices, greater shipping costs, or higher costs for bank loans—affected westerners as well. Important questions, such as slavery and the tariff, gained widespread attention throughout the West. And because their political power grew during the Age of Jackson, westerners were able to make their views toward these questions known.

Many westerners had strong ideas about the major economic questions that arose during the Age of Jackson. But they did not always agree about the answers to these questions. For example, most westerners called for low-cost government land and for government-built roads and canals. Policies such as these would lead to more widespread settlement, and in this way a stronger western economy would result. Also, westerners were generally against slavery and worked against its spread into new western states.

At the same time, many people in the West agreed with the southern belief that high tariffs were bad. This was because they felt that high tariffs caused higher prices for northern factory goods. This, in turn, raised the cost of living in the West.

Thus, westerners shared some economic goals with the North and some with the South. And during the Age of Jackson, western views toward these important questions led, in part, to the growth of sectional differences.

■ *Why did westerners become more interested in eastern economic conditions during the Age of Jackson?*

Jackson's Economic Problems. President Jackson was elected to office in 1828 and moved into the White House the following year. Jackson faced several major economic problems left by the outgoing administration of John Quincy Adams. One of the most important of these had to do with the question of tariffs.

Tariffs—taxes on overseas goods sold in America—had been used to protect the country's growing industry since 1816. The higher the tariff, the more costly overseas goods became. This helped American factory owners to sell more of their goods by lowering competition. But, because they did not have to compete for sales, factory owners could charge higher prices for their goods. Generally, the northern industrial states favored high tariffs because they were good for American business. However, many southerners and some westerners attacked tariffs because they made northern factory goods more costly to buy. For this reason, the country's sections were often bitterly divided over the tariff question throughout the 1820's.

President Adams, who had taken office in 1825, became unpopular with many American voters because of the tariff question. The chief cause of anger toward Adams was the Tariff of 1828—the highest tariff measure passed in America to that time. The Tariff of 1828 became known as the *Tariff of Abominations* because it was so widely disliked. And President Adams—an able administrator but a poor politician—was blamed because he allowed the Tariff to become law. Public dislike of the Tariff helped to bring about Adams's defeat by Jackson in 1828.

The Tariff of 1828 was widely attacked in the South. For this reason, Jackson's partner in office, Vice-President John C. Calhoun of South Carolina, worked hard to lower the tariff rate. In 1832, a lower tariff was passed by Congress. But many southerners did not feel that the new tariff was low enough. Southern anger over the tariff soon led to new troubles for Jackson.

The second Bank of the United States was another important economic question during the Age of Jackson. President Jackson believed that the second Bank had become too powerful and was no longer interested in the needs of most Americans. Many westerners did not like the Bank because it did not give low-cost loans to land buyers. President Jackson decided against a bill that would give the Bank a new twenty-year charter. When Congress passed the Bank Bill in 1832, Jackson used his *veto* power. That is, he refused to sign the bill into law and so defeated it. But the Bank Bill became a major campaign issue when Jackson ran for reelection against Henry Clay that year.

What were two major economic questions that Jackson faced between 1828 and 1832?

Jackson Meets the Issues. The tariff and the bank questions were among the most important problems of President Jackson's term. But by showing strong leadership, Jackson was able to partly overcome these problems.

Even though the Tariff of 1832 lowered the cost of overseas goods, many southerners did not believe that it was satisfactory. These people called upon President Jackson and other government leaders to cut the tariff even further. But many northerners were against another tariff cut because they wanted the prices of overseas goods to remain high.

Some southern business and government

Independence National Park Collection

The second Bank of the United States became a major campaign issue during the election of 1832. President Jackson, opposed to the idea of a federal bank, began to remove federal funds from the Bank in 1833. In 1836, the Bank's charter expired.

National Portrait Gallery, Smithsonian Institution, Washington, D.C. (Detail)

John C. Calhoun (left) led the fight against higher tariffs. President Andrew Jackson (right) was a forceful leader and was often pictured by his enemies as "King Andrew."

The Bettmann Archive

leaders stated that they would refuse to honor the tariff. Vice-President John C. Calhoun was one of the strongest enemies of the Tariff. In 1832, Calhoun resigned his office—in part because of the tariff question—and returned to South Carolina. There, he led the southern fight against the Tariff.

Calhoun wrote that no state had to follow laws passed by Congress that hurt the people of that state. Calhoun's idea was called the *doctrine of nullification.* The leaders of South Carolina's state government agreed with Calhoun. They promised to *secede*—break away—from the Union if the Tariff of 1832 was not set aside. Also, they refused to allow the tax on overseas goods to be collected in South Carolina. This dangerous situation soon came to be known as the *Nullification Crisis.*

President Jackson used the full power of his office to overcome the Nullification Crisis. He said that no state could be allowed to break away from the Union because it did not agree with certain laws. And he moved to use the United States Army to end the conflict. Henry Clay—the powerful representative from Kentucky—and other government leaders agreed with Jackson. They drew up a compromise plan that would lower the tariff over a ten-year period. South Carolina accepted this settlement, and in 1833, it was passed into law. The Nullification Crisis was ended peacefully, and the tariff was slowly lowered.

President Jackson also showed strong leadership toward the question of the second Bank of the United States. After turning down the

Bank Bill of 1832, Jackson ran for a second term in office. His opponent during the election of 1832 was Henry Clay. Clay felt that the Bank was needed to control lending and to support the value of American dollars. Clay also warned that without the Bank, a *depression*—a dangerous economic slowdown during which many businesses would be forced to close and many workers would lose their jobs—would begin in America.

President Jackson, however, was against the Bank. He did not like the fact that the public had no power to choose the Bank's officers. Jackson also felt that Bank leaders were more interested in making money than in serving public needs.

Jackson took his views to the voters. And in 1832, he was reelected in a landslide victory. Jackson won 219 electoral votes, while Clay received only 49 electoral votes. The fact that he was returned to office, Jackson said, proved that the people agreed with his ideas. But many economic problems remained when Jackson left office in 1837.

■ *What was the doctrine of nullification?*

SECTION 2 REVIEW

1. *In what ways did most westerners make their living during the Age of Jackson?*
2. *How did the tariff question encourage sectional conflicts?*
3. *Why did John C. Calhoun write the doctrine of nullification?*

3 Beginnings of Social Reform

Overview The Age of Jackson was a time when many Americans were able to improve their way of life. For some Americans, however, such as the poor and the sick, life in America was often hard and cruel. And many Americans, such as women, Indians, and blacks, also received unfair treatment. But during the years between 1828 and 1837, a growing number of people worked to correct some of these social wrongs.

Objectives After you read this section, you will be able to:

- identify the ways that ideas about America's society began to change during the Age of Jackson;
- explain how the abolitionist movement helped to bring greater justice to America;
- describe the ways life in America improved as a result of the social reform movements.

New Ideas About Society. By the 1820's, some Americans had begun to look for ways to give life deeper meaning and greater value. These people believed that the search for material wealth had caused Americans to turn against one another. They also believed that the growth of cities was a sign of dangerous social weakness. This was because city dwellers often depended upon others for many of their needs. For these reasons, some Americans decided that the way to build a better life was to live in small and simple gatherings.

During the Age of Jackson, a movement known as the *utopian movement* grew. In general, this movement was characterized by groups of people banding together to form small and ideal communities. Many such ideal—or *utopian*—communities stressed a belief in total equality. That is, members of many utopian groups viewed one another as social equals. Thus, there were no social classes. All shared equally in the work that needed to be done—raising food and building and governing the settlement. And all shared equally in the rewards.

For the most part, the utopian settlements of the Age of Jackson failed within a few years of their founding. But even though most of the utopian settlements did not last, they showed much about America. Most importantly, the utopian villages proved that Americans were trying to *reform* their society—to change it for the better.

■ *What was the most important meaning of the utopian communities of the Age of Jackson?*

Antislavery Movements. One of the most important reform movements to grow during the Age of Jackson was the battle against slavery. Throughout the 1820's and the 1830's, more and more Americans began to understand the evils of slavery. But even by 1837, much remained to be done in order to end this cruel practice.

The slave trade itself—the shipping of blacks from Africa to Europe, to the West Indies, and to America—was halted in 1808. But this did nothing to end the use of slaves already in the United States. Throughout the early 1800's, however, a growing number of people—northerners and southerners alike—acted to help black slaves. Antislavery groups were formed in the North—especially in the New England states—and in the South. And by 1820, the northern states had outlawed slavery.

After 1815, the fight to free the slaves began to take several different forms. One of these forms was seen in the small antislavery groups that slowly grew throughout the United States. Members of these groups called for the South to outlaw slavery as the North had done. For the most part, these people tried to work through the state and national laws to bring about reforms.

Another side of the antislavery battle was seen in the groups that acted to help runaway slaves escape to free northern states. These reformers did not work within the law. In fact, throughout most of the years of the antislavery battle, it was against the law to offer help to escaped slaves. Many church groups, such as the Quakers, worked in this way to end slavery. Quakers often took part in the *Underground Railroad*—the network of abolitionists that helped runaway slaves to escape north (see the feature on page 174).

During the early 1800's, the antislavery groups and the people who helped escaped slaves did their best to end slavery. They were often too few in number and in power, how-

The Granger Collection

New Harmony was a utopian community in Indiana, founded by Robert Owen in 1825.

ever, to make a great deal of difference. But during the 1830's, the abolitionists rapidly gained strength. Soon, they were able to gain the growing attention of many government leaders. This was due, in large part, to the work of outspoken abolitionist writers and newspaper reporters.

A leading abolitionist writer was William Lloyd Garrison. In 1831, Garrison printed the first copy of *The Liberator,* a powerful newspaper in the attack upon slavery. Soon, Garrison became a leader of the American Antislavery Society. Many strong and well-known abolitionists, such as Lucretia Mott and Lydia Maria Child, were members of Garrison's group. These people traveled across the country, spreading word of the growing abolitionist movement and gaining new members in the fight against slavery. During the next 10 years, groups such as Garrison's worked to bring the question of slavery to the attention of all Americans. Black abolitionists, too—such as Frederick Douglass, David Walker, and Christopher Rush—helped to lead the fight against slavery in America. Douglass and William Lloyd Garrison often traveled together throughout the North to speak against slavery. Douglass proved to be an effective speaker and writer, and his eyewitness accounts of slavery shocked many northern audiences. Because of this, many Americans became more interested in the slavery question and in other social reform movements as well.

■ *Why did the antislavery movement rapidly gain power during the 1830's?*

Other Social Reforms. The antislavery cause was not the only reform movement to gain widespread attention during the Age of Jackson. Other reform groups worked to win more rights for women, to improve public schools, and to provide better care for the sick.

Women had few real rights in America throughout the 1800's. They could not vote, they could not hold public office, and they were often not allowed to own property. But some women took the lead in working against this unfair treatment. For example, Mary Lyon acted to gain for women the right to an education. She believed that women would be better able to help themselves and to win equal treatment through education. And in 1837, Mary Lyon founded the first women's college—Mount Holyoke Seminary in Massachusetts.

Another important reform leader of the time was Horace Mann of Massachusetts. Mann led the movement to improve America's public schools. During the late 1830's, Mann won many school reforms in his home state. And these reforms slowly spread to the other states in the country. Today's ideas of tax-paid public schools are based upon the early ideas of Horace Mann.

Early reforms in the field of medical care also came about in the Age of Jackson. During this time a growing number of Americans called for improved care for the sick and for the insane. As more people became interested in these reforms, better hospitals for the sick

(Text continues on page 204.)

How does the masthead of William Lloyd Garrison's abolitionist newspaper, *The Liberator*, help to dramatize the evils of slavery?

THE LIBERATOR.

VOL. I.] WILLIAM LLOYD GARRISON AND ISAAC KNAPP, PUBLISHERS. NO. 22.

BOSTON, MASSACHUSETTS.] OUR COUNTRY IS THE WORLD—OUR COUNTRYMEN ARE MANKIND. [SATURDAY, MAY 28, 1831.

The Bettmann Archive

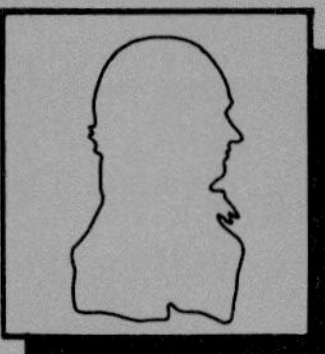

PROFILES

Dorothea Dix

Historical Pictures Service

Dorothea Dix was as born in 1802 in the frontier town of Hampden, Maine. She lived in poverty in the wilderness. At the age of 12 she left home to get an education, staying with relatives in Boston and Worchester, Massachusetts. When she was 18 she opened a school for girls and began writing books for children. She also traveled to England, supporting herself by working as a tutor.

In 1841 she accepted an invitation to teach a Sunday School class at the local jail. What she saw changed her life. What she did about it changed the lives of thousands of people. Insane or mentally ill people at that time were put in jail and often chained to walls. They lived in filth and were treated with cruelty. Dorothea knew that some European doctors had found that when the insane were treated with consistent care for their human dignity, many recovered.

She realized that if the people knew the facts, the government of the people would change how the insane were treated. Dorothea began the task of visiting the jails and asylums of Massachusetts. She wrote a record of humans "confined in cages, closets, cellars, stalls, pens... chained naked, beaten with rods." One man had been chained in a stall for 17 years. In 1843 Dorothea Dix presented her written report to the Massachusetts Legislature, and to the press.

The jail keepers called her a "snooping woman." Dorothea collected more facts. The legislature voted to build a Worchester hospital for the insane. Dorothea Dix went to 15 states to continue her study and work for reform. Her efforts led to the establishment of thirty-two new mental institutions in the young nation.

Thinking Critically

What could be some benefits of obtaining an education for a girl living in poverty?

What reasons might jailers and those who worked with the insane have to resist Dorothea Dix's "snooping"? What "right" did she have to do as she did?

Like others, Dorothea Dix came out of frontier poverty and made a difference. How can individuals make a difference in a democratic society?

and more understanding treatment for the insane slowly came about. And in the next few years, the work of reform leaders such as Dorothea Dix led to further improvements in medical care.

In the years after the Age of Jackson, real progress toward meeting some of America's social needs began to be seen. Thus, the 1820's and the 1830's marked the beginning of many important reforms in America. Because of this, the conditions of life slowly became better for people throughout the land.

■ *Who led the movement to reform public education in America during the late 1830's?*

The Bettmann Archive

William Lloyd Garrison, a New England journalist, was one of the most outspoken abolitionists of his day.

SECTION 3 REVIEW

1. *What two aspects of life in Jacksonian America did the utopian societies wish to avoid?*
2. *How were abolitionists able to gain the growing attention of many government leaders?*
3. *Why did Mary Lyon work for women's education during the Age of Jackson?*

CHAPTER 11 SUMMARY

The Age of Jackson was a time of change throughout our country. Old ideas about political rights and old social values were sometimes pushed aside during these years. In their place grew a new sense of freedom and of purpose as Americans worked together to build a stronger democracy.

Even as many Americans shared in the task of building their democracy, however, new problems helped to divide the country. Major differences among the country's sections became more clearly drawn and more troublesome. President Jackson acted to meet Americans' different needs. But his strong measures sometimes caused even greater sectional bitterness.

Throughout the Age of Jackson, a growing number of Americans tried to make their country a better place in which to live. For this reason, a new spirit of social reform came into being in the 1820's and the 1830's. Several important reform movements came about during these years and helped to bring a better life to all Americans.

CHAPTER 11 REVIEW

USING YOUR SKILLS

Studying Pictograms

The information shown below appears in the form of a *pictogram*. A pictogram is a means of illustrating and of comparing statistical data through the use of picture-symbols. The pictogram below gives statistical information on the elections of 1828 and of 1832.

1. What does each complete symbol in the pictogram represent? In general, what does each partially complete symbol represent?
2. During the election of 1828, approximately how many popular votes did Jackson receive? Approximately how many votes did Adams receive?
3. About how many votes did Jackson receive in 1832? Approximately how many votes were won by Henry Clay?
4. During which election—the election of 1828 or the election of 1832—did Andrew Jackson receive the greatest number of popular votes?
5. According to the pictogram, during which election did Jackson face the strongest challenge from an opposing candidate?
6. According to the pictogram, which of Jackson's political opponents—John Quincy Adams or Henry Clay—was most popular with the American voters?

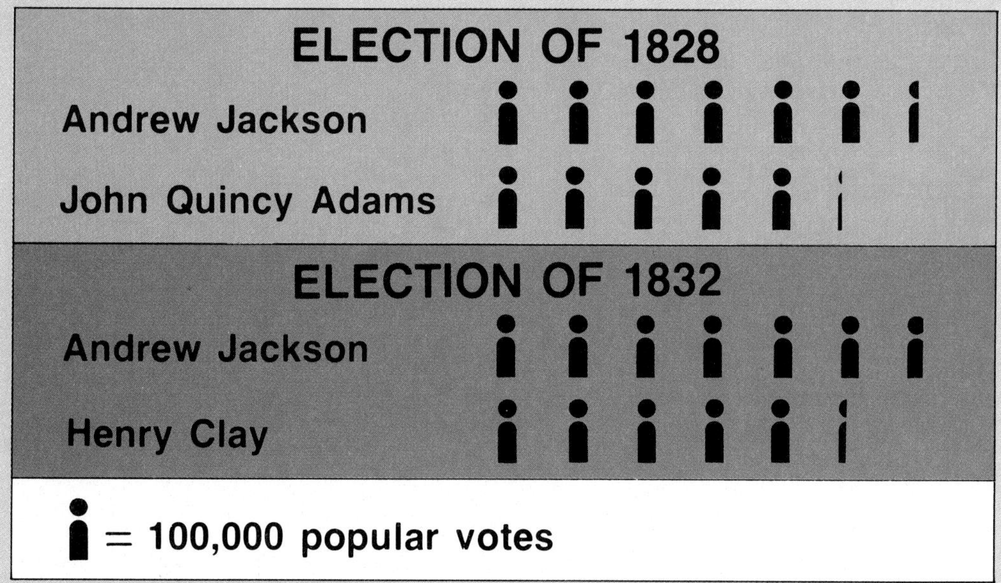

CHAPTER 11 REVIEW

YOU SHOULD KNOW

Identify, define, or explain each of the following:

suffrage
spoils system
utopian
reform

CHECKING FACTS

1. What major political goal did western farmers and northern factory workers often share during the 1820's?
2. What did the Indian Removal Law of 1830 do?
3. What were the main goals of Henry Clay's American System?
4. What was the Tariff of Abominations?
5. What state threatened to secede as a result of the Tariff of 1832?
6. What section had outlawed slavery by 1820?
7. What was the Underground Railroad?
8. What was *The Liberator*?
9. Who were Frederick Douglass, David Walker, and Christopher Rush?
10. On what are the ideas of tax-paid public schools based?

UNDERSTANDING CONCEPTS

1. How did the process of selecting presidential candidates become more democratic during the 1830's?
2. How did high tariffs work to protect America's growing industry?
3. Why did Henry Clay support the second Bank of the United States?
4. What did the utopian villages prove about many Americans during the Age of Jackson?

LEARNING FROM ILLUSTRATIONS

1. According to the illustration on page 195, what was one way that canalboats were moved along the Erie Canal?
2. Based upon your study of the cartoon on page 198, what do the symbols suggest about the artist's opinion of President Jackson?

CRITICAL THINKING

1. Do you think that President Jackson's spoils system policy was an effective way of running the government? Why do you think so?
2. In your opinion, was Jackson's Indian removal policy cruel and unfair? Give reasons for your answer.
3. Do you think the utopian belief in total equality could work in American society today? Why do you think so?

ENRICHMENT ACTIVITIES

1. A group of students might like to conduct further research on the construction and the history of the Erie Canal. Information on this topic might be found in a variety of books and encyclopedia articles. Students might then like to make a poster-size map to show the route of the Erie Canal.
2. Several students might like to find out more about the early leaders of the women's rights movement in America. Information could be found in encyclopedias, in books, and in the publications of many of today's women's rights organizations. Students might then present brief classroom reports on their findings.

CHAPTER 12

CLOSE-UP: Slavery in the American South

INTRODUCTION

By 1840, slavery had existed in America for more than 200 years. Some of the first settlements in colonial America became early centers for the Atlantic slave trade. By the mid-1700's, slavery was an accepted part of life throughout the Thirteen Colonies. At the same time, however, resistance to slavery began to spread in America. By the 1820's, slavery had ended in every northern state. But slavery continued to be widespread throughout the South until 1865.

The great majority of southerners did not own slaves. But many southerners defended slavery as an important part of life in the South. A growing number of northerners, however, attacked slavery as a cruel and unfair practice. By 1840, the people of America were bitterly divided over the question of slavery. But the Americans who suffered most from slavery were the slaves themselves.

Chapter 12 is divided into two parts. Part one tells the story of an imaginary planter and slaveholder in 1840. Part two introduces an imaginary slave, Sarah, and tells of her struggle for freedom.

1 The Life and Times of a Slaveholder

Many historians agree that the society of the *antebellum South*—the South before 1861—was shaped largely by two institutions. These two institutions were the plantation system of farming and slavery.

Most southern farmers in the 1840's were neither *planters*—great plantation owners—nor slaveholders. In fact, there were relatively few slaveholders in the antebellum South at any one time. And fewer still owned large numbers of slaves. As late as 1860, only about 10,000 southern families owned more than 50 slaves per family. Of this small number, less than 3,000 owned more than 100 slaves per family.

Southern Society in the Mid-1800's. The great majority of the large slaveholding families were of the wealthy planter class. Many owned huge plantations where cash crops, such as tobacco, rice, sugar, hemp, and especially cotton, were raised for market. And even though the planters were small in number, they controlled much of the land and the economy of the antebellum South. Thus, the powerful planter class did much to shape southern society and its view of slavery.

Southern slaveholders thought of their slaves as *chattel*—that is, as personal and private property. And until the mid–1860's, many laws were passed to uphold this view. Together, these laws formed the *slave codes*—the body of laws that governed slaves. Under the slave codes of the South, slaves had no rights or freedoms whatsoever. And like other forms of property, slaves could be bought and sold at any time. This is why slaves were legally held to be nothing more than goods to be used for their owner's gain.

Southern society during the 1840's depended in many ways upon slave labor. And as the plantation system became more important to the southern economy, the demand for slaves became greater. Throughout the early 1800's, slaves made up a growing part of the population in the antebellum South. In 1840, for example, the total southern population was less than 7 million people. Of these, almost 2.5 million—over one third—were slaves. Thus, slavery played a major role in the antebellum southern society. And it had an especially great impact upon the life-styles of plantation owners.

What group controlled much of the land and the economy of the antebellum South?

The Life of a Slaveholder. My name is Alexander Hempstead, and I own this plantation—all 2,000 acres of it. I brought my wife and my children out here to Alabama 15 years ago. Oh, yes, and we brought 8 slaves—a gift from my father. Without those 8 slaves, I could never have cleared and planted enough land to raise cotton. The slaves and I worked side by side to plant the crops, to tend them, and to bring in the harvest. But each year, we were able to open a few more acres for planting. Now, almost all the land is used to raise cotton.

I own 200 slaves today. They live in the slave quarters—those small cabins near the main house. I keep a close watch on my slaves because they're valuable property. On the slave markets in Richmond, New Orleans, and elsewhere, each one is worth between $800 and $1,200. But I don't often sell my slaves—not unless they make trouble, refuse to work, or try to run away. I need slaves to raise my cotton, to get it ready for market, and to work in my house as servants.

Perhaps I wouldn't need so many slaves if there were more free farm workers for hire. But many southern farmers don't like to work for someone else when they can own their own farms. And many people say that slaves are better able to stand our hot southern climate and to work in it. All I know is that a great number of workers are needed to run a big plantation like mine. And slavery supplies me with all the workers that I can afford.

Most of my slaves work as field hands. I have a hired *overseer*—a white man to man-

Large plantations in the southern cotton belt often spread over several thousand acres and had many slaves.

Historic New Orleans Collection, Museum/Research Center, Acc. No. 1975.93.2

This painting of a slave family returning from the fields of a cotton plantation reflects the conditions under which southern blacks worked.

age the slaves. He works the field gangs from sunrise to sunset, but I allow them 30 minutes each day for the noon meal. Also, no field work is performed on Sundays.

During the harvest, of course, the slaves must work longer hours—often until well after dark. But the cotton must be brought in as soon as it's ready, or it will rot in the fields. And the success or the failure of my plantation depends upon each year's harvest. Besides, if I didn't keep my slaves busy and well occupied, they might get into mischief or try to run away. So I make certain to allow my slaves no more spare time than is needed for proper rest. After all, my slaves' time belongs to me—as do the slaves themselves. And I have always valued my property.

■ *Why did Hempstead value his slaves?*

A Slaveholder Defends Slavery. In this year of 1840, some Americans are demanding that slavery be outlawed throughout the land. Of course, most of these people are northerners, who have no slaves of their own. There are plenty of freeborn workers—willing to work for next to nothing—in the northern factory towns. Because northerners don't need slaves, they can afford to attack our southern institutions—and many are quick to do so.

Many northerners don't understand that without slaves, our great southern plantations would no longer be able to raise crops. And if the plantation system failed, northerners and southerners alike would suffer. There would be no more cotton for cloth, no more tobacco or sugar, no more rice or hemp. These cash crops are needed by everyone. But without slavery, we planters would have to cut back on the output of our plantations. Thus, I believe that the abolitionists should mind their own business. And besides, most slaveholders agree that many blacks would not be able to care for themselves if they were not enslaved.

Some people find fault with slaveholders who think of their slaves as property—not as

The houses of slaves were of the most primitive kind. How would you describe the conditions under which slaves had to live?

Courtesy Glenbow Museum, Alberta.

fellow men and women. Yet we planters feel that the slaves should be grateful to belong to us. After all, a wise planter protects himself by taking good care of his property.

My slaves are well treated and happy. I feed and clothe them, I give them houses in which to live, and I make their decisions for them. All that I ask of my slaves is that they work for my profit. I can't understand why some of them try to run away.

I will admit that some of my neighbors may abuse their slaves from time to time. But that is the slaveholder's right because slaves are property. In my mind, however, it is foolish and wasteful to treat one's slaves badly. Slaves who can't work because they've been too badly beaten or otherwise mistreated are useless to their masters. Masters should treat their slaves as well as they treat their livestock and their household belongings. Of course, slaves who break the rules of the plantation must be quickly and sternly punished. Otherwise, the slaves may forget their proper place and begin to think of themselves as equal to their owners.

Why did Hempstead feel that slaves should not be abused by their masters?

SECTION 1 REVIEW

1. *What two institutions helped to shape antebellum southern society?*
2. *How did the planter view his slaves?*
3. *Why do you think the planter defended slavery?*

2 The Experience of Slavery

Slaveholders in the antebellum South often shared a common point of view toward slavery. Most slaves also agreed in their ideas toward slavery. But the two views—slaveholders' and slaves'—were generally much different from each other. Clearly, this was because one group—the slaveholders—had much to gain from slavery. The other group—the slaves themselves—had much to lose.

Life in Slavery. Most slaves hated slavery. They often felt anger and bitterness toward their masters, and almost all slaves longed for freedom. A leading American historian noted that even after more than 200 years of slavery, most slaves were eager for freedom. "Though the history of southern bondage," he wrote, "reveals that men *can* be enslaved under certain conditions, it also demonstrates that their love of freedom is hard to crush."

In general, slaves had good reasons for hating slavery and for dreaming of liberty. Slaves' time and skills belonged not to themselves but to their masters. But perhaps worst of all was the fact that slaves had little or no control over their own lives. Slave families could be broken up through the sale of family members. Moreover, slaves could not own property. The *slave codes*—the laws that governed slaves—stated that slaves could not own property be-

Chicago Historical Society

Slave auctions were held throughout the South during the early 1800's. Slaves had no control over a sale, which was a very degrading experience. Moreover, some slave owners did not always keep slave families together and, for many reasons, would sell one or more family members.

cause they were themselves property. And how could one form of property own another?

The slave codes that grew over the years in the antebellum South were most often cruel and unfair toward slaves. This was because such laws were based upon the idea that slaves were the *chattel*—the private property—of their owners. Thus, slaves had no more legal rights than did livestock or other personal belongings. Because of this, slaves had no way to protect themselves through the law. Moreover, slaves were not allowed to travel without passes from their masters. Slave codes also prohibited slaves from learning to read and to write. And there were many other laws that greatly limited the rights of slaves. Thus, slave codes worked to restrict slaves in every way possible.

The number of escaped slaves who were able to reach the free states of the North is not known. It is certain that throughout antebellum times, thousands of runaway slaves gained their freedom in this way. It is just as certain, however, that thousands more tried to escape and failed. Many died in the attempt to reach the North. And many others were caught and returned to their masters, only to face punishment, hardship, and possible sale. Thus, the dangers risked by runaway slaves were often very great.

■ *Why were the laws that governed slaves most often cruel and unfair?*

Escape to Freedom. My name is Sarah, and I was born into slavery on a rice plantation in Louisiana. My last master owned a large Virginia tobacco plantation. But three years ago—in 1837—I escaped from my master and made my way to the free North. Today, I live in Indiana.

My escape from slavery was carefully planned. To better prepare myself, I learned as much as possible from runaways who had been captured and returned to our plantation. They taught me how to hide from my pursuers and how to cover my trail from the dogs that would be used to hunt me. And my friends told me of some freeborn people along the route who would help me to escape.

I spent three months on the journey north. I almost starved on the way, and several times I was nearly caught by slave hunters and their dogs. Finally, I arrived at a small farmhouse in Maryland that was really a *station*—a safe house—on the *Underground Railroad.* The Underground Railroad is a network of people who help runaway slaves to escape to the North. I was passed from one member of this brave group to another until I reached Indiana. Freedom at last!

My new life in the North, however, has not been without troubles. Many northerners in this year of 1840 see nothing wrong with slavery and believe that escaped slaves should be returned to their masters. Moreover, some of the people here do not like blacks. For these reasons, it was hard for me to find work and to be accepted into the community. I lived for awhile with a Quaker family that was active in the Underground Railroad. But now I have a job as a cook in the town hotel. And I am learning how to support myself and how to live as a free person.

The greatest danger that I must still face is the fact that a *fugitive*—runaway—slave is never really safe in America. There are many people who hunt escaped slaves in order to gain the rewards offered for their return. And northern laws do little to protect captured runaways.

■ *What was the greatest threat faced by fugitive slaves in 1840?*

Why I Ran Away. Many people here in the North have asked me why I am willing to face the dangers of being a fugitive slave. It is often hard for someone who has never been a slave to understand the many answers to this question. But I will try to explain some of them.

To be a slave in America is to be thought of as property—like an animal or a piece of furniture. Because of this, slaves are viewed as things that are somewhat less than human. They are generally valued only for the amount of work they can do for their masters.

I suffered many hardships during my years as a slave. I was beaten with the whip because I did not work hard enough to suit my master and because once I "sassed" him. Also, I was sold twice—once when I was twelve and once again, six years later, when my master died. To be sold is a frightening and shameful experience. Also, it clearly shows how little control slaves have over their own lives. Four years ago, my husband and my small son were sold to pay my master's debts. I know that I will never see them again. Slave families are often broken up in this way. This is because most slave owners feel that the idea of a family has no real meaning in the world of the slaves.

I ran away because I wanted to be free and because I wanted to be treated like a person rather than a thing. I wanted to be free to raise a family and to work for my own well-being. Slavery, after all, is nothing more than a way to force one group of people to work for another group's profit. Finally I wanted to be free to live without fear of being beaten, of being sold, or of being worked until my body fails. Most slaves, I believe, feel much the same way as I do.

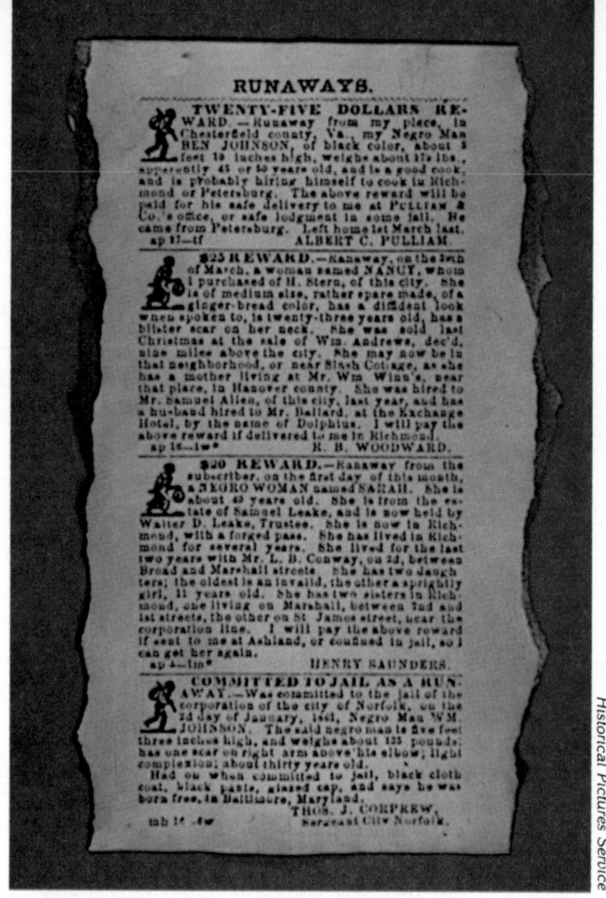
RUNAWAYS.

TWENTY-FIVE DOLLARS REWARD.—Runaway from my place, in Chesterfield county, Va., my Negro Man BEN JOHNSON, of black color, about 5 feet 10 inches high, weighs about 175 lbs., apparently 45 or 50 years old, and is a good cook, and is probably hiring himself to cook in Richmond or Petersburg. The above reward will be paid for his safe delivery to me at PULLIAM & Co.'s office, or safe lodgment in some jail. He came from Petersburg. Left home 1st March last.
ap 17—tf ALBERT C. PULLIAM.

$25 REWARD.—Runaway, on the 3rd of March, a woman named NANCY, whom I purchased of H. Stern, of this city. She is of medium size, rather spare made, of a ginger-bread color, has a diffident look when spoken to, is twenty-three years old, has a blister scar on her neck. She was sold last Christmas at the sale of Wm. Andrews, dec'd, nine miles above the city. She may now be in that neighborhood, or near Slash Cottage, as she has a mother living at Mr. Wm Winn's, near that place, in Hanover county. She was hired to Mr. Samuel Allen, of this city, last year, and has a husband hired to Mr. Ballard, at the Exchange Hotel, by the name of Dolphius. I will pay the above reward if delivered to me in Richmond.
ap 16—1w* R. B. WOODWARD.

$20 REWARD.—Runaway from the subscriber, on the first day of this month, a NEGRO WOMAN named SARAH. She is about 40 years old. She is from the estate of Samuel Leake, and is now held by Walter D. Leake, Trustee. She is now in Richmond, with a forged pass. She has lived in Richmond for several years. She lived for the last two years with Mr. L. B. Conway, on 2d, between Broad and Marshall streets. She has two daughters; the oldest is an invalid, the other a sprightly girl, 11 years old. She has two sisters in Richmond, one living on Marshall, between 2nd and 1st streets, the other on St James street, near the corporation line. I will pay the above reward if sent to me at Ashland, or confined in jail, so I can get her again.
ap 4—1m* HENRY SAUNDERS.

COMMITTED TO JAIL AS A RUNAWAY.—Was committed to the jail of the corporation of the city of Norfolk, on the 2d day of January, 1861, Negro Man WM. JOHNSON. The said negro man is five feet three inches high, and weighs about 135 pounds; has one scar on right arm above his elbow; light complexion; about thirty years old.
Had on when committed to jail, black cloth coat, black pants, glazed cap, and says he was born free, in Baltimore, Maryland.
THOS. J. CORPREW,
mh 1[illegible]—4w Sergeant City Norfolk.

Historical Pictures Service

Many slave owners offered rewards for the capture and return of runaway slaves.

What was a clear example of the lack of control that slaves had over their lives?

SECTION 2 REVIEW

1. *What were the slave codes of the antebellum South?*
2. *How did the Underground Railroad help Sarah to win her freedom?*
3. *Why did slave owners feel free to break up slave families?*

CHAPTER 12 REVIEW

SUMMARY

The South before 1861 is referred to as the antebellum South. The society of the antebellum South was largely shaped by the institutions of farming and slavery. Most southern farmers in the 1840's were neither planters—large plantation owners—nor slaveholders. The majority of large slaveholders came from the wealthy planter class. Although this class was small in number, it did much to shape southern society and its view of slavery.

Southern slaveholders looked upon slaves as chattel—private property. This view of slaves was upheld by a group of laws that are known as slave codes. Under the slave codes, slaves had no rights and could be bought and sold at any time. As the plantation system became increasingly important to the southern economy, the demand for slaves became greater. By 1840, slaves made up over one third of the southern population. As a result, slavery played a major role in antebellum southern society.

Most slaves hated slavery and dreamed of freedom. Slaves had little or no control over their lives. Slave families could be broken up through the sale of family members. Slaves could not own property because they were themselves considered property. Through the slave codes, slaves had no more legal rights than livestock or personal belongings. Slaves were not allowed to travel without passes from their masters. They were also prohibited from learning to read and write. Throughout antebellum times, thousands of slaves gained their freedom by escaping to the free states of the North. Thousands more tried to escape and failed. Those slaves who were caught were returned to their masters, only to be punished or possibly sold.

UNDERSTANDING CONCEPTS

1. What two institutions largely shaped the society of the antebellum South?
2. Why were slaves legally held to be nothing more than goods to be used for their owner's gain?
3. Why did most slaveholders believe northerners attacked the institution of slavery?
4. Why did slaves have no legal rights?
5. How did the slave codes work to restrict slaves?
6. Why were fugitive slaves in 1840 never really safe?

CRITICAL THINKING

1. Do you think most northerners would have opposed slavery if they needed slaves to work in the factories? Give reasons for your answer.
2. The typical slaveholder felt that his slaves were happy. Do you think this was true? Why do you think slaveholders felt that way?
3. If you were living in the North in the 1840's, would you have been active in the Underground Railroad? Why?

PROJECTS AND ACTIVITIES

Find out about the work of abolitionists in the United States. Use biographies, history books, and encyclopedia articles to find out about the work of one of the following abolitionists: William Lloyd Garrison, Theodore Dwight Weld, Angelina Grimke, Sara Moore Grimke, Frederick Douglass, Sojourner Truth, Christopher Rush, and Samuel Cornish. You might share your research in the form of a written report or a newspaper article.

UNIT THREE REVIEW

UNIT SUMMARY

The years from 1800 to 1815 were marked by change and by growth in America. New ways of living and of working began to appear during the early 1800's. In the North, Americans began to build industries while in the South, farming became more important than ever before. The United States grew rapidly in size as well as in power. After winning another war with Great Britain, the United States won peace with Europe and world respect as well.

Between 1815 and 1828, the people of the United States began to shape a new society. Many people in America began to take more pride in their country and in their government. New settlers moved west, and ongoing settlement of the West caused many Americans to face new economic hardships. The differences in America's three sections led to conflict between the country's sections.

During the Age of Jackson, a new sense of freedom and of purpose grew as Americans worked together to build a stronger democracy. Major differences among the country's sections became more clearly drawn. President Jackson acted to meet Americans' different needs, but sometimes his strong measures caused even greater sectional differences. Throughout the Age of Jackson, several important reform movements came about and helped to bring a better life to many Americans.

The society of the antebellum South was largely shaped by the institutions of farming and slavery. As the plantation system became increasingly important to the southern economy, the demand for slaves became greater. By 1840, slaves made up over one third of the southern population. Most slaves hated slavery and dreamed of freedom. Since slaves were considered to be property, they had no more legal rights than livestock or personal belongings.

YOU SHOULD KNOW

Identify, define, or explain each of the following:

judicial review	suffrage
secede	spoils system
embargo	reform
nationalism	antebellum South
depression	chattel

CHECKING FACTS

1. Where did industry first develop in the United States?
2. What crop became the major product of the South during the Age of Jefferson?
3. What was the purpose of the Hartford Convention?
4. What social class became the largest and most powerful of America's social classes by 1815?
5. Where did the Industrial Revolution begin in America?
6. What is an implied constitutional power?
7. What sections of the United States were angered by the Tariff of 1816?
8. What was the doctrine of nullification?
9. What reforms did Mary Lyon work for?
10. What were the slave codes?

UNDERSTANDING CONCEPTS

1. How did the North differ from the South during the early 1800's?
2. How did the Tariff of 1816 affect sectional differences in the United States?
3. How did the voting process become more democratic during the late 1820's?
4. Why did the antislavery movement gain power during the 1830's?
5. How did the slave codes work to restrict slaves?

UNIT THREE REVIEW

CRITICAL THINKING

1. Do you think that the institution of slavery could be justified in any way? Give reasons for your answer.
2. In your opinion, were all the changes that were brought about as a result of the Industrial Revolution positive ones? Give reasons for your opinion.
3. If you could live in any kind of utopian society, what kind of society would you choose? Explain your answer.

CHRONOLOGY

Arrange the following events in the order in which they happened.

a. Andrew Jackson elected President
b. John Marshall appointed Chief Justice of the Supreme Court
c. The War of 1812 begins
d. William Lloyd Garrison prints the first copy of *The Liberator*
e. Henry Clay proposes the Missouri Compromise
f. Thomas Jefferson elected President
g. Martin Van Buren elected President
h. The Louisiana Purchase is made
i. The Panic of 1819 occurs
j. The Indian Removal Act established

CITIZENSHIP IN ACTION

The Age of Jackson was a time when many Americans were able to improve their way of life. Many other Americans, however, suffered from unfair treatment. Many reforms occurred in the United States between 1828 and 1837. What problems in the United States today could reformers try to improve?

GEOGRAPHY

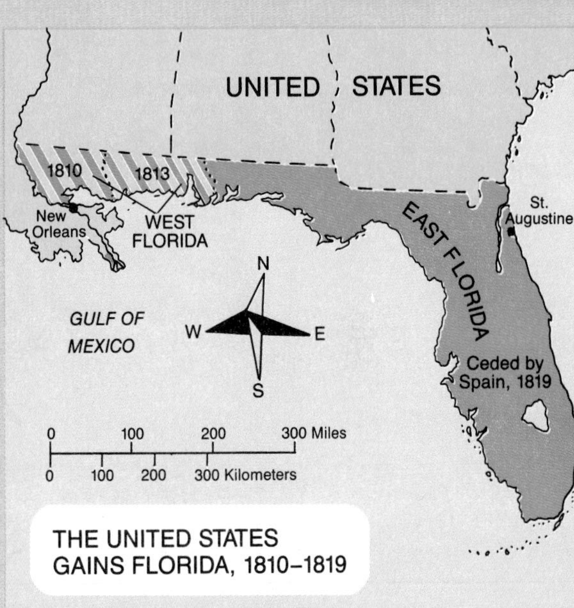

THE UNITED STATES GAINS FLORIDA, 1810–1819

1. According to the map, from what nation did the United States gain the Florida territory?
2. What part of this territory was first gained by the United States?
3. In what year was part of this territory first gained by the United States?
4. What were the two parts of the Florida territory called?
5. In what year did the United States gain the last part of this territory?

1840 1845

- 1837 Panic of 1837
- 1839 Mormon settlement established at Nauvoo, Illinois
- 1840 William Henry Harrison elected President
- 1841 Vice-President Tyler succeeds to presidency following Harrison's death
- 1844 James K. Polk elected President
- 1845 Texas annexed by United States
- 1846 War with Mexico begins; Oregon boundary dispute settled
- 1848 Zachary Taylor elected President; War with Mexico ends
- 1849 California gold rush begins

UNIT FOUR

Progress and Problems

1837 to 1860

This illustration shows gauchos—cowboys—in a horse corral in the Spanish territory that would later become Texas.

"Wall Street 1857" illustrates the bustling activity of America's financial center in the mid-1800's. Throughout the nineteenth century, America gradually changed from a primarily agricultural nation to a manufacturing and industrial power.

1850 1855 1860

- 1850 Compromise of 1850
- 1852 Franklin Pierce elected President; *Uncle Tom's Cabin* published by Harriet Beecher Stowe
- 1853 Gadsden Purchase
- 1854 Kansas-Nebraska Act; Republican Party founded
- 1856 James Buchanan elected President; Lawrence, Kansas, attacked by proslavery forces
- 1857 Dred Scott case
- 1858 Lincoln-Douglas debates
- 1859 John Brown's raid on Harpers Ferry

CHAPTERS

The United States was still a new country, a great experiment in democracy, in the years between 1837 and 1860. And like all new countries, America faced many problems as it grew and moved forward.

As America grew during the 1840's and the 1850's, so did the problem of sectionalism become larger and more dangerous. At times, the different needs and goals of the sections led to conflict among them.

America's government leaders tried to halt the slow but steady growth of sectional rivalry between 1837 and 1860. But major issues—economic, social, and political—increasingly divided the people of the different sections. And as America moved toward the 1860's, sectional differences made the likelihood of open conflict more and more real.

Runaway slave families, carrying all that they own, make their way cautiously along a road on their way to the safety of a hiding place on the Underground Railroad.

Texan military leader Sam Houston avenged the American defeat at the Alamo by leading a surprise attack on Santa Anna's army at San Jacinto in April 1836.

1835 | 1845 | 1850

- 1821 American families allowed to settle in Texas
- 1835 Texans declare independence from Mexico
- 1836 Texans defeated at the Alamo; Texas becomes Lone Star Republic
- 1837 Panic of 1837
- 1839 Mormon settlement established at Nauvoo, Illinois
- 1840 William Henry Harrison elected President
- 1841 Vice-President Tyler succeeds to presidency following Harrison's death
- 1844 James K. Polk elected President
- 1845 Texas annexed by United States
- 1846 War with Mexico begins; Oregon boundary dispute settled
- 1848 Treaty of Guadalupe Hidalgo ends War with Mexico
- 1849 California gold rush begins

CHAPTER 13

One Nation From Atlantic to Pacific

Chapter Objectives

After studying this chapter, you will be able to:

- identify the meaning and the implications of the concept of Manifest Destiny;
- contrast the principal methods followed by American settlers to acquire western territory during the 1830's and the 1840's;
- analyze the impact of westward expansion on domestic problems in America.

1 Manifest Destiny and Westward Expansion

Overview Throughout the 1840's, Americans continued to search for new lands. Our country's frontiers were steadily and rapidly pushed westward. New territories were formed, and new states were brought into the Union.

America's expansion, however, was not always a smooth or easy process. Political differences, conflicts with other countries, and growing unrest at home accompanied the nation's westward march.

Objectives After reading this section, you will be able to:

- identify the ways that Americans' views of the frontier changed during the 1840's;
- explain how the idea of Manifest Destiny helped to speed westward expansion;
- describe the major political conflicts that developed as a result of continued frontier settlement.

The Progress of Western Settlement. A growing stream of westward migration in the years after 1837 helped to speed the settlement of America's frontiers. During these years, thousands of pioneers moved into the vast and open lands of the Southwest. Thousands more poured into California and into the northwestern frontiers that stretched from the Great Lakes to the Oregon Country. By 1850, four new states—Texas, California, Iowa, and Wisconsin—had entered the Union. Moreover, huge new territories that included Minnesota, Oregon, Utah, and New Mexico were organized and prepared for statehood. Thus, between 1837 and 1850, America's borders moved steadily westward as more and more settlers reached the frontier line.

The years between 1837 and 1850 saw western settlement continue at a strong pace. Some western settlers in these years hoped to escape the long-lasting economic hardships brought about in the East by the Panic of 1837. The Panic of 1837 caused serious economic problems in the United States. Many banks and businesses throughout America were closed, and thousands of jobs were lost.

Many settlers believed that jobs and wealth could more easily be found in the growing West than in the economically troubled East. Thus, in the American mind, the frontier came to be seen as a land of hope and of opportunity.

The West, like the East, was affected by the Panic of 1837. But the frontier still offered opportunities. This was largely because land and other valuable resources were plentiful on the frontier. These resources in the West helped to encourage the growth of farming, of ranching, and of mining.

During the post-Jacksonian years between 1837 and 1850, the West became America's leading food-producing area. Large areas of the western frontier were ideally suited for farming and for the raising of livestock. As western settlement continued, the growing number of farmers and ranchers began to supply more and more of America's food needs. By about 1850, many states east of the Ohio River depended upon the West for wheat, corn, potatoes, beef, and hogs. This helped to build trade between the East and the West and to strengthen the American economy as a whole. The growth of this trade brought new economic opportunities that, in turn, helped to draw even more settlers westward.

- *When did the West become America's leading food-producing area?*

Mining and Transportation. The growth of the western mining industry also led to increased frontier settlement. Mining, however, did not develop in the West as early as did farming and ranching. It was not until 1849 and after that mining became an important frontier industry. After 1849, however, the discovery of rich mineral deposits in the West led to a rapidly growing mining and mineral industry. Gold, silver, and copper were among the first minerals to be mined in large quantities in the West. After 1850, the demand for western coal and iron ore grew slowly but steadily as America continued to industrialize.

During the 1840's, improved means of east-west travel helped to open America's frontiers to settlement and to trade. Roads and canals were built to link the East and the West, making travel easier and faster. Throughout these years, many settlers followed the great overland routes—such as the Santa Fe and

Historical Pictures Service

Many backbreaking methods were used in mining during the 1840's and the 1850's. One method of mining—known as *placer mining*—was to shovel the ore into a sluice and then to divert water from a local source and channel it over the ore. Heavy minerals, such as gold, sank to the bottom, and the remaining sludge was washed away. The miner could then recover the minerals.

the Oregon trails—that led westward. Each year, thousands of pioneers crossed to the Great Plains and beyond in wagon trains. Such trains numbered from a few wagons to dozens or even hundreds. Other settlers journeyed to the West by sea. Sailing vessels left from many eastern ports, traveling around the southern tip of South America and up the Pacific coast to California. The ocean route to the Far West took many weeks. But it was often easier and faster to travel by sea than to follow an overland trail.

Westward expansion during the late 1830's and the 1840's had a deep and powerful impact upon values and ideals throughout America. Many Americans, for example, began to feel pride in the growing size and might of their country. Some people began to believe that Americans had a natural right and a duty to settle new lands in the West.

■ *What two methods of travel were most often used by westward-bound pioneers?*

The Spirit of Manifest Destiny. As Americans pushed westward after 1837, they took pride in their country's growth. Many Americans viewed the ongoing settlement of the frontier as proof of America's social and political greatness. For this reason, the frontier became more than just a constantly changing boundary line by the 1840's. It also became a *symbol*—a sign—of American strength, bravery, and determination. Because of this, a new sense of *nationalism*—of pride and of faith in the country—grew throughout America.

The wave of nationalism that swept across America during the 1840's brought about a new idea known as *Manifest Destiny.* The term *Manifest Destiny* first appeared in a newspaper article written by John L. O'Sullivan in July of 1845. According to the article, Americans had a divine right and a mission to settle new land and to bring it into the Union. This, the writer believed, was because Americans had been chosen over all other people to enjoy the blessings of democracy. For this reason, Americans were duty-bound to spread their values and their ideals for the betterment of people throughout the continent.

The idea of Manifest Destiny became widely accepted as truth in our country during the 1840's. But it was really little more than an excuse for Americans to settle on land that in many cases belonged to others. Thus, Indian tribes throughout the West, as well as the people of neighboring countries, became victims of American land-hunger.

The beliefs expressed in the doctrine of Manifest Destiny were not new in the United States. From the earliest days of American independence, westward-bound settlers believed that they were free to take land along the country's frontiers. But the concept of Manifest Destiny stated this belief in a new and powerful way. It gave Americans a feeling that they had a right to any land that they could take. The idea of Manifest Destiny, however, soon brought the United States into dangerous conflicts with the countries that shared our borders.

■ *What did the frontier come to symbolize to Americans in the 1840's?*

The Beginnings of Texan Settlement. During the early 1800's, much of the Southwest and the Far West was owned by Spain (see map on page 224). This vast area was part of the great Spanish colony of Mexico. Spanish Mexico included the present-day states of Texas and California. It stretched as far north as the Oregon Country and as far east as the

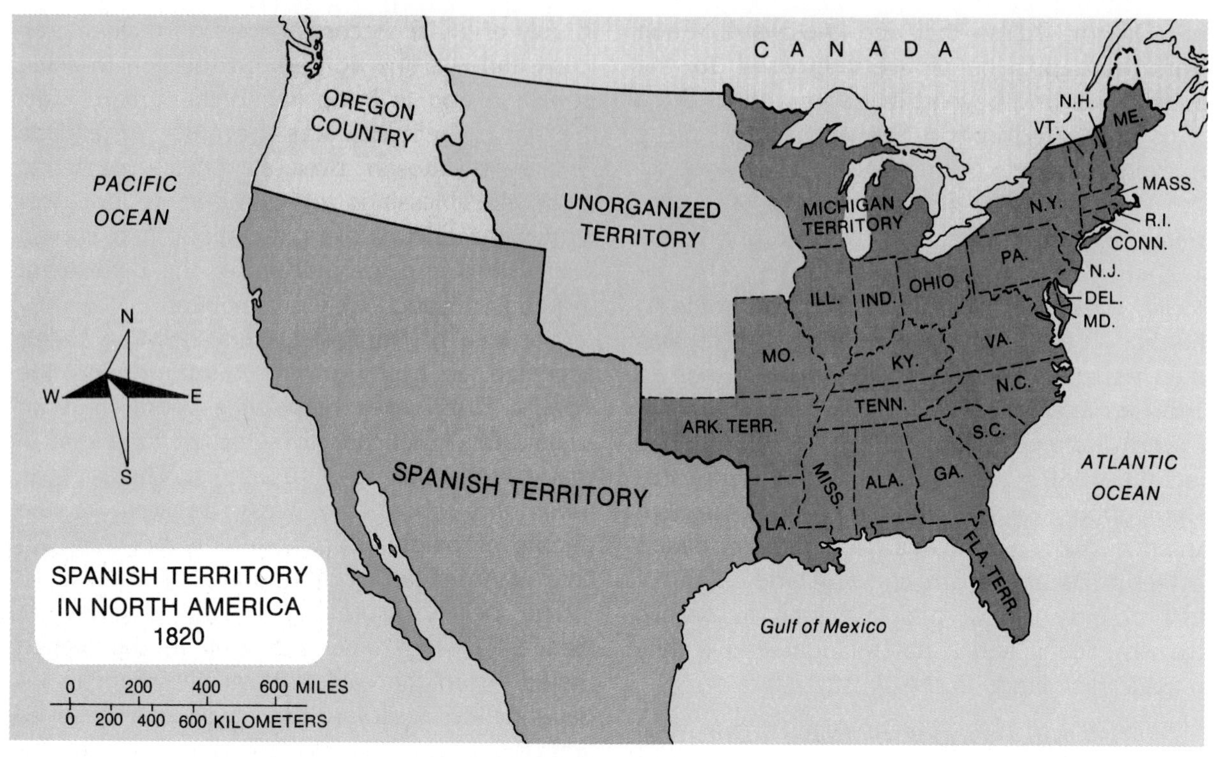

In 1820, what area bordered the Spanish territory on the north? What bodies of water bordered the Spanish territory?

borders of the old Louisiana Territory. Many Americans in the early 1800's were eager to settle these rich and open lands. But until 1821, the Spanish government did not allow citizens of the United States to own land within Mexico's borders.

Early in 1821, however, the Spanish government changed its policy toward American settlement. This change was done in order to open northeastern Mexico—what is today's Texas—to farming and to ranching. Several hundred American families, who were led by Moses Austin's son, Stephen, were allowed to settle in Texas. Each family received a gift of land from the Spanish government. In return, the settlers had to promise to become Spanish citizens and to accept Spanish laws.

Not long after Austin and his followers arrived in Texas, Mexico won its independence from Spain. The new government had many problems to face. After much controversy, the new Mexican government passed a general colonization law. Under this law, Austin's group was allowed to remain in Texas. Americans were invited to settle freely in Texas and to open the land. To attract more Americans to Texas, Mexico offered gifts of land and laws that favored the settlers' needs. But as more Americans moved into Texas, their growing power began to alarm Mexico's leaders.

In the late 1820's trouble arose between the American settlers in Texas and the new government of Mexico. The majority of the settlers in Texas, who began to call themselves Texans, were immigrants from the United States. Also, many American settlers refused to become Mexican citizens and they also paid little attention to Mexican laws.

Mexico's leaders decided that strong actions were needed to regain their control over the settlers. In 1830, they passed several laws to restrict the settlers and to bring them under government power. Many Texans were greatly angered by these new laws. They became especially bitter when slavery was outlawed throughout Texas. This was because a large number of the settlers were slaveholders from the South. Many southern slaveholders had moved to Texas during the 1820's to build cotton plantations. These Americans believed that without slaves to work in the fields, cotton could not be grown. Because of this, many Texans felt that Mexico's new antislavery law was a direct and unfair attack upon American settlers. The Texans were also angered when Mexico closed its borders in an attempt to end further American settlement. Many Texans felt that they could not continue to live under Mexican rule.

Why did Mexico act to restrict American settlers in Texas in 1830?

The Lone Star Republic. In 1835, the Texans rebelled against Mexico's rule and declared their independence. A new government was set up, and a small army was hastily gathered to defend the country from Mexican attack. But Texas was not prepared to fight powerful Mexico, and it appeared that the revolt would soon be crushed.

In March of 1836, about 190 Texans were overrun and killed at the Alamo, near the town of San Antonio. A second important battle near Goliad also ended in defeat for the outnumbered and poorly armed Texans. The Mexican ruler, General Santa Anna, then marched with his army to overcome the remaining Texans at San Jacinto. In the meantime, however, Samuel Houston took command of the new country's army. Houston was an outstanding general, and at San Jacinto, his small band of Texans won a great victory. The Mexican army was destroyed, and Santa Anna was forced to make peace with Houston and the new Texas government. In October 1836, Texas became the independent Lone Star Republic with Sam Houston as its first president.

The Texans wanted their new republic to be *annexed*—taken over—by the United States. This was because most Texans thought of themselves as American citizens. And annexation would be the first step toward statehood

DO YOU KNOW?

What is our national bird, and when was it chosen as our country's symbol?

The bald—or American—eagle was chosen as our country's national bird and symbol in 1782. The bald eagle has stirred feelings of nationalism in America ever since our country won its independence. But the eagle was chosen as the United States symbol only after a spirited debate among the new country's founders. Benjamin Franklin, for example, suggested that Congress adopt the American wild turkey as our national symbol. But the bald eagle—fierce, proud, and free—was finally accepted as the best and most visible sign of our American ideals.

Texas State Archives

Santa Anna (center) surrendered to the wounded Sam Houston following the Texan's victory at the Battle of San Jacinto.

for Texas. But the Texans' requests for annexation and for statehood met with mixed feelings throughout the United States.

■ *In what ways did Samuel Houston contribute to Texan independence?*

The Politics of Annexation. The birth of the Texas Republic helped to open large parts of the Southwest to American settlement. But it also caused anger and bad feelings to grow between the United States and Mexico. This was because the Mexican government held American land-hunger to blame for the loss of Texas. Moreover, the question of annexing Texas raised political issues in America.

After 1836, the movement to bring Texas into the Union caused feelings of nationalism to grow in the United States. Many Americans were eager to see America's borders pushed all the way to the Pacific Coast. These people felt that unlimited frontier growth was the best way to build their country's wealth and power. Moreover, many nationalists believed that Texas properly belonged to the United States because Americans had fought for the land

and won. According to this view, our country had a right to keep any land that it was strong enough to take.

Nonetheless, some Americans did not agree with the nationalist point of view and worked against the annexation of Texas. A few of these people felt that it was wrong to take land that belonged to another country, no matter what the reason. Others believed that strong feelings of nationalism in America might lead to war with neighboring countries. For these reasons, a number of Americans felt that the annexation of Texas would justly anger Mexico's government leaders. This could cause relations between the United States and Mexico—already poor—to be further weakened.

Sectionalism was another major issue that was closely tied to the Texas question. For example, southerners generally favored annexation because they knew that many Texans were slaveholders who were loyal to southern values and ideals. Thus, if Texas gained statehood, the South would gain more support in Congress.

Many northerners, on the other hand, feared that Texan annexation would destroy the balance of political power between the sections. Moreover, a growing number of northerners were against the spread of slavery to newly settled western states. These people knew that Texas wanted to enter the Union as a slave state. They felt that if slavery was allowed to grow in one western state, it could easily spread to others as well. Thus, many northerners worried that slave states might outnumber free states within a few years after Texas entered the Union. As a result, these Americans often joined their voices with those people who opposed Texan annexation on moral grounds.

By late 1836, an angry political debate had grown over the Texas question. This caused sectional differences to become more bitter and more clearly drawn throughout America. President Jackson, whose term of office was nearly over, hoped that a settlement would be reached before he left office. But as months passed, it became clear that government leaders could not agree on the issue. In order to make peace between the angry sections, Jackson decided against the immediate annexation of Texas. Texas then withdrew its request for statehood. For the time being, Texas remained an independent country with its own government and its own laws.

The question of the annexation of Texas was highly important in its own right. The Texas question also underlined two dangerous issues—nationalism and sectionalism—that faced Americans in the years after 1837.

What were the two major causes of debate over the question of Texan annexation?

SECTION 1 REVIEW

1. *What major economic problem caused many Americans to move west after 1837?*
2. *How did the idea of Manifest Destiny help to promote westward expansion?*
3. *Why did relations between Mexico and the United States become worse after the War for Texan Independence?*

2 Acquisition From Other Countries

Overview During the 1840's, America's government leaders worked to speed the course of westward settlement. Because of this, several important disputes with other countries were peacefully settled in these years. At the same time, however, new problems arose to test the power of our growing country.

Objectives After reading this section, you will be able to:

- explain how America's westward expansion led to new conflicts at home;
- analyze the ways that United States diplomacy helped to speed frontier settlement;
- describe the methods Americans used to acquire land from other countries during the 1840's.

Texas Joins the Union. Many Americans were angered when President Jackson refused to bring Texas into the Union. But Jackson's decision was a wise choice at the time, for it helped to cool the sectional debate over Texas. The issue of Texan statehood, however, remained to trouble Americans for nine more years.

President Martin Van Buren, Jackson's successor in the White House, decided not to act upon the Texas question. Van Buren knew that Mexico's leaders were angered by the loss of Texas. And he believed that any move to grant statehood to Texas would lead to war with Mexico. Because of this, Van Buren put aside the issue of Texan statehood and turned his attention to other frontier matters.

When Van Buren left office in 1841, southern leaders in Congress, such as John C. Calhoun, again called for statehood for Texas. Calhoun, like many southerners, saw the Texas question from a sectional point of view. Texan statehood would add to the political power of the South. Moreover, it would help to spread slavery in America. For these reasons, Calhoun and other southern leaders worked hard for the cause of Texan statehood.

President John Tyler, who held office from 1841 until 1845, also favored statehood for Texas. In 1844, Tyler asked Congress to accept a treaty of annexation in order to bring the Lone Star Republic into the Union. But opposition from nonslave northern states in Congress caused the measure to be turned down. The Texan bid for statehood failed once again.

The issue of Texan statehood was finally settled with the election of President James K. Polk in 1844. Polk, a member of the Democratic party, was outspokenly in favor of Texan annexation and of frontier growth in general. The fact that Polk won the election of 1844 seemed to indicate to many government leaders that most Americans wanted statehood for Texas. For this reason, Congress agreed to annex Texas. In 1845, Texas joined the United States.

The admission of Texas settled one of the major conflicts brought about by westward growth. With the Texas question finally answered, President Polk was free to give his full attention to yet another frontier issue. This had to do with American claims in the huge northwestern lands of the Oregon Country.

■ *Why did President Van Buren decide not to act upon the question of Texan annexation?*

The Oregon Country. For many years before the 1840's, America had claimed much of the great northwestern territory known as Oregon. In fact, United States claims in Oregon dated from as early as the Lewis and Clark Expedition of 1804–1806. But until about 1840, few Americans were interested in the Oregon Country. Moreover, the northern border of Oregon was a matter of long-standing dispute between the United States and Great Britain.

The Oregon Country was rich both in land and in natural resources. Large parts of Oregon were heavily forested. But the few American settlers that went to Oregon before 1840 found that much of the land could be farmed. Moreover, early trappers soon made Oregon a center for the North American fur trade. American trading companies, such as the Rocky Mountain Fur Company, helped to open the country to later settlement. The trappers who worked for these companies discovered many of the trails and the mountain passes that later made overland travel to Oregon possible.

During the early 1840's, wagon trains of American settlers reached Oregon in growing numbers. Most pioneer families followed the overland route—the Oregon Trail—across the Rocky Mountains to the Columbia River and beyond.

The trip to Oregon was long and was often filled with hardship. Disease, rugged terrain, and bad weather were among the many dangers faced by Oregon-bound settlers. But perhaps the most widely feared danger was attack by the Indians whose lands lay across the path of the Oregon Trail. During the 1840's, the western Indians learned that the growth of America threatened their homelands and their way of life. Because of this, many western Indian tribes fought against the spread of America's frontiers.

Throughout the early 1840's, about 1,000 Americans settled in Oregon each year. These

Scott's Bluff National Monument

Many Americans traveled to the Oregon Country in long trains of horse- or ox-drawn covered wagons. The settlers had to face many hardships on the long trip. What hardships are shown in this illustration?

people felt that all of Oregon below the line 54°40′ should belong to the United States. But Great Britain also claimed parts of the Oregon Country. The British held that the land north of the forty-second parallel belonged to them (see map on this page). The differences between American and British claims led to growing dispute over Oregon. Angry American settlers in Oregon called for war against Great Britain. The cry of "Fifty-four forty or fight" began to be heard throughout the United States.

Neither Great Britain nor the United States really wanted to go to war over Oregon. But both countries felt that the question of Oregon's borders should be settled once and for all. During the early 1840's, the issue grew as more and more Americans moved into Oregon.

How did early trading companies help to open the Oregon Country to American settlement?

Settlement of the Oregon Question. By 1845, a growing number of Americans no longer thought of the Oregon Country as a tiny, faraway settlement of trappers and fur traders. The American population in Oregon had grown from less than 500 in 1840 to more than 5,000 in 1845. And more settlers headed toward Oregon and the Pacific Northwest every day. It was clear to many government leaders that Oregon was well on the way

During the westward expansion of the 1840's, settlers followed many trails. What river did most of the Mormon Trail follow?

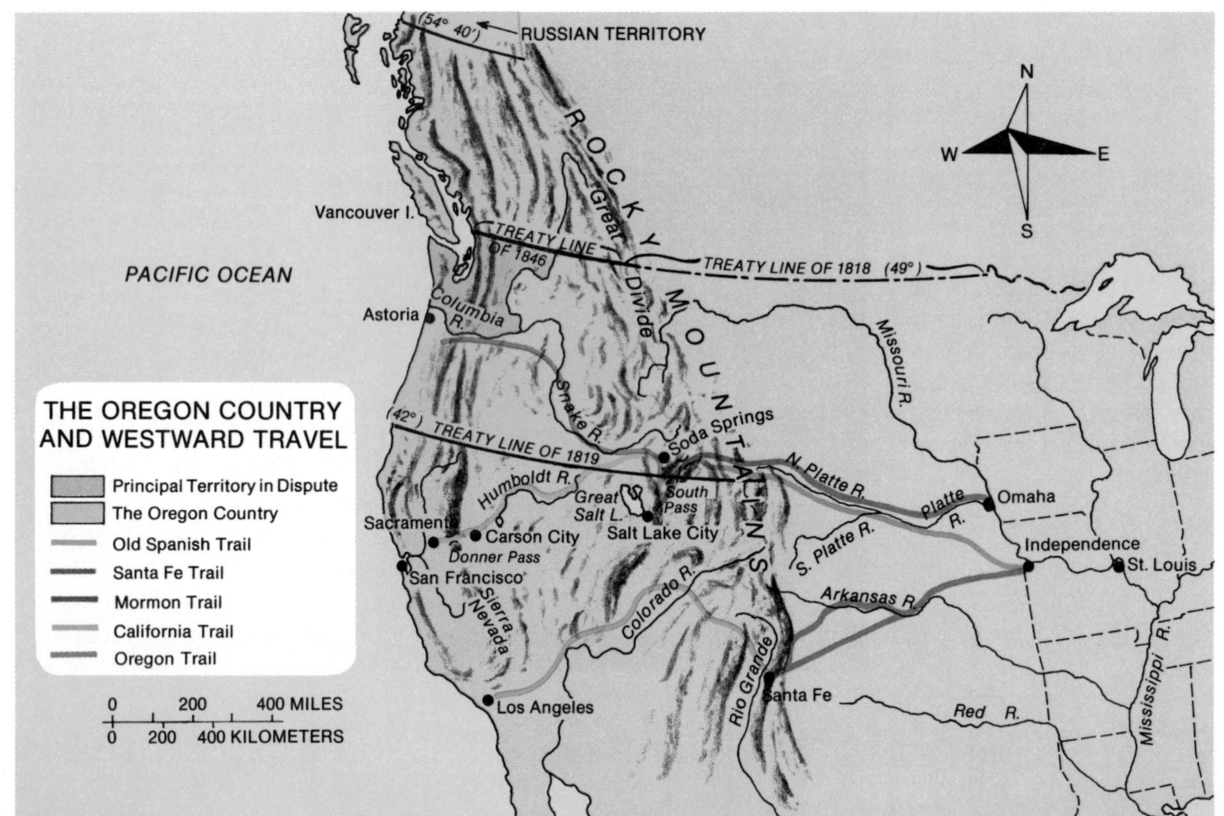

toward statehood. By the mid-1840's, the Oregon boundary question had won the attention of voters and of political leaders throughout our country.

The Oregon question became an important campaign issue during the election of 1844. James Polk, who headed the Democratic party's ticket, appealed to many Americans' sense of nationalism. Polk's victory led many people to believe that the United States was prepared to defend its claims in Oregon. President Polk seemed to agree that America would not accept any boundary settlement below the line of 54°40′.

President Polk, however, was a wise and careful leader. He did not believe that America should go to war with Great Britain over the Oregon question. Thus, Polk agreed to a *compromise* with the British government. That is, both sides gave up some of their claims in order to reach a fair settlement of the question. The Treaty of 1846 between the United States and Great Britain fixed Oregon's boundary at the forty-ninth parallel.

The Treaty of 1846 brought a peaceful settlement of the Oregon question. During the next few years, thousands of American settlers moved into the new Oregon Territory. But elsewhere along the western frontiers, Americans began to face new troubles.

■ *Why did President Polk agree to a compromise settlement of the Oregon question?*

Americans Reach the Pacific. At the same time that many Americans worked to open the Oregon Country, others moved into the lightly-settled lands of California. By the early 1840's, a handful of American pioneers had reached the Pacific coast of California. Within a few years, California had become one of the most rapidly growing of America's frontiers.

California was still a colony of Spain when the first Americans arrived there in the late 1700's. Under Spanish rule, California was allowed to remain largely unsettled. Over the years, a few important Spanish families received huge gifts of land in California. But for the most part, these great ranches were worked by native Indians rather than by Spanish settlers. Small trade centers and villages grew up around the few forts built by the Spanish government in California. But little was done to bring in settlers, and for the most part, California was unknown to Americans.

The first Americans to reach California were sailors and sea traders who came by way of the Pacific Ocean. A few of these people chose to remain in California. They became Spanish citizens and set up small businesses, mostly in trading and shipping. Slowly, stories of the opportunities and of the rich land that these Americans found in California spread eastward to the United States. By the 1820's, Americans began to become interested in the Spanish lands of the Far West.

In 1821, Mexico won independence from Spain. The Spanish holdings in the Far West then came under Mexico's rule. As they had done in Texas, Mexico's leaders opened California to limited American settlement. Over the next 20 years, a small but growing number of Americans moved into California, eager to build ranches, farms, and businesses.

There were less than 1,000 Americans in California by the early 1840's. But Mexico's leaders had learned a costly and valuable lesson from the events in Texas. They knew that even a small number of American settlers could be dangerous if the United States became interested in California. Mexico did not

Artstreet

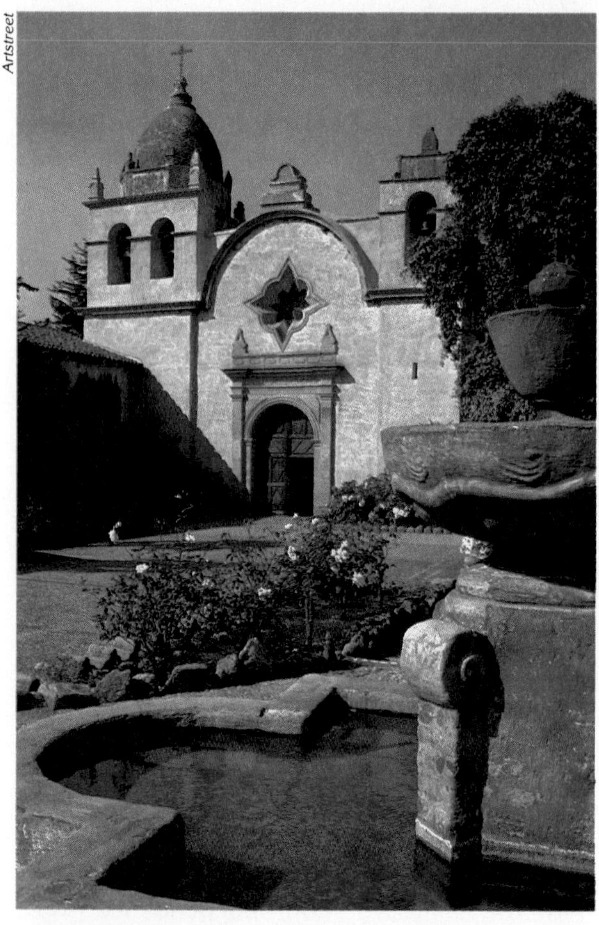

Spanish missions dotted the California coast during the 1700's. The missions were built from San Diego to San Francisco, and each mission was about one day's walk from the next.

wish to lose California in the same way that Texas was lost. Therefore, Mexico took steps to halt the entry of more American settlers into California. But this caused bad feelings to grow between the United States and Mexico.

By the mid-1840's, many Americans had begun to feel that California should belong to the United States. President Polk, who was eager to push America's borders to the Pacific Ocean, agreed with this spreading belief. Polk offered to buy California from Mexico. He also wanted to buy the area of New Mexico, with its important trading city of Santa Fe.

Mexico's leaders, however, refused to sell their country's lands in California and in New Mexico. Moreover, Mexico broke *diplomatic relations*—political ties—with the United States over this question. Some Americans then called upon President Polk to take California and New Mexico, using armed force if need be.

Thus, by the mid-1840's, another major border dispute had grown between the United States and Mexico. And by 1846, the two countries had moved to the edge of war with each other. But even as some American settlers prepared for war with Mexico, others moved west in order to find peace.

■ *How did Mexico respond to President Polk's offer to purchase California and New Mexico?*

SECTION 2 REVIEW

1. *For what reasons did John C. Calhoun work to gain statehood for Texas?*
2. *How did the Treaty of 1846 bring about a peaceful settlement of the Oregon question?*
3. *How did President Polk want to acquire California and New Mexico for the United States?*

3 The Growing Impact of the West

Overview By the mid-1840's, Americans had pushed back the country's frontiers in every direction. Texas in the southwest and the Oregon Territory in the Northwest gave settlers from the United States rich new lands to open. In the Far West, the promise of California drew eager settlers from every part of America. By 1846, the growing drive for land in the Southwest had brought the United States to war with Mexico.

Objectives After reading this section, you will be able to:

- identify the cause of the Mexican War;
- discuss the way the California gold rush helped to settle the Far West;
- explain the way westward expansion led to growing domestic problems in America.

The Mormons Settle Utah. In the early 1840's, much of the land directly to the southeast of Oregon was unknown to Americans. Most people believed that this great stretch of western land—known as the country of Utah—was little more than desert. Moreover, the Utah country in the early 1840's was hard to reach. Westward-bound settlers had to make the dangerous Rocky Mountain crossing to arrive in Utah.

Settlers often felt that there was little reason to do so, especially since Oregon and California appeared to offer so much more. For this reason, Utah was allowed to remain largely a wilderness.

During the early 1840's, however, a group of Americans was in need of just such a land to settle. These people were the *Mormons*—members of the Church of Jesus Christ of Latter-Day Saints.

The Mormons had suffered a number of hardships after their church was formed in western New York State in 1830. The founder of the Mormon faith was Joseph Smith. Throughout the 1830's, Smith and his small band of followers were subjected to bitter religious persecution. They built settlements in New York, in Ohio, and in Missouri, only to be driven out each time. Finally, the Mormons reached Illinois where, along the banks of the Mississippi River, they settled in the town of Nauvoo. But here, too, the Mormons were disliked because of their religious teachings. In 1844, a mob of citizens murdered Joseph Smith. The Mormons once again left their homes to escape religious persecution.

The new Mormon leader, Brigham Young, decided to move his followers to the Far West, out of the reach of their enemies. He also reasoned that the best way to protect his followers from further attack would be to settle on unwanted land. Thus, Young and his band set out for Utah, where they built a new Mormon city at the Great Salt Lake.

By the late 1840's, the Mormons had turned the dry and burning Utah desert into healthy farmland. Water for crops was brought down from the Rocky Mountains. Under Young's leadership, the Mormon state of Deseret was formed, with its capital at Salt Lake City. The Mormons were at last free to follow their beliefs in peace. But elsewhere along the western frontier, peace was ended as Americans entered a major new war.

■ *Why did the Mormons leave their homes in Illinois?*

The War With Mexico. During the 1840's, America's spreading frontiers had brought our country into several important disputes with its neighbors. One of these disputes—the Oregon question—was settled peacefully. Others, however, led to growing trouble for the United States. As a result, our country's long-standing boundary quarrel with Mexico finally led to war in 1846.

Feelings between Mexico and the United States had been angry and bitter since the dispute over Texas. After the Lone Star Republic was established in 1836, Mexico's leaders felt that America had acted to help Texas against Mexico. Many Mexicans saw proof of this feeling when Texas was admitted into the United States in 1845.

The bad feelings between the two countries grew even worse when President Polk offered to buy California and New Mexico. The Mexican government refused to sell these valuable lands at any price. At the same time, Mexico prepared to go to war in order to defend itself against the United States. This was because Mexico believed that the United States would soon use soldiers to take the land that it wanted.

The outbreak of war came when American soldiers under General Zachary Taylor were stationed along the banks of the Rio Grande. The United States claimed that the Rio Grande marked the true dividing line between Mexico and Texas. From the Americans' point of view, General Taylor's soldiers were still on American soil. The Mexican government, however, stated that the real border between Texas and Mexico was the Nueces River to the north. For this reason, Mexico felt that its land had been invaded by Taylor's American army. When Mexican soldiers attacked General Taylor in April 1846, the United States answered with a declaration of war.

The war between Mexico and the United States took place on several fronts. For the most part, the American army was on the attack throughout the war. Three columns of

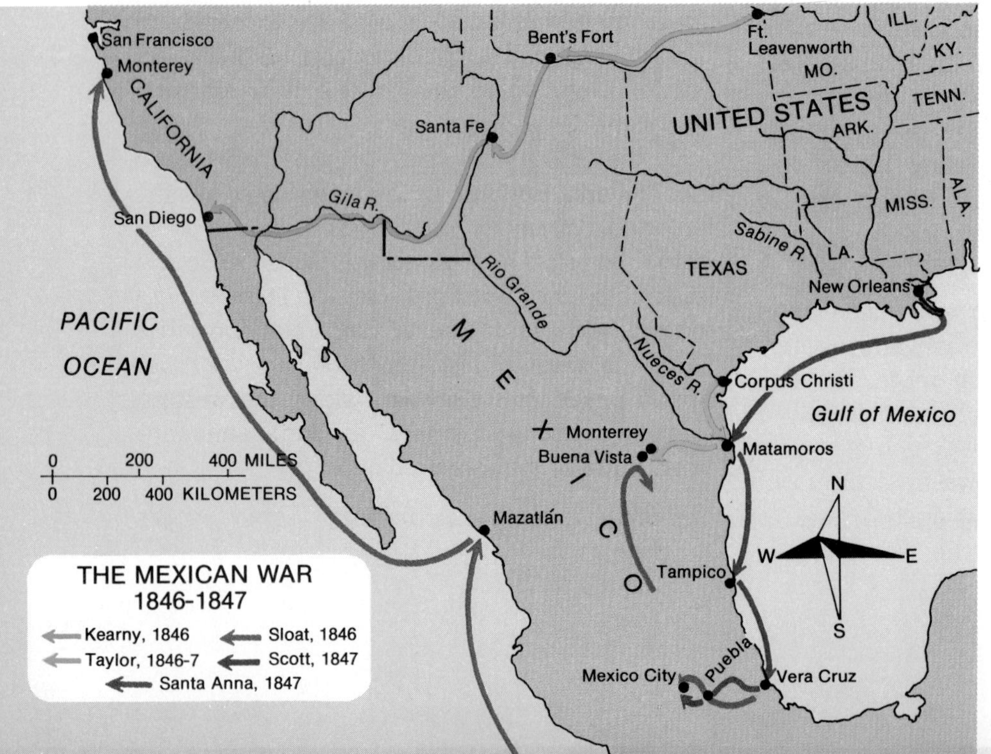

As a result of the excellent leadership of the American generals in the Mexican War, Mexico's army was quickly overwhelmed. In what city did the armies of Scott and Santa Anna meet in 1847?

U.S. soldiers moved into Mexican territory. One of these, under General Taylor, drove into Mexico from the north. In the months between September, 1846, and February, 1847, Taylor's forces won major victories at Monterrey and at Buena Vista. At about the same time, a second American column, led by Colonel Stephen W. Kearny, won control of New Mexico. Kearny then set out to take California. But American settlers in California had already overthrown their Mexican rulers. In January of 1847, the last of Mexico's soldiers were driven out, and the Republic of California was formed.

The end of the fighting in Mexico came late in 1847. A third American army, under General Winfield Scott, landed on the Mexican coast about 200 miles [320 kilometers] from Mexico City. Important battles at Vera Cruz and at Mexico City ended with American victories against heavy odds. Knowing that he was defeated, Mexico's ruler, General Santa Anna, asked for peace terms. In February 1848, the Treaty of Guadalupe Hidalgo was signed to end the war between the United States and Mexico.

The Treaty of Guadalupe Hidalgo added huge new lands to our country's growing frontiers. It was agreed that for the sum of $15 million, America would receive the Mexican provinces of California and New Mexico. This became known as the Mexican Cession of 1848. Moreover, the Rio Grande was recognized as the dividing line between Mexico and Texas. Thus, most of our country's present-day boundaries in the Southwest and in the Far West had been agreed upon by 1848. And the Mexican people who lived in the lands won by America were granted United States citizenship. These people contributed much to the richness of our country's culture.

Most Americans understood that their country had become far more wealthy because of the war with Mexico. But no one knew that the value of America's victory would soon be measured not only in land but also in gold.

■ *What new lands did America receive as a result of the Mexican Cession of 1848?*

The Gold Rush of 1849. The wealth of the new land that America gained from the Mexican War was soon matched by wealth of another kind. And because of this, the settlement of the Far West grew rapidly. At the same time, however, western settlement helped to further divide America along sectional lines.

In early 1848, gold was discovered at a sawmill belonging to John Sutter of California. Almost overnight, the news of gold in California spread throughout America. Soon, thousands of people headed westward in search of easy riches. Within a year, California was the scene of one of the greatest gold rushes in history.

Some people became rich, but most of those who went to California in the gold rush failed to find gold. Largely, this was because a great deal of money was needed to start large-scale mining. But most of the "forty-niners" had little money. They went to California hoping to find—not to spend—gold. For this reason, most of the California goldfields were soon taken over by business groups. Mining quickly became big business in California after 1849. Within a few years, millions of dollars' worth of gold was brought into the American economy by the mining companies.

The gold rush of 1849 brought thousands of Americans to the Far West in search of wealth and of opportunity. By 1850, there

(Text continues on page 237.)

RECALLING THE TIMES

Law and Order During the Gold Rush

Bayard Taylor was a journalist for the *New York Tribune* when he visited California at the height of the gold rush. He had been sent by his newspaper to write a series of articles about life in the goldfields. Taylor found that lawlessness was widespread in the mining camps. When Taylor returned to New York, he gathered his newspaper articles into a book entitled *El Dorado*. The excerpt below is taken from this book.

... In the absence of all law or available protection, the people met and adopted rules for their mutual security—rules adapted to their situation where they had neither guards nor prisons, and where the slightest license [freedom] given to crime or trespass of any kind must inevitably have led to terrible disorders. Small thefts were punished by banishment from the placers [the goldfields], while for those of large amount or for more serious crimes, there was the single alternative [choice] of hanging. These regulations, with slight change, had been continued up to the time of my visit to the country. In proportion as the emigration from our own States increased, and the digging community assumed a more orderly and intelligent aspect, their severity had been relaxed, though punishment was still strictly administered for all offences. There had been, as nearly as I could learn, not more than twelve or fifteen executions in all, about half of which were inflicted for the crime of murder. This awful responsibility had not been assumed [taken] lightly, but after a fair trial and a full and clear conviction, to which was added, I believe in every instance, the confession of the criminal.

Photri

Thinking Critically

What does Bayard Taylor describe in his article?

Why was it necessary for the miners to develop their own rules?

Do you think it was important for the miners to punish those who did not follow the rules? Why do you think so?

were well over 100,000 new settlers in California. Thus, it rapidly became clear that California would be the next state to enter the Union.

The news of California's coming statehood caused many Americans—especially southerners—to worry. California wanted to enter the Union as a free, or nonslave, state. The admission of California as a free state would upset the balance in Congress. At the time, there were 15 free states and 15 slave states in the Union. Therefore, many southerners began to believe that the war with Mexico had been a mistake for the South.

By 1850, it was clear that the discovery of gold in California had brought new riches to the United States. It had also drawn many thousands of new settlers to the growing lands of the West. But the gold rush also had caused problems. The disagreements between the sections of the country grew. And as California moved closer to statehood, these disagreements reached new and more-dangerous levels in America.

Which of America's sections feared California's coming statehood?

SECTION 3 REVIEW

1. *How did Mexico react to the stationing of American troops along the Rio Grande in 1846?*
2. *How did the gold rush of 1849 help to settle the Far West?*
3. *Why did many southerners come to feel that the war with Mexico was a mistake for the South?*

CHAPTER 13 SUMMARY

America in the years between 1837 and 1850 was in many ways a land of pioneers. During these years, the United States directed much of its attention and many of its resources toward the western frontiers. And by the early 1840's, many Americans believed that westward settlement was their country's "Manifest Destiny."

American aims in the West often led to border disputes with neighboring countries during the late 1830's and the 1840's. In some cases, border disputes brought about bad feelings and the threat of war. And as Americans moved further west, this danger became more and more real.

The settlers who reached the frontier came from many different backgrounds and for many different reasons. But most viewed the West as a land of promise and of opportunity. And many were willing to fight in order to open more of the West to settlement. In 1846, our country's expansion led to war with Mexico. Victory in the war with Mexico brought land and great wealth to our country. But western growth and settlement soon caused more unrest and trouble at home.

CHAPTER 13 REVIEW

USING YOUR SKILLS

Interpreting a Historical Map

The map below is an example of a *historical map*. Social scientists often use historical maps to learn more about the history or the political organization of an area. Historical maps can also show historical or political trends. This map shows the territorial growth of the United States from its independence to 1853. The map legend gives important information needed to fully understand the map. Study the map and answer the following questions:

1. According to the map legend, what color are the original 13 states? According to the map, what are the names of the original 13 states?
2. What color are the states of the Northwest Territory? Of the Oregon Territory? Of the Mexican Cession of 1848?
3. According to the map, what states were included in the annexation of Texas?
4. According to the map, what line separated present-day Nevada from the Oregon Territory? What treaty line separates the state of Maine from Canada?
5. According to the map legend, was the Gadsden Purchase part of the Mexican Cession of 1848? According to the map, what river marked the northern boundary of the Gadsden Purchase?

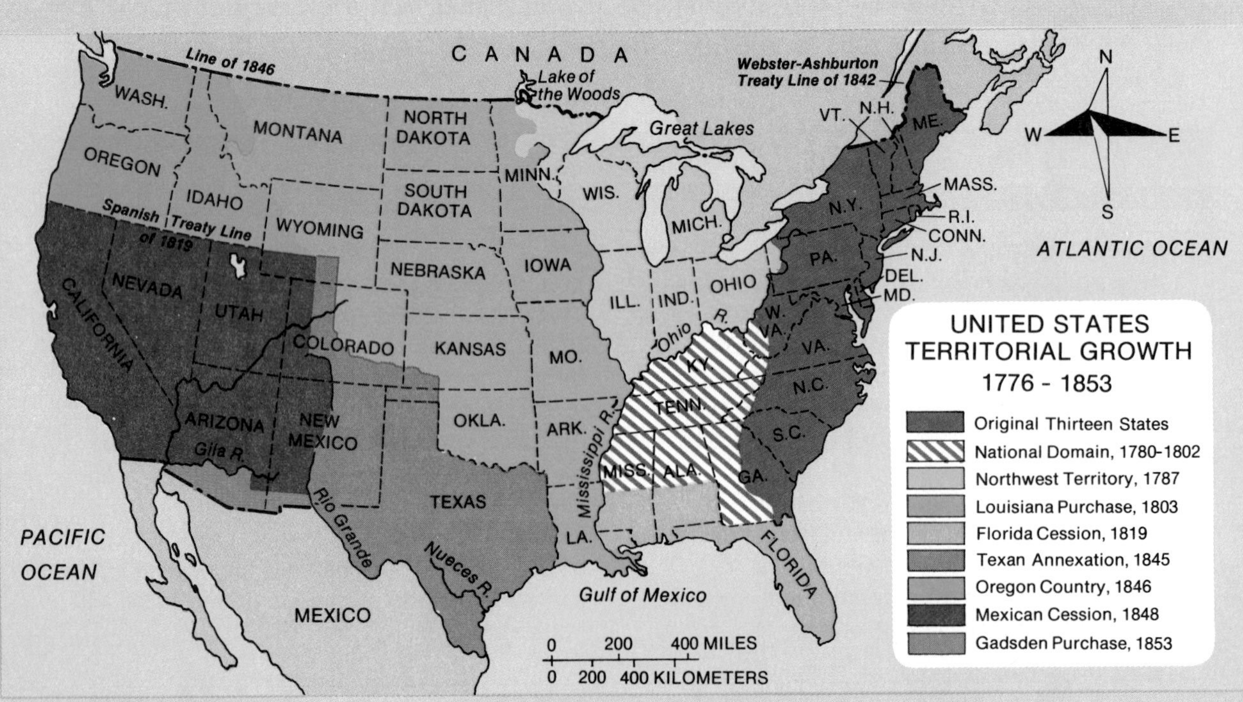

CHAPTER 13 REVIEW

YOU SHOULD KNOW

Identify, define, or explain each of the following:

symbol	Mormons
annexed	Nueces River
diplomatic relations	Mexican Cession

CHECKING FACTS

1. What three minerals were among the first to be mined in large quantities in the West?
2. When was the term *Manifest Destiny* first used in America?
3. Which group of people became the victims of America's westward expansion?
4. What country owned much of the Southwest and Far West during the early 1800's?
5. Who was Moses Austin?
6. What route did most pioneer families follow to Oregon?
7. When did Mexico win its independence from Spain?
8. Who was the leader of the Mormons who built a Mormon city at the Great Salt Lake?
9. In 1848, what river was recognized as the dividing line between Mexico and Texas?
10. What was discovered at a sawmill belonging to John Sutter of California?

UNDERSTANDING CONCEPTS

1. Why was the West able to offer settlers a new start in life?
2. In what ways was the doctrine of Manifest Destiny an expression of nationalism?
3. How was the Oregon Treaty of 1846 an example of compromise?
4. What event caused Mexico's leaders to believe that the United States had acted against their country during the War for Texan Independence?

LEARNING FROM ILLUSTRATIONS

1. Study the illustration on page 222. Why do you think the sluice was built at a downhill angle?
2. According to the map on page 230, from what two American cities did settlers traveling west probably begin their journey?

CRITICAL THINKING

1. If you had lived during the 1840's, would you have agreed with the idea of Manifest Destiny? Why or why not?
2. In your opinion, did the Mexican government have reason to refuse to sell its country's lands in California and in New Mexico to the United States government? Give reasons for your answer.
3. If you were living in 1849, would you have taken part in the gold rush? Why or why not?

ENRICHMENT ACTIVITIES

1. You might like to form a group to learn more about the "Mountain Men" who helped to open the Northwest and the Far West. Books and encyclopedia articles might have information on this topic. Your group might then prepare a poster-sized map of the Northwest and the Far West to show the trails opened by the Mountain Men.
2. You might like to find out more about some of the American soldiers who fought in the Mexican War. Information on important military figures of the Mexican War could be found in most encyclopedias. You might then present a brief classroom report.

1830 | 1840 | 1850

- 1831 William Lloyd Garrison founds the New England Anti-Slavery Society
- 1833 American Anti-Slavery Society formed
- 1846 The Wilmot Proviso defeated
- 1848 Zachary Taylor elected President
- 1850 Compromise of 1850

CHAPTER 14

The Growth of Sectionalism

Chapter Objectives

After studying this chapter, you will be able to:

- explain how the issue of slavery helped to increase sectional conflicts during the mid-1800's;
- discuss the differences between a sectional economy and a national economy;
- list the component acts of the Compromise of 1850 and its impact on sectional rivalry in the mid-1800's.

1 The Slavery Issue

Overview By about 1850, the question of owning slaves had become one of the most bitterly fought issues in our country's history. Slavery, perhaps more than any other institution, led to deep misunderstandings and to a long-lasting bitterness between the North and the South. Because slavery was largely a *southern* institution, it became a clear reminder of the differences that separated the North and the South. The slavery question made the differences between the North and South appear even greater than they really were.

Objectives After reading this section, you will be able to:

- identify the reasons that proslavery attitudes in the South became stronger between about 1820 and 1850;
- discuss the way that differing points of view helped to split the abolitionist movement;
- explain how abolitionism helped to build sectional tension in the mid-1800's.

Southern Attitudes Toward Slavery. Southern views toward slaveholding changed in many ways during the first 50 years of the 1800's. At one time, a sizable number of southerners favored the idea of *emancipation* —freedom—for slaves in America. As late as the 1820's, in fact, there were more emancipation groups in the South working to end slavery than there were in the North. At the same time, however, economic and social changes began to cause stronger proslavery feelings to spread throughout the South.

There were many reasons for the growth of southern proslavery feelings after about 1820. The need for more workers and the widespread fear of slave uprisings were among the most important of these reasons.

During the early 1800's, the South began to face a growing need for more workers. Southern plantation owners—who raised cash crops, such as cotton, tobacco, and sugar, on large farms—needed many field workers. But white southern farmers often chose to work on their own farms rather than to work for others. Moreover, the ongoing settlement of the southwestern frontier drew many southerners away from those areas of the South that most needed workers. Western settlement also helped to make southern farmers more independent and less willing to work for hire. Thus, planters had to find other, more-reliable sources of farm workers. Many planters, and factory owners as well, believed that slaveholding was the best and least costly way to meet their increased need for workers.

Early southern industry grew very slowly in the years before 1850. Nevertheless, factories and businesses that were started during this time also suffered from the need for workers. Like planters, southern business and factory owners often depended upon slaves to meet their labor needs. Many early southern factories, such as Richmond's Tredegar Iron Works, agreed to pay slave owners for the use of their slaves. Slaves also helped to build the early southern railroad network.

■ *Why did many southern factory owners favor slavery?*

Fear of Uprisings. Another cause of stronger proslavery feelings in the South after the early 1800's was the growing fear of slave uprisings. This fear was partly caused by a

Library of Congress

Illustrations, such as the one above, frequently appeared in the North during the 1850's. How did such illustrations help to influence public opinion against slavery?

bloody slave uprising that broke out in the 1790's on the French-owned island of Santo Domingo. News of the Santo Domingo uprising left a lasting impression on the minds of many southern slave owners.

Then, during the 1820's and the 1830's, word that major uprisings were being planned by American slaves spread throughout the South. Most of these stories were false, the products of fear and suspicion on the part of white slave owners. But several slave uprisings actually did take place in these years.

The fear of slave uprisings troubled many white southerners—slave owners and non-slave owners alike. Also, southern whites began to feel that slaves who gained their freedom might seek revenge against their onetime masters. The fear of slave uprisings and of revenge caused many southerners to call for greater restrictions on slaves. Because of this, harsh laws—called slave codes—were passed throughout the South after the 1820's. These laws placed strong controls upon the daily lives of all slaves. Slaveholding came to be viewed both as a system of work and as a basis for the southern way of life. And because slaveholding was seen as a way to keep the slaves under white control, proslavery feelings became stronger.

■ *Why were harsh southern slave codes passed after the 1820s?*

The Growth of Abolitionism. In the years after 1820, slavery rapidly became a fixed institution in the American South. The means used to organize slaves and to make them work differed little from one southern state to another. The state laws that governed the slaves' lives were also very much the same throughout the South. Because of this, southern slaveholding became both a system of work and a way of life for slaves and for slave owners alike. During these same years, however, opposition to slavery in America steadily became more powerful and more widespread.

The *abolitionist*—antislavery—movement began to grow in the 1830's. Among the first of the abolitionist leaders was William Lloyd Garrison of Boston. Throughout the 1830's, Garrison's newspaper, *The Liberator,* helped to spread word of the growing abolitionist movement and of its goals. And the New England Anti-Slavery Society—founded by Garrison in 1831—helped to center American's attention upon the cruelties of slavery.

Some early abolitionists, under Garrison's leadership, called for an *immediate* end to slavery. These people believed that slavery was an evil and immoral practice, one that should be outlawed without delay. Other abolitionists, however, did not agree with Garrison's demands. They felt that slavery could not be ended immediately because it was a fixed way of life in the South. These abolitionists favored the idea of a slow but steady ending of slavery. Among the most active of these gradual abolitionists were Theodore Weld and the Tappan brothers—Lewis and Arthur. In 1833, these abolitionists gathered to form the American Anti-Slavery Society.

■ *How did the New England Anti-Slavery Society work to oppose slavery?*

Split of the Abolitionist Movement. By the late 1830's, the abolitionists had become a leading American force for reform. But abolitionists were divided in their views toward emancipation. These differing views caused the abolitionist movement to divide. In 1839, those who agreed with Garrison's demands for immediate emancipation won control of the powerful American Anti-Slavery Society. This group of abolitionists became centered in the New England states. Some of its members—such as Lucretia Mott, Wendell Phillips, and Maria Chapman—made public speaking tours. They also worked to gain government support for their views.

Those abolitionists who favored more-gradual emancipation also acted to spread their beliefs. Theodore Weld, in particular, led a very able fight against slavery. Under Weld's leadership, several midwestern colleges—such as Western Reserve and Oberlin College—became centers for the abolitionist movement. Weld's teachings helped many students from these and other midwestern schools to become important members of the movement. Together with his wife, Angelina, Weld wrote *American Slavery As It Is,* a widely read attack upon slavery. And in 1850, Weld and other abolitionists were able to force Congress to outlaw the sale of slaves in Washington, D.C. This was a major victory for the abolitionists.

The work of abolitionists, such as Garrison and Weld, caused the fight against slaveholding to gain widespread public attention. Black abolitionists, such as Sojourner Truth and Frederick Douglass, helped to make this possible. Many of the black abolitionists were onetime slaves who had firsthand understanding of the evils of slavery. The movement also won growing political power, as the end of the slave trade in Washington proved. During the 1840's, the abolitionists formed the Liberty party, a political party that joined with the larger Free-Soil party in 1848. The Free-Soil

(Text continues on page 245.)

PROFILES

Henry Clay

Henry Clay was born in Virginia during the Revolutionary War. As a young man he headed for the western frontier. In 1803 he was elected to the Kentucky legislature, then to the U.S. Senate. As a Senator he battled for Federal funds for roads and canals, for Jefferson's manufacturing plans, and Madison's expansion into Florida. He switched to the House of Representatives and was elected Speaker of the House. As a "War Hawk" he pushed for the War of 1812. Clay then served on the peace negotiation committee to get the best land deal for the U.S.

The Granger Collection

By 1820 the dispute over the admission of Missouri as a slave state threatened to tear the young nation in half. Clay became famous for his ability to build the compromise of 1820. This admitted Maine as a free state and eased sectional tensions. Clay strengthened the tariffs protecting young northern and western industry, and then served as Secretary of State. In 1833 he defused the nullification crisis facing President Jackson, and in 1846 supported the Mexican War and the addition of the California territory to the country.

In 1849 the problem of extending slavery to the new territories again threatened to split the nation. Clay returned to the Senate and proposed and fought for what became known as the Compromise of 1850. Tensions eased, and civil war was postponed for a decade while northern and western industry and trade grew. Henry Clay had been making United States history for 73 years.

Thinking Critically

Why do you think Kentucky farmers and western frontiersmen would have liked what Clay did for them?

Tariffs seem like a boring subject. Why might northern and western Americans be excited about what the tariffs—taxes on foreign manufactured goods coming into the U.S.—could do for American manufacturing?

How did Henry Clay's ability to set goals and to get people to compromise make a difference in United States history?

party called for slavery to be outlawed in the western lands. Thus, by the mid-1800's, abolitionism had become a strong reform movement and a powerful political voice.

■ *In what major way did the abolitionist views of Garrison and of Weld differ?*

The Sectional Impact of Slavery. One damaging outgrowth of slavery was its tendency to destroy social and political exchange between the country's different parts. Because of this, slavery caused the sections to become more divided from one another. Moreover, Americans in one section began to hold false and unclear ideas about Americans in another section. Thus, slaveholding led to greater sectional tension and made the possibility of conflict within the country more real.

The South viewed the rise of northern abolitionism with great alarm. And by the mid-1800's, many southerners believed that the abolitionists spoke for all northerners. This widespread feeling was very dangerous. It caused southerners to feel that their way of life and their means of making a living were in danger. The abolitionists, of course, called for an end to slaveholding. But many southerners felt that the traditional life-style of the South depended upon slavery. Thus, a growing number of southerners began to think that abolitionism reflected a northern desire to destroy the South as a whole.

The abolitionist movement, however, did not speak for most northerners in the mid-1800's. By 1850, in fact, there were only about 200,000 abolitionists throughout the entire North. Most northerners either did not greatly care about slavery or believed that it would end without outside interference. Because of this, many northerners could not understand why the South felt threatened. Southern distrust and suspicion angered some northerners. Thus, more northerners began to agree with some of the abolitionists' views.

The sectional differences caused by slaveholding grew from misunderstanding and fear. Abolitionists attacked southern slavery because they believed that slaveholding was a cruel and immoral way of life. Southerners acted by defending slavery and by feeling distrust toward northerners in general. Many northerners, in turn, were angered by what they felt to be unfair southern views of the North. Thus, differing sectional feelings toward slavery caused bitterness to grow rapidly between the North and the South.

■ *How did slavery cause the sections to become increasingly isolated?*

SECTION 1 REVIEW

1. *What effect did the settlement of the southwestern frontier have upon the southern labor force between 1820 and 1850?*
2. *How did William Lloyd Garrison and his followers generally view slavery?*
3. *Why did many southerners feel that abolitionism reflected a desire on the part of the North to destroy the South?*

2 Economic Issues

Overview The economic activities of America's three sections—North, South, and West—differed in many ways during the 1840's. These differences sometimes led to cooperation and to healthy competition among the parts of the country. But at times, these differences caused anger and bitterness to grow in America.

Even with these differences, however, the American economy moved forward. Factories and farms stepped up their output to meet the growing country's needs. And important technological changes made life better for many Americans.

Objectives After reading this section, you will be able to:

- identify the factors that caused sectional economies of the early 1800's to become a single, national economy during the mid-1800's;
- describe how technological improvements helped to strengthen the economy during the 1840's;
- explain how changing economic conditions affected relations among the sections.

The Economy Before 1850. Before the mid-1800's, America's economy was really little more than a loosely knit group of sectional economies. That is, each part of the country had its own economy, largely separate from the economies of the other parts. Close trade and business ties among the sections were few. Trade was generally limited to a few kinds of raw materials, foods, and finished goods.

The United States at this time was still very much a farming country. Most Americans worked either to raise or to trade farming goods. Only in the Northeast was there any clear move away from farming, toward industry and manufacturing.

The factories of the Northeast generally made goods for local markets, rather than for sale throughout the country. Most of these northeastern factories were small, fairly simple businesses. As late as 1849, most northeastern factories employed fewer than eight workers. Often, factory owners worked beside their employees. Therefore, there was generally little real social difference between owners and their workers.

Before the mid-1800's, American trade goods sent overseas most often took the form of raw materials. Most American exports were farm goods of some sort, chiefly cotton and wheat. Most finished goods bought by Americans in the 1840's still had to be brought from overseas.

By about the mid-1840's, however, America's economy began to change. This change came about as the different parts of the country slowly began to depend upon one another for their needs. Slowly, each section began to make trade goods—food, raw materials, and finished goods—for sale throughout the country. Because of this, economic ties among the sections steadily became closer and stronger during the mid-1800's. Closer ties brought about an American economy that was national—rather than sectional—in character.

■ *What kind of economy gradually developed in America during the mid-1800's?*

Elements of a National Economy. The growth of a national economy in America was a slow but steady process, lasting many years.

I.N. Phelps Stokes Collection, Prints Division, New York Public Library, Astor, Lenox and Tilden Foundation

Utica, New York, was one of several cities along the Erie Canal that grew as a manufacturing and trade center during the mid-1800's.

As the economy became more national during the mid-1800's, several major trends began to appear. The growing importance of manufacturing, improved technology, and new business methods were among these trends.

As our country's economy became more national, its growth began to depend more upon manufacturing and less upon farming. By the late 1840's, manufacturing was rapidly becoming one of the more important parts of the United States economy. Nevertheless, most goods made in American factories during the mid-1800's were manufactured from farm crops. These included cotton cloth, flour, and ground meal. Many other important goods—such as ready-made clothing, spun wool, and lumber—also depended upon farm output for their raw materials.

However, American manufacturing could not have grown beyond a local level without an equal growth in the country's transportation network. A means of transportation was needed to bring raw materials to factories and to deliver finished factory goods to market. During the 1840's, therefore, America's rail and canal networks were greatly improved. In 1830, for example, 1,277 miles [2 043 kilometers] of canal had been built in the United States. Only ten years later, there were 3,326 miles [5 322 kilometers] of canal, with hundreds of miles more being built. Most of these canals were built in the middle Atlantic states and in the growing Midwest.

■ *Why did American manufacturing need a transportation network to grow?*

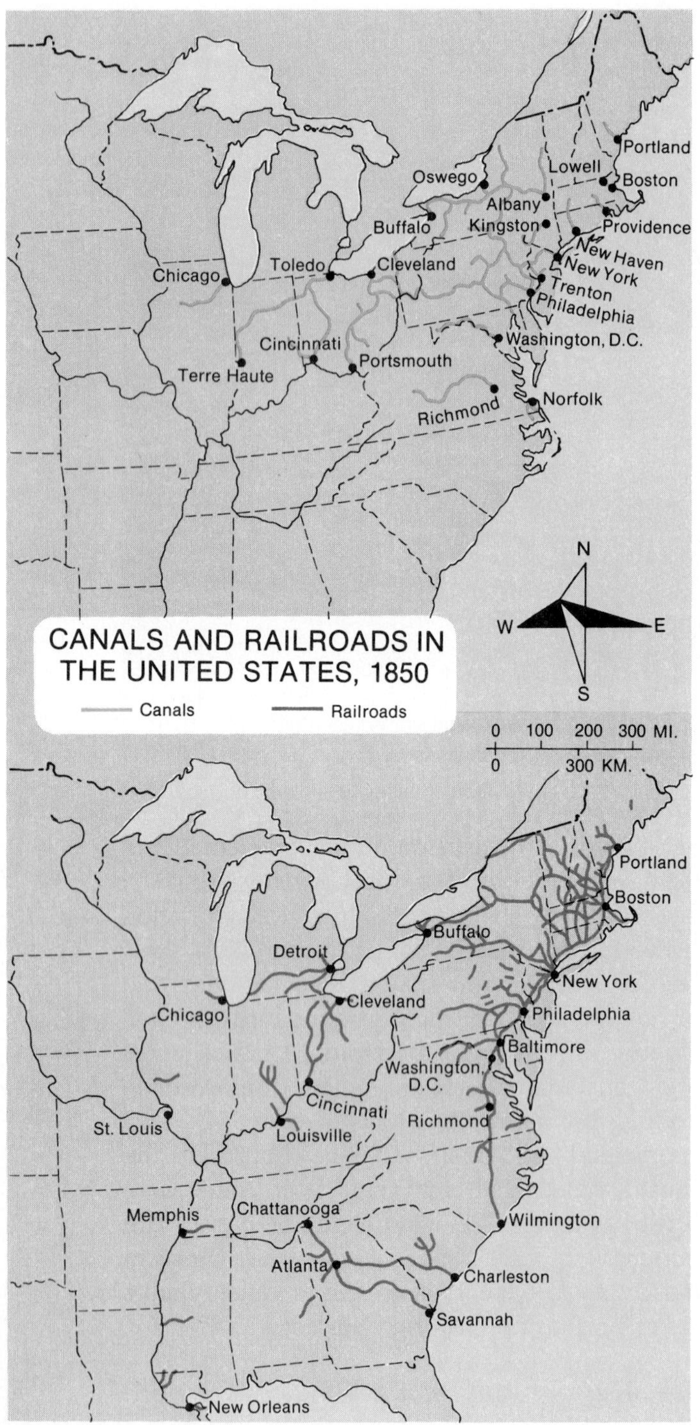

By 1850, many canals and railroads had been built in the United States. The development of these canal and rail systems helped to tie the West to the markets of the East. As a result, the South became increasingly isolated from the rest of the country. In what part of the country were most of the canals and railroads located?

America's Railroads. One of the most important improvements in American transportation was the growth of the country's railroad network. The first railroads to be built in the United States were begun in the 1820's. These were simple rail lines, often using wooden rails and horse-drawn engines and passenger cars. However, these early railroads did not compare with canals in terms of how much they could haul.

During the 1830's and the 1840's, however, railroad technology was rapidly improved. The use of iron rails, of gravel roadbeds, and of stronger steam engines added greatly to the amount of freight that railroads could carry. Improved understanding of steam power and better boiler- and engine-building techniques allowed railroads to travel over longer routes. By 1848, nearly 6,000 miles [9 600 kilometers] of railroad track had been built in the United States. Most of these rail lines were in the Northeast and in the middle Atlantic states. Within the next 10 years, however, several rail lines crossed the Mississippi River. And by 1860, Chicago had become one of America's fastest-growing rail centers.

Thus, the railroads and our canal network helped to tie the country together. And this, in turn, helped to make our American economy stronger.

Where were most rail lines built during the 1830's and 1840's?

Museum of the City of New York

Historical Pictures Service

During the mid-1800's, improved transportation methods helped to make travel easier and much faster. Wood-burning steamboats and trains made the transportation of goods and people faster and less expensive. But horsepower still remained the most common form of transportation in America.

The J.B. Speed Art Museum

Improved Business Methods. Another change that helped to speed the breakdown of sectional economic barriers was the growth of better business methods. During the 1840's, many businesses grew in size and in output. Moreover, businesses generally came to depend more upon the use of machines in these years. And they also became more *specialized.* That is, some businesses no longer made many different kinds of finished goods. Instead, they worked to make a single product in large numbers. During the 1840's, business leaders also worked to bring about new credit reporting measures. Thus, sellers would know if their customers could be trusted to repay their loans.

Improved ways of doing business led to greater exchange among business leaders throughout the country. This, in turn, helped to break down sectional barriers. But as the economy grew, different needs and goals among the country's parts once again began to lead to new troubles.

■ *How did the growth of better business methods break down sectional barriers?*

Sectional Economic Issues. The spread of America's transportation network during the mid-1800's helped to cause new sectional differences. Canals and railroads were generally built from east to west, from northern factory centers to western markets. Thus, canals and railroads helped to bring about closer trade and business ties between the North and the West. But the South did not always share in these growing ties. Fewer railroads and canals were built in the South than in the North. In some ways, the spread of a transportation network caused the South to become more economically separated from the other sections of the country.

Differences also arose over certain government economic policies. Views toward tariffs, toward the sale of public lands, and toward government domestic improvements, such as harbors and roads, differed greatly in the North, the South, and the West. This was because laws that helped one part of the country sometimes hurt the others. High protective tariffs, for example, helped the growth of northern factories and business. At the same time, however, these tariffs often caused prices to rise in the South and in the West. Because of this, most southerners and many westerners were against trade and tax laws that helped the North. Other government plans that favored one part of the country over the others also led to differences.

■ *What were two causes for the new sectional tensions of the mid-1800's?*

The Problem of Slavery. Slaveholding, however, remained the greatest cause of sectional trouble during the mid-1800's. This was because slaveholding was an economic—as well as a social—way of life. The South depended upon slave workers to provide a large part of the labor needed for its economic growth. Thus, when northern abolitionists attacked slavery, they also attacked the southern economy as a whole. This caused great bitterness on the part of slave owners. And as the attack upon slaveholding became more powerful, most southerners moved to protect their economy by defending slavery.

Looking back, it seems that slavery cost the South a great deal of money that might better have been used to help its economy grow. This was because each slave stood for a large

Some idealized illustrations of southern slave life portrayed slaves enjoying moments of relaxation with their masters. In reality, slaves were forced to spend many hours working each day, and they received few holidays.

North Carolina Museum of Art, Raleigh

outlay of the slave owner's money. This money could have been spent on new factories, on transportation, and on improved technology. Because of slaveholding, therefore, the southern economy did not have the means to move ahead and to compete with the North in many ways. This fact, too, caused ill feelings to grow between the North and the South. Within a few short years, major political differences between the two parts of the country grew.

What was probably the greatest cause of sectional trouble during the mid-1800's?

SECTION 2 REVIEW

1. *For what reasons did a national economy develop in the United States during the mid-1800's?*
2. *How did the improvement of railroads and canal networks help to make the American economy stronger?*
3. *Why were northern abolitionists attacking the southern economy when they attacked slavery?*

3 The Compromise of 1850

Overview The slavery question was clearly the most important political difference to be faced by Americans in the mid-1800's. Political ideas about slaveholding were based upon two major questions: Should slavery be allowed at all in the United States? And, if so, should it be allowed to spread freely throughout the country? By the mid-1800's, some Americans believed that the slave issue could not be settled until these two questions were finally answered.

Another political question of the mid-1800's was the matter of western settlement. Many Americans were not prepared for the political differences that arose when these new lands were brought into the Union.

Objectives After reading this section, you will be able to:

- describe how the slavery issue was tied to the problem of frontier expansion;
- explain the role that political parties played in the sectional conflict of the late 1840's;
- analyze the way that the Compromise of 1850 affected sectional rivalry in the mid-1800's.

Slavery and the West. Following the Mexican War of 1846–1848, rich new lands were opened to American settlement. Almost before the last gun was silenced, thousands of pioneer families began to pour into these huge western lands. And when gold was discovered in California in 1848, thousands more moved westward to seek their fortunes.

The settlers who flooded into the Far West and the Southwest during the late 1840's were searching for a new life. But these Americans brought old habits and old ways of life with them. In many cases, this meant that they reached the West with strongly held ideas about slavery. Some of these settlers were slave owning southerners who brought their slaves with them. Others were northern abolitionists who were willing to fight to keep slavery out of the new western lands. Most of the new settlers, however, only wanted the right to decide for themselves whether the western lands would enter the Union as free states or as slave states.

The question of slavery in the newly opened lands of the West had never been settled in a satisfactory way. The Missouri Compromise of 1820 had outlawed slavery in the lands north and west of Missouri's southern border. But this law had broken down by the 1840's. Then, the Mexican War opened the question of western slavery once again.

Soon after the Mexican War began in 1846, a bill to outlaw slave owning in any land won from Mexico came up in Congress. The author of this bill was David Wilmot, a member of Congress from Pennsylvania. The *Wilmot Proviso,* as it was called, was angrily defeated by southern leaders in the Senate. But the bill proved that some government leaders, backed by many voters, were prepared to fight against the westward spread of slavery.

The problem of western slavery gained widespread public attention after the Mexican War ended in 1848. At the heart of the matter was the question of territorial rights. Did the people of a territory have the right to decide —before statehood was granted—if they would allow slave owning? Or did the people have to wait until statehood was granted to say if their state was to be a free state or a slave state? These questions became major issues during the late 1840's.

What was the real significance of the Wilmot Proviso of 1846?

Parties and Their Leaders. The slavery question and the rights of Americans in the western lands were among the major political questions of the 1840's. Our country's government leaders and their parties worked hard to find answers to these problems. However, by the mid-1800's the major parties were deeply divided. Views toward slaveholding, western rights, and other questions differed greatly, even among members of the same party.

The two most powerful political parties of the 1840's were the Democratic party and the Whig party. The Democrats based many of their beliefs upon the ideas of Thomas Jefferson and of Andrew Jackson. But these ideas were sometimes viewed in different ways by many Democrats according to their sectional loyalties. Southern Democrats, such as John C. Calhoun, generally favored the ideas of states' rights and of a weak federal government. On the other hand, Democrats from the North and the West, such as Stephen A. Douglas of Illinois, often favored broad federal powers. In addition, the slave question sometimes divided Democrats along sectional lines.

The Bettmann Archive

The Bettmann Archive

Senator Stephen A. Douglas (top) of Illinois was a leader of northern Democrats during the 1840's and helped to frame the Compromise of 1850. During the mid-1800's, political parties became divided over sectional issues and often ran separate candidates for the presidency, as campaign posters of the period show.

DO YOU KNOW?

How did the Whig party get its name?

The Whig party in America took its name from a Scottish word—*whiggamore.* During the 1600's, British opponents of royal power were called whiggamores. These people formed a political party—the Whig party. Eventually, American colonists who wanted independence from Great Britain also became known as Whigs. The term was forgotten after the American Revolution. But in the early 1830's, President Andrew Jackson's political enemies joined forces to build a new Whig party. Jackson's opponents called themselves Whigs because they claimed that the President thought of himself as a king.

The Whig party—the second major party—had come into being during the early 1830's. From the first, the Whig party was loosely organized and was made up of voters who held widely differing political views. In general, Whigs believed in the need for a strong federal government. However, they often failed to agree on certain questions, such as tariffs and slaveholding. Among the leading Whigs of the 1840's were Henry Clay of Kentucky and Daniel Webster of Massachusetts. The Whigs—under the leadership of Clay, Webster, and others—made up a powerful force in the country's government. But during these years, the Whigs—like the Democrats—were often divided in their views toward sectional questions.

■ *What were the two leading political parties in America during the 1840's?*

Issues That Divided the Country. Most southerners in the late 1840's strongly favored the spread of slaveholding into the new western lands. They believed that the westward expansion of slavery would help to tie the West more closely to the South. Moreover, it was felt that the spread of slavery into the West would add greatly to southern political and economic power. Finally, most southern leaders believed that the territories—rather than Congress—should decide if slavery was to be allowed within their lands. This view was in keeping with the southern idea of states' rights. It also was based upon the knowledge that many southerners had settled in the new western lands. Most of these southerners were expected to vote for slavery.

Northerners, on the other hand, were more divided in their views toward the question of western slaveholding. Some thought that slavery should be allowed in the western lands, but only if the settlers themselves agreed. Others were bitterly against any westward spread of slaveholding and called for it to be outlawed in all new western lands. However, many northerners believed that Congress should settle the question through compromise. Under such a compromise, both sides would agree to give up some of their goals in return for a fair settlement.

■ *Why did most southerners favor the westward expansion of slavery in the 1840's?*

The Election of 1848. The westward spread of slavery and the rights of territorial citizens in the West were the major issues that faced American voters in 1848. But at this important crossroads in America's history, our government's leaders failed to offer sound answers to the questions.

Both the Whigs and the Democrats feared that a strong stand on these questions might anger some voters. For this reason, both parties refused to make clear statements on their views toward slaveholding and toward territorial rights. The Whigs' platform said nothing about these issues. General Zachary Taylor, the Whig candidate for office, was a hero of the Mexican War. But Taylor had no background in government, and his ideas toward the issues were largely unknown. The Democrats, on the other hand, ran Senator Lewis Cass, a westerner and a longtime government leader, for the presidency. Cass felt that western citizens should decide if slaveholding was to be allowed within their lands. But this view was not made a part of the Democratic party's platform. Thus, neither party offered real answers to the questions that faced Americans in 1848.

Many northerners were unhappy with the parties' failure to take a stand on the issues. Because of this, some northerners, in company with many abolitionists, gathered together to form the Free-Soil party. The Free-Soilers—whose real goal was to outlaw western slaveholding—called upon one-time President Martin Van Buren to serve as their candidate.

In a close race, General Zachary Taylor, the Whig favorite, won victory in the election of 1848. During his term in office, Taylor proved to be an honest President who worked to quiet

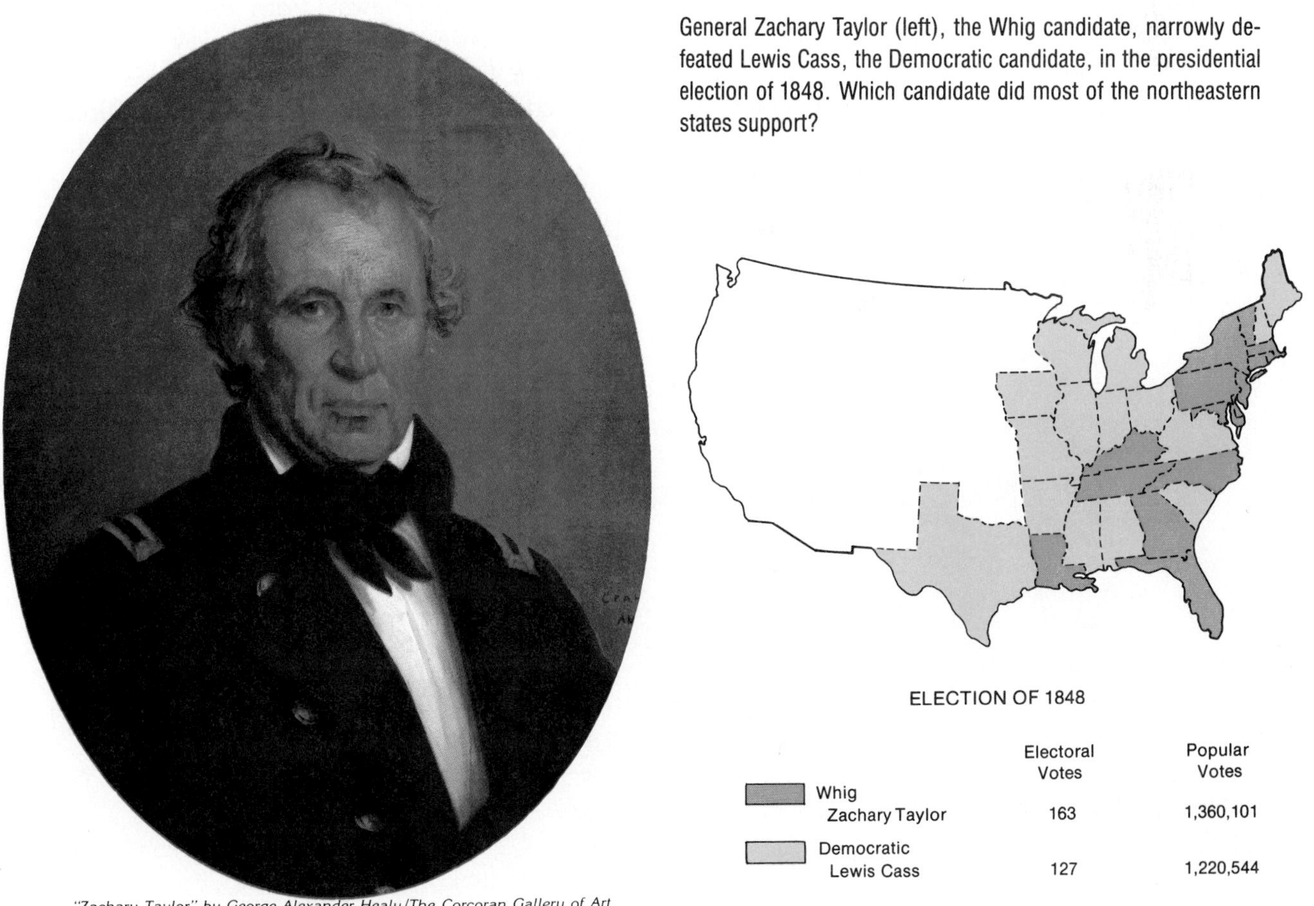

General Zachary Taylor (left), the Whig candidate, narrowly defeated Lewis Cass, the Democratic candidate, in the presidential election of 1848. Which candidate did most of the northeastern states support?

"Zachary Taylor" by George Alexander Healy/The Corcoran Gallery of Art

sectional differences. But in general, Taylor was not able to offer the strong leadership America needed to answer the slavery question. Within two years, the problem of slaveholding once again gained the attention of Americans throughout the land.

■ *What were the major issues that faced American voters in 1848?*

Compromise of 1850. The election of 1848 had failed to settle the questions of slavery and of territorial rights. But this did not mean western growth was slowed. During the next two years, thousands of Americans moved westward. California was among the most rapidly settled of the western lands, thanks in part to the gold rush of 1849. And by the end of 1849, California was prepared to enter the Union as a free state.

But California's desire to gain statehood troubled many southerners. With the entry of another free state into the Union, the balance between free states and slave states in the Senate would be upset. This would cause the South to lose its equal voice in the country's government. For this reason, southerners acted against California's call for statehood. Some southern leaders, such as John C. Calhoun, began to say that the South could protect itself only by *seceding*—breaking away—from the Union.

Southern anger over the California question led to one of the greatest dangers yet faced by the United States. Some southerners were prepared to break away from the rest of the country in order to protect their way of life. At the same time, many northerners were ready to defend California's right to enter the Union as a free state. A satisfactory agreement be-

The Compromise of 1850 allowed the westward extension of slavery into the New Mexico and Utah territories if a majority of the voters in the territories agreed. What territory was not affected by the Compromise of 1850?

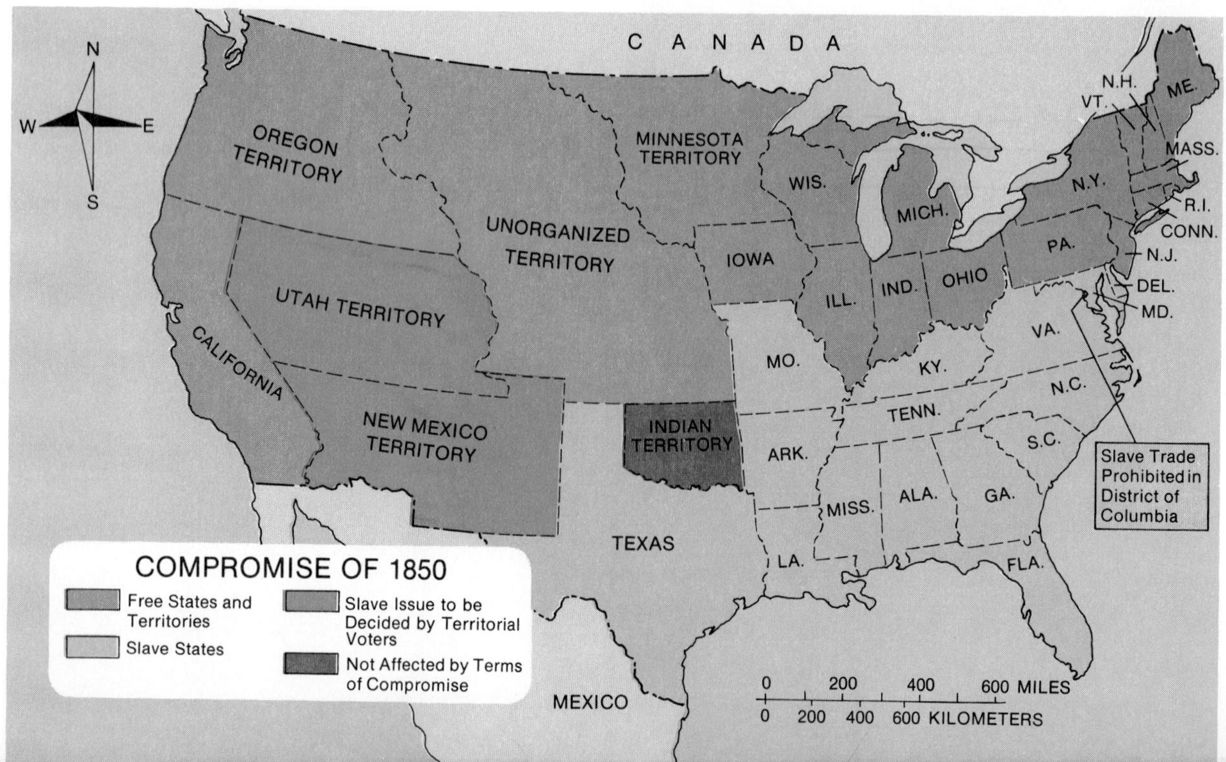

tween North and South at first seemed impossible.

But in 1850, a settlement was reached, largely through the work of Henry Clay, Daniel Webster, and Stephen Douglas. This settlement took the form of five laws passed by Congress during August and September of 1850. These laws offered some gains for both the North and the South. For example, a strong fugitive slave act was passed to stop slaves from escaping to the North. The boundaries of Texas were finally settled, with Texas receiving $10 million in payment for land given to New Mexico. At the same time, California was granted statehood as a free state. And the slave trade was outlawed in Washington, D.C. Together, these laws became known as the Compromise of 1850.

Neither the North nor the South was altogether happy with this settlement. For a time, however, the Compromise of 1850 ended talk of southern secession. The Union was saved. But deep sectional differences remained.

■ *Why did southerners feel threatened by the admission of California into the Union?*

SECTION 3 REVIEW

1. *What bill, introduced in 1846, attempted to outlaw slavery in lands won during the Mexican War?*
2. *In what ways did southern Democrats generally differ from northern Democrats during the 1840's?*
3. *How did the Compromise of 1850 attempt to solve sectional differences?*

CHAPTER 14 SUMMARY

The late 1840's were years during which the country's different sections became more sharply divided over the slave question. In fact, this question became the chief cause of sectional trouble in these years. Southerners in the 1840's began to view slaveholding as both a right and a need. A growing number of northerners, on the other hand, began to join together in the fight against slaveholding.

Despite the differences caused by the slave question, however, America's economic growth in the mid-1800's helped to draw the country together. The birth of a national economy in the 1840's led to the breakdown of some sectional barriers. But even this was not enough to erase the anger brought about by the slave question.

The ongoing settlement of the West also brought about deep sectional differences during the 1840's. As new western lands called for statehood, Americans began to fear that the balance between free states and slave states would be destroyed. The Compromise of 1850 helped to quiet these fears for a while. But it did little to settle the matter of slavery.

CHAPTER 14 REVIEW

USING YOUR SKILLS

Interpreting Circle Graphs

The circle graphs on this page illustrate one method used to visually portray statistical data. Circle graphs are often used in series to show statistical comparisons of data. In this case, each complete circle represents 100 percent of America's work force in a given year. The circles are then divided to show changes in the percentage of farm and nonfarm workers in the work force between 1820 and 1860.

1. What does each complete circle in the series of circle graphs represent? What statistical data is being compared in each circle graph?
2. Which group of workers—farm or nonfarm—made up the majority of America's labor force in 1820? Which group made up the majority of the labor force in 1840?
3. Which group of workers—farm or nonfarm—made up the minority of America's labor force in 1830? In 1850?
4. During which year portrayed by the graphs was the number of nonfarm workers the least?
5. During which year—1820 or 1860—was the number of farm workers greater? During which year portrayed by the graphs was the number of nonfarm workers the greatest?
6. According to the circle graphs, what happened to the number of farm workers in America between 1820 and 1860?

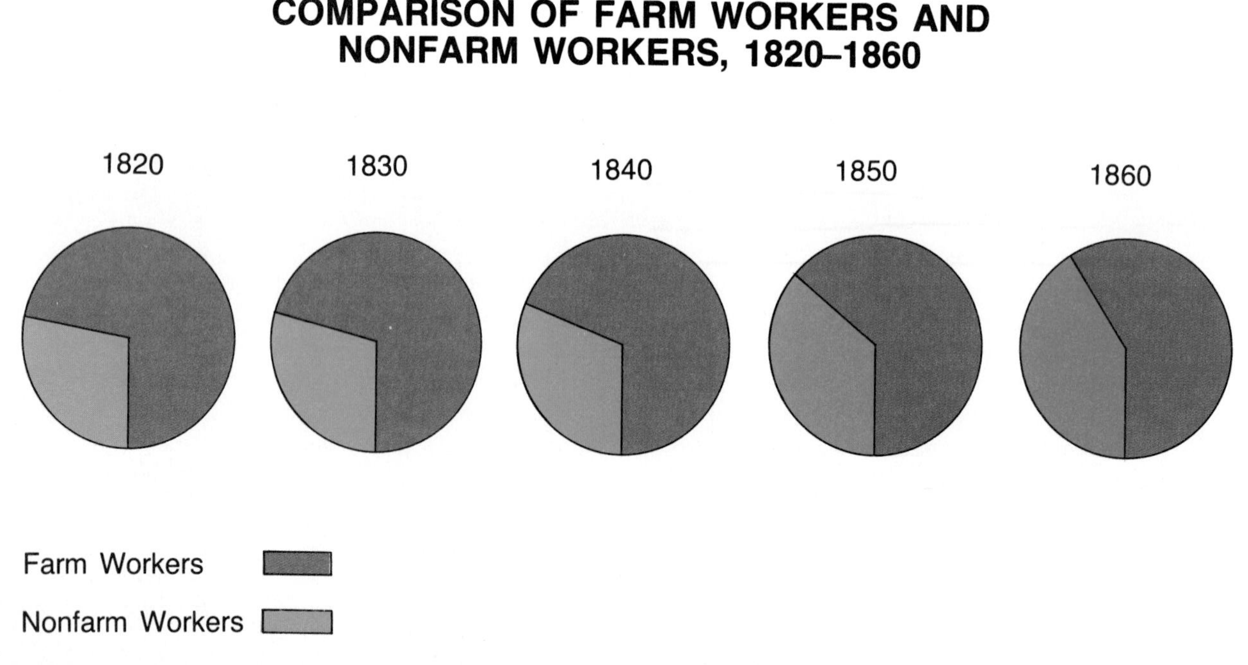

CHAPTER 14 REVIEW

YOU SHOULD KNOW

Identify, define, or explain each of the following:

emancipation	specialized
Theodore Weld	Whig party
trade goods	seceding

CHECKING FACTS

1. What did early abolitionists, under the leadership of William Lloyd Garrison, call for?
2. What kind of emancipation did Theodore Weld favor?
3. When did America's economy begin to change from a sectional economy to a national economy?
4. In what part of the country were most of the canals built in the 1840's?
5. What was one of the most important improvements in American transportation in the 1840's?
6. What part of the country favored high protective tariffs?
7. What did the Wilmot Proviso attempt to do?
8. What were the two most powerful political parties of the 1840's?
9. During which presidential election did both major political parties intentionally ignore the major issues?
10. Who were the three people involved in developing the Compromise of 1850?

UNDERSTANDING CONCEPTS

1. How did the slave revolt on the island of Santo Domingo influence southern attitudes toward slavery?
2. According to many southerners, how did the antislavery movement threaten the economy of the South?
3. What effect did the development of improved methods of transportation have upon American manufacturing?
4. Why did California's request for statehood cause some southern leaders to call for secession during the late 1840's?

LEARNING FROM ILLUSTRATIONS

1. Based on the illustration on page 242, why might you conclude that the artist did not support the Fugitive Slave Act?
2. Study the map on page 256. What territories were able to decide the issue of slavery by popular sovereignty?

CRITICAL THINKING

1. Would you have favored immediate or gradual abolition of slavery? Give reasons for your answer.
2. Do you think that the question of slavery in the territories would have best been decided by territorial voters? Why do you think so?
3. In your opinion, would stronger leadership in government have answered and resolved the slavery question in the United States in the mid-1800's? Explain your answer.

ENRICHMENT ACTIVITIES

1. You might like to form a group to conduct further research on the construction of early railroads in America. Information can be found in books and encyclopedia articles. Your group could then make a map to show railroad routes before 1850.
2. On a map of the United States, draw in the major industrial areas of the North and the major agricultural areas of the South in 1850. Display your map on the bulletin board.

1850 1855 1860

- 1852 Franklin Pierce elected President; *Uncle Tom's Cabin* published by Harriet Beecher Stowe
- 1853 Gadsden Purchase
- 1854 Kansas-Nebraska Act; Republican Party founded
- 1856 James Buchanan elected President; Lawrence, Kansas, attacked by proslavery forces
- 1857 *Dred Scott v. Sandford*
- 1858 Lincoln-Douglas debates
- 1859 John Brown's raid on Harpers Ferry

CHAPTER 15

Debate and Compromise

Chapter Objectives

After studying this chapter, you will be able to:

- list the major contrasts between northern life-styles and southern life-styles in the 1850's;
- identify the major developments that contributed to the growth of a distinctly American culture by the mid-1800's;
- explain why the Compromise of 1850 failed to resolve sectional conflicts and list the main results of this failure.

1 Society and Sectionalism

Overview The differences caused by the slavery question and by territorial rights in the West troubled and divided Americans throughout the 1850's. Changing northern and southern life-styles also pointed to the growing gulf that, more and more, separated the two sections. By the mid-1800's, life in the North was very different than life in the South in many ways.

Objectives After reading this section, you will be able to:

- identify the forces that changed northern life-styles during the mid-1800's;
- discuss how the growth of industrial prosperity influenced northern life in the 1850's;
- explain why social reforms were slower to come to the South than to the North.

Social Change in the North. In the mid-1800's, life in the North was shaped, in part, by two important forces. One of these was the ongoing rise of business. This rise brought wealth and power to the North. The other was the growing number of Europeans who came to America—chiefly to the northern states—in search of new opportunities.

The 1850's generally were good years in the North. Northern factories turned out finished goods at record rates to keep pace with the country's growing needs. The demand for goods meant that more jobs were open to workers in the North. However, working conditions in factories were poor in the 1850's. Working conditions often were dangerous and unhealthy. And the average factory worker was paid only about $260 a year.

During the 1850's, there was a greater use of machine power in northern factories. These machines helped to bring about increased rates of production. Thus, a greater number and variety of northern factory goods reached American markets in the 1850's than ever before.

What development helped to bring about increased production rates in northern factories?

The Growth of Immigration. The rise of industrialization in America drew thousands of *immigrants*—settlers from other lands—who hoped to enter the growing work force. Each year, the number of people entering the country rose to new levels. Between 1850 and 1860, more than 2 million people—largely from northwestern Europe—crossed the Atlantic to settle in America. During the same decade, nearly 35,000 people came from China to settle along the Pacific coast. Some of the new immigrants from Europe and from Asia came in search of political or religious freedom. Others came to escape the poverty and the hardships they had known in their native lands. In almost every case, these new settlers came to America to build a better life for themselves and their families.

The largest number of European immigrants settled in the North and the West. This was because factory jobs and farmland were more available in these areas than in the South, where slave labor and large plantations existed. After 1848, some Chinese immigrants came to California in search of gold, and their contribution to the mining of this new source of wealth was invaluable. Many Chinese also

Immigrants Landing at the Battery, 1885 (Detail) by Samuel Waugh, Museum of the City of New York

Many ships from Europe brought thousands of immigrants to a new life in America. Many immigrants paid fares as low as 30 dollars for the Atlantic crossing during the mid-1800's. How would you describe conditions on the ships?

came to work in other industries. The Chinese were noted for their honesty, hard work, and intelligence, and they played an important role in the development of America's western areas.

American society gained much from the immigrants who reached our shores during the 1850's. The immigrants from Asia and from Europe brought new ideas and new ways of doing things to their adopted home. Some immigrants, for example, were skilled workers or farmers. Others had been trained as teachers, as writers, or as artists. As a result, both the North and the West gained a larger work force and an improved quality of life.

From what part of Europe did most immigrants come during the 1850's?

The Impact of Industrialization. The prosperity brought about by industrialization led to many far-reaching changes in northern life during the 1850's. One of the most important of these changes was that the middle class became larger and more powerful in the North. This was because a growing number of northerners found jobs in factories, in shops, and in offices. These jobs usually paid higher wages and led to a better standard of living.

In general, it was believed that, by working hard and by learning new skills, people in the North could improve their way of life. Education, for example, was seen as one of the best ways to move up in society. This was because people who attended school were generally better able to deal with the needs of factory and office jobs. They were *literate*—able to read and to write—and they had other skills needed in an industrializing society. Not surprisingly, the number of public schools in the North grew rapidly during the 1850's.

The growth of schools in the North meant

that reading and writing were no longer for the wealthy alone. In the mid-1800's, more and more middle-class northerners began to enjoy reading—both for pleasure and for information. At the same time, better printing presses and improved bookmaking methods cut the cost of reading materials. Newspapers were highly popular during these years. The world's largest daily newspaper, the New York *Herald,* reached sales of 70,000 copies each day by 1860.

Education for young women, however, was limited. And black Americans rarely had a chance to attend school, either in the North or in the South.

■ *Why did the number of public schools in the North grow rapidly in the 1850's?*

The Results of Prosperity. By the mid-1800's, the North had become a literate society. A growing number of people were able to receive at least some amount of schooling. Theaters, libraries, and museums were more widely attended, especially in the growing northern cities.

At the same time, industrial prosperity meant that more people could live comfortably. In many cases, the growing number of factory goods found in northern markets helped people to live in greater comfort. For example, new factory methods were used to turn out machine-made furniture. Such furniture often cost less to buy than did the handmade kind. Because of this, more middle-class Americans were able to live in homes that were comfortable, pleasant, and well furnished.

Many workers, however, still held low-paying jobs. These workers did not always share in the improvements enjoyed by others.

Overall, industrialization brought about a new and better way of life in the North during the mid-1800's. Clearly, growing industrialization and immigration changed the face of northern society. At the same time, however, these changes caused the North and the South to draw ever further apart.

■ *How did industrial prosperity affect life in the North?*

(Text continues on page 265.)

Progress of Cotton #5 (Detail), Yale University Art Gallery, The Mabel Brady Collection

The plentiful supply of labor and new technology, as shown in this picture of a cotton mill, helped America become a leading industrial nation.

VIEWPOINTS DIFFER

How Did Slavery Affect the South?

Slavery, the South's "peculiar institution," set that region apart from the North and West. Most Americans today would probably agree with historian Allan Nevins's statement that "slavery was the greatest misery, the greatest wrong, the greatest curse to black and white alike..." Southerners in the 1850's, however, had differing viewpoints on the role of slavery in Southern society.

New Orleans newspaper publisher J. B. D. De Bow wrote about the positive benefits of slavery in bringing wealth to the region.

From all these dangers the conservative influence of the south has hitherto preserved the free States. Her tributes of slave-grown wealth have kept up the wages of their [northern] labor and the profits of their [northern] capital.... The southern States have peculiar and well nigh indispensable advantages in their slave institutions, which forever obliterate the division between labor and capital.... When we regard the powerful position in the world which the command of the great staple of cotton confers upon the slave States, their numerous natural advantages in climate and productions, their situation midway in the new hemisphere, holding the outlets of northern commerce, and the approaches to South America and the Pacific, through the Gulf, we cannot forbear thinking that they are destined to play a first part in the history of the world.... Divine Providence... has provided the whites of the Anglo-Norman race in the southern States with the necessary means of unexampled prosperity, with that slave labor.

A different perspective was offered by Hinton R. Helper, a Southerner who owned no slaves. His book, *The Impending Crisis of the South: How to Meet It*, was published in Baltimore in 1857.

How is it that the North, under the operations of a policy directly the opposite of ours, has surpassed us in almost everything great and good?... We are compelled to go to the North for almost every article of utility and adornment.... We have no foreign trade, no princely merchants, nor respectable artists; that, in comparison with the Free States, we contribute nothing to the literature, polite arts and inventions of the age; that... large numbers of our native population... emigrate to the West, whilst the Free States retain not only... those born within their own limits, but induce, annually, hundreds of thousands of foreigners to settle and remain amongst them.... In our opinion... the causes which have impeded the progress and prosperity of the South... may all be traced to one common source, and there find solution in the most hateful and horrible word, that was ever incorporated into the vocabulary of human economy—*Slavery*.

Think About It

1. According to Helper, what common source hindered the cultural and economic development of the South?
2. Other than slavery, what factors does De Bow believe will lead the South to "unexampled prosperity"?
3. Do you think Helper and De Bow are "sectionalists" or "nationalists"? Explain your answer.

The Leaders of Southern Society. Life in the South did not change as rapidly as did life in the North. In part, this was because the forces that changed northern life either were not present or were less powerful in the South. Also, slave owning and farming played major roles in southern life and made change slower to come about.

By the 1850's, southern society could generally be divided into four classes. The first and most powerful of these classes was that of the wealthy planters and slave owners. But only a small number of southerners belonged to the planter class. In fact, some historians feel that only about 10,000 southern families could truly be said to belong to this class by 1860.

The planters were separated from the rest of southern society for two reasons. First, planters owned large amounts of land in the South. Second, planters generally owned large numbers of slaves. Wealthy planter families owned hundreds—sometimes thousands—of slaves who were used to work the huge plantations.

The planter class held most of the economic and political power in the South during the 1850's. Also, the planters were the leaders of southern society. For these reasons, planters formed a sort of ruling class in the South.

■ *What two factors separated planters from the rest of southern society?*

The Southern Middle Class. Those who owned smaller farms made up a second social class in the South. In many cases, these southerners owned enough land to feed their families and to sometimes raise a small crop surplus. *Surplus crops*—those not used by the family—could be sold at country markets and in towns and cities.

In most cases, these farmers owned only a few slaves—generally less than five. Many owned no slaves at all. Those southerners who held small family farms made up the largest social class—in terms of numbers—in the South. These people formed the largest part of the South's middle class during the mid-1800's.

In the 1850's, most southern towns and cities did not compare in size or in activity with those of the North. Generally, southern towns and cities were market centers, where farm goods were brought for sale or for shipment. Factory towns were almost unknown in the South during these years.

Many southern city dwellers made their living as shop owners. Others worked in trades, in crafts, or in professions, such as medicine or the law. Still others were involved in the marketing of farm goods, such as cotton, tobacco, sugar, and rice. These people generally belonged to the South's middle class. In fact, southern towns and cities were slowly becoming middle-class centers in the 1850's.

Unskilled workers, farmers who had to rent their land from others, and farmers whose lands could not produce a surplus often belonged to the lower class. For these southerners, life was hard and poor. It was difficult for them to improve themselves or to move up in society. The same was true of northerners who faced similar hardships. But no matter how poor they were, white southerners enjoyed a far higher social standing than did slaves.

Slaves made up the fourth and lowest social class in the South. Southern slaves had little or no opportunity to move upward in society. They could not own land or other forms of property, nor were they allowed to improve themselves through education. Moreover, slaves had few legal rights and no political powers whatsoever. In general, they were completely at the mercy of their masters.

What group of people made up the largest portion of the southern middle class?

Southern Attitudes Toward Reform. During the mid-1800's, southern society was based, in large part, upon the way of life of the powerful planter class. The planters' values and ideals played a major role in shaping the southern life-style. And because most planters favored slavery and its spread into the West, the South in general followed these views. Moreover, the ownership of land and of slaves was an important goal of many southerners. Slaveholding and land ownership were the keys to membership in the planter class. And many middle- and lower-class southerners hoped to become planters themselves.

The number of slaves in the South continued to grow rapidly during the 1850's. By 1860, there were about 11 million people living in the southern states. Of these, 4 million—or well over one third—were black slaves. Thus, a large part of the southern population had few rights or freedoms.

Much the same thing could be said for women in America—North and South alike—in the 1850's. American women had little freedom to choose their way of life or to work to improve themselves. In general, they were not allowed to attend school, to vote, or to own property. Some work was being done in the North to improve women's rights. But in the South, this was not the case.

During these years, a growing number of northerners wanted to improve their American society. They called for better prisons, for better medical care, for more and better schools, and for more rights for women. But many southerners linked these calls for reform with the northern abolitionist movement. They believed that social reform of any kind was really a northern plan to weaken the South.

For example, northern ideas about public education were strongly attacked in some parts of the South. Many southerners believed that publicly run schools weakened individual freedom. They were also against the idea of being taxed in order to pay for public schools. For these reasons, the level of education and of literacy in the South was not as high as it was in the North during the 1850's.

Widespread feelings against reform hurt the South because such feelings slowed social progress. At the same time, they caused the North and the South to become more divided from one another than ever before.

Why were many southerners suspicious of social reforms during the mid-1800's?

SECTION 1 REVIEW

1. *What two forces were responsible, in part, for rapidly changing northern life-styles during the mid-1800's?*
2. *How did industrialization in the North affect northern ideas about education?*
3. *Why did many southerners—and especially planters—resist social reform during the mid-1800's?*

2 New Ideas and New Tensions

Overview The 1850's were years of social change, as Americans worked to improve their country. At the same time, Americans built a culture that was truly their own and that mirrored the country's values and ideals. The spirit of reform brought a new and better life for many people.

These changes were welcomed by many and feared by many others. As our country moved through the 1850's, it became more deeply divided than ever before.

Objectives After reading this section, you will be able to:

- summarize the reform movements that existed in the United States in the 1850's;
- identify the way that American culture changed during the mid-1800's;
- contrast government leaders in the 1850's with earlier American leaders.

Maryland Historical Society, Baltimore

By the mid-1800's, city dwellers in Baltimore and in other American cities faced overcrowding as a result of rapid population growth.

The Call for Reform. In the 1850's, industrialization, western settlement, and the growth of cities were slowly bringing about a new way of life in America. Some people welcomed these changes, believing that they would lead to greater progress. At the same time, however, many people understood that social changes often brought new problems.

Many of the reform movements that grew in America during the mid-1800's had their largest followings in the North. In part, this was because northerners faced a number of major social problems. These problems arose because of greater industrialization and because of greater city growth. Moreover, many reform ideals were brought to the North in the 1850's by European immigrants.

During these years, however, some Americans feared social change. They believed that such change would cause the ruin of their old way of life. Many of these people were southerners who felt that all northern reform movements were closely tied to abolitionism. Because of this, southerners in the mid-1800's were generally against the idea of broad social reform. They worked to limit the influence of outside ideas. This feeling helped to separate the South from other parts of the country. It also caused feelings of sectional rivalry to grow.

■ *Why were reform movements stronger in the North during the mid-1800's?*

Important Reform Movements. The abolitionists made up the most powerful and outspoken reform movement of the time. But throughout the 1850's, other reform groups worked equally hard to bring about a better way of life in America.

Important reforms were made in education during these years. Teachers were better trained, and schools worked to better meet the needs of their students. Under the leadership of educators such as Thomas Gallaudet and Samuel Howe schools for the deaf and for the blind were built. By 1851, schools for deaf students had been opened in 14 northern states. A growing number of Americans also called for improved care for the sick and the insane. One of the best-known leaders in the field of health care was Dorothea Dix, whose work helped all Americans.

Through the efforts of Dorothea Dix and her followers, several northern states built hospitals for the treatment of the mentally ill. Greater public understanding of the mentally ill also came about because of this important reform movement.

The *temperance*—antiliquor—movement was another of the leading reform movements of the mid-1800's. Temperance leaders believed that Americans could lead better and healthier lives by avoiding liquor. They also felt that stronger liquor laws would help to reduce crime and poverty in America. By the 1850's, the movement had led some northern states to pass laws restricting the sale and the use of liquor.

The Bettmann Archive

How did this temperance cartoon of the mid-1800's depict members of the temperance movement?

Other movements that grew during this time struggled to gain more rights for women and to bring about needed prison reforms. Even though some progress was made toward reaching these goals, much remained to be done. Nevertheless, the growth of reform movements in these years showed that many Americans wanted to build a better and healthier society.

■ *What reform movement of the mid-1800's was led by Dorothea Dix?*

An American Culture. One of the most notable changes seen during the mid-1800's was that American culture no longer reflected the culture of Europe. American writers and artists were not so ready to copy European ideas. Culture in the United States became more clearly American and less European. This showed that Americans were eager to build a way of life that was their own.

The mood of America was one of optimism and of self-confidence. Americans had a deep faith in the worth of the individual. They also believed in the qualities of truth and of goodness, and in the beauty and power of nature. American writing in these years was based largely upon these ideals.

A number of the major American writers of the period were from the New England states. Among these authors were outstanding teachers and thinkers, such as Ralph Waldo Emerson and Henry David Thoreau. Emerson and Thoreau both believed that every person was important. Both writers said that people should not be restricted by their society or by their government. Many of the essays written by these authors, such as Thoreau's *Walden,* are widely enjoyed today.

Nathaniel Hawthorne and Herman Melville were also from New England. Hawthorne and Melville agreed that the individual was the measure of all things. These authors wrote books dealing with good and evil, and with the relationship between people and their society. Among Hawthorne's best writings were *The Scarlet Letter* and *The House of the Seven Gables.* Melville was not well-known while he was alive. But his finest work, *Moby Dick,* is thought of as a major classic.

However, not all of the leading American writers of the mid-1800's came from New England. Walt Whitman, whose book of poems, *Leaves of Grass,* described his faith in ordinary Americans, was from New York. Whitman wrote in the everyday language of working Americans. In this way, he intended to give a better picture of real life in our country.

Edgar Allan Poe was one of the most original American writers of the mid-1800's. Poe was born in Boston but spent much of his life in the South. Most often writing in verse or in short-story form, Poe chose subjects based upon the strange and the frightening. Among his most widely read works were "The Raven," "The Purloined Letter," and "The Pit and the Pendulum."

The mid-1800's were years of great artistic output in the United States. The work of American authors in these years compared favorably with the finest writing of authors from anywhere in the world. Equally important was the fact that American writers were eager to describe the ideas and the life-styles of their own country. For the first time, Americans could truly be said to have a literature—and a culture—of their own.

■ *What was one of the most notable changes seen in our culture during the mid-1800's?*

Problems in Government. During these years, some Americans worked to build a freer society and a richer culture. Before these aims could be reached, however, the sectional differences that divided our country had to be settled.

Many people hoped that the Compromise of 1850 would bring about a new spirit of sectional order and harmony. But weak leadership in our country's government hindered the achievement of this goal. Because of this, the sections drifted further away from one another and moved closer to open conflict throughout the 1850's.

One of the major problems was the fact that many leaders failed to take a national point of view. Instead, they often worked for the good of their own parts of the country. By taking a broader view, these leaders might have brought the sections together. As it was, their narrow views succeeded only in causing new troubles.

The election of two weak presidents—Franklin Pierce in 1852 and James Buchanan in 1856—added to America's troubles. Both Pierce and Buchanan were Democrats, and both were northerners. But both presidents appeared to favor the South more than they did the North. And both were easily led by powerful members of Congress and by members of their cabinets. Neither Pierce nor Buchanan was able to give the country the strong leadership that it so greatly needed.

New leadership in Congress also stirred feelings of sectional anger and dislike. Earlier leaders, such as Henry Clay and Daniel Webster, had generally taken a broad view toward sectional questions. As a rule, they believed that the interests of the country should go before those of any one section. But these earlier leaders were gone by the 1850's. New government leaders—such as Stephen Douglas, Jefferson Davis, John C. Breckinridge, and Charles Sumner—were now in office.

These new leaders sometimes weakened national unity as they worked to settle sectional differences. This was because they often were less willing to agree to compromises than were earlier leaders. Moreover, they were sometimes less able to judge the feelings and the temper of people throughout the country.

■ *What was one of the major weaknesses of the federal government during the 1850's?*

Railroads and Sectionalism. In the mid-1800's, a growing number of Americans favored the building of a railroad connecting the eastern states and the West Coast. Such a *transcontinental*—cross-country—rail-

The Granger Collection

The Democratic candidate—James Buchanan—was elected President in 1856. His weak leadership aggravated sectional differences.

road would be good for America. It would speed the shipment of raw materials, food, and factory goods to the country's markets. And it would make travel and settlement both safer and faster. At the same time, a transcontinental railroad would serve to tie the country closer together.

Most Americans clearly understood the economic value of a cross-country railroad. It would bring wealth and a better way of life to people all along its route. Because of this, Americans from each part of the country wanted the railroad to be routed through their area.

President Pierce favored the idea of a southern railroad beginning in New Orleans or in Memphis. Such a route would pass through lands that, for the most part, were already organized into states and territories.

Southerners strongly agreed with Pierce's plan because it would bring about widespread economic growth in the South. But many northerners, including Senator Douglas of Illinois, were greatly angered. They wanted a route that would run through the North.

In order to reach his goal of a southern route, Pierce asked Congress to buy a large amount of land belonging to Mexico. This land, lying just to the south of the New Mexico Territory, gave easy passage through the mountains. Congress quickly agreed with this idea. James Gadsden, America's ambassador to Mexico, was told to offer the Mexican government 10 million dollars for the land. And in 1853, Mexico's leaders agreed to the sale.

The land bought from Mexico in 1853—known as the Gadsden Purchase—strengthened the case for a southern railway. But many northerners felt that they had been cheated by the President and his southern cabinet members. Sectional feelings once again divided the country.

■ *What was the advantage of a southern route for the transcontinental railroad?*

DO YOU KNOW?

Who was America's first woman physician?

In 1849, Elizabeth Blackwell became America's first woman physician. Elizabeth had to overcome many social prejudices in order to study medicine. Despite these obstacles, however, she was determined to become a practicing physician. And in 1849, Elizabeth Blackwell was graduated from the Geneva College of Medicine in New York. Four years later, Dr. Blackwell founded a hospital for women and children. Elizabeth Blackwell died in 1910, a respected member of her profession and a leader in the struggle for women's rights.

SECTION 2 REVIEW

1. *What was the most powerful reform movement in America during the mid-1800's?*
2. *How did Walt Whitman use language to portray real life in America?*
3. *How were government leaders in the 1850's different than earlier American leaders?*

3 The Breakdown of Compromise

Overview The slavery question was not the only difference that separated the country during the mid-1800's. Questions of equal government representation and of political rights in the West were also important. But America's leaders during this time could not seem to settle these differences peacefully. In addition, there was a feeling among people in each section that the government was working against their aims. For these reasons, the 1850's were years of growing sectional conflict in America.

Objectives After reading this section, you will be able to:

- identify the significance of the Kansas-Nebraska Act of 1854;
- explain how the Supreme Court heightened sectional tensions during the 1850's;
- discuss the reason why sectional conflict intensified after 1857.

Failure of the Compromise of 1850. The Compromise of 1850 was intended to settle America's sectional differences once and for all. But almost from the moment it became law, the Compromise began to break down. Because of this, the chance that America would suffer from a new outbreak of sectional trouble became far more likely.

One of the major stumbling blocks to the Compromise of 1850 was the law known as the Fugitive Slave Act. This law was supposed to stop slaves from escaping to the North. Under its terms, northerners who aided runaway slaves could be punished with fines or with jail sentences.

Southerners were pleased with the Fugitive Slave Act. They believed that it would put an end to groups, such as the Underground Railroad, that helped runaway slaves. They also hoped that the Fugitive Slave Act would weaken the abolitionist movement. Many northerners, however, were angered by the act. They viewed it as a threat to their freedom and to their ideals.

Northern anger toward the law became even greater following the publication of *Uncle Tom's Cabin* in 1852. This book, written by Harriet Beecher Stowe, pictured slave life at its worst. Moreover, it was a powerful attack upon southern values. *Uncle Tom's Cabin* heightened northern bitterness toward the Fugitive Slave Act and toward the South in general. Because of this bitterness, many northerners in the 1850's continued to help escaping slaves.

Harriet Beecher Stowe inflamed sectional differences with her book, *Uncle Tom's Cabin*.

National Portrait Gallery, Smithsonian Institution, Washington, D.C. (Detail)

Another weakness of the Compromise of 1850 had to do with slaveholding in the western territories. Two new territories—New Mexico and Utah—had been organized under the terms of the Compromise. Citizens of these new lands were given the right of *popular sovereignty* toward the slave question. This meant that territorial citizens—rather than Congress—could decide if slaveholding was to be allowed in their lands.

In the Compromise, it was agreed that these territories would have popular sovereignty so that California could enter the Union as a free state. Thus, both the North and the South made important gains. However, the granting of popular sovereignty in the new territories reopened the slave question in the West.

Many people—northerners and southerners alike—were unhappy with the Compromise of 1850. Most Americans, however, were eager to keep peace between the sections. And for a few years, the Compromise helped them to do so. But when plans were made to open more new western territories, the uneasy peace gained by the Compromise was ended.

Southerners considered *Uncle Tom's Cabin* an exaggeration of the evils of slavery.

The Bettmann Archive

■ *What effect did the publication of* Uncle Tom's Cabin *have upon the North?*

The Kansas-Nebraska Act. As you have read, when plans were begun for a cross-country railroad, questions arose over what route should be followed. Southerners backed the idea forwarded by President Pierce. Under this plan, the railroad would travel from a southern city—either New Orleans or Memphis—across the Southwest to California. Senator Douglas, however, spoke for many northerners when he called for the railroad to begin in a northern city, such as Chicago.

The drawback to Douglas's plan was the fact that a northern route would pass through unsettled western lands. These lands included present-day Kansas and Nebraska. They were not yet organized into territories. Moreover, these lands were north of the old Missouri Compromise line of 36°30′. Under the terms of the Missouri Compromise, slaveholding was outlawed in any land north of this line.

Government money was needed to build the cross-country railroad. But such money could be used only if the route passed through states or territories. Therefore, Senator Douglas wanted to organize the lands north of 36°30′ into territories. But he knew that southern lawmakers would not agree if slaveholding was outlawed in this land.

Douglas called for a law to organize the land north of 36°30′ into two new territories—Kansas and Nebraska. He also called for the end of the Missouri Compromise line that outlawed slaveholding in this land.

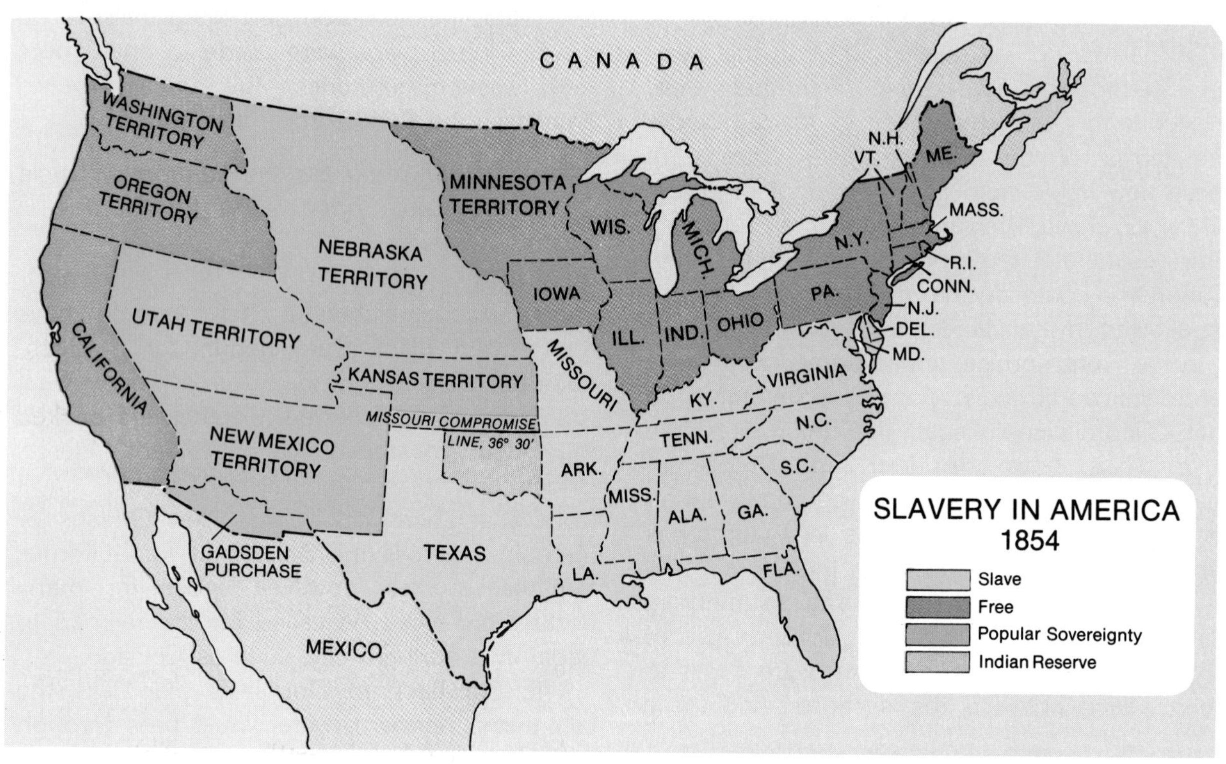

During the 1850's, federal laws opened much of the Far West to slavery. In 1854, what was the westernmost slave state?

The bill presented by Senator Douglas—known as the Kansas-Nebraska Act—was passed into law in 1854. The Kansas-Nebraska Act meant that a northern route for the cross-country railroad was possible. At the same time, however, the act brought a bitter outcry from northern abolitionists. This was because slaveholding was no longer outlawed in the land north of 36°30′. The Kansas-Nebraska Act had opened the West to slavery once again.

■ *Why did Douglas call for the end of the Missouri Compromise line of 36°30′?*

A New Political Climate. There were several important outcomes of the Kansas-Nebraska Act. It brought the slave question to the public's attention once again, and it further divided northerners and southerners.

In the North, many people believed that the Kansas-Nebraska Act was part of a southern plan to spread slavery throughout the country. And some northerners felt that the act was an attack upon the abolitionist movement and upon the North as a whole.

The Kansas-Nebraska Act also brought about major political changes. The Democratic party had won the presidential election of 1852. But by 1854, a number of Democrats had grown to dislike President Pierce. Moreover, the Democrats had become badly divided over the slave question by that year. When Senator Douglas—a powerful Democrat—called upon his party to back the Kansas-Nebraska Act, many northerners refused to follow his leadership.

The Whig party, too, had become divided over the question of slaveholding. And its defeat in the election of 1852 destroyed the party forever. By 1854, a new party—the Republican party—had come into being.

The Republicans drew their membership mainly from antislave northerners. The Republican party gained widespread attention in its fight against the Kansas-Nebraska Act in 1854.

In 1856, the Republicans' presidential candidate—John C. Frémont—was defeated by the Democrats' James Buchanan. But the young party proved that it was a major political power by winning in 11 northern states. Even while the Republicans worked to gain votes against slaveholding, however, the new territory of Kansas became a sectional battleground.

■ *From which part of the country did the Republicans draw their political support?*

Bleeding Kansas. Under the terms of the Kansas-Nebraska Act, citizens in the new territories could decide the slave question for themselves. Nebraska had been settled largely by farmers from the North and from Europe. It was certain that these people would not allow slaveholding in their land.

Kansas was at first settled largely by southerners from the neighboring slave state of Missouri. It seemed clear that slaveowners would hold power in the new territory.

Northern abolitionists quickly acted against the threat of a proslavery takeover in Kansas. Large groups of northerners rushed into the

Kansas State Historical Society

On September 13, 1856, proslavery and antislavery forces met in the Kansas Territory at the Battle of Hickory Point. Hundreds of these skirmishes helped the territory earn the name "Bleeding Kansas."

new land during the next two years. At the same time, however, southern settlers reached Kansas in growing numbers, bringing their slaves with them. Moreover, bands of armed Missourians crossed the border into Kansas to keep northerners out.

As time went on, a peaceful settlement of the slave question in Kansas became less and less likely. Newspapers in the North and in the South added to the troubles in Kansas. Writers for these papers fanned their readers' anger with false reports of terrible fighting in "Bleeding Kansas."

By 1856, the Kansas question had become a test of power between abolitionists and slaveowners. Both sides were heavily armed, and each wanted to prove that it alone stood for the majority in Kansas. In the two years between 1854 and 1856, both sides elected territorial governments. But neither was accepted by the other.

Finally, in May of 1856, real fighting broke out in Kansas. Proslavery settlers attacked the free-soil town of Lawrence. The attack caused several deaths and heavy damage to the town. In return, John Brown, an outspoken abolitionist settler, led an attack upon the proslavery village of Pottawatomie Creek. Five southern settlers were murdered. The fighting spread across Kansas and by the end of 1856, more than 200 people had been killed. But the slave question in Kansas was still not settled.

■ *In what way did northern and southern newspapers add to the troubles in Kansas?*

The Dred Scott Case. Soon after President Buchanan took office in 1857, a Supreme Court ruling helped to divide the country even further. This ruling was made in the case of *Dred Scott* v. *Sandford.*

During the 1830's, the owner of Dred Scott, a slave, had moved from the slave state of Missouri to the Wisconsin Territory. Scott had gone with his owner. But the Wisconsin Territory had outlawed slave owning within its lands. In 1846, Dred Scott brought a lawsuit to win his freedom. Because he had lived in a free territory, Scott said, he was no longer a slave. But when the case reached the Supreme Court, Justice Roger Taney felt that Scott was still a slave. The Court, influenced by Taney, ruled that a slave remained the owner's property even in a free territory.

■ *Why did Dred Scott claim that he was no longer a slave?*

The Impact of the Dred Scott Case. The Dred Scott case struck a blow against the antislavery cause. The Supreme Court's ruling meant that the Missouri Compromise was un-

In 1857, Dred Scott lost his case to become free in the U.S. Supreme Court.

Culver Pictures

constitutional. Territorial governments did not have the power to outlaw slave owning in their lands. Slave owning was legal in *any* territory.

The outcome of the Dred Scott case caused an angry public outcry across the North. Many northerners believed that Chief Justice Taney, a southerner, had used the law to help the South. The South, on the other hand, was delighted with the Dred Scott case. Southerners held that the ruling meant that slave owning was a right. And many southerners hoped that slavery would now be spread throughout the country.

The Supreme Court's ruling made little real difference in terms of slave owning in the western territories. But it added greatly to sectional bitterness in our country. After the Dred Scott case, a growing number of Americans no longer believed that the slave question could be settled in a peaceful manner.

What effect did the Dred Scott decision have upon the Missouri Compromise?

New Sectional Violence. After 1857, the country moved steadily toward an open break between the North and the South. It is possible that this could have been prevented had government leaders worked harder to more fairly settle sectional questions. But the country had few leaders who were willing to take a broad view toward the differences that divided our country.

One such leader who emerged during these years was an Illinois lawyer named Abraham Lincoln. In 1858, Lincoln—a Republican—ran for the Senate against the powerful Senator Stephen Douglas. Douglas's large following helped him to defeat Lincoln's bid for the Senate. But the Lincoln-Douglas debates during the campaign excited the country's attention. Some people began to look to Abraham Lincoln for leadership.

At the same time, however, Americans suffered from new outbreaks of sectional violence. In October of 1859, John Brown, the Kansas abolitionist, led an attack against the

Historical Pictures Service

Abraham Lincoln (standing) and Stephen A. Douglas (seated left) met in several debates during the 1858 Illinois senatorial campaign. Although Lincoln lost the election, the debates brought him national fame.

government arsenal at Harpers Ferry, Virginia. Brown's aim was to seize the weapons stored at Harpers Ferry. He planned to arm southern slaves and lead them in a general uprising.

During the attack, several soldiers were killed. John Brown and his followers were able to take the arsenal at Harpers Ferry. But within a few days, Brown and his group were captured and jailed. In December of 1859, John Brown was hanged.

Southerners were outraged by Brown's attack and by his aim of leading a slave uprising. Many northerners agreed that the act itself was wrong. But they also felt that John Brown had struck a blow for freedom. And after his death, Brown became a hero and a martyr in the eyes of some northerners.

The Kansas troubles, the Dred Scott case, and the attack upon Harpers Ferry all served to push the country closer toward war. As the 1850's ended, Americans searched for a strong leader who could bring peace to the country once again.

What did John Brown hope to achieve by attacking Harpers Ferry?

SECTION 3 REVIEW

1. *How was the Missouri Compromise line of 36°30′ affected by the Kansas-Nebraska Act of 1854?*
2. *Why was the Supreme Court's decision in the Dred Scott case a blow against the antislavery cause?*
3. *Why did conflicts between the North and the South intensify after 1857?*

CHAPTER 15 SUMMARY

Throughout the 1850's, the North and the South became more widely separated from one another. In part, this was due to growing bitterness over the slave question. But important social changes in each part of the country added to sectional differences. In the North, industrialization and immigration brought about new ways of life. In the South, however, many people worked to defend their old values and life-styles.

At the same time, a spirit of reform grew in some parts of the country. Many Americans wished to build a better way of life, not only for themselves but for others as well. These feelings helped to improve life in the United States during the mid-1800's. But they also brought about a wider and more dangerous gulf between the North and the South.

Important political changes caused sectional tensions to grow in our country. Americans hoped that the Compromise of 1850 would draw the United States together once again. But in many ways, the Compromise worked against this goal. New western settlement added to the country's growing troubles. And our government leaders could not agree on ways to meet these problems. By the late 1850's, America was on the edge of war.

CHAPTER 15 REVIEW

USING YOUR SKILLS

Reading Flow Charts

A *flow chart* is a type of chart that is often used to illustrate the various steps involved in a process. Each entry in the flow chart shows a stage of the process and the way in which any one stage is related to all the others. The flow chart below illustrates the various steps that a territory had to take in order to become a state.

1. According to the chart, what had to be done before Congress could appoint officials to govern an unorganized territory?
2. According to the chart, what requirements had to be met before a territory could be said to be "organized"?
3. When could an organized territory draft its own territorial constitution?
4. Which stage—according to the chart—came first: the drafting of a territorial constitution or the election of a territorial legislature?
5. When could a territorial legislature apply for admission into the Union?
6. What governing body had the power to grant statehood to a territory?

FROM TERRITORY TO STATE

Congress surveys the proposed territory to establish its boundaries.

The "unorganized" territory is governed by officials appointed by Congress.

When 5,000 legal voters have settled in the territory, a legislature is elected and a representative is sent to Congress. The territory is now said to be "organized."

A territorial constitution is drafted when 60,000 people have settled in the territory.

When the territorial constitution is approved, the legislature applies to Congress for statehood.

Congress votes to grant statehood to the territory, which then enters the Union as a new state.

CHAPTER 15 REVIEW

YOU SHOULD KNOW

Identify, define, or explain each of the following:

literate
surplus crops
temperance
transcontinental
popular sovereignty

CHECKING FACTS

1. Where did the largest number of European immigrants settle in the United States?
2. During the 1850's, which social class became larger and more powerful in the North?
3. For which group of people was education limited in the mid-1800's?
4. What was the most powerful social class in the South by the 1850's?
5. What kind of reform was instituted in the United States by Dorothea Dix?
6. What was the purpose of the temperance movement?
7. What was the major subject of books written by Nathaniel Hawthorne and Herman Melville?
8. What was the Gadsden Purchase?
9. What was the purpose of the Fugitive Slave Act?
10. Which Supreme Court ruling declared the Missouri Compromise of 1820 to be unconstitutional?

UNDERSTANDING CONCEPTS

1. In what way did slavery in the South influence European immigration during the mid-1800's?
2. How did the planter class affect life-styles in the South?
3. Upon what values and ideals was American writing in the mid-1800's generally based?
4. Why did many northerners oppose the Kansas-Nebraska Act of 1854?

LEARNING FROM ILLUSTRATIONS

1. Based on the illustration on page 267, what form of urban transportation appears to have been most popular during the mid-1800's?
2. Study the map on page 274. According to the map, in what territories was popular sovereignty supposed to determine the slavery question?

CRITICAL THINKING

1. During the 1850's, education was seen as the best way of moving up in society. Do you think this idea still holds true today? Why or why not?
2. The most important social reform movement in the 1800's was the abolitionist movement. Do you agree or disagree with this statement? Explain your answer.
3. Why do you think that the Compromise of 1850 failed to bring lasting political peace in the United States? Explain your answer.

ENRICHMENT ACTIVITIES

1. You might like to form a group to conduct research on northern factory conditions in the mid-1800's. Information can be found in books and in encyclopedia articles. Your group might then present a play to dramatize the problems faced by factory workers.
2. You might enjoy learning more about the famous Lincoln-Douglas debates of 1858. Use encyclopedias and other resource materials to research the different positions taken by the candidates toward the expansion of slavery in America. Then, prepare an oral report of your findings for presentation to the class.

CHAPTER 16

CLOSE-UP: The Story of the Alamo

INTRODUCTION

The town of San Antonio de Bexar, in the northeastern portion of Mexico known as Coahuila-Texas, was a scene of noise, confusion, and fear on February 23, 1836. Bexar, as it was usually called, had rarely seen such activity. The town was really little more than a frontier village. But on that day in February 1836, the armies of General Antonio López de Santa Anna—Mexico's dictator—marched into Bexar.

Santa Anna had come north from the capital of Mexico City to punish the rebellious American settlers in Mexican Texas. The Texan settlers had demanded the return of their political rights, lost when Santa Anna became dictator in 1833. By mid-1835, an armed Texan uprising had begun. The Texans simply wanted the freedoms that they had previously enjoyed under Mexican rule to be restored. But Santa Anna was determined to put down the Texan uprising.

In December of 1835, the Texans drove a large Mexican force out of Bexar and captured the town. But later that month, they learned that Santa Anna was readying a new army to march north against the settlers. Only a handful of Texans remained at Bexar to defend the town. These few soldiers decided to use an old, partly ruined mission just outside of Bexar as a fort. The old church stood near a grove of cottonwood trees. It was named the Church of San Antonio de Valero. But most people simply called the mission by the Spanish name for cottonwood—the Alamo.

1 The Background

In 1821, a young man named Stephen Austin led a group of 300 American families across the Sabine River into Texas. Austin's settlers were the first of 30,000 Americans who moved into Mexican Texas during the 1820's and the early 1830's. With Mexican help and with plenty of hard work, the Texan settlements grew and prospered. But by 1835, the Texans had to fight for the right to remain in their new homes.

Causes of the Texan Revolution. The once-strong and friendly ties between Mexico and the Texan settlers had become weakened to the breaking point by the early 1830's. There were many reasons for this. The rapidly growing number of Americans in Texas caused great alarm among Mexico's leaders. The Mexicans feared that the new Texan settlements would soon become too large to control. Moreover, the Texans wanted the right to own slaves, even though slavery was outlawed in Mexico. Throughout most of the 1820's, the government unwillingly agreed to the slave owners' demands. But in April 1830, Mexico's leaders finally moved to forbid slaveholding in

Texas. At the same time, Texas was closed to further American settlement.

The bitter Texans felt that they had been cheated by the Mexican government. A growing number of settlers began to call for a change of government leaders in Mexico. And when Santa Anna moved to win control of Mexico's government in 1833, many of the Texans supported him.

But Santa Anna proved to be the Texans' worst enemy. Elected president of Mexico in January of 1833, he soon set up a harsh dictatorship. It quickly became clear that Santa Anna planned to gather all political power into his own hands.

The new ruler sent his brother-in-law, General Cós, to destroy the state governments of Zacatecas and of Coahuila-Texas. These two states in northern Mexico were known for their democratic ideals. And Santa Anna's attack upon their governments proved that he did not intend to grant Texans the freedoms that they wanted. Thus, as General Cós moved his army northward toward Texas in mid-1835, the Texans prepared for war.

What was General Santa Anna's overall political goal?

Early Texan Victories. The first act in the Texas Revolution came in June of 1835. Santa Anna had recently sent soldiers to the army post at Anáhuac, near the Texan town of Liberty. The Texans viewed Santa Anna's action as a dangerous threat. Because of this, a young Texan army officer, William B. Travis, led an attack against the fort at Anáhuac. The Mexican soldiers were quickly defeated and driven off. Then, in October, a group of 160 settlers met and defeated a second Mexican force near Gonzales. A small battle at Goliad, 95 miles [152 kilometers] southeast of Bexar, ended in yet another Texan victory.

Colonel William Barret Travis shared command of the garrison at the Alamo in early 1836.

At the same time that the battle at Goliad took place, General Cós and 1,400 soldiers reached San Antonio de Bexar. But Cós was not a good leader, and his troops were poorly trained. A Texan army of 300, led by Stephen Austin, attacked Cós at Bexar.

Austin's Texans were eager, well armed, and confident. Among their officers were Travis and the famous knife-carrying Jim Bowie. Though they were outnumbered by almost five to one, the Texans defeated Cós after a bloody house-to-house battle and captured the town. It was December 10, 1835, and many of the Texan settlers believed that they had already won their fight for freedom. But the fighting was far from over.

Why did the Texans attack the army post at Anáhuac?

The Alamo Becomes a Fortress. By mid-January 1836, only 104 Texans remained at Bexar. These soldiers were poorly armed and supplied. They were slowly working to fortify the old mission church known as the Alamo. No one in Bexar thought that Santa Anna's army would move into Texas for many months.

The Alamo was not a good choice of places to defend. Its walls and buildings were crumbling or in ruins in many places. It was far away from the nearest large body of Texan troops. And it covered too much ground to be easily defended by the few soldiers present at Bexar.

But the old church had several advantages in the eyes of its Texan defenders. First, General Cós had left 20 cannons behind when he had withdrawn from Bexar. The Texan army was greatly in need of such guns. Second, Bexar and the Alamo lay directly between Santa Anna's army and the major Texan towns. The Mexicans would have to get past the Alamo in order to attack these settlements. It was hoped that a strong force at the Alamo might be able to stop Santa Anna's army when it came.

Why was the Alamo a poor choice of places to defend?

Problems at the Alamo. The Alamo was made up of several buildings. Among the most important of these were the ruined church, the Long Barracks, and the Low Barracks (see diagram on this page). The buildings and the mission's plaza were enclosed by a long stone wall that was roughly rectangular in shape. The wall had become weakened with age in some places and had collapsed altogether in others. Several large gaps—one

The Alamo—a century-old Spanish mission—was not designed to be a fortress and needed many modifications by the Texan defenders. What constructed feature surrounds the Alamo?

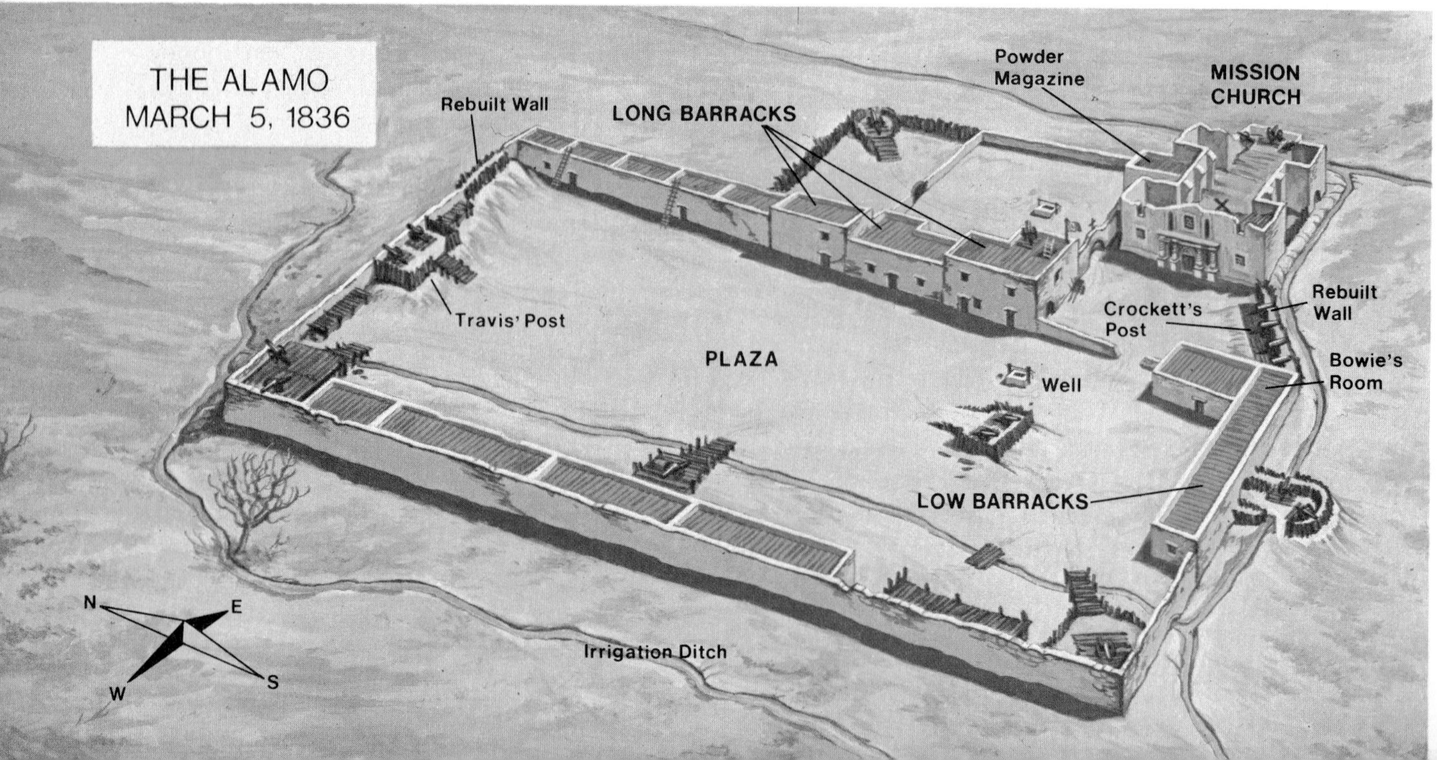

about 75 feet in length—stood where the wall was incomplete. In a letter to Sam Houston, one Texan at Bexar pointed out, "You can plainly see that the Alamo was never built by a military people for a fortress."

The Texans worked hard to make the Alamo's defenses stronger. They built walkways along its walls where soldiers could stand and fight. They set up gun positions for the cannons left behind by General Cós. Those parts of the wall that had fallen or had become too weak to withstand an attack were rebuilt. By February 1836, the Alamo had begun to look like the fort that the Texans intended it to be.

■ *In what general shape were the Alamo's walls constructed?*

SECTION 1 REVIEW

1. *What action on Santa Anna's part showed that he did not intend to grant the Texans the freedoms that they wanted?*
2. *When did the first battle of the Texas Revolution occur?*
3. *Why did the Texans decide to fortify and defend the Alamo?*

2 The Battle and Its Aftermath

In purely military terms, the Battle of the Alamo was a rather small action. Comparatively few soldiers—less than 5,000 in all—were involved in the fighting. And the battle itself was over an old, fallen-down Spanish mission outside a small frontier town. But the Battle of the Alamo marked a turning point in the Texan fight for freedom. And it proved that Americans were willing to give their lives in return for liberty.

Texans at the Alamo. While the Texans were struggling to rebuild the Alamo, a small group of 30 volunteers arrived at Bexar. They were led by Jim Bowie, a friend of Sam Houston's and one of the most famous fighting men of his day.

Bowie had been sent by Houston to withdraw the Alamo's defenders, remove its guns, and destroy the mission. But he decided against these orders. Instead, Bowie and his soldiers joined the other Texans in rebuilding the Alamo. Bowie explained his feelings when he said, "The salvation of Texas depends in great measure in keeping Bexar out of the hands of the enemy." And he added, ". . . we will rather die in these ditches than give it [the Alamo] up . . ."

During the first week of February 1836, another well-known Texan joined the Alamo's defenders. This was Colonel William Travis, who had led the Texan attack against Anáhuac the year before. Travis, a recent settler in Texas, was intensely loyal to the Texans' cause. He was also a good leader, one who would fight to the last breath for a cause in which he believed. Travis brought 25 men with him. He and Bowie agreed to share command of the Texans at the Alamo.

Finally, on February 8, another famous and colorful frontiersman—David Crockett—rode into Bexar with a small party of hard fighters. Crockett and his men were all crack shots with the long Kentucky rifles they carried. By now, the Texans at the Alamo numbered about 150. And at this point, word was received that Santa Anna had begun to march north against Texas.

■ *What two leaders shared command of the Texans at the Alamo?*

The Attack Begins. Santa Anna's powerful army reached Bexar on February 23. Surprised by the Mexicans' speedy arrival, the Texans rushed to the Alamo. Travis quickly sent a message to the Texan settlement of Gonzales, 70 miles [112 kilometers] away. He called upon the Texans to send reinforcements, and he bravely declared: ". . . We have 150 men and are determined to defend the Alamo to the last."

Soon, the Texans in the Alamo saw a large blood-red flag flying near Santa Anna's headquarters in Bexar. This was the sign of "no quarter"—the Mexicans would fight to the death. The defiant Texans answered with a shot from their largest cannon.

The next day, the Mexicans began to fire their massed cannons at the Alamo. Santa Anna kept up a devastating bombardment for days, hoping to destroy the fort and to wear down its defenders. Miraculously, no one inside the Alamo was hurt by the storm of cannon fire. But conditions inside the old fort were becoming desperate. Jim Bowie fell seriously ill and had to be hospitalized in the Low Barracks. Travis was now in full command. He sent a plea to the settlers at Gonzales and throughout Texas, asking for help. He promised that ". . . *I shall never surrender or retreat.*"

Travis's courageous words stirred the settlers. But they were far away. It would take time to send help to the Alamo. On February 29, however, a small group of Texans arrived. Crouched over their saddlebows and riding hard, they broke through the Mexican lines and raced into the Alamo. This brought the total number of defenders to 184. A number of these defenders were Mexicans who sided with the Texans' cause. Also, there were about 25 women and children in the fort. The women and children, often under heavy fire, helped to care for the wounded and to bring food, water, and gunpowder to the soldiers on the walls.

By March 5, the nerve-racking Mexican bombardment had been going on for almost two weeks. Santa Anna had also ordered several surprise attacks against the Alamo. Each time, the Mexican soldiers were driven off with heavy losses. But the Texans knew that Santa Anna would soon throw the full weight of his army against them.

■ *How did the women and children in the Alamo help to defend the fort?*

Travis's Last Warning. On the afternoon of March 5, the weary Travis called his soldiers together. He warned them to expect no further help from Texas before the final Mexican attack. Those inside the Alamo would have to fight on alone.

Then, Travis said that anyone who wished to try to escape was free to do so. Those that remained behind would fight on to the end.

Only one man wanted to leave. The other Texans decided that they would fight and die in the Alamo. They knew that they were doomed.

■ *How many Texans chose to flee from the Alamo on March 5?*

The Final Assault. At dawn of the next morning, March 6, the Mexican army made an all-out attack against the Alamo. Four strong columns, numbering perhaps 800 men each, rushed toward the fort, struggling to scale the walls. The fighting and the loss of life were terrible. Colonel Travis was among the first of the Texans to fall. "I can tell you the whole scene was one of extreme terror," a Mexican soldier wrote. He went on to say, "After some three quarters of an hour of the most horrible fire, there followed the most awful attack with hand arms."

Twice, the Mexican soldiers charged across the open ground before the Alamo. Both times, the Texans swept their lines with rifle and cannon fire. The attacks were driven back with huge losses. Finally, a third attack was made. This time, the Mexican soldiers were able to scale the walls. The fighting, now at close quarters, reached a new pitch as more and more Mexican soldiers streamed into the Alamo. The Texans, outnumbered and out of ammunition, fought back with swords, knives, and rifles used as clubs. But they were steadily pushed back, off the walls and across the plaza. It was probably at this time that Davy Crockett was killed. A Mexican soldier gave an account of the death of one Texan who might have been Crockett. ". . . Of the many soldiers who took deliberate aim at him and fired, not one ever hit him. On the contrary, he never missed a shot. He killed at least eight of our men, besides wounding several others." The Mexican soldier added, "This being observed by a lieutenant who had come in over the wall, he sprang at him and dealt him a deadly blow with his sword, . . ."

The remaining Texans were driven back to the Alamo's buildings, where they made their heroic last stand. Santa Anna's soldiers fired cannons into the buildings and then fought the Texans from room to room. Jim Bowie, a

Courtesy of Brass Door Galleries, Houston, Texas

In this idealized illustration of the fall of the Alamo, Davy Crockett, after running out of ammunition, is shown using his Kentucky long rifle to attack the Mexican soldiers.

pistol in each hand, was killed as he lay on his cot, too weak to stand.

Finally, about 90 minutes after the opening attack, the battle ended. The Alamo had fallen at last. Of the 183 Texan soldiers who had defended the old fort that morning, not one was alive. But the cost to Santa Anna's army was high. Roughly 1,500 Mexican soldiers had been lost in the attack.

■ *How many Mexican assaults were made on the Alamo during the morning of March 6?*

Aftermath of the Battle. Although every Texan soldier in the Alamo died, some Americans survived the battle. These were the women and the small children who had joined the Alamo's defenders. Santa Anna sent one of the women—Mrs. Susannah Dickerson—back to the Texan settlements in the north. He told Mrs. Dickerson to carry the story of the Alamo's fall to all the Texans. In this way, Santa Anna believed, the settlers would be warned of his anger and would end their rebellion against him.

But the story of the Alamo had a different effect than Santa Anna wished. The Texans promised to avenge their soldiers who had fallen at the old church. And six weeks later, at the Battle of San Jacinto, they kept their promise. A Texan army of 800, led by Sam Houston, surprised Santa Anna. Houston's soldiers attacked and crushed the Mexican army and won independence for Texas. The Texan battle cry at San Jacinto was "Remember the Alamo!"

Texas State Archives

Susannah Dickerson was one of only a handful of survivors at the Battle of the Alamo.

■ *Why did Santa Anna send Mrs. Dickerson back to the Texan settlements in the north?*

SECTION 2 REVIEW

1. *What were Bowie's instructions when he first reached the Alamo in mid-January 1836?*
2. *How did Santa Anna hope to destroy the Alamo and wear down its defenders?*
3. *Why did Santa Anna want the Texans to learn of the fall of the Alamo?*

CHAPTER 16 REVIEW

SUMMARY

In 1821 Stephen Austin led 300 American families across the Sabine River into Texas. These settlers were the first Americans to move into Mexican Texas during the 1820's and early 1830's. The settlement grew and prospered, but by the mid-1830's the strong and friendly ties with Mexico weakened. There were several reasons for the strained relationship between Mexico and the Texan settlement. First, the Mexicans feared that the rapidly growing population would become too difficult to control. Secondly, the Texans wanted the right to own slaves, but slavery was outlawed in Mexico. Throughout most of the 1820's, the Mexican government unwillingly agreed to the slave owners' demands. But in 1830, the Mexican government moved to outlaw slaveholding in Texas. Also, Texas was closed to further settlement.

The Texans were angry at the Mexican government. As a result, they were glad when a new ruler, Santa Anna, gained control of the Mexican government. However, Santa Anna set up a harsh dictatorship and did not intend to grant the Texans the freedoms that they wanted. He sent an army northward toward Texas, and the Texans prepared for war.

At first the Texans won the battles against the Mexican army. Although outnumbered, the Texans defeated the Mexican army at Bexar. By 1836, only 104 Texans remained at Bexar. These soldiers were poorly supplied and they decided to use the Alamo, an old Spanish mission, to defend the town.

Santa Anna's army finally reached Bexar on February 23, 1836. Surprised by the Mexicans' speedy arrival, the Texans rushed to the Alamo. There were several thousand Mexican soldiers against about 184 Texans.

On March 6, 1836, the Alamo fell. Every Texan soldier in the Alamo died. However, some of the women and children who had helped to defend the Alamo survived. Six weeks later a Texan army defeated the Mexican army at the Battle of San Jacinto and won independence for Texas. "Remember the Alamo" became the battle cry at San Jacinto.

UNDERSTANDING CONCEPTS

1. Why did friendly ties between Mexico and the Texans become weakened by the early 1830's?
2. What did Santa Anna's attack upon the state government of Texas prove?
3. Why was the Alamo not a good place to defend?
4. Why did the Texans decide to fortify and defend the Alamo?
5. Why was the Battle of the Alamo important?

CRITICAL THINKING

1. Do you think that Mexico had the right to outlaw slaveholding in the Texan settlement? Why or why not?
2. Should the Texans have used the Alamo as their fortress? Give reasons for your answer.
3. "Remember the Alamo" was the battle cry at the Battle of San Jacinto. Why do you think the battle cry was so effective?

PROJECTS AND ACTIVITIES

Prepare a biographical sketch of one of the following people involved in the Battle of the Alamo: Santa Anna, William Barret Travis, Jim Bowie, or David Crockett. Describe what the person did that was of importance in history and what finally happened to him.

UNIT FOUR REVIEW

UNIT SUMMARY

America in the years between 1837 and 1850 was in many ways a land of pioneers. By the early 1840's, many Americans believed that westward settlement was their country's "Manifest Destiny." American aims in the West often led to border disputes with neighboring countries during the late 1830's and the 1840's. In 1846, our country's expansion led to war with Mexico. Victory in the war with Mexico brought land and great wealth to our country.

The late 1840's were years during which the country's different sections became more sharply divided over the slave question. Despite the differences caused by the slave question, however, America's economic growth in the mid-1800's helped to draw the country together. The birth of a national economy in the 1840's led to the breakdown of some sectional barriers. The ongoing settlement of the West also brought about deep sectional differences during the 1840's.

Throughout the 1850's, the North and the South became more widely separated from one another. This was partly due to the slave question. But important social changes in each part of the country added to sectional differences. At the same time, a spirit of reform grew in some parts of the country. Important political changes caused sectional tensions to grow in the United States. Although the Compromise of 1850 was to draw the country together, it actually worked against this goal. By the late 1850's, America was on the edge of war.

In 1821 Stephen Austin led 300 American families into Texas. These were the first settlers to move into Mexican Texas. At first, the settlement prospered. But in the mid-1830's, the strong ties with Mexico weakened. The major problem was the fact that the Texans wanted the right to own slaves, and slavery was outlawed in Mexico. Eventually the conflict between the Texans and Mexico led to war. At the Battle of the Alamo the Mexican army greatly outnumbered the Texans, who were defeated.

YOU SHOULD KNOW

Identify, define, or explain each of the following:

symbol
diplomatic relations
emancipation
specialized businesses
seceding
literate
surplus crops
temperance
popular sovereignty

CHECKING FACTS

1. What two methods of travel were most often used by westward-bound pioneers?
2. What idea helped to increase frontier settlement during the 1840's?
3. What new lands did the United States receive as a result of the Mexican Cession of 1848?
4. What event brought thousands of Americans to the Far West in 1849?
5. What kind of economy gradually developed in America during the mid-1800's?
6. What was probably the greatest cause of sectional trouble during the mid-1800's?
7. What were the two leading political parties in the United States during the 1840's?
8. What two important forces shaped life in the North in the mid-1800's?
9. What did Dorothea Dix work for in the mid-1800's?
10. What two leaders shared command of the Texans at the Alamo?

UNDERSTANDING CONCEPTS

1. Why did the concept of Manifest Destiny help to speed frontier settlement in America?

2. How did westward expansion lead to sectional rivalry?
3. How did the rise of the abolitionist movement influence southern attitudes toward slavery?
4. Why did the Compromise of 1850 fail to settle sectional differences?
5. How did government leaders in the 1850's sometimes help to weaken American unity and to increase the chance of sectional conflict?
6. Why was the Battle of the Alamo significant?

CRITICAL THINKING

1. In defense of slavery, southerners sometimes said that the slave had a better life than the northern factory worker. Do you agree or disagree with this argument? Explain your answer.
2. The development of industrialization, the growth of cities, and improved transportation systems all brought many changes to the North in the first half of the nineteenth century. In what ways do you think these changes affected the daily lives of people in the North?
3. Do you think that the Supreme Court decision in the case of *Dred Scott* v. *Sandford* was a good decision in terms of the choices that seemed possible at the time? Why do you think so?

CHRONOLOGY

Arrange the following events in the order in which they happened.

a. California gold rush begun
b. Texas annexed by the United States
c. Compromise of 1850
d. Dred Scott case
e. John Brown's raid on Harpers Ferry
f. War with Mexico begun
g. Kansas-Nebraska Act

CITIZENSHIP IN ACTION

Many immigrants came to the United States in the mid-1800's. What rights guaranteed to all American citizens might attract modern immigrants to our country today?

GEOGRAPHY

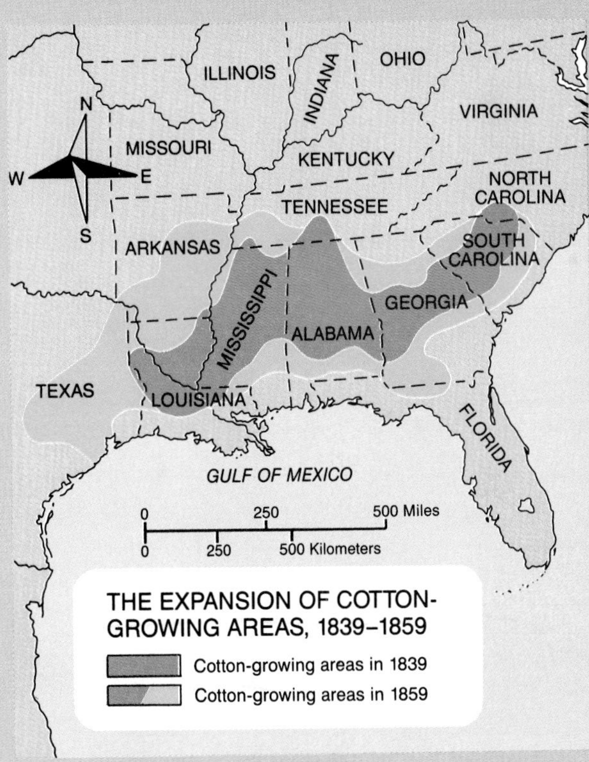

1. What does this map show?
2. According to the map, what states had cotton-growing areas in 1839?
3. What states had added the largest amount of cotton-growing areas by 1859?
4. In what direction was cotton-growing expanding?

1860

1865

- 1860 Abraham Lincoln elected President
- 1861 Confederacy formed
Fort Sumter attacked
- 1862 Battle of Antietam
- 1863 Emancipation Proclamation
Battle of Gettysburg
Siege of Vicksburg
- 1864 General William T. Sherman's troops devastate Georgia
- 1865 General Robert E. Lee surrenders at Appomattox
President Lincoln assassinated
Andrew Johnson becomes President
- 1866 Congress drafts the Fourteenth Amendment
Ku Klux Klan formed

UNIT FIVE

The Union is Tested

1860 to 1877

Conrad Wise Chapman's painting "The Flag of Sumter, October 20, 1863" shows a tattered Confederate flag over Fort Sumter, South Carolina, and a lone Confederate sentry. The painting symbolized the determination of the South to preserve its way of life.

Ex-slaves made history when they exercised their franchise after the war. The Republicans believed in strong controls to safeguard the rights of black citizens.

1870 1875

1867 Reconstruction Acts passed
Tenure of Office Act passed
Alaska purchased
Granger Movement established

1868 President Johnson impeached
Ulysses S. Grant elected President

1869 Congress drafts the Fifteenth Amendment
Knights of Labor founded
First transcontinental railroad completed

1871 Treaty of Washington signed

1873 Panic of 1873

1874 Greenback party formed

1876 Battle of Little Big Horn

1877 Rutherford B. Hayes declared President
Reconstruction ends

CHAPTERS

In 1860, the compromises that had held the North and the South together failed. Several southern states withdrew from the Union and formed the Confederate States of America. A Confederate attack on Fort Sumter started the Civil War, which lasted four bitter years. It finally ended with the Confederates' surrender in 1865.

After the Civil War the country needed rebuilding. This period of rebuilding, called Reconstruction, brought new problems, as both the President and Congress wanted to guide the course of Reconstruction. But Reconstruction did give blacks a chance to play a part in political life.

The disputed presidential election of 1876 and the Compromise of 1877 ended Reconstruction. With this, blacks lost all the rights they had worked so hard to win. But other changes were taking place.

"The Cowboy" by Frederic Remington showing bronco-busting records the spirit of the Old West.

General George Pickett's attack on the Union positions was the culmination of the three-day battle at Gettysburg. The breaking of the Union line by about 300 Confederate troops is often called the Confederate high-water mark.

1860

1865

- 1860 Abraham Lincoln elected President
- 1861 Confederacy formed
  Fort Sumter attacked
  Battle of Bull Run
- 1862 Battle of Antietam
- 1863 Emancipation Proclamation
  Battle of Gettysburg
  Siege of Vicksburg
- 1864 General William T. Sherman's troops devastate Georgia
- 1865 General Robert E. Lee surrenders at Appomattox
  President Lincoln assassinated

CHAPTER 17

The Struggle for the Union

Chapter Objectives

After studying this chapter, you will be able to:

- explain what problems the North and the South faced while fighting the war;
- describe how the war affected the North and the South;
- summarize President Lincoln's plan to restore the union.

1 The Struggle Begins—1860 to 1862

Overview Throughout the 1850's, the North and the South grew further apart. By 1860 it looked unlikely that the Union would survive. After the presidential election of 1860, South Carolina seceded—withdrew—from the Union. Efforts at compromise were made, but other states soon followed. These seceded states declared their independence and formed the Confederate States of America. A Confederate attack on the Federal troops at Fort Sumter began the Civil War. This bloody and costly war was to last for four years.

Objectives After reading this section, you will be able to:

- explain why South Carolina seceded from the Union;
- identify the incident that began the Civil War;
- compare the war plans of the North and the South.

The Election of 1860 and Secession. By 1860 the country was deeply divided by sectional differences. This was clearly apparent in the divisions within the political parties. When the Democratic party met in 1860 to choose a candidate to run for the presidency, a split developed. It could not agree on a platform for slavery in the territories. This caused the Democratic party to split into northern and southern sections. The northern section nominated Stephen Douglas for President. His view was that slavery should be decided upon by the people in the states and the territories. The southern section chose John Breckinridge of Kentucky to run for the presidency. His view was that the *Dred Scott* decision of the Supreme Court meant that all territories were open to slavery.

The leading contender for the Republican nomination for President was William Seward. However, after much discussion and bargaining at the Republican Convention in Chicago, Abraham Lincoln was nominated. Another candidate was chosen by a new party, the Constitutional Union party. This party stood for the preservation of the Union and the upholding of the Constitution. The Constitutional Union party offered no position on slavery. John Bell of Tennessee was their candidate.

In the presidential election no candidate had a majority of the popular vote. The votes in the South were split between Breckinridge and Bell. Lincoln was able to win all the northern states but one and was elected President (see map on page 296).

Before the election South Carolina had said that it would secede from the Union if Lincoln was elected President. One month after the election South Carolina seceded. Attempts at compromise were made to prevent other states from seceding. But these failed, and six more states—Georgia, Florida, Alabama, Mississippi, Louisiana, and Texas—soon followed. These seven states declared their independence and formed their own government. They called themselves the Confederate States of America. They adopted their own constitution and chose Jefferson Davis to be their president.

President Lincoln made his Inaugural Address in March of 1861. In his speech he made it clear that he believed a state had no right to secede. He also said that federal laws

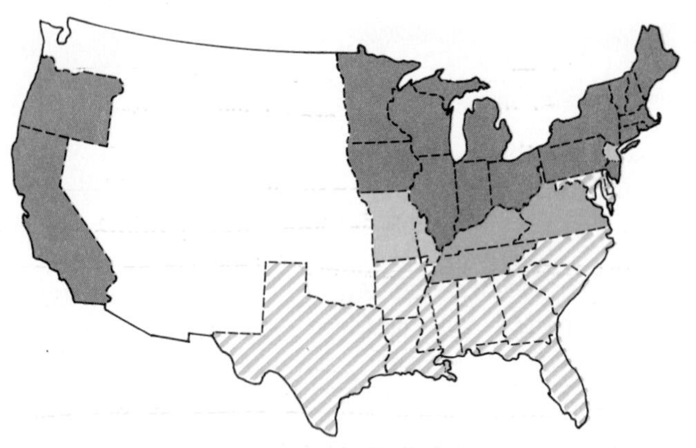

ELECTION OF 1860

	Electoral Votes	Popular Votes
Republican Abraham Lincoln	180	1,865,593
Democratic (Northern) Stephen A. Douglas	12	1,382,713
Democratic (Southern) John C. Breckinridge	72	848,356
Constitutional Union John Bell	39	592,906

Culver Pictures

Photri

The election of Abraham Lincoln (top) as President of the United States in 1860 resulted in the secession of several southern states from the Union. These states soon formed the Confederate States of America and chose Jefferson Davis (bottom) as their leader and Richmond, Virginia, as their capital.

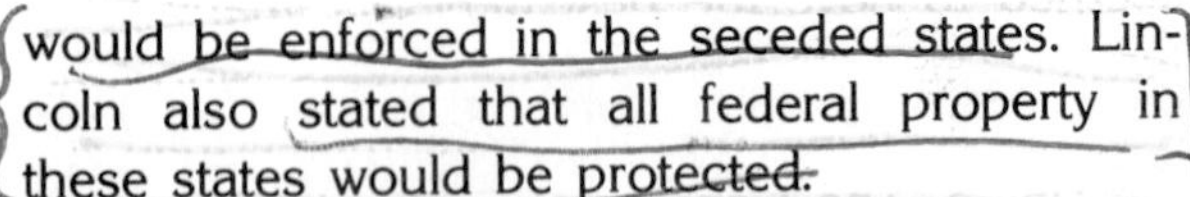

would be enforced in the seceded states. Lincoln also stated that all federal property in these states would be protected.

- *Why did the Democratic party split into northern and southern sections in 1860?*

The War Begins. By March of 1861 the Confederate states had seized most of the federal property within their boundaries. But they had not taken Fort Sumter, in Charleston Harbor. The Confederates decided to starve out the Union troops in the fort. Lincoln had to take action. His close advisers gave him many suggestions. Some said he should let the fort be taken. Others said he should send armed reinforcements. But Lincoln decided to send supplies. The Confederates decided to take the fort before it could be resupplied. If they allowed the supplies to go through, it would appear that they were accepting Lincoln's authority.

The Confederate troops, under General P.G.T. Beauregard, bombarded the fort for two days. Finally, on April 14, 1861, the Union commander, General Robert Anderson, surrendered. President Lincoln then issued a call for 75,000 volunteers to help put down the "rebellion" in the South. Within weeks four more states—Arkansas, Tennessee, North Carolina, and Virginia—seceded and joined the Confederacy.

However, not all the people in Virginia wanted to leave the Union. In the western part of Virginia most people wished to stay in the Union. This area broke away from Virginia and two years later became the state of West Virginia. Several other border states decided to remain in the Union. These were Delaware, Maryland, Kentucky, and Missouri. A similar decision had to be made by several Indian tribes. The Choctaw, Chickasaw, Creeks, Seminoles, and Cherokee all supported the Confederacy. But a group of Cherokee, led by Chief John Ross, and most of the Plains Indians favored the Union.

No major battles were fought for several months as both sides formed their armies. Then, in July 1861, the two forces met at the Battle of Bull Run (see map on page 300). This was called the Battle of Manassas by the Confederates. Many battles of the Civil War have two names. This is because the Union army named battles after the nearest river. The Confederate army, however, named battles after the nearest town.

At Bull Run, both the Union and the Confederate generals were sure that they would defeat their enemy on the first day. People in Washington were so confident the Union army would win that they took picnic baskets to the battlefield.

When the battle began, about 30,000 Union troops, led by General Irvin McDowell, faced an equal number of Confederates commanded by General P.G.T. Beauregard. The Union troops managed to break through the Confederate lines, and a Union victory looked certain. But the Confederate troops were rallied by General Thomas Jackson. A Confederate general said that Jackson stood "like a stone wall against the enemy." After the battle Jackson became known as Stonewall.

After holding their line, the Confederates mounted a counterattack. The Union troops were beaten back and began to retreat. The retreat soon turned into a rout, and the Union troops fled toward Washington.

Bull Run meant little in terms of the final outcome of the war. But it was an important battle. It boosted the Confederates' spirit, and it left the Union army dejected. The battle also showed that the war would not be won in a few days.

■ *What incident started the Civil War?*

Confederate and Union War Plans. At the outset of the war it appeared that the Union had many advantages over the Confederacy (see chart on page 298). The Union had a larger population. It also had most of the country's natural resources and industries. And the North's transportation systems were better than those in the South. The South, however, seemed to have the best generals. Many were former United States Army officers who had decided to fight for their state rather than for the Union. The Confederates also had another advantage in that often they were fighting on their home soil.

Both sides needed a plan by which to fight the war. The Confederate plan, for the most part, was to fight a defensive war. It was thought that if Union attacks could be defeated, people in the North would grow tired of fighting. President Lincoln, on the other hand, felt that the North had to fight an aggressive war—one of attack and conquer. The Union's plan, developed by General Winfield Scott, was then to attack on two fronts. One front would be in the west. The goal there would be to gain control of the Mississippi River. This would cut the Confederacy in half. The other front would be in the east, where the main goal would be the capture of Richmond, Virginia, the Confederate capital. In addition, all southern ports were to be blockaded by the Union navy. This would cut the Confederacy off from trade with other countries.

■ *What was the northern war plan?*

The Blockade. An effective blockade of southern ports was an important part of the Union war effort. However, enforcing a blockade was a difficult task. The Union navy had about 3,500 miles of Confederate coastline to patrol. But very few ships were available. At first, all types of ships were pressed into service. Later, as the war progressed, the Union was able to add more ships built specially for the blockade.

The Confederates, in turn, used specially built ships—called blockade runners—in their attempt to break the blockade. Often these ships were built in European ports.

Most of the Confederate blockade runners sailed out of Nassau, in the Bahamas. Ships from Europe brought goods to Nassau. There the goods were transferred to the blockade runners. If a blockade runner was successful, a cargo of cotton was carried on the return journey.

As the war went on, the Union tightened its blockade on most Confederate ports. In time, fewer blockade runners managed to reach the Confederate ports. By 1864 the Union blockade had effectively cut the South off from outside help.

■ *Which port did Confederate blockade runners sail from on their way to Confederate ports?*

Early Campaigns in the West. The Union plan to gain control of the Mississippi River

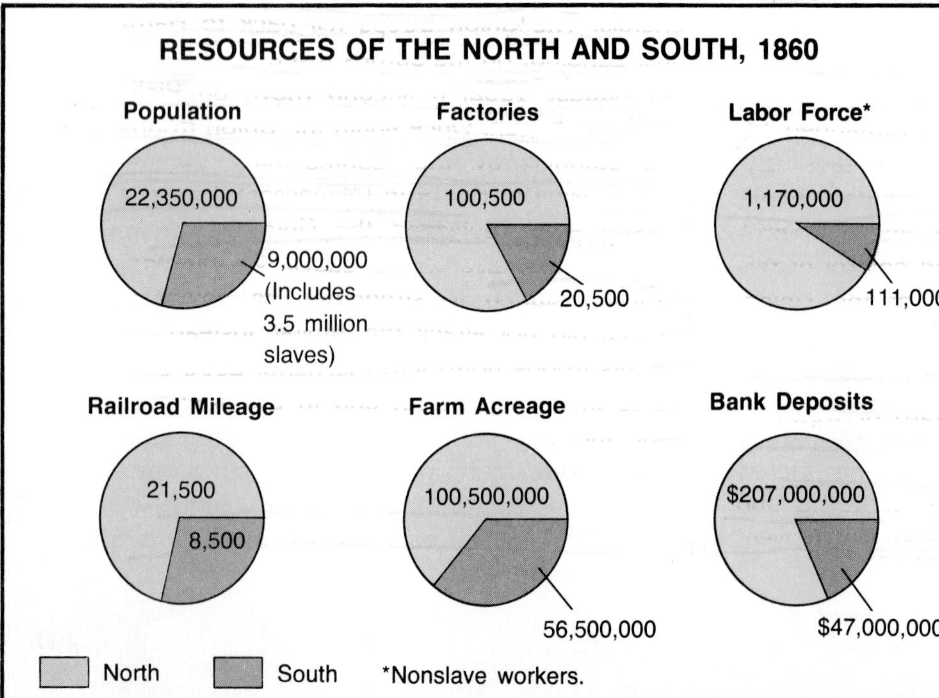

These circle graphs show a comparison of the economic resources of the Union and of the Confederacy at the start of the Civil War. These resources played a crucial role in the outcome of the war. How did the North and the South compare in terms of population, labor force, and railroad mileage?

began in 1862. In February 1862, Union troops moved south from Illinois. They were commanded by a bearded, somewhat shabbily dressed general named Ulysses S. Grant.

Grant's troops first invaded Tennessee and took Forts Henry and Donelson (see map on page 300). These were important Confederate strong points on the Cumberland and Tennessee rivers. After taking these forts, Grant wanted to move on to Corinth, Mississippi. This was an important railroad junction. But Confederate troops, led by General Albert Sidney Johnston, made a surprise attack at Shiloh. Grant was caught completely unprepared. However, he was able to hold his ground, and at the end of the day fresh Union troops arrived. The Confederates were beaten back and retreated to Corinth.

At Shiloh, Grant's troops had suffered heavy losses. General Halleck, commander of the Union troops in the west, removed Grant from the direct fighting. Some of Lincoln's advisers wanted Grant removed from the army altogether. But Lincoln had been impressed with Grant's fighting spirit. "I cannot spare this man," he said. "He fights." Shortly after this Grant was again given a battle command.

The Union campaign in the west continued. In April 1862, a Union fleet, commanded by David Farragut, captured New Orleans. By June 1862, Union troops had entered Memphis, Tennessee. But, by the end of 1862 Union forces had still not gained control of the Mississippi River. The success of the Union plan was still in the balance.

■ *Which two Confederate strongholds fell to Union forces in February of 1862?*

Early Campaigns in the East. While fighting was going on in the west, Union forces were trying to put their eastern plan into effect. The Union goal in the east was to capture Richmond. With the center of the Confederate government in Union hands, Union leaders hoped that the Confederates would stop fighting. In March 1862, the Union general George McClellan moved toward Richmond. He transported his men by water to the peninsula formed by the York and James rivers. His plan was to attack Richmond from the southeast (see map on page 300). Progress to the peninsula was delayed when the Union transport ships were attacked by the Confederate ironclad ship, the *Merrimac.* A Union ironclad ship, the *Monitor,* was sent to help. After a long fight, both ships withdrew, and the Union troops were able to move forward. way to Richmond

McClellan moved his troops slowly up the peninsula. Their progress was further slowed by a Confederate attack at Seven Pines. Confederate troops, led by General Robert E. Lee, turned back McClellan's advance at the Seven Days' Battle (June 25 to July 1, 1862). Lee, and his second in command, Stonewall Jackson, outfought and outwitted the Union generals. The Union troops fell back to Harrison's Landing, on the James River.

In August 1862, a second move on Richmond was begun. Once again the Union troops were stopped by the Confederates. At the second Battle of Bull Run (Manassas), Lee and Jackson again outwitted the Union generals. To Richmond

Fearing that Lee would attack Washington, McClellan started to strengthen its defenses. But Lee did not attack the capital. Instead, he took his troops north into Maryland. Lee's plan was to invade the North and in this way persuade the Union to end the fighting. In September 1862, McClellan brought his troops out to meet the Confederate invasion. The Confederate advance was stopped at the Battle

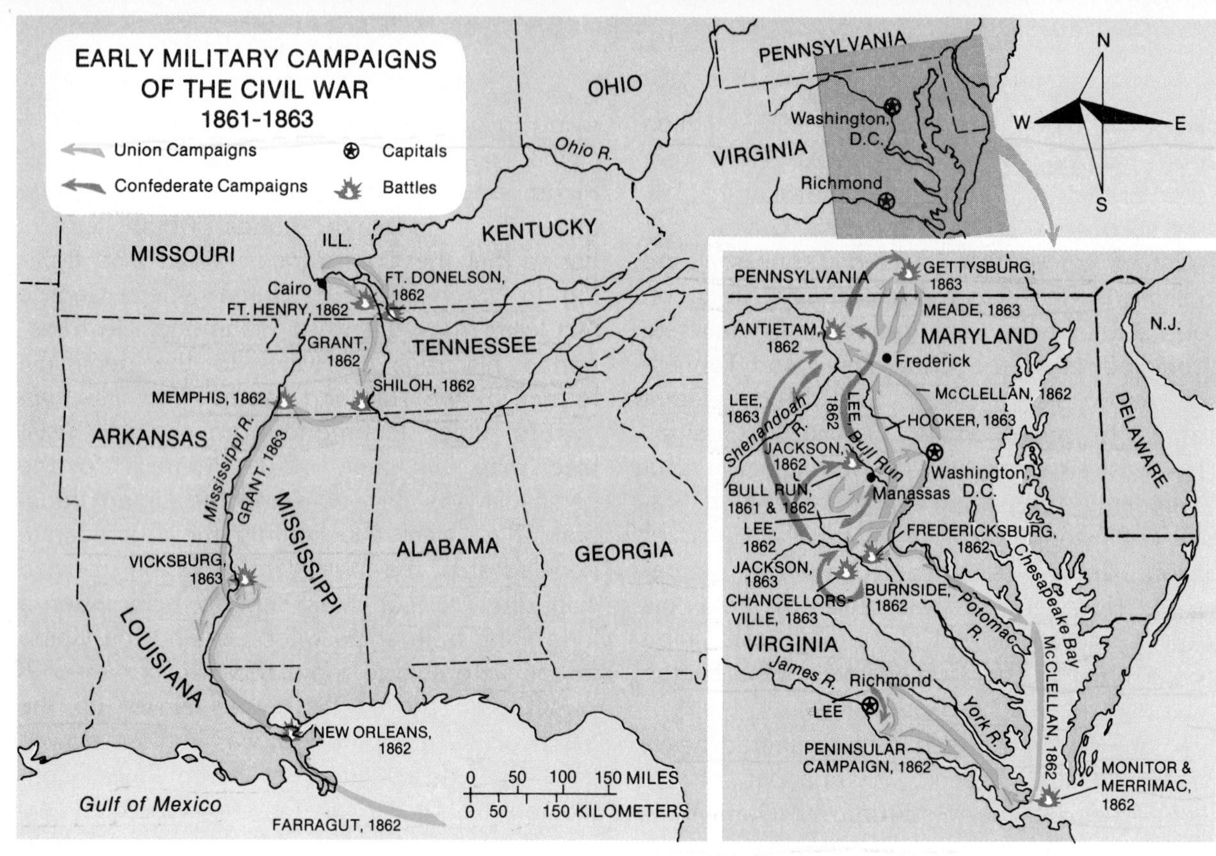

This map illustrates the early battles of the Civil War. Based on the map, what river did the Union plan to control?

of Antietam (Sharpsburg). Lee withdrew the Confederate troops and retreated southward. But McClellan hesitated and did not pursue the retreating Confederates.

Antietam was another battle where losses were great. Total losses for both sides amounted to 23,000 killed or wounded. But it was the first real Union victory in the east. People in the North were encouraged by this victory, and President Lincoln's popularity increased.

Name the two ironclad ships that fought a battle in March of 1862.

SECTION 1 REVIEW

1. *Why did South Carolina secede from the Union?*
2. *What incident began the Civil War?*
3. *How were Union and Confederate war plans different?*

2 The People at War—1862 to 1865

Overview By 1862 most people saw that the war was going to be a long and bitter struggle. Many people, both in the North and in the South, soon began to grow tired of the fighting. There was growing opposition to the way President Lincoln was handling the war. Jefferson Davis was also criticized for his war policies. The North's support for the war increased when President Lincoln issued the Emancipation Proclamation in 1862. Nine months later the turning point came with the Union victory at the Battle of Gettysburg—in July 1863. But it was nearly two more years after Gettysburg before the war finally ended.

Objectives After reading this section, you will be able to:

- discuss how the Emancipation Proclamation strengthened the northern war effort;
- summarize the problems the North and South faced during the war;
- explain why the Battle of Gettysburg was the turning point of the war.

The Emancipation Proclamation. In 1862 President Lincoln was faced with opposition to his war policies. Some people wanted the war to end immediately. They felt that too many lives and too much money had been lost already. These people demanded that President Lincoln make peace with the Confederacy as soon as possible.

President Lincoln also faced opposition from other people. Some of them were members of his own political party. These people wanted him to state that the war was being fought to end slavery. President Lincoln was unwilling to do this because some border states that had remained loyal to the Union still allowed slavery. President Lincoln feared that these states might secede if he announced that the Union was fighting to end slavery in all states.

But President Lincoln was looking for an opportunity to make a *proclamation*—an announcement—about the freeing of slaves in the seceded states. The Union victory at the Battle of Antietam, in September 1862, gave him that opportunity. He issued the Emancipation Proclamation soon after. The proclamation did not become effective until January 1, 1863. It declared that all slaves were freed in all the states that had seceded.

The Emancipation Proclamation was an important document. The North was now fighting to end slavery, as well as to preserve the Union. It lessened the opposition to President Lincoln from his own political party. And the proclamation gained for the Union the support of many people in foreign countries. Also, an

DO YOU KNOW?

Which Civil War general is popularly credited with inventing the game of baseball?

Abner Doubleday is said to have invented the game of baseball at Cooperstown, New York, in the summer of 1839.

Doubleday was a graduate of West Point. He commanded the Union gunners at Fort Sumter. He went on to fight in battles at Bull Run, Antietam, Fredericksburg, and Gettysburg.

Although modern baseball historians question whether Doubleday actually invented the game, the National Baseball Hall of Fame now stands in Cooperstown. It was dedicated in June 1939.

important result of the proclamation was that it involved many more black people in the struggle for the Union.

The extent of black involvement is not well-known. Many blacks served in the Union army. By the end of the war about 180,000 blacks had served in the Union army and navy. Generally, black soldiers were not as well treated as white soldiers. They were put into all-black regiments and were commanded by white officers. Black soldiers also received less pay than white soldiers. But these black soldiers fought very bravely. About 38,000 of them died in the war. And 21 blacks were awarded the Congressional Medal of Honor—our nation's highest award for bravery.

On what date did the Emancipation Proclamation become effective?

President Lincoln Faces More Problems. As well as having to oversee the war on the battlefield, President Lincoln faced problems on the home front. There was opposition to the way he was handling the war. Some of his top cabinet ministers, such as Secretary of State Seward and Secretary of War Stanton, were critical of his actions. The leader of the Union's army, General George McClellan, also thought that President Lincoln was unable to organize the fighting of the war.

Many members of the President's own party were unhappy with his handling of the war. These Radical Republicans formed a committee in Congress—the Joint Committee on the Conduct of the War. Through this committee the Radical Republicans held hearings that resulted in demands that President Lincoln take action to win the war quickly. In addition,

Beginning in May 1863, thousands of black Americans joined the Union army and served with distinction on many Civil War battlefields.

Chicago Historical Society

some Democrats were totally against the war. They wanted President Lincoln to end the war and make peace with the Confederacy. These Peace Democrats were called Copperheads, after a kind of poisonous snake. One outspoken Copperhead was Clement L. Vallandigham of Ohio. His criticism of the war led to his arrest and eventual banishment to the Confederacy. Other Copperheads were arrested when Lincoln suspended *habeas corpus* and declared martial law in some parts of the North. But Lincoln was often lenient in his treatment of people arrested under these conditions.

Opposition to the war also arose in some areas of the North. At the beginning of the war, the Union army had depended on volunteers to boost its size. But the number of volunteers could not replace the losses suffered in the early battles. So, in 1863, Congress passed a conscription act. This act called for the drafting of males between the ages of 25 and 40. But draftees could hire substitutes to serve for them. Or, if a draftee paid the government $300, the draftee did not have to serve at all. To many people the war appeared to be "a rich man's war, and a poor man's fight." The $300 needed to avoid the draft represented more than two thirds of the average worker's yearly earnings. As a result, most men had no choice but to fight. Because of this, riots against the draft broke out in a number of cities.

Another problem for President Lincoln was finding money to pay for the war. He did this in a number of ways. First, tariffs on all imported goods were raised. Taxes on business profits were increased, and a personal income tax was introduced. Also, government bonds were sold to banks. But even these ways could not provide enough money to meet the costs of the war. To meet these costs, President Lincoln ordered that more paper money should be printed. Soon, many people in the North lost faith in this paper money. After a short time its value decreased. The North suffered a growing inflation—rising prices.

■ *Why did the Copperheads oppose President Lincoln's war policies?*

Problems With Foreign Countries. President Lincoln also had problems with some foreign countries. He wanted to stop European countries from giving support to the Confederacy. But he also needed to trade with these countries to get guns and ammunition to fight the war. A number of bad harvests in Europe led to a shortage of food in some countries, such as Great Britain. This enabled President Lincoln to trade wheat to Great Britain in return for war materials.

But the Union's relations with Great Britain were threatened by the *Trent* Affair. Jefferson Davis had appointed James M. Mason and John Slidell to represent Confederate interests in Europe. They were to be transported to Europe on a British ship, the mail steamer *Trent.* A Union ship, the U.S.S. *San Jacinto,* stopped the *Trent* and arrested the two Confederates. Great Britain was ready to go to war over this. But President Lincoln prevented war by freeing the two Confederate representatives.

■ *Why did Great Britain need to trade with the Union during the war?*

Problems for the Confederacy. Jefferson Davis faced the same kind of problems as President Lincoln. He was criticized by many people. His vice-president, Alexander Stephens, was often critical of Davis's actions. Some state governors argued constantly with Davis over their state's rights. Also, some of Davis's closest advisers were opposed to the way he handled the war.

Davis also had problems with some foreign countries. He was interested in gaining the support of these countries. Davis considered that "cotton was king." That is, he thought that European countries, such as Great Britain, would break the Union blockade to get cotton for their textile mills. But this was not the case. These countries simply found other sources of cotton, such as Egypt.

But the Confederacy's most pressing problem was the need for money to pay for the war. The Union blockade made it difficult to raise money through import duties. Income taxes were collected, as was a tax in kind. The tax in kind amounted to about one tenth of each farmer's production. The Confederacy also had to borrow a large amount of money to pay war costs. However, like the Union, the Confederacy was forced to print large amounts of paper money. As the war went on, this paper money lost its value. As in the North, inflation ran at a high rate, and life in the Confederacy became more difficult.

Why did European countries not break the Union blockade to get Confederate cotton?

The Battles Continue. While Lincoln and Davis tried to solve these problems, the battles continued. The first major battle of 1863 was at Chancellorsville, Virginia (see map on page 300). Again, Lee mastered the Union generals, and the Confederates won another victory. But this victory was very costly. The Confederates lost more than 12,000 men, including Stonewall Jackson.

In an attempt to finish the war, Lee decided to attack the North. He thought that a Confederate victory on northern soil might force the Union to stop fighting. He took his men northward into Pennsylvania. Some of his men clashed with a unit of Union cavalry at Gettysburg. Both sides called for reinforcements. The battle raged for three days, from July 1 to July 3. The Union troops, led by General George Meade, held a strong position on high ground just outside Gettysburg. The Confederates bombarded the Union position with artillery throughout the battle. Wave after wave of infantry attacked. But the Union lines held. On July 3, a Confederate charge of 15,000 men, led by General George Pickett, was turned back.

The Confederates had suffered heavy losses. Lee re-formed his men, and they retreated southward across the Potomac. Although he held the advantage, Meade did not pursue the retreating Confederates. But the Union had won a major victory. Gettysburg marked a turning point in the war. From that time the Confederacy was always on the defensive.

The day after the victory at Gettysburg, the Union won another victory. Grant captured the town of Vicksburg, on the Mississippi River (see map on page 300). The Union now controlled all of the Mississippi River. President Lincoln rewarded Grant by giving him the command of all the Union troops in the west. Grant went on to win an important victory at Chattanooga, Tennessee, in November 1863 (see map on page 305).

Grant's successes in the west led to his appointment as leader of all Union troops in March 1864. He immediately took charge of the Union effort to capture Richmond. But Lee checked Grant's progress toward Richmond in a number of battles. Lee eventually put up strong defensive lines at Petersburg, Virginia, and Grant put the town under siege.

In August and September 1864, more Union victories were recorded. David Farragut's fleet captured the port of Mobile, Alabama. And General William T. Sherman took Atlanta, the state capital of Georgia.

Why was General Ulysses S. Grant appointed leader of all Union troops?

The Election of 1864. Sherman's victory at Atlanta came at an important time—just before the presidential election of 1864. During 1864 President Lincoln's popularity had been declining. Again people began to think that he could not win the war. Although Grant was making progress toward Richmond, he seemed unable to beat Lee in battle. Also, the war in the west appeared to be at a standstill.

In June 1864, Lincoln was nominated for President by the National Union party, an alliance of Republicans and Democrats who supported the war. Pro-war Democrat Andrew Johnson of Tennessee was chosen as Vice-President. To oppose Lincoln, the Democratic party nominated General George McClellan. Lincoln had sensed the feeling of the people in the North, and he expected to be defeated in the election. But Sherman's victory at Atlanta, and his march through Georgia to the sea, changed things. Final victory now seemed in sight. As a result in November 1864, Lincoln was easily reelected. Lincoln now began to work on a quick end to the war and a fair and lasting peace.

Who was President Lincoln's Democratic opponent in the election of 1864?

Appomattox and the End of the War. The Union army continued to march on to victory. After taking Atlanta, Sherman took his men through Georgia toward Savannah and the sea. Sherman waged a *total war.* This meant the war was being fought against civilians as well as the military. Anything that could be used for the Confederate war effort was either captured or destroyed. Sherman's troops left a 60-mile-wide trail of devastation behind them. Sherman captured Savannah on December

In the final years of the Civil War, the Union army destroyed much of the South. Where did the Union campaign head after reaching Savannah?

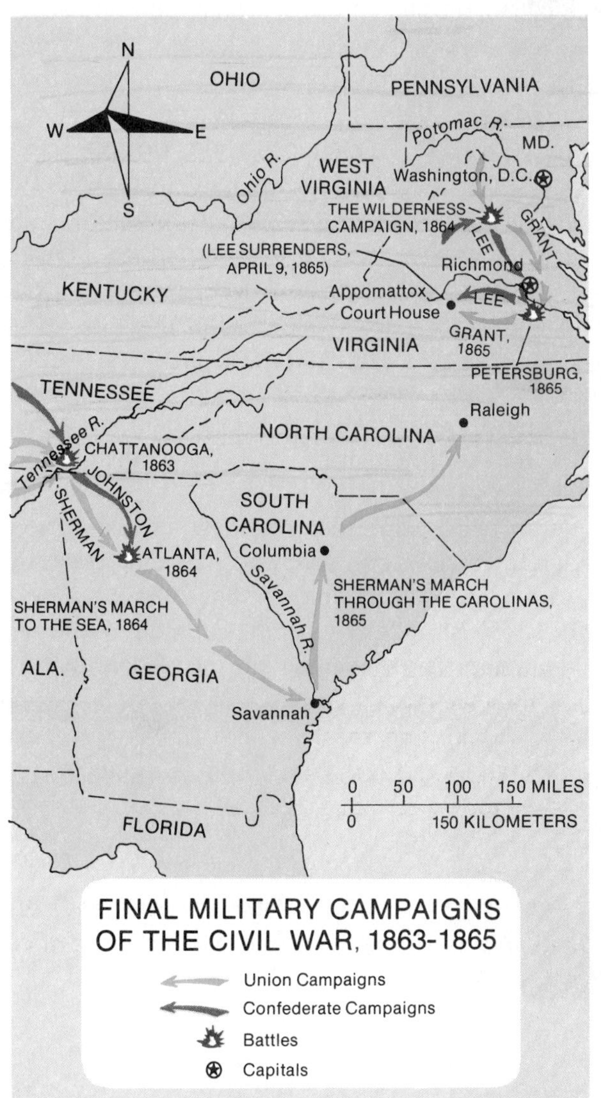

General Ulysses S. Grant earned the command of all Union armies in the spring of 1864, after major victories in the West.

Culver Pictures

21, 1864. He offered it as a Christmas gift to President Lincoln. Sherman then turned his men northward, and they began to march through the Carolinas.

In the east Grant was still laying siege to Petersburg. He did not want to make a frontal attack. Lee's position was too strong. Also, the casualties resulting from a frontal attack would be very heavy. So Grant extended his siege lines. By doing this, he hoped to stretch the Confederate defense lines to the breaking point. This he managed to do on April 2, 1865. The Confederates retreated from Petersburg. This left Richmond open to capture.

Lee's troops were now few in number. They were tired and hungry. On April 9, 1865, Lee surrendered to Grant at Appomattox Court House, Virginia. The terms of surrender were simple. Lee's troops were to lay down their guns and never take them up again to fight the Union. When they had done this, they could go home.

After Lee's surrender, the rest of the Confederate forces soon followed. General Joseph E. Johnston surrendered to Sherman on April 16, 1865, at Raleigh, North Carolina. General Kirby-Smith surrendered all the Confederate troops west of the Mississippi River on May 26, 1865. The last Confederate general to surrender was the Cherokee chief Stand Watie. He surrendered his men on June 23, 1865. The war was now over.

Which Confederate city did General Sherman offer to President Lincoln as a Christmas gift?

SECTION 2 REVIEW

1. *How did the Emancipation Proclamation strengthen the northern war effort?*
2. *What problems with foreign countries did the North and the South have to face during the war?*
3. *Why was the Battle of Gettysburg the turning point of the war?*

VIEWPOINTS DIFFER

The Civil War: Irrepressible Conflict?

William H. Seward, Senator from New York in the 1850's, spoke of an "irrepressible [inevitable] conflict" between the North and the South. Was war between them unavoidable? Historians have reached different conclusions.

Frank L. Owsley, a Southern historian writing in 1930, stressed sectional distinctions (from "The Irrepressible Conflict" in *I'll Take My Stand*):

[factors that caused the war] grew out of two fundamental differences which existed between the two sections: the North was commercial and industrial, and the South was agrarian. The fundamental and passionate ideal for which the South stood and fell was the ideal of an agrarian society.... One section with its peculiar system of society would at one time or another become dominant and control the national government.... Herein lies the irrepressible conflict, the eternal struggle between the agrarian South and the commercial and industrial North to control the government either in its own interest or... to prevent the other section from controlling it in its interests.... Slavery... was part of the agrarian system, but only one element and not an essential one.

James G. Randall, a scholar who taught at the University of Illinois, developed a "revisionist" interpretation. He laid blame for the war on a generation of blundering politicians (from: *Lincoln the Liberal Statesman*, 1947):

Let us take all the factors traditionally presented—the Sumter maneuver [attack], the election of Lincoln, abolitionism, slavery in Kansas, prewar objections to the Union, cultural and economic differences, etc.—and it will be seen that only by a kind of false display could any of these issues, or all of them together, be said to have caused the war if one omits the elements of emotional unreason and overbold leadership. If one word or phrase were selected to account for the war, that word would not be slavery, or economic grievance, or state rights, or diverse civilizations. It would have to be such a word as fanaticism (on both sides), misunderstanding, misrepresentation, or perhaps politics....

Think About It

1. For Owsley, what was the irrepressible conflict?
2. What are some of the words that Randall uses to describe the cause of the Civil War?
3. Which do you think is more directly responsible for war, impersonal forces such as differing economic or cultural systems, or the actions of individual leaders? Explain your answer.

3 The Impact of the War

Overview The Civil War ended with General Robert E. Lee's surrender at Appomattox Court House. But the war left its mark on the country. Thousands of soldiers had been killed in the bitter, four-year sturggle. The economy of the South had been almost destroyed, and plans were needed for rebuilding. President Lincoln had definite ideas about how the former Confederate states were to be readmitted to the Union. He also had plans to help the former slaves. But he was assassinated before these plans were fully put into effect.

Objectives After reading this section, you will be able to:

- recognize the effect of General Lee's surrender on the Confederacy;
- compare the impact of the war on the South and on the North;
- explain President Lincoln's Reconstruction plans.

The End of the Confederacy. General Robert E. Lee's surrender at Appomattox Court House in April 1865 signaled the end of the Confederacy. Other Confederate armies soon laid down their arms. But Jefferson Davis and some other members of the Confederate government hoped to continue the fight. When Richmond fell to Union troops, they fled southward through the Carolinas to Georgia. But in May 1865, Jefferson Davis was captured. He was taken to Virginia and imprisoned at Fortress Monroe. He was held for trial on charges of treason. During the war, northerners had threatened to hang Davis "to a sour apple tree." But after the war ill-feeling toward Davis faded. Two years after his arrest he was freed on bail. His trial was never held.

A number of other prominent southern citizens also were imprisoned for a short time. But they too were never tried. In fact, only one Confederate officer was tried for war crimes. He was Major Henry Wirz, the commandant of the prison camp at Andersonville, Georgia. He was found guilty and was executed in November 1865. At the end of the war, Confederate soldiers were allowed to return to their homes. But most returned to a land damaged by the long and bitter struggle.

■ *Where was Jefferson Davis imprisoned after his capture by Union cavalry?*

The Impact of the War in the South. Nearly everybody in the South was affected in some way by the war. About 900,000 men served as Confederate soldiers. More than 150,000 of these soldiers lost their lives during the war. The majority of the battles were fought on southern soil, and this left large areas of the South devastated. In some places the North had followed a policy of total war. Everything that could be used by the Confederate army was destroyed. For example, General William T. Sherman, in his march across Georgia in 1864, destroyed farms, factories, and railroads. In addition, retreating Confederate forces often destroyed anything that might be useful to the enemy. Richmond, Virginia, the Confederate capital, for example, was burned by retreating Confederate troops.

Thus by 1865, much of the South was in ruins. The southern economy had collapsed. It had cost the South about two billion dollars to

In early April 1865, members of the Confederate government fled Richmond, Virginia. How would you describe the city after the war?

The Bettmann Archive

fight the war. To recover from the war would take many more billions of dollars and years of work. The defeat of the Confederacy also left many people in the South feeling bitter and uncertain. Before the war, life in the South had been based on the institution of slavery. The Union's victory in the war brought an end to slavery. In the years that followed, blacks and whites had to find new ways to live together.

In which part of the country were most of the Civil War battles fought?

The Impact of the War in the North. People in the North were also affected by the war. About 1,500,000 men had served in the Union army. More than 350,000 of these soldiers died in the war. But, since few battles were fought on northern soil, the North was left in a much better condition than was the South. In some ways the North actually prospered from the war. For example, the North's industries grew during the war. New factories had been built to provide the Union army with war materials. In 1864, sixty-five new factories were opened in Philadelphia alone. New farming machinery was used to produce more food. More reapers and mowers were made during the war than in all the years between 1833 and 1860. Also, nearly 4,000 more miles [6 437 kilometers] of railroad track were laid during the war.

Although often overlooked, women played an important part in the war on both sides. Union and Confederate forces employed women as spies. Women also served as nurses in the armies. One nurse, Clara Barton, later helped to found the American Red Cross. A few women dressed as men and actually fought in some battles. But perhaps more important was that women in the North and the South often ran the farms and took jobs in factories when men left to serve in the army.

Chicago Historical Society

Belle Boyd served as a spy for the Confederacy during the early years of the Civil War.

In the North, the combined efforts of men and women led to economic growth and victory. In the South, the war left destruction in its wake. The job of rebuilding the South fell heavily upon those that remained. The Union also needed to be re-formed. This time of rebuilding is known as the *Reconstruction.*

Did the North prosper from the war?

Lincoln's Plan for Reconstruction. At the end of the war, President Lincoln was faced with two problems. First, he had to decide how the *freedmen*—former slaves—were to be helped in adjusting to freedom. Second, he had to decide how the former Confederate states were to be readmitted to the Union.

President Lincoln knew that the freedmen had to adjust to a new way of life. To help solve the problem, the Freedmen's Bureau was established. The bureau provided free food for needy freedmen after the war. The bureau also helped to set up schools for black children. It also helped many freedmen to find jobs.

To help solve the second problem, President Lincoln planned to bring the former Confederate states back into the Union as quickly as possible. In his second Inaugural Address, in March 1865, he said he hoped to treat the South "with malice toward none, with charity for all." His Reconstruction plan was simple. A former Confederate could become a United States citizen again by taking an oath. In the oath, the former Confederate would swear loyalty to the Union and to the Constitution. In addition, the Emancipation Proclamation would also have to be accepted. Then, when 10 percent of the people in the state who were eligible to vote in 1860 had taken this oath, the former Confederate state could set up a new state government. The state could then be readmitted to the Union by Congress. Tragically, President Lincoln was assassinated before his plan could be put fully into effect.

Which government agency was set up to help freedmen?

Lincoln's Assassination. The days after Lee's surrender at Appomattox were a busy time for President Lincoln. On Good Friday, April 14, 1865, he decided to relax by watching a play at Ford's Theater. During the play, John Wilkes Booth, a well-known actor and a Confederate sympathizer, shot President Lincoln once in the head. Booth then leaped to the stage, breaking his leg. But he still managed to escape. President Lincoln was taken to a house near the theater. He died early the next morning.

A wave of grief hit the country. Even those who had opposed him were shocked and saddened at President Lincoln's death. Many thousands of people viewed the funeral procession that took his body from Washington to Springfield, Illinois.

Secretary of War Stanton personally took charge of the hunt for those responsible for President Lincoln's death. A few days later, Booth was trapped in a barn and shot. A number of people stood trial for conspiring with Booth to kill the President. Four of them were executed. But, to this day, a mystery surrounds the true circumstances of the assassination of President Lincoln.

Even though the country was grief stricken, the work of Reconstruction had to go on. Vice-President Andrew Johnson was sworn in as President. He hoped to follow Lincoln's plans for Reconstruction.

Who organized the hunt for the people responsible for President Lincoln's death?

SECTION 3 REVIEW

1. *What happened to the Confederacy after General Lee surrendered?*
2. *What impact did the war have on the South?*
3. *How did President Lincoln plan to bring the former Confederate states back into the Union?*

CHAPTER 17 SUMMARY

At the time of the election of 1860, the United States was split by sectional differences. When Abraham Lincoln was elected President in 1860, South Carolina seceded from the Union. Attempts to restore the Union failed, and more southern states seceded. These states declared their independence and called themselves the Confederate States of America. When Lincoln tried to resupply Fort Sumter in Charleston Harbor, South Carolina, the Confederates bombarded the fort. The Confederate states and the Union were now at war. Most people thought that the war would be over in a matter of weeks. But it became a long and bitter struggle.

During the war, both Lincoln and the Confederate president, Jefferson Davis, faced many problems. Even their closest advisers were critical of the way Lincoln and Davis handled the war. In late 1862, Lincoln took the first step toward ending slavery by issuing the Emancipation Proclamation. This freed slaves in the seceded states. Several months later, in July 1863, the Union won a decisive victory at Gettysburg. This victory was the turning point of the war. From then on, the Confederates were always on the defensive.

The Union battle plan, a blockade of southern ports and fighting the war on two fronts, began to wear the Confederates down. General Robert E. Lee finally surrendered to General Ulysses S. Grant at Appomattox Court House in April 1865. Total war had devastated the South. President Lincoln then set about the work of Reconstruction. But he was assassinated before he could put his plans into effect.

CHAPTER 17 REVIEW

USING YOUR SKILLS

Reading Bar Graphs

Graphs enable us to compare figures easily. The bar graph below shows the number of deaths suffered by America's armed forces from the Revolutionary War to the conflict in Vietnam. Both battle deaths and deaths due to other causes, such as disease, are shown. Study the bar graph carefully; then answer the following questions:

1. In which war did the greatest number of armed-forces personnel die in battle?
2. How many members of the armed forces died of disease and other nonbattle causes in the Revolutionary War?
3. In which war did the greatest number of armed-forces personnel die from nonbattle and battle causes?
4. In which war did the least number of personnel die from all causes?
5. What changes are there in the balance between battle deaths and other deaths after World War I?
6. Why do you think battle deaths are greater than other deaths in the wars after World War I?

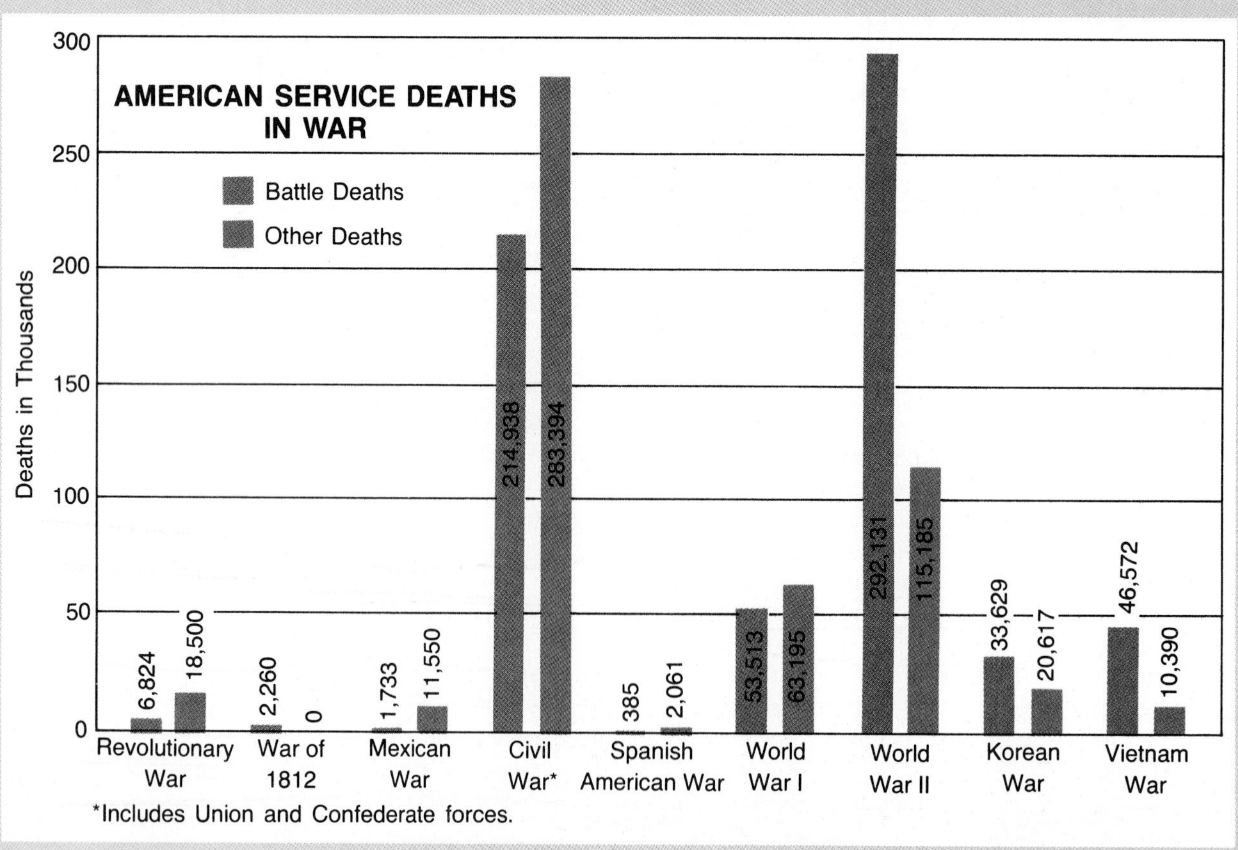

CHAPTER 17 REVIEW

YOU SHOULD KNOW

Identify, define, or explain each of the following:

Jefferson Davis	total war
proclamation	Clara Barton
Trent Affair	Reconstruction
William T. Sherman	freedmen

CHECKING FACTS

1. What four candidates ran for the presidency in 1860?
2. What was the first real Union victory in the East?
3. What did the Emancipation Proclamation state?
4. Who were the Copperheads?
5. What did the conscription act passed by Congress in 1863 call for?
6. What methods did the Union and the Confederacy use to raise money to fight the war?
7. What was the importance of the Union victory at Vicksburg?
8. Where did the Civil War end?
9. What was the Freedmen's Bureau?
10. When was President Lincoln assassinated?

UNDERSTANDING CONCEPTS

1. What were the goals of the northern war plan?
2. What was the importance of the Battle of Gettysburg?
3. What effect did General William T. Sherman's success in Georgia have on the presidential election of 1864?
4. What effect did the North's policy of total war have on the South?

LEARNING FROM ILLUSTRATIONS

1. According to the election map on page 296, how many states were won by Abraham Lincoln? How many states were won by John C. Breckinridge?
2. Study the circle graphs on page 298. What economic resources of the South were less than one fourth of the total of those resources for the United States as a whole in 1860?

CRITICAL THINKING

1. Do you think that President Lincoln's decision to send supplies to Fort Sumter was a good one? Why or why not?
2. Do you think that President Lincoln would have issued the Emancipation Proclamation had there not been a war? Why do you think so?
3. What do you think might have been the outcome of the Civil War if the Confederates had won the Battle of Gettysburg? Give reasons for your answer.

ENRICHMENT ACTIVITIES

1. Working in groups, some students might like to make a study of several Civil War battles. Each group should research and collect information about a particular battle. Information can be found in encyclopedias and historical atlases. Each group should then write a report for presentation to the class. The report should be illustrated with maps and diagrams.
2. Some students might like to draw a cartoon of President Lincoln that might have appeared in a southern newspaper or a cartoon of Jefferson Davis that might have appeared in a northern newspaper.

1865					1870

- 1865 Congress drafts the Thirteenth Amendment
  Congress establishes Freedmen's Bureau
  Vice-President Andrew Johnson becomes President
- 1866 Congress passes the Civil Rights Act
  Congress drafts the Fourteenth Amendment
- 1867 Congress passes the Military Reconstruction Act
  Reconstruction Acts passed
  Tenure of Office Act passed
  Granger movement established
  Alaska purchased
- 1868 President Johnson's impeachment trial and acquittal
  Ulysses S. Grant elected President
- 1869 Congress drafts the Fifteenth Amendment
  Knights of Labor founded
- 1871 Treaty of Washington signed

CHAPTER 18

The Impact of Reconstruction

Chapter Objectives

After studying this chapter, you will be able to:

- discuss how the plans for Reconstruction of President Lincoln and of President Johnson differed from the Reconstruction plan of Congress;
- explain how Radical Republicans in Congress put their own plan for Reconstruction into effect and impeached President Johnson;
- identify some of the problems and achievements of the United States during President Grant's first term in office.

1 The Plans for Reconstruction

Overview After the Civil War a period of reconstruction was needed. The former Confederate states had to be readmitted to the Union. The southern economy, destroyed by the war, had to be rebuilt. And a society without slavery had to be formed.

During the Civil War, President Lincoln had put forward his plan for Reconstruction. President Johnson, after Lincoln's death, tried to follow a similar plan. But Radical Republicans in Congress were not satisfied with the President's efforts. They were determined to take charge of Reconstruction themselves.

Objectives After reading this section, you will be able to:

- compare President Lincoln's and the Radical Republicans' views on Reconstruction;
- explain why Congress wanted to control Reconstruction;
- analyze the effect the congressional elections of 1866 had on Reconstruction.

Early Reconstruction. Even before the Civil War was over, people in the North were discussing what should be done with the Confederate states. President Lincoln did not look upon the Confederacy as an enemy country to be conquered and punished. He felt that all that was needed was to return the Confederate states to the Union. As early as 1863, President Lincoln had issued a proclamation that stated his plan for Reconstruction. Under Lincoln's plan a former Confederate state could set up a new state government when 10 percent of the state's voters who had voted in 1860 had taken an oath of loyalty. They also had to agree to accept the Emancipation Proclamation. With this plan, Lincoln hoped to reconstruct the Union as quickly as possible. He felt that defeat in the war would be punishment enough for the Confederate states.

It soon became clear that most Radical Republicans in Congress did not agree with President Lincoln. They were against Lincoln's plan because they thought that the Confederate states should be punished for waging war against the Union. There was also a political reason for opposition to the President's plan for Reconstruction. It arose over the question of who should take charge of Reconstruction. If President Lincoln's plan was accepted, the President would control Reconstruction, and not Congress. Therefore, the Radical Republicans in Congress put forward their own Reconstruction plan, the Wade-Davis bill.

Under the Wade-Davis bill, before a new state government could be set up in a former Confederate state, more than 50 percent of the state's voters who had voted in 1860 had to take a loyalty oath. Also, a new state constitution had to be drawn up by a state convention and accepted by Congress. The Wade-Davis bill was passed in 1864. But President Lincoln thought the terms of the bill were too harsh, and he vetoed it.

Although President Lincoln and Congress did not agree on how Reconstruction should be organized, both agreed that Reconstruction should end slavery. To this end, Congress drafted the Thirteenth Amendment to the Constitution [*97-*98] in 1865. This amendment abolished slavery throughout the United States.

President Lincoln and Congress also agreed

on the need to help former slaves once they were freed. As a result, in March 1865, Congress established the Freedmen's Bureau. It was headed by General Oliver O. Howard and was staffed by volunteers. The Freedmen's Bureau's main goals were to provide education and jobs for former slaves in the South.

Thus, by early 1865, even before the war had ended, plans for Reconstruction were under way. Although President and Congress still disagreed, three former Confederate states—Arkansas, Louisiana, and Tennessee—had formed new governments under Lincoln's plan. But in April 1865, President Lincoln was killed. At this point, Vice-President Andrew Johnson became President, and the struggle over Reconstruction began again.

■ *What did the Thirteenth Amendment to the Constitution do?*

Johnson's Plan for Reconstruction. The new President, Andrew Johnson, was a Democrat and a southerner from Tennessee. He came from humble beginnings. He never attended school and only learned to read and write after he married, when his wife taught him. But by the age of 27, he had served 3 terms as mayor of Greensville, Tennessee, and had been elected to the Tennessee legislature. In the next 20 years he served his state as governor and as a representative and a senator in the United States Congress. In 1864 he was elected Vice-President of the United States on the National Union ticket headed by Republican Abraham Lincoln.

Andrew Johnson was an able, hardworking man, but he was also very stubborn. He also was a southerner and a Democrat. Because of this, many Radical Republicans thought that he should play no part in Reconstruction. However, President Johnson fully intended to play a major part in the reconstruction of the South.

The Granger Collection

The Freedmen's Bureau helped to organize schools, like this one in Vicksburg, Mississippi, to give former slaves the formal education that had been denied them before emancipation.

Johnson's plan for Reconstruction was much like that of Lincoln. However, Johnson also wanted each new state government to ratify the Thirteenth Amendment. In addition, his plan required former Confederate army officers, government officials, and landowners with holdings worth more than $20,000 to ask for presidential pardon. This pardon was normally given freely, as Johnson, like Lincoln, did not want to punish the southern people.

By December 1865, all former Confederate states except Texas had set up new state governments. These states had also elected representatives to Congress. But Congress would not allow these representatives to take their seats. The Radical Republicans thought that Johnson's plan was not hard enough on the South. They felt that the South should be made to suffer for fighting against the Union. Congress was particularly angry because many of the new representatives elected to Congress from the South were former Confederate soldiers or officials. Even Alexander Stephens, the former Confederate vice-president, had been elected as a senator from Georgia.

The Radical Republicans were also upset about the way freedmen were being treated in the South. In many ways things were little different from the way they were during the days of slavery. Riots in cities, such as New Orleans, led to the murder of some freedmen. Also, all the former Confederate states except Tennessee had passed *Black Codes.* These were laws that restricted the rights of the freedmen. These laws made certain that whites remained in control in the South.

■ *Under President Johnson's Reconstruction plan, which former Confederates were required to ask for presidential pardon?*

Congress Takes Command. Radical Republicans in Congress would not accept President Johnson's efforts at Reconstruction. Some powerful Radical Republicans wanted to change the southern society so that blacks and whites would live together as equals. Since Johnson's plan had not achieved this goal, these Radical Republicans wanted to take charge of Reconstruction. At the same time, more moderate Radical Republicans wanted to take charge of Reconstruction because they thought that Congress, and not the President, should have control.

In December 1865, Congress took its first step to take charge by setting up the Joint Committee of Fifteen. This committee was made up of six senators and nine representatives. The most notable member of the committee was Representative Thaddeus Stevens of Pennsylvania. Stevens was against slavery, and he disliked the South. He also had strong feelings about President Johnson. He thought Johnson was a "scoundrel." The Joint Committee of Fifteen soon came to play a leading part in Congressional Reconstruction.

With the Joint Committee providing advice and guidance, Congress drafted a number of Reconstruction bills during 1866. The first was the Freedmen's Bureau bill. This extended the duties of the Freedmen's Bureau, which had been set up in 1865. Another was the Civil Rights bill. President Johnson vetoed both bills. In April 1866, Congress passed the Civil Rights Act over the President's veto. The Civil Rights Act gave citizenship to blacks and guaranteed equal civil rights to all persons born in the United States, except the American Indian.

Then, in June 1866, Congress drafted the Fourteenth Amendment [*99-*103] to the Constitution. This was a rewriting of the Civil Rights Act, since Congress feared that the courts might declare the Civil Rights Act unconstitutional. President Johnson advised the southern states not to ratify the Fourteenth Amendment. All the southern states except Tennessee followed his advice. When Tennessee ratified the Fourteenth Amendment, in July 1866, Congress readmitted Tennessee to the Union.

■ *What committee gave Congress advice and guidance on Reconstruction?*

During the 1866 congressional elections, President Johnson toured many parts of the nation in an unsuccessful campaign against the reelection of Radical Republicans.

The Granger Collection

Congressional Elections. By mid-1866, the Radical Republicans seemed to be in charge of Reconstruction. But President Johnson's veto powers stopped them from having complete control. A two-thirds majority was needed in Congress to pass a bill over the President's veto. The Radical Republicans, therefore, needed greater representation in Congress. They hoped to gain this in the congressional elections of 1866.

President Johnson played a leading part in the election campaign. He made speeches in a number of cities in the Midwest. His goal was to get backing for Democratic candidates and for his Reconstruction plan. His speaking tour began well, but things then began to go wrong. Johnson often got into arguments with hecklers. Sometimes, fighting broke out at his speeches. Johnson's tour became a disaster and actually harmed the Democratic election campaign. In the election the Radical Republicans gained control of the House of Representatives and the Senate. They were in a position to pass bills over the President's veto. By mid-1867, the Radical Republicans were in full control of Reconstruction.

How large a majority is needed in Congress to pass a bill over the President's veto?

SECTION 1 REVIEW

1. *How did Lincoln's and the Radical Republicans' views on Reconstruction differ?*
2. *Why did Congress want to control Reconstruction?*
3. *What effect did the congressional elections of 1866 have on Reconstruction?*

2 Radical Reconstruction in the South

Overview After the congressional elections of 1866, the Radical Republicans put their own Reconstruction plan—set down in the various Reconstruction acts of 1867—into effect. The Radical Republican plan was harsher than the plan of either President Lincoln or President Johnson.

Throughout the following two years, relations between President Johnson and Congress grew worse. Finally, the House of Representatives impeached the President. He was tried by the Senate in May 1868.

Republicans, supported by the presence of federal soldiers, took over the state governments in the South. Blacks played an important part in these Radical Reconstruction governments.

Objectives After reading this section, you will be able to:

- summarize the terms of Radical Reconstruction;
- explain why the House of Representatives impeached President Johnson;
- discuss which groups of Republicans controlled state governments in the South during Radical Reconstruction.

Radical Reconstruction Begins. The congressional elections of 1866 had given the Radical Republicans control of Congress and Reconstruction. They then set about the task of defeating President Johnson's plan for Reconstruction. They did this through the Military Reconstruction Act, which Congress passed in March 1867. This act placed the former Confederate states into five military districts (see map on page 320). Tennessee, which had been readmitted to the Union in 1866, was not included. Each military district was governed by a federal army general and was policed by federal soldiers.

Under the provisions of this Reconstruction act, the ten former Confederate states were to hold state constitutional conventions. Voting for delegates to these conventions was to be open to both blacks and whites. The constitutional conventions were to draw up new state constitutions that gave blacks the rights to vote and hold office. The Reconstruction act also stated that these rights should be withheld from certain classes of ex-Confederates. When a state constitution was completed, and it was found to be acceptable by Congress, that state could elect a new government. Once this was done, and once the state had ratified the Fourteenth Amendment, it could be readmitted to the Union by Congress.

However, most white southerners were unwilling to accept the Military Reconstruction Act. They feared it would replace the old ex-Confederate state officials with former slaves. Therefore, in some southern states, constitutional conventions were not called. In the other southern states some whites tried to keep blacks from registering to vote. Those blacks who were able to register often were kept from voting. To stop this, Congress passed a second Reconstruction act, also in March 1867. This act gave the army the power to register voters and to oversee the voting for delegates to state constitutional conventions.

Nevertheless, white resistance to both Reconstruction acts went on. The acts required that any new state constitution had to be approved by a majority of those registered to

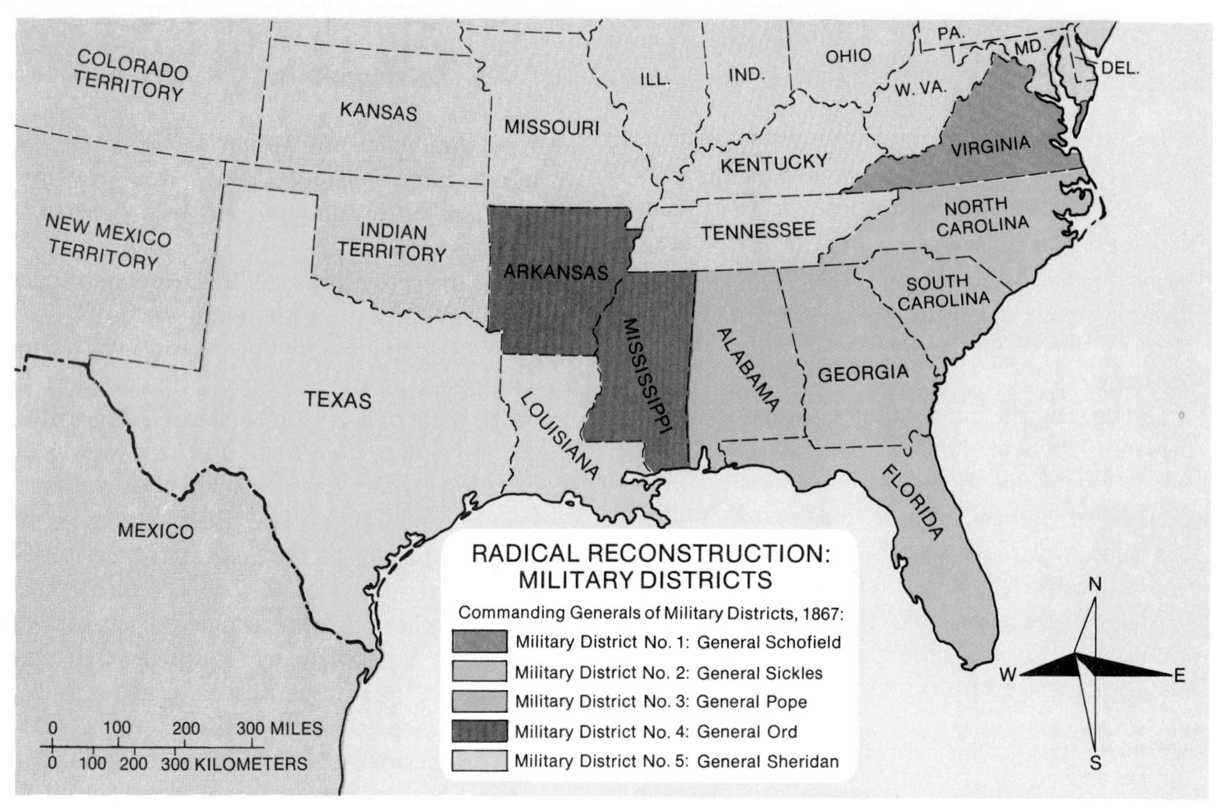

Into how many districts did the Military Reconstruction Act of 1867 group the former Confederate states?

vote. By not voting, whites found that they could block approval of the new constitutions and the progress of Reconstruction. In July 1867, Congress acted again. Yet another Reconstruction act was passed. Under this act only a majority of those voting was needed to approve new state constitutions.

■ *Why were southern whites opposed to the Military Reconstruction Act?*

The End of Radical Reconstruction. By the end of 1868, six southern states had been readmitted to the Union under the terms of the various Reconstruction acts. The remaining four—Georgia, Mississippi, Texas, and Virginia—were finally readmitted under different rules. In addition to the requirements of the Reconstruction acts, these states had to ratify the Fifteenth Amendment [*104-*105] to the Constitution. This amendment, drafted by Congress in 1869, protected the rights of blacks to vote. The Radical Republicans had proposed the Fifteenth Amendment primarily because they felt that the rights of blacks needed to be protected. But they also saw in the Fifteenth Amendment a way to strengthen the Republican party. Since the Republican party had freed the slaves, most blacks were expected to vote for Republican candidates.

Congressional Reconstruction drew to a close in July 1870, when the last former Confederate state, Georgia, was readmitted to the Union. During the period of Congressional Reconstruction, Congress had tried to increase its power and become the strongest of the three branches of government. For example, in 1868, Congress had tried to weaken the judicial branch. This was done by passing an act denying the Supreme Court jurisdiction over Reconstruction. And in the same year, Congress struck at the executive branch when an attempt was made to remove the President from office.

■ *Which former Confederate state was the last to be readmitted to the Union?*

The Impeachment of President Johnson. From the start of his presidency, Johnson's relationship with Congress had worsened. His veto of certain Reconstruction bills had upset many members of Congress. Influential members of Congress, such as Senator Charles Sumner and Representative Thaddeus Stevens, had little respect for Johnson. As a result, Sumner, Stevens, and other Radical Republicans set about to reduce the power of the President. They began by passing the Tenure of Office Act in March 1867. This act stated that a federal official who had been appointed by the President, and approved by the Senate, could not be dismissed without the Senate's permission.

In February 1868, President Johnson dismissed Secretary of War Stanton. Johnson had long thought that Stanton was sympathetic to the Radicals. The House of Representatives immediately *impeached* Johnson. To *impeach* means to charge a public official with wrongdoings. The power to impeach belongs to the House of Representatives (see Article I of the Constitution).

President Johnson was charged with "high crimes and misdemeanors." Specifically he was charged with violating the Tenure of Office Act. In keeping with the provisions of the Constitution, the Senate sat in judgment of the impeachment. Among representatives speaking for the removal of the President were Stevens; Benjamin Butler of Massachusetts; and George Boutwell, also of Massachusetts. A number of speakers made damaging remarks about Johnson's character and ability. Some even tried to connect Johnson with the assassination of President Lincoln.

President Johnson did not attend the trial, but his case was presented by a number of lawyers. Their defense was that the Tenure of Office Act was unconstitutional. In addition, they argued that the act did not even apply to Secretary Stanton, since he had been appointed by Lincoln, not by Johnson. Thirty-six votes were needed for conviction. When the vote was taken, in May 1868, seven Republican senators voted not guilty. The bid to remove the President had failed by one vote—35–19.

Many historians feel that Johnson's acquittal saved the prestige and power of the presidency. However, the impeachment and trial came in the year of a presidential election. This ended Johnson's political career. He had expected to be nominated for President by the Democrats. But, instead, they chose Horatio Seymour, a former governor of New York. The Republicans nominated Civil War hero Ulysses S. Grant. In the election, held in November 1868, Grant won an easy victory in the electoral college. But the outcome of the popular

(Text continues on page 323.)

In 1868, the dismissal of Secretary of War Stanton by President Johnson led to the impeachment of the President by the House of Representatives. In the Senate trial that followed, Senator Ross, a Republican, cast the deciding vote that led to the acquittal of President Johnson.

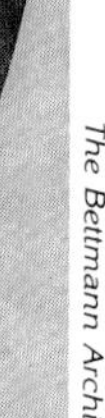

The Bettmann Archive

Thaddeus Stevens, leader of the House Republicans

Picture Collection, the Branch Libraries, New York Public Library

Edwin M. Stanton, Secretary of War

Culver Pictures

President Andrew Johnson

The Bettmann Archive

Charles Sumner, leader of the Senate Republicans

Historical Pictures Service

Edmund Ross, Republican senator from Kansas

vote was not so one-sided (see map on this page). With a Republican now in the White House, the Radical Republicans went on with their reconstruction plans unhindered.

■ *Which house of Congress has the power to impeach?*

Reconstruction Governments. As you have read, during Radical Reconstruction, Republicans had taken control of state governments in the South. The presence of federal soldiers meant that this takeover was met with little effective opposition from southern whites. There were three groups of Republicans involved in state governments at this time. One group was largely made up of former slaves—the freedmen. The other two groups were the *carpetbaggers* and the *scalawags.*

Carpetbaggers were people from the North who moved to the South after the Civil War. They got their name from the type of bag that many of them used to carry their belongings. Often, southern whites looked upon carpetbaggers as corrupt people only interested in making money. Some carpetbaggers were corrupt. But most of them were honest people who wanted to help the South. Many of them were teachers working for the Freedmen's Bureau. Other carpetbaggers were interested in developing industry in the South. For example, John Wilder and Willard Warner, both of Ohio, helped build up the iron industry in the South.

Scalawags were ex-Confederates who had joined the Republican party. People in the South usually looked upon them as traitors who had abandoned the South for their own personal gain. Some scalawags were only interested in their own gain. But many others were honest people who accepted that the war was over. They felt that working with the new state governments was the best course to take.

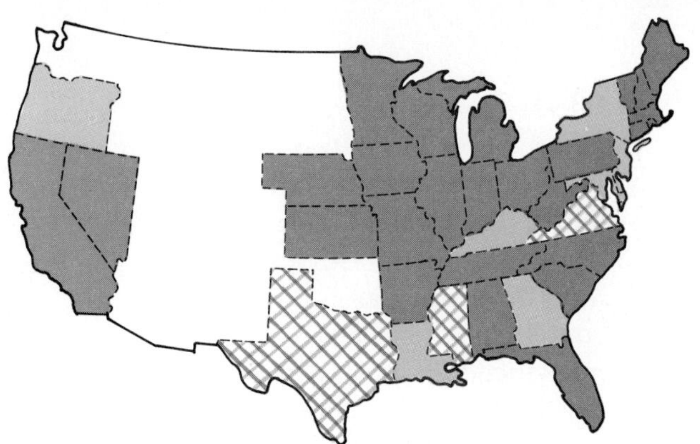

ELECTION OF 1868

	Electoral Votes	Popular Votes
Republican Ulysses S. Grant	214	3,013,421
Democratic Horatio Seymour	80	2,706,829
Not Voted*	23	

*States not readmitted to the Union before election.

In the election of 1868, how many states were not captured by Ulysses S. Grant?

General James Longstreet, for example, was one of Robert E. Lee's most able commanders. However, after the war he endorsed Radical Reconstruction and backed Grant for President in 1868.

The period of Radical Reconstruction is often called Black Reconstruction, because many blacks were involved. But none of the state governments were controlled by blacks. The only state legislature in which blacks were in a majority was in South Carolina, and that was only in the lower house. In fact, few blacks were elected to the highest state offices. And no blacks held the office of state governor, although some were elected lieutenant governor.

During Radical Reconstruction, a number of blacks served in the United States government.

Fourteen blacks were elected to the House of Representatives. And two blacks from Mississippi, Hiram R. Revels and Blanche K. Bruce, served in the United States Senate. Revels held the seat that had been held before the Civil War by Jefferson Davis.

Some black officials were uneducated and inexperienced in politics. Often these officials were under the power of unscrupulous scalawags and carpetbaggers. But many black officials proved to be of great ability and integrity. For example, Blanche K. Bruce, after serving as senator, held important posts in Republican governments until his death in 1898.

■ *Which black senator held the seat once occupied by Jefferson Davis?*

Political Corruption in the South. During the early 1870's charges arose that Republican state governments in the South were corrupt. Today we know that there was some corruption. For example, Franklin J. Moses, Jr., the scalawag governor of South Carolina, stole from the state treasury and accepted bribes. And Henry C. Warmoth, carpetbagger governor of Louisiana, awarded work contracts to those who offered him the largest bribes. On one occasion the South Carolina legislature voted an extra $1,000 to the House speaker after he lost that amount betting on a horse race.

DO YOU KNOW?

Who was the first black American to serve in the United States House of Representatives?

Joseph Hayne Rainey, Republican representative from South Carolina, took his seat in the House in 1870. Rainey was born a slave in Georgetown, South Carolina, in 1832. He served five terms in the House during the years 1870 to 1879. Although Rainey was the first black American to serve, the first black American to be elected to the House was John Willis Menard of Louisiana. But Menard's election was challenged, and he never took his seat.

However, most of the new state governments in the South were effective. Much of the war-torn South was rebuilt during the period of Radical Reconstruction. The South's railroad network was rebuilt and extended. Public education systems were established or improved. And institutions to aid the sick and the poor were built. Even though there was some corruption in Republican governments in the South, it often did not compare with the large-scale corruption in government and business in the North.

■ *What good works were done by Republican governments in the South during Radical Reconstruction?*

SECTION 2 REVIEW

1. *What were the terms of Radical Reconstruction?*
2. *Why did the House of Representatives impeach President Johnson?*
3. *Which three groups of Republicans controlled state governments in the South during Radical Reconstruction?*

3 Political Problems After the War

Overview During the first term of President Ulysses S. Grant, corruption appeared to be widespread in government and business. Grant's political inexperience only made this problem worse. There was also trouble in the field of labor relations. America's industrial development had brought with it a move toward national labor unions. Aside from these problems, there were some successes in foreign affairs in the years following the Civil War.

Objectives After reading this section, you will be able to:

- explain how President Grant's political inexperience contributed to corruption in government and business;
- summarize the aims of the early labor unions;
- discuss the successes in foreign affairs that were achieved during the period after Civil War.

Political Corruption. Some historians see the period after the Civil War as a low point in American history. This is partly because of the widespread corruption that existed in government and in business. The two terms of President Ulysses S. Grant were especially marked by corruption. President Grant was not involved directly in any of the wrongdoings. But his inexperience in politics almost certainly made the problem worse.

Grant's inexperience led to a financial scandal in 1869. In that year Jay Gould and James Fisk, stock exchange speculators, tried to gain control of the gold available on the open market. Once they had control, they planned to sell the gold to the banks at high prices. For their plan to work, they needed to stop the government from selling gold on the open market. Fisk and Gould asked Grant's brother-in-law to help them. Arguing that high gold prices would help farmers, he persuaded the President not to sell gold. Gould and Fisk netted about $11 million from their plan before Grant learned of their true intent. Grant immediately ordered Secretary of State George Boutwell to sell some of the gold held by the

(Text continues on page 327.)

The ruthless financial dealings of Jay Gould (center) and James Fisk caused many small investors to lose their life savings.

The Bettmann Archive

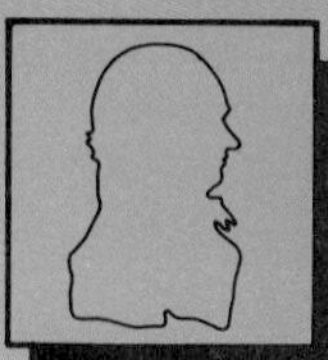

PROFILES

Horace Greeley

Horace Greeley was born on a poor New Hampshire farm in 1811. He had little schooling but enjoyed reading, learning and writing. Horace became an apprentice printer for a small Vermont paper. At the age of twenty he went to New York City to seek his fortune.

Young Greeley spent a year and a half employed as a printer. He pounced at the opportunity to edit a new magazine called *The New Yorker.* Liking his patriotic views, politicians hired him to write campaign magazines. In 1840 he was asked to write a presidential campaign weekly magazine. He called his paper the *New York Tribune.*

Greeley's editorials helped the newspaper to become the first American paper to be read in all parts of the young nation. He was strongly against slavery, but many Southerners who hated him bought his paper to see what he said. He supported Henry Clay's tariffs to promote American manufacturing, and in 1852 rallied the nation to favor homesteading. Greeley said the government should give land to people willing to farm and improve it. The Republican Party, which Greeley helped start, supported the idea. In 1862 Abraham Lincoln opened the West to homesteaders.

Greeley's editorials promoted the idea of Land Grants for education. Many schools, colleges and universities exist today because land was set aside in the 1860's for future schools. In 1865 Greeley wrote in an editorial the phrase that sent clerks and soldiers out to build America. "Go West, Young Man" has influenced American history from the 1850's through the 20th century.

The Granger Collection

Thinking Critically

Since Greeley had little schooling, what was he doing that probably kept him learning new things?

What Democratic ideals did Greeley have that are useful to build democracy today?

How valuable is Greeley's advice to young men and women of the 21st century, or is a new slogan needed?

government on the open market. With gold no longer controlled by the speculators, prices fell. But American business was scandalized. Unscrupulous financiers, playing on Grant's inexperience, had almost caused financial ruin.

During the 1860's, corruption was also found in some city governments. An example of this was the Tweed Ring in New York City. In 1869, William Marcy Tweed gained control of the New York City government. In the next three years, from 1869 to 1872, "Boss" Tweed and his partners cheated the New York taxpayers out of millions of dollars. Exactly how much the Tweed Ring stole is unknown. Some estimates run as high as $100 million. After the fraud was discovered, Tweed fled to Spain. But the Spanish government returned him to the United States to face trial. He was tried and convicted and eventually died in jail.

■ *Who attempted to gain control of the gold market in 1869?*

Culver Pictures

How does this cartoon attack Boss Tweed's use of public funds to win votes?

Corruption in Business. In business circles, corruption was probably most apparent in the railroad industry. Before the Civil War, federal and state governments had made land grants to railroad companies for the purpose of railroad construction. The railroad companies were able to sell some of the land to cover construction costs. The land was of little value when the grants were made. But, with the railroads running over it, the land gained in value. The railroads were able to charge high prices for the land and thus made large profits.

Land grants to railroad companies were ended in the early 1870's. But by then nearly 200 million acres [80 940 000 hectares] had been granted to the railroads. At one time large parts of Kansas, Minnesota, North Dakota, Washington, and other western states were controlled by the railroads. Also, land grants were often gained by bribing federal and state officials. Corruption was so great in some states that it was said that the railroads "owned" large numbers of public officials.

By the mid-1860's, through bribery and corruption, the railroad companies had become very powerful. Because so many government officials were in their pay, the railroad companies usually could operate without fear of government interference. As a result, some railroad companies were able to charge high rates for the transportation of goods. These high rates often hit farmers especially hard. Because of this, many farmers began to work together to limit the power of the railroad companies.

■ *Why was it said that railroads "owned" certain public officials?*

The Grange. For most farmers and their families, life in the 1860's was very hard. The working day was long, and the work itself was exhausting. Also, most farms were isolated. Farmers usually lived many miles from the nearest town.

Oliver Hudson Kelley, who worked for the United States Department of Agriculture, saw these problems and wanted to help farmers. So in 1867, he founded a secret society called the *Patrons of Husbandry.* Kelley's goal was to improve the lives of farmers and their families. A few local units of the Patrons of Husbandry were formed in rural areas. Through these units, lectures and debates were held to discuss new farming methods and other important matters. Picnics, concerts, and other social events also were held to bring farm families together. Each of the local units of the Patrons of Husbandry was called a Grange. Because of this the Patrons of Husbandry soon became known as the Grange.

Growth of the Grange was slow. By the end of 1868 only ten Granges had been set up. But falling prices of farm produce and high railroad transportation charges led to a rapid increase in membership. By the early 1870's the Grange was fairly strong. And, even though the Grange was a social organization, farmers began to see it as a way to air their views.

The effectiveness of the Grange was short-lived. It started to decline in the late 1870's. But many of the goals of the Grange, such as the regulation of railroads, became law in later years.

■ *Who founded the Patrons of Husbandry?*

The Granger Collection

How does this drawing of a Grange meeting in western Illinois during the summer of 1837 show the political nature of the Granger movement?

The Emergence of Labor. At about the same time that farmers were organizing, industrial workers were also looking for a way to gain their goals. The last years of the Civil War had seen rapid industrial development in the North. Not surprisingly, workers wanted to share in the profits of this development. These workers began to organize so that their views would be heard.

By the 1860's, a number of local labor unions already were in existence. Their goals had been to get a shorter workweek and higher wages. But most of these unions were small and organized only on a local level. The years after the Civil War brought efforts by workers to organize countrywide.

The first effort at national organization was the *National Labor Union.* It was formed in Baltimore, Maryland, in 1866. It was a combination of national and local unions and discontented workers. The head of the National Labor Union was William H. Sylvis. He worked to obtain better hours and more pay for his members. By 1868, the union had more than 300,000 members. But when Sylvis died in 1869, the National Labor Union declined. By the mid-1870's it had almost disappeared.

Another national union, the *Knights of Labor,* was more successful. A number of garment workers, led by Uriah Stephens, founded the Knights of Labor in Philadelphia, Pennsylvania, in 1869. In its first few years, the Knights of Labor had problems. But, because it was open to workers of all trades, both skilled and unskilled, membership began to increase. Even so, its leaders did not consider the Knights of Labor to be a union. And they were reluctant to discuss matters such as hours and wages with the employers.

These early efforts of the National Labor Union were aimed at uniting workers of all races and creeds. When the National Labor Union was formed in 1866, it was open to black and white workers. However, in 1869, delegates at the National Labor Union convention decided that blacks had to form their own separate locals. Because of this, black workers formed their own union in 1869. This was the National Colored Labor Union, which was headed by Isaac Myers of Baltimore. But the National Colored Labor Union was never very strong, and it soon ceased to exist.

The Knights of Labor also tried to unite workers of all races. The rapid growth of the Knights of Labor in the 1870's was in part due to the growth of its black membership. During the 1870's, black organizers recruited more than 60,000 black workers. But in the southern states, laws were passed against the Knights of Labor. The Knights' strikes and meetings often were broken up by violence.

The early years of labor organization were beset with problems. But from these troubled beginnings grew the strong unions that exist today. And many of the goals of these early unions, such as the eight-hour workday, have become realities.

■ *Who founded the Knights of Labor?*

Foreign Affairs. Although the years after the Civil War were beset with political corruption and labor troubles, there were some political successes. For the most part, these successes came in foreign affairs. One of these successes occurred in Mexico.

During the Civil War, Napoleon III of France had sent French soldiers to Mexico. This was against the *Monroe Doctrine,* proclaimed in 1823, which stated that European interference in the affairs of the United States or its neighbors was not welcome. Napoleon III had also installed Archduke Maximilian of Austria as emperor of Mexico. Even though the Mexican people were against this, they were unable to resist. And the United States was unable to help because of the Civil War. But as soon as the Civil War was over, President Johnson's Secretary of State, William H. Seward, sent strong protest notes to Napoleon III. Seward demanded that the French soldiers be removed from Mexico. Napoleon III did not want to fight a war with the United States, so he withdrew his soldiers. Without the backing of the French, Maximilian was soon removed from power and executed.

Seward's actions in Mexico were largely guided by his desire to strengthen the position of the United States. The presence of French soldiers in Mexico had been a threat to the security of the United States.

Seward also attempted to strengthen the United States by purchasing land from foreign powers. In 1867, Seward signed a treaty with Russia agreeing to pay $7,200,000 for Alaska. Some Americans were against the purchase. They thought that $7,200,000 was too much money for a vast expanse of barren land far to the North. These people called Alaska Seward's Folly and Seward's Icebox. Despite this opposition, Congress ratified the purchase of Alaska. But Congress later rejected Seward's attempts to make other purchases, such as Cuba and Hawaii. Today, Seward's purchase of Alaska is seen as one of the major achievements of the 1860's.

The first term of President Ulysses S. Grant (1869–1873) also brought success in foreign matters. Although President Grant did not always choose his advisers wisely, an exception to this was his Secretary of State, Hamilton Fish. Fish was successful, particularly in the settlement of a dispute between Great Britain and the United States.

Historical Pictures Service

This cartoon, published in 1867, questioned Secretary of State Seward's decision to purchase Alaska from Russia. At the time, little was known about Alaska.

The dispute arose because Great Britain had built a number of warships for the Confederacy during the Civil War. One of the warships, the C.S.S. *Alabama,* had sunk a number of Union ships. The United States demanded an apology from Great Britain. The United States also wanted Great Britain to pay compensation for the ships sunk by the *Alabama.* The Civil War ended with the dispute still not settled.

After the war, progress toward settlement was slow. But finally, in 1871, Great Britain and the United States signed the Treaty of Washington. This treaty called for an apology from Great Britain. It also set up an international commission that would decide the amount of compensation to be paid. The commission met in Geneva, Switzerland, and in 1872 decided upon the figure of $15,500,000 to be paid by Great Britain to the United States. The excellent work of Secretary of State Fish in negotiating the Treaty of Washington was a high point in the otherwise weak first term of President Grant.

■ *What dispute did the Treaty of Washington settle?*

SECTION 3 REVIEW

1. *How did President Grant's inexperience lead to a financial scandal in 1869?*
2. *Why did workers begin to organize in this period?*
3. *How did the United States and Great Britain settle the dispute over the C.S.S. Alabama?*

CHAPTER 18 SUMMARY

Much of the South had been devastated by the Civil War and needed rebuilding. A new society without slavery had to be built in the South. And a way to readmit the former Confederate states to the Union had to be worked out.

Both President Lincoln and President Johnson had put forward Reconstruction plans that were generous to the South. But the Radical Republicans in Congress wanted to control Reconstruction. They wanted to punish the South for waging war against the Union.

The Radical Republicans took control of Reconstruction after the 1866 elections. They then issued their own Reconstruction plan, which was harsher than the plans of Lincoln and Johnson. Congress and President Johnson disagreed on most matters, and the relationship between President and Congress worsened. The House of Representatives eventually impeached Johnson. He was tried by the Senate and was found not guilty.

Military occupation of the South enabled Republicans to take control of state governments. Some of these governments were found to be corrupt, but most of them did excellent work in rebuilding the South.

After the Civil War, corruption seemed to be widespread throughout government and business. These years saw the beginnings of national labor organizations. And successes were achieved in foreign affairs.

CHAPTER 18 REVIEW

USING YOUR SKILLS

Interpreting Line Graphs

Graphs help us to see and compare statistics. The graph below shows American cotton production for the years 1850 through 1870. The figures are in thousands of bales. A bale is equivalent to 500 lb (226.8 kg) of cotton. Study the graph carefully; then answer the questions that follow.

1. In which year was cotton production the highest?
2. In which year was cotton production the lowest?
3. In which two years was cotton production the same?
4. Between which two years was there the greatest decrease in cotton production?
5. In which six-year period was the increase in cotton production greatest?
6. Why do you think cotton production dropped between 1860 and 1864?

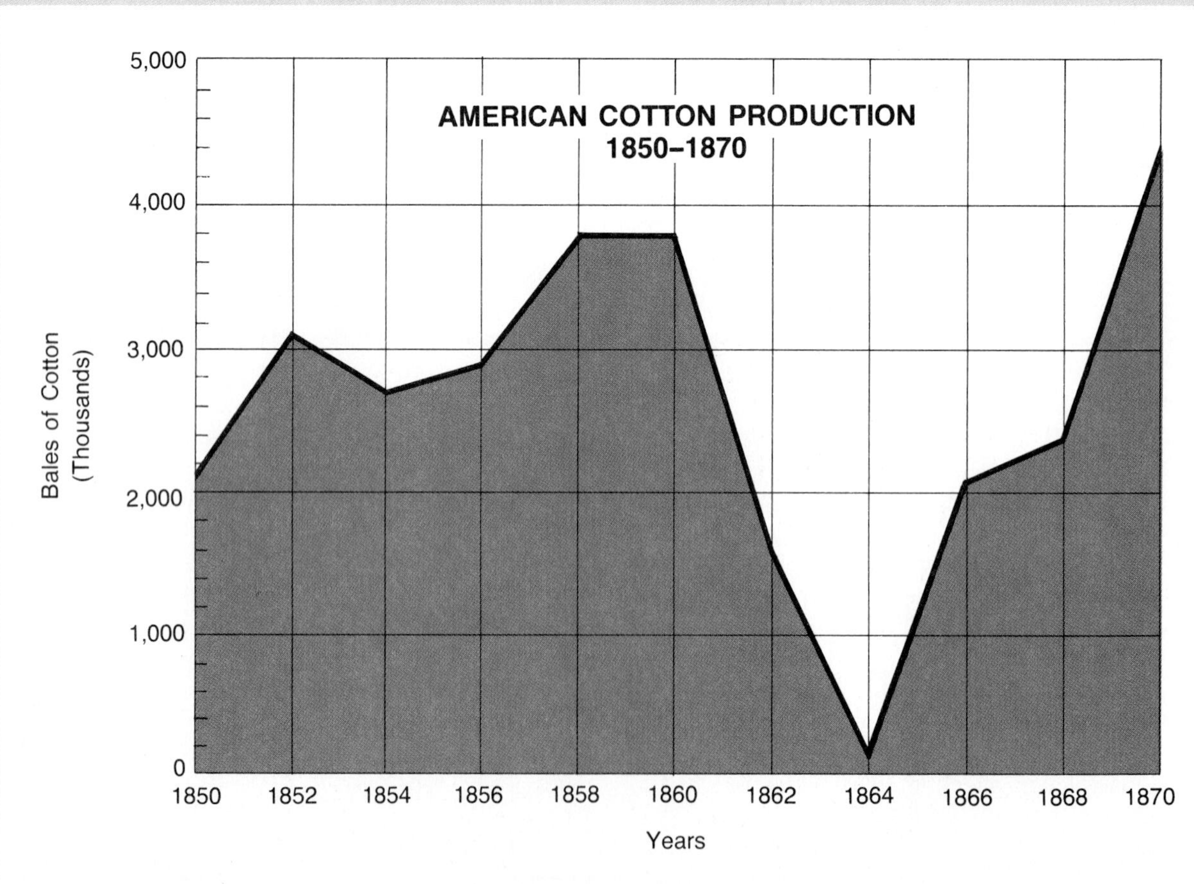

CHAPTER 18 REVIEW

YOU SHOULD KNOW

Identify, define, or explain each of the following:

Thirteenth Amendment
impeach
carpetbaggers
scalawags
Seward's Folly
Treaty of Washington

CHECKING FACTS

1. What was the Wade-Davis bill?
2. Who made up the Joint Committee of Fifteen?
3. What was the Civil Rights Act of 1866?
4. What was the Fifteenth Amendment?
5. What was the Tenure of Office Act?
6. What two blacks served in the United States Senate during Radical Reconstruction?
7. What did Jay Gould and James Fisk attempt to do?
8. What was the Tweed Ring in New York City?
9. What two national labor organizations were formed in the 1860's?
10. Who was instrumental in removing French soldiers from Mexico after the Civil War?

UNDERSTANDING CONCEPTS

1. Why did Radical Republicans object to President Johnson's plan for Reconstruction?
2. In what way did President Johnson's acquittal on impeachment charges affect the Presidency?
3. Why did the Radical Republicans think the Fifteenth Amendment to the Constitution would strengthen the Republican party?
4. Why do some historians regard the years immediately after the Civil War as a low point in American history?

LEARNING FROM ILLUSTRATIONS

1. Based on your interpretation of the political cartoon on page 325, what do you think the "moths" represent?
2. Why might you conclude that the artist of the political cartoon on page 330 probably disagreed with the purchase of Russian America—Alaska—by the United States?

CRITICAL THINKING

1. Do you think that any Reconstruction program might have been worked out to the satisfaction of a majority in Congress, the President, and the southern governments? Explain your answer.
2. Do you think that Andrew Johnson should have been removed from office? Why do you think so?
3. Why do you think political corruption was so prevalent during the years after the Civil War?

ENRICHMENT ACTIVITIES

1. A vertical time line showing the major events of Reconstruction during the years 1865 through 1872 would help students understand the sequence of these events. Information can be found in this textbook and in encyclopedias.
2. Working in small groups, some students might like to discuss how they would have run the Freedmen's Bureau. Each student could write a report of his or her findings, which could be presented to the class.

1865 1870 1875

- 1862 Homestead Act enacted
- 1869 First transcontinental railroad completed
- 1872 President Grant reelected
- 1873 Panic of 1873
- 1874 Greenback party formed
- 1876 Battle of Little Big Horn
- 1877 Georgia introduces a poll tax
  Rutherford B. Hayes declared President
  Reconstruction ends

CHAPTER 19

A New Order

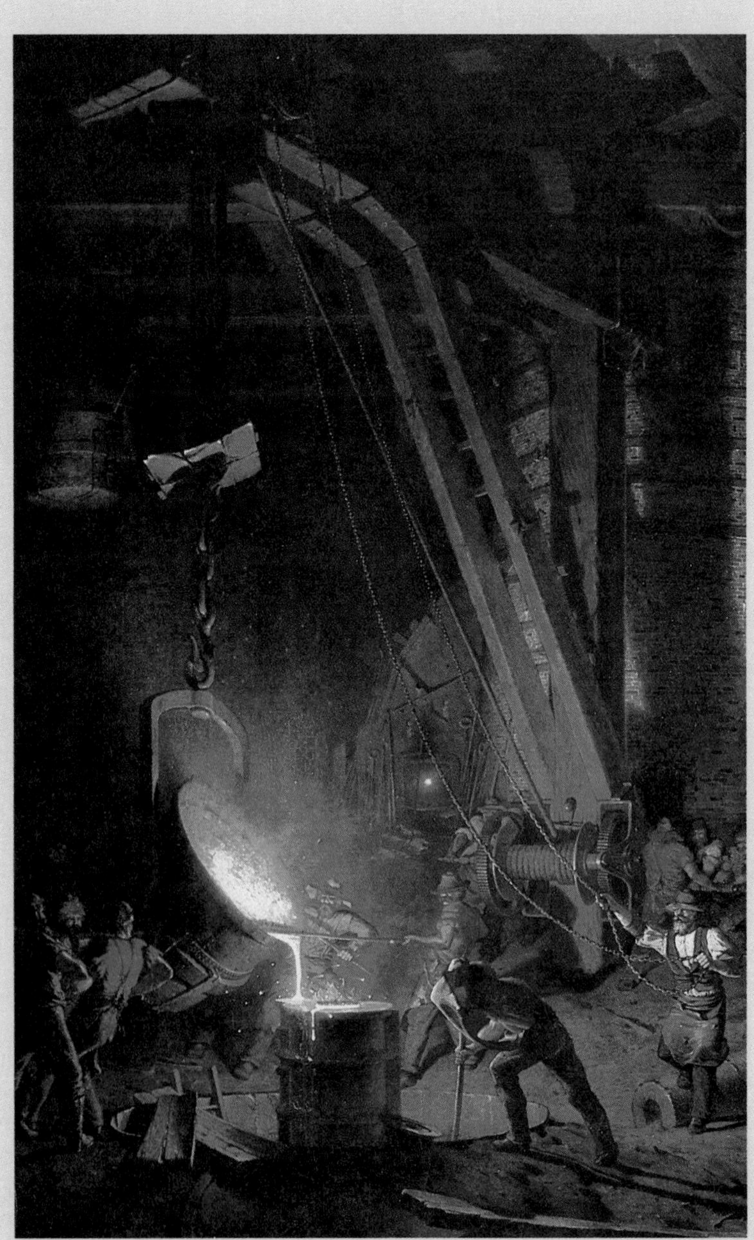

Chapter Objectives

After studying this chapter, you will be able to:

- explain the problems and changes that occurred in the North following Grant's reelection in 1872;
- identify the factors that influenced the settlement of the West;
- analyze the problems that arose in the South as Reconstruction ended.

1 Continuing Problems in the North

Overview In 1872, the United States was nearing its hundredth birthday. During nearly one hundred years of independence the entire United States had undergone rapid change. But change often brought problems. In the North, industrialization, financial difficulties, and corruption were major concerns.

Objectives After reading this section, you will be able to:

- identify the cause for the split in the Republican party in the presidential campaign of 1872;
- explain why the growth of the railroads was important to industrial development in the North;
- discuss the ways out of economic depression that were open to working people.

The Campaign of 1872. President Grant's first term in office was marked with corruption, scandal, and weakness. Even so, the Republican party nominated him for a second term in 1872. But some Republicans were against Grant's nomination. They left the Republican party and formed the Liberal Republican party. They chose Horace Greeley, editor of the *New York Tribune,* to run against Grant. Greeley was also nominated by the Democratic party.

One issue of the campaign of 1872 was corruption in government. The Liberal Republicans called for reform. And the Democrats attacked Grant because of the scandals that had come to light during his first term.

The attacks on Grant increased when the events of the Credit Mobilier scandal became known. The Credit Mobilier was the construction company for the Union Pacific Railroad Company. A newspaper, the *New York Sun,* discovered that members of the board of Credit Mobilier were also members of the board of the Union Pacific. These board members had awarded themselves large construction contracts. This allowed them to make huge profits. The *Sun* also discovered that Credit Mobilier stock had been offered to members of Congress. In return, the Union Pacific expected favorable treatment from Congress. The Credit Mobilier scandal involved members of Congress rather than Grant or his advisers. And it did not seriously affect Grant's bid for reelection.

■ *Which scandal, unearthed during the presidential campaign of 1872, involved railroad construction?*

The Election of 1872. President Grant's opponent, Horace Greeley, had been nominated by both the Liberal Republicans and the Democrats. Greeley fought a hard campaign. He attacked Grant for his weakness as President. He also made much of the scandals that came to light during Grant's first term in office. But Grant's popularity with the people proved too great for Greeley to overcome. Grant won the election by more than 750,000 votes. Tired and dejected, Greeley died just three weeks after the election.

Even though Grant had won the election easily, the corruption and scandals of his first term remained. They would remain with him throughout his second term.

■ *What was Grant's popular majority in the election of 1872?*

The Bettmann Archive

This cartoon by Thomas Nast attacked political corruption during the Grant administration.

Corruption Continues. During President Grant's second term in office it seemed that corruption was even more widespread. Customs officers from the Treasury Department pressed merchants and importers for bribes. The Navy Department gave out jobs and contracts as political favors. Secretary of War William Belknap accepted bribes from traders. In return the traders received the right to sell goods on Indian reservations and at army posts.

Perhaps the most serious scandal involving government officials was the "Whiskey Ring." The Whiskey Ring was made up of a number of midwestern whiskey distillers. Ring members bribed Internal Revenue Service officers so that they would not have to pay excise taxes. The Whiskey Ring was able to get the help of Orville Babcock, President Grant's secretary. When Grant learned of this, he ordered an investigation. But as it became clear that many of his friends and associates were involved, Grant backed down. He even kept Babcock on his White House staff.

■ *Which of President Grant's aides was involved with the Whiskey Ring?*

The Gilded Age and Civil-Service Reform. Grant's years as President, and the years immediately after, became known as the Gilded Age. The name was taken from a book written by Mark Twain and Charles Dudley Warner. The authors wrote about dishonest business leaders and politicians. But the corruption of the Gilded Age did have a positive aspect. It provided ammunition for civil-service reform.

There had long been a movement to end the spoils system in government. The political corruption that marked the years after the Civil War gave strength to this movement. The civil-service reformers pressed President Grant to change the system. They wanted government jobs to be given on merit rather than through political favor. Grant gave way and set up the Civil Service Reform Commission. He named as its chairman George William Curtis, a leading reformer and the editor of *Harper's Weekly*. But the Commission had little power and even less success. And when Grant was reelected in 1872, he lost interest in the Commission.

■ *Who was the chairman of the Civil Service Reform Commission?*

Industrialization in the North. During the Civil War, great demands had been made on northern industries to help the war effort. After the war, growth continued. The steel industry, for example, showed a very rapid growth after the war. Before and during the war, almost no steel was produced in the United States. Then during the mid-1860's, new methods of making steel, such as the Bessemer process, were put into use. These methods made the making of steel easier and cheaper. This helped the railroads since iron rails wore out rather quickly. Steel rails, on the other hand, were much stronger and longer lasting. Consequently, both the steel industry and the railroads grew rapidly in the early 1870's.

The oil industry grew rapidly during this time. Oil was discovered in Pennsylvania in 1859. Soon after, it was discovered in other parts of the eastern United States. Large oil companies were set up to make oil products that were useful to industry. These products included kerosene for lamps and lubricating oil for machinery. Within a few years many oil companies could be found around the cities of Cleveland and Pittsburgh.

Meat-packing and slaughtering also increased rapidly after the Civil War. As people moved west, great tracts of land were being opened up. These wide, open plains were ideal for raising cattle. But transporting live cattle to markets in cities in the eastern United States was costly. To get around this, slaughterhouses and meat-packing factories were built in a number of midwestern cities. Very soon, Chicago became the center of the meat-packing industry.

Industrial development would not have been so rapid without the growth of the railroads. The first transcontinental route was completed when the Central Pacific and Union Pacific railroad lines met at Promontory Point, Utah, in 1869. By 1870, most major cities in the North were served by at least one railroad line. This made the moving of raw materials and finished goods much easier. The railroads played an important part in the growth of the economy during this period. However, a severe depression hit the country in 1873 and slowed our economic growth.

■ *Why was the production of steel important to the railroads?*

Industrial Unrest. The depression of 1873 hit the working people very hard. Business failures left many people without jobs. These people received little help from government. And most labor unions could offer little aid. Only a few charitable organizations were able to help the unemployed with food and clothing.

Some workers hoped to find a way out of the depression by supporting new, independent political parties. Of these, the most successful was the Greenback, or National Independent, party. It was formed in Indianapolis, Indiana, in 1874. During this period there was much discussion on the subject of money. Some people favored the issue of more paper money. Others said that only the amount that could be backed by government gold should be issued. The Greenback party favored the

DO YOU KNOW?

What major American city was severely damaged by fire in 1871?

In October 1871, a large portion of the city of Chicago was destroyed by fire. Legend has it that the fire began when Mrs. O'Leary's cow kicked over a lighted lantern. The fire spread rapidly through the city's wooden buildings, destroying the city's downtown area. About 300 people died in the fire, and about 90,000 people were left homeless. Damage was estimated at $200,000,000.

Historical Pictures Service

The roundhouse at the Pittsburgh rail yards was burned during the railroad workers' strike of 1877.

increased issue of paper money (greenbacks) as a way to help businesses and workers to get back on their feet.

Other workers formed local groups to bring about change. In the coal-mining areas of Pennsylvania, for example, a group called the Molly Maguires was formed. It soon was accused of using violence to gain its goals. A Pinkerton detective claimed to have joined the group. Based on the detective's testimony, a number of the group's leaders were arrested. Ten of the leaders were convicted of murder and were hanged.

Another case of workers taking direct action came in the summer of 1877. Railroad managers, without warning, cut wages on most railroads by 10 percent. In July 1877, workers on the Baltimore and Ohio Railroad went on strike. Workers from other railroads soon followed. The workers took over the rail yards and refused to let any trains leave.

In some places state and local officials had difficulty handling the strikers. Violence and rioting often resulted when they tried. As a result the federal government sent in troops to end the rioting. With this, the strike ended, and the trains began to run again.

■ *What started the railroad strike of 1877?*

SECTION 1 REVIEW

1. *What caused some members of the Republican party to leave and form the Liberal Republican party?*
2. *Why was the growth of the railroads important to industrial development in the North?*
3. *Which two ways out of economic depression were open to working people?*

2 Moving Westward

Overview Since the War of Independence the American frontier had been moving westward. The search for mineral wealth had been a driving force of this movement. Miners often opened the way for permanent settlers.

The growing demand for food in the cities in the East brought about the growth of cattle-rearing on the Great Plains. And developments in agriculture made it easier to farm the dry plains. But this led to conflict between settlers and the Plains Indians.

Objectives After reading this section, you will be able to:

- explain how cattle were transported from the Texas plains to the railheads;
- discuss how the United States government tried to help small farmers;
- describe the United States government policy regarding the Plains Indians.

Mining in the West. Since the War of Independence the American frontier had been moving westward. At the forefront of this westward movement were explorers, hunters, and fur trappers. When it was realized that the lands to the west of the Appalachian Mountains were rich in minerals, miners also began to push westward. These miners were mainly prospecting for gold and silver. Whenever a discovery of gold or silver was reported, miners would rush to the area. For a while miners worked night and day in their frantic search for precious metals. New towns were built in the area to supply the miners. But when the mines were worked out, the miners moved on, and only ghost towns remained.

Most miners shared the dream of finding a large claim and getting rich quickly. But few miners realized their dream. Those few who did find a rich claim were often cheated out of it. Or they were forced to sell their claim because they could not afford to buy the tools needed to work it efficiently.

The majority of miners did little more than find the deposits of precious metals. Their claims were then bought by mining companies owned by eastern businesses. And the miners were rarely paid the true worth of the claim. For example, Henry Comstock, who gave his name to the Comstock Lode in Nevada, received only a few thousand dollars for that claim. It later produced more than $300 million in gold and silver.

Mining produced wealth that helped to strengthen the American economy. And, although miners rarely remained in one place very long, they did open up the West for settlement.

■ *Why did miners often have to sell their claims?*

Cattle on the Great Plains. Another factor that changed the western frontier was the growth of the cattle industry. By the end of the Civil War, huge herds of cattle roamed the plains areas of Texas and Mexico. They were the descendants of the long-horned cattle that had been brought to Mexico by the Spanish. These longhorns numbered in the millions and belonged to no one.

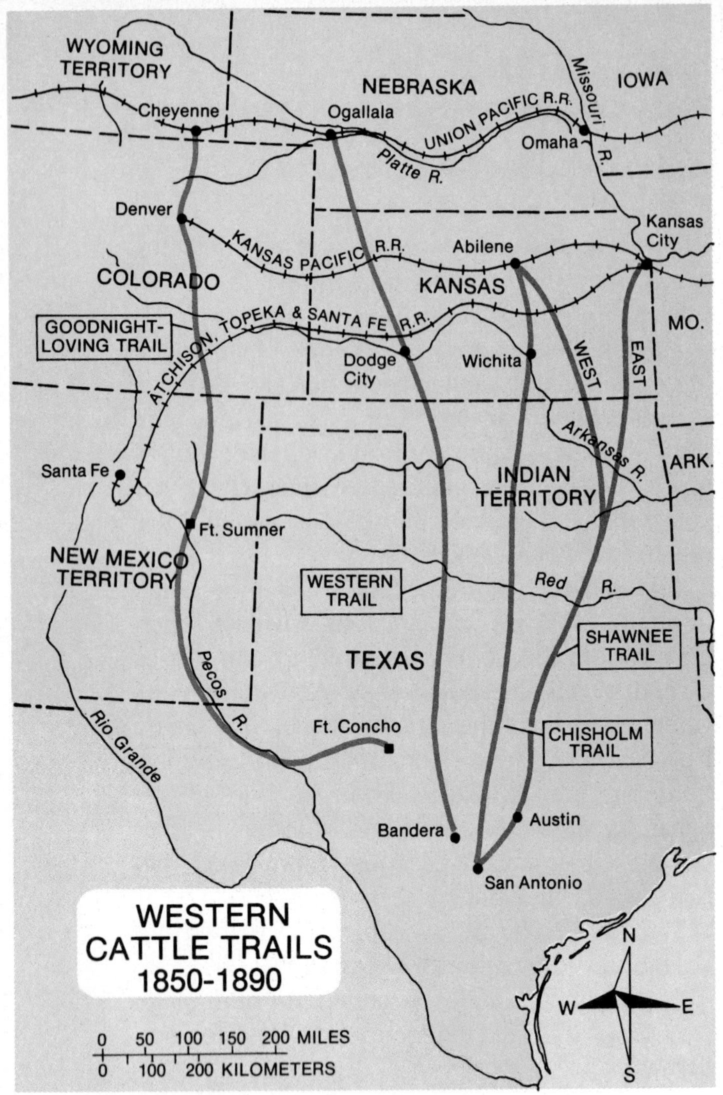

About how many miles (kilometers) did Texas ranchers have to drive cattle in order to reach Dodge City from Bandera?

Industrial growth and increasing immigration brought people to the cities in the East. The demand for food in these cities grew. Texans quickly saw that the longhorns could fill this demand, particularly since the growing network of railroads could be used to ship the cattle to the East. A number of cattle ranchers rounded up the wild longhorns and gave them their ranch brand. From these beginnings grew the huge Texas cattle ranches.

The cattle somehow had to be taken to the railheads which were far to the north. This was done by the *long drive.* Cowboys rounded up the cattle, then drove them along trails to the railheads. On the way the cattle were fattened on the rich grasses of the Great Plains.

It was soon obvious that the open expanses of the Great Plains were ideal for cattle rearing. And when it was found that the longhorns could withstand the harsh northern winters, cattle rearing spread as far north as Montana and Wyoming. Later, the extension of railroads led to the end of the long drives. But the cattle industry continued to be important.

■ *What caused the end of the long drives?*

Farmers on the Plains. Even before the Civil War there had been a movement in Congress that called for the giving of land west of the Mississippi River to people willing to settle it. But this movement was opposed by southerners in Congress. They thought that opening up the frontier to small farmers would threaten slavery. But the coming of the Civil War and the secession of the southern states removed this opposition.

In 1862, Congress passed the Homestead Act. Under this act the government would provide 160 acres [65 hectares] of land to any adult citizen. If people stayed on the land for five years and improved it, the land was free. Otherwise, the land could be purchased for $1.25 an acre.

The Homestead Act had two main goals. One was to help ease overcrowding in the big cities. But few city dwellers were attracted to

(Text continues on page 342.)

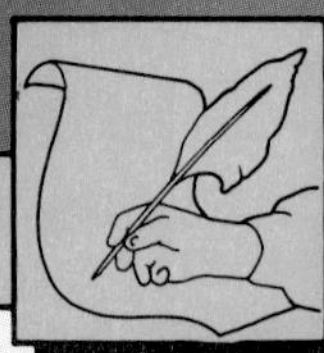

RECALLING THE TIMES

Settling the Great Plains

For farmers and their families, pioneer life on the Great Plains was not easy. But for many people, especially immigrants, who settled the plains, the struggle was worthwhile. The following is an excerpt from a letter, written in 1873, by a frontier settler to her parents in Norway:

Here, also, the crops will be poor. This spring the locusts destroyed our fields, too. In many places there will be no harvest. We did get a little, enough for our own living, but none to sell. So it will be difficult to pay our many debts. We were forced to buy our land for $480. Since we had no money, we had to borrow. Then we had other bad luck. One of our horses had a sore leg this summer. At the time when there was most work to be done we couldn't use him, so we had to buy another horse that cost $150....

Times have been hard this fall—much harder than any since we came to this land. The future is uncertain. No one knows what tomorrow will bring....

From what I have said you will see that we are not rich. But though we have no material wealth, we have nevertheless possessions of greater worth—a quiet and peaceful home with many children, all normal, gifted with health and intelligence, spirited, cheerful, and happy. We have other possessions, too. I could not name them all, but all these blessings seem to be of far greater value than money....

Solomon D. Butcher Collection/Nebraska State Historical Society

Thinking Critically

Why was life on the plains difficult for the author of this letter?

Why do you think the author of this letter considered her blessings to be of far greater value than money?

the frontier. Even though the land was free, few city dwellers could afford the cost of transportation and farm equipment. The other goal was to settle the West with many small farms. But by the 1870's it was clear that the lands west of the Mississippi River were ideal for the raising of livestock. A farm of 160 acres was too small to raise livestock with any success.

In addition, other federal legislation hurt the small farmer. For example, the Pacific Railroad Act, also passed in 1862, gave land to railroad companies on which to construct a transcontinental railroad. The railroad companies used their influence to get the best lands for themselves. The small farmers, as a result, often had to be content with land of poorer quality.

The efforts of the government to help the small farmers were largely unsuccessful. But the open spaces of the Great Plains began to be settled. The railroads began to sell their excess lands to farmers. And new developments in agriculture made farming the dry plains less difficult.

■ *What were the two main goals of the Homestead Act of 1862?*

Indians on the Plains. When the settlers came to the Great Plains, they did not find them empty. Indian civilization had been flourishing on the plains for thousands of years. For the most part, the Plains Indians lived a nomadic life, following the buffalo, which was found in large numbers on the plains. The buffalo provided the Plains Indians with the basic necessities of life—food, clothing, shelter, and tools.

Trouble between the settlers and the Indians was unavoidable. The Indians moved freely across the plains, following the buffalo. Settlers, on the other hand, wanted to put up fences and farm the land. Under pressure from the settlers, the government decided on a policy of *concentration.* Under this policy, the Indians were to be concentrated in certain areas. The rest of the Great Plains then would be opened to settlement.

Some Indians were persuaded to sign treaties that turned over large parts of their tribal lands for settlement. In return they received *reservations*—pieces of land that were reserved for them by treaty for all time. These reservations were run by agents from the federal Bureau of Indian Affairs. The agents were to see that the Indians were provided with such things as food, clothing, and ammunition for hunting. But many agents were corrupt and amassed large personal fortunes, while some Indians were given rotten food. The treaties the Indians signed were often meaningless. No sooner had the Indians been promised a piece of land for all time than settlers would move in and claim it as their own. This was often done with the federal government's protection.

■ *What policy did the government follow to end the conflict between the settlers and the Plains Indians?*

Indian Wars. In the West conflict between the Indians and whites was inevitable. As miners and settlers entered Indian lands, bitter fighting followed. The government's response was to further confine the Plains Indians. They would be moved to two reservations—one in the Black Hills of South Dakota, the other in Oklahoma. In addition, the Indians were ordered to give up their old way of life and become farmers. Some chiefs gave in to government pressure in 1868 and agreed to the confinement in return for a treaty guaranteeing

The Granger Collection

Chief Crazy Horse is shown in spotted warpaint at the top center of this illustration of the Battle of the Little Bighorn.

peace. But not all the Plains Indians accepted this treaty. Some refused to be confined and were forced to continue the fight for their land.

Then, in 1874, gold was discovered in the Black Hills. Thousands of miners poured into the area, against the treaty of 1868. The Black Hills were the sacred lands of the Sioux. So they decided to fight for their land. Joining with other Plains Indians, the Sioux set up a camp near the Bighorn River, in Montana. In 1876, the United States Army began to move against the Sioux. A detachment of cavalry, led by Colonel George Armstrong Custer, was ordered to find the Sioux camp. Instead, Custer attacked the camp. Greatly outnumbered, he and his force of 264 soldiers were killed.

Custer's Last Stand, of June 25, 1876, was a famous victory for the Sioux. But the disgrace of defeat angered the army. Their attacks on the Sioux were stepped up. By the end of 1876, most of the Sioux, starving and tired of fighting, were back on the reservation. Those who refused to surrender, led by Sitting Bull, went into exile in Canada.

■ *Where did the government plan to confine the Plains Indians?*

The End of Indian Resistance. The Plains Indians were not alone in their resistance to reservation life. In the Northwest, the Nez Percé chose resistance rather than the reservation. The Nez Percé were peace-loving people who lived in the Snake River valley region, where the states of Idaho, Oregon, and Washington meet. Their lands had slowly been taken from them by treaties. Finally, in 1877, they were ordered to leave their lands and go to the Lapwai reservation in Idaho. Chief Joseph, the Nez Percé leader, reluctantly agreed to move his people. But after some young Nez Percé killed a number of settlers who had stolen their horses, he chose to fight.

Leading his people over thousands of miles of rugged country, Chief Joseph retreated toward the Canadian border. During the retreat, the Nez Percé defeated the army in a number of battles. But, with only a few miles to go to the Canadian border, the Nez Percé were caught by soldiers led by Generals Nelson A. Miles and Oliver O. Howard. The Nez Percé were tired, cold, and hungry. So, to prevent them further suffering, Chief Joseph surrendered. Miles and Howard promised Chief Joseph that the Nez Percé would be able to return to the Northwest. But the Bureau of Indian Affairs ordered the Nez Percé to go far to the south, to the Indian Territory.

Thus, by 1878, Indian resistance was virtually at an end. Indian land had been reduced to almost nothing by unfair treaties. The buffalo, important to the life of the Plains Indians, had been almost totally wiped out by white hunters. The once-proud tribes were now confined to barren reservations.

■ *Who led the Nez Percé on a retreat to the Canadian border?*

SECTION 2 REVIEW

1. *What method did Texas cattle ranchers use to get cattle from the plains to the railheads?*
2. *How did the federal government try to help small farmers in the West?*
3. *What was the policy of the United States government toward the Plains Indians?*

3 The New South

Overview The period of Reconstruction saw many changes in the South. But the southern state governments were returning to white rule. With violence and economic pressure, southern whites stopped blacks from voting. Then with the end of Reconstruction in 1877, the progress of blacks toward full *civil rights*—rights guaranteed by the Constitution—was halted.

Objectives After reading this section, you will be able to:

- identify the change that took place in southern agriculture after the Civil War;
- describe the methods used by southern whites to stop blacks from voting;
- explain the purpose and result of the Compromise of 1877.

How does this picture illustrate the conditions faced by tenant farmers in the postwar South?

Historical Pictures Service

The End of the Plantation System. At the end of the Civil War, southern agriculture lay in ruins. Much of the region's valuable farmland had been destroyed. The main method of farming—the plantation system—was coming to an end. Before the war, plantations depended on slave labor. However, northern victory in the Civil War ended slavery. Plantation owners had to find a new source of labor. To get workers, many owners divided their plantations into a number of small lots. These they rented to *tenant farmers*—farmers who worked the land for a share of the crops. Tenant farmers soon became known as *sharecroppers.* Many freedmen became sharecroppers, working the land they had once worked as slaves.

With tenant farming, both landowners and tenants were dependent on local store owners for farm supplies, food, and clothing. Also, most tenants had very little cash. They were dependent on credit from landowners or store owners to get farming supplies. Debts were paid off with a share of the crop.

■ *Why were tenant farmers called sharecroppers?*

Tenant Farming—Advantages and Disadvantages. To be able to pay off their debts, sharecroppers had to raise a crop that could easily be sold. In the upper South this was tobacco. In the lower South it was cotton. With tenant farming, the production of both tobacco and cotton grew. This increase in production helped to restore the southern economy. But the system of tenant farming brought problems.

The need to grow a crop that could easily be sold made sharecroppers unwilling to try new farming techniques or different crops. And the continual planting of one crop on the same piece of land took important minerals from the soil. So, even though production grew, little real agricultural progress was made.

At harvest time, sharecroppers paid what they owed with a share of the crop. What was left was sold for cash. The sharecroppers were often cheated. Sometimes they were underpaid for their crop or were charged very high interest rates. Few sharecroppers made enough money to break their dependence on the landowners and the store owners.

■ *Why did sharecroppers need to raise a crop that could easily be sold?*

Industry in the South. The Civil War had destroyed many southern factories and railroads. But soon after the war had ended, enterprising people from both the North and the South began putting money into the rebuilding of southern industry.

Northern businesses put money into mining operations in the upper Tennessee Valley. Large deposits of coal and iron had been found there. The Tennessee Valley soon became an important center for mining and manufacturing. At the same time, government land grants and private investment helped in the rebuilding of the railroads in the South. The growing network of railroads, in turn, led to the development of iron manufacturing centers, such as Birmingham, Alabama.

Southern investors also played a part in the rebuilding of southern industries. The textile industry in Georgia and the Carolinas was given new life by southern investment. And the introduction of the cigarette-rolling machine revolutionized the southern tobacco industry.

■ *What invention revolutionized the tobacco industry in the South?*

Political Change in the South. As the South slowly rebuilt its economy, changes were also taking place on the political scene. When each southern state was readmitted to the Union, southern Democrats worked to gain control of the state governments. Most of these southern Democrats believed in *white supremacy*—that whites were superior to blacks. Because of this, they were against blacks playing any part in political life. But the Republican Reconstruction state governments were supported by black voters. And a number of these state governments included black representatives. Southern Democrats looked for ways to change this situation.

The Fifteenth Amendment to the Constitution had given blacks the right to vote. Southern Democrats had no legal way to stop blacks from voting. Therefore, other methods were used. White store owners withheld credit, and white landowners stopped renting land to blacks who voted. Also, blacks often lost their jobs when they voted for the Republicans. When these measures failed, violence and terror were used.

Violence against blacks in the South was most often carried out by secret organizations. The best known of these secret organizations was the Ku Klux Klan. It was originally formed as a young men's social club in Pulaski, Tennessee, in 1866. But it soon became the chief weapon of intimidation against blacks. Wearing hoods and white sheets, Klan members rode about the countryside at night, threatening blacks who dared to vote. Blacks who did not heed the threats had their property destroyed or were whipped or murdered.

Other ways were found to stop blacks from voting. In 1877, Georgia introduced a *poll tax*—a charge of two dollars when a person registered to vote. Most blacks were poor and could not afford to pay the poll tax. Those that could, for their own safety, either voted Democrat or did not vote at all.

■ *Why were most southern Democrats against blacks being involved in politics?*

Political Redemption. The southern Democrats called themselves *redeemers.* This was because in their view they were out to *redeem*—save—the state governments from Republican rule. As early as 1869, the state government of Tennessee had been "redeemed." By 1875, only the state governments of Florida, Louisiana, Mississippi and South Carolina remained in Republican hands.

The southern Democrats quickly gained control for a number of reasons. At the state level, black support for the Republicans was ended by economic pressure and violence. For a while, federal troops were able to protect the blacks. But the Indian wars in the West led to the removal of many soldiers from the South. Without army support, blacks in the South were defenseless.

While the Republicans were losing black voters, the Democrats were gaining the votes of ex-Confederates. The Amnesty Act, passed by Congress in 1872, restored the political rights of nearly all ex-Confederates. For the most part, these ex-Confederates were staunch Democrats.

At the national level, the Radical Republicans were losing power. With the deaths of such leaders as Thaddeus Stevens and Charles Sumner, the Radical Republicans lost much of their support. In addition, most people in the North had lost interest in Reconstruction. For them, business growth and westward expansion were more important. These people thought that the South should be left alone to solve its problems.

■ *Why did southern Democrats call themselves "redeemers"?*

By what year were all southern states readmitted to the Union, and by what year were the state governments controlled by the Democratic party?

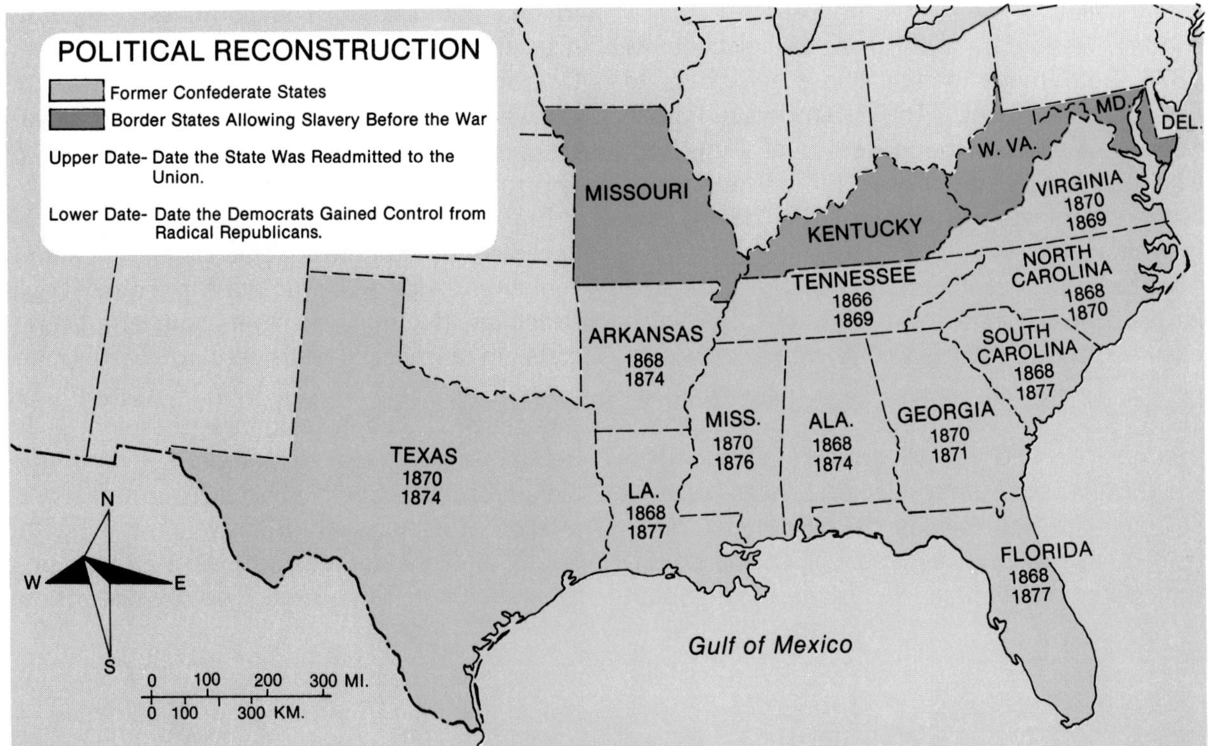

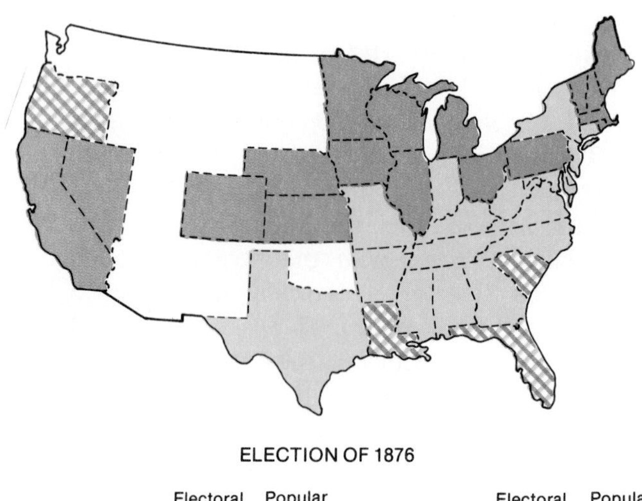

ELECTION OF 1876

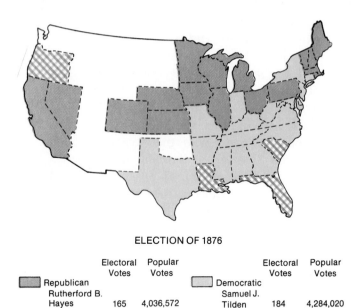

	Electoral Votes	Popular Votes		Electoral Votes	Popular Votes
Republican Rutherford B. Hayes	165	4,036,572	Democratic Samuel J. Tilden	184	4,284,020
Disputed Votes	20		Total	184	
Total	185				

The election of 1876 was resolved by the Senate, which awarded the election to Hayes.

The Election of 1876. In the election of 1876, both major parties chose reformers to run for President. The Democrats chose Samuel J. Tilden, the governor of New York who had broken the Tweed Ring. The Republicans nominated Rutherford B. Hayes, the governor of Ohio.

In the election, Tilden had a *plurality*—the largest number but not a majority of all votes cast—of more than 250,000 votes. However, neither Tilden nor Hayes had a majority of the electoral votes. Tilden had 184, one short of the 185 needed for victory. Hayes had 165 electoral votes. Twenty electoral votes were in dispute, with both parties claiming them. Nineteen of the twenty votes were from the southern states of Florida, Louisiana, and South Carolina. The remaining vote was from Oregon. Tilden needed only one of these votes to become President. Hayes needed all twenty for victory.

When Congress met to count the electoral votes, a crisis developed. Two sets of returns were sent in for the disputed votes. Congress had to decide which set of returns to accept. The Constitution [*56] gave no guidelines as to which house of Congress should count the votes. The Senate, with a Republican majority, would give all the disputed votes to Hayes. But the House of Representatives, with a Democratic majority, would give them all to Tilden. With some people talking about another civil war, it was important to find a solution to this deadlock.

■ *Why was there a question over which house of Congress should count the disputed votes?*

The Compromise of 1877. On January 29, 1877, Congress set up a special commission to end the dispute. The commission had fifteen members—eight Republicans and seven Democrats. Voting went along party lines, and all twenty disputed votes were given to Hayes. He became President by an electoral vote of 185 to Tilden's 184.

But the commission's decision had to be accepted by Congress. The House of Representatives, with a Democratic majority, could reject the decision. However, southern Democrats, in a meeting with leading Republicans, agreed to accept the decision. A compromise was reached. In return for the presidency, the Republicans agreed to withdraw federal soldiers from the South. They also promised to provide for internal improvements in the South. And they agreed to give a cabinet post to a southern Democrat. The Democrats, as well as giving the presidency to Hayes, agreed to support Republican James A. Garfield for Speaker of the House of Representatives. They also agreed to protect the rights of blacks in the South.

At first it appeared that both sides would honor the compromise. On taking office, Hayes withdrew all federal soldiers from the South. And former Confederate General David M. Key was appointed Postmaster General. But then Garfield failed to become Speaker of the House of Representatives. So Hayes withdrew his backing for bills that would have paid for internal improvements in the South. Meanwhile, the southern Democrats did little to protect the rights of blacks in the South.

The Compromise of 1877 ended Reconstruction. The withdrawal of federal soldiers allowed southern Democrats to gain power in the South. Thus the compromise had avoided another conflict. However, it also set back the progress of civil rights, as southern Democrats passed state laws that almost returned the blacks to slavery.

■ *What did the Republicans promise the southern Democrats in return for the presidency?*

SECTION 3 REVIEW

1. *What change in southern agriculture took place after the Civil War?*
2. *How did southern Democrats prevent blacks from voting?*
3. *How did the Compromise of 1877 solve the dispute over the election of 1876?*

CHAPTER 19 SUMMARY

The years after the Civil War saw rapid change in the United States. In the North there was rapid industrial development. This development gave the American economy the appearance of strength and stability. But this was a false picture. Industrial growth was too rapid, and a financial panic occurred in 1873.

During these years, the American frontier moved westward. The search for precious metals brought miners to the West. When the miners moved on, they were replaced by permanent settlers. With the introduction of new agricultural techniques, farming on the Great Plains became easier. This brought many more settlers to the open spaces of the Great Plains. But there was conflict between the settlers and the Plains Indians. Ultimately, this struggle ended the Indian way of life.

The South also changed during the years after the Civil War. With the end of slavery, the plantation system was replaced by tenant farming. Southern industry was rebuilt. And the Southern state governments were "redeemed" from Republican rule by white Democrats. With this, the progress of blacks toward full civil rights was ended.

CHAPTER 19 REVIEW

USING YOUR SKILLS

Analyzing Primary Source Materials

The following two examples of primary source material are the opinions of two people who were involved in deciding the future of the Plains Indians. Read and compare these opinions and answer the questions that follow.

1. What, according to Schurz, was the only alternative to civilization for the Indians?
2. What methods did Schurz suggest for civilizing the Indians?
3. Why, according to Chief Crazy Horse, should white men not have come to Indian lands?
4. Why did Chief Crazy Horse not want to be civilized?
5. How would Chief Crazy Horse have replied to the suggestion that he should work for a living?
6. Why, in your opinion, do the views of Chief Crazy Horse and Schurz differ so greatly?

Crazy Horse, Sioux War Chief—Early 1870's

We did not ask you white men to come here. The Great Spirit gave us this country as a home. You had yours. We did not interfere with you. The Great Spirit gave us plenty of land to live on, and buffalo, deer, antelope and other game. But you have come here; you are taking my land from me; you are killing off our game, so it is hard for us to live. Now, you tell us to work for a living, but the Great Spirit did not make us to work, but to live by hunting. You white men can work if you want to. We do not interfere with you, and again you say, why do you not become civilized? We do not want your civilization! We would live as our fathers did, and their fathers before them.

Carl Schurz, Commissioner,
Bureau of Indian Affairs—1881

... The circumstances surrounding them place before the Indians this stern alternative—extermination [death] or civilization.... To civilize them... has now become an absolute necessity if we mean to save them....

To fit the Indians for their ultimate absorption in the great body of American citizenship, three things are suggested... (1) that they be taught to work by making work profitable and attractive to them; (2) that they be educated, especially the youth of both sexes; (3) that they be individualized in the possession of property by settlement...

CHAPTER 19 REVIEW

YOU SHOULD KNOW

Identify, define, or explain each of the following:

long drive	sharecroppers
concentration	white supremacy
reservations	poll tax
tenant farmers	plurality

CHECKING FACTS

1. What was the "Whiskey Ring"?
2. What does the term Gilded Age refer to?
3. What city became the center of the meat-packing industry in the 1870's?
4. When was the first transcontinental railroad route completed?
5. What was the Homestead Act?
6. What was Custer's Last Stand?
7. Who was the leader of the Nez Percé?
8. What was the Ku Klux Klan?
9. Which southern state governments were still controlled by the Republicans in 1875?
10. Which candidate had a plurality of the popular vote in the presidential election of 1876?

UNDERSTANDING CONCEPTS

1. How did the Credit Mobilier scandal affect Grant's bid for reelection?
2. How did the federal government try to end the conflict between the Plains Indians and the settlers?
3. Why were white Democrats able to "redeem" southern state governments so easily?
4. How did the Republicans ensure that Rutherford B. Hayes became President in 1877?

LEARNING FROM ILLUSTRATIONS

1. According to the map on page 340, what city was the railhead for both the Chisholm and Shawnee cattle trails?
2. What three states, according to the map on page 347, were the last states to be "redeemed" by the southern Democratic party?

CRITICAL THINKING

1. Do you think that the Molly Maguires were justified in their actions to bring about change in the coal-mining industry? Why or why not?
2. Do you think the United States government was justified in following a policy of concentration towards the Plains Indians? Why do you think so?
3. In your opinion, was the Compromise of 1877 a failure? Give reasons for your answer.

ENRICHMENT ACTIVITIES

1. Some students might like to imagine that they were the first newspaper reporter on the scene of Custer's Last Stand. They should gather additional information about the fight and then write a newspaper article detailing the battle.
2. Some students might like to prepare an advertisement announcing the completion of the first transcontinental railroad.

CHAPTER 20

CLOSE-UP: Gettysburg— What If . . . ?

INTRODUCTION

Many historians view the Battle of Gettysburg as the turning point of the Civil War. It was the first major victory in the east for the Union army. And it was the last offensive battle fought by the Confederates. But the Battle of Gettysburg could have been a turning point of a different kind.

A number of Confederate officials were against the campaign that reached its peak at Gettysburg. They wanted most of the Confederate soldiers that were fighting in the east to be sent west. This troop movement would enable the Confederates at Vicksburg, Mississippi, to be relieved. Vicksburg had been put under siege by Union soldiers led by General Ulysses S. Grant. But General Robert E. Lee wanted to move north and try for a victory on Union ground. This victory might have relieved pressure on Vicksburg. Recognition of the Confederacy by a foreign power might have followed. And a peace agreement on Confederate terms might also have been possible.

Lee's plan was finally accepted. There were times during the campaign, and during the Battle of Gettysburg itself, when it could have been successful.

1 Gettysburg—The First Two Days

In early summer of 1863, General Robert E. Lee was leading his troops northward. He was hoping for a victory on Union soil as great as his victory had been at Chancellorsville, Virginia, earlier that year. The Union generals, however, were thinking of making another attack on Richmond, the Confederate capital. Neither they nor Lee thought that there would be a great battle at the small Pennsylvania town of Gettysburg.

Confederates Move North. In June 1863, General Robert E. Lee began to move his troops northward. Putting the Blue Ridge Mountains between himself and the Union army, Lee moved his men up the Shenandoah Valley. Crossing the Potomac River, he moved into Pennsylvania. His plan was to threaten the cities of Philadelphia and Baltimore and to cut Washington off from the rest of the country. This, he hoped, would force the Union army into attacking him and fighting a battle on his terms.

By the last week of June, Lee had most of his soldiers across the Potomac and into Pennsylvania. During this move north, Lee used his cavalry to conceal and protect his advance and to get information on the whereabouts of the Union army. Lee's chief of cavalry was General Jeb Stuart, a flamboyant but brilliant soldier. In a daring move, Stuart went to the right of the Union army, hoping to cross the Potomac to the east. But all the crossings he wanted to use were occupied by Union soldiers. He was pushed far to the east and lost contact with Lee. Lee was without

The map shows (1) Meade's headquarters; (2) Lee's headquarters; (3) Confederate artillery; (4) Culp's Hill; (5) Cemetery Hill; (6) Cemetery Ridge; (7) Round Top; (8) Little Round Top; (9) Peach Orchard; (10) Devil's Den.

Stuart's reports on the Union army for a week. Lee trusted Stuart and thought that because there was no news, the Union army was not nearby.

What led General Lee to believe that the Union army was not nearby?

Accidental Meeting at Gettysburg. On the night of June 28, Lee discovered that he was mistaken. A Confederate spy known as Harrison informed him that the Union army, led by General George Meade, was massed at Frederick, Maryland, only a few miles away. Lee's army was spread throughout Pennsylvania. He sent out messengers to call the army together. By this time the Union army had begun to move north. By chance, both armies were taking roads that would bring them to Gettysburg.

On his move north, Lee had found it necessary to cut the supply line with his home base in Virginia. But this was no hardship. His troops were living well off the rich Pennsylvania farmland. Pennsylvania, unlike Virginia, was largely untouched by the war. On June 30, 1863, Confederate soldiers were moving toward Gettysburg on the Chambersburg Road (see map on this page). They were looking for any supplies that would be useful. Also on June 30, Union cavalry was on the Chambersburg Road. The leader, General John Buford, had been ordered to locate the Confederate army. Buford found what he had been looking for. He formed a battle line west of Gettysburg and then sent messengers to call up the rest of the Union army. This battle line had to hold the Confederates until the rest of the Union army arrived.

■ *How did the Confederate and Union armies come to meet at Gettysburg?*

A Chance for Early Victory. By the morning of July 1, the first part of the Union army had arrived. These soldiers took up a position on high ground to the west of Gettysburg. Among them were some of the best soldiers in the Union army. The Confederates they faced were also tough, battle-hardened soldiers.

Quickly the fighting began. Losses were heavy on both sides. By late morning the Confederate superiority in numbers was beginning to tell. The Union battle line began to give way. Then more Confederate soldiers arrived, hitting the already weakened Union right flank. Union reinforcements finally began to come in, and this strengthened the Union line. But even more Confederates rushed in, again striking the weak Union right flank.

By now General Lee had arrived. He saw that there was a chance for an early victory. He ordered an offensive on all fronts. The Union line gave way, and the Union soldiers began to retreat through Gettysburg. This retreat was very disorganized, and many Union soldiers were taken prisoner. Those that were not taken prisoner made for an area of high ground to the south of Gettysburg, known as Cemetery Hill.

More Union troops were coming in from the south to join those who had retreated to Cemetery Hill. But even though they were increasing in numbers, they were still somewhat disorganized. General Lee saw that this was his chance for victory. He ordered one of his commanders, General Richard Ewell, to take the Union position on Cemetery Hill "if he found it practicable." But Ewell, a cautious man, hesitated. All the while the Union soldiers were growing in numbers. By late evening, Ewell felt that there were too many Union soldiers. The attack on Cemetery Hill was called off.

■ *Why did General Richard Ewell not make the attack on Cemetery Hill?*

Generals Disagree. Lee's second-in-command was General James Longstreet. He was a highly respected soldier and was well liked by his troops, who called him Old Peter. He showed his best qualities as a soldier when defending a position.

When Longstreet saw the Union army gathering on Cemetery Hill, he could not have been more pleased. He suggested to Lee that the Confederate army should move to the south around the Union position. They should

General Robert E. Lee commanded the Confederate forces during the Battle of Gettysburg.

Historical Pictures Service

then find a strong position between the Union army and Washington. The Union army would be forced to attack, and the Confederate chances for victory would be very good.

But Lee did not want to miss the chance to fight. His reply was, "They are in their position, and I am going to whip them or they are going to whip me." Longstreet dropped the subject. But he decided to bring it up again the next day.

What was General Longstreet's plan of action?

Another Chance for Victory. On the morning of July 2, Longstreet again talked of moving south around the Union position. But Lee would not hear of it. Such a move, he said, could not be made without the cavalry. Rather, the Confederates would attack the right and left flanks of the Union army. The Union army did hold a strong position. But Lee's soldiers were good fighters who were used to winning. He believed they would win again that day.

Longstreet was ordered to take his troops and attack the Union left flank. General Ewell would strike on the right flank, which the Union army had extended to Culp's Hill, east of Cemetery Hill (see map on this page). The attack was supposed to start that morning. But Longstreet was very slow to move and take up his position. The attack did not get under way until midafternoon.

The Union left was bounded by two pieces of high ground, Little Round Top and Round Top. The Union left was held by General Dan Sickles. He owed his rank to his political connections rather than to his ability as a soldier.

The Union and Confederate forces collided by chance at Gettysburg on July 1, 1863. On the following day, the two armies fought to a bloody standstill.

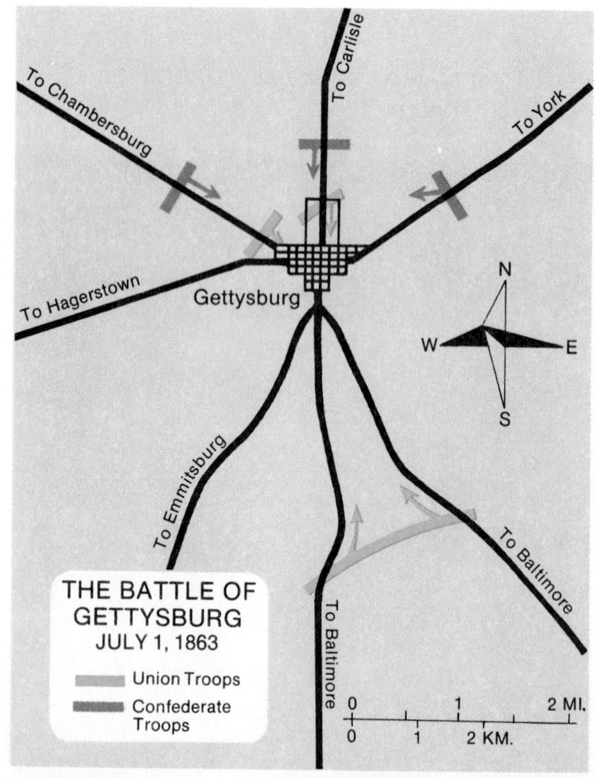

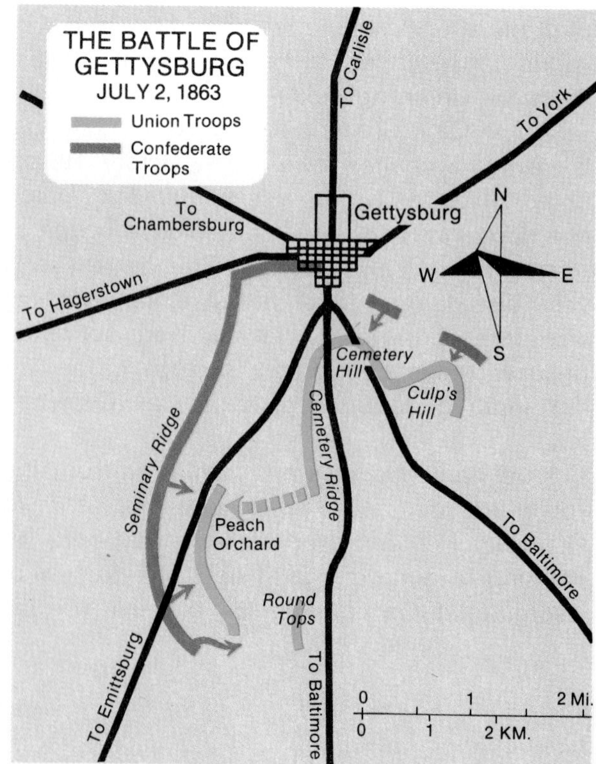

Against the orders of General Meade, Sickles moved his troops forward to some high ground in a peach orchard. When Longstreet began his attack, Sickles was surrounded, and his troops were pushed back, suffering many casualties. The fighting was fierce, and the Confederates slowly pushed their way toward the Round Tops. From there the Confederates would have a commanding view of the whole Union line.

Luckily for the Union army, a Union officer saw the importance of the Round Tops. Just in time he rushed in soldiers to defend them. The soldiers were able to beat back the Confederate attack. Bitter fighting continued all along the left flank, but the Union line held.

Ewell was also slow in getting started. But when his troops did attack, they fought fiercely. However, the Union soldiers on Culp's Hill were well dug in and were able to beat off the Confederate attacks. The Union line between Culp's Hill and Cemetery Hill was broken by the Confederates. But reinforcements did not arrive, and the Confederates had to fall back.

The second day's fighting ended with little gain for the Confederates. But if Longstreet and Ewell had attacked earlier in the day, things might have been different.

■ *What was the importance of Little Round Top and Round Top?*

SECTION 1 REVIEW

1. *What did Lee plan to do when he had moved north into Pennsylvania?*
2. *How did the battle plans of Lee and Longstreet differ?*
3. *Why did the Confederates fail to win the battle on July 2?*

2 Gettysburg—Final Day and Aftermath

At the end of the second day's fighting, General Meade called a council of war. He was not sure if he should hold his position at Gettysburg or move to another defensive position nearer Washington. His officers voted to stay and fight. Meanwhile, General Lee was planning another attack. This, he believed, would bring him final victory.

Lee and Longstreet Disagree Again. On July 3, General Lee was up well before daybreak. He was preparing to strike the blow that he believed would bring him victory. Longstreet's troops would attack the center of the Union line on Cemetery Ridge, which ran south from Cemetery Hill to the Round Tops. Ewell's troops would stage an attack on the Union right. Jeb Stuart's cavalry, which had finally arrived, would harass the Union retreat. In the unlikely event that Longstreet's attack should fail, troops led by General A. P. Hill would cover the Confederate retreat.

Shortly after sunrise, Lee met with Longstreet. Again Longstreet brought up the subject of moving around the Union left. Lee replied sharply, "The enemy is there and I am going to strike him." He then detailed his plan. Longstreet was dismayed. He felt that even with the 15,000 good soldiers he had ready, the attack could end only in disaster.

"General," he said, "I have been a soldier all my life . . . , and I should know as well as anyone what soldiers can do. It is my opinion that no 15,000 men ever arrayed for battle can take that position." But it was no good. Lee's mind was set on the attack. It would be led by General George Pickett.

Why did General Longstreet not want to make the attack on Cemetery Ridge?

Pickett's Charge struck at the center of the Union forces but failed to rout the Union army.

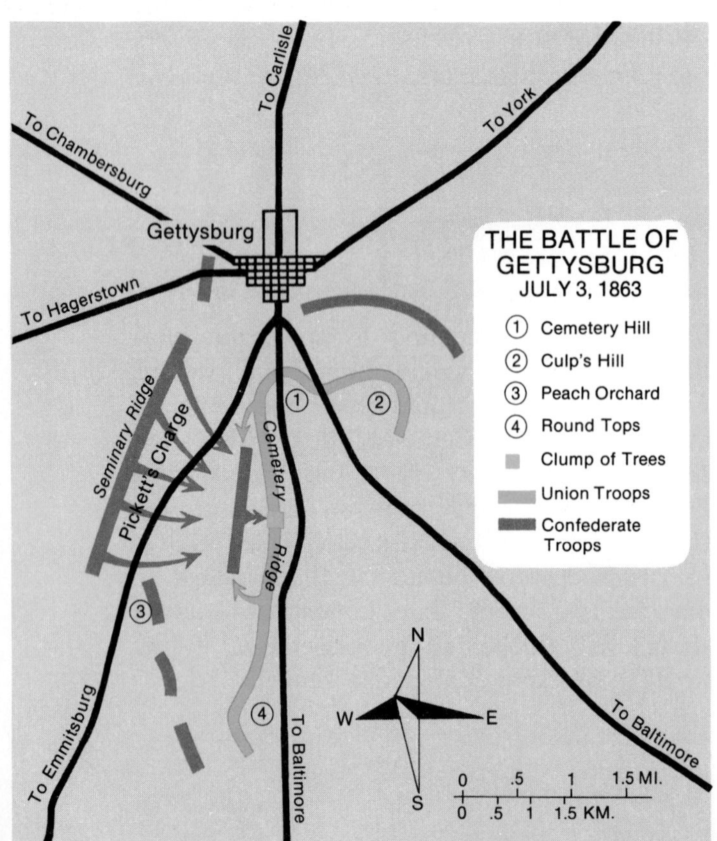

Artillery Bombards the Union Line. The third day's fighting began at one o'clock in the afternoon. The Confederates began to bombard the Union line with heavy artillery fire. This, Lee thought, would "soften up" the Union soldiers for Pickett's attack.

But the Confederate artillery was off target. The Confederates were firing over and striking behind the Union line. Most shells fell among cooks and medical orderlies, who got their first taste of battle. Even General Meade's headquarters was hit. He and his staff had to move to a safer part of the battlefield.

After nearly two hours of bombardment, the Union artillery appeared to stop returning fire. Through the smoke and haze, Confederate soldiers thought they saw Union troops falling back. Colonel E. P. Alexander, in charge of Confederate artillery, sent word to Longstreet that the attack should begin. Alexander said that he was low on ammunition. If Pickett did not move off soon, he would not be able to give him proper support.

Longstreet was surprised to hear about the lack of ammunition. Lee probably did not know of it either. If he had, he might not have ordered the attack. But it was too late to change plans. The attack had begun with Pickett's cry of, "Up, men, and to your posts! Don't forget today that you are from old Virginia!"

What fact, unknown to General Lee, might have stopped him from ordering the attack on Cemetery Ridge?

Pickett's Charge. The attack began in an orderly fashion. From their position west of the Emmittsburg Road (see map on this page), the Confederates had almost a mile of open country to cross to Cemetery Ridge. Pickett's troops were in the center of the line of attack.

With parade-ground precision, they wheeled, then marked time, waiting for the soldiers on the flanks to get into line. Then the line moved off. Its target was a small clump of trees on the brow of Cemetery Ridge.

Very soon, Union artillery began to pound the Confederate ranks. Casualties were heavy, as the ground below Cemetery Ridge offered little cover. As soldiers fell dead or wounded, the Confederate ranks closed up and kept moving forward. Union infantry, wheeling in from the left and right, put the Confederates under deadly fire from both sides. Then the Union artillery began to fire canister. The results were devastating. Hundreds of Confederate soldiers fell dead or terribly maimed. But still the Confederate ranks moved forward.

The Confederates were closing in on the Union line. They dropped to the ground, exchanging fire with the Union infantry on the line. Bullets seemed to be flying in every direction. Then, with a blood-curdling "Rebel yell," the Confederates rose and charged toward the little clump of trees.

■ *From where did Pickett's Charge begin?*

Gettysburg National Military Park, Cyclorama Center

This painting of Pickett's Charge, by Paul Philippoteaux, shows the "Confederate high-water mark" at the clump of trees (top left) and the tremendous destruction of the battle.

Confederate High-Water Mark. One of Pickett's commanders, General Lewis Armistead, was at the head of the charge. He had his hat stuck on the point of his sword as a guide for his soldiers. The Union officer commanding the defense of the line where Armistead was heading was General Winfield Scott Hancock. He and Armistead had been great friends before the war.

Armistead managed to break the Union line, followed by about 300 other Confederates. The Union soldiers broke ranks and fell back. But they were rallied by their officers, and charged back into the Confederates. The fighting was fierce and hand to hand. But there were just too many Union soldiers. Most of the Confederates who broke the Union line were killed or taken prisoner. Armistead, as he lay dying, gave a Union soldier a message for his old friend Hancock. "Tell Hancock I have done him and my country a great injustice I shall never cease to regret."

Armistead's breaking of the Union line is often called the "Confederate high-water mark." After it, the fortunes of the Confederacy seemed to decline.

Too late, Longstreet sent in reinforcements to back up the charge. But they were too few.

The charge finally broke up, and the dejected Confederates streamed back to their own line. They were met by a grieving General Lee. "It's all my fault," he said. "The blame is mine." But Lee had to prepare for the Union counterattack he expected. Seeing Pickett ride in, he told him to get his soldiers ready to fight off any attack.

"General Lee," Pickett said, the tears welling up in his eyes, "I have no division now."

■ *Which Confederate general broke the Union line on Cemetery Ridge?*

Aftermath. The attack never came. The following day, July 4, heavy rain fell. The two armies eyed each other nervously across the battlefield where nearly 50,000 soldiers were dead, wounded, or missing. Both sides had lost many of their finest and bravest soldiers. On the night of July 4, under cover of darkness, Lee began to move his army out. They set their course for Virginia.

All that was left for Lee was to try to discover why he had lost at Gettysburg. He could blame his commanders. He had often said that his army could do anything if commanded correctly. He could blame Jeb Stuart for not keeping him informed on the Union army. Or he could blame General Ewell for not pressing home the advantage on the first day. General Longstreet's late start on the second day could also be blamed. But Lee accepted that he was responsible for the defeat. "It's all my fault," he told Longstreet on July 4. He repeated this in the official report he sent to the Confederate government at the end of July.

■ *Who did Lee blame for the Confederate defeat at Gettysburg?*

Gettysburg—What If . . . ? At certain points during the Battle of Gettysburg, if things had been only slightly different, the outcome might have changed. Lee often said that if his attacks had been better organized and his commanders more forceful, he would have won.

But what would have resulted if the Confederates had won? Vicksburg might have been saved. Foreign powers, such as Great Britain and France, might have recognized the Confederacy. And a war-weary North might have accepted peace on Confederate terms.

Whatever the outcome, Gettysburg was one of the greatest and deadliest battles fought on United States soil. And Pickett's Charge was one of the most remarkable military spectacles ever seen. A foreign observer with the Confederates was moved to say, "I wouldn't have missed this for anything!"

General Longstreet replied, "The devil you wouldn't! I would like to have missed it very much."

■ *What changes did Lee think would have given him victory at Gettysburg?*

SECTION 2 REVIEW

1. *How did the third day's fighting at Gettysburg begin?*
2. *What was the Confederate high-water mark?*
3. *Why, in your opinion, did the Confederates lose at Gettysburg?*

CHAPTER 20 REVIEW

SUMMARY

In June 1863, the Confederate troops led by General Robert E. Lee began to move northward. Lee hoped for a Confederate victory on Union soil. On June 30, Confederate troops were moving toward Gettysburg on Chambersburg Road. On that same day, the Union cavalry was also on Chambersburg Road. Their leader, General John Buford, had been ordered to locate the Confederate army. When Buford found what he was looking for, he formed a battle line west of Gettysburg and then sent messengers to call up the rest of the Union army.

By the morning of July 1, part of the Union army had arrived. Fighting began quickly. The Union soldiers began to retreat and those soldiers who were not taken prisoner made for an area of high ground known as Cemetery Hill. General Lee ordered General Richard Ewell to take the Union on Cemetery Hill if possible. But Ewell felt that there were too many Union soldiers on Cemetery Hill, so the attack was called off.

General Lee's second in command, General Longstreet, wanted to take up a stronger position, nearer Washington, D.C., forcing the Union to attack. General Lee would not hear of it. On July 2, the second day of fighting, the Confederates failed to win the battle in part because Longstreet and Ewell waited until late afternoon to attack.

On July 3, General Lee and Longstreet disagreed again. Lee wanted to make the attack on the Union on Cemetery Ridge. Longstreet disagreed, but Lee ordered the attack. Hundreds of Confederate soldiers fell dead or were maimed.

Lee prepared for a Union counterattack, but the attack never came. On the night of July 4, Lee began to move his army out and set the course for Virginia. General Lee accepted responsibility for the defeat at Gettysburg.

UNDERSTANDING CONCEPTS

1. Why did General Lee believe that the Union army was not near the Confederate troops?
2. How did General Longstreet's plan of action differ from General Lee's plan?
3. Why was General Longstreet opposed to an attack on Cemetery Ridge?
4. Why was General Armistead's breaking of the Union lines called the "Confederate high-water mark?"
5. What did Lee think would have given him victory at Gettysburg?

CRITICAL THINKING

1. Do you think that General Richard Ewell should have made the attack on Cemetery Hill? Why or why not?
2. In your opinion, should General Lee have listened to General Longstreet and moved the Confederate troops south around the Union army and take a stronger position nearer Washington, D.C.? Explain your answer.
3. Do you think the South would have won the Civil War if the South would have won the Battle of Gettysburg? Why do you think so?

PROJECTS AND ACTIVITIES

The Civil War has sometimes been called the first modern war. New weapons—such as ships made of iron, observation balloons, machine guns, and submarines—were used. Use encyclopedias and other reference books to help you make drawings or models of weapons that were used during the Civil War. You might display your drawings and models in the classroom.

UNIT FIVE REVIEW

UNIT SUMMARY

During the Civil War, both Lincoln and the Confederate president, Jefferson Davis, faced many problems. In July 1863, the Union won a decisive victory at Gettysburg. The Union battle plan finally wore the Confederates down. General Robert E. Lee finally surrendered to General Ulysses S. Grant at Appomattox Court House in April 1865.

After the Civil War a period of reconstruction was needed. Both President Lincoln and President Johnson had put forward Reconstruction plans that were generous to the South. The Radical Republicans took control of Reconstruction after the congressional elections of 1866. They issued their own Reconstruction plan, which was harsher than the plans of Lincoln and Johnson. Military occupation of the South enabled Republicans to take control of state governments. In the years after the Civil War, corruption seemed to be widespread throughout government and business.

The years after the Civil War saw rapid change in the United States. In the North there was rapid industrial development. During these years, the American frontier moved westward. The South also changed during the years after the Civil War.

The Battle of Gettysburg was a terrible defeat for the Confederate army. General Lee accepted responsibility for the defeat. At certain points during the battle, if things had been only slightly different, the outcome might have changed.

YOU SHOULD KNOW

Identify, define, or explain each of the following:

proclamation	scalawags
total war	long drive
freedmen	reservations
impeach	tenant farmers
carpetbaggers	plurality

CHECKING FACTS

1. What incident started the Civil War?
2. What were the names of the two ironclad ships that fought a battle in March of 1862?
3. When and where did General Lee surrender to General Grant?
4. In which part of the country were most of the Civil War battles fought?
5. What did the Fifteenth Amendment do?
6. What good works were done by Republican governments in the South during Radical Reconstruction?
7. What two national labor organizations were formed in the 1860's?
8. What was the Homestead Act?
9. What did the Republicans promise the southern Democrats in return for the presidency in 1876?
10. Which Confederate general broke the Union line on Cemetery Ridge during the Battle of Gettysburg?

UNDERSTANDING CONCEPTS

1. What major factors led to the Union victory in the Civil War?
2. Why did Reconstruction cause disagreement between Congress and the President?
3. How did Reconstruction change the life of blacks in the South?
4. What was the importance of the railroads to industrial development in the United States?
5. How did southern industry and agriculture change after the Civil War?

CRITICAL THINKING

1. In your opinion, what was the major issue of the Civil War—preserving the Union or the question of slavery? Explain your answer.

UNIT FIVE REVIEW

2. Although President Grant was not involved in the corruption that existed during his Presidency, do you think that he was still responsible for the corruption? Why or why not?
3. If you were living in the years after the Civil War, would you have preferred to live in the West, the North, or the South? Give reasons for your answer.

CHRONOLOGY

Arrange the following events in the order in which they happened.

a. General Robert E. Lee surrendered at Appomattox
b. Abraham Lincoln elected President
c. The Battle of Little Big Horn
d. Andrew Johnson became President
e. The purchase of Alaska

CITIZENSHIP IN ACTION

The Freedmen's Bureau to help provide freed blacks and struggling white Southerners with food, clothing, medical care, legal protection, and so on. Today, how does the government help to provide these services to citizens who are in need?

GEOGRAPHY

1. What Confederate states had no major battles fought within their borders?
2. How many miles (kilometers) did Sherman's army march, from Chattanooga, Tennessee, to Raleigh, North Carolina?
3. What general led the campaign to divide the Confederacy along the Mississippi River?
4. How was the Confederacy cut off from supplies by sea?

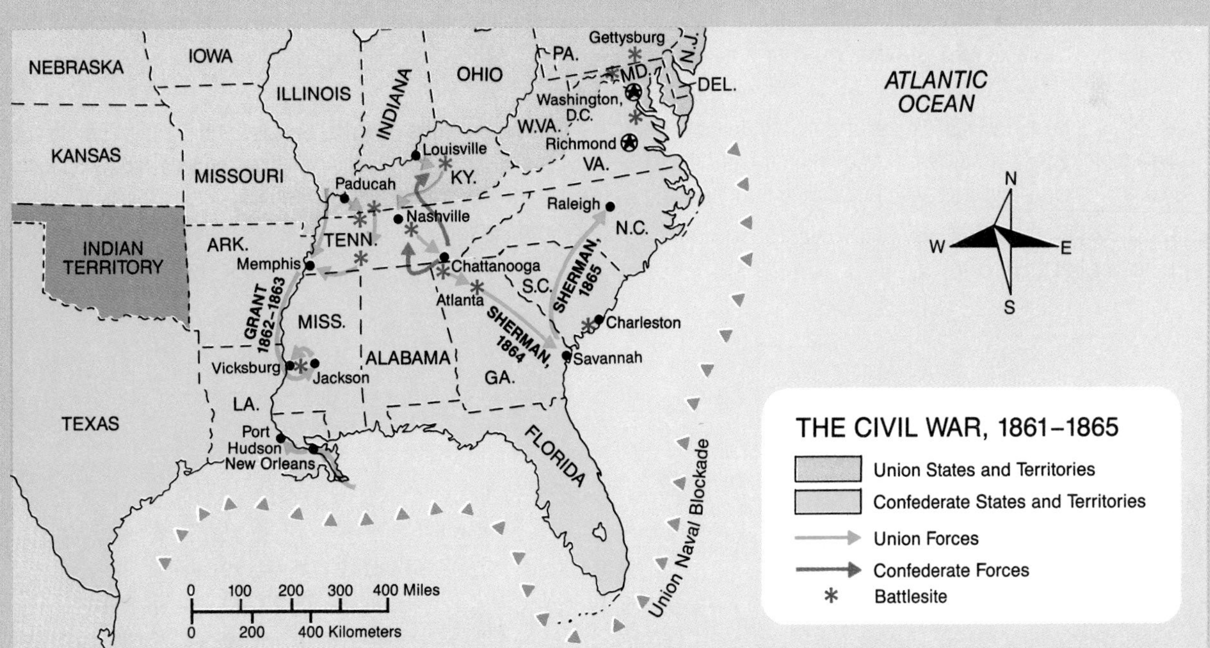

1880 | 1885

1877 Coal miners in eastern Pennsylvania go on strike
Phonograph invented

1879 Incandescent electric light invented

1882 Oriental Exclusions Act passed

1884 First skyscraper built

1886 Bombing at Haymarket Square in Chicago
American Federation of Labor founded

1887 Interstate Commerce Act passed
Dawes Act passed

UNIT SIX

The Growth of the Nation

1877 to 1900

This oil painting by Joseph Becker shows the Central Pacific Railroad through the Sierra Nevada Mountains. Chinese-American workers often cleared snow blocking the trains.

This picture shows a firing process at the Bethlehem Steel Corporation. The steel industry helped provide the foundation for industrial growth in the late 1800's.

1890 1895 1900

- 1889 Oklahoma Territory opened to settlement
- 1890 Western frontier closed
  Battle of Wounded Knee
  Sherman Antitrust Act passed
- 1891 Populist Party formed
- 1894 Pullman Strike
  Wilson-Gorman Tariff Act
- 1898 Spanish American War
- 1900 Gold Standard Act passed

CHAPTERS

During the last half of the 1800's the American West was a place of rapid change and great challenge. The population boomed in the West as men and women moved there from other states and from other countries. American Indians continued to lose their ancestral lands to farmers, ranchers, businesses, and the federal government. By 1890 white settlement spanned the North American continent.

As the frontier closed in the West, American industry underwent remarkable growth, especially in the North. Cities swelled with immigrants.

Through victory in the Spanish American War, the United States took control of some overseas lands. Thus, as the nineteenth century ended, America became a world power.

This painting of Washington Street in Indianapolis during the 1890's showed how America's cities were changing in the late 1800's as business and industry expanded.

On May 4, 1886, a violent labor demonstration was held at Chicago's Haymarket Square.

1870 1880 1890 1900

- 1869 First transcontinental railroad completed
- 1874 Barb wire invented
- 1886 Geronimo surrenders
- 1887 Interstate Commerce Act and Dawes Act passes
- 1889 Oklahoma Territory opens to settlement
- 1890 Battle of Wounded Knee
- 1891 Populist party formed
- 1894 Estelle Reel elected to state office
- 1900 Gold Standard Act passed

CHAPTER 21

The West—Progress and Problems

Chapter Objectives

After studying this chapter, you will be able to:

- identify the changes that took place and the problems that occurred on the Great Plains in the late 1800's;
- explain what factors led farmers of the Great Plains to organize into groups and to form a third political party in the late 1800's;
- enumerate the changes that indicated the frontier was ending in the 1890's.

1 Changes on the Frontier

Overview In the second half of the nineteenth century, changes took place on the western frontier. Thousands of miles of railroad tracks crossed the once-empty Great Plains. Big-business concerns moved west and, within a few years, they had taken control of much of the mining and cattle industries. Problems also began to appear. Bad weather and poor management were problems faced by most cattle ranchers. Settlers on the Great Plains found farming far from easy.

Objectives After reading this section, you will be able to:

- explain the importance of railroads for frontier settlement;
- discuss how organized mining operations affected mining communities;
- identify farming improvements that helped make the Great Plains the "breadbasket of America."

The Expanding Railroad Network. Westward travel in the first half of the nineteenth century was difficult and hazardous. But the completion of the first transcontinental railroad in 1869 made westward travel easier and cheaper. As a result, the vast expanse of the Great Plains was thrown open to settlement.

Chinese and European immigrants provided much of the labor needed to complete the first transcontinental railroad. Their efforts helped to develop the American West. Along the route from California to Utah, more than 10,000 Chinese worked long hours for little pay. Their industriousness and intelligence gained them the respect of their employers. Among the feats of these Chinese workers were tunnels carved through mountains of solid granite.

One transcontinental railroad, however, was not enough to carry all the settlers west. By 1887 there were three more transcontinental routes, one in the North and two in the South. At the same time, many small local lines were built. Railroads were slowly changing the Great Plains from open range to settled land.

The expansion of the railroads brought thousands of immigrants to settle the western frontier. These people often bought the lands granted to the railroad companies by the federal government. In return, the railroads provided a means of transportation for the products of Great Plains farmers and ranchers.

Although the railroad companies often were guilty of unfair and corrupt practices, they played an important part in the settlement of the frontier. Without the railroads, and the great achievements of the Chinese, the Irish, and others who built the rail lines, the process of settlement would have taken much longer.

■ *In what way did the railroads change the Great Plains?*

Changes in Mining. The second half of the nineteenth century also saw many changes in the mining industry. The gold rushes of the mid-1800's had been led by individual prospectors. These rugged men depended on little more than luck and hard work in their search for precious metals. They rarely made much money from their claims. And they often were cheated out of what little money they had.

This haphazard and unprofitable approach to mining was replaced by the organized methods of big business. Able to invest the large amounts of money needed for mining,

The Bettmann Archive

This painting by Charles Russell shows two prospectors panning for gold at a desert water hole.

businesses bought up claims from miners and prospectors. By the late 1870's, big-business concerns controlled nearly all the mining operations in the West. For example, by 1878, the Homestake Mining Company controlled nearly all the gold claims in the Black Hills, an area of more than 6,000 square miles [16 000 square kilometers].

The big mining companies carefully organized searches to locate minerals more efficiently. Their investments then provided the heavy machinery and large labor force needed to work a claim profitably. The big mining companies also changed the nature of mining. The individual prospectors had been mainly interested in gold. But the mining companies were just as interested in other metals, such as silver, copper, tin, and lead. These metals were then sold for industrial use.

The big mining companies had a positive effect on settlement in the West. During the days of the gold rushes, mining communities were often short-lived. The populations of whole towns frequently moved to follow the miners to places where new gold deposits had been found. Ghost towns were left where thriving communities had once existed. But with better organized and more permanent mining operations, mining communities became more stable.

■ *Why were the big mining companies able to work claims more profitably than individual miners?*

The Cattle Industry. As you have read, the cattle industry began on the southern plains of Texas. It developed in response to the need for food in our eastern cities. By the 1870's, the cattle industry had spread from Texas to as far north as the plains of Montana and Wyoming. The Great Plains area offered a vast open range for grazing. In the 1870's the only animals competing with the cattle for the grazing land were the buffalo. But the buffalo were rapidly being wiped out by buffalo hunters.

Then, as the population of the United States grew, the demand for food also increased. The increase in the demand for beef caused beef prices to rise. The opportunity to make large profits drew eastern businesses into the cattle industry. Through the investment of large sums of money, these eastern businesses soon gained control of the industry.

Profits continued to rise. In 1879, Great Plains cattle were being sold at $8 a head. Three years later, selling prices had risen to as much as $60 a head. Business was so good that the cattle industry became known as the "beef bonanza." Even European businesses were tempted to invest in the cattle industry.

Although profits were high, the cattle industry was not as healthy as it appeared. Real problems were beginning to develop on the open range.

■ *How far north did the cattle industry spread in the United States?*

Trouble for Cattle Owners. The Great Plains were public land, and any cattle owner had the right to graze cattle on it. But the rivers and lakes of the Great Plains were not part of the public land and could be owned privately. A cattle owner who gained control of a river or lake effectively controlled the surrounding land. Grazing land was useless if the animals had no water.

Cattle owners argued constantly about the ownership of water rights. These arguments were often settled by gunfights. Sometimes these gunfights developed into full-scale *range wars.* Many cowhands lost their lives in the wars over water rights.

Another problem for the cattle owners was that the Great Plains were becoming crowded. In their rush to make large profits, cattle owners had overstocked the plains. In addition, sheep had been introduced on the plains. The sheep competed with the cattle for the grazing land. The public land was also being sold off to settlers. As small farms began to appear on what was once open land, the cattle owners' open range began to diminish.

In 1874, Joseph Glidden, a farmer in De Kalb, Illinois, invented barbed wire for fences. Cattle owners saw this invention as a solution to the problems of water rights and diminishing grazing lands. But the problems grew worse.

■ *Why was the ownership of water rights important to cattle owners?*

Branding cattle was one of the many duties of cowhands in the West. The inset picture is of a black cowhand, Nat Love, who wrote a book about his life as a cowhand, *The Life and Adventures of Nat Love*.

Courtesy of Levi Strauss & Co., San Francisco, California

Library of Congress

End of the Open Range. Using barbed wire, cattle owners began to fence off the water and the land they considered their own. Disputes over water and land rights again led to gun battles. This fencing off of the Great Plains finally led to the end of the open-range cattle industry.

Left to wander across the Great Plains, cattle could normally find enough grazing land to live. They could also find shelter from the worst of the winter weather. Fenced in, however, their grazing land was limited, and little shelter from winter storms was available. The harsh winter of 1886–1887 brought disaster. Nearly 90 percent of the cattle on the Great Plains died. Most cattle owners were ruined financially. The open-range cattle industry was finished.

The cattle industry began to revive a few years later. But it was on a much smaller scale. The days of the large free-roaming herds grazing on public lands were over. The public lands were being sold and fenced off. In the future, the cattle owners would have to share the Great Plains with the sheep herders and the farmers.

■ *Which natural disaster brought about the end of the open-range cattle industry?*

Improvements in Farming. For most settlers, farming on the Great Plains was not an easy life. Most of the Great Plains area received little rainfall. A special farming method, *dry farming,* had to be used to combat this shortage of water. Dry farming was a way of plowing the land to hold the rain where it fell. The normal method of plowing allowed the rain to run off.

Dry farming proved to be the way to grow wheat. And when eastern European immigrants brought hardy strains of grain to the plains, the production and quality of wheat improved. The Great Plains soon became known as the "breadbasket of America."

As farming grew, changes in farm machinery also helped the plains farmers. Most of the farm machinery that was used on the Great Plains had been developed before the Civil War. But a number of improvements made after the Civil War made this machinery more efficient. The introduction of the Bessemer process in the 1860's made steel production easier and cheaper. Soon steel rather than iron was being used to make plows. This greatly increased the efficiency and strength of the plow. Efficiency was further increased in the late 1880's when the steam tractor began to replace the horse as a means of power.

Great Plains farmers often had to farm a large area of land just to make a little money. But with the development of mechanized planters and harvesters, the work of planting and harvesting a large area took less time and was easier. By the 1880's these machines were a common sight on the Great Plains.

The farm-machinery industry quickly grew and flourished. A number of people made vast fortunes from the sale of farm machinery. Among them was Cyrus H. McCormick, who had his company headquarters in Chicago, Illinois.

■ *How did Great Plains farmers combat the shortage of rainfall?*

Farming Becomes Big Business. As with mining and cattle ranching, big-business methods soon came to play a part in farming on the Great Plains. Most of the farms run by these methods were in the Dakotas. The successful ones were known as *bonanza farms.* The farmers applied business methods to

By the late 1800's, some farmers on the Great Plains used steam-driven tractors. At the same time, however, many plains farmers could not afford such equipment and instead relied upon their animals to pull their plows. How did the use of steam-driven tractors differ from the use of plows pulled by animals?

Albertype Collection, Wisconsin State Historical Society

International Harvester Co.

farming. One profitable crop, normally wheat, was grown. And farming was done on a large scale. The majority of bonanza farms covered thousands of acres of land.

The bonanza farmers could afford the best farm machinery. And since they bought supplies in large quantities, they could get them at wholesale rates. They could also bargain to get cheaper transportation rates. Thus, they made large profits.

The small farmers who originally settled the Great Plains could not compete with the bonanza farmers. Few small farmers made any kind of profit. Some complained that growing their crops cost more than the price for which they could sell them. They also felt that the transportation rates they paid were very high. Life for the small farmers was little more than a struggle to survive.

■ *Where were most bonanza farms to be found?*

SECTION 1 REVIEW

1. *How did the transcontinental railroads open the Great Plains to settlement?*
2. *What effect did organized mining operations have on mining communities?*
3. *Why was dry farming necessary on the Great Plains?*

2 Dissatisfaction Among Farmers

Overview Farmers on the Great Plains found work strenuous and weather and harvests uncertain. Rainfall was low, and the soil was often poor. The farmers, however, faced bigger hardships. High interest rates on bank loans and high transportation rates charged by railroads made it hard to make much money. Farmers began to organize to rid themselves of these hardships. The first effort to organize was with the Patron's of Husbandry, or the Grange. The farmers formed a third political party, the People's, or Populist party. Although the Populist party was short-lived, many of the issues it raised lived on and became law in the twentieth century.

Objectives After reading this section, you should be able to:

- identify the many problems of the Great Plains' farmers;
- explain the efforts made by the Great Plains' farmers to solve their problems;
- list the goals of the Populist party.

Life on the Plains. Life for the Great Plains farm family was not easy. It was often very lonely. Most families lived many miles away from their nearest neighbors. The nearest town was often many miles away. The feeling of isolation was worse for immigrant families. The Great Plains often were physically different from their homelands. And American customs and the English language sometimes seemed strange.

Farming the Great Plains was hard, and the working hours were long. Farm machinery was very expensive. Few farmers could afford this machinery, so they had to borrow the money from banks. The interest on these bank loans was often very high. In addition, the farmers also had to pay high transportation rates to the railroads. As a result, regardless of how hard they worked, most western farmers never made enough money to get out of debt.

The weather was another problem for western farmers. Dry spells threatened their crops. At other times, bad storms would come at harvest time and ruin the crops. On some occasions hordes of grasshoppers devoured the crops. The farmers could do little about these natural problems. But the other problems were different.

■ *Why was plains farm life especially lonely for immigrant families?*

The Farmers' Complaints. The plains farmers had many problems. But their chief complaint was that they could not get a fair price for their crops. The buyers of the crops said that this was the fault of the farmers. They had grown too much, and there was a surplus of crops. Because of this, prices were low. Few farmers believed that this *overproduction* was the cause of low prices. The blame, they said, lay with other people.

Many farmers blamed the bankers. As you have read, farmers often had to borrow from banks to pay for such things as farm machinery. The rates of interest on these loans were higher than normal. The bankers said they had to charge high interest rates to protect themselves. This, they said, was because farming was a very risky business. And the farmers had to spend most of their profits to pay back the bank loans.

Farmers also blamed the railroads. At first,

the farmers had welcomed the railroads. They saw the railroads as a cheap form of transportation. But they soon came to blame the railroads for most of their problems.

Farmers relied on the railroads to transport their crops to market. They thought that different railroads competing with one another for business would keep shipping rates low. But the railroads were only in competition for long-distance transportation. The railroads normally agreed on rates for short-distance transportation. Most farmers were only shipping their crops a short distance, and they found themselves paying very high rates. In some cases it cost more to ship crops twenty miles than it did to ship them a thousand miles. Farmers complained about this. But the railroad companies did not listen. Some railroad officials suggested that if the farmers did not like the rates, they should transport their crops by wheelbarrow!

Farmers also blamed politicians. They thought the politicians cared little about the problems of the farmers. Rather, they thought that the politicians were working with the railroad companies to keep transportation rates high. Farmers also thought that politicians were working with big-business concerns to keep tariff rates high. These high tariff rates prevented the farmers from purchasing cheap foreign-made machinery. Farmers soon came to feel that things would only improve if they helped themselves.

■ *Why did farmers criticize the railroads?*

First Efforts at Organization. As you have read, the first efforts by farmers to organize themselves came with the Patrons of Husbandry. Although the Patrons of Husbandry, or the Grange, was formed as a social organization, farmers soon saw it as a way to air their political views.

A major complaint of the farmers was the high cost of railroad transportation. Through the Grange, farmers tried to influence state governments to regulate the railroads. In 1871, the state of Illinois passed a law setting up a commission to regulate the railroads. Iowa, Minnesota, and Wisconsin soon followed with similar laws. These laws became known as the *Granger laws*.

The railroad companies refused to recognize these Granger laws. But the Supreme Court, in the case of *Munn* v. *Illinois* (1877), decided

How does this cartoon show that the Grange felt there was a need for railroad regulation?

Culver Pictures

that state governments could regulate businesses, such as the railroads, that affected the public.

The Grangers' triumph was short-lived. The railroad companies did their best to get around the Granger laws. In some cases, state governments were offered bribes to repeal the laws. And in 1886, the Supreme Court qualified its earlier decision. The Court said that state governments could not regulate traffic that crossed state lines. Only the federal government had the power to do this. In 1887, Congress passed the Interstate Commerce Act. This gave the federal government the power to regulate interstate railroad traffic. It also outlawed certain unfair practices, most notably the setting of high rates for short-haul transportation.

The Interstate Commerce Act was not a complete success. The railroad companies were normally able to ignore it. But it was important. It showed the farmers that they were able to influence federal, as well as state, government.

■ *Which Supreme Court decision said that state governments could regulate businesses that affected the public?*

Farmers in National Politics. Most farmers were not satisfied with the performance of the major political parties. To the farmers it appeared that the Democratic and Republican parties were ignoring them. But a third party emerged during the 1870's that seemed to understand the farmers' problems. This was the Greenback party.

The Greenback party took its name from the paper money that had been issued during the Civil War. The party's members felt that the country's economic problems could be solved by putting more greenbacks into circulation. Many farmers thought that this was the answer to their problems. With more money in circulation, prices for farm produce would rise. And the farmers would have more money to pay off their debts.

A large number of farmers joined the Greenback party and tried to influence the government to put more paper money into circulation. But the government would only allow that amount of paper money in circulation that could be backed by government gold. Because of this, the Greenback party began to lose its power. It faded from the political scene in the 1880's.

Although the Greenback party was not successful, it provided many farmers with useful experience. These farmers had learned how to organize in order to influence government.

■ *How did the Greenback party propose to end this country's economic problems?*

A New Political Party. In the 1880's, the farmers once again began to organize. They joined together to form *alliances.* The farmers of the northern and northwestern plains formed the Northern Alliance. Farmers in the South joined together in the Southern Alliance. Black farmers in the South formed the Colored Farmers' Alliance. These alliances did much the same as the Grange and the Greenback party had done. They supported political candidates and tried to pressure government into passing laws that would help the farmers.

The strength of the alliances grew quickly. In the elections of 1890, many candidates supported by the alliances won seats in Congress. The alliances also controlled a number of state governments. Alliance leaders began to talk about joining together to form one national alliance. With the political strength they had, this new alliance could become a third political party to challenge the Democrats and Republicans.

Most members of the Northern Alliance were in favor of forming a third party. But many farmers in the South were against it. They preferred to work through the Democratic party. They thought that a third party would split the white vote and challenge white supremacy in the South. However, northern farmers went ahead and formed a third party. In 1891, at a meeting in Cincinnati, Ohio, they announced the formation of the People's party of America, or the Populist party. They also said that they would hold a national convention the following year in Omaha, Nebraska.

■ *Why were southern farmers against forming a third political party?*

Populist Party Goals. In the summer of 1892, Populist party members met in Omaha to draw up a platform and to choose a candidate to run for President. The platform, which was adopted on July 4, 1892, called for a number of reforms.

Like the Greenback party, the Populists wanted an increase in the amount of money in circulation. But unlike the Greenbackers, the Populists wanted the "free and unlimited coinage of silver." The Populists also called for government ownership of the railroads. And they wanted the government to set up a system to store farm produce until prices rose. Farmers would be able to borrow money against the crops they had stored.

The Populist platform also included demands for political reforms. One such demand was for the direct election of United States senators. The Populists also called for the secret, or Australian, ballot. And they supported

Library of Congress

A PARTY OF PATCHES.
Grand Balloon Ascension—Cincinnati, May 20th, 1891.

How does this cartoonist view the Populist party? Why do you think, are there holes in the balloon?

the *initiative* and *referendum,* which would allow voters to take direct action on important matters.

To gain more support, the Populists included demands that would attract industrial workers. They called for a graduated income tax. This would mean that people who earned more money would pay more in taxes. The Populists supported the eight-hour workday. They were also for controls on immigration, as they feared the immigrants would take jobs from American workers.

After adopting the platform, the Populists chose General James B. Weaver as their candidate for President. They then began to plan the campaign for the 1892 elections.

■ *How did the Populists intend to increase the amount of money in circulation?*

Populist Leaders. Many colorful characters became leaders in the Populist party. These leaders were well-known for their skill in speechmaking and the almost-religious fervor with which they put over their ideas.

One of the most colorful leaders was Mary Elizabeth Lease of Kansas. She was famous for her call to farmers to "raise less corn and more hell." She was also well-known for her work in the woman suffrage movement. "Sockless" Jerry Simpson, also from Kansas, could hold a crowd spellbound with his speeches attacking eastern businesses. Ignatius Donnelly, from Minnesota, wrote novels that attacked big business. The South also produced some great leaders. Among them was Tom Watson, a Congressman from Georgia. He worked hard to unite black and white farmers in their fight against big business.

These leaders traveled all over the country. They campaigned hard, trying to get support for the candidates in the election of 1892.

■ *Which Populist leader worked to unite black and white farmers?*

The Election of 1892. The 1892 election results for the Populists were mixed. Tom Watson lost his seat in Congress. And Ignatius

The Bettmann Archive

Mary Elizabeth Lease helped campaign for the Populist party in 1892. How many electoral votes did the Populist party capture in the election of 1892?

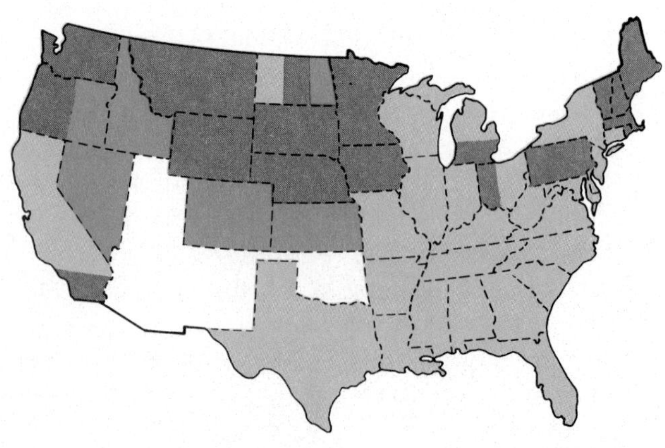

ELECTION OF 1892

	Electoral Votes	Popular Votes
Democratic Grover Cleveland	277	5,555,426
Republican Benjamin Harrison	145	5,182,690
People's (Populist) James B. Weaver	22	1,029,846

Donnelly was badly beaten in his attempt to become governor of Minnesota. But the Populists swept to power in Kansas.

Perhaps the best result the Populists achieved was the showing of General James B. Weaver in the presidential race. The Republicans had nominated incumbent President Benjamin Harrison. Against him the Democrats chose former President Grover Cleveland. The main issues in the campaign were the tariff and the increase of the amount of money in circulation. Cleveland put forward very conservative financial policies. This won him much Republican support. The popular vote in the election was close (see map on page 376). But Cleveland easily defeated Harrison in the electoral college, 277 to 145. And Weaver received over 1 million popular votes and 22 votes in the electoral college.

The mid-1890's proved to be the high point for the Populist party. It very soon became a one-issue party. This issue concerned the coinage of silver.

■ *What were the main issues in the 1892 election campaign?*

The Silver Question. Between 1892 and 1896, the coining of silver became an important question. As the election of 1896 approached, politicians began to take sides on this issue. Some Democrats were against silver coinage. These Democrats supported President Grover Cleveland. But many more Democrats were in favor of silver. A large number of them joined with the Populists to work for the coinage of silver.

This joining together of Democrats and Populists caused trouble. Many Populists were afraid that their party would become just a part of the Democratic party. These Populists would not join with the Democrats. Among them were some well-known leaders, such as Mary Elizabeth Lease. But many farmers were willing to join with the Democrats. They thought that the Populists could gain more by working with the Democrats.

Although some Republicans favored silver coinage, the Republican party was controlled by the *Gold Bugs.* These politicians were against silver coinage. At the 1896 Republican convention, Senator William McKinley of Ohio was picked to run for President. McKinley was known to be a supporter of big business. He was for a high tariff and was against the coinage of silver.

At their convention, the Democrats could not decide upon a candidate. But after Congressman William Jennings Bryan of Nebraska spoke, they nominated him. He made a rousing speech in favor of silver coinage. He answered Republican demands for a money system based on gold alone with the following words:

> Having behind us the producing masses of this nation and the world, supported by the commercial interests, the laboring interests, and the toilers everywhere, we will answer their demand for a gold standard by saying to them: You shall not press down upon the brow of labor this crown of thorns, you shall not crucify mankind upon a cross of gold!

This soon became known as the Cross of Gold speech.

The Populists also chose William Jennings Bryan as their candidate. But their choice for Vice-President was Tom Watson. Many people saw the 1896 election campaign as a fight between eastern business interests and western farming interests.

■ *Why did some Populists not want to join with the Democrats?*

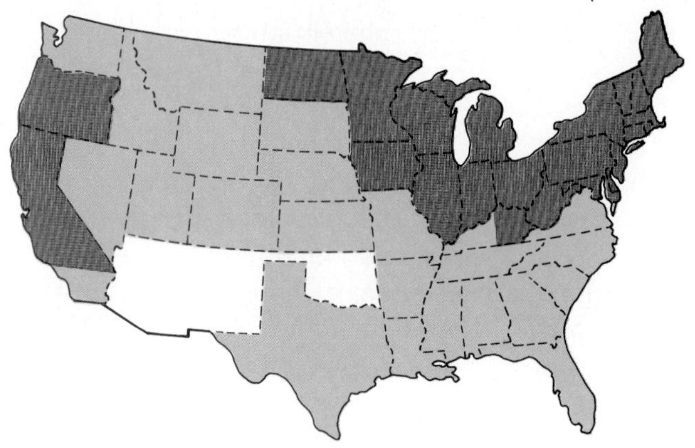

What was the difference in the electoral votes and the popular votes between McKinley and Bryan in 1896?

ELECTION OF 1896

	Electoral Votes	Popular Votes
Republican William McKinley	271	7,102,246
Democratic William J. Bryan	176	6,492,559

The Election of 1896. William Jennings Bryan campaigned vigorously. He visited 27 states and made more than 600 speeches. In contrast, William McKinley remained at his home in Canton, Ohio, and made speeches from his front porch. But McKinley had the support of the major newspapers. And his campaign funds were greater. Marcus Hanna, McKinley's campaign manager, raised more than 3.5 million dollars. Bryan raised only 300 thousand dollars.

The result of the election was an easy victory for McKinley (see map on this page). He received 271 electoral votes to Bryan's 176. The popular vote was closer, McKinley receiving 7 million votes to Bryan's 6.5 million.

The defeat of Bryan signaled the end of the power of the Populist party. The party had become identified with the silver movement. McKinley's victory was a resounding defeat for those who favored silver. The Populist party also lost power because times were better for the farmers. Bumper harvests had been gathered in 1896. And crop failures in some European countries increased the demand for American crops. Farm prices began to rise. This new prosperity caused farmers to lose interest in politics.

Although the Populist party declined as a political power, many of the issues it raised remained. Its chief issue, the adoption of silver coinage, failed. In 1900, Congress passed the Gold Standard Act, which ended the silver question. However, many other issues, such as income tax and the direct election of senators, were taken up by the Progressive party (see Chapter 25). These issues, first raised by the farmers of the plains, would influence the lives of all Americans in the twentieth century.

■ *How did the election campaigns of William McKinley and William Jennings Bryan differ?*

SECTION 2 REVIEW

1. *What was the chief complaint of the plains farmers?*
2. *How did the farmers' alliances in the 1880's help the farmers influence government?*
3. *What three political reforms did the Populist platform of 1892 include?*

3 End of the Frontier

Overview In the second half of the nineteenth century, the western plains changed from a vast wilderness to settled land. The Indians, the last barrier to settlement, were finally pushed on to small, barren reservations. The last large areas of open land were settled in the frantic "land rushes" of the 1890's. The days of the frontier were over.

Objectives After reading this section, you should be able to:

- explain why the Indians resisted the white settlers' movement westward;
- summarize the purpose of the Dawes Act of 1887;
- discuss the causes of the end of the frontier.

Indian Resistance. As the white settlers moved westward, they often clashed with the Indians already on the land. The fiercest resistance to the settlers came from the tribes of the plains. These tribes fought long and hard to keep their lands free of white settlers. But they were greatly outnumbered by the whites. The whites also had better weapons. It was only a matter of time before the Plains Indians were defeated.

After defeat, the Plains Indians saw their way of life destroyed. In the past they had roamed the plains, following the buffalo. The buffalo provided the Indians with food, clothing, shelter, and tools. But white settlers began to break up the open plains with farms and fences. White hunters also began to kill off the buffalo. These hunters used high-powered long-range rifles. With these the hunters could kill hundreds of buffalo in a day. Although some hunters killed the buffalo for meat, most were only interested in the buffalo skins. These hunters left the skinned buffalo carcasses to rot on the plains. This destruction of the buffalo, more than anything else, ended the Plains Indian way of life.

By the late 1870's, the Indian wars had ended. Most of the Indian leaders were either dead or had fled to Canada. Fighting did occasionally break out between Indians and white settlers. But no major battles were fought. The Apache leader Geronimo, however, caused trouble for the United States Army in the hills of the Southwest. He and his men would make lightning raids and then disappear into the hills. But the odds finally proved too great, and Geronimo surrendered in 1886.

DO YOU KNOW?

Where and when did Buffalo Bill Cody put on his first Wild West Show?

The first performance of William Frederick "Buffalo Bill" Cody's Wild West Show is said to have taken place at North Platte, Nebraska, on July 4, 1883. Such things as the Wild West Show and the circus became the regular Fourth of July entertainment for most plains people. The Wild West Show consisted of displays of riding and shooting skills and mock battles with Indians. For a time, one of Buffalo Bill's stars was Sitting Bull, the famous Sioux leader.

Before starting the Wild West Show, Buffalo Bill was a hunter, a scout, and an Indian fighter. Buffalo Bill took his show all over the United States and to Europe. He performed in the show up to the time of his death in 1917.

The harsh treatment that the Indians received caused concern among some whites. Helen Hunt Jackson, in her book *A Century of Dishonor,* published in 1881, wrote of the broken treaties and how the Indians had been cheated. A number of white reformers also became interested in Indian affairs. Most of these reformers felt that the problems of the Indians would be solved if the Indians followed the ways of the whites.

What brought about the destruction of the Plains Indian way of life?

The Dawes Act. The reformers' desire for the Indians to follow the ways of the whites led to the passing of the Dawes Act in 1887. These reformers believed that the Indians would never adopt the ways of the whites while the tribe, rather than individual Indians, owned the land. The Dawes Act ended tribal ownership of land. Under the act, tribal lands were broken up into small units. Individual Indians were to receive plots of land ranging in size from 40 to 160 acres [16 to 65 hectares]. After this allocation, the land left over was to be sold to whites for settlement. The money from the sale of land was to be used for Indian education. This education would be controlled by whites and would emphasize white values.

The individual ownership of land was supposed to encourage farming. But few Indians were interested in a settled life. Others found it impossible to adapt to such a foreign life-style. And, once again, the Indians found themselves cheated. Much of the land sold to the white

The Apache chief Geronimo (left) and his followers were the last Indian tribe to be confined to a reservation. The Nez Perce leader, Chief Joseph (right) and his people chose resistance rather than reservation life. Finally, in 1877 they were ordered to leave their Indian lands in the Snake River valley region and go to a reservation in Idaho.

Sophia Smith Collection

The Granger Collection

settlers was of better quality than that given to the Indians. The money from the sale of lands rarely served its intended purpose of Indian education. More often than not it went into the pockets of greedy Indian agents. Some Indians were persuaded to sell their land, often for very small sums of money. This greatly reduced the lands in Indian hands.

■ *What did the Dawes Act of 1887 end?*

The Ghost Dance. For some Indians the destruction of the old way of life was too much to bear. They looked to anyone who promised a return to the old ways. In 1889, a new belief spread among the Plains Indians. Wovoka, a Paiute from Nevada, said that the dead would return, the buffalo would be plentiful, and the whites would leave the land if the Indians did a special dance. People soon came to call this dance the Ghost Dance.

A number of Plains Indians began to follow the teachings of Wovoka. The white settlers began to worry. The army was called in, and plans were made to arrest troublesome Indian leaders. Sitting Bull, the great Sioux war chief, was shot and killed while being arrested. And a group of Indians led by Big Foot who were returning from a journey to see Wovoka were arrested at Wounded Knee Creek, South Dakota. As these Indians were being disarmed, a shot was fired. The army then opened fire. The Indians, tightly crowded together, were an easy target. As many as 300 Indians were killed. The wounded were left to freeze in the cold winter weather. This massacre at Wounded Knee in December 1890 marked the end of the Indians' resistance to settlement in the West.

■ *What did Wovoka say would be the outcome of the Ghost Dance?*

The Exodusters. Thousands of settlers moved in to take over the lands the Indians had once roamed freely. Many of these settlers were European immigrants. Some were blacks from the South.

To many blacks, it became obvious that life in the South was going to be little different from slavery days. The sharecropping system of farming made it difficult for them to make any money. Those who exercised their right to vote were often the victims of violence. Because of these things, many blacks began to think about leaving the South. Some went north to try to find work in the industrial cities. A few left the United States and went to Liberia in Africa. But the best-organized move was the black exodus—mass departure—to Kansas. Black people who joined this move became known as *exodusters.*

The two men chiefly responsible for organizing the exodusters were Benjamin "Pap" Singleton of Tennessee and Henry Adams of Louisiana. These men made it possible for thousands of black people to try for a better life on the frontier.

Southern whites were against the exodus. They thought it was a trick by northern Republicans to get black voters to where the Republicans could control them. Some southern blacks were also against the exodus. Frederick Douglass, a black leader, argued that it would harm the movement for equal rights in the South.

Regardless of the opposition, in 1879, thousands of blacks from four southern states—Louisiana, Mississippi, Tennessee, and Texas—left for Kansas. Many of them were very poor. Although they received help from charitable organizations, the early days in Kansas were hard.

Few of the exodusters made much money.

The Bettmann Archive

Oklahoma's greatest land rush took place on September 16, 1893, when 6.5 million acres [2.6 million hectares] were opened to settlers.

But they made more than they had in the South. Nevertheless, many exodusters faced racial prejudice in Kansas. However, even though life in Kansas was hard, few exodusters considered returning to the South.

■ *Why did Frederick Douglass oppose the black exodus to Kansas?*

Land Rushes. Life on the plains was hard for everyone. Bad weather, uncertain harvests, and high interest rates and transportation costs all made life difficult. These problems caused some farmers to lose their farms.

Many plains farmers used their farms as security for bank loans. In the late 1880's there were bad harvests. Some farmers made so little money they were unable to meet their loan payments. Those farmers who had used their farms as security for loans lost them to the banks, and they had to move on. Many farmers headed back east, with signs on their wagons that read "In God we trusted, in Kansas we busted." But others turned elsewhere, looking for new opportunities on the frontier.

One area where these failed farmers looked was the Oklahoma Territory. This was an area of rich land suitable for farming. The United States had seized this land from the Creek and Seminole tribes after the Civil War. This was because these two tribes had fought for the Confederates during the war.

Settlers demanded that the government open this land for settlement. People had been moving into the Oklahoma District and laying claim to parcels of land for some time. But

(*Text continues on page 384.*)

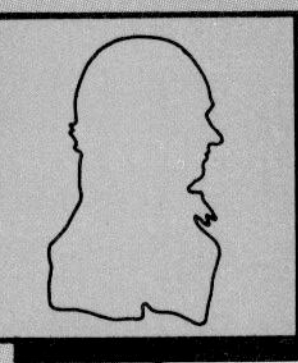

PROFILES

Sitting Bull

Sitting Bull (*Tatanka Iyotake* in his native language) was the son of a subchief of the Teton Sioux. He was born on the Grand River in South Dakota in the early 1830's. At a young age Sitting Bull distinguished himself as a fierce hunter and warrior. His first honors came when he was 14 and accompanied his father on the warpath against the Crow Indians. He became leader of the Strong Heart warrior society about 1856. Afterwards, he steadily gained influence among the Sioux as an able organizer and medicine man. Repeated treaty violations against the Sioux, beginning in 1864, led to his being on the warpath in the late 1860's and early 1870's almost constantly.

After gold was discovered on Indian land in the Black Hills in 1874, a new crisis developed. Sitting Bull became famous for his refusal to confine his nomadic band to the designated reservation. The army then began a campaign against him. Thousands of warriors joined Sitting Bull's camp, then located on the Little Big Horn River in Montana. On June 25, 1876, while Sitting Bull invoked spiritual aid, his chiefs destroyed troops from the Seventh Cavalry led by George A. Custer, killing all 211 white men. This victory was short-lived, however. The Indians broke up into smaller bands and by the following fall most of them had been forced to surrender. Sitting Bull and a few followers managed to escape into Canada. Facing starvation, they returned to the reservation in 1881.

Museum of the American Indian

Sitting Bull lived his final days on the Standing Rock reservation in North Dakota. He remained a powerful symbol of uncompromising opposition to white settlement of Indian lands. When the Ghost Dance religion threatened to stir unrest among the Dakota Sioux in 1890, Sitting Bull was perceived as a threat. When reservation police attempted to arrest him on the morning of December 15, 1890 Sitting Bull, his son, and several loyal bodyguards were shot and killed. A week later, the Wounded Knee massacre crushed the Sioux permanently and brought an end to decades of Indian warfare.

Thinking Critically

What qualities do you think might have helped Sitting Bull become a chief of the Sioux?

Was Sitting Bull successful as a military leader? Explain your answer.

Why do you think Sitting Bull became a symbol of resistance to white settlement of the northern plains?

federal troops had driven them out. However, demands for opening the land became so heavy that the government finally agreed. The land was divided into 160-acre [65-hectare] lots and was opened to settlement on April 22, 1889.

On that day, thousands of people gathered at different starting points, waiting for the gunshot that would start the land rush at noon. Some of these people were on horses; some were on foot. Some had wagons; a few even had wheelbarrows. Some people had managed to enter the territory before the starting signal and had staked their claims already. Because they had entered before the signal, these people were called sooners. But most people were kept outside the area until the starting signal was given. When this happened, there was a mad rush as the hordes of settlers set out to make their claims.

All the lots had been claimed within a few hours. By the end of the day new towns had been established. Guthrie, with a population of more than 10,000, was the largest. Other land rushes occurred in this area during the 1890's. The most famous was in 1893, when more Indian lands were thrown open to settlers. For many people, these land rushes marked the end of the frontier days.

■ *When was the Oklahoma Territory opened to settlement?*

Women and the Changing Frontier. In the early days of the frontier men greatly outnumbered women in the West. As more and more women came to the West, frontier life stabilized and became more settled. It was largely through the work of women that churches were built, schools were opened, and laws were passed and enforced. All these things helped to tame the West.

Women played a full part in life in the West. They worked as doctors, lawyers, teachers, and nurses. Some worked as miners. Farm women, as well as doing household chores and raising a family, were expected to work the land. This they did, often doing as much of the farm work as their husbands.

Throughout the West, women played a part in political life. As early as 1869, Wyoming had given women full voting rights. By the 1890's, Colorado, Idaho, and Utah had also given full voting rights to women. The women of these states led the fight for voting rights for all American women. This was finally achieved in 1920 (see Chapter 27). A number of women

Estelle Reel's election to a state office in 1894 showed the growing role of women in public affairs.

Wyoming State Archives, Museums and Historical Department

were elected to state and local government positions in the West. The first woman to be elected to state office was Estelle Reel, a Wyoming schoolteacher. She was elected state superintendent of public instruction in 1894. Women politicians helped bring law and order to the West. They played an important part in the closing of the frontier.

■ *Who was the first woman to be elected to state office?*

The End of the Frontier. By the early 1890's, the open lands of the West, for the most part, had been settled. The vast prairies were dotted with towns and farms and were broken by railroads and fences. For many people, the days of the frontier were over.

The Bureau of the Census, when reviewing the results of the 1890 census, agreed that the frontier was closed. The bureau stated that unsettled land in the West was so "broken into by isolated bodies of settlement that there can hardly be said to be a frontier line." The American people had long considered it their manifest destiny to settle the land from ocean to ocean. By the 1890's this destiny had been fulfilled. An important and colorful period in United States history had come to an end.

■ *Why did the Bureau of the Census consider the frontier to be closed?*

SECTION 3 REVIEW

1. *Why did the Indians resist the white settlers?*
2. *How did the Dawes Act encourage Indians to adopt the ways of the whites?*
3. *Why did the early 1890's mark the end of the frontier?*

CHAPTER 21 SUMMARY

The second half of the nineteenth century saw many changes in the United States. This was especially true of the West. The vast open plains were broken by thousands of miles of railroad. Big business had taken over much of the West's mining, farming, and cattle industries. The West seemed set for prosperity. But problems were beginning to grow.

Farmers in the West found farming the plains difficult. Rainfall was low, and the soil was often poor. Improvements in farming machinery and techniques helped the farmers overcome these natural problems. But other problems, such as high interest rates on bank loans and high transportation costs, proved more difficult to solve. The farmers organized and tried to change the situation. A third political party, the Populist party, was formed. But it declined after 1896, a year of bumper harvests for farmers.

The once-open plains were finally settled. The Indians, who for many years had resisted white settlement, were confined to small reservations. The final flurry of frontier settlement came with the Oklahoma land rushes. In the 1890's the Bureau of the Census declared the frontier closed. One of the most colorful periods of American history had ended.

CHAPTER 21 REVIEW

USING YOUR SKILLS

Studying a Thematic Map

The map below is a *thematic map*—it shows a particular kind of information. This map gives information on the political boundaries of an area of land. This map shows when the states west of the Mississippi River entered the Union. Study the map carefully. Then answer the questions that follow.

1. Which states have the Mississippi River as part or all of their eastern boundary?
2. How many states west of the Mississippi River were admitted to the Union before 1850?
3. Which Pacific Coast state entered the Union after 1870?
4. Which five states entered the Union between 1870 and 1889?
5. Which states were the last to enter the Union before 1900?
6. In which part of the country were most of the states that entered the Union after 1870?

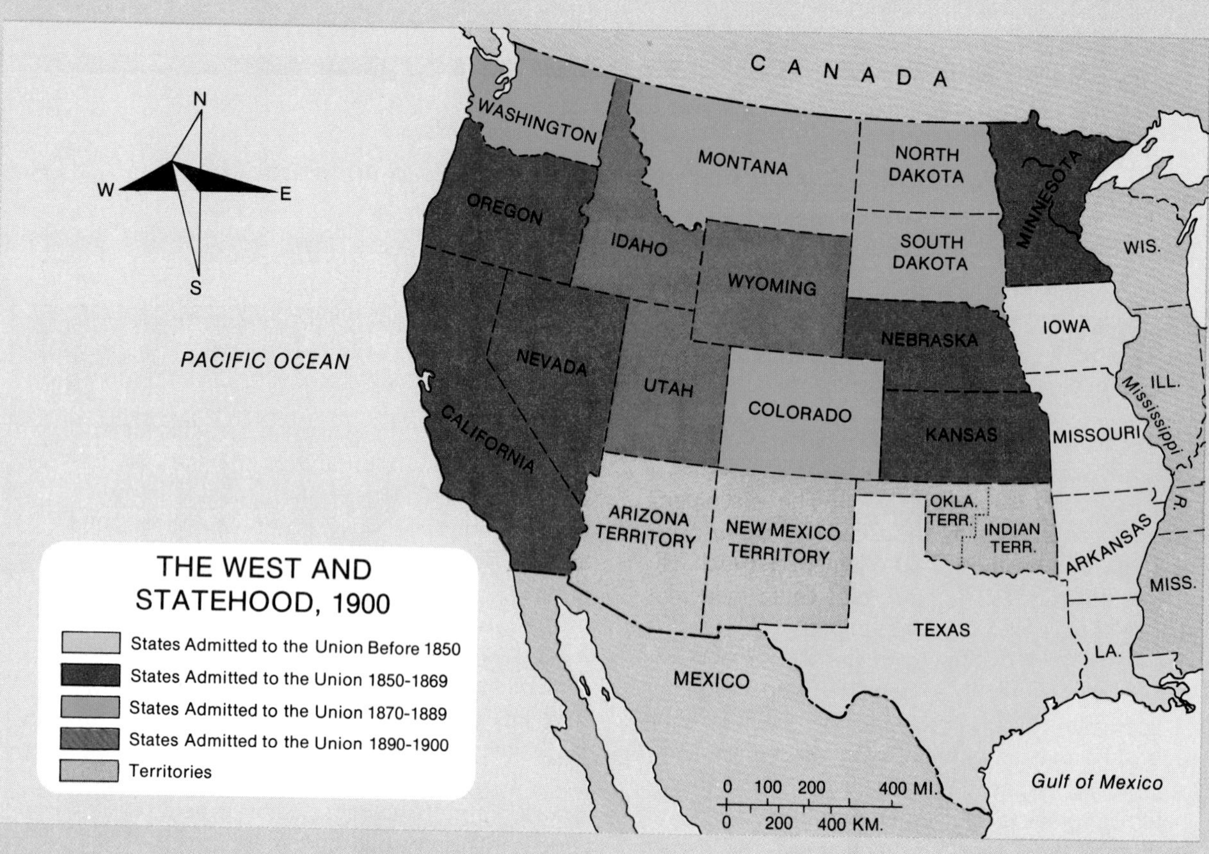

CHAPTER 21 REVIEW

YOU SHOULD KNOW

Identify, define, or explain each of the following:

range wars
dry farming
bonanza farms
Granger laws
Interstate Commerce Act
alliances
Populist party
Oklahoma Territory
exodusters
Estelle Reel

CHECKING FACTS

1. Who provided much of the labor needed to complete the first transcontinental railroad?
2. What changes took place in frontier mining in the 1870's?
3. What invention in 1874 was seen as a solution to the problems of water rights and diminishing grazing lands?
4. What was the plains farmers chief complaint?
5. What did the Supreme Court decide in the case of *Munn v. Illinois* (1877)?
6. What did many farmers learn from their experience with the Greenback party?
7. What were the goals of the Populist party?
8. What ended the Plains Indians way of life?
9. What was the Ghost Dance?
10. What were land rushes?

UNDERSTANDING CONCEPTS

1. What effect did the railroads have on frontier settlement?
2. Why did frontier farmers organize and try to influence government?
3. Why was the Populist party unsuccessful in the presidential election of 1896?

LEARNING FROM ILLUSTRATIONS

1. Examine the cartoon on page 375. What groups were shown as part of the Populist party? What do you think was the cartoonist's opinion of the Populists?
2. Study the map of the election of 1892 on page 376. What areas of the country gave the greatest support to Cleveland?

CRITICAL THINKING

1. Cattle owners argued about the ownership of water rights. Do you think people have the right to own water? Give reasons for your answer.
2. The members of the Greenback party felt that the country's economic problems could be solved by putting more greenbacks into circulation. Do you think their idea was economically sound? Why or why not?
3. Most white reformers felt that the problems of the Indians would be solved if the Indians followed the ways of the whites. Do you think these reformers were right? Give reasons for your answer.

ENRICHMENT ACTIVITIES

1. Write an "eye-witness" account of one of the Oklahoma land rushes. Information on land rushes can be found in encyclopedias and history textbooks. Share your account with the class.
2. Design a poster for the Populists' campaign for the presidential election of 1896. Your poster should include illustrations of some of the Populists' goals.

1870 1890 1910

- 1866 National Labor Union organized
- 1869 Air brake developed
- 1872 First mail-order service developed
- 1876 Telephone invented
- 1879 Incandescent electric light invented
- 1886 American Federation of Labor founded
- 1890 Sherman Antitrust Act passed
- 1894 Pullman Strike
- 1912 F. W. Woolworth Company incorporated

CHAPTER 22

The Industrialization of America

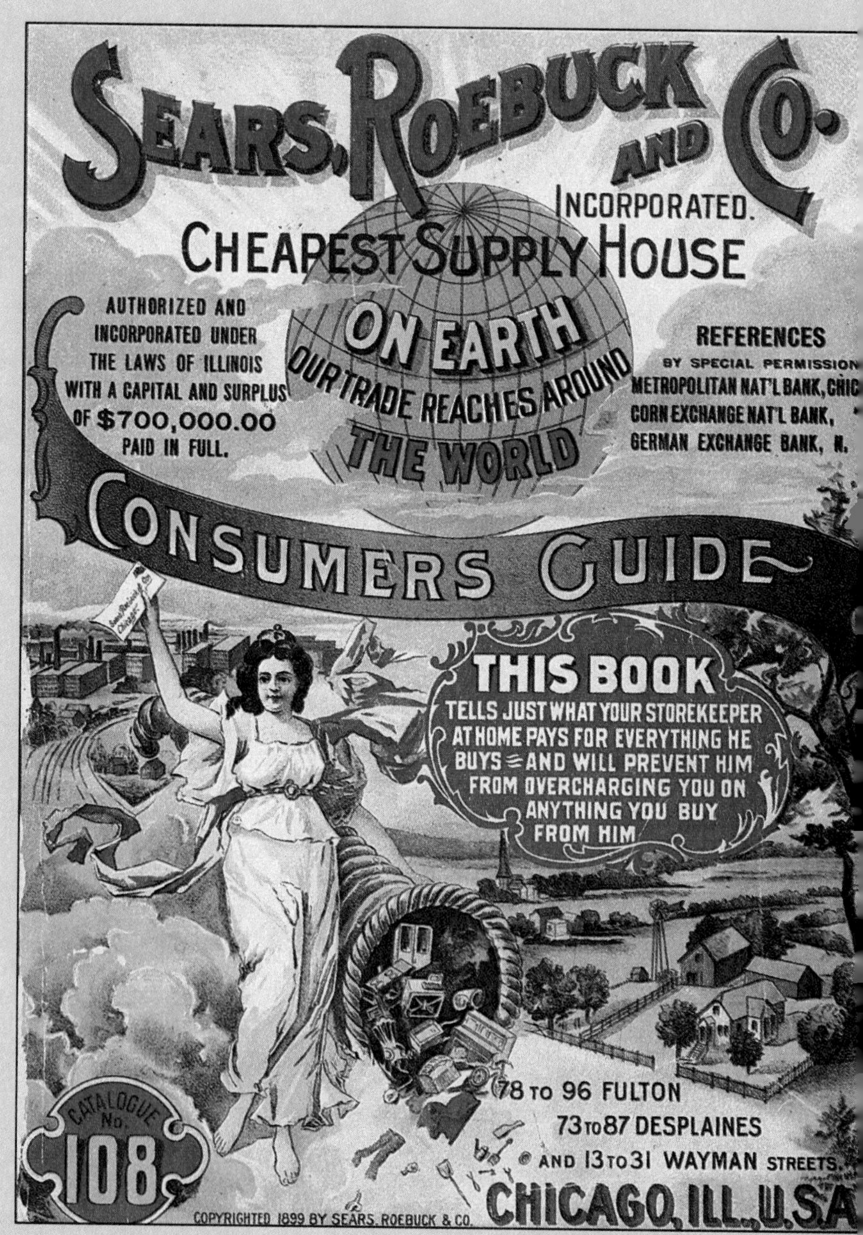

Chapter Objectives

After studying this chapter, you should be able to:

- describe how the United States was changing from an agricultural nation to an industrial nation in the late 1800's;
- explain how corporations developed and became powerful in the United States during the late 1800's;
- discuss how American workers sought to organize unions in the late 1800's to protect the interests of workers.

1 Industrial Growth

Overview Industry, including the iron, steel, and oil industries, in the United States grew rapidly in the second half of the nineteenth century. The railroad industry also showed rapid growth in this period. There were many reasons for this growth. New machinery made production quicker and cheaper. There were few government restrictions. The railroads offered a means of transportation.

Industrial growth changed the lives of most Americans. This was because the United States was changing from an agricultural country to an industrial country. Many people from farms moved to the cities. As a result, large amounts of industrial goods were needed for new construction.

Objectives After reading this section, you should be able to:

- assess the growth of industry in the United States in the second half of the nineteenth century;
- evaluate the importance of technological development in the growth of industry;
- analyze the affect that industrial growth had on the lives of Americans.

A Growing Industrial Country. The years after the Civil War were years of growth for American industry. The rate of this growth was far greater than most Americans would have thought possible.

At the outbreak of the Civil War, the United States was still an agricultural country. Many more people worked in agriculture than in industry. But in the second half of the nineteenth century, more and more workers began to work in industry. And during the years from 1860 to 1900, the value of manufactured goods in the United States grew by more than 500 percent. This growth made the United States one of the world's leading industrial countries.

The greatest growth came in the iron, steel, and oil industries. But these were not the only industries that grew during this time. Nearly all the manufacturing industries in the United States made progress in these years.

There were a number of reasons why American industry grew during this time. Raw materials were plentiful. The United States also had a large labor force and improved machinery. And our country's system of transportation helped industry to grow rapidly.

■ *Why did American industry grow during this period?*

Railroads. After the Civil War, railroads became a very important means of transportation. Railroad track mileage increased rapidly in these years. But more important than this increase in mileage was that the railroads were standardized during this time.

There were many railroad companies, and nearly every one of them used a different *gauge*—distance between rails—when laying track. So the engines and railcars of one company often could not be used on the tracks of another company. Transportation was difficult and costly if more than one company's tracks had to be used. But this was overcome by 1886, when all railroads used a standard gauge of 4 feet 8½ inches [1.44 meters]. This allowed the railroad companies to share their railcars. Long-distance transportation became easier and cheaper.

The railroads helped industry to grow in a number of ways. The railroads used large amounts of heavy industrial goods. They carried raw materials to factories and finished goods to markets. Railroads also provided many jobs for new immigrants. One estimate, for example, shows that in 1868 more than one fourth of all Chinese in America were building railroads that helped open the West.

■ *Why was the adoption of the standard gauge important to industry?*

New Technology. The growth of American industry was also the result of many inventions and developments made in the late 1800's. Some very important inventions were developed in the United States before 1850. But the pace of invention in the United States increased in the second half of the nineteenth century. For example, before 1865, only 62,000 *patents*—papers giving the right to make, use, or sell an invention—were given to American inventors. But in the years from 1865 to 1900, more than 500,000 new patents were given.

American business leaders were willing to try new ideas. Anything that would cut the time and the cost of production was considered. However, these new ideas were only used after long and careful study.

Of the thousands of inventions made during this time, a number were very important. The Bessemer process and the Siemens open-hearth system made steel production cheaper and easier. The air brake, developed by George Westinghouse in 1869, made rail travel faster and safer. And the telephone, invented by Alexander Graham Bell in 1876, made long-distance communication possible. Many inventors helped American industry. But for most Americans, Thomas A. Edison was the greatest of these inventors.

■ *When did the pace of invention in the United States increase?*

The Wizard of Menlo Park. Thomas A. Edison only had about three months of formal education. But he made a number of inventions that changed life in the United States. Edison was interested in every field of study, but most of his work was done in electricity.

In 1876, Edison opened a laboratory in Menlo Park, New Jersey. He said that he would turn out "a minor invention every ten days and a big thing every six months or so." To keep this promise, he hired many scientists. Edison was the first person to use a research team to develop new ideas.

Perhaps Edison's best-known work came in the development of the electric light bulb. A number of scientists had been working to develop an electric light bulb. The best they had managed was a bulb that burned for a few hours. After failing many times, Edison made an important breakthrough in October 1879 when he made a light bulb that burned for 40 hours. That Christmas, Edison decorated the grounds of the laboratory with a string of light bulbs. People were so surprised that they called Edison the Wizard of Menlo Park.

Edison took part in many other inventions. These included such things as the phonograph and the movie projector. Edison and other inventors played an important part in helping American industry to grow.

■ *What new approach did Edison use to solve scientific problems?*

New Management Techniques. As industries grew, new ways of managing them were needed. Workers had to be hired and trained.

Thomas Edison, shown below working on a movie machine, gave the world many inventions. How do the pictures of an early phonograph, a Beatles recording session, some scenes from the films *The Empire Strikes Back* and *Grease*, an early light bulb, and the lights of Chicago show some of the ways that Edison's ideas have been used?

And new machinery had to be used as effectively as possible. A leader in the field of new management was Frederick Winslow Taylor.

In 1878, Taylor was hired by the Midvale Steel Company of Pennsylvania as a laborer. Within five years he had risen to the position of chief engineer. During this time, Taylor introduced a number of new management ideas at Midvale. The most important of these was *time and motion study.* This involved watching workers to find ways to cut waste time and movement in their work. Time study often was resented by workers. But managers saw it as a new way to improve efficiency and production.

Time study was one of a set of ideas that Taylor called *scientific management.* Another idea was to tie workers' pay to how much they produced. In 1890, Taylor left Midvale to become a consultant. His ideas spread as he worked for a number of large companies. By the early 1900's, his ideas were so well accepted that the new management methods were called *Taylorism.*

■ *Why did managers adopt Taylor's time-and-motion-study idea?*

The management ideas of Frederick W. Taylor were widely used by businesses in the early 1900's.

The Bettmann Archive

Other Reasons for Growth. There were a number of other reasons for the growth of American industry in this period. In the second half of the nineteenth century, American cities grew rapidly. As cities grew, large amounts of industrial goods were needed for new buildings. And the people who moved to the cities needed all kinds of manufactured goods. American industry had to grow to meet this need for goods. In turn, people in the cities worked in the growing number of factories.

Another reason for growth was that there was greater investment of money in industry during this time. This was important because money was needed for such things as new machinery. The new machinery often led to greater production. This usually meant bigger profits. This made people more willing to invest. They thought they could earn more money as industries grew.

American industry also grew because our government set very few rules. Most members of government accepted the idea of *laissez-faire*—no government interference in business. In fact, government often aided business growth through land grants and loans.

The idea of laissez-faire caused some problems. Safety standards were seldom set or enforced. This meant that many workers had to work in dangerous conditions. And as there were few regulations, questionable business practices were often used.

■ *Why did the growth of American cities encourage industrial growth?*

Brown Brothers

Henry Ford changed the automobile industry by replacing hand-assembly methods with assembly-line techniques of mass production.

The Impact of Industrialization. As American industry grew, more and more machinery was used to produce goods. The use of machinery led to a greater division of labor. Rather than working on a product until it was finished, each worker would work on one part of a product. These parts would be gathered and then put together by other workers. The use of machinery and the division of labor allowed industry to *mass-produce* large amounts of goods both quickly and cheaply. But the use of machinery did put some workers out of work. However, it created other kinds of jobs.

One area where different jobs were created was in the distribution of goods. The small local general store could no longer handle the demand for mass-produced goods. Soon *department stores*—large stores that sold many kinds of goods—began to open in larger cities. *Chain stores*—stores with branches in a number of cities—also began to open. The five-and-ten-cent stores of this time were chain stores. Frank W. Woolworth first suggested the idea of selling slow-moving merchandise for 5 and 10 cents in 1878. Very soon there were 15 separate chains of five-and-ten-cent stores. These 15 chains were incorporated into the F. W. Woolworth Company in 1912.

For people who could not get to the big cities, such as farmers and their families, there was a mail-order service. These people chose goods from a catalog. They then ordered and received their goods by mail. The first mail-order service was founded by Montgomery Ward and Company in Chicago in 1872. Another well-known mail-order service—Sears, Roebuck and Company—was started in 1886.

Although industrial production increased and distribution of goods improved, the American economy was somewhat unstable. In the 25 years from 1870 to 1895 there were three major economic depressions. One occurred in 1873; another, in 1884; and the final one, in 1893. The unstable economy and changes in society made life uncertain for many working people. As you will read later, this caused some people to try to control their working conditions.

How did the division of labor affect industry?

SECTION 1 REVIEW

1. *Why did American industry grow in the second half of the nineteenth century?*
2. *How did Edison keep his promise to turn out inventions?*
3. *How did the use of machinery affect the American worker?*

2 The Rise of Big Business

Overview As American industries grew, it became clear that a new type of business organization was needed. The corporation soon became the most common form of business organization.

At first corporations competed for business. Some business leaders wanted corporations to work together rather than compete. In time, a few large corporations became very powerful.

A number of people began to work to lessen the power of these corporations. They asked the government to regulate big business.

Objectives After reading this section, you should be able to:

- explain why corporations formed in the second half of the nineteenth century;
- give examples of monopolies that existed in the late 1800's;
- assess the federal government's attempts to regulate big business.

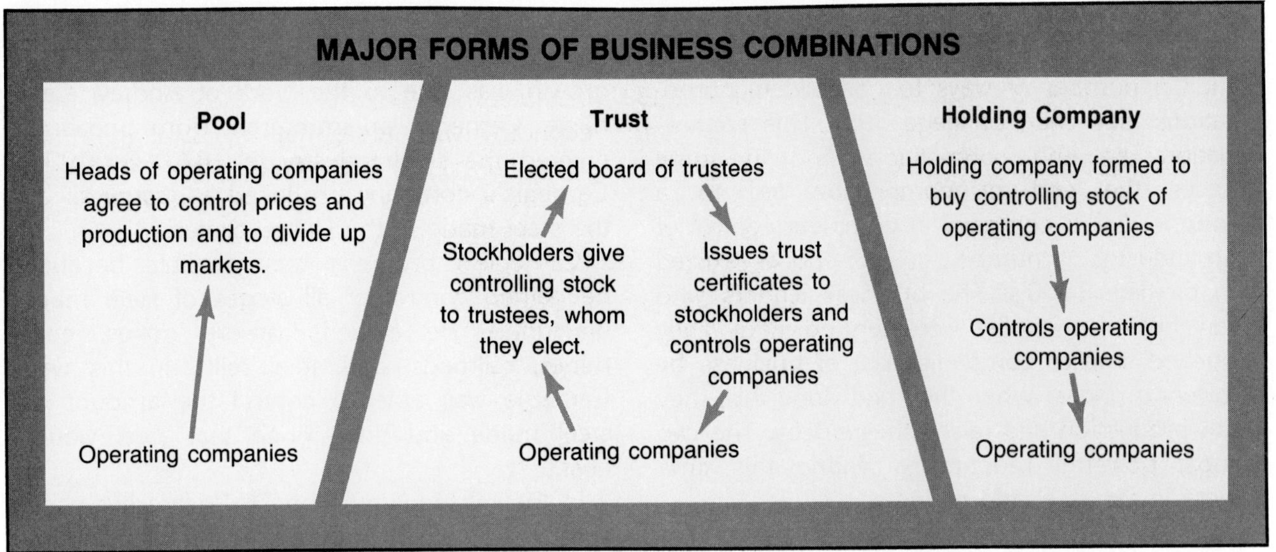
MAJOR FORMS OF BUSINESS COMBINATIONS
Pool
Heads of operating companies agree to control prices and production and to divide up markets.
Operating companies
Trust
Elected board of trustees
Stockholders give controlling stock to trustees, whom they elect.
Issues trust certificates to stockholders and controls operating companies
Operating companies
Holding Company
Holding company formed to buy controlling stock of operating companies
Controls operating companies
Operating companies

During the late 1800's and the early 1900's, businesses organized themselves into various types of large combinations in order to eliminate competition and to gain control of the market place.

New Forms of Business Organization. In the mid-1800's, most of the factories in America were owned either by individuals or by families. But as American industry expanded, these owners found it more difficult to run their factories. The size and the cost of the new, larger factories became problems. More money was needed to buy machinery. And more managers were needed to oversee the additional workers. Individual owners found it difficult to handle these problems. Thus, it became clear that a different form of business organization was needed.

During the second half of the nineteenth century, the *corporation* became the common form of business organization. A corporation is an organization that is owned by a number of *stockholders*—people who have bought shares in that organization. According to the number of shares they own, stockholders have voting rights to decide how the corporation is run.

Corporations had two big advantages over individually owned companies. One advantage was that a corporation could raise money by selling *stocks*—shares of the company. With this money the corporation could hire more workers and buy more machinery. The second advantage was that stockholders could make money if the corporation did well. If it did not do well, stockholders could lose *only* what they had invested. Stockholders were not responsible for the corporation's debts.

As corporations grew, they tried to increase their profits. Corporations in the same business competed with one another. Sometimes, this competition was so fierce that some corporations were ruined. Some business leaders began to fear that whole businesses might be destroyed. These leaders felt that the *consolidation*—the joining together—of certain corporations might be better for business.

■ *How did corporations help business to grow?*

Efforts at Consolidation. Business leaders tried a number of ways to consolidate corporations (see chart on page 395). This consolidation did end competition. And in some cases the end of competition led to a *monopoly*—a company in complete control of an industry. A number of monopolies existed in the late 1800's. The business leaders who ran these monopolies were very powerful. They pushed smaller companies out of business by lowering prices. When they had done this, they cut production and raised their prices. The two most powerful monopolies during this time were in the steel and oil industries.

■ *When does a monopoly occur?*

Industrial Monopolies. The steel industry in the United States grew rapidly in the second half of the nineteenth century. Much of this growth was due to the work of Andrew Carnegie. Carnegie, an immigrant from Scotland, entered the steel industry in 1873. By 1900, Carnegie's company produced a quarter of all the steel made in the United States.

Business leader Andrew Carnegie built a steel empire that was sold in 1901 for $447,000,000.

The Bettmann Archive

Carnegie's progress was possible because he gained control of all stages of steel manufacturing. He owned iron-ore mines, coal mines, railroads, and steel mills. In this way Carnegie was able to control the amount of steel made and how much that steel would cost.

In the oil industry John D. Rockefeller used similar methods. Rockefeller entered the oil industry in 1862. Fifteen years later his Standard Oil Company controlled nearly every stage of the oil industry. The company owned oil fields, refineries, and pipelines. And through a number of agreements, Rockefeller was able to get low railroad rates. He also built up a countrywide sales network. By 1900, Rockefeller dominated not only the American oil industry but also most of the world trade in oil.

Carnegie and Rockefeller made large fortunes. In later life, they both gave large amounts of money to good causes. Among other things, they gave money to schools, colleges, museums, and art galleries. But some people felt that business leaders like Carnegie and Rockefeller made their money through questionable methods. However, other Americans thought that the business leaders had done nothing wrong.

■ *Why was Andrew Carnegie's progress in the steel industry possible?*

The Defense of Wealth. Many people in the United States believed that life should be concerned with hard work and the accumulation of wealth. They did not question the means by which this wealth was gathered. Nor did they worry that whole industries were controlled by a few business leaders. For them, these business leaders were the hardest working and most able and therefore deserved the most wealth.

Philosophers such as Herbert Spencer defended wealth. He adapted the theories of Charles Darwin to society. In his book *Origin of Species*, Darwin said that in nature only the fittest survived in the struggle for life. Spencer said that this was the same in human society. Business leaders who made vast fortunes were the fittest in the struggle for business. In Spencer's opinion it was unfortunate that this left poor people to live unpleasant lives. But Spencer said that this was inevitable if society was to progress. Spencer's ideas became known as *social Darwinism*.

Social Darwinism squared with the feelings of a large number of Americans. But other people in the United States believed that many business leaders were guilty of wrongdoings in their gathering of wealth.

■ *Which philosophical theory supported the right of business leaders to gather wealth?*

Business Abuses. A number of industries used questionable business methods. One example was the railroad industry. At one time a number of railroad companies joined in a pool and agreed upon the transportation rates they would charge. At other times the railroad companies charged low, competitive rates for long-distance transportation. Yet they charged very high, noncompetitive short-distance rates. As you have read, this was a problem for farmers on the Great Plains.

Railroad companies were criticized for giving *rebates*. These were money refunds on shipping charges. Companies that shipped large amounts were given rebates by the railroads. But companies that shipped only small amounts were not. Small companies complained that this favored the large corporations, such as the Standard Oil Company.

The power of the Standard Oil Company was so great that it could make special arrangements with the railroad companies. One such arrangement gave money to Standard Oil when the railroads carried the oil of other companies. Standard Oil was paid 20 cents for every barrel of competitors' oil carried by the railroads.

Some efforts were made to pass laws that would require the railroads to be run for the benefit of the American people. But the railroads were able to stop these efforts by bribing politicians. Business leaders in other industries used similar methods. One writer noted that to get favorable treatment, the Standard Oil Company had done about everything to the Pennsylvania state government but "refine" it!

Through new business organization methods, such as the trust, the large corporations grew in power. The corporations set prices and the levels of production. Many Americans felt that the American economy was being controlled by a few powerful trusts. Demands were made for government to lessen the power of these trusts.

■ *What special arrangement did the Standard Oil Company have with the railroads?*

Demands for Action. There were a number of people in the United States who were worried about the power of the trusts. These people did not accept the theories of social Darwinism. Neither did they accept the idea

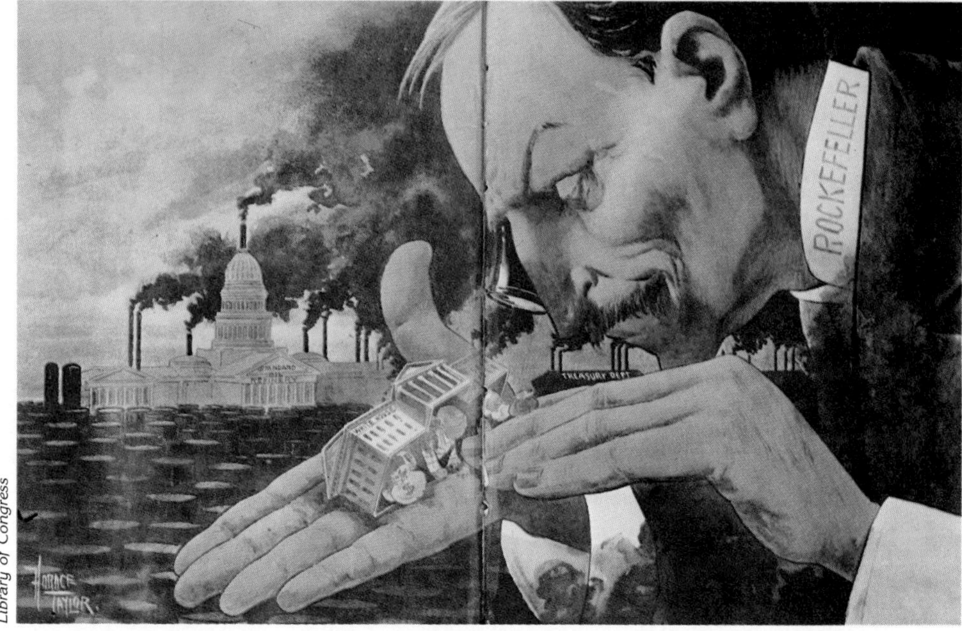

Library of Congress

A cartoonist of the early 1900's suggested the extent of John D. Rockefeller's power. What is Rockefeller holding in his hand? What does this suggest?

that what was good for the trusts was good for American society. They began to work to lessen the power of the trusts.

A number of these people were journalists. They wrote pieces for newspapers and magazines, exposing questionable business practices. One such journalist was Henry Demarest Lloyd. In 1881, *Atlantic Monthly* published a piece by Lloyd, titled "The Story of a Great Monopoly." It told of how the Standard Oil Company had gained control of the American oil industry. It was well researched and contained detailed evidence. Public interest was so great that the publishers had to issue seven reprints. Lloyd went on to write more pieces attacking monopolies in other industries.

Lloyd and other journalists led the demands for action to end the power of the trusts. They called for government to regulate questionable business practices. In time government leaders began to listen.

■ *What did Henry Demarest Lloyd attack in his articles for the* Atlantic Monthly?

Attempts at Regulation. As you learned in Chapter 21, the federal government tried to regulate the railroads by passing the Interstate Commerce Act in 1887. This set up the Interstate Commerce Commission. The commission's task was to regulate railroad shipping charges and to stop unfair business practices, such as the giving of rebates. But the commission was never given enough power to enforce the law. And the railroads eventually were able to control the commission.

Government tried to regulate other big businesses by passing the Sherman Antitrust Act in 1890. This act made it illegal for companies to join in a trust in order to control interstate trade. But the wording of the act was not clear, and it was difficult to enforce. Few trusts were convicted under the law. And in 1895, the Supreme Court further reduced the power of the Sherman Antitrust Act. In one case, the case of *United States* v. *E. C. Knight Company,* the Court said that one company buying another company to form a monopoly did not violate the Sherman Antitrust Act. After this decision, very little was done to control the trusts until President Theodore Roosevelt took office six years later.

The federal government's attempt to regulate big business failed. This came as no surprise to many people. For them it showed that government was still the friend of big business. These people had to find other ways to reduce the power of big business.

■ *What did the Sherman Antitrust Act make illegal?*

SECTION 2 REVIEW

1. *How were corporations able to help business grow?*
2. *How was John D. Rockefeller able to dominate the American oil industry?*
3. *Why did the Interstate Commerce Commission fail to regulate the railroads?*

3 The Organization of Labor

Overview The rapid industrial development during this time changed the lives of American workers. For many, working conditions were miserable and often dangerous. There were no laws to set safety standards. Factory owners did not take responsibility for injured workers. The standard of living, of large numbers of workers, however, did improve. Even so, workers began to organize for further gain. The rate of organization slowed as a result of labor unrest.

Objectives After reading this section, you should be able to:

- identify the changes in working conditions as a result of the use of machinery;
- list the goals of early labor unions;
- discuss the reasons for setbacks of labor unions.

A Changing Standard of Living. Although industrial expansion brought many problems for American workers, it also brought some benefits. Greater efficiency led to greater output. This meant that there were more goods available at lower prices. This improved the standard of living of many workers.

Those workers who gained most from industrialization were skilled workers. Their skills allowed them to ask for and receive higher pay. But unskilled workers often found it difficult to make a living wage. For example, black Americans, women, and children, who made up a large part of the working population, were paid very little. Even so, most American workers were able to improve their standard of living slightly. At the same time,

(*Text continues on page 401.*)

RECALLING THE TIMES

Child Labor

In the nineteenth century, children made up a significant part of the American work force. In the late 1890's, more than 2 million children under the age of 15 were working in industry and agriculture. They worked in conditions that were unpleasant and often dangerous. The use of child labor attracted the interest of social reformers, such as John Spargo. The writings of these reformers brought the misery of working children to the attention of the American public. Below is an excerpt from an account of Spargo's visit to a glass factory that employed children.

I shall never forget my first visit to a glass factory at night. It was a big wooden structure, so loosely built that it afforded little protection from drafts, surrounded by a high fence with several rows of barbed wire stretched across the top. I went with the foreman of the factory, and he explained to me the reason for the stockade-like fence. "It keeps the young imps inside once we've got 'em for the night shift," he said. The young imps were, of course, the boys employed, about forty in number, at least ten of whom were less than twelve years of age. It was a cheap bottle factory, and the proportion of boys to men was larger than is usual in the higher grades of manufacture. Cheapness and child labor go together—the cheaper the grade of manufacture, as a rule, the cheaper the labor employed. The hours of labor for the night shift were from 5:30 P.M. to 3:30 A.M. I stayed and watched the boys at their work for several hours and, when their tasks were done, saw them disappear into the darkness and storm of the night. That night, for the first time, I realized the tragic significance of cheap bottles.

The Bettmann Archive

Thinking Critically

In this account, Spargo says, "I realize the tragic significance of cheap bottles." What do you think he meant?

How would you compare your way of life to the way of life of children workers of a hundred years ago?

however, working conditions were getting worse.

■ *Which group of workers improved their standard of living most?*

Working Conditions. The new machines that made industrial growth possible changed the lives of most American workers. Machines often could do the work of more than ten workers. So, many workers found themselves without jobs. Those workers who managed to keep their jobs found that the use of machines made work boring and routine. Also, working with the new machines often was dangerous. At the time there were no laws calling for safety standards. When accidents happened, factory owners were not responsible for workers who were hurt or killed.

In the days when business companies were small, owners often knew all their workers well. These owners were normally interested in the well-being of their workers. And the workers felt that they could take complaints to the owners and get a fair hearing. But after industrial expansion, this relationship between owners and workers changed. Companies had become so large that the workers rarely saw the owners. And workers who had complaints were often dismissed, normally without a hearing.

Some companies owned the towns where their factories stood. After working long hours in the company factory, workers would go home to company houses. They ate food and wore clothes that were bought at company stores. Oftentimes these workers were paid with coupons that could only be spent at the company stores. Some of these workers began to feel that they were owned by the company. They also thought that although industrial expansion had brought great wealth to some, it had brought nothing to them. These workers began to organize to change these conditions.

■ *What effect did the use of machinery have on working conditions?*

Early Organization. American workers' first attempt at national organization came in 1866 with the National Labor Union. But this was short-lived. It faded soon after its founder, William Sylvis, died in 1869. At about this time, another national union, the Knights of Labor, was formed. The Knights of Labor was founded as a secret society by a number of Philadelphia garment workers led by Uriah Stephens. In 1879, Stephens was replaced as leader by Terence V. Powderly. By 1881, the Knights of Labor was no longer a secret society, and membership grew rapidly.

The Knights of Labor was open to both black and white workers. Workers of all trades—except stockbrokers, lawyers, gamblers, and liquor salesmen—were invited to

DO YOU KNOW?

Who was the first woman member of the Knights of Labor, and what was her occupation?

Mrs. Elizabeth Rodgers, a Chicago "housewife," was the first woman to join the Knights of Labor. The Knights of Labor considered "housewives" to be workers eligible for membership. Mrs. Rodgers was the mother of twelve children. When she attended the Knights of Labor national convention in 1886, she took her youngest daughter, then only two years old, with her. Mrs. Rodgers was one of the leading union organizers of the late nineteenth century, and she held a number of important offices in the Knights of Labor.

join. The Knights of Labor believed in such things as cooperative ownership of industry but were usually against the use of the strike.

Membership in the Knights of Labor grew from 19,000 in 1881 to an estimated 700,000 in 1886. But Terence Powderly was not a powerful leader. He was unable to control such a large organization. A number of local unions planned strikes. But when they received no support from the Knights of Labor, these strikes failed. And acts of violence by people linked with the labor movement, which you will read about later in this section, set the public against the Knights of Labor. Membership began to decline. By the late 1880's the Knights of Labor was no longer an important union.

■ *What brought about the decline of the Knights of Labor?*

Women, as well as minorities, were invited to join the Knights of Labor during the 1880's.

The Bettmann Archive

The American Federation of Labor. While the Knights of Labor faded, a new national union, the American Federation of Labor (AFL), began to grow. The AFL was founded in 1886. It was led by two New York cigar makers, Samuel Gompers and Adolph Strasser. The AFL consisted of a number of craft unions. The members of these unions were all skilled workers. Although these unions had joined the AFL, they were still free to run their own local affairs.

The main goals of the AFL were to get its members better pay and shorter working hours. To gain these goals, the AFL used the strike. This approach to industrial relations became known as pure and simple unionism.

With Gompers as leader, the AFL made steady progress toward fulfilling its goals. This attracted new members. By 1900, AFL membership numbered nearly 1 million workers. But some people criticized the AFL. This was because it did not allow unskilled workers to become members. Women, black Americans, and immigrants were also not welcome. Leaders of the AFL said that this was done to protect the jobs of AFL members.

■ *What was the approach of the AFL to industrial relations called?*

Working Women. In the late 1800's, women made up a significant part of the American work force. Women worked on farms, in cotton and woolen mills, in domestic service, and in the garment trades. They faced the same problems as working men. They worked for long hours, often in dangerous conditions, for little pay. Also like men, women began to organize in order to solve these problems.

In 1881, when it ceased to be a secret organization, the Knights of Labor invited women to join. In the next 5 years about

50,000 women became members. And in 1885, the Knights of Labor set up a women's department. This department hired a full-time investigator to look into the problems of working women. Leonora Barry, a hosiery worker from Amsterdam, New York, was chosen to fill this position. She worked hard to educate and organize American working women.

As you have read, the Knights of Labor did not think the strike was a good way to settle labor disagreements. Even so, some local unions that were part of the Knights of Labor did strike. Women workers often helped and supported these strikes. Women played such an important part in some of these strikes that Terence Powderly, the leader of the Knights of Labor, called them "the best men in the Order." However, after 1886, the Knights of Labor began to decline in power. Working women lost an organization through which they could air their views.

A number of women tried to become active in the AFL. But for the most part, they failed. Most working women were unskilled and as such were unable to join craft unions. Those women who were able to join craft unions did not earn enough to pay the union dues. And some unions set membership requirements that women could not meet.

Black Americans also found it difficult to join the AFL. Because of discrimination, few black Americans were hired as skilled workers. Those that were hired received lower pay than white workers. So black American workers could not afford to pay union dues. Because of this discrimination, black Americans, women, and other groups of workers looked for different ways to express their views.

■ *Why did women find it difficult to join the AFL?*

Labor Unrest. Employers often tried to stop workers from joining unions. Some workers were told that they would lose their jobs if they became union members. Others were made to sign *yellow-dog contracts*—agreements stating that they would not join a union. Workers who were union members were often *blacklisted*—put on a list of people who were not to be employed. Because of these measures, there was much labor unrest during the 1880's and 1890's.

There were a number of violent incidents during this period. One such incident occurred in Chicago in 1886. After a strike was called at the McCormick Harvesting Machine Company, the owners brought in *strikebreakers* to take the place of the striking workers. Fighting broke out between the strikers and the strikebreakers. The police were called to stop the fight. A number of people were killed. A meeting was held the following day in the Haymarket Square to protest the police action. A bomb was thrown that killed 11 people, 7 policemen among them. This incident became known as the Haymarket Riot. A number of foreign-born radicals were arrested. Eight of them were brought to trial. All were found guilty, and 7 of them were sentenced to death. Only 4 were executed (see Chapter 24). The Haymarket Riot hurt the labor movement. It also affected immigrants, as many were suspected of being troublemakers and were badly treated.

Another incident that hurt the labor movement took place in 1892 at the Homestead plant of the Carnegie Steel Company. The steelworkers' union had called a strike. But the manager of the Homestead plant, Henry Clay Frick, wanted to break the union. He brought in strikebreakers and hired Pinkerton detectives to protect them. In one clash seven detectives

The Bettmann Archive

Business leaders sometimes demanded that federal or state officials send troops to protect company property during labor disputes of the late 1800's.

were killed by the strikers. But Frick would not back down. Alexander Berkman, a radical, tried to kill Frick. But Frick survived the attack. Public sympathy was with Frick and the Carnegie Steel Company. Both the strike and the steelworkers' union were soon broken.

■ *What were yellow-dog contracts?*

The Pullman Strike. There were many labor disputes during the 1890's. Perhaps the most important was the Pullman strike of 1894. Workers at the Pullman Palace Car Factory near Chicago went on strike to protest pay cuts. Some of these workers were members of the American Railway Union. This union voted not to handle any trains with Pullman cars. Railroad traffic in and out of Chicago was completely tied up.

President Grover Cleveland sent federal troops to make sure that the mail was moved. But Governor John Peter Altgeld of Illinois said that they were not needed. He believed that President Cleveland had sent the troops to end the strike.

Eugene V. Debs, the leader of the American Railway Union, was ordered by a federal court to end the strike. However, Debs called for a nationwide strike. He was found in contempt of the court order and was jailed. This destroyed the American Railway Union. But it made Debs a national figure. After leaving jail, Debs joined the Socialist party. He went on to run for President five times on the Socialist party ticket.

■ *What reason did President Cleveland give for sending troops to the Pullman strike?*

Setbacks for Labor. Some people criticized President Cleveland for using the courts and soldiers against the Pullman strikers. But most people in the United States agreed with his actions. These people had become tired of the many strikes and the trouble that always seemed to follow. This loss of public support was a setback for labor.

The unions had worked hard to improve working conditions. And some progress had been made. But much of this hard work was wasted because of the loss of public support.

Most union members had little to do with the trouble that often accompanied strikes. It was often started by radicals who had little to do with the unions. But the unions were blamed. The general public began to think that all union members were radicals, interested only in the overthrow of the American government.

Immigrants were sometimes blamed for the labor problems of this time. Many union members disliked immigrants. This was because immigrants often were willing to work for low pay. Also, immigrants were sometimes used as strikebreakers.

The general public also distrusted immigrants. Many radicals who took part in strikes were foreign-born. Because of this, people born outside of the United States often were suspected of having radical ideas. Both the unions and the immigrants had to work hard to be accepted in the United States.

■ *Why were immigrants blamed for the labor problems of this time?*

SECTION 3 REVIEW

1. *How did the use of machinery affect the working conditions of many American workers?*
2. *What were the main goals of the AFL?*
3. *Why did the unions lose public support?*

CHAPTER 22 SUMMARY

The second half of the nineteenth century saw a rapid growth in American industry. Such things as the extension of the railroads and new technological developments made this growth possible. The United States changed from an agricultural nation to an industrial nation.

Industrial growth led to the introduction of new forms of business organization. The most common form of organization during this time was the corporation. Some corporations joined together to limit business competition. A few of these corporations became very powerful. Attempts were made by government to regulate these powerful corporations. But for the most part, these attempts failed.

Industrial growth affected the lives of most American workers. There was an improvement in the standard of living of many workers. But working conditions became unpleasant. American workers began to organize labor unions. But these efforts were slowed by labor unrest and the public's distrust of unions.

CHAPTER 22 REVIEW

USING YOUR SKILLS

Interpreting Line Graphs

Below are two line graphs that give information concerning the composition of the United States labor force during the years 1870 to 1900. Graph A shows the number of workers in the labor force involved in farming, mining and manufacturing, and other nonfarming activities. Graph B shows the percentage of the labor force involved in farm and nonfarm activities. Study the graphs carefully, then answer the questions that follow.

1. About how many farm workers were there in 1880?
2. About how many nonfarm workers were there in 1900?
3. In which decade was there a greater percentage of farm workers than nonfarm workers in the labor force?
4. In 1890, what percentage of the labor force were (a) farm workers, (b) nonfarm workers?
5. What are the main trends shown by these two graphs?
6. What, in your opinion, is the explanation for these trends?

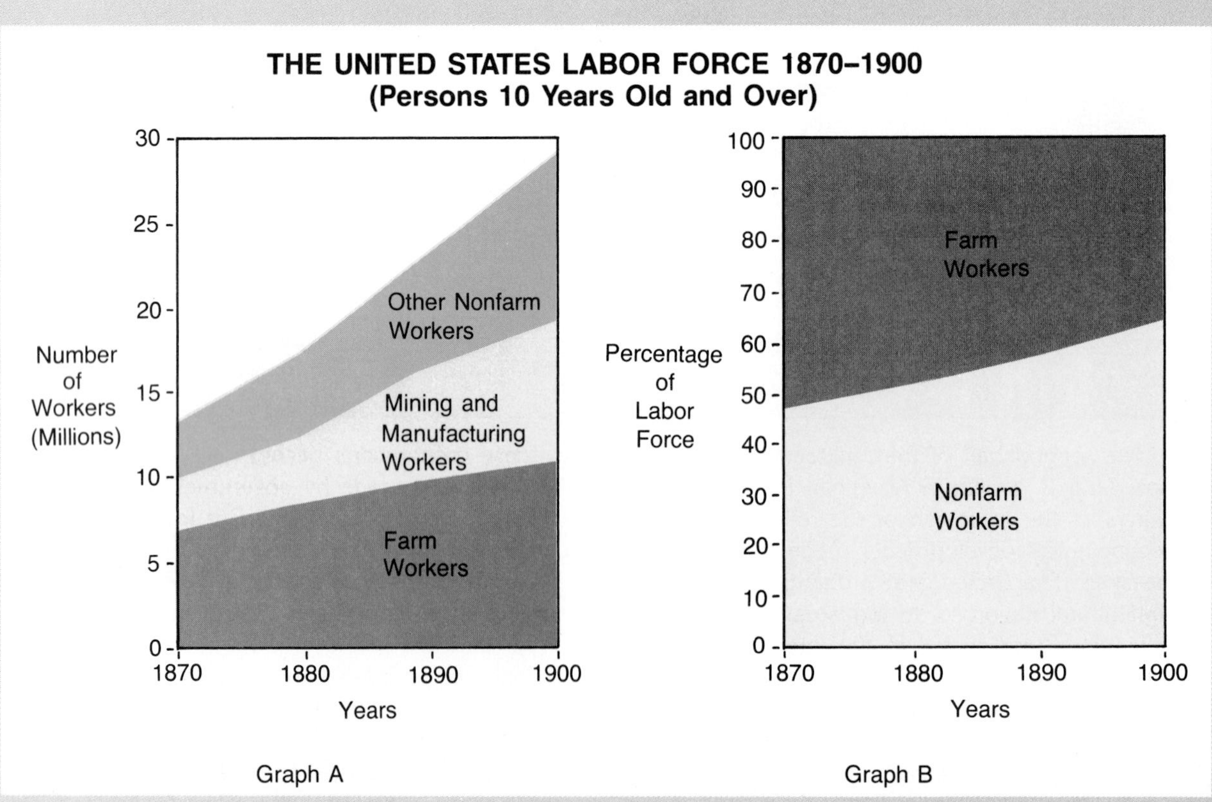

CHAPTER 22 REVIEW

YOU SHOULD KNOW

Identify, define, or explain each of the following.

gauge	social Darwinism
patents	rebates
laissez-faire	American Federation of Labor (AFL)
corporation	yellow-dog contracts
stockholders	

CHECKING FACTS

1. What three industries had the greatest growth from 1860 to 1900?
2. What allowed the railroad companies to share their railcars?
3. Name three inventions that were important for industrial development in the second half of the nineteenth century.
4. What did the management idea—time study—involve?
5. What is a monopoly?
6. What business approach did Andrew Carnegie and John D. Rockefeller use to become powerful business leaders?
7. Which Supreme Court decision weakened the Sherman Antitrust Act?
8. What caused the Knights of Labor to decline?
9. What were the two main goals of the AFL?
10. What approach did the AFL use to gain their goals?

UNDERSTANDING CONCEPTS

1. How did the railroads help industry to grow?
2. Why did government efforts to govern big business fail?
3. How did the Knights of Labor and the American Federation of Labor differ in terms of membership requirements?
4. Why did labor unions lose the support of the public?

LEARNING FROM ILLUSTRATIONS

1. Study the picture of automobile assembly operations on page 393. How would you describe these operations?
2. Look at the cartoon of John D. Rockefeller on page 398. How is the building in the background on the left labeled? How do you think that the cartoonist felt about John D. Rockefeller?

CRITICAL THINKING

1. American industry grew because our government set very few rules. Do you think the government was correct in accepting the idea of laissez-faire? Give reasons for your answer.
2. In the late 1800's, many people believed that life should be concerned with hard work and the accumulation of wealth. They did not question the means by which the wealth was gathered. Do you think many Americans believe these ideas today? Why or why not?
3. In your opinion, why would some unions set membership requirements that Black Americans and women could not meet?

ENRICHMENT ACTIVITIES

1. Design a poster advertising one of Thomas A. Edison's inventions. Your poster should stress how owning the invention would improve people's lives.
2. Research the Pullman strike of 1894. After research has been completed, the class could elect speakers for the strikers and for the Pullman Company. These speakers could then debate the issues of the strike. Write a report discussing the arguments presented by both sides.

1860 1880 1900

- 1860 Twenty percent of Americans lived in cities
- 1882 Oriental Exclusion Act passed
- 1887 American Protective Association founded
- 1889 Chicago's Hull House founded by Jane Addams
- 1890 Western frontier closed
- 1894 Wilson-Gorman Tariff Act passed
- 1898 Congress declares war with Spain
- 1900 Forty percent of Americans lived in cities
- 1901 Tenement House Law passed

CHAPTER 23

Into the Twentieth Century

Chapter Objectives

After studying this chapter, you should be able to:

- describe the problems faced by the new immigrants to America after 1890;
- identify the foremost problems that confronted American city dwellers in the late 1800's;
- analyze the factors that led America to become a world power.

1 The New Americans

Overview America's population grew rapidly in the years after the Civil War. This was mainly because millions of people from all over the world came to America in search of a better life. These immigrants faced new problems and challenges in the United States.

Objectives After reading this section, you should be able to:

- list the reasons that immigrants came to America between 1865 and 1915;
- discuss the problems the new immigrants faced in America;
- explain how schools helped the new immigrants become Americanized.

The Immigrants. After the Civil War, America's expanding industries needed millions of new workers. At the same time, problems in other lands caused many people to leave their homes. As a result, about 26 million immigrants came to America between 1865 and 1915. Before 1890 most Europeans who emigrated to America came mainly from western and northern Europe. They came from such countries as England, Ireland, Germany, and Scandinavia. Most of them spoke English. They also looked like America's first immigrants from Europe. These were relatives of earlier immigrants who had come from the same areas of Europe years before.

The pattern of immigration began to change after 1890 as more people came into the United States from eastern and southern Europe. These people have been called the new immigrants. They came from such countries as Poland, Lithuania, Russia, and Italy. Also, immigrants continued to enter the United States from other parts of the world. Many Mexican people began to come to America at this time in search of a better way of life. And after 1910, thousands of Mexicans fled the revolution in their homeland. They settled largely in California and the southwestern United States. Large numbers of Asian immigrants, mainly from China, also settled along America's west coast. In addition, after America's war with Spain in 1898, some Cubans, Puerto Ricans, and Filipinos looked to America for a new home.

Why did many immigrants come to America between 1865 and 1915?

The Immigrant Experience. Most immigrants to America in the late 1800's wanted to find a better life in the United States. Often a shortage of jobs and poor living conditions forced these people to leave their home countries. But other immigrants, such as Russian Jews, were also fleeing religious persecution in their homelands. Still other immigrants came to the United States because American businesses—especially railroads—sent agents overseas to recruit new workers. For most immigrants, America was seen as a land of opportunity. But as many of these people found out, there were many problems to be faced in their new country.

Many new immigrants were not prepared for living in America. Few could speak English. Most had little schooling, and others had no skills. And almost all of the new immigrants were very poor. Because of these problems, the new immigrants usually took the lowest-paying jobs. They worked and lived in the poorest parts of the country's largest cities, such as New York, Boston, and Chicago. In these cities these people had to put up with overcrowded housing, unhealthy living conditions, and a high crime rate. They also had to put up with unequal treatment.

Why were most immigrants of this period not well prepared for living in America?

Discrimination. Some Americans disliked the new immigrants. This was often because there were some differences between the newcomers to America and American citizens. For example, most new immigrants could not read and write. Most spoke only their native languages. Many of the new immigrants from Europe practiced the Roman Catholic religion, which differed from the Protestant faiths widely practiced in America. Some immigrants also held political ideas that were thought to be dangerous to the government of the United States. In addition, many employers felt that the newcomers were to blame for the labor unrest that was beginning to take place in the country. At the same time, many American workers blamed the new immigrants for taking their jobs. New immigrants were also given the blame for driving down wages by working for lower pay than American citizens.

New immigrants at Ellis Island in New York looked forward to a better life in America.

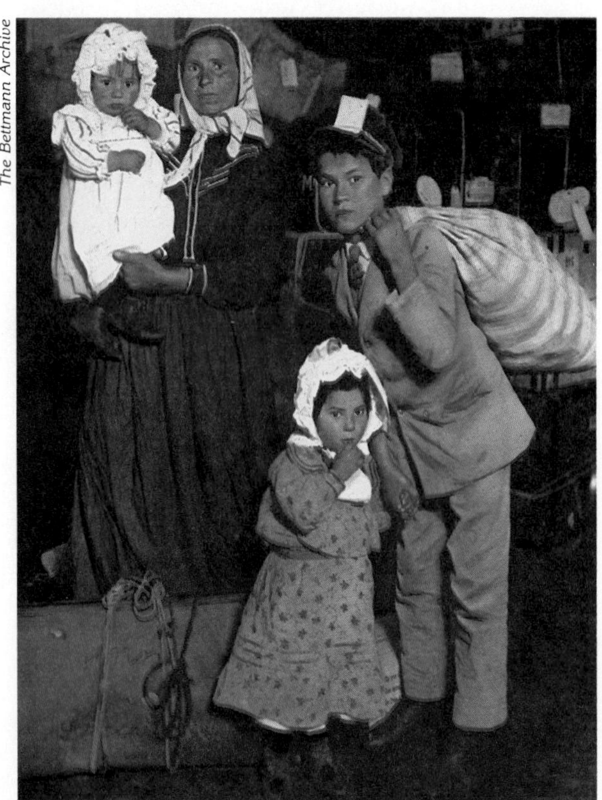
The Bettmann Archive

Because of such complaints, groups such as the American Protective Association (APA) were formed. This particular group was formed in 1887. Its purpose was to prevent Roman Catholic immigrants from coming into the country. The APA was strongest in the Midwest. In the East, Boston's Immigration Restriction League fought to keep out all immigrants who could not read and write English. In effect, this meant most new immigrants. Other groups were active on the West Coast. They often had great power among the country's leaders. For example, by an act of Congress, all Chinese and several other Asian immigrant groups were prevented from entering the country after 1882. This was called the Oriental Exclusion Act. In the same year, Congress passed the first law to limit immigration from Europe. This law was made to keep out persons who were guilty of crimes, persons not able to work, and persons suffering from mental illnesses.

Why was the Immigration Restriction League formed?

Contributions. The millions of persons who came to America in the late 1800's from all over the world brought with them the cultures and social customs of their homelands. New words, new foods, and most important, new ideas were brought to America by these people. Unskilled workers, talented artists and artisans, and people highly trained in many fields helped to build the growing American nation.

Newcomers to America at the end of the nineteenth century worked hard to become *Americanized.* That is, they wanted to become a part of American life. These immigrants and their children did this by making great contributions to the American way of life in such fields as politics, business, art, architecture, and science. Andrew Carnegie, for example, the wealthy industrial leader, was born in Scotland. Supreme Court Justice Felix Frankfurter came from Austria. Botanist Lue Gin Gong, of Chinese heritage, developed a new kind of orange. Tranquilino Luna, of Mexican heritage, represented the Territory of New Mexico in Congress in the mid-1890's.

■ *Why did many immigrants of the late 1890's work to become Americanized?*

The Fight for Equal Rights. Many groups of immigrants found it hard at first to fit into American society. For the most part, this was because of prejudice against them. This prejudice limited the jobs immigrants could get. It also limited the places where the newcomers to America could live. Many groups of immigrants were not satisfied with such conditions. They formed groups to help them adjust to living in their new land and to overcome the prejudice of the American citizens.

These groups often centered around churches and schools. Social and athletic clubs also offered meeting places for the country's newcomers. Foreign-language newspapers served as a link among the immigrants as well. In cities with large Polish populations, for example, many Polish immigrants joined the Polish National Alliance. And as greater numbers of immigrants came to America, they formed their own ethnic societies, such as German-American clubs and Slovak-American clubs. In the same way, groups such as the Italian-American Society and the National Council of Jewish Women were founded.

■ *Why were many organizations for immigrants formed in the late 1800's?*

Schools in the Late 1800's. Schooling was very important to the new immigrants and to their children. For many newcomers, schools were the only way to learn new skills and to become part of the community. However, going to school was often difficult for these people. This was because many immigrant adults and children had to work to survive in their new land. Schooling sometimes meant a loss of income. Time away from work could be a great hardship to the immigrant family. Nevertheless, schools were helpful to the American newcomers.

Schools taught the newcomers how to speak English. Some schools also helped these people to find work. This was done by teaching such subjects as carpentry and bricklaying. In this way schools became the main tool of Americanization. The number of people in American schools rose from 6.8 million in 1870 to more than 15.5 million in 1900. Immigrants and their children made up most of this increase. The amount of money spent on schooling also rose during this time, from 63 million dollars in 1870 to 214 million dollars in 1900.

Schools underwent many changes in the late 1800's. One of these changes centered on

Library of Congress

Education was the goal of many European, Asian, and Hispanic immigrants who later contributed to the growth of America.

teacher training. *Normal schools*—colleges for teacher training—were started. Better-trained teachers, it was felt, would greatly reduce the *illiteracy rate*—the number of people who cannot read and write. As a result, by 1900, the number of people in America who could not read and write English was greatly reduced from earlier rates. The new immigrants had made great progress in becoming Americanized. But it was still very hard for many of them to enter the mainstream of American society.

■ *Why was schooling very important to the new immigrants and to their children?*

SECTION 1 REVIEW

1. *Why did about 26 million immigrants come to America between 1865 and 1915?*
2. *What problems did the new immigrants face in America?*
3. *How were schools helpful to the new immigrants?*

2 Growth of the Cities

Overview American cities at the turn of the century were places of sharp contrasts. Wealthy citizens lived in large and comfortable houses. But nearby, thousands of immigrants and other poor people lived in dirty, unsafe, and overcrowded tenement buildings. Often, city governments did little to help these people.

Objectives After reading this section, you should be able to:

- list the reasons for the rapid growth of American cities after the Civil War;
- analyze the affects of rapidly growing populations on the living conditions in American cities;
- identify the technical advances and inventions that helped make American cities more livable in the late 1800's.

Reasons for Growth. The populations of many American cities grew rapidly in the years after the Civil War. In 1860 only 20 percent of the American people lived in cities. But by 1900 this percentage had doubled. In large part, the growth of the cities was brought about by the expansion of industry that was taking place in the United States at this time. Most American industries, such as steelmaking, garment making, and food processing, were set up in the country's cities. This was done in part because a larger number of workers was concentrated in cities than in rural areas.

Some American cities expanded because of their location. Cities such as Pittsburgh were located near the raw materials needed in the steel industry. Chicago, on the other hand, was well located for the country's developing transportation network.

As American cities grew, they, in turn, attracted more people who were seeking jobs and a better way of life. Some people, for example, left the country's rural areas to find work in the new factories being built in cities such as Birmingham, St. Louis, Cleveland, and Detroit. Immigrants from southern and eastern Europe, as well as from other parts of the world, also came to the country's large cities to find work. But as more people came to the cities to work and to live, problems arose.

Why were most American industries set up in the country's cities?

Living Conditions. Many American cities in the late 1800's were not able to keep up with the needs of their rapidly growing populations.

DO YOU KNOW?

When was the first skyscraper built?

The first skyscraper—so-called because it "scraped the sky"—was built in Chicago in 1884. Built as an office building for the Home Insurance Company, the skyscraper was 10-stories high. It was designed by William Le Baron Jenney. This architect used structural steel as a framework for the building. In this way more space could be put to use for living and working on scarce city land. Chicago also became the home of today's tallest skyscraper—the 110-floor Sear Tower—built in the mid-1970's. This building is 1,804 feet high [550 meters].

As more people moved to the cities, more housing was needed. Much of the housing that was provided, however, was often unsafe and unhealthy. Many newcomers to the cities often had to live in cheap, poorly constructed apartment buildings called *tenements*. This was because these people—often immigrants — were very poor. Such housing was all that these people could afford. Some of these buildings lacked running water. Others lacked heat in the winter and proper airflow in the summer. In addition, most tenements were firetraps. Nevertheless, such buildings were filled with poor people new to the cities.

Overcrowding in the cities led to other problems. The crime rate rose as more people came to the cities. Poorly trained and sometimes dishonest police officers were not always able to control lawbreaking. Environmental problems were present as well. The air in many cities, for example, was not fit to breathe. This was because factories and houses often burned coal for power and heat. The coal smoke that was given off into the air was sometimes so thick that the sun could not be seen. Many deaths were caused by such pollution. Polluted water was another cause of sickness and death. Often, raw waste from factories and houses was dumped into the lakes and rivers that provided drinking water for the cities. People who drank this water became ill. Illness then spread quickly in the cities because people lived close together. But city governments often could not control such problems. This was because many city leaders knew little about city planning. They knew even less about healthful living practices. However, a number of things took place that were to lead to improved living conditions in the cities.

Electric trolley cars helped city growth by carrying people to and from outlying areas.

The Bettmann Archive

■ *Why did many immigrants live in city tenements?*

Improving City Life. Technical advances and inventions helped to make American cities more livable in the late 1800's. The use of electricity, for example, benefited city dwellers in many ways. Electrically operated trolleys, elevated trains, and subway trains made travel within the city safer and more convenient. New means of travel allowed workers a greater area in which to choose a job. In turn, this improved the way of life of many workers. Electricity also helped to save lives. The threat of fire in overcrowded, poorly built tenements was lessened as electrical lighting replaced open-flame gaslights at the turn of the century. Brightly lighted streets also helped to reduce the crime rate.

Other innovations led to a better life in the city as well. Cleaner city water supplies be-

Museum of the City of New York

Cliff Dwellers by George Wesley Bellows, The Los Angeles County Museum of Art Los Angeles County Funds

Overcrowding, poverty, and poor sanitation were major urban problems in the late 1800's. What kinds of conditions did these city children play in?

came available in some cities as waste-disposal systems were improved. In turn, this improved the general health of the people living in the city. Developments in city services, especially within police and fire departments, also led to a safer life in the city. But these advances came about as city governments took on new powers.

■ *How did electricity help to save lives of tenement residents?*

Governing the Nation's Cities. Political power in city governments in the late 1800's was based more on the personal appeal of city leaders than on constitutional principles. This was because the United States Constitution divides power between the state and the federal governments. The Constitution does not deal with city governments. Therefore, cities could not levy their own taxes at this time. City governments had to rely on the states for tax money to support city services. Many cities were therefore not able to control their problems. Chicago, for example, could not get enough money to enlarge its water and sewer systems fast enough to serve the rapidly growing city in the 1880's and 1890's. As a result, the Chicago River became an open sewer for city and industrial waste. In turn, this hurt the general health of the city dwellers.

State legislatures in the 1880's and 1890's were often controlled by persons elected from rural areas of the state. These people cared little about city problems. They were often not willing to vote to send tax money from rural areas to help the cities. In part, many of these legislators felt that the cities were corrupt. They also believed that the cities were overrun by immigrants. Many of these lawmakers voted to spend tax money on the people from their own rural districts. Thus, little help was sent to the cities from the state governments.

■ *Why did cities have to rely on state governments for tax money?*

The Political Machines. City governments in the late 1800's were often run by political machines. These were highly structured political organizations. New York, Boston, and Chicago were among the cities run by these powerful organizations. In each city the machines gained power by providing help to the citizens and to immigrants. These organizations offered immigrants and political-party workers a job, representation, and a voice in the community. To machine leaders, the organization offered power and wealth.

The machines were led by politicians known as *city bosses.* Richard Croker, for example, was the city boss of New York City from the mid-1880's until the turn of the century. He was powerful because he controlled the money of the Democratic party in New York at Tammany Hall. This was the city's Democratic-party headquarters. Croker was not an elected official. Nevertheless, he was able to run the entire city. He did this by handing out money and favors—such as city jobs—to people who

Richard Croker in New York (inset) and other political bosses made themselves popular by arranging social events for those who lived in tenements.

Brown Brothers

The Bettmann Archive

VIEWPOINTS DIFFER

Urbanization

American cities such as Boston, New York, and Chicago grew very rapidly in the late nineteenth century. Much of this growth was the result of industrial expansion and immigration. Horace Greeley, the New York newspaper editor, noted that "We can not all live in cities, yet nearly all seem determined to do so." Some believed that cities held great promise while others viewed rapid urban growth as a threat to civilization.

F. J. Kingsbury, a noted sociologist, made this observation in 1895 (from "The Tendency of Men to Live in Cities," *Journal of Science*):

All modern industrial life tends to concentration as a matter of economy. . . . We must remember, too, that cities as places of human habitation have vastly improved within half a century. . . . I think isolated rural life, where people seldom come in contact with dwellers in large towns, always tends to barbarism. . . . It would seem, then . . . that almost everything that is best in life can be better had in the city than elsewhere, and that, with those who can command the means, physical comforts and favorable sanitary conditions are better obtained there. . . . The city is growing a better place to live in year by year. . . .

A somewhat differing perspective is offered by Josiah Strong, a Protestant clergyman and social reformer. The excerpt is from *Our Country: Its Possible Future and Its Present Crisis* (1885):

The city is the nerve center of our civilization. It is also a storm center. The fact, therefore, that it is growing much more rapidly than the whole population is full of significance. . . . The city has become a serious menace [threat] to our civilization. . . . It has a peculiar attraction for the immigrant. . . . Because our cities are so largely foreign . . . the saloon . . . is multiplied. . . . Here the sway of Mammon [materialism] is widest, and his worship the most constant and eager. . . . The rich are richer and the poor are poorer in the city than elsewhere. . . . Socialism [a political and economic system where the government owns and administers the means of production and goods] centers in the city. . . . As a rule, our largest cities are the worst governed. It is natural, therefore, to infer that as our cities grow larger and more dangerous, the government will become more corrupt, and control will pass more completely into the hands of those who themselves most need to be controlled.

Think About It

1. How does Kingsbury view rural living?
2. What factors does Strong believe contribute to the city as a "storm center"?
3. If you had the choice in 1900 to live in the country or a major city, which would you choose? Explain your answer.

needed his help. In return, Croker expected the people he had helped to back the New York City Democrats. In this way, the Democrats remained in power and in control of city jobs and money.

Political machines were often corrupt. But the country's largest cities often ran well under their leadership. Some Americans, however, were against this kind of government. These people wanted to take control of the cities away from bosses. They also wanted to lessen the growing power of immigrants within city governments. These Americans believed that cities should be run by people schooled in city planning.

■ *What group of people led political machines?*

Urban Reformers. Many important changes were made in city life in the last years of the 1800's. In part, these changes resulted from the work of reformers. Many newspapers and magazines of the time printed stories and pictures that pointed out the problems facing the cities' poor people and immigrants. Jacob Riis was one journalist who brought these problems to public attention. His pictures showed the unhealthy, overcrowded conditions in many city tenements (see the pictures on page 415). Riis's work led to housing-reform laws, the first of which in New York was the Tenement House Law of 1901. This law set up building codes for greater safety. But changes came about in other ways as well.

While some Americans worked to pass laws aimed at reform, others used more direct ways to improve life in the cities. Some Americans, particularly women, opened neighborhood centers called settlement houses. One of these houses was Chicago's Hull House. It was founded by Jane Addams in 1889. New York's Henry Street Settlement was founded by Lillian D. Wald. By 1897 more than 70 of such settlement houses had been set up in cities across the country.

These houses provided many services for the poor people of the cities. Children could learn sports, learn crafts, or study many subjects, including the English language. Settlement houses also gave children a place to spend their time constructively, under adult guidance. In so doing, these houses enabled parents to work. Settlement houses also provided programs for adults. These courses taught such things as carpentry, electrical work, and plumbing. English classes were also given without charge. By providing such services, Jane Addams and other social workers improved city life and helped to Americanize thousands of newcomers to the United States.

■ *What services did settlement houses provide for poor children?*

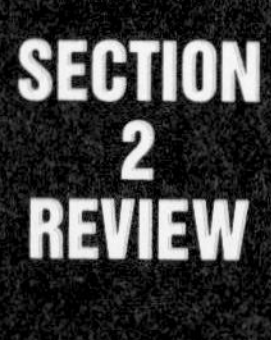

1. *Why did American cities grow rapidly after the Civil War?*
2. *How did overcrowding in the cities lead to further social problems?*
3. *What technical advances and inventions made American cities more livable in the late 1800's?*

3 America Becomes a World Power

Overview America's place among the countries of the world changed in the late 1800's. Some Americans felt that the United States had a duty to spread its way of life to other parts of the world. America's relations with other countries changed, especially with Spain. American newspapers fueled anti-Spanish feelings in the United States. Such events soon led to the Spanish American War. By the war's end, America had become a world power.

Objectives After reading this section, you should be able to:

- describe the changes in American foreign policy in the late 1800's;
- explain how American newspapers shaped American public opinion against Spain;
- discuss how the United States became a world power.

Changes in American Foreign Policy. America's relations with other countries of the world changed in the last years of the 1800's. In particular, America's relations with Spain worsened, in part, because of America's desire to set up overseas colonies. This desire for overseas growth gave new meaning to the idea of manifest destiny. Manifest destiny had been a belief of the mid-1840's that America had a God-given right to spread its way of life across North America. With the closing of the western frontier in 1890, many Americans looked overseas for room to grow.

The rapid growth of American industries in the years after the Civil War also brought changes to American foreign policy. As the industries grew, new demands arose for greater supplies of raw materials. This demand was heightened as well by the swift growth in America's population. As a result, American businesses began to seek new suppliers of raw materials, new markets for American products, and greater trading privileges. American overseas colonies seemed to be one way to satisfy these needs. However, America's actions led to strained relations with Spain—first in Cuba, then in other parts of the world.

■ *How did the closing of the western frontier affect American overseas interests?*

Relations With Cuba. As early as the 1840's some Americans had become interested in taking over Cuba. To them, Cuba was a source of necessary farm products, a source of cheap labor, and a possible new slave state. But because of sectional differences between the North and the South within the United States at the time, Cuba was never considered for statehood. Nevertheless, many wealthy Americans invested money in Cuba as well as in Puerto Rico and in other countries throughout the Caribbean area.

For the most part, American investments in Cuba were put into sugar plantations. This brought about great changes in the Cuban economy. Until this time, the Cuban economy was based on many farm crops. But as more American money was put into the Cuban sugar-growing industry, Cuba became largely a one-crop country. This meant that the main part of the Cuban economy depended upon sugar growing. And many Cuban plantation owners as well as their workers had to depend upon the American market for sale of their sugar.

This Cuban-American arrangement worked well for many years. Then, in 1890, Cuban-American trade grew even stronger. In that year Congress passed the McKinley Tariff. Because of this act, Cuban sugar could be sent to the United States free of any import duties. That is, no import duty of any kind had to be made on Cuban sugar. As a result, Cuban sugar sold well in the United States. The Cuban economy grew to an all-time high. But a greater number of Cuban workers depended totally on these sugar sales for their jobs.

Then, in 1894, Cuban-American trade nearly came to a standstill. In that year Congress passed the Wilson-Gorman Tariff Act. One part of this law put a 40 percent charge on all sugar that was brought into the United States. This was done to help American sugar growers in Hawaii and in the United States. As a result, Americans bought little Cuban sugar because its price was so high. This caused a great drop in Cuban sugar sales in the United States. It also had terrible effects in Cuba. With little demand for Cuba's one product in its only market—the United States—most Cubans had no work, no money, and little food. This led to great suffering in Cuba and to political disorder.

■ *How did the Wilson-Gorman Tariff affect American trade with Cuba?*

American Newspapers and Public Opinion. In 1895, one year after the Wilson-Gorman Tariff became law, a violent uprising against Spain broke out in Cuba, a Spanish colony. Spain had done little to help Cuba to rebuild its economy after the collapse of the Cuban-American sugar trade. Spain sent General Valeriano Weyler y Nicolau to Cuba to end the fighting. Unfortunately, General Weyler y Nicolau's ways of dealing with the Cubans were brutal. As a result, General Weyler y Nicolau became known as The Butcher. In many ways, his methods led to further discontent and violence in Cuba.

Culver Pictures

Spain's General Weyler y Nicolau was ridiculed by American cartoonists in the 1890's for his ruthless treatment of Cuban revolutionaries.

Culver Pictures

At the onset of the uprising, a few American newspapers reported on these developments. These stories seemed to stir American interest in Cuba's problems with Spain. And as the newspapers reported on the cruelty of the Spanish against the Cubans, their reading audiences grew. The country's largest newspapers discovered that stories about Spanish wrongdoing in Cuba increased the number of newspapers that were sold. In New York City, stories about the Cuban uprising became top news in the city's two leading newspapers. These were the *World*—owned by Joseph Pulitzer—and the *Journal*—owned by William Randolph Hearst. Each newspaper hoped to attract readers away from the other newspaper. Because of this competition, the newspapers told their reporters in Cuba to make their reports exciting. In story after story Americans learned about the bravery of the Cubans and about the savagery of the Spanish. Many reports compared the Cuban uprising to the American Revolution.

The sensational reports on the Cuban uprising did more than sell newspapers. The reports shaped American public opinion. Many Americans were outraged by the actions of the Spanish forces as they were reported in the newspapers. Throughout the presidential campaign of 1896 and later, groups of Americans urged government leaders in the United States to go to war with Spain. These people felt that Americans should help the Cubans. President McKinley soon found that peace was difficult to keep.

■ *Why did Spain send General Valeriano Weyler y Nicolau to Cuba?*

The Demand for War. The call for American intervention in the Cuban uprising continued to grow. More and more people began to think that the United States should help the Cubans fight for their independence from Spain. In early 1898 several events took place that pushed America closer to war. The Hearst newspapers printed a secret letter on February 9, 1898. It had been written by Dupuy de Lôme, a Spanish official in the United States. The letter stated that President McKinley was ". . . weak and a bidder for the admiration of the crowd." It went on to call the President "a would-be politician." Many Americans were outraged at Spain because of this letter.

Several days later, a tragic event brought about more anti-Spanish feelings. An American battleship, the *Maine,* exploded in Cuba's Havana Harbor. The 260 Americans on the ship were killed. A rumor spread quickly that Spain had sunk the ship. "Remember the Maine!" was heard all over the country as many Americans called for war with Spain. Only a few people questioned whether Spain was really to blame for sinking the ship. Calls for war grew quickly.

President McKinley, however, hoped to stay out of war with Spain. In March 1898 the President sent an *ultimatum* to Spain. This was a final demand that, if not carried out at once, would lead to war. The ultimatum dealt with Spain's policies toward Cuba. The Spanish agreed to carry out the American demands listed in the ultimatum. But the desire for war was so strong in Congress, in the newspapers, and among the American people that the Spanish concessions were ignored. War with Spain was declared by Congress on April 19, 1898.

■ *What two events in early 1898 pushed America closer to war with Spain?*

(Text continues on page 422.)

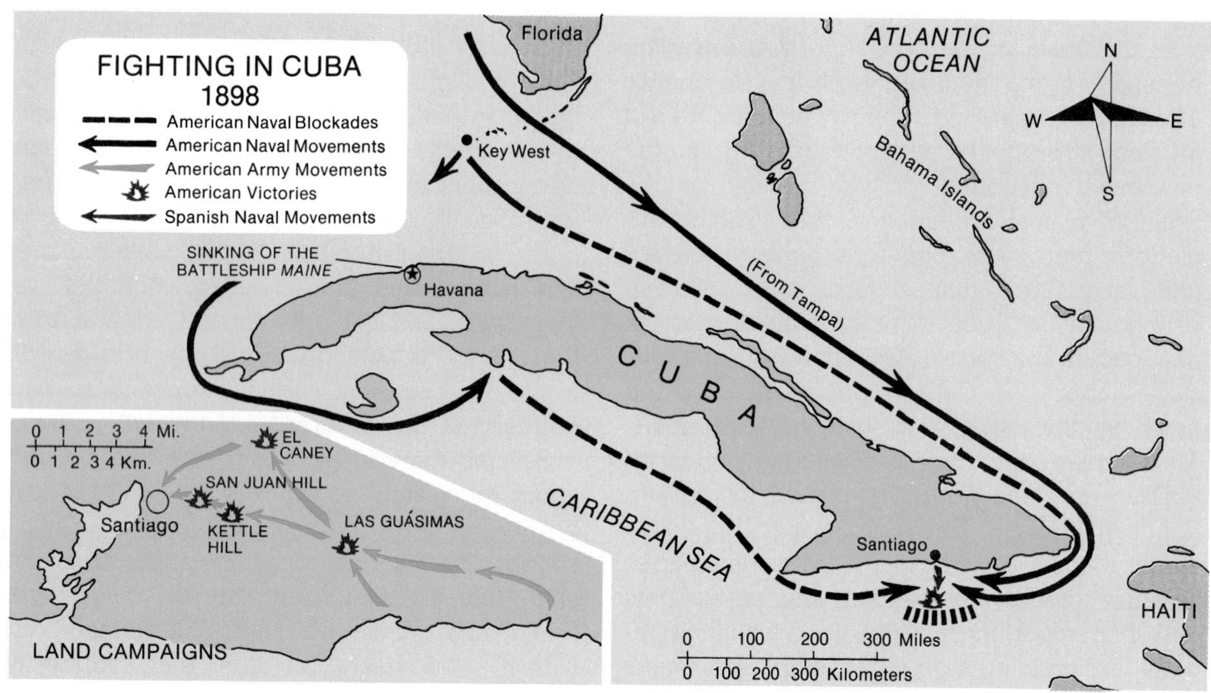

This map shows fighting in Cuba during the Spanish American War. Where did the American Navy set up blockades? How would you compare the American naval movements to the Spanish naval movements?

The War With Spain. The first fighting of the war broke out in the Spanish-ruled Philippine Islands in the western Pacific Ocean—not in Cuba. On May 1, 1898, Commodore George Dewey sailed his fleet of American warships into the harbor of Manila Bay in the Philippine Islands. The Americans easily sank the outmoded Spanish ships they found there. But Commodore Dewey had too few troops to attack the Spanish forces in the city of Manila itself. He had to wait for more American troops to join his forces.

In the meantime, Commodore Dewey gave guns, ammunition, and other war materials to anti-Spanish Filipino groups. Throughout the summer, these Filipinos fought for their independence from Spain. Thus by August, when more American soldiers were added to Commodore Dewey's command, Spanish power in the Philippine Islands was greatly weakened. The Americans easily took over the city of Manila on August 13, 1898.

Fighting the war was more difficult in Cuba itself. The American army was small. And many of the soldiers were new volunteers. They knew little of army life and ways of fighting. Furthermore, they were poorly supplied and outfitted. In fact, many new volunteers sailed to Cuba from Florida harbors in the hot spring of 1898. They wore winter uniforms made of wool. Some new soldiers were armed with little more than their own hunting gear.

Despite such problems, the most important fighting of the war took place in Cuba. The fighting broke out on June 24, 1898. American forces began to push the main Spanish army in Cuba southward to Santiago (see map on page 422). One group of American soldiers, the "Rough Riders," captured San Juan Hill in a dramatic battle in this campaign.

The American navy also entered the Caribbean Sea to fight the Spanish. On July 2, 1898, the American fleet faced what was the remaining force of the Spanish navy. Once again, the American fleet was better prepared for battle. Within hours, the American navy had sunk the last Spanish warship. The American army then advanced to Santiago. Fifteen days later, Spain surrendered.

The Spanish American War ended six months after it began. But in that short time, the United States had changed its position among the powerful countries of the world. It had become a world power. Through its victory over Spain, America gained control of Puerto Rico, Guam, Wake Island, and the Philippine Islands. Cuba also came under American protection. More important, the United States had shown its ability to stand up to a European country.

Why was Spanish power in the Philippine Islands greatly weakened by August 1898?

SECTION 3 REVIEW

1. *What effect did the growth of American industries after the Civil War have on the foreign policy of the United States?*
2. *How did American newspapers shape American public opinion against Spain?*
3. *How did the Spanish American War change the United States' position in the world?*

CHAPTER 23 SUMMARY

Millions of new immigrants, mostly from southern and eastern Europe, left their homelands in the late 1800's. They hoped to make better lives for themselves and for their children. The immigrants had to change their lives to fit into American society. But in the same way, these people contributed to the character of their new country.

The cities, where most newcomers to America settled, faced many problems in these years. Living conditions were often poor. And city services could not keep up with the increasing needs of the growing city populations. But efforts were made to better city life by city governments and by urban reformers.

America's place among the countries of the world also changed greatly. Some American business leaders were interested in Cuba, a Spanish colony. When a Cuban uprising against Spain broke out, sensational newspaper stories were printed in the United States. These stories shaped American opinion against Spain. In part, this led America into war with Spain. America won this war. It gained overseas landholdings. America entered the twentieth century as a world power.

CHAPTER 23 REVIEW

USING YOUR SKILLS

Interpreting Bar Graphs

Bar graphs are visual tools that allow us to show and compare quantity and change. In this example, the bar graph compares the populations of the nation's five largest cities and shows how they changed in the final years of the 1800's. Study the bar graph carefully. Then answer the questions that follow.

1. Which American city had the largest population in 1880?
2. Was Chicago's population in 1890 greater than or the same as Boston's in 1900?
3. Which city had the greatest population increase between 1880 and 1900?
4. Did any of the five cities shown here lose population between 1880 and 1900?
5. How many people were living in Philadelphia in 1890?
6. By what year did New York City attain a population of more than 2 million people?

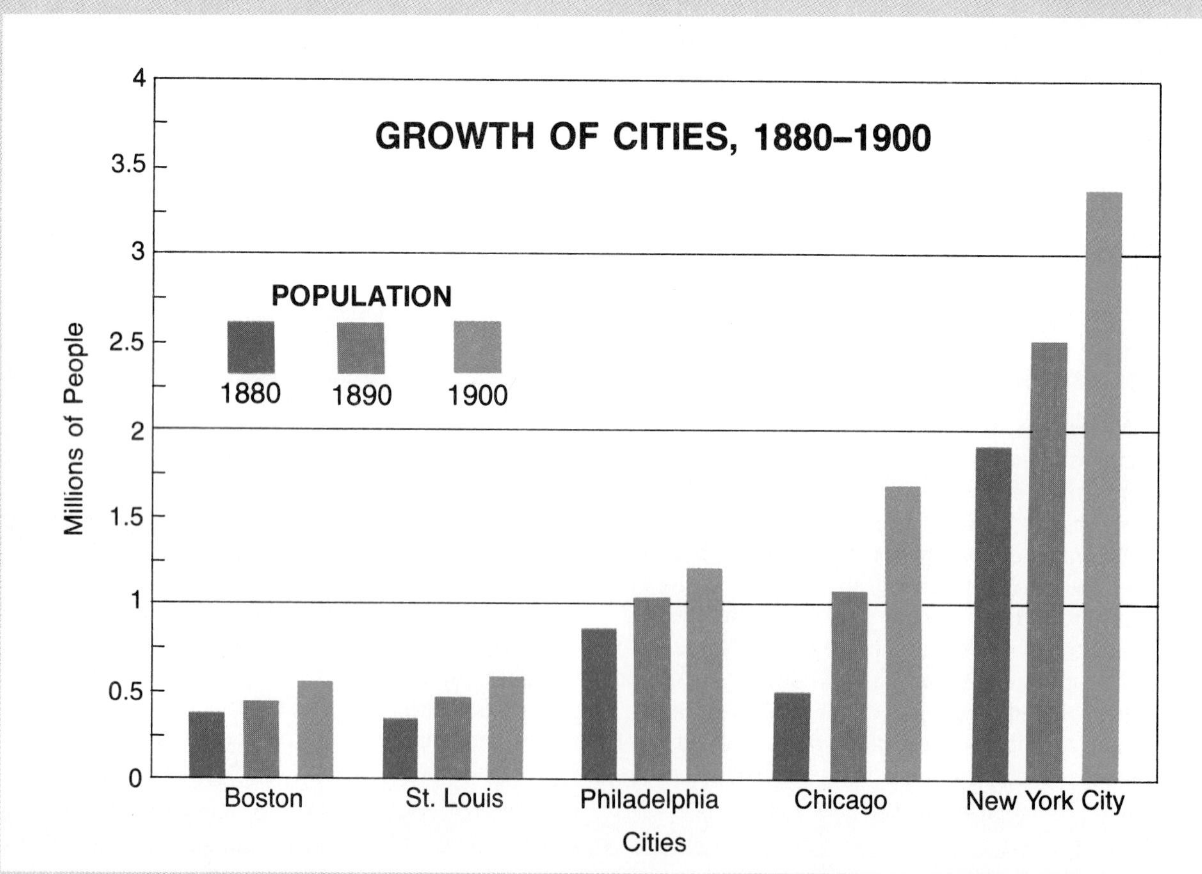

CHAPTER 23 REVIEW

YOU SHOULD KNOW

Identify, define, or explain each of the following:

Americanized
normal schools
illiteracy rate
tenements
Jacob Riis
Jane Addams
Wilson-Gorman Tariff Act

CHECKING FACTS

1. What countries did the new immigrants come from?
2. What was the purpose of the American Protective Association?
3. Name three ethnic societies that formed in the late 1800's.
4. What percent of American people lived in cities in 1860? in 1900?
5. What did the Tenement House Law set up?
6. What could children learn at settlement houses?
7. What was the idea of manifest destiny?
8. What brought about great changes in the Cuban economy?
9. What two newspapers sensationalized the Cuban uprising?
10. What islands did the United States gain control of through its victory over Spain?

UNDERSTANDING CONCEPTS

1. Why did many Russian Jews come to the United States in the late 1800's?
2. Why did Congress pass the first law to limit immigration from Europe in 1882?
3. How did polluted water affect the general health of people in American cities in the late 1800's?
4. Why were most cities not able to raise money for improvements in the late 1800's?

LEARNING FROM ILLUSTRATIONS

1. Study the two pictures on page 415. What do you think are some of the problems of city life that are shown by these pictures?
2. Study the cartoon on page 420. What do you think was the cartoonist's opinion of General Weyler y Nicolau?

CRITICAL THINKING

1. New immigrants are coming to the United States today from Central America, Europe, and Asia. What kinds of hardships do you think these new immigrants face?
2. Many American cities in the late 1800's were not able to keep up with the needs of their rapidly growing populations. What kinds of problems do American cities face today?
3. The sensational reports on the Cuban uprising shaped American public opinion. Do you think newspaper, radio, and television reports shape American public opinion today? Why or why not?

ENRICHMENT ACTIVITIES

1. To better understand your own ethnic background, talk to relatives about your family history. Try to find out in what country your family originated. Descendants of American Indians can find out about tribal history. Then draw a family tree.
2. Read two or more newspaper editorials to see what the issues are in the news. Write letters to the editors telling them how you feel about the issues.

CHAPTER 24

CLOSE-UP: The Haymarket Affair

INTRODUCTION

On a cold and bleak November day in 1887 four men walked steadily to the gallows in the Cook County Jail in Chicago. The four men were anarchists and members of the SLP—*the Socialist Labor Party. They were also well-known leaders in the fight for the eight-hour-workday movement. Each had been found guilty of murder by calling for the bombing of Chicago's Haymarket Square on May 4, 1886. But not one of them could have thrown the bomb. Their deaths touched off a controversy that has lasted for nearly a century.*

Serious labor problems had been building in Chicago and the nation for years, fueled, in part, by the SLP and other radical groups. But widespread labor unrest did not spill onto Chicago streets until the end of April 1886. On April 30 thousands of workers in Chicago and elsewhere walked off their jobs in support of the eight-hour-workday movement. Workers would no longer put up with twelve-hour to sixteen-hour workdays, low pay, and unsafe working conditions. Strikes crippled the city, disrupting food production, mail delivery, and other needed items. However, the SLP was only partly responsible for the unrest. Nevertheless, the SLP and its members received the blame for the bombing and for other Chicago labor problems. SLP members August Spies, George Engel, Adolph Fischer, and Albert Parsons went to their deaths because of their political beliefs.

1 Bombing in Haymarket Square

Chicago became the center of the *eight-hour-workday movement* shortly after the Civil War, because many of the country's largest industries were based there, employing large numbers of workers. Chicago also nurtured a largely immigrant-backed movement that came to be known as the *anarchist movement*. An event that broke out on Chicago streets and ended in a Chicago courtroom in the mid-1880's grew out of these two movements.

The First of May. Many workers in Chicago spent Saturday, May 1, 1886, rallying for the eight-hour-workday movement. More than 30,000 workers went out on strike and remained away from their jobs. One Chicago newspaper said that "no smoke curled up from the tall chimneys of the factories and mills and things had assumed a Sabbath-like appearance." Some workers stayed at home, but most took part in parades and demonstrations that were held in many parts of the city. The workers marched, usually from their job sites to wide-open areas where large groups of people listened to speakers talk about working conditions, pay, work hours, and the labor movement. "There is an eight-hour agitation everywhere," one labor newspaper noted.

The agitation died down on Sunday, May 2. There were no parades, no demonstrations—only the quiet clip-clop of horses drawing carriages on the nearly empty cobblestoned city streets. But somewhere—either in Chicago or nearby—someone was building a small package made of wadding, fuses, and dynamite.

■ *What topics were discussed by speakers during the Saturday demonstrations?*

The McCormick Riot. Sunday's calm exploded into violence on Monday, May 3. Strikers again held large rallies in many parts of the city. The largest gathering took place on Black Road near the front gates of the McCormick Harvester Machine Company. More than 6,000 strikers listened intently to 31-year-old August Spies, a member of the SLP and editor of the German-American workers' newspaper, *Arbeiter-Zeitung.* Spies told his listeners to band together and not to surrender to the pressures of their employers. But the shriek of the McCormick factory whistle midway through his speech cut him short.

The whistle signaled a change in the factory work shift. And before the first blast of the whistle had faded, about 500 men in Spies's audience left the rally and ran toward the factory.

The 500 strikers reached the factory gates as the first *scabs*—strikebreakers—were leaving for the night. Suddenly, fists were flying as strikers and strikebreakers fought each other in the street. The strikers wanted their jobs back—but on their own terms. The strikebreakers wanted jobs, too, and they were willing to work for whatever the factory owners offered them.

As the fighting spilled further down the narrow street, about 200 Chicago police officers charged into the crowd of brawling workers. The police did not rely on their nightsticks to curb the rioters. Instead, they opened fire with their service revolvers, leaving 1 striker dead

The Bettmann Archive

Attention Workingmen!

GREAT

MASS-MEETING

TO-NIGHT, at 7.30 o'clock,

AT THE

HAYMARKET, Randolph St., Bet. Desplaines and Halsted.

Good Speakers will be present to denounce the latest atrocious act of the police, the shooting of our fellow-workmen yesterday afternoon.

Workingmen Arm Yourselves and Appear in Full Force!

THE EXECUTIVE COMMITTEE

Posters announcing the workers' protest meeting at Haymarket Square were printed in both English and German because many of the strikers were of German American origin. What are working men asked to do?

and 6 others seriously wounded. Six police officers were also injured, but none had been shot.

Over the heads of his terrified and fleeing audience, Spies sighted the wisps of gun smoke curling into the night air. He heard the shouts and cries of the wounded and dying strikers. Spies immediately ran back to the office of the *Arbeiter-Zeitung*, where a poster was being printed calling on all workers in Chicago to "rise in your might.... To Arms! We call you to arms." The poster was headlined "Revenge," and it called for a mass meeting to be held the next night at the Haymarket Square on the city's West Side.

■ *Why did Spies's audience leave during his speech?*

Tuesday, May 4. The Chicago sky threatened rain most of the day, but no one was prepared for the storm that broke later in the evening. Striking workers and police had several run-ins during the day. Many workers were arrested, but no one was hurt. The upcoming Haymarket meeting, therefore, was met with a great deal of uneasiness. In fact, most workers were so worried about possible trouble at Haymarket Square that the turnout at the meeting was small. Most of the expected workers stayed home.

The Square had been chosen because it could hold about 20,000 people. But no more than 1,200 people showed up. With such a small gathering, August Spies, the first speaker, moved the meeting out of the Square and down the street to the mouth of a nearby alley, where he and the other speakers could be heard more easily.

The meeting, set to begin at 7:30 at night, started an hour later. Two speakers—Albert Parsons and Samuel Fielden—had not yet arrived when Spies began to speak. The meeting, Spies explained, was to discuss "the general situation of the eight-hour strike, and the events which have taken place in the last forty-eight hours." He was talking about the shootings at the McCormick factory. The small crowd listened quietly.

Albert Parsons began speaking at about nine o'clock. Fearing trouble, Parsons made an effort to keep his speech tame and his listeners calm. He spoke mainly about the state of labor unions in the world, adding many statistics as he spoke. When, at one point, some people in the crowd shouted their desire to hang Jay Gould, a well-known railroad owner, Parsons replied, "No! This is not a conflict between individuals, but for a change of system... [Socialism] does not aim at the life of the individual."

Chicago's Mayor Carter Harrison was in the audience, listening to the speakers. He, too, feared that trouble might break out. But he later admitted that "nothing had occurred yet, or looked likely to occur to require interference." The mayor then left the meeting and went to the Desplaines Street police station, a half block away. He told the police that the workers' meeting was peaceful. He stressed that no action needed to be taken by the police that night.

■ *Why was the meeting at Haymarket Square met with uneasiness by Chicago workers?*

The Haymarket Bombing. Parsons ended his talk about ten o'clock. He turned and introduced Samuel Fielden, the final speaker. Fielden had talked for about ten minutes when, as many people had expected, rain began to fall. Most of his audience left at that point, leaving Fielden with a crowd of only

Chicago Historical Society

Chicago's Haymarket Square was the scene of a violent labor demonstration on May 4, 1886.

about 200 people. Nevertheless, Fielden went on talking for ten minutes more. About 10:20 P.M. Fielden began to end his talk by saying, "In conclusion..." But he never finished the sentence. A team of nearly 200 police officers broke through the thinning crowd and surged toward the wagon that served as the speakers' platform. The team of police was led by Chicago police captains Ward and Bonfield, who were widely known for their strong, anti-labor-union views.

"In the name of the people of the State of Illinois," Captain Ward shouted, "I command this meeting immediately and peaceably to disperse."

"We are peaceable," Fielden replied, a look of shock on his face as he and the others on the wagon platform began to leave.

But just then a dark object rocketed through the damp night air. It made a strange hissing noise, like the sound of frying bacon. And it had an eerie glow as well, like the sputtering of a holiday sparkler. The mysterious object landed among the police, at the feet of police officer Mathias J. Degnan.

Someone had tossed a dynamite bomb into the police ranks. Chicagoans many blocks away first saw a blinding flash, followed by a deafening roar. Police officer Degnan was killed instantly. Six other police officers died soon after in a hospital. And more than 70 other police officers were seriously wounded in the blast. Two workers also died in the explosion, and 60 others were severely hurt.

The shocked crowd ran for cover as the police opened fire on them. Several workers were killed, and many more were wounded. The exact number of people killed has never been learned. The police quickly arrested a large number of workers, including Fielden and Spies. But the person most responsible for the nightmare—the bomber—was never found.

Why was Samuel Fielden unable to finish his speech?

1. *What events were held throughout Chicago on May 1, 1886?*
2. *How many strikers were killed in the McCormick Riot?*
3. *Why were many workers in Chicago on strike in early May 1886?*

2 Anarchists on Trial

Word of the Haymarket bombing traveled quickly throughout the country and the world. For the most part, business leaders who had always distrusted the labor-union movement felt that they had been proved right. Labor-union leaders and workers who backed the eight-hour-workday movement, on the other hand, were shocked and dismayed at the news. They could not believe that any labor-union member would have committed such a terrible crime.

The Trial Begins. Rumors of a plot by German Americans to destroy Chicago spread rapidly. Because of these stories and the resulting fear, the police launched a city-wide dragnet, hoping to round up as many anarchists as they could. "Make the raids first and look up the law afterward!" the state's attorney, Julius S. Grinnell, stated when asked if search warrants had been signed by a judge. About 200 people—mostly German Americans—were picked up in the raids.

By the end of May 1886 all but 31 persons had been freed from jail. The remaining suspects were charged with four separate crimes stemming from the bombing. Each was accused of conspiracy to murder police officer Mathias J. Degnan by means of a bomb, of murder by pistol shots, of being accessories to one another in carrying out Degnan's murder, and of general conspiracy to commit murder.

The state of Illinois limited its case to trying only nine of the 31 men originally charged. Each was a well-known member of the Socialist Labor Party. Each man also had taken some part in the labor-union movement. And each *defendant*—person on trial—was an admitted anarchist.

Those standing trial were August Spies, Samuel Fielden, Albert Parsons, Michael Schwab, Adolph Fischer, George Engel, Oscar Neebe, Louis Lingg, and Rudolph Schnaubelt. However, only seven defendants were in the courtroom when the trial began. Schnaubelt, released on bail, had fled the country. Parsons was hiding in Wisconsin, but he voluntarily entered the courtroom in the early afternoon of the opening day of the trial. Thus, eight men finally went to trial before Judge Joseph E. Gary in the Cook County Criminal Court in Chicago.

■ *What group of people were suspected of plotting the destruction of Chicago?*

The Verdict Is Reached. Defense attorney William Black tried to limit the scope of the case to the bombing itself. But, by Judge Gary's instructions, the state had only to prove that the men on trial were anarchists in order to find them guilty of a *capital offense*—a crime for which they could be put to death. Since each defendant admitted to belonging to the anarchist movement, the jury had little to consider. Even the courtroom bailiff could foretell the outcome of the trial as the trial began. "Those fellows are going to be hanged as certain as death..." he said. Not surprisingly, then, the hand-picked jury sided with the state after only three hours of deliberations. The twelve jurors found each of the eight men guilty as charged. And all but one of the defendants was sentenced to death. 36-year-old Oscar Neebe, against whom no evidence whatsoever was presented, was given a sentence of fifteen years in prison.

After several motions for a new trial, Judge

Gary set October 7, 1886, as the day for passing the final sentence. On that day the judge asked each defendant if he had anything to say before the sentence was read. To Judge Gary's surprise, each man had a great deal to say—so much so that the eight men spent three days talking about their beliefs and feelings and about the American system of justice.

When they had finished, Judge Gary read the sentence: "In substance and effect it is [the court's decision] that the defendant Neebe be imprisoned in the State Penitentiary at Joliet [Illinois] at hard labor for the term of fifteen years.

"And that each of the other defendants, between the hours of ten o'clock in the forenoon and two o'clock in the afternoon of the third day of December next, in the manner provided by the statute of this State be hung by the neck until he is dead. Remove the prisoners."

What did the eight convicted anarchists talk about in their courtroom speeches?

During the Haymarket trial, Judge Joseph E. Gary consistently favored the prosecution.

Culver Pictures

Final Pleas. Defense attorney Black immediately appealed the case to the Illinois Supreme Court. He was helped by Leonard Swett, who had been a friend and law partner of Abraham Lincoln.

The appeals process went on for almost a year. During that time a growing number of people began to feel that justice had not been served. Nevertheless, the Illinois Supreme Court upheld Judge Gary's rulings on September 14, 1887. A final appeal to the United States Supreme Court was turned down on November 2, 1887. Since the date of execution had been moved back during the appeals process to November 11, 1887, the condemned men had only nine days to live. Attorney Black tried to get an immediate pardon for his clients from Richard J. Oglesby, governor of Illinois, but he was only partially successful.

Black and others presented the governor with petitions signed by more than 200,000 people asking that the lives of the Chicago anarchists be spared. Well-known people, such as Samuel Gompers of the American Federation of Labor and George Bernard Shaw, a famous Irish playwright, either met with or telegraphed the governor to ask for mercy for the condemned men. Even Judge Gary and Prosecutor Grinnell had a change of heart—at least in part. Both men asked the governor to spare Fielden and Schwab from hanging.

Seventeen hours before the scheduled hanging, the governor announced that he was changing the sentences of Fielden and

Schwab to life in prison. But the others—Spies, Parsons, Engel, and Fischer—would meet the executioner as scheduled. The seventh prisoner, Louis Lingg, 22 years old, had taken his own life earlier in the day.

■ *With whose petitions of mercy did Governor Oglesby agree?*

Final Moments. Spies, Engel, Fischer, and Parsons took the news of the governor's decision well. They spent their last night in prison quietly after saying good-bye to their families. Parsons spent the long night talking with his jailers and writing a farewell letter to his two young children.

The four condemned men were handcuffed in their cells and walked to the gallows at 11:30 Friday morning, November 11, 1887—a damp, dreary day in Chicago. The men were calm, even good-humored. Fischer adjusted his noose because it was too tight. Spies thanked the executioner for making him more comfortable. But as the four stood on the gallows, each hurriedly spoke his last words. August Spies was, as usual, the first to speak: "There will come a time when our silence will be more powerful than the voices you strangle today." Albert Parsons, the last to speak out, was silenced by the hangman's rope in mid-sentence: "Let me speak, oh men of America! Will you let me speak, Sheriff Matson! Let the voice of the people be heard! Oh—"

The four Chicago anarchists died at a few minutes past noon. As the Cook County hangman pulled open the gallows' trapdoor, the Haymarket Affair was thought to have ended. To this day, it never has.

■ *How did the four condemned men spend their last night in prison?*

Randall Kryn

Many people went to the dedication of a monument for the Haymarket defendants in 1893. What saying is carved on the monument?

The Altgeld Pardon. Six years after the hanging, a new governor of Illinois, John P. Altgeld, pardoned Fielden, Neebe, and Schwab. In doing so, the governor criticized Judge Gary's courtroom procedures and the state's shoddy case against the Chicago anarchists. But such criticism almost ended the governor's own political life. By 1893 few persons objected to the governor's actions, but he was widely criticized for his reasoning. Many people agreed that the prisoners should be pardoned, but few people supported the governor's stinging criticism of the unusual

Newspaper and magazine editorial cartoons often used anarchists and their ideas as a theme for drawings during the late 1800's. Why do these men look dismayed?

The Bettmann Archive

courtroom practices that led to the anarchists' conviction.

But even before the governor's pardon was signed, several people pointed to questions about the police raids that had followed the bombing. Chicago Police Chief Ebersold, for example, stated in 1890 that Captain Michael J. Schaack—who had conducted the raids in which the eight anarchists were arrested—"wanted to keep things stirring. He wanted bombs to be found here, there, everywhere....After we got the anarchist societies broken up, Schaack wanted to send out men to organize new societies right away....He wanted to...keep himself prominent before the public."

The Haymarket Affair raises many questions about the American system of justice in the 1880's. But such an event also serves as a reminder of what can happen to our belief in fair trials when public fear and lack of courtroom fairness come together in a court of law.

Why was Governor Altgeld widely criticized for pardoning the surviving anarchists?

SECTION 2 REVIEW

1. *What evidence did the prosecution present to tie any defendant to the Haymarket bombing?*
2. *How long did the jury deliberate before reaching a verdict?*
3. *Why did people petition the governor of Illinois to spare the anarchists' lives?*

CHAPTER 24 REVIEW

SUMMARY

Many of the country's largest industries were based in Chicago in the late 1800's. These industries employed large numbers of workers. As a result, Chicago became the center of the eight-hour-workday movement. It was also the center of the anarchist movement.

On May 1, 1886, more than 300,000 workers in Chicago went out on strike in support of the eight-hour-workday movement. Many workers took part in rallies throughout the city.

On May 3, strikers held large rallies. At one rally, about 500 men left the rally to confront strikebreakers. Police officers opened fire and killed 1 striker and seriously hurt 6 others.

On May 4, a meeting of strikers was held at Haymarket Square. As about 200 police officers surged toward the speaker's platform, a bomb was thrown into the police ranks. Nine police officers and workers died, and 130 people were seriously hurt. The bomber was never found.

Rumors of a plot by German Americans to destroy Chicago spread rapidly. Because of these stories and the resulting fear, the police launched a city-wide dragnet hoping to round up as many anarchists as they could. The police arrested about 200 people in raids. Thirty-one people were charged with 4 separate crimes stemming from the bombing. Each was accused of conspiracy to murder a police officer.

Eight men finally went to trial. Each defendant was an admitted anarchist. By the judge's instructions, the state had only to prove that the men on trial were anarchists in order to find them guilty of a capital offense. The men were found guilty and sentenced to death. In the end, four of the men were executed. The Haymarket Affair raises many questions about the American system of justice in the 1880's.

UNDERSTANDING CONCEPTS

1. Why was Chicago the center of the eight-hour-workday movement?
2. What was the subject at labor rallies?
3. Why did the Chicago police launch a city wide dragnet to round up anarchists after the Haymarket bombing?
4. Why did many people from all over the world petition the governor of Illinois to spare the lives of the anarchists?
5. Why was Governor John P. Altgeld criticized for pardoning Fielden, Neebe, and Schwab?

CRITICAL THINKING

1. In May of 1886, more than 30,000 workers went on strike in Chicago in support of the eight-hour-workday movement. Do you think strikes are the best method to bring about change in working conditions? Why or why not?
2. In your opinion, were the Chicago police justified in surging the speaker's platform at the Haymarket meeting? Why or why not?
3. Do you think the police were justified in conducting raids without search warrants to round up the anarchists? Why or why not?
4. Do you think that Judge Joseph E. Gray conducted a fair trial? Give reasons for your answer.
5. What, do you think, did August Spies mean when he said "There will come a time when our silence will be more powerful than the voices you strangle today?"

PROJECTS AND ACTIVITIES

Pretend that you are a striker during the Haymarket Affair. Write a diary containing the events of May 1, 1886–May 4, 1886.

UNIT SIX REVIEW

UNIT SUMMARY

The second half of the nineteenth century saw many changes in the United States. The vast open plains were broken by thousands of miles of railroad. Big business had taken over much of the West's mining, farming, and cattle industries. Farmers in the West found farming the plains difficult. The farmers organized and tried to change the situation. The Indians were confined to small reservations. The final frontier settlement came with the Oklahoma land rushes.

This time period experienced a rapid growth in American industry. This growth changed the United States from an agricultural nation to an industrial nation. Industrial growth led to the introduction of new forms of business organization. Industrial growth affected the lives of most American workers. American workers began to organize labor unions to improve their working conditions.

Millions of new immigrants came to the United States hoping to improve their lives. These immigrants faced many problems in the United States. Living conditions were often poor.

Americá's place among the countries of the world changed. As a result of America's war with Spain, America became a world power.

Many industries employing large numbers of workers were based in Chicago. As a result, Chicago became the center of the eight-hour-workday movement. Workers on strike in support of the movement held many rallies.

YOU SHOULD KNOW

Identify, define, or explain each of the following.

dry farming	corporation
Granger laws	illiteracy rate
Populist party	tenements
exodusters	Jane Addams
laissez-faire	Haymarket Affair

CHECKING FACTS

1. What affect did big mining companies have on mining communities?
2. What was the plains farmers chief complaint in the late 1800's?
3. What was the Greenback party?
4. For what was Mary Elizabeth Lease famous?
5. Who were Gold Bugs?
6. What ended the Plains Indians' way of life?
7. What led to the passing of the Dawes Act in 1887?
8. What is a monopoly?
9. What could be learned at settlement houses?
10. What were workers striking for in Chicago on May 1, 1886?

UNDERSTANDING CONCEPTS

1. How did the railroads affect frontier settlement?
2. How did the use of machinery affect working conditions in the second half of the nineteenth century?
3. Why did the new immigrants and their children place great importance on schooling?
4. How did rapid industrial growth in the late 1800's affect living conditions in the cities?
5. Why was the eight-hour-workday movement centered in Chicago?

CRITICAL THINKING

1. Do you think the United States government was justified in seizing the Oklahoma District from the Creek and Seminole tribes because they had fought for the Confederacy during the Civil War? Give reasons for your answer.
2. The telephone, the electric light bulb, the phonograph, and the movie projector were all inventions in the late 1800's. Which invention do you think was the most important? Why?

3. In the late 1800's people living in rural areas were often unwilling to send tax money from rural areas to help the cities. Do you think the people in the rural areas had an obligation to help the cities? Why or why not?
4. Do you think the defendants in the trial of the Haymarket bombing deserved to be executed? Why or why not?

CHRONOLOGY

Arrange the following events in the order in which they occurred.

a. Dawes act passed
b. Phonograph invented
c. Spanish American War
d. Western frontier closed

CITIZENSHIP IN ACTION

Andrew Carnegie gave away millions of dollars to schools, libraries, and peace societies. Very few citizens, however, can afford to support community programs by giving away large amounts of money. What other ways can people help support community programs?

GEOGRAPHY

1. Name four cities that were major railroad centers in 1890.
2. What railroad passed through New Orleans, Houston, San Antonio, El Paso, Yuma, Los Angeles, and San Francisco?
3. What two railroads connected Helena and Duluth?

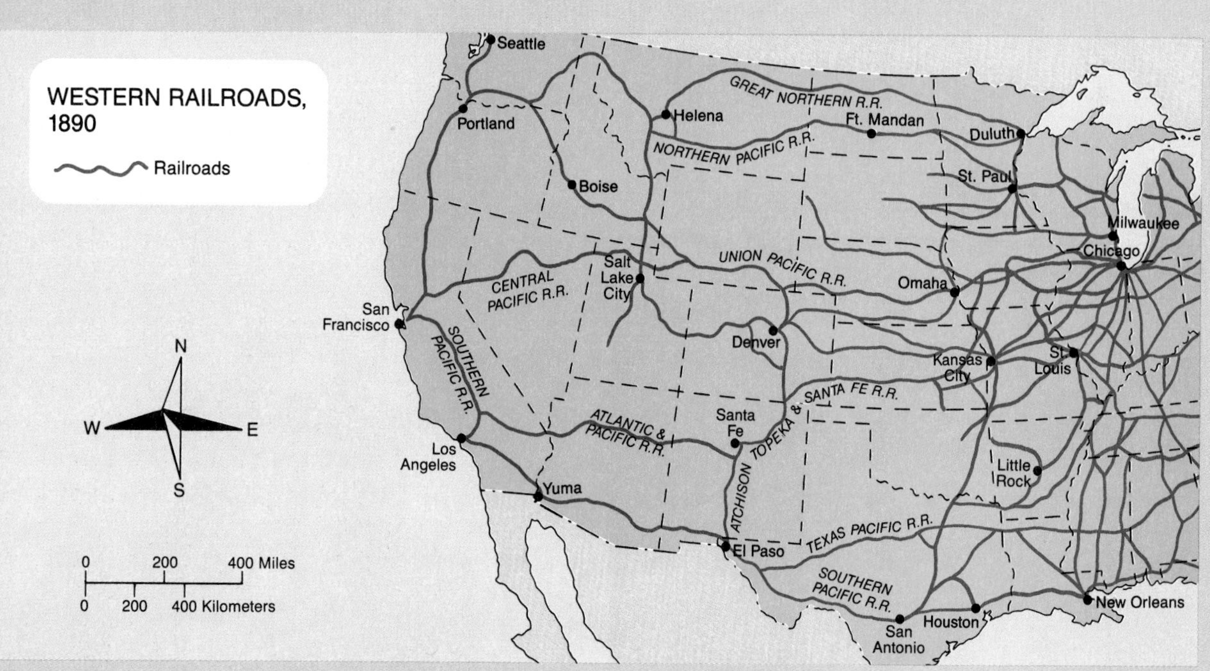

1900 — 1905 — 1910

- 1901 President McKinley assassinated, and Vice-President Theodore Roosevelt became President
- 1902 Coal miners strike in Pennsylvania
- 1905 *The Chicago Defender* started
- 1906 Pure Food and Drug Act passed
- 1908 First Model T Ford made
- 1909 Meat Inspection Act passed
NAACP was formed
- 1912 Woodrow Wilson elected President
- 1913 Federal Reserve Act passed

UNIT SEVEN

A Modern Nation in a New Century

1900 to 1929

Membership in the National Woman Suffrage Association grew from about 17,000 in 1905 to about 2 million by 1917.

This poster of Uncle Sam was widely used to encourage Americans to join the United States Army during World War I.

1915 1920 1925 1930

- 1915 *Lusitania* sunk by German submarine
- 1916 United States forces enter Mexico
- 1917 United States declares war on Germany
- 1918 World War I ended on November 11
- 1919 Women gain the right to vote
  United States rejects the Treaty of Versailles
- 1920 First radio station began broadcasting
- 1925 Scopes tried for teaching evolution
- 1927 Lindbergh crossed the Atlantic Ocean
  First sound-motion picture shown
- 1929 Stock-market crash

CHAPTERS

The United States entered the twentieth century as an industrial power with worldwide interests. When World War I began in 1914, many Americans hoped that their country would remain neutral. However, the country was too involved in world affairs to remain outside the conflict. As a result, the United States entered the war in 1917, and about two million Americans took part in military battles thousands of miles away from their homes.

Industrial growth and development caused many changes in the way Americans lived. Involvement in World War I also had a great effect on the way Americans lived. The war caused many Americans to change their ideas about our country's role in the world. The war also led to many social and economic changes. As a result, the decade after the war was marked with deep contrasts.

Charles Lindbergh is pictured with the plane in which he made the first solo flight across the Atlantic Ocean in 1927.

The Maurice Prendergast water color on paper, "Madison Square, c. 1901," shows the life-styles of the rich in Buffalo, New York.

1900 1910

- 1867 Alaska purchased from Russia
- 1898 Hawaii annexed by the United States
- 1901 President McKinley assassinated and Vice-President Theodore Roosevelt became President
- 1902 Coal miners strike in Pennsylvania
- 1905 *The Chicago Defender* started
- 1906 Pure Food and Drug Act passed
- 1909 Meat Inspection Act passed; NAACP was formed
- 1910 National Urban League formed
- 1911 Triangle Shirtwaist factory fire kills 146
- 1913 Seventeenth Amendment adopted

CHAPTER 25

A New Place in the World

Chapter Objectives

After studying this chapter, you should be able to:

- identify how the United States began to build an empire in the late 1800's;
- explain the changes that occurred in American foreign policy in the late 1800's and the early 1900's;
- list the ways by which some Americans sought to improve life in the United States through reform legislation in the early 1900's.

1 New Interests and Expanding Boundaries

Overview By the late 1800's, many Americans thought that the United States should have colonies. For this reason, the United States began to build an empire in the late 1800's.

Objectives After reading this section, you should be able to:

- explain why imperialism came about in industrialized countries of Europe in the 1800's;
- list the reasons for a growing interest in imperialism in the United States in the late 1800's;
- explain why some people in the United States were against imperialism.

Reasons for Imperialism. During the 1800's many of the powerful countries in Europe gained control of lands in other parts of the world. In this way many European countries built large empires. This buildup of empires was called *imperialism.*

Imperialism came about in the 1800's for several reasons. The rise of industry caused many countries to compete with one another for colonies. Industrialized countries, like England, France, Germany, and Italy, wanted to make sure that they could get the raw materials that were needed by their factories. These countries also needed *markets*—places to sell finished goods.

Often, the raw materials that the industrialized countries needed, such as rubber and tin, were found in lands that were unable to defend themselves against the European powers. The stronger countries did not always trade with these lands. Instead, they sometimes completely took over these parts of the world by force. Many of these lands were made into colonies.

A feeling of *nationalism*—a strong feeling of pride in one's country—was very strong in some countries in the late 1800's. This feeling, or pride, was also a cause of imperialism. Some people wanted their country to expand its power and glory by taking colonies. At this time, many military leaders believed that colonies in different places of the world were needed as naval bases. These bases were needed as *coaling stations*—places where ships could refuel.

Empires also grew out of the belief held by some people who thought that their country's type of government or laws were better than the governments or laws found in other parts of the world. Because of this, they wanted their country to spread their ways of living and governing to other countries. Also, some missionaries wanted to spread their religion to other parts of the world. Thus, some religious groups encouraged their government to set up colonies.

■ *Why did some military leaders want their country to set up colonies?*

A Growing Interest in Overseas Expansion. It was not until the late 1800's that many Americans became interested in taking colonies. This was because the United States was busy settling its own frontier until the 1890's. In the West, Americans found many valuable resources. Thus, they did not have to go overseas to get these materials. But with the closing of the frontier and with the continued growth of industry, many Americans thought it was time to expand to lands across the seas.

By 1890, the United States was rapidly becoming one of the world's leading industrial nations. American factories, like those in Europe, needed raw materials and markets. Because of this, Americans thought it was necessary to control other sources of these materials.

Many farmers also wanted the United States to expand its power overseas. During the late 1800's, the United States became the world's leading exporter of farm products. These exports included grain, livestock, and cotton. But by 1890, many other countries were selling these goods. The American farmers did not want to lose their markets. Therefore, they wanted the government to do something to protect their sales.

With the closing of the frontier, manifest destiny took on a new meaning. Some people began to think that just as the nation had expanded from the Atlantic to the Pacific, it also should expand onto other continents. In addition, many American missionaries wanted the government to help them to spread the Christian faith to other people.

Military leaders also wanted new lands. They said that in order for the United States to be strong, it must have a strong navy. And colonies would be helpful to use as naval bases and coaling stations.

Thus, by the 1890's, many Americans wanted the country to use its power to take colonies. But by this time, England, France, Germany, Italy, Spain, and Russia controlled much of the world. If the United States was to build an empire, it would have to take lands from one or more of these powers.

■ *Why did American farmers want their country to expand overseas?*

The United States Acquires an Empire. By 1900, the United States had an empire. The first distant territory to come under American control was Alaska. The United States purchased Alaska from Russia in 1867. Americans who favored the purchase of Alaska said that the United States had to expand past its borders to be a world power. Some Americans also wanted the United States to take control of the Hawaiian Islands during the 1890's. A group led by American business owners in Hawaii revolted against the Hawaiian queen in 1893 and took control of the government. They then asked Congress to make Hawaii an American colony. These business owners pointed out that Hawaii was important to Americans who traveled to China for trading. They were supported by our military leaders who wanted Hawaii as a naval base. But there was disagreement in Congress where some members did not think it was right for the United States to govern foreign people. For several years the arguments over Hawaii continued, and Hawaii remained independent.

The Hawaiian question had been settled during the Spanish American War that began in 1898. Hawaii was officially annexed by the United States that year. The islands were

The 1897 political cartoon called "The Reluctant Bridegroom," illustrates the growing movement for annexation of Hawaii to the United States. Who is the bride?

The Granger Collection

Historical Pictures Service

What flag flew over this government building in Honolulu when Hawaii was annexed in 1898?

needed as refueling stations for America's Pacific fleet. Other territory in the Pacific was added when Spain was defeated. The peace treaty ending the Spanish American War gave the United States control over Guam and the Philippine Islands. Puerto Rico was given to the United States in the same treaty.

Americans did not agree on what the country should do with the lands taken from Spain. Some people, called *anti-imperialists,* did not want the United States to hold colonies. They felt that the United States should give Guam, Puerto Rico, and the Philippine Islands complete independence. The anti-imperialists thought it would be hard to govern and to protect overseas colonies. They said that the colonies would cause new problems for the country, which, in part, was true.

Some others thought that it would be wrong for the United States to rule over people who were not represented in the Congress. Some other Americans were against making these lands part of the United States for a different reason. They thought that the people in these lands would not adapt to the American way of life. This belief was part of the reason why some Americans did not like immigrants.

However, other Americans wanted the United States to keep control over these lands. There was also a popular belief that the people in Guam, Puerto Rico, and the Philippine Islands could not govern themselves. This belief caused many Americans to feel that it was their duty to accept these lands as colonies. As a result, the United States kept control of these overseas lands. Cuba also remained under American control while it prepared for independence.

What overseas colonies did the United States control in 1900?

SECTION 1 REVIEW

1. *Why did imperialism come about in some European countries in the 1800's?*
2. *Why did Americans become interested in imperialism in the late 1800's?*
3. *Why did some Americans think that the United States should not have colonies?*

2 A New Foreign Policy

Overview After the Spanish American War, the United States had become a major colonial power. This was because American needs and interests changed. This changed the United States' relations with the rest of the world. The United States began to use its power in world affairs because of the ideas of two presidents. Both Theodore Roosevelt and William Howard Taft played major roles in shaping American foreign policy.

Objectives After reading this section, you should be able to:

- discuss the importance of the open-door policy;
- explain why the United States built the Panama Canal;
- analyze President Roosevelt's foreign policy with Latin America.

An Open Door in China. American interest in trade with China began in the late 1700's. This interest increased during the late 1800's. In part, this was because American industry was growing, and factory owners were looking for new places to sell their goods. China had a large population. Therefore many people thought it would be a rich market. Also, American farmers were interested in selling their products to China.

However, during the 1800's, America's trade with China began to decline. To a large extent, this was because England, France, Germany, and Russia had gained control of much of the trade with China. These countries did this by forcing the weak Chinese government to grant them exclusive trade rights in certain areas of China. Then in the late 1800's, some of these countries set up colonies in parts of China. At this point, many Americans began to fear that these European countries would soon control all trade with China.

Following the Spanish American War, many business leaders felt that the United States should increase trade with China. Now that America controlled Guam, the Philippine Islands, and Hawaii, trade with China was more practical and easier. Therefore the government was asked to take a strong stand against the European control of trade with China.

Secretary of State John Hay agreed that the United States should have trading rights in China. Hay, in turn, convinced President McKinley that the United States should act. Therefore, in 1899, Secretary Hay sent notes to the leaders of England, France, Germany, and Russia. His message stated that the United States wanted an *open-door policy* in China. This meant that all countries would have equal rights to trade anywhere in China. When none of the European countries objected, Hay announced that the open-door policy would be followed. However, the open-door policy was threatened just one year later.

In 1900, a group of Chinese, called the Boxers, tried to force all foreign powers out of China. The United States, England, France, Germany, Japan, and Russia sent soldiers to China to oppose the Boxers. But the United States thought that the other countries might try to take over a greater part of China. For this reason, Secretary of State Hay wrote an addition to the open-door policy. The addition stated that the United States would protect free trade in China and all of China's borders. In this way, the United States sought to protect

Many political cartoonists portrayed President Roosevelt's strong foreign policy as an attempt to police the world and to protect American colonial interests. What title does this cartoonist give to President Roosevelt?

The Granger Collection, New York

its interests in a foreign land. And by offering this protection, the United States built good relations with China.

■ *Why did some Americans want an open-door policy in China?*

The Big-Stick Policy. When President McKinley was assassinated in 1901, Theodore Roosevelt, McKinley's Vice-President, became President. President Roosevelt was interested in building the country's power in the world. President Roosevelt also believed that the United States should be firm in dealing with other countries. He said that the country must be prepared to protect its overseas lands and its worldwide trade. Roosevelt was fond of the West African saying, "Speak softly and carry a big stick; you will go far." Roosevelt's firmness in foreign affairs is why many historians refer to his foreign policy as *big-stick* diplomacy.

Theodore Roosevelt had fought in Cuba during the Spanish American War. He had also worked in the Navy Department. Because of his military experience, he knew that American ships must be able to reach distant lands rapidly. But, for American ships to get from the Atlantic Ocean to the Pacific Ocean, they had to go around South America. Obviously, a more direct route was needed. President Roosevelt decided that the United States must build a canal across Central America. He wanted it built across the Isthmus of Panama (see map on page 446). This land was owned by Colombia. In 1903, President Roosevelt offered the Colombian government 10 million dollars and a yearly rental fee in return for the right to build the canal. Colombia refused the offer. Several months later—in November 1903—a revolt against the Colombian government broke out in Panama. This revolt gave President Roosevelt a chance to act.

During the revolt, the United States stopped Colombian ships from reaching the Isthmus. As a result, the revolt succeeded; and Panama became a new, separate country. Immediately, the United States made a treaty with the new government of Panama to build the canal.

Building the canal was only one of President Roosevelt's goals. He also wanted to make sure that it would always be safe for American ships to use the canal. Roosevelt thought that to do this, the United States must guard the peace in Latin America.

At that time, many countries in Latin America had problems. And some of them owed large sums of money to European countries. President Roosevelt did not want any European country to send soldiers to collect this money. To avoid this possibility, President Roosevelt added a new part to the Monroe Doctrine. The president said that if any Latin American country was unable to keep order or to pay its debts, the United States would step in and manage that country's affairs. This is called the *Roosevelt Corollary* to the Monroe Doctrine.

■ *Why did the United States want to build the Panama Canal?*

President Taft and Dollar Diplomacy. By 1908, President Roosevelt had decided not to run for reelection. In his place the Republicans nominated William Howard Taft. Taft had been Secretary of War in Roosevelt's administration.

What were the territorial possessions of the United States in 1900, and where were they located?

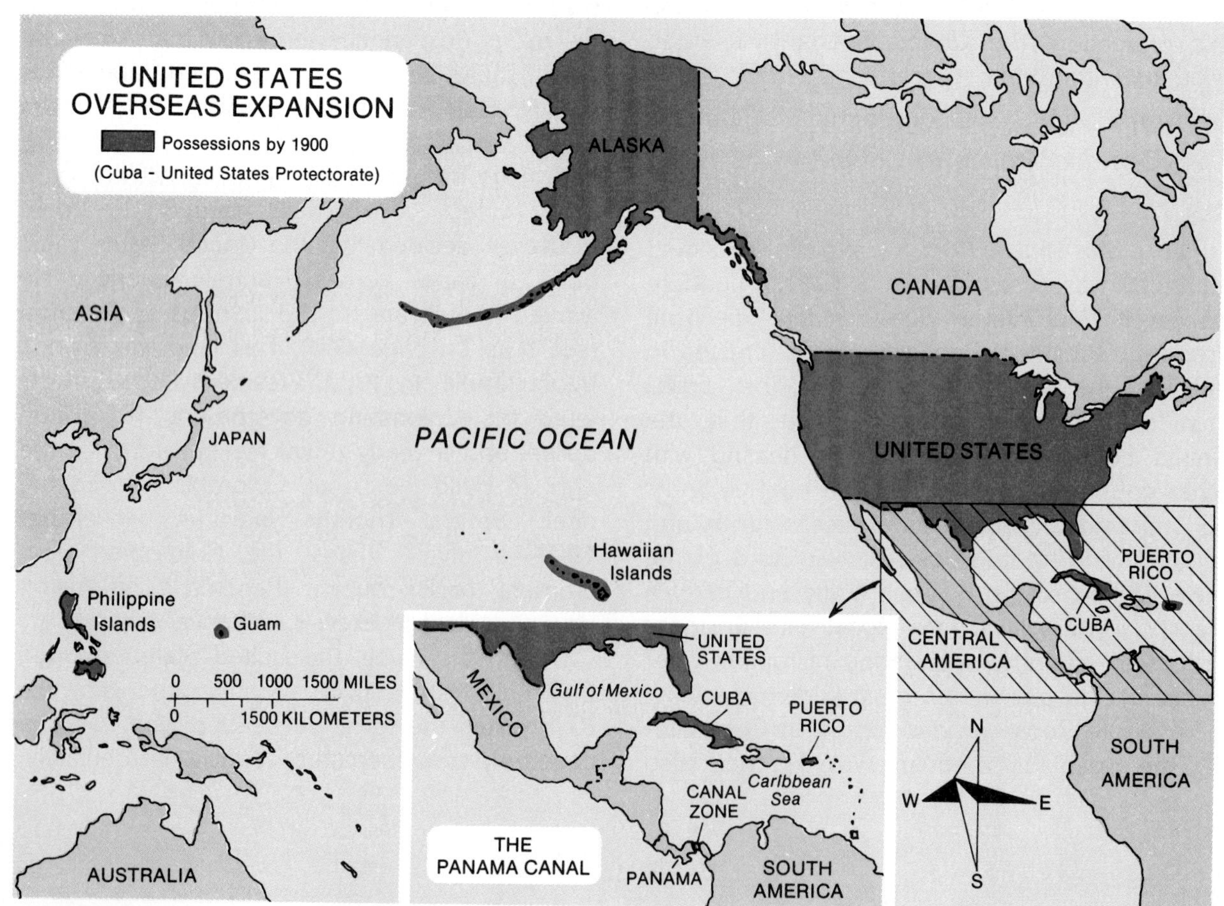

His Democratic opponent in the election was William Jennings Bryan. When the ballots were counted, Taft won the election with 7,675,320 popular votes. Bryan received 6,412,294 votes.

President Taft agreed with Theodore Roosevelt's ideas on maintaining America's strength and role in the world. He also agreed that the United States should protect the Panama Canal. President Taft wanted to make sure that the countries near the Panama Canal remained friendly to the United States.

President Taft also wanted to lessen Europe's power in these countries. However, many Latin American countries still depended on loans from Europe. Because of this, President Taft asked American bankers and business leaders to make loans and investments in Latin America. In this way, American dollars would help these countries. This policy, which was called *dollar diplomacy,* was intended to increase trade and friendly relations between the United States and Latin America.

But there were some problems with dollar diplomacy. Many people in Latin America did not want American businesses in their country. And when the United States sent soldiers to protect American property in Latin America, many people in Latin America came to dislike the United States.

■ *What was the purpose of dollar diplomacy?*

White House Historical Association

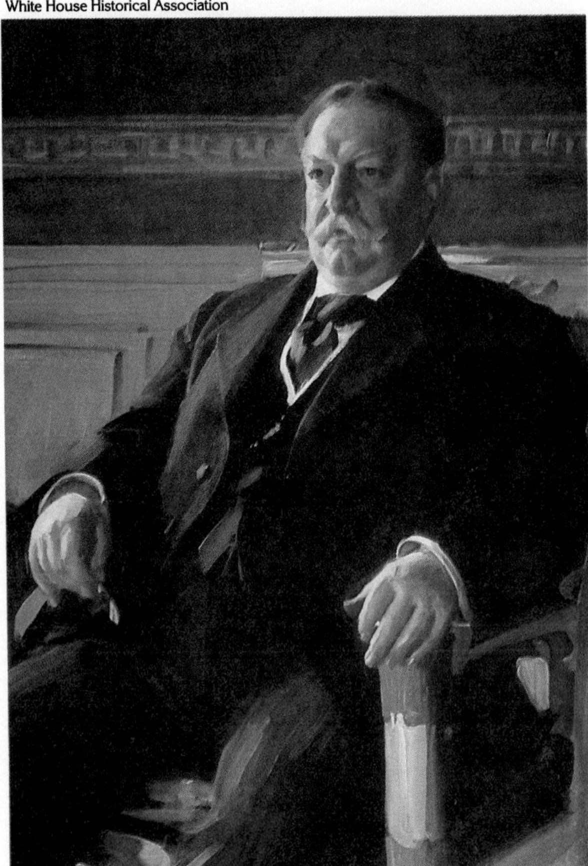

President William Howard Taft had previously served as the civil governor of the Philippines and had been President Roosevelt's Secretary of War.

SECTION 2 REVIEW

1. *What was the purpose of the open-door policy?*
2. *In what way did the outcome of the Spanish American War increase American need for a canal through Central America?*
3. *Why were the Roosevelt Corollary to the Monroe Doctrine and dollar diplomacy developed?*

3 Problems and Progress at Home

Overview By the early 1900's many Americans became more aware of the major problems in our country. Many people wanted to solve these problems in order to improve life in the United States. The people who worked for these changes were called *Progressives*. The first two Presidents of the 1900's agreed with many of the ideas of the Progressives and worked for reforms.

Objectives After reading this section, you should be able to:

- identify social problems that faced American's in the early 1900's;
- list the goals of the Progressives;
- give examples of the reforms that Presidents Roosevelt and Taft supported.

The Need for Reform. The rapid growth of American industries and cities that began in the late 1800's continued in the early 1900's. This growth changed many aspects of American life. Although some of the changes were good for the country, many of the changes also caused problems.

For example, during the late 1800's some business leaders had become very powerful by building monopolies. Some of them used their power to control politicians. Usually these business leaders supported those politicians who would put the interests of big business ahead of the interests of the majority of the people. In part, this was why little legislation was passed in the late 1800's to improve the living and working conditions of the poor in the cities. At that time, many people worked long hours under dangerous conditions for little pay in the factories. The low wages often forced many of the workers to live in crowded city slums. But because the poor had little power in the government, most lawmakers did not work to solve the problems of the poor.

■ *What problems did many American workers face in the late 1800's?*

The Muckrakers. During the late 1800's and early 1900's, some people began to write magazine articles and books about the country's problems. Their goal was to call attention to the poor living and working conditions facing many Americans, particularly in the cities. These writers were called *muckrakers.* The term came from President Roosevelt who compared these writers to "the Man with the Muckrake . . . who could look no way but downward." Some muckrakers wrote about the wrongdoings of business owners and politicians. Others wrote about child labor or about poverty.

Ida M. Tarbell was one of these writers. In 1902 and 1903 she wrote a series of articles that called attention to the unfair practices of the Standard Oil Company. As a result of the articles that exposed unfair business practices, many people began to feel that the government should put some controls on big business.

Lincoln Steffens, another muckraker, wrote articles about dishonest politicians and business leaders in the city governments. His book *The Shame of the Cities* showed that many city governments did not serve the people. However, the most famous book from these years was *The Jungle.* It was written by Upton Sinclair. *The Jungle* was a novel about the

Progressives worked hard to secure the passage of laws to regulate child labor. Before such laws were enacted, small children sometimes worked in various industries for long hours and under dangerous conditions. What conditions did these children work in?

The Bettmann Archive

Chicago stockyards. People who read *The Jungle* were shocked by the description of the dirty, dangerous conditions in the meatpacking business. As a result, many readers demanded that the government set standards for the way food was prepared and packaged.

Because of the muckrakers, Americans learned about the different problems in the country. Soon, a growing number of Americans began to call for needed reforms. The people who worked for these reforms during the early 1900's came to be known as Progressives.

■ *What was the goal of the muckrakers?*

The Progressives. The Progressives were not one unified group of people. Rather, they belonged to different groups that worked for a variety of reforms. Some worked directly to improve conditions in the cities. Others tried to make things better by backing new state laws. Still others worked for national reforms.

The Progressives included many people from the cities. In this way they were different from the *Populists.* The Populists were reformers during the 1880's. Most Populists were farmers who worked to solve the problems that affected farmers.

However, in some ways, the Progressives were similar to the Populists. Both groups believed that better laws could improve life in the United States. And both wanted to give the people more power in the government. Both groups also wanted to lessen the power of big business.

During the late 1800's the Populists had failed to gain many of their goals. In part, this was because they did not have widespread backing throughout the country. However, between 1900 and 1910, the Progressives were more successful. Their cause was helped when Theodore Roosevelt became President.

■ *What ideas did the Progressives share with the Populists?*

DO YOU KNOW?

What popular toy was named for President Theodore Roosevelt?

The teddy bear was named for President Roosevelt. Once when the President was hunting, he refused to shoot a bear cub that crossed his line of fire. After this incident, a political cartoonist began to draw cartoons of the President accompanied by two little bears. A toy maker saw these cartoons and began to make toy bear cubs named Teddy's Bears. The first teddy bears were made in either 1902 or 1903. Since then they have become popular toys in many countries.

Roosevelt the Reformer. Before entering national politics, Theodore Roosevelt had been the governor of New York. He had worked for many different reforms as governor, and he shared many ideas with the Progressives. When Roosevelt became President in 1901, many people hoped that he would continue to support reform ideas.

President Roosevelt did use the power of the federal government to bring about many reforms. For example, during the late 1800's *trusts* had grown very powerful. A trust was a combination of businesses that was formed to create a monopoly. Without competition, a trust could set prices at whatever level it wanted. Many Progressives argued that the owners of these trusts held too much power, which could be misused.

Business trusts had been made illegal by the Sherman Antitrust Law of 1896 but the law was not enforced. Therefore, trusts were allowed to continue. When Roosevelt became President, he agreed that some businesses had too much power, and he decided that some trusts should be broken up. He asked the Attorney General to file suit against the Northern Securities Company. This was a railroad business owned by J. P. Morgan, John Davison Rockefeller, James J. Hill, and E. H. Harriman. Ultimately the government won the case. The court ruled that the Northern Securities Company had to be broken up.

The Progressives were pleased with the outcome in this case. In short, the ruling warned business owners that the federal government planned to watch and to limit the activities of big business.

During his two terms, Roosevelt brought cases against 44 business trusts. In this way, he worked to limit the power of big business. This is also why President Roosevelt became known as a trustbuster.

■ *Why did the Progressives oppose trusts?*

The Coal Strike of 1902. Another goal of the Progressives was to improve life for industrial workers. President Roosevelt also shared this goal. In working toward this goal, he laid the foundations for government involvement in business when the public interest was in danger.

In May 1902, 50,000 coal miners in Pennsylvania went on strike. They asked for more pay and an 8 hour workday. These miners belonged to the United Mine Workers Union. The union leaders wanted to meet with the mine owners to settle the strike, but the mine owners refused.

The strike continued into the fall of 1902. As the weather grew colder, the country needed more coal. President Roosevelt said that it was his duty to see that Americans would have enough coal. Therefore, he wanted the strike to end. In October, Roosevelt asked the mine owners and the union leaders to meet with him in Washington. He thought that they could reach an agreement. The union leaders were willing to meet, but the owners refused. They did not want the miners to have a union.

Instead, the owners asked Roosevelt to call in the army to force the miners back to work. But Roosevelt would not do this. He told the owners that he would have soldiers go into the mines to get the needed coal. Because of Roosevelt's warning, the owners agreed to settle the matter.

Roosevelt's actions in this strike marked a new role of government. It was the first time that a President had entered a labor matter that was not directly stopping federal activities. In the view of many people, he had acted as a friend to labor.

■ *Why did President Roosevelt act to end the coal strike of 1902?*

Roosevelt's Second Term. President Roosevelt was nominated by the Republicans as their candidate in the election of 1904. He won easily over his Democratic opponent, Alton Parker. Roosevelt won 7,628,834 popular votes. The Democratic presidential nominee received 5,084,491 votes.

President Roosevelt continued to back reforms during his second term. He read *The Jungle* by Upton Sinclair. Because of this, Roosevelt wanted the government to set certain standards for businesses that took part in processing food.

Due to President Roosevelt's backing and leadership, Congress passed the Meat Inspection Act and the Pure Food and Drug Act in 1906. With these laws, the government began to inspect and regulate food and drug businesses. These were the first federal laws to protect consumers.

The Progressives also wanted the government to set standards for the operation of railroads. Many people said that the railroad rates were too high. President Roosevelt agreed that some railroads charged unfair rates. Because of this, Roosevelt favored the Hepburn Act, which was passed by Congress in 1906. It gave the government the power to set maximum railroad rates.

Roosevelt also worked to protect the country's natural resources. He tried to show the public that there was a need to save land for forests and parks.

President Theodore Roosevelt was known as a conservationist because he placed millions of acres of forestlands in federal reserves.

White House Historical Association

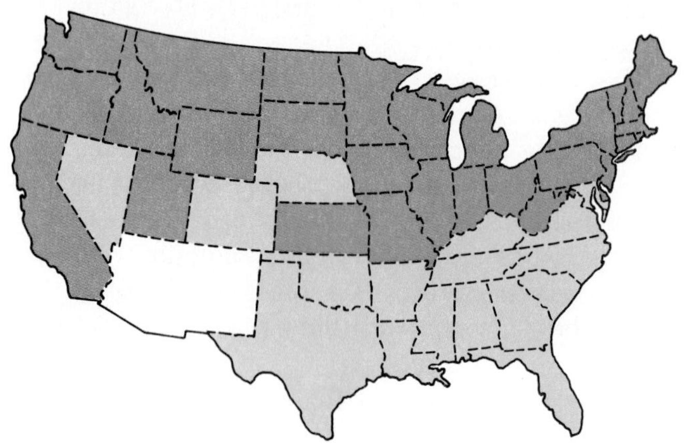

ELECTION OF 1908

	Electoral Votes	Popular Votes
Republican William Howard Taft	321	7,675,320
Democratic William Jennings Bryan	162	6,412,294

President William Howard Taft was elected in 1908 by a margin of more than 1 million popular votes. How many more electoral votes did Taft get than Bryan? 159

Roosevelt did not want to run for office again in 1908. Instead, he recommended that the Republicans nominate William Howard Taft. Roosevelt believed that Taft would follow the programs that he had begun. In 1908, Taft was nominated and elected President.

■ *What were the first federal laws to protect consumers?*

Reforms by Taft. During his time in office, President Taft also worked for reforms. He used the Sherman Antitrust Law to break up trusts. From 1909 to 1912, the government brought suits against 70 companies. Taft also backed a number of other reform measures, among which was the Mann-Elkins Act. When passed, this law gave the federal government more power to regulate railroads and telephone and telegraph companies.

Taft also favored the Sixteenth Amendment to the Constitution. This amendment gave the federal government the power to tax incomes. Many Progressives thought that a tax on income was the fairest way for the government to raise money. The Sixteenth Amendment was ratified while Taft was President.

Even though Taft worked for reforms, some people did not think that he had done enough. Former President Roosevelt also disagreed with some of Taft's decisions. Because of this, many Republicans did not want Taft to run again in 1912. They wanted Roosevelt to be their candidate instead.

■ *What was established by the Sixteenth Amendment?*

SECTION 3 REVIEW

1. *What role did the muckrakers play in the reforms of the early 1900's?*
2. *What were the goals of the Progressives?*
3. *What reforms did President Roosevelt and President Taft support?*

4 The Impact of Progressivism

Overview Between 1900 and 1912, the Progressives supported several political reforms. During this same time, women and blacks continued their struggle for equal rights.

Objectives After reading this section, you should be able to:

- list the political reforms supported by the Progressives;
- identify the problems faced by working women in the early 1900's;
- describe the injustices that blacks encountered between 1900 and 1912.

Political Reforms. Many of the Progressives believed that their state governments did not really serve the majority of the people. To solve this problem, they worked to change their state governments. They hoped to give the people more power over their government at the state level.

One change that the Progressives wanted involved the method of choosing candidates for state office. Until this time, political party leaders selected the people who ran in state elections. Often, the candidates selected were not favored by the people.

The Progressives wanted the states to use the *direct-primary* method. In a direct primary, the voters had a voice in choosing their party's candidates. The person who received the most votes in the primary election became the party's candidate in the election. Wisconsin changed to the direct-primary method in 1905. And by 1913, 13 states had direct-primary laws. With this change, the people gained more power in selecting candidates. As a result, more reform-minded politicians were elected.

Other changes were made to give the people more power over their state governments. Several states passed the *initiative* and the *referendum.* The initiative allowed voters to propose laws. In this way, voters could act if their lawmakers did not pass the laws that the voters wanted. The referendum allowed voters to accept or not accept laws passed by their local government. Between 1900 and 1912, many cities and states also adopted the *recall.* Recall made it possible to vote a person out of office.

More reform laws were passed as the people took a greater part in their government. For example, a number of state legislatures passed laws making employers responsible for accidents that happened to workers on the job. In addition some states started workers' compensation programs. These programs were insurance plans for people hurt at work. Many states also lessened the abuses of child labor. They did this by passing laws that limited the number of hours children could work daily.

The Progressives also worked for other changes. They wanted to change the way people were elected to the United States Senate. According to the Constitution, senators were to be elected by state legislatures. The Progressives wanted senators elected directly by the voters. Thus, they backed the Seventeenth Amendment. This amendment provided that senators be elected by the voters in their states. The Seventeenth Amendment was ratified in 1913.

Why did many Progressives work to change state governments?

FEDERAL PROGRESSIVE LEGISLATION 1900–1912

Date	Name of Law	What It Said
1902	Newlands Reclamation Act	Money from sale of public lands in western states would finance irrigation projects
1903	Elkins Act	Railroads must follow published rates—rebates made illegal
1906	Meat Inspection Act	Forbade interstate shipment of unhealthy animals Meat shipped interstate to be packed under clean conditions
1906	Hepburn Act	Increased power of Interstate Commerce Commission Commission could lower shipping rates upon complaint from a shipper Required railroads to use uniform method of keeping records
1906	Pure Food and Drug Act	Banned use of harmful chemicals in medicine and food shipped interstate Labels must tell contents of drugs
1910	Mann-Elkins Act	Expanded power of Interstate Commerce Commission to include supervision of telephone, telegraph, and cable companies

The work of the Progressives eventually resulted in the passage of numerous federal reform laws during the early 1900's. Which laws regulated the railroads?

Women in the Progressive Years. Between 1900 and 1912, American women carried on their fight for greater rights. By 1912 women had gained the right to vote in several states. However, they still had to face many unfair conditions.

For example, working women usually earned low pay. In particular, during the early 1900's women doing the same work as men were usually paid one half of the men's wage. Many women tried to overcome problems such as this by forming labor unions. But they faced many obstacles. Factory owners usually fired any workers who tried to start or join a union. Also, many existing labor unions were not willing to accept women as members.

Women also worked to inform the public about the terrible working conditions that women faced. Many Progressives tried to get laws passed to protect working women. However, it was not until a tragedy at the Triangle Shirtwaist Company that major actions were taken to improve the situation.

The Triangle Shirtwaist Company was a garment factory in New York City. It was on the upper floors of a large building. Most of its workers were women and children. They worked 59 hours a week. At starting time each day, the owners locked the factory doors. This was done to keep all workers in and to keep union supporters out.

In February 1909, the workers at the Triangle Shirtwaist Company went on strike. One of their demands was safer working conditions. Other garment workers in New York soon joined the strike. By late November 1909, about 20,000 garment workers, most of them women, were on strike.

The strike ended in February 1910. Many of the other garment workers made some gains from the strike. But at the Triangle Shirtwaist Company, conditions remained the same.

Then on March 25, 1911, there was a fire at the factory. The fire escape was weak, and it collapsed when the workers tried to use it. Because the factory doors were locked, many workers were trapped inside. The fire killed 146 people. As a result, the state of New York began a factory-inspection program. The tragedy led the state of New York to pass a set of factory-safety laws. Soon Progressives in other states were able to convince their legislatures of the need for similar laws.

■ *What problems were faced by working women in the early 1900's?*

Black Americans in the Progressive Years. For most black Americans, the years between 1900 and 1912 did not bring improvement. Instead, for many blacks in the South, conditions became worse as they lost the right to vote. This was done through the use of a set of laws known as *Jim Crow* laws. One such law made voters pass literacy tests. This test made it impossible for most blacks to vote, since standards were set so that most blacks would fail the test. Another type of Jim Crow law was the *poll-tax* law. A poll-tax law made people pay a tax before voting. Since most blacks were poor, they could not pay the tax. Some states passed *grandfather laws.* These laws held that people could vote only if their grandfather voted before 1865. This left out most blacks, because few blacks had been allowed to vote before 1865.

Jim Crow laws lessened the black vote greatly. For example, the number of registered black voters in Louisiana was 130,334 in 1896. By 1904, only 1,342 blacks were registered to vote.

Blacks continued to suffer from other injustices. Between 1900 and 1912, for example, there were over 1,000 lynchings in the South.

(Text continues on page 457.)

This political cartoon predicts the success of the women's rights movement. What words are written on the bell?

The Granger Collection

VIEWPOINTS DIFFER

Blacks and Progressivism

Although the Progressive movement brought about some political reforms, civil rights was not among them. In fact, race relations in the 1890s got worse. Booker T. Washington, the nation's most important black leader, outlined a "wait and work" program for blacks. It stressed economic improvement with little emphasis on political or social equality.

The following comments are from a speech Washington gave in Atlanta in 1895:

Our greatest danger is that in the great leap from slavery to freedom we [blacks] may overlook the fact that the masses of us are to live by the productions of our hands, and fail to keep in mind that we shall prosper in proportion as we learn to dignify and glorify common labor and put brains and skill into the common occupations of life.... You [Southern whites] can be sure in the future, as in the past, that you and your families will be surrounded by the most patient, faithful, law-abiding, and unresentful people that the world has seen.... In all things that are purely social we can be as separate as the fingers, yet one as the hand in all things essential to mutual progress.

Not all blacks agreed with Washington's "Atlanta Compromise." One of his most articulate critics was W. E. B. Du Bois, a professor at Atlanta University. The following excerpt is from his book, *The Soul of Black Folks*, published in 1903:

[Washington's] policy has been courageously and insistently advocated for over fifteen years, and has been triumphant for perhaps ten years. As a result of this tender [offer] of the palm branch, what has been the return? In these years there have occurred:

1. The disfranchisement [loss of the right to vote] of the Negro
2. The legal creation of a distinct status of civil inferiority for the Negro
3. The steady withdrawal of aid from institutions for the higher training of the Negro

These movements are not, to be sure, a direct result of Mr. Washington's teachings; but his propaganda has, without a shadow of doubt, helped their speedier accomplishment. The question then comes: Is it possible, and probable, that millions of men can make effective progress in economic lines if they are deprived of political rights...

Think About It

1. In general, what kind of work did Washington suggest for blacks?
2. In Du Bois's view, was Washington's program responsible for blacks losing the vote?
3. Which do you think was more important for blacks in 1900, obtaining civil rights or achieving a higher standard of living? Explain your answer.

And there were several race riots, both in the South and in the North. As a result of these race riots, many blacks were killed or injured, and some blacks lost their homes and other property. However, despite these setbacks, many blacks continued to strive for their rights.

During this time William E. B. Du Bois became a popular black leader. Du Bois thought that blacks should speak out against injustices. He wanted blacks to demand equal rights. Du Bois called a meeting of black leaders in 1905 in Niagara Falls, New York. They began the Niagara Movement—an organization to fight racial discrimination.

Many of the members and backers of the Niagara Movement became part of the National Association for the Advancement of Colored People—the NAACP. The NAACP was formed in 1909. This group was made up of both blacks and whites who shared the goal of racial equality. The members worked to end lynching. They also worked to end the laws that denied equal rights to black Americans.

Another group that was formed to fight racial discrimination was the National Urban League. It was started in 1910. This group worked to improve the working and living conditions of blacks who lived in the cities. Also active at this time were a number of black-owned newspapers that worked to help blacks who lived in the cities. For example, Robert S. Abbott started *The Chicago Defender* in 1905. It is still a powerful voice for the black community today.

■ *What organizations were formed to fight racial discrimination?*

SECTION 4 REVIEW

1. *What political reforms were supported by the Progressives?*
2. *What kinds of problems did working women face in the early 1900's?*
3. *Why were the NAACP and the National Urban League formed?*

CHAPTER 25 SUMMARY

After 1900, the United States began to play a greater role in world affairs. In part this was due to the acquisition of overseas lands. Also, as American industry grew, foreign trade became more important. The need for resources and markets caused Americans to have more interest in other countries.

At the same time, Americans worked to improve life within the country. Between 1900 and 1912, the Progressives backed a variety of reform laws. Some Progressives tried to bring government closer to the people. Some reformers worked to limit the powers of big business.

Many Americans wanted to end the injustices they saw in the country. Different groups tried to solve the problems faced by workers, consumers, women, and blacks. Through these efforts, progress was made toward ending many unfair conditions.

CHAPTER 25 REVIEW

USING YOUR SKILLS

Interpreting a Pictogram

By 1900, the United States was rapidly becoming a major industrial power. The labor force grew as industry expanded. Growing factories needed more workers. The need for workers was met by the large number of immigrants. Not only did the labor force increase, but its makeup also changed because many immigrant women took jobs in factories. The pictogram below gives statistical information on the number of men and women in the working force in 1900 and 1975. Study the pictogram and then answer the following questions:

1. How many workers does each symbol in this pictogram represent?
2. What was the total working force in the United States in 1900? How many of those workers were men? How many were women?
3. In general, how many more women were there in the labor force in 1975 than in 1900?
4. What was the total working force in the United States in 1975?
5. What percentage of the total working force did women represent in 1900? What percentage of the total working force did women represent in 1975?
6. Why do you think the percentage of women in the working force increased so greatly between 1900 and 1975?

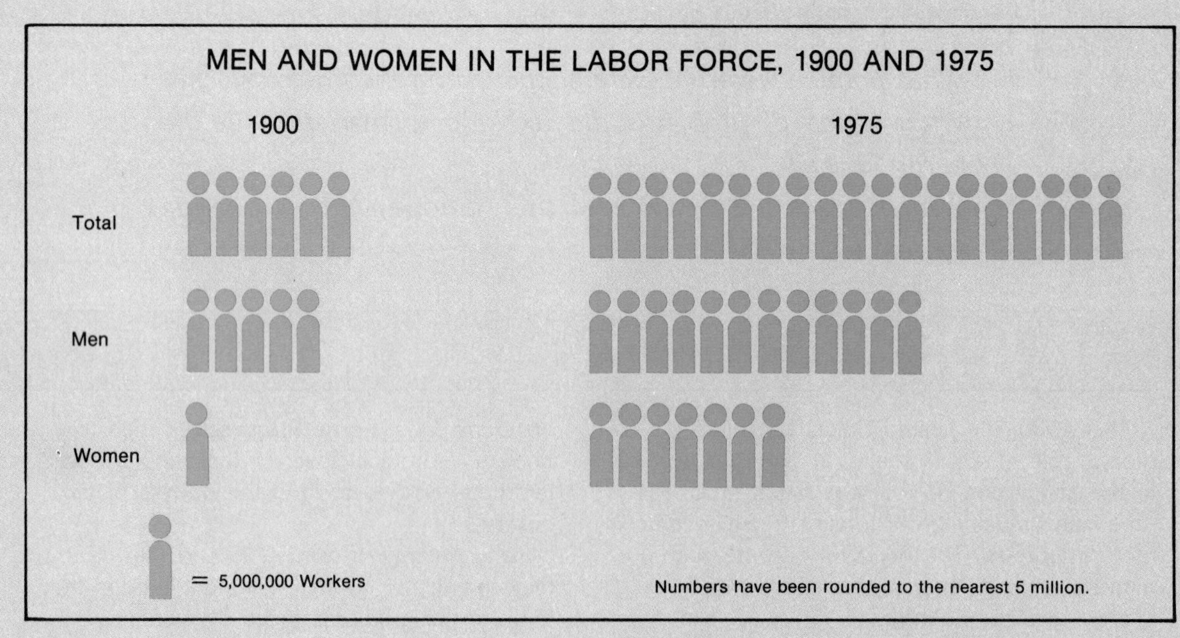

CHAPTER 25 REVIEW

YOU SHOULD KNOW

Identify, define, or explain each of the following:

imperialism	muckrakers
open-door policy	Sixteenth Amendment
dollar diplomacy	direct-primary
Progressives	Jim Crow laws

CHECKING FACTS

1. What colonies did the United States gain as a result of the Spanish American War?
2. Who were anti-imperialists?
3. What did the Boxers in China try to do?
4. What West African saying was Theodore Roosevelt fond of?
5. What was the Roosevelt Corollary to the Monroe Doctrine?
6. What was the goal of the muckrakers?
7. What did President Roosevelt do to end the coal strike of 1902?
8. What were the first federal laws to protect consumers?
9. What change in the Constitution was made by the Seventeenth Amendment?
10. What newspaper was started in 1905 to help blacks who lived in the cities?

UNDERSTANDING CONCEPTS

1. Why did different groups of Americans gain interest in overseas expansion during the late 1900's?
2. How did the United States gain the right to build the Panama Canal?
3. How were the Progressives similar to the Populists?
4. How did the Progressives achieve reforms in their states?

LEARNING FROM ILLUSTRATIONS

1. Study the cartoon on page 445. What do you think the cartoonist was trying to show about President Roosevelt and his foreign policy?
2. Look at the picture on page 449 of children working. What dangers for these children can you find in the picture?

CRITICAL THINKING

1. Some people thought it was wrong for the United States to rule over people who were not represented in the Congress. Do you think these people were right? Give reasons for your answer.
2. An addition to the open-door policy stated that the United States would protect free trade in China and all of China's borders. Do you think this was a good addition to the open-door policy? Why or why not?
3. President Theodore Roosevelt worked to protect the country's natural resources. How do people today work to protect the country's natural resources?

ENRICHMENT ACTIVITIES

1. Read some articles written by popular muckrakers of the early 1900's. Read and discuss articles from current newspapers or magazines that describe wrongs in our society today.
2. Prepare reports about the overseas lands controlled by the United States before 1900. These reports could include information on the history and geography of each area and its relationship to the United States today.

1910 1915 1920

- 1912 Woodrow Wilson elected President
- 1913 Underwood Tariff Act passed; Federal Reserve Act passed
- 1914 Clayton Antitrust Act passed; World War I started in Europe
- 1915 *Lusitania* sunk by German submarine
- 1916 United States forces enter Mexico
- 1917 People of Puerto Rico became American citizens; United States declares war on Germany; Selective Service Act passed
- 1918 World War I ended on November 11
- 1919 United States rejects Treaty of Versailles; Race riots and labor strikes

CHAPTER 26

Challenges at Home and Abroad

Chapter Objectives

After studying this chapter, you should be able to:

- explain how the New Freedom program of President Wilson was designed to bring about reforms in the United States;
- discuss how the United States became involved in World War I;
- identify the changes and problems that affected life in the United States as a result of World War I.

1 Woodrow Wilson's New Freedom

Overview In the presidential election of 1912, a split in the Republican party helped the Democrats elect their candidate—Woodrow Wilson. President Wilson was a reformer. Through his leadership, many laws were passed that were designed to help the country.

During Wilson's years in office, trouble arose in Mexico. American soldiers were sent there to protect American interests. Because of this action, friendly relations between the United States and Mexico was harmed.

Objectives After reading this section, you should be able to:

- identify the cause of the split in the Republican party in the election of 1912;
- analyze the laws that Wilson supported to improve the country;
- explain why American relations with Mexico were strained during Wilson's presidency.

The Election of 1912. Before the election of 1912, there was a split in the Republican party. This came about because of a disagreement between President Taft and former President Theodore Roosevelt. Roosevelt and his Progressive followers felt that President Taft had not backed enough reforms. These Republicans did not want Taft to be their party's candidate in 1912. Instead, they wanted to nominate Roosevelt.

However, at the party's convention, the majority of Republicans backed Taft, and he was selected as the party's candidate. But the Republicans who favored Roosevelt would not support Taft. They left the Republican party and formed a new party—the Progressive party. Former President Roosevelt became their candidate for the presidency.

The Democrats chose Woodrow Wilson—the governor of New Jersey—as their candidate. Governor Wilson was a reformer who favored strong antitrust laws. In his campaign for the presidency, Wilson said that the government should cut down on the power of big business in the country. Wilson called his reform plans the *New Freedom.*

Woodrow Wilson won the election with 6,293,453 votes. The Republican vote was divided between Theodore Roosevelt and William Howard Taft. Roosevelt came in second with 4,119,538 votes. Taft received 3,484,980 votes. Wilson was the first Democrat to be elected President since 1892.

■ *Who were the three major candidates in the election of 1912?*

New Freedom Reforms. Wilson believed that the President should take an active part in shaping the country's laws. On his first day in office, he went before Congress to explain what laws he thought were needed.

One of President Wilson's main goals was to lower the *tariff*—the tax collected on goods from other countries. High tariffs raised the prices that Americans paid for imported goods. This kept cheaper foreign goods from competing with American goods. Wilson believed that the present tariff offered unfair advantages to certain businesses by keeping prices high. Thus, he backed the Underwood Tariff Act, which was passed by Congress in 1913. This law cut tariffs for the first time since the Civil War. It lowered the cost of many goods in America.

White House Historical Association

Woodrow Wilson was an idealistic President who expanded the powers of his office.

President Wilson also worked with Congress to reform the country's banking system. Some Americans felt the New York bankers had too much power over the country's money supply. Business owners in the West and in the South often found it hard to borrow money. Also, some banks were not sound. People often lost money when these banks failed. Therefore, public opinion tended to back President Wilson's plans to correct the weaknesses in our country's banking and money systems.

Following President Wilson's leadership, Congress passed the Federal Reserve Act in 1913. This law set up a new banking system. All national banks were required to join the system. State banks and trust companies could also become members. The country was divided into 12 banking districts. A Federal Reserve Bank was opened in each district. These banks supervised the activities of member banks. They also controlled credit by raising and lowering interest rates. This system helped to make our currency more sound. It also was designed to make it easier for Americans in all parts of the country to borrow money.

Under President Wilson, the federal government took steps to end some unfair business practices. An important step was made when the Clayton Antitrust Act was passed in 1914. This law clearly listed the things that businesses were not allowed to do, such as fix prices. To enforce this law, Congress set up the Federal Trade Commission. This commission investigated business activities to end unfair methods of competition. The Federal Reserve System and the Federal Trade Commission still serve our country today.

President Wilson also backed new laws to meet the special needs of certain Americans. Farmers were helped by the Federal Farm Loan Act. President Wilson also supported a law that set the workday of railroad workers at 8 hours. In the past, some railroad workers had to work 12 hours or more in one day.

The New Freedom also included reforms for America's overseas lands. In 1916, Congress passed a law that gave the Philippine Islands more self-government. And in 1917, the people of Puerto Rico became American citizens.

■ *What is the purpose of the Federal Trade Commission?*

Wilson Faces Foreign Problems. President Wilson wanted the United States to build friendships with the countries of Latin America. However, he found this difficult when conditions in some of these countries threatened American interests. As a result, President Wilson sent American soldiers into Nicaragua, Haiti, and the Dominican Republic. These actions angered many people in Latin America.

From the beginning of his term, President Wilson faced troubled relations with Mexico. Mexico was torn by revolution. There were several leaders who wanted to rule Mexico. Each of these leaders had an army of followers that fought to gain power in the country.

Many Americans were very interested in the outcome of these events in Mexico. This was because over 40,000 Americans lived in Mexico. Also, American businesses had invested about 1 billion dollars in Mexico.

In 1913, General Victoriano Huerta took power in Mexico. Huerta was disliked by many Mexican leaders because he would not back reforms. President Wilson also disliked Huerta. This was because Huerta had used violence to gain his power. As a result, President Wilson refused to recognize Huerta as the rightful leader of Mexico. Instead, President Wilson backed one of Huerta's enemies—Venustiano Carranza. President Wilson helped Carranza by allowing him to buy weapons from the United States. The President hoped that Carranza would be able to defeat Huerta.

Then, in April 1914, the United States was almost drawn into war against Huerta's government. Several American sailors were arrested in Mexico for entering a port that was off limits. They were quickly released. Yet, President Wilson was still angered. He wanted Huerta to apologize by saluting the American flag. When Huerta refused, Wilson ordered the United States navy to take over the Mexican port of Veracruz. Both Huerta and Carranza objected to this use of American troops in their country.

Meanwhile, Huerta's enemies grew stronger and forced him from power. Carranza took over, and President Wilson recognized him as the head of Mexico. But the trouble did not end. Another leader—Pancho Villa—began a revolt against Carranza. Villa believed that Carranza had not done enough to help the poor people of Mexico.

Villa considered the United States to be his

Venustiano Carranza led a successful struggle to bring constitutional government to Mexico.

The Bettmann Archive

Culver Pictures

Francisco "Pancho" Villa (at center) and Emiliano Zapata (to the right of Villa) were popular leaders during the Mexican Revolution. They combined their forces to help overthrow the Huerta government. This picture was taken in Mexico City's National Palace soon after soldiers under Villa and Zapata occupied the Mexican capital in 1914.

enemy because President Wilson supported Carranza. In March 1916, Villa crossed into New Mexico and killed 17 Americans. This caused President Wilson to order American soldiers into Mexico to capture Villa. But Villa could not be easily caught. Many Mexicans favored Villa and helped him to hide from the Americans. Because of this, by April 8, 1916, about 6,000 American soldiers were in Mexico trying to locate and capture Villa.

Although Carranza did not like Villa, he disliked having American troops in Mexico even more. Therefore, he asked President Wilson to withdraw the soldiers from Mexico. For some time, it seemed that the United States and Mexico might go to war over this matter. However, at this same time, America was being drawn into the war in Europe. Faced with the problems in Europe, President Wilson withdrew the American army from Mexico in January 1917.

Why did President Wilson send American troops into Mexico during 1916?

SECTION 1 REVIEW

1. *What caused the split in the Republican party in the election of 1912?*
2. *How did the Federal Reserve Act change banking?*
3. *Why were American relations with Mexico strained during Wilson's presidency?*

2 World War I

Overview In 1914, World War I broke out in Europe. President Wilson planned to keep the United States out of the war. However, as the war continued, the United States moved closer to the Allied side. In 1917, Germany's use of submarines caused the United States to declare war on Germany.

Americans quickly prepared for war. American factories and farms increased production in order to supply more goods. By the spring of 1918, American troops were ready to take part in the fighting. American soldiers played an important part in defeating the German army.

Objectives After reading this section, you should be able to:

- explain why American ties with the Allies became stronger as the war continued;
- discuss why the United States declared war on Germany;
- describe how the United States helped the Allies in World War I.

War Breaks Out in Europe. There were many causes for World War I. Beginning in the late 1800's, relations among the major countries of Europe became more and more strained. Each of these countries wanted to be stronger than its neighbors. These countries also competed for colonies in order to have markets, raw materials, and glory. Fearing one another's growing power, several major European countries prepared men and machines for war.

This competition led to a system of alliances. Countries that formed alliances made certain agreements. In some alliances, if one member became involved in a war, the other members would have to go to its aid. By 1914 there were two major alliances in Europe. Great Britain, France, and Russia formed one group. Germany and Austria-Hungary belonged to another (see chart on this page). Other agreements linked the smaller countries of Europe to these larger groups. Therefore, a war between two countries might involve many countries of Europe.

The incident that brought Europe to war happened on June 28, 1914. A young Serbian student killed the archduke and archduchess of Austria-Hungary. The killer was caught and brought to trial. However, the leaders of Austria-Hungary were not satisfied. They blamed Serbia for the murders. Therefore,

The Triple Entente and the Triple Alliance included countries that had signed agreements, treaties, or military pacts with one another prior to World War I.

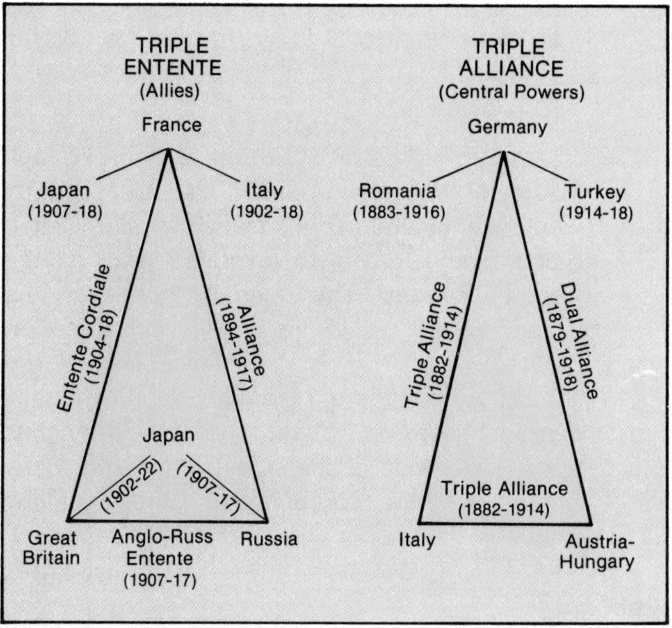

Austria-Hungary declared war on Serbia. Germany honored its promise to Austria-Hungary and entered the war. Russia then came to the defense of Serbia. Within days, most European countries were at war. The countries that backed Germany and Austria-Hungary came to be known as the Central Powers. The other side, known as the Allied powers or Allies, was led by Great Britain, France, and Russia.

Germany had planned for an easy victory. This was because Germany planned to use its strong army to defeat France. To do this, the Germans marched through Belgium and into France in August 1914. They were not stopped until they reached the Marne River. There, the fighting on the western front became a *stalemate*—a standstill. For three years, soldiers fought from 2 facing lines of trenches. Millions of men were killed or wounded in battles that gained only a few feet of land. For example, in 1916, a battle was fought on a 20-mile [32-kilometer] front near Verdun, France. Nearly 1 million men were killed in the fighting. In 10 months the front line had moved less than 4 miles [6.4 kilometers].

■ *What incident in 1914 led to World War I?*

American Neutrality. When war broke out, President Wilson announced that our country would be neutral. This meant that the United States would try not to favor the Allies or the Central Powers. This also meant that the United States would trade with countries on both sides.

Most Americans agreed with the President's decision. However, it was hard for Americans not to favor one of the sides in the war. Many Americans had come from Europe. Many more had family members or friends living in Europe. Overall, however, the United States had more ties with the Allies than with the Central Powers. For example, our ideas about government were similar to those in Britain and in France. The United States had also done more trading with the Allies than with the Central Powers.

As the war continued, American ties with the Allies became stronger, while our ties with the Central Powers became weaker. In part, this was because the Allies used the powerful British navy to blockade the Central Powers. With this blockade, the Allied leaders planned to stop the Central Powers from receiving any goods that could help them in the war. British ships would not allow many American ships to deliver goods to the Central Powers. Although this violated America's rights as a neutral country, President Wilson did not take any steps to end the British action. Therefore, American trade with the Central Powers was cut back. At the same time, the Allies were buying more goods from the United States. Americans were also making large loans to the Allies. In this way, business ties between the United States and the Allies grew stronger.

The Central Powers wanted to end the British blockade. They also wanted to stop the flow of goods to the Allies. The sea power of the Central Powers was based on a new weapon—the submarine. In 1915, Germany declared all the waters around Great Britain to be a war zone. It was announced that German submarines would sink any Allied ships in the zone. Germany warned neutral ships to stay out of these waters. Germany also warned that Americans would be in danger if they traveled on Allied ships.

President Wilson did not like Germany's plan. He knew that it put American lives in

Historical Pictures Service

Germany relied upon submarine warfare to offset Great Britain's powerful surface fleet and to cut Allied supply lines. Later, as the war continued, new naval tactics were developed that reduced the effectiveness of the submarine.

danger. The President also believed that Americans had the right to travel on Allied ships without fearing a submarine attack. Because of this, he said that Germany would be held responsible for any loss of American lives.

On May 7, 1915, there were 128 Americans among the 1,198 people killed when a German submarine sank the *Lusitania.* The *Lusitania* was a British passenger ship. It also carried explosives. However, the Allies denied that there were war materials on board. Americans were shocked that Germany would sink a passenger ship.

President Wilson was angered by this act. However, he still hoped to avoid war. He called for an end to submarine warfare. In reply, Germany agreed to limit its use of submarines.

In 1916, Wilson ran for reelection. In the campaign, the President's backers boasted of Wilson's record of neutrality. They used the slogan "He kept us out of war." The Republican candidate was Supreme Court Justice Charles Evans Hughes. President Wilson won in a close election. He received 9,127,695 popular votes, while candidate Hughes received 8,533,507 votes.

■ *How did Great Britain violate America's rights as a neutral country?*

The United States Enters the War. Even before the 1916 election, President Wilson thought that the country might be drawn into the war. Because of this, he asked Congress to improve our army and navy. The President wanted the country to be prepared to fight if necessary.

In January 1917, Germany announced that its submarines would once again attack all ships in the waters around Great Britain. This would put American lives in danger.

In late February, the United States learned about a message sent from a German leader, Arthur Zimmermann, to Mexico. The message asked Mexico to go to war against the United States. Germany also noted that Mexico might be able to get back the lands that had become Texas, Arizona, and New Mexico.

President Carranza of Mexico refused Germany's offer. The Zimmermann note caused more Americans to want to go to war against Germany. This feeling grew in March 1917 when several American trading ships were sunk by German submarines. Therefore, on April 2, 1917, President Wilson asked Congress to declare war. Congress agreed, and on April 6, 1917, the United States declared war on Germany.

■ *What important announcement did Germany make in January of 1917?*

The Country at War. The United States was immediately able to aid the Allies in several ways. The American navy was used to protect Allied ships from German submarines. Our government helped the Allies with loans. The United States also brought its industrial strength to the Allied side. Factories and farms increased production. The federal government set up the War Industries Board to direct factories in making war goods. The Food Administration was given the power to set food prices and to limit the amount of food sold at home. As a result, our government was able to ship millions of tons of food to the Allies.

To raise an army, Congress passed the Selective Service Act in May 1917. This law gave the federal government the power to draft men into the army. These men had to be trained and outfitted. Because of this, large numbers of American soldiers did not reach France until 1918. By the end of the war, in November 1918, 4 million American men had served in the armed forces. About one-half had been sent overseas.

The war caused a shortage of workers in the United States. Because of this, more women entered the industrial work force. Many black Americans from the South moved to northern cities because of more job openings. Many Mexicans migrated to the United States to take jobs.

The government raised money for the war through taxes and by borrowing from the people. The government borrowed money by selling Liberty bonds. Millions of Americans bought bonds to help the war effort.

To make sure that all Americans backed the war effort, the Committee on Public Information was set up. This group printed millions of booklets to explain why the United States was fighting the war. Congress also passed laws that outlawed disagreement with the war. Under these laws, some people who were against the draft or against the war were put in jail.

Some Americans turned their dislike for the German government into a distrust of German Americans. Anti-German feelings took many forms. Some schools stopped teaching the German language. Libraries took books by German authors off their shelves. And some people would not use German-sounding words. For example, sauerkraut became known as liberty cabbage.

■ *How did the United States raise money for the war?*

American Troops at War. Germany knew that it would take a long time before American soldiers could be sent to France. The German army believed it could defeat the Allies before American soldiers reached the front. Because of this, Germany planned a series of attacks beginning in March 1918.

In part, this plan was possible because Russia had left the war. A revolution forced the Russian *czar*—emperor—to give up his power in early 1917. Later that year, the *Bolshe-*

viks—the Communists—took over the Russian government. The Communist government concluded a peace treaty with Germany in March 1918. With peace on the eastern front, Germany was then able to move more soldiers west to France. By this time, the Allied forces were badly weakened after three years of trench warfare.

However, by early 1918, the United States was prepared to send soldiers overseas. About 85,000 American soldiers arrived in France in March 1918. In April, 120,000 more troops were sent. Thereafter, an average of 200,000 American soldiers arrived in France each month for the next 6 months.

American soldiers poured toward the front to help stop the German attack. In May 1918, American and Allied forces won an important battle at Château-Thierry. This victory ended the German advance.

With the help of American troops, the Allies were able to launch a counterattack against the German army in July 1918. American soldiers attacked the German line at Saint-Mihiel, France. Germany had held this town since 1914. The Americans, however, forced the Germans to retreat. Less than two weeks later, Americans were involved in more fighting. This battle, at Meuse-Argonne, lasted more than six weeks. There were heavy losses on both sides. In the end, the Germans were defeated.

By October 1918, the German army had been beaten by the Allies. The German government asked for an *armistice*—an end to the fighting—in November. On November 11, 1918, the fighting stopped after an armistice was signed.

Photri

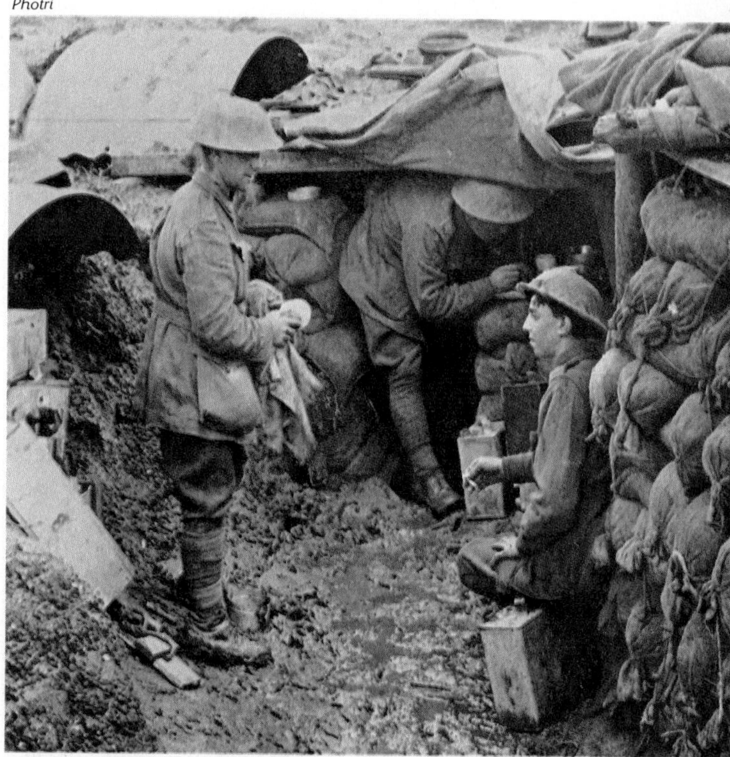

Huge networks of trenches crossed the battlefields of Europe as the war reached a bloody stalemate. What were living conditions like for soldiers in the trenches?

Why was Germany able to transfer troops to the western front in 1917?

SECTION 2 REVIEW

1. *Why did American ties with the Allies become stronger as World War I continued?*
2. *Why did the United States declare war on Germany?*
3. *How did the United States help the Allies in World War I?*

3 The Impact of World War I

Overview After World War I, the Allies wrote the peace terms. The treaty included President Wilson's plans for a league of nations. However, many Americans did not like many parts of the treaty. Because of this, the United States Senate rejected the treaty. Therefore, the United States never joined the League of Nations.

As Americans returned to peacetime, they found that the war had brought about many changes in the United States. Many Americans faced hard times in the years after the war. In some cases, postwar problems caused fear and distrust between different groups of Americans.

Objectives After reading this section, you should be able to:

- evaluate President Wilson's plans for peace;
- explain how the Red Scare affected labor unions;
- discuss how postwar problems in the United States faced black Americans.

The Cost of the War. World War I caused great losses to each country that took part in the fighting. In Europe, large areas of land and much property had been destroyed. More important, however, was the loss of human life. In all, more than 10 million soldiers were killed in World War I. Another 20 million soldiers were wounded. In addition, about 10 million civilians died because of the war. These deaths were caused by fighting or from famine or disease.

After the fighting ended in November 1918, many people were wondering what had caused the war. Many people also wanted to know how future wars could be prevented. President Woodrow Wilson of the United States offered a plan for world peace.

- *About how many soldiers and civilians died as a result of World War I?*

President Wilson's Peace Plans. President Wilson explained his ideas for world peace in January 1918. The President said that when the war was over, the countries of the world should work together to build a lasting peace. The President's guidelines for peace became known as the *Fourteen Points* (see chart on page 471).

The Fourteen Points were designed to improve relations among countries. For example, one point stated that all countries should have freedom of the seas. Other points called for the end to secret treaties and a limit on the size of armies and navies. The President believed that these plans would remove some of the causes of war. In the final point, President

DO YOU KNOW?

Who was the leading American flying ace in World War I?

Eddie Rickenbacker became the leading air ace by shooting down 22 enemy planes and 4 enemy balloons. Before entering the army in 1917, Rickenbacker had become an expert at automobile mechanics and racing. In the army, Rickenbacker became a member, then later the commander, of the leading United States flying groups. Rickenbacker reached the rank of captain and became a national hero through his exploits.

THE FOURTEEN POINTS

1 Agreements between nations should be made public. There should be no secret treaties or alliances.

2 There should be freedom of the seas in wartime and in peacetime.

3 Barriers to free trade between nations should be removed.

4 Nations should reduce the size of their armies to the level needed for domestic safety.

5 Colonial claims should be settled in such a way as to recognize the interests of the colonial population and the interests of the governing nation.

6 Russia should be welcomed as a free nation. Russia should be able to determine its own course of development.

7 Belgium should be a free, sovereign nation.

8 German troops should be removed from French lands. Germany should return the area known as Alsace-Lorraine to the French.

9 The Italian frontiers should be readjusted along the lines of nationality.

10 The people of Austria-Hungary should be allowed to develop self-government.

11 German troops should be removed from Romania, Serbia, and Montenegro. Serbia should be given access to the sea. The Balkan countries should be independent.

12 Turkey should be an independent country. However, people of other nationalities living in Turkey should be allowed their rights. The Dardanelles should be permanently opened as a free passage for ships of all nations.

13 Poland should be an independent country.

14 A general association of nations should be formed under certain agreements. The purpose of this association will be to ensure the independence and the security of "great and small states alike."

According to the Fourteen Points, when should there be freedom of the seas?

Wilson called for an organization of the world's countries to prevent future wars. He believed that this would make it easier for countries to settle their differences and to avoid wars. This organization was later known as the League of Nations.

President Wilson believed that when the peace terms were written at the end of the war, they should be based on his Fourteen Points. He said that the peace treaty must be fair to all nations, including the defeated ones. Many German people had heard of President

Wilson's plans for peace. They expected these ideas to be the basis of the peace settlement. However, the leaders of France, Great Britain, and Italy did not fully agree with President Wilson's ideas. This was because they held different ideas on how war could be prevented. Disagreements among the countries surfaced when these leaders met to work out the peace terms.

■ *What was the purpose of President Wilson's Fourteen Points?*

The Treaty of Versailles. Representatives from the Allied countries met in Versailles, France, in the spring of 1919. They came together to write a peace treaty. President Wilson led the American delegation to the talks. Prime Minister David Lloyd George headed the British group. Premier Georges Clemenceau led the French representatives, and Premier Vittorio Orlando led the Italian delegation. Italy had joined the Allies in 1915.

When the talks began, it soon became clear that the European leaders did not agree with President Wilson's plans. They wanted a peace treaty that would benefit their own country and also one that would punish Germany for starting the war. Their goal was to draw up a treaty that would weaken Germany. They believed that this was the way to ensure future peace.

Foremost in President Wilson's mind was

The Treaty of Versailles changed the map of Europe as new nations were formed. Germany and Russia lost valuable lands. What new and independent nations were formed from the Austro-Hungarian Empire?

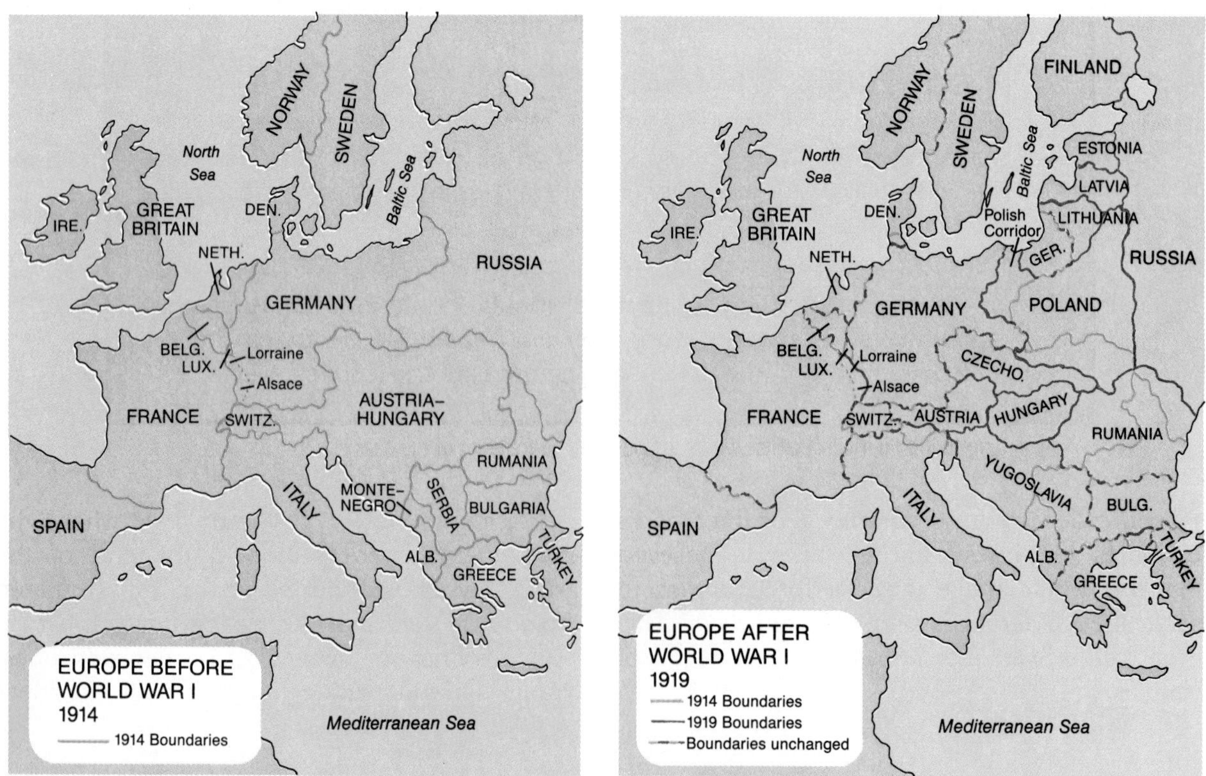

the creation of the League of Nations. To gain support for this goal, Wilson was forced to compromise on other points. As a result, a rather harsh treaty was drawn up. Germany was blamed for the war and was required to pay for damages caused by the war. Also, the treaty changed European boundaries and formed some new nations (see maps on page 472). Through these changes, Germany lost some valuable land and part of its population.

President Wilson thought that the harsh terms of the treaty could cause future problems. However, he believed that these matters could be worked out through the League of Nations.

Every country that signed the treaty agreed to become a member of the League of Nations. But according to our Constitution the Senate must *ratify*—vote to accept—all treaties. Therefore, when the President returned from France in June 1919, he took the treaty to the Senate for its approval.

■ *What were the goals of the European leaders who met to write the treaty after World War I?*

The United States Rejects the Treaty. Many Americans did not like the Treaty of Versailles. Some people did not like the harsh terms that the treaty forced on Germany. However, most of those who disliked the treaty did so because they were opposed to the plan for the League of Nations. Some of these people thought that the league would involve the United States in future European wars. Others said that if the United States joined the league, our country would no longer be free to make its own decisions in foreign affairs. A number of United States senators shared these beliefs.

One group of senators refused to approve the treaty unless changes were made in the plans for the League of Nations. This group was led by Senator Henry Cabot Lodge of Massachusetts. Senator Lodge said that without these changes, the league might pull the United States into a new war.

President Wilson refused to accept any changes in the treaty. He believed that if the people knew more about the league, they would urge their senators to approve the treaty. Therefore, in September 1919, President Wilson began a speaking tour that would take him across the United States. His goal was to go directly to the people to gain public support for the treaty and for the League of Nations. But within a short time, his busy schedule put a strain on his health. In late September, President Wilson became so ill that he was forced to end the tour.

Discussion over the treaty continued in the United States Senate. The Senate voted twice on the treaty. Neither time did the treaty receive enough votes for approval. As a result, the United States did not join the League of Nations. In part, this was because many Americans wanted to turn their attention away from the problems of other countries.

■ *For what reason did Senator Henry Cabot Lodge object to the League of Nations?*

Postwar Problems. When the war in Europe ended, many Americans wanted to return to the way of life they had had before the war. In most cases, however, this was not possible. The war had brought about many great changes in the United States and in the world.

American workers faced some major problems when the war ended. During the war, the great need for goods had enabled workers to earn more money. However, once the war was over, fewer goods were needed. As a result,

Gallery 9

IF YOU WANT
To
FIGHT!
JOIN THE MARINES

During World War I many women contributed to America's war effort. This poster encouraged women to join the marines.

some workers lost their jobs, while other workers had to accept lower pay. At the same time, Americans found that the cost of living was rising. In part, this was because the government had ended its controls on prices when the war ended.

Thousands of soldiers returned home from Europe in 1919. The government did little to help these veterans find new jobs. Many veterans and their families soon faced hard times. In addition, many women lost the jobs that they had held during the war. This caused further hardships for some people.

These problems and others caused many workers to go on strike. In 1919, for example, there were about 3,000 strikes in the United States. More than 4 million workers took part in these strikes. However, most workers made few gains from these strikes.

What one problem did many returning soldiers face after World War I?

The Red Scare. The Red Scare was a fear of communism that swept the United States after World War I. This fear came about because the Communists in Russia had called for workers everywhere to revolt. To many Americans, the labor strikes of 1919 appeared to be the work of Communists. Due to this fear, many people turned against labor unions. This destroyed many of the gains that unions had made in the late 1800's.

The fear that Communists were working against the United States became stronger when several bombings occurred in 1919. In some cases, bombs were set off to destroy property. In other cases, bombs were directed against public officials. Several other bombs were found in the mail by postal workers. And one bomb went off in front of the house of Attorney General A. Mitchell Palmer. This caused many people to think that Communist agents were plotting against the United States.

Attorney General Palmer used his authority to round up those people who he thought might harm the country. In what later became known as Palmer Raids, thousands of men and women were arrested. Most of the people were released after spending a few weeks in jail. There were, however, a number of aliens—immigrants who were not citizens—among the suspects. They were deported to the countries from which they had come.

Some Americans began to think that people

from other countries might cause problems for the United States. This, in turn, caused some people to believe that immigration should be limited or stopped altogether. At the same time, problems grew between different groups of Americans.

■ *What was the Red Scare?*

Problems for Black Americans. In the years after the war, black Americans continued to face injustices. Over 100,000 black Americans were among the troops who had served in France during World War I. The French people had treated them as equals. These black soldiers looked forward to better times when they returned home. However, they found that things had not improved. In some ways, conditions had become worse. Faced with prejudice and discrimination, many blacks were not willing to accept things as they were. Blacks had a new pride in themselves, and they were willing to fight for their rights.

As postwar problems increased, racial problems also increased. Fewer jobs led to job competition between blacks and whites. Housing shortages and discrimination made it difficult for blacks to find a decent place to live. Additional problems arose in 1919 when some black workers were hired to replace striking workers. This led to further distrust between whites and blacks.

Many whites came to resent the advances that blacks had made during the war. Some of these whites joined the new Ku Klux Klan. This secret society had been reorganized in 1915. In the years immediately after the war, the Klan gained strength in the South as well as in the North. Klan members acted not only against blacks but also against Jews, Catholics, and immigrants. Klan members and other whites often used violence in their attacks on blacks. For example, in 1919, 83 blacks were lynched. Ten of these victims were soldiers in

(Text continues on page 477.)

Curt Teich Postcard Collection, Lake County Museum

Although many black Americans worked and fought for their country during World War I, they continued to face social and economic injustice after 1918. The rise of the Ku Klux Klan, with its activities directed against racial and religious minorities, added to the hardships suffered by black Americans after the war. How would you describe the clothes worn by Klan members?

RECALLING THE TIMES

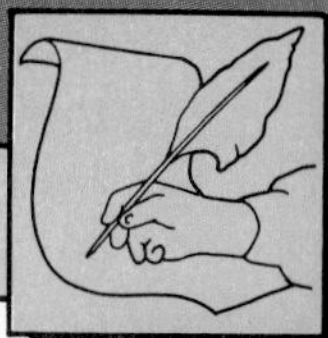

Harlem Hell Fighters

The all-black 369th Infantry Regiment was one of the most highly decorated American units in World War I. Two of its members were the first Americans to receive the French Croix de Guerre for gallantry in action. Later, the entire 369th Infantry Regiment received the award. The 369th Regimental Band had also become famous in Europe. It is credited with introducing jazz music to Europe.

The following is an account by a student who was in the crowd of New Yorkers who welcomed back the 369th Infantry Regiment.

... Even before the troops appeared, the sidewalks were jammed from buildings to curbs with spectators....

... Back from the Rhine to get the applause of their city and of Harlem were the troops known in France as the 369th U.S. Infantry, but known in New York as the Harlem Hell Fighters....

The 369th was marching in a formation unfamiliar to most American troops... Because the 369th had been segregated from the rest of the American forces and had served under the French command, they were marching in the extraordinarily dramatic Phalanx formation of the French Army. Shoulder to shoulder, from curb to curb, they stretched in great massed squares, thirty-five feet wide by thirty-five feet long, of men, helmets, and bayonets. Through the newly erected Victory Arch at 25th Street and Fifth, they tramped far up the Avenue in an endless mass of dark-skinned, grim-faced, heavy-booted veterans of many a French battlefield.

National Archives

Then we heard the music! Somewhere in the line of march was Jim Europe and his band... the fantastic sixty-piece band... beating out those rhythms that could be heard all the way down at our end of the parade. As Major Little said later, on the "17th of February, 1919, New York City knew no color line."

Thinking Critically

Why, do you think, was the 369th segregated from the rest of the American forces?

Do you think the members of the 369th Infantry Regiment were right in looking forward to better times when they returned home? Why or why not?

uniform. In some cases, these attacks on blacks led to riots.

A major riot began in Chicago on July 28, 1919. The trouble began when a black swimmer was attacked by whites on a Lake Michigan beach. The swimmer drowned. Other blacks who saw what happened were angered when the police refused to arrest anyone for the murder. Rumors about the incident quickly spread throughout the city. This sparked street fighting that lasted for 13 days. Mobs of whites entered black neighborhoods and shot at any blacks they saw. Blacks were attacked while traveling between their homes and their jobs. Many blacks responded with violence. In the end, 15 whites and 23 blacks had been killed. About 500 people had been injured. Also, more than 1,000 families, mostly black, had their homes destroyed by the riot.

Between June and December of 1919, there were 25 riots in the United States. Violence against blacks continued into the 1920's. In spite of this, black Americans remained determined to fight for equal rights, and black leaders became more outspoken against racial discrimination.

■ *How did the postwar job shortage cause problems between blacks and whites?*

SECTION 3 REVIEW

1. *What ideas did President Wilson have for the Treaty of Versailles?*
2. *In what way did the Red Scare affect labor unions in the United States?*
3. *Why did tension increase between blacks and whites in the United States after World War I?*

CHAPTER 26 SUMMARY

Woodrow Wilson—a Democrat—won the presidential election of 1912. President Wilson intended to use his office to work for reform laws. His New Freedom program brought many improvements to the United States. However, events in other countries drew his attention from these matters.

The President felt it was necessary to send American troops into Latin America. This action caused many Latin Americans to distrust the United States.

World War I broke out in Europe in 1914. The President and most Americans wanted the United States to stay out of the war. Nevertheless, this became impossible, and in 1917 the United States entered World War I. The war brought about many long-lasting changes in our country. Some of these changes caused problems after the war ended in November 1918. Many Americans, for example, disagreed with President Wilson's ideas for the League of Nations.

CHAPTER 26 REVIEW

USING YOUR SKILLS

Analyzing Primary Sources

An analysis of primary source material—letters, diaries, documents, and firsthand accounts—helps historians learn about people and their times. Below are three letters written to the *Chicago Defender,* a newspaper published by black Americans. These letters were written by blacks in 1917, a time when thousands of blacks moved from the South to the North. Study these letters and answer the questions that follow.

1. Drawing from the first two letters, explain one reason why southern blacks wrote to the *Defender* in 1917.
2. Why did the writer of the first letter want to leave the South?
3. According to the third letter, how did some northern employers encourage blacks to move north?
4. Using these letters as evidence, what would you say about the kinds of job skills that blacks from the South had to offer to northern employers during 1917?
5. Drawing from these letters, explain why southern blacks moved to the North in 1917.

My dear Sir: I have been reading your paper for some time... I have read a few letters in your paper asking for help of securing a position in the North. I am trying to make a man of myself... in the South and owing to prejudice I can't get a start. I am 18 years of age weighs 152 lbs.... I am asking how can I get transportation from here [and if] it can be deducted from [my] salary... I will certainly appreciate any thing you do for me...

Dear Sir: I have learned of the splendid work which you are doing in placing colored men in touch with industrial opportunities. I therefore write you to ask if you have an opening anywhere for me. I am a college graduate and understand Bookkeeping. But I am not above doing hard labor in a foundry or other industrial establishment. Please let me know if you can place me.

Dear Sir:... In reading the Defenders want ad I notice there is lots of work to be had and if I haven't miscomprehended I think I also understand that the transportation is advanced to able bodied working men who... desire work... with the understanding that those who have been advanced transportation [costs]... same will be deducted from their salary after they have begun work....

CHAPTER 26 REVIEW

YOU SHOULD KNOW

Identify, define, or explain each of the following:

New Freedom
Federal Trade Commission
stalemate
armistice
ratify
Ku Klux Klan

CHECKING FACTS

1. Who were the three presidential candidates in the election of 1912?
2. What was the purpose of the Federal Reserve Act?
3. What Mexican leader revolted against Venustiano Carranza?
4. What incident brought Europe to war in 1914?
5. What country was responsible for sinking the *Lusitania*?
6. In what two ways did the American government raise money to pay for World War I?
7. When was the armistice that ended World War I?
8. What was President Wilson's guideline for peace after World War I?
9. What was President Wilson's foremost goal of the peace treaty?
10. What was the Red Scare?

UNDERSTANDING CONCEPTS

1. Why did the United States become involved in Mexico during President Wilson's term of office?
2. Why was it difficult for Americans to remain neutral during World War I?
3. Why did some Americans oppose the Treaty of Versailles?
4. How did postwar problems lead to increased tensions between blacks and whites?

LEARNING FROM ILLUSTRATIONS

1. Look at the picture on page 467. What dangers for the survivors of the torpedoed ship can you find in the picture?
2. Study the maps on page 472. What new countries can you find that were set up in Eastern Europe after World War I under the terms of the Treaty of Versailles?

CRITICAL THINKING

1. President Wilson disliked General Huerta of Mexico because Huerta had used violence to gain his power. As a result, Wilson helped one of Huerta's enemies—Venustiano Carranza—by allowing him to buy weapons from the United States. Do you think that the President of the United States has the right to do that? Give reasons for your answer.
2. To make sure that all Americans backed the war effort, Congress passed laws that outlawed disagreement with the war. Do you think these laws were fair? Why or why not?
3. Review the chart on page 471 of the Fourteen Points. Do you think these points would have helped improve relations among countries? Why or why not?

ENRICHMENT ACTIVITIES

1. Listen to recordings of songs that were popular during World War I. Then, discuss the role of music during wartime.
2. To learn more about the home front during World War I, investigate the work of the Creel Committee on Public Information, the Food administration, and Liberty Loan drives. Make posters showing the work of these groups.

1910 | 1920 | 1930

- 1908 First Model T Ford made
- 1919 Eighteenth Amendment adopted; Nineteenth Amendment adopted
- 1920 First radio station began broadcasting; Warren G. Harding elected President
- 1923 President Harding died and Vice-President Calvin Coolidge became President
- 1925 John Scopes tried for teaching evolution
- 1927 Lindbergh crossed the Atlantic Ocean; First sound-motion picture shown
- 1929 Stock-market crash
- 1932 Amelia Earhart crossed the Atlantic Ocean

CHAPTER 27

Prosperity and Poverty

Chapter Objectives

After studying this chapter, you should be able to:

- list the factors involved in America's economic growth during the 1920's;
- describe how the prosperity of the 1920's affected the way Americans lived;
- identify the relationship between the economic problems of the 1920's and the stock-market crash in 1929.

1 New Industries and New Prosperity

Overview During the 1920's, the country as a whole was richer than it had been in earlier years. Rapidly growing businesses, such as the automobile industry, led to growth in many other businesses. Most Americans felt certain that business would continue to grow. The presidents of the 1920's believed that the government should not interfere with business. They believed that continued business growth would bring lasting prosperity to the United States.

Objectives After reading this section, you should be able to:

- give examples of how the automobile industry changed other American businesses in the 1920's;
- explain why Americans bought stock during the 1920's;
- summarize President Coolidge's ideas about government and business.

The Automobile. The automobile brought about great changes in the United States during the 1920's. Automobiles made it easier for Americans to travel and to learn more about one another. They brought farmers in closer touch with the people who lived in the cities. Workers no longer had to live near their jobs. As a result, suburbs sprang up as more people moved out of the city. However, the automobile's strongest impact during the 1920's was on the economy.

The mass-production methods developed by Henry Ford in his automobile factory became important in many industries. Ford used standard parts and assembly lines to cut the time and cost needed to build cars. Each worker on an assembly line completed one step in building a car. The car moved from worker to worker on a slow-moving belt. This method cut production costs greatly. For example, when Henry Ford made his first Model T Ford in 1908, it sold for \$950. But in 1925, improved production methods made it possible for him to sell Model T Fords for \$290. *Mass production*—making large amounts of the same good—also made it possible for many Americans to purchase items that they might not otherwise have been able to buy.

In 1919 there were 6,771,000 cars in service in the United States. By 1929, there were about 23,121,000 cars. Building and operating these cars required many different goods and services. For example, large quantities of glass, steel, and rubber were needed. Road building created new demands. Thus, the *boom*—sudden growth—of the automobile industry spread to other businesses.

Greater use of the automobile also caused part of the construction boom that happened during the early 1920's. More people were interested in living in the *suburbs*—small communities on the outskirts of large cities. More tourist cabins and resorts were built as Americans began to enjoy automobile travel. Garages and service stations were needed.

The popularity of automobiles also changed the buying habits of many Americans. People no longer limited themselves to buying only what they could pay for in cash. *Installment buying*—paying for something in small sums of money over a set length of time—became more widely used.

■ *What is mass production?*

Electric Power and Radio. The electric light and power industry grew rapidly during the 1920's. In 1920, only 34 percent of all American homes had electric service. By 1930, however, electricity was used in 68 percent of all homes.

As electricity became more available, more Americans bought electrical laborsaving tools for their households. This led to a greater production of refrigerators, vacuum cleaners, toasters, washing machines, and many other electrically powered goods. Electric power was used in factories to produce more goods in a shorter period of time. The use of electricity also gave rise to some important new industries during the 1920's.

The first radio station—KDKA—began broadcasting in Pittsburgh, Pennsylvania, in 1920. One year later about 50,000 Americans owned radios. In 1922, this number had grown to about 600,000. By 1929, about 10 million radios and about 750 radio stations were in operation in the United States alone.

Radio informed, entertained, and helped to bring Americans closer together. It also added to the growth of many other businesses through advertising.

■ *What percent of American homes had electric service in 1920?*

Air Travel. Although airplanes had been used in World War I, it was not until the 1920's that air travel became popular. One pilot—Charles Lindbergh—was most responsible for this new interest. On May 20, 1927, Lindbergh took off from New York in his plane the *Spirit of St. Louis.* When he landed in Paris 33½ hours later, Lindbergh became the first man to fly nonstop across the Atlantic Ocean alone. Lindbergh quickly became a world hero. Five years later, in 1932, Amelia Earhart became the first woman to fly across the Atlantic Ocean alone.

After these famous flights, air travel became more widely used for business and for pleasure. About 6,000 passengers had flown during 1926. In 1930, about 418,000 passengers

Photri

In the early days of broadcasting, radio studios were frequently cluttered with equipment. Despite primitive conditions, radio broadcasts grew in popularity and became sources of news and of entertainment.

The Bettmann Archive

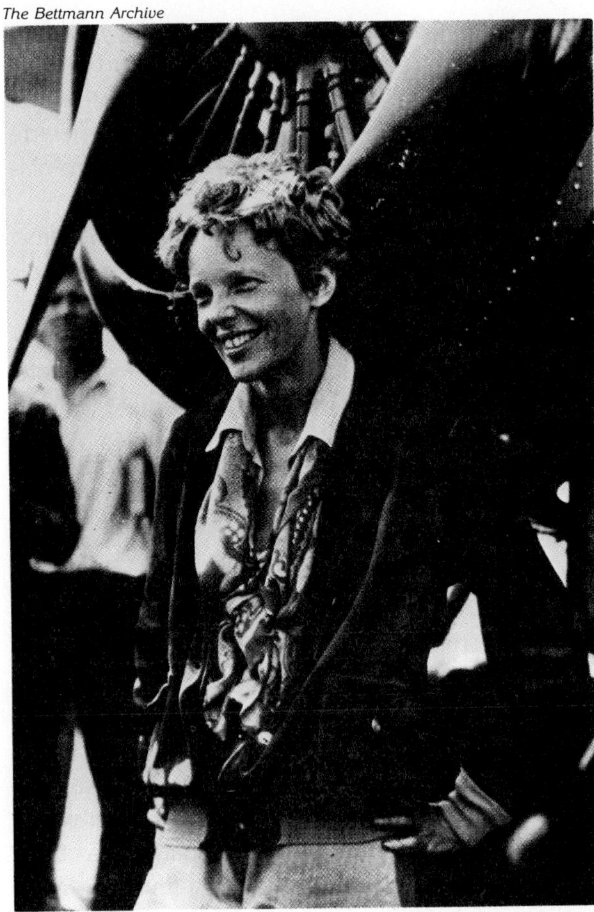

Amelia Earhart disappeared in the southwest Pacific in 1937 while attempting to fly around the world. Her fate has remained a mystery.

used the airlines for business or personal travel. In addition, air-mail service was greatly expanded during the 1920's.

■ *What flight made Charles Lindbergh a hero in 1927?*

Confidence in Business. Improved production methods combined with the growth of new industries helped to make the 1920's prosperous years for many Americans. Wages went up for many workers. Profits climbed for business owners and investors as their companies produced more goods at a cheaper rate in a shorter period of time.

Many workers were able to purchase cars, refrigerators, radios, or other luxury goods during the 1920's. They bought these goods with their savings or through installment buying. They were willing to go into debt to make these purchases because they felt certain that their jobs were secure. They were confident that they could make future payments. Well over a million Americans also used their money to invest in business. The most popular way of investing was by buying *stock*—shares in a company.

During the 1920's, many people used their savings and borrowed money to buy stock. Some people bought stock as a long-term investment. Many others did not expect to own their stock for a long time. They hoped to become rich quickly by selling their stock for a price higher than what they had paid. It became common to hear stories of persons who had become wealthy through the stock market.

The hope of making a fortune drew many people into the stock market. As more Americans wanted to buy stock, stock prices rose at a great rate. These high prices reflected the common feeling that American businesses were sound and would continue to grow.

■ *Why did many people buy stock during the 1920's?*

A Republican Victory. Many voters turned away from the Democratic party in the presidential election of 1920. There were two major reasons for this change. First, many Americans blamed President Wilson for the problems that faced our country during 1919 (see Chapter 26). Second, other Americans would not accept President Wilson's demand that the United States play a leadership role in the world. They felt that the Republican party's candidate, Warren G. Harding, would bring the country back to the simpler ways enjoyed before the war. In a campaign speech, Harding said that the country should return to "normalcy." This appealed to many voters.

The Democrats chose James M. Cox as their presidential candidate in 1920. However, the mood of the day gave the Republicans a sweeping victory. Harding won the election with 16,143,404 votes. Cox received 9,130,328 votes.

What two reasons caused many voters to favor the Republican party in the 1920 election?

Presidents Harding and Coolidge. President Harding was a popular, well-liked President.

This cartoon shows President Calvin Coolidge turning down a third term as President.

The Granger Collection

During his term of office the country pulled out of the business depression that had begun after World War I. However, in many ways, President Harding was a weak leader. He made some poor decisions that scarred his administration.

Some of the men whom President Harding had appointed to high government offices took bribes. One of these officials was Secretary of Interior Albert B. Fall. Secretary Fall secretly leased government-owned oil lands to private companies. One of these oil reserves was in Teapot Dome, Wyoming. A long series of investigations later found that Secretary Fall had accepted large sums of money for granting these leases.

President Harding and the country were just beginning to learn about these wrongdoings when Harding died suddenly in August 1923. Vice-President Calvin Coolidge then became President.

President Coolidge believed that the country's prosperity was made possible because the government did not interfere with business. Because of this, he was against laws that would restrict business. He also favored laws that would help business. To encourage business growth, President Coolidge cut taxes and reduced government spending. He also continued the high tariff.

What kinds of laws did President Coolidge think would keep our nation prosperous?

The Election of 1924. In 1924, President Coolidge received the Republican nomination to run for his own term in office. However, some Republicans would not back Coolidge. They said that he favored business but did not deal with some problems faced by farmers and by workers. Because of this, some Repub-

Brown Brothers

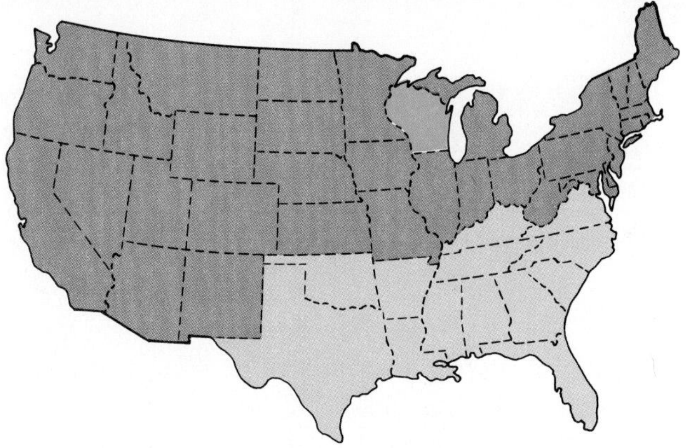

ELECTION OF 1924

	Electoral Votes	Popular Votes
Republican Calvin Coolidge	382	15,718,211
Democratic John W. Davis	136	8,385,283
Progressive Robert M. LaFollette	13	4,831,289

Calvin Coolidge, pictured at the left, opened the baseball season in 1925 by throwing out the first ball. According to the map above, what state did the Progressive party win in the election of 1924?

licans left the party. They then formed a third party, the Progressive party. The Progressives selected Robert La Follette as their candidate. The Democrats chose John W. Davis as their presidential candidate.

The Republicans campaigned by taking credit for the country's prosperity. Most Americans seemed to agree with this and elected Coolidge by a large margin. President Coolidge received 15,718,211 votes, while the Democratic candidate Davis received 8,385,283. La Follette received 4,831,289 votes. This was the highest number of votes ever given to a third-party candidate up to this point in America's history.

■ *Why did some Republicans leave the party in the election of 1924?*

SECTION 1 REVIEW

1. *How did the automobile industry change other American businesses in the 1920's?*
2. *Why did many Americans buy stock during the 1920's?*
3. *Why did President Coolidge lower taxes and reduce government spending?*

2 Culture During the 1920's

Overview The prosperity and industrial growth of the 1920's caused many changes in American life. Many Americans had more free time and more American women took a greater part in activities outside of their homes. Many Americans, particularly those in rural areas, did not like the way the country was changing. They favored a number of laws aimed at bringing the country back to more-traditional ways.

Objectives After reading this section, you should be able to:

- explain how the prosperity of the 1920's changed the way of life of many Americans;
- list the political and social freedoms gained by American women in the 1920's;
- assess the intolerance of many Americans during the 1920's toward people with new or unusual ideas or customs.

Leisure Activities. The prosperity of the 1920's brought more leisure time to many Americans. At the same time, new pastimes were becoming popular. Americans were introduced to sports and to new forms of comedy and music through their radios.

Spectator sports gained thousands of new fans. During the 1920's, baseball became known as the national pastime. Baseball star Babe Ruth became well-known as he set new records for hitting home runs. Talented football players, such as Red Grange, also became popular heroes. Tennis attracted new fans and players. Americans Helen Wills and Bill Tilden became world-famous tennis champions during the 1920's. Prizefighting also drew a large following. Tens of thousands of fans attended boxing matches involving champions Jack Dempsey and Gene Tunney.

Movie stars became popular as the motion-picture industry grew during the 1920's. By 1922, about 40 million people saw a film each week. Throughout the decade the number of movie fans increased greatly each year. Huge, deluxe theaters were built to show the films of such film stars as Rudolph Valentino, Joan Crawford, and Clara Bow. Until 1927, all films

During the 1920's and the 1930's, Helen Wills repeatedly won tennis championships in the United States and in Europe.

The Bettmann Archive

were silent. However, in that year, the first motion picture with sound joined with film—*The Jazz Singer*—was shown. The "talkies" drew even larger audiences, and by 1930, movies drew about 90 million viewers each week.

Listening to music and dancing were also very popular during the 1920's. Two new forms of music—jazz and the blues—swept the country. Both were created by black musicians. Jazz and the blues brought fame to many black Americans. W. C. Handy wrote the "St. Louis Blues"; and musicians such as Louis Armstrong, Duke Ellington, and singer Bessie Smith were among those who developed and played this solely American music.

■ *What two new forms of music were popular during the 1920's?*

New York Historical Society

Fads and Fashions. The fun-seeking mood enjoyed by those who prospered during the 1920's gave rise to many different fads. Some people tried to set records by performing unusual feats. For example, "Shipwreck" Kelly sat high atop a flagpole for days at a time. Throughout the country, dance marathons drew hundreds of participants. Couples would dance for days, even weeks, in the hopes of outlasting all others who entered the dance.

Personal fashions also changed rapidly. The younger generation set new trends in dress. For men, it was stylish to wear baggy trousers, bow ties, and slicked-back hair. Women's fashions also changed. In some ways, these new fashions reflected several changes in women's roles during the 1920's.

■ *What was the challenge of a dance marathon?*

The 1920's were years of great change for Americans. What popular 1920's dance is shown in the picture at the left? In the picture below, the dancer in the center is "*Duke*" Ellington, who later became a famous jazz musician.

The Bettmann Archive

DO YOU KNOW?

Who was the first woman to be elected governor in the United States?

Nellie Tayloe Ross was elected governor of Wyoming in 1924. On the same day, Miriam A. Ferguson was elected governor of Texas. Nellie Ross, however, was inaugurated governor of Wyoming three days before Miriam Ferguson took office in Texas. Nine years later, in 1933, Nellie Tayloe Ross became the first woman director of the United States Mint. She was appointed to this federal office by President Franklin Delano Roosevelt.

Changes for Women. American women gained some political and social freedom during the 1920's. The presidential election of 1920, for example, was the first one in which American women were eligible to vote. This was made possible by the Nineteenth Amendment, which was ratified in 1919. It opened the way for women to take a greater part in American government. In many ways, this expanded political role was based on countless other changes that were happening in women's lives.

Many of the women who took jobs outside the home during World War I continued to work after the war. Women's employment became even greater during the 1920's. In part, this was made possible by a growing independence from housekeeping. Laborsaving devices, such as vacuum cleaners and washing machines, cut the time needed to care for the home. Canned foods and electric refrigerators cut the time needed to shop for foods and to prepare meals.

Women's earnings increased family incomes. This made it possible for more families to enjoy the newly available consumer goods. However, in some other families, women's wages were needed for the family to meet basic expenses. Thus, women worked for many reasons. By 1930, about 25 percent of the work force was made up of women.

■ *What was provided for by the Nineteenth Amendment?*

Prohibition. The movement to end the use of alcohol in the United States began before the Civil War. However, it did not gain widespread support until World War I. Most of those persons who favored *prohibition laws*—laws to end the use of alcohol—believed that drunkenness was the cause of many of our country's problems. Many of those who wanted a national prohibition law lived on farms or in small towns. These people often disliked the way the country was changing. In particular, they disliked the rapid growth of cities. They believed that the cities were centers of immorality where long-standing American values and ways of life were being lost. Many of those who held this view also believed that drinking and visiting saloons were corrupting practices.

Some people favored prohibition during World War I for other reasons. For example, many people believed that grain should not be used to make alcohol when our Allies were depending on our grain shipments for food. For this reason, the federal government took steps to limit the manufacture of alcohol.

Those who were against liquor continued their drive for a constitutional amendment to outlaw its manufacture, sale, or transportation. This goal was met in 1919 when the Eighteenth Amendment—called the prohibition amendment—was added to our Constitution.

(Text continues on page 490.)

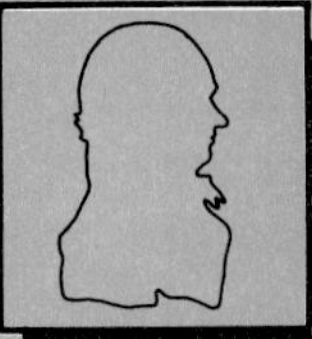

PROFILES

Jane Addams

Jane Addams was the daughter of an 1840's Illinois settler who built a mill, started a bank, formed the "Addams Guards" in the Civil War, and served eight terms as State Senator. Young Jane grew up learning she had a duty to use her ability to serve humanity. She went to college at a time when few men and far fewer women even went to high school. In 1883 at the age of 23 she sailed to Europe to travel and study.

In Europe she was shocked by the poverty of the workers coming to the cities to seek employment. At Toynbee Hall in England she saw wealthy young men and women trying to teach the poor to read and to discuss ideas, so the poor would have the skills to succeed in an industrial society. Jane felt that she could help the poor in urban America. She returned to Chicago to find a house where she could do her work. She was able to acquire Hull House, in 1889 an old Mansion in an area taken over by poor immigrants—Italians, Jews, Irish, Germans, and Black Americans moving out of the South. Jane Addams defined "social work" before there was such an occupation. She taught people to help themselves, and to work together.

University of Illinois at Chicago

Jane Addams fought for pioneer welfare laws, juvenile laws, apartment regulations, women's rights, the eight hour work day, factory inspections, and workman's compensation. In 1908 she was a member of the group that set up the National Association for the Advancement of Colored People. In 1931 she won the Nobel Peace Prize. Her books and articles taught millions that one person can make a difference.

Thinking Critically

In your opinion, would Jane Addam's father have taught her that success in America depended on luck, or effort?

Jane Addam's horrified "Society" by moving into the slums to work with "those people." But she made helping fashionable. Can individuals still make a difference? Defend your opinion.

What stereotypes might hinder anyone who believes in reforming society, today or in Jane Addam's time?

Congress then passed the Volstead Act. This law gave the Bureau of Internal Revenue power to enforce the amendment.

However, many Americans were against the prohibition amendment and were not willing to obey it. They felt that the government did not have the right to tell them that they were not allowed to drink alcohol. *Bootlegging*—smuggling liquor—became a money-making business. Because of this, *gangsters*—people involved in organized crime—took over the liquor trade in some cities. Sometimes gangs fought one another for power over the bootleg business in a city. At times, gangs carried out these wars on city streets.

Many Americans broke the prohibition law. Some people made liquor at home, and others visited *speakeasies*—places where liquor was sold. Therefore, this law did not bring the reforms its backers had expected. Instead, it led to more crime.

■ *What was the Volstead Act?*

Immigration Restriction. Some Americans who disliked the way our country was changing during the 1920's blamed the immigrants for causing these changes. For years, some Americans had thought that the United States should put limits on immigration. Several reasons caused this idea to gain more support during the 1920's.

A number of union leaders believed that continued open immigration would cause problems for American workers. These leaders wanted immigration to be limited to prevent unemployment or lower wages. Other Americans said that immigrants from certain countries were not easily "Americanized." Some people argued that foreigners had political ideas that were dangerous to our form of government.

These arguments led Congress to pass laws that restricted immigration. These laws set the number of persons that would be allowed to move to the United States from each foreign country. Newcomers from Great Britain, Ireland, and Germany were favored. This was done by allowing large numbers of people from these countries to come to the United States. However, immigrants from eastern and southern European countries were less favored by these laws. These laws also reflected a discrimination against Asians by completely barring immigration from Asia.

■ *Why did some labor leaders want the government to limit immigration?*

Intolerance and the Courts. Two famous court cases of the 1920's show that some Americans had become intolerant toward those persons who held unpopular views. Also, the reaction to these cases shows that other Americans would not accept the limits of this intolerance. One case was the trial of Bartolomeo Vanzetti and Nicola Sacco, two Italian immigrants. They were charged with the murder of a payroll guard in a robbery attempt. The evidence that tied them to the murder was very weak. However, Sacco and Vanzetti held radical ideas about government. They were anarchists—they believed that people should overthrow the government and live without laws. Both men had refused to serve in World War I because they did not agree with its aims.

Even though the case against them was weak, Sacco and Vanzetti were found guilty. However, their case received national and worldwide attention. Many people protested the court's decision. They felt that Sacco and Vanzetti had been convicted because they were immigrants and because of their political

The trial of John Scopes for violating a state law by teaching about evolution aroused the nation. Scopes was brilliantly defended by Clarence Darrow, shown leaning on the table. How would you describe the atmosphere in this courtroom?

The Bettmann Archive

views. Nevertheless, they were executed for the crime.

The other case involved a conflict between scientific theories and religious teachings. During the 1920's, some Americans believed that our country was becoming an evil place because religion was becoming less important. Therefore, they favored laws that would stop this trend. One such law was passed in Tennessee. It forbade public-school teachers to teach about the *theory of evolution*—the idea that humans developed from lower forms of life. Teaching about evolution was outlawed because it went against the story of creation told in the Bible.

At the same time, however, other Americans disagreed. Many of them did not think that religion should be allowed to limit education. Among this group was John Scopes, a biology teacher in Tennessee. Scopes deliberately broke the law by teaching his class about evolution. He did this to test the law by bringing the country's attention to the issue. In his trial, Scopes was defended by Clarence Darrow, a famous lawyer. The prosecution was led by former presidential candidate William Jennings Bryan. The case became one of the most popular news stories of 1925. Many Americans saw the trial as a contest between the forces of tradition and the forces of progress. In the end, Scopes lost the case and was fined for breaking the law. The Tennessee law remained on the books. However, the case had made it clear that the country was changing. Some Americans welcomed the changes, while others wanted to carry on in more-traditional ways.

■ *What law did John Scopes violate?*

SECTION 2 REVIEW

1. *How did the prosperity of the 1920's change the way of life of many Americans?*
2. *Why were women freer to take jobs during the 1920's than ever before?*
3. *What laws passed during the 1920's reveal an intolerance toward people with new or unusual ideas or customs?*

3 An Uneven Prosperity

Overview Not all Americans shared in the prosperity of the 1920's. Many farmers faced hard times. Workers in some industries faced problems as these businesses became troubled. Workers in other industries also faced rising unemployment as new machines were brought into factories.

At the same time, a small group of Americans were making large profits from their business investments. This encouraged further investments. Because of this, stock prices rose. However, businesses found that they were turning out more goods than Americans could buy. In 1929, these problems reached Wall Street, where stock prices crashed.

Objectives After reading this section, you should be able to:

- explain why some industries experienced problems during the 1920's;
- analyze the affect of installment buying on the production of goods during the 1920's;
- identify the causes of the stock-market crash on October 29, 1929.

The Nonpartisan Leader

NATIONAL EDITION MAY 30, 1921

The Granger Collection

Industries boomed during the 1920's; but farmers did not share in this prosperity, as the price of farm products declined.

Farm Problems. Unlike many other Americans, farmers did not enjoy prosperity during the 1920's. During World War I, there had been a large demand for farm products. This caused prices of farm products to go up. These higher prices led many farmers to increase their production. To do this, many farmers hired more workers and bought extra land and new equipment. Farmers often took out loans to make these purchases.

However, the demand for farm products went down after the war. In part, this happened because American exports were no longer needed by other countries. Yet, at the same time, new machines increased farm production. As a result, supply went up while demand dropped. Thus, crop prices fell sharply in 1920. At the same time, the prices of manufactured goods needed by farmers were rising. Soon, it became difficult for farmers to pay off their debts. When they could not meet their loan or mortgage payments, farmers lost their farms.

During the 1920's, farmers looked to the federal government for help. President Coolidge, however, did not think the federal government should aid the farmers. Because of this belief, more farmers found it increasingly difficult to make a living.

■ *Why did the demand for American farm products drop after World War I?*

Other Troubled Industries. In addition to agriculture, a number of other American industries faced major problems during the 1920's. In some cases, business problems in one industry affected whole communities. Thus, during the 1920's, some American towns and regions were depressed—experiencing a period of lowered trade, production, employment, and income.

The coal industry, for example, suffered heavily during the 1920's. High wartime demand for coal had led to the opening of many new mines. At the same time, more-efficient equipment was developed. Therefore, larger amounts of coal were produced. However, the need for coal dropped greatly during the 1920's. In part, the lesser need for coal was caused by the rising use of other fuels, such as oil, natural gas, and electricity.

Greater coal production combined with the lesser demand led to *overproduction*—making more goods than could be used. This caused the price of coal to go down. In 1920, for example, the price of coal to railways had been $4.20 a ton. By 1929, the railways were paying only $2.40 a ton.

As coal prices fell, mineowners began to cut their costs. Thousands of workers were laid off from their jobs. Other workers had to accept wage cuts in order to keep their jobs. The eight-hour workday and some safety requirements that miners had gained in earlier years were also lost as operating budgets were cut. Hundreds of towns, dependent on local coal mines as their main industry, fell into poverty.

The cotton-textile industry experienced similar overproduction problems during the 1920's. Due to lowered sales, thousands of textile-mill workers faced hard times. Many towns in the South and in New England had been built around textile mills. When these mills faced poor business conditions, these towns faced poverty.

■ *Why did the demand for coal drop during the 1920's?*

Productivity and Profits. A large part of the prosperity of the 1920's was due to increased *productivity*—the ability to turn out more goods. In many cases, this was made possible through the use of new machines. These machines often replaced workers and cut production time. Factories were able to turn out more goods at lower costs in shorter periods of time. This brought about an increase in business profits.

Business profits also became greater because taxes were lowered during the 1920's. Because high profits were being made, some Americans increased their investments in business through the purchase of stocks and bonds. These investments helped businesses to grow and to increase productivity further. In this way, even more goods were made.

Low taxes and increased productivity brought high returns to business investors. These high gains, however, were made by a very small group of people. This small group was becoming much wealthier than most other Americans. By 1929 the richest 5 percent of all American families received about 30 percent of all income. Furthermore, over one half of the income in 1929 went to only 20 percent of the people.

■ *What were two causes of increased business profits during the 1920's?*

Wage Earners During the 1920's. Wages, in general, also went up during the 1920's. However, workers' earnings usually did not rise at the same rate as did production and profits. This meant that factories were soon turning out more goods than workers could afford to buy. However, this overproduction was not immediately obvious. This was because many workers were buying goods on the installment plan. Overproduction became more apparent after 1925 when many workers began to cut their spending to hold down their debts.

At the same time, a growing number of Americans had little or no buying power. This included farmers and workers in troubled industries such as textiles. This also included workers who lost their jobs when new machines were brought into factories. These people were unable to buy on credit. As a result, the number of Americans who could afford to buy houses, automobiles, and furniture became smaller.

■ *Why was it not immediately apparent that many American manufacturers were overproducing during the 1920's?*

Warning Signs. In addition to the problems facing farmers, miners, and textile workers, other problems arose. By the mid-1920's, there were signs that several other industries had reached their peak.

By the mid-1920's the demand for new housing had fallen. Since construction was one of the businesses that had caused the boom of the early 1920's, cutbacks in this field also affected many other businesses. Car sales also fell sharply in 1926. And although the automobile business improved in the following year, it never again grew at the rate of the early 1920's. Therefore, automobile makers cut back their purchases of materials. This, in turn, meant that there would be less business for those who made steel, glass, rubber, and other goods.

By 1928 a growing number of manufacturers found that they were left with surpluses—goods not sold. These surpluses, in most cases, could not be exported. In part, this was because of our high tariff. The high tariff made it difficult for foreign countries to sell their goods in the United States. Thus, they did not have American dollars to use to buy our products. In addition, some countries had reacted to our tariff by imposing high taxes on American goods.

Despite these declines in sales, Americans, in general, remained confident that our economy was healthy. They continued to invest money in the stock market. These investors believed that business was sound and that profits would keep on rising.

■ *What two important industries experienced lowered demand by the mid-1920's?*

The Election of 1928. In August 1927, President Coolidge announced that he would not run for office again. Nevertheless, the Republican party seemed certain to win the election. The Republicans claimed credit for the peace and prosperity enjoyed by Americans since 1920.

The Republicans chose Herbert C. Hoover as their candidate in the election of 1928. Hoover was already known to many Americans. He had been in charge of the food relief

program in Europe during and after World War I. He had also served as Secretary of Commerce under President Harding and President Coolidge.

At the same time, the Democratic party was weakened by a split in its ranks. In part, this was because the Democratic party included a wide range of Americans with many different interests. For example, many working-class people from the northern cities belonged to the Democratic party. Often, they favored laws that were opposed by the Democrats from the more rural South.

Governor Alfred E. Smith of New York won the Democratic party's nomination for President in 1928. In many ways, however, Governor Smith represented only one part of the party. He was a Roman Catholic from New York City. There was opposition to Smith from those Americans who distrusted Catholics and people from big cities. Furthermore, Smith was against prohibition. This stand also cost him votes.

Hoover won the election easily. Hoover received 21,391,993 votes. Smith received 15,016,169. It was the third straight presidential election won by the Republican party.

President and Mrs. Hoover traveled around the country on a whistle-stop tour during the election campaign of 1928. According to the map below, how would you describe Hoover's victory over Democrat Alfred E. Smith?

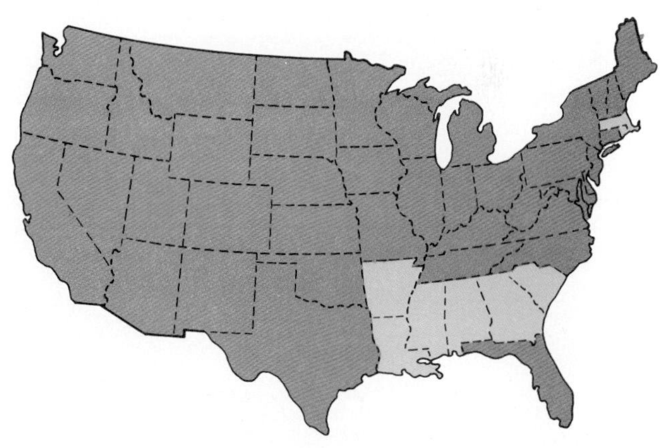

ELECTION OF 1928

	Electoral Votes	Popular Votes
Republican Herbert C. Hoover	444	21,391,993
Democratic Alfred E. Smith	87	15,016,169

However, Smith did receive a great number of votes in the large cities. This seemed to show that the Democrats might find their future support in the rapidly growing cities.

■ *What three characteristics of candidate Alfred E. Smith were disliked by some voters?*

The Stock-Market Crash. In the first few months of President Hoover's term, American prosperity seemed unlimited. However, within nine months after the inauguration, stock prices crashed. Throughout the 1920's, stock prices had climbed upward. This trend continued even after production cutbacks in key industries. After President Hoover's election, stock prices reached new heights. Much of the leap was caused by *speculators*—investors willing to take a high risk with the hope of making large profits. Most speculators bought their stock on *margin*—borrowing money from a bank to pay for the stock. With stock prices rising, speculators were able to hold their stock for a short time before selling it at a price higher than what they paid. Thus, the speculators could repay the bank loan and still be left with a profit.

While speculators were driving stock prices upward, profits in some industries were dropping. More and more Americans were buying fewer new homes and consumer goods than they had bought in the early 1920's. As sales fell, manufacturers cut production. They were forced to lay off some workers. Thus, rising

Wall Street in New York City was the scene of great confusion during the last week of October 1929, as crowds of people reacted to the dramatic collapse of prices on the stock market.

The Bettmann Archive

stock prices did not reflect the real business situation. In fact, many investors were buying shares in worthless companies.

In September 1929, stock prices began to fall. Some stock prices recovered, but toward the end of October, prices again dropped. This time they dropped drastically. Wall Street, the home of the New York Stock Exchange, became the scene of growing confusion. A group of the country's most powerful bankers tried to stop the prices from falling. However, their investments only delayed the crash. Stock prices dropped further each day.

On October 29, 1929, the stock market crashed. Many investors who had bought their stock on margin rushed to sell their stock. As more and more stockholders tried to sell, prices were driven down. About 16 million shares of stock were sold that day. Thousands of men and women lost everything they owned within a matter of hours. They could not pay back the money they had borrowed to buy stocks. Banks had also invested in the stock market. Falling stock prices caused these investments to lose value. As a result, banks started to close. Hard times spread as more banks and businesses failed. Within a few years, the country had entered a full-scale depression.

■ *How did most speculators obtain money to buy stocks?*

SECTION 3 REVIEW

1. *Why did the coal industry suffer heavily during the 1920's?*
2. *Why were manufacturers unaware, at first, that they were overproducing?*
3. *Why did the high level of stock prices continue even after some industries had faced lowered profits and production cutbacks?*

CHAPTER 27 SUMMARY

For many Americans, the 1920's were a time of prosperity. Much of this wealth was caused by the growth of new industries. These businesses also caused other changes.

During the 1920's, many Americans began to spend more time and money on entertainment. However, at the same time, some other Americans were in a more serious mood. These Americans felt that important parts of American life were being threatened. This concern led some Americans to work for laws that would preserve established traditions.

In the 1920's business growth was uneven. Some Americans faced hard times, while others made large fortunes. However, the economy was not sound. By the late 1920's, many businesses were making more goods than Americans could afford to buy. The problem of overproduction faced by a few industries in earlier years soon spread to other industries. Stock prices began to fall. Then, in October 1929, the stock market crashed. Business failures increased, and the nation slipped into a full-scale depression.

CHAPTER 27 REVIEW

USING YOUR SKILLS

Interpreting Circle Graphs

The Immigration Act of 1924 was passed to limit the number of persons who could immigrate to the United States from each country outside of the western hemisphere. These limits were made through a quota system. Quotas for each country were based on the number of persons of that national origin who were living in the United States in 1890. By using 1890 as the base year, the law discriminated against nationalities that had not immigrated to the United States in large numbers until after 1890. For example, the quota for immigrants from Ireland was set at 28,567, while the quota for Greece was only 100. The circle graphs below illustrate how immigration to the United States changed under the new law. Study the graphs and then answer the following questions:

1. How many fewer immigrants came to the United States in 1925 than in 1924?
2. What percentage of all immigrants to the United States came from northern and northwestern Europe in 1924 and in 1925?
3. What percentage of all immigrants to the United States came from southern and eastern Europe in 1924 and in 1925?
4. From what world area did the smallest percentage of immigrants arrive in both 1924 and 1925?
5. The percentage of immigrants arriving from which areas dropped by more than half between 1924 and 1925?
6. Drawing information from these two graphs, describe five changes that occurred in immigration to the United States between 1924 and 1925.

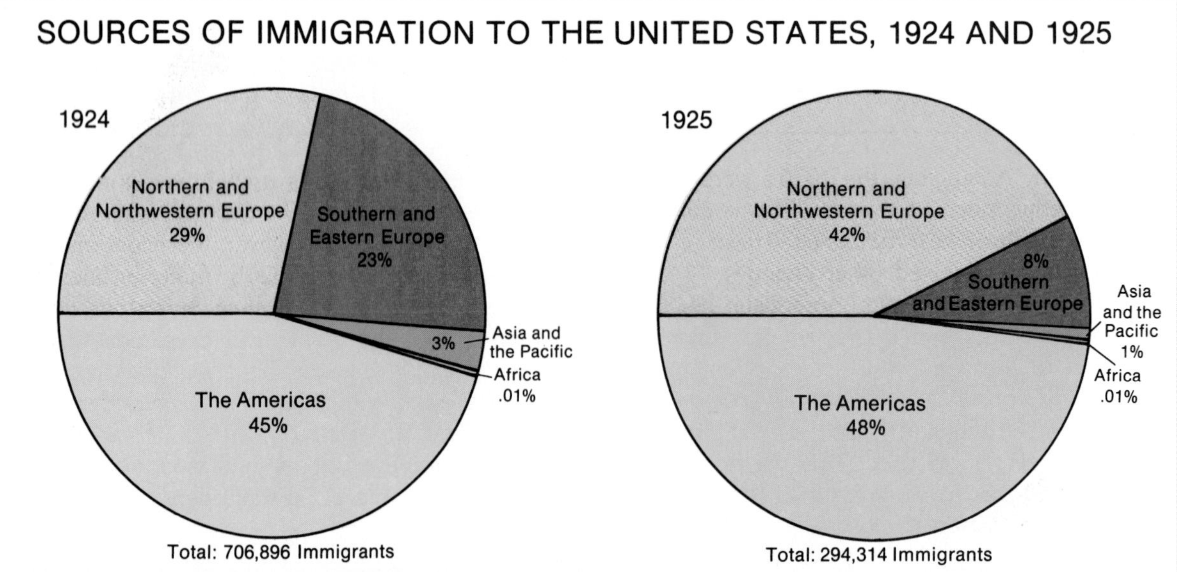

CHAPTER 27 REVIEW

YOU SHOULD KNOW

Identify, define, or explain each of the following:

suburbs
installment buying
prohibition laws
bootlegging
theory of evolution
overproduction
productivity
speculators

CHECKING FACTS

1. When did the first radio station begin broadcasting?
2. Who was the first man to fly across the Atlantic Ocean?
3. What third party did some Republicans form in 1924?
4. What was the national pastime during the 1920's?
5. What was the first motion picture with sound?
6. What two new forms of music developed in the 1920's?
7. What amendment gave women the right to vote?
8. What were two causes of increased business profits during the 1920's?
9. Who was the Republican candidate for President in 1928?
10. Who was the Democratic candidate for President in 1928?

UNDERSTANDING CONCEPTS

1. How did the boom in the automobile industry after World War I cause an increase in other businesses?
2. How did the government encourage business growth during the 1920's?
3. What laws and events of the 1920's show that some Americans did not like some of the changes that were occurring?
4. How was the prosperity of the 1920's an uneven prosperity?

LEARNING FROM ILLUSTRATIONS

1. Look at the cartoon on page 492. What do you think was the cartoonist's opinion of middle men?
2. Study the election map on page 485. What area of the nation voted solidly for the Democratic candidate in 1924?

CRITICAL THINKING

1. Installment buying became widely used in the 1920's. What kinds of things are bought today using installment buying?
2. How do you spend your leisure time? What does this tell you about what is important to you?
3. President Coolidge did not think the federal government should aid farmers. Do you think Coolidge was right? Why or why not?

ENRICHMENT ACTIVITIES

1. Trace the history of the Nineteenth Amendment. Share your findings with the class through reports or by reproducing posters, leaflets, or other media used in the campaign.
2. Examine the history of jazz music. Listen to some recordings of jazz music to enrich your study.
3. Learn more about the stock market. Daily prices of stocks are recorded in many newspapers. Watch the price of a certain company's stock over a period of time. Make a line graph showing the changes in the price of the stock.

CHAPTER 28

CLOSE-UP: American Royalty—The Rich

INTRODUCTION

The American dream for many people was to get rich. Certainly luck played its part in such dreams, especially for the forty-niners in the gold fields of California. Traditionally, American wealth was measured by the amount of land one controlled or inherited. But the Civil War set the stage for accumulation of great wealth based on money, not property. America's population, which stood at slightly more than 31 million in 1860, more than doubled by 1900. More people meant greater consumption of products, cheaper labor to produce them, and larger profits. Entrepreneurs, *people who start and manage their own businesses, were free to pursue business opportunities without government interference. They invested in and promoted new industries.*

America came to view the increasing wealth of certain individuals as the benefits of God, given to those who deserved it. Principles of social Darwinism and survival of the fittest were readily adopted by businessmen and laborers alike. For the next eighty years, until the stock-market crash of 1929, America's great fortunes developed. Those who possessed these fortunes became America's answer to the aristocracy of Europe.

1 Establishing the Great Fortunes

The Civil War set the stage for industrialization and profit. Both North and South needed huge amounts of equipment to carry on the war. Price was of little concern, and both sides provided large profits for manufacturers. When the war ended, profits were available to be used for speculation and investment. No longer divided, the nation was on the verge of tremendous expansion, and businessmen were eager to be a part of it.

Where the Great Fortunes Were Made. The railroad industry was the first to experience massive growth. In 1865, only about 35,000 miles (56 326 kilometers) of railroads existed, mainly in the East. By 1900, railroad lines had increased to nearly 200,000 miles (321 869 kilometers). Farsighted railroad men, like Cornelius Vanderbilt, began organizing railroad companies that produced enormous profits.

Expansion of the railroads was due largely to improvements in the quality of the rails on which they rode. Steel became the standard material used in the making of the rails. As the miles of track grew, so did the steel industry that produced them. With the business skills of men like Andrew Carnegie, steel became as profitable as railroads.

Investors rushed to the newly developing industries especially steel. Bankers, such as J. P. Morgan, were eager to own and consolidate the many separate companies that made up the industry. With large amounts of cash to invest, they began buying up stock and eventually took control of entire industries.

The oil industry during the late nineteenth century and the early twentieth century was a source of great wealth for people such as John D. Rockefeller.

In 1870, John D. Rockefeller organized the Standard Oil Company of Ohio. At this time, oil was heavily used for machinery and medicine. By 1877, Rockefeller controlled 95 percent of the oil production in the United States.

What three industries produced great wealth following the Civil War?

The Founders of the Great Fortunes. When Cornelius Vanderbilt entered the railroad business, he combined existing railroad companies. By doing so, he eventually controlled over 4,500 miles (7 242 kilometers) of track. When he died he left nearly $200 million to his immediate family. He gave control of the New York Central Railroad to his son William Henry Vanderbilt. Since income and inheritance taxes were not in effect until 1913, the inheritance represented nearly unimaginable wealth.

While Vanderbilt expanded the railroad empire, Andrew Carnegie developed the steel industry. Between 1889 and 1899 his profits averaged over $7 million dollars a year. In 1900, with no taxes to pay, he made $40 million. The following year his holdings were sold to an investor group, headed by J. P. Morgan, for over $400 million.

John Pierpont Morgan, the son of J. P. Morgan, was a New York financier involved in railroads, insurance companies, and banking. By 1900, Morgan was investing in the steel industry. A personal fortune, at least equal to that of Carnegie, allowed Morgan to put together a group of investors to create an all-powerful steel company. After successfully buying out Carnegie, the Morgan group began United States Steel—America's first billion dollar corporation.

John D. Rockefeller used the years following the formation of Standard Oil to gain control of all aspects of oil-refining. Although he never quite became a billionaire, his fortune reportedly amounted to almost $816 million dollars.

Henry Ford amassed his fortune through the invention and development of the automobile. His mass-production techniques made it possible to produce many automobiles quickly. This process made it possible to sell the automobiles much more cheaply, thereby allowing more people to afford them.

Around 1900, there were approximately four thousand millionaires in the United States. The United States Senate alone, with only ninety members in 1900, had 25 millionaires. By the early 1900's nearly seven-eighths of America's wealth was owned by one percent of its families. In the early 1900's, the wealthy began to view their money in two distinctively different ways. On the one hand, money was meant to be squandered and used in as showy a way as possible. On the other hand, with wealth came social responsibility. Both ideas were carried out during the next thirty years.

Through what industry did Henry Ford amass his fortune?

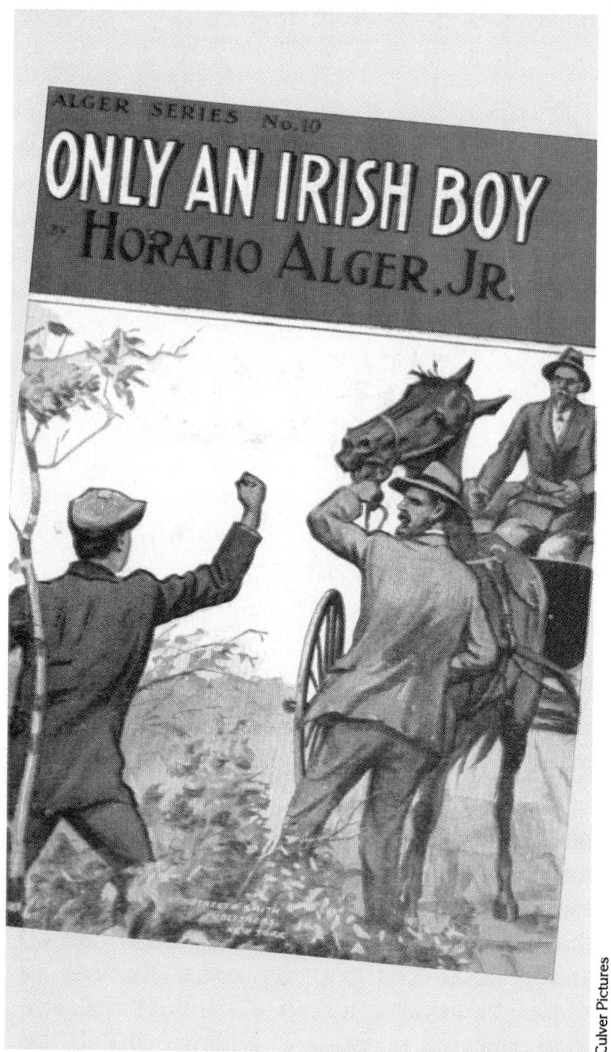

Culver Pictures

In Horatio Alger's book *Only an Irish Boy* a poor boy who by hard work, honesty, and a little luck becomes a rich man. Alger used this same theme in more than 100 books. Alger's popular books helped legitimize and justify great wealth.

With Money Comes Responsibility. America in 1900 was a vast quilt work of the incredibly wealthy and the terribly poor. Often the very wealthy, especially the newly rich, looked on the poor with contempt. Since many of the newly rich had been poor themselves, they felt those who stayed poor must be lazy.

The super rich, like Andrew Carnegie, did not apologize for their wealth. In 1900, Carnegie wrote in *The Gospel of Wealth* that great riches were no crime. In fact, he was convinced that a law of nature gave him the right to his enormous fortune. However, he believed that wealth, once accumulated, should be used to benefit humanity. The pleasure of riches, according to Carnegie and others, was not in having them, but in *philanthropy*—giving wealth away to benefit society. Between 1900 and 1919, Carnegie donated nearly $250 million to establish over 2,800 public libraries.

After 1890, John D. Rockefeller provided money to establish the University of Chicago and numerous other educational activities. He soon realized that in order to spend money wisely he needed assistance. So numerous independent foundations were set up to oversee his donations.

Rockefeller's son, John D. Rockefeller, Jr., devoted most of his life to helping others. In 1901, he provided funds to set up the Rockefeller Institute for Medical Research. In 1913, the Rockefeller Foundation to support research began. In 1920 alone, John D. Rockefeller, Jr., donated nearly $64 million to various charities. His total donations exceeded $474 million. To date, the Rockefeller contributions to society are in excess of $1 billion.

With the leadership of Carnegie and the Rockefellers, many other millionaires returned large parts of their fortunes to society. In nearly all cases, these people provided money for the cultural, scientific, and educational benefits of society.

Not all of the super rich felt the same way as Carnegie or the Rockefellers. Some thought money that was spent on others was wasted, while money spent on themselves was the fulfillment of the natural rights of the rich.

■ *What did most of the donations of the millionaires provide for?*

SECTION 1 REVIEW

1. *How did the Civil War set the stage for industrialization and profit?*
2. *How did Cornelius Vanderbilt amass his wealth?*
3. *Why did Andrew Carnegie give away some of his wealth?*

2 Life-Styles of the Rich

In 1900, the average American worker earned between $400 and $500 per year. By modern standards that seems to be an incredibly small amount. But with prices far lower than today, this amount was sufficient to live reasonably well. In that same year, Andrew Carnegie earned $10 million or about 20,000 times as much as the average American.

American workers were fascinated by the great fortunes of the super rich. When Carnegie and Rockefeller donated millions of dollars, workers were struck by their generosity. But it was the goings-on of the selfish super rich that provided the real fascination. From the mansions of the Vanderbilts, to lavish New York dinners, the rich *flaunted*—displayed for public notice—their good luck and vast fortunes.

Look at That House. By far the most impressive show of wealth were the houses built by the rich. The Vanderbilt family set the standard for opulence, or abundance of wealth. By 1903, there were seven great Vanderbilt houses, representing a total value of nearly $35 million, within a seven block area of Fifth Avenue in New York. Although not very impressive from the outside, these houses were filled with rare statues, furniture, books, and art. American millionaires wanted to live like foreign royalty. So they purchased and imported their art from royalty and castles in Europe.

One of the most incredible houses of all was built by George W. Vanderbilt at Ashville, North Carolina. For three years, three hundred stonemasons worked to complete the house, which he named *Biltmore*. The house had 40 master bedrooms and an equal number of smaller bedrooms. It had a banquet hall that could seat 300 guests and a library of 250,000 books. A staff of 65 people served Vanderbilt and his guests, making *Biltmore* equal to many European castles. The house was surrounded by an estate that eventually grew to 203 square miles (526 square kilometers) and was tended by hundreds of full-time workers.

Although the Vanderbilts represented the ultimate builders of expensive homes, they were not alone. Throughout the United States, great homes with marble floors, carved ceilings, mural paintings, and innumerable servants, housed the wealthy. John D. Rockefeller did not build on the scale of the Vanderbilts, but his home was only one of more than 75

Maurice Prendergast. *Madison Square*. c1901. watercolor on paper. 15" × 16½". Collection of Whitney Museum of American Art. Joan Whitney Payson Bequest 76.14

How does Maurice Prendergast portray the rich in this water color painting?

buildings on his estate. During the summer the estate employed 1,500 people to maintain Rockefeller's 70 miles (113 kilometers) of private roads and a personal eighteen-hole golf course.

By comparison, Henry Ford lived rather simply in his 55 room mansion outside of Detroit. Yet, it took 60 employees to tend the gardens, a private lake, and a power plant that provided heat and electricity.

Perhaps the all-time winner for showy dwellings was Charles M. Schwab, a manager at one time or another for both Carnegie and Morgan. His $8 million mansion had 3 elevators, a private telephone switchboard, a freezer to hold 20,000 pounds (9 072 kilograms) of meat, and 3 full-time chefs on duty around the clock. In addition to its 75 rooms, Schwab's house contained a gymnasium, a 65-foot (20-meter) heated swimming pool, 8 bowling alleys, and a billiard room with 12 tables.

J. P. Morgan spent only a few million on his New York homes. Instead, he purchased rare books, manuscripts, and paintings. Next to his house in Manhattan he built a Renaissance palace to hold his collection.

Other super rich bought entire rooms, paneling and all, from European castles and homes. Then they shipped these rooms to the United States where they were reconstructed. In the 1920's, William Randolph Hearst, a New

This Vanderbilt house is called "The Breakers." It was the largest of the Vanderbilt houses, and resembled an oversized Italian villa.

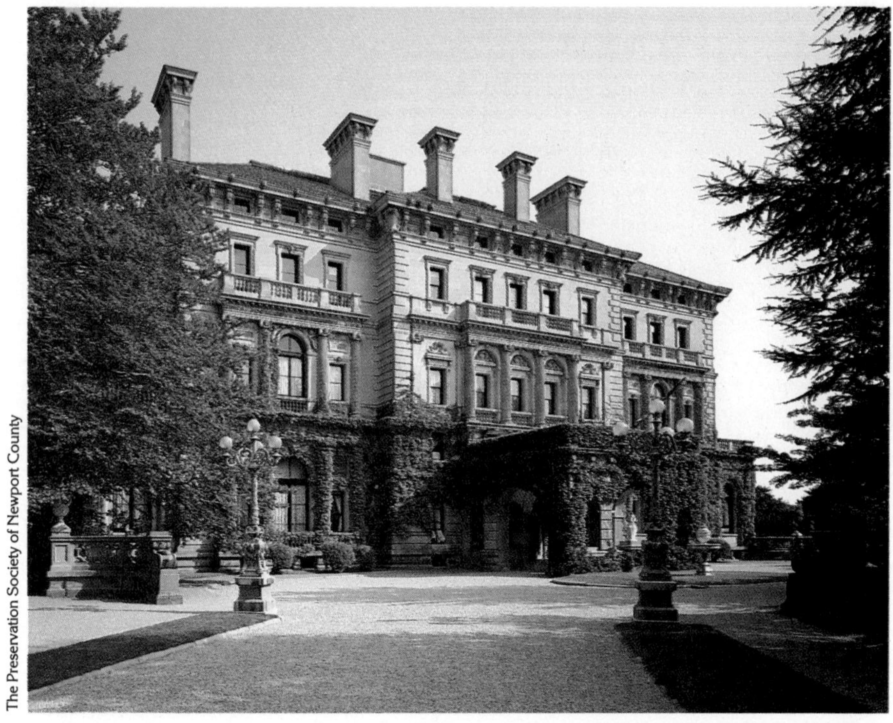
The Preservation Society of Newport County

York newspaper owner, even went so far as to purchase an entire Welsh castle and move it to California. At one time, Hearst even attempted to convince the Egyptian government to sell one of the minor pyramids, but that deal fell through.

What was the most impressive show of wealth by the rich?

On the Society Trail. Although houses and furnishings provided an outlet for the super rich, these things were not a real social activity. It was the parties and formal balls and dinners that brought the wealthy together to impress one another. In the early 1900's, New York City was the capital of society in America. The social elite were represented by a group known as the Four Hundred. This number was considered to be the number of socially acceptable people in New York. No cost was too great in order to establish a family's reputation as one of the leaders of the social set.

In 1897, Mrs. Bradley Martin, who arrived in New York City from upstate New York, wanted to impress society. So she invited the Four Hundred for an evening of dinner and dancing. She spent over $1 million for this occasion. She used 6 thousand orchids and 10 thousand roses to cover tables, walls, and ceilings. She hired five orchestras. The largest one, a fifty-piece military band, was on loan from the National Guard. She served supper from midnight until two-thirty in the morning. Supper included whole English suckling pigs, sides of beef, lobster, and pheasants. She hired four hundred carriages to pick up and return guests to their homes.

The guests at such occasions competed with one another for the most expensive clothing and jewelry. Mrs. Bradley Martin wore a $10 thousand dress and about $100 thousand worth of jewelry. She was outshone, however, by Mrs. Astor, another super rich woman. Mrs. Astor came wearing $250 thousand worth of diamonds.

It was not always necessary to give a grand party in order to fulfill social obligations. Dinners at home, with a dozen guests attended by several servants, were acceptable. Ten-course meals with seven or eight fine wines were normal for such home entertaining. Hostesses prided themselves on their ability to feed several dozen guests on short notice. Guests expected fine China and crystal. They also expected solid silver and gold place settings. A meal at home could easily cost the host $500 to $700 per guest. Yet the social prestige gains from such affairs were thought to be well worth the cost.

How did the wealthy impress one another?

Yachts and Trains. The super rich were fascinated with travel, and they expected to travel in luxury. They often traveled in private yachts and train cars. Yachts were very large and were equipped with a large crew. Yachts were stocked with fine wines and excellent food. Expensive rugs covered the decks and costly draperies hung over port holes. Often, a piano was available in the cabin. J. P. Morgan's yacht, the *Corsair III*, was equipped with a crew of thirty people. Morgan also built a steamer for travel on the Nile River, just in case he ever decided to visit Egypt.

Many of the super rich traveled in private railroad cars. These cars were often fitted with carved paneling, gold fixtures, linen sheets, and tapestries. Meals were prepared aboard a private dining car, and were served by waiters who also doubled as butlers. It was common for regularly scheduled locomotives to be sidetracked while private trains passed.

When automobiles appeared on the market, the super rich had them first. They impressed one another by driving down streets of New York City, Newport, and Chicago with their horseless carriages. At Newport, during the early 1900's, there were parades of automobiles decorated with flowers. The super rich passengers were almost as dressed up as their automobiles. For the first few years after the invention of the automobile, only the super rich could afford automobiles because only the super rich could afford the upkeep.

What were some means of transportation used by the super rich?

Showy Wealth Goes Into Hiding. When the stock market collapsed in 1929, most of the super rich were unaffected. The Vanderbilts, Fords, and others simply had too much money to be hard pressed by the events faced by the rest of the nation. However, the crash signaled the end of an era. While most Americans struggled to find a job, pay the rent, or have enough to eat, the wealthy changed their life-styles very little.

The parties continued, only on a much quieter and less grand scale. Fewer new houses were built, but art collections continued to grow. The second, third, and fourth generations of wealthy were not nearly as interested in showing off their fortune. Many devoted most of their time to supporting causes that helped others. Others invested in new businesses to increase family wealth even more. The days of the flashy fortunes were over, but what an incredible time it had been.

What event brought about the end of an era for the super rich?

The Granger Collection

A favorite leisure-time activity of the rich was tennis. Notice how the people dressed for a game of tennis.

SECTION 2 REVIEW

1. *How did the average American workers feel about the super rich?*
2. *Why did American millionaires import their art from royalty and castles in Europe?*
3. *Why did showy wealth become less apparent after 1929?*

CHAPTER 28 REVIEW

SUMMARY

The American dream of wealth began in earnest following the Civil War. Large profits from the war allowed investors to support growing industries such as the railroads and steel. It was common for fortunes to be acquired by obtaining control of vast segments of an industry.

While Cornelius Vanderbilt gained control over much of the nation's railroads, Andrew Carnegie acquired vast holdings in the steel industry. When John Pierpont Morgan bought out Carnegie, the first billion dollar corporation, United States Steel, was formed.

John D. Rockefeller dominated the oil industry by controlling 95 percent of all oil production and distribution. Later, the inventor Henry Ford built an automobile that was affordable to the common person.

Some of the super rich felt an obligation to return some of their wealth to society. Andrew Carnegie gave millions to the creation of public libraries, while the Rockefellers established foundations to carry on research and encourage learning.

Unfortunately, not all of the super rich were as generous as Carnegie and Rockefeller. The magnificent homes of the Vanderbilts, Ford, Schwab and others were clear examples of the showy use of wealth.

Equally showy displays of wealth were the fabulous parties and dinners given by the wealthy. No expense was too outrageous when comfort and style were the goal. On the yachts of the super rich, luxury was just as apparent as in their homes. Railroad cars were just as spectacular as the yachts. At the beginning of the age of the automobile, the super rich were the only people who could afford to keep up an automobile.

The depression of 1929 lessened the obvious excesses of the wealthy. Fewer new houses were built and parties were given on a less grand scale. However, art collections continued to increase in these households. Many of the later generations of the super rich turned to the work of helping others. They reestablished the idea that with wealth comes responsibility. The depression of 1929 lessened the obvious excess of the wealthy.

UNDERSTANDING CONCEPTS

1. Why was the United States ready for the establishment of vast fortunes following the Civil War?
2. Why did rich people like Carnegie and the Rockefellers establish various foundations?
3. How did average American workers react to the incredible wealth of the super rich?
4. Why did the super rich import many items from Europe for their houses in the United States?

CRITICAL THINKING

1. In your opinion, was the concentration of vast wealth in the hands of a few people good or bad for the United States? Give reasons for your answer.
2. Do you think that rich people have a responsibility to help the less-fortunate members of society? Why do you think so?
3. Are you impressed by showy displays of wealth? Why or why not?

PROJECTS AND ACTIVITIES

Use the library to find *Fortune* magazine's annual list of the wealthiest Americans. Explain how most of these people acquired their wealth. Choose one of these people, and use encyclopedias and other sources to write a short biography. Share your biography with the rest of the class.

UNIT SEVEN REVIEW

UNIT SUMMARY

After 1900, the United States began to play a greater role in world affairs. This was due to the acquisition of overseas lands, the growing importance of foreign trade, and the need for resources and markets. At the same time, Americans worked to improve life within the country. Between 1900 and 1912, the Progressives backed a variety of reform laws. Through these efforts, progress was made toward ending many unfair conditions.

President Woodrow Wilson's New Freedom Program brought many improvements to the United States. However, events in other countries drew his attention from these matters. The President felt it was necessary to send American troops into Latin America. Then in 1917 the United States entered World War I. The war brought about long-lasting changes in our country.

For many Americans, the 1920's were a time of prosperity. Many Americans began to spend more time and money on entertainment. At the same time, some other Americans felt that important parts of American life were being threatened, and they worked for laws that would preserve established traditions. In the 1920's some Americans faced hard times, while others made large fortunes. However, the economy was not sound. Stock prices began to fall. In October, 1929, the stock market crashed. Business failures increased, and the nation slipped into a full-scale depression.

The American dream of wealth began in earnest following the Civil War. Large profits from the war allowed investors to support growing industries such as the railroads and steel. It was common for fortunes to be acquired by obtaining control of vast segments of an industry. Some of the super rich felt an obligation to return some of their wealth to society.

YOU SHOULD KNOW

Identify, define, or explain each of the following:

imperialism	ratify
direct-primary	overproduction
Jim Crow laws	speculators
armistice	entrepreneurs

CHECKING FACTS

1. What colonies did the United States gain as a result of the Spanish American War?
2. What was the open-door policy in China?
3. What was dollar diplomacy?
4. Who were muckrakers?
5. What program did the Triangle Shirtwaist Company tragedy lead to?
6. What were Wilson's New Freedom reforms?
7. What incident led Europe to war in 1914?
8. What was the Fourteen Points?
9. What was provided for by the Nineteenth Amendment?
10. To what charities did Andrew Carnegie donate money?

UNDERSTANDING CONCEPTS

1. Why did the United States become more involved in world affairs after 1900?
2. How did the political reforms that were achieved between 1900 and 1929 give Americans greater control over the government?
3. How did our country's participation in World War I affect all Americans?
4. How did President Theodore Roosevelt's ideas about government and business compare with those of President Coolidge?
5. What social and economic problems existed during the 1920's?

UNIT SEVEN REVIEW

CRITICAL THINKING

1. Why, do you think, did American business owners in Hawaii want the United States to take control of the Hawaiian Islands?
2. In your opinion, how would World War I have ended if the United States had remained neutral?
3. How would your life be different if there were no automobiles?
4. Andrew Carnegie wrote in the *Gospel of Wealth* that great riches were no crime. In fact, he was convinced that a law of nature gave him the right to his enormous wealth. However, he believed that wealth, once accumulated, should be used to benefit humanity. Do you agree or disagree with Andrew Carnegie's ideas? Give reasons for your answers.

CHRONOLOGY

Arrange the following events in the order in which they happened.

a. Federal Reserve Act passed
b. *The Chicago Defender* started
c. Stock-market crashed
d. Women gained the right to vote
e. First radio station began broadcasting
f. First Model T Ford made
g. Lindbergh crossed the Atlantic Ocean
h. President McKinley assassinated 1901
i. NAACP formed
j. World War I ended

CITIZENSHIP IN ACTION

Many American soldiers died in World War I fighting for freedom. How do people in our country honor the memory of those who died in World War I?

GEOGRAPHY

1. What countries were neutral nations?
2. Was the Ottoman Empire one of the Allies or one of the Central Powers?
3. Were the following countries of North Africa—Algeria, Libya, French Morocco, and Egypt—part of the Allies or part of the Central Powers?
4. What were the advantages of the Central Powers' location?
5. What were the advantages of the Allies location?

1930

1935

- 1930 Hawley-Smoot Tariff signed
- 1932 Franklin Delano Roosevelt elected President
- 1933 First fireside chat by FDR; New Deal begun; Tennessee Valley Authority created
- 1934 Indian Reorganization Act passed; Dust storms swept through parts of the country; Platt Amendment repealed
- 1935 Second New Deal begun; Social Security Act passed; National Recovery Act declared unconstitutional; Congress of Industrial Organization founded
- 1936 General Motors strike in Flint, Michigan; Olympics held in Berlin, Germany

UNIT EIGHT

The Depression and World War II

1930 to 1945

The picture entitled, "The Unemployment Agency," by Isaac Soyer shows the anxiety and despair of the unemployed during the Great Depression.

Dorothea Lange's well-known photograph, "Migrant Mother," became an image of the suffering experienced by many people during the Great Depression.

1940

1939 World War II began in Europe

1940 President Roosevelt elected to third term

1941 Pearl Harbor attacked by Japan
United States declared war on Japan, Germany, and Italy

1945

1944 Allies invaded France

1945 FDR died
Vice-President Harry Truman became President
Germany surrendered
First atomic bomb dropped
Japan surrendered

CHAPTERS

Even though the federal government took steps to halt the depression, the economy did not improve in the early 1930's. Many Americans blamed President Hoover for the hard times. This helped Franklin D. Roosevelt to be elected President in 1932.

President Roosevelt believed that the federal government needed to act quickly to fight the depression. He started a plan to help the economy. It was called the New Deal. This plan greatly expanded the activities of the federal government.

World War II broke out in Europe in 1939. The United States hoped to stay out of the fighting. However, our country became involved after Pearl Harbor was attacked by Japan in 1941. The United States fought on the side of the Allies to defeat Germany, Italy, and Japan—the Axis powers. World War II finally ended in 1945 after atomic bombs were used for the first time in a war.

On two occasions during World War II, the Big Three—Churchill, Roosevelt, and Stalin—met to try to settle differences about the nature of the postwar world.

Black Americans achieved great successes at the 1936 Olympics held in Berlin, Germany. Jesse Owens (left) and Ralph Metcalfe (right) were outstanding Olympic athletes.

1930 — 1935

- 1930 Hawley-Smoot Tariff signed
- 1932 Reconstruction Finance Corporation established; Franklin Delano Roosevelt elected President
- 1933 Twentieth amendment became law; First fireside chat by FDR; New Deal begun; Federal Emergency Relief Administration set up; Civilian Conservation Corp set up; National Industrial Recovery Act passed; Tennessee Valley Authority created
- 1934 Indian Reorganization Act passed

CHAPTER 29

The Great Depression

Chapter Objectives

After studying this chapter, you should be able to:

- identify the basic causes of the depression;
- describe how the depression disrupted the living patterns of many Americans;
- identify several significant programs initiated by President Roosevelt.

1 The Country Slips Into Depression

Overview During 1930, unemployment in the United States rose greatly. Before long the United States was suffering from the worst depression in its history.

Objectives After reading this section, you should be able to:

- assess the affect that unemployment in some businesses had on other businesses;
- give examples of the ways in which President Hoover used the federal government to end the depression;
- explain why President Hoover lost the election of 1932.

Hard Times Spread. The American economy slumped after 1929, and as business activity declined, more workers lost their jobs. Many of those who continued to work had their earnings cut. Millions of families had to cut back their spending. This led to even more unemployment because fewer goods were being bought. Therefore, fewer goods were produced.

Conditions worsened as banks began to fail. In 1930 alone, over 1,000 banks closed. During the next year, over 2,000 banks suspended their operation. This caused thousands of depositors to lose their savings.

Americans who had taken out loans or mortgages during the more prosperous 1920's found it difficult to continue making payments. Thousands of families lost their homes when they could not pay their mortgages. Furniture and automobiles were *repossessed*—taken back by the seller—when buyers failed to make their installment payments. As more factories and banks were forced to close, Americans wondered when business would get started again and bring an end to the depression.

■ *Why did many Americans lose their homes during the early years of the depression?*

President Hoover's Stand. President Hoover believed that the federal government should play only a small role in business matters. He felt confident that the American economy was basically secure. Because of this, he believed that Americans could work out ways to end the business setback. He used his office to encourage many groups to cooperate in solving the country's problems.

President Hoover met with business leaders and asked them to keep wages and prices stable. He asked labor leaders to agree not to strike. President Hoover also asked the states to undertake public building projects in order to provide more jobs for the unemployed. He also led the federal government in its largest construction program in history.

The President recognized that many Americans were in great need. He urged private groups and local governments to do their best to provide *relief*—aid—for the poor. He would not, however, back any relief program that would give federal money directly to the poor. President Hoover believed that this would be an improper use of federal power. He also felt that Americans would be giving up part of their freedom if they began to depend on aid from the federal government.

The President worked out a number of programs designed to help the country return to prosperity. One plan was designed to help farmers by keeping the price of crops steady. Also, in 1930, the President asked Congress to use $150 million for new public buildings. This would provide more jobs.

President Hoover also favored raising the tariff as a way to help our country's businesses. He backed the Hawley-Smoot Tariff of 1930. This act made most imported goods more expensive for Americans. However, instead of helping business, this high tariff worked against American industry. It led a number of other countries to place tariffs on American-made goods. This lessened the amount of American goods sold in these countries.

■ *What did President Hoover believe to be the proper role of government in business matters?*

The Depression Worsens. Despite President Hoover's efforts, the depression grew worse. Each day more Americans lost their jobs. Breadlines and soup kitchens became crowded as more Americans had to turn to charities for their food.

Thousands of families could no longer pay their rents or mortgages. Hundreds of homeless families were drawn to *Hoovervilles*—slums made up of shacks built from any available material. In these shacks people lived without heat, electricity, or water. Thousands of other homeless and jobless Americans wandered from city to city looking for work. A large number of these drifters were young people whose parents could no longer support them.

The depression was particularly severe for those who had faced hardships during the more prosperous 1920's. With fewer jobs

A. Devaney, Inc.

In the early 1930's, slums of makeshift shacks—called *Hoovervilles*—grew up around the country, as nearly 1 million unemployed Americans wandered the country in search of work. What unsafe living conditions are shown in this picture?

available, black Americans, for example, found it almost impossible to keep their jobs because of discrimination. Working women also faced unfair treatment. Many employers assumed that women did not need their jobs. In some cases, women were paid less than 25 cents an hour. Thousands of women had to depend on low incomes to support themselves and, in some cases, to provide for their families.

As the depression continued, American farmers slipped further into poverty. President Hoover's program failed to keep crop prices up. Farm owners had to lay off their hired help in an effort to lower farm costs. As prices of farm products continued to drop, farmers could not pay their debts. Banks began to take possession of farms when owners could not repay their loans.

The continuing depression caused President Hoover to change some of his ideas about government and business. In 1932 he backed the establishment of the Reconstruction Finance Corporation (RFC). Through the RFC, the federal government provided money for banks, railroads, and other large industries. It was hoped that this money would give business the spark needed for recovery. President Hoover also favored programs that would make loans to farmers and would spend more money on public works. Never before had the government played such a large part in the country's economy. However, President Hoover would not change his ideas on one important matter. He stood firm on his view that the federal government should not give relief money directly to citizens.

The President did not recognize that local relief agencies could no longer meet the needs of the unemployed. By the fall of 1931 several large cities had no more money to use

DO YOU KNOW?

When was the "Star-Spangled Banner" adopted as the national anthem?

On March 3, 1931, President Hoover signed an act passed by Congress that made the "Star-Spangled Banner" our national anthem. The lyrics had been written over 100 years earlier by Francis Scott Key during the War of 1812. Key had witnessed the all-night British bombardment of Fort McHenry, Maryland. The next morning, when the smoke and haze finally cleared, Key saw that the American flag was still flying at the fort. This scene inspired Key to write the words of the song, which became our national anthem.

for aid to the poor. As the number of jobless continued to climb, more and more Americans began to demand that the federal government take action to help those in need. In addition, more Americans began to blame President Hoover for the hard times.

■ *What was the purpose of the Reconstruction Finance Corporation?*

The Bonus Army. President Hoover's popularity dropped to a low point in the summer of 1932. In part, this was because of the way in which he handled the bonus army. The bonus army was a group of about 15,000 World War I veterans. Many of these veterans were jobless and could not support their families.

Each veteran was due to receive a bonus payment in the 1940's. However, the veterans thought that this money should be given to them immediately. They marched to Washington to make their demand heard. Many of them brought their families. In Washington,

Wide World

In 1932, World War I veterans crowded into Washington, D.C., to persuade Congress to approve the early payment of their war bonuses.

they camped in tents and shacks. Some of them moved into empty government buildings.

The Senate would not approve the early payment for the bonuses. Instead, the veterans were offered free railroad tickets home. Most of the marchers accepted these tickets and left Washington. However, about 2,000 veterans stayed on.

On July 28, 1932, the United States Army joined the Washington police to remove the remaining veterans from the city. Tanks and tear gas were used to drive them out. Americans were shocked when they learned that our government had used the army against jobless veterans and their families. President Hoover appeared insensitive for ordering this action. It now seems clear that the commanding officer, General Douglas MacArthur, was not obeying orders when he drove the bonus army from Washington. This was not known at the time. Therefore, the public blamed President Hoover.

■ *Why did World War I veterans march to Washington in 1932?*

The Election of 1932. The Republican party chose President Hoover to run for office again in 1932. However, the Democratic party seemed sure of victory. This was because most Americans were disappointed with President Hoover's leadership.

The Democratic party selected Franklin Delano Roosevelt as its candidate. During his campaign, Roosevelt did not present a clear-cut plan for ending the depression. However, unlike Hoover, Roosevelt seemed willing to try new things. As a result, Roosevelt won an overwhelming victory with 22,809,638 popular votes. Hoover received only 15,758,901 votes.

According to the Constitution, Roosevelt would not begin his term until March 1933.

In what part of the country was Hoover most popular?

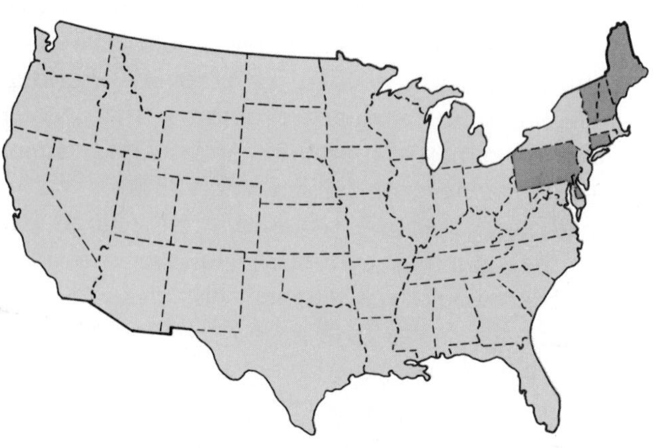

ELECTION OF 1932

	Electoral Votes	Popular Votes
Democratic Franklin D. Roosevelt	472	22,809,638
Republican Herbert Hoover	59	15,758,901

This was the last time in our history that the President's inauguration was held so long after the election. In 1933, the Twentieth Amendment [*115-*120] became law, changing Inauguration Day to January 20.

Between Roosevelt's election and his inauguration, the country slipped further into depression. About 16 million workers, almost one third of the work force, were jobless. In addition, a banking crisis began when Americans became afraid that more banks would fail. This led people to withdraw their money from the banks. Many banks were left without enough money to continue doing business. By the time the new President took office, conditions all across the nation seemed desperate.

■ *How many American workers were unemployed when Roosevelt took office?*

SECTION 1 REVIEW

1. *How did unemployment in some businesses lead to cutbacks in other businesses?*
2. *How did President Hoover use the federal government in an effort to end the depression?*
3. *Why was President Hoover defeated in the election of 1932?*

2 A New Deal for Americans

Overview When he entered office, President Roosevelt told the nation to remain confident in the country's future. He said, "The only thing we have to fear is fear itself." President Roosevelt worked with the Congress on a wide range of measures aimed at providing all Americans with a "new deal."

Objectives After reading this section, you should be able to:

- list the goals of the New Deal;
- explain the New Deal plans for farm recovery;
- discuss the New Deal plans for the recovery of industry.

A Bold Leader. Franklin Delano Roosevelt was known as a bold leader even before he entered the White House. Roosevelt—or FDR as he was called—had been the governor of New York since 1928. As governor, he had backed state aid for the jobless. He also led the state government in undertaking a number of reforms. In addition, FDR worked for laws that would protect natural resources.

In his personal life, FDR had shown that he would work hard to overcome problems. In 1921 he had become very ill with polio—a disease that left him partially paralyzed. Although he never regained full use of his legs, he did not let this interfere with his activities.

Many voters had backed Roosevelt for

President because he seemed to be open-minded and hopeful about our country's future. During the campaign, he promised a "new deal" to lead the nation out of the depression. In his inaugural address on March 4, 1933, President Roosevelt told the nation to remain confident in the country's future. He promised to undertake bold, new actions against the country's problems. His pledge for action helped Americans to believe that the United States could overcome the depression.

■ *What public office did FDR hold before becoming President?*

Beginning the New Deal. President Roosevelt kept his promise to take immediate action against the country's problems. To do this, he called Congress to meet in a special session. He then asked the lawmakers to pass laws aimed at three goals. First, relief laws were necessary to meet the needs of those Americans who were without food, housing, and other basic needs. Second, recovery laws were needed to help business and agriculture start up again. Third, reform laws were needed to solve the country's economic problems. President Roosevelt's plans for these three goals became known as the *New Deal* (see chart on page 521).

During President Roosevelt's first week in office he worked out a way to end the banking crisis. The President closed every bank in the country by declaring a bank holiday. Government inspectors were put in charge of deciding which banks were sound.

The President then held a radio broadcast called a *fireside chat* to explain these actions. He told the nation that only sound banks would be allowed to reopen. The President was successful in ending the banking crisis. He convinced Americans once again to trust banks with their savings.

President Roosevelt's fireside chats explained his policies and actions and helped to restore public confidence in the American economy and government. Roosevelt's wife, Eleanor, became involved in public affairs and developed a public personality independent of her husband.

The Granger Collection

Franklin D. Roosevelt Library

SOME NEW DEAL LAWS AND PROGRAMS

Name	Date	Purpose
Agricultural Adjustment Act	May 1933	Set up system to advise and assist farmers Aimed at controlling crop prices
Farm Credit Act	June 1933	Provided credit to farmers Offered mortgages on farm property
National Recovery Administration	June 1933	Allowed businesses to plan together to make codes for industries Set up a public-works program
Federal Emergency Relief Act	May 1933	Provided money to the states for relief programs
Civilian Conservation Corps	March 1933	Gave jobs to young men from poor families
Public Works Administration	June 1933	Set up public-works projects to provide jobs and to stimulate business
Federal Deposit Insurance Corporation	June 1933	Insured bank accounts
Truth in Securities Act	May 1933	Required the sellers of stocks and bonds to disclose important information about these securities
Securities and Exchange Commission	June 1934	Regulated the stock exchange
Homeowners Loan Corporation	June 1933	Made mortgage loans to homeowners
Federal Housing Administration	June 1934	Insured mortgages and provided funds for home improvements
Beer Act	March 1933	Legalized the sale and manufacture of weak beer and wine—a step toward the end of Prohibition that came with an amendment in December 1933
Reciprocal Trade Agreements	June 1934	Made it possible for the Secretary of State to work out trade agreements with other countries to increase American exports

According to the table above, what laws and programs were passed to help farmers? To help homeowners? To help the unemployed?

More importantly, President Roosevelt had shown many Americans that the government would act quickly to strengthen our economy. His later fireside chats convinced many Americans that the President would keep in touch with the citizens.

The special session of Congress continued until June 16, 1933. This lawmaking session is often called the *Hundred Days.* During this period, the Congress passed 15 major New Deal laws. During the Hundred Days, President Roosevelt and his advisers worked with the

Congress to find ways to aid the millions of suffering Americans.

■ *What were the three goals of the New Deal?*

Providing Relief. President Roosevelt believed that the federal government had to act to provide food for the hungry and jobs for the unemployed. The Congress agreed that this relief was needed. As a result, the lawmakers passed laws that set up a number of aid programs.

President Roosevelt and Congress worked together to set up the Federal Emergency Relief Administration in May of 1933. This office was given a budget of $500 million. The money was given out to the states to use for their aid programs.

President Roosevelt and his advisers favored relief programs that gave jobs to the unemployed. They felt that American workers would feel better about themselves if these workers were doing a job rather than just taking money from the government.

One of the most popular work relief programs of the New Deal was the Civilian Conservation Corps (CCC). It was aimed at helping young men from poor families. The CCC set up work camps in rural parts of the country. Young men who joined the CCC lived in these camps and worked to protect and restore our natural resources.

The CCC was in operation between 1933 and 1940. During those years, about 2.5 million youths earned money and gained job skills through the CCC.

The New Deal included other job programs. Through the Civil Works Administration (CWA), for example, about 4 million Americans found jobs during the winter of 1933–1934. The CWA offered many different jobs. It also left the country with many long-lasting improvements. Roads, schools, and airports were built

The Bettmann Archive

FDR (in first car) was photographed during a tour of a Civilian Conservation Corps camp. During its first year, the CCC gave jobs to about 250,000 young men in 1,500 camps across the nation. Members of the CCC planted trees, worked to prevent soil erosion, and built public parks over a span of 7 years.

and repaired by CWA workers. The CWA also provided jobs for writers and for artists.

The CWA was followed by other work relief programs. These programs, however, were seen only as emergency measures. The President's goal was for business to recover and to begin hiring more workers.

The New Deal also provided relief for property owners who could not pay their regular mortgage payments. Thousands of Americans kept their homes and their farms because of these programs. At the same time, the government tried new ways to bring economic recovery to American farmers.

■ *What is a work relief program?*

Plans for Farm Recovery. American farmers were among those hardest hit by the depression. Crop prices had fallen greatly after World War I. Corn, for example, had sold for about $1.23 a bushel during World War I. By the early 1930's, corn was selling for about $0.50 a bushel. Overproduction was the major cause of low crop prices.

One of the goals of the New Deal, therefore, was to raise crop prices by ending overproduction. To do this, Congress passed the Agricultural Adjustment Act (AAA) in May 1933. This law gave the Secretary of Agriculture the power to pay farmers to lower their crop output. In some cases, farmers were paid to destroy crops.

The AAA had several shortcomings. For example, many persons thought it was wrong for food to be wasted while many Americans were hungry. However, the President knew that farmers would continue to face hard times until crop prices were raised.

Another problem with the AAA was that it aided only farm owners. Many other persons who made their living from farming were hurt by the program. Sharecroppers and hired farm workers, for example, often lost their means of earning a living when farm owners cut their crop output. Large numbers of blacks in the South and Mexican Americans in the Southwest faced this problem.

Like many parts of the New Deal, the AAA was an experiment. Although it caused some problems, the policy of limiting output did raise crop prices.

■ *How did the New Deal try to end the overproduction of farm crops?*

Recovery for Industry. In 1930, far more Americans were earning their living through industry than through farming. Thus, industry had to recover if the depression was to be ended. To get business going again, Congress passed the National Industrial Recovery Act in June of 1933. With this law, Congress gave the President great powers over business.

The law set up the National Recovery Administration (NRA). The NRA was in charge of approving *codes*—rules—for each industry. The codes were to be written by business leaders from each industry. One aim of the NRA was to end unfair competition. To do this, the codes set the amount of goods that each business would be allowed to make. Also, the codes set minimum prices for goods.

The NRA codes were also aimed at helping industrial workers. For example, the codes set the maximum hours to be worked each week. In addition, each industry had to agree on *minimum wages*—the lowest pay that would be given to workers. Workers were also promised the right to bargain collectively.

During the summer of 1933, the Blue Eagle—the emblem for the NRA—became a well-known sight. Many Americans backed this New Deal experiment. Union leaders believed the NRA would help unions to become stronger. The NRA rules were also helping to end child labor. Many business owners also backed the NRA as a way to end the depression. This hopeful outlook, however, did not last long.

Within a year, it became clear that the NRA had many weaknesses. Small businesses, for example, charged that big businesses had too much power in writing the codes. Because of this, small businesses were not being treated fairly. Consumers also charged that big businesses were given too much power under the NRA. Also, it became impossible to see that codes were carried out. Thus, President Roosevelt and the Congress had to work out other ways to meet the goals of the NRA.

In what three ways did the NRA codes aid industrial workers?

SECTION 2 REVIEW

1. *What were the goals of the New Deal?*
2. *How did the Agricultural Adjustment Act raise crop prices?*
3. *How did the NRA codes aid industrial workers?*

3 New Deal Reforms

Overview The New Deal promised many reform programs. One program was begun to improve an entire region. Other programs were geared to help the economy and to help minority groups.

Objectives After reading this section, you should be able to:

- explain why the TVA was created;
- discuss how the New Deal helped American minorities;
- describe the pressures on President Roosevelt to change the New Deal.

The TVA. One of the broadest reforms of the New Deal was the Tennessee Valley Authority (TVA). Even before the depression, the people of the Tennessee Valley had lived in terrible poverty. The valley was rich in natural resources. However, much of this wealth was lost because of floods, erosion, or poor farming methods. The TVA was aimed at ending these problems. Its major goal, however, was to provide electricity at low rates to the people of the Tennessee Valley.

One of the main backers of the TVA was Senator George Norris of Nebraska. For many years he had been asking the federal government to build a power plant on the Tennessee River in Muscle Shoals, Alabama. Senator Norris believed that the government should also undertake similar projects in other parts of the country.

During the 1920's, Senator Norris's plan for the Tennessee Valley was passed twice by the Congress. The first time the plan was passed, it was vetoed by President Coolidge. After its second passage, it was vetoed by President Hoover. Neither President wanted the government to enter into the electric-power business.

Senator Norris finally received approval for his plan from President Roosevelt. Roosevelt had a strong interest in the TVA. He saw it as a means of conserving and developing the natural resources of the Tennessee Valley.

Congress created the TVA in May 1933. For the first time in American history, a region extending into several states (see map on this page) was brought under the power of one government office. Headquarters for the TVA was set up in the Tennessee Valley, not in Washington, D.C. From this location, the TVA could better make its decisions in cooperation with people from the area and with local governments.

The TVA built dams and power plants on the Tennessee River and on its branches. This provided electric power for the residents. This electricity also attracted more businesses to the valley. In addition, the TVA provided the area with flood control and other conservation projects.

The TVA undertook many other tasks as well. For example, TVA workers improved rivers for navigation. They also taught the people of the area better ways of farming. The TVA has been very important in bringing long-lasting improvements to the Tennessee River valley area.

■ *What was the main goal of the TVA?*

Other Reforms. Several New Deal laws were aimed at correcting shortcomings in the economy. As you have read, President Roosevelt took steps to aid the country's banks during his first days in office. In the following months, Congress passed laws to change banking practices. Through the Glass-Steagall Banking Reform Act of June 1933, the government took greater control over the country's banks. This law also provided savers with federal insurance on their savings accounts. This insurance was to be handled by the Federal Deposit Insurance Corporation (FDIC). Because of the FDIC, savings could never again be completely wiped out, as they were in the early years of the depression.

New laws were also passed that regulated the sales of stocks and bonds. Other New Deal laws were aimed at helping minority groups.

■ *What was the purpose of the FDIC?*

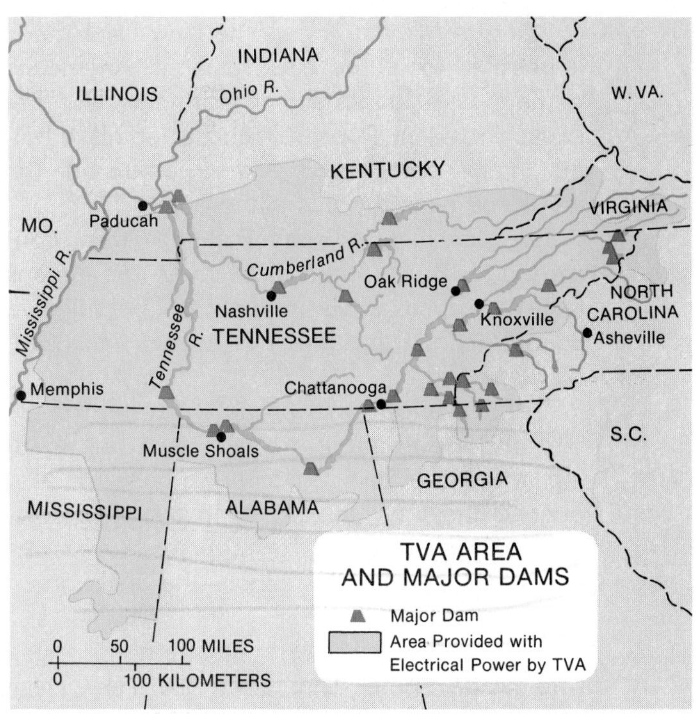

Which states are provided with electrical power from the TVA?

Reforms for Minorities. The New Deal made it possible for some disadvantaged Americans to gain fairer treatment. In part, this was because President Roosevelt chose for his advisers many persons who were aware of the hardships faced by minority groups.

The President's wife, Eleanor, was concerned with the hardships some Americans faced because of discrimination. She made a special effort to advance equal rights for blacks.

President Roosevelt brought several blacks into the government to take part in shaping the New Deal. President Roosevelt also opened the way for women to take a greater part in government. He appointed Frances Perkins as Secretary of Labor—the first woman cabinet member.

American Indians were also among those who made some gains from the New Deal.

Frances Perkins, the first woman in a President's cabinet, served from 1933 to 1945.

Photo Trends

President Roosevelt named two persons to office who were sensitive to the problems faced by American Indians. One of them was Secretary of Interior Harold Ickes. The other was John Collier—Commissioner of Indian Affairs.

Collier and Ickes worked for the passage of the Indian Reorganization Act of 1934. Before this law, the government had taken steps to break up Indian tribes and to distribute land owned by the tribes. The 1934 law changed this by reorganizing and encouraging tribal unity. It also protected tribal ownership of lands.

Despite these efforts, the hard times seemed to fall most heavily on minority groups. Discrimination, even by the federal government, continued. For example, black youths in the CCC worked in all-black camps. In the Southwest, several states tried to cut down on the number of jobless by returning illegal Mexican aliens to Mexico. Large numbers of persons of Mexican descent, including many American citizens, were forced to leave the United States.

Therefore, for many Americans, the New Deal did not go far enough in ending hardships. However, some other Americans held a different view of the New Deal. They felt that the New Deal had already made too many changes in government and in business.

■ *Who was Frances Perkins?*

Pressures on the President. By 1935 there was growing pressure on the President to change the New Deal. Part of this pressure was brought on by business owners. Many of them felt that the New Deal was harming the American economy. They claimed that President Roosevelt was using the government to change the free enterprise system. They called for lower government spending and for

(Text continues on page 528.)

VIEWPOINTS DIFFER

The New Deal: Revolutionary or Conservative?

Historians have been curious, and divided, on the role of the New Deal in American life. Was Roosevelt's "reform" program an extension of the liberal Populist and Progressive traditions? Or did it represent a dramatic break from the mainstream of American history?

Louis Hacker, a historian writing in the 1940s, referred to the New Deal as the "third American Revolution." The following passage is from his book, *Shaping of the American Tradition* (1947):

... A Revolution was started by the New Deal—not a revolution in the violent... sense, but a revolution nevertheless. The whole concept [idea] of the state, or national government, underwent a metamorphosis [change]. The state had previously been a passive [inactive] or impartial force,... Now it became the interventionist state. It imposed on the free business enterpriser [business person] all sorts of controls... it entered openly into business itself... it used its great... financial [money] powers to redistribute wealth and to create income; it committed itself to an elaborate [sweeping] program of social security that offered protection, in time, to the whole population against the mischances of unemployment, invalidity, and sudden death, and from the cradle to the grave...

Henry Steele Commager, one of America's most respected historians, understood the New Deal somewhat differently. For him it represented another phase in democracy's struggle against privilege and special interests. The connection between the New Deal and earlier reform movements seemed obvious (from: "Twelve Years of Roosevelt," *American Mercury* April, 1945)

What was really but a new deal of the old cards looked... like a revolution for two reasons: because it was carried through with such breathless rapidity, and because in spirit at least it contrasted [differed sharply]... with what immediately preceded [came before].... Actually, precedent [guidelines] for the major part of the New Deal legislation was to be found in... earlier periods. Regulation of... business dated back to the Interstate Commerce Act of 1887... The farm relief program of the Populists, and of [Woodrow] Wilson, anticipated much that the Roosevelt administrations enacted.... Labor legislation had its beginnings in such states as Massachusetts... while much of the program of social security was worked out in Wisconsin and other states during the second and third decades of the new century.

Think About It

1. What evidence does Hacker cite to justify his claim that the New Deal was revolutionary?
2. At what point before the New Deal does Commager believe the federal government began to regulate big business?
3. Do you think that Hacker and Commager might define the term revolution differently? Explain your answer.

lower taxes. These business leaders also wanted the President to keep the government out of business matters.

President Roosevelt answered these attacks by saying that a main goal of the New Deal was to maintain the American business system. Because of this, he would not accept these ideas for changing the New Deal.

Some other Americans charged that the New Deal did not do enough for workers or for the jobless. Three popular leaders with this viewpoint were Senator Huey Long, Francis Townsend, and Father Charles E. Coughlin. By early 1935, each of these men had built up a large following. These followers held views that were very different from those held by business leaders. These Americans wanted the New Deal to go even further in providing Americans with money to live on.

A ruling from the Supreme Court also served to put pressure on the New Deal. In May 1935, the Court struck down the National Recovery Administration (NRA). In the ruling, the Court said that Congress could not give its lawmaking powers to the President. Then, in January 1936, the Court ruled that the Agricultural Adjustment Act (AAA) was unconstitutional. Thus, while a growing number of Americans were asking more from the New Deal, the Court was acting to limit President Roosevelt's actions. As hard times continued and the election of 1936 neared, President Roosevelt had to choose a course for the future.

What two New Deal programs did the Supreme Court declare to be unconstitutional?

SECTION 3 REVIEW

1. *Why was the Tennessee Valley Authority created?*
2. *How did the Indian Reorganization Act reform the government's policy toward Indians?*
3. *Why did business leaders want President Roosevelt to change the direction of the New Deal?*

CHAPTER 29 SUMMARY

At the onset of the depression, President Hoover believed that business would soon recover. The President used his office to speed this recovery. Despite these efforts, conditions became worse. As unemployment skyrocketed, Americans began to blame the President for the continuing hardships. Because of this, President Hoover was defeated in the election of 1932. Franklin Delano Roosevelt was elected President.

President Roosevelt promised to undertake bold steps to end the depression. His plans for relief, recovery, and reform became known as the New Deal. The New Deal was, in many ways, an experiment. It included a wide range of programs aimed at meeting many different goals.

Some parts of the New Deal succeeded, while others failed. By 1935, there was growing criticism of the New Deal. Also, the Supreme Court made two decisions that forced the President to change his program.

CHAPTER 29 REVIEW

USING YOUR SKILLS

Interpreting Statistics

In the study of history, we often use statistical information to learn more about our subjects. To understand the problems of the depression, for example, it is necessary to know how many Americans could not find jobs during those years. The chart below lists the number of persons who were unemployed during each year between 1929 and 1935. The same information is plotted on the graph. Study the chart and the graph and then answer the questions.

1. How many Americans were unemployed during the year of the stock-market crash?
2. In what year between 1929 and 1935 did unemployment peak?
3. Between which two consecutive years did the largest increase in unemployment take place?
4. Between which two consecutive years did the number of unemployment change the least?
5. Between which two years did the number of unemployed begin to decrease?
6. What conclusions can you make about unemployment between 1929 and 1935?

Year	Number of Unemployed
1929	1,550,000
1930	4,340,000
1931	8,020,000
1932	12,060,000
1933	12,860,000
1934	11,340,000
1935	10,610,000

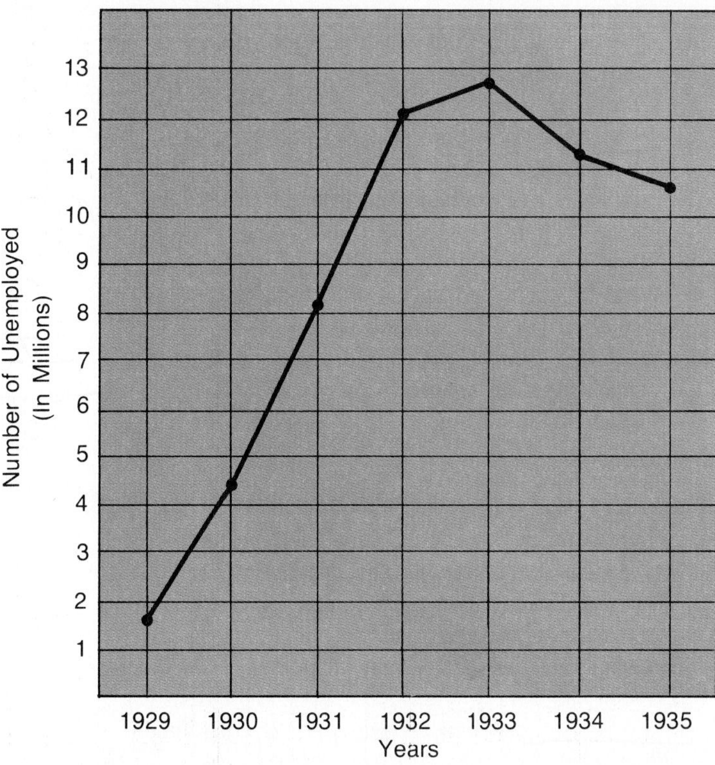

CHAPTER 29 REVIEW

YOU SHOULD KNOW

Identify, define, or explain each of the following:

repossessed
relief
Hoovervilles
New Deal
fireside chat
Hundred Days
codes
minimum wages
TVA
Frances Perkins

CHECKING FACTS

1. How many banks closed in 1930?
2. What was the result of the Hawley-Smoot Tariff of 1930?
3. Which Americans were hardest hit by the depression?
4. What was the purpose of the Reconstruction Finance Corporation?
5. What were the three goals of the New Deal?
6. What were two work relief programs of the New Deal?
7. What was the goal of the National Industrial Recovery Act?
8. What was the major goal of the TVA?
9. What law provided savers with federal insurance on their savings accounts?
10. What two New Deal programs were declared unconstitutional by the Supreme Court?

UNDERSTANDING CONCEPTS

1. Why did many Americans lose their homes during the early years of the depression?
2. Why was President Hoover against using federal money for relief programs?
3. How did the New Deal help farmers?
4. In what different ways did the New Deal help minority groups? Fail to help minority groups?
5. What were the main criticisms of the New Deal?

LEARNING FROM ILLUSTRATIONS

1. Based on the illustration on page 516, what types of materials do you think were used to build Hoovervilles?
2. Look at the table on page 521. What New Deal laws and programs listed were aimed at helping businesses?

CRITICAL THINKING

1. If you had been a voter in the election of 1932, who would have been your choice for President? Why?
2. What do you think President Roosevelt meant when he said, "The only thing we have to fear is fear itself?"
3. How did the Indian Reorganization Act of 1934 compare to the Dawes Act of 1887?

ENRICHMENT ACTIVITIES

1. Make a list of questions you have about life during the Great Depression and the New Deal. Your list might include questions such as the following: How did the Great Depression affect your way of life? What kinds of leisure-time activities did you enjoy during the Great Depression? Did the New Deal help improve living conditions for you and your family? Did you take part in any New Deal programs? If so, what were they? Then, interview individuals who remember the Great Depression and the New Deal. Discuss your interviews with the class.
2. Write a report about the popular forms of entertainment enjoyed by Americans during the Depression. Music, plays, movies, radio shows, and sports are among the topics that can be investigated. Present your report to the class.

1934

1937

- 1934 Dust storms swept through parts of the country
Platt Amendment repealed
- 1935 Second New Deal begun
Social Security Act passed
National Recovery Act declared unconstitutional
Wagner Act passed
Congress of Industrial Organizations founded
- 1936 General Motors strike in Flint, Michigan
- 1937 Ohio River flooded killing 250 people
Farm Security Administration set up

CHAPTER 30

The New Deal and the Continuing Depression

Chapter Objectives

After studying this chapter, you should be able to:

- enumerate the reasons why President Roosevelt shifted the direction of the New Deal in 1935;
- list the programs undertaken by the government to solve problems in American farm areas;
- identify the major economic problems facing the countries of Europe after World War I.

1 The Second New Deal

Overview Beginning in 1935, President Roosevelt backed a number of new reform laws. These laws became known as the *Second New Deal*. Some of these laws brought long-lasting changes to the United States. The Second New Deal also encouraged the growth of labor unions.

Objectives After reading this section, you should be able to:

- identify the main reason for President Roosevelt to change the direction of the New Deal;
- discuss the purpose of the Social Security Act;
- explain the changes in American labor unions during the 1930's.

Changing the New Deal. In 1935, President Roosevelt shifted the direction of the New Deal. There were three main reasons for this change. First, the United States was still in the midst of the Great Depression. The New Deal had not yet achieved its goals. Second, many business leaders had withdrawn their support from the President. They said that the New Deal would destroy the American business system. In many cases, they were openly critical of the New Deal. President Roosevelt was surprised and bothered by these remarks. Many of his New Deal programs had been aimed at helping business. President Roosevelt thus decided in 1935 that he could no longer count on the backing of business leaders. He would look elsewhere for future support.

The third reason for change was that the American public was making more demands on the government. Having suffered through nearly five years of the depression, large numbers of Americans began to think that the government should be doing more to help the average citizen. Congress and the President began to move in this direction with a number of new laws in 1935. This has become known as the Second New Deal. The laws of the Second New Deal emphasized reform. They also called for greater government spending.

■ *Which group of Americans no longer supported President Roosevelt in 1935?*

The Works Progress Administration. One of the main programs of the Second New Deal was the Works Progress Administration (WPA). The WPA was a huge work-relief program. Between 1935 and 1938, the WPA put over 3 million Americans to work. The WPA undertook a large number of public building projects. It also included projects for jobless artists, writers, musicians, and actors. The work produced by these WPA workers brought some

DO YOU KNOW?

What radio show led Americans to believe that martians were invading the country?

A Halloween radio broadcast of H. G. Wells's *The War of the Worlds* on October 30, 1938, led a number of Americans who missed the show's introduction to believe that creatures from Mars were invading earth. Orson Welles, the radio announcer, wanted the story to sound as real as possible. So, he began the show with music and conversation but interrupted the program with new bulletins about martian landings in New Jersey. Welles was so convincing that some radio listeners panicked.

excellent entertainment, literature, and artwork to the public.

One branch of the WPA was aimed at helping the millions of young Americans who could not find jobs. This office was called the National Youth Administration (NYA). It served both men and women between the ages of 16 and 25. The NYA made it possible for thousands of young people to stay in school by offering them part-time jobs.

The WPA helped millions of Americans. Yet, it was not a permanent solution to the problems of unemployment. It was clear that a large number of persons would remain without jobs even when prosperity returned. The Second New Deal addressed this matter by passing the Social Security Act.

■ *What was the purpose of the National Youth Administration?*

Bettmann Archive

What kind of project are these WPA workers working on?

Social Security. The Social Security Act of 1935 was one of the most far-reaching laws of the New Deal. With this law, the government took over new responsibilities for the well-being of citizens. One of the goals of the law was to protect workers against poverty during unemployment and after retirement.

The Social Security Act set up a government-run system of old-age insurance. The program put a payroll tax on workers and on their employers. This money was put into a fund that would be used to give pensions—retirement incomes—to these workers after they reached the age of 65. Disabled workers could also draw money from this fund. In addition, this program provided for incomes to be paid to the families of workers who died.

The Social Security Act also set up guidelines for a system of unemployment insurance. For the most part, the states were allowed to develop their own plans for giving payments to those who were out of work for a short time.

The social security programs were not open to all American workers. Farm workers, household servants, and public employees were among those who were left out. In later years, the programs were changed to cover most American workers. The social security system continues today.

■ *What was the purpose of the Social Security Act?*

Encouraging Unions. Workers had been promised the right to form unions under the National Recovery Act of 1933. However, this law was declared unconstitutional by the Supreme Court in May 1935. Thus, unions lost the protection of the law. After this court decision, President Roosevelt decided to back a law that had been put forth earlier by Senator Robert Wagner of New York.

The Wagner Act—also called the National Labor Relations Act—became law in July 1935. This law gave protection to the organized labor movement. It did this by guarding the right of workers to form unions. The act outlawed certain antiunion practices.

The National Labor Relations Board (NLRB) was set up to oversee the act. One of its duties was to give workers a fair chance to decide which union, if any, would represent them. To do this, the NLRB would hold elections in which workers voted by secret ballot.

The Wagner Act gave organized labor the backing of the federal government. Many business owners, however, did not like the new law. Some business leaders believed that the Supreme Court would declare that the Wagner Act was unconstitutional.

■ *What was one duty given to the National Labor Relations Board?*

Union Growth and Change. America's labor unions drew many new members after the Wagner Act was passed. Workers in several large industries—such as steel and automobile making—wanted to join a union. However, the craft union did not suit the many unskilled workers in these factories.

Craft unions were made up of workers who shared the same skill, such as carpenters or bakers. During the 1930's many labor leaders backed a different kind of union—the industrial union. These unions were formed by joining all workers in an industry. Both skilled and unskilled workers could become members.

When did union membership begin to increase? In what years was union membership greatest?

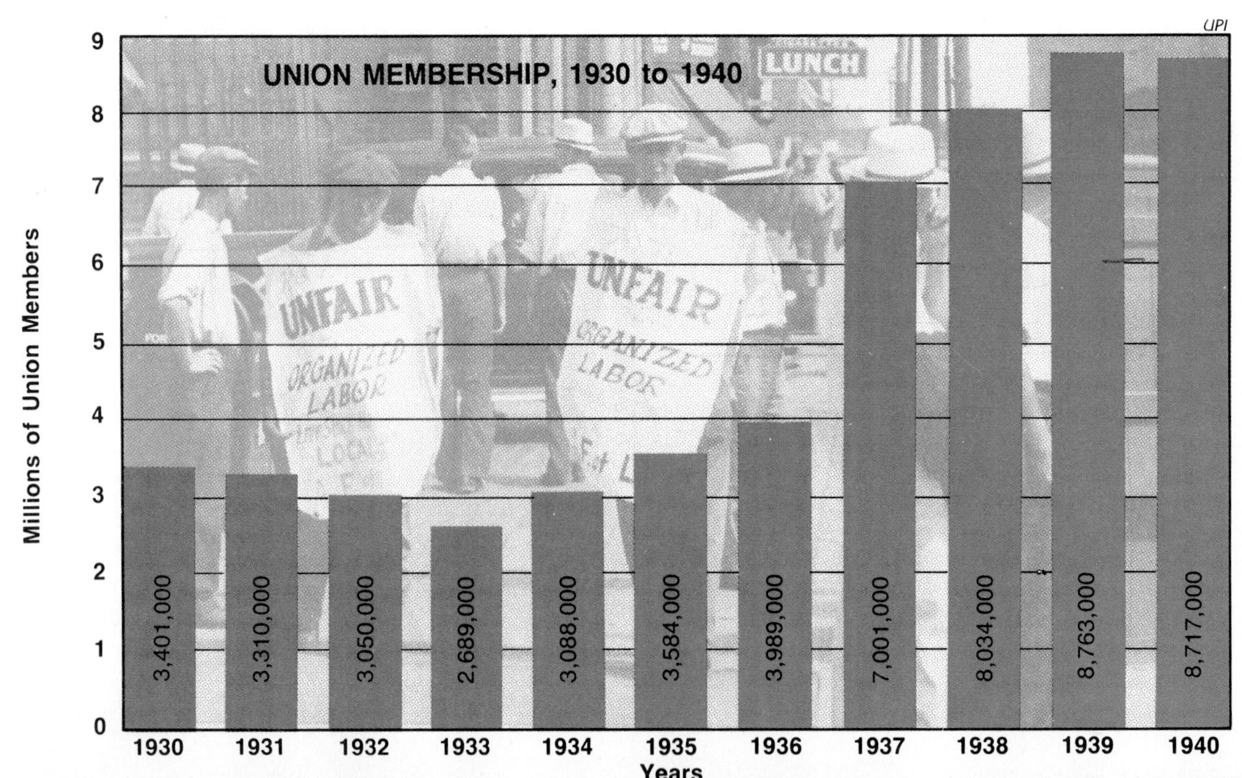

One labor leader who favored the formation of industrial unions was John L. Lewis. Lewis was the leader of the United Mine Workers. In 1935, he wanted the American Federation of Labor (AFL) to take a stronger stand in favor of the new unions. The AFL was based on craft unions. When the AFL refused to move toward industrial unions, John L. Lewis founded the Congress of Industrial Organizations. The CIO's goal was to organize all the workers in the country's largest businesses. Among the targets were the steel, automobile, tire, and rubber industries.

■ *What is an industrial union?*

The Sit-Down Strike. In its fight for recognition, the CIO developed a new weapon—the sit-down strike. In a sit-down strike, workers stopped working but stayed at their posts. This prevented the factory owners from hiring strikebreakers to take the place of striking workers.

The first large sit-down strike was staged by union members at the General Motors automobile factory in Flint, Michigan. The strike began on December 28, 1936. It lasted six weeks. The strike forced the company to accept the union as the employees' representative.

The Wagner Act came under attack soon after it was passed. But, in April 1937 the Supreme Court upheld the Wagner Act. Thus, the court agreed that the government could protect the rights of workers to join unions. With this protection, the AFL and the CIO both began drives to get more members.

By forming industrial unions, the CIO brought the benefits of organization to many American workers who had been left out of craft unions. Black workers in coal mining, in the textile industry, and in the steel industry joined CIO unions. The CIO took a part in the fight for equal rights for blacks.

■ *What was a sit-down strike?*

The Election of 1936. The Republican party needed a strong candidate to run against Roosevelt in the election of 1936. Governor Alfred M. Landon of Kansas was the party's choice. Landon had a good record in state government. In the campaign, Landon and Roosevelt called for similar programs. Landon, however, claimed that he would also balance the government's budget.

The outcome of the election showed that President Roosevelt had built a wide base of support. President Roosevelt received the electoral votes of all but two states. In his victory, President Roosevelt received an overwhelming number of votes from workers, farmers, the jobless, and the elderly.

■ *Who was the Republican candidate in the election of 1936?*

SECTION 1 REVIEW

1. *Why did President Roosevelt change the New Deal?*
2. *What was the purpose of the Social Security Act?*
3. *Why did some labor leaders favor the organization of industrial unions?*

2 Roosevelt's Second Term

Overview As President Roosevelt began his second term, the country was showing some signs of recovery. There remained, however, many problems to be solved. Millions of Americans were still out of work. Also, natural disasters added to the hardships faced by Americans during these years. President Roosevelt believed that the programs of the New Deal were necessary for helping the country. His determination to carry out these programs led him into a confrontation with the Supreme Court.

Objectives After reading this section, you should be able to:

- discuss why President Roosevelt proposed a law that would change the court system;
- analyze the causes of the Dust Bowl;
- give examples of government programs aimed at solving farm problems in the 1930's.

Challenging the Supreme Court. Early in his second term, President Roosevelt undertook an action that challenged the Supreme Court. During 1935 and 1936, the Court had declared that several New Deal laws were unconstitutional. With these decisions, the Supreme Court ended two major New Deal programs—the AAA and the NRA. President Roosevelt did not agree with these decisions. Furthermore, he did not want the Court to make any more decisions that would limit the New Deal. The President was particularly concerned about the Social Security Act. President Roosevelt believed that this program was a major achievement of his presidency.

President Roosevelt wanted to appoint some new justices to the Supreme Court who would favor the New Deal. However, there were no vacancies to be filled. President Roosevelt came up with a plan that would allow him to name new members to the Court even though there were no openings.

In early 1937, the President asked Congress to pass a law that would have changed the court system. President Roosevelt pointed out that 6 of the 9 Supreme Court justices were over 70 years old. He claimed that these elderly members could not keep up with the work load. Because of this, Roosevelt wanted to name an additional member to the Court for each justice who stayed on the bench past the age of 70. President Roosevelt suggested that

Brown Brothers

The advanced age of several Supreme Court justices was sometimes the subject of editorial cartoons in the mid-1930's. How does the cartoonist show the advanced ages of some of the Supreme Court justices?

up to 6 new Supreme Court members be added in this way.

The law called for by President Roosevelt suggested that the entire federal court system needed more judges. However, the President's true aim was easily seen. President Roosevelt wanted to "pack" the Supreme Court with justices who would stand behind the New Deal.

The "court-packing" plan was met with strong opposition. Even some longtime backers of the President were against the plan. They thought it was wrong for the President to want this power over the Supreme Court.

The law called for by President Roosevelt was never passed. However, no more New Deal laws were struck down by the Court. In addition, five of the nine seats on the Supreme Court became vacant during Roosevelt's second term. This gave President Roosevelt the opportunity to name five of his own choices to the Court.

■ *What was the real reason why President Roosevelt wanted to add more justices to the Supreme Court?*

Disasters in Farm Areas. Natural disasters added to the problems faced by many American farmers during the depression. During the early 1930's there was a *drought*—dry spell—on the Great Plains. For many years, farmers had overworked the land in this area. Too many animals had been allowed to graze on the wild grasses. In addition, homesteaders and farmers had cut down trees and had raised crops without concern for the erosion of the soil.

These poor farming methods combined with the drought and unusually high winds led to terrible dust storms beginning in 1934. High winds swept the topsoil from huge sections of land in Kansas, Arkansas, Oklahoma, New Mexico, Texas, and Colorado. The area became known as the Dust Bowl during the mid-1930's.

During the storms, thick clouds of dust filled the air. The dirty air was dangerous to breathe. Farmers in the Dust Bowl could no longer make a living from the damaged land. Thousands of families including former farm owners, tenant farmers, and laborers left the area in search of jobs. This added to the already large number of unemployed workers created by the hard times of the depression. Many of these families headed west to California, Washington, and Oregon.

Many of these farm families joined the thousands of workers who took short-term jobs on large farms. They were hired for low wages to work during planting and harvesting. These families lived in shacks and tents without running water. Many persons became very ill in these unclean conditions. When the work ran out, they had to move to another area. In most cases, these families were not helped by state welfare offices. This was because they had not lived in the state long enough.

The increase in the number of farm workers added to the hardships faced by Mexican Americans in the area. For many years, Mexican Americans had filled these difficult, low-paying farm jobs. However, they were denied even these jobs when families from the Dust Bowl moved west.

As the dust storms blew across the plains, the eastern states faced destructive floods. The worst flood came in 1937 when the Ohio River rose high above its banks. About 250 persons were killed in this flood. Hundreds of thousands of Americans were left homeless. Farms and other businesses were damaged by the waters. In most cases, local resources could

(Text continues on page 539.)

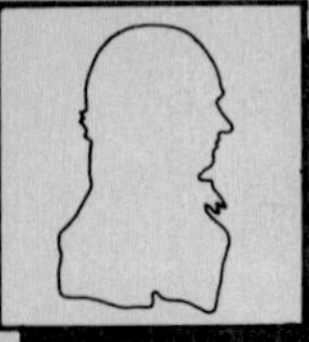

PROFILES

Woody Guthrie

The manager of the electric plant was "not happy at all" that the government was going to name the new 1966 substation after some songwriter. Then he heard Woody Guthrie's songs; "This land is your land," "Roll on Columbia," "So long, it's been good to know ya." "I'm proud of the name," sang the manager.

Woody Guthrie was born in Oklahoma in 1912. His family faced one disaster after another. Their house burned and the next one was ripped apart by a tornado. Woody's sister was killed in a stove explosion and his father went bankrupt. When he was 13, Woody shined shoes, delivered milk, and lived with a neighborhood family. He found an old guitar and taught himself to play it. He grew up playing at Saturday dances and working as a sign painter.

During the Depression of the 1930's, dust storms and drought wiped out hope in farm communities. Woody then began to write songs about people sticking together. He traveled to California as a migrant worker, singing live on radio shows. In 1940 he went east and wrote "This land is my land, This land is your land, from California to the New York Island."

Woody wrote songs of unions and working men and women and racial equality and freedom. "Reuben James," "Pretty Boy Floyd," "Hard, Ain't it Hard," "This Train is Bound for Glory," and "Blowin in the Wind" are now national possessions. Woody died in 1967 but his dreams of human accomplishment live on in America's music.

The Bettmann Archive

Thinking Critically

What feelings might Guthrie's music have created to make the manager proud of the name of the power substation?

Guthrie's songs celebrate working together, fighting for what's right, and the grandeur of nature's beauty. Why are these concerns not simply the product of the Dust Bowl and the Depression?

Guthrie's music goes beyond entertainment. His songs lift and unite the nation's spirit. What popular music today does the same?

not meet the needs created by these disasters. Citizens looked to the federal government for help.

■ *What conditions created the Dust Bowl?*

Government Action. The natural disasters of the 1930's made clear the need for conservation programs. The government began to work out ways to prevent such full-scale damage in the future. For example, farmers were taught ways to deal with erosion. Projects were undertaken to restore the fertility of farmland. Dams were built and trees were planted to protect soil from the harmful effects of wind and water. The second Agricultural Adjustment Act, passed in 1938, was also aimed at protecting the country's farmland. It helped farmers who practiced soil conservation. Farmers were given payments for not planting certain crops on part of their land. This land would be planted with crops that restored the soil.

The New Deal also took steps to meet the needs of the rural poor. The Farm Security Administration (FSA) was set up in 1937 to help tenant farmers, sharecroppers, and migrant farm workers. The FSA offered these persons low-cost loans to help them buy farms. The FSA also built housing camps for migrant farm workers.

It is hard to judge the New Deal. Some programs did ease many of the hardships of the depression. Other laws, such as the Social Security Act, brought long-lasting changes to the United States. In 1938, however, the country was still in the depression. About 10 million Americans were out of work. New Deal critics called for the President to abandon his programs. At the same time, international affairs demanded the President's attention. The depression had greatly changed America's relations with other countries.

L.C./F.S.A. Files—Photographer Jack Delano

The average tenant farmer could afford few material comforts during the 1930's.

■ *What groups of Americans were aided by the Farm Security Administration?*

SECTION 2 REVIEW

1. *Why did President Roosevelt propose a law to change the Supreme Court?*
2. *How did poor farming practices help to create the Dust Bowl?*
3. *What programs did the government undertake to solve the problems in farm areas?*

3 Foreign Relations During the Depression

Overview During the 1920's, American prosperity had helped to ease the economic problems facing many other countries. This changed, however, when the United States entered the depression. The depression became a worldwide problem as international loans and trade were cut back. The United States took steps to improve relations with countries during the 1930's. Ties with Japan, however, became strained.

Objectives After reading this section, you should be able to:

- list the economic problems in Europe after World War I;
- give examples of ways the United States worked to improve relations with its neighboring countries;
- explain why some Americans wanted the United States to remain isolated during the 1930's.

A Worldwide Depression. The depression of the 1930's was a worldwide problem. The unemployment and poverty that faced Americans during these hard times also troubled the people of other countries. The roots of these problems are found in World War I.

The war left the countries of Europe with many problems. Houses, farms, and factories had been destroyed. Several countries were in debt for large loans they had taken out during the war. In addition, Germany was expected to pay the Allies $32 billion in *reparations*—payments for war damages. High unemployment troubled many countries.

The Bettmann Archive

After World War I, German refugees often found their homes and businesses in ruins. Thus the German government faced the problem of rebuilding the country while trying to pay Germany's war debts.

During the 1920's, however, all of Europe did not suffer the full impact of these problems. In part, this was because of the economic boom enjoyed by the United States. During the prosperous 1920's, the American government and private American investors made loans to foreign nations. Also, the United States imported large amounts of goods from other countries. These loans and purchases helped many foreign countries.

However, during the late 1920's, American investors became less willing to make loans to other countries. Moreover, after the stock-market crash of October 1929, American loans dropped even more.

Many foreign countries were further hurt when the United States passed the Hawley-Smoot Tariff in 1930. This raised the tariff on most imports. It was hoped that by cutting imports, Americans would buy American-made goods and business would improve. However, other countries replied by raising their own tariffs. High tariffs, in turn, led to a great cutback in world trade. As a result, business declined and the depression spread and brought hardships to countries all over the world. Faced with this situation in 1932, President Roosevelt set forth to work out a foreign policy for the country.

■ *In what two ways did the prosperous American economy benefit other countries during the 1920's?*

The Good-Neighbor Policy. During the 1930's, the United States enjoyed generally good relations with the countries of North and South America. The foundation for these friendly terms was laid by President Coolidge and President Hoover during the 1920's. These presidents led the United States away from the practice of interfering in the affairs of Latin America. They also began the withdrawal of American troops from Latin America. When President Roosevelt took office, he stated that he would lead the country with a *good-neighbor policy.*

In 1933 the United States made a joint agreement with the other countries of the Americas. Together the nations declared that no country would intervene in the affairs of another country. The United States took steps to carry through with this promise. In 1934, for example, the United States changed its relationship with Cuba by repealing the Platt Amendment. Through the repeal, the United States announced that it no longer claimed the right to interfere with Cuban affairs.

The United States also built friendlier ties with its neighboring countries during the 1930's through trade agreements. These pacts increased trade by reducing tariffs. These trade agreements showed many countries that the United States was willing to cooperate with its neighbors.

■ *What agreement did the United States make with its American neighbors in 1933?*

Relations With the Soviet Union. In 1933, the United States *recognized*—opened relations with—the Soviet Union. Between 1917 and 1933 the American government did not have any official dealings with the Soviet government. This was because the United States did not like the communist form of government of the Soviet Union.

A number of reasons led President Roosevelt to change this firm stand against the Soviet Union. One of the major reasons was the belief that the Soviet Union would buy large amounts of American goods. This trade,

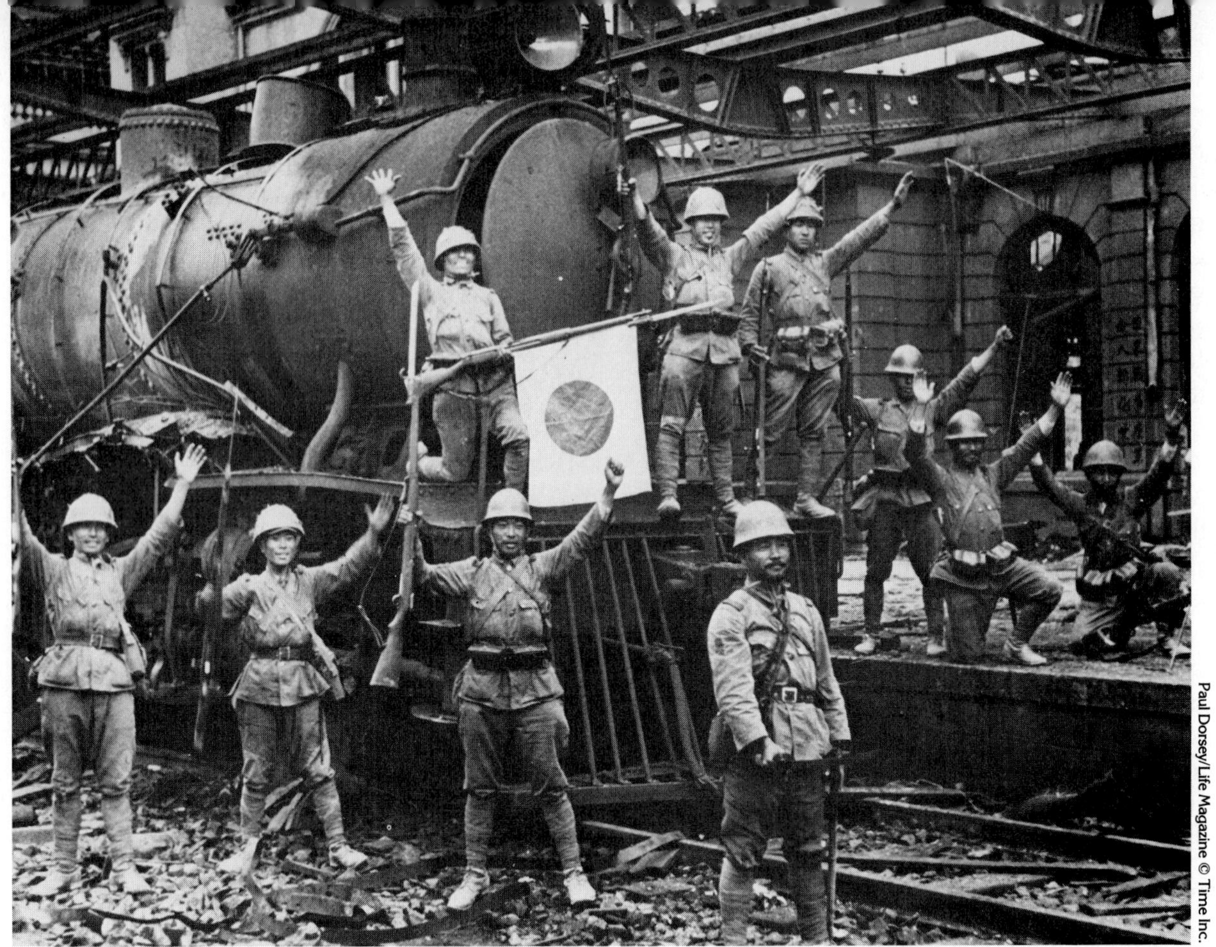
Paul Dorsey/Life Magazine © Time Inc.

The Japanese conquered Manchuria in 1932 and then worked to expand their influence to other parts of China in the late 1930's.

it was hoped, would then create jobs and help to reduce unemployment in the United States.

What was one of the major reasons that led the United States to recognize the Soviet Union?

American Relations With Japan. During the 1930's relations between the United States and Japan were weak. This was because the United Sates objected to Japanese *aggression*—use of power over other lands—throughout Asia.

By 1930 a group of military leaders had become very powerful in Japan. They wanted Japan to build an overseas empire. While President Hoover was in office, Japanese armies attacked Manchuria, the northern province of China. This land was rich in the natural resources needed by Japan. Japan then renamed this land Manchukuo and set up a government there.

This Japanese attack on China was against the open-door policy (see Chapter 25). It also violated other peace treaties that Japan had signed. In January 1932 the American secretary of state, Henry L. Stimson, sent a note to Japan to protest this attack. This, however, was the strongest action the United States was willing to undertake. This was largely because there was a widespread desire in the United States for *isolationism*—staying out of the affairs of other countries. Americans wanted to be isolated for a number of different reasons. Some felt that nothing had been gained in the world war that the United States had entered in 1917. Other people wanted the United States to give its full attention to ending the depression.

Japan continued to use armed force against China. At times, American citizens in China were treated poorly in these incidents. Then, on December 12, 1937, Japanese planes bombed an American gunboat, the *Panay*, on the Yangtze River in China. Three American oil tankers were also bombed. Two Americans were killed, and about 30 others were wounded in the attack. The American government demanded that the Japanese government apologize for the incident. The United States also demanded payment and a promise that such an incident would never happen again. The Japanese quickly met these demands. By taking no further action, the Americans showed how strongly they wanted to stay out of war. Before long, however, world events showed Americans that they could not remain isolated.

■ *What is isolationism?*

SECTION 3 REVIEW

1. *What economic problems faced Europe following World War I?*
2. *How did the United States change its relationship with Cuba in 1934?*
3. *Why did some Americans want their country to remain isolated during the 1930's?*

CHAPTER 30 SUMMARY

As the depression continued into 1935, President Roosevelt backed a number of new laws. Among them were the Social Security Act and the Wagner Act. Overall, these new laws expanded the activities of the federal government. They brought long-lasting changes to the country.

President Roosevelt was reelected in 1936 with a large majority of the votes. During this term, the President tried to expand his power over the Supreme Court. The Congress, however, refused to pass the President's "court-packing" plan.

During the depression, the United States worked toward better relations with the other countries of the Americas. The United States also opened relations with the Soviet Union. At the same time, relations between Japan and the United States were strained as Japan invaded China.

USING YOUR SKILLS

Interpreting Political Cartoons

Political cartoonists often use humor or emotion to comment on someone or something in the news. Both of the cartoons that appear below were first printed during the depression. They express two distinct points of view. Examine the cartoons carefully and then answer the questions that follow.

1. Whom do the characters used in these cartoons represent?
2. How would you describe the action depicted in each of these cartoons?
3. Which of the cartoons expresses a favorable view of the New Deal?
4. What do you think was the main message communicated in each of these cartoons?

Historical Pictures Service

Tom Howard/The Columbus Dispatch

CHAPTER 30 REVIEW

YOU SHOULD KNOW

Identify, define, or explain each of the following:

pensions
drought
reparations
good-neighbor policy
recognized
aggression
isolationism

CHECKING FACTS

1. What was the Works Progress Administration?
2. What was one of the goals of the Social Security Act?
3. What did the Wagner Act guard?
4. What was the CIO's goal?
5. What part of the United States became known as the Dust Bowl?
6. What conditions caused the Dust Bowl?
7. Who did the Farm Security Administration help?
8. What was a major reason that led the United States to recognize the Soviet Union?
9. What did the United States do to protest Japan's attack on China?
10. What was the *Panay*?

UNDERSTANDING CONCEPTS

1. Why was the direction of the New Deal changed in 1935?
2. How did the American labor movement change during the 1930's?
3. Why did President Roosevelt try to change the Supreme Court?
4. What events demonstrated America's desire for isolation during the 1930's?

LEARNING FROM ILLUSTRATIONS

1. Study the graph on page 534. According to the graph, in what year was union membership lowest? How many union members were there in 1940?
2. Look at the cartoon on page 536. What do you think the artist was trying to portray about the Supreme Court?

CRITICAL THINKING

1. How did the General Motors strike in 1936 compare to the Pullman Strike in 1894?
2. In your opinion, which of the New Deal programs was the most successful? Why do you think this was so?
3. If you had been a citizen of the United States in the late 1930's, would you have encouraged the country to be isolated? Why or why not?

ENRICHMENT ACTIVITY

Prepare a short lesson on the development of the American labor movement. Divide into small groups to investigate separate topics. Then, report to the class. Possible projects include biographies of labor leaders, interviews with union members, accounts of famous strikes, charts and graphs to show union membership in the past and in the present, and an examination of laws that concern labor unions. Some famous strikes that might be investigated are the McCormick Harvesting Machine Company strike in 1886, the Pullman strike in 1894, the coal strike in 1902, the Triangle Shirtwaist Company strike in 1909–1910, and the General Motors strike in 1936–1937.

1937

1945

- 1937 Rome-Berlin-Tokyo Axis pact signed
- 1939 World War II began in Europe
- 1940 President Roosevelt elected to third term
- 1941 Pearl Harbor attacked by Japan
  United States declared war on Japan, Germany, and Italy
- 1944 Allies invaded France
- 1945 FDR died
  Vice-President Harry Truman became President
  Germany surrendered
  First atomic bomb dropped
  Japan surrendered

CHAPTER 31

The Second World War

Chapter Objectives

After studying this chapter, you should be able to:

- identify the causes of World War II;
- list the major causes that moved the United States away from neutrality;
- explain President Truman's main reasons for ordering the use of the atomic bomb against Japan.

1 The Origins of the War

Overview During the 1930's, many Americans' desire for isolation was weakened. This happened because Japan, Italy, and Germany began to invade other countries. By early 1941, the United States was heading toward war.

Objectives After reading this section, you should be able to:

- list the causes of World War II;
- explain the purpose of the neutrality laws passed by Congress between 1935 and 1937;
- discuss why the United States moved away from neutrality.

Government Changes in Europe. During the 1920's and the 1930's, the people of Europe looked for ways to end the problems caused by war and a major depression. Many people lost confidence in their governments. Some turned to new political parties that demanded major changes in the government.

In Italy, the Fascist party gained many members after World War I. Benito Mussolini was the party's leader. He promised the Italian people that the Fascists would bring glory and wealth to Italy. In 1922, Mussolini became the head of the Italian government. He guarded his powers by outlawing all other parties. Mussolini became a *dictator*—a leader who holds total power within a country. In a dictatorship, schools, newspapers, businesses, and even social clubs fall under the control of the dictator.

During the 1930's, Adolf Hitler became the dictator of Germany. Hitler was the head of the National Socialist German Worker's party. This group was also known as the Nazi party. Hitler was a powerful speaker. In his speeches, he told the people of Germany that they had been wronged by many enemies. Hitler promised that he would make Germany a world power.

In their rise to power, both Hitler and Mussolini promised to make their nations rich and strong. They promised jobs for the unemployed. They also promised to rid their countries of people who they said would harm their nation. In working toward these goals, these leaders showed no regard for the rights of individuals.

Other European countries were also under the hold of dictators during the 1930's. Joseph Stalin held all power in the Soviet Union. And, in 1936, General Francisco Franco led a rebellion against the government of Spain. Like Hitler and Mussolini, Franco did not believe in democracy. Circumstances led Franco into an alliance with these dictators. These two leaders aided Franco in this civil war against the government of Spain. As a result, Franco gained full control of Spain in 1939.

■ *What four European nations were ruled by dictators during the 1930's?*

Building Armies for Conquests. Both Hitler and Mussolini built strong armies for their countries. As these leaders rebuilt their military forces, they created jobs and also helped many businesses within Italy and Germany. These military forces were to be used to conquer other lands. Hitler and Mussolini claimed that their nations had to expand to get the resources they needed. They declared that such conquests would bring pride and glory to their countries.

Mussolini began to build what he called the

Second Roman Empire in 1935. Italian forces attacked Ethiopia—an African nation. The Ethiopian soldiers had poor equipment and little training. They could not stop the Italian invasion. No other country helped Ethiopia defend itself against Italy.

Hitler had violated the Treaty of Versailles by building up the German army. Then, in 1936, Germany went against the treaty again when its soldiers marched into the Rhineland. This was a part of Germany that bordered on France. According to the Treaty of Versailles, no German troops were to enter this area. No action was taken by France or any other country to force Hitler to remove these soldiers from the Rhineland. With this move, Hitler and the Nazis had begun working toward their goal of a German empire.

■ *In what two ways did Hitler violate the Treaty of Versailles?*

This poster advertises the anti-Jewish film "The Eternal Jew."

The Holocaust. Hitler and the Nazi party believed that all enemies of the state and other "undesirables" should be removed from Germany. These undesirables included persons who held opposing political ideas as well as members of minority religious and ethnic groups. Jews, in particular, were singled out for persecution. The Nazis blamed the Jews for many of Germany's problems.

During their early years in power, the Nazis made laws that stripped Jews of their rights. It soon became difficult for Jews to earn a living in Germany. Yet, it was also difficult for most of them to move to other countries. In part this was because most countries, including the United States, had laws that limited immigration.

As the years passed, Nazi treatment of Jews and other groups worsened. After war broke out in 1939, the Nazis began to kill these people. This *holocaust*—mass murder—was carried out in concentration camps built for this purpose. Over 6 million Jews were killed by the Nazis before 1945. Unknown numbers of religious leaders, gypsies, and other people were also put to death.

■ *What groups of people were considered as undesirable by the Nazis?*

Forming the Axis. In 1937, Japan, Italy, and Germany signed an agreement. The pact between them became known as the Rome-Berlin-Tokyo Axis. Each member of the Axis had plans to extend its power over other lands.

DO YOU KNOW?

Who was the only American President to be elected to four terms in office?

Franklin D. Roosevelt was the only American to win four presidential elections. He served as President for more than twelve years, from 1932 to 1945. He died a few months after his fourth inaugural. In 1951, the United States Constitution was amended to limit the years a person could serve as President of the United States to ten. No person can now be elected to more than two full terms in office.

In doing so, the Axis powers would go against the rights of other nations and threaten world peace.

While the Axis powers planned their future conquests, other countries were working out ways to avoid wars. In the United States, Congress passed laws aimed at keeping the United States out of foreign wars.

■ *What countries formed the Axis?*

From Neutrality to Involvement. Between 1935 and 1937, Congress passed several neutrality laws. These laws cut off the sale of American weapons to all countries at war. Within a few years, however, aggression from the Axis countries led the United States to change its neutral stand.

In March 1938 Austria was joined to Germany. Hitler announced that Germany and Austria would be unified under his rule. Later that year, Hitler turned his attention to Czechoslovakia. Over 3 million German-speaking people lived in the western part of Czechoslovakia. Hitler demanded that this land—known as the Sudetenland—be joined with Germany. Hitler promised that this would be

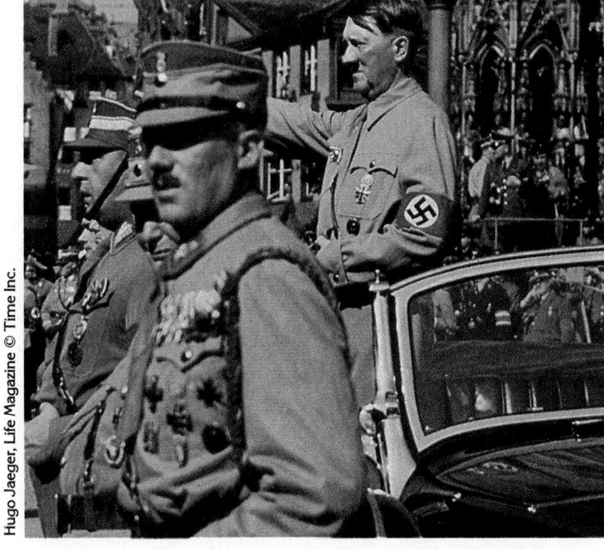

Hugo Jaeger, Life Magazine © Time Inc.

Adolf Hitler is standing in a car receiving the salutes of columns of soldiers.

the last demand for land that he would make. The leaders of Great Britain and France met with Hitler in September 1938. Their desire to avoid war with Germany led them to accept Hitler's demand for the Sudetenland.

By the spring of 1939 it was clear that Hitler had plans for taking over more countries. In March the Germans took control of Czechoslovakia. At the same time, Mussolini's army invaded Albania. Hitler then made demands on Poland. Great Britain and France stated that they would back Poland against Germany. Thus, when Germany attacked Poland on the morning of September 1, 1939, Great Britain and France declared war on Germany. World War II had begun.

Germany's powerful army easily overpowered other countries. By late April 1940, Germany controlled Denmark, Norway, the Netherlands, and Luxembourg. German troops were in northern France, and it appeared that all of France would soon fall to the Germans. At the same time, the Soviet Union—then a German ally—took over Latvia, Lithuania, and Estonia. Italy moved into Eastern Europe and North Africa.

When the war in Europe began, the American Congress changed the neutrality laws. First, Congress made it possible for Britain and France to buy American arms on a cash-and-carry basis. After Germany defeated France in June 1940, President Roosevelt made it even easier for Great Britain to receive American war materials.

While still hoping to avoid war, the American public backed President Roosevelt in his decision to aid Great Britain. President Roosevelt ran for reelection in 1940. By defeating his Republican opponent, Wendell Willkie, Roosevelt became the first President to be elected to a third term.

What did Hitler promise when he met with the leaders of Great Britain and France in 1938?

The United States and Japan. As war raged in Europe, Japan continued to take over more lands in Asia. At this time, several European countries held colonies in Asia. The war with Germany, however, made it difficult for these colonial powers to guard their overseas holdings. The United States wanted to stop Japan from taking over these resource-rich lands.

The United States had been aiding China in its struggle against Japan since 1938. In 1940, the United States blocked Japan's aggressions by cutting off the sale of war materials to Japan. Other countries followed and cut their trade with Japan. By June 1941, for example, Japan was cut off from almost all sources of oil. Without oil for energy, the Japanese could not carry out their plans for expansion.

Communications between the United States and Japan showed that each country stood firm with its demands. The United States would not reopen trade with Japan until Japan withdrew from the lands it occupied. Japan maintained that it could not accept these terms.

At the same time, the United States was moving closer to war with Germany. American ships were assisting the British fleet in the Atlantic. Also, the United States was sending war goods to the Soviet Union after Germany invaded that country in June 1941. These events caused growing tension between the United States and Germany.

President Roosevelt hoped that the United States and Japan could settle their differences without war. Thus, on December 6, 1941, President Roosevelt sent a message to the emperor of Japan. He asked Emperor Hirohito to withdraw Japanese troops from Indochina.

How did the United States try to stop Japan's aggressions in Asia in 1940?

SECTION 1 REVIEW

1. *Why did Hitler and Mussolini build strong armies for their countries?*
2. *What was the aim of the neutrality laws passed by Congress between 1935 and 1937?*
3. *What caused the United States to move away from neutrality?*

2 The United States at War

Overview The emperor of Japan did not reply to President Roosevelt's message of December 6, 1941. Instead, the Japanese carried out a surprise attack on the American military base at Pearl Harbor in Hawaii. This drew the United States into war. The war affected all Americans in some way.

Objectives After reading this section, you should be able to:

- explain why the United States entered World War II;
- assess the affect of our country's involvement in World War II on industry;
- analyze the affect of World War II on Americans.

The Attack on Pearl Harbor. Early in the morning of December 7, 1941, the Japanese attacked the United States with an air raid on Pearl Harbor. Pearl Harbor was the site of a major American naval and air base in Hawaii. Unprepared for an attack, the United States suffered heavy losses. More than 2,000 members of the military were killed as well as 68 Hawaiian civilians. Over 1,000 people were injured.

The Japanese goal was to cripple America's power in the Pacific. This would make it possible for Japan to continue its expansion in Asia without American interference. In the Pearl Harbor attack, the Japanese destroyed about 170 American planes. In addition, 18

The surprise attack by Japan on Pearl Harbor in 1941 caught America's military forces off guard. Japanese dive-bombers and torpedo planes caused great loss of life and inflicted heavy damage on America's Pacific fleet. However, no American aircraft carriers were in port at the time of the attack. Thus, the Japanese victory was not complete. How does this picture indicate that the Japanese attack on Pearl Harbor was successful?

Photri

American ships were either sunk or badly damaged.

Americans were shocked by the attack. On the following day, Congress declared war against Japan. Great Britain joined the United States and declared war on Japan. Then, on December 11, 1941, Germany and Italy entered the war against the United States. Thus, the United States was involved in a war that was being carried out in Asia, Europe, and Africa.

The Japanese followed their raid on Pearl Harbor with attacks on other bases in the Pacific. Japanese conquests of Guam, Wake Island, Hong Kong, and the Philippine Islands gave the Axis powers the upper hand in the Pacific Ocean. At the same time the Axis was taking a greater hold of Europe. The United States and the other anti-Axis countries—together called the *Allies*—met to plan their military strategy. Together they decided to first put their major efforts into defeating the Axis in Europe.

What event led the United States to declare war against Japan?

Women pilots contributed to the war effort by flying planes from America to bases overseas.

Photri

America's Armed Forces. The United States had begun to build up its military forces before the attack on Pearl Harbor. In September 1940, the threat of war had led the Congress to pass the first peacetime draft law in American history. Because of this, about 1.6 million Americans were in the army when the United States entered the war. Thereafter, the size of America's armed forces grew quickly.

Americans from all groups and backgrounds made up the 15 million who served in the armed forces before the war ended. American women began to play a larger part in the country's defense with the formation of several all-women military corps. Limited to noncombat jobs, women served as mechanics, drivers, pilots, clerks, cooks, and medical experts.

Early in the war the military followed strict segregation practices. Black Americans, Mexican Americans, and Japanese Americans were put into separate military units. About 1 million black Americans entered the military during the war. Most of these recruits were limited to certain jobs and kept out of advanced training programs. As the war progressed, however, segregation was slightly eased.

Why did the United States enact its first peacetime draft?

War Production. Millions of Americans worked on the home front to contribute to the total war effort. Workers in industry, agriculture, and science produced the goods needed for war. American farmers, for example, had to increase their farm output. The greater use of machines made it possible to produce more food even though the number of farm workers declined.

America's industries were rapidly converted to meet the needs of wartime. Unemployment had been dropping since the war began in Europe in 1939. The Great Depression ended when the United States had begun to supply goods to warring countries. At the same time, the United States was building up its own military supplies. After the United States entered the war, the need for workers became even greater. Labor shortages developed. In many cases, the need for workers broke down the barriers that had kept blacks, women, and other Americans from certain jobs.

Most wartime industries were located in cities in the North and West. Blacks from the South and Mexican Americans from the Southwest moved to these cities to fill jobs. This often caused overcrowding, which led to disagreements among residents. Riots broke out in several cities during the war.

■ *Where were most industries located during World War II?*

Government Controls. During the war, the government put greater controls on the everyday lives of all Americans. Most of these actions were taken to mobilize the country's resources behind the war effort. To prevent problems that might be caused by shortages, the government undertook a program of *rationing*—limiting the purchase of certain products. Many foodstuffs—including coffee, butter, sugar, tea, and meats—were rationed. Automobile driving was cut back greatly because gasoline was rationed. Furthermore, no new automobiles for civilian use were built during the war. This was because materials and production facilities were needed for the war effort.

Library of Congress

Women workers were vital to America's war production. They helped to build all types of military equipment, from tanks to airplanes.

Other nonrationed goods came into short supply during the war. This happened because workers were earning high wages and could therefore afford more luxury goods. To prevent prices from rising as shortages occurred, the government set price limits on many goods. In this way the government hoped to curb *inflation*—ever-rising prices. Congress also gave the President the power to fight inflation by freezing wages, salaries, and rents. The government also used its taxing power to check inflation.

■ *What is rationing?*

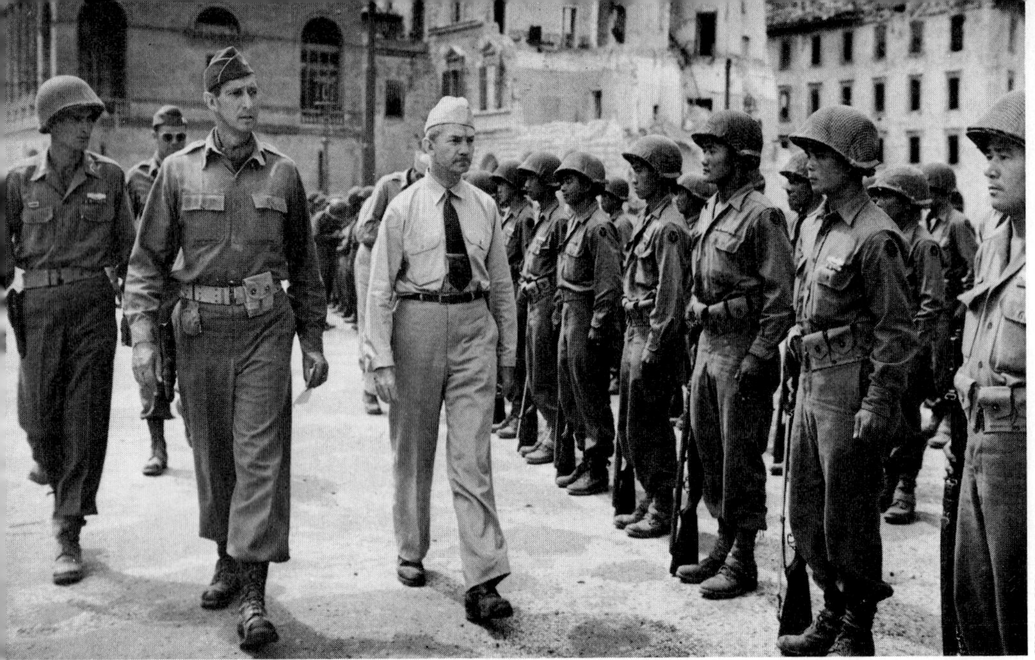
Photo Trends

General Mark Clark (left center) and Secretary of the Navy James V. Forrestal (center) review an honor guard of Japanese American soldiers. More than 33,000 Japanese Americans served in the armed forces of the United States during World War II.

Civil Rights Denied. The rights of one group of Americans were severely limited by the government during World War II. After the bombing of Pearl Harbor, Japanese Americans were distrusted by many other Americans. In part, this was because some Americans feared that Japan might attack America's West Coast. Some people believed that enemy agents might be hiding among the Japanese Americans who lived on the West Coast.

This fear led to a widespread mistreatment of Japanese Americans. In February and March of 1942 the federal government carried out the forced relocation of over 100,000 Japanese Americans. The government claimed it was a military necessity to move these people inland. They were housed in camps. In most cases, these camps were overcrowded. There was little privacy or recreation for the residents. Furthermore, relocation caused these people to lose their jobs and their property.

Despite this poor treatment, Japanese Americans remained loyal to the American government. For example, the all-Japanese American 442nd Regimental Combat Team became one of the most highly decorated combat units in World War II.

After the war, in 1948, the federal government took steps to compensate Japanese Americans for the property losses they suffered because of the wartime relocation. The money set aside for this purpose was very small in comparison to the actual losses. Thus, the Japanese Americans never regained all their property.

Why did the federal government force over 100,000 persons to relocate?

SECTION 2 REVIEW

1. *Why did the United States declare war against Japan?*
2. *How did the war change American industry?*
3. *How did labor shortages affect minority groups?*

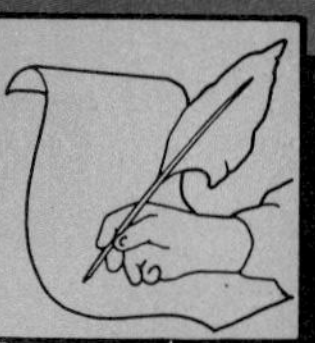

RECALLING THE TIMES

Japanese Relocation

Between March and August of 1942, the government removed over 100,000 persons of Japanese birth and ancestry from their homes on the Pacific Coast. They were forced to leave behind their homes and businesses and to move into poorly constructed relocation centers. Jeanne Wakatsuki was seven years old when her family was taken to Manzanar—a relocation center—where they spent three and a half years. The following excerpt is from a book about Jeanne Wakatsuki's experiences at Manzanar.

... The shacks were built of one thickness of pine planking covered with tarpaper. They sat on concrete footings, with about two feet of open space between the floorboards and the ground. Gaps showed between the planks, and as the weeks passed and the green wood dried out, the gaps widened. Knotholes gaped in the uncovered floor.

Each barracks was divided into six units, sixteen by twenty feet, about the size of a living room, with one bare bulb hanging from the ceiling and an oil stove for heat. We were assigned two of these for the twelve people in our family group; ... We were issued steel army cots, two brown army blankets each, and some mattress covers, which my brothers stuffed with straw....

... It was bitter cold when we arrived, and the wind did not abate.

National Archives

Thinking Critically

Imagine that you had been sent to a relocation center like the one Jeanne Wakatsuki was sent to. What would you have missed most about the way of life you left behind? How would you have felt toward the American government?

3 Victory for the Allies

Overview By early 1942, the Axis powers controlled large parts of the globe. However, in late 1942, the Allies won some important victories. The increased production of war goods in the United States gave the Allies an advantage over the Axis. After years of fighting, the Allies were victorious in Europe and in the Pacific.

Objectives After reading this section, you should be able to:

- explain the significance of the Declaration of the United Nations;
- discuss the military action of World War II;
- analyze Truman's decisions to use the atom bomb against Japan.

Allied War Aims. The United States and its allies worked together to defeat the Axis powers. Just two weeks after the Japanese attacked Pearl Harbor, leaders from several countries met in Washington, D.C. There they agreed on common war plans and goals. The result of the meeting was the *Declaration of the United Nations.* Representatives from 26 countries at war against the Axis powers signed this statement. They pledged full cooperation in the war effort. They also agreed not to make a separate peace with the Axis and to work for lasting world peace once the war ended.

England, the Soviet Union, and the United States were called the *Big Three* among the Allied powers. The Big Three were the largest suppliers of goods and troops to the Allied war effort. Leaders from the Big Three met a number of times during the war. They played a major part in making military plans. They also worked out plans for dealing with the problems that would follow the war.

■ *What nations made up the Big Three?*

The War in Europe. The Allies decided that they had to take control of North Africa before undertaking the war in Europe. German troops had conquered much of North Africa by 1942. These troops were led by Field Marshall Erwin Rommel. The German goal was to capture Egypt and the Suez Canal—a vital waterway.

In late October 1942 the British, led by Field Marshall Bernard Law Montgomery, stopped Rommel's advance. Troops from other Allied countries, including American General George S. Patton's troops, joined in this struggle to clear the Axis from North Africa. In early May 1943, the Germans and Italians in North Africa were forced to surrender. This victory opened the Mediterranean Sea to the Allies. The next step was the Allied invasion of Sicily and Italy.

The Italian armies were quickly defeated by the Allies. Faced with defeat, Mussolini, the Italian dictator, was forced to resign. The new government of Italy surrendered to the Allies in early September 1943. Fighting in Italy continued, however. German armies moved into Italy and carried on the war against the Allies.

As Allied forces fought the German army in Italy, Soviet soldiers battled the Germans on the eastern front. Germany had invaded the Soviet Union in June 1941. The Germans had inflicted great damage and suffering in the Soviet Union. However, in August 1942, the five-month battle of Stalingrad began. The Soviet victory in this battle marked a turning point in the fighting between these two armies. The Soviets ended the German advance and forced the German army into a steady retreat.

In 1943 the British and Americans began working on plans for an invasion of German-occupied France. This invasion—known as Operation Overlord—would aid the Soviet army in the east by opening a second front against the Germans. It was planned that on *D day*—the day set for the invasion—the Allies would land on the beaches of Normandy in France. In preparation for D day, Allied bombers dropped tons of bombs on Germany and on German-occupied lands. In these raids, as in others throughout the war, the American air force played an important part in weakening the Axis.

D day took place on June 6, 1944. General Dwight D. Eisenhower served as supreme commander of the Allied forces in Europe. The invasion force was followed by hundreds of thousands of additional Allied troops.

The Allies pushed the German army eastward toward Germany. In December 1944, the Germans staged their last major strike with the *Battle of the Bulge.* The Allied victory in this battle forced the Germans to retreat into Germany.

The Soviet army forced the Germans out of eastern Europe by early 1945. The Soviet army then prepared to invade Germany from the east. In the spring of 1945, the Soviets carried on this advance while the other Allies invaded Germany from the west. Hitler,

The war in Europe was fought on several fronts. By the end of the war, the Axis Powers had almost totally been overrun by the Allies.

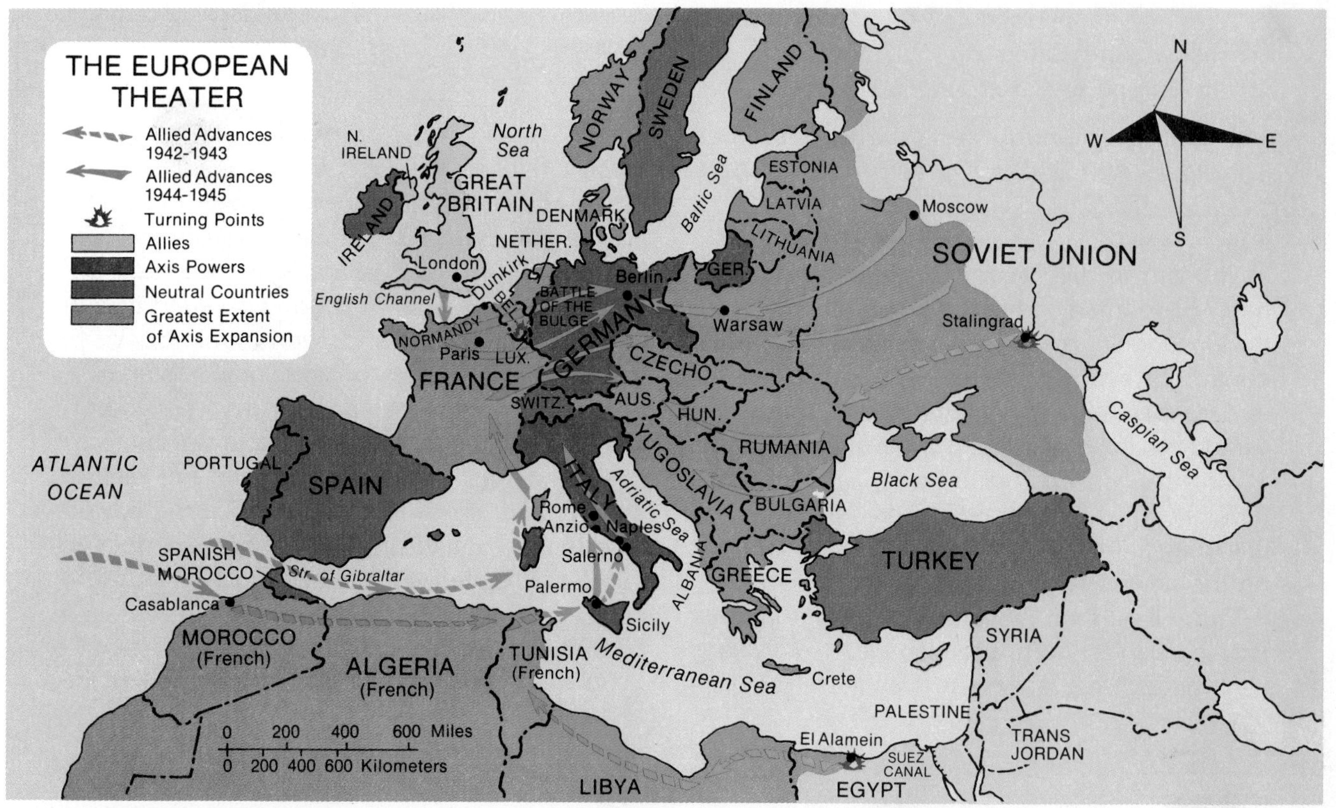

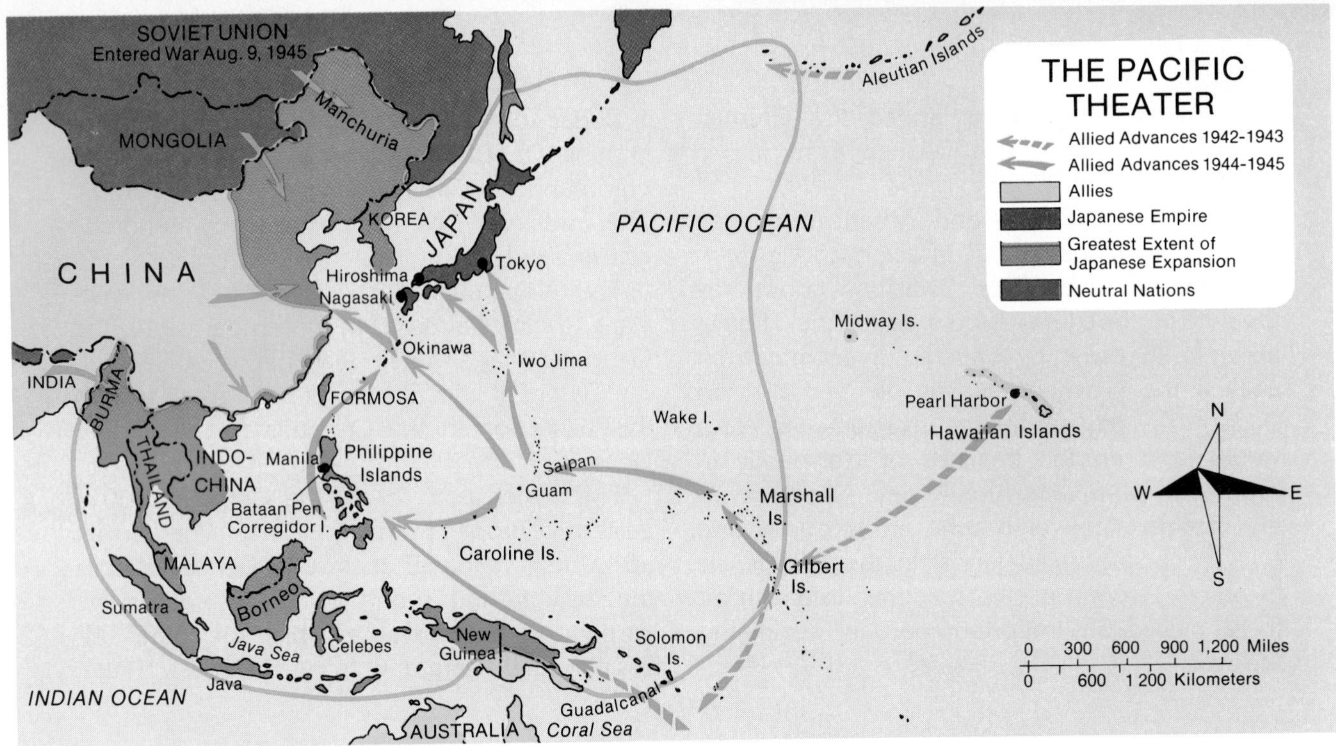

Allied strategy in the Pacific involved fighting an island-hopping campaign. Eventually this strategy allowed the Allies to strike at Japan itself.

the German dictator, took his own life as the Soviets pressed toward Berlin. Finally, Germany surrendered on May 7, 1945. The war in Europe was over.

- *Why did fighting continue in Italy even after the Italian government surrendered?*

The War in the Pacific. By early 1942, Japan had made many important conquests in the Pacific and in Asia. The Japanese had taken control of many vital resources including oil and rubber. In mid-1942, however, the Allies were able to stop Japan's advance. In June 1942, the United States won an important naval battle near Midway Island (see map on this page). For the first time, Japan was put on the defensive.

The Allies then began to retake important Pacific islands from the Japanese. This was very difficult because the Japanese soldiers usually refused to surrender. The Allies, however, carried through with their plans for *island hopping.* This meant that they would attack only key islands and skip over less important islands. This method succeeded in cutting off supplies and communications to the Japanese soldiers on the smaller islands.

America's industrial power was very important in gaining the upper hand in the war against Japan. Increased production of aircraft carriers and airplanes gave America the advantage in the air and on the sea. For example, in 1939 the United States had built only 5,856 airplanes. In 1943, Americans produced 85,898 airplanes.

By the spring of 1945, the Allies had made

great progress in the Pacific. Americans had retaken the Philippines after more than two years of Japanese occupation. Moreover, the Americans took Iwo Jima and Okinawa from the Japanese. The Allies then made final plans to invade the main islands of Japan.

What was the importance of the battle near the Midway islands?

The Atomic Bomb. President Truman had been in office for only a few months when he had to make major decisions concerning the war against Japan. Truman had become President after Franklin Roosevelt's sudden death in April 1945. In July 1945, President Truman met with the leaders of the Soviet Union and England in Potsdam, Germany. At this time, the Allies held the upper hand in the war against Japan. From Potsdam, the Allied leaders gave the Japanese a final warning to surrender. The Japanese rejected this warning.

President Truman then decided to use a new weapon—the atom bomb—against Japan. The President believed that the bomb was so destructive that it would force the Japanese to surrender. In this way, the Americans would be spared the further loss of life that would be suffered in an invasion of the Japanese islands.

On August 6, 1945, an atom bomb was dropped on Hiroshima, a Japanese city. More than 90,000 people were killed or missing after the blast. Despite these heavy losses the Japanese did not surrender. Thus, on August 9, 1945, a second bomb was dropped on a Japanese city. It fell on Nagasaki, killing about 40,000 people. Faced with total destruction, the Japanese government asked the Allies for peace. On September 2, 1945, the Allies accepted Japan's formal surrender. World War II was over.

What was one reason why President Truman decided to use the atom bomb?

Culver Pictures

Thousands of Japanese at Hiroshima died from the intense heat and radiation caused by the blast of the first atom bomb. Thousands more died from the fires that were ignited by the bomb's gigantic fireball.

The Aftermath of War. The war caused changes and problems that affected all nations long after the fighting ended. It is estimated that about 50 million people died because of the war. About 400,000 Americans had been killed in the war. And more than 600,000 Americans were wounded.

The United States emerged from the war as a world leader. Americans began to make major decisions about the future of countries all over the globe. The American military, for example, remained posted in several countries throughout the world.

Even before the war was over, the United States had joined with other countries in forming the United Nations (UN). After the war, the UN faced many important tasks. Cities and farmlands in many countries had been destroyed in the war. Many governments had fallen, leaving a need for leadership and direction. The UN began programs to help the millions of people who were left in need by the war. The United States played a large part in these and other programs to rebuild war-damaged countries.

What was the goal of the programs started by the United Nations?

SECTION 3 REVIEW

1. *What did the countries that signed the Declaration of the United Nations pledge to do?*
2. *How did the Battle of the Bulge mark a turning point in the war?*
3. *Why did President Truman decide to use the atomic bomb?*

CHAPTER 31 SUMMARY

September 1, 1939, marked the beginning of World War II in Europe. The United States hoped to remain neutral in the war. But the Axis powers—Germany, Italy, and Japan—invaded lands in several parts of the globe. This led the United States to aid those countries that were fighting against the Axis powers.

The United States was drawn into the war when Japan attacked Pearl Harbor on December 7, 1941. Jobs and daily living habits were changed as industry changed over from peacetime needs to war production. The government increased its controls over citizens' everyday activities.

The Allied powers first gave their attention to ending the Axis hold on Europe. Victory in North Africa brought about the Allied landing in Italy in 1943. This then led to the Allied invasion of western Europe on D day—June 6, 1944. The Allies landed in France and began to push the Germans eastward. Germany was forced to surrender in May 1945. The war in the Pacific ended in August 1945 after America dropped two atomic bombs on Japan.

CHAPTER 31 REVIEW

USING YOUR SKILLS

Interpreting a Thematic Map

Maps are valuable tools to use to organize many different types of information. The following map contains information on state population changes between 1940 and 1950. A color code is used to indicate how each state's population changed during this period. Using a map for this information makes it possible to see the change in each state as well as sectional changes. Study this map and the color key. Then, answer the questions that follow.

1. How many states experienced an overall population loss during these years?
2. Which north central state experienced the highest rate of population growth?
3. By what percentage did the population of Florida change during these years?
4. Which section of the country contained the most states with a population growth of over 30 percent?
5. What reasons would you give to explain why the American population shifted in these ways during the 1940's?

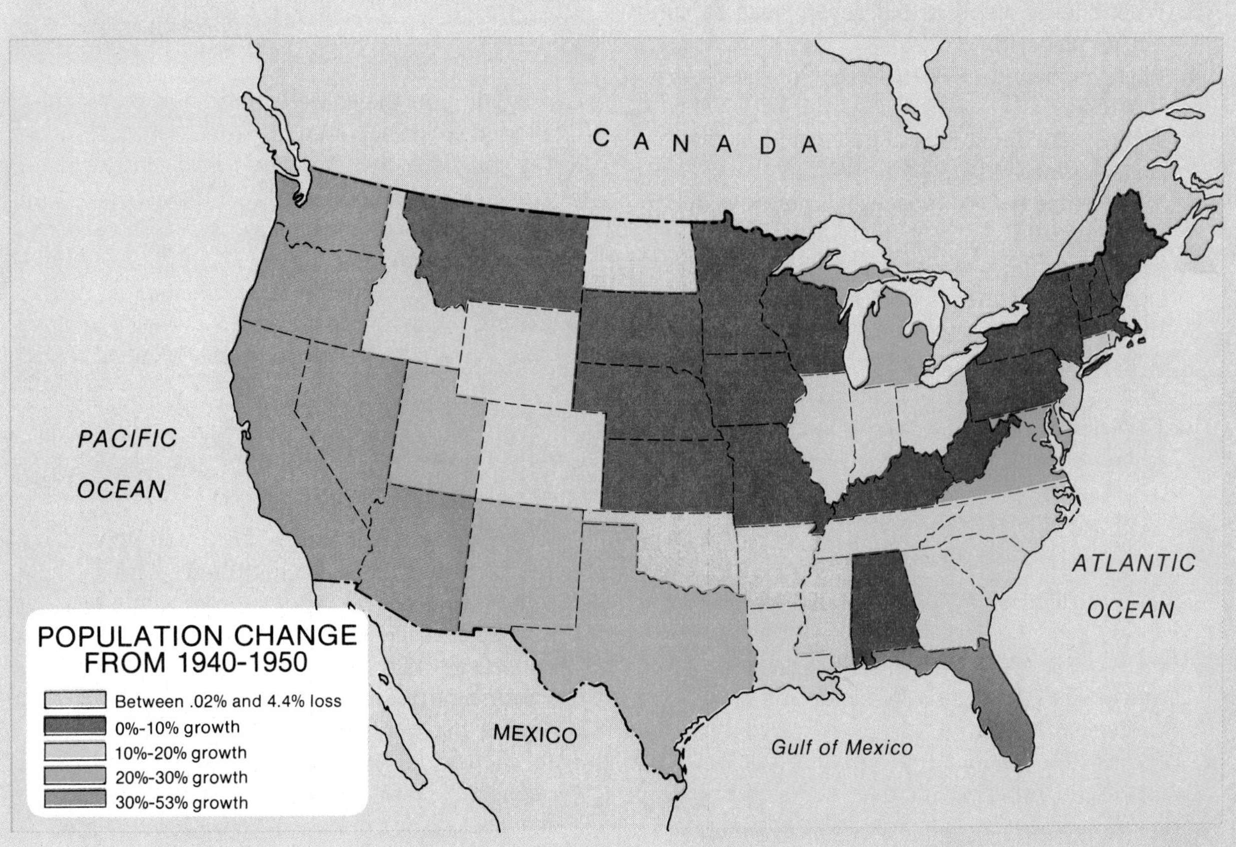

CHAPTER 31 REVIEW

YOU SHOULD KNOW

Identify, define, or explain each of the following:

dictator	inflation
holocaust	Big Three
Allies	D–day
rationing	island hopping

CHECKING FACTS

1. What four dictators ruled in European nations during the 1930's?
2. Who were the "undesirables" in Germany?
3. What energy resource did Japan need to carry out its plans for expansion?
4. What happened at Pearl Harbor on December 7, 1941?
5. Where were most industries located in the United States during World War II?
6. What happened to Japanese Americans during World War II?
7. What were the war plans and goals of the Declaration of the United Nations?
8. What was the German goal in North Africa?
9. What marked the turning point in the fighting between the Soviets and the Germans?
10. What kinds of programs did the United Nations begin as a result of World War II?

UNDERSTANDING CONCEPTS

1. Why did Hitler and Mussolini build strong armies?
2. Why did the leaders of Great Britain and France agree to Hitler's demands for the Sudetenland?
3. Why did the American government put more controls on American citizens during the war?
4. How did American industry aid our country's efforts during World War II?
5. Why was the atom bomb used against Japan?

LEARNING FROM ILLUSTRATIONS

1. Study the map on page 558. How far east did Japanese power extend when Japan's empire was at its greatest height?
2. Look at the picture on page 559. What does this picture show about the effects of the atom bomb dropped on Hiroshima?

CRITICAL THINKING

1. Why, do you think, were Hitler and Mussolini allowed to gain power in their countries?
2. Do you think that America's involvement in World War II helped ease the depression in the United States or made it worse? Give reasons for your answer.
3. If it had been your decision whether or not to use the atom bomb to end the war, would you have used it? Give reasons for your answer.

ENRICHMENT ACTIVITIES

1. Learn more about World War II through personal interviews. Gather information by interviewing people who remember the war. Be sure to investigate activities on the home front as well as military operations. Present this information to your class.
2. During the war, posters were frequently used to encourage Americans to find ways to support the war effort. Find reproductions of the posters in books. Then, make copies of these posters for your classroom.

CHAPTER 32

CLOSE-UP: The 1936 Berlin Olympics

INTRODUCTION

The 1936 Olympic Games had already been planned for Berlin, Germany, when Hitler and the Nazis took full control of the country in 1933. At first, there was disagreement among the Nazis concerning the Games. After long discussions, however, Hitler decided that Germany would go ahead and hold the Games in Berlin. Hitler and the Nazis planned to use the Olympics as an opportunity to impress the world. To do this, the Nazis spent millions of dollars to build a magnificent Olympic complex. The Nazis also undertook extensive training to prepare their "all-Aryan" Olympic team.

At the same time, athletes from all parts of the United States were training for the Olympic team. Many of the top track-and-field athletes were black; among them was Jesse Owens—an extraordinary runner. According to Nazi beliefs, blacks were not as good as Aryan Germans.

1 Preparations for the 1936 Olympics

The Olympic Games, held every four years, bring together athletes from all parts of the world. Two of the purposes of the Games are to promote amateur athletics and to encourage world peace. In 1936, however, the Olympic hosts had other goals in mind.

Decisions for Berlin. In 1931, the International Olympic Committee selected Berlin, Germany, as the site for the 1936 Olympics. The German people were happy and excited with this decision. Germany had never before hosted the Olympics.

In 1933, however, events took place that threatened to keep the Games out of Germany. In that year Adolf Hitler and his Nazi party took full control of the German government. Some Nazis believed that Germany should not be the site of the Olympics. They argued that it would cost too much money to host the Games. Even worse, they feared that the Olympics would draw hundreds of foreign reporters to Germany. They did not want these reporters digging into the activities of the Nazi government.

Another Nazi, however, had different ideas about the upcoming Olympics. Joseph Goebbels, one of Hitler's top aides, wanted the Nazis to go ahead with the Olympic plans. Goebbels pointed out that the Nazis would benefit from the worldwide attention that would be drawn by the Games. Goebbels explained that the Nazis could show to the world only what they wanted the world to see. With a good show, they could have it appear that their way of governing was the best way. Hitler agreed with Goebbels. He believed the world would see that German athletes as well as the German nation were superior to all others.

■ *Why did Hitler decide that the Olympics would be staged in Berlin?*

Nazi Discrimination. Hitler believed that some people were superior to others. He claimed that the "Aryan race" was above all other groups of people. He said that the fair-skinned people of northern Europe were members of this race. Hitler told the people of Germany that they were the best examples of Aryans. He also claimed that many of Germany's problems were caused by people who were not Aryans.

Hitler told his followers that Germany could achieve glory only if non-Aryans were not allowed to interfere with the country's rise. Thus, non-Aryans were stripped of their rights as citizens. As you read in Chapter 31, Jews were the main target of Hitler's race laws. These rules entered into Germany's preparations for the Olympics.

■ *Who, according to Hitler, belonged to the Aryan race?*

Germany's Olympic Team. Hitler believed that only Aryan athletes should be allowed to represent Germany in the Olympics. At the same time, he wanted to avoid any problems with the International Olympic Committee. If the committee learned that Jews would not be allowed on Germany's teams, the committee might decide to hold the Games in some other country. Because of this, Hitler looked for indirect ways to keep Jews and other non-Aryans off the German team.

In April 1933, for example, the German boxing federation announced that Jewish fighters could no longer take part in its matches. Then in June 1933, Jews were dropped as members in all athletic clubs in Germany. Without the practice, training, and coaching offered in clubs, Jews were not able to qualify for the German Olympic team.

■ *How did the Nazis prevent Jews from qualifying for the 1936 Olympics?*

Protests Against Germany. As early as 1933, some people were aware of Nazi Germany's unfair treatment of Jews and other religious groups. They urged the Olympic committee to remove the upcoming Games from Germany. The committee agreed to look into the matter. When faced with the committee's questions, the Nazis invited two Jewish

Culver Pictures

Adolf Hitler is leading the parade at the 1936 Olympics opening ceremony in Berlin, Germany.

athletes to be on the German team. The Olympic officials were satisfied by this action.

But the movement against the Nazi Olympics did not end there. Many Americans did not agree with the Olympic committee's decision to keep the Games in Germany. Large numbers of Americans, including athletes, thought that the United States should boycott—not attend—the Olympics. There were several reasons for this. Most important was the Nazi mistreatment of Jews and other citizens. Furthermore, some members of the American team were Catholics, blacks, and Jews. Many people wondered if these athletes would receive fair treatment in Germany. Beyond this, many Americans believed that the Olympics should be free of politics. They objected to the ways in which the Nazis were using the Olympics to further their own political position in the world. After much discussion, however, it was decided that the United States team should take part in the Games.

- *What was the main reason why some Americans wanted the United States team to boycott the 1936 Olympics?*

SECTION 1 REVIEW

1. *What are two of the purposes of the Olympic Games?*
2. *In what ways did the Nazis prevent Jews from qualifying for the Olympic team?*
3. *Why did the Nazis invite two Jewish athletes to join the German Olympic team?*

2 The Berlin Olympics

Hitler planned to awe the world with the grandness of the 1936 Olympics. He also expected Germany's Aryan athletes to demonstrate superiority over contestants from other countries. As the Games unfolded, however, the Nazis were shocked by the results.

The Nazi Olympic Spectacle. Hitler's government spent over 30 million dollars on the 1936 Olympic Games. Over 4,000 German workers had spent two years building the elaborate Olympic complex. The main stadium that they built was the largest in the world. It provided seating for 100,000 spectators.

A closed-circuit television system was set up in Germany. This was the first time that the Olympics were carried over television. The Nazis also built very modern press facilities and gave special treatment to reporters. Every possible effort was made to see that reporters enjoyed their stay in Germany.

Hitler also wanted a permanent record to capture the glory of the 1936 Olympics. For this he called upon Leni Riefenstahl, a top

Süddeutcher Verlag

Leni Riefenstahl was well-known for her films dramatizing the power of the Nazi movement.

German film director. Her task was to make the official film of the Games.

The city of Berlin was polished for Germany's guests during the Games. In particular, the anti-Jewish posters that were common to Berlin streets before the Games opened were removed.

What were two preparations made for the Berlin Olympics?

Hosting the Athletes. Male and female athletes were not treated equally during the Olympics. Male athletes who were competing in the Games were given very comfortable living quarters in the Olympic Village. Almost 4,000 men from 50 different countries were housed in the Olympic Village. The Nazis had undertaken extensive planning to impress these athletes with the excellence of Nazi organization. German cooks, for example, had been taught how to prepare hundreds of different foreign dishes. Because of this, each athlete staying in the Olympic Village was served the foods that were common in his own country. Other steps were taken to make these athletes feel "at home." In some cases, special bedding was imported from an athlete's home country to aid his rest.

Female athletes, however, did not receive the pampering that was extended to male athletes. In part, this was because women's sports did not receive the attention that was given to men's sports at the time. The Nazis housed women athletes in dormitories and served them all the same, plain food.

How many athletes were housed in the Olympic Village?

The Olympics Open. As head of the host country, Adolf Hitler opened the 1936 Olympics. Hitler approached the microphone and said, "I announce as opened the Games of Berlin, celebrating the eleventh Olympiad of the modern era." The thrilled crowd roared in excitement. More fabulous ceremonies then followed. Music, parades, and rallies were carried beyond the stadium into all parts of Berlin.

The reporters who were covering the 1936 Olympics sent home accounts of Berlin's festive mood. The world was told of the wonderful achievements of Hitler and the Nazis. For the most part, the darker side of Nazi rule was overlooked. Therefore, the Nazis had succeeded in one part of their plan for showing their greatness. They also expected that Germany's Aryan athletes would be the most outstanding Olympic stars.

■ *What did the Nazis expect the results of the Games would be?*

The Competition Begins. On the first day of the Games, it appeared that the Nazis' claims of athletic superiority might be true. First, Hans Wölke won a gold medal for Germany when he set a new Olympic record in the shot put. Later in the day, Tilly Fleischer of Germany won a gold medal in the javelin throw. Fleischer broke the record that had been set by the American "Babe" Didrickson in the 1932 Olympics.

German fans were pleased by the achievements of Tilly Fleischer in the 1936 Olympics.

Wide World

The German fans were very excited by these two early victories. Germany had taken only one gold medal in the 1932 Olympics. The Nazis pointed out that under their direction, the 1936 German team passed that mark in only one day. Furthermore, these were the first Olympic medals ever won by Germans in track-and-field meets—the most popular Olympic sports.

Adolf Hitler was very proud of these German athletes. After their victories, Hitler had them brought to his stadium box for personal congratulations. Throughout the day, Hitler met with each German who won an Olympic medal—either gold, silver, or bronze. In addition, Hitler gave his personal congratulations to three athletes from Finland who took all three medals in the 10,000-meter run. Hitler left the stadium, however, without congratulating the three Americans who placed first, second, and third in the men's high-jump event. Two of these three men were black. Many people believed that Hitler left the stadium because he was not willing to shake hands with black athletes.

■ *In what event did Americans win all three medals?*

The Games Continue. On the second day of the Games, Hitler was once again in his stadium box. However, he would no longer invite any winning athletes to his box. One of the Olympic officials pointed out that it was wrong for Hitler to meet with some winners but not to meet with others. Because of this, Hitler decided that he would not congratulate any of the winners.

It was on the second day of the Olympic Games that Jesse Owens, a black American athlete, began to draw the crowd's attention. Owens tied the Olympic record as he placed

Helen Stephens (left) and Jesse Owens (right) relaxed between events during the 1936 Olympics. These outstanding American athletes each won gold medals for their achievements during the summer Olympics in 1936.

first in the 100-meter dash. Then, on the next day, Owens took part in the broad-jump competition.

Owens's main competitor in this event was Luz Long of Germany. Although they were competitors, Owens and Long had become friends during the qualification trials. This friendship upset the Nazis, who believed that Long, an Aryan, was of a better race than Owens.

Hitler was not in his box to see the final competition between Owens and Long. Some people believed that he did not want to see a German compete with a black. But the audience proved that all Germans did not feel the same way. The crowd cheered both Long and Owens as they each broke the Olympic record.

Jesse Owens won the final competition with a jump that measured 8.06 meters (26 feet 5⁵⁄₁₆ inches). Luz Long won a silver medal for second place. Later that same day, other black Americans won gold medals in major events. German athletes were also winning many gold medals, but most of their victories came in less-popular events.

■ *Who were the main competitors in the broad-jump event?*

Olympic Hero Owens. The claims of Aryan supremacy were overshadowed as Jesse Owens emerged as the hero of the 1936 Olympics. On the fourth day of the Berlin Games all eyes were on Jesse Owens as he entered his third event—the 200-meter dash. The crowd roared with enthusiasm when Owens crossed the finish line first. In his victory, Owens had set another world record and had won his third gold medal.

Four days later, Owens was selected to run on the American team in the 400-meter relay. This team won the race with a time that set a new world record. This victory gave Jesse Owens his fourth gold medal.

The German audience, unlike the Nazi newspapers, cheered Owens's extraordinary achievements. Even Germany's Aryan athletes crowded around Owens to shake his hand. No other athlete in the 1936 Olympics had won more than one gold medal in track-and-field events. Furthermore, Owens had set three incredible Olympic records. To Hitler's disappointment, it was Owens—a black American—who ranked above all others in the Berlin Olympics.

■ *What achievement made Jesse Owens the hero of the 1936 Olympics?*

Wide World

Helen Stephens, standing on the platform, won the 100-meter dash during the 1936 Olympics.

The Results of the Games. Grand ceremonies were held in the Olympic Stadium on August 16, 1936, to mark the end of the Berlin Olympics. According to the Nazi newspapers, the Germans were the overwhelming winners in the Games. These newspapers ignored the accomplishments of Owens and other black athletes. This was because the Nazis continued to claim that the Aryan athletes were the best in the world. Many of the people who had seen the Olympics, however, did not see it this way.

German athletes had done very well in the 1936 Games. In fact, Germany led all other countries in total gold medals. Most of the German victories, however, took place in the less popular Olympic events. On the other hand, many of the medals won by the so-called "non-Aryans" were in the high-interest sports. For example, in addition to Jesse Owens, four black athletes from the United States won gold medals in track-and-field events. Black Americans also won several silver and bronze medals.

Through the Olympics, the Nazis had impressed the world with many of their achievements. The Olympic buildings and ceremonies were certainly outstanding. The Nazis failed, however, in their overall goal. This was because Jesse Owens and other nonwhite athletes showed the world that there was not one super race of humans.

How many black Americans won gold medals in track-and-field events?

SECTION 2 REVIEW

1. *Who was Leni Riefenstahl?*
2. *How did Jesse Owens's friendship with Luz Long go against Nazi beliefs?*
3. *Why did Nazi newspapers play down the achievements of Jesse Owens?*

CHAPTER 32 REVIEW

SUMMARY

In 1931, Berlin, Germany, was chosen as the site of the 1936 Olympics. In 1933, some Nazis did not want the Olympics to be held in Germany. They felt that the Olympics would be too costly. They also feared that foreign reporters would look into the activities of the Nazi government. One of Hitler's top aides, however, wanted the Nazis to go ahead with the Olympic plans. He believed that the world would see that German athletes as well as the German nation were superior to all others.

Many people were aware of Nazi Germany's unfair treatment of Jews and other religious groups. They wanted the Olympics to be held elsewhere. Many Americans felt that the United States should boycott the Olympics. In the end, the 1936 Olympics were held in Berlin, Germany, and the United States team participated.

Hitler's government spent over 30 million dollars building the Olympic complex. Reporters from all over the world were given special treatment. The reporters sent home accounts of the wonderful achievements of Hitler and the Nazis.

At first, Hitler met with all the Aryans who won medals. However, he left the stadium when three black Americans won the medals in the high-jump event. On the second day of the games, Jesse Owens, a black American, won the 100-meter dash. Hitler would not meet with Owens. In the end, Owens set three Olympic records and won 4 gold medals. Owens ranked above all others in the Berlin Olympics. The Nazis failed to prove that the Aryans were the superior race.

UNDERSTANDING CONCEPTS

1. Why did some Nazis believe that Germany should not be the site of the 1936 Olympics?
2. Why did Hitler agree to go ahead with the Olympic plans?
3. How were German Jews prevented from qualifying for the Olympics?
4. Why did many Americans want to boycott the 1936 Olympics?
5. How were male and female athletes treated at the Berlin Olympics?
6. Why was Jesse Owens the hero of the 1936 Olympics?
7. How did the Nazis fail their overall Olympic goals?

CRITICAL THINKING

1. Hitler believed that only Aryan athletes should be allowed to represent Germany in the Olympics. Do you think any government has the right to keep athletes from competing in the Olympics because of their religion or their race? Give reasons for your answer.
2. Many Americans thought that the United States should boycott the Olympics because of the Nazi mistreatment of Jews and other citizens. If you had been a member of the United States Olympic team in 1936, would you have been for or against a boycott? Give reasons for your answer.
3. In your opinion, how was television important to the 1936 Olympics?

PROJECTS AND ACTIVITIES

The two main goals of the Olympics are to promote amateur athletics and to encourage world peace. In 1980 the Olympics held in Moscow were boycotted by 62 countries, including the United States. Do research to find out why these countries boycotted the 1980 Olympics. The 1984 Olympics held in Los Angeles were boycotted by the Soviet Union and several eastern European countries. Do research to find out why these countries boycotted the 1984 Olympics.

UNIT EIGHT REVIEW

UNIT SUMMARY

President Hoover believed that business would soon recover from the depression. Conditions, however, became worse. Because of this, President Hoover was defeated in the election of 1932 by Franklin Delano Roosevelt. President Roosevelt promised to undertake bold steps to end the depression. His plans for relief, recovery, and reform became known as the New Deal. Some parts of the New Deal succeeded, while others failed.

As the depression continued into 1935, President Roosevelt backed a number of new laws that brought long-lasting changes to the country. President Roosevelt was reelected in 1936. During this term, the President tried to expand his power over the Supreme Court. During the depression, the United States worked toward better relations with the other countries of the Americas and with the Soviet Union.

September 1, 1939 marked the beginning of World War II in Europe. The United States hoped to remain neutral in the war, however, it was drawn into the war when Japan attacked Pearl Harbor on December 7, 1941. Jobs and daily living habits were changed as industry changed over from peacetime needs to war production. On D day—June 6, 1944, the Allies landed in France and began to push the Germans eastward. Germany was forced to surrender in May 1945. The war in the Pacific ended in August 1945 after America dropped two atomic bombs on Japan.

The Nazis hoped that the world would see that German athletes as well as the German nation were superior to all others as a result of the 1936 Olympics in Berlin, Germany. Although many Aryans won medals, Jesse Owens—a black American—ranked above all others in the Berlin Olympics. The Nazis failed to prove that the Aryans were the superior race.

YOU SHOULD KNOW

Identify, define, or explain each of the following:

repossessed
relief
minimum wages
pensions
drought
reparations
isolationism
dictator
inflation
D Day

CHECKING FACTS

1. What did the Hawley-Smoot Tariff do?
2. What were Hoovervilles?
3. What did the New Deal hope to achieve?
4. What did the TVA accomplish?
5. What was the goal of the Social Security Act?
6. What was the good-neighbor policy?
7. What was the holocaust?
8. What goods were rationed in the United States during World War II?
9. What programs did the United Nations begin as a result of World War II?
10. What were two Nazi goals of the Olympics?

UNDERSTANDING CONCEPTS

1. How did President Hoover feel about the federal government being involved in business matters?
2. How did the Civilian Conservation Corps (CCC) help young Americans during the depression?
3. Why was the Social Security Act one of the most far-reaching laws of the New Deal?
4. In the 1930's, why did many Americans believe that the United States should follow a policy of isolationism?
5. Why did the United States stop selling war materials to Japan in 1940?
6. How did the Japanese attack on Pearl Harbor affect public opinion in the United States?
7. Why did many people think the 1936 Olympics should not be held in Berlin, Germany?

UNIT EIGHT REVIEW

CRITICAL THINKING

1. Do you think the government has a responsibility to help homeless people? Why or why not?
2. Many Americans felt that the New Deal was harming the American economy. They felt that President Roosevelt was using the government to change the free enterprise system. Do you agree or disagree with the way these Americans felt? Explain your answer.
3. During World War II, Japanese Americans were forced to move to poorly constructed relocation centers. Do you think this was fair? Why or why not?

CHRONOLOGY

Arrange the following events in the order in which they occurred.

a. World War II began in Europe
b. Germany surrendered
c. Japan surrendered
d. Pearl Harbor was attacked by Japan
e. United States enters World War II
f. First fireside chat by FDR
g. Olympics held in Berlin, Germany
h. Social Security Act passed
i. Dust storms swept through parts of country
j. Allies invade France

CITIZENSHIP IN ACTION

Mussolini and Hitler were dictators of their countries. Why do you think citizens allow dictators to gain control of their countries? What rights do citizens living in a dictatorship give up? Do you think American citizens would allow a dictator to gain control of the United States? Why or why not?

GEOGRAPHY

1. How was the location of the Axis Powers in Europe advantageous?
2. What country was occupied by Italy in 1939?
3. What territories were occupied by Germany in 1939?
4. What territories were occupied by Germany in 1938?
5. What territory was remilitarized by the Axis powers in 1936?

1945 — 1950 — 1955

- 1945 World War II ended
- 1946 Beginning of cold war era; Truman Doctrine announced
- 1948 European Recovery Program begun; Soviet blockade of Berlin
- 1949 "Fair Deal" program begun
- 1950 Korean War begun
- 1952 Dwight Eisenhower elected President
- 1954 *Brown v. Board of Education of Topeka*; Senator Joseph McCarthy censured
- 1955 Montgomery bus boycott

UNIT NINE

Conflict and Change

1945–1965

During the 1950's, many Americans were able to afford the newest appliances.

Dwight D. Eisenhower won the nomination for President of the United States at the Republican Convention in 1956. Ike went on to win the presidential election.

1960

1965

- 1957 Economic recession
- 1958 *Explorer I* launched into space
- 1960 John Kennedy elected President; Civil Rights Act of 1960
- 1962 Cuban Missile Crisis
- 1963 President Kennedy assassinated; Vice-President Lyndon Johnson became President
- 1964 Lyndon Johnson elected President; Expanded U.S. military role in Republic of South Vietnam; Civil Rights Act of 1964
- 1965 "Great Society" programs begun; Dr. Martin Luther King, Jr. awarded Nobel Peace Prize

CHAPTERS

The United States emerged from World War II a far stronger country, both at home and overseas. The rapidly growing postwar economy brought a better life for millions of Americans. At the same time, our country accepted new global responsibilities as the price of world leadership. But the growth of east-west rivalry gave birth to a dangerous new era—the cold war.

Throughout these years, our federal government worked to overcome major social problems caused by poverty and by inequality. By the 1950's, however, many Americans were still unable to share in the affluence and freedom of our society. But as more people became aware of these problems, demands for equality and for justice—especially for blacks—grew louder. By the 1960's, our country had undertaken broad new social and political reforms.

Our country grieved over the death of President John F. Kennedy in November, 1963. Many people worried about the change in presidential power.

On July 20, 1969, Neil A. Armstrong became the first person to walk on the moon.

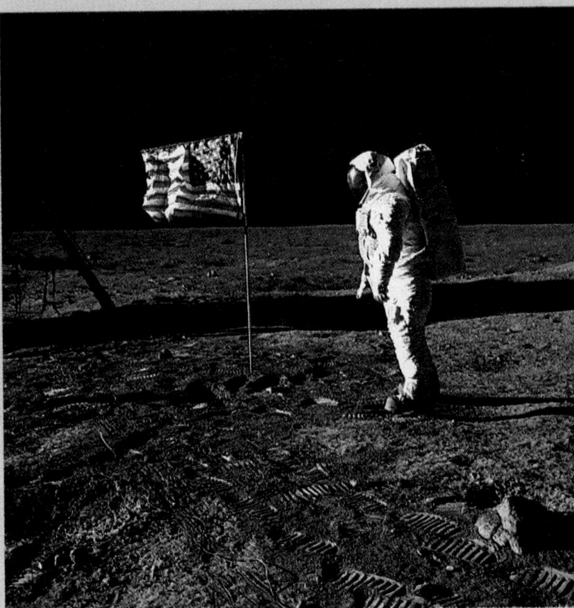

1945 ... 1950

- 1945 World War II ended
- 1946 Beginning of cold war era; Truman Doctrine announced
- 1947 Taft-Hartley Act passed
- 1948 Soviet blockade of West Berlin; European Recovery Program (Marshall Plan) begun
- 1949 "Fair Deal" program begun
- 1950 Korean War begun

CHAPTER 33

From World War to Cold War

Chapter Objectives

After studying this chapter, you should be able to:

- enumerate America's postwar economic problems and describe the solutions that were found to overcome these problems;
- explain the significant ways in which America's postwar society differed from the society of earlier years;
- describe the major international challenges faced by America's postwar leaders.

1 Adjustment to a Peacetime Economy

Overview The defeat of the Axis powers in mid-1945 allowed Americans to turn their attention to peacetime economic needs. But after four years at war, our economy was based upon the meeting of wartime goals. Now, Americans faced the task of adjusting to a peacetime economy.

Objectives After reading this section, you should be able to:

- explain why America's economy became a planned economy;
- discuss how demobilization after World War II threatened the American economy;
- assess America's postwar foreign policy.

End of the Wartime Economy. The end of World War II in August 1945 brought the return of global peace for the first time in more than six years. Much of Europe and Japan lay in smoking ruins. Food, medicine, and factory goods were in short supply. Famine and disease threatened to take hold in many of the world's war-torn countries. The need to begin rebuilding was great.

The American economy had changed dramatically since the start of the war. America's economic might had become one of our country's strongest weapons in the fight against the Axis powers. But in order to make the best use of this weapon, the government had taken control of nearly every part of our economy. Controls had been placed upon wages, the length of the workweek, and the kinds and numbers of goods produced. Moreover, the use of natural resources—such as rubber, iron ore, coal, and oil—was controlled by the government. America's economy had become a *planned economy*—the government largely controlled production and the living standards of its citizens.

The fall of Japan in August 1945 ended the need for strong economic controls to meet the country's war goals. Americans, who had suffered much to win the war, were eager to return to a peacetime way of life. They wanted to spend their wartime savings on goods—such as new housing, automobiles, and appliances—that were difficult to buy during the war. When the war ended, Americans felt that such consumer goods should be made available once again.

■ *Why were government economic controls thought necessary during World War II?*

The Economic Impact of Peace. To return America's economy to a peacetime footing, defense spending had to be cut. But this spending had to be reduced without causing a depression. Care had to be taken so that workers did not lose their jobs.

Another major problem was the return of our soldiers and sailors from their posts in Europe and in the Pacific. At the end of the war, over 12 million Americans were in our armed forces. Many millions of these men and women were stationed overseas. Most wanted to come home and to take up peacetime life once again. But if these millions of Americans entered the job market all at once, there would not be enough jobs to go around. Unemployment could be widespread. And this, in turn, might lead to a new economic depression.

President Truman also believed that the lifting of wartime controls could cause prices to

Wide World

New Yorkers enthusiastically celebrated the news of Japan's surrender in August 1945.

rise. American consumers had money to buy needed goods. But at war's end, the supply of such goods was far less than the number of buyers. Economists feared that because the demand for goods was greater than the supply, prices would rise sharply. The result would be a dangerous *inflation.* Rapidly rising prices would cause the buying power of the dollar to fall.

■ *Why did the President believe that economic controls should be lifted gradually?*

Demobilization and Inflation. To help meet our country's problems, President Truman decided to slowly cut the size of America's armed forces. A slow cutback, he felt, would help the country's job market to absorb returning veterans. At the same time, Truman planned to remove economic controls in stages instead of all at once. In this way, price rises, shortages, and overall inflation might not come about.

After four years at war, however, the American public was eager to return to peacetime conditions. Americans in the armed forces wanted to come home. And consumers and business leaders alike wanted economic restrictions to be lifted. For these reasons, President Truman and the Congress were forced to set aside their plans for a slow economic adjustment. By late 1946, over 10 million Americans had left the military. And government leaders, bowing to the wishes of voters, had removed most of the economy's wartime restrictions. The fear of runaway inflation and of growing joblessness increased.

The widespread joblessness expected by some Americans, however, failed to come about. Returning veterans had little trouble finding work in businesses, in factories, or on farms. In part, this was because almost 9 million veterans were helped by the *Servicemen's Readjustment Act*—the GI Bill—between 1946 and 1949. This act helped onetime soldiers and sailors to find low-cost loans with which to buy houses and to start businesses. The GI Bill also helped many veterans to further their education by paying part of their school costs.

However, the country did suffer from a growing inflation. Sharp price rises and troublesome shortages of consumer goods appeared as economic controls were lifted.

■ *How did the Servicemen's Readjustment Act assist veterans after World War II?*

Postwar Labor Problems. For the most part, America's return to a peacetime economy went smoothly. Inflation troubled the country.

But in the years after 1945, overall raises in wages helped to offset higher prices.

Trouble between business and labor, however, became a major problem in the postwar years. During the war, union members worked hard to meet the country's defense needs. Most workers agreed not to strike, and most accepted fixed pay ceilings. But after 1945, workers were faced with higher prices for manufactured goods and for food. Moreover, many workers faced cutbacks in overtime pay, as businesses returned to peacetime working hours. For these reasons, many workers in postwar America suffered from a loss of real earning power.

As a result, workers called for higher pay scales and for better working conditions. To gain these goals, thousands of workers turned to their most powerful bargaining weapon—the strike. In 1946 alone, more than 5,000 strikes were called. Over 4.5 million workers went on strike. Many of the country's largest industries—such as steel, coal, railroads, food packing, and automobiles—were hit by strikes. Because of this, America's economic growth was slowed.

■ *What powerful bargaining weapon was often used by organized labor after 1945?*

Government and Organized Labor. President Truman generally backed the aims of organized labor. He felt that workers should be free to bargain for a better life for themselves and for their families. But President Truman was against strikes that damaged the country as a whole. In several cases, he used his presidential powers to end such strikes.

Many Americans were deeply angered by the growing use of strikes by workers in the postwar years. Some voters began to call for government control of unions. Congress acted to answer these calls by passing the Labor-Management Relations Act of 1947—often called the *Taft-Hartley Act.* This act gave the President the right to halt economically damaging strikes for an 80-day "cooling off" time. The Taft-Hartley Act controlled union powers in many other ways as well.

Passage of the Taft-Hartley Act raised a loud outcry from organized labor. President Truman was also against the act. He felt that the act gave government leaders too much power over unions. But even though unions came under greater government control after 1947, they continued to make important gains for their members.

■ *How did Congress act to control organized labor during the postwar years?*

John L. Lewis rose through union ranks to become president of the United Mine Workers. During the 40 years that he was in office, Lewis worked to improve mine safety standards.

United Mine Workers Union Photo Archives

The Postwar Economy. The years between 1946 and 1953 were generally times of strong economic growth in America. During these years, however, the economy suffered from dangerous rates of inflation. Between 1946 and 1948, for example, prices rose by about 30 percent. Then, between 1948 and 1949, Americans were faced with a mild recession. But by and large, times were good for most people. Business boomed as rates of production and of sales rose rapidly. It was also a time when American farmers raised and sold more crops than ever before.

Consumers, too, found that they had a broader choice of goods to buy. Wages generally improved during these years. And America's *Gross National Product* (GNP)—the value of goods and services produced each year—nearly doubled. The swift rise in the GNP proved that our economy was healthy and strong.

Industrial output in America rose greatly in the years between 1946 and 1953. In part, this was because Americans had more money to spend on factory goods and services. Moreover, our country became a leader in the fight to rebuild war-torn nations throughout the world. Americans spent billions of tax dollars to aid countries in Europe, in Asia, and in the Middle East. Money, food, medicine, and factory goods from the United States helped many countries along the road to postwar recovery. The flow of American aid to war-torn countries around the world also spurred factory output at home. And this, in turn, helped to build a stronger American economy.

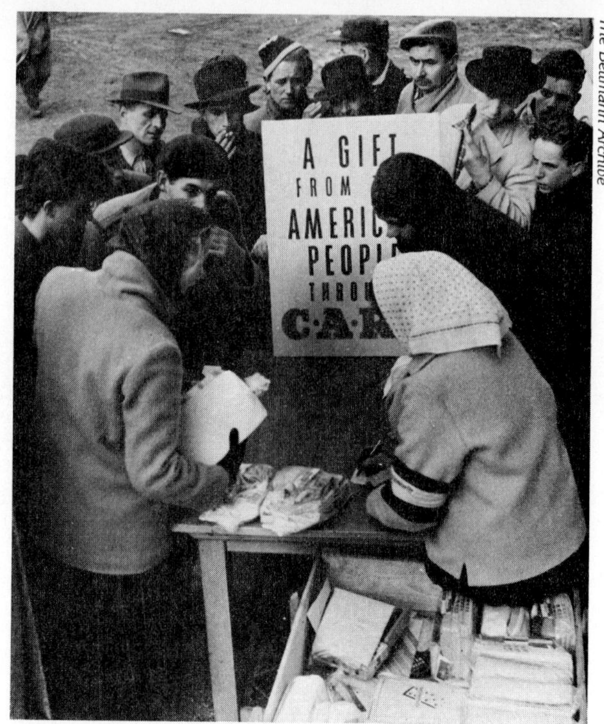

The Bettmann Archive

Americans aided the people of war-torn Europe with packages of food, medicine, and clothing.

What did the swift rise in America's GNP prove about our postwar economy?

SECTION 1 REVIEW

1. *Why did America's economy become a planned economy after World War II?*
2. *How did President Truman intend to avoid widespread unemployment and runaway inflation following the war?*
3. *Why did America's postwar foreign policy help to strengthen the overall economy?*

2 Postwar Society

Overview The return to peacetime in 1945 brought about lasting changes in our American way of life. Many people wanted to increase their material possessions, and others wanted to move upward in society. And still others faced the loss of social gains made during the war years.

Objectives After reading this section, you should be able to:

- describe the affect of postwar prosperity upon the way of life of Americans;
- evaluate the influence that the rising level of American education had on Americans' standard of living;
- discuss the lack of upward mobility that faced minorities in the postwar years.

Social Goals in Postwar America. Americans in the postwar years faced major social—as well as economic—changes. People were eager to return to a peacetime life. Moreover, World War II marked the end of the Great Depression and the return of full prosperity. Americans intended to use their newfound wealth to build a better life for themselves.

In the years after 1945, *social mobility*—movement from one social class to another—became more widespread in America. This meant that people had a better chance to move upward in society. Upward social mobility became a major aim of many Americans.

There were several reasons for the rise of social mobility in America. One of the most important was based upon postwar economic growth. Business and industry were booming. As a result, more jobs became open.

Another cause of greater social mobility in postwar America was the growing power of the labor movement. In the years after 1945, unions won higher wages and improved working conditions for their members. Between 1946 and 1953, millions of workers shared in the gains made by America's unions.

Education also was a key to upward social mobility in postwar America. The growth of business and of industry opened many new jobs. But many of these new jobs called for specialized training. People who attended school in order to gain such training were in growing demand on the American job market. And because they had the needed skills to offer, well-educated workers could expect better jobs and higher pay.

■ *What were three causes of increased social mobility in postwar America?*

Changing American Life-styles. Our American way of life changed greatly between 1946 and 1953. In part, this was due to changing values and goals. But postwar changes also came about as our population grew and moved.

The number of Americans rose sharply during the postwar years. In 1940, for example, about 132 million people lived in the United States. By 1946, our population was up to 141 million. Then, only eight years later, our population reached well over 150 million, a gain of over 18 million people since 1940.

One reason for the sudden population growth in America was the postwar "baby boom." Veterans returning from the war wanted to settle down and begin their families. Moreover, the prosperity of the postwar years caused many people to think that times would be good for raising children. Finally, after the war, many people left their homes in war-torn countries overseas. Thousands came to America in search of peace and of freedom.

As our postwar society became larger, it also became more urban. One reason for this was because businesses and industries were found mostly in or near cities. The promise of office and factory jobs drew thousands of Americans to the cities.

Another cause of city growth in postwar America had to do with the improved productivity of farmers. Machine power and new planting and harvesting ideas allowed fewer farmers to raise more food. Because of this, the need for farm workers dropped greatly after the war. Unemployed farm workers and their families moved to America's cities to find new jobs and to reach new goals.

■ *How did postwar prosperity in America affect our country's population growth?*

New Educational Opportunities. Americans in the postwar years became not only more prosperous but better educated as well. This was made clear by the growing number of students who attended American colleges between 1946 and 1953. In 1946, for example, college students numbered 1.7 million throughout America. But by 1950, this number had risen to 2.7 million.

There were many reasons for the sharp rise in the number of college students during the postwar years. The growth of prosperity in our country was one important cause. More American families could afford to send their children to college.

Changing business and industrial needs also helped to explain the rise in college attendance. A growing number of office and factory jobs took specialized training. And many young job seekers found that the best way to gain such training was by attending college.

Another major cause of growing college enrollment in the postwar years was the GI Bill of Rights. Under the GI Bill, veterans who wished to return to school received government aid to help meet their college costs. More than 9 million veterans had received some form of government aid through the GI Bill by 1950. Many of these veterans used the help offered by the GI Bill to return to school.

The rising level of education in our country during the postwar years changed life in America for the better. Highly trained workers found better jobs with better pay. And their skills and ideas led to new products and serv-

Wide World

Millions of veterans took advantage of the GI Bill of Rights to further their education. This law provided federal grants to help veterans pay college expenses.

ices. Because of this, many Americans were able to enjoy a higher standard of living in the years after 1945.

■ *How did changing business and industrial needs influence college attendance?*

Postwar Advances in Health Care. Economic growth and broader educational opportunities brought about a better life for millions of Americans. Nowhere during the postwar years was this more true than in the field of health care and medicine.

Technological discoveries, improved medicines, and ongoing research were important keys to better health care in postwar America. By the early fifties, these advances had led to vaccines against such feared diseases as yellow fever and polio. Greater understanding of medicines, such as sulfa drugs and penicillin, brought about new treatments for many other illnesses. And because Americans were generally wealthier in these years, they could afford better—but more costly—care.

Outstanding postwar improvements in the field of health care helped many Americans to enjoy longer, fuller lives. Because of these improvements, the average American could expect to live 68 years by 1950. Work in the health care field made our postwar society stronger and richer. But much remained to be done if all Americans were to share equally in these and other improvements.

■ *What were three important keys to improved health care in postwar America?*

The Struggle for Equality. Postwar social improvements helped many Americans to build a better way of life. But minorities and women were still subjected to unfair economic, political, and social treatment.

By the end of World War II, women filled many of the jobs left empty by our fighting men. By entering the work force in large numbers, women had won greater economic power. Moreover, women had shown that they could work equally hard and equally well.

After the war, many women discovered that their gains had been only temporary. And although American women had been voting since 1920, very few held government offices.

Blacks, American Indians, Hispanics, and Asian Americans also found that the small gains they had made during the war were temporary. Many of them had taken wartime jobs in businesses and in factories. In Hawaii, for example, Japanese Americans made up one third of the work force. And members of many racial and ethnic groups served in our armed forces with distinction. One example was the Japanese Americans who served with the 442nd Regimental Combat Team.

(Text continues on page 585.)

DO YOU KNOW?

How was polio conquered?

Dr. Jonas Salk developed a vaccine for preventing polio. Many Americans had suffered from this disease. President Franklin D. Roosevelt was a polio victim. In 1938, the National Foundation for Infantile Paralysis was founded in Roosevelt's name. Its purpose was to raise money to find a cure or way of preventing polio. Dr. Jonas Salk conducted one of the studies at the foundation. After many tests, Dr. Salk's vaccine was declared safe on April 12, 1955. Young people were quickly vaccinated and polio began to disappear. Dr. Salk received the Congressional Gold Medal for his work.

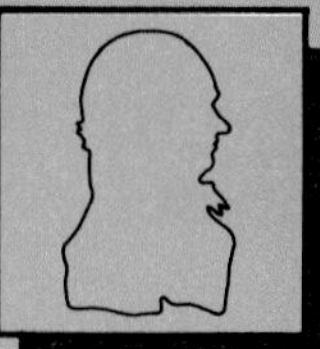

PROFILES

Jackie Robinson

Jackie Robinson believed in liberty and justice for all, and he believed in standing up for his rights. His mother worked hard to get enough money to raise him and his brothers and sister during the 1920's in California. Theirs was the only black family on a street of Anglos, Hispanics, and Orientals. When Jackie was ten years old a man insulted him with racial slurs and threw rocks at him. Little Jackie fired rocks right back while the neighbors ducked for cover. The man was forced to retreat.

Jackie's athletic drive lead him to star in college sports—track, basketball, and football. In 1942 he entered the Army as a private. By 1943 he was an officer. One night a civilian bus driver demanded that Robinson sit in the back of the bus. Robinson refused. The driver called the Military Police and falsely accused Jackie with being drunk and disorderly. Robinson stood up for his rights and was acquitted in a court–martial.

In 1947 Robinson was chosen as the person best able to integrate major league baseball. He joined the Dodgers. Jackie knew he would have to play fantastic ball every day. In 1949 he won the National League Batting Championship and the most valuable player award. Slowly, other black players began to be admitted to major league teams. Jackie was a leader on the field and off the field he fought for civil rights.

In 1959, along with Dr. Martin Luther King, he received an Honorary Doctorate. He was named to the Baseball Hall of Fame for his hitting, fielding, and leadership. Jackie Robinson demonstrated that pledging allegiance to liberty and justice for all is not a belief, it's an activity.

Wide World Photos

Thinking Critically

What evidence is there that Jackie Robinson believed in fighting for justice before he became a famous ballplayer?

In your opinion, why did Jackie Robinson purposely not fight vocally for civil rights his first few years in the major leagues?

How does it matter whether "Liberty and Justice for All" is a belief or an activity?

The return to peacetime, however, saw many minority group members lose the jobs that they had held during the war. Others had to settle for jobs that offered less pay and poorer conditions.

Job discrimination kept most American minorities on the bottom rung of the postwar social and economic ladder. Moreover, these Americans did not have an equal chance to gain a good education. Because of this, upward social mobility was almost unknown among postwar American minorities. And because they had little earning power, these people had fewer chances to enjoy good housing or good health care.

■ *How did American women win more economic power during the war years?*

SECTION 2 REVIEW

1. *What impact did economic growth and prosperity have upon social mobility in postwar America?*
2. *How did the rising level of American education influence standards of living in our country?*
3. *Why were most minorities unable to share in the advances made in our country during the postwar years?*

3 The Truman Years

Overview The postwar years were often troubled times for the United States. President Truman's strong leadership helped our country to move ahead during these years. However, a new kind of war—a cold war—faced the country with many dangers.

Objectives After reading this section, you should be able to:

- summarize the goal of President Truman's Fair Deal plan;
- identify the causes of the cold war;
- explain why the United States became involved in the Korean conflict.

The President's Postwar Goals. President Truman had several major postwar goals. First, he wanted to bring about a smooth changeover from wartime to peacetime in America. To meet this need, Truman felt, inflation and the jobless rate had to be kept as low as possible. Moreover, growing peacetime consumer needs had to be met. President Truman believed that the government should play a leading role in the effort to reach these important economic goals.

Second, Truman wanted to keep many of the social programs that made up Roosevelt's New Deal. Some changes in these programs had to be made. But the aim of Truman's social legislation package—called the *Fair*

One of President Truman's major goals while in office was to ensure that all Americans enjoyed equal civil rights.

Deal—remained the same. That is, Truman—like Roosevelt—believed that a better society could be built through direct government action.

Another of President Truman's postwar goals had to do with America's role in world affairs. President Truman intended to protect America's interests at home and overseas. He also wanted to further the cause of world peace and freedom. The best way to meet these aims, the President felt, was to take a strong international stand.

■ *Why did President Truman favor greater American participation in world affairs?*

Birth of the Cold War. During World War II, the United States and the Soviet Union worked together for the defeat of the Axis. Soon after the Allied victory, however, relations between the two countries began to cool. Confrontations between the Western democracies—led by America—and the Soviets and their Communist friends spread throughout the postwar world. This east-west competition became known as the *cold war.*

The cold war between the United States and the Soviet Union most often took a political form. The Soviets eagerly worked to gain power and influence in other countries. The United States, on the other hand, tried to check the spread of Soviet power. Cold war rivalry was generally peaceful. But it was always backed by the threat of armed might.

■ *What was a major America goal during the cold war?*

Causes of the Cold War. There were many important reasons for the coming of the cold war. One of these had to do with differing American and Soviet ideas about political rights and freedoms. In a democracy, such as that of the United States, all political power rests in the hands of the people. But under communism, the government is all-powerful. Citizens of a Communist government have few political rights and little freedom. Clearly, the two forms of government—democracy and communism—are based upon conflicting ideals. The cold war was, in large part, brought about by this conflict.

Postwar Soviet takeovers in several Eastern European countries also helped to bring about the cold war. In each of these countries, Communist governments were set up under Soviet leadership. The countries then became *satellites* of the Soviet Union. That is, they were largely under Soviet control.

The Soviet Union's leaders believed that

their Communist system would one day destroy the Western democracies. In order to reach their goal, Soviet leaders undertook a huge postwar arms buildup. Russian armies occupied much of Eastern Europe. And in 1949, the Soviets built their first atomic bomb. Now, both the United States and the Soviet Union were nuclear powers. The United States moved to counter growing Soviet might with an arms-building program of its own. This dangerous and costly arms race was yet another major cause of cold war tension.

■ *Why did the Soviets work to become more powerful than the United States?*

The Truman Doctrine. Many Americans believed that the postwar spread of Soviet power was a direct threat to our country's safety and freedom. President Truman strongly agreed with this view. And when the Soviets moved to overthrow governments that were friendly to America, Truman decided to act.

Soviet leaders badly wanted to gain Mediterranean seaports for their navy vessels. In order to reach their goal, the Soviet leaders worked to set up Communist governments in Greece and in Turkey. These governments, the Soviets believed, would then allow the Russian navy to use their seaports.

In answer to the Soviet move, President Truman asked Congress to give money and arms to Turkey and to Greece. Truman stated that the United States should help any country that was in danger of a Communist takeover.

Truman's belief that the United States should work to halt the spread of communism became known as the *Truman Doctrine.* In order to put this aim into action, government leaders in our State Department developed the *containment policy.* Under this plan, countries threatened with Communist takeovers would be given American economic and military aid. In this way, the spread of communism would be checked or contained.

■ *What was the aim of the Truman Doctrine?*

Strengthening the Free World. During the postwar years, the Soviet Union tested America's willingness to back the containment policy in many ways. One of the most dangerous of these tests took place in postwar Germany.

Following the war, Germany was divided into eastern and western zones of occupation. Eastern Germany was held by the Soviets. Control of western Germany was shared by

Following World War II, Germany was divided and occupied by the major Allied powers.

America, Great Britain, and France. The same was true of Berlin, Germany's largest city. The Soviets agreed to grant free American, British, and French access to West Berlin.

In 1948, however, the people of war-torn West Berlin were gravely threatened by a Soviet blockade of their city. America countered the Soviet move by airlifting thousands of tons of food, medicine, and clothing into West Berlin. In less than a year, the Soviets were forced to lift their blockade.

American leaders believed that a stronger Europe would help stop the spread of Soviet power and of communism. For this reason, Secretary of State George Marshall called upon the United States to help rebuild war-torn Europe. In 1948, the European Recovery Program, better known as the Marshall Plan, was begun. Under the Marshall Plan, 14 billion dollars were spent on economic aid to Europe. The Marshall Plan was costly. But it helped to block the threat of communism and to build a stronger free world.

The United States also acted to guard the political safety of the free world. Under American leadership, free world countries joined together to defend one another in case of attack. Strong treaty organizations, such as the North Atlantic Treaty Organization (NATO) and the Organization of American States (OAS), were formed. These treaty groups protected the freedom of member countries.

■ *What was the purpose of the Marshall Plan?*

Conflict in Korea. The most dangerous postwar test of America's containment policy came not in Europe but in the Far East. The country of Korea had been held by the Japanese during World War II. After the war, the United Nations (UN) decided to divide Korea along the line of the 38th parallel. With Soviet backing, the new government of North Korea became communistic. The government of South Korea, on the other hand, was against communism and was aided by the United States.

In June 1950, the army of North Korea suddenly attacked the South Koreans. After early setbacks, the United States and the UN rushed to help South Korea. By the end of

After World War II, Korea was a divided country. North Korea was communist while South Korea was an anticommunist republic.

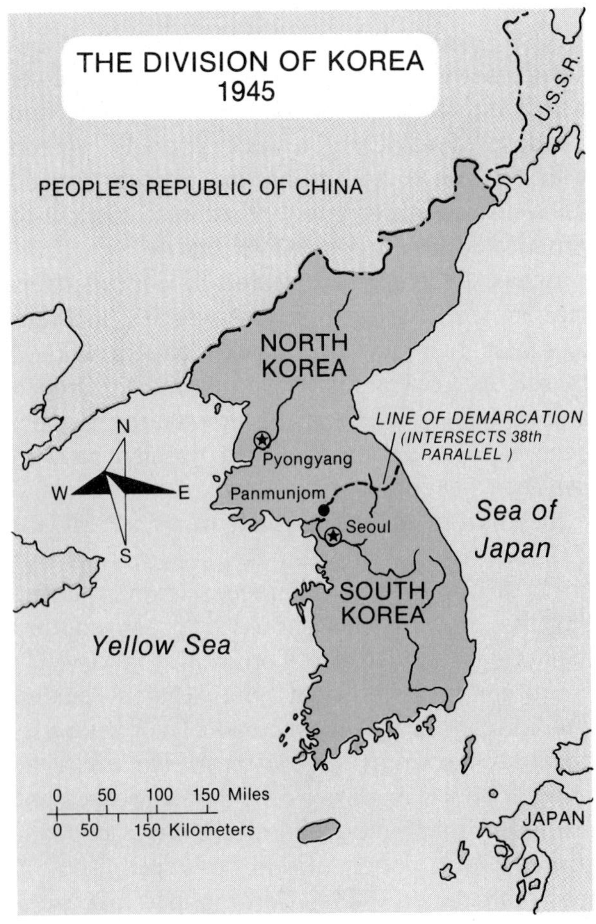

1950, the North Korean army had been pushed back to the Yalu River (see map on page 588). At that point, however, Communist China entered the war on the side of the North Koreans.

In November 1950, a huge Chinese counterattack surprised the UN army, led by America's General Douglas MacArthur. MacArthur's soldiers were thrown back into South Korea. The UN army fought bravely and hard, however, and halted the Chinese advance.

By mid-1951, peace talks were under way in Korea. In July 1953, a peace settlement between North Korea and South Korea was finally reached.

In terms of gains, neither side won a great deal from the war. Korea remained divided. At the same time, however, South Korea was saved from a Communist takeover. The spread of communism was halted on yet another front.

■ *In what ways did the governments of North Korea and of South Korea differ?*

SECTION 3 REVIEW

1. *What was the overall aim of President Truman's Fair Deal plan?*
2. *How did the postwar arms race help to build cold war tensions?*
3. *Why did the United States become militarily involved in the Korean conflict?*

CHAPTER 33 SUMMARY

The postwar years were times of major economic growth and change in America. War-weary Americans turned to the new task of building peacetime prosperity. But troubles sometimes arose, such as those that grew between business and labor. Americans also were faced with sharp rises in prices and in the overall cost of living. By and large, however, the postwar years were times when many Americans could afford a better way of life.

Life in America also underwent many changes during the postwar years. A rapidly growing population brought about new trends in America. One of the most important of these trends was seen in the overall growth of our cities. Many Americans were able to improve their standards of education and of living in general. But some others were not able to share in these gains.

President Truman brought outspoken leadership to our country during the postwar years. The President called for direct government action to improve life in our country. Also, Truman believed that America should take a strong stand in world affairs. During the postwar years, government did have a more powerful effect upon the American way of life. Moreover, our country became the free world's leader during a time of growing east-west competition.

CHAPTER 33 REVIEW

USING YOUR SKILLS

Interpreting a Secondary Source

The secondary source below illustrates the way that historians analyze and describe a historical event or trend. Secondary sources are not firsthand observations. Therefore, they are sometimes of less value than primary sources. But they do help to provide interpretations or evaluations of important events and trends. The secondary source below is taken from the book *An Unsettled People* by Rowland Berthoff. The author gives his view of the impact of economic prosperity on postwar American society. Read the excerpt and then answer the questions that follow.

1. According to the author of the excerpt, what did postwar prosperity enable most individuals in our society to do?
2. Why did many rural southerners migrate to America's cities following the war?
3. According to the author, what happened to old industrial centers as new ones grew during the postwar years?
4. What was the impact of postwar industrial automation upon unskilled and semiskilled workers in America?
5. In what way did the proportion of white-collar workers in the postwar labor force change?
6. In general, what important social changes does the author of the excerpt describe?

Prosperity after 1945 enabled most individuals to advance steadily in occupational status, income, and property.... Rural Southerners, both black and white, continued to respond to the call of the cities for labor after the war, especially since cotton-cultivating and picking machines were replacing many of them anyway.... The industrial labor force also was more mobile than ever, as whole new major industries sprang up... As new [industrial] centers grew, old ones declined; coal-mining regions decayed and lost population as petroleum and natural gas were piped throughout the country for industrial and domestic fuel.

... "Automation," the early final phase of the technological side of the Industrial Revolution, displaced unskilled and semiskilled labor, wiping out the hoped-for jobs of many new migrants from the country.... On the other hand, anyone already qualified for the white collar of a salaried professional, technical, or clerical position could rise as the proportion [balance in number] of such middle-class workers in the labor force increased;...

CHAPTER 33 REVIEW

YOU SHOULD KNOW

Identify, define, or explain each of the following:

planned economy
social mobility
Fair Deal
cold war
satellites
Truman Doctrine

CHECKING FACTS

1. What was one of America's strongest weapons in the fight against the Axis powers?
2. How many Americans were in the armed forces by the end of World War II?
3. What right did the Taft-Hartley Act give to the President?
4. What were three reasons for the rise of social mobility in postwar America?
5. What did the "baby boom" help cause?
6. Name three reasons for the sharp rise in college enrollment during the postwar years.
7. What was the aim of the Fair Deal?
8. Who led the western democracies in the cold war?
9. What was the purpose of the European Recovery Program?
10. What kind of government does North Korea have?

UNDERSTANDING CONCEPTS

1. Why did many government leaders wish to maintain economic controls in postwar America?
2. How did consumer demand and the supply of consumer goods influence the postwar economy?
3. In what ways did organized labor help to improve the social mobility of its members?
4. How did the European Recovery Program help to build a stronger free world after 1948?

LEARNING FROM ILLUSTRATIONS

1. Look at the picture on page 576. What event do you think that the artist is trying to portray? Support your answer.
2. Study the map on page 587. According to the map, what country controlled East Germany in 1945? What four countries had zones of occupation in Germany in 1945?

CRITICAL THINKING

1. Do you think the President should have the right to halt economically damaging strikes for a "cooling off" time? Give reasons for your answer.
2. Job discrimination and lack of educational opportunities left most American minorities from sharing in postwar prosperity. Do you think the government should have done something to help American minorities share in the postwar prosperity? Why or why not?
3. The dangerous and costly arms race increased the cold war tension. Do you think the United States could have countered the growing Soviet might in some other way? Why or why not?

ENRICHMENT ACTIVITIES

1. Research the cost of the postwar arms race. Many books and periodicals contain this information. Make a line graph showing your findings.
2. Learn more about the political career of President Harry Truman. Many helpful biographies and articles are available. Present a biographical report on President Truman's life to the class.

1950		1955		1960
1950 McCarthyism era begun	1952 Dwight D. Eisenhower elected President	1954 Economic recession Senator Joseph McCarthy censured *Brown v. Board of Education of Topeka*	1956 War between Egypt and Israel Worldwide oil shipments disrupted	1957 Economic recession Eisenhower Doctrine announced

CHAPTER 34

The Eisenhower Years

Chapter Objectives

After studying this chapter, you should be able to:

- enumerate America's postwar economic problems and describe the solutions that were found to overcome these problems;
- describe the major international challenges faced by America's postwar leaders;
- explain the significant ways in which Americans' postwar society differed from the society of earlier years.

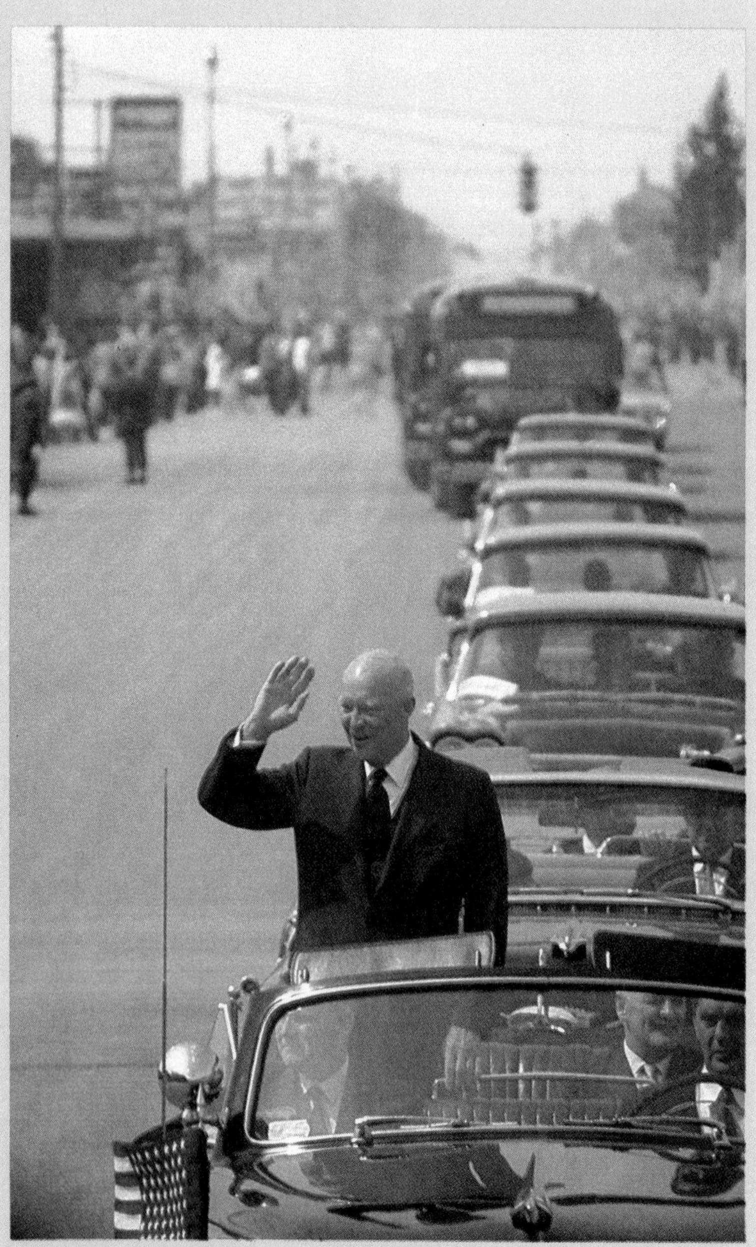

1 Political Change in the Fifties

Overview In 1952, General Dwight D. Eisenhower, a famous wartime leader, became our thirty-fourth President. President Eisenhower believed that the federal government had become too large and too powerful during the 1930's and 1940's. He wanted to limit the government's growth and power. At the same time, he tried to protect America's overseas interests by building stronger free world alliances.

Objectives After reading this section, you should be able to:

- explain the changes in government aims during the Eisenhower administration;
- discuss the economic policies of President Eisenhower;
- identify the problems of farmers during the 1950's.

A Changing Political Order. The election of 1952 saw the end of the Democratic party's twenty-year control of the presidency. In that year, General Dwight D. Eisenhower, a popular wartime hero, became our country's first Republican President since 1932.

President Eisenhower was voted into office with a large majority. He defeated his Democratic opponent—Governor Adlai Stevenson of Illinois—by a popular vote of 33.9 million to 27.3 million. Moreover, Eisenhower won all but nine states (see election map on this page).

The new President's strong showing proved that he enjoyed widespread support throughout the country. Eisenhower's victory also showed that some voters no longer accepted the more liberal ideals followed by Presidents Roosevelt and Truman. Some newspapers and political writers stated that Eisenhower's election would bring an end to "big government" in America.

As he entered the White House in 1953, President Eisenhower faced many grave challenges. Chief among these was the need to win a lasting world peace, free from the danger of nuclear war. The President said he wanted to build greater public confidence in our federal government. He also said he wanted to restore a spirit of self-reliance in all Americans.

In some cases, President Eisenhower's political aims were much the same as those of

In 1952, Republican Dwight D. Eisenhower scored an impressive victory over his Democratic opponent, Adlai Stevenson. What was the difference in electoral votes for the two candidates?

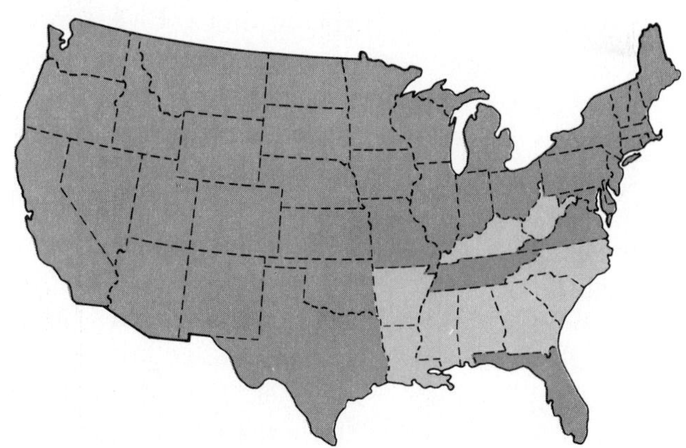

ELECTION OF 1952

	Electoral Votes	Popular Votes
Republican Dwight D. Eisenhower	442	33,936,234
Democratic Adlai E. Stevenson	89	27,314,992

earlier Presidents. But there were important differences as well. And these differences brought about changes in our country's political order.

What was the major challenge facing President Eisenhower after his election?

New Federal Philosophies. President Eisenhower felt that his election was a sign that many Americans favored new political goals. The President tried to take these new expectations into account as he formed his governmental policies.

Throughout his campaign, Eisenhower had said that our government had become too large and too powerful. He also stated that the executive branch—the presidency—had gained dangerous influence over daily life in America. For these reasons, Eisenhower believed, the government no longer served the people's best interests. He also felt that the presidency had grown too powerful.

President Eisenhower worked to share federal power more fully among all three branches of government. At times, Eisenhower acted strongly to win the cooperation of congressional and judicial leaders. In other cases, however, he followed a hands-off policy toward Congress and the courts. Moreover, Eisenhower tried to *delegate*—spread—his own presidential powers among his White House staff.

Some critics of Eisenhower's policies have stated that he was a weak leader and a do-nothing President. They felt that by sharing power with others, Eisenhower failed to take full responsibility for his actions.

Others have viewed the Eisenhower philosophy of government in a different light. These observers believe that President Eisenhower helped to rebuild federalism in our country. They also feel that by sharing his authority, Eisenhower acted to return political power to the people themselves. In any case, it is clear that President Eisenhower intended to halt the trend toward centralized government in America.

How did Eisenhower work to share federal power more fully?

New Economic Policies. Another promise made by President Eisenhower during his campaign was to bring greater economy to government. He wanted to encourage business growth in America. To reach these goals, Eisenhower followed economic policies that differed from those of the Roosevelt and the Truman years.

A major step in lowering the cost of government, Eisenhower believed, was balancing the federal budget. This meant that the government would spend only as much each year as it earned in taxes and other income. Cutbacks in federal spending would force government leaders to use money more wisely. In addition, less government spending would build a stronger dollar by lowering the rate of inflation.

President Eisenhower also wanted lower taxes for businesses and for individual taxpayers. Lower taxes would place more money in the hands of America's consumers. And this, in turn, would help to bring about more spending, greater production, and more jobs. Tax cuts would also help to lower government spending.

Another Eisenhower policy called for fewer government controls and for less federal economic activity. The President aimed to weaken the government's influence over our economy. He believed that America's free-market system should be subjected to as little government regulation as possible. The government's main economic duties should be to uphold the law, to encourage private enterprise, and to protect free-market conditions.

■ *Why did President Eisenhower favor a balanced federal budget?*

Continuing Economic Troubles. The Eisenhower years were generally prosperous times in America. Many people were able to afford a better way of life. Our gross national product (GNP) rose for the most part. This was seen as a sign of America's growing wealth. Consumer spending reached new heights as Americans in record numbers bought new houses, automobiles, and other market goods. The average family's income grew steadily throughout the 1950's.

During these same years, however, the country was troubled by several *recessions*—economic slowdowns. The worst of these took place in 1954 and again in 1957. These recessions, caused in part by cutbacks in government spending, temporarily weakened our economy. They also brought about higher unemployment.

Another ongoing economic problem had to do with government spending. President Eisenhower and his Secretary of the Treasury, George Humphrey, worked to trim government spending wherever possible. But rising costs for some government programs, such as defense, school aid, and social security, kept spending levels high.

For two years—1956 and 1957—President Eisenhower was able to balance our country's budget. But in other years, the President had to meet growing needs with greater spending. This was most true during times of recession, when more welfare spending was needed.

■ *What was one cause of the recessions of 1954 and 1957?*

Problems for Farmers. As a group, America's farmers faced major economic setbacks during the 1950's. Throughout these years,

President Eisenhower (left), Secretary of State Dulles (center), and Adlai E. Stevenson (right) are shown during a meeting at the White House.

Photo Trends

The Bettmann Archive

Farm machinery helped farmers produce record crops. But during the 1950's, farmers faced economic problems as crop surpluses caused farm prices to decline. At the same time, prices for farm equipment, like this grain rake, increased.

farmers were hard hit by rising costs for machinery, land, and equipment. This meant that farmers had to spend more money to raise crops and to prepare them for sale.

At the same time, the prices for farm goods went down. Improved farming methods and greater crop-raising efficiency led to the overproduction of farm goods. Crop surpluses—caused in part by lower world food demands—soon appeared. These surpluses drove farm prices sharply downward.

In 1956, Congress passed a new farm bill. Under this act, farmers agreed to lower their production levels by using only part of their land to raise crops. Only the land needed to meet the market's needs was to be used. The remaining lands were set aside in a *soil bank.* The government paid the farmers to put their land in the soil bank. In this way, our government leaders believed that America's farm surplus would be cut back and that prices would rise.

The soil-bank plan enjoyed some success after 1956. But the plan did not erase the problem of crop surpluses. Because of this, farmers continued to be economically hard pressed during the late 1950's.

■ *What were two causes of farm overproduction during the 1950's?*

SECTION 1 REVIEW

1. *Why did Eisenhower work to share federal power more fully among all three branches of government?*
2. *Why did Eisenhower want lower taxes for business and for individual taxpayers?*
3. *Why did the prices for farm goods go down during the 1950's?*

2 America and the World

Overview New ideas about the United States world role grew during the Eisenhower years. During these years, some Americans were slow to accept their country's responsibilities as a world power. But others called for stronger American leadership to keep peace and order in the world. President Eisenhower gave much attention to forming our country's foreign policies. But fear of communism at home and growing unrest overseas caused some people to question the President's work.

Objectives After reading this section, you should be able to:

- assess the influence of McCarthyism on America's foreign policies;
- discuss the goals of Eisenhower's foreign policy;
- explain the aims of the Eisenhower Doctrine.

The Impact of McCarthyism. The early years of the 1950's were troubled times in America. The Korean War and questions about our country's proper role in world affairs were major causes of this unrest. Another important cause was the growing fear of communism.

Beginning in 1950, Joseph McCarthy—then a little-known senator from Wisconsin—charged that our government had been infiltrated by Communists. McCarthy's charges were based largely upon suspicion rather than fact. But they helped to fan the public's fear. In turn, McCarthy won a great deal of attention and power.

Between 1950 and 1954, Senator McCarthy brought accusations of disloyalty against hundreds of government workers and leaders. Some Americans were angered by the senator's methods and by his charges. But many citizens accepted McCarthy's word. A wave of *McCarthyism*—an unreasoning fear of communism and suspicion toward those who held different views—swept across our country.

Many people believed that McCarthy's downfall came in 1954. During that year, Senator McCarthy charged that the United States Army had been infiltrated by Communists. Hearings on McCarthy's charges were held by the Senate and were televised throughout the country. Viewing the telecasts, Americans gained a firsthand view of McCarthy's attacks and of his damaging use of power. Strong public feelings against the senator soon spread across the land. Later that year, the Senate voted to censure McCarthy.

Feelings of McCarthyism slowly died in America. But the public's faith in our government had been badly shaken.

■ *How did the public respond to McCarthy's tactics during the 1954 army hearings?*

Eisenhower and Dulles. McCarthyism, the Korean War, and the growth of Soviet power led many Americans to favor stronger foreign policies. One of President Eisenhower's first goals was to end the war in Korea. Within a few months of his inauguration, the President was able to arrange a truce in the war-torn land. With the coming of peace in Korea, Eisenhower turned his attention to forming new world policies for America.

President Eisenhower's main foreign-policy goal was to build a lasting world peace. At the

(*Text continues on page 599.*)

VIEWPOINTS DIFFER

McCarthyism

Senator Joseph McCarthy's senational charges—communists had infiltrated the State Department—brought about public fear. Although no Communist party members were ever found, several communist sympathizers, liberals, and noncomformists lost their government jobs.

In the following passage, McCarthy defends his tactic of "guilt through association."

One of the safest and most popular sports engaged in today by every politician and office seeker is to "agree with McCarthy's aim of getting rid of Communists in government," but at the same time to "condemn his irresponsible charges and shot-gun techniques." It is a completely safe position to take ..

The fact that... [certain government employees] have not been convicted of treason or of violating some espionage [spy] laws is no more a valid argument that they are fit to represent this country... than the argument that a person who has a reputation of consorting [associating] with criminals... is fit to act as your babysitter because he has never been convicted of a crime.

We are not concerned with GUILT by association because here we are not concerned with convicting an individual of any crime. We are concerned with the question of whether the individual who associates with those who are trying to destroy this nation, should be admitted to the high councils of those planning [government] policies...

Few members of Congress challenged McCarthy's reckless tactics directly. One who did so was Senator Margaret Chase Smith of Maine:

Those of us who shout the loudest about Americanism in making character assassinations are all too frequently those, who, by our own words and acts, ignore some of the basic principles of Americanism—

The right to criticize.

The right to hold unpopular beliefs.

The right to protest.

The right to independent thought.

The exercise of these rights should not cost one single American citizen his reputation or his right to a livelihood, not should he be in danger of losing his reputation or livelihood merely because he happens to know someone who holds unpopular beliefs.

Think About It

1. Why is Senator McCarthy not concerned about guilt by association?
2. Are the rights listed by Senator Smith protected by the Constitution?
3. McCarthy seems to be making a case for "innocence by association." Do you think this is a valid concept? Explain your answer.

same time, he intended to protect countries friendly to the United States. In this way, Eisenhower reasoned, our country's security would be made stronger.

Eisenhower's world goals were shared by his Secretary of State, John Foster Dulles. Secretary Dulles enjoyed the President's trust. For this reason, Dulles was given much of the day-to-day responsibility for directing America's overseas affairs. He also worked closely with the President to form our country's long-term foreign-policy plans. The strong working partnership between Eisenhower and Dulles gave the secretary unusually broad powers to act on his own.

Secretary Dulles had great faith in the power of personal diplomacy. The secretary believed that this was the best way to build better world understandings. He traveled tirelessly in order to meet face-to-face with chiefs of state in other countries.

■ *What type of diplomacy was favored by Secretary Dulles?*

The Eisenhower Doctrine. President Eisenhower and Secretary Dulles gave much of their attention to forming a new foreign policy for America. Their overall goal was to make the United States and the free world stronger and more secure. To reach this goal, Eisenhower and Dulles knew that the worldwide spread of Soviet power had to be checked.

Throughout the 1950's, the United States received a growing share of its energy needs from oil-rich Middle Eastern countries. At the same time, however, the Soviet Union worked to build closer ties with several Arab states. Among these were Egypt, Syria, and Iraq. By the mid-1950's, the Soviet Union had poured huge amounts of military aid into these countries.

The growing Soviet-Arab partnership was viewed by many as a danger to American safety. The flow of Middle Eastern oil to the United States and to other free-world countries could be cut off. This danger became more real in 1956, when war broke out between Egypt and the American-backed country of Israel. The Israeli-Egyptian war was quickly settled. But worldwide oil shipments had been badly disrupted. Many Americans felt that Soviet actions in the Middle East had led to the outbreak of trouble.

In 1957, President Eisenhower warned

The Bettmann Archive

Secretary of State John Foster Dulles worked to insure the peace and the safety of the United States and of its allies through strong armed forces. He helped to formulate the Eisenhower Doctrine.

against further Soviet buildups in the Middle East. Moreover, he stated that American troops would be used to protect friendly Middle Eastern countries from Communist takeovers. Eisenhower's promise to guard peace in the Middle East became known as the *Eisenhower Doctrine.* This new American stand proved that our country intended to play a stronger role in Middle Eastern events.

■ *Why was the Soviet Union's presence in the Middle East a threat to America?*

New Threats to World Peace. The American desire to protect world peace and to halt the spread of communism was often tested during the 1950's. At times, the United States was drawn into dangerous crises far from home. At other times, new trouble spots arose closer to our own shores.

The Communist takeover in mainland China during the late 1940's was seen as a major threat to world peace. This threat became more real when China attacked the United Nations soldiers fighting in Korea in 1950. Moreover, the Communist Chinese wished to move against the small Pacific island of Formosa (Taiwan). This island was held by Chinese who had fled from the Communists' takeover in 1949.

The Chinese government of Formosa was led by Chiang Kai-shek with strong American backing. President Eisenhower warned that any attack against Formosa would be treated as an attack against the United States. This policy helped to protect the safety of Chiang's government and of the Chinese on Formosa. But the Communist Chinese repeatedly made clear their aim to destroy Chiang and his people. This danger caused grave unrest in Asia and throughout the world during the Eisenhower years.

Closer to home, a new Communist danger arose in the Caribbean island of Cuba. In 1959, a Cuban civil war ended in victory for Fidel Castro. At first, the new Cuban leader

UPI

General George C. Marshall (left) visited the Chinese leader Generalissimo Chiang Kai-shek (right) and his wife Madame Chiang (center) at their home in Nanking, China. Chiang later set up a government on Formosa after being forced out of mainland China by the Communists in 1949.

promised to bring freedom and democracy to his people. Americans welcomed Castro's victory.

But Castro soon declared himself to be a Communist. He quickly asked for aid and weapons from the Soviet Union. By 1960, Cuba had become an important Soviet military base. Later, events in Castro's Cuba would push the world to the edge of nuclear war.

■ *Why did Americans first welcome Castro's takeover in Cuba?*

SECTION 2 REVIEW

1. *How did McCarthyism influence America's foreign policies?*
2. *In what way did President Eisenhower intend to strengthen America's security?*
3. *Why was the Eisenhower Doctrine formulated?*

3 Affluence and Anger

Overview Americans' world outlook changed greatly during the 1950's, as new needs arose. The growing economy offered many Americans new chances to build better lives. But some people believed that our society had grown weaker as it became more interested in material wealth. Throughout these years, however, many citizens undertook the long and bitter struggle to win equal civil rights.

Objectives After reading this section, you should be able to:

- analyze the affect of America's growing affluence on society;
- discuss how some Americans reacted to the country's affluent society;
- evaluate the strengths of the civil rights movement during the 1950's.

An Affluent Society. Society in America became far more *affluent*—materially wealthy—during the 1950's than ever before. There were many reasons for our country's growing wealth. The American population grew rapidly after World War II. More people meant wider markets for factory goods and for business services. And new markets, in turn, meant more jobs for American workers.

Family income levels also rose during the 1950's. Many new jobs offered higher pay and better chances to move ahead. Millions of Americans found it easier to pay for basic needs—such as housing, food, and clothing. Because of this, they were able to spend more of their earnings on goods that would once have been luxuries.

As consumer buying reached new heights in America, business leaders worked to win a greater share of the market. In many cases, this competition led to a wider variety of high-quality goods.

America's rapidly growing wealth meant that more people were able to build a life of material comfort. Our middle-class society enjoyed living standards that, in many countries, could only be found among the very rich. At the same time, however, hardship and poverty were still widespread in many parts of America.

■ *What was one result of growing business competition in America during the 1950's?*

Continuing Social Problems. Poverty remained a leading weakness of America's society during the Eisenhower years. In many cases, poor Americans lacked the training or the education needed to find good jobs. These people often had to accept low-paying jobs that did not allow them to build a better life. In other cases, changing consumer needs caused sudden joblessness and loss of income. Many farm workers and Appalachian coal miners were among those who were hard hit by changing market needs.

Another social weakness was America's failure to offer an equal education to all of its citizens. Without a good education, people had fewer chances to build a better life for themselves and their families. The lack of good schools was felt most among members of minorities and among many city dwellers.

The spread of inner-city slums was yet another social danger in the 1950's. Throughout these years, thousands of poor Americans were trapped in crumbling slum neighborhoods. Many of these people could not pay for better housing. Slum dwellers faced cruel daily hardships, such as overcrowding, high crime rates, and lack of good schools.

The 1950's were years of growing social affluence in our country. But for many Americans, the 1950's were times of hardship, poverty, and hopelessness.

■ *Why were many poor Americans unable to find good jobs during the 1950's?*

Paul S. Conklin

While the 1950's were generally prosperous years, some Americans lived in areas that were affected by a changing economy. These people faced poverty, unemployment, and difficult living conditions as they tried to adjust to these economic problems. How would you describe the living conditions of these people?

Critics of Affluence. A growing number of writers and critics believed that America's old values had been weakened by rising affluence. These observers charged that Americans had lost their spirit of independence and their eagerness to help others.

Some writers felt that success in America depended upon one's willingness to conform. Businesses, for example, sometimes favored those who dressed and behaved in certain ways. Sloan Wilson's book *Man in the Gray Flannel Suit* pictured business people whose working lives were empty and machinelike. Wilson's book became a best-seller and helped to make clear the dangers of overconformity in America.

In 1958, John Kenneth Galbraith, a leading economist, wrote *The Affluent Society.* Galbraith stated that America had become a land of great material wealth. But this came about at the cost of growing personal selfishness.

Galbraith warned that more public attention had to be given to meeting our society's needs. Otherwise, life in our country would become poorer for all Americans in the years ahead.

Galbraith, Wilson, and other leading writers of the 1950's helped to build greater social awareness in America. But much remained to be done in order to build a truly equal American society.

■ *According to Galbraith, what was the cost of great material wealth in America?*

Equality and the Courts. For years, the civil rights movement had fought against laws and court rulings that limited black freedom in America. In many cases, these laws and rulings helped to *segregate*—separate—blacks from white society.

DO YOU KNOW?

What was the first play to appear on Broadway that was written by a black woman?

The long-running play *A Raisin in the Sun* was the first play to appear on New York's Broadway that was written by a black woman. The play was written by Lorraine Hansberry. Writer Hansberry was only 29 years old when her play reached Broadway in March 1959. *A Raisin in the Sun* was an immediate success, and both the play and its author received widespread critical acclaim. After 530 performances and nearly 16 months on Broadway, the drama was made into a major motion picture.

One such court ruling, in the case of *Plessy* v. *Ferguson,* dated from 1896. The Supreme Court decided in favor of the idea of "separate but equal" public facilities for blacks. But the court's ruling was unfair to black Americans. Often, fewer tax dollars were spent on blacks' public facilities. Because of this, black public schools and other facilities were generally of poor quality.

In 1954, however, the Supreme Court moved to overturn its earlier ruling. In the case of *Brown* v. *Board of Education of Topeka,* the Court ruled against the "separate but equal" idea. This case proved that blacks had an equal right to use *the same* public schools and other facilities as whites. The Supreme Court's ruling was a turning point in black Americans' struggle for equal civil rights.

Another Supreme Court ruling in 1955 ordered schools throughout America to end segregation "with all deliberate speed." But some state governments refused to follow this order.

In 1957, the President used soldiers to protect blacks entering Central High School in Little Rock, Arkansas. Eisenhower showed that strong measures would be followed whenever needed to keep peace and to open the schools. Because of this, school desegregation was speeded and the black civil rights movement pushed ahead.

■ *Why was the "separate but equal" ruling clearly unfair to blacks?*

Blacks Join Together. The civil rights movement took another major step forward in 1955. Blacks in Montgomery, Alabama, acted together to boycott their city's segregated bus lines. A young black minister, Dr. Martin Luther King, Jr., gave strong leadership to the boycott. And the National Association for the Advancement of Colored People (NAACP) joined with Montgomery's blacks to fight against unfair treatment.

In November 1956, the NAACP won a major court victory against segregated buses and other forms of public transportation. And that December, blacks in Montgomery gained the right to equal use of the city's transportation network.

The Montgomery bus boycott, like *Brown* v. *Board of Education of Topeka,* was a milestone in America's civil rights movement. The boycott proved that when black Americans worked as a group, the cause of civil rights was furthered. Moreover, by working together, blacks were able to win greater political power. For these reasons, more black Americans began to fight for equal rights. And new black leaders, such as Dr. Martin Luther King, Jr., led the struggle.

In the years ahead, the black civil rights movement reached many of its goals. And all Americans gained a society that was more free and more democratic.

■ *What did the Montgomery boycott prove?*

Women in Mid-Century. American women made some social and economic gains during the Eisenhower years. One means used by

Wide World

During the 1950's two prominent black ministers—the Reverend Ralph Abernathy (left) and Dr. Martin Luther King, Jr. (center)—worked to end all segregation on the public bus system of Montgomery, Alabama.

women in America to move ahead was through education. In 1957, for example, almost 138,000 women earned college degrees. This was over 20 percent more than the number of women who had received degrees ten years earlier.

Many kinds of jobs, however, remained closed to women throughout the 1950's. Most factory jobs, for example—including jobs that women had filled during wartime—were controlled by men during these years. Moreover, women still lacked an equal voice in our country's government. Although they could and did vote, few women in these years were able to run for public office. And women who held government jobs generally had little or no decision-making powers.

During the Eisenhower years, women took some important steps toward reaching full equality in America. But it was not until the 1960's that women began to gain a real voice in our country.

What was one means used by women in America to move ahead during the 1950's?

SECTION 3 REVIEW

1. *In what way did America's growing affluence change the standard of living in our country?*
2. *How did leading writers and social critics affect American society in the 1950's?*
3. *Why did the Supreme Court's decision in* Plessy v. Ferguson *lead to social unrest among black Americans?*

CHAPTER 34 SUMMARY

The Eisenhower years marked a time of changing political goals in America. The President hoped to cut the size and the influence of our federal government. He also worked to build the economy by lowering taxes and government spending. In this way, the President hoped to give citizens more control over their own lives and fortunes. But Eisenhower found that strong government action was needed to overcome the problems faced by some Americans.

Fear of communism at home and of growing Soviet power overseas shaped new attitudes toward our country's world role. New American policies grew out of changing conditions in Asia and in the Middle East. President Eisenhower and Secretary of State Dulles tried to build a lasting world peace. But throughout the 1950's, Americans faced many dangers that were brought about by the changing world order.

The 1950's were years of growing material wealth in the United States. But not all Americans had an equal chance to share in their country's rising affluence. Poverty was still widespread. And the issue of black civil rights caused new unrest in America.

CHAPTER 34 REVIEW

USING YOUR SKILLS

Interpreting Statistical Data

The table and the line graph on this page illustrate two different ways that social scientists can portray the same statistical data. Tables are often used to accurately list and categorize data. Line graphs, on the other hand, are useful in providing visually clear comparisons for easy reference. Both the table and the graph show total government defense budgets for the years 1953 through 1960. They also compare the amount spent each year on defense needs with the amount spent on veterans' benefits and services. Study the table and the graph and then answer the questions that follow.

1. How does the information given in the table compare with the data shown on the graph? In what general way do the table and the graph differ?
2. According to the table, which category of our total defense budget received the largest amount of money between 1953 and 1960? Which received the least?
3. According to the graph, in which year was our total defense budget highest? In which year was the budget lowest?
4. Between which two consecutive years did spending on national defense increase the most? Between which two consecutive years did it decrease the most?
5. According to the graph, did spending for veterans' benefits and services generally increase or decrease after 1953?
6. In comparison, which of the two methods—tables or line graphs—is best for determining exact dollar amounts? Which is best for determining trends?

FEDERAL SPENDING FOR NATIONAL DEFENSE AND VETERANS BENEFITS AND SERVICES, 1953–1960
(in billions of current dollars)

Year	Total Defense Budget Spending*	National Defense	Veterans Benefits and Services
1953	74.1	50.4	4.4
1954	67.5	47.0	4.3
1955	64.4	40.7	4.5
1956	66.2	40.7	4.8
1957	69.0	43.4	4.9
1958	71.4	44.2	5.2
1959	80.3	46.5	5.3
1960	76.5	45.7	5.3

* Includes nonmilitary defense spending administered by departments and agencies other than the Department of Defense and the Veterans Administration.

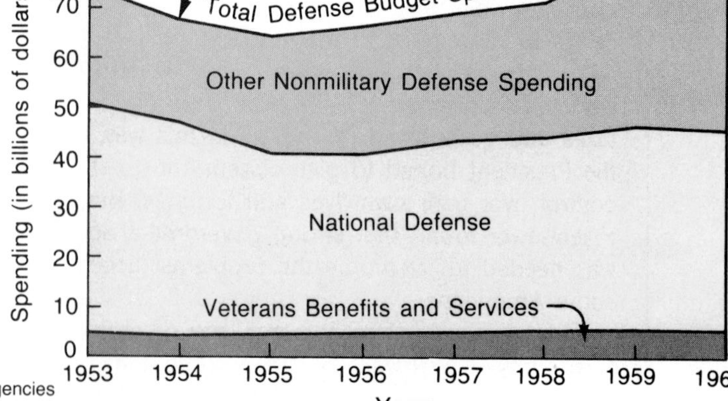

CHAPTER 34 REVIEW

YOU SHOULD KNOW

Identify, define, or explain each of the following:

delegate
recessions
soil bank
McCarthyism
affluent
segregate

CHECKING FACTS

1. What main challenge faced President Eisenhower after his election?
2. What did Eisenhower believe was a major step in lowering the cost of government?
3. What happened to the GNP during the Eisenhower years?
4. What happened to unemployment during the recessions of the 1950's?
5. Upon what were McCarthy's communism charges based?
6. Who led the Chinese government on Formosa?
7. What Caribbean island became an important Soviet military base by 1960?
8. What kinds of hardships did slumdwellers face in the 1950's?
9. Who wrote *The Affluent Society*?
10. What Supreme Court ruling outlawed segregated public schools?

UNDERSTANDING CONCEPTS

1. Why did Dwight Eisenhower win the 1952 presidential election?
2. Why did McCarthyism lead to a loss of public confidence in our federal government?
3. Why was America threatened by the Soviet Union's presence in the Middle East during the 1950's?
4. What was the impact of *Brown v. Board of Education of Topeka* on America's democracy?

LEARNING FROM ILLUSTRATIONS

1. Look at the election map on page 593. What area of the country gave the greatest support to Adlai E. Stevenson in 1952?
2. Study the picture on page 602. What does the picture show about the conditions in which the people of the area were living?

CRITICAL THINKING

1. Eisenhower's economic policies included balancing the federal budget. In order to do this, money for government programs had to be cut. If you were asked to trim government spending, in which of the following areas would you cut expenses: defense, school aid, social security, foreign aid, farm aid, veterans' programs, welfare programs, or space programs? Give reasons for your choices.
2. John Kenneth Galbraith warned that more public attention had to be given to meeting our society's needs. Otherwise, the quality of life would become poorer for all Americans in the years ahead. What do you think Galbraith meant by this?

ENRICHMENT ACTIVITIES

1. To learn more about America's economy, form a group to conduct research on the growth of our gross national product during the Eisenhower years. Your group could then make a poster-sized graph that compares our GNP in the 1950's with the GNP in the 1980's.
2. To better understand the civil rights movement in America, study the writings, speeches, and biographies of black leaders, such as Dr. Martin Luther King, Jr. Report your findings to the class.

1960

1965

- 1958 *Explorer I* launched
- 1960 John F. Kennedy elected President
- 1961 Equal Opportunity Commission set up; Bay of Pigs invasion
- 1962 Cuban Missile crisis; John Glenn, Jr. orbited the earth
- 1963 President Kennedy assassinated; Vice-President Lyndon B. Johnson became President
- 1964 Twenty-fourth Amendment passed; Civil Rights Act of 1964 became law; Johnson's War on Poverty begun; Lyndon Johnson elected President
- 1965 "Great Society" programs begun

CHAPTER 35

The Kennedy–Johnson Years

Chapter Objectives

After studying this chapter, you should be able to:

- enumerate the economic problems President Kennedy faced upon becoming President and the steps he took in dealing with them;
- list the several major causes of the continuance of the cold war between the United States and the Soviet Union;
- compare and contrast the political beliefs held by the two major candidates for the presidency in the 1964 election.

1 The New Frontier

Overview The newly elected President, John F. Kennedy, wanted to bring peace throughout the world in the early 1960's. The President wanted to make gains in civil rights, to strengthen the economy, to lower unemployment, and to promote the exploration of space. Continuation of the cold war, however, blocked the President's efforts to meet many of his goals.

Objectives After reading this section, you should be able to:

- discuss the legislation that Kennedy proposed to improve American society;
- enumerate the advances in the civil rights movement in the early 1960's;
- give examples of the ways President Kennedy worked to fight inflation.

The Election of 1960. Senator John F. Kennedy of Massachusetts won the presidency in 1960 over his Republican opponent Richard M. Nixon by a slim margin of votes (see map on this page). Senator Lyndon B. Johnson of Texas became the Vice-President.

The presidential campaign was highlighted by a series of televised debates between the two major candidates. These broadcasts played a large part in Kennedy's victory. Kennedy's youth, sense of humor, and appearance appealed to many voters. Nevertheless, Senator Kennedy had to overcome two large political problems during the campaign. First, he had to convince many voters that he had the experience to lead the nation. This was because he would become—at forty-three years of age—the youngest person to be elected President. Second, Kennedy had to convince some people that his Roman Catholic religion should not be an issue in the campaign nor should it have any influence on his presidency.

What two political problems did Senator Kennedy face during the campaign in 1960?

Camelot. The Kennedy presidency brought a feeling of change to the United States. During his 1960 campaign, Kennedy promised to lead America to a "New Frontier." This frontier, he said, was in the world at large, within

What was John F. Kennedy's margin of victory in popular votes in the 1960 election?

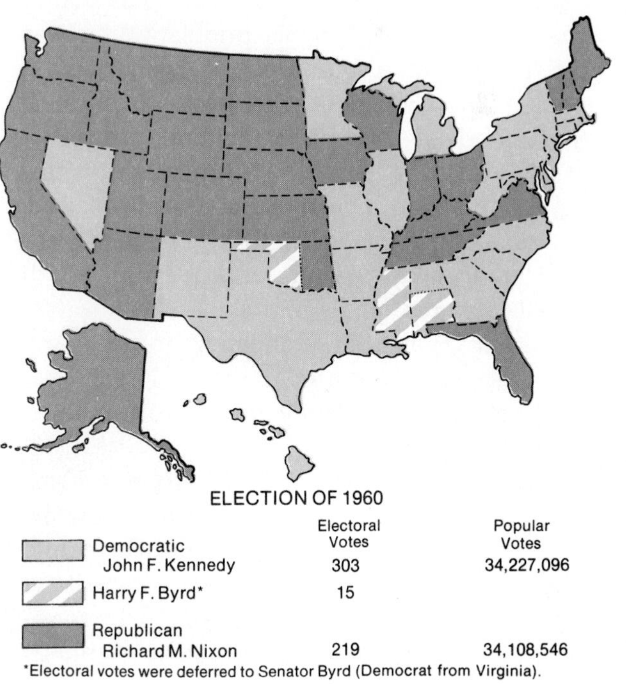

the country itself, and in outer space. "The New Frontier of which I speak is not a set of promises—it is a set of challenges," the President said.

Historian Theodore White later compared the Kennedy presidency to the legend of Camelot. Camelot was the name of the mythical court of King Arthur in ancient England. The knights of the Round Table were the best and the brightest in the land. And the goal of King Arthur and his knights—like the goal of President Kennedy and his staff—was to serve the people of their land as best they could. Many of President Kennedy's goals—such as an American moon landing within ten years—stirred the country's imagination. And many of his social programs offered new hope for a better life to many Americans. With other programs, the President planned to lead the United States in helping people in other parts of the world.

President Kennedy was popular with young Americans. Because of his popularity, he was able to influence the lives of many young people. The President's interest in physical fitness and in America's cultural life influenced the lives of many Americans. New interest in good health practices developed. This was largely because the President enjoyed swimming, hiking, and playing touch football with his family and staff. The fine arts in America, including theater, music, and films, received increased support largely because of the President's interest in cultural events. This interest was shown at President Kennedy's Inauguration. Poet Robert Frost was asked to read a piece from his work. Other artists, such as violinist Isaac Stern and cellist Pablo Casals, were often invited to perform at the White House. To many Americans, the young and active Kennedy administration opened a new era for the United States.

Why did support for the fine arts in America increase in the early 1960's?

New Frontier Legislation. The presidency of John F. Kennedy helped to bring about changes in American society and throughout the world. In his first year in office, the new President sent 25 major bills to Congress. In these bills, the President had outlined his plans for improving American society. President Kennedy also issued an executive order on March 6, 1961. This order set up the Equal Opportunity Commission. This government agency worked to make certain that every American was given an equal chance to obtain government employment.

The President was also concerned about America's role in aiding other countries. He set up the Peace Corps in March 1961. Young Americans were sent to developing countries to teach modern methods of farming, building, and health care to the people of these lands. In the same month, President Kennedy set up the Alliance for Progress. This was a ten-year plan to help Latin American countries undertake many reforms and fight poverty among their people.

Why was the Equal Opportunity Commission established?

The Civil Rights Movement. Equal rights was the major social issue of the early 1960's. New leaders and new organizations called for an end to racial discrimination. Groups such as the Congress of Racial Equality (CORE) and the National Association for the Advancement of Colored People (NAACP) undertook peaceful marches and

Dr. Martin Luther King, Jr., (center foreground) gained the respect and admiration of many people for his peaceful efforts to end racial discrimination in the United States. Dr. King is shown leading a civil rights march from Selma, Alabama, to the state capital in Montgomery during the mid-1960's. How would you describe the size of the civil rights march? Were all the marchers black?

Wide World

other nonviolent demonstrations. These actions focused attention on racial problems throughout the country. Both groups believed in peaceful protest to achieve their goals.

Another important organization in the civil rights movement at this time was the Southern Christian Leadership Conference (SCLC). This group was founded by Dr. Martin Luther King, Jr., a Baptist minister. Dr. King became world famous for his strong leadership in the civil rights movement and for his firm belief in peaceful protest to bring about social change.

But social change came slowly for many black Americans. Gradually, however, many black men and women began to benefit from the equal rights movement. James Meredith was a black student. He entered the University of Mississippi in October 1962. There he was protected by federal officers. Federal soldiers also guarded the school grounds. His enrollment broke down an educational barrier for many black people in Mississippi. Meredith's action also showed that the federal government would uphold the rights of black Americans anywhere in the country.

President Kennedy and his administration responded to the call for racial equality. In June 1963 the President asked for congressional action on far-reaching equal rights laws. Following the President's example, thousands of Americans became involved in the equal rights movement as well. In August 1963 more than 200,000 people took part in

(Text continues on page 613.)

RECALLING THE TIMES

King's Dream

Dr. Martin Luther King, Jr., was one of the most famous civil rights leaders of the 1960's. His idea of using peaceful demonstrations to gain equal rights for black Americans won the respect of many people. In August 1963 Dr. King spoke at a large civil rights gathering in Washington, D.C. In that speech he told of his hope for future racial peace in the United States.

I say to you today, my friends, that in spite of the difficulties and frustrations of the moment I still have a dream. It is a dream deeply rooted in the American dream.

I have a dream that one day this nation will rise up and live out the true meaning of its creed: "We hold these truths to be self-evident; that all men are created equal."

I have a dream that one day on the red hills of Georgia the sons of former slaves and the sons of former slaveowners will be able to sit down together at the table of brotherhood....

I have a dream that my four little children will one day live in a nation where they will not be judged by the color of their skin but by the content of their character....

When we let freedom ring, when we let it ring from every village and every hamlet, from every state and every city, we will be able to speed up that day when all of God's children, black people and white people, Jews, Protestants, and Catholics, will be able to join hands and sing in the words of the old Negro spiritual, "Free at last! free at last, thank God almighty, we are free at last!"

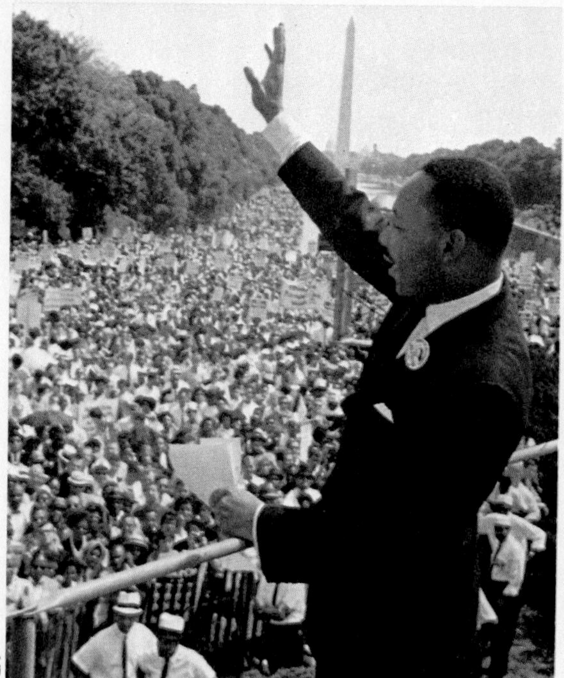

UPI

Thinking Critically

What do you think King is referring to when he says, "the table of brotherhood"?

Do you think the time has come when "all God's children" are able to join hands and sing in the words of the old Negro spiritual, "Free at last, free at last, thank God almighty, we are free at last"?

a march in Washington, D.C. The marchers wanted to show their support for the goals of the peaceful equal rights movement.

What was the major social issue during the early 1960's?

Economic Growth. President Kennedy faced many challenges upon becoming President. The economy of the country was particularly troublesome. The nation's economy was slowing down when President Kennedy took office in January 1961. By February, Kennedy's Secretary of Labor, Arthur Goldberg, stated that the country was in the middle of a "full-fledged recession." Also, the rate of unemployment climbed to its highest level since 1941. More than one million American workers did not have jobs.

In May 1961 Congress approved President Kennedy's plan to increase the minimum hourly wage from $1.00 to $1.25. This helped many Americans to buy more products. In turn, businesses began to make more goods. This created a need for more workers. Thus, the increase in the minimum hourly wage helped to lower unemployment among adult workers. Therefore, some economic problems were eased. At the same time, however, *inflation*—rapidly rising prices—became a greater problem.

President Kennedy worked hard to fight inflation. In early 1962 the President personally praised the country's major steel companies and their workers. The steelworkers had agreed to their industry's offer of greater benefits—such as better insurance and more vacation time—instead of an increase in pay. The President felt that this would hold down inflation. One month later, however, the United States Steel Corporation—the industry leader—increased the price of steel by six dollars a ton. The President publicly criticized this action as inflationary.

Soon after the President made this statement, prices on the New York Stock Exchange dropped to their lowest level since the stock-market crash of 1929. Many business leaders blamed the drop in trading on President Kennedy. They felt that the President did not strongly support American business. The President answered this criticism by taking actions to boost the economy. In January 1963 he sent a 13.6-billion-dollar tax-reduction plan to Congress. Such a plan was to give tax relief to American businesses and to American workers. Later in the year, the President approved the sale of extra American wheat to the Soviet Union. This increased the earnings of American wheat farmers. It also promoted foreign trade and stimulated the American economy.

What effect did the increase in the minimum hourly wage have on American buyers?

SECTION 1 REVIEW

1. *Why did Kennedy set up the Equal Opportunity Commission?*
2. *How did the enrollment of James Meredith at the University of Mississippi help the civil rights movement?*
3. *How did Kennedy promote foreign trade and stimulate the American economy?*

2 Cold-War Politics

Overview Shortly after 12:30 P.M. on Friday, November 22, 1963, it was reported that President Kennedy had been shot in Dallas, Texas. Minutes later a shocked world was told of his death. Kennedy's presidency had lasted 1,000 days. In that time the cold war had continued between the Soviet Union and the United States. And several crises between the world's two most powerful countries had taken place. A "Space Race" developed that led to many scientific discoveries and, eventually, to the landing of an American astronaut on the moon.

Objectives After reading this section, you should be able to:

- discuss the foreign policy of the United States in the early 1960's;
- explain the involvement of the United States in Cuban affairs;
- compare and contrast the space programs of the United States and the Soviet Union.

Continuation of the Cold War. United States foreign policy in the early 1960's was based on the belief that no more nations should fall under Communist control. It was feared that if one country fell under Communist control, other countries in the same area would become Communist as well. This belief was called the *domino theory.* This theory led to confrontations and competition between the United States and the Soviet Union—the world's most powerful Communist country.

Both the United States and the Soviet Union wanted to control important military locations in Europe and in the Middle East. These two countries also competed for the resources of developing countries in Africa, in Southeast Asia, in Central and South America, and in the Caribbean area. Both of these world powers wanted to guard their interests throughout the world. Growing tensions between the United States and the Soviet Union could be seen when problems developed in Berlin, Germany, and in Cuba.

What belief formed the basis of American foreign policy in the early 1960's?

The Berlin Crisis. Germany had been a trouble spot between the United States and the Soviet Union since the end of World War II. After the war Germany was divided into two countries. East Germany took on a Communist form of government. It became an ally of the Soviet Union. West Germany became an ally of the United States, Great Britain, and France. Berlin, the capital of Germany before the war, was located in East Germany. Because of postwar agreements, Berlin was divided into four sectors. These sectors were controlled by France, Great Britain, the United States, and the Soviet Union.

In June 1948 the Soviet Union set up a blockade of Berlin. In this way the Soviets blocked all land traffic from traveling between West Germany and Berlin. This was done to force the withdrawal of the United States, Great Britain, and France from the divided city. The United States responded to this crisis by airlifting enough supplies every day to help the 2 million people stranded in Berlin's American sector. The Soviet blockade ended in mid-1949. Nevertheless, Berlin remained a divided city.

In 1961, Berlin, Germany, was divided from one end to the other by a wall built along the border of the Soviet-controlled sector of the city. Guards were stationed along the wall to help prevent people from crossing into West Berlin from East Berlin. What kind of material was used to make the wall?

Photo Trends

Berlin was still a trouble spot when President Kennedy took office in 1961. The President met with Soviet Premier Nikita Khrushchev in Vienna, Austria, in June 1961. During this meeting Khrushchev demanded the American withdrawal from Berlin. President Kennedy refused. Communist East Germany then built a wall between the Soviet sector and the other parts of the city. This was done to stop East Germans from freely moving into the American, British, and French sectors. Armed guards were stationed along the length of the wall. The divided city has remained a world trouble spot to this day.

■ *What did Soviet Premier Khrushchev demand of President Kennedy during their meeting in Vienna, Austria, in 1961?*

The Cold War and Cuba. Military and political changes on the Caribbean island of Cuba were of great interest to the United States. This was mainly because the island was only 90 miles from the United States. A revolution had taken place in Cuba in the late 1950's. As a result of the revolution, Fidel Castro, a popular young leader, came to power.

At first, the United States hoped to support the new Cuban government under Fidel Castro. But in 1960 Castro stated that he had become a Communist. In response, the United States broke off diplomatic relations with the Castro government in January 1961. At the same time, the United States took in thousands of Cubans who left their homeland because of the changes Castro was making.

Some of these people planned to return to Cuba to overthrow the Castro government. The United States Central Intelligence Agency secretly trained a group of these Cubans to take part in an attack on Castro's army. On April 17, 1961, an invasion force of American-trained Cubans invaded their homeland at the Bay of Pigs. The invasion was quickly beaten back. The invaders suffered

Andrew St. George/Magnum

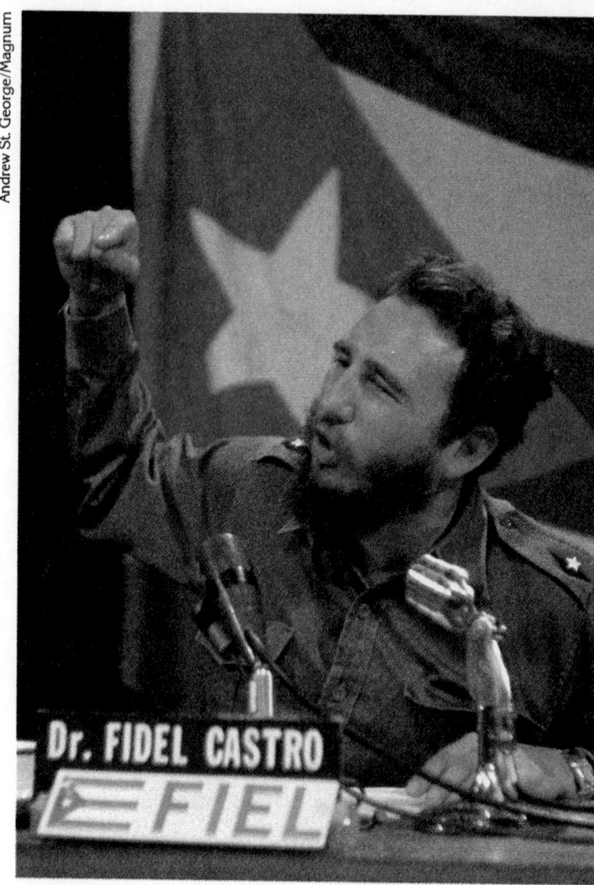

Fidel Castro became the leader of Cuba in 1959 after he led a successful revolt against the military dictatorship that ruled the island.

heavy losses. And the United States—as well as President Kennedy, who had approved the attack—lost the world's respect. This was because many countries felt that the United States had no right to interfere in Cuban affairs. Later developments in Cuba brought the United States and the Soviet Union to the brink of nuclear war.

The Soviet Union had been supplying Cuba with defensive weapons for several months. In the early fall of 1962, however, the United States noticed that missile sites were being built on the island. These particular missiles, President Kennedy knew, were capable of attacking the United States. The President immediately ordered a naval blockade of Cuba. This action cut off all shipments to Cuba except shipments of food and medicine. At the same time, the President demanded that Soviet Premier Nikita Khrushchev have the missiles removed from Cuba. The world waited to see what would happen in this confrontation between the United States and the Soviet Union. After several tense days, the Soviet leader agreed to President Kennedy's demand. Premier Khrushchev ordered the Soviet missiles out of Cuba. He also said that the United Nations could oversee the operation. President Kennedy ended the naval blockade of Cuba. The crisis ended without war.

■ *Why did the United States end diplomatic relations with the Cuban government in 1961?*

The Space Race. The cold war between the United States and the Soviet Union was carried beyond the earth into outer space during the Kennedy years. The Soviet Union had been the first country to put unmanned space satellites into space. These were scientific instruments made to orbit the earth. The Space Age had begun, in fact, with the launching of the Soviet Union's first satellite, *Sputnik I,* in October 1957. This caused many Americans to ask that a greater effort be made to develop America's space technology. It also led other Americans to say that American schools should spend more time teaching science. The first American satellite, *Explorer I*, was rocketed into space in January 1958.

The Soviet Union took the early lead in manned spaceflight. Soviet cosmonaut Yuri

Gagarin became the first person to orbit the earth in April 1961. However, less than one month later American astronaut Alan B. Shepard, Jr., rocketed into space. Commander Shepard did not orbit the earth, however. But within a year, the United States was able to put astronaut John Glenn, Jr., into three orbits around the earth. This was a spaceflight of nearly five hours. Nevertheless, this achievement was still well behind Soviet records for manned spaceflight.

The space race between the Soviet Union and the United States was not limited to manned spaceflights. Both countries sent rockets to explore the moon and nearby planets. Both countries also launched navigational, communications, and weather satellites. The United States sent almost 20 satellites into space between 1958 and the end of 1963. Some of these were used to send television broadcasts between Europe and North America. These satellites also gathered weather information and made important scientific discoveries. Later American advances in space technology led to the American lead in the space race by the mid-1960's.

■ *What country took the early lead in the space race?*

Death of a President. President Kennedy traveled to Texas in November 1963 to lay the groundwork for his upcoming reelection campaign. Texas was an important state because of its large voting population. It was also the home state of Vice-President Lyndon Johnson.

The President visited three Texas cities before flying on to Dallas on November 22, 1963. The President was joined on this trip by Vice-President Johnson and by Texas Governor John Connally. President Kennedy and First Lady Jacqueline Kennedy were met by large, friendly crowds in each city. In Dallas, the President rode in a motorcade through the city to the place where he was to speak in the early afternoon.

At 12:30 P.M. the President's open-topped car passed a schoolbook warehouse. Suddenly, several shots rang out. The President was fatally wounded. Governor Connally was seriously wounded. The Vice-President, riding in a car behind the President's, was not hurt. Both the President and the governor were rushed to a nearby hospital. The President was pronounced dead at Dallas's Parkland Hospital at 1:00 P.M. The governor later recovered. Secret Service agents rushed the Vice-President to the Dallas airport. There, at 2:39 P.M., Lyndon B. Johnson became the nation's new President.

■ *Why was President Kennedy visiting Texas in November 1963?*

SECTION 2 REVIEW

1. *Why did the domino theory lead to confrontations and competition between the United States and the Soviet Union?*
2. *Why did the United States and President Kennedy lose the world's respect because of the Bay of Pigs invasion of Cuba?*
3. *What effect did the launching of the Soviet satellite,* Sputnik 1, *have upon many Americans?*

3 Beginnings of the Great Society

Overview The nation's new President, Lyndon B. Johnson of Texas, promised to carry out many of the programs planned by President Kennedy. These programs were planned to improve education and to end poverty in the United States. In addition, President Lyndon Johnson worked actively to bring full civil rights to all Americans.

Objectives After reading this section, you should be able to:

- give examples of President Johnson's support for the civil rights movement;
- describe the state of the economy of the United States in 1964;
- discuss the issues in the 1964 election for President of the United States.

The Torch Is Passed. Vice-President Lyndon B. Johnson became the nation's thirty-sixth President shortly after President Kennedy's death. The oath of office was given by Sarah T. Hughes, a judge of the United States district court in Texas. The power of the presidency was given over to the Vice-President because of Article II of the United States Constitution [*59]. This article states that if the office of President becomes open for any reason, the Vice-President will become the President. This article was later added to by the Twenty-fifth Amendment [*130–134].

The smooth changeover in presidential power was important to the country. President Johnson eased the worries of many Americans when he became President. He did this by promising to keep the goals set by President Kennedy. President Johnson also planned to carry out President Kennedy's plans for social change.

Why did Lyndon B. Johnson become President upon the death of President Kennedy?

President Johnson and Civil Rights. President Johnson was a firm believer in equal rights for all Americans. He actively worked for the advancement of civil rights. He did this by supporting many of President Kennedy's plans. He also developed his own legislation—bills—to send to Congress.

President Kennedy had sent 25 major bills to Congress during his first year in office. Congress, however, did not pass all of these bills at that time. This was partially because Kennedy was not effective in dealing with members of Congress. President Johnson, on the other hand, was able to have these same bills passed in the Congress. This was largely because he had spent many years in Congress himself and had a great deal of personal influence among the legislators.

Early in 1964 the Twenty-fourth Amendment to the United States Constitution was signed into law by President Johnson [*128–129]. This amendment had been favored by President Kennedy. The poll-tax amendment, as it was called, made it illegal for states to place a tax on voting in federal elections. As a result, many more people—especially in the rural South—were given their civil right to vote. These people no longer had to pay to take part in the election of their country's leaders.

In July 1964 President Johnson signed into

law the greatest civil rights law written to that time. The Civil Rights Act of 1964 stated that equal service must be given to all people in any business that served the public. This included hotels, restaurants, buses, movies, and so on. This law also said that a person's race could have no bearing on job hiring.

How did President Johnson show his support for the civil rights movement?

Meeting Human Needs. President Johnson knew that millions of Americans were trapped in poverty and ignorance. These people lacked schooling. They therefore had little chance to better their lives or their children's futures. In response, President Johnson started a large-scale effort to end poverty and to promote education in the country. On January 8, 1964, the President delivered his State of the Union message to Congress and the country. In it, President Johnson declared a "War on Poverty." He asked Congress to pass laws that would make certain that every American had enough to eat, a place to live, and a job to do.

President Johnson's War on Poverty program was sent to Congress in mid-March 1964. By the end of the year two bills had passed that took care of many human needs. The Food Stamp Bill became law on August 31, 1964. This bill allowed poor people to obtain government coupons to pay part of their food costs. Two days later, the President signed a bill into law that provided more than 1 billion dollars for the building of housing for the nation's poor people. It also helped to pay for *urban renewal.* This was the large-scale repair and upkeep of the country's large cities.

What name was given to President Johnson's effort to end poverty?

The Nation's Economy. The economy throughout 1964 was strong. The country was prosperous and at peace. Most Americans were earning and saving more money than ever before. They were also spending more money. This led many businesses to increase output and to hire more workers. Unemployment dropped for most groups of workers. But unemployment was still high for people with little education and for minority groups.

Elliot Erwitt/Magnum

Partly because of his long experience in the legislative branch, Johnson was more successful in pushing his programs through Congress than Kennedy had been.

DO YOU KNOW?

What American civil rights leader won the Nobel peace prize in 1964?

Martin Luther King, Jr., a Baptist minister, won the Nobel peace prize in 1964 for his work in furthering the civil rights of black Americans through peaceful means. Dr. King's belief in nonviolence stemmed, in part, from his religious views. His thinking was also influenced by the writings of Mahatma Gandhi and of Henry David Thoreau. Dr. King founded the Southern Christian Leadership Conference (SCLC). This group believed in using peaceful protest to bring about changes in American society.

The cost of living rose by less than 1 percent during the year. And the buying power of money fell only slightly. There were several reasons for this prosperity.

Both President Kennedy and President Johnson had urged American businesses to operate at full strength. In addition, federal tax cuts in early 1963 and in early 1964 put more money into circulation. By March 1964 more than 800 million dollars a month was added to the take-home pay of American workers. President Johnson took a chance by lowering government spending while making a tax cut. Most of the time, such action would bring on a downturn in the economy. In 1964, however, the high rate of consumer spending kept the economy strong.

■ *What was the state of the nation's economy in 1964?*

The Election of 1964. President Johnson was elected to a full, four-year term as President in the 1964 presidential election. His running mate, Senator Hubert H. Humphrey of Minnesota, became the Vice-President. Voters chose President Johnson over the Republican candidate, Senator Barry Goldwater of Arizona, by a large margin (see map on this page). There were several reasons for this great victory.

A large number of voters admired the way President Johnson took control of the government immediately after President Kennedy's death. Many voters also wanted to give President Johnson the chance to put his own plans into effect. In addition, the economy was strong, and the country was not involved in large-scale fighting, although American troops were carrying on limited fighting in Southeast Asia. During his campaign the President pointed out that he had taken steps to lessen the threat of nuclear war. He also noted that he had lowered taxes and had signed into law the Civil Rights Act of 1964.

How would you describe Democrat Lyndon Johnson's victory in the 1964 election?

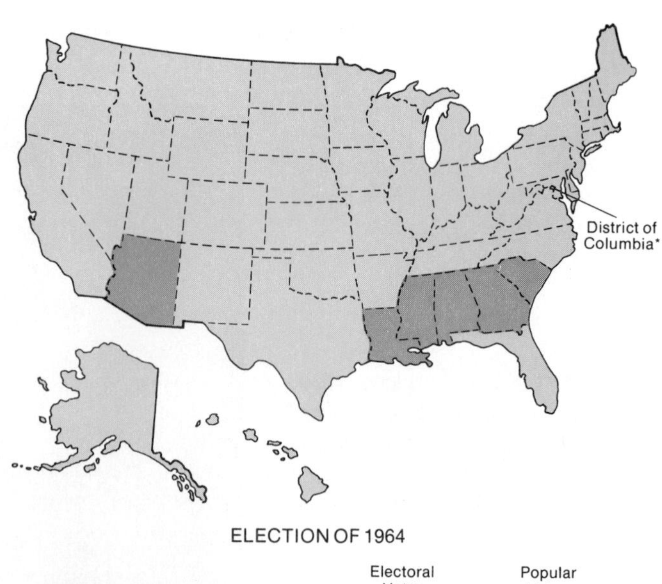

ELECTION OF 1964

	Electoral Votes	Popular Votes
Democratic Lyndon B. Johnson	486	46,676,220
Republican Barry Goldwater	52	26,860,314

*Washington, D.C. voters took part in presidential election for first time.

The beliefs of the two major candidates presented clear choices to the voters in the 1964 election. Senator Goldwater was a conservative Republican. He believed that the federal government was becoming too involved in the everyday life of the American people. He felt that state governments or people themselves should take care of most problems. For example, Senator Goldwater believed that the goals of the civil rights movement could best be reached by community action and through state governments. He felt that federal laws would not bring about better opportunities for black Americans.

President Johnson, on the other hand, was a liberal Democrat. He believed that the federal government should take even further actions to better American society. In May 1964, during the campaign, the President first spoke of the "Great Society." This was the name he gave to his plans for a better life for all Americans. These plans included federal civil rights laws and bills to boost the country's economy. With his election in 1964, President Johnson's Great Society was begun.

In what ways did Senator Goldwater's views on civil rights differ from President Johnson?

SECTION 3 REVIEW

1. *How did Johnson actively work for the development of civil rights?*
2. *Why did the federal government increase the amount of money in circulation in 1964?*
3. *Why did President Johnson win the election of 1964 by such a large margin?*

CHAPTER 35 SUMMARY

President Kennedy's New Frontier brought a sense of excitement to American life in the early 1960's. Great strides were made by the civil rights movement as new organizations and leaders broke through old social barriers. At the same time, many Americans began to take an interest in recreation and in good health practices.

President Kennedy could not end the cold war between the Soviet Union and the United States. Confrontations arose over several issues. The space race was another aspect of the competition between these countries. President Kennedy did not live to see America pull ahead in the space race. He was killed in Dallas, Texas, on November 22, 1963.

Vice-President Lyndon Johnson became President shortly after President Kennedy's death. President Johnson then carried out many of President Kennedy's planned programs, as well as his own. These programs set out to better the lives of all Americans. President Johnson was elected for a full, four-year term in the election of 1964.

CHAPTER 35 REVIEW

USING YOUR SKILLS

Interpreting a Flow Chart

A number of volunteer groups were established in the early 1960's. These groups included the Peace Corps, Volunteers in Service to America (VISTA), and the Foster Grandparent Program (FGP). In 1971 these groups and others, such as the Retired Senior Volunteer Program (RSVP), The Senior Companion Program (SCP), and the National Student Volunteer Program (NSVP), were combined in an independent federal agency named ACTION. The organizational chart below shows the structure and the relationships among the offices that make up ACTION. Study the chart carefully and then answer the questions below.

1. How many offices report directly to the Office of the Director?
2. Which of the offices in ACTION controls the operations of VISTA?
3. Which of the offices in ACTION controls the operations of the Peace Corps?
4. Which of the offices in ACTION enables private citizens to advise the director?
5. How can you tell that ACTION has offices in foreign countries?
6. What on the chart indicates that some programs exist in various states?

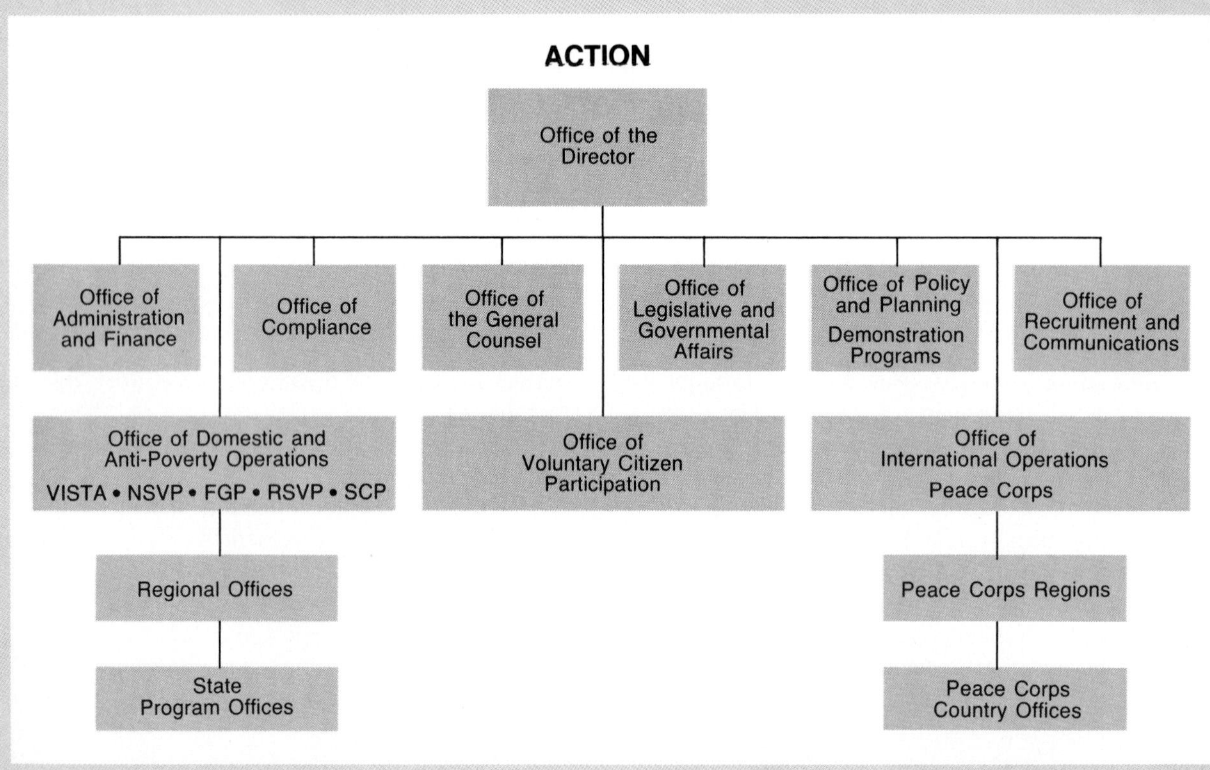

CHAPTER 35 REVIEW

YOU SHOULD KNOW

Identify, define, or explain each of the following:

Peace Corps
domino theory
Explorer I
War on Poverty
urban renewal
Great Society

CHECKING FACTS

1. Who was the Republican candidate for President in 1960?
2. What did President Kennedy mean when he spoke of a New Frontier?
3. What was the Alliance for Progress?
4. What civil rights organization was established by Martin Luther King, Jr.?
5. How did the United States respond to the Soviet blockade of Berlin?
6. How far is Cuba from the United States?
7. Who was the first American astronaut in space?
8. What did the Twenty-fourth Amendment make illegal?
9. How did the Food Stamp Bill help poor people?
10. Who was Johnson's running mate in 1964?

UNDERSTANDING CONCEPTS

1. How did the increase in the minimum hourly wage in 1961 affect the American economy?
2. Why were military and political changes in Cuba of great interest to the United States?
3. How did Americans react to the launching of *Sputnik I*?
4. What was one result of the passage of the Twenty-fourth Amendment?
5. How did Senator Goldwater and President Johnson's views on civil rights differ?

LEARNING FROM ILLUSTRATIONS

1. Study the election map on page 609. What areas of the country gave the most support to John F. Kennedy?
2. Look at the picture on page 615. What does the picture show that indicates that the Berlin wall would be difficult to cross?

CRITICAL THINKING

1. President Kennedy set up the Peace Corps in 1961 to help people in other countries. If you were to join the Peace Corps, what country would you hope to go to and what would you like to teach the people?
2. What does the Berlin wall tell you about communism?
3. From what you know of society today, do you think President Johnson won the War on Poverty? Give reasons for your answer.

ENRICHMENT ACTIVITIES

1. Illustrate the space race by making picture collages, by drawing posters, or by making plastic or wooden models of early American and Soviet spacecraft. Display your work in your classroom.
2. During the early 1960's, many Americans feared the outbreak of nuclear war and took steps to protect themselves. To better understand this period, interview your parents and others who remember the national interest in civil defense. Discuss your findings with the class.

CHAPTER 36

CLOSE-UP: Space— The Last Frontier

INTRODUCTION

On the morning of October 5, 1957, America awoke to newscasts of a satellite circling the earth. The Soviet Union had beaten the United States into space with the launch of Sputnik I. *It was only twenty-three inches around and weighed 184 pounds.* Sputnik I *was man's first successful attempt to place an object in space. Governments and amateur radio operators everywhere tracked its distinctive "beep-beep" signal. Newspapers carried front page stories describing the object and its launch. Radio talk shows and television news devoted extra time to the event.*

To America in 1957 the Soviet challenge was clear. Space, "The Last Frontier," awaited the nation with the greatest talents and commitment to succeed. Americans wanted, and expected, the United States to win the space race.

1 America's Quest for Space

Although caught off guard by the success of *Sputnik*, America was not totally unprepared. For decades, American scientists had been working on rockets, with the dream of using them to launch objects into space. The next decade saw those dreams come true. The United States space program began with the successful launch of *Explorer I* in 1958.

United States Rocketry Before *Sputnik*. During World War I, a physicist from Clark College, Robert H. Goddard, began experimenting with rocket propellants. In 1926, he launched the world's first liquid propellant rocket near Auburn, Massachusetts. By 1929, he had moved to New Mexico to establish an experimental station to build rockets. At the New Mexico site, Goddard developed many of the basic ideas of modern rocketry. Among his over 200 patents was one for a multistage rocket, the basic idea behind modern launch rockets.

NASA

At a very young age, Robert H. Goddard became fascinated by rockets and their potential for flight into space. In a report published in 1919, Goddard predicted the development of rockets capable of traveling to the moon and beyond.

While Goddard worked alone in the desert, a small group of graduate students at the California Institute of Technology (CalTech) began experimenting with rockets. Unlike today, when researchers receive millions of dollars in government funds, these pioneers often spent weekends searching junkyards for equipment. Experiments were sometimes funded with money from second jobs. Paperwork was even done in the back seat of automobiles because office space cost too much. Early failures and lack of funds were discouraging. The handful of students and enthusiastic amateurs persisted, hoping for better days.

The increasing threat of world war put new importance on the development of rockets. When the military decided to provide money for rocket research, testing equipment improved, results got more predictable, and rocketry became respectable. On July 1, 1944, the CalTech scientists began operating under a new name, Jet Propulsion Laboratory. American rocketry was beginning to move forward and hope for the conquest of space was heightened.

■ *What did Robert H. Goddard do?*

Formation of NASA. When the Soviet Union stunned the world with the launch of *Sputnik*, American confidence in its technical superiority was temporarily shattered. In one editorial the Russian newspaper *Pravda* wrote, "The so-called system of free enterprise is turning out to be powerless in competition with socialism." For a time, with one failure after another, some Americans wondered if the Soviets might be right.

American political leaders did not miss the importance of the Soviet accomplishment and reaction of the world. The Soviet feat detracted from the American image as a technological leader. It also gave substance to the Soviet claim that they could build intercontinental ballistic missiles (ICBMs). The threat to the security of the United States was obvious. Additional pressure developed when the Soviets launched *Sputnik II* on November 3, 1957, carrying a live dog named Laika.

Finally, United States scientists, led by Wernher Von Braun, managed to launch a satellite into orbit on February 7, 1958. It was clear, however, that the American space effort needed guidance. On July 29, 1958, President Eisenhower signed the law that created the National Aeronautics and Space Administration (NASA). NASA's purpose was simple—coordinate America's space program and regain the technological lead from the Soviet Union.

■ *Why was the successful launch of* Sputnik *seen as a threat to the United States?*

Unmanned Space Flights Lead to Americans in Space. In the fall of 1958, NASA began the Mercury program to develop a spacecraft that would take an American *astronaut*—a person who travels in space—beyond the earth's atmosphere. The first seven astronauts—Gordon Cooper, Scott Carpenter, John Glenn, Alan Shepard, Gus Grissom, Walter Schirra, and Deke Slayton—were introduced to the public in 1959. By 1961, the United States was closing the gap on the Soviet Union even more. On January 31, 1961, a chimpanzee named Ham went into Earth orbit for a week. The Soviets responded by launching a man, Yuri Gagarin, into a one-orbit pass around the Earth on April 12, 1961.

NASA

These men composed the first group of astronauts announced by the National Aeronautics and Space Administration. The men are, front row, left to right, Walter M. Schirra, Jr., Donald K. Slayton, John H. Glenn, Jr., and M. Scott Carpenter. Back row, left to right, are Alan B. Shepard, Jr., Virgil I. Grissom, and L. Gordon Cooper, Jr.

The race tightened on May 5, 1961, when Alan B. Shepard, Jr., took his Mercury capsule *Freedom 7* higher than any other American. The flight, which lasted some fifteen minutes, rose to 117 miles above the Atlantic Ocean. In July 1961, the second successful suborbital flight by an American took Virgil Grissom sixteen minutes into space.

By early 1962, the United States was ready to go into orbit. On February 20, 1962, John H. Glenn, Jr., circled the Earth three times in the *Friendship 7* capsule. The space race was dead even, but clearly the United States was on the verge of pulling ahead.

Who was Alan B. Shepard?

SECTION 1 REVIEW

1. *How did the scientists at CalTech support their experiments?*
2. *What was the purpose of NASA?*
3. *When did the first American circle the Earth, and who was he?*

2 An American Man-in-the-Moon

By spring 1961, it was clear that the quest for space had reached a crossroad. American astronauts were flying in the near heavens, but a long-range goal for future missions was missing. Directions and priorities for the remainder of the century and beyond needed defining. Space exploration, while in its infancy, was maturing rapidly.

President Kennedy Points the United States at the Moon. When Alan Shepard splashed down, few Americans realized the long-range importance of the event. Certainly, the United States was back on the space track with the Soviets. In what direction that track led was not clear.

President John Kennedy set the national priority in a speech on May 25, 1961. He declared that an American should land on the moon by the end of the decade. For a nation that had only just launched a man into suborbital flight, this was a nearly inconceivable idea. With the nation and aerospace industry thus committed, NASA set out on the most difficult venture yet attempted.

NASA originally announced the Apollo program in 1960, intending it to take America into sub-orbital and then orbital flight. With the nation's new quest for the moon, the program was expanded. To be sure the mission would succeed, three new spacecraft were needed. A *command module* to carry three astronauts to and from the moon was the first developed. The *service module*, a flying warehouse used to contain various propulsion, power, and environmental systems, was the second priority. The final stage was a *lunar module* to take two astronauts to and from the moon's surface.

A further complication was the need for a rocket that could deliver astronauts, modules, and equipment into and back from lunar orbit. The Atlas rockets used to launch the Mercury capsules were only able to lift about 2,000 pounds into low orbit. The lunar mission required an explosive charge of nearly 100,000 pounds. The Saturn rocket, was built to propel the lunar craft.

NASA, the President, and the American people were confident that the moon was attainable. But more development and a great deal of luck were still needed.

What new spacecrafts were needed for the lunar missions?

The "Step" Between. As development of the lunar modules went forward, three more Mercury flights were launched. Between May 1962, and May 1963, Scott Carpenter, Walter

NASA

Gemini 7 had a successful liftoff.

Schirra, and Gordon Cooper completed the single astronaut phase of the Apollo program.

The second phase of the Apollo program began with the successful launch of two astronauts in *Gemini 3* during March 1965. NASA saw the Gemini program as a step between the Mercury flights and the lunar mission. The basic purpose was to gain experience in the operations necessary to land on the moon. Gemini astronauts were to "walk in space," practice maneuvering spacecraft, rendezvous with other spacecraft, and control reentry.

Of the ten Gemini missions, the second provided the most excitement. On June 3,

1965, Edward H. White, II, became the first American to walk in space. He maneuvered outside the orbiting Gemini 4 capsule for twenty minutes. During Gemini 8, a docking was accomplished with an unmanned target capsule, *Agena*. By November 1966, the Gemini program concluded. Confidence and success was running high at NASA. The next stage, Apollo/Lunar, was ready. America was poised for the final step.

■ *What were the major purposes of the Gemini missions?*

"All Is Not Lost." The beginning of the new year 1967 saw the United States holding a slight lead in the space race. The first two phases of the Apollo program were complete, and the few minor technical problems were solved. Then disaster struck.

On January 27, 1967, NASA conducted a routine test of the three-man Apollo capsule. Roger B. Chaffee, Virgil "Gus" Grissom, and Edward H. White, II were the first astronauts scheduled to fly in this final stage of the Apollo program. Several minutes after testing began, a flash fire, probably caused by an electrical malfunction, engulfed the cabin in flames. The nation received the news with shocked disbelief. For the first time Americans had died in the pursuit of space travel.

Many called for a halt of the lunar mission. NASA delayed the program while it investigated the cause of the fire and carried out several new safety measures. Criticism grew, but there were far more supporters than detractors. Supporters argued that sacrifices in talent and life went with all great human achievements. America's quest for the moon was no different. The program continued with a renewed commitment to succeed.

■ *What did NASA do following the Apollo fire?*

America Closes in on the Moon. Several unmanned Apollo flights followed the disastrous fire of January 27. By October 1967, NASA was ready to launch *Apollo 7* with a crew of three. In addition to accomplishing a variety of technical maneuvers, the flight was the longest of any American flight to date—eleven days.

With the success of *Apollo 7*, a series of preliminary flights to circle the moon began. *Apollo 8* lifted off from Cape Kennedy in December 1968. When Frank Borman, James Lovell, Jr., and William Anders reached lunar orbit on December 24, they became the first Americans to circle the moon. From an altitude of seventy miles they described and photographed the details of the moon's surface.

Apollo 9 and *Apollo 10* continued the circumlunar exploration of the moon. During both flights American astronauts practiced docking, guidance, and observation techniques. During *Apollo 10*, the lunar module, nicknamed *Snoopy*, flew within 50,000 feet of the moon's surface. The mission photographed the planned landing site for the lunar landing and returned to the command module, nicknamed *Charlie Brown*, successfully. All was ready for the flight of *Apollo 11*.

■ *What happened during the flight of Apollo 10?*

NASA

Edwin E. Aldrin, Jr., took the lunar lander, *Eagle*, to the surface of the moon.

"The *Eagle* Has Landed." As over one million spectators waited in the morning sun and millions more sat by televisions, *Apollo 11* prepared for launch. America was ready to fulfill the dream of mankind throughout history—to travel to the moon.

Apollo 11, with its capsule *Columbia*, lifted off from launch complex 39 at Cape Kennedy on July 16, 1969. The mission proceeded perfectly, with the astronauts relaying regularly scheduled television broadcasts back to Earth. By July 20, all systems were tested, and the landing module prepared. Mission Control granted permission to begin the lunar descent.

While Michael Collins remained in the command module, Neil Armstrong and Edwin Aldrin took the lunar lander, *Eagle*, to the surface of the moon. As untold millions listened, Neil Armstrong reported, "Tranquility Base here. The *Eagle* has landed."

The plan was to check all systems on *Eagle*, eat, rest, and then move out of the lander. With mounting excitement, the two *Eagle* crewmen asked to skip the rest time and go onto the lunar surface. As Neil Armstrong reached the second rung of the descent ladder, he paused to release a remote television camera. At 10:56:20 Eastern Standard Time, July 20, 1969, the words "That's one small step for a man, one giant leap for mankind" echoed around the world.

When Edwin Aldrin joined Armstrong, they took photos and explored the area with childlike fascination. Soon after stepping out, they erected a metallic United States flag near the landing craft. Using the television camera to show the area to viewers back on Earth, the astronauts focused on the flag and then a plaque. The plaque read:

HERE MEN FROM THE PLANET EARTH
FIRST SET FOOT UPON THE MOON
JULY 1969, A.D.
WE CAME IN PEACE FOR ALL MANKIND

The plaque, signed by the astronauts and President Richard M. Nixon, was left behind for future explorers to read.

Five more Apollo flights, and twelve Americans finally walked on the moon. But *Apollo 11* was the turning point in our country's quest for space travel. The American space program now turned to the development of a reusable space shuttle.

■ *What was the purpose of Apollo 11?*

NASA

In 1975, crews from the United States and from the Soviet Union linked up in space, conducted experiments, and held a joint news conference.

America's Future in Space. In 1971 the United States sent a space probe to Mars. This probe carried instruments and cameras to gather information about Mars. This information was sent back to the earth. And in 1972 a space vehicle was sent toward Jupiter to gather information.

In 1973 a space station, called *Skylab*, was placed in orbit around the earth. Astronauts lived and worked in this station for several months. They carried out experiments to help scientists learn more about exploring space.

A new era in America's space program began with the plans for a space shuttle. It could carry cargo and passengers into and back from space. Unlike rockets and capsules in use up to that time, the shuttles were to be reusable. The first successful space shuttle flight occurred on April 12, 1981, when *Columbia* completed a two-day mission.

During the next five years Americans became accustomed to the launch and return of a growing shuttle fleet. The shuttle *Challenger* began flights in early 1984, *Discovery*

NASA

In 1983, Sally K. Ride became the first American woman astronaut, when she flew on *Challenger*, the second space shuttle.

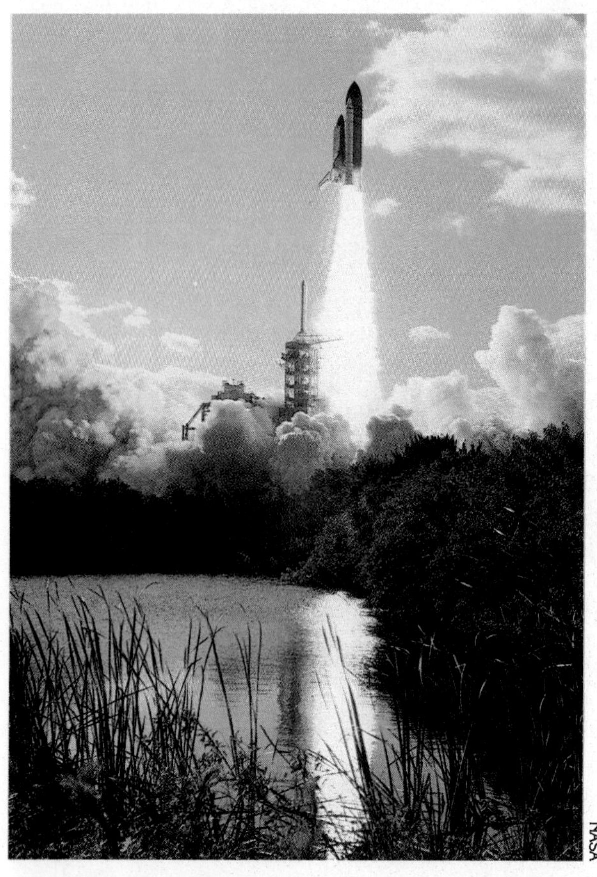
NASA

The space shuttle *Challenger* exploded after takeoff on January 28, 1986. The crew members were Francis R. Scobee, Michael J. Smith, Ronald E. McNair, Ellison S. Onizuka, Judith A. Resnik, Gregory B. Jarvis, and Sharon Christa McAuliffe.

first flew in summer 1984, and *Atlantis* took off in October 1985. The promise of a safe, reliable shuttle program was a reality. Between 1981 and January 1986, twenty-four shuttles entered and returned from space.

The worst moment in the history of the U.S. space program was yet to come. At 11:39 A.M. on January 28, 1986, barely one minute into its flight, the shuttle *Challenger* exploded. The tragedy was especially shocking because of the routine success the shuttle program had come to expect. The disaster touched even more Americans since it was viewed by millions of school children because a teacher, Christa McAuliffe, was aboard.

As it had done before, NASA moved quickly to find the cause of the accident and correct the problem. In the fall of 1988, after a delay of over two years, the shuttle program resumed with the successful launch of *Discovery.*

With the launch of *Discovery* American confidence returned and the space program turned once more toward the future. For the 21st century NASA has plans for space stations and probes to the furthest extents of the universe. The space race will undoubtedly continue, and yet, the ultimate beneficiaries will be mankind.

What was the name of the first successful space shuttle?

SECTION 2 REVIEW

1. *What did President Kennedy announce in 1961?*
2. *Why were the Gemini missions so important?*
3. *Why was the space shuttle program considered a new era in America's space program?*

CHAPTER 36 REVIEW

SUMMARY

Americans were shocked when the Soviet Union successfully placed a satellite into orbit in 1957. The event sparked the imagination of the world and a space race began that continues today.

The United States worked on rocket development as early as the 1920's, but had little money to carry on serious research. The launch of *Sputnik* brought national attention and money to an American space program.

NASA was formed in 1958 to coordinate the American efforts in space. In that same year, the Mercury program introduced the nation to its first astronauts. John H. Glenn, Jr., became the first American to orbit the Earth in February 1962.

In 1961, President John Kennedy challenged the nation to land a man on the moon by the end of the decade. The Apollo program focused on the need for new machinery and techniques to reach the lunar surface.

The Gemini program was designed to provide a step between the low-orbit flights of the Mercury capsules and the lunar mission. In June 1965, Edward H. White, II became the first American to walk in space.

By 1967, Gemini was finished and the lunar series of Apollo flights began. As millions of people waited, *Apollo 11* landed on the moon in July 1969. Neil Armstrong stepped onto the moon several hours later saying, "That's one small step for a man, one giant leap for mankind."

In 1972, the space shuttle program began. The shuttles acted as reusable spacecrafts and flew twenty-four successful missions. In January 1986, a tragic explosion destroyed the shuttle *Challenger*, temporarily halting NASA's programs. Finally, in the fall of 1988, the shuttles began to fly once more and Americans were back in space.

UNDERSTANDING CONCEPTS

1. Why was the United States shocked at the success of the Soviet launch of *Sputnik*?
2. How was the United States' space program given a clear direction in the early 1960's?
3. What was the significance of the Apollo flight immediately before *Apollo 11*?
4. How did the United States react to the Apollo and *Challenger* disasters?

CRITICAL THINKING

1. In your opinion, why were the Soviets able to gain an early advantage in the space race?
2. What was the significance of the Soviet successes in space for the success of the American space program?
3. Why is a long-range plan for space exploration so important to the success of future missions?

PROJECTS AND ACTIVITIES

1. Use an encyclopedia or other books about space to write a brief biography of one of the astronauts mentioned in this chapter. Then share your biography with your classmates.
2. Use an encyclopedia to make a chart comparing the dates, number of astronauts, and time in flight for the Soviet and American space programs from 1957 to 1961. Share your chart with your classmates.
3. Use the school or public library to make a list of books dealing with space and space exploration. Then choose one of the books to read. Write a book report about the book. Share your report with your classmates.

UNIT NINE REVIEW

UNIT SUMMARY

The postwar years were times of major economic growth and change in America. War-weary Americans turned to the new task of building peacetime prosperity. By and large, the postwar years were times when many Americans could afford a better way of life. President Truman brought outspoken leadership to our country during the postwar years. Our country became the free world's leader during a time of growing east-west competitions.

The Eisenhower years marked a time of changing political goals in America. The President hoped to cut the size and the influence of our federal government. He also worked to build the economy by lowering taxes and government spending. Fear of communism at home and of growing Soviet power overseas shaped new attitudes toward our country's world role. The 1950's were years of growing material wealth in the United States. But not all Americans shared equally in the affluence.

President Kennedy's New Frontier brought a sense of excitement to American life in the early 1960's. Great strides were made by the civil rights movement as new organizations and leaders broke through old social barriers. President Kennedy could not end the cold war between the Soviet Union and the United States. Confrontations between these powerful countries arose over several issues. Vice-President Lyndon Johnson became President shortly after President Kennedy's death. President Johnson then carried out many of President Kennedy's planned programs as well as his own. These programs set out to better the lives of all Americans.

The space race between the United States and the Soviet Union began in 1957. It was in that year that the Soviets successfully placed a satellite in orbit. In 1958, NASA was formed to coordinate the American efforts in space. In 1969, the United States landed a man on the moon. Although the United States has had many successful space missions, there have been many challenging problems to solve. The space race continues between the United States and the Soviet Union.

YOU SHOULD KNOW

Identify, define, or explain each of the following:

social mobility
cold war
recessions
McCarthyism
segregate
Peace Corps
domino theory
urban renewal
Great Society

CHECKING FACTS

1. What is a planned economy?
2. What caused city growth in postwar America?
3. What was the aim of the Fair Deal?
4. What was a major goal of America during the cold war?
5. What was the Truman Doctrine?
6. What was the main challenge facing President Eisenhower after his election?
7. What was the Supreme Court ruling in *Brown v. Board of Education of Topeka*?
8. What is the NAACP?
9. What was the United States' response to the Soviet blockade of Berlin?
10. What was *Skylab*?

UNDERSTANDING CONCEPTS

1. How was the postwar economy influenced by the supply of consumer goods and consumer demand?
2. What were the major causes of the cold war after 1945?
3. How did the civil rights movement strengthen America's democracy?

4. How did the belief in the domino theory affect our foreign policies during the early 1960's?
5. Why was the 1964 election an overwhelming victory for President Johnson?

CRITICAL THINKING

1. Why was organized labor against the Taft-Hartley Act?
2. Compare and contrast World War I's postwar economy with World War II's postwar economy in the United States.
3. In your opinion, how was the Red Scare similar to McCarthyism? How was it different?
4. Why was President Johnson viewed as a reform President?

CHRONOLOGY

Arrange the following events in the order in which they happened.

a. Dwight Eisenhower elected President
b. "Great Society" programs begun
c. John Kennedy elected President
d. "Fair Deal" program begun
e. Montgomery bus boycott
f. Cuban Missile crisis
g. World War II ended
h. President Kennedy assassinated
i. Dr. Martin Luther King awarded Nobel Peace Prize

CITIZENSHIP IN ACTION

Many citizens in America work to bring about changes for the common good, that is, for the good of all Americans. During the last 30 years, how have Americans worked to improve life in the United States? What changes must they continue to work on in the future?

GEOGRAPHY

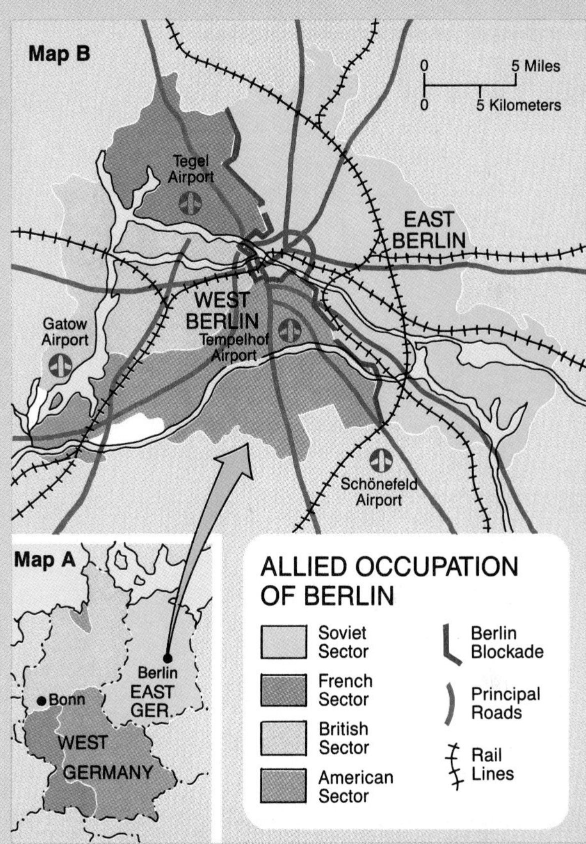

1. According to Map A, the smallest sector of occupation was held by what country?
2. Why were the Soviets able to halt the flow of supplies from Schönefeld airfield to West Berlin during the blockade of 1948–1949?
3. Why do you think the people attempting to flee from East Berlin to West Germany did not go around the Berlin Wall to reach West Germany?
4. In which sectors of Berlin were the following airports located: Tempelhof Airport, Gatow Airport, and Tegel Airport?
5. How many airports are in the Soviet sector?

1965 | 1970 | 1975

1965 Medicare bill signed by President Johnson

1966 First black cabinet member, Robert C. Weaver, appointed to head the Department of Housing and Urban Development

1968 President Johnson decided not to seek reelection
Richard Nixon elected President

1969 American astronauts landed on the moon

1972 Senate approved women's rights amendment
President Nixon reelected

1973 Vice-President Agnew resigned
Vietnam War ended for United States

1974 President Nixon resigned
Gerald R. Ford became President

UNIT TEN

America Faces New Challenges

1965 to the Present

American soldiers in South Vietnam had to adapt to the adverse conditions of jungle warfare.

President Nixon made a historic trip to the People's Republic of China in 1972. For the first time in more than 20 years, Chinese and American leaders met to discuss their differences.

1980 1985

1976 Jimmy Carter elected President

1977 Alaska pipeline opened
Energy Department added to the cabinet

1978 Senate ratified Panama Canal treaties

1979 Diplomatic relations established with People's Republic of China
Americans held as hostages in Iran

1980 Ronald Reagan elected President

1984 Congresswoman Geraldine Ferraro chosen as the first female vice-presidential candidate on a major party ticket
President Reagan reelected

1988 George Bush elected President

CHAPTERS

There have been many challenges for the people of the United States since 1965. Since 1965, our country has worked to improve its relations with other countries. The economy was affected by inflation, recession, and a growing deficit in the federal budget.

George Washington's America was an agricultural society. Two centuries after George Washington's presidency, George Bush became President of an information society. In the information society in which you will work, your job will be to gather, organize, and distribute information to other human beings. Reading, scanning, researching, and accurately gathering information are skills needed to get and hold a job in an information society. Writing, listening, speaking, and proofreading are basic skills needed in an information society.

In 1979 President Carter (center) brought together the Egyptian president Anwar el-Sadat (left) and the Israeli prime minister Menachem Begin (right) to Camp David to negotiate peace in the Middle East.

The United Nations Building is located in New York, New York. The flags of the member nations are displayed in front of the building.

1965 1970 1975

- 1965 Department of Housing and Urban Development added to the cabinet
- 1966 Department of Transportation added to the cabinet; American involvement in South Vietnam increased
- 1967 Twenty-fifth Amendment added to the Constitution
- 1968 Civil Rights Act of 1968 passed; President Johnson did not seek reelection; Richard Nixon elected President
- 1972 Senate approved women's rights amendment

CHAPTER 37

Years of Turmoil

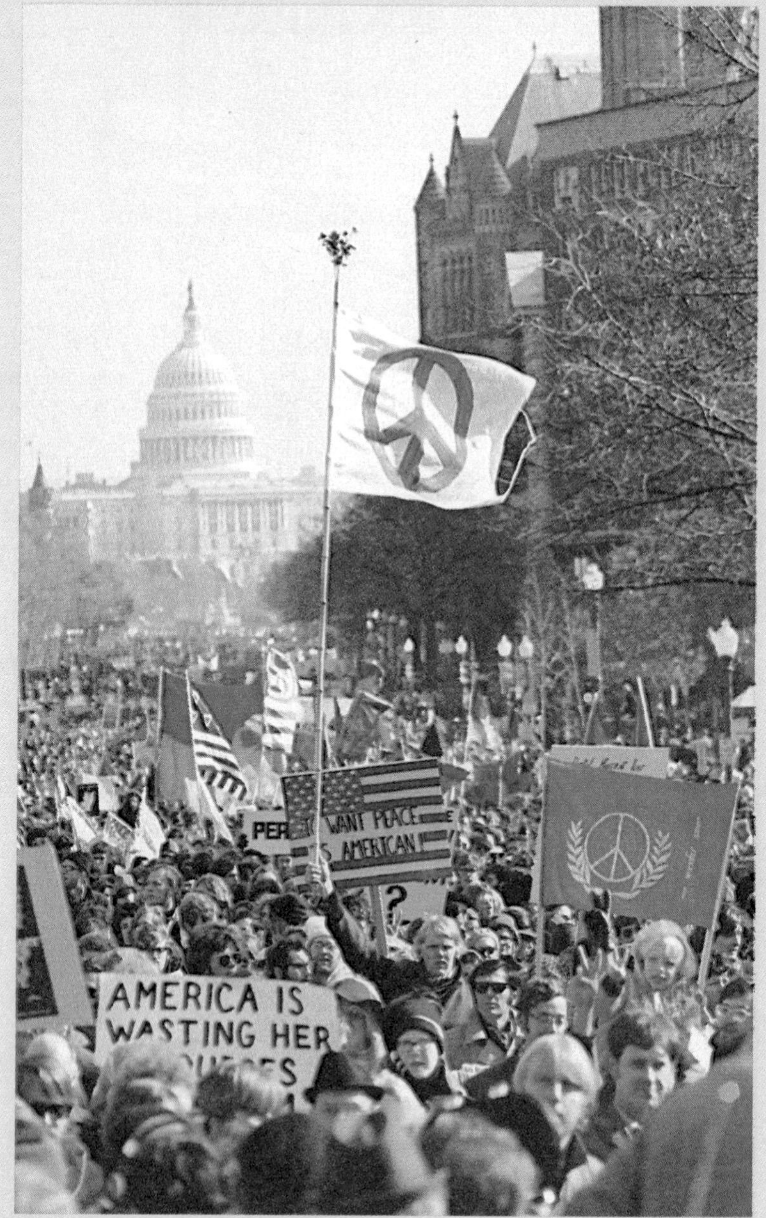

Chapter Objectives

After studying this chapter, you should be able to:

- identify the social changes that took place in the United States following President Johnson's election in 1964;
- explain how American involvement in the war in South Vietnam increased while President Johnson was in office;
- discuss how American involvement in the war in South Vietnam caused problems in the United States.

1 A Changing Society

Overview Many changes took place in American society after President Johnson was elected to a full term in 1964. Some of these changes were due to the President's efforts to improve the quality of life for all Americans. President Johnson believed that the federal government should try to improve life for all Americans. Other social changes came from important decisions by the Supreme Court. Social changes also took place as groups of Americans worked together for social improvements.

Many of the social changes of the mid-1960's helped specific groups of Americans. For example, older Americans, black Americans, American Indians, Hispanics, and women were helped by many of the laws passed while President Johnson was in office.

Objectives After reading this section, you should be able to:

- give examples of President Johnson's programs to help improve life for all Americans;
- explain how some Supreme Court decisions affected American society in the 1960's;
- discuss the affect of social changes during the 1960's upon special groups in the United States.

Laws to Improve Society. President Johnson began his first full term in office in January 1965. The President believed that the federal government should try to improve life for all Americans. To reach that goal, the President asked Congress to pass a number of new laws. President Johnson's program for laws to help Americans improve their lives became known as the *Great Society.* The term came from an expression used by the President in several of his speeches.

One important part of the Great Society was *medicare.* This was a plan to help people over the age of 65 pay for hospital and doctors' services and for certain other health needs. Many Americans needed the help that was given by the medicare program. That was because many older people often found their retirement income was not enough to cover both living costs and the high costs of health care.

Some other Great Society programs helped different groups of Americans. For example, the Neighborhood Youth Corps was set up to help teenagers who were out of work. Other programs were started to give money to schools to improve education. The Model Cities program was set up to provide money for rebuilding slum areas of cities. The goal of these and of other Great Society programs was to improve the quality of life for all Americans.

While President Johnson was in office, changes were also made in the government. In 1965 the Department of Housing and Urban Development was added to the President's cabinet. The next year the Department of Transportation was also added to the cabinet. These offices handled the problems of cities and the problems of transportation.

In 1967 a new amendment was added to the Constitution. This amendment, known as the Twenty-fifth Amendment, stated what steps the government should follow if either the President or Vice-President died or could not serve [*130–*134].

What was the Great Society?

Society and the Supreme Court. The Supreme Court also made several rulings during the 1960's that changed life for many Americans. In 1962 and 1963, for example, the Supreme Court upset some Americans by deciding that prayers said in public schools were against the Constitution. The Court said that the government could neither help nor oppose religion. Therefore, prayers could not be said in public schools, since public schools were a part of local government.

Another important ruling of the Supreme Court had to do with election districts for Congress and for state legislatures. Over the years, most states had not changed the lines dividing their election districts. In the meantime, many people moved to cities. But as the cities grew, they did not get more representatives in Congress or in the state legislatures. This meant that people in cities had fewer representatives than they should have had. This problem was corrected in 1964 when the Supreme Court ruled that each election district had to have about the same number of people. This ruling helped cities to be better represented at the different levels of government.

How does the cartoon illustrate the underrepresentation of urban areas in Congress and in state legislatures?

"There are some surpluses I don't mind."/Straight Herblock *(Simon & Schuster, 1964)*

The Supreme Court also made several rulings protecting the rights of people suspected of breaking the law. In 1964 the Court said that a confession could not be used against a person if the police had not let the person see a lawyer first. In another case, the Supreme Court said suspects had to be told their constitutional rights before being questioned by police.

Many Americans did not like these rulings. Some people were upset because the Court wanted to keep religion out of public schools. Other people felt that the Court was going too far to protect people suspected of breaking the law. And some Americans were angry because President Johnson agreed with many of the Court's findings. While the Supreme Court was influencing life in the United States, other social changes were affecting black Americans.

- *What were some of the important rulings made by the Supreme Court in the 1960's?*

Changes in Black Americans. In the early 1960's social conditions for blacks in the United States seemed to be improving. The federal courts and the federal government were working to protect the civil rights—rights guaranteed by the Constitution—of all Americans. But laws and court rulings could not

During the 1960's, discrimination forced many blacks to live in run-down neighborhoods that offered few recreational facilities for children. But social conditions slowly improved for some black Americans during this time. What kind of living conditions did these black children live with?

Tom Stack/Tom Stack & Associates

overcome some of the problems facing black Americans. Because of discrimination, blacks in cities often had to live in crowded neighborhoods with run-down housing. Schools in these areas were often poor. As a result, many blacks did not receive the kind of education that would enable them to get good jobs. This, in turn, led to high unemployment among black Americans.

Between 1965 and 1967, riots broke out in the black neighborhoods of several cities. One of the worst of these riots took place in 1965 in a black neighborhood of Los Angeles called Watts. The rioting lasted for 6 days and left 34 people dead and over 800 people wounded. At the same time millions of dollars' worth of property was destroyed. There was more rioting in black neighborhoods in 1968 following the assassination of the civil rights leader, Dr. Martin Luther King, Jr. An investigation of these outbreaks showed that many blacks felt trapped by the poor conditions in which they lived and worked. Sometimes small incidents led to serious problems because of the frustration felt by many blacks.

Black leaders could not agree on how to solve these problems. Some black leaders spoke of using *black power.* That usually meant giving black people power over matters relating to black neighborhoods. The term also meant teaching blacks to be proud of their culture.

Black Americans did make some important gains during the 1960's. A black senator, Edward W. Brooke of Massachusetts, was elected to the Senate. In 1967 Richard G. Hatcher was elected mayor of Gary, Indiana. Hatcher was one of the first blacks to be elected mayor of a major American city. Blacks were also elected to several state legislatures.

Under President Johnson's leadership, a new civil rights law was passed. The Civil Rights Act of 1968 said people could not be treated unfairly because of race when trying to find housing. The law also made it a crime to interfere when a person was voting or campaigning in any election in the United States.

What were some of the major causes of the urban riots in the 1960's?

Other Groups in American Society. The civil rights efforts of black Americans caused other groups, such as American Indians and Hispanics—Spanish-speaking Americans—to work for improved social conditions. Each of these groups wanted to gain better living conditions and better job opportunities for their people.

American Indians had faced difficult social conditions for many years. Many Indians still lived on reservations. However, some Indians had moved to cities because they believed life there would be better. But Indians in cities often could not get jobs. In some cases this was due to discrimination. In other cases, it was because some Indians had not received the training needed for many jobs. As a result, most Indians in city areas were poor and could not afford good housing.

During the 1960's, groups, such as the American Indian Movement (AIM), were set up by Indians to help solve some of their problems. These groups worked to improve education and job opportunities for Indians.

Hispanics in the United States also found living conditions difficult. These people were the descendants of the early Spanish settlers of California, of immigrants from Mexico, and of migrants from Puerto Rico.

Hispanics were often the victims of discrimination. This meant that those in cities could only find housing in run-down neighborhoods where there were fewer educational opportunities. Many Hispanics were not taught English. The lack of education and inability to speak English made it hard for most Hispanics to get good jobs.

These problems led to the formation of groups to help Hispanics. César Chávez formed the United Farm Workers as a union for those Hispanics who were farm workers. The union was able to gain better pay and better working conditions for its members. Other gains were also made by Hispanics.

During the 1960's several Hispanics were given important jobs with the federal government. President Johnson made Vicente T. Ximenes the chairman of the President's Cabinet Committee on Mexican-American Affairs. Dr. Hector García was chosen to be a member of the United States delegation to the United Nations. And Raul H. Castro was made United States ambassador to El Salvador. While some progress was being made by Hispanics, women also began working to change ideas about their place in society.

How did the civil rights efforts of black Americans influence American Indians and Hispanics?

Women in the 1960's. For many years women workers in the United States had not been treated fairly. Sometimes women doing the same work as men were paid less. In addition, many jobs that were open to men were not open to women.

Ideas about the place of women in our society began to change in the 1960's. Special women's organizations were formed to work for an end to the unfair treatment of women. These groups also worked to let the public know about the problems faced by women.

(*Text continues on page 644.*)

The 1960's were years of change for America's women. Protest rallies focused attention on discrimination against women. In addition, new job opportunities opened for women in industry and in professions such as pharmacy, law, and medicine.

Elizabeth Crews/Stock, Boston

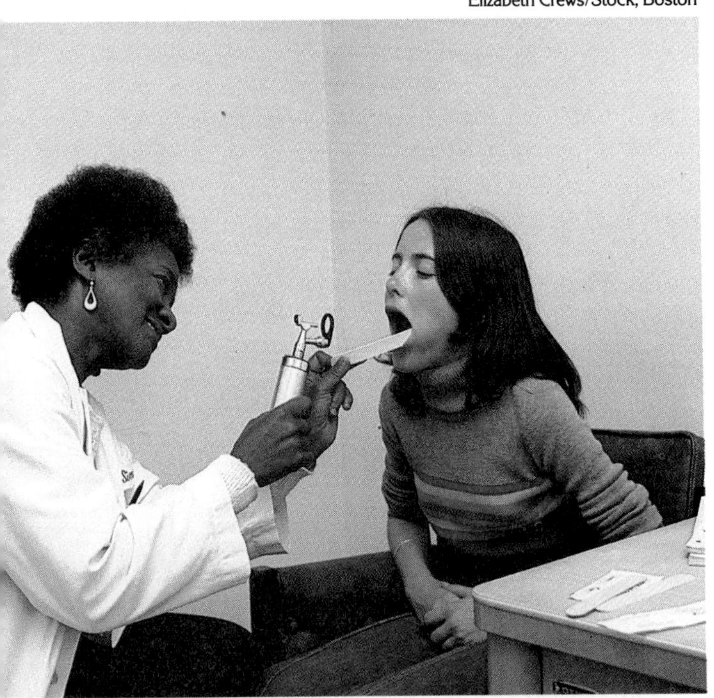

Bill Gillette/Stock, Boston

Photri

Bob Daemmrich/Stock, Boston

The National Organization for Women (NOW) was set up in 1966. This group and other groups worked to see that women were paid the same as men when doing the same kind of work. The groups also asked for public support for child day-care centers and for equal job opportunities for women.

The work of these women's groups helped women get jobs once open only to men. Women became police officers, construction workers, and business leaders. Women were also elected to Congress and to state and local government offices during the 1960's. In the early 1970's Congress passed an amendment to the Constitution that would prevent a person from being treated unfairly because of the person's sex. Those who favored this law had until 1982 to gain the approval of the required number of 38 states.

■ *What was the National Organization for Women (NOW)?*

SECTION 1 REVIEW

1. *Why was medicare an important part of the Great Society?*
2. *For what reason did the Supreme Court rule in the early 1960's that prayers could not be said in public schools?*
3. *Why were special women's organizations set up during the 1960's?*

2 The Challenge of Foreign Affairs

Overview Foreign relations caused many problems for the United States during the 1960's. There were difficulties in Latin America, the Middle East, Eastern Europe, and Southeast Asia.

One of the most serious foreign problems during that time was American involvement in a war in Southeast Asia. South Vietnam came to depend on American aid as Communist rebels fought to take over the country. When the war grew worse, the United States was drawn into the fighting.

Objectives After reading this section, you should be able to:

- describe the foreign relations problems the United States encountered in Latin America during the mid-1960's;
- discuss the changes in foreign relations between the United States and the Soviet Union while President Johnson was in office;
- summarize the United States involvement in the war in South Vietnam between the years of 1965 and 1968.

In the early 1960's the United States began to increase its military aid to South Vietnam. That was because the war with the Vietcong was being lost. At the same time, the government of South Vietnam did not have widespread popular support. The government there changed many times as new leaders tried to bring stability to the country. However, each new government was able to stay in power only because of military support from the United States. Thus, by the end of 1963 over 16,000 Americans were serving in South Vietnam. But these Americans acted only as military advisers and, at that time, did not fight against the Vietcong.

Then in August 1964, two United States warships reportedly were attacked by North Vietnamese torpedo boats in the Gulf of Tonkin. President Johnson ordered American planes to bomb North Vietnam. At the same time, Congress passed the *Gulf of Tonkin Resolution.* This allowed the President to take whatever steps were needed to stop the attacks on American soldiers and to prevent aggression in South Vietnam. More soldiers were sent to South Vietnam, and by the end of 1965 over 180,000 American soldiers were stationed in the country. By that time, American troops had been ordered to fight against the Vietcong. Thus, the role of the United States in the war rapidly expanded.

■ *What is guerrilla warfare?*

Growing Involvement. President Johnson believed that the war in South Vietnam could be ended if the United States sent enough military aid to the country. As a result, the number of American soldiers and the amount of war goods sent to South Vietnam increased between 1965 and 1968. In addition, American planes bombed North Vietnam, areas of South Vietnam held by the Vietcong, and supply routes used by the Vietcong. By the end of 1968, more bombs had been dropped on North and South Vietnam than had been dropped during all of World War II. And by 1968 over 500,000 American soldiers were taking part in the fighting in South Vietnam.

The use of so much military power was designed to show the Vietcong and their ally, North Vietnam, that they could not win the war. President Johnson felt that when the Vietcong and North Vietnam knew they were facing overwhelming American power, they would negotiate a settlement of the war. But this plan did not work.

Communist forces went on fighting, even though they suffered heavy losses. Their losses in military goods were replaced by the Soviet Union and by communist China. The Vietcong and North Vietnam refused to talk about peace terms until the United States stopped its bombing raids and left South Vietnam. As the war grew more serious, some people began to question America's involvement in South Vietnam.

■ *Why did the United States use so much military power in South Vietnam?*

Public Opinion and the War. The war in South Vietnam deeply divided the people of the United States. Those who supported the war were called *hawks,* while those who opposed the war were known as *doves.*

The hawks supported the war for two reasons. One reason was the domino theory. This was the belief that communism would spread to other countries in Southeast Asia if South Vietnam was defeated by Communist forces. It was believed that if we failed to stop the Communists, they would take over other countries in the area. The second reason for

Photri

During the Vietnam War, American troops faced difficult jungle conditions as they battled communist Vietcong rebels.

our involvement in South Vietnam was that the United States had promised to help South Vietnam resist being taken over by outside forces. Therefore, the United States had a duty to help South Vietnam since it was fighting the Vietcong, who were aided by North Vietnam.

On the other hand, the doves used several arguments to support their belief that the United States should leave South Vietnam. One idea stressed by the doves was that the war was a civil war between opposing groups in South Vietnam. Therefore, the doves said, the war did not concern the United States. Other doves believed that the war was harming South Vietnam. These people said that there was not much sense in destroying the country to save it from communism. Some doves also argued that the United States could not win a guerrilla war where the enemy made surprise attacks and then hid. Since the Vietcong rarely fought in open combat, it was believed that the superior military power of the United States was almost useless against the Communist forces.

Thus, American society was divided by different viewpoints about the war. In time, the government of the United States began changing its policy in South Vietnam.

■ *What was the domino theory?*

A New Policy. The criticism of American policy in South Vietnam grew as the war went on. Some members of Congress and other well-known Americans spoke against any further American involvement in the fighting. There were antiwar marches in several major American cities. For example, a large antiwar meeting was held in Washington, D.C., in October 1967. There was also strong opposition to the war among college students. Part of the reason for this was because people of college age could be drafted for military service.

Then, early in 1968, the Vietcong and the North Vietnamese began a surprise offensive. There was much destruction and loss of life in South Vietnam. The attacks showed that American power had failed to weaken the Communists to any great extent. The attacks also showed the determination of the Communists to carry on the war. However, the Communists failed to win their military objectives, and they suffered heavy losses.

A short time after the Communist offensive was stopped, the United States began to change its policy in South Vietnam. President Johnson realized that a military victory was not possible unless the United States was willing to fight a full-scale war.

In March 1968, President Johnson announced that he was taking steps to cut down the war in Vietnam by ordering a halt to most of the bombing of North Vietnam. The President hoped this would cause North Vietnam to begin peace talks to end the war. As a result, representatives of North Vietnam and of the United States began peace talks in Paris within a few months.

At the same time, the President stated that he would not seek reelection in 1968. This decision was based partly on the growing public criticism of our country's policy in South Vietnam. The President's popularity had dropped since the election of 1964. That was because many Americans blamed the President for getting the United States into the war in South Vietnam.

■ *What was one reason that President Johnson did not run for reelection in 1968?*

SECTION 2 REVIEW

1. *Why did President Johnson send American troops into the Dominican Republic in 1965?*
2. *Why did the United States and the Soviet Union seem to be moving toward friendlier relations in the late 1960's?*
3. *Why did American policy in South Vietnam begin to change in 1968?*

3 Problems at Home

Overview The United States faced a number of domestic problems during the 1960's. One of these problems was inflation. There were also other problems as the election of 1968 drew near. President Johnson decided not to run again in 1968. This influenced several well-known Democrats to decide to run for President. But there was fighting during the Democratic convention. This happened when groups protested against the war in Vietnam. Following the election campaign, the Republicans won the presidency. However, the Democrats held both houses of Congress.

Objectives After reading this section, you should be able to:

- assess the government's steps to control inflation while President Johnson was in office;
- discuss the events at the Democratic convention in 1968;
- identify the main problems facing the country during the 1968 campaign.

War and the Economy. During the late 1960's the American economy was greatly affected by spending for the war in South Vietnam and for the programs of the Great Society. This led to a growing demand for goods which, in turn, caused prices to rise. As prices rose, workers asked for higher wages. But when workers were given higher pay, producers raised prices to make up for higher labor costs. Thus, inflation became a growing economic problem.

President Johnson knew that one way to deal with inflation was to raise taxes. When taxes are raised, people have less money to spend for goods, so demand drops. And often when demand drops, prices go down. But the President and Congress moved slowly. That was because they knew that higher taxes were not popular.

In 1966 the President asked the American people to cut down their buying as one way of lowering demand. At the same time, some cuts were made in spending by the government.

The government also worked to slow inflation by encouraging higher interest rates. This was done in the hope of lowering demand by making borrowing cost more. But the higher interest rates only led to a slowdown in the construction industry. That was because many building projects were paid for by borrowing. The slowdown also caused some people to lose their jobs. This happened because many construction workers were laid off.

Even with these changes by the government, high prices were still a problem. So in 1968 a 10 percent income-tax *surcharge*—an extra tax—was passed by Congress. President Johnson hoped that the extra tax would lower spending and demand. The President believed that in time this would help to slow inflation. However, by 1968, inflation had been growing for some time. As a result, the extra tax did not slow inflation the way the government expected. Inflation only added to the growing political problems as the 1968 presidential election drew near.

■ *For what reason did President Johnson and Congress move slowly in raising taxes to control inflation?*

Political Turmoil. As you have read, President Johnson had decided not to run again in 1968. Since the President was a Democrat, the Democratic party faced the task of choosing someone else to run for President. The choice would be made at the Democratic party's convention during the summer. Among those who hoped to be chosen were Senator Eugene J. McCarthy of Minnesota, Senator Robert F. Kennedy of New York, and Vice-President Hubert H. Humphrey.

Senator McCarthy and Senator Kennedy were backed by many young people who opposed the war in South Vietnam. Both senators had often spoken against President Johnson's policy in South Vietnam. To gain support among Democrats in each state, the two senators traveled around the country during the spring of 1968. But in June of that year, Senator Kennedy was killed in California by an assassin.

Following Senator Kennedy's death, Vice-President Humphrey faced no strong opposition in his bid to be nominated for President. That was because the Vice-President had more support among the delegates to the Democratic convention than did Senator McCarthy.

In August 1968, the Democrats met in

(*Text continues on page 652.*)

VIEWPOINTS DIFFER

The Role of China in the Vietnam War

The line of debate over the American tragedy in Vietnam have not been clearly drawn. One early issue that surfaced was the extent to which China was behind the actions of the North Vietnamese.

William P. Bundy, Assistant Secretary of State for Far Eastern Affairs, presented the Johnson administration's position in 1966:

There is today in Communist China a government whose leadership is dedicated to the promotion of communism by violent revolution . . .

We have seen . . . in the contrast between what the Soviets have done in Eastern Europe and behavior of predecessor [previous] regimes, that there is a Communist logic that does insist on total control, that will not tolerate anything other than the imposition [established by force] of the full Communist totalitarian system . . .

. . . important to Peking is its encouragement and support of Communist Asian regimes in North Korea and North Vietnam. What is now happening in Vietnam is basically the result of Hanoi's ambitions and efforts. [But] Peking might wish eventually to dominate North Vietnam or a united Vietnam under Hanoi's initial control.

John Kenneth Galbraith, an economist, former ambassador to India, and critic of American policy in Vietnam offers a different perspective.

The Communist world has come to pieces along national lines. The two great centers during the past years [the U.S.S.R. and China], on occasion, have been close to diplomatic breach.

China, which the proponents of the Vietnam conflict for a while bravely pictured as the *deus ex Machina* [controlling influence] is rent within itself. Its assumed puppet in Hanoi, like its earlier puppet in North Korea, has publicly asserted its independence. Not even the most ardent defender of the [Vietnam] war can now believe that Hanoi wants to be part of a Chinese-led empire.

Think About It

1. Bundy compared China's domination of Asian communist states to the Soviet Union's domination of what region?
2. What evidence does Galbraith offer in order to conclude that North Vietnam was not a puppet state of China?
3. Which viewpoint, Bundy or Galbraith, might be used to justify a strong American military role in Vietnam? Explain your answer.

Chicago for the party convention. Many antiwar groups came to the city at the same time. They planned to demonstrate against the war in South Vietnam. These groups clashed with the National Guard and with the police during the convention. The antiwar demonstrations were shown on television. And many Americans were shocked by what they saw.

When the convention ended, Vice-President Humphrey had been chosen to run for President by the Democratic party. Senator Edmund S. Muskie of Maine had been chosen to run for Vice-President. However, these two people faced a hard election campaign. That was partly because of the public's dislike of what was shown on television during the convention.

For what reason did many antiwar groups come to Chicago during the Democratic convention in 1968?

A Political Challenge. The Republican party also held its convention in August 1968. Several well-known Republicans hoped to gain the nomination for President. But former Vice-President Richard M. Nixon was favored by most of the convention delegates. As a result, Nixon was chosen to run for President on the first ballot. Governor Spiro T. Agnew of Maryland was chosen to run for Vice-President.

In addition to the two major political parties, a third party was formed in 1968. The American Independent party chose former Governor George C. Wallace of Alabama to run for

De Wys, Inc.

Robert Kennedy (center, standing) was a leading contender for the 1968 Democratic presidential nomination until his assassination. In the election, Republican Richard M. Nixon carried most of the states of the West and of the Midwest. By how many popular votes did Nixon win?

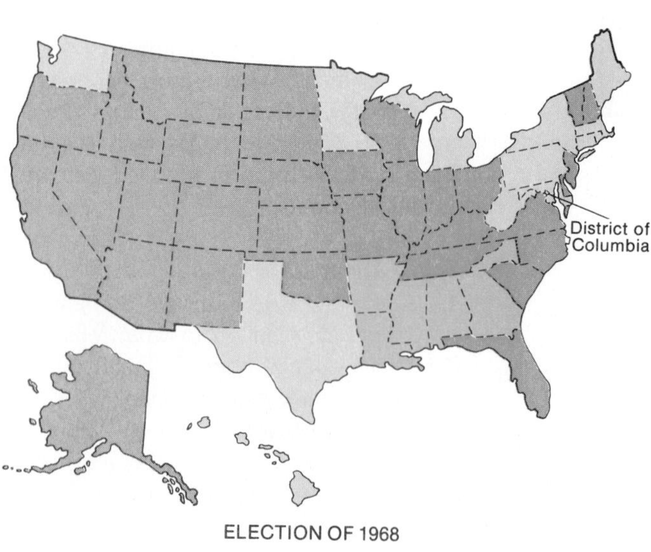

ELECTION OF 1968

	Electoral Votes	Popular Votes
Republican Richard M. Nixon	301	31,770,237
Democratic Hubert H. Humphrey	191	31,270,533
American Independent George C. Wallace	46	9,906,141

President. General Curtis E. LeMay, a former Air Force Chief of Staff, was chosen to run for Vice-President. Some voters liked the American Independent party because of Governor Wallace's views. Wallace favored states' rights. He also was against the civil rights policies of the federal government.

The 1968 campaign centered on the main problems facing the country in the late 1960's. Among these were the war in South Vietnam and law and order in the United States. To win votes, the candidates traveled around the country and appeared on television. During these appearances, the voters were told how each candidate would deal with the problems of the times if elected to office.

Richard Nixon won the election in 1968. But Vice-President Humphrey did much better than had been expected. Governor Wallace's total vote was far behind that of the two major candidates. Even though the Republicans won the White House, the Democrats carried both houses of Congress. This meant the new President faced working with a Democratic Congress.

■ *What third political party was formed in 1968?*

SECTION 3 REVIEW

1. *What serious problem developed during the 1960's while President Johnson was in office?*
2. *In what way did the antiwar demonstrations at the Democratic convention in 1968 affect the presidential-election campaign of 1968?*
3. *Why did some voters support the American Independent party in 1968?*

CHAPTER 37 SUMMARY

Many changes took place in American life while President Johnson was in office. One change was that the government and different groups of people worked for changes to improve life for all Americans.

While these changes were taking place, the United States faced problems in dealing with other countries. One important problem was the growing American involvement in a war in South Vietnam. As the United States entered the fighting, some people began to criticize the government. In time, the American people became sharply divided over to what extent the United States should take part in the war in South Vietnam.

The war grew more serious, and inflation became a problem in the United States. During the summer of 1968, political candidates were chosen to run for the presidency. A third political party was formed. This group also chose a presidential candidate. Following the campaign in the fall of 1968, Americans chose Republican Richard M. Nixon to be the new President.

CHAPTER 37 REVIEW

USING YOUR SKILLS

Interpreting a Political Cartoon

Political cartoons are often used to express ideas about important problems of the times. Below are two cartoons showing how the war in South Vietnam affected the United States. Study the two cartoons, and then answer the questions below.

1. In Cartoon A, what does the animal following President Johnson represent?
2. What do the babies being carried by President Johnson in Cartoon A represent?
3. What does Cartoon B seem to show about the size of the federal budget?
4. What does the person in Cartoon B represent?
5. What do you think Cartoon A and Cartoon B are trying to show about how the war in South Vietnam influenced affairs in the United States?

CHAPTER 37 REVIEW

YOU SHOULD KNOW

Identify, define, or explain each of the following:

Great Society
medicare
Vietcong
guerrilla warfare
Gulf of Tonkin Resolution
income-tax surcharge

CHECKING FACTS

1. What was the Model Cities program?
2. What did the Twenty-fifth Amendment state?
3. What did an investigation of riots in black neighborhoods show?
4. What did the American Indian Movement (AIM) work to improve?
5. Who replaced Nikita Krushchev as the premier of the Soviet Union?
6. What country had ruled Indochina from the 1800's until after World War II?
7. What was a cause of Johnson's drop in popularity since the 1964 election?
8. What industry was affected by the higher interest rates in the late 1960's?
9. Who was nominated at the 1968 Democratic Convention?
10. Who was chosen to run for President by the American Independent party?

UNDERSTANDING CONCEPTS

1. Why were some Americans upset by Supreme Court rulings during the 1960's?
2. Why did President Johnson increase the number of soldiers and the amount of war goods sent to South Vietnam between 1965 and 1968?
3. How was American public opinion affected by the war in South Vietnam?
4. How was the economy affected by the war in South Vietnam?

LEARNING FROM ILLUSTRATIONS

1. Examine the picture on page 648. What were some of the difficult conditions that American troops faced?
2. Study the map on page 652. From what area of the country did George C. Wallace receive his strongest support?

CRITICAL THINKING

1. How would you compare the demonstrations by blacks in the early 1960's with the demonstrations by blacks between 1965 and 1967?
2. The war in Vietnam deeply divided the people of the United States. Would you have been a hawk or a dove? Give reasons for your answer.
3. How, do you think, did television affect the election of 1968?

ENRICHMENT ACTIVITIES

1. Research how North Vietnam and South Vietnam became countries. Information might be found in books on Asia, in newsmagazines, and in encyclopedias. Report to the class about these countries. You might draw a map showing Indochina and how it was divided into four countries including the two Vietnams.
2. Find out about third parties in presidential elections. Information might be found in encyclopedias and in American-history books. Make a chart listing the third parties. Show when they ran candidates, and give the major points in each party's platform.

1970 1975

- 1969 United States and Soviet Union began to hold SALT
- 1971 National Women's Political Caucus set up; Voting age lowered to 18
- 1972 President Nixon met with leaders of Communist China; President Nixon visited Soviet Union; President Nixon reelected
- 1973 Vietnam War ended for United States; Vice-President Spiro Agnew resigned; Gerald R. Ford appointed Vice-President
- 1974 President Nixon resigned; Gerald R. Ford became President
- 1975 Draft requirement ended
- 1976 United States bicentennial; James E. "Jimmy" Carter elected President

CHAPTER 38

Years of Change

Chapter Objectives

After studying this chapter, you should be able to:

- explain how American involvement in the war in South Vietnam ended;
- identify the changes that occurred in American foreign relations while President Nixon was in office;
- discuss the problems and changes that took place while President Ford was in office.

1 The Nixon Years

Overview When President Nixon took office in 1969, the war in South Vietnam was still going on. The President worked to cut down America's role in the war. An agreement to end the fighting was signed in 1973.

During the early 1970's, changes were also taking place in our country's relations with other countries. President Nixon visited China and the Soviet Union in 1972. Such visits helped to improve relations between the United States and these communist countries.

President Nixon was reelected in 1972. Later, Americans were shocked by a serious political scandal involving the White House. Because of the scandal, President Nixon resigned in 1974. Gerald R. Ford became President.

Objectives After reading this section, you should be able to:

- discuss the ways the United States tried to end the war in South Vietnam;
- analyze the foreign relations of the United States with China and the Soviet Union;
- describe how the United States was affected by a major political scandal in the 1970's.

The Continuing War in South Vietnam. One of the most difficult problems facing President Nixon was the undeclared war in South Vietnam. The President hoped to end American involvement in the war through a policy called *Vietnamization.* This meant that American forces were to be slowly taken out of South Vietnam. At the same time, the South Vietnamese army was to be trained and equipped to take over the job of defending the country. As a result, over 60,000 American soldiers left South Vietnam in 1969.

In another move to reduce the fighting, President Nixon ordered American forces to use a tactic called *protective reaction.* This meant that American soldiers were to fight only when attacked or threatened by an attack.

While these efforts were taking place in South Vietnam, peace talks were begun in Paris. However, the talks made little progress toward ending the war. That was because neither side seemed willing to compromise.

■ *What was protective reaction?*

The End of the War. There was a new development in the war in April 1970. At that time American soldiers were ordered into Cambodia. This was done to destroy supply bases used by North Vietnam and by the Vietcong to attack South Vietnam.

The war dragged on during 1971. Then in March 1972, North Vietnam launched heavy attacks on South Vietnam. President Nixon ordered more bombing of North Vietnam and air strikes on enemy bases in Laos and Cambodia. The President also ordered that mines be placed in North Vietnamese harbors. This was done to reduce the supplies that North Vietnam was receiving by sea.

At the same time, Henry Kissinger, a foreign-policy adviser to President Nixon, worked to break the deadlock at the Paris peace talks. After many meetings a cease-fire was finally arranged in January 1973.

Following the agreement, American soldiers were quickly withdrawn from South Vietnam. But North Vietnam continued to attack South

Vietnam at different times during the next two years. Without American help, South Vietnam could not stop these attacks. As a result, South Vietnam was forced to surrender to North Vietnam in April 1975.

More than 50,000 Americans were killed in the war in South Vietnam. In addition, the war cost the United States billions of dollars. Most Americans hoped that the United States would never again be involved in such a long and unpopular war.

For what reason were American soldiers ordered into Cambodia in April 1970?

Changing Foreign Relations. While the war in South Vietnam was going on, other important events were taking place that affected the foreign relations of the United States. For example, our country became more friendly with Communist China—the People's Republic of China. In 1949, when the Communists took over China, the former government leaders fled to Taiwan—an island off the coast of China. The United States continued to look upon these noncommunist leaders as the government of China.

President Nixon toured the Great Wall of China during his visit to Communist China in 1972.

Wide World

Then in 1971, the People's Republic of China was admitted to the United Nations. The following year President Nixon went to Communist China to meet with its leaders. The purpose of this meeting was to improve relations between the two countries.

Our country also moved toward friendlier relations with the Soviet Union during the years that President Nixon was in office. That was a time of *détente*—a relaxing of tensions between the two countries. In 1969 the United States, the Soviet Union, and a number of other countries had signed the Nuclear Nonproliferation Treaty. These countries agreed not to give nuclear weapons to any country that did not already have them. Also in 1969 the Soviet Union and the United States had begun to hold talks to find ways to limit nuclear weapons. These talks were called the Strategic Arms Limitation Talks, or SALT.

Relations between the United States and the Soviet Union remained friendly in the early 1970's. President Nixon visited the Soviet Union in May 1972. During this visit the President held a number of meetings with Soviet leaders. As a result, several agreements were signed between the United States and the Soviet Union. For example, the two countries agreed to limit certain kinds of weapons. The United States and the Soviet Union also agreed to work together on health and environmental problems and to share certain kinds of information.

For what reason did President Nixon go to China in 1972?

The 1972 Election. In the spring of 1972 several well-known Democrats hoped to be chosen as their party's candidate for President. However, by the time the Democratic party met in July 1972, Senator George S. McGovern of South Dakota had gained the lead. He was chosen to run for President on the first ballot. But some Democrats were upset by the choice of Senator McGovern. These people felt that some of McGovern's ideas were too radical. He opposed the war in Vietnam and favored what some people felt were extreme social changes.

The Republican party met in August 1972. President Nixon was chosen to run for a second term. There was little opposition to this choice.

The 1972 campaign centered on the problems of inflation, civil rights, and the war in South Vietnam. Political corruption was also talked about during the campaign. Part of the reason for this was because several people were caught during the summer of 1972 breaking into the headquarters of the Democratic party in the Watergate building in Washington, D.C. The people involved in this crime were thought by some to be working for the Nixon administration. As you will read, investigations of this break-in led to a major political scandal in 1973. But at the time, the public paid little attention to the event.

President Nixon was reelected by a landslide vote. He received the electoral vote of every state except Massachusetts and the District of Columbia (see map on this page). However, the voter turnout was the lowest in over 20 years. Only 55 percent of those eligible to vote did so.

■ *For what reason were many Democrats upset when the party chose Senator McGovern to run for President in 1972?*

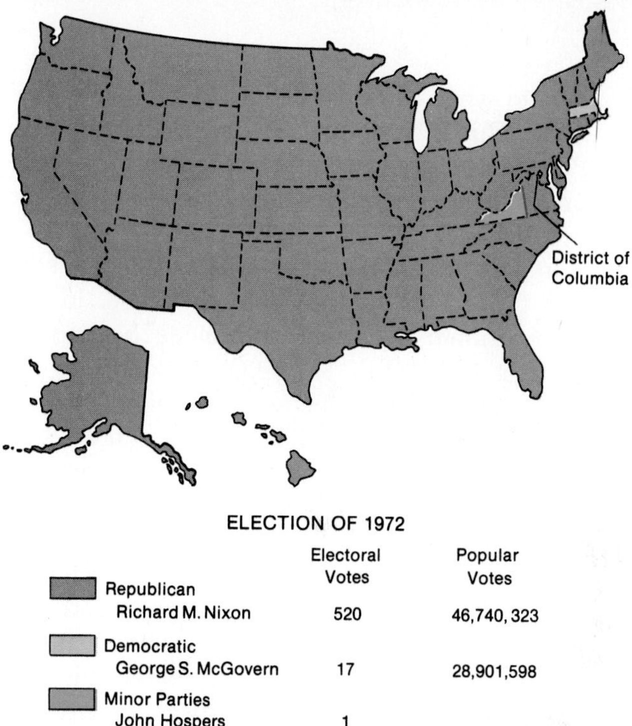

ELECTION OF 1972

	Electoral Votes	Popular Votes
Republican Richard M. Nixon	520	46,740,323
Democratic George S. McGovern	17	28,901,598
Minor Parties John Hospers	1	

What was President Nixon's margin of victory in popular votes in the 1972 election?

The Watergate Affair. The break-in at the Democratic party headquarters in the Watergate building did not affect the election of 1972. But soon after President Nixon began his second term in office, the break-in began to take on greater importance.

The people who broke into the Democratic headquarters were trying to hide listening devices in these offices. Seven people were found to be involved in the crime. In early 1973 they were tried, convicted, and sent to prison. During the trial it became known that some of these people were connected to the White House and also to a committee that had been set up to help reelect President Nixon. More investigations into the break-in were begun. In March 1973 the President told the public that no one in the White House had taken part in what came to be called the Watergate Affair. But in late April 1973, several aides to President Nixon resigned because they were under investigation for being involved in the scandal.

In May 1973, President Nixon asked a special prosecutor to look into the case. In the same month a Senate committee headed by Senator Sam Ervin, Jr., began looking into the Watergate Affair. One of President Nixon's aides, John W. Dean III, told the group that the President had known of the efforts of some people in the White House to cover up the break-in.

Later, the Senate committee learned that President Nixon made secret tape recordings of most conversations that took place in the White House. The Senate committee and the special prosecutor asked for these recordings. However, President Nixon refused to give up the tapes on the grounds of *executive privilege.* This meant that the President believed the separation of powers between the branches of government allowed the executive branch to keep some information secret.

Then in October 1973, President Nixon fired the special prosecutor. That was because the prosecutor had tried to get the tape recordings and other facts about Watergate from the White House. This event became known as the Saturday Night Massacre because the President also fired other high government officers at the same time. These people had disagreed with the President about firing the special prosecutor. Many Americans were angry at President Nixon for this move. The President then allowed some tapes to be given to the groups looking into Watergate. But many of the recordings had sections missing and were hard to understand.

In the same month, Vice-President Spiro Agnew left office after being charged with failing to pay income taxes. Earlier, charges were made that the Vice-President had been paid bribes while governor of Maryland. Gerald R. Ford, a member of Congress from Michigan, was appointed as the new Vice-President. The resignation of Vice-President Agnew along with Watergate led to a further decline in President Nixon's popularity.

■ *For what reason did Vice-President Agnew resign in October 1973?*

The Resignation of a President. In November 1973 a new prosecutor was chosen by President Nixon to carry on the Watergate investigation. A month later the House of Representatives began to look into the possible impeachment of President Nixon.

As the different Watergate investigations went on, the President was asked for more tapes of White House conversations. Again, President Nixon refused on the grounds of executive privilege. The special prosecutor then asked a federal court to order President Nixon to give up the tapes. In July 1974, the Su-

DO YOU KNOW?

Do you know who became our President in the 1970's even though he was never elected as Vice-President or President?

Representative Gerald R. Ford of Michigan was appointed Vice-President in 1973 by President Nixon after Vice-President Spiro T. Agnew resigned. Then in August 1974, President Nixon resigned because of the Watergate scandal. As a result, Gerald R. Ford became the 38th President without being elected to either the vice-presidency or the presidency.

L. P. Laffont/Sygma

Fred Ward/Black Star

After resigning from office, President Nixon and his wife (left) left the White House by helicopter. A short time later, President Ford (right) was sworn into office as his wife watched the ceremony.

preme Court ruled that President Nixon had to give the tapes to the groups looking into Watergate.

By this time the House Judiciary Committee had begun impeachment hearings. After the tapes were made public, they showed that President Nixon knew about the cover-up of the Watergate break-in. As a result, in July 1974, the committee passed three articles charging that President Nixon had committed impeachable acts.

Faced with impeachment and possible removal from office, President Nixon resigned on August 9, 1974. Vice-President Ford was sworn in as President at noon on the same day. About a month later President Ford gave former President Nixon a full pardon for any crimes that he might have committed while in office. Some Americans were angry with President Ford for pardoning Mr. Nixon. These Americans felt that the pardon was wrong since many of the people close to President Nixon had been sent to prison for their part in Watergate.

For what reason did some Americans become angry with President Ford a short time after he became President?

SECTION 1 REVIEW

1. *In what way did President Nixon believe that Vietnamization would help to end American involvement in South Vietnam?*
2. *How did relations between the United States and China change in the early 1970's?*
3. *Why did President Nixon resign in August 1974?*

2 Economic Problems

Overview Inflation was a serious economic problem when President Nixon took office in 1969. The President worked to slow the rise in prices without having the economy go into a recession. However, business did slow down in late 1969. Nevertheless, prices continued to rise. In early 1972, government controls on wages, prices, and rents helped to slow inflation.

The problems of inflation were made worse in 1973 when some Arab countries stopped shipping oil to the United States. There was a fuel shortage, and the price of oil went up sharply.

Objectives After reading this section, you should be able to:

- analyze the problems with the American economy in the early 1970's;
- discuss Nixon's steps to bring inflation under control;
- explain how the American economy was affected by a war between Israel and some Arab countries in 1973.

President Nixon and the Economy. When President Nixon took office in 1969, inflation was the most serious economic problem in our country. Part of the cause for the rise in prices was due to an increase in government spending for the Vietnam War and for the Great Society.

President Nixon hoped to slow the rise in prices by cutting government spending. However, the President wanted to cut spending for such programs as education, social welfare, housing, and urban renewal. This upset some members of Congress. These people felt that domestic programs should not be cut unless there was also a cut in defense spending.

President Nixon also looked for other ways to control rising prices. But the President had to move slowly in trying to check inflation. That was because the country could move into a recession if steps to slow the economy were taken too quickly.

In late 1969 and early 1970 the economy did go into a recession, as President Nixon had feared might happen. Stock prices and

AVERAGE RETAIL PRICES IN DOLLARS FOR SELECTED FOODS, 1969–1974

	Years					
	1969	1970	1971	1972	1973	1974
Bread (One-Pound Loaf)	$ .23	$ .24	$ .25	$ .25	$ .28	$ .35
Pork Chops (One Pound)	1.12	1.16	1.08	1.25	1.56	1.57
Sugar (One Pound)	.12	.13	.14	.14	.15	.32
Eggs (One Dozen)	.62	.61	.53	.52	.78	.78
Milk (One-Half Gallon)	.55	.57	.59	.60	.65	.78
Chocolate Bar (One Ounce)	.06	.07	.07	.07	.07	.10

Inflation was a serious economic problem in the United States during the 1970's. According to this chart, which food items increased in price between 1969 and 1974? In what year did the prices of some food items decrease from the year before?

business profits went down. At the same time, the number of people out of work went up. However, even with the downturn of the economy, prices continued to go up.

■ *What was the most serious economic problem in our country when President Nixon took office in 1969?*

A Troubled Economy. In August 1971, President Nixon took further steps to slow inflation. At that time the President ordered wages, prices, and rents frozen for 90 days. During that time wages, prices, and rents could not be raised. The President hoped this step would help bring inflation under control. When the 90 days ended, wages, prices, and rents were allowed to rise. But increases were held down by guidelines set by the government. Workers and businesspeople were asked to accept these guidelines to help fight inflation.

President Nixon's actions did help to slow the rise in prices. Many people did not like the controls on wages and prices. But in general, most Americans accepted the government's plans. As a result, by early 1972, the economy was improving.

Then in late 1973 the economy again moved into a recession. By that time the Watergate investigations were taking much of President Nixon's time. As a result, the President did not have enough time to work on some of the country's other important problems.

■ *For what reason did President Nixon order wages, prices, and rents frozen for 90 days in August 1971?*

Fuel and Inflation. Over the years our country's need for fuel, especially oil, had been growing. But the sources of oil in the United States were not large enough to meet these growing needs. As a result, the United States came to depend on other countries for some of its oil. Among the countries from which our country bought oil were several countries in the Middle East.

In the fall of 1973 war broke out again in

Tom McHugh/Photo Researchers

The energy crisis of 1973 caused many people to wait in lines such as those pictured above for gasoline.

(Text continues on page 665.)

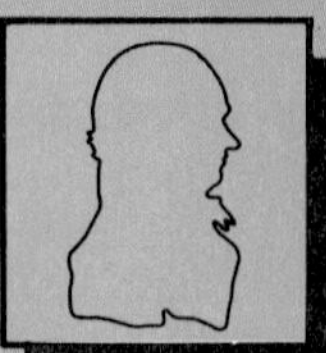

PROFILES

Cesar Chavez

Cesar Chavez was born in Arizona and moved to California with his parents during the Depression of the 1930's. There he saw the difficult life of migrant farm workers. The fruits and vegetables of America's tables still begin their journey from field to store to table in the hands of such daily laborers. By the 1960's these farm workers still didn't have typical labor safeguards. They had no right to organize a union, no minimum wage and no federally guaranteed guidelines for insurance or poison and pesticide protection. As an adult, Chavez decided to do something about those conditions.

Cesar persuaded impoverished farm workers not to pick grapes for farm owners who would not guarantee them a minimum wage or health protection. In 1965, his National Farm Workers Union went on strike. College students, Black civil rights workers and Catholic clergy who supported the picketers were attacked by local rural police. Chavez then asked the clergy to urge churchgoers nationwide not to buy grapes.

By not getting grapes, many people who were not politically active felt they too could make a difference in expanding democratic reforms. An estimated 17 million Americans stopped consuming grapes. The four largest growers then signed contracts with Chavez' U.F.W. From 1964 to 1980 the U.F.W. helped increase real wages 70%, improved pension plans, disability insurance and credit union and health care. Chavez received no salary for this. He has been strongly criticized for being a bad administrator. As an American, however, when he decided to make a difference, he did.

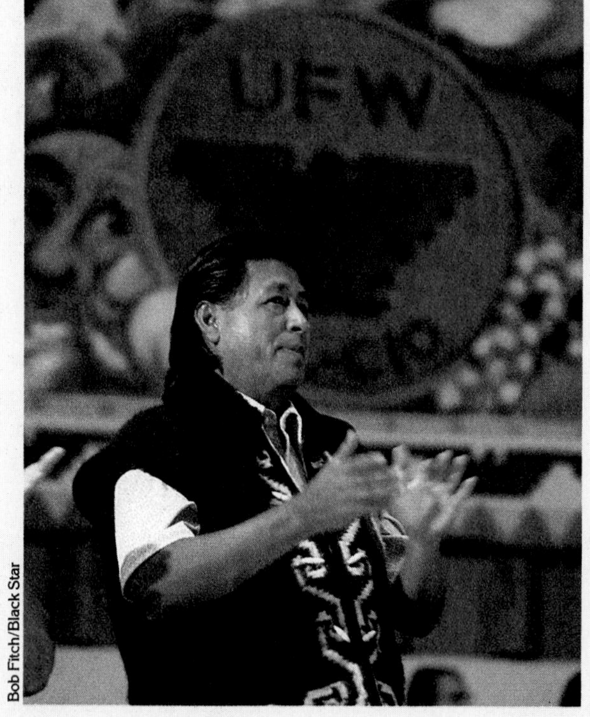

Bob Fitch/Black Star

Thinking Critically

A strike fails if other people supply the labor that is being withheld. In your opinion, what other groups would want starting farm laborer's positions?

What democratic values do you think Chavez appealed to in order to affect both production and market demand in America's free economy?

Chavez has been criticized as a poor administrator. Does a voluntary leader in a democracy have a responsibility to be an effective administrator?

the Middle East between Israel and a number of Arab countries. The United States and the Soviet Union used their influence to get Israel and the Arab countries to accept a cease-fire. In the meantime, however, the Arab countries stopped shipping oil to the United States and to several other industrialized countries. This was done because these countries were friendly toward Israel.

The action of the Arab countries caused a fuel crisis in the United States. There was a shortage of gasoline and of heating oil. To save fuel, President Nixon asked Americans to drive slower and to use public transportation whenever possible. The fuel shortage caused the price of gas and of other oil products to go up. The high cost of gas and oil added to the growing inflation in our country. The fuel crisis also affected business in the United States. Car sales went down. As a result, many workers in the automobile industry were laid off.

The Arab countries agreed to sell oil to the United States again in March 1974 after the fighting in the Middle East was stopped. However, some Americans began to think about ways to save fuel, since the United States was becoming increasingly dependent on oil from other countries.

■ *For what reason did Arab countries stop shipping oil to the United States and to several other industrialized countries in the fall of 1973?*

SECTION 2 REVIEW

1. *What happened to the American economy in late 1969 and early 1970?*
2. *How did most Americans feel about the controls placed on wages, prices, and rents by the government during the early 1970's?*
3. *How was the American economy affected by a war between Israel and some Arab countries in 1973?*

3 Society and Change

Overview While President Nixon was in office, many changes took place in American society. For example, the President worked to change and improve the way the government helped needy people. Some Americans, however, felt that President Nixon did not do enough to promote civil rights. There were some gains toward full equality for all Americans while President Nixon was in office.

As President Nixon tried to end American involvement in South Vietnam, protests against the war went on. One reason for the protests was the way the government chose people for the armed services. Many protests were peaceful, but at times these protests became violent.

Objectives After reading this section, you should be able to:

- discuss President Nixon's plans to help needy Americans;
- assess the progress made in the field of civil rights while President Nixon was in office;
- list the contributions of Asian Americans to our country.

Help for Needy Americans. The federal government had begun to help needy Americans in the days of the Great Depression. One kind of help given by the government was called public assistance or welfare. This help was in the form of direct payments to people in need. During the 1960's the government's welfare programs were expanded.

President Nixon felt that changes were needed in the country's welfare programs. That was because the President believed some of the welfare plans started under President Johnson had not worked well. As a result, some of these programs were ended.

One of President Nixon's ideas was a plan to share federal tax money with state and local governments. These governments could then decide how to use this money. Part of the money was to be used by state and local governments to help their people who were in need. The plan was called *revenue sharing.* The plan was passed by Congress in 1972.

Another idea of President Nixon's was the Family Assistance Plan. Under this plan, the federal government would give a yearly minimum payment to families with low incomes. However, the plan did not have enough support to get through Congress and did not become law.

Social security is another way that the federal government helps people. This is a social-insurance plan paid for by taxes from workers and from employers. The major purpose of social security is to pay a small monthly income to older people who no longer work. While President Nixon was in office, the amount of money received each month by those under social security was raised.

■ *What is revenue sharing?*

Civil Rights. In general, most black leaders were disappointed with the civil-rights record of President Nixon. For example, in 1969, the White House tried to give southern schools more time to end public-school *segregation*—the practice of separating people by race. However, the Supreme Court ruled that there could be no further delays in ending segregation.

Then in 1971, the Supreme Court ruled that pupils could be moved or bused to different schools to achieve a racial balance. But President Nixon was against the busing of pupils. The President felt that pupils should attend schools in their own neighborhood rather than be bused to schools that were faraway. But in some cases, the use of neighborhood schools helped segregation to go on since many of these schools were in minority neighborhoods. Therefore, some black leaders felt that President Nixon was not helping civil rights.

The President did, however, take some steps to help minorities gain equal job opportunities. During the first year that President Nixon was in office, the government began using what was known as the *Philadelphia Plan.* Under

Representative Shirley Chisholm of New York was the first black woman elected to Congress.

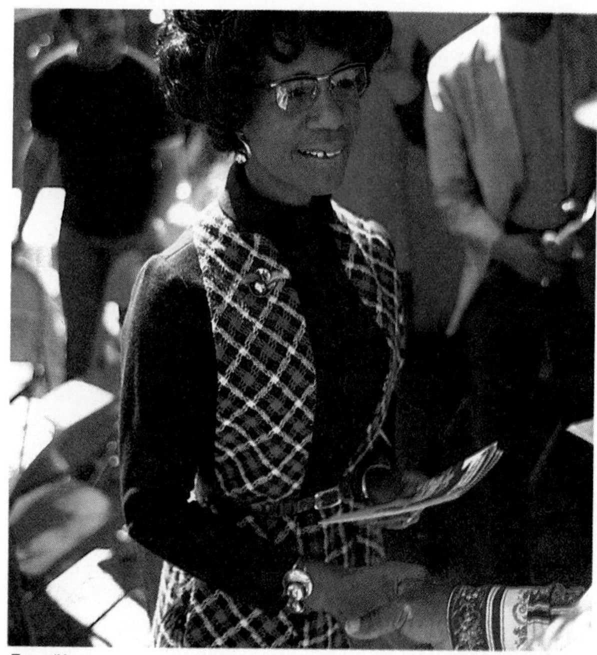
Fusco/Magnum

this plan, builders working on federal building jobs had to promise to try to hire a certain number of minority workers.

While black Americans were unhappy with President Nixon's efforts for civil rights, the federal government also worked to help American Indians. In the summer of 1970, President Nixon said the government should change its policy toward the American Indian. Under the new plan, Indians were to be given control over federal money spent for Indian housing, schools, health care, public works, and economic development.

■ *In what way did the federal government work to see that minorities had equal job opportunities while President Nixon was in office?*

Women's Rights. Women also made gains during the years that President Nixon was in office. In 1971 the National Women's Political Caucus was set up. One goal of this group was to have more women go to the national political conventions in 1972. The group also wanted to have more women serve in the government. As a result of working for these goals, more women than ever before went to the presidential nominating conventions in 1972.

Also in 1972 a national women's group complained to the federal government about American television programs. The group felt that many programs shown during the day for women viewers were of little value.

In 1973, 20 women were named to the Women's Hall of Fame in Seneca Falls, New York. This was the town where the first important women's rights meeting was held in the mid-1800's. In late 1974 women made another important gain. At that time 18 women were elected to the United States House of Representatives.

■ *What important political gain was made by women in late 1974?*

Social Unrest. President Nixon worked to end American involvement in South Vietnam after taking office in 1969. However, protests against the war went on while the President tried to end the fighting. Many of these protests were organized by college students. But there were also other groups of Americans who were against the war. Antiwar demonstrations took place in several American cities in October and November of 1969.

Then in April 1970, American soldiers were sent into Cambodia. This caused antiwar protests to be held at many colleges in the United

States. Unfortunately, some of these protests led to violence. For example, in May 1970, four students were killed at Kent State University in Ohio when the National Guard fired into a crowd. Many college students across the United States were outraged by these deaths. And a number of colleges closed for a time in protest against the shootings.

■ *For what reason did many colleges in the United States close for a time in the spring of 1970?*

Changes in the Early 1970's. One reason for the protests by college students was the *draft.* This was the means used by the government to choose people for the armed services. Many young Americans who believed the United States should get out of South Vietnam also believed that drafting people was wrong.

In 1970 President Nixon asked a group of people to study the draft. This group reported that our country should work toward having all-volunteer armed forces. In 1973 the United States stopped drafting people after the cease-fire in South Vietnam ended American involvement there. Then the United States began depending on volunteers to meet the country's military needs. And in 1975 the United States stopped requiring young people to even register for the draft.

Another change that affected American society was an amendment to the Constitution passed in 1971. This change allowed more young Americans to take part in electing people to office. The Twenty-sixth Amendment lowered the voting age to 18 [*135-*136]. As a result, over 11 million young Americans were given the right to vote.

■ *In what way did the Twenty-sixth Amendment change the Constitution?*

Antiwar demonstrations spread throughout the country into the 1970's. Thousands of Americans expressed their opposition to continued American participation in the Vietnam conflict.

Constantine Manos/Magnum

The Achievements of Asian Americans. Throughout much of our history, Asian Americans have been the victims of racial discrimination and prejudice. Despite these obstacles, however, Asian Americans have made outstanding contributions to American life.

Since World War II, Asian Americans have served their country, holding political offices at the local, state, and national levels. Notable among them have been Hiram L. Fong, Daniel K. Inouye, and Spark M. Matsunaga in the Senate, and Patsy Takemoto Mink, Norman Y. Mineta, and Robert T. Matsui in the House. March Fong Eu was the first woman to be elected secretary of state of California.

In business, the arts, science, and education, Asian Americans have contributed to our country's growth and prosperity. For example, Wang Laboratories was begun by An Wang and today ranks among the largest of America's corporations. And in New York stands the World Trade Center, the creation of Minoru Yamasaki, one of the leading architects in America. In every aspect of life, Asian Americans are playing an increasing role in America's progress.

■ *Who was the first woman elected secretary of state of California?*

SECTION 3 REVIEW

1. *What was revenue sharing?*
2. *How did President Nixon feel about the busing of pupils to achieve a racial balance in public schools?*
3. *How have Asian Americans contributed to our country's growth and prosperity?*

4 The Ford Administration

Overview President Ford worked to build public trust in the government after taking office in 1974. Many Americans had lost faith in the government of our country as a result of the Watergate Affair. The President also tried to solve some of the problems facing our country. Inflation and recession were serious problems when Ford took office. In addition, President Ford tried to build friendship with other countries.

While the Watergate affair was ending, changes were taking place in the field of civil rights. Women benefited from these changes. Hispanics, Indians, and blacks were also helped by some of these changes.

President Ford was defeated in the race for the presidency by Jimmy Carter, Jr. Several public debates had been held between these two candidates.

Objectives After reading this section, you should be able to:

- list some of the problems facing President Ford after taking office in 1974;
- discuss the changes that took place in foreign affairs while President Ford was in office;
- explain how women, Hispanics, Indians, and blacks were affected by civil rights changes in 1974 and 1975.

Domestic Problems. After taking office in 1974 following President Nixon's resignation, President Ford faced many problems. One problem had to do with the Watergate Affair. This scandal had caused many Americans to lose faith in the government of our country. So President Ford worked to restore people's trust in the government.

President Ford also had problems in dealing with Congress. For example, the President and Congress did not agree on how to deal with our country's energy problems. There were also differences between President Ford and Congress over social welfare laws. Part of the reason for these differences was because President Ford was a Republican, while the majority of the members of Congress were Democrats.

In September 1975, two unsuccessful attempts were made to assassinate President Ford. Later, the President cut back on some of his travel plans because of these incidents.

■ *What problem did President Ford face as a result of the Watergate Affair?*

President Ford and the Economy. When President Ford took office in 1974, inflation and recession were serious economic problems in our country. By the end of the year about 6.5 million Americans were out of work. Car production was down, and fewer new homes were being built. But even though business activity was declining, prices were rising. Part of the reason for the growing inflation was because the price of oil had been raised by the countries who sold oil to the United States. Also, food prices had gone up because of poor crops in the United States in 1974.

President Ford developed a program to deal with inflation. His program was called WIN—Whip Inflation Now. President Ford believed that one way to fight inflation was to hold down government spending. As a result, the President vetoed many bills passed by Congress that involved spending large amounts of money. President Ford felt such spending would raise the demand for goods and, thus, cause prices to rise.

Toward the end of 1974, President Ford began to think about trying to stimulate the economy. One way to do this was by lowering taxes. If taxes were cut, people would have more money to spend. As this money was spent, the demand for goods would go up, and this would help business to grow. In early 1975, a bill lowering taxes temporarily was passed by Congress. Inflation began to slow. However, by 1975, unemployment remained high. More than 9 percent of the American work force was unemployed.

■ *In what way did President Ford want to stimulate the economy?*

President Ford and Foreign Affairs. After taking office in 1974, President Ford let other countries know that the foreign policy of the United States would not change. In November 1974, President Ford went to Japan, South Korea, and Vladivostok in the Soviet Union. At Vladivostok, the President met with Soviet Leader Leonid Brezhnev. A tentative arms limitation agreement was reached at this meeting. But the next year the United States and the Soviet Union failed to reach any further agreement on how to limit arms.

Dennis Brack/Black Star

In 1974, President Ford met with Leonid Brezhnev in Vladivostok in the Soviet Union to discuss arms limitation agreement.

In the summer of 1975, President Ford attended a meeting in Helsinki, Finland. Leaders from the Soviet Union and 33 other nations also attended the meeting. These leaders signed the Helsinki Accord. These nations agreed to work together for world peace. They also agreed to improve human rights.

While President Ford was in office, the United States also helped to ease some of the tensions in the Middle East. In September 1975 Israel and Egypt agreed to settle differences over some lands that had been taken by Israel in earlier fighting with Egypt. The agreement was reached with the help of the American Secretary of State, Henry Kissinger. Part of the agreement called for Americans to be stationed in the Middle East to make certain that both sides were following the agreement. Some people feared this might lead to another Vietnam-type of involvement for the United States. However, this did not happen.

In December 1975 President Ford visited China. This trip helped to improve relations between the United States and China.

■ *How did the United States help to ease tensions in the Middle East in 1975?*

Civil Rights. At the same time that the Watergate Affair was coming to an end in our country, changes were also taking place in the field of civil rights. For example, in 1974 the Supreme Court upheld a law that required that women be paid the same as men when doing the same work. Also in 1974, laws were passed to see that women were treated the same as men when trying to borrow money.

Black Americans also made political gains in 1974. Black mayors were elected in more than 100 American cities. However, there were racial problems in some cities in 1974. This happened when children were bused to schools to balance racial groups.

Early in 1975 President Ford signed a law that gave Indians greater control of their affairs. But there was fighting in 1975 between some Indian groups and law officers. This happened when the Indians took over certain lands and buildings to bring attention to the problems facing Indians. However, some Indian leaders believed that Indians should use the courts to further the cause of Indian rights.

A special bicentennial celebration took place in New York harbor.

In July 1975 Congress renewed the Voting Rights Act of 1965. The law was also extended to protect the voting rights of Hispanics and of Indians. This law outlawed the use of literacy tests to keep people from voting.

In what ways were women protected by a Supreme Court ruling in 1974?

The Bicentennial. While President Ford was in office, our country celebrated its two-hundredth birthday, or *bicentennial*. Special events were held all over the United States during 1976. On July 4, 1976, the Liberty Bell in Philadelphia was struck 13 times in remembrance of the original Thirteen Colonies.

During the bicentennial many countries sent their leaders or high-ranking diplomats to visit the United States. These people traveled around our country bringing greetings and good wishes to the American people. As the bicentennial celebrations ended, many Americans turned their attention to the coming presidential election of 1976.

For what reason were celebrations held throughout our country in 1976?

The Campaign and Election of 1976. In the spring and summer of 1976, American political parties began preparing to choose someone to run for President. During that time, party elections were held in each state. The members of each party voted for a person that they thought would be a good candidate for

In the 1976 election, Democrat Jimmy Carter received the greatest support from the South and from several states in the Northeast.

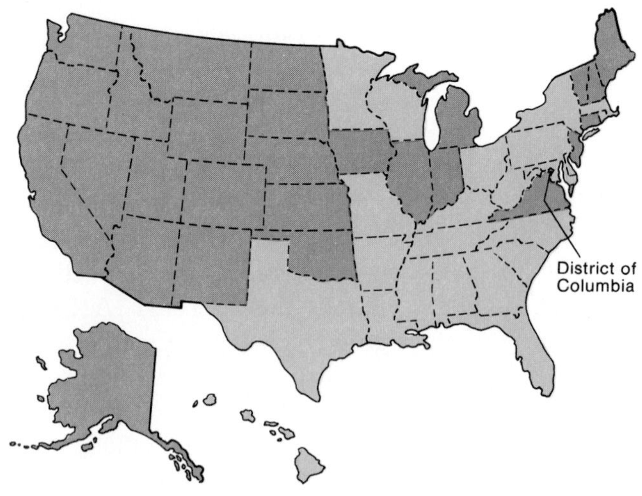

ELECTION OF 1976

	Electoral Votes	Popular Votes
Democratic James E. Carter	297	40,827,394
Republican Gerald R. Ford	241	39,145,977

President. These elections are called *primary elections*.

When the Democratic party met in July, James E. "Jimmy" Carter, Jr., a former governor of Georgia, had won most of the state primaries. As a result, Carter was chosen by the Democratic party to run for President. Senator Walter F. Mondale of Minnesota was chosen to run for Vice-President on the ticket with Carter.

The Republican party met in August 1976. Ronald Reagan, a former governor of California, challenged President Ford's bid to become the party's presidential nominee. Even though Reagan had strong support, the party chose President Ford to run for President. Senator Robert J. Dole of Kansas was chosen to run for Vice-President.

By the time the campaign started, inflation and recession were again causing problems in the American economy. The campaign centered on these problems as well as on foreign affairs. Several public debates were held between President Ford and Jimmy Carter.

The election in November was very close. Jimmy Carter won the election with a little more than 50 percent of the popular vote (see map on page 672).

■ *What were some of the problems upon which the 1976 presidential election campaign was centered?*

SECTION 4 REVIEW

1. *What was one reason that President Ford had problems in dealing with Congress while he was in office?*
2. *How did President Ford work to improve our country's relations with other countries?*
3. *Why did some Indian groups take over certain lands and buildings in 1975?*

CHAPTER 38 SUMMARY

Many changes took place in the relations of the United States with other countries while President Nixon was in office. In 1973 our country ended its part in the war in South Vietnam. The United States also improved its relations with China and with the Soviet Union. However, a serious political scandal involving the White House was made public in the early 1970's. As a result, President Nixon resigned in August 1974.

There were also economic problems in the United States during the early 1970's. In order to solve these problems, President Nixon tried to slow rising prices without causing a business slowdown. But inflation and recession continued to be economic problems.

President Ford worked to restore public trust in the government following the Watergate scandal. The President also tried to overcome economic problems and to build friendship with other countries.

CHAPTER 38 REVIEW

USING YOUR SKILLS

Interpreting a Bar Graph

Graphs are often used to show information about changes that affect the economy of a country. Below is a graph showing how the price of oil per barrel changed between December 1970 and January 1974. Study the graph and then answer the questions.

1. What was the price of a barrel of oil on June 1, 1971?
2. How much did the price of a barrel of oil change between December 31, 1970, and January 1, 1974?
3. According to the graph, during what year did the greatest number of changes take place in the price of a barrel of oil?
4. Based on the graph, what happened to the price of oil between October 16 and December 1, 1973?
5. Based on the graph, what was the lowest price charged for a barrel of oil?
6. According to the graph, what would probably be the trend of the price of oil in the years after 1974?

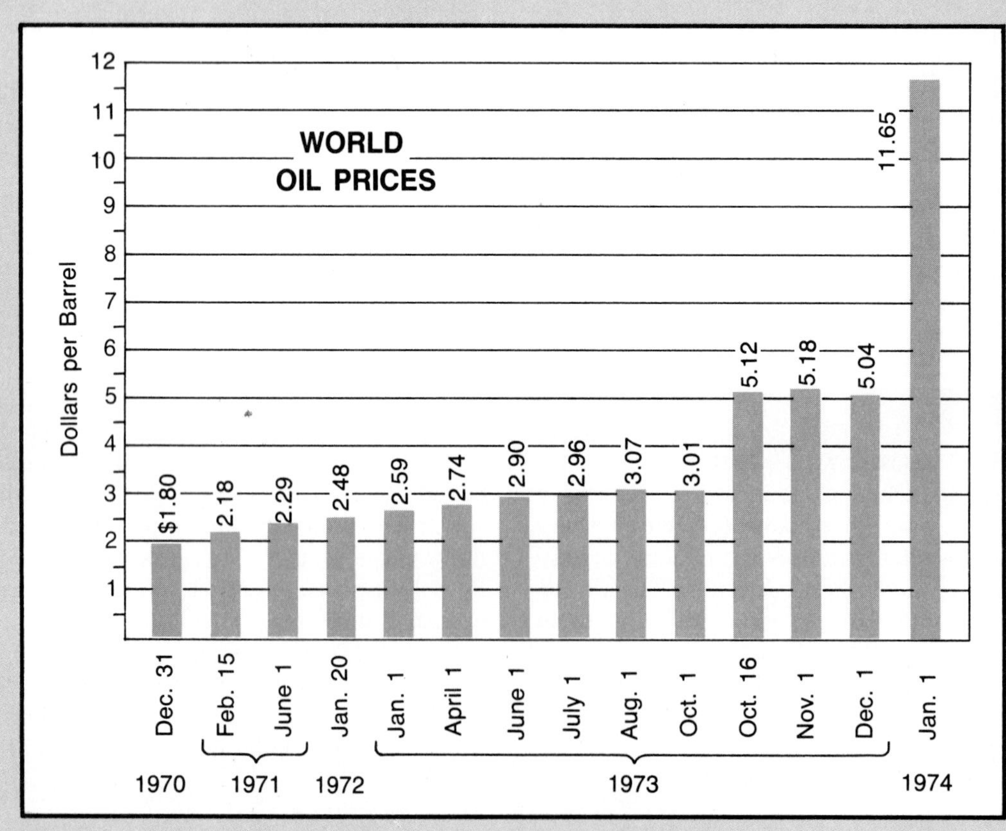

CHAPTER 38 REVIEW

YOU SHOULD KNOW

Identify, define, or explain each of the following:

Vietnamization
détente
executive privilege
revenue sharing
segregation
draft
bicentennial
primary elections

CHECKING FACTS

1. Who was the foreign-policy adviser to President Nixon?
2. What did the United States and the Soviet Union agree to when they signed the Nuclear Nonproliferation Treaty?
3. What was the Watergate Affair?
4. What steps did President Nixon take to slow inflation in 1971?
5. What caused a fuel crisis in the United States in 1973?
6. What was the Family Assistance Plan?
7. What was the goal of the National Women's Political Caucus?
8. What did the Twenty-sixth Amendment do?
9. What two economic problems did President Ford face in 1974?
10. In 1974, how were women protected by a Supreme Court ruling?

UNDERSTANDING CONCEPTS

1. Why did President Nixon visit the People's Republic of China in 1972?
2. Why did President Nixon resign in 1974?
3. How did the fuel shortage that began in the summer of 1973 affect the American economy?
4. Why were most black leaders disappointed with President Nixon's efforts for civil rights?
5. Why did President Ford want to lower taxes in 1975?

LEARNING FROM ILLUSTRATIONS

1. Study the map on page 659. According to the map, how many states supported Democrat George McGovern?
2. According to the chart on page 662, what food item increased in price the most between 1969 and 1974? What food item increased in price the least between 1969 and 1974?

CRITICAL THINKING

1. What, do you think, was President Nixon's greatest accomplishment as President of the United States? Why do you think this is so?
2. Some Americans were angry with President Ford for pardoning former President Nixon. Do you think President Ford was right or wrong for pardoning former President Nixon? Give reasons for your answer.
3. President Nixon felt that pupils should attend schools in their own neighborhoods rather than be bused to schools that were far away in order to achieve racial balance. How do you feel about the issue of busing?

ENRICHMENT ACTIVITIES

1. Research how relations between the United States and China have changed since President Nixon's visit there in 1972. Information might be found in encyclopedias and in newsmagazines. Then hold a discussion about the advantages and disadvantages of improving our country's relations with China.
2. Make a chart showing the effects of inflation during the 1970's. The chart should show the trends of prices of a number of standard items in recent years. Then discuss the effects of inflation with the class.

1980 1984 1988

- 1977 Department of Energy added to the cabinet
- 1979 Camp David Accords
  Americans held as hostages in Iran
- 1980 Ronald Reagan elected President
- 1983 United States invaded island of Grenada
- 1984 Congresswoman Geraldine Ferraro chosen as the first female vice-presidential candidate on a major party ticket
  President Reagan reelected
- 1987 Hearings held into the Iran-contra affair
- 1988 President Reagan and Mikhail Gorbachev held summit meeting in Moscow
- 1989 Vice-President George Bush elected President

CHAPTER 39

America: Yesterday, Today, and Tomorrow

Chapter Objectives

After studying this chapter, you will be able to:

- explain the domestic and foreign problems that affected our country after President Carter was elected President;
- discuss President Reagan's economic and foreign policies;
- analyze the challenges and problems faced by the United States in the late 1980's.

1 The Carter Years

Overview After taking office, President Carter faced many problems. There was a growing energy shortage, and the economy was in trouble. During the late 1970's, many changes took place in foreign affairs. Our country signed new treaties dealing with the Panama Canal. And the United States set up diplomatic relations with Communist China. But there were problems with other countries.

Objectives After reading this section, you will be able to:

- identify the economic problems that developed in our country during the 1970's;
- explain how President Carter tried to improve relations between the United States and other countries;
- discuss the difficult foreign problems faced by our country in 1980.

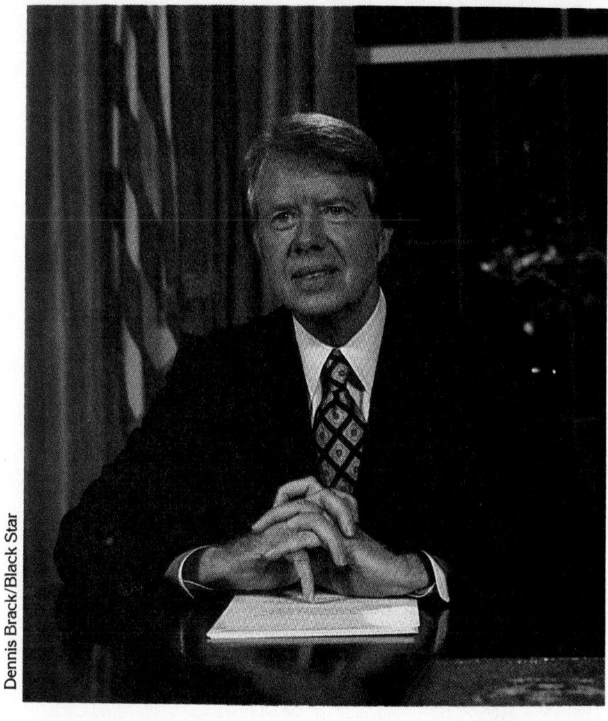

Dennis Brack/Black Star

After his election, Jimmy Carter pledged to restore people's confidence in the national government.

President Carter and Domestic Affairs. One problem that President Carter faced after taking office was the growing energy shortage in our country. In 1977, the United States continued to import more than 40 percent of its oil needs of nearly 18 million barrels a day. Most of this oil came from the Organization of Petroleum Exporting Countries (OPEC). A number of OPEC members had increased the price of oil by 400 percent since 1973. The high cost of oil added to inflation and weakened the American dollar.

Early in 1977, President Carter sent an energy plan to Congress. This plan was changed many times before it was passed. The energy bills that Congress finally passed in October 1978 provided incentives for increased production aimed at the oil and gas industry. The bills also provided incentives for homeowners who took energy-saving measures. The Department of Energy was set up in 1977. This new department tried to find ways to meet the country's future energy needs.

In January 1979, an energy crisis once again affected all Americans. A revolution in Iran toppled the government of Shah Mohammad Reza Pahlavi. Within a few weeks, Iranian production and shipment of oil stopped. At

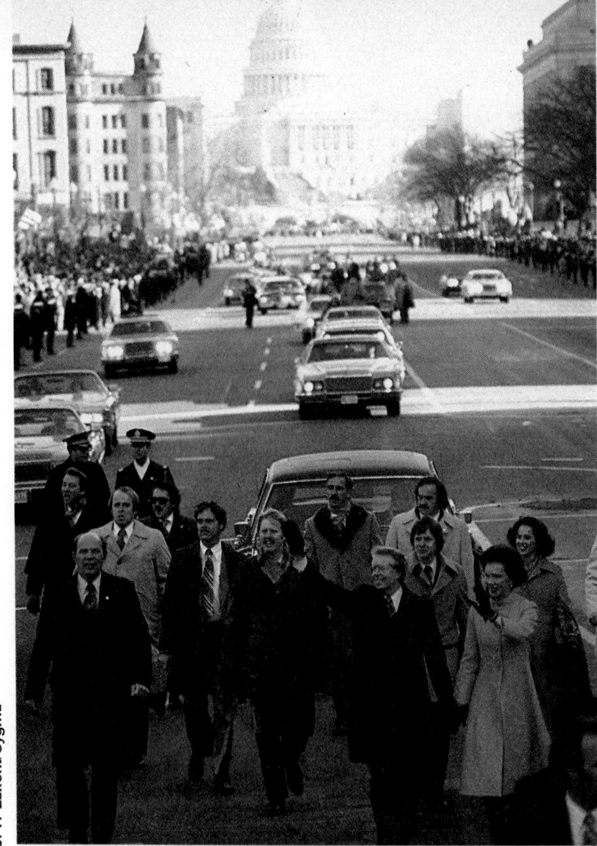

J. P. Laffont/Sygma

President Carter began his administration with acts of informality in an effort to remain close to the people of the nation. After he took the oath of office, Carter and his wife, Rosalynn, and their daughter walked down Pennsylvania Avenue to the White House rather than riding in a limousine.

that time, Iran accounted for about ten percent of the world's production of crude oil.

Because of the problem in Iran and the oil shortage that resulted, the demand for oil on the world market was greater than the supply. In the United States, the cost of gasoline and of all other oil products rose. As a result, in July 1979 President Carter sent another energy plan to Congress. One part of this plan called for a corporation to be set up to develop new ways to make fuel from coal and from oil-rich shale rock.

President Carter also worked to help the schools of our country. In October 1979, a new cabinet office, the Department of Education, was set up. The Secretary of Education, Shirley M. Hufstedler, promised that the new department would help schools raise their academic standards.

■ *What was the purpose of the Department of Energy that was set up in 1977?*

Economic Problems for President Carter. At the time President Carter took office in 1977, the United States continued to face the problems of high unemployment and rising inflation. Nearly 7 percent of the labor force was out of work. The cost of living was rising at an annual rate of about 6 percent. At the same time, our country faced a record trade deficit. That is, the United States was importing more goods than it was exporting. The trade deficit was largely the result of huge imports of steel, automobiles, textiles, shoes, and especially oil.

To solve the problem of unemployment, Congress passed a multibillion-dollar program to create thousands of jobs and, at the same time, to cut taxes to increase consumer spending. Congress also increased the minimum wage. These measures, however, produced only limited results.

The rise in government spending to fight unemployment helped to increase inflation. In order to deal with the rising inflation, President Carter changed his economic plans. Part of his plans called for Congress to cut spending for domestic programs and to limit the increases in defense spending.

But Carter's anti-inflation plans were unsuccessful. By 1979, inflation had grown worse. Prices were about 13 percent higher than they had been at the end of 1978. Then in 1980, the economy moved into a recession. Housing construction and automobile production went down. As workers in these industries were laid off, unemployment rose. By mid-1980, about 8 percent of the work force was unemployed. In the fall of 1980, however, there were signs that the economy was improving.

■ *What happened to the economy in 1980?*

Civil Rights Developments. The late 1970's were years when civil rights groups kept working toward the goal of fair treatment for all Americans. In 1978, the deadline for passing the Equal Rights Amendment (ERA) to the Constitution was extended to 1982.

There were also some improvements for American Indians during the late 1970's. As energy problems grew worse, a number of Indian tribes found that their lands had become very valuable. That was because these lands contained such resources as coal. And while President Carter was in office, a Blackfoot Indian, Forrest G. Gerard, was chosen to be assistant secretary of the interior for Indian affairs.

But problems continued for America's minority groups. In May 1980, riots broke out in Miami, Florida. The violence left a number of people dead and destroyed many businesses. The direct cause of the disorder was anger over police treatment of blacks. But outrage among blacks over unemployment and inflation was a deeper cause of the riots.

■ *What victory was achieved by women's rights groups in 1978?*

DO YOU KNOW?

Who was the first black woman to be appointed to the President's cabinet?

The first black woman to be appointed to the President's cabinet was Patricia Roberts Harris. In 1977 she was appointed the Secretary of Housing and Urban Development in President Carter's cabinet. When President Carter made several changes in the cabinet in 1979, Ms. Harris was made the new head of the Department of Health, Education, and Welfare. Earlier, while President Johnson was in office, Ms. Harris was appointed as the American ambassador to Luxembourg. Thus, Ms. Harris was also the first black woman to serve as an ambassador to another country.

Liaison Agency

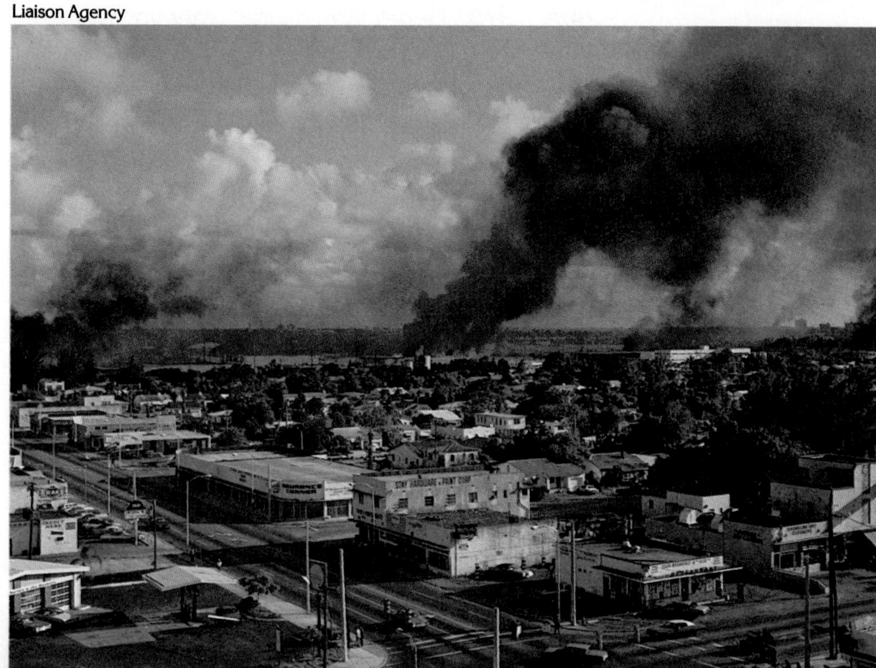

Riots in Miami during the spring of 1980 involved a 240-square-block area known as Liberty City. Fires continued burning in the area on the morning after the outbreak of violence.

Efforts to Improve Foreign Relations. From the beginning of his administration, President Carter tried to set a different tone for the conduct of American foreign policy. He spoke out strongly for the cause of human rights throughout the world. Carter criticized *apartheid*—racial segregation—by the governments of South Africa and Rhodesia. President Carter also criticized the harsh treatment of Soviet *dissidents* by the Soviet government. Dissidents are opponents to a government's policies. In some cases, Carter restricted or cut off military aid and trade with nations accused of violating human rights.

Shortly after taking office in 1977, President Carter stated the goals of his foreign policy. One of these goals was to reach a new agreement with Panama over the Panama Canal. In September 1977, President Carter and the chief of the government of Panama, Brigadier General Omar Torrijos Herrera, signed two new treaties relating to the canal. In these treaties, the United States agreed to give complete control of the canal to Panama by the year 2000. Both countries also agreed that the United States would have the right to protect the neutrality of the canal. The treaties were approved by the Senate in 1978.

Another change relating to foreign policy took place in January 1979. At that time the United States set up diplomatic relations with the People's Republic of China—Communist China. Our country had been moving toward closer ties with Communist China since the early 1970's.

During 1979, President Carter also signed a second Strategic Arms Limitation Treaty, known as SALT II, with the Soviet Union. The idea behind SALT II was to reach a balance of nuclear weapons so that neither nation would attack the other. However, the treaty met with opposition in the Senate from those who believed that the United States had made too many concessions. But when the Soviet Union invaded Afghanistan in December 1979, the hopes for Senate ratification ended.

■ *How did the treaties signed in 1977 by the United States and Panama affect the Panama Canal?*

Camp David Accords. As President Carter took office in 1977, conflict in the Middle East continued. Then in November 1977, President Anwar el-Sadat of Egypt and Israeli Prime Minister Menachem Begin laid the groundwork for peace negotiations between the two countries. But troubles in the peace negotiations soon developed.

At this point, President Carter directly intervened and invited Sadat and Begin to meet with him at Camp David. After several days of talks the three leaders announced that they had come to an agreement that would provide a framework for peace. This agreement was known as the Camp David Accords. Then in April 1979, Begin and Sadat met in Washington to sign a peace treaty. This treaty ended the state of war that had existed between the two countries for thirty years. Egypt became the first Arab nation to formally recognize Israel's right to exist.

President Carter was praised for his efforts to bring peace to the Middle East. However, most Arab nations rejected the Camp David Accords. They also denounced Egypt for entering into this agreement. So by the end of 1979, hopes for peace in the Middle East had faded.

■ *What was the result of the Camp David Accords?*

Abbas/Magnum

Public demonstrations in the streets of Tehran supporting the Ayatollah.

Peter Marlow/Magnum

In January 1981, the 52 American hostages received a warm and happy homecoming.

Foreign Problems. One of the most important foreign problems for the United States began in 1979. Early that year, the *shah*—the king—of Iran, Shah Mohammad Reza Pahlavi, was forced from power. A religious leader, Ayatollah Khomeini, became the leader of the country. Then, in November 1979, several hundred Iranians took over the American Embassy in the capital city, Tehran. More than 50 Americans were taken hostage. The Iranians were angry at the United States for allowing the shah to come to our country for medical treatment. At first, there was strong public support for President Carter in his efforts to free the hostages. The President's popularity went up. Then, in April 1980, the United States tried to free the hostages by force. But the rescue mission failed. As the crisis dragged on, it became an issue in the 1980 election. Finally, a settlement with Iran was arranged, and the hostages were released on January 20, 1981.

Another problem for the United States began in late 1979. The Soviet Union invaded Afghanistan in December. In protest, the United States and a number of other countries boycotted the 1980 summer Olympic Games held in Moscow. The United States also cut back its trade with the Soviet Union. At the same time, the United States moved to strengthen its armed forces. In July 1980, young men were once again required to register for the draft. This was done to increase America's military preparedness. As the presidential election of 1980 drew near, most Americans knew that whoever was chosen faced many challenging foreign problems.

■ *Why did the United States boycott the 1980 summer Olympic Games?*

The 1980 Presidential Election. During the summer of 1980, the two major parties held conventions to choose presidential candidates.

The Republicans met in Detroit in July. Former Governor Ronald Reagan of California was supported by most members of the party. He was chosen by the Republicans to run for President. George Bush was chosen to run for Vice-President.

The Democrats met in New York City in August. Senator Edward Kennedy of Massachusetts tried to gain the nomination. But President Carter won the party's nomination for a second term. Vice-President Walter Mondale was chosen as President Carter's running mate.

One interesting feature of the 1980 campaign was the emergence of another important presidential candidate. John Anderson, a member of Congress from Illinois, had hoped to be chosen by the Republican party to run for President. But when Ronald Reagan gained the support of most Republicans, Anderson decided to run as an independent, third-party candidate. In August, Anderson chose former Wisconsin Governor Patrick Lucey as a vice-presidential running mate.

The election campaign centered on economic problems—inflation and recession—and on foreign affairs. Two public debates were held. The candidates presented ideas on how to deal with the problems facing our country. In the November election, Ronald Reagan overwhelmingly defeated President Carter, while John Anderson ran far behind (see map on this page). However, none of the candidates seemed able to inspire all the voters. As a result only 54 percent of those 18 or older voted in the 1980 election.

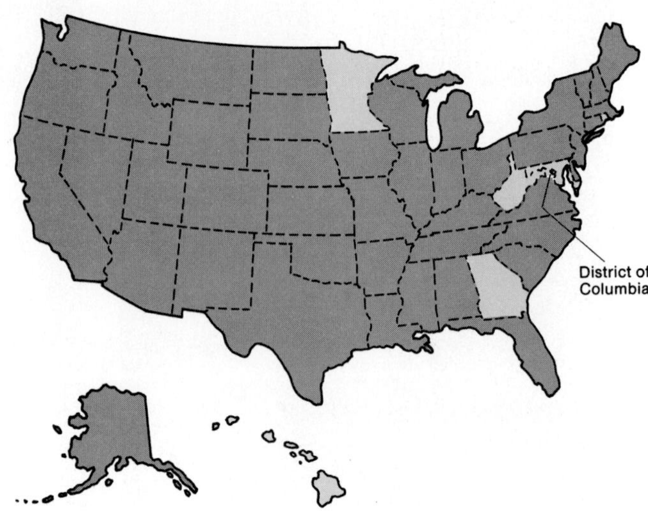

ELECTION OF 1980

	Electoral Votes	Popular Votes
Republican Ronald W. Reagan	489	43,899,248
Democratic James E. Carter	49	35,481,435

Republican Ronald Reagan defeated President Carter in the 1980 election by winning large popular-vote majorities in all sections of the country.

■ *Who were the presidential candidates in the 1980 election?*

SECTION 1 REVIEW

1. *What were President Carter's plans to help solve unemployment in the late 1970's?*
2. *How did President Carter try to improve relations between the United States and Communist China?*
3. *Why did Iranians take 50 Americans hostages in November 1979?*

2 The Reagan Administration

Overview President Reagan faced serious economic problems when he took office in 1981. The President called for a plan consisting of tax cuts and spending cuts to deal with these problems. By the end of his second term, the economy began to show some signs of stability.

President Reagan took a strong stand in dealing with the Soviet Union and built up America's military power. Although relations with the Soviet Union were strained during the President's first term, by the end of his administration they improved greatly. The President also faced problems with other foreign countries during his administration.

Objectives After reading this section, you will be able to:

- identify the economic problems the United States faced during President Reagan's administration;
- evaluate the relations between the United States and the Soviet Union during the 1980's;
- discuss the problems the United States faced in Central America and in the Middle East during the 1980's.

President Reagan's Economic Policy. At the time President Reagan took office in 1981, the economy suffered from high unemployment and severe inflation. The President quickly proposed a plan to Congress to deal with these problems. This plan called for large tax cuts in both personal and business income. It called for cuts in federal job programs and other federal social programs. The plan also called for a large increase in defense spending. The President's economic program was called Reaganomics.

Congress passed most of President Reagan's economic plan by August 1981. President Reagan also took other measures to try to improve the nation's economy. For example, he lifted some government regulations on business that he believed led to more costs than benefits for both business and consumers. The President also opened up some public lands for private development by mining, lumber, and oil companies. Some business groups felt that this step would help ease the energy shortage and create new jobs. Other groups, however, feared that the private development of public lands might harm the environment.

■ *Why were some groups opposed to the private development of public lands?*

A Troubled Economy. Despite President Reagan's efforts to stimulate the economy, the country was in a deep recession by the summer of 1982. Thousands of businesses failed and unemployment reached nearly 12 percent of the work force. The construction of new housing and the production of automobiles fell to their lowest levels in several years.

During the recession, high unemployment led to a sharp loss in tax revenue. Because many federal social programs had been cut, the increase in the number of unemployed workers strained the ability of state and local governments to provide help. At the same time, government spending for defense increased greatly. This led to a growing deficit in the federal budget. In order to lower the deficit, Congress raised taxes in the late summer of 1982. The federal deficit, however, continued to grow throughout 1983 and 1984.

Steve Kelley/The San Diego Union

This cartoon shows what many business and financial leaders feel is a threat to the nation's continued economic recovery.

The bright spot in the nation's economy during these years was a drop in the rate of inflation. This decline, which was partly due to a fall in the price of oil, helped spark an economic recovery. By early 1984, interest rates had declined somewhat, consumer spending had increased, and unemployment had dropped. Moreover, the output of goods and services expanded and stock prices rose.

President Reagan hoped to reduce the huge federal deficit. However, economic growth was slow. This resulted in another record deficit in 1986 that exceeded $200 billion. In 1986, Congress followed up on President Reagan's plan to establish a new, simplified tax system. This system included lower tax rates on individual and corporation income taxes.

The economy suffered a severe setback on October 19, 1987. On that day, Black Monday, the stock market recorded its largest one-day loss ever. Several reasons were given for the 1987 stock-market crash. Some analysts concluded that the stocks were simply overvalued and just ready for a fall. Other analysts, however, believed that the crash was the result of government policies. They pointed to the growing federal deficit. Some economists predicted that the prices of stock would continue to fall and that the economy would plunge into a recession. But the prices of stock did not continue to fall, and the economy did not enter into a recession. By the end of 1988, unemployment had decreased to a 14-year low, and inflation remained low.

■ *What happened to the stock market on October 19, 1987?*

Assassination Attempt. In March 1981, President Reagan was shot as he left a hotel in Washington, D.C., where he had addressed a labor meeting. The President's press secretary and two other persons were also wounded in the attack. Vice-President George Bush, who had been in Texas at the time of the shooting, returned immediately to Washington to take charge during the emergency.

By the end of April, President Reagan had fully recovered from his wounds and had resumed his duties as President. After a trial that lasted several weeks, the accused assailant was found not guilty by reason of insanity. He was sent to a mental hospital in Washington, D.C.

■ *What happened to President Reagan's accused assailant?*

The 1984 Election. The two major political parties held conventions during the summer of 1984 to nominate presidential candidates. The Democrats nominated former Vice-President Walter Mondale. In a historic step, Mondale picked Congresswoman Geraldine Ferraro of New York as his running mate. This was the first time in American history that a woman was chosen as a vice-presidential candidate on a major party ticket. President Reagan easily won the Republican party's nomination for a second term. Vice-President George Bush was again chosen as Reagan's running mate. The campaign focused on issues such as the federal budget deficit and arms control.

In November, President Reagan won the election by an overwhelming landslide. The President, however, did not sweep other Republican candidates into office on his coattails, as some Republican party leaders had hoped for. The balance of power in the Congress remained much the same as it had been in the last Congress, with the Republicans controlling the Senate and the Democrats controlling the House of Representatives. Despite massive voter-registration drives by both major political parties, only about 53 percent of those 18 or older voted in the 1984 election.

Who was chosen as Walter Mondale's running mate in the 1984 presidential campaign?

Relations With the Soviet Union. One of the major goals of President Reagan's foreign policy was to take a strong stand in dealing with the Soviet Union. President Reagan believed that the Soviet Union held a military advantage over the United States in terms of the number and the power of its weapons. So the President called for a quick buildup of America's military power. Our country's forces were strengthened and modernized, and new weapons, such as the neutron bomb and the MX missile, were built.

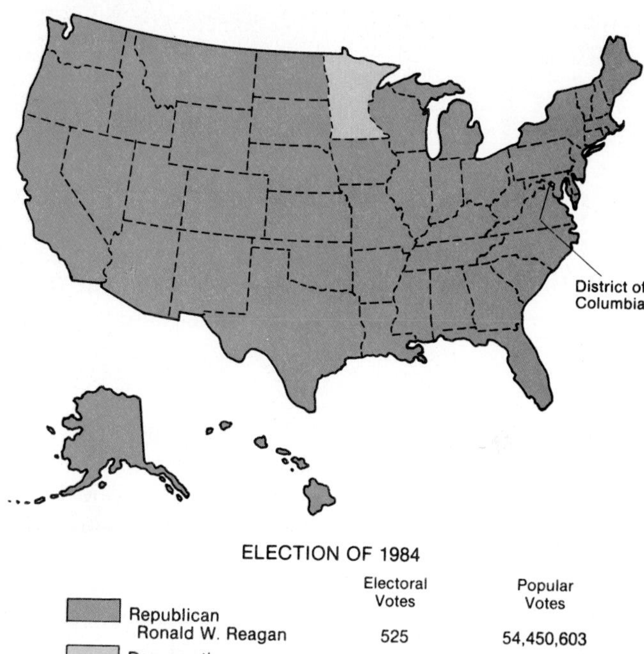

ELECTION OF 1984

	Electoral Votes	Popular Votes
Republican Ronald W. Reagan	525	54,450,603
Democratic Walter F. Mondale	13	37,573,671

President Ronald Reagan won an impressive victory over Democratic challenger Walter Mondale in the 1984 election.

During President Reagan's first term, relations between the United States and the Soviet Union grew colder. The two countries, however, continued to discuss ways to limit nuclear weapons. President Reagan proposed a plan for new arms talks—called the Strategic Arms Reduction Talks (START)—between the United States and the Soviet Union. This plan called for both countries to cut back their arsenal of nuclear weapons. The talks were held in Geneva, Switzerland, in June 1982, but they ended before any agreements between the two countries were reached. In December 1983, the Soviets left the talks in protest over the

RECALLING THE TIMES

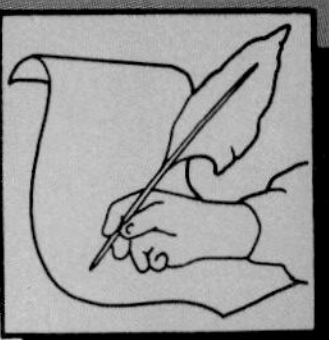

An Historic Moment

Walter Mondale, the Democratic nominee for President in 1984, announced his decision to pick Congresswoman Geraldine Ferraro of New York as his running mate on Thursday, July 12, 1984. The following excerpt, from the July 23, 1984, issue of *Time* magazine, describes the historic announcement and the country's reaction to it:

"One last point," he [Mondale] says, his voice making its usual high climb but betraying no awareness that he is about to deliver the line of his life: "This is an exciting choice." Quickly he looks down at the rostrum, hunting for the next sentence in the speech. He continues: "I want to build a future." Wait. The audience is clapping. Walter Mondale appears surprised. They seem to be giving an ovation to his previous remark. Perking up like a bird, he acknowledges the woman standing to his right, as if seeing her for the first time. He smiles, she smiles back. The applause grows loud. "Let me say that again," says the delighted Mondale. "*This* is an *exciting* choice!" The crowd goes wild. Mondale is clapping too. Does he know yet what he has done?

Does *anyone* know what happened midday last Thursday in the Minnesota statehouse? If this were Great Britain or India, whose pulse would race? But *here*? It couldn't happen here. The professionals think they can explain it.... Of course, the gender gap is the key to everything: more women, more votes. Got it. But wasn't something else involved in Mondale's decision to propose a woman for Vice President of the United States? Or did we

L. Walker/Gamma-Liaison

only imagine that the nation whooped, quaked, froze, beamed?

But in the long run, what happened in Minnesota was not just politics. The selection of Ferraro will affect not only the woman in the voting booth. It will be equally felt by the man who—today, next month, next year—stares across his desk, dining-room table or bed sheets and sees someone as if for the first time. There is no analogue to lean on, no sentimentalization to rely on, nothing Americans can do now but work the matter out for themselves and see where the rejiggled republic stands. The world's most powerful nation may be ready to be led by a woman, and any woman at all may prepare herself to lead it. This is an exciting choice.

Thinking Critically

Why do you think Walter Mondale's choice for running mate was called "an exciting choice?"

In your opinion, will the United States have a female President in the near future? Give reasons for your answer.

American decision to put nuclear weapons in West Germany for the defense of Western Europe.

In 1985, President Reagan and Soviet leader Mikhail Gorbachev met in Geneva, Switzerland. This meeting helped to ease the tensions between the two countries. The Soviet Union and the United States agreed to educational, scientific, and cultural exchanges. In 1986, the two leaders met in Reykjavik, Iceland. The purpose of this meeting was to discuss arms reductions, but no agreement was reached. In June 1988, President Reagan and Mr. Gorbachev held a summit meeting in Moscow. The two leaders signed two accords on nuclear tests. They also signed agreements on cooperation in scientific, cultural, and transportation affairs.

■ *What was the result of the Moscow summit meeting between the Soviet Union and the United States in June 1988?*

Problems in Central America. The United States faced difficult problems in Central America during the early 1980's. In 1979, a leftist government came to power in Nicaragua. This government began sending arms to leftist guerrillas who were trying to set up Communist governments in El Salvador and in other Central American countries. As a result, our government cut off all economic aid to Nicaragua and began supporting a group of Nicaraguans, called *contras*, who sought to overthrow the Nicaraguan government.

In 1983 and in 1984 the United States aided the contras in placing mines in the Nicaraguan harbors. The Reagan administration had hoped the mines would slow arms shipments to El Salvador. Some people opposed United States aid to the contras. In 1984 Congress voted against further aid, but restored the aid in 1986.

In October 1983, the United States invaded the Caribbean island of Grenada, mainly to protect Americans on the island after leftist rebels overthrew the government. Moreover, President Reagan charged that the Soviet Union and Cuba were preparing to use Grenada as a military base. American troops won control of the island after three days. The Grenadian people then made plans to form a new government. Most of the American forces were withdrawn a few months later.

■ *Why did President Reagan send troops to Grenada?*

Tension in the Middle East. Conflicts in the Middle East continued in the early 1980's. In June 1982, Israel invaded Lebanese territory after suffering repeated attacks by Palestine Liberation Organization (PLO) groups based in Lebanon. The PLO represents the Palestinian Arabs. Its chief goal is to form a separate Palestinian state from territory controlled by Israel. After a cease-fire arrangement between the Israeli army and members of the PLO had been worked out, President Reagan sent U.S. marines to Lebanon as part of a multinational peacekeeping force. This peacekeeping force was to help the government in Lebanon restore its authority and was to help with the withdrawal of all foreign troops. In October 1983, however, terrorists bombed the U.S. marine headquarters in Lebanon, killing 241 Americans. As a result, President Reagan decided to pull all American forces out of Lebanon in March 1984.

■ *Why did President Reagan send marines to Lebanon in the early 1980's?*

Combating Terrorism. President Reagan tried to stop increasing terrorism in the world. In October 1985 Palestinian terrorists hijacked the Italian cruise ship *Achille Lauro* and killed an American passenger before surrendering to Egyptian authorities. President Reagan ordered the U.S. Navy jets to stop the Egyptian airliner carrying the terrorists. The U.S. jets forced the airliner to land in Sicily. There the hijackers were arrested.

In April 1986, a U.S. serviceman was killed and others were hurt when terrorists bombed a nightclub in West Berlin. U.S. officials believed that agents of Libya were involved. Reagan then ordered U.S. air strikes against military centers and suspected terrorist centers in the Libyan cities of Tripoli and Benghazi.

■ *Why did President Reagan order air strikes against two Libyan cities in 1986?*

The Iran-Contra Affair. The Reagan administration came under criticism in November 1986. It was then that the American public learned that the United States illegally sold weapons to Iran and used the profits to help the Nicaraguan contras. At first, both activities were secret operations. The arms sales were done to win the freedom of several Americans held hostage by Lebanese terrorists friendly to Iran. But at the time, the United States had a policy that prohibited the sale of weapons to Iran and other nations that were considered to be supporters of terrorists. Many countries friendly to the United States criticized the arms sale.

The transfer of funds to support the contras occurred in the mid-1980's. At that time Congress prohibited aid to the contras. However, President Reagan said that he did not know about the fund diversion. Both the arms sale and the fund transfer were carried out by some members of the National Security Council (NSC), a White House agency. In 1987, Congress held televised hearings into what became known as the Iran-contra affair. These hearings pointed to an attempt by members of the NSC to keep the fact of the arms sale and the aid to the contras from Congress.

Sherbell/Picture Group

One of the highlights of the hearings into the Iran-contra affair was the testimony of Lieutenant Colonel Oliver North, a member of the National Security Council staff.

■ *Why did the United States begin to sell arms to Iran?*

The 1988 Election. During the summer of 1988 the two major political parties held conventions to nominate presidential candidates. The Democrats met in Atlanta in July. Governor Michael Dukakis of Massachusetts won the party's nomination for President. Senator Lloyd Bentsen of Texas was chosen as Governor Dukakis's running mate. The Republicans held their convention in New Orleans in August. Vice-President George Bush was chosen to run for President. Senator Dan Quayle of Indiana was chosen to run for Vice-President.

The election campaign centered on issues such as the economy, defense spending, and the federal deficit. Two public debates were held by the presidential candidates, and one debate was held by the vice-presidential candidates.

An interesting feature of the 1988 campaign was the importance of the media. As in 1960, television was an important factor in the 1988 campaign. However, the candidates generally stayed away from spontaneous contact with the press. Rather, their appearances were staged so as to present the most positive image. The press was criticized for not pointing out exaggerations and distortions brought out by each candidate about the other one's record.

In the November election, Vice-President George Bush defeated Governor Michael Dukakis (see map on this page). Voter turnout in the 1988 election was very low. Only 50 percent of the qualified voters took part in the election.

After the election, Vice-President George Bush proceeded to prepare for his presidency. By December 1988 he had appointed several cabinet members. These included James A. Baker III for Secretary of State, Nicholas Brady for Treasury Secretary, Jack Kemp for Housing and Urban Development, Elizabeth Dole for Secretary of Labor, and Louis Sullivan for Health and Human Services. Then on January 20, 1989, George Bush was inaugurated as the forty-first President of the United States.

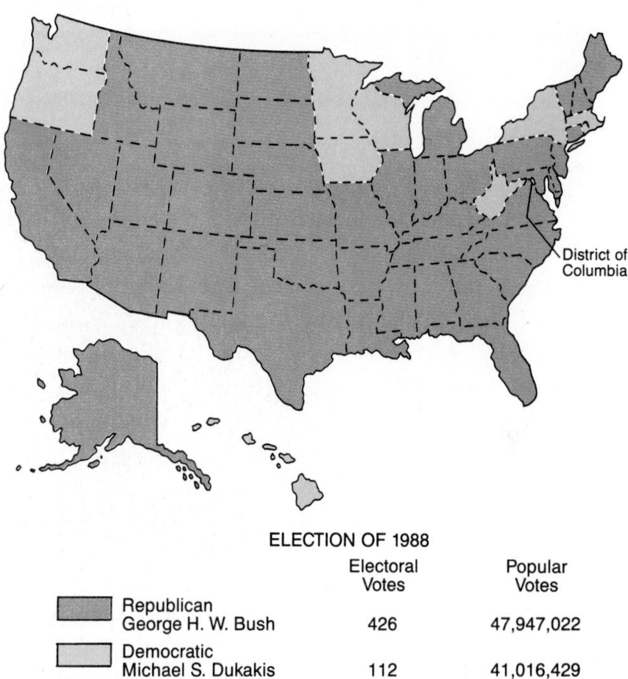

ELECTION OF 1988

	Electoral Votes	Popular Votes
Republican George H. W. Bush	426	47,947,022
Democratic Michael S. Dukakis	112	41,016,429

What was Vice-President George Bush's margin of victory in electoral votes in the election of 1988?

■ *What factor played an important part in the 1988 campaign?*

SECTION 2 REVIEW

1. *What reasons did some analysts give for the October 1987 stock market crash?*
2. *How did the meetings in 1986 and in 1988 between the Soviet Union and the United States end?*
3. *Why did the United States cut off all economic aid to Nicaragua in the 1980's?*

3 American Society in Transition

Overview Technology has changed rapidly in recent years. Communication advances, computer technology, and medical advances have changed the way people live. The United States faced many challenges by the late 1980's. Among the challenges were energy issues, pollution, and the problems of a changing population. Poverty, low incomes, and an increase in homelessness presented serious problems for our country.

Objectives After reading this section, you will be able to:

- identify some of the changes brought about by advances in communication, computer technology, and medicine;
- discuss some of the challenges facing the United States in terms of energy, pollution, and a changing population;
- analyze the causes of poverty and homelessness in the United States today.

Advances in Communication. Space technology has been important in providing information about neighboring planets and distant galaxies. In addition, space technology has resulted in advances in communication. Today radio waves, telephone calls, and television images can be bounced off satellites in space. This allows almost instant communication between any two points on earth. Television viewers in our country can watch news events as they happen halfway around the world. Television weather reports include images from weather satellites. These images have brought greater accuracy in weather forecasting.

Television has become an important influence on Americans' lives. More than 98 percent of the homes in the United States have at least one television set. Television has become a major way of reaching people through advertising messages. In the mid-1980's, over $18 billion dollars was spent on television advertising in the United States. In addition, television advertising has greatly affected the way public officials are elected to office. Before television, political candidates relied on public appearances to get votes. Today, candidates rely heavily on television to communicate with voters.

Video cassette recorders (VCRs), which are devices that record visual images and sound on magnetic tape, have become an important part of home entertainment systems in the 1980's. People use VCRs to tape television programs while they are away or while they are watching a program on another channel. People rent or buy prerecorded cassettes of sports events, movies, and other programs. People also use portable videotape recorders, which include a video camera, to make home movies.

What do political candidates today rely on to communicate with voters?

The Computer Age. The 1980's saw advances in computer technology. These advances have resulted in creating hundreds of thousands of new jobs in the areas of computer design, programming, repair, and selling. Computers are a multibillion-dollar business, and therefore play an important part in the American economy. The use of computers is likely to grow in the future.

Computers have changed the way people live. Today many American homes have computers and computer-controlled devices. Computer games and computer-aided teaching machines have become popular. Many Americans have personal computers, which are desk-top or portable computers. These kinds of computers are designed for general-purpose use, such as keeping account of household expenses and storing income tax information. Many Americans also own microwave ovens and other appliances equipped with computing devices. In the mid-1980's, the number of personal computers used for educational purposes in public elementary and secondary schools has increased greatly.

The sales of personal computers for use in the home have fallen somewhat in the late 1980's. This is due in large part to an oversupply of products and an overcrowding of companies into the market. Some people are questioning the usefulness of a home computer. Many people feel that it is more efficient to keep hand-written records for things such as grocery lists, recipes, and check books.

Why do computers play an important part in the American economy?

Medical Advances. The 1980's saw many advances in medicine. The *laser*—energy released as a highly concentrated beam of light—can burn away harmful tissue. As a result, the laser has become an important tool in surgery. Radioactive elements have been used successfully in treating some cancers. Also, *organ transplants*—the substitution of a healthy organ, such as a heart or kidney, for an unhealthy one—have become very common. But advances in medicine have made medical care very expensive. Few people today can afford the best medical care without some kind of financial aid.

On the other hand, because of advances in medical technology, Americans have been living longer and healthier lives. In addition, advances in medicine have brought about a change in the makeup of the American population. People are living longer and, at the same time, American families are tending to have fewer children. As a result, the proportion of Americans who are over 65 years old is growing.

What advances in medical technology have been made in recent years?

Energy Issues. One of the most important challenges facing the United States today is energy development. Americans are dependent on fossil fuels—oil, coal, and natural gas—for their energy needs. But fossil fuels may be exhausted in the future if Americans continue to use these fuels at the present rate. The United States has a large supply of coal. But the greater use of coal to meet energy needs would add to our country's pollution problems.

Nuclear energy is a possible replacement for fossil fuels as a source of energy. Nuclear power plants can produce a large amount of the electrical energy our country requires. But the use of nuclear power has created problems. The major problem is safety. Although a nuclear explosion at a nuclear power plant is highly unlikely, an accident can cause radioactivity to be released into the air. The radioactivity causes concern for people's safety. Another danger of nuclear power is the disposal of radioactive waste from nuclear power plants. Some of this waste has been buried in the ground. Some of it has been dumped into the sea. Much of this waste will remain dangerous for years to come. The fear is that the material may, in time, seep out of its containers, risking people's safety. Because of these problems, the future of nuclear power is doubtful.

An accident at the Three Mile Island nuclear plant near Harrisburg, Pennsylvania, in April 1979 caused many Americans to question the safety of nuclear power.

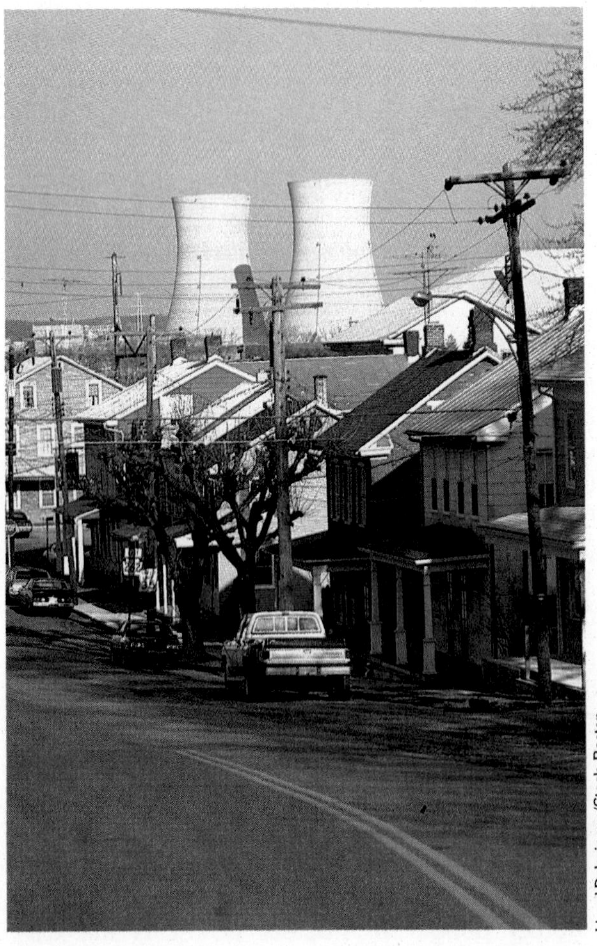
Lionel Delevingne/Stock, Boston

The depletion of fossil fuels and the dangers of nuclear energy make it necessary to look for alternative sources of energy. These sources of energy include *solar power*—power using the sun's energy—waterpower, wind power, and *geothermal power*. Geothermal power is power created from the heat that exists beneath the earth's surface.

The United States must find solutions to its energy problems. These solutions are necessary if the United States is to keep its position as a highly industrial power. These solutions are also necessary if the American people are to maintain their standard of living. In addition to finding alternative energy sources, the American public will need to conserve energy in order to avoid an energy crisis. Many homeowners today are insulating their homes more effectively. Manufacturers are making heating equipment that uses energy more efficiently.

■ *What are some alternative sources of energy?*

Environmental Problems. A serious environmental problem in the United States today is pollution. The burning of fossil fuels causes most air pollution. Homes, businesses, and motor vehicles that burn such fuels are the major sources of air pollution. The most harmful result of air pollution is its effect on people's health. Air pollution can worsen some respiratory diseases. Air pollution can also cause other diseases, such as cancer. Waste products from industries and untreated sewage is a major source of water pollution. Solid wastes are a major source of land pollution.

Many industrial processes create toxic or hazardous wastes. Some of these wastes are

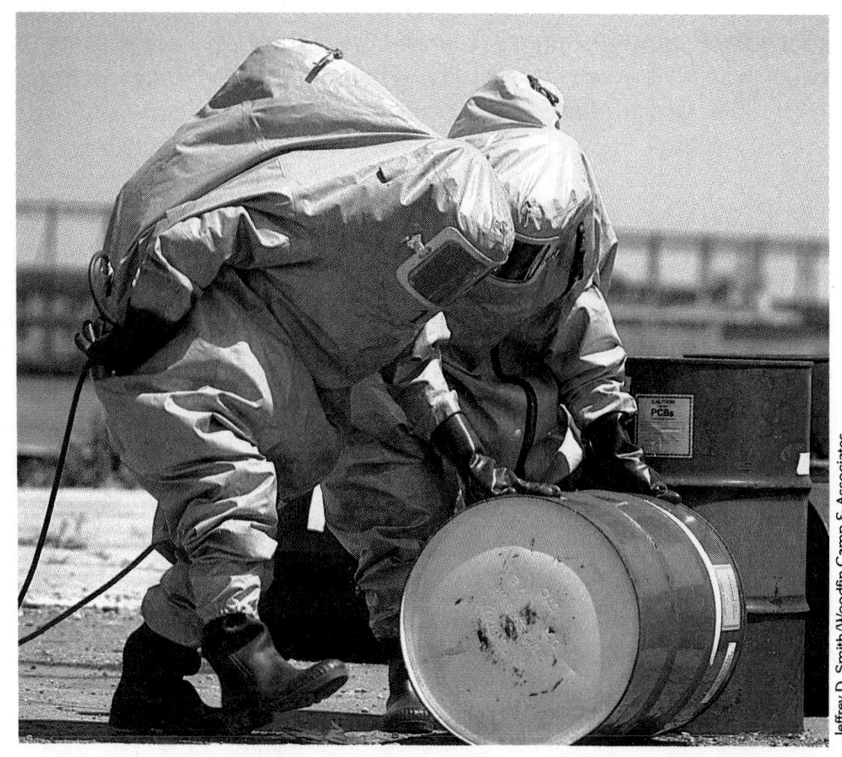

Jeffrey D. Smith/Woodfin Camp & Associates

The disposal of toxic wastes has become a major problem in many states. In this illustration, workers wearing gas masks walk through a toxic waste dump.

dumped into streams, rivers, and lakes. These toxic wastes can contaminate drinking water. The toxic wastes can also contaminate fish, which may then be eaten by humans. Many of the by-products of industry contain waste material that does not naturally break down into safer substances. As a result, these waste materials may endanger humans years after the materials have been disposed of. *PCBs*—chemicals used in making plastics—have been banned by the government since 1979. Yet large amounts of PCBs remain in the environment, still toxic.

Today steps are being taken to find solutions to the problem of pollution. Federal, state, and local governments have taken steps to control all types of pollution. Laws have been passed that limit the amount of pollution that automobiles and industries can put into the environment. The use of some chemicals has been banned. Funds have been established in order to conduct research into ways of controlling pollution. More attention is being paid to the handling and disposal of toxic wastes. This includes more secure packaging and less dumping of these wastes in heavily populated areas. Scientists are also looking for ways in which harmful chemical compounds can be broken down so they do not remain toxic.

■ *What are the major sources of air pollution?*

A Changing Population. During the late 1980's, millions of Americans continued to be on the move. Today people are leaving areas of the Northeast and the Midwest and moving to the South and West. According to the estimates of the Census Bureau, by the year 2010 an additional 16 million people will have moved to the South. An additional 10 million people will have moved to the West. The Northeast and the Midwest will continue to lose population. In the late 1980's, the greatest movement was to the Sunbelt. Newcomers accounted for the rapid growth in Arizona, California, Florida, and Texas. Job opportunities and a good climate lured many people to these states. Also, retirement communities in these areas attracted many older people.

Much of the movement to the South and West was to the urban areas. These large population shifts have brought old problems to new areas. These problems include traffic jams, air pollution, water shortages, and strained sewer systems.

In addition to the shift of the American population to the South and West, large numbers of people continue to move from the cities to the suburbs. Most of the people who live in suburbs also work there rather than commute to jobs in the city. This is due to the fact that suburbs have managed to attract businesses away from the cities.

By the mid-1980's, American society was getting older. There were more people over the age of 65 in the United States than there were teenagers. An increase in life expectancy

Chinese Americans are part of a diverse ethnic group of Asian Americans that includes Filipinos, Indians, Vietnamese, Kampucheans, Koreans, and other groups, as well as Japanese Americans.

George Gardner/The Image Works

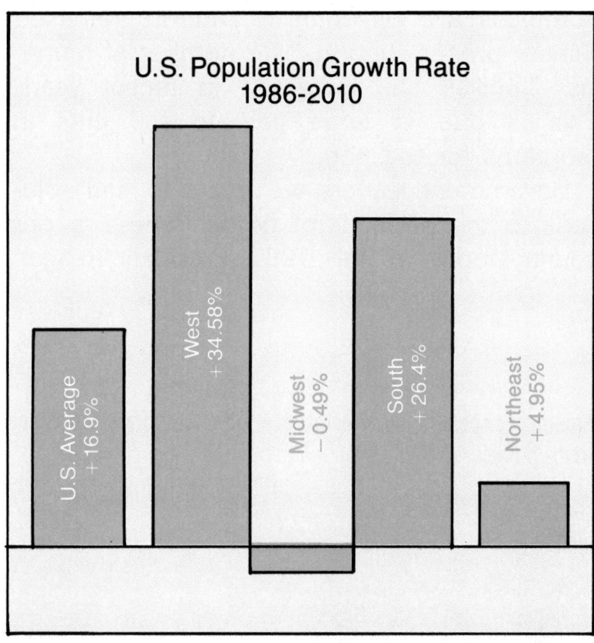

Which United States region is expected to have the highest percentage of population increase by 2010?

and a decrease in the birthrate were two reasons for the aging population. The aging trend should continue as the baby boom generation approaches middle age during the 1990's.

A maturing population creates new problems. As the proportion of Americans over 65 increases, the costs of social security and health care will also increase. An aging population might also have an impact on the labor force. As more workers reach middle age, there will be fewer chances for promotions. This, in turn, could result in greater job dissatisfaction and more career changes. On the other hand, the economy could benefit from an aging population. This is because a larger number of workers will be in their productive years.

What regions in the United States are expected to gain in population as a result of migration from other regions?

Working for Equal Rights. The American nation in the 1980's is one of racial, ethnic, and cultural diversity. The power and influence of minorities has grown with their increase in population. Today over 12 percent of the population is black—over 29 million people. About 66 percent of the black population is registered to vote. Hispanic Americans are the second largest minority group in America today. They make up about 7 percent of the population—over 18 million people. Around 40 percent of Hispanic Americans are registered to vote. Many blacks and Hispanics today believe that the best way to achieve economic and social equality is through political action.

Asian Americans are the fastest growing ethnic group in America. Like blacks and Hispanics, Asian Americans have often been the victims of prejudice and discrimination. But like these other minorities, they have made many contributions to American society.

American Indians have also grown in number and in political power. Tribal leaders have become active in representing the interests of the tribes in Washington, D.C. American Indians have successfully defended their rights on reservations through the court system. They have also won awards of payments from broken treaties.

In 1982 the Equal Rights Amendment (ERA) failed to gain ratification because of the lack of state adoptions. By the late 1980's, many gains had been made in insuring equal opportunity for women. However, many gains still need to be made. Although women make up almost half of the labor force, relatively few hold executive or managerial positions. Women receive only about 60 percent of the pay that men receive for the same jobs. Only about 15 percent of physicians, 18 percent of lawyers, and 6 percent of engineers are women. But today more women than ever graduate from professional schools and go on to careers in traditionally male fields.

■ *What is the fastest growing ethnic group in America today?*

Social Concerns. Poverty and low incomes continue to be important concerns in America today. A large number of blacks, Hispanics, Asians, and women live in poverty. While about 11 percent of whites live in poverty, about 31 percent of blacks and 27 percent of Hispanics live in that condition. Women head about 50 percent of all low-income families. Many minority workers continue to lack the skills needed for well-paying jobs in a high-technology economy.

Homelessness has become a serious problem in the United States today. The number of homeless people range from 250,000 to 3 million. This is because homelessness occurs in a number of ways. Some people are homeless for a short time. Some are homeless for a number of times. Other homeless people remain homeless permanently. The main causes of homelessness in the United States are unemployment, shortages of low-income housing, widespread poverty, and untreated mental illness. Drug abuse, divorce, and other personal difficulties are also causes of homelessness in the United States.

Many of the homeless are young, unemployed minority men. Large numbers are women who cannot afford housing. Some homeless are psychiatric patients released without proper support. The number of homeless families has increased in recent years. This is due in large part to the cuts in programs for the poor.

Government leaders are trying to find solutions to the problem of homelessness in our country today. In July 1987, President Reagan

Emergency shelters, such as this one, offer temporary assistance to the homeless.

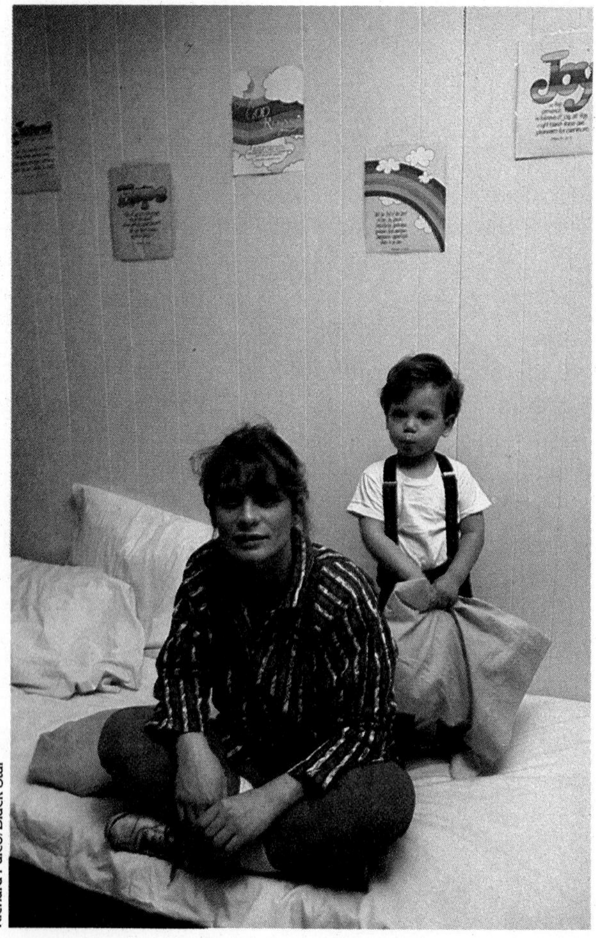

Richard Falco/Black Star

signed a bill providing the homeless with emergency aid. The bill provided for an agency to be created to coordinate federal programs for the homeless. The agency would also determine the extent of the problem in America. State and city governments planned to provide more low-income housing and emergency shelters. Job training, counseling, and medical and psychiatric care are also needed by the homeless.

■ *How are government leaders dealing with the problem of homelessness in the United States?*

SECTION 3 REVIEW

1. *How has television affected the way that public officials are elected to office?*
2. *What problems have been created by a maturing population?*
3. *What factors have contributed to the increased number of homeless people in the United States today?*

CHAPTER 39 SUMMARY

President Carter faced many problems during his term in office. There was a growing energy shortage. The economy suffered higher unemployment rates and an increased rate of inflation. President Carter worked for the cause of human rights throughout world. President Carter helped to reach an agreement between Egypt and Israel. A peace treaty ending the state of war that existed between the two countries was signed in 1979. One of the most important foreign problems faced by President Carter was the takeover of the American embassy in Iran and the taking of 50 Americans as hostages in November 1979.

During the early 1980's President Reagan tried to improve our nation's economy. The economy faced several setbacks. But by the late 1980's, unemployment and inflation remained low. Relations between the United States and the Soviet Union improved considerably during President Reagan's second term. Problems in Central America and the Middle East continued throughout the Reagan administration. President Reagan took several actions to stop increased terrorism in the world. Vice-President George Bush was elected President in the 1988 election.

By the late 1980's, several technological advances changed the way people in the United States lived. The United States faced challenges in the area of energy development, environmental problems, and changing population patterns. The United States also faced the serious problems of poverty and homelessness.

CHAPTER 39 REVIEW

USING YOUR SKILLS

Evaluating Public Opinion Polls

A *public opinion poll* is a survey taken to find out the beliefs or opinions of a large number of people. Only a small number of the large group are actually questioned. If these people are carefully chosen, their opinions will generally accurately reflect the opinion of the entire group. Polls are generally taken by private polling companies, university research centers, and government agencies. Polls may ask many kinds of questions. Before an election, a poll may ask people whom they plan to vote for. Computers generally tabulate the responses to the questions. How reliable a poll is depends on the size of the group of people that are questioned. It also depends on how these people are chosen. Also, polls that have been sponsored by a person who has something to gain by a certain outcome may not be very reliable. Below are some questions asked in a public opinion poll taken prior to the November 1988 election. Study the questions given in the poll, and then answer the questions that follow.

1. According to the poll, what percentage of people questioned in July 1988 would have voted for George Bush?
2. How did public opinion about who's the most decisive leader change between August and September 1988?
3. How did most people who were interviewed feel about Bush's choice of Senator Dan Quayle as his running mate?
4. What did the majority of people interviewed think about Dukakis's experience in foreign affairs?
5. Based on the above responses, what reasons might have accounted for George Bush's increased popularity between July and September 1988?

■ Now, between Dukakis and Bush, who do you think is the more decisive leader?

	Sept. '88	Aug. '88
Dukakis	40%	50%
Bush	46%	39%
Neither and not sure	14%	11%

■ Now let me read you some statements about each of the candidates for President. For each, tell me if you tend to agree or disagree.

Governor Dukakis is too soft on crime

	Total
Agree	43%
Disagree	41%
Not sure	16%

■ Bush demonstrated poor judgment in the way he picked Senator Dan Quayle as his running mate

	Total
Agree	51%
Disagree	42%
Not sure	7%

■ Michael Dukakis is too inexperienced in foreign affairs

	Total
Agree	63%
Disagree	28%
Not sure	9%

■ If you had to choose, would you vote for Bush or Dukakis?

Sept. '88	Total
Bush	50%
Dukakis	44%
Aug. '88	
Bush	45%
Dukakis	51%
July '88	
Bush	47%
Dukakis	50%

CHAPTER 39 REVIEW

YOU SHOULD KNOW

Identify, define, or explain each of the following:

apartheid	laser
dissidents	organ transplants
shah	solar power
contras	geothermal power

CHECKING FACTS

1. What percent of its oil did the United States import in 1977?
2. What was the direct cause of the riots that broke out in Miami in May 1980?
3. What change took place in American relations with Communist China while President Carter was in office?
4. What two leaders met with President Carter at Camp David in 1979?
5. What was President Reagan's economic program called?
6. With what Soviet leader did President Reagan meet in Geneva, Switzerland, in 1985?
7. The agents of what country were suspected in the bombing of a nightclub in West Berlin that killed a U.S. serviceman?
8. What percent of American homes have at least one television set?
9. What are two major problems created by nuclear power?
10. What is the second largest minority group in the United States today?

UNDERSTANDING CONCEPTS

1. Why did several hundred Iranians take over the American Embassy and hold Americans hostage in 1979?
2. Why did President Reagan and Mikhail Gorbachev meet in Reykjavik, Iceland, in 1986?
3. How did President Reagan attempt to stop increasing terrorism in the mid-1980's?
4. What are the main causes of homelessness in the United States today?

LEARNING FROM ILLUSTRATIONS

1. Look at the political cartoon on page 684. What two factors threaten our nation's continued economic recovery?
2. Look at the graph on page 695. What region shown on the graph is expected to lose population between 1986 and 2010?

CRITICAL THINKING

1. Terrorism has become a serious problem in the world today. Do you think governments should ever give in to terrorist demands? Why or why not?
2. Banning the private use of automobiles would help to solve both energy and pollution problems. Why is this alternative unlikely to be accepted by Americans? Should it be accepted? Give reasons for your answers.
3. It has been said that we are all responsible for our environmental problems. Do you agree or disagree? Explain your answer.

ENRICHMENT ACTIVITIES

1. Research the current state of the economy. Find out about inflation, unemployment, and other economic indicators. Then make graphs showing the information you found.
2. Using this book and other resources, make a chart of environmental problems. Use separate columns to state each problem, its sources, its effects, and possible solutions. Display your chart on the bulletin board.

CHAPTER 40

CLOSE-UP: The United States and The World

INTRODUCTION

What will it be like to live in the United States in the future? No one knows for sure. It is certain, however, that many of the problems Americans face are also important to citizens of other countries. In many ways America's future is tied to peaceful relationships and cooperation with other countries.

George Washington advised his generation of Americans not to become entangled in world affairs. Two bloody and costly world wars in this century, however, have made America a world power and leader. Most Americans do not believe it desirable or possible to return to isolationism.

Since World War II, a cold war with the Soviet Union and later Communist China shaped American foreign policy. This meant that the United States and our allies sought to stop communist influence around the world. Sometimes this policy resulted in armed conflict, as in the Korean and Vietnam wars. There were also moments of sharp confrontation, for example, the Cuban Missile crisis in October, 1962.

Still, various American presidents have worked to cooperate with the Soviet Union and its allies. President Eisenhower invited the Soviet Premier Khrushchev to tour the United States in 1959. President Kennedy set up a direct telephone line with Kremlin leaders to avoid accidental nuclear war. President Nixon visited both the Soviet Union and China in 1972 in an effort to ease tensions. Various cultural, scientific, and educational exchanges with China and the Soviet Union have also taken place. In the late 1980's there are hopeful signs that signal an end to the cold war.

1 Challenges, Today and Tomorrow

Today our country faces the challenge of living in a new world. This challenge is not new in the sense that Columbus brought the discovery of a "new world" to Europe. It is new because the problems of the 1990's and beyond are unlike those in America's past. Industrial pollution threatens to upset the world's delicate ecosystem. Many people around the world do not have enough to eat. In many countries,. the people are also very poor and often cannot find productive work. Money spent for more and more weapons threatens better living conditions. Solutions to these problems must be found, or the planet itself may be destroyed.

The Global Village. Americans live in a land of great wealth and beauty. They live in a free nation with a proud heritage. But they also live in a *global village*. This means that technological advances have made the world seem smaller. The time required to travel from one place to another is shorter. Communication by means of space satellites is very rapid.

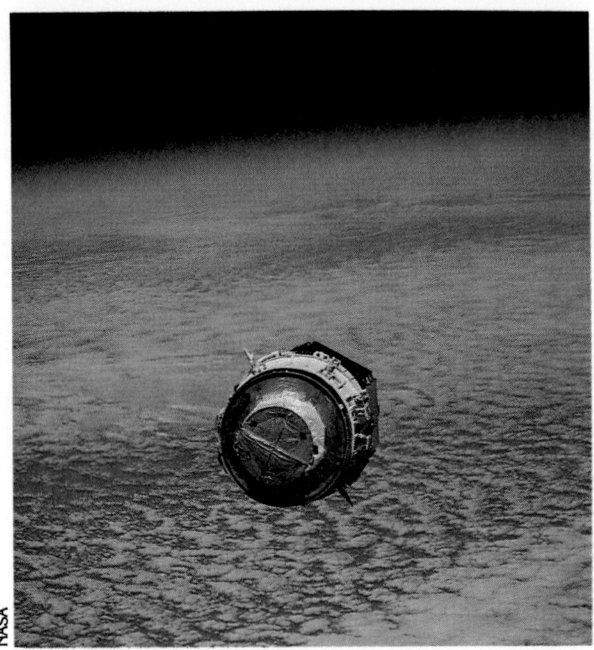

This space satellite makes communication very rapid making the world seem smaller than it seemed years ago.

For example, news from any part of the earth can be known the world over in a few seconds. Television viewers in Moscow, in Beijing, and in capital cities across the globe can receive Cable News Network (CNN) based in Atlanta, Georgia. Farmers on several continents can receive up to the minute data from the Chicago, Illinois, Board of Trade by using a telephone and a computer. Within hours of an earthquake or other natural disaster in a remote region, appeals can be made and relief supplies speedily sent. No country or people needs to be isolated from the world community.

The rapid changes in communications technology have helped the peoples of the world better understand that they share a common humanity. They also share the same planet.

Consider another example. Imagine if the world were a global village of 100 people. In this village only 6 of the residents would be Americans. Approximately 70 villagers would be unable to read; only one would have a college education. Over 50 would suffer from some form of malnutrition and over 80 would live in substandard housing. Within the village, 7 or 8 people would control half the village's resources and income. The remaining villagers would exist on the other half.

This is a troubling picture. There is a new urgency to the idea that common solutions must be found to common problems. Responsible world leaders have urged that we "think globally, act locally."

How can news and information from one country be shared around the world within seconds?

Protecting the Environment. Environmental issues, for example, are not unique to our country. All industrialized countries have poisoned the air, polluted major rivers and streams, and outgrown facilities for safe garbage disposal. Many countries have exploited the earth's resources, including precious metals, without regard for future generations. Energy needs use up precious fossil fuels such as coal, natural gas, and oil. Fresh water supplies are dangerously low.

Acid rain—pollution caused by the burning of gas, oil, or coal mixed with water vapor—is a serious problem for the eastern United States and Canada. Fish in hundreds of lakes and forest trees are being killed by this type of pollution. Coal burning factories and electrical power stations in the American Midwest appear to be the major source for acid rain pollution. Canadian and United States of-

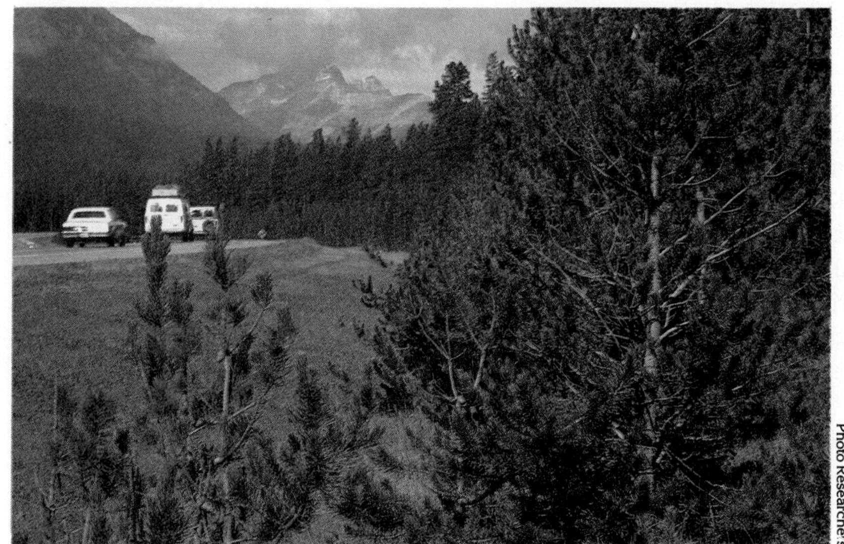

Photo Researchers

Dying lakes and forests are often hundreds of miles or kilometers from large cities and factories. Scientists have discovered that the dying lakes and forests lay directly in the path of wind currents blowing over large cities in the United States and Canada.

ficials are cooperating on efforts to solve this problem.

Scientists the world over are concerned about the *greenhouse effect*. When fossil fuels such as oil and coal are burned, they release carbon dioxide gas into the atmosphere. The gas allows sunlight to reach the earth but prevents some surface heat from leaving the atmosphere. As a result, many scientists believe the earth is getting warmer. This could have devastating geographic, economic, and political effects. Sea levels could rise from melting polar ice caps, flooding coastal cities. Productive farmlands could also be reduced.

A related issue is loss of the ozone layer—a gas in the upper atmosphere. Some scientists fear that it is being depleted as a result of air pollution. This is important because ozone screens out much of the harmful ultraviolet radiation from the sun. Increased ultraviolet radiation could cause more skin cancer and birth defects. It also slows some types of food crop production.

How can the ozone layer be protected and other environmental challenges be met? Several industrial countries, including the United States, have banned propellants used in aerosol cans. These propellants, called chlorofluorocarbons or CFCs, are known to deplete ozone. Another source of CFCs is freon, a gas used to cool refrigerators and air conditioners. These manufacturing uses of CFCs are largely unregulated.

To be effective, preventing pollution of the air as well as oceans and fresh water systems will require international action. Most countries, however, have shown little interest in making the necessary commitment of resources. In 1972 the United Nations sponsored a Global Conference on the Human Environment in Stockholm, Sweden. The conference recognized the need for international cooperation. It also established a system for monitoring conditions of the global environment.

■ *What is acid rain?*

The Food Crisis. Many people are poor and starving in the world today. At least a third of the world's five billion people are poor and undernourished. At least a half million people each day do not consume enough calories to be able to carry on normal life.

Throughout the non-industrialized world, food production cannot keep up with population increases. In these countries the land is often poor and primitive farming techniques are used. The good land is used to raise high demand export crops, such as coffee or bananas, even flowers. These crops generate cash for the economy but not food that can be consumed locally.

Other problems leading to world food shortages include natural disasters such as flooding or drought. Harsh civil wars in Ethiopia, Cambodia, and Sudan in the 1970's and 1980's have also contributed to widespread scarcity of food. In the Sahel regions of northern Africa, a devastating famine in 1972–1974 brought the food crisis to the attention of the world.

How can this challenge be met? A World Food Conference was held in Rome, Italy, in 1974 to explore possible action. Although delegates pledged to end hunger and malnutrition within a decade, the situation has actually grown worse. During the late 1980's global production of cereal grains, such as wheat and rice, was down. At the beginning of 1990, food reserves are at their lowest levels since the early 1970's. Famine conditions continue to exist in parts of Africa and Asia.

Many industrial countries are responding to the food crisis by working at ways to increase crop production. The *green revolution*—the development of high-yield crops through hybrid seeds, special fertilizers, and improved farming methods—has had an important impact. Bangladesh, once thought without hope in the struggle to become self-sufficient in rice

W. Campbell/Sygma

Many children, like the ones shown in this picture, are starving. These people are in a refugee camp in Ethiopia.

Tom Bytes/Sygma

Thousands of people attended the Live-Aid concert held in Philadelphia.

production, made steady progress in the late 1970's. Devastating floods in 1988, however, destroyed much of this effort.

Americans have always been a generous people. Through a Food for Peace program of the federal government, over $30 billion worth of agricultural products have been sent to countries in need since the mid 1950's. Private charities have also played an important role. Rock stars and movie stars have given concerts and benefits to aid hunger victims. In 1985 "Live Aid"—a live 17 hour rock concert televised from Philadelphia and London—was broadcast to over 150 countries. It raised over $70 million for famine relief in Africa.

The real solution to the food crisis, however, is probably not increased foreign aid, or increased food production. Both are needed. World agriculture has never produced as much per person as it does today. There are also more well-fed people on earth today than ever before.

Instead, the answer to solving the food shortage lies in a complex tangle of distribution and supply problems, international politics, and local traditions. Sometimes when international aid arrives, there is not adequate transportation to take the supplies where they are needed. Rival donor countries have competed with local political leaders on relief programs. Local customs or religious traditions may prevent acceptance of food resources. It will take increased international goodwill and determination to resolve these issues.

What is the green revolution?

Arms Control. For centuries, most countries have believed that the best way to prevent war is to arm themselves. Since the late 1950's, the United States and the Soviet Union have been engaged in a policy of MAD—mutually assured destruction. Both governments know that no matter how strong a nuclear attack might be made, the other side can counterattack with a fatal blow. Since neither can defeat the other without being defeated, an uneasy truce is maintained.

The MAD *deterrence*—a strategy for preventing hostile actions—has led to the largest arms race in world history. It is an unparalleled race because of the sheer number of weapons involved, their technological capability, and their destructive power. Both nations have nuclear weapons systems powerful enough to destroy the other several times over. And more are being built.

The cost of this arms race is staggering. The annual defense budget of the United States is approaching $300 billion. Many resources, such as precious metals, are put into weapons systems that will likely never be used. Moreover, technological advances increase the cost of weapons systems each year. For example, during World War II and for several years afterwards, the basic weapon for fighter airplanes was the machine gun. A burst of

U.S. Airforce

The United States has added the F-16 fighter planes, the stealth bombers, and the Trident submarine to its defense arsenal.

U.S. Airforce

U.S. Navy

machine gun fire in a dogfight cost about $20. In modern fighter planes, these weapons have been replaced with sophisticated heat-seeking air-to-air missiles. These missiles cost over $300,000 per round.

The new American fleet of 132 stealth bombers will cost an estimated $500 to $850 million per plane. Estimates on the Strategic Defense Initiative (SDI or "Star Wars")—a laser satellite defense system—run into the hundreds of billions of dollars.

Many people feel that the United States and the Soviet Union can no longer afford such an expensive arms race. This is also true for other countries as well. Yet many nations arm themselves far beyond what is needed for their adequate defense. A 1989 United Nations report stated that the health of the world's children was in decline for the first time in recent years. A major factor for the decline was that resources previously used for health care and education were being diverted to military spending.

Other than cost, perhaps the single greatest danger from the arms race between the United States and the Soviet Union is accidental nuclear war. Several precautions are built into America's defenses to insure that a crisis will be dealt with slowly. On the other hand, this policy makes the country more vulnerable to a surprise attack. Some military leaders have argued for a "launch on warning" response to an attack warning. This means that missiles would not be destroyed in their bases from the incoming attack. But if the warning were a false alarm, it would be too late. This type of defense is highly prone to accident.

The super powers—the United States and the Soviet Union—are in the process of negotiating ways to limit the arms race. The SALT treaties of the 1970's paved the way for a new treaty that bans intermediate nuclear forces (INF) in 1988. Both the Americans and the Soviets are now ready to negotiate reductions in strategic, or long range, nuclear weapons.

What is the single greatest danger from the arms race between the United States and the Soviet Union?

SECTION 1 REVIEW

1. *Why is there growing international concern over the ozone layer?*
2. *What are some of the problems that contribute to world hunger?*
3. *What are some of the dangers of the nuclear arms race between the United States and the Soviet Union?*

2 International Cooperation

If nations are to live in peace with one another, it is necessary to find ways to cooperate and work together on common problems. One way to do this is through international organizations in which all countries may participate. The United Nations is one such organization. Another way to bring about world stability is through reform and peaceful initiatives taken by the major powers.

The United Nations. Immediately after World War II, in June 1945, the Allied powers worked together to create the United Nations. Fifty-one nations signed the UN charter. The world had been torn apart by war. There was widespread destruction and suffering throughout Europe and Asia. World leaders were hopeful that ways could be found to prevent future wars. Today the United Nations continues to search for peaceful solutions to international problems. Membership in the UN has increased dramatically; by 1990 there were 159 member states.

The United Nations has several interrelated parts, including many specialized agencies. A Secretary General serves as the chief administrative official. Since 1982, this office has been held by Javier Perez de Cuellar of Peru.

The United Nations General Assembly consists of representatives from each member country. Each country gets one vote. The General Assembly debates various issues important to the member nations and adopts resolutions. The member countries, however, are not required to follow the General Assembly's decisions.

One important function of the General Assembly is to approve the UN's budget. It was

UNITED NATIONS DUES BY COUNTRY, 1988–89

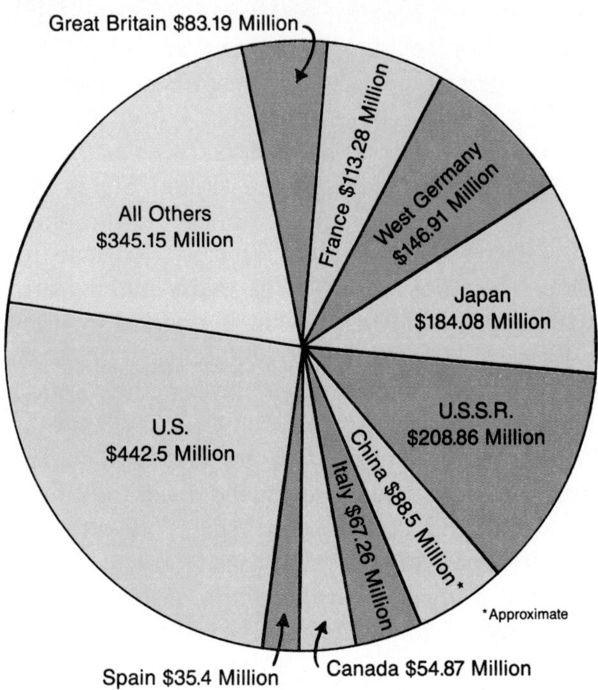

Which four countries contribute the most to United Nations' budget?

$1.77 billion for 1988–89. A dues formula agreed upon in the 1970's allocates dues according to national wealth. The United States pays 25 percent of the total UN budget. The Soviet Union pays 11.3 percent; Japan, 8.7 percent; and West Germany 7.8 percent. Great Britain, China, and France each pay about 5 percent. All other members make up the remaining contributions.

The United Nations Security Council is specifically charged with maintaining peace and international security. The Council consists of fifteen members, five of whom are permanent—the United States, the Soviet Union, China, France, and Great Britain. For an important decision to be made by the Security Council, all the permanent members must vote for it. This arrangement effectively gives any of the permanent powers a veto.

Originally it was thought that the Security Council would keep peace through *collective security*. This means that if one UN member state is threatened, all or most member nations are pledged to come to its defense. This system has not worked well. The permanent members of the Security Council have been unable to agree on what actions to take. As an alternative, the General Assembly has authorized special "peace-keeping" forces in crisis situations. These forces do not involve troops from either the United States or the Soviet Union. UN forces have gathered information and monitored ceasefire agreements, primarily in the Middle East.

Specialized and Related Agencies are another important feature of the United Nations. These 27 semi-independent organizations work in several areas to improve living conditions around the world. The International Monetary Fund (IMF), for example, promotes increased world trade. The United Nations Children's Fund (UNICEF) provides aid to needy children and their mothers in poor countries. The World Health Organization (WHO) helps plan for the future by working to improve health care for all people. WHO studies different diseases and sets up health care centers.

The United Nations serves to increase international cooperation in other ways. For example, the UN headquarters in New York City is a place where diplomats from various countries can meet. Diplomats can exchange views and present their country's position on issues. *Good offices*—a method of settling disputes using a neutral third party to negotiate differences—of the Secretary General has also helped to end armed conflicts. In 1988, Perez de Cuellar was instrumental in bringing about a cease fire in the Iran-Iraq war.

■ *What countries are permanent members of the Security Council?*

Glasnost and Perestroika. Organizations such as the United Nations work effectively only if the member countries are willing to get along. Sometimes, internal reforms within a country, or a shift in political power, can signal a desire for change.

When Mikhail Gorbachev came to power in the Soviet Union in 1985, he inherited a troubled economy and a bureaucracy resistant to change. He viewed President Reagan as a reckless, gunslinging cowboy. For his part, Reagan described the Soviet Union as an "evil empire."

Gorbachev quickly moved to begin new, reform policies at home and abroad. *Glasnost*, or "openness," and *perestroika*, a term for "restructuring" the government and economy, describe this effort. As a result of these policies, the Soviet Union has begun a new relationship with the world and with her own people. To Americans, these changes appear dramatic, but they have proceeded slowly. This is because it has taken a few years for Gorbachev to secure his power base in the *politburo*—the highest political authority in the Soviet Union.

A few examples of this "openness" will illustrate how dramatically the Soviet Union is changing. Newspapers may now print articles criticizing official government policy. News about airplane crashes, earthquakes, shipwrecks, hijackings and similar incidents are being reported for the first time. Even unfavorable news about the government is now being heard on radio and television and reported in the press.

Gorbachev has also begun the process of changing the structure of Soviet government. The Supreme Soviet—the national legislature—enacted a series of sweeping constitutional reforms in 1988 at Gorbachev's request. These reforms strengthened the legislature and created the office of President. Multi-candidate elections were held in 1989, the first in Russia since the 1917 Communist Revolution. Internal controls over citizens have also been eased. Political and religious dissidents have been released from jail or exile. Some dissidents have been allowed to emigrate. Corrupt officials have been fired and senior officials identified with previous regimes have been forced to retire.

On the international scene, Gorbachev has enjoyed tremendous popularity. He announced an end to the nine year war between Soviet troops and rebel factions in Afghanistan. He also initiated new diplomatic initiatives with several western countries and Japan. Gorbachev and President Reagan met three times between 1986 and 1988 to explore arms reductions and other issues.

Strained Soviet tensions with China also show signs of easing. An official summit between the Chinese and the Soviet Union, the first in 30 years, will be held in 1989. Gorbachev plans on visiting Chinese leader Deng Xiaoping.

There is a human interest side to *glasnost* as well. Three grey whales became stranded in 1988 off the coast of northern Alaska. Ice trapped them from swimming to warmer waters. In a gesture of friendship, a Soviet icebreaker worked with American officials to help the animals escape. Two of the whales were freed. Later that year a devastating earthquake struck the Soviet Republic of Armenia. Thousands of people were killed and cities destroyed. Many countries, warmed by the idea by *glasnost*, generously responded with food, clothing, and medical supplies.

Koch/Contrasto/Picture Group

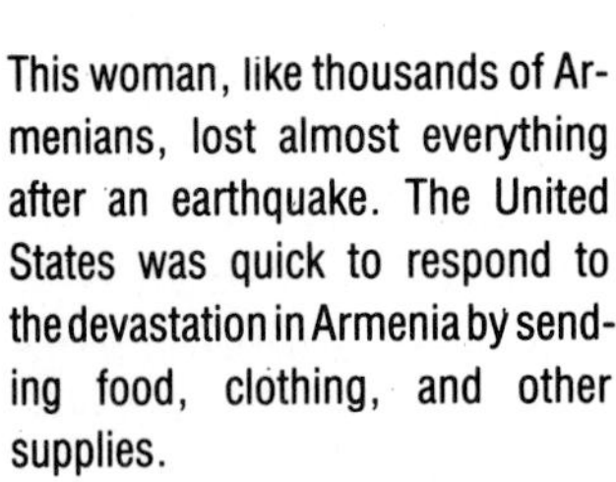

This woman, like thousands of Armenians, lost almost everything after an earthquake. The United States was quick to respond to the devastation in Armenia by sending food, clothing, and other supplies.

In a surprising speech to the United Nations General Assembly in December, 1988, Gorbachev offered a vision for "a new world order." Military force, he suggested, should no longer be a tool of foreign policy. "Closed societies," he said, don't work. *Ideology*—a political belief system—should cease to dominate international affairs as it had for the past forty years. These points were then followed up by his stunning announcement of plans to cut total Soviet military personnel 10 percent within two years. This includes 50,000 Soviet troops from Eastern Europe, and reduction by half of the Russian tank divisions in East Germany, Czechoslovakia, and Hungary. These cuts, significant as they may be, still leave NATO and the western allies at a disadvantage. Eastern Europe and Soviet troops, tanks, and planes remain numerically superior.

Many leaders in western Europe and North America remain suspicious of Soviet intentions. They argue that no Communist leader can be trusted. The evidence is mounting, however, that *glasnost* and *perestroika* are not just policies to buy time for the Soviet economy to improve. Rather, they represent fundamental changes in Soviet society and government.

What troop reductions did Gorbachev offer the United Nations during his speech there in 1988?

Signs of Hope. As the final decade of the 20th century began, several longstanding conflicts appeared to be easing. In many of these problem areas, the United States has sought to achieve negotiated settlement.

The Reagan administration negotiated an agreement leading to the creation of an independent African state of Namibia, beginning April 1, 1990. This territory in southwest Africa was the last remaining colony on that continent. South Africa, who governed the territory since the end of World War II, agreed to pull out its troops. Angola, Namibia's neighbor, had been supporting a civil war against the South Africans with the aid of Cuban troops. Angola and Cuba also agreed to a cease fire and the withdrawal of Cuban soldiers. The signing ceremony took place at the United Nations in New York. The UN will send peace keeping troops to Angola to monitor the Cuban withdrawal.

In Central America, the difficult civil war in Nicaragua appears to be near an end. President Reagan had hoped to topple the leftist Sandinista government by supplying the contra resistance movement. On several key votes, however, the United States Congress voted for humanitarian aid—but not military aid—for the contras. Without military supplies, the armed conflict has dwindled.

Still another sign of hope was a breakthrough in the Middle East stalemate between Israel and the Palestine Liberation Organization (PLO). The PLO views itself as the sole legitimate representative of the Palestinian people. In late 1988, the PLO National Council moved to declare an independent Palestinian state. With this action came a clear recognition of Israel's right to exist and a rejection of terrorist activities.

Once the United States was satisfied that PLO leader Yasser Arafat had renounced terrorism, a diplomatic dialogue between the United States and the PLO began. This move ended thirteen years of American diplomatic isolation. Only Israel stands alone in rejecting all contact with the PLO. The opportunity is at hand for the United States to negotiate a lasting Middle East settlement.

The United States Navy escorted oil tankers through the Persian Gulf to protect the tankers from attack by Iranians.

In late 1988, the guns finally were silent in the Iraq-Iran war. This war was fought through much of the 1980's but quickly reached a stalemate. Both Iraq and Iran are oil producing countries and the war widened into the Persian Gulf in 1984. A large international fleet of American, British, French, and Soviet warships was drawn to the Gulf in order to protect vital oil shipping lanes. The United States escort ships were the object of bitter attacks by the Iranians. The cease-fire was arranged through the efforts of the Secretary General of the United Nations.

There are other international warming trends. Vietnam has announced plans to pull back its troops from neighboring Kampuchea (Cambodia). This withdrawal ends ten years of occupation. The United States and Canada have agreed to a new free trade treaty that will be signed in 1990. The countries of the European common market are also making progress toward their long-sought-after goal of a full European economic union.

As the last decade of the 20th century dawns, the peoples of the world are taking small steps toward understanding each other. There is a clear movement toward political and economic openness. Only with such understanding and openness will the earth's rich resources be managed, hungry people fed, and the arms race reduced. The 1990's are a decade for hope in humankind.

What led to a winding down of the civil war in Nicaragua?

SECTION 2 REVIEW

1. *What conditions led to the creation of the United Nations?*
2. *What are the meanings of glasnost* and *perestroika?*
3. *What is the last African colony to achieve independence?*

CHAPTER 40 REVIEW

SUMMARY

In the 1990's and beyond, America will be faced with new challenges. Many of these challenges will require that countries work together to find acceptable solutions. Countries can no longer live in isolation; they are dependent on each other in several ways. Pollution of the environment through acid rain and the greenhouse effect, for example, are not problems for the United States alone. Likewise, the food shortage is not limited to a single country or region. If the deadly arms race between the super powers leads to accidental nuclear war, the results would be disasterous for all countries.

International organizations can help countries work on common problems. The United Nations is one such organization that promotes better understanding. It also provides the setting for settling conflicts peacefully. The United States helped to found the UN in 1945 and occupies a permanent seat on the Security Council. Much of the everyday work of the UN is done through specialized agencies, such as UNICEF and the WHO.

Sometimes, however, a positive change in the foreign policy of one or two major powers can significantly ease international tensions. Internal reforms within the Soviet Union during the late 1980's illustrate this point. Through a policy of openness and restructuring of the government and economy, many changes have been made. These changes include a willingness to negotiate longstanding differences with other countries. There is also a freer flow of news and information both inside and outside the Soviet Union. The United States has welcomed these reforms. As the 21st century approaches, there is good reason to hope that pressing world issues may be one step closer to peaceful resolution.

UNDERSTANDING CONCEPTS

1. How might the greenhouse effect damage the environment in the United States?
2. What are some problems that contribute to the world food shortage?
3. What are some of the major problems for the United States caused by the arms race with the Soviet Union?
4. What is the purpose of the UN Security Council?
5. How has the structure of the Soviet government changed under Gorbachev?

CRITICAL THINKING

1. Do you think the concept of the world as a "global village" is important to understanding world problems? Why or why not?
2. Has the United Nations been an effective organization for promoting peace and understanding since 1945? Why or why not?
3. In what ways have *glasnost* and *perestroika* contributed toward an easing of Soviet tensions with the United States? Explain your answer.

PROJECTS AND ACTIVITIES

1. Write to the UN Office of Public Information (United Nations, New York, NY 10017) and ask for literature on UN efforts to solve the world food crisis. Make a scrapbook of this information and share it with your class.
2. Prepare a chart of United States spending for the arms race from 1950 to 1990. Use this book, encyclopedias, almanacs, and other library resources to collect information. What trends do you see? Display your chart on a bulletin board.

UNIT TEN REVIEW

UNIT SUMMARY

Many changes took place in American life while President Johnson was in office. The government and different groups of people worked for changes to improve life for all Americans. The United States was faced with the growing involvement in a war in South Vietnam. In time, the American people became sharply divided over to what extent the United States should take part in the war in South Vietnam. The war grew more serious, and inflation became a problem in the United States. In 1968, Richard M. Nixon was chosen President.

In 1973, our country ended its part in the war in South Vietnam. The United States improved its relations with the Soviet Union. However, a serious scandal involving the White House was made public in the early 1970's. As a result, President Nixon resigned in August 1974. Gerald Ford became President. President Ford worked to restore public trust in the government following the Watergate scandal.

During President Carter's term in office, our country faced a growing energy shortage, high unemployment rates, and an increased rate of inflation. During President Reagan's term in office, unemployment and inflation remained low. By the late 1980's, the United States faced challenges in the area of energy development, environmental problems, and changing population patterns. Poverty and homelessness became growing problems.

YOU SHOULD KNOW

Identify, define, or explain each of the following:

medicare	draft
guerilla warfare	apartheid
Vietnamization	dissidents
détente	contras
segregation	glasnost

CHECKING FACTS

1. What was the purpose of the Twenty-fifth Amendment?
2. In the late 1960's, what industry was affected by high interest rates?
3. Who was nominated at the 1968 Democratic Convention?
4. What was the purpose of the Nuclear Nonproliferation Treaty?
5. What caused a fuel crisis in the United States in 1973?
6. What is revenue sharing?
7. What caused the riots in Miami, Florida, in May 1980?
8. What was Reaganomics?
9. What new problems does a maturing population create?
10. Who are the homeless people in the United States?

UNDERSTANDING CONCEPTS

1. Why did President Johnson increase military aid to South Vietnam between 1965 and 1968?
2. How did the war in South Vietnam affect the economy of the United States?
3. How did the war between Israel and some Arab countries in 1973 affect the American economy?
4. Why did the United States boycott the 1980 summer Olympic Games held in Moscow?
5. Why did the United States government support the contras?
6. How did the American people help the Armenian people after the earthquake?

CRITICAL THINKING

1. How were the Great Society programs endangered by America's foreign policy?

2. When Gerald R. Ford was sworn in as President after Nixon resigned, Ford said, "Our Constitution has worked. . . . Here the people rule." What did Ford mean by those words?
3. Homelessness is a serious problem in the United States. How do you think this problem could be solved?

CHRONOLOGY

Arrange the following events in the order in which they occurred:

a. President Nixon resigned
b. President Johnson decided not to seek reelection
c. Americans held as hostages in Iran
d. Senate approved women's rights amendment
e. American astronauts land on the moon
f. American involvement in South Vietnam increased
g. Gerald R. Ford became President

CITIZENSHIP IN ACTION

In this unit you read about the dreams that some American leaders had for groups of people or for the nation in the future. What kind of dream would you like to see the United States fulfill in the future?

GEOGRAPHY

1. What two states are the least-densely populated?
2. What two states are the most-densely populated?
3. How would you describe the population density of the central part of the country?
4. What is the population density of the area where you live?

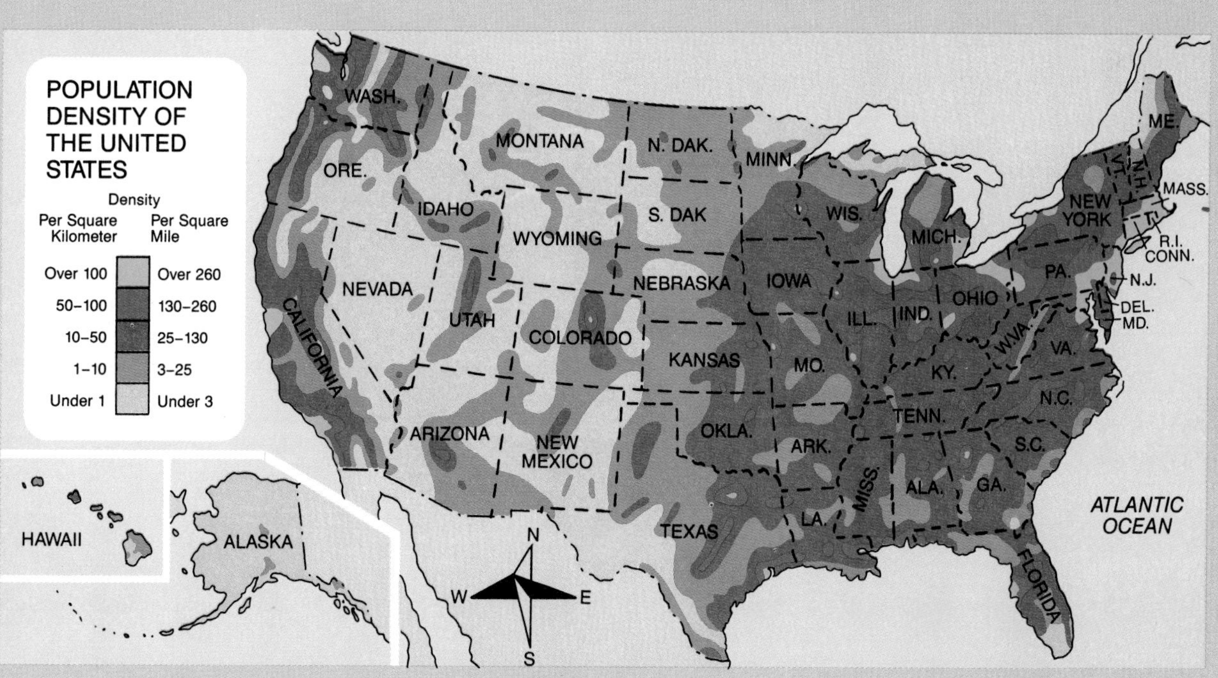

REFERENCE MATERIALS

PRESIDENTS OF THE UNITED STATES

The information beside each portrait gives the President's name and the years of the President's birth and death. In addition, the years that each President served are given, as well as the state where the President was born, the President's political party, and the name of the Vice-President(s) who served with each President.

All Photos Library of Congress

1. George Washington
(1732–1799)
Served 1789–1797
Virginia
Unopposed
John Adams

3. Thomas Jefferson
(1743–1826)
Served 1801–1809
Virginia
Democratic-Republican
Aaron Burr
George Clinton

2. John Adams
(1735–1826)
Served 1797–1801
Massachusetts
Federalist
Thomas Jefferson

4. James Madison
(1751–1836)
Served 1809–1817
Virginia
Democratic-Republican
George Clinton
Elbridge Gerry

5. James Monroe
(1758–1831)
Served 1817–1825
Virginia
Democratic-Republican
Daniel D. Tompkins

10. John Tyler
(1790–1862)
Served 1841–1845
Virginia
Whig
....

6. John Quincy Adams
(1767–1848)
Served 1825–1829
Massachusetts
Democratic-Republican
John C. Calhoun

11. James K. Polk
(1795–1849)
Served 1845–1849
North Carolina
Democrat
George M. Dallas

7. Andrew Jackson
(1767–1845)
Served 1829–1837
South Carolina
Democrat
John C. Calhoun
Martin Van Buren

12. Zachary Taylor
(1784–1850)
Served 1849–1850
Virginia
Whig
Millard Fillmore

8. Martin Van Buren
(1782–1862)
Served 1837–1841
New York
Democrat
Richard M. Johnson

13. Millard Fillmore
(1800–1874)
Served 1850–1853
New York
Whig
....

9. William Henry Harrison
(1773–1841)
Served 1841–1841
Virginia
Whig
John Tyler

14. Franklin Pierce
(1804–1869)
Served 1853–1857
New Hampshire
Democrat
William R. King

15. James Buchanan
(1791–1868)
Served 1857–1861
Pennsylvania
Democrat
John C. Breckinridge

16. Abraham Lincoln
(1809–1865)
Served 1861–1865
Kentucky
Republican
Hannibal Hamlin
Andrew Johnson

17. Andrew Johnson
(1808–1875)
Served 1865–1869
North Carolina
Democrat
. . . .

18. Ulysses S. Grant
(1822–1885)
Served 1869–1877
Ohio
Republican
Schuyler Colfax
Henry Wilson

19. Rutherford B. Hayes
(1822–1893)
Served 1877–1881
Ohio
Republican
William A. Wheeler

20. James A. Garfield
(1831–1881)
Served 1881–1881
Ohio
Republican
Chester A. Arthur

21. Chester A. Arthur
(1829–1886)
Served 1881–1885
Vermont
Republican
. . . .

22. Grover Cleveland
(1837–1908)
Served 1885–1889
New Jersey
Democrat
Thomas A. Hendricks

23. Benjamin Harrison
(1833–1901)
Served 1889–1893
Ohio
Republican
Levi P. Morton

24. Grover Cleveland
(1837–1908)
Served 1893–1897
New Jersey
Democrat
Adlai E. Stevenson

25. William McKinley
(1843–1901)
Served 1897–1901
Ohio
Republican
Garret A. Hobart
Theodore Roosevelt

30. Calvin Coolidge
(1872–1933)
Served 1923–1929
Vermont
Republican
Charles G. Dawes

26. Theodore Roosevelt
(1858–1919)
Served 1901–1909
New York
Republican
Charles W. Fairbanks

31. Herbert C. Hoover
(1874–1964)
Served 1929–1933
Iowa
Republican
Charles Curtis

27. William Howard Taft
(1857–1930)
Served 1909–1913
Ohio
Republican
James S. Sherman

32. Franklin D. Roosevelt
(1882–1945)
Served 1933–1945
New York
Democrat
John N. Garner
Henry A. Wallace
Harry S Truman

28. Woodrow Wilson
(1856–1924)
Served 1913–1921
Virginia
Democrat
Thomas R. Marshall

33. Harry S Truman
(1884–1972)
Served 1945–1953
Missouri
Democrat
Alben W. Barkley

29. Warren G. Harding
(1865–1923)
Served 1921–1923
Ohio
Republican
Calvin Coolidge

34. Dwight D. Eisenhower
(1890–1969)
Served 1953–1961
Texas
Republican
Richard M. Nixon

35. John F. Kennedy
(1917–1963)
Served 1961–1963
Massachusetts
Democrat
Lyndon B. Johnson

36. Lyndon B. Johnson
(1908–1973)
Served 1963–1969
Texas
Democrat
Hubert H. Humphrey

37. Richard M. Nixon
(1913–)
Served 1969–1974
California
Republican
Spiro T. Agnew
Gerald R. Ford

38. Gerald R. Ford
(1913–)
Served 1974–1977
Nebraska
Republican
Nelson A. Rockefeller

39. James E. Carter, Jr.
(1924–)
Served 1977–1981
Georgia
Democrat
Walter F. Mondale

40. Ronald W. Reagan
(1911–)
Served 1981–1989
Illinois
Republican
George H. W. Bush

41. George H. W. Bush
(1924–)
Served 1989–
Massachusetts
Republican
J. Danforth Quayle

42. Bill Cliton

FACTS AND FIGURES ABOUT THE UNITED STATES

State	Year of Entry Into Union	Population (1988 Census Bureau Estimates)	State Capital	Area (in sq mi)
Alabama	1819	4,127,000	Montgomery	51,609
Alaska	1959	513,000	Juneau	586,412
Arizona	1912	3,466,000	Phoenix	113,909
Arkansas	1836	2,422,000	Little Rock	53,104
California	1850	28,168,000	Sacramento	158,693
Colorado	1876	3,290,000	Denver	104,247
Connecticut	1788	3,241,000	Hartford	5,009
Delaware	1787	660,000	Dover	2,057
Florida	1845	12,377,000	Tallahassee	58,560
Georgia	1788	6,401,000	Atlanta	58,876
Hawaii	1959	1,093,000	Honolulu	6,450
Idaho	1890	999,000	Boise	83,557
Illinois	1818	11,544,000	Springfield	56,400
Indiana	1816	5,575,000	Indianapolis	36,291
Iowa	1846	2,834,000	Des Moines	56,290
Kansas	1861	2,487,000	Topeka	82,264
Kentucky	1792	3,721,000	Frankfort	40,395
Louisiana	1812	4,420,000	Baton Rouge	48,523
Maine	1820	1,206,000	Augusta	33,215
Maryland	1788	4,644,000	Annapolis	10,577
Massachusetts	1788	5,871,000	Boston	8,257
Michigan	1837	9,300,000	Lansing	58,216
Minnesota	1858	4,306,000	St. Paul	84,068
Mississippi	1817	2,627,000	Jackson	47,716
Missouri	1821	5,139,000	Jefferson City	69,686
Montana	1889	804,000	Helena	147,138
Nebraska	1867	1,601,000	Lincoln	77,227
Nevada	1864	1,060,000	Carson City	110,540
New Hampshire	1788	1,097,000	Concord	9,304
New Jersey	1787	7,720,000	Trenton	7,836
New Mexico	1912	1,510,000	Santa Fe	121,666
New York	1788	17,898,000	Albany	49,576
North Carolina	1789	6,526,000	Raleigh	52,586
North Dakota	1889	663,000	Bismarck	70,665
Ohio	1803	10,872,000	Columbus	41,222
Oklahoma	1907	3,263,000	Oklahoma City	69,919
Oregon	1859	2,741,000	Salem	96,981

State	Year of Entry Into Union	Population (1988 Census Bureau Estimates)	State Capital	Area (in sq mi)
Pennsylvania	1787	12,027,000	Harrisburg	45,333
Rhode Island	1790	995,000	Providence	1,214
South Carolina	1788	3,493,000	Columbia	31,055
South Dakota	1889	715,000	Pierre	77,047
Tennessee	1796	4,919,000	Nashville	42,244
Texas	1845	16,780,000	Austin	267,339
Utah	1896	1,691,000	Salt Lake City	84,916
Vermont	1791	556,000	Montpelier	9,609
Virginia	1788	5,996,000	Richmond	40,817
Washington	1889	4,619,000	Olympia	68,192
West Virginia	1863	1,884,000	Charleston	24,181
Wisconsin	1848	4,858,000	Madison	56,154
Wyoming	1890	471,000	Cheyenne	97,914
District of Columbia		620,000		69
Total		245,807,000		3,615,125

TERRITORIES, POSSESSIONS, AND COMMONWEALTHS OF THE UNITED STATES

Territory, Possession, or Commonwealth	Year of Acquisition	Population (1987 Census Bureau Estimates)	Capital	Area (in sq mi)
American Samoa	1900	38,400	Pago Pago	76
Guam	1899	130,400	Agana	212
Midway Island	1867	2,200	....	2
Northern Marianas	1947	20,300	Saipan	184
Puerto Rico	1899	3,292,000	San Juan	3,435
Trust Territories of Pacific Islands	1947	140,000	....	700
Virgin Islands	1917	106,100	Charlotte Amalie	133
Wake Island	1899	1,600	....	3

Greenland (DEN.)
ICELAND
Alaska (U.S.)
NORTH AMERICA
CANADA
UNITED KINGDOM
IRE.
London
Paris
FRANCE
Montreal
UNITED STATES
Chicago
New York
ATLANTIC OCEAN
SPAIN
PORT.
Madrid
Los Angeles
MOROCCO
30° N
Tropic of Cancer
BAHAMAS
Western Sahara (MOROCCO)
MAURITANIA
MALI
MEXICO
CUBA
HAITI
DOM. REP.
Hawaii (U.S.)
Mexico City
BELIZE
JAM.
Puerto Rico (U.S.)
GUAT.
HOND.
EL SAL.
NIC.
COSTA RICA
PAN.
VENEZUELA
GUYANA
SURINAME
Fr. Guiana
SENEGAL
GAMBIA
GUINEA BISSAU
GUI.
SIERRA LEONE
LIBERIA
IVORY COAST
GHANA
BURKINA FASO
Bogota
COLOMBIA
0° Equator
ECUADOR
SOUTH AMERICA
BRAZIL
PACIFIC OCEAN
PERU
Lima
BOLIVIA
PAR.
Rio de Janeiro
Tropic of Capricorn
CHILE
ARGENTINA
30° S
UR.
Santiago
Buenos Aires
0 1,000 2,000 Miles
0 1 000 2 000 Kilometers
60° S
Antarctic Circle
90° N
180°
120° W
60° W
0°
60° N
90° S
WORLD:POLITICAL
★ Capitals • Major cities

ARCTIC OCEAN
SOVIET UNION
ASIA
EUROPE
AFRICA
NORWAY
SWEDEN
FINLAND
Leningrad
Moscow
POL
E GER
Berlin
CZECH
HUNG
ROM
BUL
YUGO
ITALY
Rome
GREECE
Istanbul
TURKEY
MONGOLIA
Beijing
N KOREA
Seoul
S. KOREA
JAPAN
Tokyo-Yokohama
CHINA
Shanghai
TAIWAN
Hong Kong
AFGHANISTAN
PAKISTAN
Karachi
Delhi
INDIA
Bombay
Calcutta
NEPAL
BHUTAN
BANGLADESH
BURMA
LAOS
VIETNAM
THAILAND
Bangkok
PHILIPPINES
Manila
SRI LANKA
MALAYSIA
SINGAPORE
INDONESIA
Jakarta
PAPUA NEW GUINEA
PACIFIC OCEAN
INDIAN OCEAN
AUSTRALIA
Sydney
Melbourne
NEW ZEALAND
IRAN
Tehran
IRAQ
Baghdad
SYRIA
LEB
ISRAEL
JORDAN
KUWAIT
BAHRAIN
QATAR
UAE
OMAN
SAUDI ARABIA
Riyadh
YEM.
P.D.R. OF YEM.
DJIBOUTI
Cairo
EGYPT
LIBYA
TUNISIA
Algiers
ALGERIA
NIGER
CHAD
SUDAN
ETHIOPIA
SOMALIA
NIGERIA
BENIN
TOGO
Lagos
CAMEROON
CEN. AFR. REP
EQUAT. GUI.
GABON
CONGO
UGANDA
KENYA
Nairobi
RWANDA
BURUND
ZAIRE
TANZANIA
SEYCHELLES
ANGOLA
ZAMBIA
MALAWI
COMOROS
MOZAMBIQUE
MADAGASCAR
ZIMB
BOTS.
SOUTH-WEST AFRICA (Namibia)
SWAZILAND
Johannesburg
REP. OF S. AFR.
LESOTHO
ANTARCTICA
30° N
0° Equator
30° S
60° S
90° N
90° S
180°

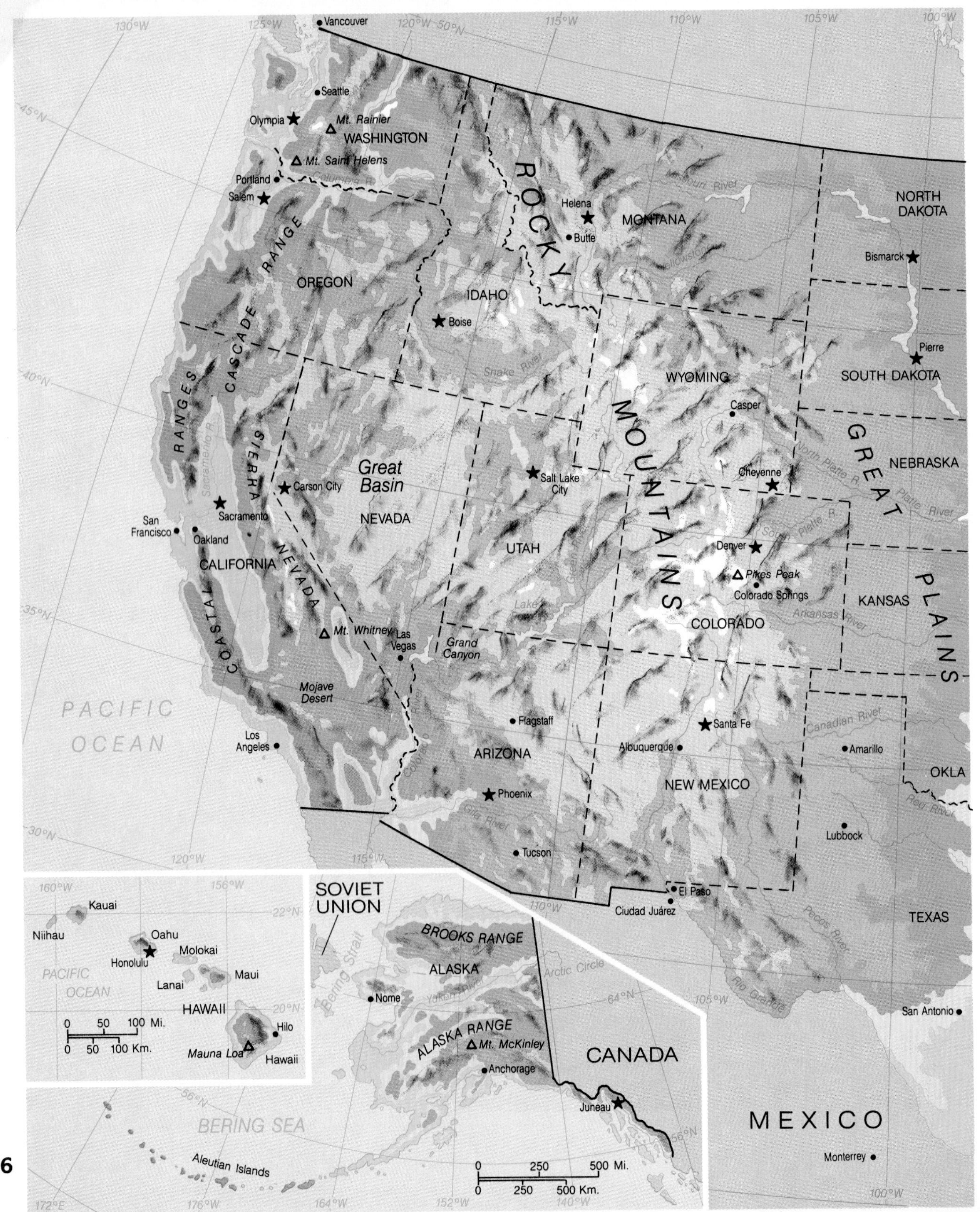
PACIFIC OCEAN
WASHINGTON
OREGON
CALIFORNIA
NEVADA
IDAHO
MONTANA
WYOMING
UTAH
COLORADO
ARIZONA
NEW MEXICO
NORTH DAKOTA
SOUTH DAKOTA
NEBRASKA
KANSAS
OKLA
TEXAS
MEXICO
CANADA
SOVIET UNION
ALASKA
HAWAII
ROCKY MOUNTAINS
GREAT PLAINS
CASCADE RANGE
COASTAL RANGES
SIERRA NEVADA
Great Basin
Mojave Desert
Grand Canyon
BROOKS RANGE
ALASKA RANGE
BERING SEA
Aleutian Islands
Bering Strait
Arctic Circle
Vancouver
Seattle
Olympia
Mt. Rainier
Mt. Saint Helens
Portland
Salem
Columbia R.
Helena
Butte
Missouri River
Yellowstone
Bismarck
Pierre
Boise
Snake River
Casper
North Platte R.
Platte River
South Platte R.
Cheyenne
Denver
Pikes Peak
Colorado Springs
Arkansas River
Salt Lake City
Green River
Lake Powell
Carson City
Sacramento
Sacramento R.
San Francisco
Oakland
Mt. Whitney
Las Vegas
Los Angeles
Colorado River
Flagstaff
Phoenix
Gila River
Tucson
Santa Fe
Albuquerque
Canadian River
Amarillo
Red River
Lubbock
El Paso
Ciudad Juárez
Pecos River
Rio Grande
San Antonio
Monterrey
Kauai
Niihau
Oahu
Honolulu
Molokai
Lanai
Maui
Hilo
Mauna Loa
Hawaii
PACIFIC OCEAN
0 50 100 Mi.
0 50 100 Km.
Nome
Yukon River
Mt. McKinley
Anchorage
Juneau
0 250 500 Mi.
0 250 500 Km.
130°W
125°W
120°W
115°W
110°W
105°W
100°W
50°N
45°N
40°N
35°N
30°N
160°W
156°W
22°N
20°N
64°N
56°N
172°E
176°W
164°W
152°W
140°W

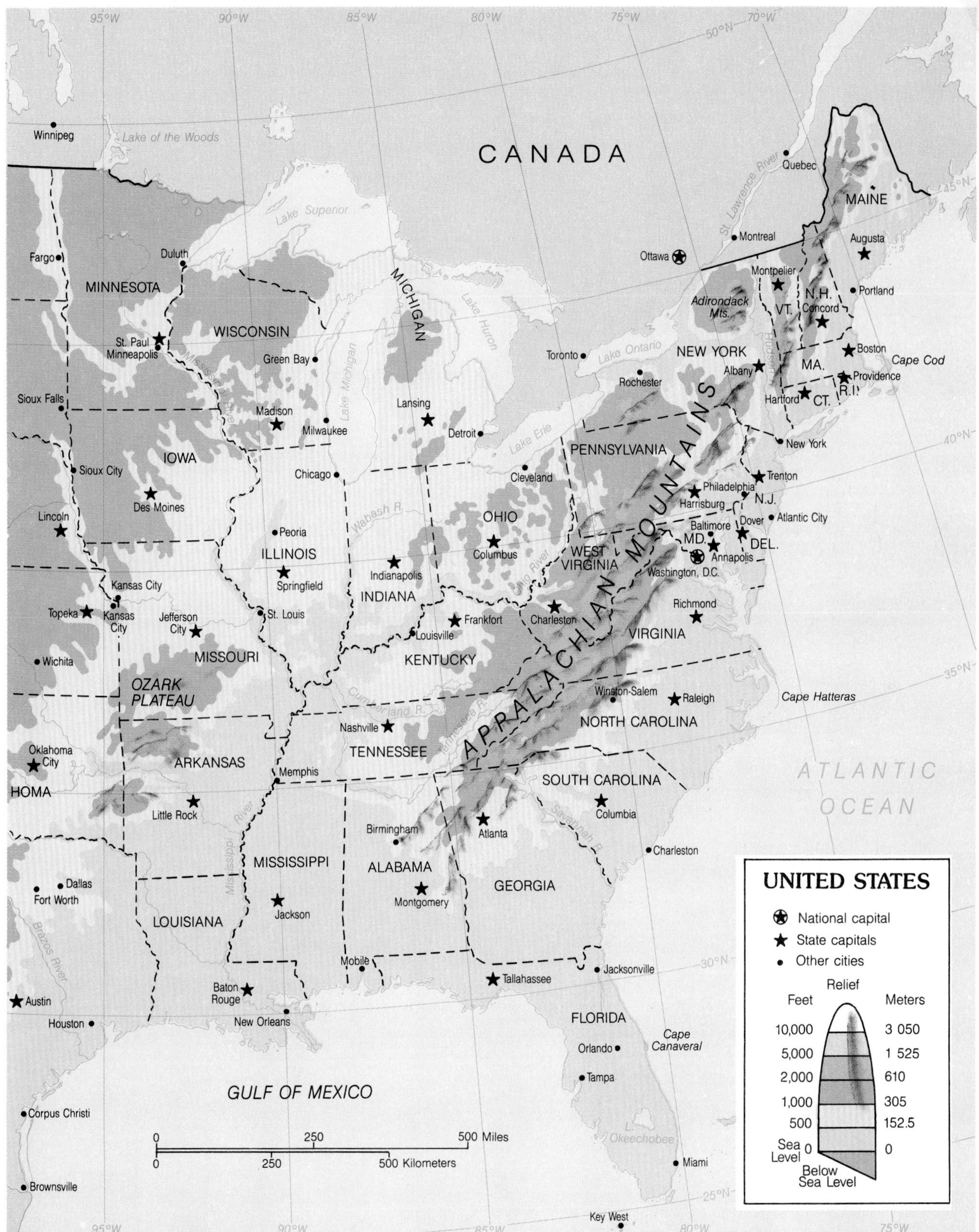
CANADA
UNITED STATES
National capital
State capitals
Other cities
Relief
Feet
Meters
10,000
3 050
5,000
1 525
2,000
610
1,000
305
500
152.5
Sea Level 0
0
Below Sea Level
APPALACHIAN MOUNTAINS
OZARK PLATEAU
Adirondack Mts.
ATLANTIC OCEAN
GULF OF MEXICO
Cape Cod
Cape Hatteras
Cape Canaveral
Lake of the Woods
Lake Superior
Lake Michigan
Lake Huron
Lake Ontario
Lake Erie
L. Okeechobee
St. Lawrence River
Mississippi River
Ohio River
Wabash R.
Cumberland R.
Tennessee R.
Savannah R.
Hudson R.
Brazos River
MAINE
N.H.
VT.
MA.
R.I.
CT.
NEW YORK
PENNSYLVANIA
N.J.
DEL.
MD.
WEST VIRGINIA
VIRGINIA
NORTH CAROLINA
SOUTH CAROLINA
GEORGIA
FLORIDA
ALABAMA
MISSISSIPPI
TENNESSEE
KENTUCKY
OHIO
INDIANA
ILLINOIS
MICHIGAN
WISCONSIN
MINNESOTA
IOWA
MISSOURI
ARKANSAS
LOUISIANA
HOMA
Winnipeg
Quebec
Montreal
Ottawa
Toronto
Augusta
Portland
Montpelier
Concord
Boston
Providence
Hartford
Albany
Rochester
New York
Trenton
Philadelphia
Harrisburg
Atlantic City
Dover
Baltimore
Annapolis
Washington, D.C.
Richmond
Raleigh
Winston-Salem
Columbia
Charleston
Atlanta
Jacksonville
Tallahassee
Orlando
Tampa
Miami
Key West
Cleveland
Columbus
Detroit
Lansing
Charleston
Frankfort
Louisville
Indianapolis
Chicago
Peoria
Springfield
St. Louis
Milwaukee
Madison
Green Bay
Duluth
St. Paul
Minneapolis
Fargo
Sioux Falls
Sioux City
Des Moines
Lincoln
Kansas City
Topeka
Kansas City
Jefferson City
Wichita
Oklahoma City
Little Rock
Memphis
Nashville
Birmingham
Montgomery
Jackson
Mobile
Baton Rouge
New Orleans
Dallas
Fort Worth
Austin
Houston
Corpus Christi
Brownsville
0
250
500 Miles
0
250
500 Kilometers
95°W
90°W
85°W
80°W
75°W
70°W
50°N
45°N
40°N
35°N
30°N
25°N

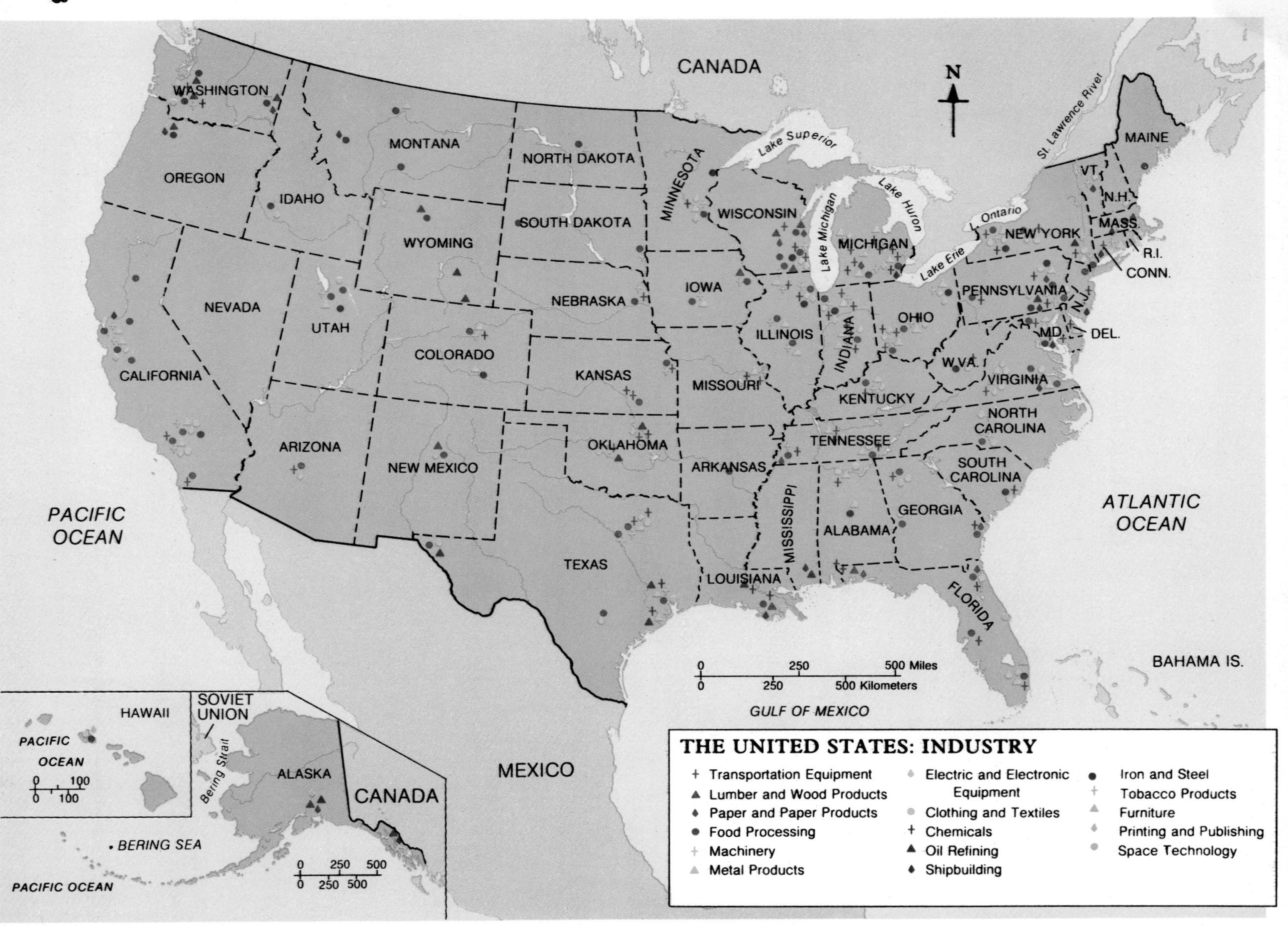
THE UNITED STATES: INDUSTRY
Transportation Equipment
Lumber and Wood Products
Paper and Paper Products
Food Processing
Machinery
Metal Products
Electric and Electronic Equipment
Clothing and Textiles
Chemicals
Oil Refining
Shipbuilding
Iron and Steel
Tobacco Products
Furniture
Printing and Publishing
Space Technology
CANADA
MEXICO
PACIFIC OCEAN
ATLANTIC OCEAN
GULF OF MEXICO
BAHAMA IS.
St. Lawrence River
Lake Superior
Lake Michigan
Lake Huron
Lake Erie
Ontario
WASHINGTON
OREGON
CALIFORNIA
IDAHO
NEVADA
MONTANA
WYOMING
UTAH
ARIZONA
COLORADO
NEW MEXICO
NORTH DAKOTA
SOUTH DAKOTA
NEBRASKA
KANSAS
OKLAHOMA
TEXAS
MINNESOTA
IOWA
MISSOURI
ARKANSAS
LOUISIANA
WISCONSIN
ILLINOIS
MICHIGAN
INDIANA
OHIO
KENTUCKY
TENNESSEE
MISSISSIPPI
ALABAMA
GEORGIA
FLORIDA
SOUTH CAROLINA
NORTH CAROLINA
VIRGINIA
W.VA.
PENNSYLVANIA
NEW YORK
MD.
DEL.
N.J.
CONN.
R.I.
MASS.
VT.
N.H.
MAINE
N
0 250 500 Miles
0 250 500 Kilometers
HAWAII
PACIFIC OCEAN
0 100
0 100
SOVIET UNION
Bering Strait
ALASKA
CANADA
BERING SEA
PACIFIC OCEAN
0 250 500
0 250 500

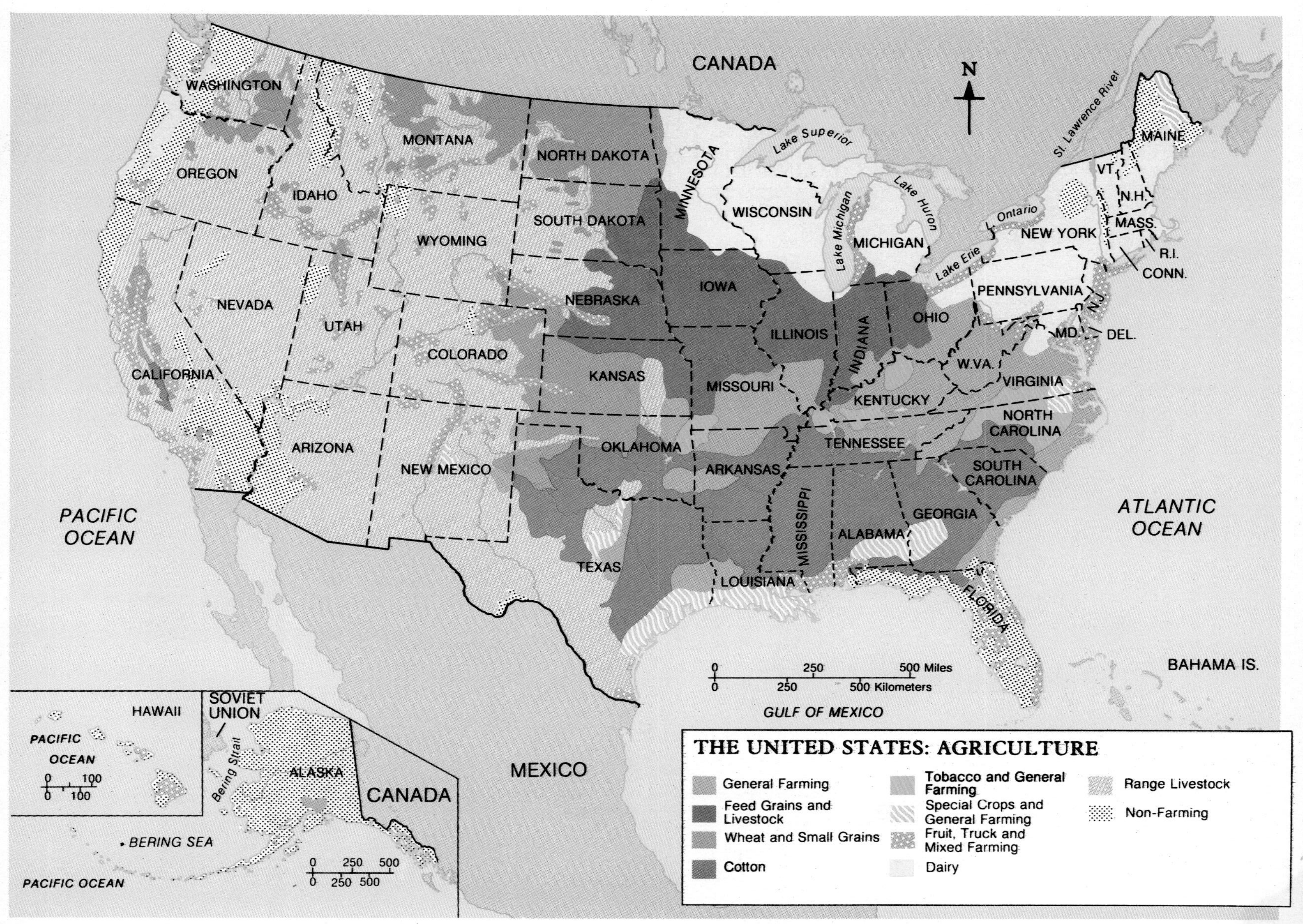
THE UNITED STATES: AGRICULTURE
General Farming
Feed Grains and Livestock
Wheat and Small Grains
Cotton
Tobacco and General Farming
Special Crops and General Farming
Fruit, Truck and Mixed Farming
Dairy
Range Livestock
Non-Farming
N
CANADA
WASHINGTON
OREGON
IDAHO
MONTANA
NORTH DAKOTA
SOUTH DAKOTA
WYOMING
NEVADA
UTAH
CALIFORNIA
COLORADO
NEBRASKA
KANSAS
ARIZONA
NEW MEXICO
OKLAHOMA
TEXAS
MINNESOTA
WISCONSIN
IOWA
MISSOURI
ARKANSAS
LOUISIANA
ILLINOIS
MICHIGAN
INDIANA
OHIO
KENTUCKY
TENNESSEE
MISSISSIPPI
ALABAMA
GEORGIA
FLORIDA
SOUTH CAROLINA
NORTH CAROLINA
VIRGINIA
W.VA.
PENNSYLVANIA
NEW YORK
MD.
DEL.
N.J.
CONN.
R.I.
MASS.
N.H.
VT.
MAINE
Lake Superior
Lake Michigan
Lake Huron
Lake Erie
Ontario
St. Lawrence River
ATLANTIC OCEAN
PACIFIC OCEAN
BAHAMA IS.
GULF OF MEXICO
MEXICO
0 250 500 Miles
0 250 500 Kilometers
HAWAII
PACIFIC OCEAN
0 100
0 100
SOVIET UNION
Bering Strait
ALASKA
CANADA
BERING SEA
PACIFIC OCEAN
0 250 500
0 250 500

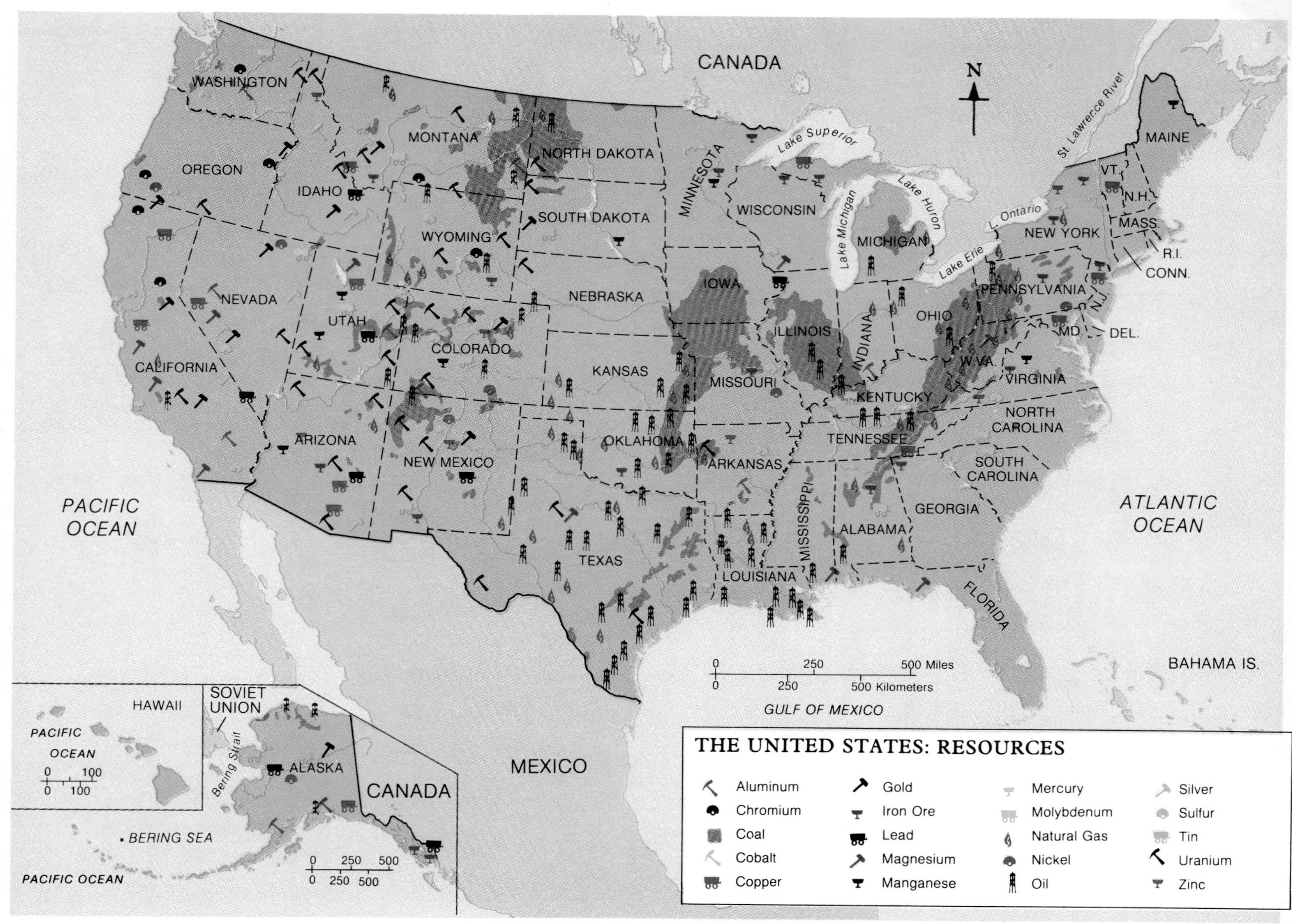
THE UNITED STATES: RESOURCES
Aluminum
Chromium
Coal
Cobalt
Copper
Gold
Iron Ore
Lead
Magnesium
Manganese
Mercury
Molybdenum
Natural Gas
Nickel
Oil
Silver
Sulfur
Tin
Uranium
Zinc
CANADA
N
MAINE
VT.
N.H.
MASS.
R.I.
CONN.
NEW YORK
PENNSYLVANIA
N.J.
DEL.
MD.
W.VA.
VIRGINIA
NORTH CAROLINA
SOUTH CAROLINA
GEORGIA
FLORIDA
OHIO
MICHIGAN
INDIANA
ILLINOIS
KENTUCKY
TENNESSEE
ALABAMA
MISSISSIPPI
LOUISIANA
ARKANSAS
MISSOURI
IOWA
WISCONSIN
MINNESOTA
NORTH DAKOTA
SOUTH DAKOTA
NEBRASKA
KANSAS
OKLAHOMA
TEXAS
MONTANA
WYOMING
COLORADO
NEW MEXICO
IDAHO
UTAH
ARIZONA
WASHINGTON
OREGON
NEVADA
CALIFORNIA
St. Lawrence River
Lake Superior
Lake Michigan
Lake Huron
Lake Erie
L. Ontario
ATLANTIC OCEAN
BAHAMA IS.
GULF OF MEXICO
MEXICO
PACIFIC OCEAN
0 250 500 Miles
0 250 500 Kilometers
HAWAII
PACIFIC OCEAN
0 100
0 100
SOVIET UNION
Bering Strait
ALASKA
CANADA
BERING SEA
PACIFIC OCEAN
0 250 500
0 250 500

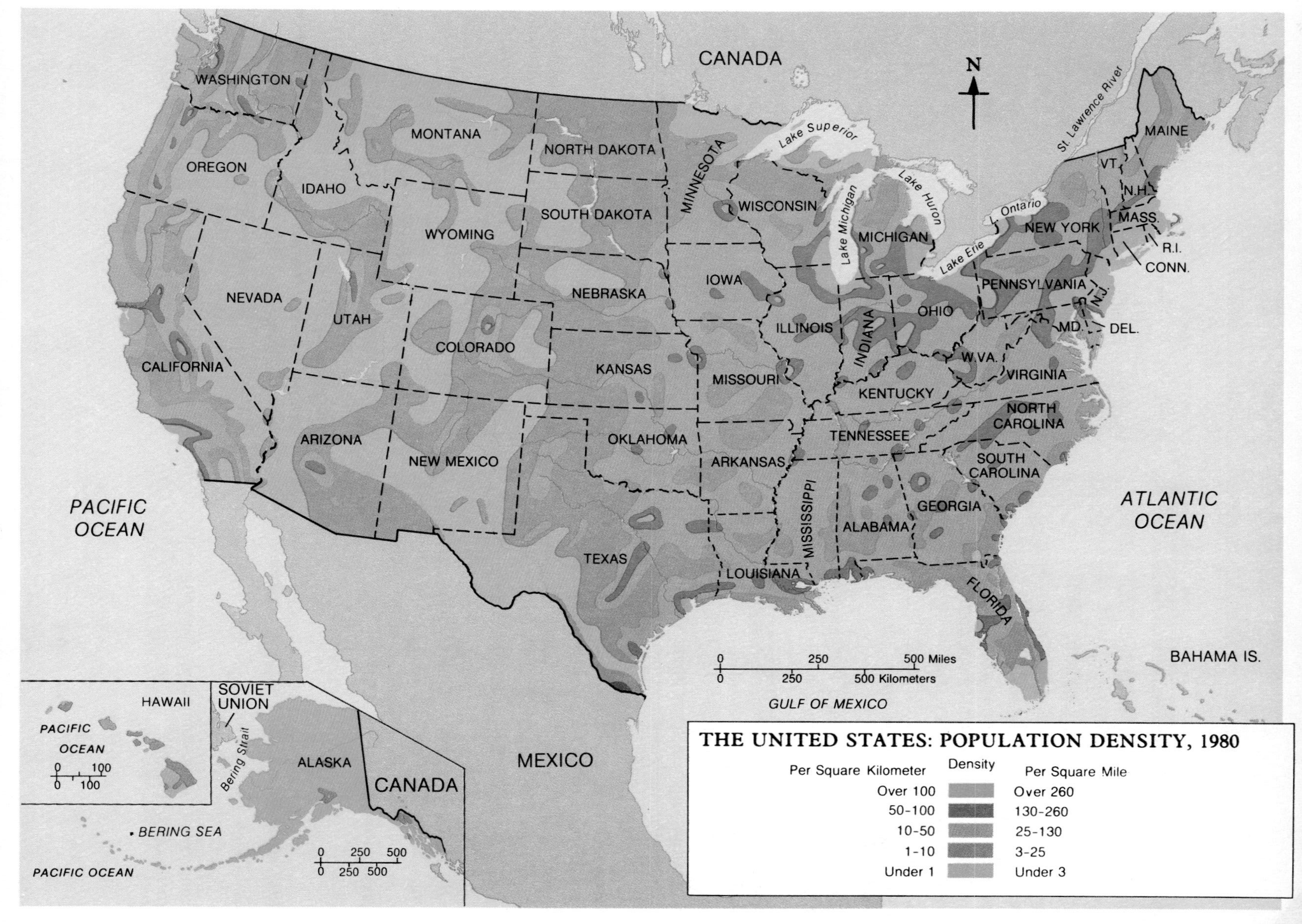
CANADA
N
St. Lawrence River
Lake Superior
Lake Huron
Lake Michigan
L. Ontario
Lake Erie
WASHINGTON
MONTANA
NORTH DAKOTA
MINNESOTA
MAINE
VT.
N.H.
MASS.
R.I.
CONN.
OREGON
IDAHO
SOUTH DAKOTA
WISCONSIN
MICHIGAN
NEW YORK
WYOMING
NEVADA
UTAH
NEBRASKA
IOWA
PENNSYLVANIA
N.J.
OHIO
INDIANA
ILLINOIS
MD.
DEL.
COLORADO
CALIFORNIA
KANSAS
MISSOURI
W.VA.
VIRGINIA
KENTUCKY
NORTH CAROLINA
ARIZONA
OKLAHOMA
TENNESSEE
NEW MEXICO
ARKANSAS
SOUTH CAROLINA
MISSISSIPPI
ALABAMA
GEORGIA
TEXAS
LOUISIANA
FLORIDA
PACIFIC OCEAN
ATLANTIC OCEAN
BAHAMA IS.
0 250 500 Miles
0 250 500 Kilometers
GULF OF MEXICO
MEXICO
HAWAII
PACIFIC OCEAN
0 100
0 100
SOVIET UNION
Bering Strait
ALASKA
CANADA
BERING SEA
PACIFIC OCEAN
0 250 500
0 250 500
THE UNITED STATES: POPULATION DENSITY, 1980
Per Square Kilometer
Density
Per Square Mile
Over 100
Over 260
50-100
130-260
10-50
25-130
1-10
3-25
Under 1
Under 3

GAZETTEER

A

Afghanistan Country in central Asia, south of the Soviet Union. **(p. 680, 681)**

Alabama Southern state. **(pp. 295, 346)**

Alamo Spanish mission and fort in San Antonio, Texas. 29°N 99°W **(pp. 225, 282–288)**

Alaska Largest state of the United States, in land size. Smallest in population. Most northern state. **(pp. 181, 330, 442)**

Albany Capital of New York State. The Dutch of New Netherland called it Fort Orange. 43°N 74°W **(p. 69)**

Antietam Creek in Maryland that flows into the Potomac River. Site of early battle of the Civil War. **(pp. 299–300)**

Appalachian Mountains Mountain system of eastern North America, extending from Canada to central Alabama. **(pp. 91–92, 110, 113)**

Appomattox Virginian town where General Lee surrendered to General Grant on April 9, 1865. 37°N 79°W **(pp. 306, 308)**

Arizona Southwestern state. Southern part of state borders Mexico. Grand Canyon State. **(p. 694)**

Arkansas South-central state. Eastern border is Mississippi River. **(pp. 189, 297, 316, 537)**

Atlanta Capital and largest city of Georgia. 34°N 84°W **(p. 305)**

Austria-Hungary Former monarchy in central Europe. A Central Power in World War I. Divided into several countries as a result of the Treaty of Versailles. **(pp. 465–466, 472)**

B

Bay of Pigs Bay in southern Cuba. 22°N 81°W **(pp. 615–616)**

Bering Strait Strait connecting Asia and North America. **(pp. 17, 20)**

Berlin Former capital of Germany, which has been divided into East Berlin and West Berlin since 1945. East Berlin is the capital of East Germany. 53°N 13°E **(pp. 564–571, 588, 614–615)**

Boston Port city and capital of Massachusetts. 42°N 71°W **(pp. 103, 104, 140–147, 155)**

Breed's Hill Hill near Boston Harbor. Site of fighting during the Revolutionary War. 42°N 71°W **(p. 104)**

Buffalo Industrial and port city in New York State on Lake Erie. 43°N 79°W **(pp. 26, 342, 344, 368, 379)**

Bull Run Stream in northeastern Virginia. Site of fighting during the Civil War. 39°N 78°W **(pp. 297, 299)**

Bunker Hill Hill near Boston Harbor. Site of fighting during the Revolutionary War. 42°N 71°W **(p. 104)**

C

California Western state borders Pacific Ocean. Most-populated state. Ceded to the United States by Mexico in 1848. **(pp. 221, 223, 231–232, 233, 235–237, 252, 256, 257, 273)**

Cambodia Country in Southeast Asia, south of Thailand. Known today as Democratic Kampuchea. **(pp. 657, 667, 668, 712)**

Canada Country in North America, whose northern-most part is Cape Columbia. **(pp. 48–49, 51)**

Central America Narrow southern portion of North America connecting that continent with South America. **(pp. 29–33, 42–44, 181, 687, 711,–712)**

Charleston Port city in South Carolina. 33°N 80°W. **(pp. 106–107, 110)**

Château Thierry Site of a battle in northeastern France during World War I. 49°N 3°E **(p. 469)**

Chesapeake Bay Large inlet of the Atlantic Ocean in Virginia and Maryland. **(p. 163)**

Chicago Major industrial and port city in Illinois. 42°N 88°W **(pp. 264, 489)**

China Country in eastern and central Asia, known officially as the People's Republic of China. **(pp. 444–445, 542–543, 550, 657, 658, 671, 680)**

Colorado West-central state. Western half of state has high ranges of Rocky Mountains. **(p. 537)**

Comstock Lode Gold and silver mine near Virginia City, Nevada. 39°N 120°W **(p. 339)**

Concord Village near Boston, Massachusetts. The first battle of the Revolutionary War took place here. 43°N 71°W **(p. 103)**

Connecticut New England state in the northeastern part of the country. One of the original 13 states. **(p. 57)**

Cowpens Site of a battle in South Carolina during the Revolutionary War. 35°N 82°W **(p. 110)**

Cuba Island in the West Indies. **(pp. 418–419, 420–423, 541, 600–601, 615–616, 682)**

Czechoslovakia Country in central Europe, south of Poland. **(pp. 549, 646)**

D

Dallas Major industrial and commercial city in Texas. 33°N 97°W **(p. 617)**

Delaware Eastern state. Located in Delmarva Penins ula. **(pp. 58, 297)**

Denmark Country in northwestern Europe, between the Baltic and North seas. **(p. 549)**

Dominican Republic Country in the West Indies on the eastern part of Hispaniola Island. **(pp. 463, 645)**

Dust Bowl Area in the United States hit by severe drought and wind storms in the 1930's. The area included land in Kansas, Arkansas, Oklahoma, New Mexico, Texas, and Colorado. **(p. 537)**

E

Egypt Country in northern Africa on the Mediterranean Sea, known officially as the Arab Republic of Egypt. **(pp. 599, 671, 680)**

El Salvador Country in Central America, southwest of Honduras. **(p. 687)**

England Southern part of the island of Great Britain, excluding Wales. **(pp. 17, 40, 50–52, 55–69, 73–78, 83, 85–99, 103–111, 140–146, 441, 442)**

Erie Canal Connected the Hudson River in the eastern part of New York with Lake Erie in the western part of New York. **(pp. 194, 195)**

F

Far East Countries of East Asia and the Malay archipelago. **(p. 39)**

Florida Southern state. Located on peninsula between the Atlantic Ocean and the Gulf of Mexico. **(pp. 135, 295)**

Fort Sumter Located at the entrance to Charleston harbor in South Carolina. 33°N 80°W **(pp. 295, 296)**

France Country in Western Europe, south of the English Channel. **(pp. 17, 40, 47–49, 108, 111, 134–135, 158–159, 162–163, 329–330, 441, 442, 465, 466, 549–550, 646)**

G

Gadsden Purchase Land bought from Mexico in 1853. Now part of New Mexico and Arizona. **(p. 271)**

Georgia South Atlantic state. One of the 13 original states. **(pp. 58, 295, 305–306, 320, 321, 346)**

Germany Former country in central Europe. Divided into two republics—East Germany and West Germany—since 1949. **(pp. 261, 441, 442, 465–473, 540, 547–550, 556–558, 564–570, 587–588, 614–615)**

Gettysburg Small town in southern Pennsylvania. Site of Civil War battle. 40°N 77°W **(pp. 301, 304, 353–360)**

Goliad Texas town near San Antonio. 29°N 97°W **(p. 283)**

Gonzales Texas city near San Antonio. 30°N 97°W **(p. 283)**

Great Britain Island country of Western Europe. Includes England, Scotland, Wales, and Northern Ireland. **(pp. 85, 134–135, 162–164, 229–231, 331, 465–473, 549–557)**

Great Plains The continental slope extending through the United States and Canada. **(pp. 223, 339–340, 342)**

Great Lakes The chain of five lakes between the United States and Canada. The Great Lakes include Lakes Ontario, Huron, Erie, Michigan, Superior. **(p. 67)**

Greece Country in southern Europe, on the Balkan Peninsula. **(p. 587)**

Grenada Island nation in the Caribbean. **(p. 687)**

Guam Island territory of the United States in the western Pacific Ocean **(pp. 423, 443, 444, 552)**

Gulf of Tonkin Gulf Southeast of North Vietnam. **(p. 647)**

H

Haiti Country on Hispaniola Island in the West Indies. **(p. 463)**

Harpers Ferry Town in northeastern West Virginia. 39°N 78°W **(p. 278)**

Hawaii A state that is a chain of volcanic and coral islands in the north central Pacific Ocean. **(pp. 442–443, 444)**

Hiroshima Port city on the Japanese island of Honshu. 34°N 132°E **(p. 559)**

Hudson Bay Inland sea in the Northwest Territories of Canada. **(p. 40)**

Hudson River Large river in New York State. **(p. 49)**

I

Idaho Northwestern state. **(p. 343)**

Illinois North-central state. **(p. 233)**

Indiana North-central state. **(p. 364)**

Iowa Central state. **(p. 221)**

Iran Southwest Asian country that was formerly named Persia. **(pp. 677–678, 681, 688, 712)**

Iraq Southwest Asian country, south of Turkey. **(pp. 599, 712)**

Israel Country in southwest Asia, south of Lebanon. **(pp. 599, 645–646, 671, 680, 712)**

Italy Southern European country, south of Switzerland and east of France. **(pp. 441, 442, 547–549, 556)**

Iwo Jima Small island south of Japan's main islands. **(p. 559)**

J

Jamestown Located in Virginia on the James River. First permanent English settlement in North America. 37°N 77°W **(pp. 55, 58)**

Japan Country in East Asia, consisting of four large islands of Hokkaido, Honshu, Shikoku, and Kyushu, plus thousands of small islands. **(pp. 542–543, 547–552, 554–559)**

K

Kansas Central state. **(pp. 273–276, 381–382)**

Kentucky East-central state. **(pp. 158, 297)**

L

Laos Southeast Asian country, south of China and west of Vietnam. **(p. 657)**

Latin America The land directly south of the United States where Spanish-speaking and Portuguese-speaking people live. **(pp. 445–446, 447, 541, 610, 645)**

Lebanon Country on the Mediterranean Sea, south of Syria. **(p. 687)**

Lexington Site of the first fight between the minutemen and the British troops in 1775. Located near Boston, Massachusetts. 42°N 71°W **(pp. 98–99, 103)**

Libya North African country on the Mediterranean Sea, west of Egypt. **(p. 688)**

Louisiana Southern state. **(pp. 48, 295, 316)**

Louisiana Purchase Region between the Mississippi River and the Rocky Mountains purchased from France in 1803. **(pp. 158–160)**

M

Maine Northeastern state. **(p. 185)**

Maryland Eastern state. One of the original 13 states. **(pp. 57, 297)**

Massachusetts Northeastern state. One of the original 13 states. **(pp. 57, 97, 115, 185)**

Mexican Cession Lands acquired by the United States from Mexico under the Treaty of Guadalupe Hidalgo in 1848. **(p. 235)**

Mexico Country in North America south of the United States. **(pp. 223–228, 231–232, 271, 282–288, 329–330, 463–464)**

Mexico City Capital and most-populous city of Mexico. 24°N 104°W **(p. 235)**

Michigan North-central state. **(p. 189)**

Middle East Region that includes the countries of southwest Asia and northeast Africa. **(pp. 599–600, 645–646, 663, 665, 671, 680, 687)**

Minnesota North-central state. **(p. 343)**

Mississippi Southern state. **(pp. 295, 320)**

Mississippi River Large river system in the central United States that rises from Lake Itasca, Minnesota, and flows southward into the Gulf of Mexico. **(pp. 48, 135, 158–159, 298, 304)**

Missouri Central state. **(pp. 184–185, 297)**

Montana Northwestern state. **(pp. 343, 368)**

Montreal Major city in Quebec, Canada, on the St. Lawrence River. 46°N 74°W **(pp. 49, 68)**

N

Nagasaki Port city of Japan. 33°N 130°E **(p. 559)**

Nebraska Central state. **(pp. 273–275)**

Nevada Western state. **(p. 339)**

New Amsterdam Dutch settlement on Manhattan Island. Now known as New York City. 41°N 74°W **(p. 50)**

New England Region that includes the states from Maine to Connecticut. **(pp. 155–156, 160–161, 165, 175, 190–191)**

New France The French Empire in North America. It consisted of present-day Canada and most areas of the central part of North America. **(pp. 47–49)**

New Jersey Eastern state. **(pp. 57–58)**

New Mexico Southwestern state. **(pp. 221, 232, 235, 257, 273, 464)**

New Orleans Major port and transportation center on the Mississippi River in Louisiana. 30°N 90°W **(pp. 135, 158, 165)**

New Spain Land in North America claimed by the Spanish. New Spain included parts of what is now the Southeast, the Southwest, and the West in the United States. **(pp. 44–46)**

New York Northeastern state. One of the original 13 states. **(pp. 49–50, 57, 155–156, 194)**

New York City Seaport at the mouth of the Hudson River and the largest city in the United States. 41°N 74°W **(pp. 326, 327)**

Nicaragua Country in Central America, south of Honduras. **(pp. 463, 687, 711)**

North Carolina Eastern state. **(pp. 58, 73, 75, 78, 297)**

North Korea Country in East Asia. Divided at the 38th parallel from South Korea. **(pp. 588–589)**

Northwest Territory Lands north of the Ohio River and east of the Mississippi River. **(pp. 115–116, 135, 164)**

O

Ohio Eastern state. **(p. 158)**

Okinawa Small island southwest of Japan. **(p. 559)**

Oklahoma South-central state. **(p. 342, 382, 384)**

Oregon Northwestern state. **(pp. 160, 221, 223, 228–231, 233, 234)**

Oregon trail Overland route from Independence, Missouri to the Columbia River valley. **(pp. 222–223, 229, 230)**

P

Panama Country in Central America, on the Isthmus of Panama. **(pp. 445–446, 645, 680)**

Panama Canal Located on the Isthmus of Panama. Connects the Pacific and Atlantic oceans. **(pp. 445–446, 447, 677, 680)**

Pearl Harbor American naval base near Honolulu. 21°N 158°W **(pp. 551–552, 556)**

Pennsylvania Northeastern state. One of the original 13 states. **(pp. 58, 155–156, 338)**

Persian Gulf Major sea route for ships carrying oil exports from the Middle East. **(p. 712)**

Philadelphia Port city in southeastern Pennsylvania. 40°N 75°W **(pp. 98, 103)**

Phillipine Islands Country in the Pacific Ocean, southeast of Asia. **(pp. 422, 443, 444, 462, 552)**

Plymouth Colony founded by Pilgrims in New England. 42°N 71°W **(pp. 56, 57)**

Poland Country on the Baltic Sea in Eastern Europe. **(p. 549)**

Portugal Country on the Iberian Peninsula south and west of Spain. **(p. 39)**

Promontory Point Place where the Central Pacific and Union railroads were joined. Just north of the Great Salt Lake. 42°N 112°W **(p. 337)**

Puerto Rico Island in the West Indies that is part of the United States. **(pp. 423, 443, 462, 474)**

Q

Quebec Located on the St. Lawrence River in eastern Canada. 47°N 71°W **(pp. 47, 51, 68)**

R

Republic of South Africa Country at the southern tip of Africa. **(pp. 680, 711)**

Rhode Island Northeastern state. One of the original 13 states. **(pp. 57, 66, 121)**

Richmond Located on the James River in Virginia. 38°N 78°W **(pp. 298, 299, 304, 306, 353)**

Rio Grande River that forms the boundary between Texas and Mexico. **(p. 234)**

Rocky Mountains Mountain system in western North America extending from the Arctic to Mexico. **(p. 233)**

S

Salt Lake City Capital of Utah. 41°N 112°W **(p. 233)**

San Antonio City in southern Texas. Site of the Alamo. 29°N 99°W **(p. 225)**

Santa Fe trail Overland trail from Independence, Missouri, to Santa Fe, New Mexico. **(pp. 222–223)**

Saratoga City in eastern New York. 43°N 75°W **(p. 108)**

Savannah Oldest city in Georgia. 32°N 81°W **(pp. 305–306)**

South Carolina Southeastern state. One of the original 13 states. **(pp. 58, 106, 110, 198, 295)**

South Dakota Northwest-central state. **(pp. 342–343)**

South Korea Country in Asia on the Korean Peninsula between the Yellow Sea and the Sea of Japan. **(pp. 588–589)**

Soviet Union Country in eastern Europe and Asia. Officially known as the Union of Soviet Socialist Republics. **(pp. 541–542, 547, 550, 556–558, 599–600, 601, 614–617, 625–633, 645–646, 658, 670–671, 680, 681, 685, 687, 706, 707, 710–711)**

Spain Country on the Iberian Peninsula. **(pp. 17, 39, 41–46, 158, 181, 223–224, 231, 365, 418–423, 443, 444, 547)**

T

Taiwan Island Off the southeast coast of China, and the seat of the Chinese Nationalist Government. **(pp. 600, 658)**

Tehran Capital of Iran. 36°N 52°E **(p. 681)**

Tennessee Southeastern state. **(pp. 158, 297, 316, 317, 319, 346)**

Texas Southern state. **(pp. 189, 221, 223–228, 233, 234, 317, 320, 368)**

U

Utah Western state. **(pp. 221, 233, 273)**

V

Valley Forge Located near Philadelphia, Pennsylvania. 40°N 76°W **(p. 109)**

Vermont Northeastern state. **(p. 158)**

Vietnam Southeast Asian country, east of Laos and Democratic Kampuchea. **(pp. 644, 646–649, 665, 667–668)**

Virginia Eastern state. One of the original 13 states. **(pp. 55–56, 58, 297, 320)**

W

Washington, D.C. Capital of the United States, in the District of Columbia, which was set aside for this purpose. 39°N 77°W **(pp. 132, 165, 243)**

West Indies Islands in the Caribbean Sea, between North America and South America. **(p. 62)**

West Virginia Eastern state. **(p. 297)**

Wisconsin North central state. **(pp. 189, 221, 277)**

Wyoming Northwestern state. **(p. 368)**

Y

Yorktown Town in Virginia. 37°N 76°W **(pp. 110–111)**

THE DECLARATION OF INDEPENDENCE

WITH COMMENTS

The Declaration of Independence is printed on the following pages in the left-hand columns. In the right-hand columns are comments which tell in everyday language what the writers of the Declaration of Independence said in more formal language. The comments will help you understand the meaning of each paragraph.

In Congress, July 4, 1776
The Unanimous Declaration of the Thirteen United States of America

When, in the course of human events, it becomes necessary for one people to dissolve the political bands which have connected them with another, and to assume, among the powers of the earth, the separate and equal station to which the laws of nature and of nature's God entitle them, a decent respect to the opinions of mankind requires that they should declare the causes which impel them to the separation.

The American people have decided to break away from England. We will now form a separate nation. We should tell the world why we are doing so.

We hold these truths to be self-evident: That all men are created equal; that they are endowed by their Creator with certain unalienable rights; that among these are life, liberty, and the pursuit of happiness. That, to secure these rights, governments are instituted among men, deriving their just powers from the consent of the governed; that, whenever any form of government becomes destructive of these ends, it is the right of the people to alter or to abolish it, and to institute new government, laying its foundation on such principles, and organizing its powers in such form, as to them shall seem most likely to effect their safety and happiness. Prudence, indeed, will dictate that governments long established should not be changed for light and transient causes; and accordingly all experience hath shown that mankind are more disposed to suffer, while evils are sufferable, than to right themselves by abolishing the forms to which they are accustomed. But when a

We think that everyone can see that God has given to all people certain basic rights. Among these are life, liberty, and the right to seek happiness. We believe, too, that people set up governments to protect such rights. In exchange, they agree to give these governments certain powers.

The people have a right to act when a government begins to destroy their rights. They can change the government, or do away with it. Then they can form a new government that will do what they want it to do.

We realize that a government that has lasted a long time should not be changed or done away with for some small reason. But what can we do when a government takes away our rights time after time? What can we do when it shows that it wants to crush the people? It is our duty to declare ourselves

long train of abuses and usurpations, pursuing invariably the same object, evinces a design to reduce them under absolute despotism, it is their right, it is their duty, to throw off such government, and to provide new guards for their future security. Such has been the patient sufferance of these colonies; and such is now the necessity which constrains them to alter their former systems of government. The history of the present King of Great Britain is a history of repeated injuries and usurpations, all having in direct object the establishment of an absolute tyranny over these states. To prove this, let facts be submitted to a candid world.

free of that government. It is our right to set up one that will protect our rights.

As English subjects, we in the colonies have patiently suffered unfair treatment by the king. He has tried to rule us like a tyrant. Here is a list of facts that proves this statement.

He has refused his assent to laws the most wholesome and necessary for the public good.

The king has refused to approve good laws that we needed.

He has forbidden his governors to pass laws of immediate and pressing importance, unless suspended in their operation till his assent should be obtained; and, when so suspended, he has utterly neglected to attend to them.

He has not allowed the colonial governments to pass needed laws; he has delayed the passage of such laws.

He has refused to pass other laws for the accommodation of large districts of people, unless those people would relinquish the right of representation in the legislature,—a right inestimable to them, and formidable to tyrants only.

In some places we have lost the right to send representatives to our own governments. The king has demanded that we give up this right before he would pass laws we have needed. This important right is feared only by tyrants.

He has called together legislative bodies at places unusual, uncomfortable, and distant from the depository of their public records, for the sole purpose of fatiguing them into compliance with his measures.

He has called meetings of our assemblies at places distant from where their governments usually meet. He has done this to wear out our representatives and make them do as he wishes.

He has dissolved representative houses repeatedly, for opposing, with manly firmness, his invasions on the rights of the people.

He has refused, for a long time after such dissolutions, to cause others to be elected, whereby the legislative powers, incapable of annihilation, have returned to the people at large for their exercise; the state remaining, in the meantime, exposed to all the dangers of invasion from without and convulsions within.

The king has often closed down our legislatures (assemblies). He has done this because such an assembly is against his attempts to take away our rights. Then he has tried to prevent us from electing a new assembly to take its place. Meanwhile, the colony was unprotected.

He has endeavored to prevent the population of these states; for that purpose obstructing the laws for naturalization of foreigners, refusing to pass others to encourage their migration hither, and raising the conditions of new appropriations of lands.

He has tried to keep the colonies from growing. He has not allowed people from other lands to become citizens of the colonies. He has not allowed more people to come to America. He has made it hard for

He has obstructed the administration of justice, by refusing his assent to laws for establishing judiciary powers.

He has made judges dependent on his will alone for the tenure of their offices, and the amount and payment of their salaries.

He has erected a multitude of new offices and sent hither swarms of officers to harass our people and eat out their substance.

He has kept among us in times of peace, standing armies, without the consent of our legislatures.

He has affected to render the military independent of, and superior to, the civil power.

He has combined with others to subject us to a jurisdiction foreign to our constitution and unacknowledged by our laws, giving his assent to their acts of pretended legislation:

For quartering large bodies of armed troops among us;

For protecting them, by a mock trial, from punishment for any murders which they should commit on the inhabitants of these states;

For cutting off our trade with all parts of the world;

For imposing taxes on us without our consent;

For depriving us, in many cases, of the benefits of trial by jury;

For transporting us beyond seas, to be tried for pretended offenses;

For abolishing the free system of English laws in a neighboring province, establishing therein an arbitrary government, and enlarging its boundaries, so as to render it at once an example and fit instrument for introducing the same absolute rule into these colonies;

For taking away our charters, abolishing our most valuable laws, and altering, fundamentally, the forms of our governments;

For suspending our own legislatures, and declaring themselves invested with power to legislate for us in all cases whatsoever.

newcomers from other lands to get land in the colonies.

The king has not let us pass laws that would give us our own courts. He has decided for us how long our judges can hold office. He has insisted that he alone can decide what a judge's salary can be and when it should be paid.

He has set up many new offices and sent officers to fill them. These officers bother our people. We have to pay their salaries and the cost of what they do.

The king keeps an army in our land in times of peace. He does this without asking the consent of our assemblies. In this way, he keeps us under military rule.

The king, his ministers, and the British Parliament have tried to rule us by laws that are completely different from our own laws. Here is a list of some of the things such laws have tried to do.

These laws would make us house and feed many armed soldiers.

The king's laws would allow his soldiers to murder us without their being punished.

We would be taxed without our consent.

In many cases these laws would take away our right to be tried before a jury. In other cases we would have to go to England for a trial.

The king's laws would do away with Canada's laws. They would set up a government run by England. The king's laws would also enlarge Canada. Parliament might try to do the same to us next.

These laws would take away our charters. They would end some of our most valuable laws. They would change the form of our governments and stop our legislatures from meeting. Instead, the king says he and Parliament have the power to make all laws for us.

He has abdicated government here, by declaring us out of his protection and waging war against us.

The king has given up his right to govern us. He has done this by stating that we are out of his protection. He has also gone to war against us.

He has plundered our seas, ravaged our coasts, burned our towns, and destroyed the lives of our people.

He has attacked our coasts; he has burned our towns; he has killed our people.

He is at this time transporting large armies of foreign mercenaries to complete the works of death, desolation, and tyranny already begun with circumstances of cruelty and perfidy scarcely paralleled in the most barbarous ages, and totally unworthy the head of a civilized nation.

The king has hired large armies of foreign soldiers. He is sending them to our country. With them, he intends to complete the work of ruling us like a tyrant.

He has constrained our fellow-citizens, taken captive on the high seas, to bear arms against their country, to become the executioners of their friends and brethren, or to fall themselves by their hands.

He has forced American citizens, taken prisoner at sea, to fight against other Americans.

He has excited domestic insurrection among us, and has endeavored to bring on the inhabitants of our frontiers the merciless Indian savages, whose known rule of warfare is an undistinguished destruction of all ages, sexes, and conditions.

The king has stirred up quarrels among us. He has also tried to get the Indians to kill all the Americans on the frontier.

In every stage of these oppressions we have petitioned for redress in the most humble terms; our repeated petitions have been answered only by repeated injury. A prince whose character is thus marked by every act which may define a tyrant is unfit to be the ruler of a free people.

When the king does something wrong, we ask him to correct it. Then he only injures us again. A king who acts like a tyrant is not fit to rule a free people.

Nor have we been wanting in our attentions to our British brethren. We have warned them, from time to time, of attempts by their legislature to extend an unwarrantable jurisdiction over us. We have reminded them of the circumstances of our emigration and settlement here. We have appealed to their native justice and magnanimity; and we have conjured them, by the ties of our common kindred, to disavow these usurpations, which would inevitably interrupt our connections and correspondence. They, too, have been deaf to the voice of justice and consanguinity. We must, therefore, acquiesce in the necessity which denounces our separation, and hold them, as we hold the rest of mankind, enemies in war, in peace, friends.

From time to time we have warned the people of Great Britain, that the Parliament is unjust in the way it rules us. We have reminded them of our reasons for settling here. We have asked them, as a just and fair people, to speak out against what Parliament and the king have been doing to us. They have not listened to us.

We must therefore look at the British people as our enemies in case of war and as our friends in times of peace. They are the same as our people in this way.

We, therefore, the representatives of the United States of America, in General Congress, assembled, appealing to the Supreme Judge of the world for the

We have stated the facts. We, the representatives of the United States, knowing that God is our judge, declare that these colonies are

rectitude of our intentions, do, in the name and by authority of the good people of these colonies, solemnly publish and declare, That these united colonies are, and of right ought to be, free and independent states; that they are absolved from all allegiance to the British crown, and that all political connection between them and the state of Great Britain is, and ought to be, totally dissolved; and that, as free and independent states, they have full power to levy war, conclude peace, contract alliances, establish commerce, and to do all other acts and things which independent states may of right do. And, for the support of this declaration with a firm reliance on the protection of Divine Providence, we mutually pledge to each other our lives, our fortunes, and our sacred honor.

free and independent states. They no longer owe any loyalty to England or its king. Our free states now have all the powers that any free state has. We can depend on God's protection. With it, and with the knowledge that what we are doing is right, we pledge all that we have in support of this declaration of independence—our lives, our fortunes, and our sacred honor.

John Hancock

New Hampshire
Josiah Bartlett
Wm. Whipple
Matthew Thornton

Massachusetts-Bay
Saml. Adams
John Adams
Robt. Treat Paine
Elbridge Gerry

Rhode Island
Step. Hopkins
William Ellery

Connecticut
Roger Sherman
Sam'el Huntington
Wm. Williams
Oliver Wolcott

New York
Wm. Floyd
Phil. Livingston
Frans. Lewis
Lewis Morris

Pennsylvania
Robt. Morris
Benjamin Rush
Benja. Franklin
John Morton
Geo. Clymer
Jas. Smith
Geo. Taylor
James Wilson
Geo. Ross

Delaware
Caesar Rodney
Geo. Read
Tho. M'Kean

Georgia
Button Gwinnett
Lyman Hall
Geo. Walton

Maryland
Samuel Chase
Wm. Paca
Thos. Stone
Charles Carroll of Carrollton

Virginia
George Wythe
Richard Henry Lee
Th. Jefferson
Benja. Harrison
Ths. Nelson, Jr.
Francis Lightfoot Lee
Carter Braxton

North Carolina
Wm. Hooper
Joseph Hewes
John Penn

South Carolina
Edward Rutledge
Thos. Heyward, Junr.
Thomas Lynch, Junr.
Arthur Middleton

New Jersey
Richd. Stockton
Jno. Witherspoon
Fras. Hopkinson
John Hart
Abra. Clark

THE CONSTITUTION OF THE UNITED STATES

WITH COMMENTS

The Constitution is printed on the following pages in the left-hand columns. Each paragraph is numbered for easy reference. Those parts of the Constitution which have been set aside or changed by the adoption of amendments are crossed out. In the right-hand columns are comments which tell in everyday language what the writers of the Constitution said in more formal language. Bracketed numbers are used for reference purposes. The comments are intended to help you understand the wording of each article and section, but are not intended to interpret or explain the Constitution. Only the Supreme Court has the authority to make final interpretations of the Constitution.

PREAMBLE

We The People of the United States, in Order to form a more perfect Union, establish Justice, insure domestic Tranquility, provide for the common defence, promote the general Welfare, and secure the Blessings of Liberty to ourselves and our Posterity, do ordain and establish this Constitution for the United States of America.

The writers of our Constitution knew they needed a stronger central government than was possible under the Articles of Confederation. That is why they thought out and wrote the Constitution you are about to read. Notice that this is a government of the people.

ARTICLE I

1 **Section 1.** All legislative Powers herein granted shall be vested in a Congress of the United States, which shall consist of a Senate and House of Representatives.

1 *The power to make laws shall be given to a Congress made up of two houses: a Senate and a House of Representatives.*

2 **Section 2.** The House of Representatives shall be composed of Members chosen every second Year by the People of the several States, and the Electors in each State shall have the Qualifications requisite for Electors of the most numerous Branch of the State Legislature.

2 *Representatives shall be elected every two years by those voters in each state who are qualified to vote for representatives in the larger branch of that state's legislature.*

3 No Person shall be a Representative who shall not have attained to the Age of twenty-five Years, and been seven Years a Citizen of the United States, and who shall not, when elected, be an Inhabitant of that State in which he shall be chosen.

3 *A representative shall be at least twenty-five, shall have been a citizen for at least seven years, and shall live in the state from which he or she is elected.*

4 Representatives and ~~direct Taxes~~ shall be apportioned among the several States which may be included within this Union, according to their respective Numbers, ~~which shall be determined by adding to the whole Number of free Persons, including those bound to Service for a Term of Years~~, and excluding Indians not taxed, ~~three fifths of all other~~

4 *The number of representatives shall be in proportion to the state's population, except that only three fifths of the slaves shall be counted. Direct taxes shall be levied in the same proportion. See Article XIV [100] and Article XVI [106].*

Persons. The actual Enumeration shall be made within three Years after the first Meeting of the Congress of the United States, and within every subsequent Term of ten Years, in such Manner as they shall by Law direct. The Number of Representatives shall not exceed one for every thirty Thousand, but each State shall have at Least one Representative; ~~and until such enumeration shall be made, the state of New Hampshire shall be entitled to chuse three, Massachusetts eight, Rhode Island and Providence Plantations one, Connecticut five, New York six, New Jersey four, Pennsylvania eight, Delaware one, Maryland six, Virginia ten, North Carolina five, South Carolina five, and Georgia three.~~

The American people shall be counted every ten years. There shall not be more than one representative for every thirty thousand persons, but a state without that many people shall have one.

Until the people are counted the first time, there shall be this many representatives from each state. The number of representatives allowed in each state is now in accordance with the provisions of Article XIV, Section 2 [100].

5 When vacancies happen in the Representation from any State, the Executive Authority thereof shall issue Writs of Election to fill such Vacancies.

5 A state's governor shall call a special election to fill a vacancy in the House.

6 The House of Representatives shall chuse their Speaker and other Officers; and shall have the sole Power of Impeachment.

6 Only the House may call an official of the United States to trial, or impeach the official.

7 **Section 3.** The Senate of the United States shall be composed of two Senators from each State, ~~chosen by the Legislature thereof~~, for six Years; and each Senator shall have one Vote.

7 Today senators are elected by the voters in each state, not by the legislatures. See Article XVII [107].

8 Immediately after they shall be assembled in Consequence of the first Election, they shall be divided as equally as may be into three Classes. The Seats of the Senators of the first Class shall be vacated at the Expiration of the second Year, of the second Class at the Expiration of the fourth Year, and of the third Class at the Expiration of the sixth Year, so that one third may be chosen every second Year; ~~and if Vacancies happen by Resignation, or otherwise, during the Recess of the Legislature of any State, the Executive thereof may make temporary Appointments until the next Meeting of the Legislature, which shall then fill such Vacancies.~~

8 This arrangement was made so that there would always be experienced senators. After the first session, the Senate membership would never be entirely new.

The governor of a state shall appoint someone to fill a vacancy in a Senate seat of that state until an election can be held. See Article XVII [108].

9 No person shall be a Senator who shall not have attained to the Age of thirty Years, and been nine Years a Citizen of the United States, and who shall not, when elected, be an Inhabitant of that State for which he shall be chosen.

9 A senator shall be at least thirty, a citizen for at least nine years, and shall live in the state from which he or she is elected.

10 The Vice President of the United States shall be President of the Senate, but shall have no Vote, unless they be equally divided.

10 The Vice-President's vote has sometimes been important.

11 The Senate shall chuse their other Officers, and

11 The Senate shall choose its officer, but it

also a President pro tempore, in the Absence of the Vice President, or when he shall exercise the Office of President of the United States.

cannot elect its leader except under these conditions.

12 The Senate shall have the sole Power to try all Impeachments. When sitting for that Purpose, they shall be on Oath or Affirmation. When the President of the United States is tried, the Chief Justice shall preside: And no Person shall be convicted without the Concurrence of two thirds of the Members present.

12 Only the House can impeach or call an officer of the United States to trial, but only the Senate can conduct the trial.

13 Judgment in Cases of Impeachment shall not extend further than to removal from Office, and disqualification to hold and enjoy any Office of honor, Trust or Profit under the United States: but the Party convicted shall nevertheless be liable and subject to Indictment, Trial, Judgment and Punishment, according to Law.

13 In an impeachment trial, punishment can go no further than to remove a person from office and disqualify the person for any federal office. The person found guilty may then be tried in regular courts.

14 **Section 4.** The Times, Places and Manner of holding Elections for Senators and Representatives, shall be prescribed in each State by the Legislature thereof; but the Congress may at any time by Law make or alter such Regulations, except as to the Places of chusing Senators.

14 A state legislature may say when, where, and how its senators and representatives will be elected. Congress can change these regulations except to say where they shall be elected.

15 The Congress shall assemble at least once in every Year, ~~and such Meeting shall be on the first Monday in December, unless they shall by Law appoint a different Day.~~

15 The Twentieth Amendment [116] changed this date to January 3.

16 **Section 5.** Each House shall be the Judge of the Elections, Returns and Qualifications of its own Members, and a Majority of each shall constitute a Quorum to do Business; but a smaller Number may adjourn from day to day, and may be authorized to compel the Attendance of absent Members, in such Manner, and under such Penalties as each House may Provide.

16 Each house may decide whether its members are elected properly.
More than half the members of a house must be present in order to do business.

Each house may make its own rules about compelling members to attend.

17 Each House may determine the Rules of its Proceedings, punish its Members for disorderly Behavior, and, with the Concurrence of two thirds, expel a Member.

17 Each house is responsible for keeping itself and its members in order.

18 Each House shall keep a Journal of its Proceedings, and from time to time publish the same, excepting such Parts as may in their Judgment require Secrecy; and the Yeas and Nays of the Members of either House on any question shall, at the Desire of one fifth of those Present, be entered on the Journal.

18 With occasional exceptions, the record of what is said and done in both houses shall be published for all to read.

19 Neither House, during the Session of Congress, shall, without the Consent of the other, adjourn for more than three days, nor to any other Place than that in which the two Houses shall be sitting.

20 **Section 6.** The Senators and Representatives shall receive a Compensation for their Services, to be ascertained by Law, and paid out of the Treasury of the United States. They shall in all Cases, except Treason, Felony and Breach of the Peace, be privileged from Arrest during their Attendance at the Session of their respective Houses, and in going to and returning from the same; and for any Speech or Debate in either House, they shall not be questioned in any other Place.

21 No Senator or Representative shall, during the Time for which he was elected, be appointed to any civil Office under the Authority of the United States, which shall have been created, or the Emoluments whereof shall have been encreased during such time; and no Person holding any Office under the United States, shall be a Member of either House during his Continuance in Office.

22 **Section 7.** All Bills for raising Revenue shall originate in the House of Representatives; but the Senate may propose or concur with Amendments as on other Bills.

23 Every Bill which shall have passed the House of Representatives and the Senate, shall, before it become a Law, be presented to the President of the United States; If he approve he shall sign it, but if not he shall return it, with his Objections to that House in which it shall have originated, who shall enter the Objections at large on their Journal, and proceed to reconsider it. If after such Reconsideration two thirds of that House shall agree to pass the Bill, it shall be sent, together with the Objections, to the other House, by which it shall likewise be reconsidered, and if approved by two thirds of that House, it shall become a Law. But in all such Cases the Votes of both Houses shall be determined by yeas and Nays, and the Names of the Persons voting for and against the Bill shall be entered on the Journal of each House respectively. If any Bill shall not be returned by the President within ten Days (Sundays excepted) after it shall have been presented to him, the Same shall be a Law, in like Manner as if he had

19 *Once a session of Congress has begun, it must continue in the same place for the regular term, except as noted.*

20 *The members of Congress shall be paid for their services. They cannot be arrested, except for the crimes mentioned, while attending a session of the Senate or the House.*

The members of Congress shall not be questioned for what they say while speaking in either house.

21 *During his or her term of office, no member of Congress may take a position that Congress created or for which it raised the pay during that time.*

No one holding a federal position may be a member of Congress at the same time.

22 *All tax bills start in the House, but the Senate may propose changes in them.*

23 *All bills passed by both houses must be sent to the President before they can become law.*

The President signs bills which he or she approves, but the President may refuse to sign a bill.

The President's objections in each case are written into the Congressional Record, and Congress reconsiders the bill.

The rejected bill may become law without the President's signature if two thirds or more of the members of each house vote yes and their votes are recorded.

If the President does not return a bill to Congress within the time shown here, it becomes law without his or her signature unless Congress prevents return of the bill by adjourning.

signed it, unless the Congress by their Adjournment prevent its Return, in which Case it shall not be a Law.

24 Every Order, Resolution, or Vote to which the Concurrence of the Senate and House of Representatives may be necessary (except on a question of Adjournment) shall be presented to the President of the United States; and before the Same shall take Effect, shall be approved by him, or being disapproved by him, shall be repassed by two thirds of the Senate and House of Representatives, according to the Rules and Limitations prescribed in the Case of a Bill.

24 Other acts of Congress which require agreement of both houses (except motions to adjourn) must also be sent to the President. These take effect under the same conditions as bills.

25 **Section 8.** The Congress shall have Power To lay and collect Taxes, Duties, Imposts and Excises, to pay the Debts and provide for the common Defence and general Welfare of the United States; but all Duties, Imposts and Excises shall be uniform throughout the United States;

25 This section states the eighteen powers of Congress that are sometimes called enumerated powers.
Congress has the power to tax and to use such taxes for our welfare. Taxes shall be the same throughout the country.

26 To borrow Money on the credit of the United States;

26 Congress may borrow money.

27 To regulate Commerce with foreign Nations, and among the several States, and with the Indian Tribes;

27 Congress may regulate trade. This commerce clause is used in many ways to promote the general welfare.

28 To establish an uniform Rule of Naturalization, and uniform Laws on the subject of Bankruptcies throughout the United States;

28 Congress may set up rules by which people can become citizens, and for people who owe debts they cannot pay. These rules must be the same for all.

29 To coin Money, regulate the Value thereof, and of foreign Coin, and fix the Standard of Weights and Measures;

29 Congress shall coin money and decide its value. It shall also fix the standards by which things are weighed and measured.

30 To provide for the Punishment of counterfeiting the Securities and current Coin of the United States;

30 Congress makes laws by which counterfeiters may be punished.

31 To establish Post Offices and post Roads;

31 It builds post offices and roads.

32 To promote the Progress of Science and useful Arts, by securing for limited Times to Authors and Inventors the exclusive Right to their respective Writings and Discoveries;

32 It protects the rights of authors and inventors.

33 To constitute Tribunals inferior to the supreme Court;

33 It sets up courts that are lower than the Supreme Court.

34 To define and punish Piracies and Felonies committed on the high Seas, and Offences against the Law of Nations;

34 Congress may handle problems of this sort in connection with foreign trade.

35 To declare War, grant Letters of Marque and Reprisal, and make Rules concerning Captures on Land and Water;

35 It can declare war and make rules about privateering.

36 To raise and support Armies, but no Appropriation of Money to that Use shall be for a longer Term than two Years;

36 *Congress raises and maintains armies.*

37 To provide and maintain a Navy;

37 *It creates and supports a navy.*

38 To make Rules for the Government and Regulation of the land and naval Forces;

38 *Congress makes the rules by which the armed forces are regulated.*

39 To provide for calling forth the Militia to execute the Laws of the Union, suppress Insurrections and repel Invasions;

39 *It calls out the militia when needed for certain purposes.*

40 To provide for organizing, arming, and disciplining, the Militia, and for governing such Part of them as may be employed in the Service of the United States reserving to the States respectively, the Appointment of the Officers, and the Authority of training the Militia according to the discipline prescribed by Congress;

40 *Congress has certain control over the militia, but reserves other powers to the states.*

41 To exercise exclusive Legislation in all Cases whatsoever, over such District (not exceeding ten Miles square) as may, by Cession of particular States, and the Acceptance of Congress, become the Seat of the Government of the United States, and to exercise like Authority over all Places purchased by the Consent of the Legislature of the State in which the Same shall be, for the Erection of Forts, Magazines, Arsenals, dock-Yards, and other needful Buildings;—And

41 *The federal government can buy or receive land from the states for certain purposes. Congress can make laws for these areas, including the capital.*

42 To make all Laws which shall be necessary and proper for carrying into Execution the foregoing Powers, and all other Powers vested by this Constitution in the Government of the United States, or in any Department or Officer thereof.

42 *Congress can pass all the laws that are necessary and proper to carry out all the powers the Constitution says Congress has. This is the "elastic clause."*

43 **Section 9.** ~~The Migration or Importation of such Persons as any of the States now existing shall think proper to admit, shall not be prohibited by the Congress prior to the Year one thousand eight hundred and eight, but a Tax or duty may be imposed on such Importation, not exceeding ten dollars for each Person.~~

43 *"Such Persons" were slaves. Congress could not prohibit the importing of slaves before 1808, but the states could be taxed up to ten dollars for each slave imported.*

44 The Privilege of the Writ of Habeas Corpus shall not be suspended, unless when in Cases of Rebellion or Invasion the public Safety may require it.

44 *A writ of habeas corpus is an order which protects people against illegal imprisonment.*

45 No Bill of Attainder or ex post facto Law shall be passed.

45 *No law shall be passed that pronounces a person guilty of some crime (usually treason) without a proper trial, nor any law passed that punishes an action that took place before the law was passed.*

46 No Capitation, or other direct, Tax shall be laid, unless in Proportion to the Census or Enumeration herein before directed to be taken.

46 Any federal tax on individuals must be in proportion to the population of the state. See Article XVI [106].

47 No Tax or Duty shall be laid on Articles exported from any State.

47 Goods shipped out of a state cannot be taxed.

48 No Preference shall be given by any Regulation of Commerce or Revenue to the Ports of one State over those of another: nor shall Vessels bound to, or from, one State, be obliged to enter, clear, or pay Duties in another.

48 Laws dealing with tariffs or commerce must treat all states alike. Interstate shipping may not be taxed.

49 No Money shall be drawn from the Treasury, but in Consequence of Appropriations made by Law; and a regular Statement and Account of the Receipts and Expenditures of all public Money shall be published from time to time.

49 A law is needed to allow funds to be taken from the federal Treasury. A statement of federal income and spending must be published.

50 No Title of Nobility shall be granted by the United States: And no Person holding any Office of Profit or Trust under them, shall, without the Consent of the Congress, accept of any present, Emolument, Office, or Title, of any kind whatever, from any King, Prince, or foreign State.

50 No titles of nobility may be given. No federal officer may accept a title, position, or gift from a foreign government unless Congress gives its approval.

51 **Section 10.** No State shall enter any Treaty, Alliance, or Confederation; grant Letters of Marque and Reprisal; coin Money; emit Bills of Credit; make any Thing but gold and silver Coin a Tender in Payment of Debts; pass any Bill of Attainder, ex post facto Law, or Law impairing the Obligation of Contracts, or grant any Title of Nobility.

51 This section makes it unlawful for state governments to do certain things. A state cannot make treaties, issue money, set aside federal laws dealing with money, or weaken the promises made in contracts.

52 No State shall, without the Consent of the Congress, lay any Imposts or Duties on Imports or Exports, except what may be absolutely necessary for executing its inspection Laws: and the net Produce of all Duties and Imposts, laid by any State on Imports or Exports, shall be for the Use of the Treasury of the United States; and all such Laws shall be subject to the Revision and Controul of the Congress.

52 Unless Congress approves, no state may tax imports or exports except to get those taxes needed to cover costs of inspection.

Any net gain must be paid to the federal Treasury.

53 No State shall, without the Consent of Congress, lay any Duty of Tonnage, keep Troops, or Ships of War in time of Peace, enter into any Agreement or Compact with another State, or with a foreign Power, or engage in War, unless actually invaded, or in such imminent Danger as will not admit of Delay.

53 No state may tax ships, keep an army or navy in peacetime, or make treaties with other states and nations, unless Congress agrees.

No state may go to war unless invaded or in grave danger.

ARTICLE II

54 **Section 1.** The executive Power shall be vested in a President of the United States of America. He

54 This section sets up the offices of President and Vice-President and makes their

shall hold his Office during the Term of four Years, and, together with the Vice President, chosen for the same Term, be elected, as follows

terms of office four years.

55 Each State shall appoint, in such Manner as the Legislature thereof may direct, a Number of Electors, equal to the whole Number of Senators and Representatives to which the State may be entitled in the Congress: but no Senator or Representative, or Person holding an Office of Trust or Profit under the United States, shall be appointed an Elector.

55 *The President and Vice-President shall be chosen by electors. Each state may appoint as many electors as it has members in Congress. No federal officer may be an elector.*

56 The Electors shall meet in their respective States, and vote by Ballot for two Persons, of whom one at least shall not be an Inhabitant of the same State with themselves. And they shall make a List of all the Persons voted for, and of the Number of Votes for each; which List they shall sign and certify, and transmit sealed to the Seat of the Government of the United States, directed to the President of the Senate. The President of the Senate shall, in the Presence of the Senate and House of Representatives, open all the Certificates, and the Votes shall then be counted. The Person having the greatest Number of Votes shall be the President, if such Number be a Majority of the whole Number of Electors appointed; and if there be more than one who have such Majority, and have an equal Number of Votes, then the House of Representatives shall immediately chuse by Ballot one of them for President; and if no person have a Majority, then from the five highest on the List the said House shall in like Manner chuse the President. But in chusing the President, the Votes shall be taken by States, the Representation from each State having one Vote; A quorum for this Purpose shall consist of a Member or Members from two thirds of the States, and a Majority of all the States shall be necessary to a Choice. In every Case, after the Choice of the President, the Person having the greatest Number of Votes of the Electors shall be the Vice President. But if there should remain two or more who have equal Votes, the Senate shall chuse from them by Ballot the Vice President.

56 *Electors shall meet in their own state and vote for two persons. At least one of these must be from another state.*

Results of the balloting shall be sent to Congress, and there the votes of all the states shall be counted.

Whoever has received the largest majority is President.

If two persons with a majority tie for first place, the House shall choose one as President.

If no person has a majority, the House must choose a President from the five highest on the list.

When the House ballots, each state gets one vote. Representatives from two thirds of the states must be present when the vote is taken.

After the President is chosen, the person with the most electoral votes becomes Vice-President.

If two are tied for Vice-President, the Senate chooses one of them by ballot. The Twelfth Amendment [96] changed the way in which the President and Vice-President are elected.

57 The Congress may determine the Time of chusing the Electors, and the Day on which they shall give their Votes; which Day shall be the same throughout the United States.

57 *Congress may name the day when electors are chosen and the day when electors will vote.*

58 No Person except a natural born Citizen, or a Citizen of the United States, at the time of the Adoption of this Constitution, shall be eligible to the Office of President; neither shall any Person be eligible to that Office who shall not have attained to the Age of thirty five Years, and been fourteen Years a Resident within the United States.

58 To be eligible for President, a person must be a native citizen, at least thirty-five years old, and shall have lived in the United States at least fourteen years.

59 In Case of the Removal of the President from Office, or of his Death, Resignation, or Inability to discharge the Powers and Duties of the said Office, the Same shall devolve on the Vice President, and the Congress may by Law provide for the Case of Removal, Death, Resignation or Inability, both of the President and Vice President, declaring what Officer shall then act as President, and such Officer shall act accordingly, until the Disability be removed, or a President shall be elected.

59 If the office of President becomes vacant, the Vice-President shall take over the office.

If neither the President nor Vice-President can serve, Congress may decide by law who will act as President.

60 The President shall, at stated Times, receive for his Services, a Compensation, which shall neither be encreased nor diminished during the Period for which he shall have been elected, and he shall not receive within that Period any other Emolument from the United States, or any of them.

60 The President receives a regular salary, which cannot be changed during his or her term of office. The President may not receive any other pay from a state or the federal government.

61 Before he enter on the Execution of his Office, he shall take the following Oath or Affirmation:—"I do solemnly swear (or affirm) that I will faithfully execute the Office of President of the United States, and will to the best of my Ability, preserve, protect and defend the Constitution of the United States."

61 Before a President can take office, he or she must take this oath that he or she will carry out the President's duties and uphold the Constitution.

62 **Section 2.** The President shall be Commander in Chief of the Army and Navy of the United States, and of the Militia of the several States, when called into the actual Service of the United States; he may require the Opinion, in writing, of the principal Officer in each of the executive Departments, upon any Subject relating to the Duties of their respective Offices, and he shall have Power to grant Reprieves and Pardons for Offences against the United States, except in Cases of Impeachment.

62 The President is commander in chief of our armed forces.

The President has a right to get written opinions from cabinet members.

The President can suspend punishment for offenses against the United States, except as noted.

63 He shall have Power, by and with the Advice and Consent of the Senate, to make Treaties, provided two thirds of the Senators present concur; and he shall nominate, and by and with the Advice and Consent of the Senate, shall appoint Ambassadors, other public Ministers and Consuls, Judges of

63 The President may make treaties, choose foreign representatives, appoint Supreme Court judges, and fill federal posts which may be established later, but the Senate must approve each act.

the supreme Court, and all other Officers of the United States, whose Appointments are not herein otherwise provided for, and which shall be established by Law: but the Congress may by Law vest the Appointment of such inferior Officers, as they think proper, in the President alone, in the Courts of Law, or in the Heads of Departments.

Congress may say who shall appoint minor officers.

64 The President shall have Power to fill up all Vacancies that may happen during the Recess of the Senate, by granting Commissions which shall expire at the End of their next Session.

64 *When the Senate is not in session, the President may make appointments to vacant federal offices to last until the end of the next Senate session.*

65 **Section 3.** He shall from time to time give to the Congress Information of the State of the Union, and recommend to their Consideration such Measures as he shall judge necessary and expedient; he may, on extraordinary Occasions, convene both Houses, or either of them, and in Case of Disagreement between them, with Respect to the Time of Adjournment, he may adjourn them to such Time as he shall think proper; he shall receive Ambassadors and other public Ministers; he shall take Care that the Laws be faithfully executed, and shall Commission all the Officers of the United States.

65 *The President must keep Congress informed on the nation's progress and propose to Congress laws he or she thinks are needed.*
The President may call an emergency session of one or both houses of Congress.
If the two houses disagree on when to adjourn, the President may adjourn them to a future date.
The President must meet representatives of foreign governments.
The President must see that federal laws are carried out. The President authorizes all federal officers to take their positions.

66 **Section 4.** The President, Vice President and all civil Officers of the United States, shall be removed from Office on Impeachment for, and Conviction of, Treason, Bribery, or other high Crimes and Misdemeanors.

66 *The President and all civil officers shall be removed from office when impeached and found guilty of treason, bribery, or other major crimes.*

ARTICLE III

67 **Section 1.** The judicial Power of the United States, shall be vested in one supreme Court, and in such inferior Courts as the Congress may from time to time ordain and establish. The Judges, both of the supreme and inferior Courts, shall hold their Offices during good Behavior, and shall, at stated Times, receive for their Services, a Compensation, which shall not be diminished during their Continuance in Office.

67 *The judicial authority of the United States shall belong to the Supreme Court and to any lower courts established by Congress.*
Judges of federal courts shall hold their offices so long as they act properly.
They shall be paid a salary which cannot be reduced while they are in office.

68 **Section 2.** The judicial Power shall extend to all Cases, in Law and Equity, arising under this Constitution, the Laws of the United States, and Treaties made, or which shall be made, under their Authority;—to all Cases affecting Ambassadors, other public Ministers and Consuls;—to all Cases of admiralty and maritime Jurisdiction;—to Controversies to

68 *Federal courts shall decide all cases that come under the laws or authority of the federal government.*

which the United States shall be a Party;—to Controversies between two or more States;~~—between a State and Citizens of another State~~;—between Citizens of different States,—between Citizens of the same State claiming Lands under Grants of different States, ~~and between a State, or the Citizens thereof, and foreign States, Citizens or Subjects~~.

Federal courts also shall decide all cases that do not come within the jurisdiction of any individual state. See Article XI [95].

69 In all Cases affecting Ambassadors, other public Ministers and Consuls, and those in which a State shall be Party, the supreme Court shall have original Jurisdiction. In all the other Cases before mentioned, the supreme Court shall have appellate Jurisdiction, both as to Law and Fact, with such Exceptions, and under such Regulations as the Congress shall make.

69 *Cases that involve diplomats or one of the states should be taken straight to the Supreme Court.*

The Supreme Court shall have power to review and reverse the decisions on cases heard in the lower courts. Congress may make rules for handling these cases.

70 The Trial of all Crimes, except in Cases of Impeachment, shall be by Jury; and such Trial shall be held in the State where the said Crimes shall have been committed; but when not committed within any State, the Trial shall be at such Place or Places as the Congress may by Law have directed.

70 *A criminal case (except an impeachment trial) must be tried by jury in the state where the crime was committed.*

Congress may decide where trials shall be held for crimes that were not committed within any state.

71 **Section 3.** Treason against the United States, shall consist only in levying War against them, or in adhering to their Enemies, giving them Aid and Comfort. No Person shall be convicted of Treason unless on the Testimony of two Witnesses to the same overt Act, or on Confession in open Court.

71 *Treason is the act of making war on the United States or helping its enemies.*
No one can be found guilty of treason unless the act was witnessed by two persons or is confessed in court.

72 The Congress shall have Power to declare the Punishment of Treason, but no Attainder of Treason shall work Corruption of Blood, or Forfeiture except during the Life of the Person attained.

72 *Congress has power to fix the penalty for treason, but the traitor's family cannot be punished.*

ARTICLE IV

73 **Section 1.** Full Faith and Credit shall be given in each State to the Public Acts, Records, and judicial Proceedings of every other State. And the Congress may by general Laws prescribe the Manner in which such Acts, Records and Proceedings shall be proved, and the Effect thereof.

73 *The official acts of a state must be recognized by the other states.*

Congress may decide which acts should be recognized, and to what extent they are binding in other states.

74 **Section 2.** The Citizens of each State shall be entitled to all Privileges and Immunities of Citizens in the several States.

74 *A citizen of one state shall enjoy all the rights of citizenship when he or she goes to another state.*

75 A person charged in any State with Treason, Felony, or other Crime, who shall flee from Justice, and be found in another State, shall on Demand of the executive Authority of the State from which he

75 *If a person charged with a crime escapes to another state, the accused shall be returned to the state from which he or she fled if the governor of that state requests it.*

fled, be delivered up, to be removed to the State having Jurisdiction of the Crime.

76 ~~No person held to Service or Labour in one State, under the Laws thereof, escaping into another, shall, in Consequence of any Law or Regulation therein, be discharged from such Service or Labour, but shall be delivered upon Claim of the Party to whom such Service or Labour may be due~~.

76 Persons in bondage cannot be freed by a state to which they may escape. They must be returned to their masters. This section no longer has any force. See Article XIII [97].

77 **Section 3.** New States may be admitted by the Congress into this Union; but no new State shall be formed or erected within the Jurisdiction of any other State; nor any State be formed by the Junction of two or more States, or Parts of States, without the Consent of the Legislatures of the States concerned as well as of the Congress.

77 Congress may admit new states to the Union, but new states cannot be formed out of existing states unless Congress and the legislatures of the states concerned approve.

78 The Congress shall have Power to dispose of and make all needful Rules and Regulations respecting the Territory or other Property belonging to the United States; and nothing in this Constitution shall be so construed as to Prejudice any Claims of the United States, or of any particular State.

78 Congress can make the necessary rules for managing federal lands and property.

Nothing in the Constitution denies any claims the states or the United States may have.

79 **Section 4.** The United States shall guarantee to every State in this Union a Republican Form of Government, and shall protect each of them against Invasion; and on Application of the Legislature, or of the Executive (when the Legislature cannot be convened) against domestic Violence.

79 The nation guarantees a republican form of government and protection against invasion to every state.

The federal government will protect a state against riots if the legislature or governor asks for such aid.

ARTICLE V

80 The Congress, whenever two thirds of both Houses shall deem it necessary, shall propose Amendments to this Constitution, or, on the Application of the Legislatures of two thirds of the several States, shall call a Convention for proposing Amendments, which, in either Case, shall be valid to all Intents and Purposes, as Part of this Constitution, when ratified by the Legislatures of three fourths of the several States, or by Conventions in three fourths thereof, as the one or the other Mode of Ratification may be proposed by the Congress; ~~Provided that no Amendment which may be made prior to the Year One thousand eight hundred and eight shall in any Manner affect the first and fourth Clauses in the Ninth Section of the first Article~~, and that no State, without its Consent, shall be deprived of its equal Suffrage in the Senate.

80 Congress can propose constitutional amendments by a two-thirds vote of both houses, or shall, if the legislatures of two thirds of the states so request, call a national convention to propose amendments.

Amendments become law when approved by the legislatures or by special conventions in three fourths of the states.

Congress shall decide which method to use. Until the year 1808 no amendment may affect the existing law on importing slaves nor the law that direct taxes must be in proportion to population. No amendment can deprive any state of its equal representation in the Senate unless the state permits it.

ARTICLE VI

81 All Debts contracted and Engagements entered into, before the Adoption of this Constitution, shall be as valid against the United States under this Constitution, as under the Confederation.

81 This Constitution does not cancel the existing debts and agreements of the nation.

82 This Constitution, and the Laws of the United States which shall be made in Pursuance thereof; and all Treaties made, or which shall be made, under the Authority of the United States, shall be the supreme Law of the Land; and the Judges in every State shall be bound thereby, any Thing in the Constitution or Laws of any State to the Contrary notwithstanding.

82 This Constitution, plus the laws and treaties made in using it, is the highest law in the land.

The judges in every state are bound by the Constitution even though some state laws conflict with it.

83 The Senators and Representatives before mentioned, and the Members of the several State Legislatures, and all executive and judicial Officers, both of the United States and of the several States, shall be bound by Oath or Affirmation, to support this Constitution; but no religious Test shall ever be required as a Qualification to any Office or public Trust under the United States.

83 All legislative, executive, and judicial officers, federal and state, must swear to support the Constitution.

Religion shall never be a qualification for public office.

ARTICLE VII

84 The Ratification of the Conventions of nine States, shall be sufficient for the Establishment of this Constitution between the States so ratifying the Same.

Done in Convention by the Unanimous Consent of the States present the Seventeenth Day of September in the Year of our Lord one thousand seven hundred and Eighty seven and of the Independence of the United States of America the Twelfth. In witness whereof We have hereunto subscribed our Names . . .

84 When this Constitution is ratified by nine or more states, it will go into effect in those states.

The signatures of thirty-nine delegates witness that the Constitution was approved on September 17, 1787, by all the states then represented in the Constitutional Convention.

AMENDMENTS TO THE CONSTITUTION

ARTICLE I (1791)

85 Congress shall make no law respecting an establishment of religion, or prohibiting the free exercise thereof; or abridging the freedom of speech, or of the press; or the right of the people peaceably to assemble, and to petition the Government for a redress of grievances.

85 Congress may not establish a religion or interfere with freedom of worship.

Congress cannot abridge our freedom to speak, to print, or to meet and ask the government to correct what is wrong.

ARTICLE II (1791)

86 A well regulated Militia, being necessary to the

86 Congress cannot take away a citizen's

security of a free State, the right of the people to keep and bear Arms, shall not be infringed.

right to serve in a state militia or to keep arms.

ARTICLE III (1791)

87 No Soldier shall, in time of peace be quartered in any house, without the consent of the Owner, nor in time of war, but in a manner to be prescribed by law.

87 In peacetime, soldiers cannot be lodged in any house against the owner's will. In wartime, it can be done only under special laws.

ARTICLE IV (1791)

88 The right of the people to be secure in their persons, houses, papers, and effects, against unreasonable searches and seizures, shall not be violated, and no Warrants shall issue, but upon probable causes, supported by Oath or affirmation, and particularly describing the place to be searched, and the persons or things to be seized.

88 People, houses, and possessions cannot be searched or seized without a sworn warrant that tells exactly what place to search and what person or thing to seize.

ARTICLE V (1791)

89 No person shall be held to answer for a capital, or otherwise infamous crime, unless on a presentment or indictment of a Grand Jury, except in cases arising in the land or naval forces, or in the Militia, when in actual service in time of War or public danger; nor shall any person be subject for the same offence to be twice put in jeopardy of life or limb; nor shall be compelled in any criminal case to be a witness against himself, nor be deprived of life, liberty, or property, without due process of law; nor shall private property be taken for public use, without just compensation.

89 No person can be tried for a major crime unless a grand jury says that it sees grounds for a trial. This rule does not apply to the armed forces.

If acquitted, a person cannot be tried again for the offense.

No one can be forced to testify against himself or herself.

Life, liberty, and property can be taken only through regular legal processes.

If private property is taken for public use, a fair price must be paid for it.

ARTICLE VI (1791)

90 In all criminal prosecutions, the accused shall enjoy the right to a speedy and public trial, by an impartial jury of the State and district wherein the crime shall have been committed, which district shall have been previously ascertained by law, and to be informed of the nature and cause of the accusation; to be confronted with the witnesses against him; to have compulsory process for obtaining witnesses in his favor, and to have the Assistance of Counsel for his defence.

90 A person accused of crime has the right to a prompt trial by an impartial jury from the state and district where the crime is said to have taken place.

The accused must be told the crime and the evidence and must be present during testimony. Witnesses whose help the accused needs must be brought to court. The accused has a right to expert legal defense.

ARTICLE VII (1791)

91 In suits at common law, where the value in con-

91 Parties to a lawsuit can demand a jury

troversy shall exceed twenty dollars, the right of trial by jury shall be preserved, and no fact tried by a jury shall be otherwise re-examined in any Court of the United States, than according to the rules of the common law.

trial when more than twenty dollars' value is involved.

A case once tried by a jury cannot be retried in any court in a way that would set aside a person's legal rights.

ARTICLE VIII (1791)

92 Excessive bail shall not be required, nor excessive fines imposed, nor cruel and unusual punishments inflicted.

92 *The Supreme Court makes the final decision regarding what is excessive, cruel, or unusual.*

ARTICLE IX (1791)

93 The enumeration in the Constitution, of certain rights, shall not be construed to deny or disparage others retained by the people.

93 *The mention of certain rights in this Constitution does not mean that rights not spoken of are taken away from the people.*

ARTICLE X (1791)

94 The powers not delegated to the United States by the Constitution, nor prohibited by it to the States, are reserved to the States respectively, or to the people.

94 *The states, or the people, possess all the rights that the Constitution does not assign to the federal government or deny to the states.*

ARTICLE XI (1798)

95 The Judicial power of the United States shall not be construed to extend to any suit in law or equity, commenced or prosecuted against one of the United States by Citizens of another State, or by Citizens or Subjects of any Foreign State.

95 *Federal courts have no power to try cases in which a state is sued by citizens of another state, or by citizens of a foreign country.*

ARTICLE XII (1804)

96 The Electors shall meet in their respective states, and vote by ballot for President and Vice-President, one of whom, at least, shall not be an inhabitant of the same state with themselves; they shall name in their ballots the person voted for as President, and in distinct ballots the person voted for as Vice-President, and they shall make distinct lists of all persons voted for as President, and of all persons voted for as Vice-President, and of the number of votes for each, which lists they shall sign and certify, and transmit sealed to the seat of the government of the United States, directed to the President of the Senate;—The President of the Senate shall, in presence of the Senate and House of Representatives, open all the certificates and the votes shall then be counted;—The person having the greatest number of votes for President, shall be the President, if such number be a majority of the whole number

96 *Electors shall meet in each state and vote for President and Vice-President on separate ballots.*

At least one of those voted for shall be from outside the electors' own state.

The votes for each office shall be counted and listed separately. The results, signed and sealed, shall be sent to the President of the Senate. At a joint session of Congress, he or she will open the lists and have the votes counted.

Whoever receives more than half of the electoral votes for President shall have that office. If no one has a majority, the House shall

of Electors appointed; and if no person have such majority, then from the persons having the highest numbers not exceeding three on the list of those voted for as President, the House of Representatives shall choose immediately, by ballot, the President. But in choosing the President, the votes shall be taken by states, the representation from each state having one vote; a quorum for this purpose shall consist of a member or members from two-thirds of the states, and a majority of all states shall be necessary to a choice. And if the House of Representatives shall not choose a President whenever the right of choice shall devolve upon them, before the fourth day of March next following, then the Vice-President shall act as President, as in the case of the death or other constitutional disability of the President.—The person having the greatest number of votes as Vice-President, shall be the Vice-President, if such a number be a majority of the whole number of Electors appointed, and if no person have a majority, then from the two highest numbers on the list, the Senate shall choose the Vice-President; a quorum for the purpose shall consist of two-thirds of the whole number of Senators, and a majority of the whole number shall be necessary to a choice. But no person constitutionally ineligible to the office of President shall be eligible to that of Vice-President of the United States.

elect as President one of the three candidates having the most votes.

Each state shall have one vote in the House balloting. At least two thirds of the states must be represented. The winner must receive the votes of a majority of the states.

When the House must elect a President and it fails to do so before the following March 4, the Vice-President shall serve until a President is elected.

Whoever receives more than half of the electoral votes for Vice-President shall have that office.

If no one has a majority, the Senate shall elect as Vice-President one of the two candidates having the most votes. Two thirds of the senators must be present and voting. The winner must receive the votes of a majority of all the senators.
A person not legally qualified for President cannot be Vice-President.

ARTICLE XIII (1865)

97 **Section 1.** Neither slavery nor involuntary servitude, except as a punishment for crime whereof the party shall have been duly convicted, shall exist within the United States, or any place subject to their jurisdiction.

98 **Section 2.** Congress shall have power to enforce this article by appropriate legislation.

97 *Neither slavery nor forced labor shall exist within the United States or its possessions except as a punishment for one convicted of a crime.*

98 *Congress may make laws to enforce this article.*

ARTICLE XIV (1868)

99 **Section 1.** All persons born or naturalized in the United States, and subject to the jurisdiction thereof, are citizens of the United States and of the State wherein they reside. No State shall make or enforce any law which shall abridge the privileges or immunities of citizens of the United States; nor shall any State deprive any person of life, liberty, or prop-

99 *All those born or naturalized in the United States and subject to its laws are citizens of the nation and of the state where they live.*
No state can make or enforce a law that deprives a citizen of his or her rights. No state can take away a person's life, liberty, or

erty, without due process of law; nor deny to any person within its jurisdiction the equal protection of the laws.

property except by legal means, nor refuse anyone the full protection of the law.

100 **Section 2.** Representatives shall be apportioned among the several States according to their respective numbers, counting the whole number of persons in each State; excluding Indians not taxed. But when the right to vote at any election for the choice of electors for President and Vice President of the United States, Representatives in Congress, the Executive and Judicial officers of a State, or the members of the Legislature thereof, is denied to any of the male inhabitants of such State, being twenty-one years of age, and citizens of the United States, or in any way abridged, except for participation in rebellion, or other crime, the basis of representation therein shall be reduced in the proportion which the number of such male citizens shall bear to the whole number of male citizens twenty-one years of age in such State.

100 *The number of representatives for each state in the House of Representatives shall be in proportion to its population.*

But if a state denies any citizen over twenty-one the right to vote in state or federal elections, its representation in the House shall be cut down.

In that case, a state will lose representatives in proportion to the proportion of citizens over twenty-one years of age who are denied the right to vote.

101 **Section 3.** No person shall be a Senator or Representative in Congress, or elector of President and Vice President, or hold any office, civil or military, under the United States, or under any State, who, having previously taken an oath, as a member of Congress, or as an officer of the United States, or as a member of any State legislature, or as an executive or judicial officer of any State, to support the Constitution of the United States, shall have engaged in insurrection or rebellion against the same, or given aid or comfort to the enemies thereof. But Congress may by a vote of two-thirds of each House, remove such disability.

101 *No one can hold any state or federal office who, as a federal or state officer, once swore to support the Constitution and later rebelled against the United States or helped its enemies.*

Congress can remove this penalty by a two-thirds vote of both houses.

102 **Section 4.** The validity of the public debt of the United States, authorized by law, including debts incurred for payment of pensions and bounties for services in suppressing insurrection or rebellion, shall not be questioned. But neither the United States nor any State shall assume or pay any debt or obligation incurred in aid of insurrection or rebellion against the United States, or any claim for the loss or emancipation of any slave; but all such debts, obligations and claims shall be held illegal and void.

102 *The federal government shall pay all its debts, including debts contracted in putting down rebellion.*

But neither federal nor state governments may pay debts contracted by aiding a rebellion against the United States, nor pay anyone for the loss of slaves.

103 **Section 5.** The Congress shall have power to enforce, by appropriate legislation, the provisions of this article.

103 *Congress can pass laws for carrying out this article.*

ARTICLE XV (1870)

104 **Section 1.** The right of citizens of the United States to vote shall not be denied or abridged by the United States or by any State on account of race, color, or previous condition of servitude.

104 *Neither federal nor state governments can deny any citizen the right to vote because of race or color, or because the citizen was once in bondage.*

105 **Section 2.** The Congress shall have power to enforce this article by appropriate legislation.

105 *Congress can pass laws for carrying out this article.*

ARTICLE XVI (1913)

106 The Congress shall have power to lay and collect taxes on incomes, from whatever source derived, without apportionment among the several States, and without regard to any census or enumeration.

106 *Congress can levy and collect taxes on income of any kind. Such taxes need not be apportioned among the states nor be based upon the census.*

ARTICLE XVII (1913)

107 The Senate of the United States shall be composed of two senators from each State, elected by the people thereof, for six years; and each Senator shall have one vote. The electors in each State shall have the qualifications requisite for electors of the most numerous branch of the State legislature.

107 *The Senate shall consist of two senators from each state elected by the people to serve six years. Each senator has one vote.*
Citizens who can vote for members of the larger branch of their state legislatures can vote for United States senators.

108 When vacancies happen in the representation of any State in the Senate, the executive authority of such State shall issue writs of election to fill such vacancies: Provided, That the Legislature of any State may empower the executive thereof to make temporary appointments until the people fill the vacancies by election as the Legislature may direct.

108 *If one of its Senate seats becomes empty, the governor of a state shall order an election.*
The legislature may allow the governor of a state to appoint a senator until one is elected by orders of the legislature.

109 This Amendment shall not be so construed as to affect the election or term of any senator chosen before it becomes valid as part of the Constitution.

109 *Senators elected before this amendment becomes effective will not be affected by it.*

ARTICLE XVIII (1919)

110 ~~After one year from the ratification of this article, the manufacture, sale, or transportation of intoxicating liquors within, the importation thereof into, or the exportation thereof from the United States and all territory subject to the jurisdiction thereof for beverage purposes is hereby prohibited.~~

110 *One year after this amendment is ratified it will be illegal to manufacture, sell, move, export, or import intoxicating liquor for use as a beverage anywhere in the United States or its territories. This amendment was repealed. See Article XXI [121].*

111 ~~The Congress and the several states shall have concurrent power to enforce this article by appropriate legislation.~~

111 *Both Congress and the states can pass laws to enforce this article.*

112 ~~This article shall be inoperative unless it shall have been ratified as an amendment to the Constitution by the legislatures of the several states, as provided in the Constitution, within seven years from the~~

112 *Congress put a time limit on the process of ratification.*

~~date of the submission hereof to the States by the Congress.~~

ARTICLE XIX (1920)

113 The right of the citizens of the United States to vote shall not be denied or abridged by the United States or by any States on account of sex.

114 The Congress shall have power by appropriate legislation to enforce the provisions of this article.

ARTICLE XX (1933)

115 **Section 1.** The terms of the President and Vice-President shall end at noon on the twentieth day of January, and the terms of Senators and Representatives at noon on the third day of January, of the years in which such terms would have ended if this article had not been ratified; and the terms of their successors shall then begin.

116 **Section 2.** The Congress shall assemble at least once in every year, and such meeting shall begin at noon on the third day of January, unless they shall by law appoint a different day.

117 **Section 3.** If, at the time fixed for the beginning of the term of the President, the President-elect shall have died, the Vice-President-elect shall become President. If a President shall not have been chosen before the time fixed for the beginning of his term, or if the President-elect shall have failed to qualify; then the Vice-President-elect shall act as President until a President shall have qualified; and the Congress may by law provide for the case wherein neither a President-elect nor a Vice-President-elect shall have qualified, declaring who shall then act as President, or the manner in which one who is to act shall be selected, and such person shall act accordingly until a President or Vice-President shall have qualified.

118 **Section 4.** The Congress may by law provide for the case of the death of any of the persons from whom the House of Representatives may choose a President whenever the right of choice shall have devolved upon them, and for the case of the death of any of the persons from whom the Senate may choose a Vice-President whenever the right of choice shall have devolved upon them.

113 Neither federal nor state governments can deny citizens the right to vote because of their sex.

114 Congress can pass laws for carrying out this article.

115 The President's and Vice-President's terms shall end at noon, January 20. Senators' and representatives' terms end at noon, January 3. The year in which these terms are to end is not affected by this amendment.

New terms for the above offices shall begin as old terms end.

116 Congress must meet at least once a year. Unless Congress rules otherwise, the session shall begin at noon, January 3.

117 If a President-elect dies before inauguration, the Vice-President-elect shall become President.

If no President has been elected or if the President-elect has failed to qualify, the Vice-President-elect shall act as President until a President qualifies for the office.

Congress may decide by law who will serve as President, or how he or she will be chosen, if neither a President-elect nor a Vice-President-elect qualifies by inauguration day. The person thus chosen shall serve until a President or Vice-President qualifies.

118 Congress may decide what to do if, when the House is to choose a President, one of those eligible has died.

Congress may likewise decide what to do when the Senate is to select a Vice-President and one of those eligible has died.

119 **Section 5.** Sections 1 and 2 shall take effect on the 15th day of October following the ratification of this article.

119 *New dates on which the terms of President, Vice-President, and members of Congress are to begin and Congress is to meet, will be effective on the October 15 following ratification of this article.*

120 **Section 6.** This article shall be inoperative unless it shall have been ratified as an amendment to the Constitution by the legislatures of three-fourths of the several States within seven years from the date of its submission.

120 *Congress put a time limit on the process of ratification.*

ARTICLE XXI (1933)

121 **Section 1.** The eighteenth article of amendment to the Constitution of the United States is hereby repealed.

121 *The Eighteenth Amendment is repealed.*

122 **Section 2.** The transportation or importation into any State, Territory, or Possession of the United States for delivery or use therein of intoxicating liquors, in violation of the laws thereof, is hereby prohibited.

122 *It is unlawful to bring intoxicating liquors into any state or territory to be left or used there contrary to the laws of that state or territory.*

123 **Section 3.** This article shall be inoperative unless it shall have been ratified as an amendment to the Constitution by conventions in the several States, as provided in the Constitution, within seven years from the date of the submission hereof to the States by the Congress.

123 *Congress put a time limit on the process of ratification.*

ARTICLE XXII (1951)

124 **Section 1.** No person shall be elected to the office of the President more than twice, and no person who has held the office of President, or acted as President for more than two years of a term to which some other person was elected President shall be elected to the office of the President more than once. But this Article shall not apply to any person holding the office of President when this Article was proposed by the Congress, and shall not prevent any person who may be holding the office of President, or acting as President, during the term within which this Article becomes operative from holding the office of President or acting as President during the remainder of such term.

124 *No person can be elected President more than twice.*
A person cannot be elected President more than once if he or she has already served more than two years of someone else's presidential term.
This amendment does not apply to the President in office at the time this amendment is proposed by Congress.
The person serving as President when this amendment is ratified will not be prevented from finishing his or her term.

125 **Section 2.** This article shall be inoperative unless it shall have been ratified as an amendment to the Constitution by the legislatures of three-fourths of the several states within seven years from the date of its submission to the states by the Congress.

125 *Congress set a time limit for the ratification of this amendment.*

ARTICLE XXIII (1961)

126 **Section 1.** The District constituting the seat of Government of the United States shall appoint in such manner as the Congress may direct:

A number of electors of President and Vice-President equal to the whole number of Senators and Representatives in Congress to which the District would be entitled if it were a State, but in no event more than the least populous State; they shall be in addition to those appointed by the States, but they shall be considered, for the purposes of the election of President and Vice-President, to be electors appointed by a State; and they shall meet in the District and perform such duties as provided by the twelfth article of amendment.

126 *People living in the District of Columbia can vote for the President and Vice-President.*

127 **Section 2.** The Congress shall have power to enforce this article by appropriate legislation.

127 *Congress can pass laws for carrying out this article.*

ARTICLE XXIV (1964)

128 **Section 1.** The right of citizens of the United States to vote in any primary or other election for President or Vice-President, for electors for President or Vice-President, or for Senator or Representative in Congress, shall not be denied or abridged by the United States or any state by reason of failure to pay any poll tax or other tax.

128 *This amendment stipulates that no state can prescribe a poll tax as a qualification for voting for members of Congress and electors of the President and Vice-President.*

129 **Section 2.** The Congress shall have power to enforce this article by appropriate legislation.

129 *Congress can pass laws for carrying out this article.*

ARTICLE XXV (1966)

130 **Section 1.** In case of the removal of the President from office or of his death or resignation, the Vice President shall become President.

130 *The Vice President becomes President if the President is removed from office, dies, or resigns.*

131 **Section 2.** Whenever there is a vacancy in the office of the Vice President, the President shall nominate a Vice President who shall take office upon confirmation by a majority vote of both Houses of Congress.

131 *The President nominates a Vice President should there be a vacancy in the office of the Vice President.*

132 **Section 3.** Whenever the President transmits to the President pro tempore of the Senate and the Speaker of the House of Representatives his written declaration that he is unable to discharge the powers and duties of his office, and until he transmits to them a written declaration to the contrary, such powers and duties shall be discharged by the Vice President as Acting President.

132 *The Vice President acts as Acting President if the President writes to the President pro tempore of the Senate and the Speaker of the House that he or she is unable to perform his or her duties and the Vice President will continue as Acting President until the President writes to the President pro tempore and Speaker that he or she is again able to discharge the duties of President.*

133 **Section 4.** Whenever the Vice President and a majority of either the principal officers of the executive departments or of such other body as Congress may by law provide, transmit to the President pro tempore of the Senate and the Speaker of the House of Representatives their written declaration that the President is unable to discharge the powers and duties of his office, the Vice President shall immediately assume the powers and duties of the office as Acting President.

133 *The Vice President assumes the powers and duties of Acting President if he or she and a majority of the principal officers of the executive departments—or some other body as Congress may by law provide—send a written declaration to the President pro tempore of the Senate and the Speaker of the House of Representatives that the President is unable to perform his or her duties.*

134 Thereafter, when the President transmits to the President pro tempore of the Senate and the Speaker of the House of Representatives his written declaration that no inability exists, he shall resume the powers and duties of his office unless the Vice President and a majority of either the principal officers of the executive department or of such other body as Congress may by law provide, transmit within four days to the President pro tempore of the Senate and the Speaker of the House of Representatives their written declaration that the President is unable to discharge the powers and duties of his office. Thereupon Congress shall decide the issue, assembling within forty-eight hours for that purpose if not in session. If the Congress, within twenty-one days after receipt of the latter written declaration, or, if Congress is not in session, within twenty-one days after Congress is required to assemble, determines by two-thirds vote of both houses that the President is unable to discharge the powers and duties of his office, the Vice President shall continue to discharge the same as Acting President; otherwise, the President shall resume the powers and duties of his office.

134 *If the President then writes a declaration to the President pro tempore of the Senate and the Speaker of the House of Representatives that he or she is able to perform his or her duties then he or she resumes those duties—unless the Vice President and a majority of the principal officers of the executive departments—or some other body as Congress may by law provide—send a written declaration that the President is not able to perform his or her duties. If this happens, Congress meets to determine the issue. If both Houses decide by a two-thirds vote that the President is not able to discharge his or her duties, the Vice President shall act as Acting President. If a two-thirds vote is not given, the President resumes his or her duties.*

ARTICLE XXVI (1971)

135 **Section 1.** The right of citizens of the United States, who are eighteen years of age or older, to vote shall not be denied or abridged by the United States or by any State on account of age.

135 *No citizen eighteen years of age or older can be denied the right to vote on the basis of age.*

136 **Section 2.** The Congress shall have power to enforce this article by appropriate legislation.

136 *Congress can pass laws for carrying out this article.*

REFERENCE BIBLIOGRAPHY

UNIT ONE A NEW LAND, A NEW PEOPLE

Alderman, Clifford Lindsey. *The Story of the Thirteen Colonies.* New York: Random House, Inc., 1966.

The reasons why the settlers of each colony came to the New World are discussed along with political and social developments leading to the Revolution.

Baker, Betty. *Walk the World's Rim.* New York: Harper & Row Pubs., Inc., 1965.

The journey from Texas to Mexico made by a young Indian boy in a party with explorer Cabez de Vaca is told in this fiction story set against a background of southwest Indian life of the time.

Clapp, Patricia. *Constance: A Story of Early Plymouth.* New York: Lothrup, Lee & Shepard Bks., 1968.

A young girl's journal records the pleasures and hardships of her voyage from England to the colonies and her life in early Massachusetts in this fiction story.

Daugherty, James. *The Landing of the Pilgrims.* New York: Random House, Inc., 1950.

Based on the writings of William Bradford, Governor of Plymouth Colony, this is an account of the first three years of the colony.

Edmonds, Walter. *The Matchlock Gun.* New York: Dodd, Mead & Co., 1941.

A young boy grows in courage and responsibility protecting his mother and sisters from Indians in the early days of the Hudson Valley settlement in this fiction story of the French and Indian Wars. A Newbery Medal winner.

Fritz, Jean. *The Double Life of Pocahontas.* New York: Putnam Publishing Group, 1983.

This telling of the life of the Indian princess who wed an early settler of the Virginia colony, John Rolfe, is based on known incidents to give sympathetic insights into the relations between the two groups.

Irwin, Constance. *Strange Footprints on the Land: Vikings in America.* New York: Harper & Row Pubs., Inc., 1980.

Evidence of Viking settlements in North America is examined along with counter-arguments to encourage thoughtful conclusions about Norse exploration.

Meyer, Carolyn and Charles Gallenkamp. *The Mystery of the Ancient Maya.* New York: Atheneum Pub., 1985.

What has been learned by explorers, scientists, and amateurs about the Mayan civilization is examined in the form of a mystery investigation.

O'Dell, Scott. *The King's Fifth.* Boston: Houghton Mifflin Co., 1966.

Gold fever takes hold in the life of a young mapmaker diverting him from his quest for knowledge in this fiction story.

Speare, Elizabeth. *The Witch of Blackbird Pond.* Boston: Houghton Mifflin Co., 1958.

A determined young woman stands up for herself and must bear the consequences in Puritan colonial Connecticut. A Newbery Medal winner. Fiction.

Tunis, Edwin. *Tavern at the Ferry.* New York: Harper & Row Pubs., Inc., 1973.

Frontier American living is described in the period preceeding the Revolution using the activities involved in running the enterprises of the title which were situated on the Delaware River.

UNIT TWO A NEW NATION IS ESTABLISHED

The American Revolutionaries: A History In Their Own Words, 1750–1800. New York: Thomas Y. Crowell Junior Books, 1987.

The words of the common folk of the era are assembled from letters, diaries, journals, memoirs, and newspapers to give the rebel point of view.

Avi. *The Fighting Ground.* New York: Harper & Row Pubs., Inc., 1984.

One day tells the story of a thirteen-year-old boy who changes his view of war when he is involved in a skirmish near his farm home, is captured, and escapes in this fiction adventure set in the Revolution.

Brandt, Keith. *John Paul Jones, Hero of the Seas.* Mahwah, N.J.: Troll Assocs., 1983.

The life of this hero of the early days of the United States is examined as he worked his way up through various jobs that led to a naval career and his contributions to his country.

Clapp, Patricia. *I'm Deborah Sampson.* New York: Lothrop, Lee & Shepard Bks., 1977.

This is a fictionalized first-person account of the true story of a girl who served in the Continental Army during the Revolution disguised as a boy.

Collier, James L. and Christopher Collier. *My Brother Sam Is Dead.* New York: Four Winds Press, 1974.

A true incident in the early days of a New England community is the basis for this fiction story of a family whose sons declare opposing loyalties during the Revolutionary War.

Forbes, Esther. *Johnny Tremain.* Boston: Houghton Mifflin Co., 1943.

A young boy apprenticed to a silversmith in colonial Boston is caught up in the turmoil leading to the American Revolution.

Foster, Genevieve. *Year of Independence, 1776.* New York: Charles Scribner's Sons, 1970.

The quarrels between England and her American colonies which led to the outbreak of war and eventual formation of the United States are described along with other changes in the world involving the sciences, arts, and politics.

Fritz, Jean. *Shhh! We're Writing the Constitution.* New York: The Putnam Publishing Group, 1987.

The differences in viewpoint among the men who wrote the Constitution are portrayed as well as details about the time in which they lived.

Giblin, James Cross. *Fireworks, picnics, and flags.* Boston: Houghton Mifflin Co., 1983.

Events leading to the signing of the Declaration of Independence are described, and the meaning of many national symbols as well as early celebrations of this event are highlighted.

Hauptly, Denis. *"A Convention of Delegates": The Creation of the Constitution.* New York: Atheneum Pubs., 1987.

The personalities involved in the Constitutional Convention of 1787 are portrayed in a straightforward manner which also reveals key figures in the important roles they played.

Hilton, Suzanne. *We the People: the Way We Were, 1783–1793.* Philadelphia: Westminster Pr., 1981.

Personal accounts from many sources describe the daily life of people building the new United States during the first ten years after becoming independent.

Phelan, Mary Kay. *The Story of the Boston Massacre.* New York: Thomas Y. Crowell Junior Bks., 1976.

The arrival of British troops in Boston and the Massacre and trial which followed are described and highlighted with quotations from original sources.

UNIT THREE THE GROWING REPUBLIC

Blos, Joan. *A Gathering of Days: A New England Girl's Journal, 1830–1832.* New York: Charles Scribner's Sons, 1979.

The fourteenth year of a girl growing up in New England in the 1830's is told in diary form while the issues of the day unfold through her observations in this fiction story. A Newbery Medal winner.

Blumberg, Rhoda. *The Incredible Journey of Lewis and Clark.* New York: Lothrop, Lee & Shepard Bks., 1987.

The expedition to explore the vast and unknown region of western America in the early 19th century is described with much detail in this account without diminishing the excitement of the adventure.

Bohner, Charles. *Bold Journey: West with Lewis and Clark.* Boston: Houghton Mifflin Co., 1985.

A young man travels west with Lewis and Clark in this fictionalized telling of the adventure.

Marrin, Albert. *1812, The War Nobody Won.* New York: Atheneum Pubs., 1985.

An account of the everyday life of the Americans, British, and Indians who fought on land and at sea is given in a manner that reveals the moments of glory as well as disappointment.

O'Dell, Scott. *Island of the Blue Dolphins.* Boston: Houghton Mifflin Co., 1960.

A young Indian girl accidentally left on a remote island off the California coast in the 1800's manages to survive and find some beauty in her lonely habitat. A Newbery Medal winner. Fiction.

———. *Streams to the River, River to the Sea: A Novel of Sacagawea.* Boston: Houghton Mifflin Co., 1986.

A fiction telling of Lewis and Clark through the eyes of the young Indian woman who was their interpreter and guide.

Steele, William O. *The Lone Hunt.* San Diego, CA.: Harcourt Brace Jovanovich, Inc., 1976.

In early Tennessee a young boy, yearning to be independent, is determined to continue the hunt for the last buffalo seen in the area.

Tunis, Edwin. *Frontier Living.* New York: Thomas Y. Crowell Junior Bks., 1961.

Daily living is described and illustrated as settlers move westward.

Yates, Elizabeth. *Amos Fortune, Free Man.* New York: E. P. Dutton, 1950.

After forty years as a slave brought from Africa to the young United States, a black man is able to buy his freedom and help other slaves. A Newbery Medal winner.

UNIT FOUR PROGRESS AND PROBLEMS

Baker, Olaf. *Where the Buffaloes Begin.* New York: Frederick Warne & Co., Inc., 1981.

A legend of the American Indian is retold and illustrated in this short tale of a boy who leads a stampeding herd of buffalo away from his people.

Bealer, Alex W. *Only the Names Remain: The Cherokees and the Trail of Tears.* Boston: Little, Brown & Co., 1972.

The history of the Cherokee Indians with emphasis on their exile west of the Mississippi in 1839.

Bierhorst, John. *The Mythology of North America.* New York: William Morrow & Co., Inc., 1985.

An anthology of selected myths considered to be "old, sacred, or true" by the tellers summarizes major themes in the mythology of North American Indians.

Black Americans: A History in Their Own Words, 1619–1983. New York: Thomas Y. Crowell Junior Bks., 1984.

The social history of Black Americans is dramatically told in their own words.

De Angeli, Marguerite. *Thee Hannah!* New York: Doubleday & Co., Inc., 1940.

The youngest in a large Quaker family loves fine things and has trouble fitting into the conservative pattern of her elders.

Fox, Paula. *The Slave Dancer.* New York: Bradbury Pr., 1973.

A young boy is kidnapped and taken aboard a slave ship to work during the early days of slave trade in America. A Newbery Medal winner.

Fritz, Jean. *Stonewall.* New York: The Putnam Publishing Group, 1979.

This biography gives a realistic and honest portrayal of a complex character who played an important role in the early United States.

Hamilton, Virginia. *The People Could Fly: American Black Folktales.* New York: Alfred A. Knopf, Inc., 1985.

Representative folktales are retold to depict the black slaves' struggles for survival in the early years of this country.

Native American Testimony: An Anthology of Indian and White Relations, First Encounter to Dispossession. New York: Thomas Y. Crowell Junior Bks., 1978.

In a mature book of readings, Indian and white relations are presented through excerpts from speeches, writings, and stories by native Americans.

Petry, Ann. *Harriet Tubman, Conductor on the Underground Railroad.* New York: Thomas Y. Crowell Junior Bks., 1955.

A dramatic and stirring biography of an indomitable woman also gives insight into the workings of the complex escape route to the North for slaves.

Rounds, Glen. *The Prairie Schooners.* New York: Holiday House, Inc., 1968.

The daily life on a wagon train in 1843 from Missouri to the Oregon Territory is described.

Steele, William O. *The War Party.* San Diego, CA: Harcourt Brace Jovanovich, Inc., 1978.

The reality of war is experienced by a young Indian brave when he is wounded in his first battle.

UNIT FIVE THE UNION IS TESTED

Avi. *Emily Upham's Revenge.* New York: Pantheon Bks., 1978.

An adventure tale set in early Massachusetts imitates the style of morality stories of the time.

Beatty, Patricia. *Charley Skedaddle.* New York: William Morrow & Co., Inc., 1987.

A young boy from New York joins the Union Army to avenge his fallen brother but flees from the horror of war, much to his shame.

———. *Turn Homeward, Hannalee.* New York: William Morrow & Co., Inc., 1984.

A group of southern mill workers become displaced persons during the Civil War.

Crane, Stephen. *The Red Badge of Courage.* New York: Bantam Bks., Inc., first published in 1894.

The state of mind of a young soldier is portrayed during the action of the Battle of Chancellorsville in this fiction story for mature readers.

Freedman, Russell. *Lincoln: A Photobiography.* Boston: Houghton Mifflin Co., 1987.

Material gathered from Lincoln's writings and speeches enhances this realistic portrayal that picks fact from fiction, moving from childhood through early businesses to his political career and assassination. A Newbery Medal winner.

Hunt, Irene. *Across Five Aprils.* New York: Ace Bks., 1964.

The Civil War becomes a reality when a young farm boy in southern Illinois sees his family pulled apart as his brothers join opposing armies.

Katz, William Loren. *An Album of the Civil War.* New York: Franklin Watts, Inc., 1974.

Many old photographs and prints illustrate the chronological events of the Civil War.

Keith, Harold. *Rifles for Watie.* New York: Thomas Y. Crowell Junior Bks., 1957.

A young Union soldier fighting the Civil War in the Western states is assigned as a spy and loses his carefree attitude as he learns the depth of convictions of others. A Newbery Medal winner.

Lens, Sidney. *Strikemakers and Strikebreakers.* New York: Lodestar Bks., 1985.

A well researched history of the labor movement in the United States is presented.

O'Dell, Scott. *Sing Down the Moon.* Boston: Houghton Mifflin Co., 1970.

The forced march of Indians to Fort Sumner in 1864 is told by a young Navajo girl in this fiction account.

Steele, William O. *The Perilous Road.* San Diego, CA: Harcourt Brace Jovanovich, Inc., 195.

A yankee-hating mountain boy learns the futility of war during the Civil War in Tennessee.

UNIT SIX THE GROWTH OF THE NATION

Asimov, Isaac. *The Golden Door: The United States from 1865 to 1918.* Boston: Houghton Mifflin Co., 1977.

The important events during the period from after the Civil War to just before the outbreak of World War I are highlighted to give a feeling of the times and political trends.

Beatty, Patricia. *Hail Columbia.* New York: William Morrow & Co., Inc., 1970.

Oregon of the 1890's is the unlikely setting for a visit from a suffragist Aunt to the delight of her nieces in this fiction story.

Calvert, Patricia. *The Snowbird.* New York: Charles Scribner's Sons, 1980.

An orphaned brother and sister must find their way to their uncle who homesteads in the Dakota Territory and is married to a woman who does not welcome them in a tale set in 1883.

Conrad, Pam. *Prairie Songs.* New York: Harper & Row Pubs., Inc., 1985.

At the turn of the century, a frail, young wife struggles with the harshness of life on the prairie.

Freedman, Russell. *Cowboys of the Wild West.* Boston: Houghton Mifflin Co., 1985.

Portraying real cowboys of the Old West, this descriptive account highlighted with many period photographs gives the history of cattle ranching.

Keith, Harold. *The Obstinate Land.* New York: Harper & Row Pubs., Inc., 1977.

The hostile land of the Cherokee Strip is the setting for this realistic story of a family's struggle to make their living.

UNIT SEVEN
A MODERN NATION IN A NEW CENTURY

Beatty, Patricia. *Eight Mules from Monterey.* New York: William Morrow & Co., Inc., 1982.

A new librarian travels the mountain trails by mule to deliver books to remote communities in this story of early twentieth century California.

Edmonds, Walter. *Bert Breen's Barn.* Boston: Little, Brown & Co., 1975.

To help his family's desperate circumstances, this quiet story tells of a boy determined to raise a barn on their land.

Lasky, Kathryn. *The Night Journey.* New York: Frederick Warne & Co., Inc., 1981.

A grandmother tells her great granddaughter the story of the dangerous journey she took to escape from Russia during the reign of the Czar.

Sebestyen, Ouida. *Words by Heart.* Boston: Little, Brown & Co., 1979.

The problems of the only black family in an all-white community in the Southwest are told in this story set in the Reconstruction period.

Skurzynski, Gloria. *The Tempering.* Boston: Houghton Mifflin Co., 1983.

The conditions in an early twentieth century Pennsylvania steel town shape the lives of three young men.

Rostkowski, Margaret I. *After the Dancing Days.* New York: Harper & Row Pubs., Inc., 1986.

A young girl helping her doctor father in a veteran's hospital after World War I learns that not all soldiers die gloriously when she befriends a horribly burned and bitter young man.

Yep, Laurence. *Dragonwings.* New York: Harper & Row Pubs., Inc., 1975.

A young Chinese boy adjusts to life in San Francisco and the western world in this story set at the turn of the century.

UNIT EIGHT
THE DEPRESSION AND WORLD WAR II

Armstrong, William. *Sounder.* New York: Harper & Row Pubs., Inc., 1969.

Harsh customs and harsh circumstances cripple the bodies of a dog and its master in this story of the South. A Newbery Medal winner.

Greene, Bette. *Summer of My German Soldier.* New York: Dial Bks. for Young Readers, 1973.

In this story set in a small southern town during World War II a young girl hides an escaped German prisoner of war, and she and her family suffer.

Hooks, William H. *Circle of Fire.* New York: Atheneum Pubs., 1982.

A young boy struggles with his conscience when he suspects that his father is part of the Ku Klux Klan in this story set in North Carolina.

Hunt, Irene. *No Promises in the Wind.* Chicago: Follett Pub. Co., 1970.

In a story that takes place during the Great Depression, a boy finds he must quickly learn to make his own way in life.

Lawson, Don. *F.D.R.'s New Deal.* New York: Harper & Row Pubs., Inc., 1979.

A picture of the times in the United States from 1929 to the start of World War II is given through highlights of the most important people and events.

Paterson, Katherine. *Jacob Have I Loved.* New York: Harper & Row Pubs., Inc., 1980.

The Chesapeake Bay region is the setting for this story of rivalry between two sisters and the social expectations of the 1940's.

Taylor, Mildred. *Roll of Thunder, Hear My Cry.* New York: Dial Bks. for Young Readers, 1976.

This story takes place in rural Mississippi during the Great Depression and tells of a black family's struggle to remain independent and stay on their land. A Newbery Medal winner.

Uchida, Yoshiko. *Journey Home.* New York: Atheneum Pubs., 1978.

The struggle to return to a normal life is told in this story of a Japanese-American family released from an internment camp after World War II.

UNIT NINE CONFLICT AND CHANGE

Archer, Jules. *The Incredible Sixties: The Stormy Years that Changed America.* San Diego, CA: Harcourt Brace Jovanovich, Inc., 1986.

Social conditions and issues of the day are presented with many photographs in an undemanding style for popular reading.

Bridgers, Sue Ellen. *All Together Now.* New York: Alfred A. Knopf, Inc., 1979.

A young girl spends a summer with her grandparents in a small North Carolina town while her father is with the military forces in Korea.

Killian, James. *Sputnik, Scientists, and Eisenhower.* Cambridge, MA: MIT Pr., 1977.

Written by Eisenhower's Science Advisor, this is a memoir of the early United States' space program and the founding of N.A.S.A.

Haskins, James and Kathleen Benson. *The 60's Reader.* New York: Viking Penguin, Inc., 1988.

The political and social unheavals of the 1960's are recalled through speeches, essays, and writings of the times.

Hauptly, Denis J. *In Vietnam.* New York: Atheneum Pubs., 1985.

The history of Vietnam and American's foreign policy of the time are used to give an account of America's involvement in the Vietnam conflict.

King, Martin Luther. *Stride Toward Freedom.* New York: Harper & Row Pubs., Inc., 1958.

The bus boycott that took place in Montgomery, Alabama, in 1955–56 is described by the leader of the American Civil Rights movement.

Life in Rural America. Washington, DC: National Geographic Society, 1974.

Many color photos accompany descriptions of farm life, small town and ranch life, and country living.

Walter, Mildred Pitts. *The Girl on the Outside.* New York: Lothrop, Lee & Shepard Bks., 1982.

In this story of the 1957 integration of Little Rock High School in Arkansas, a black girl and a white girl each tells about it from her own point of view.

UNIT TEN
AMERICA FACES NEW CHALLENGES

Ashabranner, Brent. *Dark Harvest: Migrant Farmworkers in America.* New York: Dodd, Mead & Co., 1985.

The world of migrant workers is explored with information and photographs interwoven with personal interviews.

Cleaver, Vera and Bill Cleaver. *Queen of Hearts.* Philadelphia: Lippencott, 1978.

A young girl must take care of her ailing grandmother and finds that she is not the only one who is angry over circumstances which she cannot control.

Hamilton, Virginia. *Sweet Whispers, Brother Rush.* New York: The Putnam Publishing Group, 1982.

Part of a fatherless family with a working mother, a young girl finds an unusual way to deal with her frustration at having to care for her brother when they are left alone.

Highwater, Jamake. *Eyes of Darkness.* New York: Lothrop, Lee & Shepard Bks., 1985.

Based on the life of Charles Alexander Eastman, an Indian doctor and writer, this is the story of a young man who tries to integrate his traditional heritage with the white man's world.

Paterson, Katherine. *Come Sing, Jimmy Jo.* New York: Lodestar Bks., 1985.

A young boy who is at an age of much change in his personal development must also adjust to becoming a successful country music singer in this story of a West Virginia family.

Pringle, Laurence. *Nuclear War: From Hiroshima to Nuclear Winter.* Hillside, NJ: Enslow Pubs., Inc., 1985.

The effects of nuclear war on the world are considered in this detailed history of nuclear warfare.

———. *Restoring Our Earth.* Hillside, NJ: Enslow Pubs., Inc., 1987.

The study of how various organizations work to restore the earth's resources is presented here along with possible solutions to environmental problems.

Taylor, L. B. *The New Right.* New York: Franklin Watts, Inc., 1981.

This is a overview of the Christian Right movement along with opposing views where applicable.

Weiss, Ann. *Good Neighbors?* Boston: Houghton Mifflin, Co., 1985.

Key factors in the history of United States and Latin American relationships which lead to current situations are presented.

GLOSSARY

This glossary contains brief definitions of certain words and terms used in this book and brief descriptions of certain events that are important in American history. The boldface number **(123)** listed after each definition indicates the page where the word or term is first used. You may find additional meanings of words by using your dictionaries.

Some of the words in this glossary are respelled in a special way to help the reader say them. The respelling of a word appears in parentheses.

When a word has two or more syllables, the syllables are not usually given equal stress. In the respelling of a word, the syllable or syllables with the most stress are printed in large capital letters. Syllables that are not stressed are printed in small letters. Words that have only one syllable are printed in small capital letters.

Below is a list of special letters and letter groupings used for the respelling of words. A description of the way the letter or letters are said and an example of a respelled word follow each letter or letter grouping.

a	*a* in *trap* [TRAP]
ah	*a* in *far* [FAHR]
	o in *hot* [HAHT]
aw	*a* in *all* [AWL]
	o in *order* [AWRD-uhr]
ay	*a* in *face* [FAYS]
e	*e* in *let* [LET]
	a in *care* [KER]
ee	*e* in *equal* [EE-kwuhl]
	i in *ski* [SKEE]
i	*i* in *trip* [TRIP]
	e in *erase* [i-RAYS]
iy	*i* in *kite* [KIYT]
	y in *sky* [SKIY]
oh	*o* in *rodeo* [ROHD-ee-OH]
	ow in *slow* [SLOH]
oo	*oo* in *food* [FOOD]
	u in *rule* [ROOL]
ow	*ou* in *out* [OWT]
oy	*oi* in *voice* [VOYS]
th	*th* in *thin* [THIN]
th (underlined)	*th* in *that* [THAT]
u	*u* in *put* [PUT]
	oo in *foot* [FUT]
uh	*u* in *cup* [KUHP]
	a in *asleep* [uh-SLEEP]
	e in *term* [TUHRM]
	i in *bird* [BUHRD]
	o in *word* [WUHRD]
z	*s* in *atoms* [AT-uhmz]
zh	*s* in *measure* [MEZH-uhr]
	z in *azure* [AZH-uhr]

A

Abolitionist (AB-uh-LISH-uhn-uhst). A person who wanted to end slavery. **(173)**

Acid rain. Rainwater that is made much more acidic than normal by atmospheric pollutants from the burning of fossil fuels such as coal and oil. **(702)**

Allied powers. In World War I, the nations that fought against the Central Powers. In World War II, the nations that fought against the Axis powers. The United States was a member of the Allied powers in both wars. **(466)**

American Federation of Labor (AFL). A union of skilled workers founded in 1886 by Samuel Gompers. This union worked to gain higher pay and shorter working hours for its members. **(402)**

Americanization. The process by which people from other countries sought to fit into American life in the late 1800's and early 1900's. **(411)**

American System. A plan by Henry Clay in the 1820's that called for the federal government to use high tariffs to protect America's growing trade and manufacturing. The plan also called for the government to build roads and canals to make trade and travel easier. **(181)**

Anarchist (AN-uhr-kist). A person who believes that a society should have no government and no laws. **(427)**

Annexation (AN-EK-SAY-shuhn). A joining or adding, especially of new territory. **(225)**

Antebellum (ANT-i-BEL-uhm) **South.** The term used when referring to the South in the years before the Civil War. **(208)**

Anti-Federalist party. The name of a political party formed in 1787 to oppose the ratification of the Constitution. Anti-Federalists believed that approving the Constitution would make the national government too powerful. **(123)**

Apartheid (uh-PAHR-TAYT). A policy of racial segregation and economic and political discrimination against non-Europeans in the Republic of South Africa. **(680)**

Archaeologist (AHR-kee-AHL-uh-juhst). A scientist who studies the way of life of past peoples by examining remains, fossil relics, artifacts, and the monuments left by such peoples. **(19)**

Armistice (AHR-muh-stuhs). An agreement to end the fighting in a war. **(469)**

Articles of Confederation. The plan of government of 1781, under which the thirteen original states formed a loose union. **(112)**

B

Bicameral (biy-KAM-uh-ruhl) **legislature.** The name given to a lawmaking body that is composed of two houses. **(122)**

Big-stick diplomacy. The name of the foreign policy of President Theodore Roosevelt. Under this policy, the United States sought to be firm in its dealings with other countries. **(445)**

Big Three. The name used when referring to England, the Soviet Union, and the United States during World War II. **(556)**

Bill of Rights. The name given to the first ten amendments to the Constitution, which guarantee certain rights and freedoms to individuals. **(124)**

Black Codes. The term for harsh local and state laws passed to control blacks in the South after the Civil War. **(317)**

Blacklisted. Put on a list of known union members who are not to be employed because of their union activities. Such lists were often used by antiunion businesses in the late 1800's and early 1900's. **(403)**

Black power. The term for the use of political and economic power by blacks to further the cause of racial equality. **(641)**

Bleeding Kansas. The term used to describe conditions in the territory of Kansas in the 1850's, as proslavery and antislavery groups fought for control of the territory. **(276)**

Blockade runner. A specially built ship designed to break through the northern blockade of southern ports during the Civil War. **(298)**

Bolshevik (BOHL-shuh-VIK). A member of the Communist party that seized power in Russia in 1917. **(468)**

Boycott. The term for an organized refusal to buy goods or services. **(94)**

C

Cabinet. A group made up of the heads of the executive departments of the federal government. The members of the cabinet act as advisers to the President. Through customs, the cabinet has become an accepted part of the government, although it is not provided for in the Constitution. **(130)**

Carpetbagger. A northerner who went to the South after the Civil War and entered politics or business there, sometimes for personal gain. **(323)**

Caucus (KAW-kuhs). A meeting of the members of Congress or of a legislature who belong to the same political party. Such meetings were once used to nominate presidential candidates. **(189)**

Cede (SEED). To give up something, such as land, through a treaty. **(158)**

Central Powers. The nations that fought against the Allied powers during World War I. Germany and Austria-Hungary were the two most powerful members of the Central Powers. **(466)**

Chattel (CHAT-uhl). A piece of personal property such as money or goods. The term was often applied to slaves in the South. **(208)**

Checks and balances. The system provided for in the Constitution that allows each branch of the federal government to act as a check on the power of the other two branches. **(128)**

City bosses. Politicians who headed the political organizations in many large American cities in the late 1800's and early 1900's. These organizations usually controlled the city government. **(416)**

Civil rights. The term for the rights of personal liberty that are guaranteed to American citizens by the Constitution. **(640)**

Cold war. The struggle between the United States and the Soviet Union following the end of World War II. This struggle was carried on mainly through propaganda and by political and economic means rather than through actual warfare. **(586)**

Compromise (KAHM-pruh-MIYZ). The term used when dispute is settled by each side's giving up some of its demands. **(121)**

Compromise of 1850. A plan worked out by several members of Congress that let California into the Union as a free state and provided for the passage of several other laws that were wanted by the North and the South. **(257)**

Concentration (KAHN-suhn-TRAY-shuhn). A policy followed by the federal government after the Civil War, by which the Plains Indians were brought together in certain areas so that the rest of the Great Plains could be opened for settlement. **(342)**

Concurrent (kuhn-KUHR-uhnt) **powers.** The term for those powers that may be exercised by both the federal government and the state governments, such as the power to build roads and the power to levy and to collect taxes. **(127)**

Congress of Industrial Organizations (CIO). The national organization of industrial unions. The union was founded in 1935 by John L. Lewis, and it merged with the AFL in 1955. **(535)**

Conspiracy (kuhn-SPIR-uh-see). The act of working with others secretly to commit an unlawful act. **(431)**

Constitutional supremacy (soo-PREM-uh-see). The principle that the Constitution of the United States is the highest law in the country and that any laws passed by state and local governments must agree with the Constitution. **(127)**

Containment policy. A plan followed by the United States after World War II to check the spread of communism. The United States gave economic and military aid to countries that were threatened with a Communist takeover. **(587)**

Contras. The name for Nicaraguans who seek to overthrow the Nicaraguan government. **(687)**

Copperheads. The name given to Democrats from the North who were opposed to the Civil War and who wanted President Lincoln to end the war by making peace with the South. **(303)**

Corporation (KAWR-puh-RAY-shuhn). A business organization that is owned by people who have bought shares in the organization. **(395)**

Culture (KUHL-chuhr). The common customs, beliefs, and practices of a society that are passed from one generation to another. **(22)**

D

Debtor (DET-uhr). A person who owes something to another person. **(58)**

Declaration of Independence. The document by which the Thirteen Colonies declared that they were free and independent of Great Britain. **(105)**

Delegated powers. The powers given to the federal government by the Constitution. **(127)**

Democratic party. One of the two major American political parties. The origins of the Democratic party go back to the Democratic-Republican party, led by Thomas Jefferson. The present name was adopted during the administration of Andrew Jackson. **(231)**

Depression. A period of low economic activity characterized by high unemployment, low prices, and a general lack of buying power. **(199)**

Détente (DAY-TAHNT). The relaxing of tensions between two countries. **(658)**

Deterrence (di-TUHR-uhns). A strategy for preventing war by building up vast military power and maintaining large stocks of weapons. **(706)**

Dictator (DIK-TAYT-uhr). A leader who rules the political, social, and economic life of a country with absolute power. **(547)**

Diplomatic relations. The process of conducting formal affairs between nations. **(232)**

Direct primary. A preliminary election to choose party candidates to run in regular elections. **(453)**

Dissidents (DIS-uhd-uhnts). People who disapprove of and protest against policies of their government. **(680)**

Domino theory. The belief that if one country in Southeast Asia was taken over by the Communists, neighboring countries would also be taken over by Communists. **(614)**

Draft. A method used by the federal government to select people for the armed services. **(668)**

Duty. The term for a tax on goods coming into a country from another country. **(90)**

E

Economy. The system through which goods are made, divided, and used by people. **(31)**

Eisenhower Doctrine. A foreign policy position taken by the United States under President Eisenhower. This country promised to use American forces to protect friendly Middle Eastern countries from a Communist takeover. **(600)**

Elastic clause. A section of the Constitution that stretches the power of the federal government. This clause gives Congress the power to make all laws that are necessary and proper to carry out its other delegated powers. **(129)**

Emancipation (i-MAN-suh-PAY-shuhn) **Proclamation.** President Lincoln's order of 1862 freeing the slaves in those states still in rebellion against the Union as of January 1, 1863. **(301)**

Embargo (im-BAHR-goh). A government order that prevents trading ships from leaving ports controlled by that government. **(163)**

Empire. A group of countries and territories united under one rule, as the British Empire. **(30)**

Enumerated (i-NOO-muh-RAYT-uhd) **powers.** The special powers given to the President by the Constitution of the United States. **(127)**

Era of Good Feelings. The name for the period from the end of the War of 1812 to the middle 1820's. It was a time of little political conflict, since the Federalist party had disappeared and the Democratic-Republican party was supreme. **(178)**

Excise (EK-SIYZ) **tax.** A tax on goods made and sold within a country. **(134)**

Executive privilege. A belief that the separation of powers between the branches of government allows one branch to keep certain kinds of information from another branch. **(660)**

Expressed powers. The specific powers of the federal government that are written into the Constitution. **(127)**

F

Fair Deal. The name for President Truman's social-legislation program, which was designed to improve society through direct government action. **(585)**

Federalist party. The name of a political party organized in 1787 to bring about the ratification of the Constitution. Federalists favored a strong national government. **(123)**

Fireside chats. The name for the radio talks by President Franklin D. Roosevelt to the American people, explaining the government's plans for dealing with the depression. **(520)**

Fourteen Points. The name given to President Wilson's plan for building permanent world peace after the end of World War I. **(470)**

Freedman. The term used when referring to a person who had been a slave. **(316)**

Freedmen's Bureau. An agency of the federal government set up in 1865 to help former slaves and other persons who were suffering from the effects of the Civil War. **(316)**

Free-Soil party. A political party organized in the 1840's to oppose the extension of slavery into the territories. **(255)**

G

Gadsden Purchase. An area of land, now part of southern Arizona and New Mexico, that the United States purchased from Mexico in 1853. Some Americans wanted this land for a cross-country railroad. **(271)**

Geothermal (JEE-oh-THUHR-muhl) **power.** Power produced by the use of heat from the earth's interior. The power is generated when water comes into contact with underground rocks and turns into steam. **(692)**

Gilded Age. The name given to the years of Grant's presidency and the years immediately after. The term came from a book by Mark Twain and Charles Dudley Warner. **(336)**

Glasnost (GLAHZ-nohst). Russian for "openness." The term describes the Soviet leader Mikhail Gorbachev's policy of open information, which allows the Soviet media to report fully about events at home and abroad and to criticize the government. **(710)**

Global village. The term used for the idea that modern advances in transportation and communication have made the world seem no larger than a village. **(701)**

Good-neighbor policy. The popular term for the Latin American policy followed by President Franklin D. Roosevelt. In the early 1930's the United States worked to promote better relations with Latin American countries. **(541)**

Grandfather laws. The term for laws enacted in several southern states between 1895 and 1910 with the purpose of preventing blacks from voting. These laws limited the right to vote to those people who had voted on January 1, 1865, or to the descendants of those who had voted on that date. **(455)**

Grange. An organization of farmers, formed in 1867 to further their interests. **(328)**

Granger laws. Laws passed by a number of states to regulate railroads in the late 1800's. These laws were passed as a result of the influence of farmers through the Grange. **(373)**

Great Society. The name given to the legislative program of President Johnson for laws to help Americans improve their lives. **(621)**

Green revolution. The term for the use of new crop varieties, fertilizers, and farming methods to greatly increase food production. **(704)**

Greenback party. A third political party that developed in the 1870's. This group believed that the country's economic problems could be solved by putting more paper money into circulation. **(337)**

Greenhouse effect. The result of an increase of carbon dioxide gas in the earth's atmosphere. The gas traps heat that would otherwise escape into space and causes a warming of the earth. **(703)**

Gross National Product (GNP). The term for the total value of all goods and services produced by a country within a certain time. **(580)**

Guerrilla warfare. The waging of war through surprise attacks by small groups. **(646)**

Gulf of Tonkin Resolution. A resolution passed by Congress in 1964 that authorized President Johnson to take whatever steps were needed to stop attacks on American soldiers and to stop further aggression in South Vietnam. **(647)**

H

Hispanics. People in the United States who are Spanish-speaking Americans. **(642)**

Holocaust (HAHL-uh-KAWST). The term used for the mass murder of Jews and other groups by the Nazis during World War II. **(548)**

Home rule. The right of a group, such as a colony or town, to govern itself. **(65)**

Homestead Act. A federal law passed in 1862 that gave 160 acres (65 hectares) of land west of the Mississippi River to the head of a family, providing the person would settle and cultivate the land for 5 years. **(340)**

Hoovervilles. The name for the slum settlements in which homeless people lived during the worst days of the depression in the 1930's. **(516)**

House of Burgesses. A group of Virginia landowners who formed the first lawmaking body in the English colonies in 1619. **(65)**

I

Ideology (IYD-ee-AHL-uh-jee). A system of beliefs, theories, and political aims for society. **(711)**

Immigrant (IM-i-gruhnt). A person born in one country who enters another country to become a permanent resident. **(136)**

Impeach. To charge a public official with wrongdoing while in office. The method for removing federal officers is provided for in Article 1 of the Constitution. **(321)**

Imperialism (im-PIR-ee-uh-LIZ-uhm). The foreign policy of extending the control of one nation over the political and economic life of other areas around the world. **(441)**

Implied powers. The powers that are not expressly stated in the Constitution but that are reasonably suggested by the powers that are stated. **(179)**

Inauguration (in-AW-guh-RAY-shuhn). The ceremony in which a person is formally installed in a political office. **(135)**

Indentured servant. A person who promised to work without pay in the English colonies for a certain length of time to pay for the cost of the trip to the colonies. **(63)**

Industrialize (in-DUHS-tree-uh-LIYZ). To build up a country's manufacturing and business activities. **(155)**

Industrial union. A union formed by the joining of all the workers in a given industry. **(534)**

Inflation. The term used to describe the economic situation in which prices rise, and thus the value of money decreases. **(553)**

Initiative (in-ISH-uht-iv). A method by which voters are given the power to propose or to enact laws directly. **(453)**

Isolationism (IY-suh-LAY-shuh-NIZ-uhm). The term for America's foreign policy after World War I and before World War II. Under this policy, the United States sought to avoid involvement in the affairs of other countries. **(543)**

J

Jim Crow laws. Legislation passed by some states, which discriminated against blacks. **(455)**

Judicial review. The power of the Supreme Court to decide whether acts of Congress and of the states are in agreement with the Constitution. **(154)**

K

Kansas-Nebraska Act. An act of 1854 that created the territories of Kansas and Nebraska and permitted both antislavery and proslavery groups to practice their beliefs in those territories. **(274)**

Knights of Labor. A national labor union that was formed in 1869 and included both skilled and unskilled workers. **(329)**

Ku Klux Klan (KOO-KLUHKS-KLAN). A secret society formed in the South during Reconstruction that terrorized blacks in order to prevent them from exercising their civil rights. A second organization, the Knights of the Ku Klux Klan, formed in 1914, opposed Catholics and Jews as well as blacks. **(346)**

L

Laissez-faire (LES-AY-FAR). A policy whereby the government does not interfere in the business affairs of a nation. **(392)**

Laser (LAY-zuhr). A device that creates a narrow beam of very intense light going in only one direction. **(691)**

League of Nations. A world organization, based on President Wilson's ideas, that was set up after World War I to preserve world peace. **(471)**

Louisiana Purchase. The purchase from France by the United States in 1803 of the land between the Mississippi River and the Rocky Mountains and between Canada and the Gulf of Mexico. **(158)**

Loyalist. A colonial who remained loyal to the king of England during the American Revolution; also called a Tory. **(95)**

M

McCarthyism. During the early 1950's, the name given to an unreasoning fear of communism and to the feelings of suspicion toward people who held views different from those of the majority. **(597)**

Manifest Destiny. A popular American belief of the 1830's and 1840's that the United States had a right and a mission to extend its boundaries to the Pacific Ocean. **(223)**

Marshall Plan. The popular name for the European Recovery Program, by which American economic aid was given to European countries to help them recover from the effects of World War II. **(588)**

Mayflower Compact. An agreement signed by the Pilgrims in 1620. It was the first written agreement about self-government in America. **(56)**

Medicare. A plan set up in 1965 to help elderly people pay for hospital and doctor's services and for certain other health needs. **(639)**

Mercantilism (MUHR-kuhn-TEE-LIZ-uhm). A system by which countries sought to gain wealth by acquiring colonies. These colonies provided raw materials for the home country. The colonies also served as markets for goods from the home country. **(60)**

Mercenary (MUHR-suh-NER-ee). A soldier hired by a foreign country to fight in its army. **(106)**

Mexican Cession (SESH-uhn). The western lands, including the territories of California and New Mexico, gained by the United States from Mexico as a result of the Mexican War. **(235)**

Minutemen. The name for colonists who were trained to fight the British at a minute's notice at the time of the American Revolution. **(98)**

Missouri Compromise. An act of Congress in 1820 that admitted Missouri to the Union as a slave state and Maine as a free state. **(185)**

Monroe Doctrine. A foreign policy statement made by the United States in 1823 that told European powers they were no longer free to take land in the Western Hemisphere. **(181)**

Muckrakers (MUHK-RAY-kuhrz). A group of journalists of the Progressive era who wrote about the social, political, and economic evils of the late 1800's and early 1900's. **(448)**

N

Nationalism. The feelings of pride and loyalty that a people have toward their nation. **(177)**

Navigation Acts. Laws passed by the English government in the 1600's and 1700's that protected English businesses from competition with other countries and with the English colonies. **(60)**

Nazi (NAHT-see) **party.** The name for the National Socialist German Worker's Party. Adolf Hitler was the leader of the party in the 1930's. **(547)**

Neutrality (noo-TRAL-uht-ee). The policy of favoring neither one side nor the other in a dispute, conflict, or war. **(163)**

New Deal. The name given to the program of President Franklin D. Roosevelt to lead the United States out of the depression. **(520)**

New Freedom. The name of President Wilson's program of legislative reforms. **(461)**

New Frontier. The name given to the legislative program of President Kennedy. **(609)**

North Atlantic Treaty Organization (NATO). An alliance set up after World War II by the United States and other free-world countries. The members of this alliance agreed to defend one another in case of attack by another nation. **(588)**

Nullification (NUHL-uh-fuh-KAY-shuhn). The idea that a state did not have to follow laws passed by Congress if those laws hurt the people of the state. **(198)**

O

Open-door policy. A policy suggested by Secretary of State John Hay of the United States in 1899 that said all nations should have equal trading rights in China. **(444)**

Overseer (OH-vuhr-SIR). A person who was hired by a slave owner to direct slaves while they worked in the fields. **(209)**

Ozone (OH-ZOHN) **layer.** A layer of atmospheric gases high above the earth. The layer contains ozone, an unstable form of oxygen, which protects the earth from solar ultraviolet rays. **(703)**

P

Palestine Liberation Organization (PLO). An organization that represents the Palestinian Arabs. Its chief goal is to destroy Israel in order to form a separate Palestinian country. **(687)**

Patent (PAT-uhnt). An official document, issued by the government, that gives an inventor the exclusive right to make, use, and sell an invention for a term of years. **(390)**

Patriot (PAY-tree-uht). The name given to American colonists who wanted to be free of British rule and who joined the colonial side during the American Revolution. **(95)**

Peace Corps. An organization set up by President Kennedy to aid developing countries. American volunteers were sent to these countries to teach modern farming methods, to provide health care, and to help construct buildings. **(610)**

Perestroika (PER-uh-STROY-kuh). A Russian word for "restructuring." The term describes the economic and political reforms begun by Mikhail Gorbachev to make the Soviet economy more productive and the government more democratic. **(710)**

Planned economy. The situation within a country in which the government controls every part of the nation's economy. This was the case in the United States during World War II. **(577)**

Planters. The small but powerful social class that held most of the economic and political power in the South before the Civil War. **(61)**

Poll tax. A tax once required to be paid before a person could vote. Poll taxes are now illegal. **(346)**

Popular sovereignty (SAHV-ruhn-tee). The doctrine in American history that the people of each territory had the right to decide whether slavery would be allowed in their territory. **(273)**

Populist party. A third party organized in 1891 by farmers, westerners, workers, and small-business people. The party supported such reforms as public ownership of railroads, direct election of United States senators, and a graduated income tax. **(372)**

Potlatch. A celebration among several tribes of northwestern Indians that lasted for many days. The celebration was held to prove the wealth and social standing of the Indians giving the celebration. **(27)**

Precedent (PRES-uhd-uhnt). The term for something that may serve as an example or rule to follow in future situations. **(130)**

Primary election. An election in each state by which the members of political parties choose people to run for office. **(453)**

Progressives. A group of reformers who were active between 1890 and World War I. These people worked for many reforms to overcome the problems caused by industrialism. **(449)**

Prohibition (PROH-uh-BISH-uhn) **laws.** Laws passed during World War I, designed to control and to end the use of alcoholic beverages. **(488)**

Protective tariff. A high tax placed on goods made outside a country in order to protect the industries within that country from foreign competition. **(178)**

R

Radical (RAD-i-kuhl) **Republicans.** The name for a group in Congress who wanted to deal harshly with the defeated South after the Civil War. **(315)**

Radiocarbon dating. A method of determining the age of things that were once alive. **(19)**

Range wars. The name given to the fighting that broke out between cattle owners in the late 1800's over water rights on the Great Plains. **(369)**

Ratification. The term for approving or accepting a legal document such as a treaty or an amendment. **(123)**

Rebate (REE-BAYT). A practice once used by railroads of returning part of the shipping costs to large shippers. **(397)**

Recall. The procedure by which the people can remove a public official from office. **(453)**

Recession. A time when there is a slowdown in business activity within a nation. **(595)**

Reconstruction (ree-kuhn-STRUHK-shuhn). The period of time following the end of the Civil War, during which the governments of the former Confederate states were reorganized and those states were readmitted to the Union. **(310)**

Referendum (REF-uh-REN-duhm). A method by which laws passed by a legislative body can be referred to the people for their approval or rejection. **(453)**

Reaganomics. The name given to President Reagan's economic program. **(683)**

Renaissance (REN-uh-SAHNS). A period in European history between the 14th and 17th centuries. During that time there was a revival of interest in the classical arts and literature. Modern science also had its beginning at that time. **(39)**

Repeal (ri-PEEL). The term for ending a law by legal means. **(93)**

Republican party. One of our two major political parties. It was founded in the 1850's to oppose the spread of slavery. **(275)**

Reserved powers. The term for the powers that are not granted to the federal government nor denied to the states, but that are given to the people or to the state governments by the Constitution. **(127)**

Revenue sharing. A plan that provides for the sharing of federal tax money with state and local governments for certain projects. **(666)**

Roosevelt Corollary (KAWR-uh-LER-ee). President Theodore Roosevelt's addition to the Monroe Doctrine, in which he stated that the United States would, on occasion, intervene in Latin American affairs to preserve stability in that part of the world. **(446)**

S

Satellite (SAT-uh-LIYT). A small, weak nation that is dominated by a stronger nation. **(586)**

Scab. A derisive term used by union members for a worker who takes the place of a striking worker. **(428)**

Scalawag (SKAL-i-WAG). A southern white who supported Reconstruction and who sometimes used political power for personal gain. **(323)**

Secede (si-SEED). To withdraw from an organization such as a nation or a political party. **(161)**

Segregation (SEG-ri-GAY-shuhn). The practice of separating people in public places by race. **(666)**

Separation of powers. The system by which the powers of the federal government are divided among the three branches of government. **(127)**

Servicemen's Readjustment Act (GI Bill). A law enacted after World War II that provided benefits to war veterans. These veterans were given financial help to buy homes, to start businesses, and to further their education. **(578)**

Seward's Folly and **Seward's Icebox.** The terms jokingly used to describe the purchase of Alaska in 1867 from Russia, arranged by Secretary of State William H. Seward. **(330)**

Shaman (SHAHM-uhn). The term for the medicine man of the Indians of the Eastern Woodland area. This medicine man also had political and social power among the Indians. **(25)**

Sharecropper. A farmer who pays a landlord with a part, or share, of crops that have been raised. Many blacks and poor whites became sharecroppers in the South following the Civil War. **(345)**

Slave codes. The body of laws that regulated slave life. These laws were passed by the southern states before the Civil War. **(208)**

Social Darwinism. A social theory, developed by Herbert Spencer, that applied Darwin's ideas about the survival of the fittest to human society. To some people, the adaptation of this theory to the business world explained why some business leaders were successful and made great fortunes. **(397)**

Social mobility. The term used for the ability to move from one social class to another. **(64)**

Social Security Act. An act passed in 1935 to provide old-age pensions and several other social benefits for certain groups of Americans. **(533)**

Social status. The term for a person's rank or place in society. **(64)**

Societies. The term used when referring to groups of people who share the same traditions, institutions, and interests. **(23)**

Soil bank. The term for setting aside farmlands and not using them to grow crops. This idea was used while President Eisenhower was in office as a way of lowering crop production in the hope of raising crop prices. **(596)**

Solar power. The term for the use of the energy from sunlight to generate power. "Solar panels" are used to convert the sun's energy to heat. Devices called solar cells convert the sun's energy to electricity. **(692)**

Space satellite. A space vehicle containing scientific instruments that orbits the earth to gather different kinds of information. **(616)**

Specie (SPEE-shee). A term sometimes used when referring to gold or silver coins. **(115)**

Speculator (SPEK-yuh-LAYT-uhr). A person who buys or sells property or goods in the hope of making a profit from changing market conditions. **(496)**

Spoils system. The practice of removing public officeholders of a defeated party and replacing them with faithful members of the victorious party. **(192)**

States' rights. The political doctrine that upholds the powers of the states as opposed to the powers of the national government. **(154)**

Strategic Arms Limitations Talks (SALT). The name given to the conferences held by the United States and the Soviet Union to find ways to limit nuclear weapons. **(658)**

Strategic Arms Reduction Talks (START). The name given to the conferences held by the United States and the Soviet Union to find ways to reduce nuclear weapons. **(685)**

Strategic Defense Initiative (in-ISH-uht-iv) **(SDI).** A United States research-and-development program designed to create a defense against nuclear-missile attack by means of ground- and satellite-based lasers and particle beams. Enemy missiles would be destroyed by these beams before they could reach their targets. **(707)**

Strikebreakers. Workers who take the place of striking union workers in a labor dispute. **(403)**

Subsistence farming. A kind of farming whereby farmers grow only enough food to meet the basic needs of their families. **(61)**

Suburb (SUHB-UHRB). A community located next to a city, with a different government from that of the central city. **(481)**

Suffrage (SUHF-rij). The term used for the right to vote. **(189)**

T

Tax surcharge. An extra tax that is sometimes collected by a government. **(650)**

Technology (tek-NAHL-uh-jee). The term for the knowledge and skills used to provide objects necessary for human survival and comfort. **(22)**

Temperance (TEM-pruhns) **movement.** A reform movement of the mid-1800's that sought to convince Americans to avoid the use of liquor. **(268)**

Tenements (TEN-uh-muhnts). A term for apartment buildings, especially those with low standards of safety and comfort. **(414)**

Terrorism. The use of violent means—such as kidnapping, murder, random bombings, and hijacking—to achieve a political purpose. **(688)**

Total war. The term for fighting a war by destroying everything of use to the enemy. This way of fighting involves waging war on civilians as well as on military forces. The Civil War was one of the first wars that was a total war. **(305)**

Transcontinental (TRANS-KAHNT-uh-NENT-uhl). Extending across a continent. **(270)**

Tribe. A group of people who share a common characteristic such as language or religion or who live in the same general area. **(24)**

Truman Doctrine. The belief that the United States should work to halt the spread of communism following World War II. This was done mainly through the means of economic aid to countries threatened by a Communist takeover. **(587)**

Trust. A combination of businesses with similar operations, formed in the same industry and operated as a single unit. The purpose of a trust is usually to end competition and to create a monopoly so that the trust can control prices. **(450)**

U

Ultimatum (UHL-tuh-MAYT-uhm). The term used for the final demand, especially for a demand by a party in a conflict. **(421)**

Underground Railroad. A system that helped runaway slaves escape from the South into the North or into Canada. **(173)**

United Nations. A world organization established in 1945 for the purpose of maintaining international peace. **(560)**

Urban (UHR-buhn). The term used when referring to towns or cities, especially those with populations of 2,500 or more. **(155)**

Urban renewal. The term for projects undertaken to repair and to maintain run-down areas of our nation's large cities. Such projects are usually financed by the federal government. **(619)**

Utopian (yoo-TOH-pee-uhn) **movement.** A movement during the Age of Jackson that was characterized by groups of people banding together to form small ideal communities. **(200)**

V

Veto (VEET-oh). The act of refusing to approve or to accept something, especially the action of a legislative body. **(128)**

Vietcong. The name for Communist rebels who fought to overthrow the government of South Vietnam. **(646)**

Vietnamization. A policy used by the United States in South Vietnam, whereby American forces were slowly taken out of the country while the South Vietnamese army was trained and equipped to take over the job of defending the country. **(657)**

W

Wampum (WAHM-puhm). The term for the beads and trinkets used for money and ornaments by many Indian groups of North America. **(50)**

War on Poverty. The name given to President Johnson's program to overcome the problems of poverty in the United States. **(619)**

Whig party. An anti-Jackson political party that was organized in the 1830's. **(254)**

Whiskey Rebellion. An armed uprising against the federal government in 1794 by Pennsylvania farmers who refused to pay an excise tax on whiskey. **(134)**

White supremacy (su-PREM-uh-see). A belief among white people of the South following the Civil War that whites were superior to blacks. **(346)**

Wilmot Proviso (pruh-VIY-zoh). A part of a bill introduced in the House of Representatives in 1846 that said any territory gained as a result of the Mexican War should not be open to slavery. The bill was defeated in the Senate. **(252)**

Writs (RITS) **of Assistance.** The name of court orders that allowed British soldiers to search colonial homes, ships, and warehouses for smuggled goods. **(92)**

Y

Yellow-dog contract. An agreement between an employer and an employee, in which the worker promised not to join a union. **(403)**

INDEX

The following abbreviations are used in this index: *c.*, chart; *cart.*, cartoon; *exc.*, excerpt; *g.*, graph; *ill.*, illustration; *m.*, map; *q.*, quotation; and *t.*, table.

A

B

C

D

E

F

G

H

I

J

K

L

N

O

P

Q

R

S

T

Photography Credits—i, v: Kenneth Garrett. vi–13: Kenneth Garrett. 16L: Olaf Soot/Tony Stone Worldwide. 16R: Bettmann Archive. 17L: "Jamestown about 1614" (detail), National Park Service, Jamestown. 17R: Princeton University Library. 36: National Maritime Museum, Greenwich. 54: "Baltimore in 1752," (detail), Maryland Historical Society, Baltimore. 72: British Museum. 82L: "Back of the State House," William Birch, Historical Society of Pennsylvania. 82R: "Surrender of Lord Cornwallis at Yorktown" (detail), John Trumbull, Yale University Art Gallery. 83L: "Signing of the Constitution" (detail), Howard Christy, Architect of the Capitol. 83R: Concord Museum. 84: "Pulling Down the Statue of George III," Private Collection. 102: "Declaration of Independence" (detail) by John Trumbull, Architect of the Capitol. 120: "Signing of the Constitution" (detail) by Howard Christy, Architect of the Capitol. 139: The Granger Collection. 150L: "Second Street North from Market Street with Christ Church" by William Birch and Son (detail), Historical Society of Pennsylvania. 159R: "The Lackawanna Valley" (detail) by George Inness, National Gallery of Art, Washington, D.C., Gift of Mrs. Huttleston Rogers. 151L: "Election Day at the Statehouse" (detail) by John Lewis Krimmel, Historical Society of Pennsylvania. 151R: "Underground Railroad" (detail) by Charles T. Webber, Cincinnati Art Museum, Subscription Fund Purchase. 152: The Granger Collection. 170: "Cincinnati Public Landing" (detail) by J. C. Wild. Courtesy of the Cincinnati Historical Society. 188: "Portrait of General Andrew Jackson, President of the United States, 1833" by Ralph Earl, Memphis Brooks Museum of Art, Memphis, TN, Memphis Park Commission Purchase 46.0. 207: The Granger Collection. 218L: "Gauchos in a Horse Corral by James Walker, The Thomas Gilcrease Institute of American History and Art, Tulsa, OK. 218R: "Wallstreet, 1857," (detail) Museum of the City of New York. 219L: "On to Liberty" (detail) by Kaufman, The Metropolitan Museum of Art, 1982.443.3. 219R: "Dawn at the Alamo" (detail) by H. A. McArdle, Courtesy, Archives Division, Texas State Library. 220: Artstreet. 240: "Broadway, New York" by Thomas Hornor, New York Public Library. 281: The San Jacinto Museum of History Association, Houston, TX. 292L: "The Flag of Sumter, October 20, 1863" (detail), by Conrad Wise Chapman, The Museum of the Confederacy, Richmond, VA, photo by Katherine Wetzel. 292R: The Granger Collection. 293L: "The Cowboy," by Frederic Remington, Courtesy Amon Carter Museum, Fort Worth. 293R: Gettysburg National Military Park. 294: "A Rainy Day in Camp" (detail), by Winslow Homer, Metropolitan Museum of Art, Gift of Mrs. William F. Milton, 23.77.1. 314: The Bettman Archive. 334: "The Gun Foundry" by John Ferguson Weir, Putnam County Historical Society, Cold Spring, NY. 352: The Granger Collection. 364L: "Snowsheds on the Central Pacific Railroad" by Joseph Becker, The Thomas Gilcrease Institute of American History and Art, Tulsa, OK. 364R: Bethlehem Steel Corp. 365L: "Washington Street, Indianapolis at Dusk," (detail), 72.133, © Indianapolis Museum of Art, Gift of a Couple of Old Hoosiers. 365R: The Granger Collection. 366: "On the Road" 1860 (detail) by Thomas Otter, The Nelson-Atkins Museum of Art, Kansas City, Missouri (Nelson Fund). 388: Sear Archives. 408: "The Bowery at Night" (detail) by W. Louis Sonntag, Jr., Museum of the City of New York. 426: The Bettmann Archive. 438L: Culver Pictures. 438R: The Granger Collection. 439L: The Bettmann Archive. 439R: "Madison Square," 1901 (detail). Collection of Whitney Museum of American Art. Joan Whitney Payson Bequest 76.14. 440: The Granger Collection. "Allies Day" by Childe Hassam, National Gallery of Art, Washington, gift of Ethelyn McKinney in memory of her brother, Glenn Ford McKinney. 480: "The Great White Way" by Howard Thain, New York Historical Society. 500: "Family Group" by Albert Herter, Three Lions. 512L: "Employment Agency. (detail). 1937. Oil on canvas. 34½ × 45 inches. Collection of Whitney Museum of American Art. Purchase 37.44. 512R: Historical Pictures Service, Chicago. 513L: Franklin D. Roosevelt Library. 513R: The Bettmann Archive. 514: Dorothea Lange Collection, The Oakland Museum. 531: Library of Congress. 546: "Tori" by Victor Gunnis, The U.S. Marine Corps Museum, Washington, D.C. 563: The Granger Collection. 574L: Curt Teich Postcard Collection, Lake County Museum. 574: Wide World Photos. 575L: Fred Ward/Black Star. 575R: NASA. 576: "Homecoming GI" by Norman Rockwell, Library of Congress. 592: Wayne Miller/Magnum. 608: Wayne Miller: Magnum. 625: NASA. 636L: C. Simonpietri/Sygma. 636R: Magnum. 637L: Owen/Black Star. 637R: Joe Sohn/The Image Works. 638: Wide World Photos. 656: Lizabeth J. Menzies/The Image Works. 676: Hank Morgan/Rainbow. 700: Dennis Brack/Black Star.